Axis I

DISORDERS USUALLY FIRST DIAGNOSED IN INFANCY, CHILDHOOD, OR ADOLESCENCE

Learning Disorders
Reading Disorder / Mathematics Disorder / Disorder of Written Expression

Motor Skills Disorder
Developmental Coordination Disorder

Pervasive Developmental Disorders
Autistic Disorder / Rett's Disorder / Childhood Disintegrative Disorder / Asperger's Disorder

Attention-deficit and Disruptive Behavior Disorders
Attention-deficit/Hyperactivity Disorder / Oppositional Defiant Disorder / Conduct Disorder

Feeding and Eating Disorders of Infancy or Early Childhood
Pica / Rumination Disorder / Feeding Disorder of Infancy or Early Childhood

Tic Disorders
Tourette's Disorder / Chronic Motor or Vocal Tic Disorder / Transient Tic Disorder

Communication Disorders
Expressive Language Disorder / Mixed Receptive/Expressive Language Disorder / Phonological Disorder / Stuttering

Elimination Disorders
Encopresis / Enuresis

Other Disorders of Infancy, Childhood, or Adolescence
Separation Anxiety Disorder / Selective Mutism / Reactive Attachment Disorder of Infancy or Early Childhood / Stereotypic Movement Disorder

DELIRIUM, DEMENTIA, AMNESTIC AND OTHER COGNITIVE DISORDERS

Delirium
Delirium Due to a General Medical Condition / Substance-intoxicated Delirium / Substance-withdrawal Delirium / Delirium Due to Multiple Etiologies

Dementias
Dementia of the Alzheimer's Type; with Early Onset: if onset at age 65 or below; with Late Onset: if onset after age 65 / Vascular Dementia / Dementias Due to Other General Medical Conditions / Substance-induced Persisting Dementia / Dementia Due to Multiple Etiologies

Amnestic Disorders
Amnestic Disorder Due to a General Medical Condition / Substance-induced Persisting Amnestic Disorder (refer to specific substance for code)

SUBSTANCE-RELATED DISORDERS

Alcohol-related Disorders
Amphetamine-related Disorders
Caffeine-related Disorders
Cannabis-related Disorders
Cocaine-related Disorders
Hallucinogen-related Disorders
Inhalant-related Disorders
Nicotine-related Disorders
Opioid-related Disorders
Phencyclidine (or Related Substance)-related Disorders
Sedative, Hypnotic, or Anxiolytic-related Disorders
Polysubstance-related Disorder

SCHIZOPHRENIA AND OTHER PSYCHOTIC DISORDERS

Schizophrenia
Paranoid Type / Disorganized Type / Catatonic Type / Undifferentiated Type / Residual Type
Schizophreniform Disorder
Schizoaffective Disorder
Delusional Disorder
Brief Psychotic Disorder
Shared Psychotic Disorder (Folie à Deux)
Psychotic Disorder Due to a General Medical Condition
with delusions / with hallucinations / Substance-induced Psychotic Disorder

MOOD DISORDERS

Depressive Disorders
Major Depressive Disorder / Dysthymic Disorder
Bipolar Disorders
Bipolar I Disorder / Bipolar II Disorder (Recurrent Major Depressive Episodes with Hypomania) / Cyclothymic Disorder
Mood Disorder Due to a General Medical Condition
Substance-induced Mood Disorder

ANXIETY DISORDERS

Panic Disorder
without Agoraphobia / with Agoraphobia
Agoraphobia without History of Panic Disorder
Specific Phobia
Social Phobia (Social Anxiety Disorder)
Obsessive-Compulsive Disorder
Posttraumatic Stress Disorder
Acute Stress Disorder
Generalized Anxiety Disorder
Anxiety Disorder Due to a General Medical Condition
Substance-induced Anxiety Disorder

SOMATOFORM DISORDERS

Somatization Disorder
Conversion Disorder
Hypochondriasis
Body Dysmorphic Disorder
Pain Disorder

FACTITIOUS DISORDERS

Factitious Disorder

DISSOCIATIVE DISORDERS

Dissociative Amnesia
Dissociative Fugue
Dissociative Identity Disorder (Multiple Personality Disorder)
Depersonalization Disorder

SEXUAL AND GENDER IDENTITY DISORDERS

Sexual Dysfunctions
Sexual Desire Disorders: Hypoactive Sexual Desire Disorder; Sexual Aversion Disorder / Sexual Arousal Disorders: Female Sexual Arousal Disorder; Male Erectile Disorder / Orgasmic Disorders: Female Orgasmic Disorder (Inhibited Female Orgasm); Male Orgasmic Disorder (Inhibited Male Orgasm); Premature Ejaculation / Sexual Pain Disorders: Dyspareunia; Vaginismus / Sexual Dysfunction Due to a General Medical Condition / Substance-induced Sexual Dysfunction
Paraphilias
Exhibitionism / Fetishism / Frotteurism / Pedophilia / Sexual Masochism / Sexual Sadism / Voyeurism / Transvestic Fetishism
Gender Identity Disorders
Gender Identity Disorder: in Children; in Adolescents or Adults (Transsexualism)

EATING DISORDERS

Anorexia Nervosa
Bulimia Nervosa

SLEEP DISORDERS

Primary Sleep Disorders
Dyssomnias: Primary Insomnia; Primary Hypersomnia; Narcolepsy; Breathing-related Sleep Disorder; Circadian Rhythm Sleep Disorder (Sleep-Wake Schedule Disorder) / Parasomnias; Nightmare Disorder (Dream Anxiety Disorder); Sleep Terror Disorder; Sleepwalking Disorder / Sleep Disorders Related to Another Mental Disorder
Sleep Disorder Due to a General Medical Condition
Substance-induced Sleep Disorder

IMPULSE CONTROL DISORDERS NOT ELSEWHERE CLASSIFIED

Intermittent Explosive Disorder
Kleptomania
Pyromania
Pathological Gambling
Trichotillomania

ADJUSTMENT DISORDERS

Adjustment Disorder
with Anxiety / with Depressed Mood / with Disturbance of Conduct / with Mixed Disturbance of Emotions and Conduct / with Mixed Anxiety and Depressed Mood

Axis II

Mental Retardation
Mild Mental Retardation / Moderate Mental Retardation / Severe Mental Retardation / Profound Mental Retardation

PERSONALITY DISORDERS

Paranoid Personality Disorder
Schizoid Personality Disorder
Schizotypal Personality Disorder
Antisocial Personality Disorder
Borderline Personality Disorder
Histrionic Personality Disorder
Narcissistic Personality Disorder
Avoidant Personality Disorder
Dependent Personality Disorder
Obsessive-Compulsive Personality Disorder

OTHER CONDITIONS THAT MAY BE A FOCUS OF CLINICAL ATTENTION

Psychological Factors Affecting Medical Condition
Medication-induced Movement Disorders
Relational Problems
Relational Problem Related to a Mental Disorder or General Medical Condition / Parent-Child Relational Problem / Partner Relational Problem / Sibling Relational Problem
Problems Related to Abuse or Neglect
Physical Abuse of Child / Sexual Abuse of Child / Neglect of Child / Physical Abuse of Adult / Sexual Abuse of Adult
Additional Conditions That May Be a Focus of Clinical Attention
Bereavement / Borderline Intellectual Functioning / Academic Problem / Occupational Problem / Child or Adolescent Antisocial Behavior / Adult Antisocial Behavior / Malingering / Phase of Life Problem / Noncompliance with Treatment / Identity Problem / Religious or Spiritual Problem / Acculturation Problem / Age-related Cognitive Decline

DSM-IV Multiaxial Classification System

Axis I	Axis II	Axis III
Clinical syndromes:		
Disorders Usually First Diagnosed in Infancy, Childhood, or Adolescence	Mental Retardation Personality Disorders	General Medical Conditions
Delirium, Dementia, Amnestic and other Cognitive Disorders		
Substance-related Disorders		
Schizophrenia and Other Psychotic Disorders		
Mood Disorders		
Anxiety Disorders		
Somatoform Disorders		
Factitious Disorder		
Dissociative Disorders		
Sexual and Gender Identity Disorders		
Eating Disorders		
Sleep Disorders		
Impulse Control Disorders Not Elsewhere Classified		
Adjustment Disorders		

Axis IV
Psychosocial and Environmental Problems

Check:

_____ Problems with primary support group. Specify:

_____ Problems related to the social environment. Specify:

_____ Educational problem. Specify:

_____ Occupational problem. Specify:

_____ Housing problem. Specify:

_____ Economic problem. Specify:

_____ Problems with access to health care services. Specify:

_____ Problems related to interaction with the legal system/crime. Specify:

_____ Other psychosocial and environmental problems. Specify:

Axis V

Global Assessment of Functioning Scale (GAF Scale)

Consider psychological, social, and occupational functioning on a hypothetical continuum of mental health/illness. Do not include impairment in functioning due to physical (or environmental) limitations.

Code

Code	Description
100 | 91	Superior functioning in a wide range of activities, life's problems never seem to get out of hand, is sought out by others because of his many positive qualities. No symptoms.
90 | 81	Absent or minimal symptoms (e.g., mild anxiety before an exam), good functioning in all areas, interested and involved in a wide range of activities, socially effective, generally satisfied with life, no more than everyday problems or concerns (e.g., an occasional argument with family members).
80 | 71	If symptoms are present, they are transient and expectable reactions to psychosocial stressors (e.g., difficulty concentrating after family argument); no more than slight impairment in social, occupational, or school functioning (e.g., temporarily falling behind in school work).
70 | 61	Some mild symptoms (e.g., depressed mood and mild insomnia) OR some difficulty in social, occupational, or school functioning (e.g., occasional truancy, or theft within the household), but generally functioning pretty well, has some meaningful interpersonal relationships.
60 | 51	Moderate symptoms (e.g., flat affect and circumstantial speech, occasional panic attacks) OR moderate difficulty in social, occupational, or school functioning (e.g., no friends, unable to keep a job).
50 | 41	Serious symptoms (e.g., suicidal ideation, severe obsessional rituals, frequent shoplifting) OR any serious impairment in social, occupational or school functioning (e.g., no friends, unable to keep a job).
40 | 31	Some impairment in reality testing or communication (e.g., speech is at times illogical, obscure, or irrelevant) OR major impairment in several areas, such as work or school, family relations, judgment, thinking, or mood (e.g., depressed man avoids friends, neglects family, and is unable to work; child frequently beats up younger children, is defiant at home, and is failing at school).
30 | 21	Behavior is considerably influenced by delusions or hallucinations OR serious impairment in communication or judgment (e.g., sometimes incoherent, acts grossly inappropriately, suicidal preoccupation) OR inability to function in almost all areas (e.g., stays in bed all day; no job, home, or friends).
20 | 11	Some danger of hurting self or others (e.g., suicide attempts without clear expectation of death, frequently violent, manic excitement) OR occasionally fails to maintain minimal personal hygiene (e.g., smears feces) OR gross impairment in communication (e.g., largely incoherent or mute).
10 | 1	Persistent danger of severely hurting self or others (e.g., recurrent violence) OR persistent inability to maintain minimal personal hygiene OR serious suicidal act with clear expectation of death.
0	Inadequate information.

Note: Reprinted with permission from the Criteria of DSM-IV, 1994 American Psychiatric Association.

Jennifer Johnson, Esq.
553-4996

Exploring Abnormal Psychology

Exploring Abnormal Psychology

John M. Neale
State University of New York at Stony Brook

Gerald C. Davison
University of Southern California

David A. F. Haaga
American University

John Wiley & Sons, Inc.
New York   Chichester   Brisbane   Toronto   Singapore

Cover	Paul Klee, "Captive"
	©1995 Artists Rights Society,
	New York/VG Bild-Kunst, Bonn
Acquisitions Editor	Chris Rogers
Director of Development	Johnna Barto
Marketing Manager	Rebecca Herschler
Senior Production Editor	Katharine Rubin
Text Designer	Laura Ierardi
Manufacturing Manager	Mark Cirillo
Photo Editor	Lisa Passmore
Illustration Coordinator	Rosa Bryant
Illustrators	J/B Woolsey Associates; Precision Graphics

This book was set in 10/12 Palatino by Digitype and printed and bound by Von Hoffmann Press. The cover was printed by Phoenix Color.

Recognizing the importance of preserving what has been written, it is a policy of John Wiley & Sons, Inc. to have books of enduring value published in the United States printed on acid-free paper, and we exert our best efforts to that end.

The paper in this book was manufactured by a mill whose forest management programs include sustained yield harvesting of its timberlands. Sustained yield harvesting principles ensure that the number of trees cut each year does not exceed the amount of new growth.

Library of Congress Cataloging in Publication Data:
Neale, John M., 1943–
    Exploring abnormal psychology / John M. Neale, Gerald C. Davison,
David A. F. Haaga
        p.   cm.
    Includes bibliographical references.
    ISBN 0-471-59673-6 (alk. paper)
    1. Psychology, Pathological.   I. Davison, Gerald C.   II. Haaga,
David A. F.   III. Title.
RC454.N39   1995
616.89—dc20   95-20152
                                                                              CIP

Printed in the United States of America
10   9   8   7   6   5   4   3   2   1

To Gail and Sean
     (JMN)

To Aaron and Ida
     (GCD)

To Candice, Kevin, and Megan
     (DAFH)

About the Authors

John M. Neale is Professor of Psychology at the State University of New York at Stony Brook. He received his B.A. from the University of Toronto and his M.A. and Ph.D. from Vanderbilt University. His internship in clinical psychology was as a Fellow in Medical Psychology at the Langley Porter Neuropsychiatric Institute. In 1975 he was a Visiting Fellow at the Institute of Psychiatry, London, England. In 1974 he won the American Psychological Association's Early Career Award for his research on cognitive processes in schizophrenia. In 1991 he won a Distinguished Scientist Award from the American Psychological Association's Society for a Science of Clinical Psychology. He has been on the editorial boards of several journals and has been associate editor of the *Journal of Abnormal Psychology*. Besides his numerous articles in professional journals, he has published books on the effects of televised violence on children, research methodology, schizophrenia, case studies in abnormal psychology, and psychological influences on health. His major research interests are schizophrenia and the relationship of stress and coping to health.

Gerald C. Davison is Professor of Psychology at the University of Southern California, where he was also Director of Clinical Training from 1979 to 1984 and Chair of the Department from 1984 to 1990. Previously he was on the psychology faculty at the State University of New York at Stony Brook (1966–1979). He received his B.A. from Harvard and his Ph.D. from Stanford. He is a Fellow of the American Psychological Association and has served on the Executive Committee of the Division of Clinical Psychology, on the Board of Scientific Affairs, on the Committee on Scientific Awards, and on the Council of Representatives. He is also a Charter Fellow of the American Psychological Society, a member of APS's Publications Committee, a past president of the Association for the Advancement of Behavior Therapy, and was Publications Coordinator of that organization. He served two terms on the National Academy of Sciences Committee on Techniques for the Enhancement of Human Performance. In 1988 Davison received an outstanding achievement award from APA's Board of Social and Ethical Responsibility, in 1989 was the recipient of the Albert S. Raubenheimer Distinguished Faculty Award from USC's College of Letters, Arts and Sciences, and in 1993 won the university-wide USC Associates Award for Excellence in

Teaching. His book *Clinical Behavior Therapy*, co-authored in 1976 with Marvin Goldfried and reissued in expanded form in 1994, is one of two publications that have been recognized as Citation Classics by the Social Sciences Citation Index. He is on the editorial board of *Behavior Therapy, Cognitive Therapy and Research, Journal of Cognitive Psychotherapy*, and *Journal of Psychotherapy Integration*. His current research program focuses on the relationships between cognition and a variety of behavioral and emotional problems. In addition to his teaching and research, he is a practicing clinical psychologist.

*D*avid A. F. Haaga is Associate Professor of Psychology at the American University. He received his B.A. from Harvard and his M.A. and Ph.D. from the University of Southern California. He completed a postdoctoral fellowship at the Center for Cognitive Therapy, University of Pennsylvania. Dr. Haaga is Associate Editor of *Cognitive Therapy and Research*. In 1992 he received the New Researcher Award from the Association for Advancement of Behavior Therapy and the Faculty Honor Award for excellence in teaching from the Graduate Student Council of the American University. Dr. Haaga's research interests include cognitive assessment, depression, and cigarette smoking.

Preface

In contemporary abnormal psychology there are few hard and fast answers. Indeed, the very way the field should be conceptualized and the kinds of questions that should be asked are hotly debated issues. In *Exploring Abnormal Psychology* we have tried to present glimpses of possible answers to two primary questions: *What causes psychopathology?* and *Which treatments are most effective in preventing or reducing psychological suffering?*

▶ Goals of the Book

Our intent is to communicate to students (and faculty as well) our own excitement about our discipline, particularly the puzzles that challenge researchers and therapists in their search for the causes of psychopathology and for ways to prevent and ameliorate it. In doing so, we aimed to meet the needs of students who may never take another psychology course, as well as the needs of psychology majors who may be planning a career in a mental health profession.

Professors often find that they face a difficult choice. As professionals they want to select a comprehensive text that covers current research and social issues pertinent to the field as well as one that offers lucid discussion of disorders. As teachers, they recognize that what many of their students need most is a text tailored toward making them informed citizens who are better prepared to face mental health issues in their own lives and in society. Yet, these same professors do not wish to give up the sense of accuracy, scientific rigor, and concern for social issues that excite them as professionals. We have tried in this book to find a means of letting professors have it both ways.

Scientific and Accessible

Like our other text, Davison and Neale's *Abnormal Psychology*, the present effort emphasizes that the field of abnormal psychology is a scientific one. In this shorter (16 rather than 21 chapters) book, however, we tried to make the benefits of that bigger text more accessible to a wider range of students. We are also mindful of the time constraints many professors face in teaching this course, especially in schools on the quarter system. We have, therefore, reduced the amount of detail in some of our discussions of research and therapy procedures. Nevertheless, major points are represented, and selected issues are presented in sufficient detail to illustrate the ways professionals approach a problem. For example, a Focus Box in Chapter 4 considers the possible advantages of dimensional rather than categorical schemes for classifying mental disorders, and Chapter 16 describes several ambiguities in the interpretation of meta-analytic reviews of the effectiveness of psychotherapy.

Up-to-Date DSM-IV Criteria and Research

Besides condensing and simplifying the information covered in Davison and Neale's *Abnormal Psychology*, we have thoroughly updated our coverage relative to the 1994 edition of that text. For example, diagnostic criteria throughout the book are based on the published Fourth Edition of the *Diagnostic and Statistical Manual of Mental Disorders* (American Psychiatric Association, 1994), and prevalence data for most disorders are based on the recently published National Comorbidity Survey. We have expanded coverage of other particularly active research areas such as the application of the Five Factor Model of normal personality to an understanding of personality disorders (Chapter 11), the effectiveness of the nicotine patch for cigarette smokers (Chapter 12), and the possible role of the mass media in eating disorders (Chapter 14).

Multicultural Issues

Finally, we have enhanced our discussion of multicultural and diversity issues in the study of psychological disorders. We address cultural considerations in detail in assessment (Chapter 5) and intervention (Chapter 16). Also, throughout the text we discuss how cultural and historical issues shed light on our understanding of the entire field of abnormal psychology, beginning in Chapter 1 with an examination of whether *ataque de nervios* (a syndrome originally identified in Puerto Rico) is equivalent to panic disorder and ending in Chapter 16 with an essay on the history of treatments for gay people as an example of the role of values in psychotherapy.

Multiple Perspectives

An overall goal of the book is the integration of major perspectives in abnormal psychology. Our experience in teaching undergraduates has made us very much aware of the importance of making explicit the unspoken assumptions underlying any quest for knowledge. In our handling of the perspectives (paradigms), we have tried to make their premises clear. Long after specific facts are forgotten, the student should retain a grasp of the basic problems in the field of psychopathology and should understand that the answers one arrives at are, in an important but often subtle way, constrained by the questions one poses and the methods employed to ask those questions. Throughout the book we discuss four major perspectives: *psychodynamic, behavioral, cognitive,* and *biological.* When therapy is discussed, we also describe the *humanistic and existential* perspective.

We are convinced that each perspective makes valuable contributions. Rather than force an entire field into, for example, a biological perspective, we argue from the available information that different problems in psychopathology are amenable to analyses within different frameworks. For instance, biological processes must be considered when examining mental retardation and schizophrenia, but for other disorders a cognitive or behavioral theory is useful, and for still others psychodynamic theories can enhance our understanding.

Moreover, combining the perspectives in a pluralistic manner is often the best approach. In Chapter 5 we illustrate this principle with a critical thinking piece on how projective testing from the psychodynamic perspective can enhance the usefulness of the data obtained from more straightforward psychological measures usually favored by adherents of other perspectives. Similarly, the importance of a *vulnerability-stress perspective* on the causes of disorders has become more and more evident in recent years. Emerging data indicate that many, perhaps most, disorders arise from subtle interactions between somatic or psychological predispositions (diatheses) and stressful life events. Our coverage continues to reflect these hypotheses and findings.

Student-Focused Presentation

Exploring Abnormal Psychology is not simply an updated and condensed version of Davison and Neale, nor is it quite like any of the other excellent abnormal psychology textbooks now available. In writing this new book we incorporated several new features with the student reader in mind.

Extended Case Studies

First, we wanted to give students a more vivid sense of the effects of psychological disorders on *people*, beyond the usual neatly-summarized cases. The abstract lists of characteristics and perspectives on causes and treatment, important as they are, can obscure the real people and their families affected by psychological disorders. An extended case opens each disorder chapter and is revisited later in the chapter. The broader scope of this case enables us to bring in social background and family situations as well as the course of treatment from both the clinician's and the patient's point of view.

Critical Thinking Emphasis

We also enhanced our emphasis on the critical thinking skills that serve science and scientists so well and that can provide student readers with the tools they need to become more thoughtful consumers of psychological information in the popular press. Whereas the entire text *models* (we hope) critical thinking skills as theories and data are reviewed, each chapter also includes an explicit, extended "Applying Critical Thinking Skills" feature. In these sections, we show how an important issue relevant to the chapter topic can be considered from multiple points of view and how evidence can be gathered to help choose the most useful explanations for a given phenomenon.

These critical thinking pieces often focus on a particular research finding and illuminate the ways in which a detailed analysis of one result can often lead to further refinements in subsequent research. Critical thinking is not for researchers or readers of published studies only, however. For example, we show in Chapter 4 (a case of blood phobia) and Chapter 6 (a case of social phobia) how critical thinking about individual case studies can generate hypotheses about classification of disorders and theories of psychotherapy.

Legal, Ethical, Social Issues

Besides consuming research reports or clinical case reports, many students will encounter the principles and methods of abnormal psychology through their knowledge of current events or in the personal experiences of their families or friends. To foster students' ability to make such connections, we included Legal, Ethical, and Social Issues essays on such topics as the psychological effects of various nursing home environments (Chapter 15), mainstreaming in the public school system (Chapter 14), and deinstitutionalization and homelessness (Chapter 9). Also, while the text is not a self-help book, we suggest guidelines for choosing a therapist in Focus Box 16.3.

Effective Study Aids

The scientific basis, human impact, social issues, and critical thinking features of this book are effective only if the student actually reads the book and remembers its contents. We therefore placed great emphasis throughout the development of this text on using understandable language, illustrating concepts with examples, and linking ideas within and between chapters. In addition, we have added three new pedagogical features to our efforts at making the main points of the material clear and memorable.

First, important technical terms are defined the first time they are used and are included in a *running glossary* in the margins of the text. Thus, students can consult a formal definition of each term without disrupting their reading to check the main glossary at the end of the text.

Second, each major section of a chapter is followed by an interim summary, labelled *"To Recap"*, which reviews the main issues just discussed and gives the student a cue and an opportunity to consolidate the material before moving forward.

Most important, the chapter ends with a unique *visual summary* depicting the core concepts of the chapter and their interrelationships. Reviewers of the text in its earlier drafts noted that these summaries are likely to be especially useful for the many students who show a strongly visual learning style.

Organization

We have followed the traditional order of opening with an overview of historical and scientific considerations. Next, we have devoted two pivotal chapters to a discussion of the different perspectives—Chapter 2, Psychodynamic, Humanistic/Existential, and Biological and Chapter 3, Behavioral, Cognitive, and Vulnerability-Stress—to lay the foundation for a study of the various disorders. Then we have addressed classification, diagnosis, and clinical assessment.

Chapters 6 through 15 describe the different pathologies, presenting what is known about their causes and about treating and preventing them. While some books devote separate chapters to descriptions and treatment of disorders, we have discussed descriptions, causes, and treatment within the chapter for each specific disorder. Indeed, the extended case studies that begin each pathology chapter, and are revisited later in the chapter, include descriptions of symptoms, social history, and treatment. We believe this organization gives the student a coherent overview. Chapter 16 covers more generically relevant issues in intervention.

Separate chapters are devoted to anxiety disorders, dissociative and somatoform disorders, stress and health, schizophrenia, mood disorders, personality disorders, substance-related disorders, sexual and gender identity disorders, developmental and eating disorders, and aging and psychological disorders.

Supplements

To help support the teaching and learning of the basics of abnormal psychology, a variety of ancillary materials are available from the publisher. In addition to pedagogical aids included in this text, a *Study Guide* is provided to help the student comprehend the concepts presented in the text and prepare for examinations.

For the instructor an extensive *Instructor's Manual* includes lecture support materials. A comprehensive *Test Bank* provides aid in preparing examinations. Computerized versions for IBM-compatibles and Macintoshes are also available.

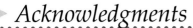

Acknowledgments

It is a pleasure to acknowledge the contributions of a number of colleagues. Their thoughtful comments have helped us to refine the manuscript and improve the book.

Survey Respondents

When we began this project, we surveyed more than 330 abnormal psychology instructors concerning their classroom experiences with textbooks. Their comments and suggestions helped us to develop a text tailored for the typical classroom.

Manuscript Reviewers

During the development phase, a number of instructors read and commented on the manuscript. We would like to acknowledge the contributions made by the following reviewers:

Gisele M. Casanova
Purdue University Calumet

Andrew L. Dickson
University of Southern Mississippi

Richard M. Eisler
Virginia Tech

Linda E. Flickinger
St. Clair County Community College

Travis Langley
Troy State University

John T. Lung
Mount San Antonio College

Martin Pearlman
Middlesex County College

Sarah L. McAuley
University of Central Arkansas

Maribeth Palmer-King
Broome Community College

Paula Pile
Guilford Technical Community College

Mary Prieto-Bayard
California State University at Long Beach

Ronald Ribble
University of Texas at San Antonio

Katherine Elaine Royal
Middle Tennessee State University

Scott Hunter
University of Illinois

Sandra T. Sigmon
University of Maine

Charles L. Spirrison
Mississippi State University

Darryl T. Stevens
Mount Saint Mary's College

Soren Svanum
Indiana University—Purdue at Indianapolis (IUPUI)

Inger C. Thompson
Glendale Community College

Michael W. Vasey
Ohio State University

Michael E. Wells
Surry Community College

Michael J. Zborowski
SUNY College of Buffalo

In addition we are grateful to research assistants Wilson McDermut and Elisha Tarlow for their help in the preparation of this book.

Our book profited from the skills and dedication of numerous John Wiley & Sons Staff, especially Johnna Barto, Karen Dubno, Chris Rogers, Kaye Pace, Rebecca Herschler, Lisa Passmore, Katharine Rubin, Madelyn Lesure, Rosa Bryant, and Pui Szeto. Special thanks go to Leslie Carr, who provided many helpful editing suggestions as we attempted to produce a readable and engaging text without sacrificing scientific accuracy or professional responsibility.

Finally, the authors are grateful for the loving support of their families: Gail and Sean (JMN), Kathleen, Eve, and Asher (GCD), and Candice, Kevin, and Megan (DAFH).

John M. Neale
Stony Brook, NY

Gerald C. Davison
Los Angeles, CA

David A.F. Haaga
Washington, DC

Brief Contents

Contents

▶ *Chapter 7*

Dissociative and Somatoform Disorders 164

▶ *Chapter 8*

Stress and Health 188

▶ *Chapter 9*

Schizophrenia 216

▶ *Chapter 13*

Sexual and Gender Identity Disorders   358

▶ *Chapter 14*

Developmental Disorders and Eating Disorders   399

To the Student: *A User's Guide*

Our goals in writing *Exploring Abnormal Psychology* are not only to present theories, research, and therapies of abnormal psychology but also to convey some of the intellectual excitement that is associated with the search for answers to some of the most puzzling questions facing humankind.

Several features of this book were designed to make it easier to master and enjoy the material—elements intended to make it more "user friendly." It is worthwhile to take some time now to get familiar with the special features of the book. If these elements are employed systematically, this book will help ensure your enjoyment and success in the course.

Chapter 6

Anxiety Disorders

The Case of Karen Rusa

Phobias

Panic Disorder

Generalized Anxiety Disorder

Obsessive-Compulsive Disorder

Focus Box 6.1: Comorbidity in the Anxiety Disorders

Posttraumatic Stress Disorder

Focus Box 6.2: Posttraumatic Stress Disorder and the Vietnam War

Perspectives on the Causes and Treatment of Anxiety Disorders

Applying Critical Thinking Skills: Therapy for Social Phobia

The Case of Karen Rusa Revisited

Chapter Outline
Provides a general overview of the organization of the chapter. At a glance the chapter is broken down by section. The outline also shows where cases and special topics appear.

...ness experienced by Paula is characteristic of ...is chapter we examine dissociative disorders as ...ers, which create physical disabilities or cause ...e symptoms of these disorders and then discuss ...sing in more depth on those disorders about

...sorders

... the individual experiences disruptions of con- We will address four dissociative disorders— ... fugue, depersonalization disorder, and disso- ...own as multiple personality disorder. People ...ble to recall important personal events or may ... or even, as in the case of Paula, assume a new ...ess from the more specific, less complex disso- ...and complicated problem posed by those, like ...ted.

...**sia** is suddenly unable to recall important per- ...some stressful event such as witnessing the ...emory is too extensive to be explained by ordi- ... memory loss is for all events during a limited ...tic experience. Far less frequently, the amnesia ... a period of distress, or it is total, covering the ...riod of amnesia, the person's behavior is other- ...e memory loss may bring some disorientation ...e case of total amnesia, the patient does not rec- ...retains the ability to talk, read, and reason and ...reviously acquired knowledge of the world and ...c episode may last several hours or as long as ...rs as suddenly as it came on, with complete re- ...recurrence. ...in many organic brain disorders as well as in ...amnesia can be fairly easily distinguished from ...ative brain disorders memory fails slowly over ...ain injury (e.g., after an automobile accident) or ...nked to the accident or the substance being

dissociative disorders Disorders in which the normal integration of consciousness, memory, or identity is suddenly altered; *dissociative amnesia, dissociative fugue, depersonalization disorder, and dissociative identity disorder.*

dissociative amnesia A *dissociative disorder* in which the person suddenly becomes unable to recall important personal information to an extent that cannot be explained by ordinary forgetfulness.

In the film Regarding Henry *Harrison Ford played the role of a man who experienced amnesia as a result of brain trauma suffered when he was shot in the head. In this scene he was still unable to remember his family members.*

If a person not only becomes totally amnesic but suddenly moves away from home and work and assumes a new identity, the diagnosis of **dissociative fugue** is made. Sometimes the assumption of the new identity can be quite elaborate, with the person taking on a new name, new home, new job, and even a new set of personality characteristics. The individual may succeed in establishing a fairly complex social life, all without questioning the inability to remember the past. More often, however, the new life does not develop to this extent, and the fugue consists for the most part of limited, but apparently purposeful, travel, during which social contacts are minimal or absent. (The word *fugue* comes from the Latin *fugere*, "to flee.") Fugues typically occur after a person has experienced

dissociative fugue A *dissociative disorder* in which the person forgets important personal information and assumes a new identity, moving to a new location unexpectedly.

Marginal Glossary
Defines important terms when they first appear in text for immediate reinforcement. All highlighted terms also appear in alphabetical order in an end-of-book glossary for easy reference.

134   Chapter 6   Anxiety Disorders

▶ The Case of Karen Rusa

Karen Rusa was a thirty-year-old married woman and the mother of four children. Although she had been having anxiety-related problems for a number of years, she had never sought professional help. In the past several months, she had been experiencing intrusive, repetitive thoughts about her children's safety. She frequently found herself imagining that a serious accident had occurred, and she could not put the thought out of her mind. One day she imagined that her son Alan had broken his leg playing football at school. There was no reason to believe that there had been an accident, but Karen brooded about it until she finally called the school to see if Alan was all right. Even after receiving their reassurance that he had not been hurt, she described herself as being surprised when he later arrived home unharmed.

Karen's daily routine included performing an extensive series of counting rituals. Specific numbers had come to have a special meaning for her. For example, when she was grocery shopping, numbers affected Karen's selection of an item, such as a box of cereal. Karen believed that if she took the first one on the shelf, something terrible would happen to her oldest child; if she selected the second item, some unknown disaster would befall her second child; and so on.

When she was occasionally in too great a hurry to observe the rituals, Karen experienced considerable anxiety. She described herself as tense, jumpy, and unable to relax during these periods. Her fears were usually confirmed, because something unfortunate invariably happened to one of the children within a few days after each such "failure." The fact that minor accidents are likely to occur at a fairly high rate in any family of four children did not change Karen's belief that her failure to follow the numerical rules caused the accident.

In addition to these obsessive ideas and compulsive behaviors, Karen reported dissatisfaction with her marriage and problems in managing her children. Her husband, Tony, had been placed on a complete physical disability about a year earlier. Although he was only thirty-two years old, he suffered from a very serious heart condition that made physical exertion potentially dangerous. Since leaving his job as a clerk at a plumbing supply store, he had spent most of his time at home watching television, and he performed few household chores or family errands. The inequity of this situation was apparent to Karen, and extremely frustrating, yet she found herself unable to handle it effectively.

The children were also clearly out of her control. Robert, age six, and Alan, age eight, were very active and mischievous. Neither responded well to parental discipline, which was inconsistent at best. Both had been noted to be behavioral problems at school. On one occasion, Karen had been called to take Alan home early after he kicked the school principal and told him to "go to hell." The girls were also difficult to handle. Denise, age nine, and Jennifer, age eleve[...] [...]guing with each other. During the past several we[...] and more time crying and hiding alone in her bed[...]

anxiety An unpleasant feeling of fear and apprehension accompanied by increased physiological arousal and avoidance behavior.

Anxiety, that unpleasant feeling of fear [...] abnormal psychology familiar to mos[...] psychopathologies and is a principal [...] in this chapter. Yet anxiety plays an importa[...] people as well, for very few of us go throu[...] experiencing some anxiety or fear. Indeed i[...] fear. If you were swimming in the ocean and [...] healthy, motivating response. But the anxiet[...] people is usually brief and in response to obj[...]

---

158   Chapter 6   Anxiety Disorders

tives offer contrasting views of how anxiety disorders might best be treated. A brief review of the key features of each perspective is provided in the chapter summary.

▶ The Case of Karen Rusa Revisited

We began this chapter with the case of Karen Rusa, whose anxiety took the form of obsessive thoughts and fears that centered on the health of her children. Her compulsive behaviors fall into a special type of checking ritual known as repeating. Repeaters perform an action, often a particular magical number of times, in an effort to prevent disastrous events from happening. Clearly, Karen's case exemplifies OCD.

The actual treatment process in any given case always depends on more than just making the diagnosis and looking up what is the best-supported treatment for this disorder. To illustrate such considerations and strategies more vividly, here and in subsequent chapters we discuss the selected case in more detail, beginning with a consideration of the patient's background and moving on to the treatment procedures used, their effects, and discussion of what alternative approaches might have been considered.

SOCIAL HISTORY

Karen was raised in New York City by Italian immigrant parents who were devout Roman Catholics. She attended parochial schools, and her memories of the severe practices of the church and school authorities were vivid. The formal rituals of the church played an important role in her life, as they did for the rest of her family. Beginning at a very early age, Karen was taught that she had to follow many specific guidelines that governed social behavior within the church (not eating meat on Fridays, going to confession regularly, etc.). She was told that her strict adherence to these norms would ensure the safety of her immortal soul and, conversely, that transgressions would be severely punished.

Karen remembered her parents as having been very strict disciplinarians. Her mother was apparently a cold, rigid person who had insisted on the maintenance of order and cleanliness in their household. When the children deviated from these guidelines, they were severely punished. Karen's most positive recollections of interaction with her mother centered on their mutual participation in prescribed church functions. She did not remember her parents ever demonstrating affection for each other in front of their children.

Shortly after she graduated from high school, Karen married Tony. He was two years older than she and had been working as a stock boy at a department store. Their courtship was hurried, and Karen became pregnant two months after their marriage. In retrospect, Karen wondered whether her interest in Tony had been motivated by a desire to escape from the confines of her parents' home.

Karen began experiencing repetitive, intrusive thoughts about injuring herself as a result of an accident she witnessed at about this time. While Karen was chatting with a friend, the woman's one-year-old daughter crawled off the porch and was run over by another child riding a bicycle. The girl was seriously injured and remained in the hospital for several weeks. Shortly thereafter, at unpredictable but frequent intervals throughout the day, Karen would find herself thinking about jumping out windows, walking in front of cars, and other similar dangerous behaviors. She attempted to get rid of these thoughts by quickly repeating a short prayer that she had learned as a child. This procedure was moderately successful as a temporary source of distraction, but it did not prevent the recurrence of a similar intrusive thought several hours later. These thoughts of self-injury gradually disappeared after the birth of her first child, Jennifer.

When Jennifer was nine months old, Karen once again became pregnant. She and

---

Case Studies

Bring psychological disorders to life. All the disorder chapters (6–15) begin with a vivid description of a real person suffering from one of the psychological disorders discussed in the chapter. Later in the chapter, in the *Case Revisited*, the person's background and course of treatment are reviewed in light of the information about the disorder presented in the chapter. It may be useful to review the Case Study from different perspectives.

Applying Critical Thinking Skills

Encourage thoughtful evaluation of evidence. These sections include questions to show how an important issue in human behavior can be considered from multiple points of view and how material can be gathered to help choose the most useful explanations.

To Recap

Provides periodic review of key concepts. At the end of each major section a brief summary serves as a checkpoint before moving to a new topic.

Dependent Personality Disorder

The **dependent personality** lacks self-confidence and self-reliance. Such individuals passively allow their spouses or partners to assume responsibility for deciding where they should live, what jobs they should hold, with whom they should be friendly. They agree with others even when they know others are wrong, and they have difficulty initiating any activities on their own. Dependent personalities feel uncomfortable when alone and are often preoccupied with fears of being left to take care of themselves. They are unable to make demands on others, and they subordinate their own needs to ensure that they do not break up the protective relationships they have established. When close relationships end, they urgently seek another relationship to replace the old one.

Dependent personality overlaps strongly with borderline and avoidant personality disorders (Morey, 1988) and is linked to several Axis I diagnoses, notably depression (Bornstein, 1992), as well as to poor physical health (Greenberg & Bornstein, 1988).

dependent personality Lacking in self-confidence, people with a dependent personality passively allow others to run their lives and make no demands on them so as not to endanger these protective relationships.

APPLYING CRITICAL THINKING SKILLS

SEX DIFFERENCES IN DEPENDENCY

Sex differences in dependency traits vary with the method of assessment. Women score higher than men on objective self-report tests of dependency (see Chapter 5). That is, women are more likely to agree with such statements as "I easily get discouraged when I don't get what I need from others" (Hirschfeld et al., 1977). But on projective tests of dependency men and women score equally on average (Bornstein, Manning, Krukonis, Rossner, & Mastrosimone, 1993). For example, they are equally likely to see in Rorschach cards (see Chapter 5) images of gift giving or food and drink, which are linked with dependency in psychoanalytic theory.

▶ *What conclusion does the evidence seem to support?* Men and women may have equivalent psychological dependency needs, just as we are all biologically dependent at the start of life. These needs are reflected in their responses to subtle projective tests that have no apparent (to the test taker) relevance to dependency. Men, or at least those who endorse traditionally masculine sex roles, may be less willing to admit dependency (Bornstein, 1992). Therefore, they score lower on transparent questionnaire measures.

▶ *What other interpretations are plausible?* It may be that projective tests are not valid measures of dependency and therefore do not show the (true) sex difference revealed by objective tests.

▶ *What other information would help choose among the alternative interpretations?* If the second interpretation is correct, that projective tests are invalid and objective tests are valid, then the projective tests should fare worse in predicting dependency-related behaviors, dependency-related psychological and physical disorders, and so forth. Moreover, objective and projective tests of dependency should correlate poorly with one another.

If the first interpretation (men are just as dependent, but unwilling to admit it) is accurate, then objective dependency test scores should be correlated with sex-role attitudes. People who endorse traditionally masculine sex roles should score low on objective tests of dependency.

Research along these lines so far favors the first interpretation. Specifically, objective dependency test scores correlate positively with feminine sex-role orientation and negatively with masculine orientation, among both male and female subjects (Bornstein, 1992). In other words, people with a high "masculine" score

---

Perspectives on the Causes and Treatment of Anxiety Di[sorders]

TO RECAP

Anxiety is experienced as an unpleasant feeling of fear. Anxiety disorders inv[olve] excessive, lasting anxiety about matters that do not warrant such concern. A p[hobia] is an excessive, unrealistic fear, out of proportion to the danger actually associ[ated] with what is feared. Specific phobias concern particular objects or situations; [ago-] raphobia involves fear of being in public places, especially on one's own, fro[m] which it would be difficult to escape; and social phobia is an irrational fear of [situ-] ations in which one must interact with strangers or is otherwise subject to scr[utiny] and evaluation by other people. People with panic disorder experience repeat[ed] panic attacks, consisting of a sudden surge of intense anxiety along with mult[iple] physical symptoms, such as heart palpitations, dizziness, or nausea, and thou[ghts] of going crazy or even dying. Agoraphobia is a common complication of pani[c dis-] order.

Chronic worry is the core of generalized anxiety disorder (GAD). The patie[nt is] frequently tense and apprehensive about one or more situations or responsibi[li-] ties. The GAD patient finds worry difficult to manage and as such is subject to multiple physical symptoms of tension and anxiety. People with obsessive-compulsive disorder (OCD) suffer from obsessions (intrusive, recurring thoughts, impulses, or images that seem uncontrollable) or compulsions (repetitive behaviors or mental acts that the person feels driven to perform in order to reduce distress or ward off disaster) or both. Common obsessions include doubts about whether a task was actually completed. Common compulsions include cleaning rituals and checking many times whether something was done. Posttraumatic stress disorder (PTSD) is an extreme response to a severely stressful event. To be diagnosed with PTSD, this response must last more than one month and include (a) reexperiencing the traumatic event, (b) avoiding stimuli associated with the trauma, and (c) signs of increased arousal, such as an exaggerated startle response.

Perspectives on the Causes and Treatment of Anxiety Disorders

Psychodynamic Perspectives: Conflict Between Id and Ego

Psychoanalytic theory regards anxiety as the result of an unconscious conflict between the ego and id impulses. The impulses, usually sexual or aggressive in nature, are struggling for expression, but the ego cannot allow their expression because it unconsciously fears that punishment will follow. Since the source of the anxiety is unconscious, the person experiences apprehension and distress without knowing why.

As we have seen, anxiety disorders vary. If unconscious conflict is the source of maladaptive anxiety, what would determine whether someone has, for instance, OCD versus a specific phobia? Two possibilities are the psychosexual stage at which the person's development is fixated and the nature of the defense mechanism the person employs in keeping the conflict unconscious.

OCD is believed to reflect fixation at the anal stage of development. Obsessions and compulsions are viewed as similar, resulting from instinctual sexual or aggressive forces that are not under control because of overly harsh toilet training. The symptoms observed represent the outcome of the struggle between the id and the defense mechanisms; sometimes the id predominates, sometimes the defense mechanisms. For example, when obsessive thoughts of killing intrude, the forces of the id are dominant. More often, however, the observed symptoms reflect the partially successful operation of one of the defense mechanisms. For example, an individual fixated at the anal stage may use the defense of reaction formation to resist the urge to soil, instead becoming compulsively neat, clean, and orderly.

FOCUS BOX 6.2

Posttraumatic Stress Disorder and the Vietnam War

During war, military personnel must contend with devastating stress, and some of them break down. In World War I the term used was *shell shock*, reflecting the somatogenic belief that the soldier's brain suffered chronic concussions through the sudden and severe atmospheric pressure changes from nearby explosions. In World War II and the Korean War the great weariness of soldiers, their sleeplessness, tendency to startle at the

thousand, and many more seriously wounded and permanently maimed. Military personnel, after their oneyear tour of duty, returned home alone and quickly, by jet. There were no battalions of soldiers arriving stateside together at war's end, no parades, no homecomings, indeed, none of the grateful celebration that all of us have seen in newsreels showing the end of World War II and, more recently, the Persian Gulf War. To

LEGAL, ETHICAL, AND SOCIAL ISSUES

Dissociative Identity Disorder (Multiple Personality Disorder) and the Insanity Defense

The **insanity defense** is the legal argument that a defendant should not be held responsible for an illegal act if his or her conduct is attributable to mental illness that interferes with rationality or that results in some other excusing circumstance, such as not knowing right from wrong. A staggering amount of material has been written on the insanity defense, even though it is pleaded in only about 2% of all cases that reach trial and is rarely successful (Steadman, 1979). For a person to be found not guilty by reason of insanity (NGRI) he or she must be so impaired as to be unable to exercise free will and thus to be responsible for his or her actions. Such impairment is difficult to prove.

The grounds accepted for establishing insanity defenses have changed many times. In the past decade there has been a new effort in the United States to clarify the legal defense of insanity. This effort was fueled by the controversy created by the NGRI verdict in the highly publicized trial of John Hinckley Jr. for attempted assassination of President Ronald Reagan. The judge who presided over the trial received a flood of mail. People were outraged that a would-be assassin of a U.S. president had not been held criminally responsible and had only been committed to an indefinite stay in a mental hospital until he was deemed mentally healthy enough for release.

Because of the publicity of the trial and the public outrage at the NGRI verdict, the insanity defense became a target of criticism. As a consequence of political pressures to get tough on criminals, Congress enacted in October 1984 the Insanity Defense Reform Act, addressing the insanity defense for the first time. This new law, which has been adopted in all federal courts (though not by every state), contains several provisions.

▸ The defendant must be found unable to appreciate the wrongfulness of his or her conduct.
▸ The mental disorder must be "severe." This has the effect of excluding insanity defenses on the bases of nonpsychotic disorders, such as antisocial personality disorder.
▸ Defenses relying on "diminished capacity" or "diminished responsibility," based on such mitigating circumstances as extreme passion or "temporary insanity," were ruled as inadmissible.

insanity defense   The legal argument that a defendant should not be held responsible for an illegal act if the conduct is attributable to mental illness.

Successful use of the ins
Jr., for attempting to ass
prompted criticism of la
ultimately a revision of

▸ The burden of
than with the p
prosecution's ha
was sane beyon
the crime (the
with the consti
considered inno
must prove tha
must do so with
less stringent bu
designed to mak
dant of moral an
▸ If the person jud
covered from m
ing release from
carceration can
allowable for the

As you read thes
multiple personalit
agnoses that could
Defense Reform Ac
MPD (now known
may not have been
criminal act, but ma

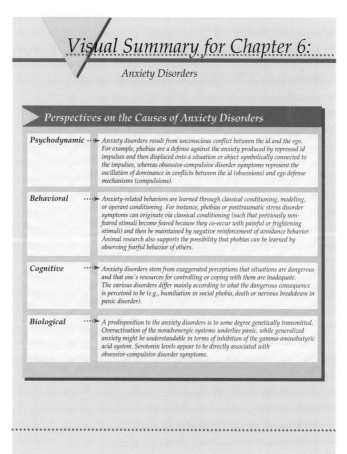

Visual Summary for Chapter 6:

Anxiety Disorders

Perspectives on the Causes of Anxiety Disorders

Psychodynamic ⤑ Anxiety disorders result from unconscious conflict between the id and the ego. For example, phobias are a defense against the anxiety produced by repressed id impulses and then displaced onto a situation or object symbolically connected to the impulses, whereas obsessive-compulsive disorder symptoms represent the oscillation of dominance in conflicts between the id (obsessions) and ego defense mechanisms (compulsions).

Behavioral ⤑ Anxiety-related behaviors are learned through classical conditioning, modeling, or operant conditioning. For instance, phobias or posttraumatic stress disorder symptoms can originate via classical conditioning (such that previously nonfeared stimuli become feared because they co-occur with painful or frightening stimuli) and then be maintained by negative reinforcement of avoidance behavior. Animal research also supports the possibility that phobias can be learned by observing fearful behavior of others.

Cognitive ⤑ Anxiety disorders stem from exaggerated perceptions that situations are dangerous and that one's resources for controlling or coping with them are inadequate. The various disorders differ mainly according to what the dangerous consequence is perceived to be (e.g., humiliation in social phobia, death or nervous breakdown in panic disorder).

Biological ⤑ A predisposition to the anxiety disorders is to some degree genetically transmitted. Overactivation of the noradrenergic systems underlies panic, while generalized anxiety might be understandable in terms of inhibition of the gamma-aminobutyric acid system. Serotonin levels appear to be directly associated with obsessive-compulsive disorder symptoms.

Focus Boxes
Allow exploration of a specialized topic without detracting from the flow of the text. These sections expand on a point of view or provide additional detail to deepen your understanding of important and sometimes controversial issues.

Legal, Ethical, Social Issues
Enhance your understanding of complex issues. These special essays deal with applications of abnormal psychology to current societal concerns.

Visual Summary
Serves as a road map to the main concepts covered in the chapter. Every chapter concludes with this unique feature which gives an immediate sense of what you have learned and enhances your understanding of the relationship of the various topics. This is a key element in reviewing material for an exam.

Chapter 1

Introduction: Historical and Scientific Considerations

The Case of Ernest H.

Slumping in a comfortable leather chair, Ernest H., a thirty-five-year-old city police officer, looked skeptically at his therapist as he struggled to describe a series of problems. His recent inability to maintain an erection when making love with his wife was the immediate reason for his seeking therapy, but after gentle prodding from the therapist Ernest listed many other difficulties, some dating from his childhood, but most of them having begun in the past few years.

Ernest's childhood had not been happy. His mother, whom he loved dearly, died suddenly when he was only six, and for the next ten years he lived either with his father or with a maternal aunt. His father drank so heavily that he seldom managed to get through any day without alcohol. Moreover, the man's moods were extremely variable; he had even spent several months in a state hospital with a diagnosis of manic-depressive psychosis. The father's income was irregular and never enough to pay bills on time or to allow them to live in any but the most run-down neighborhoods. At times Ernest's father was totally incapable of caring for himself, let alone his son. Ernest would then spend weeks, sometimes months, with his aunt in a nearby suburb.

Despite these apparent handicaps, Ernest completed high school and entered the tuition-free city university. He earned his living expenses by waiting tables at a small restaurant. During college his psychological problems began to concern him. He often became extremely depressed for no apparent reason, and these periods of sadness were sometimes followed by times of manic elation. His lack of control over these mood swings troubled him greatly, for he had observed this same pattern in his father. Ernest also felt highly self-conscious when he was around people with authority over him— his boss, his professors, and even some of his classmates, with whom he compared himself unfavorably. He was especially sensitive about his clothes, which were old and worn compared with those of wealthier students.

It was on the opening day of classes in his junior year that he first saw his future wife. When the tall, slender young woman moved to her seat with grace and self-assurance, his were not the only eyes that followed her. He spent the rest of that semester watching her from afar, taking care to sit where he could glance over at her without being conspicuous. Then one day, as they were leaving class, they bumped into each other quite by accident. Her warmth and charm emboldened him to ask her to join him for some coffee. When she said yes, he almost wished she had not. Amazingly enough, as he saw it, they soon fell in love, and before the end of his senior year they were married. Ernest could never quite believe that his wife, as intelligent a woman as she was beautiful, really cared for him. As the years wore on, his doubts about himself, and about her feelings toward him grew.

He hoped to enter law school, and both his grades and law school boards made these plans a possibility, but he decided instead to enter the police academy. His reasons, as he told his therapist, were doubts about his intellectual abilities and an increasing uneasiness in situations in which he felt himself being evaluated. Seminars had become unbearable for him in his last year in college, and he had hopes that the badge and uniform of a police officer would give him the instant recognition and respect that he seemed incapable of earning on his own.

To help him get through the academy, his wife quit college at the end of her junior year, against Ernest's pleas, and obtained a secretarial job. He felt that she was far brighter than he and saw no reason for her to sacrifice her potential to help him make his way in life. But at the same time he recognized the fiscal realities and grudgingly accepted her financial support.

The police academy proved to be even more stressful than college. Ernest's mood swings, although less frequent, still troubled him. And like his father, who was now confined to a state mental hospital, he drank to ease his psychological pain. He felt that his instructors considered him a fool when he had difficulty standing up in front of the class to give an answer that he himself knew was correct. But he made it through the academy and was assigned to foot patrol in one of the wealthier sections of the city.

Now thirty-two years old, with a fairly secure job that paid reasonably well, he began to think of starting a family. His wife wanted this as well, and it was then that his problems with sexual functioning began. He thought at first it was the alcohol—he was drinking at least six ounces of bourbon every night, except when on the swing shift. Soon, though, he began to wonder whether he was actually avoiding the responsibility of having a child, and he began to doubt that his wife really found him attractive and desirable. The more understanding and patient she was about his sometimes frantic efforts to consummate sex with her, the less "manly" he felt himself to be. The less often they made love, the more suspicious he was of his wife. She had become even more beautiful and vibrant as she entered her thirties. In addition, she had been promoted to the position of administrative assistant at the law firm where she worked. She would mention—perhaps to taunt him—long, martini-filled lunches with her boss.

The incident that finally convinced Ernest to see a therapist was an ugly argument with his wife one evening when she came home from work after ten. Ernest had been agitated for several days. To combat his fear that he was losing control, he had drunk almost a full bottle of bourbon each night. By the time his wife walked in the door on that final evening, Ernest was already very drunk, and he attacked her both verbally and physically about her alleged infidelity. In her own anger and fear, she questioned his masculinity in striking a woman and taunted him with the disappointments of their lovemaking. Ernest stormed out of the house, spent the night at a local bar, and the next day somehow pulled himself together enough to seek professional help.

This case study is open to a wide range of interpretations. No doubt you have some ideas about how Ernest's problems developed, what his primary difficulties are, and perhaps even how you might try to help him. We know of no greater intellectual or emotional challenge than deciding how to conceptualize the life of a person with psychological problems and how best to treat him or her. In Chapters 2 and 3 we will refer to the case of Ernest to illustrate how workers from different theoretical perspectives might interpret his situation and try to intervene.

Every day we try to understand other people. Figuring out why others act or feel the way they do is not easy. Indeed, we do not always understand why we feel and behave as we do. Understanding normal behavior is hard enough; understanding human behavior beyond the normal range, such as that of the police officer just described, is even more difficult.

This book deals with all aspects of abnormality—describing it, explaining it, treating it, and preventing it. To study abnormal psychology requires tolerance for ambiguity. As you will see, the human psyche remains elusive; we know with certainty much less about our field than we might hope. Nevertheless, in many areas exciting progress is made each year. We hope to communicate both what is known and what is unknown, as well as the methods by which therapists and researchers attempt to improve our understanding of abnormal behavior.

One of the challenges of studying abnormal psychology is the difficulty of remaining open-minded and objective about such a personal subject. Abnormal behavior affects us all. Who, for example, has not experienced irrational thoughts and feelings? Or who has not known someone, a friend or perhaps a relative, whose behavior seemed "crazy"? If you have, you realize how frustrating and frightening it is to try to understand and help a person suffering psychological difficulties. Even if you have not been personally affected, the media keep frightening images of unusual behavior in focus. Hardly a week passes without a violent act, such as an ax murder or multiple slayings, being reported. The assailant is diagnosed by a police officer or mental health authority as mentally disturbed.

Sometimes we learn that the person has previously been confined in a mental hospital.

All of us bring to our study of abnormal behavior preconceived notions of what the subject matter is. For example, a student who has volunteered in a day-care center might be inclined to see early childhood experiences and parent–child relationships as the most important influences on development. Another person, who lives in a neighborhood ruled by gangs and overrun with drugs, might view a wider environment outside the family as the key influence. As we will see, many factors may influence abnormal behavior.

In the next section we turn to another challenge in studying abnormal psychology, the question of how to define "abnormal." After a brief description of the types of professionals currently working to understand and treat abnormal behavior, we shall examine how views of abnormality have evolved throughout history. Finally, this introductory chapter describes (a) the main methods used in contemporary research to try to increase knowledge about abnormal behavior and (b) some of the habits of critical thinking a person needs to be a wise consumer of the results of research using these methods.

What Is Abnormal Behavior?

Abstract terms are more difficult to define than you might think. If you want to give someone a hard time, ask for a precise, complete definition of some everyday concept. What is a "chair," for instance? If your friend says, "a piece of furniture designed for a person to sit on," you could respond, "So is a couch a chair?" If the other person replies, "It is a piece of furniture designed for one person to sit on, and it has four legs and a seat and a back," you might ask, "What about a beanbag chair? What about a bar stool?" If your friend is still speaking to you, you might at least be able to agree that finding a formal definition seems surprisingly awkward, given that most people go about their daily lives without a great deal of confusion about the chairs they encounter.

One possible response to the difficulty of finding an agreeable definition for a term is to throw up your hands and say, "I can't define abnormal behavior. It's like pornography—I know it when I see it." But this reply does not always suffice. Many socially relevant questions depend on our having a better definition of abnormality than just "I know it when I see it." Is homosexuality abnormal? Is alcoholism a disease? Should insurance companies cover the costs of treatment for unhappy marriages? Each of these issues in one way or another hinges on our efforts to define **abnormal behavior**. Even if no one criterion is perfect, several criteria taken together help: statistical infrequency, unexpectedness, violation of norms, personal distress, and disability or dysfunction.

Statistical Infrequency

One component of abnormal behavior is that it is *infrequent*. One does not often encounter people who believe that the CIA is communicating with them through their television sets. Those who focus on this statistical aspect of abnormal behavior typically measure specific characteristics of people, such as personality traits, and the distribution of these characteristics in the population. One type of population distribution, the **normal curve** (Figure 1.1), depicts the majority of people as being in the middle as far as any particular characteristic is concerned; that is, very few people fall at either extreme. Saying that someone is normal in this sense implies that he or she does not deviate much from the average.

Statistical infrequency is used explicitly in diagnosing mental retardation. Figure 1.1 gives the normal distribution of intelligence quotient measures in the

abnormal behavior   Patterns of emotion, thought, and action deemed pathological for one or more of the following reasons: infrequent occurrence, violation of norms, personal distress, disability or dysfunction, and unexpectedness.

normal curve   As applied in psychology, the bell-shaped distribution of a measurable trait depicting most people in the middle and few at the extremes.

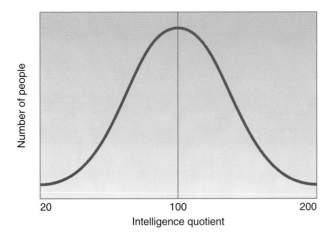

Figure 1.1 *The intelligence distribution among adults, illustrating a normal, or bell-shaped, curve.*

population. Although it is not the only measure, low intelligence (defined here as an intelligence quotient below 70) is a key criterion in the diagnosis of mental retardation (see Chapter 14).

Infrequency is relevant to defining a behavior as abnormal, perhaps even necessary (it is hard to imagine considering a behavior abnormal if 90% of humans engage in it, no matter how irrational or puzzling it might otherwise seem). However, infrequency by itself is not enough. Great athletic ability, for instance, is infrequent but not abnormal. We need to supplement frequency information to determine whether a behavior is abnormal. The remaining features of the definition of abnormality are intended to help us decide *which* infrequent characteristics are abnormal.

Unexpectedness

We need to consider whether, in view of the circumstances a person faces, that person's behaviors or feelings are *unexpected*. Hunger is an expected response to not eating and thus would not be considered abnormal. In contrast, many forms of abnormal behavior are unexpected responses to situations. For example, anxiety disorders are diagnosed when the anxiety occurs in response to a safe situation, as when people worry continually about their financial situation even though they are well-off.

Violation of Norms

Another view is that abnormal behavior is whatever *violates social norms* and threatens or makes anxious those observing it. The sometimes wild behaviors of manic patients and the strange antics of schizophrenic patients fit this definition. This component explicitly makes abnormality historically and culturally relative; depending on current cultural norms, a particular behavior might or might not be considered abnormal. Homosexuality, for example, was considered a psychological disorder prior to the early 1970s, but now it is not.

The Effects of Culture in Defining Abnormality

In addition to highlighting the likelihood that beliefs about what is abnormal may change over time, the violation-of-norms component of the definition is useful because it draws attention to the role of culture in defining and classifying abnormal behavior. As the United States has become an increasingly multicultural nation, the degree to which the criteria for defining and describing abnormality

Attending class in the nude, as this Berkeley student did in 1992, is a clear norm violation but does not necessarily indicate psychopathology.

are shaped by cultural norms has received more attention from professionals. To cite one example, studies in Puerto Rico have identified the syndrome of *ataque de nervios* ("attack of nerves") (Guarnaccia, Canino, Rubio-Stipec, & Bravo, 1993). This syndrome often occurs at a funeral or in the wake of significant stress, such as family conflict; the person suffering *ataque de nervios* may experience sweating, heart palpitations, and a sense that he or she is going crazy, and may become hysterical, shouting at others or even hitting them.

A study conducted in New York at an anxiety disorders clinic found *ataque de nervios* equally common among Dominican as Puerto Rican patients and more common among women than men (Liebowitz et al., 1994). Especially important is that the symptoms of *ataque de nervios* appeared to overlap somewhat, but not completely, those officially recognized as leading to a diagnosis of panic disorder (see Chapter 6). Whether *ataque de nervios* is essentially the same thing as panic disorder (the same subjective and biological phenomena, but with different behaviors depending on a person's cultural background) and therefore likely to need the same kinds of treatment remains an open question. In general, learning more about how abnormal behavior is expressed and interpreted by people from a variety of cultural backgrounds is critical for accurate assessment and diagnosis of patients, and therefore for successful treatment. We shall explore the issue of cultural influences on assessment and diagnosis in more detail in Chapters 4 and 5.

Although helpful in clarifying the historical and cultural relativity of definitions of abnormality, violation of norms, like statistical infrequency, is not sufficient as a definition. Some behaviors, such as prostitution or robbery, violate social norms but are not generally considered part of the domain of abnormal psychology.

Personal Distress

Abnormality can also be defined in part by *personal distress*. People's behavior is abnormal if it creates great suffering and torment in them. Many of the forms of abnormality addressed in this book, such as anxiety disorders and depression, involve considerable personal suffering. Ernest, the police officer whose case opened

Grief is an expected response to losing a loved one. However, personal distress that is not expected in a given situation is part of the definition of abnormal behavior.

this chapter, is certainly suffering. But some disorders do not cause distress. The psychopath, for example, treats others coldheartedly but without experiencing any guilt or anxiety whatsoever. Furthermore, some forms of distress, such as that caused by a painful injury, do not seem to belong to the field. Another difficulty in using personal discomfort as a defining characteristic is that it is subjective and idiosyncratic. Degrees of personal distress are difficult to compare, for people's standards for defining their own psychological states can vary greatly.

Disability

Another component of abnormal behavior is *disability*, that is, the inability to pursue some goal because of the abnormality. Substance related disorders, for example, are defined principally by how the substance abuse creates social or occupational disability (e.g., poor work performance, serious arguments with one's spouse). Similarly, a phobia could indicate both distress and disability if, for example, a severe fear of flying prevented someone from taking a job promotion (see Wakefield, 1992). As with suffering, however, disability applies to some, but not all, disorders. It is not clear, for example, whether voyeurism (obtaining sexual gratification by watching others undress or engage in sexual relations without their awareness or consent) is necessarily a disability. Most transvestites are married, lead conventional lives, and usually cross-dress in private. Also, characteristics that might in some circumstances be considered disabilities—being short if you want to be a professional basketball player—do not fall within the domain of abnormal psychology.

Alcohol abuse is considered abnormal in part because it causes disability in the form of work-related problems and physical health problems.

Thus no one feature perfectly defines a behavior as abnormal and permits us easily to reach agreement when considering new or controversial categories of behavior as possible psychological disorders (e.g., compulsive gambling). What we present in this book is a list of conditions, called disorders, that are currently considered abnormal. As has happened before, the disorders in the list will undoubtedly change with time, as social norms, cultural values, and scientific knowledge evolve.

To Recap

Like many abstract concepts, abnormal behavior is difficult to define. No single criterion is perfect for distinguishing abnormal from normal behavior, but several criteria seem to capture at least part of the definition of abnormality: statistical infrequency, unexpectedness, violation of social norms, personal distress, and disability. Consideration of social norms in particular makes it clear that our ideas about what qualifies as abnormal are to a degree influenced by our culture and time.

The Mental Health Professions

A wide variety of professionals are authorized to diagnose and treat psychological disorders. The training for each is different. A **clinical psychologist** requires a Ph.D. or Psy.D. degree, which entails a minimum of four years of graduate study in psychology, more commonly five to seven, as well as a year or two of supervised postdoctoral work experience and a passing score on a licensing examination.

Training for the Ph.D. in clinical psychology is much like that for the other fields of psychology, with a heavy emphasis on scientific research. Candidates are required to research and write a lengthy dissertation on a specialized topic. Further, candidates in clinical psychology are distinguished from other Ph.D. candidates in psychology in that they also learn applied skills in two areas. First, they learn techniques of assessment and diagnosis of mental disorders. Second, they learn how to practice **psychotherapy**, a primarily verbal means of helping troubled people. Students take courses in which they master specific techniques of diagnosis and psychotherapy under close professional supervision; then, during an intensive internship and perhaps formal postdoctoral training, they gradually assume increasing responsibility for the care of patients.

Other clinical graduate programs are more focused on practice. These programs offer the relatively new degree Psy.D. (doctor of psychology). The curriculum is generally the same as that available to Ph.D. students, but there is less emphasis on research and more on clinical training. The thinking behind these programs is that clinical psychology has advanced to a level of knowledge and certainty that justifies—even requires—intensive training in specific techniques of assessment and therapy rather than combining training in practice with research.

A **psychiatrist** holds an M.D. degree and has had postgraduate training, called a residency, in which he or she has received supervision in diagnosis and psychotherapy. By virtue of the medical degree, and in contrast with psychologists, psychiatrists can also continue functioning as physicians—giving physical examinations, diagnosing medical problems, and the like. However, the only aspect of medical practice in which most psychiatrists engage is prescribing the various drugs that have been developed to treat specific psychological disorders.

A **psychoanalyst** has received specialized training at a psychoanalytic institute. The program usually involves several years of clinical training as well as an in-depth psychoanalysis of the trainee. Although Sigmund Freud held that psychoanalysts do not need medical training, until recently most psychoanalytic institutes required of their graduates an M.D. and a psychiatric residency. Today, however, many institutes offer psychoanalytic training to clinical psychologists and social workers.

A **psychiatric social worker** obtains an M.S.W. (master of social work) degree. Master's and doctoral programs for **counseling psychologists** are somewhat similar to graduate training in clinical psychology but usually have less emphasis on research and more emphasis on skills needed to consult with healthy clients facing difficult decisions (e.g., career planning) rather than with those experiencing psychological disorders.

---

clinical psychologist A specialist in the area of psychology concerned with the study of *psychopathology*, its causes, prevention, and treatment.

psychotherapy A primarily verbal means of helping troubled individuals change their thoughts, feelings, and behavior to reduce distress and to achieve greater life satisfaction.

psychiatrist A physician (M.D.) who has taken specialized postdoctoral training, called a residency, in the diagnosis, treatment, and prevention of mental and emotional disorders.

psychoanalyst A therapist who has taken specialized postdoctoral training in psychoanalysis after earning either an M.D. or a Ph.D. degree.

psychiatric social worker A mental health professional who holds a master of social work (M.S.W.) degree.

counseling psychologists Mental health professionals whose training is similar to that of *clinical psychologists*, though usually with less emphasis on research and *psychopathology*.

The term **clinician** is often applied to people who, regardless of professional degree, offer diagnostic and therapeutic services to the public. Thus, clinicians can include Ph.D.'s in clinical or counseling psychology, Psy.D.'s, holders of an M.S.W. degree, and psychiatrists. A highly diverse group of people can be called **psychopathologists**. These people conduct research into the nature and development of the various disorders that their therapist colleagues try to diagnose and treat. Psychopathologists come from any number of disciplines; although some are clinical psychologists, their educational backgrounds may range from biochemistry to developmental psychology. What unites them is their commitment to the study of how abnormal behavior develops. Since we still have much to learn about abnormality, the diversity of backgrounds and interests is an advantage, for it is too soon to be certain in which area major advances will be made.

clinician A health professional authorized to provide diagnostic and therapeutic services.

psychopathologists Mental health professionals who conduct research into the nature and development of mental and emotional disorders.

To Recap

Several disciplines, including medicine, psychology, and social work, provide training for those who wish to study abnormal behavior (psychopathologists) and/or to diagnose and treat it (clinicians). Psychologists hold Ph.D. or Psy.D. degrees, while psychiatrists hold M.D. degrees. Within psychology, different degree programs vary mainly according to the degree of emphasis they place on training in practical clinical skills or in research methods.

Clinicians come from diverse degree programs, but all are trained in psychotherapy and diagnosis.

History of Psychopathology

The study of the nature and development of mental disorders, or **psychopathology**, has a long history. Mental disorders have been seen as evidence of possession by demons, as a medical problem involving imbalance of bodily fluids, as an indication that a person is a witch, as a result of too much blood in the brain, and so on. The major points of view generally vying for attention have been biological (accounting for mental disorders in terms of physical malfunction) and psychological (explaining mental disorders with reference to such factors as social stress or moral failings). Treatments have varied accordingly.

psychopathology The study of the nature and development of mental disorders.

Early Demonology

Before the age of science, anything that seemed beyond the control of humankind—eclipses, earthquakes, storms, fire, disease, the passing of the seasons—was regarded as supernatural. The earliest writings of the philosophers, theologians, and physicians who studied the troubled mind considered abnormality a reflection of the displeasure of the gods or possession by demons. The doctrine that an evil being, such as the devil, can live within a person and control his or her mind and body is called **demonology**. The ancient Babylonians had in their religion a specific demon for each disease. Examples of demonological thinking can be found in the records of the early Chinese, Egyptians, and Greeks as well. Among the Hebrews, deviancy was attributed to possession of the person by bad spirits, after God in his wrath had withdrawn protection. Christ is reported to have cured a man with an unclean spirit by casting out the devils from within him and hurling them onto a herd of swine (Mark 5:8–13).

demonology The doctrine that a person's abnormal behavior is caused by an evil spirit.

Exorcism, the casting out of evil spirits by ritualistic chanting or torture, typically took the form of elaborate prayer rites, noisemaking, forcing the afflicted to drink terrible-tasting brews, and on occasion more extreme measures, such as flogging and starvation, to make the body uninhabitable by the devil.

exorcism The casting out of evil spirits by ritualistic chanting or torture.

Early Physiological Explanations in Ancient Greece and Rome

In the fifth century B.C. Hippocrates, often regarded as the founder of modern medicine, distinguished medicine from religion, magic, and superstition. Hippocrates rejected the prevailing Greek belief that the gods sent serious physical diseases and mental disturbances as punishment. He insisted instead that such illnesses had natural causes and should be treated like other, more common maladies, such as colds. Hippocrates regarded the brain as the organ of consciousness, of intellectual life and emotion, and it followed that if someone's thinking and behavior were deviant, there was some kind of brain pathology. He is considered one of the earliest proponents of **somatogenesis**—the notion that something wrong with the *soma*, or body, disturbs thought and action. In contrast, **psychogenesis** is the belief that something is due to psychological origins.

somatogenesis Development from bodily origins as distinguished from psychological origins.

psychogenesis Development from psychological origins as distinguished from somatic origins.

Hippocrates classified mental disorders into three categories: mania; melancholia; and phrenitis, or brain fever. Through his teachings the phenomena of abnormal behavior became more clearly the province of physicians than of priests. For melancholia Hippocrates prescribed tranquillity, sobriety, care in choosing food and drink, and abstinence from sexual activity. Such a regimen was assumed to have a healthful effect on the brain and the body. Because Hippocrates believed in natural rather than supernatural causes, he depended on his own keen observations and made a valuable contribution as a clinician. He kept remarkably detailed records describing many of the symptoms now recognized in epilepsy, alcoholic delusion, stroke, and paranoia.

Hippocrates' physiology was rather crude, however, for he conceived of normal brain functioning, and therefore of mental health, as based on a delicate balance among four humors, or fluids of the body: blood, black bile, yellow bile, and phlegm. An imbalance produced disorders. If a person was sluggish and dull, for example, the body supposedly contained a preponderance of phlegm (hence the word *phlegmatic*, meaning slow or sluggish). A preponderance of black bile was the explanation for melancholia; too much yellow bile explained irritability and anxiousness; and too much blood, changeable temperament. Hippocrates' humoral pathology did not withstand later scientific scrutiny. His basic premise, however, that normal and abnormal behaviors are markedly affected by physiology, was prophetic. In the next seven centuries, Hippocrates' naturalistic approach to disorder was generally accepted by other Greeks as well as by the Romans.

The Greek physician Hippocrates held a somatogenic view of abnormal behavior, considering insanity a disease of the brain.

The Dark Ages and the Return of Demonology

The death of Galen (A.D. 130–200), a second-century Greek regarded as the last major physician of the classical era, is sometimes regarded as marking the beginning of the Dark Ages for all medicine and for the treatment and study of abnormal behavior in particular. Over several centuries of decay, Greek and Roman civilization declined. During the Middle Ages and the Renaissance (A.D. 400–1500), the churches gained in influence, and Christian monasticism, through its missionary and educational work, replaced classical culture. The view that mental disorder was due to spiritual disorder again took hold.

Monks cared for the mentally disordered by praying over them and touching them with relics or by making fantastic potions for them to drink in the waning phase of the moon. The families of the mentally ill might take them to shrines or sometimes disavowed them because of fear and superstition. Many disturbed people roamed the countryside, losing more and more of their faculties.

The Mentally Ill as Witches

During the thirteenth and the next few centuries, a populace already suffering from social unrest and recurrent famines and plagues became obsessed with the devil. Faced with unexplained and frightening events, people tend to seize on whatever explanation is available. The times conspired to heap enormous blame on those considered to be witches. Witchcraft, viewed as instigated by the powerful Satan of the heretics, was a heresy and denial of God.

In 1484 Pope Innocent VIII urged the clergy of Europe to leave no stone unturned in the search for witches. He sent two Dominican monks to northern Germany as inquisitors. Two years later they issued a comprehensive manual, *Malleus Maleficarum* ("the witches' hammer"), to guide the witch hunts. This legal and theological document came to be regarded by Catholics and Protestants alike as a textbook on witchcraft. It described various signs by which witches could be detected, such as red spots or areas of insensitivity on the skin, supposedly made by the claw of the devil when touching the person to seal a pact. Those accused of witchcraft were to be tortured if they did not confess; those convicted and penitent were to be imprisoned for life; and those convicted and unrepentant were to be handed over to the law for execution. The manual specified that a person's sudden loss of reason was a symptom of demonic possession and that burning was the usual method of driving out the supposed demon.

Witch-hunting declined gradually in the seventeenth and eighteenth centuries. In Spain in 1610, the inquisitor Alonso Salazar y Frías concluded that most of the accusations in Logroño, Navarre, had been false. He ordained that accusations must be accompanied by independent evidence, that torture could not be used, and that the property of the convicted would not be confiscated. Thereafter accusations of witchcraft dropped sharply in Spain. In Sweden in 1649 Queen Christina ordered that all prisoners accused of witchcraft be freed except those clearly guilty of murder. In France witchcraft trials declined after an edict was issued by Louis XIV in 1682. The last execution of a witch was in Switzerland in 1782.

For some time the standard historical interpretation has been that all the mentally ill of the later Middle Ages were considered witches (Zilboorg & Henry, 1941). In their confessions the accused sometimes reported having had intercourse with the devil and having flown to sabbats, the secret meetings of their cults. These reports have been interpreted by contemporary writers as delusions or hallucinations and thus are taken to indicate that some witches were psychotic. Moreover, to identify people with the Devil's mark, an area of insensitivity to pain, professional witch prickers went from town to town sticking pins into

In the dunking test, if the woman did not drown, she was thought to be in league with the devil.

FOCUS BOX 1.1

The Salem Incident: Witchcraft or Poisoning?

In December 1691 eight girls who lived in or near Salem Village were afflicted with "distempers," which called for medical attention. Physicians, however, could find no cause for their disorderly speech, strange postures and gestures, and convulsive fits. One of the girls was the daughter of the minister, Samuel Parris, another his niece. A neighbor soon took it upon herself to have Parris's Barbados slave, Tituba, concoct a "witch cake" of rye meal and the urine of the afflicted and feed it to a dog to determine whether witchcraft was indicated. Shortly thereafter, in February 1692, the girls accused Tituba and two elderly women of witchcraft, and the three were taken into custody.

Accusations began to fly as well from other residents of the village. The jails of Salem, of surrounding towns, and even of faraway Boston filled with prisoners awaiting trial. By the end of September, nineteen people had been sent to the gallows, and one man had been pressed to death. The convictions were all obtained on the bases of spectral evidence—an apparition of the accused had appeared to the accuser—and the test of touch—an accuser's fit ceased after he or she was touched by the accused. The afflicted girls were present at the trials and often disturbed the proceedings with their violent fits, convulsions, and apparent hallucinations of specters

During the Salem witch trials, many women were accused of witchcraft. The afflictions of the accused may have been caused by ergot poisoning.

the bodies of the accused. The fact that some "witches" did not respond to the prickings has been considered evidence of their madness.

More careful analyses of the witch-hunts, however, reveal that although some accused witches were mentally disturbed, many more sane than insane people were tried. Confessions were typically obtained during brutal torture and at the suggestion of the torturers. Indeed, in England, where torture was not allowed, the confessions did not usually contain descriptions indicative of delusions or hallucinations. Similarly, insensitivity to pain has many causes, including organic dysfunctions. More important, there are documented cases of deliberate trickery. Often during pricking a needle was attached to a hollow shaft so that it did not actually puncture the skin, although to observers it appeared to be penetrating deeply (Schoeneman, 1977; Spanos, 1978).

An examination of the records from lunacy trials in Britain during the Middle Ages showed that at least by then witchcraft was not used as the explanation for abnormal behavior (Neugebauer, 1979). Beginning in the thirteenth century, these trials were held to determine a person's sanity. A judgment of insanity allowed and familiars. (Familiars are spirits, often in animal form, who are believed to act as servants to a witch.)

In January 1693 a superior court convened and received fifty new indictments for witchcraft that had been made by a grand jury. It tried twenty persons, acquitted seventeen, and condemned three, although they were never executed. In May 1693 Governor Phips ordered a general reprieve; about 150 suspected witches were released, ending the strange episode.

These events in Salem have often been presented as an illustration of how the mentally ill of the era were mistreated through the widespread belief that they were possessed, although the accused witches were for the most part persons of good reputation in the community. The episode is sometimes seen as an instance of mass hysteria; the witchcraft accusation, once made, mushroomed for some reason. Earlier accusations of witchcraft in Puritan communities of New England had never had such an outcome, however.

A different proposed explanation is that the accusers in Salem were suffering from ergot poisoning (Caporael, 1976). Ergot, a parasitic fungus, grows on cereal grains, mainly rye, and its development is fostered by warm, rainy growing seasons. Several of the alkaloids of ergot contain lysergic acid, from which LSD is synthesized. Ingestion of food made from flour contaminated with ergot can cause crawling sensations on the skin, tingling in the fingers, vertigo, headache, hallucinations, vomiting, diarrhea, and convulsions. The alkaloids of ergot can also induce delirium and mood changes, such as mania and depression.

Could ergot poisoning account for the events in question? First, the behavior of the initial accusers is indeed similar to the known effects of ergot poisoning. The girls did report having hallucinations; they also vomited, had convulsions, and said that they felt as though they were being choked and pricked with pins. Second, rye was a well-established crop in Salem, and there had been heavy rains in 1691, which would promote the growth of the fungus. Rye was usually harvested in August and threshed in the late autumn. The onset of the girls' strange behavior occurred at about the time they would be beginning to eat food made from the new grain. The accumulating accusations of witchcraft apparently came to an abrupt halt in the following autumn, when a new supply of grain, grown during a dry 1692, became available. After that time the afflictions of the girls and those of others in Salem were not mentioned in accounts of the period.

Why, then, did only some people feel that their bodies had been possessed? Caporael argues that the western portion of Salem Village, where the ground is lower and the meadows are swampy, would be the most likely source of contaminated grain. The pattern of residence of the young girls and of the other accusers fits this hypothesis; they were more likely to live in or to eat grain grown in the western fields. Most of the accused witches and their defenders lived in the eastern section of the village.

Caporael has presented a compelling set of arguments for her ergot-poisoning hypothesis, although direct proof of what happened three hundred years ago is, of course, hard to come by.

the Crown to become guardian of the lunatic's estate. The trials looked at the defendant's orientation, memory, intellect, daily life, and habits. Strange behavior was typically explained by physical illness or injury or some emotional shock, indicating a more enlightened view of mental disorders than previously thought. In all the cases examined by Neugebauer only *one* referred to demonological possession. Focus Box 1.1 presents in a new light the most famous episode of witchcraft in the United States, the Salem incident.

Development of Asylums During the Renaissance

In Europe, the mentally ill began to be separated from society in earnest in the fifteenth and sixteenth centuries. **Asylums**, refuges established for the confinement and care of the mentally ill, took in a mixed lot of disturbed people and beggars. These institutions had no specific regimen for their inmates other than to get them to work. But during the same period hospitals geared more specifically for

asylums Refuges established in western Europe in the fifteenth century to confine and care for the mentally ill; the forerunners of the mental hospital.

A tour of St. Mary's of Bethlehem (Bedlam) provides amusement for these two upper-class women in Hogarth's eighteenth-century painting.

the mentally ill also appeared. The Priory of St. Mary of Bethlehem was founded in 1243, and in 1547 Henry VIII handed it over to the city of London, thereafter to be a hospital solely for the mentally ill. The conditions in Bethlehem were deplorable. Over the years the word *bedlam*, a contraction and popular name for this hospital, became a descriptive term for a scene of wild uproar and confusion. Bethlehem eventually became one of London's great tourist attractions. Even as late as the nineteenth century, viewing the violent patients and their antics was considered entertainment, and tickets of admission to Bedlam were sold.

The Reform Movement and Moral Treatment in Europe and the United States

In 1793, while the French Revolution raged, Philippe Pinel was put in charge of a large asylum in Paris known as La Bicêtre.

> [The patients were] shackled to the walls of their cells, by iron collars which held them flat against the wall and permitted little movement. . . . They could not lie down at night, as a rule. . . . Oftentimes there was a hoop of iron around the waist of the patient and in addition . . . chains on both the hands and the feet. . . . These chains [were] sufficiently long so that the patient could feed himself out of a bowl, the food usually being a mushy gruel—bread soaked in a weak soup. Since little was known about dietetics, [no attention] was paid to the type of diet given the patients. They were presumed to be animals . . . and not to care whether the food was good or bad. (Selling, 1940, p. 54)

Pinel (1745–1826) is considered a primary figure in the movement for humanitarian treatment of the mentally disordered. He was allowed to remove the chains of the people imprisoned in La Bicêtre and to treat them as sick human beings rather than as beasts. Many who had been completely unmanageable became calm. Formerly considered dangerous, they strolled through the hospital and grounds with no inclination to create disturbances or to harm anyone. Light and airy rooms replaced their dungeons. Some who had been incarcerated for years were restored to health and were eventually discharged from the hospital.

Freeing the patients of their restraints was not the only humanitarian reform

Pinel's freeing the patients at La Bicêtre is the event often considered to mark the beginning of more humanitarian treatment of the insane.

advocated by Pinel. Consistent with the egalitarianism of the new French Republic, he believed that mental patients were essentially normal people who should be approached with compassion and understanding and treated with dignity as individuals. Their reason supposedly having left them because of severe personal and social problems, it might be restored to them through comforting counsel and purposeful activity.

For all the good Pinel did for the mentally ill, he was not completely enlightened and egalitarian. The more humanitarian treatment he reserved for the upper classes; patients of the lower classes were still subjected to terror and coercion as a means of control (Szasz, 1974).

The first mental hospital in the United States was founded in Williamsburg, Virginia, in 1773. Here as well, inclusion of abnormal behavior within the domain of hospitals and medicine did not guarantee that more humane and effective treatment would be offered. Benjamin Rush (1745–1813), who began practicing medicine in Philadelphia in 1769, is considered the father of American psychiatry. He believed that mental disorder was caused by an excess of blood in the brain. Consequently, his favored treatment was to draw great quantities of blood, as much as six quarts over a period of a few months. Little wonder that patients so treated became less agitated—anyone would be weak from the loss of that much blood (Farina, 1976)! Rush entertained another hypothesis, that many "lunatics" could be cured by frightening them. In one recommended procedure the physician was to convince the patient of her or his impending death. A New England physician of the nineteenth century implemented this prescription in an ingenious manner. "On his premises stood a tank of water, into which a patient, packed into a coffin-like box pierced with holes, was lowered. . . . He was kept under water until the bubbles of air ceased to rise, after which he was taken out, rubbed, and revived—if he had not already passed beyond reviving!" (Deutsch, 1949, p. 82).

The sympathetic and attentive treatment introduced by Pinel was adopted by several small, private American hospitals. In accordance with this approach, which became known as **moral treatment**, patients had close contact with attendants, who talked and read to them and encouraged them to purposeful activity. Residents led lives as normal as possible and in general took responsibility for themselves as much as possible.

In 1844 superintendents of some of these hospitals formed an organization

moral treatment A therapeutic regimen, introduced by Philippe Pinel during the French Revolution, whereby mental patients were released from their restraints and treated with compassion and dignity.

Dorothea Dix, a nineteenth century advocate of social reform, promoted the development of institutions to provide specialized care for the mentally ill.

called the Association of Medical Superintendents of American Institutions for the Insane, a forerunner of today's American Psychiatric Association, to lobby politicians for funding of an expansion of the apparently successful moral treatment approach (A. B. Johnson, 1990). Their efforts dovetailed with those of their contemporary, the social reformer Dorothea Dix (1802–87). Outraged by the degrading conditions of care for the mentally ill in prisons and poorhouses, she advocated the creation of specialized, publicly funded institutions for the treatment of mentally ill people.

Moral treatment had to be abandoned in the second half of the nineteenth century. The staffs of the large, public mental hospitals built to take in the many patients for whom the private ones had no room could not provide the individual attention mandated by the moral treatment approach (Bockhoven, 1963). Moreover, extension to public facilities meant that moral treatment had to serve a less select population—immigrants who did not speak English, demented elderly patients, and chronic alcoholics, among other challenging groups—and the treatment was not readily or successfully adapted to serve such patients (A. B. Johnson, 1990).

To Recap

Many ancient civilizations considered abnormal behavior a reflection of the displeasure of the gods or possession by demons. In the fifth century B.C. Hippocrates introduced a medical perspective on abnormality, attributing mental disorders to imbalance among bodily fluids and prescribing such treatments as changes in diet. The details of this approach have not survived, but the overall idea that abnormality might have something to do with the body foreshadowed later trends. The Middle Ages brought a return to demonology, including the labeling of some of the mentally ill as witches. A more humanitarian view began in Europe and then spread to the United States in the late eighteenth and in the nineteenth centuries. According to this view, typified by Pinel's moral treatment approach, severe personal and social problems led otherwise normal people to become irrational, and compassionate, attentive treatment and purposeful activity could restore health. It proved impossible, however, to transport the moral treatment approach to the large mental hospitals built in the second half of the nineteenth century in the hope of extending humane care for the mentally ill to more difficult cases.

Foundations of Contemporary Concepts of Abnormal Behavior

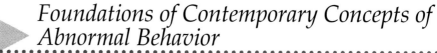

A Return to Somatogenesis

After the fall of Greco-Roman civilization, the writings of Galen were the standard source of information about both physical and mental illness. Not until the Middle Ages did new facts begin to emerge. One development that fostered progress was the discovery by Vesalius (1514–64) that Galen's presentation of human anatomy was incorrect. Galen had presumed that human physiology mirrored that of the apes he had studied. A more scientific approach to abnormal behavior received another boost from the efforts of the famous English physician Thomas Sydenham (1624–89). Sydenham advocated an empirical approach to classification and diagnosis that subsequently influenced those interested in mental disorders.

One of these was a German physician, Wilhelm Griesinger, who insisted that any diagnosis of mental disorder specify a physiological cause, a clear return to the somatogenic views first developed by Hippocrates. His follower Emil Kraepelin (1856–1926) wrote a textbook of psychiatry first published in 1883 and provided a classification system to help establish the organic nature of mental illnesses. Kraepelin saw in mental disorders a tendency for a certain group of symptoms, called a **syndrome,** to appear together regularly enough to be regarded as having an underlying physical cause, much as a particular medical disease and its syndrome may be attributed to a physiological dysfunction. He regarded each mental illness as distinct from all others, having its own cause, symptoms, course, and outcome. Even though cures had not been worked out, at least the course of the disease could be predicted. Kraepelin proposed two major groups of severe mental diseases: dementia praecox, an early term for schizophrenia, and manic-depressive psychosis. He believed that a chemical imbalance caused schizophrenia and that an irregularity in metabolism caused manic-depressive psychosis. Kraepelin's scheme for classifying these and other mental illnesses became the basis for the present diagnostic categories, which will be described more fully in Chapter 4.

> **syndrome** A group of *symptoms* that tend to occur together in a particular disease.

Much was learned about the nervous system in the second half of the nineteenth century. Perhaps the most striking medical success was the discovery of the full nature and origin of syphilis, a venereal disease that had been recognized for several centuries. Since 1798 it had been known that a number of mental patients manifested a syndrome characterized by a steady deterioration of both physical and mental abilities and that these patients suffered multiple impairments, including delusions of grandeur and progressive paralysis. Soon after these symptoms were recognized, people realized that these patients never recovered. In 1825 this deterioration in mental and physical health was designated a disease, **general paresis.** Although in 1857 it was established that some patients with paresis had earlier had syphilis, there remained many competing theories of the cause of paresis. For example, in attempting to account for the high rate of the disorder among sailors, some supposed that seawater might be the cause.

> **general paresis** Infection of the central nervous system by a spirochete which destroys brain tissue; marked by eye disturbances, tremors, and disordered speech as well as severe intellectual deterioration and *psychotic* symptoms.

Then in the 1860s and 1870s Louis Pasteur established the **germ theory** of disease, the view that disease is caused by infection of the body by minute organisms. It then became possible to demonstrate the relation between syphilis and general paresis. In 1897 Richard von Krafft-Ebing inoculated paretic patients with matter from syphilitic sores. The patients did not develop syphilis, indicating that they had been infected earlier. Finally, in 1905, the specific microorganism that causes syphilis was discovered. A causal link had been established between infection, destruction of certain areas of the brain, and a form of psychopathology. If one type of psychopathology had a biological cause, so could others. Somatogenesis gained credibility, and the search for more biological causes was off and running.

> **germ theory (of disease)** The general view in medicine that disease is caused by infection of the body by minute organisms and viruses.

Advances in Psychogenesis

The search for somatogenic causes dominated psychiatry until well into the twentieth century, no doubt partly because of the stunning discoveries made about general paresis. But in other parts of western Europe, in the late eighteenth and throughout the nineteenth century, mental illnesses were attributed to psychological malfunctions. For reasons not entirely clear to us even today, many people in western Europe were at that time subject to hysterical states: they suffered from physical incapacities, such as blindness or paralysis, that did not have a biological cause (see p. 179).

Various psychogenic explanations for these occurrences were developed. For example, Franz Anton Mesmer (1734–1815), an Austrian physician, believed that hysterical disorders were caused by a particular distribution of a universal magnetic fluid in the body. Moreover, he felt that one person could influence the fluid of another to bring about a change in the other's behavior. He conducted meetings, cloaked in mystery and mysticism, during which afflicted

The French psychiatrist Jean Charcot lectures on hysteria in this famous painting. Charcot was an important figure in reviving interest in psychogenesis.

Josef Breuer, the Austrian physician and physiologist, collaborated with Freud in the early development of psychoanalysis. He treated Anna O. by the cathartic method he originated.

patients sat around a covered tub, with iron rods protruding through the cover from bottles of various chemicals beneath. Mesmer, clothed in rather outlandish garments, would enter the room, take various rods from the tub, and touch afflicted parts of his patients' bodies. The rods were believed to transmit animal magnetism and adjust the distribution of the universal magnetic fluid, thereby curing the patients. Whatever we may think of what seems today to be a questionable theoretical explanation and procedure, Mesmer apparently helped many people overcome their hysterical problems. He is generally considered one of the earlier practitioners of modern-day hypnosis, which is discussed in more detail in Chapter 7 (p. 173). The word *mesmerize* is the older term for *hypnotize.*

Although Mesmer was regarded as a quack by his contemporaries, the study of hypnosis gradually became respectable. A great Parisian neurologist, Jean Martin Charcot (1825–93), also studied hysterical states, not only anesthesia and paralysis, but blindness, deafness, convulsive attacks, and gaps in memory brought about by hysteria. Charcot initially advocated a somatogenic point of view. One day, however, some of his enterprising students hypnotized a normal woman and suggested to her certain hysterical symptoms. Charcot was deceived into believing that she was an actual hysterical patient. When the students showed him how readily they could remove the symptoms by waking the woman, Charcot changed his mind about hysteria and became interested in nonbiological interpretations of these very puzzling phenomena.

In Vienna, toward the end of the century, a physician named Josef Breuer (1842–1925) treated a young woman who had become bedridden with a number of hysterical symptoms. Her legs and right arm and side were paralyzed, her sight and hearing were impaired, and she often had difficulty speaking. She also sometimes entered a dreamlike state, or "absence," during which she mumbled to herself, seemingly preoccupied with troubling thoughts. During one treatment session Breuer hypnotized Anna O. and repeated some of her mumbled words. He succeeded in getting her to talk more freely and ultimately with considerable emotion about some very upsetting past events. On awakening from these hypnotic sessions, she frequently felt much better.

With Anna O. and other hysterical patients Breuer found that relief of symptoms seemed to last longer if under hypnosis they were able to recall the precipitating event for the symptom and if, furthermore, their original emotion was expressed. Reliving the upsetting event and releasing the emotional tension produced by previously forgotten thoughts about it was called catharsis. Breuer's method became known as the **cathartic method**. In 1895 one of his colleagues joined him in the publication of *Studies in Hysteria*, a milestone in abnormal psychology. In the next chapter we will continue to examine this early therapy, particularly as it relates to the thinking of Breuer's collaborator, Sigmund Freud.

To Recap

The foundations of some of the main contemporary perspectives on abnormal psychology are rooted in the late nineteenth century. Kraepelin noted that certain symptoms occurred together often enough to suspect that they represented syndromes with underlying physical causes. His classification system for these syndromes, coupled with the success of Pasteur's germ theory in general and the identification of a biological cause of general paresis in particular, fostered the ongoing search for biological causes of mental disorders. The psychogenic point of view also evolved in the nineteenth century, partly through the study of hysterical states. Several variations of hypnosis were useful in showing that the power of suggestion could influence physical disabilities that had developed without a biological cause. Breuer laid the groundwork for later approaches to psychotherapy by observing that the effectiveness of hypnosis was increased if patients expressed the emotions experienced in reaction to the events that had upset them originally.

cathartic method A therapeutic procedure introduced by Breuer and developed further by Freud in the late nineteenth century whereby a patient recalls and relives an earlier emotional catastrophe and reexperiences the tension and unhappiness, with the goal of relieving emotional suffering.

The Research Methods of Abnormal Psychology

Today abnormal psychology is an area of scientific study. Although, as we shall see in the next two chapters, the women and men who work as researchers and therapists may take different approaches, all share a commitment to finding dependable answers to questions about abnormal behavior. As with any science, the goal is to use observation of abnormal behavior systematically to acquire and evaluate information and develop general theories that explain the information. These observations should be reproducible (not flukes), and the explanations should be testable (not taken on faith alone).

All scientific research entails the collection of data. Sometimes research remains at a purely descriptive level. In the field of abnormal psychology there is a large descriptive literature concerning the typical symptoms of people who have been diagnosed as having particular disorders. These symptoms can be related to other characteristics, such as gender or social class: for example, attention-deficit/hyperactivity disorder is more common in boys than in girls. This information, too, is descriptive, in this case describing the nature of the relation between two or more characteristics. It says nothing about what causes the relation—why, for instance, boys are more likely to be hyperactive and have difficulty sustaining attention. Other studies are aimed at identifying such causes.

In this section we describe the most commonly used research methods in the study of abnormal behavior: the case study; epidemiological research; the correlational method; and the experiment. The methods vary in the degree to which they permit the collection of adequate descriptive data and the extent to which they produce results that tell us something about the causes of mental disorders.

The Case Study

The most familiar method of observing others is to study them one at a time and record detailed information about them. A clinician prepares a **case study** by collecting historical and biographical information on a single individual, often including experiences in therapy. A comprehensive case study covers family

case study The collection of historical or biographical information on a single individual, often including experiences in therapy.

history and background, medical history, educational background, jobs held, marital history, and details concerning development, adjustment, personality, life course, and current situation. The discussion of Ernest with which this chapter began is a case study.

Case studies provide a detailed picture of one person's mental disorder. Their detail makes them a rich source of **hypotheses**, tentative explanations of behavior that have yet to be proven or disproven (Lazarus & Davison, 1971). Through exposure to the life histories of a great number of patients, clinicians gain experience in understanding and interpreting them. Eventually clinicians may notice similarities of circumstances and outcomes and formulate important hypotheses that would not likely have been uncovered in a more controlled investigation. For example, in his clinical work with disturbed children, Leo Kanner (1943) noticed that some of them showed a similar constellation of symptoms, including failure to develop language and extreme isolation from other people. He therefore proposed the existence of a new diagnosis—infantile autism—which was subsequently confirmed by larger scale research (see Chapter 14).

However, case studies are very limited and cannot provide compelling proof of the *causes* of behavior. Let us consider a clinician who has developed a new treatment for depression, tries it out on a client, and observes that the depression lifts after six weeks of the therapy. Although it would be tempting to conclude that the therapy worked, such a conclusion cannot be drawn because several other factors could also have produced the change. A stressful situation in the patient's life may have resolved itself, or perhaps (and there is evidence for this) episodes of depression are naturally time limited. Thus, several plausible alternative explanations or rival hypotheses could account for the clinical improvement. The data yielded by the case study do not allow us to determine the true cause of the change. However, if a patient, such as Breuer's Anna O., seems to improve as a result of re-experiencing particularly emotional life events, it might be possible to develop a hypothesis—or several hypotheses—about why this occurred.

Case histories can also provide especially telling instances that *negate* an assumed universal relationship or law. Consider, for example, the proposition that episodes of depression are *always* preceded by an increase in life stress. Finding even a single case in which this is not true would disprove the theory and, at the least, force it to be changed to assert that only *some* episodes of depression are triggered by stress.

hypothesis What the investigator believes will happen in a scientific investigation if certain conditions are met or particular variables are manipulated.

In some epidemiological research, interviewers go to homes in a community to determine the rates of different disorders.

epidemiology The study of the frequency and distribution of illness in a population.

prevalence In *epidemiological* studies of a disorder, the percentage of a population that has it at a given time.

incidence In *epidemiological* studies of a particular disorder, the rate at which new cases occur in a given period of time.

risk factors Conditions or variables that, if present, increase the likelihood of developing a disorder.

Epidemiological Research

Epidemiological research lies at the opposite end of the spectrum from the case study. While the case study examines a mental disorder in depth as it occurs in one individual, **epidemiology** is the study of the frequency and distribution of a disorder in an entire population. In epidemiological research, data are gathered about the rates of disorder and the factors that may influence them in a large sample or population. This research looks at the **prevalence** of mental disorders, the proportion of a population that has a particular disorder at a given point or period of time. For example, epidemiological research gives us information about how prevalent depression is. It also examines **incidence**, the number of new cases of a disorder that occur in some period, usually a year, and any **risk factors**, or the conditions or variables that, if present, increase the likelihood of developing the disorder. For example, epidemiological research might uncover a rise in the incidence of stress-related disorders (Chapter 8) and then set about trying to find any common risk factors (perhaps unemployment) contributing to this rise.

In psychopathology, knowledge of rates of various diagnoses is important for planning health care facilities. Such information was collected in a significant

Table 1.1 ▶ *Lifetime Prevalence of Several DSM-III Diagnoses*

	Percentage of Sample		
Diagnosis	*New Haven*	*Baltimore*	*St. Louis*
Alcohol abuse/dependence	11.5	13.7	15.7
Schizophrenia	1.9	1.6	1.0
Manic episode	1.1	0.6	1.1
Major depressive episode	6.7	3.7	5.5
Phobia	7.8	23.3	9.4
Panic disorder	1.4	1.4	1.5
Obsessive-compulsive	2.6	3.0	1.9
Somatization	0.1	0.1	0.1
Anorexia	0.0	0.1	0.1
Antisocial personality	2.1	2.6	3.3

Source: After Myers et al. (1984).

large-scale study, The Epidemiological Catchment Area (ECA) study, which was conducted in three cities—Baltimore, St. Louis, and New Haven (Myers et al., 1984). In each city a careful plan was developed for sampling residents and interviewing them using an interview specially constructed to formulate diagnoses. More than three thousand people were interviewed at each site. Some data from the ECA study are displayed in Table 1.1. The table presents what are called **lifetime prevalence rates**, the proportion of the sample that had ever experienced a disorder up to the time of the interview. We will make use of the data from the ECA study and those of a follow-up project, The National Comorbidity Survey (Kessler et al., 1994), throughout this book.

lifetime prevalence rates The proportion of a sample that has ever had a disorder.

Epidemiological research can also contribute to understanding the causes of illness. During an outbreak of cholera in London, John Snow was able to determine how the disease had spread and, finally, how to stop it using epidemiological information. He examined the cases and learned that most victims had drunk water from one source, the Broad Street pump. He then hypothesized that cholera was transmitted by contaminated water. He investigated further and showed that rates of the disease were higher in London than in upstream communities, where the water was cleaner. Numerous contemporary examples also attest to the importance of epidemiological research in understanding disease. As we will see in Chapter 8, the various risk factors for heart disease (e.g., smoking, high cholesterol) were discovered in large-scale studies comparing rates of disease in persons with and without the risk factor.

The Correlational Method

The **correlational method** establishes whether there is a relation between or among two or more variables. Numerous examples can be drawn from everyday life. Income correlates positively with the number of luxuries purchased: the higher the income, the more luxuries purchased. Height tends to be positively correlated with weight: taller people are usually heavier.

correlational method Research that establishes whether two or more variables are related.

The correlational method is often employed in epidemiological research as well as in other studies that use smaller samples. Correlational studies address questions of the form "Are variable X and variable Y associated in some way so that they vary together (co-relate)?" In other words, questions are asked concerning relationships; for example, "Are scores obtained on college examinations related to anxiety?"

The correlational method is widely used in abnormal psychology. Whenever we compare people given one diagnosis with those given another or with normal people, the study is correlational. For example, normal people and people with an anxiety disorder may be compared to see how much stress each group experienced recently.

The correlational method, although common, has an important disadvantage. It does *not* allow us to determine cause–effect relationships because of two major problems of interpretation, the directionality problem and the third-variable problem. The **directionality problem** is that a correlation between two variables tells us that they are related or tend to co-vary with each other, but we do not really know which is cause and which effect. For example, correlations have been found between the diagnosis of schizophrenia and social class; lower-class people are more frequently diagnosed as schizophrenic than are middle- and upper-class people. One possible explanation is that the stresses of living in the lower social classes produce schizophrenic behavior. But a second and perhaps equally plausible hypothesis has been advanced: it may be that the disorganized behavior patterns of schizophrenic individuals cause them to lose their jobs and thus to become impoverished.

As for the **third-variable problem**, it may be that neither of the two variables studied in a correlation produces the other. Rather, some other variable or process may be responsible for the correlation. In psychopathology research there are numerous examples of third variables. For instance, biochemical differences between schizophrenics and normals have frequently been reported. These differences could reflect different diets or the fact that the patients are taking medication for their condition—the differences may not therefore reveal anything informative about the nature of schizophrenia.

directionality problem A difficulty in the *correlational method* of research whereby it is known that two variables are related, but it is unclear which is causing the other.

third-variable problem The difficulty in the *correlational method* of research whereby the relationship between two variables may be attributable to a third factor.

The Experiment

The factors causing the associations revealed by correlational research cannot be determined with absolute certainty. As we have seen, correlation does not imply causation. The **experiment** is generally considered to be our most powerful tool for determining causal relations between events. As an introduction to the basic components of experimental research, let us consider the major aspects of the design and results of a study of how expressing emotions about past traumatic events is related to health (Pennebaker, Kiecolt-Glaser, & Glaser, 1988). Fifty undergraduates participated in a six-week study, one part of which entailed coming to a laboratory for four consecutive days. Half the subjects were required, on each of the four days, to write a short essay about a past traumatic event. They were instructed as follows:

experiment The most powerful research technique for determining causal relationships, requiring the manipulation of an *independent variable*, the measurement of a *dependent variable*, and the *random assignment* of subjects to the several different conditions being investigated.

> During each of the four writing days, I want you to write about the most traumatic and upsetting experiences of your entire life. You can write on different topics each day or on the same topic for all four days. The important thing is that you write about your deepest thoughts and feelings. Ideally, whatever you write about should deal with an event or experience that you have not talked with others about in detail.

The remaining students also came to the laboratory each day, but wrote essays describing such things as their daily activities, a recent social event, the shoes they were wearing, and their plans for the rest of the day. Information about how often the participating undergraduates used the university health center was available both for the fifteen-week period before the study began and for the six weeks after it began. These data are shown in Figure 1.2. As the figure shows, members of the two groups had visited the health center about equally prior to the experiment. After writing the essays, however, the number of visits declined

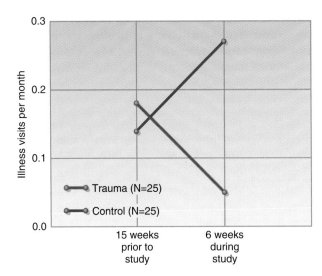

Figure 1.2 *Health center illness visits for the periods before and during the experiment. After Pennebaker et al. (1988).*

for students who wrote about traumas and increased for the remaining students. (This increase may have been due to seasonal variation in rates of visits to the health center. The second measure of number of visits was taken in February, just before midterm exams.) From these data the investigators concluded that expressing emotions has a beneficial effect on health.

Basic Elements of Experimental Design

The researcher typically begins with an **experimental hypothesis**, what he or she assumes will happen when a particular variable is manipulated. In the student-health experiment just described, Pennebaker and his colleagues hypothesized that expressing emotion about a past event would improve health. Then the investigator chooses an **independent variable**, some factor that will be under the control of the experimenter. In the student-health experiment some students wrote about past traumatic events and others about mundane happenings.

The researcher also arranges for the measurement of a **dependent variable**, which is expected to depend on or vary with manipulations of the independent variable. The dependent variable in this study was the number of visits to the health center. When differences between groups are found to be a function of variations in the independent variable, the researcher is said to have produced an **experimental effect**.

An important feature of any experimental design is the inclusion of at least one **control group** which does not receive the experimental treatment (the independent variable). A control group is necessary if the effects in an experiment are to be attributed to the manipulation of the independent variable. In this study, the data from the control group provided a standard against which the effects of expressing emotion could be compared. In the Pennebaker et al. study the control group wrote about mundane events. Because it is important to ensure that experimental and control subjects do not differ from one another before the introduction of the independent variable, they are put in groups according to **random assignment**, a procedure that ensures that each subject has the same chance as any other subject to be assigned to the experimental or to the control group.

Even with a control group and random assignment, experiments are not always conclusive. We do not always know that results would be similar, for instance, in settings outside the experimenter's control. One concern is that merely knowing that one is a subject in a psychological experiment often alters behavior, and thus results produced in the laboratory may not be produced in "real life."

experimental hypothesis   What the investigator believes will happen in a scientific investigation if particular variables are manipulated.

independent variable   In a psychological *experiment*, the factor, experience, or treatment that is under the control of the experimenter and that is expected to have an effect on the subjects as assessed by changes in the *dependent variable*.

dependent variable   In a psychological *experiment*, the behavior that is measured and expected to change with manipulation of the *independent variable*.

experimental effect   A difference between groups experiencing different manipulations of the *independent variable*.

control group   The subjects in an *experiment* who form a baseline against which the effects of the manipulation of the experimental group can be evaluated.

random assignment   A method of assigning subjects to groups in an *experiment* that gives each subject an equal chance of being in each group.

In the 1950s Harry Harlow examined the effects of early separation from the mother on infant monkeys. This now famous experiment is analogue research. Harlow found that even a cloth surrogate mother is better than isolation for preventing subsequent emotional distress and depression.

analogue experiment An experimental study of a phenomenon different from but related to the actual interests of the investigator.

Researchers must be continually alert to the extent to which they claim generalization for findings, for there is no entirely adequate way of dealing with this issue. The best that can be done is to perform similar studies in new settings with new participants so that the limitations, or the generality, of a finding can be determined.

Analogue Experiments

The experiment is judged to be the most telling way to determine cause–effect relationships. The effectiveness of treatments for psychopathology is usually evaluated by the experimental method, for it has proved a powerful tool for determining whether a therapy reduces suffering. However, it is seldom used by those seeking the causes of abnormal behavior. There is a good reason for this. Suppose that a researcher has hypothesized that a child's emotionally charged, overdependent relationship with his or her mother causes schizophrenia. An experimental test of this hypothesis would require assigning infants randomly to either of two groups of mothers! The mothers in one group would undergo an extensive training program to ensure that they would be able to create a highly emotional atmosphere and foster overdependence in children. The mothers in the second group would be trained not to create such a relationship with the children under their care. The researcher would then wait until the subjects in each group reached adulthood and determine how many of them had become schizophrenic. Consider the ethics of such an experiment. Would the potential scientific gain of proving that an overdependent relationship with a person's mother brings on schizophrenia outweigh the suffering that would surely be imposed on some of the participants? In almost any person's view it would not.

In an effort to take advantage of the power of the experimental method, research on the causes of abnormal behavior has sometimes taken the format of an **analogue experiment**. Investigators attempt to bring a *related* phenomenon, that is, an analogue, into the laboratory for more intensive study. Some of the animal experiments we examine in later chapters are analogue in nature, with their results generalized to human beings. It is important to keep in mind that we are arguing by analogy when, for example, we attempt to relate stress reactions of white rats to anxiety in people.

To Recap

Scientific research on abnormal behavior involves the collection of data in order to improve description, explanation, and treatment of mental disorders. Researchers use various methods to achieve these goals. Case studies are useful for disconfirming supposedly universal laws or for suggesting hypotheses that can be tested later through controlled research. Epidemiological research gathers information about the prevalence of disorders and about risk factors that increase the probability of a disorder. Correlational studies allow us to determine the extent to which two or more variables correlate or co-vary, and are frequently employed in abnormal psychology. In most cases, conclusions drawn from correlational studies cannot be legitimately interpreted in cause–effect terms, however, because either variable may be causing the other, or a third may be causing them both to co-vary. The experiment is the best method for determining if one variable *causes* a particular effect—and it is not always conclusive either. Experiments entail the manipulation of independent variables and the careful measurement of their effects on dependent variables. Subjects are generally assigned to one of at least two groups: an experimental group, which experiences the manipulation of the independent variable, and a control group, which does not. If subjects are randomly assigned and differences between the experimental and control groups are observed on the dependent variable, we can conclude that the manipulation of the independent variable does have an effect.

> ## APPLYING CRITICAL THINKING SKILLS

RESEARCH METHODS

As we have seen, the history of attempts to understand abnormality reveals disagreements about where the answers will be found—in the bodily fluids, in the brain, in the soul?—and psychopathologists have developed and evaluated a number of ways to try to reduce these uncertainties and increase knowledge. The core purpose of these techniques and methods of investigation is to assist **critical thinking**, a habit you can apply in daily life and as a student of abnormal psychology regardless of whether you ever treat a patient or publish the results of a formal research project. Different educators define critical thinking in a variety of ways (R. H. Johnson, 1992), but in general they emphasize a thought process that involves:

> questioning assumptions
> exploring alternative conclusions
> being routinely skeptical of claims about what is true that are based on personal authority, anecdotes, and the like (Brookfield, 1987).

critical thinking　A habit of thinking involving questioning assumptions, evaluating the soundness of evidence for claims people make, and exploring alternative hypotheses.

Thinking critically about the validity of what you hear or read is very important in everyday life, as we are all bombarded daily by the claims of politicians, teachers, authors, journalists, advertisers, and peers, often with conflicting messages about what to do or what to believe. Fostering critical thinking has become a major concern of educators (Brookfield, 1987), in part because it is widely recognized that there is simply too much information for any of us to be expert in all fields. Furthermore, some of what is presented as fact rests on flimsy data or on data subject to a wide variety of interpretations. Critical thinking skills can help us be better consumers of information in abnormal psychology as well as in other areas by enabling us to better evaluate new claims we come across in books (including this one), newspaper articles, or elsewhere.

To illustrate the process of critical thinking, and particularly the crucial habit of considering alternative explanations and using evidence to evaluate them, we will from time to time throughout this book select a particular argument or piece of research to subject to a critical analysis. This analysis will take the form of considering the answers to a series of questions. We begin with a relatively easy hypothetical example (adapted from Neale & Liebert, 1986), which illustrates the limitations of correlational studies and shows how critical thinking helps scientists and the rest of us avoid jumping to faulty conclusions.

Suppose the newspaper reports a "very high" positive correlation between the number of churches in a city and the number of crimes committed in the city. In other words, the more churches within a city, the more crimes are committed in that city.

> *What conclusion does the evidence seem to support?* On the face of it, it seems alarming that the number of churches and the number of crimes are positively correlated. Perhaps religion fosters crime, and religious influences on values and education in our schools need to be seriously reconsidered.

> *What other interpretations are plausible?* Perhaps as criminals are overcome with remorse at their acts, they seek forgiveness and peace through organized spirituality. More likely, perhaps neither crime nor religion causes the other. The correlation of the two may instead be driven by a third variable, such as population. That is, bigger cities tend to have more churches and bigger cities tend to have more crime (and more banks, more stores, etc.) than smaller cities, but this does not mean that the number of churches and the number of crimes were themselves causally related.

> *What other information would help choose among the alternative interpretations?* Sorting out causal from noncausal relations might best be

accomplished by conducting experiments, but that is unrealistic in this case. No one would be able or willing to randomly assign a given number of churches or a given number of crimes to particular cities to see if one causes the other. A next-best strategy would be to identify pairs of cities of about the same size that nevertheless vary in the number of churches. If churches cause crime, the city in each pair with more churches will have more crime. If the third variable of population is the real explanation for what is going on, then we should see no systematic relation; in some pairs the high-church city will have more crime, and in others the low-church city will have more crime.

As you read arguments or descriptions of the results of studies in the chapters to follow, you may find it helpful to your understanding of the material to challenge yourself with questions like those just discussed. This will give you practice in the art of critical thinking, which is more subtle than it might first appear. Asking yourself the second question (What other interpretations . . . ?) helps you avoid being a passive, mindless receptacle of others' possibly unfounded opinions. Equally important, though, the third question (What other information . . . ?) helps you avoid the opposite extreme of being nihilistic (". . . you could lay a thousand psychologists end to end and never reach a conclusion") because it forces you to think in terms of *testable* interpretations of the evidence. Untestable, vague, alternative interpretations ("maybe this study was bogus; they're always coming up with new things that cause cancer") are easy to think up, but do not tend to promote advances in understanding.

Visual Summary for Chapter 1:

Historical and Scientific Considerations

What is abnormal behavior?

It is statistically infrequent (high-jumping 7 feet does not count).
The infrequent behavior should also have one or more of these properties:
•*Unexpected* •*Violates Norms* •*Distressing* •*Disabling*

What are the mental health professions?

Title	Degree	Training and Special Skills
Clinical psychologist	Ph.D. or Psy.D.	Graduate school and supervised postdoctoral work. General psychology, research, psychotherapy, assessment.
Psychiatrist	M.D.	Medical school and residency. Can prescribe drugs to treat mental disorders.
Psychoanalyst	Various	Extensive clinical training in psychoanalysis and their own personal analysis. A specialized form of therapy developed by Sigmund Freud.
Psychiatric Social Worker	M.S.W.	Psychotherapy techniques.
Counseling Psychologist	M.A. or Ph.D.	Psychotherapy and counseling techniques.

A Timeline of Psychopathology

Demonology	Hippocrates introduces somatogenesis	Demonology returns; witch-hunts	Asylums used to separate the insane	Pinel introduces humanitarian treatment of the insane	Moral treatment tried in small, private American hospitals
Ancient	5th century B.C.	400–1500 A.D.	15th century	1793	mid 19th century

Research methods in abnormal psychology:

Method	Features	Strengths	Limitations
Case study	Detailed description of individual patient.	Suggests new hypotheses. Can disprove "universal" laws.	Not enough control to draw strong conclusions.
Epidemiology	Analyzes rates of disorder in large, representative samples of whole populations. May provide information on cultural, gender, and racial differences.	Identifies those most needing mental health services, and extent of needs. Provides clues to causes of disorders.	Usually not conclusive as to causes of disorder. Need to study large samples usually limits search for correlates to demographics.
Correlational method	Two or more variables studied to see if they co-vary in a positive or negative relationship.	Can study any suspected causes.	Describes the relationship between variables, not causes, though it may suggest them.
Experiment	Independent variable manipulated and effect on dependent variable measured. Results compared against those of a control group.	Can infer which is cause and which is effect, within the study, with confidence.	No guarantee that same cause–effect process operates outside the context of experiment.

Moral treatment abandoned by large state hospitals	Mesmer, Charcot, Breuer, Freud and others show promising results with hypnosis and cathartic method, advancing psychogenic perspective on mental disorders	Kraepelin publishes classification scheme for mental disorders	Specific microorganism causing syphilis and thereby general paresis identified, encouraging search for biological causes
late 19th century	late 19th century	1883	1905

Chapter 2

Psychodynamic, Humanistic/ Existential, and Biological Perspectives

When the *Viking 1* and *Viking 2* landed on Mars and began to look for life, scientists repeatedly cautioned against concluding that there was no life on Mars just because instruments failed to detect any. These scientists realized they were in a bind. Life on another planet can be looked for only with the instruments they themselves have developed, and these devices are limited not only by the technology available, but also by scientists' preconceptions. The tests run on Mars made assumptions about the nature of living matter that may not match what has evolved there. In a similar way, our search for the causes of and effective treatments for mental disorders is and has been limited by the means currently available as well as by our preconceptions regarding abnormal behavior.

Subjectivity in Science: The Role of Perspectives

We believe that the informed use of the research methods and critical thinking habits introduced in Chapter 1 is the best way to make progress in learning to understand, treat, and prevent psychological disorders. Still, it is important to appreciate that, even with these methods, science is not a completely objective enterprise. Scientific observation is a human, fallible endeavor. Scientists can design only instruments to make observations about which they have some initial idea. They realize (though it is easy to forget at times) that certain observations are not made simply because we do not know everything we should look for.

Subjective factors, especially the researcher's theoretical perspective, can influence scientific inquiry by affecting her or his guesses about what to seek. The broad conceptual framework or approach within which a scientist works is the scientist's *perspective*—or a set of basic assumptions that specify both the kinds of concepts considered legitimate and the methods to be used in collecting and interpreting data. (A fancier work for *perspective* is *paradigm*, a term widely used in discussions of philosophy of science [Kuhn, 1962].) There are several major perspectives on abnormal behavior, and the work of many clinicians and researchers is grounded in one (or sometimes more) of them.

In this chapter and the next we will look at the current major perspectives on abnormal behavior. Each perspective suggests different approaches to studying the causes and treatments of the psychological disorders presented in Chapters 6 through 15. We will discuss six perspectives on abnormal psychology: psychodynamic, humanistic and existential, and biological in this chapter; and behavioral, cognitive, and vulnerability-stress in Chapter 3. The particular perspective that guides a professional's research or practice has important consequences for the way in which abnormal behavior is defined, investigated, and treated.

Psychodynamic Perspectives

psychodynamic perspectives A general view that *psychopathology* results from the interplay among *unconscious* forces.

psychoanalytic theory Sigmund Freud's theory of the way in which *psychodynamics* influence normal and abnormal behavior.

Psychodynamic perspectives stem from Sigmund Freud's (1856–1939) theory and practice of psychoanalysis. Since Freud's time many other therapists and theorists have elaborated on his **psychoanalytic theory**. They share a belief that human behavior is the product of the interaction or dynamics of conscious and unconscious thoughts and feelings within the individual and the view that we must turn to the unconscious to understand both human behavior in general and psychopathology in particular. They also emphasize the important role that early experiences play in personality development.

Psychoanalytic Theory

In the popular press, the term *psychoanalysis* usually refers to a method of treatment in which the patient lies on a couch and talks for hundreds of hours to an analyst about whatever comes into his or her head. Though this is the treatment Freud developed, psychoanalysis is also an unusually comprehensive psychological theory, encompassing descriptions of normal personality functioning and personality development in childhood as well as explanations of how these processes can go awry and lead to psychopathology. We begin with Freud's description of normal personality functioning, his analysis of the structure of the mind.

Structure of the Mind

Freud divided the mind, or the psyche, into three main parts: id, ego, and superego, each representing specific functions. The **id** is present at birth and accounts for all the energy needed to run the psyche. It consists of the basic urges for food, water, elimination, warmth, affection, aggression and sex. Freud, trained as a neurologist, regarded the source of all energy of the id as biological; it is later converted by some means into psychic energy, all of it unconscious, below the level of awareness.

The id operates on what Freud called the **pleasure principle**. That is, it seeks immediate gratification of needs. When the id is not satisfied, tension is produced, and the id strives to eliminate this tension as quickly as possible. For example, an infant feels hunger, an unpleasant drive, and is impelled to move about, sucking, in order to reduce the tension arising from the unsatisfied drive. This is one means by which the id obtains gratification; it represents the person's first interaction with the environment. The other means of obtaining gratification is **primary process** thinking, generating images or fantasies of what is desired. The infant who wants mother's milk imagines the mother's breast and thereby obtains some short-term satisfaction through a wish-fulfilling fantasy.

The second structure of the personality that Freud identified, the **ego**, is primarily conscious and begins to develop from the id during the second six months of life. The task of the ego is to deal with reality. Since fantasy alone will not keep a person alive, the ego does not employ primary process thinking. Through its planning and decision-making functions, which Freud called **secondary process** thinking, the ego realizes that operating on the pleasure principle at all times, as the id would like to do, is not the most effective way of maintaining life. The ego thus operates on the **reality principle** as it mediates between the demands of reality and the immediate gratification desired by the id. In the breast-feeding example, secondary process thinking could involve the baby deciding that he or she is not really hungry but just needs to suck, in which case a rattle or pacifier might do. Or such thinking could entail planning a way to get the mother to appear, for example, by crying.

The **superego**, the third structure of the personality, is generally equivalent to what we call conscience. It is the carrier of society's moral standards as interpreted by the child's parents. The superego develops through the resolution of the oedipal conflict, to be discussed shortly. When the id pressures the ego to satisfy its needs, the ego must cope not only with the constraints of reality, but also with the right–wrong moral judgments of the superego. For example, a child may judge that it is possible to cheat on a test because the teacher has left the room, but refrains from doing so because of the guilt he or she would feel as a result of being dishonest.

According to Freud, then, behavior is a complex interplay of three psychic systems, all vying for the achievement of goals that cannot always be reconciled.

Sigmund Freud was the founder of the psychoanalytic perspective, both proposing a theory of the causes of mental disorder and devising a new method of therapy.

id In *psychoanalytic theory*, that part of the personality present at birth, composed of all the energy of the mind and expressed as biological urges that strive continually for gratification.

pleasure principle In *psychoanalytic theory*, the demanding manner by which the *id* operates, seeking immediate gratification of its needs.

primary process In *psychoanalytic theory*, one of the *id's* means of reducing tension, by imagining what it desires.

ego In *psychoanalytic theory*, the predominantly conscious part of the personality responsible for decision making and for dealing with reality.

secondary process The reality-based decision-making and problem-solving activities of the *ego*.

reality principle In *psychoanalytic theory*, the manner in which the *ego* delays gratification and otherwise deals with the environment in a planned, rational fashion.

superego In *psychoanalytic theory*, the part of the personality that acts as the conscience and reflects society's moral standards.

psychodynamics In *psychoanalytic theory*, the interplay of mental and emotional forces and processes that develop in early childhood and affect behavior and mental states.

unconscious In *psychoanalytic theory*, the repository of instinctual forces and emotions of which the person is unaware.

psychosexual stages (psychosexual development) In *psychoanalytic theory*, critical developmental phases through which an individual passes, each stage characterized by the body area providing maximal erotic gratification. The adult personality is formed by the pattern and intensity of instinctual gratification at each stage.

oral stage In *psychoanalytic theory*, the first *psychosexual stage*, extending into the second year, during which the mouth is the principle erogenous zone.

anal stage In *psychoanalytic theory*, the second *psychosexual stage*, occurring during the second year of life, during which the anus is considered the principal site of gratification.

phallic stage In *psychoanalytic theory*, the third *psychosexual stage*, extending from ages three to six, during which maximal gratification is obtained from genital stimulation.

latency period In *psychoanalytic theory*, the years between ages six and twelve, during which *id* impulses play a minor role in motivation.

genital stage In *psychoanalytic theory*, the final *psychosexual stage*, reached in adulthood, in which heterosexual interests predominate.

The interplay of these forces is referred to as the **psychodynamics** of personality. Freud considered most of the important determinants of behavior to be **unconscious**, inaccessible to awareness. Both the id instincts and many of the superego's activities are not known to the conscious mind. The ego is primarily conscious, having to do with thinking and planning. But the ego, too, has important unconscious aspects, the defense mechanisms, that protect it from anxiety; these will be discussed shortly.

Stages of Psychosexual Development

Freud believed that we develop through a series of four separate **psychosexual stages**, so called because at each stage a different part of the body is the most sensitive to sexual excitation and therefore the most capable of providing satisfaction to the id. Infants derive maximum gratification of id impulses from excitation of the sensory endings around the mouth. Sucking and feeding are the principal pleasures of the **oral stage,** which occurs during infancy. In the second year of life the child enters the **anal stage,** as enjoyment shifts to the anus and the elimination and retention of feces. In the **phallic stage,** which extends from age three to age five or six, maximum gratification comes from stimulation of the genitalia. Between ages six and twelve the child is in a **latency period,** which is not considered a psychosexual stage. The child behaves asexually, although according to Freud's theoretical scheme all behavior is driven basically by the sexual and aggressive id impulses. The final and adult stage is the **genital stage,** during which sexual interests again predominate.

During each stage the growing person must resolve the conflicts between what the id wants and what the environment will provide; how this is accomplished determines basic personality traits that will last throughout the person's

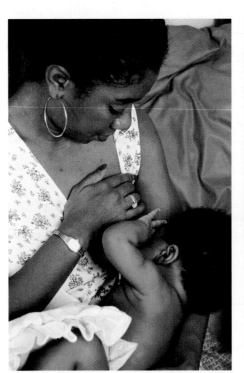

The oral stage is the first of Freud's psychosexual stages. During this stage maximum gratification of id impulses comes from sucking.

During the anal stage the site of pleasure shifts to the anus and toilet training typically begins.

life. For example, a child who in the anal stage is made to feel overly concerned with not messing or soiling herself or himself or is not at all encouraged to assume control of his or her bodily functions would become **fixated** at this psychosexual stage. As adolescents and adults such people are likely to regress to this stage when under stress; this type of person is sometimes called an **anal personality**. An anal retentive personality can be created when parents' reactions to toilet training cause a child to worry about letting go and becoming soiled. This personality is considered stingy and sometimes obsessively clean. These traits, even among adults, can be traced back to early events and to the manner in which gratification was provided or denied the child.

Perhaps the most important crisis of development occurs during the phallic stage, around age four. Then, Freud asserted, the child is overcome both with sexual desire for the parent of the opposite sex and with angry, hostile feelings toward the parent of the same sex. Fearing that the same-sex parent feels similarly competitive and angry, the child feels acutely the threat of dire punishment from that parent. The child thus avoids the entire conflict by repressing it, pushing it into the unconscious. This desire and repression are referred to as the **Oedipus complex** for a boy and the *Electra complex* for a girl. The dilemma is usually resolved through increased identification with the parent of the same sex and through the adoption of society's mores, which forbid a child to desire his or her parent. Through the learning of these moral values, the superego develops.

Defense Mechanisms

According to Freud and elaborated by his daughter, Anna (A. Freud, 1966), the discomfort experienced by the ego when confronted with urges such as the desire for an unattainable parent can be reduced in several ways. A **defense mechanism** is an unconscious strategy that protects the ego from anxiety. Perhaps the most important defense mechanism is **repression**, which pushes impulses and thoughts unacceptable to the ego into the unconscious. Repression not only prevents awareness but also keeps buried desires from growing up (Wachtel, 1977). By remaining repressed, these infantile memories cannot be corrected by adult experience and therefore retain their original intensity.

Several defense mechanisms are defined and illustrated in Table 2.1. In each case there is some misperception or misrepresentation of reality, e.g., in **denial** an objective event is not recalled and in **rationalization** the reason for an action is misrepresented, with a socially acceptable reason offered instead of the real reason. Being mistaken about reality in order to protect oneself from anxiety sounds on the face of it unhealthy, hence the lay Freudian epithet "you're being defensive." However, Freud considered defenses a potentially healthy way of managing conflict and stress.

Contemporary psychodynamic theorists and researchers agree that defenses can be either healthy or pathological (Vaillant, 1994). One consideration is time. A brief period of denial while one adjusts to a major life change such as bereavement may be a reasonably healthy means of keeping the anxiety and grief to manageable levels. But if someone literally believes their spouse is still alive ten years later, that would not be a good sign.

Neo-Freudian Psychodynamic Theories

The significance of Freud's theories was widely recognized by his contemporaries. Several met with Freud periodically to discuss psychoanalytic theory. Some theorists who shared Freud's position that psychodynamics are critical in determining behavior nonetheless came to disagree with him on specific aspects of psychoanalytic theory, such as the relative importance of id versus ego, of biological, instinctual drives versus sociocultural factors, of the earliest years of life

---

fixated (fixation) In *psychoanalytic theory*, arrested *psychosexual* development at a particular stage because of too much or too little gratification at that stage.

anal personality In *psychoanalytic theory*, an adult whose traits, such as stinginess, are assumed to be caused by *fixation* through either excessive or inadequate gratification of id impulses during the *anal stage* of *psychosexual development*.

Oedipus complex In Freudian theory, the desire and conflict of the four-year-old male child, who wants to possess his mother sexually and eliminate the father rival. The threat of punishment from the father causes *repression* of these *id* impulses. Girls have a similar sexual desire for the father, which is repressed in analogous fashion, called the *Electra complex*.

defense mechanism In *psychoanalytic theory*, reality-distorting strategies unconsciously adopted to protect the *ego* from anxiety.

repression A *defense mechanism* whereby impulses and thoughts unacceptable to the *ego* are pushed into the *unconscious*.

denial *Defense mechanism* in which objective events are kept out of conscious awareness.

rationalization A *defense mechanism* in which a socially acceptable reason is unconsciously invented by the *ego* to protect itself from confronting the real reason for an action, thought, or emotion.

Anna Freud, daughter of Sigmund Freud, made major contributions in detailing the role of ego defense mechanisms in psychological functioning.

Table 2.1 ▶ Selected Ego Defense Mechanisms

Defense Mechanism	Definition	Example
Repression	Keeping unacceptable impulses or wishes from conscious awareness.	A professor starting a lecture she has dreaded giving says "In conclusion. . . ."
Denial	Keeping objective events from conscious awareness.	A victim of incest in childhood cannot recall the incident(s) as an adult.
Projection	Attributing to someone else one's own thoughts or feelings	Someone who hates members of a racial group believes that it is they who dislike him or her.
Displacement	Deflecting feelings from their original target to someone else.	A boy gets mad at his brother but then acts angrily toward his friend.
Rationalization	Offering socially acceptable explanations that are not the real reasons for behavior.	A parent berates a child out of anger and impatience, then indicates that she did so to "build character."
Reaction formation	Unacceptable wishes or impulses are transformed into their opposite.	A person with sexual feelings toward children leads a campaign against child sexual abuse.
Sublimation	Aggressive or sexual impulses are diverted into prosocial behaviors.	Someone who has aggressive feelings toward his father becomes a surgeon.

in contrast with adult experiences, of whether sexual urges are at the core of motives and actions that are themselves not obviously sexual; and of unconscious processes versus conscious ones.

To elaborate on some of these themes, we outline the major ideas of two of the most influential of the theorists who adapted Freud's ideas in forging approaches of their own—Carl Jung and Erik Erikson. Other theorists are discussed in the chapters that address the particular disorders to which they gave the most attention. For example, object relations theories proposed by Otto Kernberg, Heinz Kohut, and others have been influential in understanding the personality disorders, especially narcissism (see Chapter 11).

Jung's Analytical Psychology

One of Freud's closest associates and at one time his heir apparent, Carl Jung (1887–1961), a Swiss psychiatrist, broke with Freud in 1914. Jung proposed ideas radically different from Freud's, ultimately establishing **analytical psychology**. Although he continued to believe that our motives are often unconscious, Jung deemphasized the importance of biological drives as the main causes of behavior and focused on the concept of self-actualization, a state of fulfillment that occurs when a person balances and gives expression to all aspects of his or her personality.

Jung hypothesized that, in addition to our personal unconscious, which Freud stressed, our **collective unconscious** contains information from the social history of humankind. The collective unconscious is the store of all the experiences people have had over the centuries. Unlike Freud's idea of the unconscious, it contains positive and creative forces instead of serving as a site for conflict and aggressive desires. Jung also asserted that each of us has masculine and feminine

analytical psychology A variation of Freud's *psychoanalysis* introduced by Carl Jung and focusing less on biological drives and more on such factors as self-fulfillment, *collective unconscious*, and religious symbolism

collective unconscious Jung's concept that every human being has inherited the wisdom, ideas, and strivings of those who have come before.

traits, the *animus* and *anima*, that can be blended to forge a creative personality and that people have spiritual and religious needs that are as basic as their sexual ones. He catalogued various personality types, perhaps the most important of which is *extraversion* (the tendency to be gregarious, obtaining satisfaction from other people) versus *introversion* (the tendency to be somewhat shy and reserved). In addition, Jung wrote at length on religious symbolism and the meaning of life, and as a consequence became popular among mystics, novelists, and poets. Finally, whereas Freud regarded current and future behavior as determined primarily by the past, Jung focused on purpose, decision making, and goal setting. According to Jung, then, to understand people we have to appreciate their dreams and aspirations, not just the effects of their past experiences, as important as those may be (Jung, 1928).

Carl Jung was the founder of analytical psychology, a blending of Freudian and humanistic concepts.

Erikson's Psychosocial Stages of Development

Like Freud, Erik Erikson was interested in the psychodynamics that formed the basis for personality development. Whereas Freud believed that development essentially ended early in life, Erikson emphasized the idea that people continue to change through middle age and into their senior years.

Erikson proposed eight **psychosocial stages of development** through which people progress, each characterized by a particular challenge or crisis. The resolution of the crisis affects how the individual deals with each subsequent developmental stage (Table 2.2). If a crisis is not adequately handled, then, according to Erikson, the resolution of subsequent crises is hampered.

To illustrate, let us look at the fifth stage, perhaps the most important one,

psychosocial stages of development In Erik Erikson's theory, phases of personality development, each of which is associated with a particular challenge or crisis.

Table 2.2 ▶ *Erikson's Eight Stages of Psychosocial Development*

Stage and Approximate Age Range	Psychosocial Crisis	Major Developments
Infancy, 0–1	Trust vs. mistrust	In the caregiver—baby relationship, the infant develops a sense of trust or mistrust that basic needs such as nourishment, warmth, cleanliness, and physical contact will be provided for.
Early childhood, 1–3	Autonomy vs. shame, doubt	Children learn self-control as a means of being self-sufficient, e.g., toilet training, feeding, walking, or developing shame and doubt about their abilities to be autonomous.
Play age, 3–6	Initiative vs. guilt	Children are anxious to investigate adult activities, but may also have feelings of guilt about trying to be independent and daring.
School age, 7–11	Industry vs. inferiority	Children learn about imagination and curiosity, develop learning skills, or develop feelings of inferiority if they fail—or if they think they fail—to master tasks.
Adolescence, 12–20	Identity vs. identity confusion	Adolescents try to figure out who they are, how they are unique, if they want to have a meaningful role in society, how they can establish sexual, ethnic, and career identity. Feelings of confusion can arise over these decisions.
Young adulthood, 20–30	Intimacy vs. isolation	The wish to seek companionship and intimacy with a significant other, or avoid relationships and become isolated.
Adulthood, 30–65	Generativity vs. stagnation	The need to be productive—for example, to create products, ideas, or children—or to become stagnant.
Mature age, 65+	Integrity vs. despair	A review and effort to make sense of one's life, reflecting on completed goals or doubts and despair about unreached goals and desires.

Erik Erikson emphasized the importance of psychosocial development throughout the life span. He was more optimistic than Freud about people's continuing capacity for growth.

identity crisis   A developmental period in adolescence marked by concerns about who one is and what one is going to do with his or her life.

psychoanalysis   A term applied primarily to the therapeutic procedures pioneered by Freud.

in which Erikson introduces a term for which he is famous, **identity crisis**. This crisis, said to occur between the ages of twelve and twenty, reflects the transition from childhood to adulthood, a period when we develop a sense of self, both the kind of psychological beings we are and the kind of lives we plan to forge for ourselves (Erikson, 1959). Although the choice of an occupation, role, or profession is important—physician, lawyer, construction worker, parent, and so on—a person's identity is said to go much deeper. We are concerned with the direction of our lives: what things are going to be important and sought after, what kinds of compromises we are prepared to make to achieve our goals, what kind of people we want to be—in general all the things that constitute our sense of self as developing adults who are responsible for ourselves and who are ready to make commitments to goals and to other human beings. It is a tumultuous time, considering that young people are simultaneously trying to come to terms with their sexuality.

Therapy Based on Psychodynamic Perspectives

Freud's approach to treatment has been modified by other psychodynamic clinicians through the years, just as his original theory of personality and psychopathology has been modified. We begin by describing the original methods of psychoanalysis, and we then consider subsequent modifications.

Psychoanalysis

At the heart of classical **psychoanalysis** is the therapeutic attempt to identify and remove repressions that have prevented the ego from helping the individual grow into a responsible, healthy adult. Psychopathology is assumed to develop when people remain unaware of their true motivations and fears. They can be restored to healthy functioning only by becoming conscious of what has been repressed. When people can understand what is motivating their actions, they have a greater number of choices. The ego—the primarily conscious, deliberating, choosing portion of the personality—can better guide the individual in rational, realistic directions if unconscious conflicts (conflicts repressed from consciousness) are at a minimum.

To a psychodynamic therapist or analyst, the proper focus of therapy is not the symptom or problem the patient reports as a reason for seeking therapy, for example, being beset with time-consuming and meaningless rituals such as

In a typical psychoanalytic therapy session, the patient reclines on a couch and the analyst sits out of the patient's view.

compulsive hand washing. Instead the focus is the unconscious conflicts originating in childhood that presumably underlie the current problems. Only by lifting the repression can the person confront the underlying problem and reevaluate it in the context of adult life. Several techniques are used in psychoanalysis to try to reveal and clarify the meaning of these unconscious conflicts.

Free Association.   Perhaps the most important psychoanalytic technique is **free association**. The patient, reclining on a couch, is encouraged to give free rein to thoughts and feelings and to verbalize whatever comes to mind. The assumption is that through free association unconscious connections will surface, leading to the uncovering of unconscious material. The patient reports thoughts and feelings immediately, without thinking about them and screening out the elements that might seem unimportant, unintelligent, or shameful. Freud assumed that thoughts and memories occurred in associative chains and that recent ones reported first would ultimately trace back to earlier, crucial ones. In order to get to these earlier events, however, the therapist has to be careful not to guide or direct the patient's thinking or influence the patient nonverbally. Thus, the analyst usually sits behind the patient and refrains from making many comments.

> *free association* A key psychoanalytic procedure in which the patient is encouraged to give free rein to thoughts and feelings, verbalizing whatever comes into the mind without monitoring its content. The assumption is that, over time, hitherto *repressed* material will come forth for examination by the patient and analyst.

Resistance.   Blocks to free association do arise, however. Patients may suddenly change the subject or be unable to remember how a long-ago event ended. They may try any tactic to interrupt the session, or they may remain silent, get up from the couch, look out the window, or make jokes and personal remarks to the analyst. Patients may even arrive late or "forget" sessions altogether. Such obstacles to free association—**resistances**—were noted by Freud and contributed to his development of the concept of repression. He asserted that these moments of interference with free association most often resulted from unconscious control over sensitive areas. Because resistances provide crucial information about the patient, it is precisely these areas that psychoanalysts want to probe. For example, resistance would be inferred if a patient often came late to appointments with the therapist. The analyst might hypothesize that the patient has problems dealing with authority figures, stemming from unresolved conflicts with his or her father.

> *resistances* During *psychoanalysis*, the defensive tendency of the unconscious part of the *ego* to ward off from consciousness particularly threatening *repressed* material.

Analysis of Dreams.   In addition to free association and watching for resistances, psychoanalysts use **dream analysis**. The analyst guides the patient in remembering and later analyzing his or her dreams. Freud called dreams the "royal road to the unconscious" because he believed that during sleep ego defenses are lowered, allowing repressed material to come forth, usually in disguised form. The issues concerning the patient are often expressed in symbols (**latent content**) to help protect the conscious ego from the significance of dream material. The **manifest content** of dreams—what is immediately apparent— may be regarded as a compromise between repression of true meaning and a full expression of unconscious material. For example, a patient struggling to figure out what he or she wants to do in life might have a dream in which he or she cuts down a tall tree. Under these circumstances, this manifest content might symbolize the patient's anger toward his or her father (latent content). The content of dreams, then, is both shaped by unconscious thoughts and feelings and somewhat distorted by defense mechanisms. Never completely abandoned, even in sleep, defense mechanisms continue their fight to protect the ego from repressed impulses.

> *dream analysis* A key psychoanalytic technique in which the unconscious meanings of dream material are uncovered.
>
> *latent content* In dreams, the presumed true meaning hidden behind the *manifest content*.
>
> *manifest content* The immediately apparent, conscious content of dreams. Compare with *latent content*.

Interpretation.   As unconscious material begins to appear, another psychoanalytic technique, **interpretation**, comes into play. At the right time the analyst begins to point out the patient's defenses and the underlying meaning of his or her

> *interpretation* In *psychoanalysis*, a key procedure in which the *psychoanalyst* points out to the patient where *resistances* exist and what certain dreams and verbalizations reveal about impulses repressed in the *unconscious*.

dreams, feelings, thoughts, and actions. The analyst must time this carefully. The patient must evidence enough awareness of his or her situation to be able to tolerate hearing what the therapist says. Otherwise the patient's defenses and resistance may be so strong that he or she may reject the interpretation and leave treatment. To be effective, the analyst's interpretations should reflect insights that the patient is on the verge of making; the patient can then regard these insights as his or her own, rather than viewing them as coming from the analyst.

Interpretation is the analyst's principal weapon against the continued use of unhealthy defense mechanisms. The analyst may point out how certain statements by the patient relate to repressed material or suggest what the manifest content of dreams truly means. Interpretations may be particularly helpful in establishing the meaning of the resistances that disturb the patient's free association. The analyst may, for example, point out how the patient tends to avoid a particular topic or how the tone of voice changes when discussing a particular person or issue.

If an interpretation is timed correctly, the patient starts to examine the repressed impulse in the light of present-day reality. In other words, the patient begins to realize that he or she no longer has to fear the awareness of the impulse. For example, a college student can begin to realize that disagreement with his or her parent will not bring the world to an end. It is common, however, for patients to deny that the interpretation is accurate. A dilemma for analysts lies in how to interpret this denial. One possibility is that the patient is right and the interpretation is inaccurate; certainly dream analysis is not an exact science, and psychotherapists of any theoretical perspective are subject to forming hypotheses about a patient that miss the mark.

On the other hand, the denial may simply be evidence of defense mechanisms at work. The psychoanalytic theory of personality, as noted earlier, provides a rationale for being skeptical about whether people really know their own most important wishes and motivations. Therefore, analysts must also consider the possibility that a denied interpretation is correct, but premature in the sense that the patient is not yet ready to acknowledge it. Only through repeated confrontation, often emotional, with disturbing inner conflicts can the patient gradually acknowledge and then understand them. Determining whether an interpretation denied by the patient is incorrect or simply too threatening for the time being is one of the biggest technical challenges in psychoanalysis. Even if the patient agrees with the interpretation consciously, it is likely that he or she will need to encounter it several times during the course of analysis before being able to fully understand the conflict.

Transference.   One of the phenomena most helpful to understanding unconscious conflicts is **transference**, whereby the patient transfers onto the analyst attitudes or responses toward key individuals (chiefly parents) in his or her life. Freud noted that his patients sometimes acted toward him in an emotion-charged and unrealistic way. For example, a patient much older than Freud would behave in a childish manner during a therapy session. Sometimes these reactions were positive and loving, but many times they were quite negative and hostile. Since these feelings seemed out of character with the ongoing therapy relationship, Freud assumed that they were relics of attitudes transferred to him from those held in the past toward important people in the patient's history, primarily parents. That is, Freud believed that patients responded to him as though he were one of the important people in their past. Freud used this transference of attitudes, which he came to consider a valuable and inevitable aspect of psychoanalysis, as a way to reveal to patients the childhood origin of many of their concerns and fears. As patients saw themselves through the transference they came to understand the roots of their behavior in childhood. In psychoanalysis, trans-

transference The venting of the patient's emotions, either positive or negative, by treating the analyst as the symbolic representative of someone important in the past. An example is the patient's becoming angry with the analyst to release emotions actually felt toward his or her father.

ference is regarded as essential to a successful analysis. Indeed, it is precisely when analysts notice transference developing that they take hope that the important repressed conflict from childhood is getting closer to the surface.

To encourage the development of transference, analysts intentionally remain distant and therefore somewhat mysterious to patients. In this way an analyst ensures that a patient's reaction to him or her is largely a result of transference rather than a result of something that the analyst has said or done. Besides literally sitting behind the patient while the patient free-associates, analysts try to reveal little of their personal lives and to behave in a neutral manner, serving in effect as blank screens on which important persons in the patient's life can be projected.

EXCERPT FROM A PSYCHOANALYTIC SESSION: AN ILLUSTRATION OF TRANSFERENCE

PATIENT (*A fifty-year-old male business executive.*): I really don't feel like talking today.

ANALYST (*Remains silent for several minutes, then.*): Perhaps you'd like to talk about why you don't feel like talking.

PATIENT: There you go again, making demands on me, insisting I do what I just don't feel up to doing. (*Pause.*) Do I always have to talk here, when I don't feel like it? (*Voice becomes angry and petulant.*) Can't you just get off my back? You don't really give a damn how I feel, do you?

ANALYST: I wonder why you feel I don't care.

PATIENT: Because you're always pressuring me to do what I feel I can't do.

This patient had been in therapy for about a year, complaining of depression and anxiety. Although extremely successful in the eyes of his family and associates, he felt weak and incompetent. Through many sessions of free association and dream analysis, the analyst had begun to suspect that the patient's feelings of failure stemmed from his childhood experiences with a punitive and critical father, a man even more successful than the client, who never seemed satisfied with his son's efforts. The exchange quoted was later interpreted by the analyst as an expression of resentment by the patient of his father's pressures on him and had little to do with the analyst himself. The patient's tone of voice (petulant) and his overreaction to the analyst's gentle suggestion that he talk about his feelings of not wanting to talk were clues leading to this interpretation.

Countertransference.   Therapists must also work to remain aware of **countertransference**, the attitudes and feelings of the analyst toward the patient that stem from the analyst's own emotional vulnerabilities and predispositions. A goal of psychoanalysis is to keep these feelings from interfering with treatment.

In order to know what aspects of their reactions to a patient reflect countertransference, analysts must have an unusually high degree of self-awareness. All analysts must undergo a training analysis, in which the trainee is psychoanalyzed by a senior analyst, as a formal part of their education. Although many therapists of different theoretical perspectives consider it useful to have been in therapy themselves, it is required for psychoanalysts.

Detachment.   As important as what analysts do is what they do not do. Most notably, psychoanalysts do not become actively involved in helping the patient deal with everyday problems, usually refraining, for instance, from making direct suggestions about how to behave in a troublesome situation. The problem with giving direct advice is that the patient may gain short-term relief, which would reduce her or his motivation to endure the discomfort associated with uncovering repressed conflicts and thereby attaining lasting benefits.

countertransference Feelings that the analyst unconsciously directs to the patient, stemming from his or her own emotional vulnerabilities and unresolved conflicts.

Brief Dynamic Therapies

Psychoanalysis evolves as a slow process. It involves establishing trust, analyzing resistances and transference, assimilating interpretations, and finally integrating the understanding of formerly unconscious conflicts into one's life. As a result, analysis usually takes from two to five or more years and generally requires a minimum of two or three sessions per week.

Over the past forty or so years, several approaches to psychodynamic therapy have developed that differ from psychoanalysis as advocated by Freud. These **brief dynamic therapies** are shorter, informed by such Freudian concepts as defense mechanisms and unconscious motivation, but without relying on the couch and the time-consuming techniques of free association and dream analysis. Such therapy is more active and directive than is psychoanalysis and is focused more on present problems and relationships than on childhood conflicts.

One example of brief dynamic therapy is Interpersonal Therapy (IPT), developed by Myrna Weissman and Gerald Klerman (Klerman et al., 1984). IPT (discussed further in Chapter 10) concentrates on current interpersonal difficulties and on discussing with the patient—even teaching the patient directly—better ways of relating to others. The kind of major personality change sought by classical psychoanalysis is not a goal of IPT.

brief dynamic therapies Short-term therapy approaches based on such Freudian concepts as *defense mechanisms*, but with a more active approach and more attention to present problems and relationships.

▶ The Case of Ernest H. Revisited

APPLYING PSYCHODYNAMIC PERSPECTIVES

We now return to the case of Ernest H., the police officer, with which this book began. The information provided on Ernest is open to a number of interpretations, depending on the perspective adopted. Throughout this chapter and the next we will illustrate the perspectives by sketching how they might be applied in treating Ernest. It may be helpful to return to page 2 to review Ernest's case.

A therapist working from the psychoanalytic point of view might hypothesize that Ernest has blamed his father for his mother's early death. Such strong anger at the father has been repressed, but Ernest has not been able to regard him as a competent, worthwhile adult and to identify with him. Fixation at the oedipal stage of psychosexual development may have made Ernest anxious about authority and kept him from functioning as an adult. The therapist would probably look for this theme to surface as part of Ernest's transference. He or she would also look for evidence of Ernest's resistance to approaching certain ideas, such as his competitiveness with other men. These elements, coupled with dream analysis and free association, would help Ernest lift his repressions and deal openly and consciously with his buried anger toward his father.

Evaluating Psychodynamic Perspectives

Perhaps no investigator of human behavior has been honored and criticized as much as Freud. During the last years of the nineteenth century and the beginning years of this century, when he was first espousing his view of infantile sexuality, he was personally vilified. At that time sexuality was little discussed among adults. How scandalous, then, to assert that infants and children were also motivated by sexual drives! Psychoanalysis was an original and creative theory, proposed and defended in the face of severe criticism.

The merits of psychoanalysis as a theory of personality and psychopathology are mixed. The biggest criticism facing this perspective is that psychoanalytic theory is based on clinical observations of adult patients and those patients' recollections of what happened during childhood. Psychoanalytic theories are therefore based on very few data, and by current scientific standards, uncontrolled case-study data are too limited and subjective to provide sufficient evidence on which to evaluate the theories (see Chapter 1).

A complication in trying to test the theory more conclusively is that some of the concepts, such as the unconscious or defense mechanisms, are difficult to study scientifically. Consider the idea of reaction formation (see Table 2.1). The possibility that an unconscious impulse can be, but need not be, manifested as its opposite would seem to mean that any behavior at all could confirm predictions made by the theory, a "heads I win, tails you lose" situation. Accordingly, some scholars have argued that psychoanalysis should not be evaluated on the basis of scientific criteria but rather as work in the arts and humanities might be evaluated. Just as we would not ask whether a particular interpretation of a short story by William Faulkner is true, but rather whether it makes sense, is internally consistent, is aesthetically pleasing, and seems to lead to new self-understanding, so too we could ask similar questions of psychoanalytic arguments (Spence, 1982).

Many psychoanalytically oriented theorists and investigators, however, believe that the challenge lies in finding ways to test these claims that are adequate to the complexity of the theory. In recent years several studies have found some empirical support for predictions based on the psychoanalytic theory of personality (Westen, 1990). In particular, psychoanalytic theory has made a strong contribution to psychology by focusing attention on unconscious processes. The details of the nature and contents of the unconscious as described by Freud (such as the specific thematic relations between present-day unconscious conflicts and earlier fixations in psychosexual development) have not necessarily been verified. However, the basic point that much of what drives our behavior is inaccessible to awareness is now widely accepted and owes its roots in psychology largely to psychoanalytic theory (Greenwald, 1992). Focus Box 2.1 describes some of the basic psychological research leading to this acceptance.

Freud's ideas about treatment have had a mixed fate. On the negative side, traditional, long-term psychoanalysis has not been shown to be any more effective with problems such as anxiety and depression than is briefer, more supportive dynamic therapy (Koss & Butcher, 1986). Perhaps making what is implicit in a person's behavior explicit so that it can be dealt with in a more rational, mature manner is a worthy goal, but not one that is well met by techniques such as free association (Bornstein, 1993).

Brief dynamic therapy is currently the subject of more extensive research than is traditional psychoanalysis. Brief dynamic approaches have been found effective in treating a variety of problems, including stress and bereavement (Marmar, Horowitz, Weiss, Wiiner, & Kaltreider, 1988), late-life depression (Thompson, Gallagher, & Breckenridge, 1987), mood and personality disorders (Marziali, 1984), and several anxiety disorders (Koss & Shiang, 1994), including posttraumatic stress disorder (Horowitz, 1988). Interpersonal therapy is perhaps the best-validated variation on psychodynamic therapies; as such, it was included in a major research project on the treatment of depression (see Chapter 10). Its effectiveness was equal to cognitive therapy (to be discussed in Chapter 3), which is sometimes considered the best available psychotherapy for depression. A general summary review of well-controlled studies of brief dynamic therapy suggested that it is more effective than no treatment and equally effective as the other psychotherapies to which it was compared (Crits-Christoph, 1992).

To Recap

According to Freud's psychoanalytic theory, behavior is a dynamic interplay of the id, the ego, and the superego. The id seeks immediate gratification of basic urges; the ego seeks to mediate between reality constraints and the id's desires; and the

◤ FOCUS BOX 2.1

Awareness, the Unconscious, and Behavior

Much of the working of the mind takes place without our awareness. Consider an example. A common method of studying selective attention is to play separate tapes to each ear and ask subjects to attend to only one. Usually subjects later report little knowledge of the sounds directed to the unattended ear, yet these unattended stimuli can affect behavior. This indicates they are perceived and processed unconsciously, thus providing some scientific evidence for the existence of an unconscious.

After people had listened to a human voice played into one ear while tone sequences were played in the unattended ear, they reported having heard no tones (W. R. Wilson, 1975). Furthermore, in a memory task in which they listened to tone sequences that had been played earlier and others that had not been played, subjects were unable to distinguish between the two sequences. Despite this demonstration that the subjects did not recognize tone stimuli played previously, another measure revealed a startling result. When subjects were asked to rate how much they liked a series of tone sequences, they preferred those that had been presented earlier to the unattended ear over novel sequences. Some aspects of the tone sequences played initially must have been absorbed, even though subjects said that they had not heard them and demonstrated that they did not recognize them.

It is known that familiarity affects judgments of tone stimuli similar to those used by Wilson. Familiar sequences are preferred to novel ones.

Awareness, as measured by verbal report, is not always a very accurate indication of the effect of stimuli on behavior (Nisbett & Wilson, 1977). In one study, subjects memorized a list of word pairs. For some subjects the word pairs were specially constructed so that they would be likely to affect the subjects' performance in the second part of the study. For example, one of the word pairs these subjects first memorized was "ocean–moon." This pair was expected to make subjects more likely to respond "Tide" when later asked to name a detergent. The results agreed with expectation: subjects who had memorized the special word pairs gave twice the number of expected associations given by subjects who had not memorized those pairs. Right after the second part of the test, subjects were asked why they had given their particular responses. Even though they could still recall the word pairs, subjects almost never said that the word pairs had brought their responses to mind. Instead, they gave reasons such as "My mother uses Tide" or "Tide is the most popular detergent." They were not aware of the effect that the memory test had had on their behavior.

These studies provide laboratory evidence for the operation of unconscious processes. But do they generalize to more naturalistic dependent variables? A study by Bornstein, Leone, and Galley (1987) indicates that the answer is yes. They investigated whether exposure to a picture of a person's face for such a brief time that a subject would not recognize the image would nonetheless influence subsequent interactions with that person. Groups of a subject and two confederates of the experimenter had to read ten poems and as a group decide on the sex of the author of each poem. By arrangement the two confederates disagreed on seven of the ten, putting the subject in the role of tie breaker. Prior to judging the poems, half the subjects viewed, for four milliseconds, five presentations of a slide of one of the confederates. The other half saw a slide of the other confederate. Previous research had shown that exposures like these could not be discriminated from blank flashes of light. Consistent with the hypothesis of the study, subjects agreed with the confederate whose slide they had seen twice as often as they agreed with the other confederate.

These experiments, which are but a small sampling of research making a similar point, are closely related to the psychoanalytic concept of the unconscious. Contemporary investigators have begun to verify Freud's view that some human behavior is determined by unconscious processes. Many of these researchers interpret such processes in a different way than did Freud, however (Kihlstrom, Barnhardt, & Tataryn, 1992). Freud postulated the existence of *the* unconscious, a repository of instinctual energy and repressed conflicts and impulses. Most current researchers reject the idea of an energy reservoir, holding more simply that we are not aware of everything going on around us nor of some of our cognitive processes. At the same time, these stimuli and processes of which we are unaware can affect behavior powerfully. This research highlights the difficulty of understanding the causes of human behavior. Merely to ask someone, "Why did you do that?" may yield information about that person's own psychological theories, which may be intriguing in their own right (Furnham, 1988), but will not likely serve as a comprehensive explanation.

superego represents the constraints of conscience. These systems develop through a sequence of psychosexual stages of child development, and problems at these stages can lead to related personality deficiencies in adulthood. Freud considered the primary determinants of behavior, including abnormal behavior, to be unconscious. The main goal of psychoanalytic therapy is to use such tools as dream analysis and analysis of the transference relationship with the analyst to make unconscious conflicts conscious. Subsequent therapies have adopted Freud's general perspective on psychodynamics but altered some of the techniques, especially by taking a more active, briefer approach, and these appear to be no less effective.

Humanistic and Existential Perspectives

Humanistic and existential perspectives share with psychodynamic perspectives the view that a person's psychological well-being can be enhanced by increasing awareness of motivations and needs. However, these perspectives contrast markedly with regard to their views of human nature and the interaction of the person and society. Whereas psychoanalytic theory assumes that human nature, embodied in the sexual and aggressive impulses of the id, is something in need of restraint, humanistic and existential perspectives propose that human nature is essentially good. When distorted by social pressure, however, mental disorders can develop. Humanistic and existential therapies also emphasize people's freedom of choice. They view free will as our most important characteristic, for our choices determine how we grow and enrich our lives.

humanistic and existential perspectives A generic term for theories that emphasize the individual's subjective experiences, free will, and ever-present ability to decide on a new life course.

Carl Rogers's Person-Centered Theory

Carl Rogers (1902–87) was an American psychologist whose theorizing about personality and psychotherapy grew out of years of clinical and teaching experience (Rogers, 1951, 1961). His theory and the therapy he developed became known as **person-centered**, for he believed that to understand individuals we must look at the way they experience events rather than at the events themselves. Each person's own perceptions and feelings are the major determinants of his or her behavior and make that person unique. Rogers also stressed that when people are not concerned with the evaluations, demands, and preferences of others, their lives are guided by an innate tendency for **self-actualization**, the realization of their fullest potential. To this end they are inherently purposive and goal

person-centered A theory and *humanistic-existential therapy* developed by Carl Rogers that emphasizes the importance of the therapist's understanding a person's subjective experiences and assisting him or her to reduce anxieties as well as fostering actualization of the person's potential.

self-actualization Fulfilling one's potential as an always growing human being; believed by *person-centered therapists* to be the master motive.

Carl Rogers, a humanistic therapist, proposed that the key ingredient in therapy is the attitude and style of the therapist rather than specific techniques.

directed; only when others (parents, peers, social mores, environmental pressures) influence their inner drives do they lose their way.

Person-Centered Therapy

Assuming that a mature and well-adjusted person makes judgments based on what is intrinsically satisfying and actualizing, Rogers avoided imposing goals on the client during therapy. Rogers believed that the client should take the lead and direct the course of the session; the therapist's job is to remain empathic and supportive so that during their hour together, the client can rediscover his or her basic nature and begin to make choices regarding which course of life is intrinsically gratifying. Because of his very positive view of people, Rogers assumed that their decisions would not only make them happy with themselves, but would also turn them into good, civilized people.

According to Rogers and other humanistic and existential therapists, people must take responsibility for themselves, even when they are troubled. It is often difficult for a therapist to refrain from giving advice, from taking charge of a client's life, especially when the client appears incapable of making his or her own decisions. But Rogerian therapists hold steadfastly to the rule that a person's innate capacity for growth and self-direction will assert itself, provided that the therapeutic atmosphere is warm, attentive, and receptive. Indeed, they believe that if the therapist steps in, the process of growth and self-actualization will only be thwarted. Whatever short-term relief might come from the therapist's intervening will sacrifice long-term growth. The therapist must not become yet another person whose wishes the client strives to satisfy.

Rogers's approach thus places greater emphasis on the attitude and emotional style of the therapist than on the use of specific intervention procedures (Rogers, 1951). The therapist should have three core qualities: genuineness, unconditional positive regard, and accurate empathic understanding.

Genuineness refers to spontaneity, openness, and authenticity. The therapist has no phoniness and no professional facade, disclosing feelings and thoughts informally and candidly to the client. In a sense the therapist, through honest self-disclosure, provides a model for what the client can become by being in touch with feelings and able to express them and accept responsibility for doing so. The therapist has the courage to present himself or herself to others as he or she really is.

Second, the successful therapist is able to extend **unconditional positive regard**. Other people set what Rogers called conditions of worth—I will love you if. . . . The person-centered therapist prizes clients as they are and conveys unpossessive warmth for them, even if he or she does not approve of their behavior. People have value merely for being people, and the therapist must care deeply for and respect a client, for the simple reason that the client is another human being, engaged in the struggle of growing and being alive.

The third quality, **accurate empathic understanding**, is the ability to see the world through the eyes of clients from moment to moment, to understand the feelings of clients, both those of which they are aware and those of which they may be only dimly aware.

Empathy is conveyed through the therapist's acceptance, recognition, and clarification of the client's feelings. It is the basic technique of Rogerian therapy. An analysis of ten detailed studies of what was actually said in person-centered therapy sessions indicated that reflections (usually of the client's emotions) constituted about three-fourths of the therapist's comments (Greenberg, Elliott, & Lietaer, 1994). Within the context of a warm therapeutic relationship, the therapist encourages the client to talk about his or her most deeply felt concerns and attempts to restate the emotional aspects, not just the content, of what the client says.

---

genuineness In *person-centered therapy*, an essential quality of the therapist, referring to openness and authenticity.

unconditional positive regard According to Rogers, a crucial attitude for the *person-centered* therapist to adopt toward the client, who needs to feel complete acceptance as a person in order to evaluate the extent to which current behavior contributes to *self-actualization*.

accurate empathic understanding In person-centered therapy, an essential quality of the therapist, referring to the ability to see the world through the client's eyes.

Because their feelings are mirrored by the therapist without judgment or disapproval, clients can review them, clarify them, and accept them. Feared thoughts and emotions previously too threatening to enter awareness can become part of the self-concept. If therapeutic conditions allowing self-acceptance are established, clients begin to talk in a more honest and emotional way about themselves. Rogers assumed that such talk in itself is primarily responsible for changing behavior.

Showing empathy as it is described in person-centered therapy is sometimes mistakenly assumed to be an easy, straightforward matter, but it is not; it requires much subtlety. The therapist is not limited to merely finding words for the emotional aspects of what the client says, but also, in *advanced empathy*, considers what is believed to lie behind the client's observable behavior and most obvious thoughts and feelings. The therapist makes an inference about what is troubling the client and interprets what the client has said in a way that seems different from the client's actual statements, as illustrated in the following transcript.

EXCERPT FROM A PERSON-CENTERED THERAPY SESSION

CLIENT (*An eighteen-year-old female college student.*): My parents really bug me. First it was Arthur they didn't like, now it's Peter. I'm just fed up with all their meddling.

THERAPIST: You really are angry at your folks.

CLIENT: Well, how do you expect me to feel? Here I am with a 3.5 GPA, and providing all sorts of other goodies, and they claim the right to pass on how appropriate my boyfriend is. (*Begins to sob.*)

THERAPIST: It strikes me that you're not just angry with them. (*Pause.*) Maybe you're worried about disappointing them.

CLIENT (*Crying even more.*): I've tried all my life to please them. Sure their approval is important to me. They're really pleased when I get A's, but why do they have to pass judgment on my social life as well?

Although the emotion expressed initially was one of anger, the therapist believed that the client was really fearful of criticism from her parents. She therefore made an advanced empathic statement in an effort to explore with the client what was only implied but not expressed. Previous sessions had suggested that the client worked hard academically primarily to please her parents and to avoid their censure. She had always been able to win their approval by getting good grades, but more recently the critical eye of her mother and father were directed at the young men she was dating. The client was beginning to realize that she had to arrange her social life to please her parents. Her fear of disapproval from her parents became the focus in therapy after the therapist had helped her see beyond her anger.

Thus, in **primary empathy**, the therapist tries to restate to clients their thoughts, feelings, and experiences from their own point of view: the therapist views the client's world from the client's perspective and then communicates to the client that this frame of reference is understood and appreciated. In **advanced empathy**, the therapist generates a view that takes the client's world into account but with the goal of conceptualizing things in a more constructive way. The therapist presents to the client a way of considering himself or herself that may be quite different from the client's accustomed perspective (Egan, 1975).

primary empathy A form of empathy in which the therapist understands the content and feeling of what the client is saying and expressing from the client's point of view.

advanced empathy A form of empathy in which the therapist infers concerns and feelings that lie behind what the client is saying.

Existential Perspectives on Abnormality

Existentialism, like humanism, emphasizes personal growth and choice. The existential point of view, however, is gloomier, having grown out of a European philosophical movement influenced by the horrors of World War II and based on the writings of Sartre, Kierkegaard, and Heidegger. Although existentialism shares the view that people strive to develop their potential, it stresses the anxiety that is inevitable in making such important choices, the choices on which existence depends, such as staying or not staying with a spouse, with a job, or in your hometown. Hamlet's famous soliloquy, beginning "To be, or not to be—that is the question" (act III, scene 1), is a classic existential statement. To be truly alive is to confront the anxiety that comes with existential choices.

Existential anxiety derives from several sources (Tillich, 1952). Perhaps its most profound source is the awareness that one day we shall die. We are also aware of our helplessness against chance circumstances that can forever change our lives, such as a disabling automobile accident. The existentialist view emphasizes that people are alone and must ultimately make decisions, act, and live with the consequences. So must we also create the meaning of our lives. This responsibility for endowing our world and our lives with substance and purpose is another source of existential anxiety. According to the existential perspective, psychopathology arises when people elect to avoid choices and pretend that they do not have to be made. This course may protect them from anxiety, but it also deprives them of living a meaningful life. Thus, whereas the humanistic message is upbeat, the existential is tinged with sadness and anxiety, but not despair, unless the exercise of free will and the assumption of responsibility that accompanies it are avoided.

Existential Therapy

Like the humanistic, person-centered therapist, the existential therapist offers support and empathy through the adoption of the individual's frame of reference. The therapist then helps the individual explore his or her behavior, feelings, and relationships, and what life means. The therapist encourages the client to confront and clarify past and present choices. Present choices are considered the most important.

Another goal of the existential therapist is to help the individual relate authentically to others. People are assumed to define their identity and existence in terms of their personal relationships; a person is threatened with nonbeing—or alienation—if isolated from others. Even a person who is effective in dealing with other people and with the world can become anxious if deprived of open and frank relationships. Hence, although the existential view is a highly subjective one, it strongly emphasizes relating to others in an open, honest, spontaneous, and loving manner.

Although existentialism asserts that we must relate authentically to others, the paradox of life is that at the same time, each of us is ultimately alone. Separate from others, we must create our own existence in the world alone.

The existential therapist strives to make the therapeutic relationship an authentic encounter between two human beings so that the client has some practice in relating to another individual in a straightforward fashion. The therapist, through honesty and self-disclosure, helps the client learn authenticity. This can take the form of the therapist's openly expressing strong disapproval of what the client is doing—but without rejecting the client as a worthwhile human being.

The ultimate goals of existential therapy are to make the client more aware of his or her own potential for choice and growth and to make existential anxiety bearable. People must be encouraged to accept responsibility for their own existence and to realize that, within certain limits, they can redefine themselves at any moment and behave and feel differently, despite the anxiety they may face.

Even in relation to person-centered therapy, which places less emphasis on technique than do other forms of psychotherapy, existential therapy is vague about what therapeutic techniques will help the client grow. Indeed, a reliance on technique may be seen as counterproductive, an objectifying process in which the therapist acts on the client as though he or she were a thing to be manipulated (Prochaska, 1984). As such, the existential approach is best understood as a general attitude taken by certain therapists toward human nature, rather than as a set of therapeutic techniques.

The Case of Ernest H. Revisited ◄

Applying Humanistic and Existential Perspectives

A person-centered therapist might see the early death of Ernest's mother and the erratic parenting style of his father as having deprived him of an early experience of unconditional positive regard. Ernest may have developed the notion that he is not acceptable just for who he is, that his worth is conditional on performance. The highly competitive environments in which he has worked (college, police academy, police work) may have fostered this view as well. In this light, having difficulty performing sexually becomes more than an unpleasant or dissatisfying situation; it might seem to Ernest more proof that he is not worth much as a human being. The therapist would want to provide Ernest a far different experience by being nonjudgmental in therapy and by not structuring the therapy as an arena in which he needs to perform techniques and learn skills. By reflecting Ernest's feelings and accepting him unconditionally, the person-centered therapist would hope to show him that he is understood, and in principle he can then accept himself and therefore not have to try so desperately for acceptance from others and lash out when he does not get it.

Evaluating Humanistic and Existential Perspectives

Research on person-centered therapy has focused principally on relating outcome to the personal qualities of therapists (empathy, genuineness, and warmth) and has yielded inconsistent results (Beutler, Crago, & Arizmendi, 1986). Interestingly, these therapist qualities appear to be more closely related to therapy outcome if they are rated by the patients rather than by independent observers (Beutler et al., 1986). In other words, if patients feel that their therapists are genuine and empathic, they tend to get better. On the negative side, this result could indicate that the therapist's actual (objectively rated) level of, say, genuineness is irrelevant: regardless of what therapists do, patients who are doing well will say good things about them and those who are not getting any benefits will say negative things about them. Alternatively, the results may be consistent with Rogers's theorizing. Perhaps what is real and influential is how the patient experiences the therapist's style, but this experience may not be apparent to observers of a therapy session because it may depend on subtle, individual-specific cues. The therapist's behaviors and feelings that convey empathy to one patient may seem patronizing to another, even if they look the same to a third party. If so, this explanation would imply that it is important to convey the qualities Rogers emphasized, but that how to do so cannot be a straightforward matter of following the same therapeutic guidelines with all patients.

The therapist's attitudes stressed in person-centered therapy, by themselves, may not be sufficient to help clients change. Rogers developed his ideas about therapy in the course of working with people who were only mildly disturbed. As a way to help unhappy but not severely disturbed people understand themselves better, person-centered therapy may very well be appropriate and effective. It may not, however, be appropriate for a severe psychological disorder, as Rogers himself warned.

Existential therapy, by contrast, has not been the subject of controlled psychotherapy research, primarily because existentialism lacks the definable, concrete operations on which scientific research can be conducted. Moreover, existential therapists tend to see contemporary science as dehumanizing and hence to be avoided. They believe that applying science to individuals denies their unique humanness.

Neither humanistic nor existential perspectives have contributed much to the description or explanation of psychopathology, as opposed to its treatment. They have focused their attention more on personal growth and development than on specific psychological disorders. As such, these perspectives are included in this chapter because of their historical and current influence on counseling and psychotherapy, but they will not be a main emphasis in Chapters 6 through 15 on psychological disorders.

Before leaving the topic of humanistic and existential perspectives, it is important to note that some creative research has been conducted in recent years on one of their core concepts, free will.

► APPLYING CRITICAL THINKING SKILLS

RESEARCH ON FREE WILL

Free will has not traditionally been a subject of scientific research. Science is generally about deterministic cause–effect relations. Two-pound bricks fall from the top of the Empire State Building at a given speed because that is how gravity works, not because they choose that speed. Likewise, most researchers believe that a real science of human behavior should be able to identify the causes of our actions without reference to free will. However, for most humanistic and existential therapists, free will is a starting assumption, not a hypothesis to be tested.

George Howard and Christine Conway believed, though, that it should be possible to test the impact of free will on behavior, rather than assume on the basis of an overall theoretical perspective that it is or is not influential. The method they came up with was ingenious. Twenty-two undergraduate students volunteered to participate in a study of the extent to which they could control their peanut-eating behavior. Each day a subject received a sixteen-ounce jar of peanuts and one of four sets of instructions: (a) keep the jar in sight in the dormitory room and "eat as many peanuts as you wish," (b) keep the jar in sight and "try not to eat any peanuts," (c) put the jar out of sight and eat as many peanuts as desired, or (d) keep the jar out of sight and try not to eat any peanuts. The external, situational variable (whether the jar was in or out of sight) had only a small effect on eating, but the free will variable (try vs. try not to eat) had a very large effect. With the peanuts in sight, for instance, subjects ate about nine times as many peanuts on days when they were trying to eat peanuts as on days when they were trying not to (Howard & Conway, 1986, Study 1).

Let us examine this study from the standpoint of applying critical thinking skills.

► *What conclusion does the evidence seem to support?* Howard and Conway (1986) interpreted the large effect of whether or not subjects were trying to eat peanuts, both in an absolute sense and in relation to the situational factor of in sight/out of sight, as evidence that free will, or volition, is an important influence on human behavior, just as humanistic and existential theorists have argued, and that it is amenable to scientific investigation.

► *What other interpretations are plausible?* But other conclusions can account for the peanut-eating results. Perhaps in sight versus out of sight was the wrong situational variable to study as a contrast for the try/try not manipulation. Free will might have little noticeable impact if pitted against the most powerful environmental variables in predicting behavior, whatever they might be.

Peanut eating is also a relatively trivial behavior. Perhaps people can exercise free choice in regard to fairly inconsequential issues but not more important ones.

It is possible, too, that because the subjects were instructed to try or try not to eat the study might show only that subjects complied with the experimenters' choice of goals, not their own (Hayes, 1987). People tend to be rewarded for complying with directives from authorities and punished for not doing so. It is not necessary to attribute this effect to free will.

▶ *What other information would help choose among the alternative interpretations?* These findings regarding the impact of free will have been replicated for more important outcomes, such as number of heterosexual social interactions (among students desiring more such interactions) (Howard & Conway, 1986, Study 3) and amount of physical exercise (Howard & Myers, 1990). Moreover, these studies have shown that try/try not instructions have a greater impact than other factors specifically selected by the individual subject as relevant to her or his behavior. For example, one person might select day of the week as a major determinant of level of exercise, while another might select the weather (Howard & Myers, 1990). Thus, the free will effect does not appear to be limited to trivial issues or to comparisons with ill-chosen environmental factors.

What about the point that the effect might be seen as simply complying with the experimenter's instructions? Howard and Conway (1986, Study 2) tried to address this alternate interpretation by letting some subjects choose their instructions for each day (try to eat vs. try not to eat peanuts) and record them privately (not telling the experimenter), whereas other subjects flipped a coin to determine what instructions to follow (again, not telling the experimenter whether they had decided that heads or tails would indicate try vs. try not instructions for the day). Again, subjects ate much more on days on which they were to try to eat (the instructions this time being administered by themselves, or by a coin flip whose rules they had chosen). Whether or not this follow-up study seems decisive may depend on one's theoretical perspective. For example, Hayes (1987) noted in rebuttal that eventually the experimenter would know (at the end of the study) whether on a given day the subject had been in the try or try not condition. Thus, despite the time delay, this can still be seen as compliance with social pressure to do what the experiment calls for you to do.   ◢◣

TO RECAP

Humanistic and existential perspectives hold that people have a capacity to exercise free will, that they are not programmed by their genes or their early experiences or social environments. These perspectives emphasize the unique humanity of each person and thus place little emphasis on psychological disorders or categories. Particularly in the existential approach, specific therapeutic techniques and controlled research on their effects take a back seat to therapists' helping clients gain in awareness, self-acceptance, and capacity to relate in a genuine manner to others. Carl Rogers's person-centered therapy has been more open to research, with mixed results but some support for his view that therapists' attitudes, such as unconditional positive regard for the client, are helpful.

▶ *Biological Perspectives*

As discussed in Chapter 1, it has long been believed that complete understanding of abnormal behavior must take into account somatic or bodily factors. The **biological perspective** on abnormal behavior is a broad theoretical point of view holding that mental disorders are caused by biological processes or mechanisms that have gone awry. As our knowledge of these processes and

biological perspective A broad theoretical view that holds that mental disorders are caused by some aberrant bodily process or defect.

Behavior genetics studies the degree to which characteristics, like physical resemblance or psychopathology, are shared by family members.

behavior genetics The study of individual differences in behavior that are attributable in part to differences in genetic makeup.

genes Ultramicroscopic areas of the *chromosome*. The gene is the smallest physical unit of the DNA molecule that carries a piece of hereditary information.

genotype An individual's unobservable, physiological genetic constitution; the totality of *genes* possessed by an individual.

phenotype The totality of observable characteristics of a person.

heritability The extent to which *genes* contribute to the likelihood that a person will develop a particular disorder or condition.

family studies A research strategy in *behavior genetics* in which the frequency of a trait or of abnormal behavior is determined in relatives who have varying percentages of shared genetic background.

twin study A research strategy in *behavior genetics* in which *concordance* rates of *monozygotic twins* and *dizygotic twins* are compared.

monozygotic (MZ) twins Genetically identical siblings who have developed from a single fertilized egg; sometimes called identical twins.

mechanisms has increased, the links between mental functioning and biological functioning have become clearer. We will review evidence indicating that heredity probably predisposes a person, through physiological malfunction, to develop schizophrenia (see Chapter 9). It appears that some forms of depression may result from a failure of the usual processes of neural transmission (Chapter 10). In these and other instances, a type of psychopathology is viewed as caused by the disturbance of some biological process.

Researchers and clinicians who view abnormal behavior from a biological perspective have focused their inquiries on two particularly promising areas, behavior genetics and neurochemistry.

Behavior Genetics

Behavior genetics is the study of individual differences in behavior that are attributable in part to differences in genetic makeup. When the ovum, the female reproductive cell, is joined by the male's spermatozoon, a zygote, or fertilized egg, is produced. It has forty-six chromosomes (twenty-three contributed by the mother and twenty-three by the father), the number characteristic of a human being. Each chromosome consists of thousands of **genes**. The genes carry the genetic information (DNA) that is passed from parents to child. Each cell of the human body contains a full complement of chromosomes and genes in its nucleus.

The total genetic makeup of an individual, consisting of inherited genes, is referred to as the **genotype**. The **phenotype** refers to all the person's observable characteristics. The phenotype reflects interactions between the genotype and the environment. The basic question addressed in behavior genetics research is whether and to what extent individual differences in phenotype (in the case of behavior genetics research in psychopathology, differences in abnormal behavior) are associated with variability in genotype. For example, are the panic attacks that some people experience (Chapter 6) to some degree inherited? To what degree?

It is critical to keep in mind that psychopathology (or any other behavior) is not inherited in the same way as is eye color. Rather, when we speak of genetic influences on psychopathology, we mean that the genotype increases a person's liability or risk of developing some form of abnormality. Behavior is always due to *both* genes and environment. The extent to which genes contribute to the likelihood that a person will develop a disorder is referred to as the **heritability** of the disorder.

Studying Mental Disorders in Families

In order to address the question of heritability, researchers capitalize on what is known about genetic similarity among related individuals, make observations about behavioral similarity, and see if there is any correlation between the two. **Family studies** are based on the fact that the average number of genes shared by two blood relatives can be determined. For example, children receive half their genes from one parent and half from the other. Thus, on the average, siblings are identical in 50% of their genetic background. In contrast, relatives not as closely related share fewer genes. For example, nephews and nieces share 25% of the genetic makeup of an uncle. If a predisposition for a mental disorder can be inherited, a study of the family of someone with the disorder should reveal a correlation between the number of shared genes and the prevalence of the disorder in relatives. In other words, the disorder would appear more often in those closely related than in those distantly related.

Studying Mental Disorders in Twins

A special kind of family study, called the **twin study**, has been particularly helpful in studying genetic contributions to mental disorders. In a twin study, the similarity in abnormal behavior of identical twins, or **monozygotic (MZ) twins,** is compared to that of fraternal twins, or **dizygotic (DZ) twins**. Identical, MZ twins develop from a single fertilized egg and are genetically the same. DZ pairs develop from separate eggs and on the average are only 50% alike genetically, no more alike than any two siblings. MZ twins are always the same sex, but DZ twins can be either the same sex or opposite in sex. Twin studies begin with diagnosed cases and then search for the presence of the disorder in the other twin; if the other twin has the disorder also, the pair is said to be concordant. To the extent that a predisposition for a mental disorder can be inherited, **concordance** should be greater in MZ pairs than in DZ pairs because the MZ pairs are more similar genetically. As we will see in Chapter 9, twin studies have been used extensively to examine the genetic component involved in schizophrenia. In one famous case, that of the Genain quadruplets, all four identical sisters developed forms of schizophrenia.

Family and twin studies are useful, but not always easy to interpret. Assume for instance that a family study finds more children with anxiety disorders in the families of anxious parents than in the families of their anxious parents' cousins who do not have anxiety disorders. Does this mean that a predisposition to develop anxiety disorders is genetically transmitted? Not necessarily. Maybe these children learned extremely fearful behaviors by observing their anxious parents.

Environmental Influences versus Genetic Influences

It is very difficult to determine where genetic influences end and environmental influences begin. Children are more likely to be living with their siblings than with their second cousins, for instance, and for that reason alone may be more alike on whatever environmental factors might affect psychopathology as well as more similar genetically. Likewise, MZ twins might be treated more similarly than are DZ twins. These environmental similarities could account for any findings that MZ twins are more similar in behavior than are DZ twins.

To avoid this environmental variable, behavior genetics researchers sometimes study adopted children. A study that showed that the biological children of alcohol-dependent fathers are especially likely to develop alcohol problems, even if they are adopted early in life and raised by nondrinking adoptive parents, would provide stronger evidence of a genetic effect than would an ordinary family study. Similarly, a study that showed that MZ twins separated in infancy and reared in separate adoptive homes are more similar with respect to whether or not they develop panic disorder than are DZ twins reared together (who are higher in environmental similarity) would be a clearer indication that genetics has some role in the onset of panic disorder.

dizygotic (DZ) twins Birth partners who have developed from separate fertilized eggs and who are only 50% alike genetically, no more so than siblings born from different pregnancies; sometimes called fraternal twins.

concordance As applied in *behavior genetics*, the similarity in psychiatric diagnosis or in other traits within a pair of twins.

Twins play an important role in behavior genetics research as investigators try to determine the extent to which psychological disorders are hereditary.

Neurochemistry

Another area in which work from the biological perspective has been fruitful is the study of the biochemical mechanisms that underlie behavior. It now appears that some abnormal behaviors result from a breakdown of one or more biochemical processes.

neuron A single nerve cell.   The nervous system is composed of billions of neurons. Although differing in some respects, each **neuron** has four major parts (Figure 2.1): (1) the cell body; (2) several dendrites, its short and thick extensions; (3) one or more axons, but usually only one, long and thin, extending a considerable distance from the cell body; and (4) terminal buttons on the many end branches of the axon. When a neuron is appropriately stimulated at its cell body or through its dendrites, a

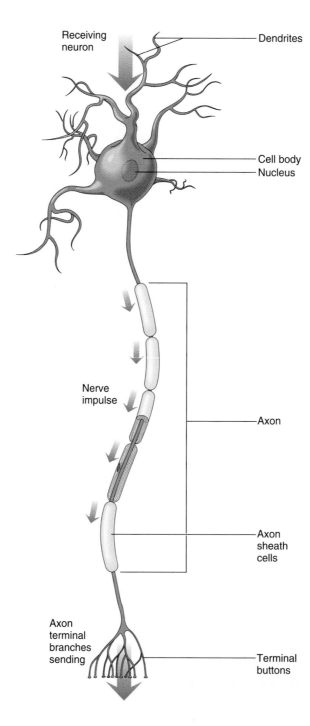

Figure 2.1   *The neuron, the basic unit of the nervous system.*

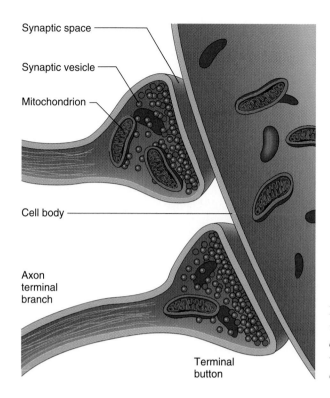

Synaptic space

Synaptic vesicle

Mitochondrion

Cell body

Axon
terminal
branch

Terminal
button

Figure 2.2 *A synapse, showing the terminal buttons of two axon branches in close contact with a very small portion of the cell body of another neuron.*

nerve impulse, a change in the electric potential of the cell, travels down the axon to the terminal endings. Between the terminal endings of the sending axon and the receiving neurons there is a small gap, the **synapse** (Figure 2.2).

Chemical Messengers: Neurotransmitters

For a nerve impulse to pass from one neuron to another, it must have a way of bridging the synaptic space. The terminal buttons of each axon contain synaptic vesicles. These small structures are filled with **neurotransmitters**, chemical substances important in transferring a nerve impulse from one neuron to another. A neuron synthesizes and stores only one principal neurotransmitter. When the nerve impulse reaches the terminal button, the synaptic vesicles release the neurotransmitter. The neurotransmitter crosses the synapse and stimulates another neuron by interacting with **receptors**, proteins embedded in the membrane of the postsynaptic cell. Each neurotransmitter is synthesized in the neuron through a series of metabolic steps, usually beginning with an amino acid. Each of the reactions along the way to producing an actual transmitter is catalyzed by an enzyme.

Several principal neurotransmitters have been identified and implicated in psychopathology, including norepinephrine, epinephrine, dopamine, serotonin, and gamma-aminobutyric acid (GABA). Theories linking neurotransmitters to the various psychopathologies usually propose that a given disorder is due to either too much of a particular transmitter (e.g., schizophrenia results from too much dopamine) or too little (e.g., anxiety results from too little GABA). Several explanations for these imbalances are possible. Too much or too little of a particular transmitter could result from an error in its synthesis. Similar disturbances in the amounts of specific transmitters could result from changes in the usual processes by which transmitters are deactivated after being released into the synapse. Generally, when a neurotransmitter has been released into the synapse, not all of it interacts with the receptors. What is left over needs to be cleaned up to restore the synapse to its prior state. Some of this excess transmitter is pumped back into the presynaptic neuron and some is deactivated by enzymes. A failure

nerve impulse A change in the electric potential of a *neuron*; a wave of depolarization spreads along the *neuron* and causes the release of the *neurotransmitter*.

synapse A small gap between two *neurons* where the nerve impulse passes from the axon of the first to the dendrites, cell body, or axon of the second.

neurotransmitters Chemical substances important in transferring a *nerve impulse* from one *neuron* to another.

receptors Proteins embedded in the membrane covering a neural cell that interact with one or more *neurotransmitters*.

of either of these processes could result in a neuron firing too easily and thus would be similar to a state of excess transmitter. Finally, the receptors could be at fault. If the receptors on the postsynaptic neuron were too numerous or too easily excited, for example, the result would be akin to having too much transmitter released. *Any of these deviant biochemical processes could produce abnormal behavior.*

Therapy Based on Biological Perspectives

An important implication of the biological perspective is that altering bodily functioning may be effective in treating or even preventing certain psychological disorders. In some cases, when a deficiency in a particular biochemical substance is found to contribute to some problem, it makes sense to attempt to correct the imbalance by providing appropriate doses of the deficient chemical. Clearly in this instance there is a reason to view a disorder as a biological defect and to attempt to correct the fault through a biological intervention.

Phenylketonuria (PKU) is a form of mental retardation caused by a genetically determined enzyme deficiency that makes the body unable to metabolize the amino acid phenylalanine into tyrosine. As we discuss in Chapter 14, state laws require routine testing of an infant's blood for excess phenylalanine; if the test is positive, a specific diet low in the amino acid is prescribed. Children otherwise doomed to profound mental deficiency can thereby be brought closer to the normal range of intelligence. This is an example of successful prevention via correcting a biological anomaly.

Some biological interventions are used to treat existing disorders rather than to prevent future ones. In some severe cases in which less-invasive procedures have already failed, brain surgery may be attempted (e.g., with obsessive-compulsive disorder; see Chapter 6). The predominant biological intervention, however, is drugs; they are in widespread use for disorders such as anxiety, depression, and schizophrenia. Lithium is the most frequently used drug in the treatment of bipolar disorder, and stimulants are often employed in treating children with attention-deficit disorder. Biological intervention strategies are somewhat more specific to particular disorders than are some psychological therapies (notably psychodynamic, humanistic, and existential approaches), so the particulars of these therapies are described in more detail in Chapters 6 through 15 on specific psychopathologies.

The Case of Ernest H. Revisited

APPLYING BIOLOGICAL PERSPECTIVES

A clinician working from a biological point of view would be attentive to the similarity between Ernest H.'s alternate manic and depressed states and the cyclical mood swings suffered by his father. Mindful of the research (to be reviewed in Chapter 10) that suggests a genetic factor in mood disorders, the therapist would likely hypothesize that some inherited, probably biochemical, defect predisposes him to break down under stress. Depending on his or her conclusions after extensive examination, the therapist might prescribe lithium carbonate, a drug that is generally helpful in reducing the magnitude of mood swings in bipolar disorder.

Evaluating Biological Perspectives

Biological perspectives on the causes and treatment of psychological disorders have made striking advances in the past several decades. There is strong evidence that genetics plays a role in establishing vulnerability to certain types of alcohol dependence among men (Chapter 12), autism (Chapter 14), and schizo-phrenia (Chapter 9), among other disorders. Likewise, biochemical research has suggested a role for neurotransmitters in several disorders. Therapeutically effective drugs have been developed for many disorders, including some of the most debilitating (e.g., schizophrenia, bipolar disorder, panic disorder, and major depression).

Biological research tends to have a far more scientific veneer than do the efforts of those working from other perspectives, making use, for instance, of highly sophisticated technologies. Furthermore, discussions of the biology of abnormal behavior seem more concrete; whatever their other disagreements, most clinicians and researchers at least recognize terms such as *gene, chromosome,* and *serotonin* as meaning the same thing in one lab as in another. The same cannot be said for some of the constructs (such as "repression" or "self-actualization") central to alternative perspectives on abnormal behavior. The image of science makes it all too easy to overlook limitations of the biological perspective, to assume that all its products represent definite, replicable facts, and that we are just around the corner from a biological cure for or prevention of all our troubles.

In this context it becomes particularly important to think critically and examine the evidence with a skeptical eye. Details are pursued in subsequent chapters, but for illustrative purposes we mention here three considerations:

▶ *Early findings of specific, single genes accounting for the heritability of mental disorders, such as bipolar disorder, have turned out to be difficult to replicate in subsequent research* (Reiss, Plomin, & Hetherington, 1991). Media accounts of biological research often give more prominent attention to the initial, promising findings than to subsequent failures to replicate them, leading to perhaps exaggerated perceptions of how solid the results are.

▶ Although studies show sound evidence that vulnerability to many disorders is to some extent heritable, the very same *behavior genetic studies actually provide some of the best evidence that biology alone is not the whole story*, that the development of psychological disorders also depends greatly on environmental factors (Reiss et al., 1991).

▶ *Medications for many disorders are effective only so long as the patient keeps taking them; they suppress symptoms but do not cure the disorder* or teach the patient skills for remaining well in the face of subsequent stress; therefore, relapse is a major problem when medication is discontinued (e.g., Michelson & Marchione, 1991).

TO RECAP

Those who view mental dysfunction from biological perspectives contend that psychological disorders stem from one or another faulty biological structure or mechanism. Behavior genetics research, particularly studies of monozygotic and dizygotic twins, has established that many psychological disorders are at least partly heritable. Research on neurochemistry has determined that several neurotransmitters play a role in various psychopathologies as well. Biological treatment in the form of medication has proven useful in controlling the symptoms of disorders but often does not provide a lasting cure. Thus patients are subject to a high risk of relapse when medication is discontinued.

Visual Summary for Chapter 2:

Psychodynamic, Humanistic/Existential and Biological Perspectives

Perspectives influence the hypotheses researchers test in searching for the causes of psychopathology and the methods therapists use in treating it.

Psychodynamic

Ideas About Causes of Mental Disorder	Methods of Treatment	Comments
Unconscious conflicts among id, superego, and ego can lead to unhealthy defensiveness, and, ultimately, maladaptive behavior.	Patient's free associations coupled with information in their dreams, and therapist's analysis of the transference of old relationships to the patient–analyst setting, enable the therapist to offer interpretations with the aim of making the unconscious conflicts conscious and thereby more easily replaced by healthier, more mature coping styles. Some recent variants are briefer and more directive.	Creative theory; fostered recognition of the importance of influences outside of awareness. Specific predictions are difficult to test scientifically.

Humanistic

Ideas About Causes of Mental Disorder	Methods of Treatment	Comments
Only conditional love and acceptance from parents or others leads a person to try to meet with approval rather than to accept the self as is and do what is intrinsically gratifying.	Therapist behaves in a genuine manner. Unconditionally prizes client; helps client achieve self-understanding by reflecting expressed and implicit feelings.	Results ambiguous in studies of therapy theory. May not be enough for more disturbed clients. Little impact on the search for causes of specific disorders.

Existential

Ideas About Causes of Mental Disorder	Methods of Treatment	Comments
Failure to cope with the anxiety that stems from being basically alone and aware of mortality leads a person to avoid the need to make his or her own choices and thus take responsibility for creating meaning in life.	*Encourage client to accept responsibility, explore choices, and relate authentically to others.*	*Vague as to how therapist is to achieve these goals. Little research on either causes or treatment*

Biological

Ideas About Causes of Mental Disorder	Methods of Treatment	Comments
Aberrant biological processes, such as genetically transmitted vulnerabilities to specific disorders, or too much or too little of a given neurotransmitter.	*Manipulation of the aberrant process, possibly through diet or surgery, but most often via medication.*	*Rapid recent progress in finding neurochemical mechanisms of pathology has helped development of effective drugs to ease some symptoms of disorder. However, genes' interaction with environment is also a factor in pathology. Drugs often provide temporary relief of symptoms, but not a cure.*

Chapter 3

Behavioral, Cognitive, and Vulnerability-Stress Perspectives

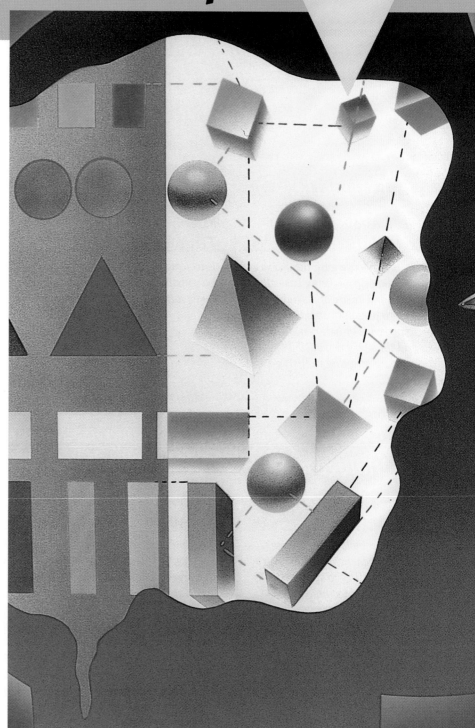

*I*n this chapter we complete our survey of major perspectives on abnormal behavior by discussing the behavioral, cognitive, and vulnerability/stress perspectives.

Behavioral Perspectives

The idea central to any **behavioral perspective**, that psychologists should restrict themselves to observable behavior, came about partly in response to dissatisfaction with the scientific status of structuralism, which dominated early twentieth-century psychology and held that the proper subject of study was mental functioning and structure. The goal of psychology, then a very new discipline, was to learn more about what goes on in the mind by analyzing the contents of conciousness. To do this, experimental psychologists such as Wilhelm Wundt (1882–1920), who founded the first formal psychological laboratory in Leipzig in 1879, and Edward Titchener (1867–1927), whose laboratory was at Cornell University, devised elaborate training procedures to teach subjects to report on the most basic aspects of their experiences while being exposed to stimuli. Through painstaking **introspection,** self-observation of mental processes, subjects attempted to uncover the building blocks of experience and the structure of consciousness. For example, Wundt's subjects listened to a metronome set to click usually slowly and sometimes fast, sometimes sounding only a few times and then many. The subjects looked within themselves and reported that a fast series of clicks made them excited, a slow series relaxed. Just before each click they were conscious of a slight feeling of tension, and afterward, slight relief.

After several years, many in the field began to lose faith in the ability of introspection to obtain useful knowledge about people because different laboratories using the introspective method were yielding conflicting data. It appeared that introspection was not clarifying the answers to any questions. This dissatisfaction was brought to a head by John B. Watson (1878–1958), who in 1913 revolutionized psychology with statements such as the following:

> Psychology as the behaviorist views it is a purely objective experimental branch of natural science. Its theoretical goal is the prediction and control of behavior. Introspection forms no essential part of its methods, nor is the scientific value of its data dependent upon the readiness with which they lend themselves to interpretation in terms of consciousness. (p. 158)

To replace introspection, Watson looked to the experimental procedures of the psychologists who were investigating learning in animals. Because of his efforts, the focus of psychology changed from thinking to learning and consequently behavior. The task of psychology became to find out which stimuli would elicit which directly observable responses as an animal learned new habits. With such objective stimulus–response information, psychologists hoped that human behavior could be both predicted and controlled. **Behaviorism** can be defined as an approach that focuses on the study of observable behavior rather than of consciousness.

Pavlov: Classical Conditioning

Several types of learning attracted the research efforts of psychologists. The first type, classical conditioning, was discovered quite by accident by the Russian physiologist Ivan Pavlov (1849–1936) at the turn of the century. In his studies of the digestive system, a dog was given meat powder to make it salivate. Before long, Pavlov's laboratory assistants became aware that the dog began salivating

behavioral perspective As applied in abnormal psychology, a set of assumptions that *abnormal behavior* is learned in the same way as other human behavior.

introspection A procedure whereby trained subjects are asked to report on their conscious experiences. This was the principal method of study in early twentieth-century psychology.

John B. Watson, American psychologist, was the major figure in establishing psychology as the study of observable behavior rather than an investigation of subjective experience.

behaviorism The school of psychology associated with John B. Watson, who proposed that observable behavior, not consciousness, is the proper subject matter of psychology.

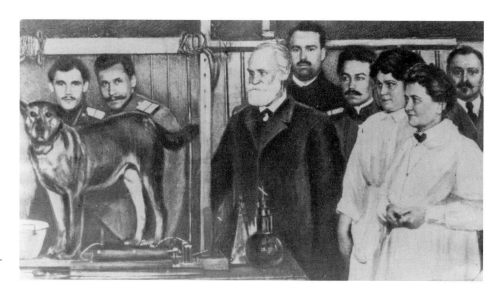

Pavlov's studies of dogs provided a foundation for understanding classical conditioning, one of the fundamental processes of learning.

when it saw the person who fed it, and as the experiment continued, the dog began to salivate even earlier, when it heard the footsteps of its feeder. Pavlov was intrigued by these findings and decided to study the dog's reactions systematically. In the first of many experiments, a bell was rung behind the dog, and then the meat powder was placed in its mouth. After this procedure had been repeated a number of times, the dog began salivating as soon as it heard the bell ring and before meat powder was given.

classical conditioning A basic form of learning, sometimes referred to as Pavlovian conditioning, in which a neutral stimulus is paired with another stimulus (called the *unconditioned stimulus, or UCS)* that naturally elicits a certain desired response (called the *unconditioned response or UCR)*. After repeated trials the neutral stimulus becomes a *conditioned stimulus (CS)* and evokes the same or a similar response, now called the *conditioned response (CR)*.

Classical conditioning can be defined as a process by which a neutral stimulus comes to elicit a response by virtue of being associated with a stimulus that automatically elicits the response even in the absence of prior learning. In Pavlov's experiment, because the meat powder automatically elicits salivation, with no prior learning, the powder is termed an **unconditioned stimulus (UCS)** and the response of salivation an **unconditioned response (UCR)**. When the offering of meat powder is preceded several times by a neutral stimulus, the ringing of a bell (Figure 3.1), the sound of the bell alone (the **conditioned stimulus, CS**) is able to elicit the salivary response (the **conditioned response, CR**). As

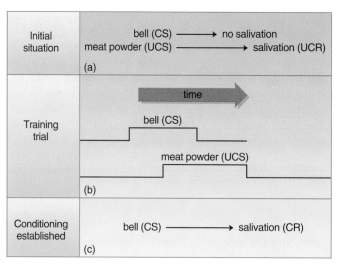

Figure 3.1 *The process of classical conditioning. (a) Before learning, the meat powder (UCS) elicits salivation (UCR), but the bell (CS) does not. (b) A training or learning trial consists of presentations of the CS, followed closely by the UCS. (c) Classical conditioning has been accomplished when the previously neutral bell elicits salivation (CR).*

the number of paired presentations of the bell and the meat powder increases, the number of salivations elicited by the bell increases. When the repeated soundings of the bell are later not followed by meat powder, fewer and fewer salivations are elicited, and the CR gradually disappears. This process is called **extinction**.

Another famous experiment, questionable from an ethical point of view, was conducted by John Watson and Rosalie Rayner (1920). They introduced an eleven-month-old boy, Little Albert, to a white rat. The child indicated no fear of the animal and appeared to want to play with it. But whenever he reached for the rat, the experimenter made a loud noise (the UCS) by striking a steel bar behind Albert's head, causing him great fright (the UCR). After five such experiences Albert became very frightened (the CR) by the sight of the white rat, even when the steel bar was not struck. The fear initially associated with the loud noise had come to be elicited by the previously neutral stimulus, the white rat (now the CS). This study suggests the possible relationship between classical conditioning and the development of certain emotional disorders, in this instance a phobia.

Thorndike and Skinner: Operant Conditioning

The second principal type of learning drew primarily on the work of Edward Thorndike (1874–1949). Rather than investigate stimuli and the responses they elicit, as Pavlov did, Thorndike was interested in the effect that consequences have on behavior. He had observed that alley cats, angered by being caged and making furious efforts to escape, would eventually and accidentally hit the latch that freed them. Recaged again and again, they would soon come to touch the latch immediately and purposefully. Based on these observations Thorndike formulated the **law of effect**: behavior that is followed by consequences satisfying to the organism will be repeated, and behavior that is followed by noxious or unpleasant consequences will be discouraged. Thus the behavior or response that has consequences serves as an instrument, encouraging or discouraging its own repetition. For this reason, learning that focuses on consequences was first called instrumental learning.

Some years later, B. F. Skinner (1904–90) introduced **operant conditioning**, a term that highlights behavior that operates on the environment. He reformulated the law of effect by shifting the focus from the linking of stimuli and responses—S–R connections—to the relationships between responses and their consequences. The distinction is subtle, but it reflects Skinner's contention that stimuli do not so much get connected to responses as they become the occasions for responses to occur if, in the past, they have been reinforced. For example, we all come to learn that if we tell a server in a restaurant what we want to eat, the request will usually be reinforced by eating. In this instance the server is what Skinner called a **discriminative stimulus**—an event that, in effect, tells an organism that if it performs a certain behavior, a certain consequence will follow.

Renaming the "law of effect" the "principle of reinforcement," Skinner distinguished two types of reinforcement. **Positive reinforcement** refers to the strengthening of a tendency to respond by virtue of the presentation of an event, called a positive reinforcer. For example, a hungry person will tend to repeat behaviors (operants) that are followed by the availability of food. **Negative reinforcement** also strengthens a response, but it does so via the removal of an unpleasant or aversive event rather than the addition of a positive one. If a child stops whining when attended to by a parent, the whining is a *negative reinforcer* of the parent's behavior. That is, the parent's tendency to attend to the child is increased, because doing so causes the unpleasant behavior to stop. Note that negative reinforcers are aversive consequences that, because they are removed by

extinction The elimination of a classically *conditioned response* by the omission of the *unconditioned stimulus*. In *operant conditioning*, the elimination of the *conditioned response* by the omission of *reinforcement*.

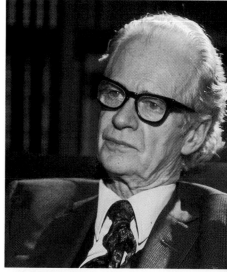

B. F. Skinner was responsible for the study of operant behavior and the extension of this approach to education, psychotherapy, and society as a whole.

law of effect A principle of learning that holds that behavior is acquired by virtue of its consequences.

operant conditioning The acquisition or elimination of a response as a function of the environmental contingencies of *reinforcement* and *punishment*.

discriminative stimulus An event that informs an organism that if a particular response is made, *reinforcement* will follow.

positive reinforcement The strengthening of a tendency to behave by virtue of the fact that previous responses in that situation have been followed by presentation of a desired reward.

negative reinforcement The strengthening of a tendency to behave by virtue of the fact that previous responses in that situation have been rewarded by the removal of an aversive stimulus.

punishment In psychological experiments, any noxious stimulus imposed on the animal or person to reduce the probability that it will behave in an undesired way.

Babies are experts at evoking caretaking behaviors, which they often go on to negatively reinforce by calming down.

a response, increase the likelihood of that response to recur. They differ from **punishment**. A punishment is any consequence that decreases the probability of the response occurring in the same situation in the future.

Skinner argued that all behavior is determined by the reinforcers provided by the social environment. The goal of Skinner (1953) and his followers, like that of Watson, was the prediction and control of behavior. The behaviorists hope that by analyzing behavior in terms of observable responses and reinforcement, they will be able to determine when certain behavior will occur. The information gathered should then help indicate how behavior is acquired, maintained, changed, and eliminated.

In the Skinnerian approach, abstract terms and concepts are avoided. For example, in contrast to Freud's theories, references to thoughts, needs, motivation, and wants are conspicuously absent in Skinnerian writings. To provide an entirely satisfactory account of human behavior, Skinner believed that psychology must restrict its attention to directly observable stimuli and responses and to the effects of reinforcement.

As an example of how operant conditioning can be applied to understanding the cause of a form of abnormality, let us consider depression. Behavioral researchers would not focus their theory on the mood state itself, because depressed mood is not directly observable. Rather, they might focus on something observable, such as how much the depressed person moves around (generally little). Lewinsohn (1974) proposed that depression results from a low level of positive reinforcement. When the amount of reinforcement decreases, the person emits fewer responses, the amount of reinforcement decreases further, and depression finally results. Lewinsohn's theory is relatively straightforward to describe, but more complicated to test, as discussed in the following critical thinking exercise.

> ### APPLYING CRITICAL THINKING SKILLS

PLEASANT EVENTS AND DEPRESSION

Outside the laboratory it is very difficult to observe directly the extent to which someone's actions result in positive reinforcement over a period of time. As a way to estimate positive reinforcement, MacPhillamy and Lewinsohn (1974) asked people to indicate how often (if at all) in the past month each of 320 events had occurred. The list of events was developed by asking earlier samples of people what sorts of events provided them pleasure and included items such as "talking about sports, playing in a musical group, being with their grandchildren" (MacPhillamy & Lewinsohn, 1974, p. 652). Depressed people reported fewer such events in the past month than did either people with other psychological disorders or nondistressed people.

▷ *What conclusion does the evidence seem to support?* The lower frequency of pleasant events supports the idea that depressed people experience less positive reinforcement, which can maintain their depression and may even have caused it in the first place.

▷ *What other interpretations are plausible?* Depressed people also tend to think negatively, as is emphasized by the cognitive perspective discussed later in this chapter. Perhaps depressed people experience just as many pleasant events as do other people, but they have a harder time remembering the positive events and an easier time remembering negative events.

▷ *What other information would help choose among the alternative interpretations?* Measuring the occurrence of events by asking depressed and nondepressed people what happened to them in the past month cannot distinguish actual differences in what happened from memory biases. One option would be to ask a friend who knows the subject well to report on what the subject has experienced.

If depressed people really engage in fewer pleasant events, this difference from nondepressed people should be evident in their friends' reports about them also. If MacPhillamy and Lewinsohn's results came about because of the effect of depression on memory, then friends' reports will not reveal an especially low rate of pleasant events for depressed people. Finally, it is possible that both points of view are partly correct. That is, depressed people may engage in fewer pleasant events than nondepressed people, but they may exaggerate this deficit by selective forgetting of positive experiences. This possibility would be supported if the study of friends' reports showed smaller, but still noticeable, differences in pleasant events, with the nondepressed subjects scoring higher.

Modeling

The behavioral perspective also emphasizes a third type of learning, **modeling**, sometimes called observational learning. Modeling involves learning new behaviors by watching and imitating others. Experimental work has demonstrated that witnessing someone perform certain activities can increase or decrease diverse kinds of behavior, such as sharing, aggression, and fear (e.g., Bandura & Menlove, 1968). For example, a child might learn to fear and avoid large dogs by witnessing a parent acting fearfully in their presence.

modeling Learning by observing the behavior of others.

Children can learn new behaviors, for better or worse, by watching and imitating others.

Therapy Based on Behavioral Perspectives

Several therapeutic techniques have been developed as an outgrowth of behavioral perspectives. The term **behavior therapy** is often applied to these techniques. Depending on the results of an initial behavioral assessment (see Chapter 5), the behavior therapist, together with the patient, targets behaviors to be increased (for example, expressing one's feelings clearly to friends) or decreased (smoking cigarettes) and develops a strategy for achieving this behavior change.

behavior therapy A branch of *psychotherapy* relying mainly on the application of learning principles to the alteration of clinical problems.

Counterconditioning

Classical conditioning principles have been used to break the connection between conditioned responses such as fear and anxiety and the conditioned stimuli, such as dogs or snakes or airplanes, that provoke those responses. The association of fear and dogs, for example, can be eliminated by pairing the conditioned stimulus (the dog) with new, nonfearful responses. Referred to as **counterconditioning**, this principle of behavior change holds that a response to a given stimulus can be eliminated by eliciting a new response in the presence of that stimulus, as diagrammed in Figure 3.2. For example, if a child is afraid of a harmless animal, the therapist might attempt to elicit a playful reaction in the presence of the animal. This counterconditioning, or substitution of a playful response, can eliminate fear.

counterconditioning Relearning achieved by eliciting a new response in the presence of a particular stimulus.

An early clinical demonstration of counterconditioning was reported by Mary Cover Jones (1924). She successfully eliminated a little boy's fear of rabbits by feeding him in the presence of a rabbit. The animal was kept several feet away at first, and then it was moved gradually closer on successive occasions. In this fashion the fear produced by the rabbit was crowded out by the stronger positive feelings associated with eating.

Systematic Desensitization

In his work with fearful adults, Joseph Wolpe (1958) employed techniques similar to those used by Jones. He found that many of his clients could be encouraged to expose themselves gradually to the situation or object they feared if they were at the same time engaging in behavior that inhibited anxiety. Rather than have his patients eat, however, Wolpe taught these adults deep muscle relaxation. Many of the fears felt by Wolpe's patients were so abstract—for example, fear of criticism and fear of failure—that it seemed impractical to confront them with real-life situations that would evoke these fears. Therefore, Wolpe reasoned that he might have fearful patients imagine what they feared.

Joseph Wolpe, one of the pioneers in behavior therapy, is known particularly for systematic desensitization, a widely applied behavioral technique.

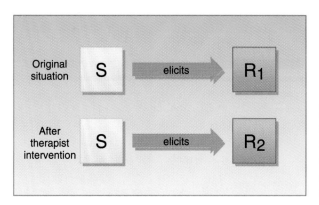

Figure 3.2 *Schematic diagram of counterconditioning. An original response (R_1) to a given stimulus (S) is eliminated by evoking a new response (R_2) to the same stimulus.*

Thus he formulated a new technique, **systematic desensitization**, in which a deeply relaxed person is asked to imagine a series of increasingly anxiety-provoking situations; the relaxation tends to inhibit any anxiety that might otherwise be elicited by the imagined scenes. If relaxation does give way to anxiety, the client signals to the therapist by raising an index finger, stops imagining the situation, rests, reestablishes relaxation, and then reimagines the situation. If anxiety drives out relaxation again, the client goes back to an earlier situation and later tries to handle the more difficult one. Over successive sessions a client is usually able to tolerate increasingly more difficult scenes as he or she climbs the hierarchy in imagination. The ability to tolerate stressful imagery in therapy sessions is usually accompanied by reduced anxiety in real-life situations. To move their adjustment from imagination to reality, clients are generally instructed to place themselves in progressively more frightening real-life situations between therapy sessions.

Systematic desensitization appears deceptively simple. However, as with any therapy for people in emotional distress, its application is a complicated affair. For one thing, the clinician must determine, by means of a comprehensive behavioral assessment, that the situations creating anxiety in the client do not warrant such fearful reactions. If a person is anxious because he or she lacks the skills to deal with a given set of circumstances, desensitization is not appropriate; for example, to be anxious about piloting an airplane is logical when you don't know how to operate an aircraft!

systematic desensitization A major *behavior therapy* procedure in which a fearful person, while deeply relaxed, imagines a series of progressively more fearsome situations. The two responses of relaxation and fear are incompatible, and fear is dispelled.

Relaxation training is the first step in systematic desensitization. Once clients master relaxation, they begin to imagine scenes from the anxiety hierarchy.

The thirty-five-year-old substitute mail carrier who consulted us had dropped out of college sixteen years ago because of crippling fears of being criticized. Earlier, his disability had taken the form of extreme tension when faced with tests and speaking up in class. When we saw him, he was debilitated by fears of criticism in general and of evaluations of his mail sorting in particular. As a consequence, his everyday activities were severely constricted and, though highly intelligent, he had apparently settled for an occupation that did not promise self-fulfillment.

After the client agreed that a reduction in his unrealistic fears would be beneficial, he was taught over several sessions to relax all the muscles of his body while in a reclining chair. We then created for him a list of anxiety-provoking scenes.

You are saying "Good morning" to your boss.
You are standing in front of your sorting bin in the post office, and your supervisor asks why you are so slow.
You are only halfway through your route, and it is already 2:00 P.M.
As you are delivering Mrs. Mackenzie's mail, she opens her screen door and complains about how late you are.
Your wife criticizes you for bringing home the wrong kind of bread.
The officer at the bridge toll gate appears impatient as you fumble in your pocket for the correct change.

These and other scenes were arranged in an *anxiety hierarchy*, from least to most fear-evoking. Desensitization proper began with the client instructed first to relax deeply as he had been taught. Then he was to imagine the easiest item, remaining as relaxed as possible. When he had learned to confront this image without becoming anxious, he went on to the next scene, and so on. After ten sessions the man was able to imagine the most distressing scene in the hierarchy without feeling anxious and gradually his tension in real life became markedly less.

Though outcomes of single cases do not prove anything, this early case of one of the authors just happened to turn out exceptionally well. Freed of his social evaluative anxieties, this client went on to finish college, then earned a Ph.D., and is now a tenured professor. Would that all our clients fared as well.

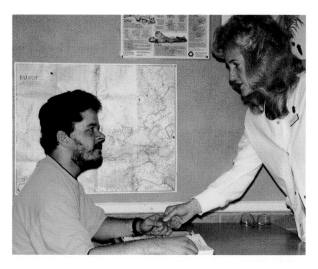

Shown here is a token economy conducted by the Social-Learning Program at Fulton State Hospital, Fulton, Missouri. The patient is receiving a token and verbal praise from the staff member for actively participating in an academic class.

Token Economies

In the 1950s, several investigators suggested that therapists should try to apply Skinner's (1953) work on operant conditioning and shape overt behavior in humans through the use of reinforcement and punishment. An early example of this work is the **token economy**, a procedure in which tokens (such as poker chips or stickers) are given for desired behavior. The tokens can later be exchanged for desirable items and activities.

token economy A *behavior therapy* procedure, based on *operant conditioning* principles, in which patients are given tokens, such as poker chips, for desired behaviors. The tokens can be exchanged for desirable items and activities.

In one study, an entire ward of a mental hospital was set aside for a series of experiments (Ayllon & Azrin, 1968). The forty-five female patients, who averaged sixteen years of hospitalization, were systematically rewarded for such activities as making their beds and combing their hair. The rewards were plastic tokens that could later be exchanged for special privileges, such as listening to records, going to the movies, renting a private room, or enjoying extra visits to the canteen. The rules of the token economy—the medium of exchange, the chores and self-care rewarded and by what number of tokens, the items and privileges that could be purchased and for how many tokens—were carefully established and posted. Even markedly disturbed adult hospital patients were taught to do such things as arrive on time for meals and eat with utensils.

Time-out is an operant procedure wherein the consequence for misbehavior is removal to an environment with no positive reinforcers.

Using Modeling in Therapy

Behavior therapists can employ modeling in changing behavior, often in a manner similar to systematic desensitization. For example, phobics have been shown films of people confronting whatever it is that the phobic patient fears—snakes, hospitals, dogs, dental work—even sex. In these films the actors, or models, gradually move closer to the feared animal or situation. With this treatment the fears of the patients are decidedly reduced (e.g., Bandura, Blanchard, & Ritter, 1969; Hill, Liebert, & Mott, 1968; Roberts, Wurtele, Boone, Ginther, & Elkins, 1981; Melamed, Hawes, Heiby, & Glick, 1975). Tastefully designed explicit films of people touching themselves, masturbating, and having intercourse have helped inhibited adults become more comfortable with their sexuality (McMullen & Rosen, 1979).

Assertiveness Training. An important application of modeling is in the area of **assertiveness training**, which may begin with conversations in which the therapist tries to get the client to distinguish between assertiveness and aggression. People who are submissive may feel that they are being hostile even when making a reasonable request or refusing a presumptuous one. Next, the therapist usually provides sample situations that require that the client stand up for himself or herself—otherwise the client would feel put upon.

The therapist discusses and models appropriate assertiveness and then has the client role-play situations. Improvement is rewarded by praise from the therapist or from other members of an assertiveness-training group. Graded homework assignments, such as asking a mechanic to explain the latest bill for repairs or telling a relative that his or her constant criticisms are resented, are given as soon as the client has acquired some degree of assertiveness through session work.

assertiveness training Behavior therapy procedures that attempt to help a person express more easily thoughts, wishes, beliefs, and legitimate feelings of resentment or approval.

The Case of Ernest H. Revisited ◄

APPLYING BEHAVIORAL PERSPECTIVES

A therapist working from a behavioral perspective would want to obtain more information about the conditions in which Ernest H. feels especially anxious about being evaluated by others. The therapist might employ systematic desensitization, teaching Ernest to relax deeply as he imagines a hierarchy of these situations. A behavioral therapist would also probably use modeling to teach Ernest more constructive behaviors (to replace verbal and physical abuse) to use in situations in which he doubts his wife's fidelity. Once communication has improved in the relationship, any sexual problems that remain might be treated by developing a series of undemanding but increasingly more intimate sexual encounters with his wife.

Evaluating Behavioral Perspectives

Because it calls attention to the importance of the immediate situation or environmental factors (such as discriminative stimuli or the reinforcing effects of how other people respond to one's behavior), the behavioral perspective complements the psychodynamic perspective's detailed attention to internal and unconscious processes. Moreover, the roots of the behavioral perspective in the psychology of learning have raised the standards of science in abnormal psychology. Behavior therapists have been especially diligent in subjecting their treatment techniques to the test of controlled research.

Specifying the nature of the treatment, a requirement for research, is relatively easy in a medication study, for example, of the effects of 250 milligrams of a chemical compound given once a day. It is quite difficult, however, in studying psychotherapies, which take place in the context of interpersonal relationships and conversations that do not follow mechanical, standardized scripts. Nevertheless, attempting to be more concrete and detailed about which therapeutic methods were used is necessary if therapists want others to be able to test (or simply use) a treatment technique. The use of treatment manuals by behavior therapists in this respect has been adopted by psychodynamic, cognitive, and humanistic therapists as well (Luborsky & DeRubeis, 1984).

Another important contribution made by the behavioral perspective is that it has greatly expanded the scope of psychotherapy. Two differences from psychoanalysis as developed by Freud are noteworthy here. First, operant behavior therapy techniques rely on changing the environment, not solely on changing the patient. Second, interventions based on learning principles tend to be shorter because they are more active, directive and goal-focused than classical psychoanalysis (this contrast is less sharp when newer psychodynamic perspectives are considered; see Chapter 2).

These features of behavior therapy make effective psychological intervention accessible to many people for whom long-term, insight-oriented techniques are not economically feasible, or at least not efficient. Behavior therapy has been applied with success to improve the social skills of chronic schizophrenic patients and the communication skills of autistic children, to cite just two examples. The range of childhood behavior problems that are treated, often successfully, through operant conditioning is broad, including bed-wetting, thumb sucking, nail biting, aggression, tantrums, hyperactivity, disruptive classroom behavior, poor school performance, language deficiency, extreme social withdrawal, and asthmatic attacks (Nemeroff & Karoly, 1991).

In spite of these accomplishments, the behavioral perspective also shows significant limitations. Its commendable emphasis on scientific evaluations of therapy outcome has made clear that the methods, while useful, do not lead to complete and lasting cures in all, or depending on the disorder, in even a majority of cases. Also, though its achievements in the area of treatment have been strong, the behavioral perspective has been less successful as an explanation of the causes of psychopathology. Abnormality has not yet been convincingly traced to particular learning experiences. Consider how difficult it would be to show that depression results from a particular reinforcement history. A person would have to be continually observed over a period of years while his or her behavior was recorded and occurrences of reinforcement noted.

Moreover, the fact that therapeutic methods derived from learning principles are effective does not prove that the particular deviant behavior was learned in the first place (Rimland, 1964). (Similar logic applies for the other perspectives. If a medication is helpful, for instance, this in itself does not mean that the problems must have been caused in the way predicted by the theory that led to using medication. Likewise, a nonbiological therapy might work even if the original source of the problem was biological.) It does not even prove that improvement came about by virtue of the learning mechanisms hypothesized to underlie the treatment. Systematic desensitization, for instance, has been shown to reduce anxiety in many controlled studies. Some investigators believe, however, that counterconditioning is not necessarily the best explanation of why the method works. They believe it may be exposure to what the person fears that creates the change. Relaxation may be merely a useful way to encourage a frightened individual to confront what he or she fears (Wilson & Davison, 1971) rather than a means of providing a new, conditioned response.

TO RECAP

The behavioral perspective is concerned with how behaviors are learned and how maladaptive learned behaviors can be changed through new learning. Classical conditioning involves changes in the connection between antecedent conditions and behaviors. Operant conditioning involves the effect of positive and negative consequences on behavior. Modeling refers to direct imitation of behaviors. Each of these mechanisms of learning has spawned a number of treatment techniques. Behavior therapy has been applied to a wide array of psychological problems, with considerable success. However, the behavioral perspective's contributions to our understanding of the causes of psychopathology have been less extensively validated in research than the effectiveness of the treatments based on them.

Cognitive Perspectives

We have seen that behavioral perspectives emphasize aspects of a person's situation or environment as a cause of abnormal behavior or behavior change, whereas the psychodynamic and humanistic perspectives focus almost exclusively on the patient's inner conflicts, thoughts, and feelings. Some researchers and therapists sympathetic to the behavioral emphasis on controlled research nevertheless believe that principles of conditioning and modeling alone could not adequately account for therapeutic change.

Research began to suggest that achieving behavior change required attending not only to the consequences of behavior, but also to such issues as patients' attitudes toward their problems, beliefs about their therapists and whether they should adhere to their therapists' influence, and so forth. In short, the patient's thinking, or cognition, was part of the picture along with the actual details of the situations the patient confronted. For example, a child's success or lack of it in school came to be seen as a product not just of the rewards received, but also of the child's expectations as well as those of the teachers.

Cognition is a term that groups together the mental processes of perceiving, recognizing, conceiving, judging, and reasoning. The **cognitive perspective** focuses on how people—and animals—structure their experiences, how they make sense of them, transforming environmental stimuli into information that is usable. Cognitive psychologists regard the learner as aware and actively interpreting a situation in the light of past experience and expectations about the future.

The learner fits new information into an organized network of already accumulated knowledge, often referred to as a **schema** (Neisser, 1976). New information may fit the schema; if not, the learner reorganizes the schema to fit the information. The following situation illustrates how a schema, or cognitive set, may alter the way in which information is processed and remembered.

cognition The process of knowing; the thinking, judging, reasoning, and planning activities of the human mind.

cognitive perspective General view that people can best be understood by studying how they perceive and structure their experiences.

schema A mental structure for organizing information about the world (*Pl.* schemata)

> The man stood before the mirror and combed his hair. He checked his face carefully for any places he might have missed shaving and then put on the conservative tie he had decided to wear. At breakfast, he studied the newspaper carefully and, over coffee, discussed the possibility of buying a new washing machine with his wife. Then he made several phone calls. As he was leaving the house he thought about the fact that his children would probably want to go to that private camp again this summer. When the car didn't start, he got out, slammed the door and walked down to the bus stop in a very angry mood. Now he would be late. (Bransford & Johnson, 1973, p. 415).

Now read the excerpt again, but add the word "unemployed" before the word "man." Now read it a third time, substituting "stockbroker" for "man." Notice how differently you understand the passage. Ask yourself what parts of the newspaper these men read. If this query had been posed on a questionnaire, you

Aaron Beck developed a cognitive therapy for the cognitive biases of depressed people.

might have answered "the want ads" for the unemployed man and "the financial pages" for the stockbroker. Actually, the passage does not specify which part of the paper was read. Your answers would have been wrong, but in each instance the error would have been a meaningful, predictable one.

The most recent of the perspectives covered in this book, cognitive viewpoints have become widespread and influential but without really substituting for psychoanalytic and behavioral points of view (Friman, Allen, Kerwin, & Larzelere, 1993). The emphases of contemporary cognitive theorists vary somewhat, but all link mental disorders to maladaptive thought patterns and misjudgments.

In this section we review the two best-known theories from the cognitive perspective in abnormal psychology, the cognitive theory and therapy of Aaron T. Beck and the rational-emotive theory and therapy developed by Albert Ellis.

Beck's Cognitive Theory

Cognitive theory has been applied to the explanation of many psychological disorders. At the most general level, the theory holds that how a person thinks about the negative events that befall her or him are the most critical causes of negative emotions and dysfunctional behaviors. In analyzing thinking, cognitive theory distinguishes between automatic thoughts and dysfunctional beliefs. **Automatic thoughts** are negative and unrealistic conscious thoughts and images that appear to come on involuntarily and are not readily dismissed by the person. **Dysfunctional beliefs** are tacit attitudes that constitute vulnerability to psychopathology and are often not obvious to the person. For example, a parent hears a child say that he or she failed a test at school and experiences the automatic thought "What a lousy parent I am." Underlying this and related automatic thoughts may be the dysfunctional belief that the parent is completely responsible for the happiness and welfare of the entire family.

In contrast to automatic thoughts, dysfunctional beliefs are not expected to be readily accessible, particularly when things are going well. That is, people do not walk around thinking "I must make sure that everyone in my family is successful and happy" or "Everybody must love me, or else I am worthless." Adherence to

automatic thoughts In Beck's theory, the things people picture or tell themselves as they make their way in life.

dysfunctional beliefs In Beck's theory, attitudes, of which a person may be unaware, that constitute vulnerability to *psychopathology*.

these beliefs becomes apparent only when they are challenged by negative events (e.g., clear indications of failure or of rejection). The negative automatic thoughts and emotions that result from such events become active and therefore more obvious.

An important aspect of Beck's theorizing is that each psychological disorder is characterized by a particular type of thought pattern (Beck, 1976). Automatic thoughts centering on themes of loss and failure, accompanied by globally negative evaluations of the self, characterize depression, for instance. The thought patterns of those with anxiety disorders are characterized by a preoccupation with danger. These patients may be overly sensitive to feelings of nervousness or excitement or pay so much attention to these normal feelings that they come to seem overwhelming. For others, external situations, such as crowds or bridges, are perceived as threats, signals of imminent catastrophe.

Cognitive Therapy: Changing Maladaptive Interpretations

The overall goal of Beck's **cognitive therapy (CT)** is to provide the client with experiences, both in and outside the consulting room, that will alter automatic thoughts and dysfunctional beliefs in a favorable way. Thus a client who, based on an ineptness belief, bemoans his or her witlessness for burning a roast, is encouraged to view the failure as regrettable, but discouraged from overgeneralizing and concluding that he or she can do nothing right on future occasions.

cognitive therapy (CT) A therapy associated with the psychiatrist Aaron T. Beck, concerned with changing negative *schemata* and certain cognitive biases or distortions that underlie and reinforce the person's symptoms.

Attempts to change negative thinking are made at both the behavioral and the cognitive levels. One behavioral technique, useful for clients who are convinced that they are depressed all the time and who become still more deeply depressed because of this belief, is to have them record their moods at regular intervals during the day. If it turns out that these reports show some variability, as indeed often happens even with very depressed people, this information will challenge their general belief that life is always miserable. This change in thinking can then serve as the basis for a change in behavior, such as getting out of bed in the morning, doing a few chores, or even going to work.

Similarly, depressed clients often do very little because tasks seem to them insurmountable and thus they believe they can accomplish nothing. To test this belief, the therapist breaks down a particular task into small steps and encourages the client to focus on just one step at a time. If this tactic is skillfully handled—if, for example, the therapist has developed a sufficient rapport or relationship with the patient to suggest that the shy, depressed patient simply go get a cup of coffee or dessert—the patient finds that he or she can, in fact, accomplish something. These small accomplishments are then discussed with the therapist as inconsistent with the notion that tasks are beyond the patient's ability. As the patient's view of the self begins to change, more difficult tasks will appear less forbidding, and success can build on success, with still further beneficial changes in the client's beliefs about the self and his or her world.

In Beck's therapy, therapist and patient work as co-investigators to uncover and examine any maladaptive interpretations of the world that may be aggravating the patient's depression and general life condition. They try to uncover both automatic thoughts and dysfunctional beliefs. Even though automatic thoughts are in principle readily accessible, most of us are not in the habit of monitoring and evaluating them. Clients therefore usually need practice in taking note of such thoughts and images, especially the ones that are associated with depressed mood. The therapist helps the client monitor such thoughts, and together they examine their validity. Why should your child's problems at school mean that you are a bad parent? What else affects your youngster and determines whether he or she does well at school? In this fashion the therapist teaches the client to check his or her thoughts against the available information and to entertain hypotheses that might attribute the child's failure on the test to factors other than having a bad parent.

This phase of identifying and modifying automatic thoughts is followed by a more subtle phase, the identification of underlying dysfunctional assumptions or beliefs. How can the therapist help the individual alter dysfunctional assumptions? In addition to verbal persuasion, the therapist may encourage the client to behave in a way inconsistent with these assumptions. For example, a person who believes it is necessary to please everyone at the office can decline the next unreasonable request and see whether, as he or she was assuming, the sky falls.

Ellis's Rational-Emotive Theory

irrational beliefs Self-defeating assumptions that are assumed by *rational-emotive* therapists to underlie psychological distress.

rational-emotive theory (RET) The model that explains *psychopathology* as a result of negative experiences occurring to someone who holds *irrational beliefs* about their implications.

Another cognitive theory and therapy views **irrational beliefs** as the source of mental dysfunction. This idea, put forth by Albert Ellis (1962) and called **rational-emotive theory (RET)**, proposes that when negative events occur, people who hold rational beliefs will experience normal negative emotions such as sorrow, concern, and frustration. People who subscribe to irrational beliefs, such as having to be perfect in everything they do, however, will feel unhealthy levels of depression, anxiety, and anger and will behave in a self-defeating manner. RET emphasizes three main categories of irrational belief, each having particular consequences:

1. "I must be thoroughly competent, adequate, achieving, and lovable at all times, or else I am an incompetent, worthless person." This belief is expected to lead to feelings of panic and depression.
2. "Other significant people in my life must treat me kindly and fairly at all times, or else I can't stand it and they are bad, rotten, and evil persons who should be severely blamed, damned, and vindictively punished for their horrible treatment of me." This belief is expected to lead to feelings of anger and to aggressive behavior.
3. "Things and conditions absolutely must be the way I want them to be and must never be too difficult or frustrating. Otherwise, life is awful, terrible, horrible, catastrophic, and unbearable." This belief is hypothesized to create self-pity and low frustration tolerance, as well as procrastination (Kendall, et al., 1995).

Rational-Emotive Therapy: Disputing Irrational Beliefs

rational-emotive therapy (RET) A therapy introduced by Albert Ellis and based on the assumption that much disordered behavior is rooted in absolutistic demands that people make on themselves. The therapy aims to alter the unrealistic, self-defeating goals individuals set for themselves, such as "I must be universally loved."

The aim of **rational-emotive therapy (RET)** is to eliminate irrational beliefs and thus self-defeating emotions and behaviors. After becoming familiar with the client's problems, the therapist presents the basic theory of rational-emotive therapy so the client can understand and accept it. Once the client is persuaded that his or her emotional problems will benefit from rational examination, the therapist proceeds to teach the person to identify and challenge irrational beliefs. Exactly how this is done varies a great deal from one RET therapist to another. Some rational-emotive therapists, like Ellis himself, argue with clients, cajoling and teasing them, sometimes in very blunt language. Others operate more subtly. They invite clients to discuss their own irrational thinking and then gently lead them to discover more rational ways of regarding the world, thus encouraging them to change themselves (Goldfried & Davison, 1976).

Once a client verbalizes a more rational belief during a therapy session, it must be made part of everyday thinking. Homework assignments can provide opportunities for the patient to experiment with the new belief and to experience the positive consequences of viewing life in less catastrophic ways and acting accordingly.

Because they emphasize changing overt behavior, both CT and RET are similar to behavior therapies. The overlap of these perspectives is shown by the fact that behavior therapy conventions, books, and journals routinely include information on CT and RET, and vice versa. Indeed, CT is sometimes referred to as "cognitive behavior therapy" (Hollon & Beck, 1986), and Ellis (1993) recently began calling RET "rational emotive behavior therapy."

In keeping with the RET emphasis on underlying beliefs rather than on automatic thoughts in the stream of consciousness, patients are first encouraged to learn to question their overall philosophies rather than their reading of what is going on in the specific situation. Suppose you feel bad because someone you know had a party and did not invite you, which you interpreted as a personal rejection. In Beck's cognitive therapy you would first be encouraged to consider (and collect evidence relevant to evaluating) alternative interpretations (maybe they called to invite you, but your machine malfunctioned, and you never got the message; maybe the party was only for people they knew from work; etc.). In RET the preferred tactic would be to ignore the possible misinterpretation and target your belief about its meaning (Say you're right—they intentionally left you out because they think you're boring and no fun. Where is it written that they have to like and admire you? In fact, go out and court rejection by trying to date attractive people who don't know you so that you can see it is not the end of the world.). Only if this tack did not work would an RET therapist revert to questioning interpretations.

Both approaches convey the message that people can change their psychological predicaments by thinking differently. They emphasize that the way people think about themselves and their world is a major determinant of the kind of person they will be—and people can *choose* to think about things differently.

Albert Ellis, a cognitive behavior therapist, has focused on the role of irrational beliefs as causes of abnormal behavior.

The Case of Ernest H. Revisited

APPLYING COGNITIVE PERSPECTIVES

Working from the cognitive perspective, a therapist might focus on Ernest's self-consciousness at college, which seems related to the fact that, compared with his fellow students, he grew up with few advantages. Economic insecurity and hardship may have made him unduly sensitive to criticism and rejection. He regards his wife as warm and charming, a belief that highlights his perception that he lacks social skills. Alcohol has been his escape from such tensions. But heavy drinking, coupled with persistent doubt about his own worth as a human being, has interfered with sexual functioning, worsening an already deteriorating marital relationship. Depending on the level of confrontation the therapist felt appropriate, he or she might use rational-emotive therapy to challenge Ernest's implicit irrational beliefs (such as that he needs universal approval for every undertaking and that his wife's advancement means he will be left behind).

The rational-emotive therapist believes that a person's reluctance to interact with others at a party is due to anxiety caused by the belief that everyone at the party must like them.

Evaluating Cognitive Perspectives

Like behavioral perspectives, cognitive perspectives draw heavily on basic experimental psychology and demand rigorous standards of proof. Accordingly, they have generated extensive research, particularly Beck's theory and therapy.

Descriptive research supports many aspects of Beck's account of the thinking patterns of depressed people. As mentioned earlier, depressives tend to think, "I have always been a failure," while those suffering from anxiety think, "What if I can't cope with all this?". The discrimination between anxiety and depression is particularly impressive given that these disorders overlap a great deal and often occur in the same people (Haaga, Dyck, & Ernst, 1991).

However, there is little compelling evidence that the cognitive perspectives are accurate in delineating the initial causes of psychopathology (Costello, 1993). To some degree, this lack results from problems in defining and developing valid measures of such key variables as irrational beliefs (T. W. Smith, 1989). Most important, however, critical terms, such as *schema*, have not always been defined in a clear, consistent manner.

A more positive evaluation may be made of the cognitive perspectives as they relate to treatment. With respect to depression and several of the anxiety disorders, there are clear indications that CT is an effective treatment, as effective as behavioral treatment of anxiety disorders or medication treatment of major depression. Patients treated with CT seem to maintain the improvements made in therapy longer than do those in comparison treatments, even treatments that work well in the short term (Chambless & Gillis, 1993; Evans et al., 1992). It thus appears that CT teaches skills that patients are later able to use effectively on their own, though measuring and verifying the nature of these skills have proven difficult (Barber & DeRubeis, 1989).

TO RECAP

According to the cognitive perspectives, dysfunctional thought patterns are at the heart of many mental disorders. Two major cognitive approaches are Beck's cognitive theory and therapy and Ellis's rational-emotive theory and therapy. Aaron Beck's cognitive theory places its emphasis on misperceptions of, or exaggerated negative interpretations about the significance of, negative events. Albert Ellis's rational-emotive therapy focuses more on irrational beliefs that conditions or people, including the self, "must" be other than what they are before a person can be happy. Both approaches have some research support, especially cognitive therapy, which appears to result in prolonged improvement after the end of treatment for a sizable proportion of patients.

Vulnerability-Stress Perspectives

vulnerability-stress perspective As applied in *psychopathology*, a view that assumes that individuals predisposed toward a particular mental disorder will be particularly affected by stress and will then manifest *abnormal behavior.*

The **vulnerability-stress perspective** is more general than the other perspectives we have discussed. It links biological, psychological, and environmental influences on mental disorders and is not limited to one particular school of thought, such as behavioral, cognitive, or psychodynamic. This perspective focuses on the interaction between a predisposition toward disease—the vulnerability—and environmental, or life, disturbances—the stressors. Vulnerability refers to any characteristic or set of characteristics of a person that increases that person's chance of developing a disorder. This could be biological, as in genetically transmitted vulnerabilities discussed in Chapter 2. Or it could be psychological, for example, the tacit dysfunctional beliefs that the cognitive perspective sees as making a person vulnerable to depression.

Possessing the vulnerability for a disorder increases a person's chance of developing it but does not by any means guarantee that the disorder will develop. The stress part of vulnerability-stress refers to a condition of a person's environment that causes difficulty. It could be an academic test, damage done by a flood, effects of prejudice, or a host of other events. The presence of such conditions, called stressors, may cause a person's vulnerability to be translated into an actual disorder. In this sense, the vulnerability-stress perspective is more comprehensive than perspectives that describe vulnerability factors but do not explain why one person with the vulnerability develops a disorder while another does not.

Stressors can be either biological or psychological. Oxygen deprivation at birth or poor nutrition during childhood are examples of biological stressors that can lead to brain dysfunction. Psychological stressors include terribly traumatic events, such as rape or the death of a spouse, as well as more mundane occurrences that many of us experience, such as not achieving goals we have set for ourselves. Stress need not refer only to single events, either. More chronic conditions, such as poverty, also contribute to psychological distress (Gotlib & Avison, 1993).

According to this perspective, both vulnerability and stress are necessary in the development of disorders. For example, some people have inherited a biological predisposition that places them at high risk for schizophrenia (see Chapter 9). Given sufficient stress, they stand a good chance of becoming schizophrenic. Other people, those at low genetic risk, are not likely to develop schizophrenia, regardless of how difficult their lives are.

Therapy Based on Vulnerability-Stress Perspectives

Because it is a more general, inclusive framework than the other perspectives, there is no single therapy uniquely associated with the vulnerability-stress perspective. Depending on the nature of the vulnerability and the stressor(s), any of a wide variety of interventions might be suitable. Perhaps the most valuable implication of the vulnerability-stress perspective for treatment is that it directs our attention to multiple options for intervention. One treatment approach related to this interdependent view is **family systems therapy**. In this therapy the problems of individual members of the family are explored and treated within the context of the family as a whole. We discuss this form of therapy in more detail in Chapter 14. Another approach is to attempt to reduce stress, for example, by working to decrease the number of critical comments directed by family members at the vulnerable individual. Or, the therapist might try to reduce vulnerability and thereby increase resilience to the very same stress by teaching skills for coping with stressful events. Often both approaches are combined.

family systems therapy A general approach to treatment that focuses on the complex interrelationships within families.

Evaluating Vulnerability-Stress Perspectives

A limitation of the vulnerability-stress perspective is that it lacks the specificity associated with theories such as psychoanalysis. This perspective depends on other perspectives for its content. What aspects of functioning are likely to serve as vulnerabilities? What sorts of stressors would be apt to play a role in abnormal behavior? Clues to filling in these details must be obtained from the other perspectives discussed in this and the prior chapter.

Conversely, a notable advantage of the vulnerability-stress perspective is that it is pluralistic. This view explains why all children of alcohol-dependent individuals do not grow up to abuse alcohol, why everyone living in poverty does not show high levels of depressive symptoms, or why every young woman living in a culture obsessed with thinness does not develop an eating disorder. It assumes that no one risk factor or type of environmental pressure accounts for psychological disorders by itself.

To Recap

The vulnerability-stress perspective proposes that disorders are caused by the interaction of a predisposition toward the disorder and the occurrence of stressors. It is a pluralistic perspective, for the vulnerability can take diverse forms (such as biological, cognitive, psychodynamic), and the stressors can be chronic conditions, acute events, or even biological stressors, such as malnutrition. There is therefore no one therapy associated with this perspective.

Consequences of Adopting a Perspective

We have now surveyed the main theoretical perspectives on psychological disorders and their treatment. Although each perspective is useful in that it highlights certain causes to look for or techniques that might be helpful in treatment, we have seen that each can be limiting as well. More generally, the mere act of adopting a particular perspective causes a researcher to make a decision concerning what kinds of data will be collected and how they will be interpreted. Thus a researcher may very well ignore possibilities and overlook other information in advancing what seems to be the most probable explanation.

For example, a behaviorist is prone to attribute the high prevalence of schizophrenia in lower-class groups to the lack of social rewards that these people have received, the assumption being that normal development requires a certain amount and patterning of reinforcement. A biologically oriented theorist will be quick to remind the behaviorist of the many deprived people who do *not* become schizophrenic. He or she might suggest that certain biological factors that predispose people both to schizophrenia and to deficiencies in the intellectual skills necessary to maintain occupational status account for the observed correlation between social class and schizophrenia. The behaviorist will be entirely justified in reminding the biological theorist that these alleged factors have yet to be found. The biological theorist might rightfully answer, "Yes, but I'm placing my bets that they are there, and if I adopt *your* behavioral perspective, I may not look for them." To which the behaviorist may with justification reply, "Yes, but *your* assumption regarding biological factors makes it less likely that you will look for and uncover the subtle reinforcement factors that in all probability account for both the presence and the absence of schizophrenia."

The fact is that both are in a sense correct and in another sense incorrect. They are both correct in asserting that certain data are more likely to be found through work done within a particular perspective. But they are incorrect to become unduly agitated because each and every social scientist is not assuming that one and the same factor will ultimately be found crucial in the development of all mental disorders.

Abnormal behavior is much too diverse to be explained or treated adequately by any one of the current perspectives alone. As we subsequently examine various categories of psychopathology, we will find substantial differences in the extent to which biological and behavioral perspectives, as well as the others discussed in this chapter and the previous one, are applicable. It is probably to our advantage that psychologists do *not* agree on which perspective is the best. We know far too little to make hard-and-fast decisions on the exclusive superiority of any one perspective, and there is enough important work to go around. We will often see, too, that a plausible way of looking at the data is to assume multiple causes. This practice again highlights the usefulness of the pluralistic approach associated with the vulnerability-stress perspective.

The same reasoning applies to treatment. We examine in more detail later the effectiveness of specific treatments for specific disorders (Chapters 6 through 15) and across the board (Chapter 16). It is important to note from the outset, though, that just as no one perspective has all the answers about what causes abnormal behavior, so, too, no one perspective on treatment holds all the answers. Such a conclusion has gained widespread acceptance among practicing clinicians confronted with the remarkable diversity of psychological problems. Indeed, most therapists subscribe to **eclecticism**, employing ideas and techniques from a variety of schools of thought (Garfield & Kurtz, 1974). In Chapter 16 we examine some of the ways in which contemporary therapists attempt to blend the various theoretical perspectives in order to maximize their effectiveness.

eclecticism In psychology, the view that more is to be gained by employing concepts from various theoretical systems than by restricting oneself to a single theory.

To Recap

Adopting a particular perspective on abnormal behavior sensitizes psychopathologists and clinicians to some likely causes and effective treatment methods, but biases them against finding possible causes or therapy techniques not consistent with their perspectives. Complete elimination of bias is unlikely, so it is healthy for the field that widely differing perspectives are represented. Many therapists explicitly recognize the value of multiple perspectives by practicing in an eclectic manner, drawing techniques and concepts from more than one approach.

Visual Summary for Chapter 3:

Behavioral, Cognitive, and Vulnerability–Stress Perspectives

Perspectives influence the hypotheses researchers test when searching for causes of psychopathology and the methods therapists use in treating it.

Behavioral

	Ideas About Causes	Methods of Treatment	Comments
Classical Conditioning	History of association between previously neutral stimulus and a stimulus that automatically elicits negative reaction such as fear.	Eliminate unhealthy response by counter-conditioning a healthy response (e.g., relaxation) to the conditioned stimulus.	Strong emphasis on research. Wide application. Less success in explaining causes of disorders than in treating them.
Operant Conditioning	Dysfunctional behaviors have been reinforced and/or healthier ones punished.	Manipulate consequences of behavior (e.g., tokens for desired behavior).	
Modeling	Imitation of others, such as witnessing a parent behave as if anxious.	Deliberate demonstration of more positive behavior, such as assertive communication.	

Cognitive

	Ideas About Causes	Methods of Treatment	Comments
Beck	Misperceptions or biased interpretations of events, stemming from dysfunctional beliefs about the self or the environment (e.g., that signs of anxiety are dangerous, that a single setback means one is a failure).	Collaboration between therapist and patient to master the habit of questioning negative assumptions and collecting evidence on their accuracy.	Good results in treating and describing anxiety and depression. Less so in explaining disorders.
Ellis RET	Irrational beliefs that one must be perfect and universally loved, or that conditions must be easy, or that others must be fair and kind.	Disputation of irrational beliefs via questioning their logic and utililty.	Applied primarily to anxious, inhibited patients.

Vulnerability–Stress

Ideas About Causes	Methods of Treatment	Comments
Interaction of a personal vulnerability, putting one at risk, with the occurrence of a stressor.	Various. Anything that would reduce risk, reduce stress, or improve ability to manage stress.	Somewhat nonspecific but has the benefit of being open to multiple possible causes. Fosters eclectic thinking.

Chapter 4

Classification and Diagnosis

*D*iagnosis is a critical aspect of abnormal psychology, just as it is of general medicine. Physical ailments are diagnosed on the basis of patients' reports of symptoms, physicians' observations, and the results of medical tests. Likewise, psychological disorders are diagnosed according to patients' reports, clinicians' observations, and the results of relevant tests. In both general medicine and psychopathology, diagnosis serves several important purposes. To the extent that standard diagnostic criteria are used in making diagnoses, the diagnoses provide an efficient way for professionals to communicate accurately with one another about the types of cases they are treating or studying. Also, for the practicing clinician, a diagnosis may be helpful in indicating what might have caused the patient's problems, whether the problems are likely to resolve with time or persist, and what treatments might prove helpful.

The current official system of diagnostic categories widely employed by mental health professionals is the *Diagnostic and Statistical Manual of Mental Disorders,* Fourth Edition, commonly referred to as **DSM-IV** and published by the American Psychiatric Association in 1994. We will be looking at how the DSM has evolved, and the strengths and weaknesses of the current system.

DSM-IV   The current *Diagnostic and Statistical Manual of the American Psychiatric Association.*

A Brief History of Classification

By the end of the nineteenth century, medicine had progressed far beyond its practice during the Middle Ages, when bloodletting was at least part of the treatment of virtually all physical problems. Gradually, people recognized that different illnesses required different treatments. Diagnostic procedures were improved, diseases classified, and applicable remedies administered. Impressed by these successes, investigators of abnormal behavior also tried to develop classification schemes that would lead to progress in studying and treating mental disorders.

But during the nineteenth century, and indeed into the twentieth as well, there was great inconsistency in the classification of abnormal behavior. This inconsistency was recognized as a serious problem that impeded communication among people in the field. In the United States the American Psychiatric Association published its *Diagnostic and Statistical Manual* (DSM) in 1952 in an effort to systematize the diagnosis of mental disorders. This was followed by the DSM-II in 1968 and, in 1980, by an extensively revised diagnostic manual, DSM-III. A somewhat revised version, DSM-III-R, appeared in 1987. The two DSM-IIIs represented a significant departure from the first two DSMs in that they relied less on vaguely defined and highly abstract theoretical terms and more on concrete behavioral information in describing the disorders.

In 1988 the American Psychiatric Association appointed a task force to begin work on DSM-IV, which was published in 1994. Working groups of mental health professionals reviewed sections of DSM-III-R, examined relevant scientific research, and collected new data if needed. Perhaps the most important feature of the process was a change in the way in which diagnostic criteria could be altered. Changes had to be supported on the basis of an explicit statement of the reasoning behind them and by empirical evidence, collected by reviews of the literature or by focused reanalysis of existing data or data collected for this purpose in field trials (Widiger, Frances, Pincus, Davis, & First, 1991). In previous versions of the DSM, the evidence supporting diagnostic changes was not always made explicit.

Thus, both the content of the diagnostic manuals, and the procedures used in revising them, have evolved considerably, and further changes will no doubt occur as more is learned about psychological disorders. Therefore, while it is important for clinicians and students of abnormal psychology to know the DSM-IV, described in the next section, it is also important to critically evaluate current diagnostic practices and the basis for controversies about them, as we shall see later in this chapter.

To Recap

Historically, there has been a lack of consensus on how to classify abnormal behavior, and vague criteria have made communication among researchers and clinicians difficult. Recent editions of the *Diagnostic and Statistical Manual of Mental Disorders* (DSM), published by the American Psychiatric Association, represent current efforts to make diagnostic criteria clearer and the process of revising them more scientific. The current revision of the DSM, DSM-IV, states that any proposed revisions to existing diagnostic criteria must be based on explicit arguments and evidence.

The Diagnostic System of the American Psychiatric Association

The Axes

As we mentioned, the third edition of the DSM was the groundbreaking edition. DSM-III employed **multiaxial classification** for the first time. With this classification system, each person being diagnosed with a mental disorder is rated on five separate dimensions, or axes (Table 4.1). The multiaxial system forces the diagnostician to consider a broad range of information, including the environment in which the patient lives. Axis I comprises all the various categories of mental disorders except for the personality disorders and mental retardation, which make up Axis II. Personality disorders were separated from the clinical disorders of Axis I so that in making a diagnosis attention is not focused solely on the current episode of distress or dysfunction, but the possible presence of long-term disturbances in personality are considered as well. For example, a person who is a heroin addict would be diagnosed on Axis I as having a substance-related disorder; he or she might also have a long-standing antisocial personality disorder, which would be noted on Axis II.

The remaining three axes are not needed to make the actual diagnosis but are included because factors other than a person's symptoms should be considered in an assessment. On Axis III the clinician indicates any general medical conditions believed to be relevant to the mental disorder in question. For example, having a serious disease like cancer would be relevant to the overall diagnostic picture. Axis IV gives the clinician the opportunity to note any psychosocial and environmental troubles, for example, occupational problems such as unemployment, economic difficulties, and conflicts with family members, that the person has been experiencing that may be contributing to the disorder. Finally, on Axis V, the clinician indicates the person's current level of adaptive functioning, taking into account the severity of psychological symptoms as well as the quality of social relationships, occupational functioning, and use of leisure time.

Table 4.2 shows how the case of Ernest H., with which we opened this book, might look in DSM-IV terms. Ernest's sense of inferiority, concerns about being shamed or ridiculed by others, and avoidance of occupational activities, such as law school, his fear of criticism and interpersonal rejection, all dating back to early adulthood, justify the diagnosis of Avoidant Personality Disorder. Disruption of his family life by estrangement from his wife justifies the Axis IV code of Problems with Primary Support Group for Ernest.

A rating of 55 on the 0–100 Global Assessment of Functioning (GAF) scale (Axis V) puts Ernest in the middle of a range (51–60) characterized by moderate

multiaxial classification Classification having several dimensions, each of which is employed in categorizing; the *DSM-IV* is an example.

Table 4.1 ▸ **DSM-IV Multiaxial Classification System**

Axis I	Axis II	Axis III
Clinical disorders: Disorders Usually First Diagnosed in Infancy, Childhood, or Adolescence Delirium, Dementia, Amnestic, and Other Cognitive Disorders Substance-Related Disorders Schizophrenia and Other Psychotic Disorders Mood Disorders Anxiety Disorders Somatoform Disorders Factitious Disorder Dissociative Disorders Sexual and Gender Identity Disorders Eating Disorders Sleep Disorders Impulse-Control Disorders Not Elsewhere Classified Adjustment Disorders	Personality Disorders: paranoid, schizoid, schizotypal, antisocial, borderline, histrionic, narcisstic, avoidant, dependent, obsessive-compulsive Mental Retardation	General Medical Conditions

Axis IV
Psychosocial and Environmental Problems

Check:

_____ Problems with primary support group. Specify: _____

_____ Problems related to the social environment. Specify: _____

_____ Educational problems. Specify: _____

_____ Occupational problems. Specify: _____

_____ Housing problems. Specify: _____

_____ Economic problems. Specify: _____

_____ Problems with access to health care services. Specify: _____

_____ Problems related to interaction with the legal system/crime. Specify: _____

_____ Other psychosocial and environmental problems. Specify: _____

symptoms or moderate difficulty in functioning. The next lower range (41–50) lists "unable to keep a job" and "no friends" (American Psychiatric Association, 1994, p. 32) as examples of the degree of impairment of functioning, which appears too harsh for Ernest's case. Conversely, the next higher GAF range (61–70) depicts "mild symptoms" or "some difficulty" in functioning but "generally functioning pretty well, has some meaningful interpersonal relationships" (American Psychiatric Association, 1994, p. 32), which seems too positive an evaluation of the current functioning of a person who shows up for treatment on the heels of getting drunk, verbally and physically abusing his wife for an alleged affair, and then spending the night in a bar licking his wounds.

The Major Diagnostic Categories of DSM-IV

The major diagnostic categories of Axes I and II are summarized in this section. An overview of the entire DSM appears inside the front and back covers of this book for quick reference. Most of these categories are represented in the chapters that follow, although not in the same order in which they are discussed here.

(Table 4.1 continued)

Axis V
Global Assessment of Functioning (GAF) Scale

Consider psychological, social, and occupational functioning on a hypothetical continuum of mental health–illness. Do not include impairment in functioning due to physical (or environmental) limitations.

Code (**Note:** Use intermediate codes when appropriate, e.g., 45, 68, 72.)

100 Superior functioning in a wide range of activities, life's problems never seem to get out of hand, is sought
91 out by others because of his or her many positive qualities. No symptoms.

90 Absent or minimal symptoms (e.g., mild anxiety before an exam), good functioning in all areas, interested
and involved in a wide range of activities, socially effective, generally satisfied with life, no more than every-
81 day problems or concerns (e.g., an occasional argument with family members).

80 If symptoms are present, they are transient and expectable reactions to psychosocial stressors (e.g., difficulty
concentrating after family argument); no more than slight impairment in social, occupational, or school func-
71 tioning (e.g., temporarily falling behind in schoolwork).

70 Some mild symptoms (e.g., depressed mood and mild insomnia) OR some difficulty in social, occupational, or
school functioning (e.g., occasional truancy, or theft within the household), but generally functioning pretty
61 well, has some meaningful interpersonal relationships.

60 Moderate symptoms (e.g., flat affect and circumstantial speech, occasional panic attacks) OR moderate diffi-
51 culty in social, occupational, or school functioning (e.g., few friends, conflicts with peers or co-workers).

50 Serious symptoms (e.g., suicidal ideation, severe obsessional rituals, frequent shoplifting) OR any serious im-
41 pairment in social, occupational, or school functioning (e.g., no friends, unable to keep a job).

40 Some impairment in reality testing or communication (e.g., speech is at times illogical, obscure, or irrelevant)
OR major impairment in several areas, such as work or school, family relations, judgment, thinking, or
mood (e.g., depressed man avoids friends, neglects family, and is unable to work; child frequently beats up
31 younger children, is defiant at home, and is failing at school.)

30 Behavior is considerably influenced by delusions or hallucinations OR serious impairment in communication or judgment (e.g., sometimes incoherent, acts grossly inappropriately, suicidal preoccupation) OR inability
21 to function in almost all areas (e.g., stays in bed all day; no job, home, or friends).

20 Some danger of hurting self or others (e.g., suicide attempts without clear expectation of death; frequently violent; manic excitement) OR occasionally fails to maintain minimal personal hygiene (e.g., smears feces) OR
11 gross impairment in communication (e.g., largely incoherent or mute).

10 Persistent danger of severely hurting self or others (e.g., recurrent violence) OR persistent inability to main-
1 tain minimal personal hygiene OR serious suicidal act with clear expectation of death.

0 Inadequate information.

Source: DSM-IV, 1994 American Psychiatric Association

Table 4.2 ▷ *Example of a DSM-IV Multiaxial Diagnosis: Ernest H.*

Axis I: 303.90 Alcohol Dependence
V61.1 Partner Relational Problem
291.8 Alcohol-Induced Sexual Dysfunction, with Impaired Arousal
296.46 Bipolar I Disorder, Most Recent Episode Manic, In Full Remission

Axis II: 301.82 Avoidant Personality Disorder

Axis III: None

Axis IV: Problems with Primary Support Group

Axis V: GAF = 55 (current)

Disorders Usually First Diagnosed in Infancy, Childhood, or Adolescence

Within this broad-ranging category are the intellectual, emotional, and physical disorders that usually begin in infancy, childhood, or adolescence. Some of the problems described are *separation anxiety disorder* (anxiety about being away from home or separated from those to whom the child is attached, beyond what is expected for the child's age); *conduct disorder* (consistently behaving in a way that violates others' rights or basic societal norms); *attention-deficit/hyperactivity disorder* (great difficulty sustaining attention and an impulsive, excessively active pattern of behavior); *mental retardation* (subaverage intelligence with impaired social adjustment and identified at an early age, coded on Axis II); *autistic disorder* (severe impairment in social and intellectual functioning and communication, diagnosed before age 3); and *learning disorders*, which cover delays in the acquisition of speech, reading, arithmetic, and writing skills. We discuss these disorders in Chapter 14.

Substance-Related Disorders

For people diagnosed within this category the ingestion of various substances—alcohol, opiates, cocaine, amphetamines, and so on—has changed their behavior enough to impair their social or occupational functioning. They may be unable to control or stop their use of the substance and may be physically addicted to it. Substance abuse can also cause the symptoms of other mental disorders; such *substance-induced mental disorders* are categorized in the DSM along with the other disorders whose symptoms they share. For example, excess intake of caffeine may cause extreme anxiety and panic; this caffeine-induced anxiety disorder would be classified as an anxiety disorder. The substance-related disorders themselves are examined in Chapter 12.

Schizophrenia and Other Psychotic Disorders

For people with *schizophrenia*, the ability to care for themselves, relate to others, and work has deteriorated, often severely. Their language, thought, and communication are disordered, and they may shift from one subject to another completely unrelated one. They commonly experience delusions, such as believing that thoughts not their own have been placed in their heads; in addition, they may suffer hallucinations, such as hearing voices that come from outside themselves. Their emotions may be blunted or flattened, or they may be highly inappropriate. Such people have lost contact with the world and with others. These serious mental disorders are discussed in Chapter 9.

Like schizophrenia, the other disorders in this category feature delusions or hallucinations, the "psychotic" symptoms that reflect a loss of contact with reality. For example, the most obvious symptoms of people with *delusional disorders* are their false beliefs of being persecuted. This diagnosis can also be applied to extreme and unjustified jealousy, as when a spouse becomes convinced, without reasonable cause, that his or her partner is unfaithful. Although schizophrenics may also experience delusions, DSM-IV distinguishes delusional disorders from *schizophrenia, paranoid type*, by noting that in schizophrenia, delusions tend to be more bizarre and fragmented; the schizophrenic person also has hallucinations and is generally more disturbed. Delusional disorders are discussed in Chapter 9.

Mood Disorders

As the name implies, this category of DSM-IV is concerned with disorders that affect people's emotional states. In *major depressive disorder* the person is deeply sad and discouraged and experiences a loss of pleasure from usual activities. Clinically depressed people often have trouble sleeping, are likely to lose weight,

Alcohol is the most frequently abused substance.

and lack energy. They may have suicidal thoughts. Someone suffering *mania* may be described as exceedingly elated, more active and in less need of sleep than usual, distractible, and with unrealistically great self-esteem. *Bipolar disorder* is diagnosed if the person experiences episodes of mania or of both mania and depression. Mood disorders are surveyed in Chapter 10.

Anxiety Disorders

Unreasonable, often paralyzing, fear is the central quality running through the category of anxiety disorders. People with a *specific phobia* fear an object or situation so intensely that they must avoid it, even though they know that their fear is unreasonable. In *panic disorder* the person is subject to sudden but brief attacks of intense apprehension, so upsetting as to cause trembling and shaking, dizziness, and difficulty breathing. Panic disorder may also be accompanied by *agoraphobia*; in this case the person is afraid to leave familiar surroundings (usually for fear of the embarrassment of experiencing a panic attack in public). The anxiety of *generalized anxiety disorder* is pervasive and persistent. People are jumpy and may feel a lump in their throat and a pounding heart. They fret chronically and have a hard time controlling their worries. People with *obsessive-compulsive disorder* are subject to recurrent, unwanted thoughts, ideas, and images (obsessions). They may experience a compulsive urge to perform an act repetitively to try to ward off the feared situation. For example, people who worry about germs obsessively may also wash their hands compulsively. People with *post-traumatic stress disorder* (PTSD) suffer from a variety of anxiety symptoms following exposure to a life-threatening or other extreme event that evoked great horror or helplessness in them. The anxiety disorders are reviewed in Chapter 6.

Fear of contamination and excessive hand washing are frequent in obsessive-compulsive disorder.

Somatoform Disorders

The physical symptoms of somatoform disorders have no known physiological cause but seem to serve a psychological purpose. Persons with *somatization disorder* have a long history of multiple physical complaints. In *conversion disorder* the person reports the loss of motor or sensory function, such as a paralysis or blindness. Individuals with *pain disorder* suffer from severe and prolonged pain believed to result in part from psychological factors. *Hypochondriasis* is the misinterpretation of minor physical sensations as serious illness. People with *body dysmorphic disorder* are preoccupied with an imagined defect in their appearance. These disorders are covered in Chapter 7.

Dissociative Disorders

This category of DSM-IV includes disorders in which psychological dissociation, a sudden change in consciousness affecting memory and identity, plays a large part. Persons with *dissociative amnesia* may forget their whole past or more selectively lose memory for a particular time period. With *dissociative fugue* people suddenly and unexpectedly travel to a new locale, start a new life, and are amnesic for their previous identity. The person with *dissociative identity disorder* possesses two or more distinct personalities, with one dominant at a time. This disorder used to be known as multiple personality disorder. *Depersonalization disorder* is a severe and disruptive feeling of self-estrangement or unreality. These disorders are examined in Chapter 7.

Sexual and Gender Identity Disorders

The sexual disorders section of DSM-IV includes three main subcategories. In paraphilias, such as exhibitionism (exposing one's genitals to a stranger), voyeurism (observing unsuspecting naked people, typically strangers), and sex-

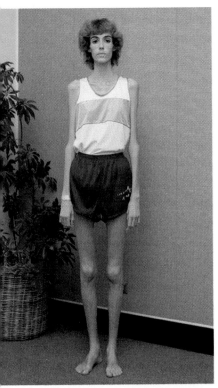

Anorexia, involving severe weight loss and extreme fear of becoming fat, is one of the eating disorders.

ual masochism (being humiliated or made to suffer as a way of becoming sexually aroused), the sources of sexual gratification are unconventional. Persons with *sexual dysfunctions* (e.g., premature ejaculation, inhibition of orgasms) are unable to complete the usual sexual response cycle. People with *gender identity disorders* feel extreme discomfort with their anatomical sex and usually identify themselves as members of the opposite sex. These disorders are studied in Chapter 13.

Sleep Disorders

Two major subcategories of sleep disorders are distinguished. In the *dyssomnias*, sleep is disturbed in amount (e.g., the person is unable to maintain sleep or sleeps too much), quality (the person does not feel rested after sleep), or timing (e.g., the person is unable to sleep during conventional sleep times). In the *parasomnias*, an unusual event occurs during sleep (e.g., nightmares, sleepwalking).

Eating Disorders

This DSM category considers extreme eating patterns an expression of psychological distress. In *anorexia nervosa* the person avoids eating and becomes emaciated, often because of an intense fear of becoming fat. In *bulimia nervosa*, there are frequent episodes of binge eating coupled with compensatory activities such as self-induced vomiting or laxative use. These disorders are discussed in Chapter 14.

Factitious Disorder

This diagnosis is applied to people who intentionally produce or complain of either physical or psychological symptoms, apparently because of a psychological need to assume the role of a sick person.

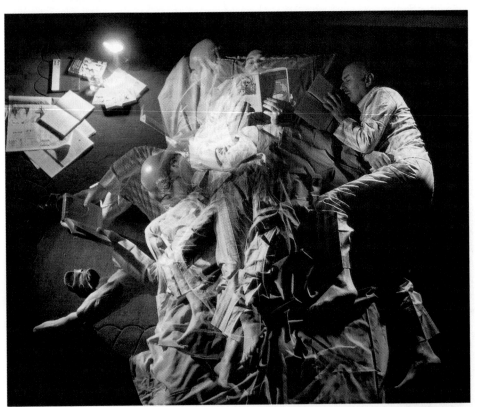

An example of dyssomnia is insomnia, a recurrent difficulty in falling asleep or staying asleep. A multiple-exposure image portrays the restless night of one insomnia sufferer as he tosses and turns, interspersed with periods of reading.

Adjustment Disorders

This diagnosis refers to the development of emotional or behavioral symptoms following the occurrence of a major stressful event. However, the symptoms are not severe enough to meet the diagnostic criteria for any Axis I diagnosis. Someone experiencing anxiety and sadness associated with entering college, for example, might be diagnosed as having an adjustment disorder.

Impulse-Control Disorders Not Elsewhere Classified

This category includes a number of conditions in which the person's behavior is inappropriate and seemingly out of control. For example, in *intermittent explosive disorder* the person has episodes of violent behavior that result in destruction of property or injury to another person. In *pathological gambling* the person is preoccupied with gambling, is unable to stop, and gambles as a way to escape from problems. Those suffering from *trichotillomania* are impelled to pull out their hair, often to such an extent that they have to wear a wig to avoid attracting attention.

Personality Disorders

People with personality disorders show a lasting pattern of behavior and subjective experience that is quite different from what is expected in their culture, is inflexible, affects many areas of life, starts in adolescence or early adulthood, and leads to distress or impairment. Recall that these disorders are listed on Axis II. Ten distinct personality disorders make up the category. In *schizoid personality disorder*, the person is aloof, has few friends, and is indifferent to praise and criticism. The individual with a *narcissistic personality disorder* has an overblown sense of self-importance, requires constant attention, and is likely to exploit others. Someone diagnosed as having an *antisocial personality disorder* exhibited antisocial behavior before the age of fifteen through truancy, running away from home, delinquency, and general belligerence. In adulthood the person is indifferent about holding a job, acting responsibly, planning for the future, and staying on the right side of the law. Also called psychopaths, those with antisocial personal-

Gambling is considered a psychological disorder when the person cannot stop gambling even though it is causing financial or interpersonal problems.

Memory loss, especially for recent events, is the most critical symptom of Alzheimer's disease and other dementias.

ity disorder do not feel guilt or shame for transgressing social mores. Chapter 11 covers these and other personality disorders, with an emphasis on antisocial personality disorder.

Delirium, Dementia, Amnestic, and Other Cognitive Disorders

Delirium is a clouding of consciousness, wandering attention, and an incoherent stream of thought. Usually reversible, it may be caused by several medical conditions as well as by poor diet or substance abuse. *Dementia*, a typically irreversible deterioration of mental capacities, especially memory, is associated with Alzheimer's disease, stroke, several other medical conditions, and substance abuse. Delirium and dementia are discussed in Chapter 15. *Amnestic syndrome*, an impairment in memory when there is no delirium or dementia, is considered in Chapter 12, because it is often linked to alcohol abuse.

Other Conditions That May Be a Focus of Clinical Attention

This broad category is for conditions that are not regarded as mental disorders but still may be a focus of attention or treatment. If an individual's medical illness appears to be caused in part or exacerbated by a psychological condition, the diagnosis is *psychological factors affecting physical condition*; these conditions are reviewed in Chapter 8. Among the other conditions in this category are academic problems, marital problems, occupational problems, and physical or sexual abuse.

To Recap

A novel feature of the DSM is multiaxial organization; every time a diagnosis is made, the clinician is to describe the patient's condition according to each of five axes, or dimensions. Axes I and II encompass the mental disorders per se; Axis II covers specifically personality disorders and mental retardation. Any physical disorders believed to bear on the mental disorder in question are listed on Axis III. Axis IV is used to indicate the psychosocial and environmental problems that the person has been experiencing; and Axis V rates the person's current level of adaptive functioning.

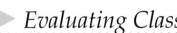

Evaluating Classification and Diagnosis

The major categories of abnormal behavior will be examined in more detail throughout this text. On the basis of this brief overview, however, we will examine here the usefulness of the current diagnostic system, focusing first on the pros and cons of classifying abnormal behavior at all and second on the merits of the DSM system in particular.

Advantages and Disadvantages of Classification

We begin by describing the needs that a classification system is meant to satisfy. It systematizes diagnosis; it enables professionals to talk to one another by creating a shared language; it helps create specific and empirically based descriptions of disorders; and it may guide treatment planning or predictions of the course of symptoms to be expected. But some believe that classifying mental disorders is not worth the risk. Those opposed to any attempt to classify make two main points. First, classification may stigmatize a person, and second, it pigeonholes unique individuals unfairly. Consider how you might be affected by being told that you are a schizophrenic. You might become guarded and suspicious lest someone recognize your disorder. Furthermore, the fact that you are a "former mental patient" could have a great impact on your life. Friends and loved ones now treat you differently, and employment may be difficult to obtain.

There is little doubt that diagnosis can have such negative consequences. The public tends to hold a very negative view of mental patients, and patients and their families believe that such stigmatizing commonly leads to negative effects (Rabkin, 1974; Wahl & Harrman, 1989). And yet, documenting the actual negative consequences of diagnosis has been difficult. Gove and Fain (1973) followed up a large sample of patients one year after discharge from a hospital. The former patients were interviewed about jobs, social relationships, and outside activities. The patients' descriptions of how they were functioning at that time and how they had functioned in the past were not very different. Thus, although we must recognize and guard against the possible social stigma of a diagnosis, the problem may not be as common as we might think.

The second argument against diagnosis is that whenever we classify, we lose information and overlook some of the uniqueness of the person being studied. This argument is intuitively appealing. Who really believes that his or her own personality and psychological functioning can be accurately summed up in a single categorical label, whether it be in the normal range (such as "frat type," "gossip," "nerd") or the abnormal (such as "panicker" or "psychopath")?

However, just because some information is lost when we categorize does not necessarily mean that classification is a bad idea. It is important to bear in mind that a diagnosis is the beginning, not the end, of psychological evaluation. It is used for communicating in general terms about a patient or group of patients (as in a sample of patients studied in research). In-depth assessment of a patient for the purposes of planning treatment goes beyond diagnosis alone and takes into account the patient's circumstances. Axis IV was also developed to alleviate this concern.

And too, sometimes the information we lose when categorizing is irrelevant, or at least irrelevant for the purpose at hand. If I am trying to make a world-class apple pie, it might be extremely important to know whether the object in front of me is a Jonathan apple or a Granny Smith apple, what part of the country it comes from, when it was harvested, and so forth. Just knowing that it is a fruit will not do. On the other hand, if my concern is whether I can allow my son to put the object in his mouth, the type of apple does not matter; all I care about is whether it fits the category of "fruit" or the category of "poison."

Furthermore, if members of a category share important characteristics, then determining whether someone fits the category can provide useful information for clinicians and researchers. To take an example, a form of mental retardation, phenylketonuria, is caused by a deficiency in the metabolism of the protein phenylalanine, resulting in the release of incomplete metabolites that injure the brain (see p. 56). A diet drastically reduced in phenylalanine prevents some of this injury. In this case the diagnostic label distinguishing this particular form of mental retardation made effective treatment possible.

Classification can therefore be helpful if it directs our attention to important features that patients in a category share but away from the unique aspects of each member of the category that might be less clinically relevant. However, we should remember that a diagnosis is not a complete description of a real person experiencing distress and disability. Accordingly, each of the chapters covering specific mental disorders in this book includes a detailed look at a person who has been diagnosed as having one of the disorders in the category covered in that chapter. We hope that this will make the effects of these disorders on real people clearer to you.

Reliability and Validity in Diagnosis

If classification in general is neither all good nor all bad, the question becomes how to evaluate the actual categories and criteria currently used for classification and diagnosis of abnormal behavior. To review this issue we need first to introduce the concepts of reliability and validity, which are the most common criteria by which psychologists evaluate measurement procedures (see Chapter 5) and diagnoses.

In the most general sense, **reliability** refers to the consistency with which a measurement procedure measures something, while **validity** concerns the extent to which a procedure is measuring what we intend it to measure. Consider a bathroom scale. If you step on it three times in a row, and it reads 150 each time, this result supports the conclusion that it is a reliable scale, but it may not be a valid reading. Suppose you have ten friends whose weights you happen to know with very high confidence (say, from a trip to a physician's office the previous day). If each gets on the scale (one at a time), and the scale's readings reflect those of the day before, this result supports the validity of the scale.

Validity, in particular, is sometimes difficult to comprehend if you are new to studying social sciences. In dealing with measurement in our daily lives, we sometimes have to cope with unreliability but rarely stop to think about validity. Is this thermometer really a measure of body temperature or of something else? Is this yardstick measuring length or something else? What else could they be measuring? In psychology it is not so simple. The stuff we are trying to measure (personality, mental illness, etc.) is less tangible, and it is possible to be misled, as we discuss in more detail in Chapter 5.

One way to think about reliability and validity is that reliability concerns whether a given measurement procedure is insensitive to differences in circumstance that should *not* matter in view of what you are trying to measure, while validity relates to whether the measure is sensitive to differences in circumstance that *should* matter. Consider the grading procedure for a final essay exam in a course. The grade should ideally be insensitive to, among other things, which teaching assistant happened to read the essay, whether it was graded on Wednesday when the professor was in a good mood or Friday when she or he was not, and so forth. If scores for similar essays are indeed consistent across these variations, the exam was graded reliably. However, grades should *vary* depending on whether what the student wrote was logical and detailed or not. If the superior essay received the better grade, then the exam was graded validly.

Reliability of a Diagnosis

Because the value of a diagnosis depends on its being reliable—not subject to the whims of the diagnostician or influenced by the weather or day of the week—several types of reliability evaluations are commonly made for diagnoses. They all relate to consistency of measurement in the face of irrelevant changes of circumstance, but they differ with respect to *what* changes in circumstance are being evaluated.

Interrater reliability refers to the extent to which multiple judges agree about what they are judging. For example, suppose you want to know if a veteran or rape victim meets the criteria for a diagnosis of posttraumatic stress disorder. You could have the person interviewed and diagnosed by two clinicians, in separate meetings, unaware of each other's conclusions. The extent to which the raters agree would be an index of interrater reliability. Clearly, for a classification system to be useful, those applying it must be able to agree on who does and does not fit the category. The popularity of seeking second opinions suggests that many consumers of health care realize that interrater reliability is not perfect in medical diagnosis or in the diagnosis of psychological disorders.

Retest reliability measures the extent to which people being diagnosed twice, perhaps several weeks or months apart, are rated in the same way. This kind of reliability is important to evaluate only if it is safe to assume that people do not

---

reliability The extent to which a test, measurement, or classification system is consistent in that it produces the same observation each time it is applied.

validity The extent to which a test or diagnosis measures what it is intended to measure.

Observers do not always see the same event the same way. To ensure that a diagnosis is dependable, it is important to evaluate interrater reliability by seeing if multiple clinicians agree on whether or not someone has a particular disorder.

interrater reliability The relationship between the judgments that at least two raters make independently about a phenomenon.

retest reliability The relationship between the scores that a person achieves when he or she takes the same test at two separate times.

really change much over the time interval between evaluations. How safe this assumption is depends on how long the time interval is and what diagnosis is being evaluated (Nelson-Gray, 1991). Diagnoses of personality disorders, for example, would be expected to show retest reliability over longer intervals than the Axis I disorders.

Finally, **internal consistency reliability** relates to whether different parts of a measure, in this case individual diagnostic criteria, tend to go together in the same people. For example, is someone with one symptom of schizophrenia (hallucinations, say) more likely than others to have the other symptoms of schizophrenia? Every person with a disorder will not have all its symptoms, but unless the symptoms go together to some degree it would not make much sense to consider them part of the same syndrome.

internal consistency reliability The extent to which scores on different parts of a measure, such as different test items or diagnostic criteria, are consistent with one another.

Validity of a Diagnosis

It is also extremely important for a diagnosis to be valid; that is, use of the criteria should actually tell us something about the person being diagnosed that corresponds to the disorder we claim to be measuring. Like reliability, the question of validity can be addressed in many ways. Some of the ways are sufficiently common that they have taken on their own names as subtypes of validity. Especially important in studying diagnoses are content validity and criterion-related validity.

Content validity concerns whether a measure includes, in appropriate proportions, all the major aspects of the domain being measured. An abnormal psychology knowledge test with twenty questions about personality disorders and none about Axis I disorders, for instance, would lack content validity. In the case of diagnostic categories, the issue is whether the official criteria of a disorder adequately represent the symptoms associated with that disorder.

content validity The extent to which all important aspects of the characteristic are included in appropriate proportions in a measure.

Criterion-related validity refers to whether scores on a measure are systematically related to other important information about a person (the criteria). If, for instance, ratings made after a job interview were high for those who went on to do well in the job and low for those who did poorly (assuming for the moment that they were hired anyway), it would indicate that the interview had some criterion-related validity.

criterion-related validity The extent to which diagnostic criteria or scores on a test are systematically related to other important information about a person (the criterion).

The criterion-related validity of a diagnosis is often divided according to whether the outcome is evaluated at the same time as the diagnosis (**concurrent validity**) or later (**predictive validity**). The example just described illustrates predictive validity. A finding that patients diagnosed with major depressive disorder are much more likely to be in distressed marriages than are patients with an adjustment disorder diagnosis would support concurrent validity. A common test of predictive validity that is useful for clinicians in planning treatment is to see if a diagnosis is valid for predicting response to therapy. If the diagnosis of major depressive disorder enabled you to predict that someone would benefit from a particular treatment, whereas patients with adjustment disorders and other diagnoses would benefit more from a different treatment, this situation would exemplify predictive validity—making the diagnosis helps you predict a fact not yet revealed (response to treatment). The following section gives an example of a diagnostic subcategory, blood phobia, validated in large part on the basis of its predicting response to a specific type of treatment.

concurrent validity A kind of *criterion-related validity*, the extent to which common current features are found (e.g., the same socioeconomic status) among patients with the same diagnosis.

predictive validity A kind of *criterion-related validity*, the extent to which being diagnosed in a particular way predicts some future criterion such as response to treatment.

> **APPLYING CRITICAL THINKING SKILLS**

A CASE OF BLOOD PHOBIA

Andrew F., a first-time father-to-be, was attending a series of classes on childbirth, preparing for his role as coach during labor and delivery. During a class devoted to information about medical interventions that might be used during delivery, the nurse-teacher described an episiotomy, a surgical procedure to widen the opening through which the baby's head passes during delivery. Somewhat squeamish for most of his life, Andrew found this talk unsettling and began to feel anxious. The room seemed to grow hotter and stuffier by the minute.

Reasoning that there was nothing to fear in the mere discussion of an episiotomy that would not even be happening to him if it should occur at all, Andrew tried to calm down, using muscle-relaxation procedures that are often helpful as part of the treatment of specific phobias (see Chapter 6). The next thing he was aware of was being prone, with a throbbing headache, and hearing people ask, "Is he okay?" The nurse informed him that he had fainted and fallen out of his chair, hitting his head.

Before the next class session, Andrew read about *blood phobia* ("the fear and avoidance of situations involving direct or indirect exposure to blood, injuries [and] wounds," Ost, 1992, p. 68) and learned that trying to relax may have been ill-advised. When confronted with the phobic situation, blood phobics typically experience an initial burst of sympathetic hyperactivity but then a *decrease* in heart rate and blood pressure (McGrady & Bernal, 1986). Because of this sudden drop in blood pressure, blood phobics are at risk for fainting. A majority (70%) of blood phobics requesting treatment in an outpatient clinic had fainted at least once (the average was eleven times) in the phobic situation, the social consequences of which many of them feared more than fainting itself (Ost, 1992). Thus, his ill-timed attempt to relax, perhaps lowering his blood pressure further, may have increased his chances of fainting.

At the next class session Andrew was prepared. When the talk came around to medical interventions during delivery, he began to feel hot and light-headed again. This time, he deliberately *tensed* his muscles until the feeling passed, and he did not faint.

Let us analyze this case example from the standpoint of applying critical thinking skills.

▶ *What conclusion does the evidence seem to support?* Andrew's far different experiences in otherwise similar situations seem to indicate that tensing rather than relaxing one's muscles is the best way to cope with fears induced by blood phobia. More generally, the distinctive treatment response illustrated here supports the predictive validity of blood phobia and suggests that it should be a separate diagnosis from other specific phobias.

▶ *What other interpretations are plausible?* At least three other explanations can make sense out of what happened to Andrew. First, perhaps the two situations were not identical; the nurse might have gone into gorier detail the first time the subject was discussed, for instance. If so, then Andrew might have done better the second time whether he tensed his muscles or not, just because it was a milder situation. Second, even if the two discussions were the same, maybe Andrew was more used to it by the second class and knew what to expect, so that it did not bother him as much. Again, he would have been fine regardless of how he chose to cope. Finally, Andrew might be unusual; maybe other blood phobics would respond better to relaxation than to tension, just like people with other specific phobias. If so, the diagnostic distinction would not be supported.

▶ *What other information would help choose among the alternative interpretations?* The first two alternatives (situations differed in fearfulness; the second went better only because of getting used to it) could be tested by conducting a more systematic study of Andrew's case in the form of a single-case experiment (Hersen & Barlow, 1976). We might, for instance, give the nurse-teacher a standard script, to ensure that the details of episiotomies are presented in a similar manner each time. Also, it would be important for Andrew's strategy to switch back and forth from muscle tension to muscle relaxation from one class meeting to the next. If muscle tension is truly superior, then he will have problems, perhaps even faint again, when he goes back to using relaxation. On the other hand, if repeated exposure to the topic and getting used to it are the key, then he will continue to improve even on the days he uses relaxation.

The third explanation (Andrew is unusual in his response to treatment) could be tested by including more blood phobics in the study; some would use muscle tension and others relaxation. If Andrew's case is typical, then those using muscle tension will fare better on average. In fact, such research has been done and shows that Andrew's case is not unusual (Ost, Sterner, & Fellenius, 1989). The distinctive treatment response of blood phobics is one of the reasons the DSM-IV lists it as a distinct type of specific phobia (blood-injection-injury type), to be noted in making the diagnosis.

Interrelation of Reliability and Validity

Ordinarily, high reliability is necessary but not sufficient for validity. If a diagnostic category cannot be judged consistently by different clinicians, changes from day to day, or includes criteria that have nothing to do with one another, we are unlikely to be able to make valid statements about that category. For this reason, the poor reliability of pre-DSM-III diagnostic categories sparked a much greater concern throughout the 1960s and 1970s with improving reliability than with improving validity (Blashfield & Livesley, 1991). It is important to bear in mind, though, that high reliability is not a guarantee of high validity. It is even possible that trying at all costs to improve reliability can actually decrease validity. Consider the following (hypothetical) proposal for a DSM-V criterion:

▷ All patients more than six feet tall will be assigned the diagnosis of specific phobia.
▷ All patients under five feet eight inches tall will be assigned the diagnosis of alcohol dependence.

These criteria could no doubt be applied with near-perfect interrater reliability. Provided that we were working at an adult clinic, retest reliability would also be excellent, and internal consistency reliability would be irrelevant, since only one judgment would need to be made. Most assuredly, though, the validity of the diagnoses specific phobia and alcohol dependence would decrease if this change were made!

This example shows the theoretical possibility that increasing reliability could decrease validity, but it is, of course, unrealistic. A possible real-world example is provided by antisocial personality disorder, considered in more detail in Chapter 11. The DSM-III-R excluded traits previously considered important, such as being manipulative, glib, and superficial, in favor of more reliably identifiable behaviors, such as failing to honor financial obligations. In the process it may have defined a less valid category (Hare, Hart, & Harpur, 1991) that is too closely linked to criminal behavior. DSM-IV criteria for antisocial personality disorder reflect some changes away from this exclusive focus on high reliability. Failure to sustain a monogamous relationship, for example, was deleted from the list of criteria, even though it can be rated reliably, because it appeared to detract from the validity of antisocial personality disorder diagnoses.

To Recap

Depending on the relevance of the information and its purpose, the loss of unique information about a person in the course of classification can be good or bad. How well a diagnostic scheme (or any other measurement procedure) actually works is evaluated in psychology according to whether it is reliable (consistent in measuring something) and valid (actually measures what we want to measure). Aspects of diagnostic reliability include interrater reliability (agreement among different judges about what diagnosis should be applied); retest reliability (consistency over

time in what diagnosis someone receives); and internal consistency reliability (whether the symptoms believed to constitute a disorder actually go together in the same people).

Aspects of diagnostic validity include content validity (whether the important features of the disorder are represented in the diagnostic criteria) and criterion-related validity (whether the diagnosis predicts other important facts about people, such as what treatment would benefit them). High reliability is usually necessary for high validity, but it does not guarantee high validity, and trying above all to increase reliability can even lower validity.

Strengths and Weaknesses of Current DSM Categories

Clarification of Criteria

Thomas Widiger, an expert on classification and on personality disorders, coordinated efforts to use research findings in establishing DSM-IV criteria for mental disorders.

Prior to DSM-III, interrater reliability was not acceptable primarily because the criteria for making a diagnosis were not presented clearly (Ward, Beck, Mendelson, Mock, & Erbaugh, 1962). Too often, different clinicians arrived at different diagnoses for the same patient. Beginning with DSM-III and DSM-III-R, the diagnostic categories were devised to be more reliable. Each diagnostic category in Axes I and II was described much more extensively than it was in DSM-II.

Specific diagnostic criteria for the category are now spelled out in a more precise fashion—these are the symptoms and other facts that must be present to justify the diagnosis—and the clinical symptoms that constitute a diagnosis are defined in a glossary. Efforts are made to ensure that these criteria are as concrete and descriptive as possible, not based on abstract inferences that assume that one particular perspective for studying abnormal psychology is correct in its analysis of the disorder.

Having specific criteria is helpful for differential diagnosis, which means distinguishing a diagnosis from others. In a sense, all diagnosis is differential diagnosis; to say that a patient qualifies for one diagnosis and not others necessarily means that the clinician differentiated among the possible diagnoses to be given. But the term is usually used to refer to the more difficult distinctions, selecting one diagnosis instead of others with which it might have much in common. For instance, if a patient is afraid of, and therefore avoids, eating in restaurants, this behavior would be ambiguous and would require a differential diagnosis. The behavior "may be based on concerns about negative evaluation from others (i.e., Social Phobia) or concerns about choking (i.e., Specific Phobia)" (American Psychiatric Association [APA], 1994, p. 409).

Table 4.3 compares the descriptions of a manic episode given in DSM-II with the diagnostic criteria given in DSM-IV. The bases for making diagnoses are decidedly more detailed and concrete in DSM-IV. Accordingly, interrater reliability for most current diagnostic categories appears to be good. On the other hand, the interrater reliability of diagnoses may not always be as high in everyday usage, for diagnosticians may not adhere as precisely to the criteria as do those whose work is being scrutinized in formal studies (e.g., Jampala, Sierles, & Taylor, 1988).

Improved Consistency

In addition to advances in clarifying criteria, progress has also been made in dealing with a second source of diagnostic disagreements, inconsistency on the part of the diagnostician. The use of standardized interview techniques for evaluating whether patients meet the criteria (see Chapter 5) may help avoid inconsistencies, although there is no well-controlled research evidence supporting this hypothesis at present (Williams et al., 1992).

Table 4.3 ▶ *Description of Manic Disorder in DSM-II versus DSM-IV*

DSM-II

Manic-depressive illness, manic type. This disorder consists exclusively of manic episodes. These episodes are characterized by excessive elation, irritability, talkativeness, flight of ideas, and accelerated speech and motor activity. Brief periods of depression sometimes occur, but they are never true depressive episodes.

DSM-IV
Criteria for Manic Episode

A. A distinct period of abnormally and persistently elevated, expansive, or irritable mood, lasting at least 1 week (or any duration if hospitalization is necessary).

B. During the period of mood disturbance, three (or more) of the following symptoms have persisted (four if the mood is only irritable) and have been present to a significant degree:
   (1) inflated self-esteem or grandiosity
   (2) decreased need for sleep (e.g., feels rested after only 3 hours of sleep)
   (3) more talkative than usual or pressure to keep talking
   (4) flight of ideas or subjective experience that thoughts are racing
   (5) distractibility (i.e., attention too easily drawn to unimportant or irrelevant external stimuli)
   (6) increase in goal-directed activity (either socially, at work or school, or sexually) or psychomotor agitation
   (7) excessive involvement in pleasurable activities that have a high potential for painful consequences (e.g., engaging in unrestrained buying sprees, sexual indiscretions, or foolish business investments)

C. The symptoms do not meet criteria for a Mixed Episode (see p. 335).

D. The mood disturbance is sufficiently severe to cause marked impairment in occupational functioning or in usual social activities or relationships with others, or to necessitate hospitalization to prevent harm to self or others, or there are psychotic features.

E. The symptoms are not due to the direct physiological effects of a substance (e.g., a drug of abuse, a medication, or other treatment) or a general medical condition (e.g., hyperthyroidism).

Note: Manic-like episodes that are clearly caused by somatic antidepressant treatment (e.g., medication, electroconvulsive therapy, light therapy) should not count toward a diagnosis of Bipolar I Disorder.

Source: DSM-II (APA, 1968, p. 36); DSM-IV (APA, 1994, p. 332).

Internal consistency reliability of mental disorder diagnoses has received less research attention than have other forms of reliability, especially interrater reliability, but there is some evidence to suggest that the personality disorder categories show positive, but modest internal consistency (Morey, 1988). Major depressive disorder criteria, on the other hand, appear to be highly internally consistent (Buchwald & Rudick-Davis, 1993).

Cross-cultural and Other Influences on Validity in DSM-IV

Although the improvements in some aspects of reliability of the DSM *may* lead to more validity, there is no guarantee that they will. Content validity in particular has not been the focus of much systematic research. For the most part, it is simply assumed that appointing professionals with acknowledged expertise in a given area to the DSM subcommittees responsible for developing the criteria for each disorder will ensure that the criteria adequately reflect the symptoms of the disorders (Blashfield & Livesley, 1991).

For some diagnoses there is substantial evidence of other aspects of validity, however. Bipolar disorder patients, for example, tend to respond well to a drug called lithium carbonate (see p. 276). The fact that this drug does not work well for people in most other diagnostic classes supports the predictive validity of the bipolar diagnosis. Even in the case of categories such as bipolar disorder, though, where it seems safe to say that the disorders have some degree of validity, it is unclear whether the precise rules for making diagnostic decisions in DSM-IV are ideal. We see from Table 4.3 that for patients to be diagnosed as suffering from mania, they must have three symptoms from a list of seven, or four if their mood is irritable. But the reason for requiring three symptoms rather than two or five is unknown (Finn, 1982).

More generally, not all DSM categories are supported by extensive evidence of validity at all, as will become evident when we review the specific disorders in subsequent chapters. Several aspects of the DSM system and the way in which it has been developed might play a role in limiting validity.

First, the DSM is a **categorical classification**, a yes–no approach. Is the patient schizophrenic or not? This type of classification is convenient in the sense that it simplifies communication. However, if abnormal and normal behavior differ only in degree (like height), not in kind (like biological sex), then the use of a categorical approach may be misleading and oversimplifying (see Focus Box 4.1 for a discussion of **dimensional classification**.)

Second, the DSM is largely based on clinical and research experience in Western cultures and as such might not be reflective of the forms and expressions of psychopathology unique to other cultures. Evidence on the cross-cultural applicability of standard diagnostic criteria is limited, but for the two disorders that have been most thoroughly studied (schizophrenia and depression), it appears that the core symptoms are similar cross-culturally. Some differences exist, however. For example, guilt is a frequent symptom of depression in Western society, but an infrequent symptom in Japan and Iran (Draguns, 1989). Also, other disorders may be more subject to misdiagnosis as a result of ignorance of cultural issues. Recognizing this possibility, the DSM-IV includes as one of the basic considerations for defining personality disorder that the pattern of experience and behavior "deviates markedly from the expectations of the individual's culture" (APA, 1994, p. 629). A difficulty in trying to apply such a principle is that research focused specifically on delineating the psychological characteristics of healthy, well-functioning members of particular minority groups is sparse (Uba, 1994).

Third, mental disorder categories have proliferated throughout the process of revising the DSMs. DSM-I, for instance, had 108 categories, while DSM-III-R contained 297 (Sprock & Blashfield, 1991). Some critics contend that there is little justification for many of the new categories, that more stringent criteria should be adopted for determining when a new disorder is justified, and even that some of the old categories should be eliminated (Blashfield, Sprock, & Fuller, 1990).

The difficulty stems in part from the many purposes of a diagnostic system, as illustrated by debates over the inclusion in DSM-IV of premenstrual dysphoric disorder. In this disorder, a variant of "Depressive Disorder Not Otherwise Specified," depressed or anxious mood occurs during the last week of the luteal phase in most menstrual cycles that is sufficiently severe to interfere significantly with a person's usual activities. Some argue that there is little sys-

categorical classification An approach to assessment in which the basic decision is whether a person is or is not a member of a discrete grouping.

dimensional classification An approach to assessment according to which a person is placed on a continuum.

The extraordinary position attained by this yoga practitioner from India illustrates a behavior unusual in some cultures but not to be considered abnormal.

Categorical and Dimensional Classification

DSM IV and its precursors are all **categorical classification systems.** But this is not the only method of classification, or necessarily the best one. Some clinicians favor a dimensional system for classifying mental disorders. When you ask someone how tall he or she is, the answer is seldom simply, "tall" or "short." You are more apt to hear something like "five feet eleven and a half inches." Why? Because everyone knows that height varies on a continuum, rarely is there anything to be gained (and there may be considerable detail to be lost) by reducing the information on someone's height to a yes–no categorical analysis.

Conversely, when you ask whether someone is pregnant, you probably anticipate hearing yes or no, not "somewhat," "more so than average," or "68%." While some of the details of pregnancy (how many months since conception, etc.) vary on a continuum, the basic fact is well described by a categorical rating of pregnant or not pregnant.

Thus, depending on the circumstances, categorical classification might or might not be ideal. Diagnosis of mental disorders has traditionally used a categorical system, as does the DSM for Axes I, II, III, and IV (though Axis V does not). Some investigators believe that this aspect of the DSM should be changed. It might be more appropriate, in other words, to describe patients in terms of *how* depressed they are, just as we typically evaluate weight, blood pressure, or body temperature along continuous dimensions, rather than select an arbitrary cutoff for deciding whether someone is or is not depressed.

A **dimensional classification** scheme avoids the problem of arbitrary and possibly misleading cutoffs. The entities or objects being classified must be ranked on a quantitative dimension (e.g., a 1 to 10 scale of anxiety, where 1 represents minimal and 10 extreme). Classification would be accomplished by assessing patients on the relevant dimensions and perhaps plotting the location of the patient in a system of coordinates defined by his or her score on each dimension.

Many investigators believe that a dimensional system could be applied to most of the symptoms that constitute the diagnoses of the DSM—anxiety, depression, and the many personality traits that are included in the personality disorders. Using complex mathematical procedures for analyzing the degree to which features of the disorder occur together (Meehl & Golden, 1982), one study suggested that borderline personality disorder would be better described by a dimensional system than by a categorical yes–no system (Trull, Widiger, & Guthrie, 1990).

Based on such evidence and arguments, DSM-IV now mentions several possible dimensional classifications of personality disorders, including one based on a five-factor model of normal personality that we present in Chapter 11. These dimensional schemes are not officially part of the DSM-IV Axis II, however. If implemented more completely in future versions of the DSM, this change might improve diagnostic reliability. Categorical evaluations of personality disorder are less reliable than are dimensional judgments, perhaps because even small differences of opinion between raters can lead to different yes–no conclusions if a patient's symptoms are quite close to the cutoff used in assigning a particular diagnosis (Heumann & Morey, 1990).

tematic research on this diagnosis and that its inclusion might serve to reinforce negative stereotypes and to stigmatize large numbers of women as having a mental disorder. Thus this diagnosis could negatively affect women in employment or child-custody decisions. Others suggest that the diagnosis is justified because it officially acknowledges an important, possibly treatable form of distress, and it provides explicit criteria to guide research on its causes and treatment (Span, 1993).

Throughout this book, as we present the literature on various disorders, there will be further opportunities both to describe the strengths and weaknesses of this effort of health professionals to categorize mental disorders and to consider how DSM-IV may deal with some of the problems that still exist. What is most heartening about the DSM is that its attempts to be explicit about the rules for diagnosis make it easier to detect problems in the diagnostic system. We can expect more changes and refinements over the next several years.

To Recap

Because recent versions of the DSM are far more concrete and descriptive than earlier ones, diagnoses based on them are improved in interrater reliability. In some categories, however, validity remains an open question. That is, it is too soon to know how much useful knowledge about psychopathology, its prevention and treatment, will be gained through widespread use of DSM-IV. Some possible limitations of the DSM are its (a) use of a categorical classification system, (b) being based largely on experience in Western, industrialized cultures, and (c) inclusion of an ever-expanding list of disorders, some with little research foundation.

Visual Summary for Chapter 4:

Classification and Diagnosis

Diagnostic classification schemes are intended to provide a standard language for professional communication about psychological disorders and clues for the clinician about the likely causes, course, and treatment response of a patient's problems.

The Five Axes of the Current Official Diagnostic System, DSM-IV (1994)

		Examples
I	**Clinical Disorders**	panic disorder, schizophrenia
II	**Personality Disorders / Mental Retardation**	antisocial, narcissistic
III	**General Medical Conditions**	prostate cancer, if believed to be relevant to the mental disorder
IV	**Psychosocial and Environmental Problems**	divorce, threat of job loss
V	**Global Assessment of Functioning**	1–100 rating of overall mental health, considering psychological, social, and occupational functioning

Using a Diagnostic Scheme for Mental Disorders

Disadvantages	Possible Rebuttals	Advantages	Possible Rebuttals
Diagnostic label (e.g., schizophrenia) can be stigmatizing.	Research does not support this as a major cause of patients' problems.	A standardized scheme provides for clear communication among professionals.	Not if it changes every few years, and not if practicing clinicians use the scheme erratically.
Classification always means losing information about the unique person being diagnosed.	Information is indeed lost, but if the diagnosis conveys important information (e.g., how patients are likely to do in a particular kind of therapy) and discards information unimportant for mental health care (like shoe size), that is fine.	A diagnosis helps with the search for causes and treatment of people's problems.	Only if it is reliable and valid.

Aspects of Reliability and Validity Applied to Diagnostic Categories

Reliability (Consistency of Measurement)	Term	Definition	Sample Question
	Interrater Reliability	Consistency of judgment across raters.	If one clinician says the patient has schizophrenia, what is the probability that a second would agree?
	Retest Reliability	Consistency of ratings of the same person across time.	If your diagnosis today is social phobia, what is the probability that an evaluation one month from now would lead to the same diagnosis?
	Internal Consistency Reliability	Consistency of ratings of the same person at the same time across the various criteria in a diagnostic category.	If a child has one feature of attention-deficit/hyperactivity disorder, what is the probability that he or she has the others?

Validity (Success in Measuring Characteristic Intended)	Term	Definition	Sample Question
	Content Validity	Inclusion and proportionate representation of the major aspects of disorder, exclusion of criteria that do not belong.	Are all the main features of depression, as judged by experts or as revealed by research, included in the criteria for a major depressive episode?
	Concurrent Validity	Diagnosis relates to other important information about the person, collected at the same time.	Are people with specific phobias lower in occupational status than are nonphobic people?
	Predictive Validity	Diagnosis relates to other important information about the person, collected later.	Do people diagnosed before treatment with panic disorder subsequently get more benefit from Xanax than do people with generalized anxiety disorder?

Chapter 5

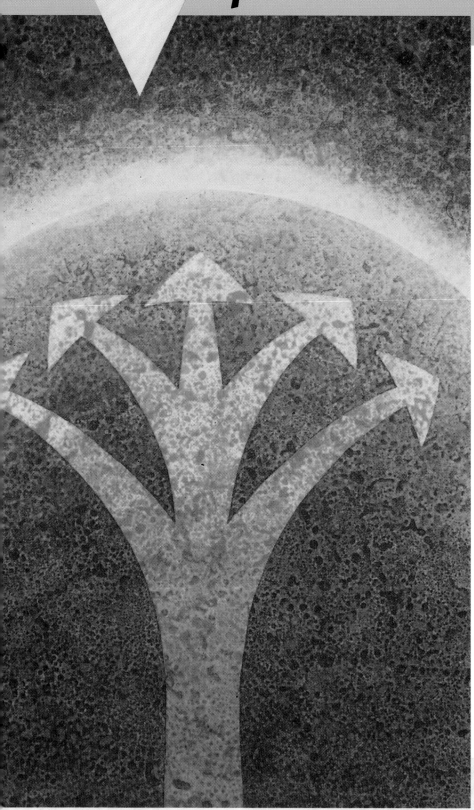

Clinical
Assessment
Procedures

With mental disorders as with physical disorders, before a treatment can begin, a thorough assessment of the patient must be made. Some clinical assessment procedures are used to help in making the DSM-IV diagnoses discussed in the previous chapter. Most of the clinical assessment procedures reviewed in this chapter, however, are not specifically intended to provide a diagnosis. But they do help clinicians and researchers find out what is wrong with a person, what may have caused the problems, and what might be done to resolve them. Some of these procedures are also used to evaluate the effects of therapy. In this chapter we review the types of clinical assessment currently in widespread use. The chapter concludes with a consideration of how cultural diversity can and should be taken into account in clinical assessment.

Psychological Assessment

Numerous psychological assessment methods are available. Generally speaking, we can find out about people by asking them (or others who know them well) what they are like or by observing their behavior in real or contrived situations. Although we will describe the methods individually, note that these procedures are by no means mutually exclusive. Many clinicians believe that using a combination of assessment procedures of different types yields the most useful overall picture. Indeed, most patients treated in therapy or studied in research complete a multifaceted set of assessments.

Interviews

Most of us have probably been interviewed at one time or another, although the conversation may have been so informal that we did not regard it as an interview. An **interview** is any interpersonal encounter, conversational in style, in which one person, the interviewer, uses language as the principal means of finding out about another, the interviewee. Thus a Gallup pollster who asks a college student whom she will vote for in an upcoming presidential election is interviewing with the restricted goal of learning which candidate she prefers. A clinical psychologist who asks a patient about the circumstances of his most recent hospitalization is similarly conducting an interview.

interview Any conversation in which one person uses language to find out about another.

Unstructured Clinical Interviews

clinical interview General term for conversation between a clinician and a patient, aimed at determining diagnosis, history, causes of problems, and possible treatment options.

One way in which a **clinical interview** differs from a political poll is the attention the interviewer pays to *how* the interviewee answers questions—or does not answer them. For example, a client who does not seem upset while describing recent marital conflicts would be evaluated differently from one who cried while discussing a similar situation.

An interviewer's perspective influences the type of information sought and obtained. A psychoanalytically trained clinician can be expected to inquire in detail about the person's childhood history and to be sensitive to changes in topics that might reflect repression of unpleasant memories. A behavioral clinician is likely to focus on current environmental conditions that can be related to changes in the person's behavior, for example, the circumstances under which the person becomes anxious. Thus the unstructured clinical interview does not follow a prescribed course, but varies with the perspective adopted by the interviewer.

Great skill is necessary to carry out good clinical interviews, for they are conducted with people who are often under considerable stress. Even a client who sincerely wants to tell a professional about intensely personal problems may not be able to do so without assistance. Clinicians, regardless of their theoretical perspectives, recognize the importance of establishing rapport with the client. They empathize with their clients in an effort to draw them out, to encourage them to elaborate on their concerns, and to examine different facets of a problem. A simple summary statement of what the client has been saying can help sustain the momentum of talk about painful and possibly embarrassing events and feelings, and an accepting attitude toward personal disclosures dispels the fear that revealing terrible secrets to another human being will have disastrous consequences.

Structured Interviews

Thus, the unstructured clinical interview is an art form. Guided by personal experience, theoretical perspective, and the content and manner of the patient's responses to questions, the clinician decides which areas to pursue and which to ignore. At times, though, mental health professionals need to ensure that certain bases are covered in a standard way, particularly when trying to decide on a DSM-IV diagnosis. To meet this need, investigators have developed **structured interviews**, in which the sequence and wording of questions is prearranged rather than left to the judgment of the interviewer.

structured interview An *interview* in which the sequence and wording of questions is prearranged.

Some structured interviews are disorder specific, such as the Anxiety Disorders Interview Schedule—Revised (ADIS-R; DiNardo & Barlow, 1988). Others attempt to cover most of the main diagnostic categories listed in Chapter 4. The Structured Clinical Interview for DSM-III-R (SCID) (Spitzer, Williams, Gibbon, & First, 1992), for instance, is a branching interview in which the client's response determines the next question, with detailed instructions for the interviewer concerning when to probe in detail and when to go on to questions about another diagnosis. Most symptoms are rated on a three-point scale of severity, with instructions for directly translating the symptom ratings into diagnoses. As with the unstructured clinical interview, evaluation of responses requires both listening to what the interviewee says and observing how she or he acts in the interview. For some diagnostic criteria (such as the lack of emotional expressiveness characteristic of schizophrenia or the slowed motor activity of major depression) the interviewer is in at least as good a position as the interviewee to observe whether the interviewee shows the characteristic.

The initial questions used on the SCID for diagnosing obsessive-compulsive disorder (discussed in Chapter 6) are presented in Figure 5.1. The interviewer begins by asking about obsessions. If the responses elicit a rating of 1 (absent), the interviewer turns to questions about compulsions. If the patient's responses again elicit a rating of 1, the interviewer is instructed to go to the questions for generalized anxiety disorder. On the other hand, if the symptoms are present, the interviewer continues with further questions about obsessive-compulsive disorder. The SCID is an important tool for collecting information to make diagnoses. The increasing use of structured interviews may be a major factor in the improvement of diagnostic reliability described in Chapter 4.

Strengths and Weaknesses of Interviews

The unstructured clinical interview can be a source of considerable information to the clinician. But, it does have limitations. Clinicians may overlook *situational* factors in the interview that may influence what the patient says or does. Consider how a teenager is likely to respond to the question "How often have you used illegal drugs?" when it is asked by a young, informally dressed psychologist and again when it is asked by a sixty-year-old psychologist in a business suit. In the usual clinical scenario, a clinician has no opportunity to see how the client might respond under such different conditions. More generally, as noted earlier, the way in which the unstructured clinical interview is conducted differs from one interviewer to another, perhaps on the basis of theoretical perspective. Thus the information collected is left largely up to the particular interviewer. To the ex-

Interview					Obsessive-Compulsive Disorder Criteria
		Rating Scale			
I would like to ask you if you have ever been bothered by thoughts that kept coming back to you even when you tried not to have them?	?	1	2	3	Obsessions: (1) Recurrent, persistent ideas, thoughts, impulses, or images that are experienced as intrusive, unwanted, and senseless or repugnant (at least intially).
IF YES: DISTINGUISH FROM BROODING ABOUT PROBLEMS (SUCH AS HAVING A PANIC ATTACK) OR ANXIOUS RUMINATION ABOUT REALISTIC DANGERS: What were they?	?	1	2	3	(2) The individual attempts to ignore or suppress them or to neutralize them with some other thought or action.
(What about awful thoughts, or thoughts that didn't make any sense to you–like actually hurting someone even though you didn't want to, or being contaminated by germs or dirt?)	?	1	2	3	(3) The individual recognizes that they are the product of his or her own mind and not imposed from without (as in thought insertion).

GO TO COMPULSIONS   DESCRIBE OBSESSIONS

Interview					Obsessive-Compulsive Disorder Criteria
Was there anything that you had to do over and over again and couldn't resist doing, like washing your hands again and again, or checking something several times to make sure you'd done it right?	?	1	2	3	Compulsions: (1) Repetitive, purposeful and intentional behavior that is performed according to certain rules or in a stereotyped fashion.
IF YES: What did you have to do? (What were you afraid would happen if you didn't do it?) (How many times did you have to ____? How much time did you spend each day ____?)	?	1	2	3	(2) The behavior is not an end in itself, but is designed to neutralize or prevent extreme discomfort or some dreaded event or situation. However, either the activity is not connected in a realistic way with what it is designed to neutralize or prevent or it is clearly excessive.

GO TO GENERALIZED ANXIETY DISORDERS SECTION   DESCRIBE COMPULSIONS

Key to rating scale
? = Inadequate information
1 = Absent or false
2 = Subthreshold
3 = Threshold or true

Figure 5.1   *Sample item from the SCID.*

tent that an interview is unstructured, the interviewer must rely on intuition and general experience in deciding how to ask questions and interpret the responses. This situation may well limit reliability and therefore validity of assessment. Diagnoses based on interview methods that vary from one clinician to another may not be reliable.

Thus, as useful as unstructured interviews can be, more formal and systematic methods of assessment are also needed. Structured interviews can help increase reliability by ensuring that clinicians ask about all pertinent diagnostic criteria in a standard way. There are, though, important areas (such as brain functioning or unconscious processes) about which people cannot report, regardless of the nature of the interview process, so other means of assessment are needed.

Assessment of Intelligence

Alfred Binet, a French psychologist, originally constructed mental tests to help the Parisian school board predict which children were in need of special schooling. Intelligence testing has since developed into one of the largest psychological industries. An **intelligence test**, sometimes referred to as an **aptitude test**, is a standardized means of assessing a person's current mental ability. The Scholastic Aptitude Test, the Graduate Record Examination, and individually administered tests such as the Wechsler Adult Intelligence Scale and the Stanford-Binet, are all based on the assumption that a detailed sample of an individual's current intellectual functioning can predict how well that individual will perform in school.

These tests have other uses as well. In conjunction with achievement tests, they help diagnose learning disorders and identify areas of strengths and weaknesses for academic planning. They can also be used to identify intellectually gifted children so that appropriate instruction can be provided them in school. And, when used as part of neuropsychological evaluations, periodic testing of a person believed to be suffering from dementia can track the deterioration of mental ability over time. The Wechsler Adult Intelligence Scale (WAIS) is often used as part of a battery, or series, of neuropsychological tests, an area of assessment discussed later in this chapter. A Spanish-language version of the WAIS has been available for almost thirty years (Wechsler, 1968) and can be useful in assessing the intellectual functioning of people from Latino cultures (Gomez, Piedmont, & Fleming, 1992; Lopez & Taussig, 1991). The use of intelligence tests in the diagnosis of mental retardation is discussed in Chapter 14.

Strengths and Weaknesses of Intelligence Tests

Intelligence tests typically have very good retest reliability and internal consistency reliability. Concurrent validity is also strong. For example, the fourth edition of the Stanford–Binet, published in 1986, readily distinguishes among intellectually gifted, learning disordered, and mentally retarded individuals (Thorndike, Hagen, & Sattler, 1986). Similar data are available on the revised version of the Wechsler scale (e.g., Matarazzo, 1972). However, predictive validities of these scales are more problematic, a seeming irony considering that the original Stanford–Binet was designed to predict future performance.

It is important to keep in mind that these tests measure only what a psychologist considers intelligence to be. The tasks and items on an intelligence test were, after all, invented by psychologists—they did not come to us inscribed on stone tablets. In addition, factors other than what we think of as pure intelligence play an important role in how people do in school, for example, family and personal circumstances, motivation, and the difficulty of the curriculum. Though intelligence test scores and school performance are correlated, measured intelligence is only a small part of the picture of school performance.

intelligence test A standardized means of assessing a person's current mental ability, for example, the Stanford–Binet test and the Wechsler Adult Intelligence Scale.

aptitude test An assessment of a person's intellectual functioning that is supposed to predict how he or she will perform at a later time; well-known examples include the Scholastic Aptitude Test and the Graduate Record Examination.

In the Block Design subtest of the Wechsler IQ test the blocks are to be arranged to match the design in the examiner's booklet.

Projective Personality Tests

In addition to unstructured clinical interviews, many clinicians use one or more personality tests in making assessments. These tests help clinicians begin to zero in on the specific aspects of a patient's **personality**—his or her characteristic ways of feeling, thinking, and behaving—that are leading to problems. Personality tests are administered under the same conditions and with the same instructions to many people at different times. The responses collected are analyzed to indicate how certain kinds of people tend to respond. This process, called **standardization**, enables statistical norms for the tests to be established. The responses of a particular patient can then be compared with these norms. In this section we examine a special kind of personality test, the projective test.

A **projective test** is a psychological assessment device in which a set of standard stimuli, ambiguous enough to allow wide variation in perception and interpretation, is presented. Because the stimuli are ambiguous, the patient's impressions are assumed to reflect unconscious processes and to reveal his or her true attitudes, motivations, and modes of behavior. Projective tests are especially favored by clinicians and researchers with psychodynamic perspectives. In a sense, the test stimuli are seen as functioning like a traditional psychoanalyst. Just as a patient is believed, as part of the transference (see Chapter 2), to project unconscious assumptions or attitudes onto a neutral analyst, so the test taker projects unconscious attitudes onto ambiguous stimuli.

Perhaps the best-known projective tests are the **Rorschach Inkblot Test** and the **Thematic Apperception Test (TAT)**. In the Rorschach test, the subject is shown ten inkblots, one at a time, and asked to tell what figures or objects he or she sees in each of them. Half the inkblots are in black, white, and shades of gray; two add red splotches; and three are in pastel colors. Traditionally, Rorschach responses have been interpreted in terms of their content and the unconscious conflicts that might therein be reflected. If a patient reports seeing eyes on the Rorschach, for example, the hypothesis might be that the patient is experiencing paranoia. Alternatively, the responses can be interpreted on the basis of their

personality A person's habitual ways of feeling, thinking, and acting.

standardization The process of constructing an assessment procedure so that norms can be established and research conducted on its *reliability* and *validity*. Test administration procedures and instructions are fixed.

projective test A psychological assessment device employing a set of standard but ambiguous stimuli on the assumption that such material will allow unconscious motivations and conflicts to be uncovered. The *Rorschach* series of inkblots is an example.

Rorschach Inkblot Test A *projective test* in which the examinee is instructed to interpret a series of ten inkblots reproduced on cards.

Thematic Apperception Test (TAT) A *projective test* consisting of a set of black-and-white pictures reproduced on cards, each depicting a potentially emotion-laden situation. The examinee, presented with the cards one at a time, is instructed to make up a story about each situation.

In the Rorschach test, the client is shown a series of inkblots and is asked what he or she sees in each of them.

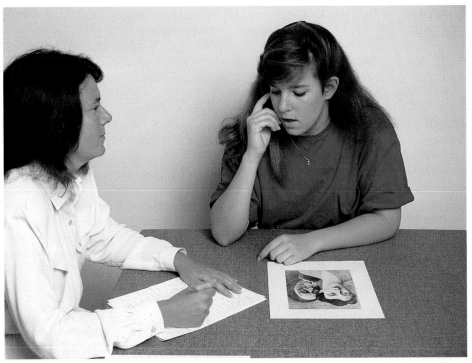

A client relates a story in response to one of the cards from the Thematic Appreciation Test. Like the Rorschach, this projective test is designed to reveal unconscious conflicts and concerns.

form, as a clue to how the person perceptually and cognitively organizes real-life situations (Exner, 1978, 1986). For example, respondents who see human figures in motion in their Rorschach responses tend to use inner resources when coping with their needs, whereas those whose Rorschach responses can be characterized as involving color are more likely to seek interaction with the environment (Erdberg & Exner, 1984).

In the Thematic Apperception Test (Murray, 1943), the examinee is shown, one by one, a series of black-and-white pictures representing various scenes and asked to tell a story related to each. The clinician then interprets the responses. For example, a patient might be shown a picture of a prepubescent girl looking at nattily attired mannequins in a store window and then tell a story that contains angry references to the girl's parents. In this case the clinician may infer that the patient resents his or her parents and is projecting this resentment onto the girl in the picture.

Strengths and Weaknesses of Projective Personality Tests

Early research on the Rorschach suggested a number of problems (Anastasi, 1988). Five quite different systems for administering, scoring, and interpreting the test were in widespread use, making it difficult to know whether results were actually comparable and had the same meaning in different clinics or different studies. Also, it turned out that people could alter their Rorschach responses so as to create a more favorable impression (Masling, 1960). Though this is true of most psychological tests, one of the goals of projective testing in particular is to prevent the possibility of faking in this sense. Moreover, factors that should ideally be irrelevant appeared to influence Rorschach results, including whether the person administering the test behaved in a warm or cold manner (Masling, 1960). Finally, and most crucially, good, extensive norms were not collected on the Rorschach such that one could really tell, say, whether seeing a crab in card 10 was unusual or not.

During a ride in the country with his two children, Herman Rorschach (1884–1922), Swiss psychiatrist, noticed that what they saw in the clouds reflected their personalities. From this observation came the famous inkblot test.

The TAT also lacks extensive normative information and standardized scoring procedures. Indeed, not only are scoring systems diverse, but even the series of cards differs greatly across clinicians and research studies (Keiser & Prather, 1990). Accordingly, it is difficult to compare results across studies and generate a solid base of information about what aspects of personality relevant to psychopathology the test validly measures.

With the Rorschach, however, the situation has improved in recent years, largely through the work of John Exner (1986) and his associates. They compiled features from the existing scoring systems that were reliably scorable and appeared to be supported by at least some evidence of validity. The Exner system is now the dominant one used in Rorschach research and in graduate school instruction on the Rorschach. Exner and his associates have gathered extensive clinical and nonclinical norms for the variables scored in their system. Perhaps most important, they have made the system responsive to research findings. For example, they made changes in the procedure for assessing depression on the basis of Rorschach responses when they found that many people otherwise known to be depressed failed to be detected as depressed by the Rorschach scoring system (Exner, 1991).

One unresolved difficulty with the test is that people are allowed to, and do, offer different numbers of responses to each card. It is unknown what, if any, significance different response frequencies hold for understanding personality. However, they greatly influence scores on many variables derived from the Rorschach and used in comparing a patient's performance to established norms (such as the number of responses that involve the white space on a card or the number of responses that feature human movement) (G. J. Meyer, 1992). This ambiguity was highlighted in a review of seven studies comparing Rorschach results of African-Americans with those of whites. Overall, scores were similar. The only consistent difference was that African-American people gave fewer responses. Other differences that appeared in the studies involved variables that are influenced by the number of responses, so the implications of the differences are unclear (G. Frank, 1992).

A possible solution to this problem would be to structure the test so that everyone would be encouraged to give, but would be limited to, say, two responses per card. This change, though, would have the potential disadvantage of obtaining scores that would not be comparable to norms derived from administrations of the test that did not limit the number of responses. More research is needed on whether such a change would improve validity of the Rorschach (G. J. Meyer, 1992).

Personality Inventories

personality inventory A self-report questionnaire by which an examinee indicates whether statements assessing habitual tendencies apply to him or her.

Another psychological assessment tool, the personality inventory or questionnaire, is less open-ended than the projective test. In a **personality inventory**, people indicate whether statements about characteristic tendencies apply to them. For example, they might be asked to indicate to what extent they agree with statements such as "I tend to enjoy trying new hobbies." These questionnaires typically meet the general requirements of test construction and standardization. It is therefore rare for a personality inventory to lack reliability. Validity, however, still presents a problem in many instances.

Some personality questionnaires are perspective specific. The Purpose in Life (PIL; Crumbaugh, 1968) test, for example, was designed to measure Viktor Frankl's concept of an "existential vacuum," a feeling of emptiness and boredom stemming from the failure to find meaning in one's life. The PIL consists of twenty items, each of which the subject rates on a 1-to-7 scale (such as "If I should die today, I would feel that my life has been worthwhile"). The PIL shows high internal consistency reliability and correlates with therapist ratings of purpose and meaning (Crumbaugh & Maholick, 1964).

Similarly, therapists and investigators working from the cognitive perspective often use questionnaires to tap a wide range of cognitions, such as fears of negative evaluation, a tendency to think irrationally, and a tendency to make negative inferences about life experience. For example, to assess depressive attitudes, Weissman and Beck (1978) devised the Dysfunctional Attitude Scale (DAS). This questionnaire contains such items as "People will probably think less of me if I make a mistake." The DAS has shown concurrent validity in the sense that it can differentiate between depressed and nondepressed people.

The MMPI

Other personality questionnaires are used by clinicians and researchers of diverse perspectives. Perhaps the best known of these is the **Minnesota Multiphasic Personality Inventory (MMPI)**, developed in the early 1940s by Hathaway and McKinley (1943) and revised in 1989 (Butcher, Dahlstrom, Graham, Tellegen, & Kraemer, 1989). The MMPI is intended to be an inexpensive means of detecting psychopathology. It is called multiphasic because it was designed to detect several psychiatric problems. Over the years, the MMPI has been widely used to screen large groups of people, such as military personnel, for whom clinical interviews are not feasible.

To develop the test, investigators began with factual statements considered by clinicians to be indicative of various mental problems. These items were rated as self-descriptive or not both by patients already diagnosed with particular disorders and by a large group of people considered normal. If patients in one clinical group responded to an item in a particular way more often than did those in other groups, it was selected for the test. With additional refinements, sets of these items were established as scales for determining whether or not a respondent should be diagnosed in a particular way. If a person answered a large number of the items in a scale in the same way that people in a certain diagnostic group answered, his or her behavior was expected to resemble the behavior of people with that diagnosis.

The MMPI scales at first related reasonably well to psychiatric diagnoses, but related less well as the DSM classification system changed. For example, Winters, Weintraub, and Neale (1981) found that the MMPI did very poorly in predicting the DSM-III diagnosis of schizophrenia.

The revised MMPI-2 (Butcher et al., 1989) has several noteworthy improvements. The original sample fifty years ago lacked representation of racial minorities, such as African-Americans and Native Americans, restricting its standardization sample to white men and women, essentially, rural Minnesotans. The new version was standardized with a much larger sample that was more similar to 1980 U.S. census figures.

Some revisions served the purpose of updating the content of the MMPI. A number of items containing allusions to sexual adjustment, bowel and bladder functions, and excessive religiosity were removed, for example, because they were judged in some testing contexts to be needlessly intrusive and objectionable. Sexist wording was eliminated along with outmoded idioms.

Other revisions have extended the range of the test. Several new items deal with substance abuse, Type A behavior (see p. 203), eating disorders, and interpersonal relationships. MMPI-2 is otherwise quite similar to the original; it has the same format, yields the same scale scores and profiles (Ben-Porath & Butcher, 1989; Graham, 1988), and in general provides continuity with the vast literature already existing on the original MMPI (Graham, 1990). Early research on the new instrument demonstrates good retest and internal consistency reliability (Butcher et al.,1989) and also suggests adequate concurrent validity with criteria such as

Minnesota Multiphasic Personality Inventory (MMPI) A lengthy *personality inventory* by which individuals are diagnosed through their true–false replies to groups of statements that indicate states such as *anxiety, depression,* and *paranoia.*

behavioral ratings by spouses and symptom ratings by clinicians (Graham, 1988). Items similar to those on the various scales are presented in Table 5.1.

Strengths and Weaknesses of Personality Inventories

One difficulty with personality inventories is that, unlike projective personality tests, they are often transparent. That is, it is clear to the subject what is being measured. Transparent questionnaire measures are susceptible to deliberate manipulation or faking on the part of the respondent. For example, even seriously disturbed people know that if they wish to be regarded as normal they must not admit to worrying a great deal about germs on doorknobs. Or, a person who wants to be hired by a police department that is under attack for incidents of police brutality knows better than to endorse a statement such as "When I am angry, I tend to lash out at other people." There is evidence that these tests *can* be "psyched out." In most testing circumstances, however, people do not *want* to falsify their responses, because they want to be helped.

Also, in creating the MMPI, special precautions were taken to try to identify people giving false responses. The test designers included several so-called validity scales designed to detect deliberate faking (see Table 5.1). In one, the lie scale, a series of statements sets a trap for the person who is trying to look too good. An item on the lie scale might be "I read the newspaper editorials every night." The assumption is that few people would be able to endorse such a statement honestly. Thus persons who endorse a large number of the statements in the lie scale might well be attempting to present themselves in a particularly good light. Their scores on other scales would therefore be viewed with more than the usual skepticism.

Besides deliberate, conscious faking, personality inventories may yield misleading results if people unconsciously deny, even to themselves, undesirable characteristics, such as severe distress. People who are genuinely well adjusted look the same on a transparent measure as those who are greatly distressed but not consciously aware of it, so results are ambiguous. One approach to clarifying the results of personality inventories involves combining them with projective tests to obtain a fuller picture. A study suggesting that this combination could be useful is examined in the following critical thinking exercise.

> APPLYING CRITICAL THINKING SKILLS

USING PROJECTIVE PERSONALITY TESTS IN COMBINATION WITH STRAIGHTFORWARD MEASURES

In one study, heart rate and blood pressure were measured at rest and during a number of psychologically stressful tasks, such as counting backward in one's head as fast and accurately as possible (Shedler, Mayman, & Manis, 1993). Cardiovascular reactivity was measured by noting the increase in blood pressure and heart rate in response to these stressful tasks. In a separate part of the research project, subjects completed a straightforward questionnaire measuring self-perceived mental health. There was no systematic correlation between scores on the mental health questionnaire and cardiovascular reactivity.

▶ *What conclusion does the evidence seem to support?* At least within this sample (twenty-three-year-olds participating in an ongoing longitudinal study of many areas of psychological functioning), mental health was independent of cardiovascular health as reflected in reactivity to stressors encountered in the laboratory.

▶ *What other interpretations are plausible?* The researchers reasoned that mental health might indeed be related to cardiovascular reactivity to stressors. The

Table 5.1 ▶ *Typical Clinical Interpretations of Items Similar to Those on the MMPI-2*

Scale[a]	Sample Item	Interpretation
? (cannot say)	This is merely the number of items left unanswered or marked both true and false.	A high score indicates evasiveness, reading difficulties, or other problems that could invalidate the results of the test. A very high score could also suggest severe depression or obsessional tendencies.
L (Lie)	I approve of every person I meet. (True)	Person is trying to look good, to present self as someone with an ideal personality.
F (infrequency)	Everything tastes sweet. (True)	Person is trying to look abnormal, perhaps to ensure getting special attention from the clinician.
K (Correction)	Things couldn't be going any better for me. (True)	Person is guarded, defensive in taking the test, wishes to avoid appearing incompetent or poorly adjusted.
1. Hs (Hypochondriasis)	I am seldom aware of tingling feelings in my body. (False)	Person is overly sensitive to and concerned about bodily sensations as signs of possible physical illness.
2. D (Depression)	Life usually feels worthwhile to me. (False)	Person is discouraged, pessimistic, sad, self-deprecating, feeling inadequate.
3. Hy (Hysteria)	My muscles often twitch for no apparent reason. (True)	Person has somatic complaints unlikely to be due to physical problems; also tends to be demanding and histrionic.
4. Pd (Psychopathy)	I don't care about what people think of me. (True)	Person expresses little concern for social mores, is irresponsible, has only superficial relationships.
5. Mf (Masculinity–Femininity)	I like taking care of plants and flowers. (True, female)	Person shows traditional gender characteristics, e.g., men with high scores tend to be artistic and sensitive; women with high scores tend to be rebellious and assertive.
6. Pa (Paranoia)	If they were not afraid of being caught, most people would lie and cheat. (True)	Person tends to misinterpret the motives of others, is suspicious and jealous, vengeful and brooding.
7. Pt (Psychasthenia)	I am not as competent as most other people I know. (True)	Person is overanxious, full of self-doubts, moralistic, and generally obsessive-compulsive
8. Sc (Schizophrenia)	I sometimes smell things others don't sense. (True)	Person has bizarre sensory experiences and beliefs, is socially reclusive.
9. Ma (Hypomania)	Sometimes I have a strong impulse to do something that others will find appalling. (True)	Person has overly ambitious aspirations and can be hyperactive, impatient, and irritable.
10. Si (Social introversion)	Rather than spend time alone, I prefer to be around other people. (False)	Person is very modest and shy, preferring solitary activities.

Source: Hathaway and Mckinley (1943); reused in Butcher et al. (1989).

[a] The first four scales assess the validity of the test; the numbered scales are the clinical or content scales.

problem with the study could be in the way in which mental health was measured. Straightforward assessment methods, such as structured interviews and personality or mental health questionnaires, can reveal only what the patient is aware of and is willing to report, which may be only the more socially acceptable aspects of her or his personality. Shedler and his colleagues (1993) reasoned that *low* scores on questionnaire measures of distress might be especially ambiguous. Most people who acknowledge significant distress on such measures are probably indeed experiencing distress. However, those who report that all is well might be genuinely mentally healthy or they might be using the defense mechanism of denial (see Chapter 2) to maintain an "illusion of mental health" (Shedler et al., 1993, p. 1117).

▶ **What other information would help choose among the alternative interpretations?** If the first interpretation is correct, then mental health will be unrelated to cardiovascular measures no matter how you slice it. If the second interpretation, that some of those who report low distress are actually denying their genuine feelings, is correct, then projective testing should clarify matters. To distinguish those who showed "illusory mental health," Shedler and his associates used projective tests. Subjects were asked to respond to a series of questions about the earliest memory they could recall, as well as other early memories about happy and unhappy childhood experiences, their parents, and themselves, to augment the data on cardiovascular reactivity and stress.

A psychoanalytically trained clinician, unaware of the scores on other measures, rated the subjects on the basis of their reports of early memories as relatively mentally healthy or relatively fragile and susceptible to negative reactions to stress. Subjects with illusory mental health (low reported distress, but judged to be unhealthy on the basis of projective testing) showed significantly higher cardiovascular reactivity to stress than did either *genuinely* mentally healthy subjects (who looked healthy on both straightforward and projective testing) or *manifestly distressed* subjects (who looked unhealthy on both measures).

The results were consistent with the view that defensive denial of psychological distress takes a toll on physical well-being. From an assessment point of view, the study suggests that projective testing may be especially useful for identifying those who report high levels of well-being on straightforward tests but are actually distressed. In clinical practice, one of the biggest assessment challenges is this very process: thinking critically about the meaning of one set of test results and using other tests to select among the multiple interpretations consistent with the first set of results. In this case, without projective tests, a clinician might overlook the psychological components contributing to cardiovascular reactivity.   ◀

In addition to allowing possible unconscious or conscious misrepresentation of the person's inner experience, personality inventories have been criticized for ignoring the relevance of situational influences on human behavior. Consider the self-report inventories measuring cognition. When patients are asked about their thoughts on such measures, they have to reflect backward in time and provide a retrospective and rather general report of their thoughts in certain situations. "When someone criticizes you in class, do you tend to think, 'I'm such a failure'?" is a question they might be asked, for example. People's responses to such questions about thoughts in certain past situations may well be different from what they would report were they able to do so in the immediate circumstance. In response to these concerns, researchers have been working on ways to measure subjects' immediate and ongoing thought processes when confronted with particular circumstances (Parks & Hollon, 1988) (see Focus Box 5.1).

Researchers and clinicians from the behavioral perspective have been particularly critical of the neglect of situational factors on the part of personality inventories. By emphasizing standardization of test content and testing conditions so as to obtain the most readily interpretable indication of what a person's inner self is like, these tests intentionally downplay environmental factors. From a behavioral point of view this is a serious limitation that restricts the usefulness of the tests, particularly for planning treatment.

The idea that traditional approaches to personality assessment place too much

Specialized Approaches to Cognitive Assessment

Questionnaires such as the *Dysfunctional Attitude Scale* are useful measures of general beliefs about life, other people, or the self. Other questionnaires concerning cognition measure the thoughts we typically have in a general class of situations (e.g., "when I am the focus of attention"). These tests can be informative, but more situation-specific information is also desirable for testing theory and planning treatment from a cognitive perspective. Can we show, for example, that a socially anxious person does in fact, as rational-emotive theory would predict, view criticism from others as catastrophic, whereas someone who is not socially insecure does not?

The *Articulated Thoughts in Simulated Situations* (ATSS) method (Davison, Robins, & Johnson, 1983) is an example of research that assesses immediate thoughts. In this procedure, a subject pretends to be a participant in a situation, such as listening to a teaching assistant criticize a term paper. Presented on audiotape, the scene pauses every ten or fifteen seconds. During the ensuing thirty seconds of silence, the subject talks aloud about whatever he or she is thinking in reaction to the words just heard. Then the audiotaped scene continues, stopping after a few moments so that the subject can articulate his or her thoughts again. One taped scene in which two pretend acquaintances criticize the subject includes the following segments.

> **First Acquaintance:** He certainly did make a fool of himself over what he said about religion. I just find that kind of opinion very close-minded and unaware. You have to be blind to the facts of the universe to believe that. (*Thirty-second pause for subject's response.*)
> **Second Acquaintance:** What really bugs me is the way he expresses himself. He never seems to stop and

think, but just blurts out the first thing that comes into his head. (*Thirty-second pause.*)

Subjects readily become involved in the pretend situations, regarding them as credible and realistic. The following cognitive patterns have emerged from a few of the studies conducted thus far.

1. Socially anxious therapy patients articulated thoughts of greater irrationality than did nonanxious control subjects (Bates, Campbell, & Burgess, 1990; Davison & Zighelboim, 1987), which supports concurrent validity.
2. In a predictive validity study, recent ex-smokers who would relapse within three months had fewer negative expectations about the consequences of smoking than did those who would still be abstinent three months later (Haaga, 1989).
3. In an experiment that directly compared ATSS data with overt behavior, the more anxiously subjects were observed to behave when giving a speech, the less capable they felt themselves to be while articulating thoughts in a stressful, simulated speech-giving situation (Davison, Haaga, Rosenbaum, Dolezal, & Weinstein, 1991) .

This pattern of results indicates that the ATSS method ferrets out people's thinking about both inherently bothersome and objectively innocuous situations.

Other cognitive assessment methods have also proved useful. For example, *thought listing* has the person write down thoughts prior to or following an event of interest, such as entering a room to talk to a stranger, as a way to determine the cognitive components of social anxiety (Cacioppo, Glass, & Merluzzi, 1979).

---

emphasis on inner traits and not enough on behavior in specific situations gained considerable credibility from a book published by Walter Mischel, *Personality and Assessment* (1968). Mischel argued that personality traits such as those measured in personality inventories are not important determinants of behavior. Trait theorists believe that human beings can be described as having a certain amount of a characteristic, such as stinginess or obsessiveness, and that their behavior in a variety of situations can be predicted reasonably well by the degree to which they possess this characteristic. This position implies that people will behave fairly consistently in a variety of situations—a highly aggressive person, for example, will be more aggressive than someone low in aggression at home, at work, and at play. After reviewing the evidence bearing on this question, Mischel concluded that the behavior of people is often not very consistent from situation to situation.

The work of the prominent psychologist Walter Mischel stimulated the current debate concerning whether personality traits or situations are the most powerful determinants of behavior.

Mischel's attack on trait theory may have been overstated. It ignored the possibility that clinical problems, unlike the normal personality variations studied in most of the research he reviewed, may be associated with rigidity in the face of changing conditions (Wachtel, 1977). Also, standard psychology experiments on the consistency of behavior across situations tell us only about how people react to the situations in which the experiment places them. By contrast, one way in which people express their personality consistency in the real world is to *elicit* certain kinds of reactions from their surroundings. The paranoid individual may not only perceive people as threatening, but may make them so by attacking them first. In effect, he or she transforms different situations into similar and dangerous ones. As a result, the paranoid's own behavior may vary little.

Some of the most promising contemporary research on personality development is based directly on this idea that personality consistency must be considered in an environmental context. For example, Caspi and Herbener (1990) divided a sample of married couples into subgroups according to how similar the husband and wife were to one another in personality. The more similar the couples, the more stable was the individual personality of each partner over the ten years of the longitudinal study. It appeared that each spouse served as a mini-environment, modeling and reinforcing continuity of the same personality characteristics in the another.

Even if too extreme in downgrading the importance of traits, Mischel's critique nonetheless was valuable. It provoked personality assessors to consider more seriously the situations in which behavior is observed, rather than to assume that traditional methods would reveal all they needed to know about someone's personality (Kenrick & Funder, 1988).

Direct Observation of Behavior

Partly in response to Mischel's critique of personality traits, interest has been growing in assessing people's actions by observing them directly in specific situations. In other words, instead of (or in addition to) describing individual differences in traits, many therapists consider it important to observe behavior directly in real-life settings or contrived situations. It can be informative to bypass people's verbal summaries of their behavior ("I tend to shout a lot when angry") and see for yourself how they act in relevant conditions, just as in assessing cognition it can be informative to measure specific thoughts in specific situations (see Focus Box 5.1). It is also important to observe the consequences that follow a patient's behavior. Consider the following example excerpted from a case report (Patterson, Ray, Shaw, & Cobb, 1969), which describes an interaction between a boy named Kevin and his mother, father, and sister Freida.

> Kevin goes up to father's chair and stands alongside it. Father puts his arms around Kevin's shoulders. Kevin says to mother as Freida looks at Kevin, "Can I go out and play after supper?" Mother does not reply. Kevin raises his voice and repeats the question. Mother says, "You don't have to yell; I can hear you." Father says, "How many times have I told you not to yell at your mother?" Kevin scratches a bruise on his arm while mother tells Freida to get started on the dishes, which Freida does. Kevin continues to rub and scratch his arm while mother and daughter are working at the kitchen sink. (p. 21)

This informal description could probably be provided by any observer. But in formal behavioral observation, the observer divides the uninterrupted sequence of behavior into various parts. Because the therapist in this case is behaviorally oriented and approaches therapy from the perspective that behaviors are learned, he applies terms that make sense within a learning framework. "Kevin begins the exchange by asking a routine question in a normal tone of voice. This

Behavioral assessment often involves direct observation of behavior, as in this case where the observer is behind a one-way mirror.

ordinary behavior, however, is not reinforced by the mother's attention, for she does not reply. Because she does not reply, the normal behavior of Kevin ceases and he yells his question. The mother expresses disapproval—punishing her son—by telling him that he does not have to yell. And this punishment is supported by the father's reminding Kevin that he should not yell at his mother" (Patterson et al., 1969). This behavioral rendition acknowledges the consequences of ignoring a child's question. At some point the behavior therapist will undoubtedly advise the parents to attend to Kevin's requests when expressed in an ordinary tone of voice, lest he begin yelling.

It is difficult to observe most behavior as it actually takes place, and little control can be exercised over where and when it may occur. For this reason, many therapists contrive artificial situations in their consulting rooms or in a laboratory so that they can observe how a client or a family acts under certain conditions. For example, Barkley (1981) had a mother and her hyperactive child spend time together in a laboratory living room, complete with sofas and television set. The mother was given a list of tasks for the child to complete, such as picking up toys or doing arithmetic problems. Observers behind a one-way mirror watched and rated the child's reactions to the mother's efforts to control as well as the mother's reactions to the child's compliant or noncompliant responses. These assessment procedures yielded data that showed that, compared with children who had been given placebo medications, hyperactive children who were being treated with methylphenidate (Ritalin) were more obedient to their mothers, who, in turn, were more positive in their reactions to their children (Barkley & Cunningham, 1979). In this case the treatment was being assessed as much as the patient.

Direct observations can also be made by significant others in the client's natural environment. For example, the Conners Teacher Rating Scale (Conners, 1969) enables teachers to provide reliable behavioral assessment data on children in classrooms, and the Achenbach Child Behavior Checklist (Achenbach & Edelbrock, 1983) has parents or teachers rate children's behavior. Finally, therapists can ask individuals to observe their own behavior and keep track of various *self-monitoring* A procedure whereby the individual observes and reports certain aspects of his or her own behavior, thoughts, or emotions.

kinds of responses. This approach, called **self-monitoring**, has been used to evaluate efforts to reduce smoking as well as to treat eating disorders and other problems.

Strengths and Weaknesses of Direct Observation of Behavior

The example of Kevin and his family illustrates one important strength of direct observation, its link to *treatment*. Actually seeing the problematic behavior is much more likely than retrospective interviews or questionnaires or tests of mental ability to yield information about its antecedents and (sometimes subtle) consequences. Therefore, direct observation is more likely to suggest ways of changing the problem behavior. Some advocates of behavioral assessment have suggested that a key bottom-line consideration is often overlooked in evaluating traditional measures. **Treatment utility** refers to whether having the results of an assessment procedure improves treatment outcome relative to not having these data (Hayes, Nelson, & Jarrett, 1987). Treatment utility is distinct from reliability and validity. It is possible to have highly reliable and valid information on, say, the verbal ability of a patient, but this information might not enhance the therapist's ability to treat the patient.

treatment utility The extent to which knowing the results of an assessment procedure improves the outcome of treatment.

A limitation of direct observation methods is that they tend to be obtrusive. If you have ever attempted as part of a behavior change program to write down every hour of studying accomplished, or every piece of food consumed, you may have noticed the effects of this obtrusiveness. Research on self-monitoring shows that behavior may be altered by the very fact that it is being self-monitored (Haynes & Horn, 1982). **Reactivity** of behavior is the phenomenon of behavior changing because it is being observed. Although reactivity is a complication from the point of view of finding out what the patient typically does when not being formally assessed, therapeutic interventions can take advantage of reactivity. It appears that the eye of the beholder usually affects the beauty in a favorable manner. Desirable behavior, such as engaging in social conversation, often increases in frequency when it is self-monitored (Nelson, Lipinski, & Black, 1976), whereas undesirable behavior, such as smoking cigarettes or overeating, diminishes (Baker & Kirschenbaum, 1993; McFall & Hammen, 1971).

reactivity (of behavior) The phenomenon whereby the object of observation is changed by the very fact that it is being observed.

To Recap

Clinical interviews differ from other interviews in that much attention is paid to how someone answers a question, not just what is said. Good clinical interviewing requires the ability to empathize with the client so as to encourage her or him to speak openly about personal information and feelings. However, different interviewers may obtain different results. Diagnoses are therefore typically made on the basis of structured interviews that dictate the sequence and wording of questions.

Some important psychological data cannot be verbally reported. Intelligence testing involves a detailed sample of the person's current intellectual functioning and is useful for predicting school performance, diagnosing learning disorders and mental retardation, and tracking the course of dementias. Personality testing includes projective tests, which assume that unconscious processes are best revealed in people's perceptions of ambiguous situations.

More straightforward personality inventories, such as the MMPI, provide an efficient, usually reliable means of assessing personality. To the degree that the traits being measured are accessible to awareness and the person is motivated to report accurately, validity is high. However, these tests may fail to take situational influences on behavior sufficiently into account. Direct observation or self-monitoring of behavior is used to identify more precisely how someone acts in particular situations and what the consequences of those actions are, which should prove useful for planning treatment.

Biological Assessment

Many mental disorders have a biological component, whether it is a cause, as in phenylketonuria, or an effect, as in the nutritional deficits suffered by many people who have eating disorders. Thus psychotherapists often recommend that patients have a full physical examination to determine if any physical health problems might be contributing to their psychological difficulties. For many years, researchers and clinicians have also attempted to use observations about the functioning of the brain and other parts of the nervous system and their connection to behavior in an effort to understand normal and abnormal psychological functioning (see Focus Box 5.2). Recent technological advances in brain imaging have begun to make this possible.

Brain-Imaging Techniques

Many behavioral problems can be brought on by brain abnormalities. Neurological tests, such as checking the reflexes or examining the retina for any sign of blood vessel damage, are among the biological assessment techniques useful in determining possible sources of abnormality in brain dysfunction.

Computerized axial tomography, the **CAT scan**, and positron emission tomography, the **PET scan**, are recent advances in assessing brain abnormalities. In the CAT scan (see Figure 5.4) a moving beam of X rays passes into a horizontal cross section of the patient's brain, scanning it through 360 degrees. The moving X-ray detector on the other side measures the amount of radioactivity that penetrates and thus detects subtle differences in tissue density. The computer uses the information to construct a two-dimensional, detailed image of the cross section. The patient's head is then moved, and the machine scans another cross section of the brain. The resulting images can show the enlargement of ventricles, signaling degeneration of tissue, and also the locations of tumors and blood clots.

Nuclear magnetic response imaging (NMR), also known as MRI (for magnetic resonance imaging), is superior to CAT scans because it produces pictures of higher quality and does not rely on even the small amount of radiation that CAT requires. In NMR the person is placed inside a large, circular magnet, which causes the hydrogen atoms in the body to move. When the magnetic force is turned off, the atoms return to their original positions and thereby produce an electromagnetic signal. These signals are read by the computer and translated into black-and-white pictures of brain tissue.

In PET scanning (see Figure 5.5), a more expensive and invasive procedure, a substance used by the brain is labeled with a short-lived radioactive isotope and injected into the bloodstream. The radioactive molecules of the substance emit a particle called a positron, which quickly collides with an electron. A pair of high-energy light particles shoot out from the skull in opposite directions and are detected by the scanner. The computer analyzes millions of such recordings and converts them into a motion picture of the functioning brain in horizontal cross section, projected onto a television screen. The images are in color; fuzzy spots of lighter and warmer colors are areas in which metabolic rates for the substance are higher. Moving visual images of the working brain can indicate sites of epileptic seizures, brain cancers, strokes, and trauma from head injuries, as well as the distribution of psychoactive drugs in the brain. The PET scanner is also being used to study possible abnormal biological processes underlying disorders (e.g., lower levels of glucose metabolism in the dorsolateral prefrontal cortex of people with schizophrenia; see Chapter 9).

CAT scan Computerized axial tomography, a method of assessment employing X rays taken from different angles and then analyzed by computer to produce a representation of the part of the body in cross section. Often used on the brain.

PET scan Computer-assisted motion pictures of the living brain, created by analysis of radioactive particles from isotopes injected into the bloodstream.

nuclear magnetic response imaging (NMR) A biological assessment that entails placing a person inside a large magnet. When force is turned on, hydrogen atoms move; when force is turned off they return to their original positions. This process produces an electromagnetic signal that a computer can translate into black-and-white pictures of living tissue.

Structure and Function of the Human Brain

The brain is located within the protective coating of the skull and is enveloped with three layers of nonneural tissue, membranes referred to as **meninges**. Viewed from the top, the brain is divided by a midline fissure into two mirror-image **cerebral hemispheres**, which together constitute most of the cerebrum. The major connection between the two hemispheres is a band of nerve fibers called the **corpus callosum**. Figure 5.2 shows the surface of one of the cerebral hemispheres.

The upper, side, and some of the lower surfaces of the hemispheres constitute the **cerebral cortex**. The cortex consists of tightly packed neuron cell bodies with many short, interconnecting processes. These neurons, estimated to number ten to fifteen billion, make up a thin outer covering, the so-called gray matter of the brain. The cortex is vastly convoluted. The ridges are called **gyri** and the depressions between them **sulci** or fissures. Deep fissures divide the cerebral hemispheres into several distinct areas, called lobes. The **frontal lobe** lies in front of the central sulcus; the **parietal lobe** is be-

hind it and above the lateral sulcus; the **temporal lobe** is located below the lateral sulcus; and the **occipital lobe** lies behind the parietal and temporal lobes. Different functions tend to be localized in particular areas of the lobes—vision in the occipital; discrimination of sounds in the temporal; reasoning and other higher mental processes, plus the regulation of fine voluntary movement, in the frontal; initiation of movements of the skeletal musculature in a band in front of the central sulcus; reception of sensations of touch, pressure, pain, temperature, and body position from skin, muscles, tendons, and joints in a band behind the central sulcus.

The two hemispheres of the brain have different functions. The left hemisphere generally controls the right half of the body by a crossing over of motor and sensory fibers. It is responsible for speech and, according to some neuropsychologists, for analytical thinking in right-handed people and in some left-handed people as well. The right hemisphere controls the left side of the body, discerns spatial relations and patterns, and is involved in emotion and intuition. But analytical thinking cannot be located exclusively in the left hemisphere or intuitive and even creative thinking in the right—the two hemispheres communicate with each other constantly via the corpus callosum. Localization of apparently different modes of thought is probably not as clear-cut as some people believe.

If the brain is sliced in half, separating the two cerebral hemispheres (Figure 5.3), additional important features can be seen. The gray matter of the cerebral cortex does not extend throughout the interior of the brain. Much of the interior is **white matter** consisting of large tracts or bundles of myelinated (sheathed) fibers that connect cell bodies in the cortex with those in the spinal cord and in other centers lower in the brain. These centers are additional pockets of gray matter, referred to as *nuclei*. The nuclei serve both as way stations, connecting tracts from the cortex with other ascending and descending tracts, and as integrating motor and sensory control centers. Four masses, collectively called the basal ganglia, are deep within each hemisphere. Also deep within the brain are cavities, called *ventricles*, which are continuous with the central canal of the spinal cord and are filled with cerebrospinal fluid.

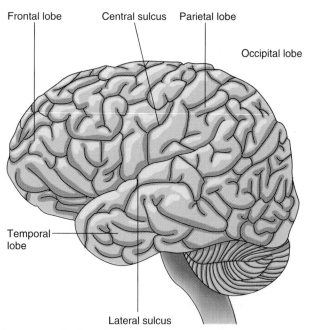

Frontal lobe   Central sulcus   Parietal lobe

Occipital lobe

Temporal lobe

Lateral sulcus

Figure 5.2   *Surface of the left cerebral hemisphere, indicating the lobes and the two principal fissures of the cortex.*

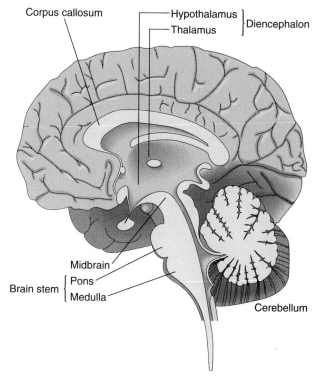

Corpus callosum

Hypothalamus
Thalamus   } Diencephalon

Midbrain
Brain stem { Pons
           Medulla

Cerebellum

Figure 5.3 *A cross section of the brain through the medial plane, showing the internal structures.*

Figure 5.3 shows four important functional areas or structures.

1. The **diencephalon**, connected in front with the hemispheres and behind with the midbrain, contains the *thalamus* and the **hypothalamus**, which consist of groups of nuclei. The thalamus is a relay station for all sensory pathways except the olfactory. The nuclei making up the thalamus receive nearly all impulses arriving from the different sensory areas of the body before passing them on to the cerebrum, where they are interpreted as conscious sensations. The hypothalamus is the highest center of integration for many visceral processes. Its nuclei regulate metabolism, temperature, water balance, sweating, blood pressure, sleeping, and appetite.
2. The **midbrain** is a mass of nerve-fiber tracts connecting the cerebral cortex with the pons, the medulla oblongata, the cerebellum, and the spinal cord.
3. The **brain stem** is made up of the **pons** and **medulla oblongata** and functions primarily as a neural relay station. The pons contains tracts that connect the cerebellum with the spinal cord and with motor areas of the cerebrum. The medulla oblongata serves as the main line of traffic for tracts ascending from the spinal cord and descending from the higher centers of the brain. At the bottom of the medulla, many of the motor fibers cross to the opposite side. The medulla also contains nuclei that maintain the regular life rhythms of the heartbeat, of the rising and falling diaphragm, and of constricting and dilating blood vessels. In the core of the brain stem is the reticular formation, sometimes called the reticular activating system because of the important role it plays in arousal and in the maintenance of alertness. The tracts of the pons and medulla send in fibers to connect with the profusely interconnected cells of the reticular formation, which in turn send fibers to the cortex, the basal ganglia, the hypothalamus, the septal area, and the cerebellum.
4. The **cerebellum**, like the cerebrum, is made up for the most part of two deeply convoluted hemispheres with an exterior cortex of gray matter and an interior of white tracts. The cerebellum receives sensory nerves from the vestibular apparatus of the ear and from muscles, tendons, and joints. The information received and integrated relates to balance and posture and equilibrium and to the smooth coordination of the body when in motion.

A fifth important part of the brain, not shown in Figure 5.3, is the **limbic system**, structures that are continuous with one another in the lower cerebrum and that developed earlier than did the mammalian cerebral cortex. The limbic system controls the visceral and physical expressions of emotion—quickened heartbeat and respiration, trembling, sweating, and alterations in facial expressions—and the expression of appetitive and other primary drives—hunger, thirst, mating, defense, attack, and flight. This system is made up of cortex that is phylogenetically older than the so-called neocortex, which covers most of the hemispheres.

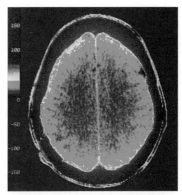
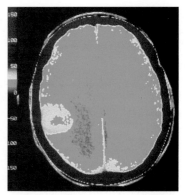

Figure 5.4   *These two CAT scans show a horizontal slice through the brain. The brain on the left is normal; that on the right has a tumor on its left side.*

Neurochemical Assessment

It might seem that assessing the amount of a particular neurotransmitter or the quantity of its receptors in the brain would be straightforward. But it is not. Only recently has PET scanning allowed an assessment of receptors in a living brain. Therefore, most of the research on neurochemical theories of psychopathology has relied on indirect assessments.

In postmortem studies the brains of deceased patients are removed, and the amount of specific neurotransmitters in particular brain areas can then be directly assayed. Different brain areas can be infused with substances that bind to receptors, and the amount of binding can then be quantified; more binding indicates more receptors.

Another common method of assessment is to analyze the metabolites of neurotransmitters that have been broken down by enzymes. A metabolite, typically an acid, is produced when a neurotransmitter is deactivated. For example, the major metabolite of dopamine is homovanillic acid and of serotonin, 5 hydroxyindoleacetic acid. The metabolites can be detected in urine, blood, and cerebrospinal fluid (the fluid in the spinal column and the brain's ventricles). A high level of a particular metabolite indicates a high level of a transmitter.

Neuropsychological Assessment

Long before the development of new technologies such as brain-imaging techniques, neurologists and neuropsychologists were working in different ways to learn how the central nervous system functions and how to detect and treat prob-

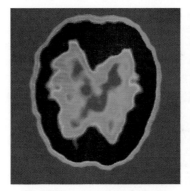
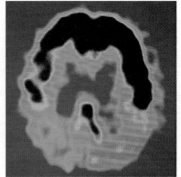

Figure 5.5   *The PET scan on the left shows a normal brain; the one on the right shows the brain of a patient with Alzheimer's disease.*

lems caused by disease or injury to the brain. A **neurologist** is a physician who specializes in medical diseases that affect the nervous system, such as muscular dystrophy or cerebral palsy. A **neuropsychologist** is a psychologist who studies how dysfunctions of the brain affect the way we think, feel, and behave.

We might reasonably assume that neurologists, with the help of such procedures as PET and NMR scans, can observe the brain and its functions directly and thus assess brain abnormalities. Many brain abnormalities and injuries, however, involve changes in structure or function so subtle or slight that they cannot be detected by direct physical examination.

Because the way in which the person functions is the problem—what he or she does, says, thinks, or feels—neuropsychologists have developed several tests that assess behavioral disturbances caused by brain dysfunctions. Research indicates that these **neuropsychological tests** have some validity in the assessment of brain damage. They are often used in conjunction with the brain-scanning techniques described in the previous section.

One such procedure is the Halstead–Reitan battery or group of tests (Reitan & Wolfson, 1985). The concept of using a battery of tests, each evaluating different functions, is critical, for only by studying a person's pattern of performance can an investigator adequately judge whether the person has suffered brain damage. But the Halstead–Reitan battery can do even more: it can sometimes help locate the area of the brain that has been affected. Three of the tests included in the Halstead–Reitan battery are:

1. **Tactile Performance Test—Time.** While blindfolded, the subject tries to fit variously shaped blocks into spaces of a form board, first using the preferred hand, then the other, and finally both. The purpose is to measure the person's motor-speed response to the unfamiliar.
2. **Tactile Performance Test—Memory.** After completing the timed test, the subject is asked to draw the form board from memory, showing the blocks in their proper location. Both this and the timed test are sensitive to damage in the right parietal lobe.
3. **Speech Sounds Perception Test.** Subjects listen to a series of nonsense words consisting of two consonants with a long *e* sound in the middle. They then select the "word" they heard from a set of alternatives. This test measures left-hemisphere function, especially temporal and parietal areas.

neurologist A physician who studies the nervous system, especially its structure, functions, and abnormalities.

neuropsychologist A psychologist concerned with the relationships among cognition, affect, and behavior on the one hand, and brain function on the other.

neuropsychological tests Psychological tests, such as the *Luria–Nebraska*, that can detect impairment in different parts of the brain.

Neuropsychological tests assess various performance deficits in the hope of detecting a specific area of neural malfunction. Shown here is the tactile performance test.

The Luria–Nebraska battery (Golden, Hammeke, & Purisch, 1978), based on the work of the Russian psychologist Aleksandr Luria (1902–77), is also in widespread use (R. L. Kane, Parsons, & Goldstein, 1985). This battery of 269 items is divided into 11 sections to determine basic and complex motor skills, rhythm and pitch abilities, tactile and kinesthetic skills, verbal and spatial skills, receptive speech ability, expressive speech ability, writing, reading, arithmetic skills, memory, and intellectual processes. The pattern of scores helps reveal damage to the frontal, temporal, sensorimotor, or parietal-occipital area of the right or left hemisphere.

Strengths and Weaknesses of Biological Assessment

Brain-imaging techniques represent a considerable advance in the possibilities for expanding knowledge. These tools provide startling pictures of internal organs and permit the gathering of information about living tissue, including the brain. Clinicians and researchers in many disciplines are currently using these techniques both to discover previously undetectable organic problems and to study the neural bases of thought, emotion, and behavior.

Indirect methods of neurochemical assessment have been useful, but they also have limitations. The main problem with postmortem studies is that most research subjects have been treated for years with various medications that may have caused whatever neurochemical abnormalities are observed. For example, the drugs commonly used to treat schizophrenic patients are known to increase the number of dopamine receptors. The primary limitation of metabolite studies is that amounts of neurotransmitter in the brain must be inferred from analysis of metabolites in the *periphery*. For example, serotonin is a neurotransmitter in the brain, but it is much more prevalent in the gut, where it regulates peristalsis. Therefore, analyzing serotonin metabolites in blood may not provide a good indication of serotonin levels in the brain. Because cerebrospinal fluid fills the ventricles of the brain, metabolites found in the fluid are more likely to reflect actual brain functions, but only if the fluid is from an area surrounding the ventricles.

Neuropsychological tests have proven quite useful. The Luria–Nebraska battery, for instance, can be scored in a highly reliable manner (Maruish, Sawicki, Franzen, & Golden, 1984) and is believed to show effects of brain damage that are not (yet) detectable by neurological examination (Moses, 1983). A particular advantage of the Luria–Nebraska tests is that it is possible to control for educational level, so that a less-educated person does not receive a lower score solely because of limited educational experience (Brickman, McManus, Grapentine, & Alessi, 1984). A children's version (Golden, 1981), for ages eight to twelve, has also been found useful in diagnosing brain damage and in evaluating educational strengths and weaknesses (Sweet, Carr, Rossini, & Kasper, 1986).

Interpretation of findings from neuropsychological tests or from brain scans is complicated. There is no one-to-one relationship between such findings and psychological dysfunctions. Assessment is especially difficult in the case of chronic brain damage present for years before the assessment is conducted. Functioning may be affected by how the patient has reacted to and coped with the losses brought about by the brain damage, how people in the patient's social environment have reacted and tried to help, and so forth. Similarly, neuropsychological assessors attempting to understand the consequences of any brain-injuring event need to take into account the abilities of the patient prior to that event (Boll, 1985). This straightforward truth brings to mind the story of the man who, recovering from an accident that broke all the fingers in both hands, earnestly asked the surgeon whether he would be able to play the piano when his wounds had healed. "Yes, I'm sure you will," said the surgeon. "That's wonderful," exclaimed the man, "because I don't even know how to play the piano *now*!"

To Recap

Biological assessments include computer-controlled brain-imaging techniques. CAT scans and NMR imaging yield pictures of brain tissue and can illuminate the locations of tumors, the extent of enlargement of ventricles, and so forth. PET scanning is a more functional approach. A substance used by the brain is labeled with a short-lived radioactive isotope and injected into the bloodstream. A window on brain functioning is provided by observing the pattern of metabolic rates of the substance.

Neurochemical assessment procedures include postmortem studies of the brains of dead patients, as well as the analysis of metabolites of neurotransmitters. These indirect methods are somewhat ambiguous. The deceased patients may have taken medications that created neurochemical abnormalities, and the level of metabolites in the periphery may not reflect the level of neurotransmitters in the brain.

Neuropsychological tests, such as the Halstead–Reitan battery, are often used along with brain-imaging techniques. They are useful for identifying the presence and location of brain damage based on the person's pattern of performance on tests sensitive to behavioral disturbances caused by brain dysfunction.

▶ *Cultural Diversity and Clinical Assessment*

Up to this point we have discussed diagnosis (Chapter 4) and various modes of clinical assessment (this chapter) as though the methods apply equally well to everyone. However, what if a clinician is trying to evaluate psychological problems in a member of a minority group? Is it in patients' best interests for assessment to take into consideration cultural factors that may distinguish them from the majority culture where they live? If, for instance, the clinician is assessing an Asian-American man who is emotionally withdrawn, should the clinician consider that lower levels of emotional expressiveness in men are positively sanctioned among Asian-Americans as compared with the culture that predominates in the United States at this time?

Official diagnostic criteria historically have made little mention of cultural considerations. An examination of eleven widely used diagnostic criteria sets and structured interviews for schizophrenia, affective disorders, and personality disorders revealed minimal mention of cultural variables (Lopez & Nunez, 1987). The DSM-III contained only one cultural reference in the criteria for these three sets of disorders (DSM-IV pays more attention to cultural diversity, as noted in Chapter 4). Overall, although eight of the eleven instruments studied did consider culture, they referred to it infrequently, revealing an insensitivity to cultural differences in psychopathology.

What are the consequences of considering, or not considering, culture in clinical assessment? We examine this issue with reference to specific minority groups in the following subsections.

Assessment of Latinos/Latinas

Cultural and linguistic biases have been found when clinicians use established tests and instruments with Latino/Latina clients (Malgady, Rogler, & Constantino, 1987). If the patient does not speak English, for example, emotional problems can be underestimated because of the way an interpreter translates between the English-speaking clinician and the Spanish-speaking patient (Sabin, 1975). Different cultural norms can also set the stage for misjudgments. The belief that evil spirits can possess a person is not, in the Puerto Rican culture, a sign of schizophrenia. Rather, it is consistent with the spiritualism prevalent in Puerto Rico, whereby people are believed to be surrounded by invisible spirits (Rogler &

Assessment must take into account the person's cultural background. Believing in possession by spirits is common in some cultures and thus should not always be taken to mean that the believer is psychotic.

Hollingshead, 1985). Other difficulties arise because Latinos/Latinas may disclose less about themselves than do Anglo patients to non-Latino/Latina clinicians (Levine & Padilla, 1980). Also, Latinos/Latinas who are not fluent in English may become even less so under stressful circumstances (Peck, 1974). Consider the difficulty you may have experienced traveling in a foreign country, phrase book in hand, simply trying to catch a bus. Now imagine how much more daunting it would be to have to respond in a second language to highly personal questions from a clinician. In addition, the very term *Latino/Latina* subsumes several differing cultures, including Mexican-American, Cuban, Puerto Rican, and Central American, and these differences are also likely to be overlooked.

Assessment of Native Americans

Although, as noted earlier in this chapter, the MMPI-2 was developed using samples more representative of the overall U.S. population than those used for the original MMPI, only seventy-seven Native Americans were included (Butcher et al., 1989). These people were all from a single tribe; thus differences among Native American tribes were overlooked. Furthermore, no validation studies have been conducted with Native Americans, even though the MMPI is the most frequently used psychological assessment technique with this group (Manson, Walker, & Kivlahan, 1987).

The situation is similarly problematic for virtually all other psychological tests. Most approaches to Native Americans and native Alaskans have been ethnocentric and unappreciative of their particular cultures and life circumstances (Dauphinais & King, 1992). Native American children may lack interest in the individualistic, competitive nature of an intelligence test because of the cooperative, group-oriented values instilled by their culture (O'Conner, 1989). Their performance on such a test may therefore underestimate their intellectual abilities. Furthermore, as with other minority groups that are overrepresented in the lower socioeconomic classes, Native Americans' intelligence test scores may reflect deprived conditions, and so interpretation of their scores should be informed by the conditions in which they have grown up. It should not be assumed that below-average test performance means that these children are unable to learn (National Commission on Testing and Public Policy, 1990).

Assessment of African-Americans

Research on clinical evaluation has illustrated several potential pitfalls in taking culture into account. These can be described with reference to African-Americans. A survey of a large sample of mental health practitioners in California found that clinicians sometimes minimized the seriousness of a patient's problems by attributing them to a subcultural norm (Lopez & Hernandez, 1986). To **minimize** means to underestimate the psychopathological significance of a behavior because it is seen as normal in the patient's subculture. By being mindful of cultural differences—and believing that what is abnormal in one culture may be normal in another—clinicians can err on the side of minimizing problems and hence reduce the chances of providing appropriate professional intervention.

minimize To underestimate the severity of a clinical problem by attributing the problem behavior to the patient's cultural background.

On the other hand, clinicians can also **overpathologize**, a different kind of diagnostic bias in which a normal behavior is misinterpreted as pathological because of a failure to take cultural differences into account. For example, based on the same case summary, some clinicians did not make a diagnosis of schizophrenia when the patient was described as white, but did make the diagnosis when the patient was described as African-American (Blake, 1973).

overpathologize To misinterpret a normal behavior as pathological by ignoring the patient's cultural background.

Including cultural factors in diagnosis and clinical assessment of minority patients is a challenge. If clinicians are sensitive to cultural differences, they might interpret a given unusual behavior as a reflection of a cultural difference and therefore not a sign of psychopathology—a minimizing bias. If they overlook or downplay the significance of cultural factors when diagnosing a minority client, they may be prone to overpathologizing minority patients, attributing subculturally normative behavior to mental disorders (Lopez, 1989). Only with more extensive research on cultural variation in the expression of psychopathology will we be able to strike an informed balance between these potential problems and provide optimal assessment and treatment for people of all backgrounds.

To Recap

Standard diagnostic criteria and methods traditionally have paid little attention to cultural factors that may be relevant when assessing members of ethnic minorities. Minority group members have also been underrepresented at times in the research leading to the development of standard assessment methods, so that it is impossible to know whether published norms are valid for them. Language differences and different subcultural norms for behaviors and experiences also complicate the evaluation of minorities. These complications can result in clinicians' minimizing problems (as when a symptom of a psychological disorder is written off as normative within the minority patient's subculture) or overpathologizing (as when a normal difference from the majority culture is misinterpreted as pathological).

Visual Summary for Chapter 5:

Clinical Assessment Procedures

Clinical assessment procedures may provide information useful for making a diagnosis, for identifying causes of a patient's problems, and for planning or evaluating treatment. Depending on the assessor's theoretical perspective, the nature of the problems, and the goals of the assessment process, one or more of the following main types of assessment may be conducted.

Types of Assessment

	Definition	Example	Comments
Unstructured Clinical Interview	Conversation in which assessor finds out about patient via language, including how the questions are answered.	Initial therapy session	Type of questions asked, and inferences drawn from the responses, highly variable and depend to some degree on theoretical perspective. Too unreliable for most research and diagnostic purposes, but indispensable means of finding out details about someone and establishing therapy relationship.
Structured Interview	Interview in which the sequence and wording of questions is fixed, not determined by clinician's choices or style.	Structured Clinical Interview (SCID)	Enhances diagnostic reliability by ensuring consistency of the procedure for gathering information. Insufficient for comprehensive assessment because some hypothesized causes of disorders are not accessible to verbal report.
Intelligence Test	Standard tasks used to sample current mental ability.	WAIS-R, Stanford–Binet	Contributes to diagnosis of mental retardation, monitoring of neuropsychological problems, prediction of school performance. Highly reliable. As long as results are not overinterpreted as reflection of all competencies, tests serve their purpose well.
Projective Personality Tests	Presentation of ambiguous stimuli allowing for range of interpretations, which should reveal unconscious processes.	Rorschach Inkblot Test, TAT	Can be difficult to score reliably, though recent systems have improved. Validity constrained by lack of information on how to interpret some nonstandard aspects (such as number of responses on Rorschach). Can help in identifying problems or conflicts patient is unable or unwilling to report directly.
Personality Inventories	Questionnaires calling for the respondents to indicate to what degree various characteristics apply to themselves.	MMPI	In most circumstances, straightforwardness and ease of interpretation are helpful. Transparency is a problem when defensiveness or even lying is to be expected. May underestimate situational influences on behavior.

	Definition	Example	Comments
Direct Observation of Behavior	Therapist, peer, teacher, or even the patient watches and rates the patient's actions in everyday environment or in a staged role play.	Self-monitoring the nature and frequency of exercise behavior	Useful for planning and evaluating treatment. Third party may be able to see patterns in behavior (for example, only if I pout do you pay atttention) that elude the participants. Often reactive (being observed changes the person's behavior).
Brain Imaging	Computer-based devices for seeing into the living brain to evaluate structure or functioning.	PET scan	Uniquely useful for discovering organic problems and identifying the neural bases of thought, emotion, and behavior. Interpretation of functional significance of results may be complicated by the history of the patient's efforts to cope with problems.
Neurochemical Assessments	Methods of evaluating the amount of a neurotransmitter or the number of its receptors.	Postmortem brain assays	Complicated by medication history as a possible explanation of the findings.
Neuropsychological Tests	Tasks used to evaluate behavioral disturbances caused by brain dysfunction.	Halstead–Reitan battery	Can help in identifying presence and location of slight brain damage that could elude direct physical examination. Emphasis on behavioral, functional impact complements results of neurological assessment.

Cultural Diversity and Clinical Assessment

Assessment of people from subcultures, races, or countries other than the assessor's may be complicated by misunderstanding of cultural norms. Little research has examined specifically whether findings from the main clinical assessment procedures have the same meaning in all subcultures. Potential pitfalls in interpretation include:

• Minimizing the psychopathological implications of a behavior because the clinician mistakenly considers it a normal manifestation of the patient's cultural background.

• Overpathologizing what is actually a normal behavior given the patient's background because the clinician misapplies majority culture standards in evaluating the behavior.

Chapter 6

Anxiety Disorders

The Case of Karen Rusa

Karen Rusa was a thirty-year-old married woman and the mother of four children. Although she had been having anxiety-related problems for a number of years, she had never sought professional help. In the past several months, she had been experiencing intrusive, repetitive thoughts about her children's safety. She frequently found herself imagining that a serious accident had occurred, and she could not put the thought out of her mind. One day she imagined that her son Alan had broken his leg playing football at school. There was no reason to believe that there had been an accident, but Karen brooded about it until she finally called the schoo to see if Alan was all right. Even after receiving their reassurance that he had not been hurt, she described herself as being surprised when he later arrived home unharmed.

Karen's daily routine included performing an extensive series of counting rituals. Specific numbers had come to have a special meaning for her. For example, when she was grocery shopping, numbers affected Karen's selection of an item, such as a box of cereal. Karen believed that if she took the first one on the shelf, something terrible would happen to her oldest child; if she selected the second item, some unknown disaster would befall her second child; and so on.

When she was occasionally in too great a hurry to observe the rituals, Karen experienced considerable anxiety. She described herself as tense, jumpy, and unable to relax during these periods. Her fears were usually confirmed, because something unfortunate invariably happened to one of the children within a few days after each such "failure." The fact that minor accidents are likely to occur at a fairly high rate in any family of four children did not change Karen's belief that her failure to follow the numerical rules caused the accident.

In addition to these obsessive ideas and compulsive behaviors, Karen reported dissatisfaction with her marriage and problems in managing her children. Her husband, Tony, had been placed on a complete physical disability about a year earlier. Although he was only thirty-two years old, he suffered from a very serious heart condition that made physical exertion potentially dangerous. Since leaving his job as a clerk at a plumbing supply store, he had spent most of his time at home watching television, and he performed few household chores or family errands. The inequity of this situation was apparent to Karen, and extremely frustrating, yet she found herself unable to handle it effectively.

The children were also clearly out of her control. Robert, age six, and Alan, age eight, were very active and mischievous. Neither responded well to parental discipline, which was inconsistent at best. Both had been noted to be behavioral problems at school. On one occasion, Karen had been called to take Alan home early after he kicked the school principal and told him to "go to hell." The girls were also difficult to handle. Denise, age nine, and Jennifer, age eleven, spent much of their time at home arguing with each other. During the past several weeks, Karen had been spending more and more time crying and hiding alone in her bedroom.

anxiety An unpleasant feeling of fear and apprehension accompanied by increased physiological arousal and avoidance behavior.

*A*nxiety, that unpleasant feeling of fear and apprehension, is one aspect of abnormal psychology familiar to most of us. Anxiety can occur in many psychopathologies and is a principal element of the disorders considered in this chapter. Yet anxiety plays an important role in the psychology of normal people as well, for very few of us go through even a week of our lives without experiencing some anxiety or fear. Indeed it would be abnormal never to feel fear. If you were swimming in the ocean and saw a shark nearby, fear would be a healthy, motivating response. But the anxiety experienced by mentally healthy people is usually brief and in response to objectively dangerous situations. Anxiety disorders, like Karen's concern about her children's safety and her superstitious counting rituals, involve excessive, lasting anxiety about matters that do not warrant such a high level of concern.

Anxiety disorders are classified in DSM-IV in six principal categories: phobias, panic disorder, generalized anxiety disorder, obsessive-compulsive disorder, posttraumatic stress disorder, and acute stress disorder. We turn now to an examination of the defining characteristics of each of the anxiety disorders, followed by theories of their causes and treatment.

anxiety disorders Disorders in which fear or tension is overriding and the primary disturbance: *phobias, panic disorder, generalized anxiety disorder, obsessive-compulsive disorder, post-traumatic stress disorder,* and *acute stress disorder.*

Phobias

A **phobia** is a disrupting, fear-based pattern of avoidance, out of proportion to the danger posed by a particular object or situation and, indeed, recognized by the sufferer as groundless. For example, some people are extremely afraid of heights, even in cases of minimal danger, such as being on the tenth floor of a building. These people will go out of their way to avoid heights, even if it means that they cannot visit a good friend who lives in a high-rise apartment. People with phobias realize that their fear is excessive and unrealistic. Yet they feel that they cannot cope with it and must instead avoid its source.

phobia An *anxiety disorder* in which there is intense fear and avoidance of specific objects and situations, recognized as irrational by the individual.

The term *phobia* is derived from the name of the Greek god Phobos, who frightened his enemies. Today we name these unwarranted fears and avoidance patterns by placing the Greek word for the feared object or situation in front of the suffix *-phobia*. Some of the more familiar phobias are *claustrophobia*, fear of closed spaces; *agoraphobia*, fear of public places; and *acrophobia*, fear of heights. More exotic fears have also been given Greek-derived names, for example, *ergasiophobia*, fear of writing; *taphephobia*, fear of being buried alive, and even *Anglophobia*, fear of England.

Some specific fears do not cause enough hardship to compel an individual to seek treatment, however. For example, a person with an intense fear of snakes who lives in a metropolitan area will probably have little direct contact with

Fear and avoidance of heights is classified as a specific phobia. Other specific phobias include fears of animals, injections, and enclosed spaces.

snakes and may therefore not believe that anything is seriously wrong. The term *phobia* usually implies extreme discomfort or some kind of social or occupational impairment as a result of the anxiety. Phobias are divided into three main groups: specific phobias, agoraphobia, and social phobia.

Specific Phobias

specific phobias An unwarranted fear and avoidance of a specific object or circumstance, for example, fear of nonpoisonous snakes or fear of heights.

Specific phobias are unwarranted fears caused by the presence or anticipation of a specific object or situation. The most common sources of these phobias are animals (e.g., dogs, snakes, insects), heights, closed spaces, air travel, and blood and injections. Specific phobias are common. Lifetime prevalence is estimated at 16% for women and 7% for men (Kessler et al., 1994). The majority of these phobias begin in early childhood (Marks & Gelder, 1966). Specific phobias may not be a homogeneous category, however. The age of onset appears to differ across four major groupings of phobias: animal phobias develop earliest, around age seven; blood phobias develop around age nine; dental phobias tend to begin around age twelve; and claustrophobia, around age twenty (Ost, 1987).

Agoraphobia

agoraphobia A cluster of fears centering on being in open spaces and leaving the home.

A complicated syndrome, **agoraphobia** (from the Greek *agora*, "place of assembly," "marketplace") is a cluster of fears centering on public places and being unable to escape or find help should one suddenly become incapacitated. Fears of shopping, encountering crowds, and traveling are often a part of agoraphobia. One study found that 93% of a sample of agoraphobics also reported fears of heights and enclosed spaces such as subways and elevators (Buglass, Clarke, Henderson, Kreitman, & Presley, 1977). Nevertheless, many agoraphobics have good days when they can move about with relative ease. Being with a trusted companion can also help them leave the house.

Examination of the psychophysiological responses of agoraphobics confirms the clinical impression that unlike people with specific phobias, they are subject to a rather diffuse, nonspecific anxiety. Readings of the autonomic activity of agoraphobics usually show high levels of arousal, even when they are supposedly relaxing (Marks, 1969).

For reasons that are not yet fully understood, agoraphobia is more commonly diagnosed in women. The majority of sufferers develop their problems in adolescence and early adulthood. Agoraphobia is an especially distressing condition. Consider how limiting it must be to be afraid of leaving the house. Perhaps for this reason agoraphobia is the most common phobia seen by therapists, constituting roughly 60% of all phobias examined. In DSM-IV, agoraphobia can be diagnosed as occurring with or without a history of panic disorder (discussed later). In some people it develops as a consequence of panic attacks.

Animals are among the most commonly feared objects by people with specific phobias.

Social Phobia

social phobia Persistent, irrational fear of situations in which one is exposed to scrutiny by others or interaction with unfamiliar people.

A **social phobia** is a persistent, irrational fear of situations in which one is exposed to scrutiny by other people or interaction with unfamiliar people. While many of us may experience some anxiety when giving a speech or meeting new people, social phobics often fear a broad class of situations, including speaking or performing in public, eating in public, writing in front of others (even signing a check to pay for something in a store), or using public restrooms. Virtually any activity that might be carried out in the presence of others can elicit extreme anxiety. A common theme is fear that one will act in an embarrassing manner or will display symptoms of anxiety that will be noticed by others. The DSM-IV notes that in some cultures, such as Japan and Korea, the concern may be one of inadvertently giving offense to others.

Social phobia can be an extremely debilitating condition. Living arrangements, career choices, hobbies, and of course social life can all be restricted if a person is unduly concerned about, and therefore avoids whenever feasible, the possibility of being embarrassed. Social phobias are common, with a lifetime prevalence of 11% for men and 16% for women (Kessler et al., 1994). Onset is generally during adolescence, when social awareness and interaction with others assume increasing importance in a person's life.

In making the DSM-IV diagnosis of social phobia, clinicians indicate not only whether the criteria are met, but also if the condition is generalized. Generalized social phobia involves fear of most social situations and is difficult to distinguish from avoidant personality disorder (see Chapter 11), a pervasive, typically lifelong pattern of social inhibition and hypersensitivity. Other social phobics do not show such a generalized impairment, fearing a more limited set of situations, for example, public speaking.

People with agoraphobia fear leaving a safe place such as the home and entering public places from which escape might be difficult. Often they have experienced panic attacks in the past.

Panic Disorder

In **panic disorder** the person experiences recurrent, sudden, and often inexplicable attacks of a host of jarring symptoms—difficulty breathing, heart palpitations, chest pain, feelings of choking and smothering; dizziness, nausea, sweating, and trembling; and intense apprehension, terror, and feelings of impending doom. **Depersonalization**, a feeling of being outside the body; **derealization**, a feeling that the world is not real; and fears of losing control, going crazy, even dying may overwhelm the patient. Panic attacks occur frequently, perhaps once weekly or more often. They usually last minutes, rarely hours, and they are sometimes linked to specific situations, such as driving a car. When associated with situational triggers, they are referred to as cued panic attacks. They

panic disorder An *anxiety disorder* in which the individual has sudden and inexplicable attacks of jarring symptoms, such as difficulty breathing, heart palpitations, dizziness, trembling, terror, and feelings of impending doom. In DSM-IV, said to occur with or without *agoraphobia*.

depersonalization An alteration in perception of the self in which the individual loses a sense of reality and feels estranged from the self and perhaps separated from the body.

derealization Loss of the sense that the surroundings are real.

Public speaking is unsettling for many people, but especially distressing for those with social phobia, an intense fear of situations in which one is exposed to the scrutiny of others.

can also occur in what seem to be benign situations, such as relaxation, in sleep, and in unexpected situations. In these cases they are referred to as uncued attacks. Recurrent uncued attacks are required for the diagnosis of panic disorder. Having only cued attacks more likely reflects the presence of a phobia.

The lifetime prevalence of panic disorder is about 2% for men and 5% for women (Kessler et al., 1994). It typically begins in early adulthood, and its onset is associated with stressful life experiences (Pollard, Pollard, & Corn, 1989).

In DSM-IV, panic disorder is diagnosed as either with or without agoraphobia, but most frequently panic disorder is accompanied by agoraphobia. Patients with panic disorder typically avoid the situations in which a panic attack could be dangerous or embarrassing. If the avoidance becomes widespread, panic with agoraphobia is the result.

Generalized Anxiety Disorder

The patient, a twenty-four-year-old mechanic, had been referred for psychotherapy by his physician, whom he had consulted because of dizziness and difficulties in falling asleep. He was visibly distressed during the entire initial session, gulping before he spoke, sweating, and continually fidgeting in his chair. Although he first described his physical concerns, a more general picture of pervasive anxiety soon emerged. He reported that he nearly always felt tense. He seemed to worry about anything and everything. He reported a long history of difficulties in interpersonal relationships, which had led to his being fired from several jobs. As he put it, "I really like people and try to get along with them, but it seems like I fly off the handle too easily. Little things they do upset me too much. I just can't cope unless everything is going exactly right."

generalized anxiety disorder (GAD) One of the *anxiety disorders*, where worry is chronic, uncontrollable, and excessive. The individual is jittery and strained, distractible, and apprehensive that something bad is about to happen. A pounding heart, fast pulse and breathing, sweating, flushing, muscle aches, a lump in the throat, and an upset gastrointestinal tract are some of the bodily indications of this disorder.

The individual with **generalized anxiety disorder (GAD)** is persistently anxious. Chronic, uncontrollable, excessive worry about all manner of things is the hallmark of GAD. So pervasive is this distress that it is sometimes referred to as freefloating anxiety. Physical complaints—sweating, flushing, pounding heart, upset stomach, diarrhea, frequent urination, cold, clammy hands, dry mouth, a lump in the throat, shortness of breath—are frequent and reflect hyperactivity of the autonomic nervous system. The patient is easily startled, fidgety, restless, and sighs often. As for the state of mind, the person is generally apprehensive, often imagining and worrying about impending setbacks, such as losing control, having health problems, or experiencing financial difficulty. Impatience, irritability, angry outbursts, insomnia, and distractibility are also common, for the person is always on edge.

The lifetime prevalence of GAD is estimated at 4% for men and 7% for women (Kessler et al., 1994). Stressful life events appear to play some role in its onset (Blazer, Hughes, & George, 1987). Most (90%) people with GAD also meet criteria for at least one other lifetime diagnosis, commonly major depression or another anxiety disorder (Wittchen, Zhao, Kessler, & Eaton, 1994). Characteristics associated with increased likelihood of GAD include being at least twenty-five years old, being unemployed, being previously married (separated, widowed, or divorced), and living in the northeast region of the United States (Wittchen et al., 1994). About one-half of people with GAD have sought professional care for their condition; if no other disorder is present, this treatment is more likely to come from a general medical facility than from a mental health specialty clinic. Many anxious patients see nonpsychiatric physicians to obtain antianxiety medication (Wittchen et al., 1994).

Obsessive-Compulsive Disorder

Obsessive-compulsive disorder (OCD) is an anxiety disorder in which the mind is flooded with persistent and uncontrollable thoughts (obsessions) or the individual is compelled to repeat certain acts again and again (compulsions), causing significant distress and interference with everyday functioning.

Obsessions are intrusive and recurring thoughts, impulses, and images that arise unintentionally and uncontrollably. Karen's fears for her children's safety were obsessional. Whereas many of us may have similar fleeting experiences, such as wondering whether we turned off the lights, the obsessive individual has them with such force and frequency that they interfere with normal functioning. Obsessions may also take the form of extreme doubting, procrastination, and indecision. The patient may be unable to come to a conclusion and stop considering an issue (Salzman & Thaler, 1981). A very common obsession is the persistent thought that a completed task was not actually completed. For example, one twenty-eight-year-old student began obsessively asking himself, "Did I lock the door? Am I sure?" each time he left his room despite clearly remembering having done so (Akhter, Wig, Varma, Pershad, & Varma, 1975, p. 343). Less common are obsessive impulses, urges to perform certain actions, ranging from rather trivial whims to grave and assaultive acts. For example, a lawyer was obsessed by the desire to drink from his ink pot, an act he knew would be absurd. This lawyer also had the serious urge to strangle his only son, although apparently he loved him (Akhter et al., 1975).

While an obsession is a thought that creates anxiety, a **compulsion** is a repetitive behavior or mental act that one feels driven to perform in order to reduce distress or prevent some disaster from occurring. Karen's counting rituals are examples. The compulsion is not realistically connected with its apparent purpose and is clearly excessive. Often an individual who continually repeats some action fears dire consequences if the act is not performed. The sheer frequency with which an act is repeated may be staggering. Extreme cleanliness and orderliness are frequently reported compulsions and are often achieved only by elaborate ceremonies that take hours and even most of the day. Some people wash their hands dozens of times each day. Others rely on repetitive "magical" protective practices, such as counting, saying particular numbers, or touching a talisman or

obsessive-compulsive disorder (OCD) An *anxiety disorder* in which the mind is flooded with persistent and uncontrollable thoughts or the individual is compelled to repeat certain acts again and again, causing significant distress and interference with everyday functioning.

obsession Intrusive and recurring thought that seems irrational and uncontrollable to the person experiencing it.

compulsion The irresistible impulse to repeat an irrational behavior or mental act over and over again.

Howard Hughes, the famous industrialist, suffered from an obsessive fear of contamination. Here, on a trip to London, Hughes had the windows of his Rolls-Royce lined with newspaper to protect himself from unclean air.

a particular part of the body to allay their fear. Still other kinds of compulsions focus on checking, with the compulsive going back seven or eight times to make certain that lights, gas jets, or faucets are turned off, windows are fastened, doors are locked. Sometimes compulsions take the form of performing an act, such as eating, extremely slowly.

A frequent consequence of obsessive-compulsive disorder is damage to the individual's relations with other people, especially with members of the family. People saddled with the irresistible need to wash their hands every ten minutes or count every tile in a bathroom floor are likely to cause concern and even resentment in spouses, children, friends, or coworkers. These feelings in turn are likely to have additional consequences for the obsessive-compulsive person, engendering feelings of depression and generalized anxiety and setting the stage for even further deterioration of personal relationships. Thus, as with Karen Rusa, patients with OCD often have other problems, such as depression. The co-occurrence of multiple psychological disorders is explored in Focus Box 6.1.

OCD affects between 1% and 3% of the population (Myers et al., 1984). It usually begins in early adulthood, often following some stressful event, such as pregnancy, childbirth, family conflict, or difficulties at work (Kringlen, 1970). Early onset is more common among men and is associated with checking compulsions; later onset is more frequent among women and is linked with cleaning compulsions (Noshirvani, Kasvikis, Marks, Tsakiris, & Monteiro, 1991).

▶ *Posttraumatic Stress Disorder*

posttraumatic stress disorder (PTSD) An *anxiety disorder* in which a particularly stressful event, such as military combat, rape, or a natural disaster, brings in its aftermath intrusive reexperiencings of the trauma, a numbing of responsiveness to the outside world, estrangement from others, a tendency to be easily startled, and nightmares, recurrent dreams, and otherwise disturbed sleep.

A twenty-seven-year-old singer was referred by a friend for evaluation. Eight months before, her boyfriend had been stabbed to death during a mugging from which she escaped unharmed. After a period of mourning she appeared to return to her usual self. She helped the police in their investigation and was generally considered an ideal witness.

Nevertheless, shortly after the arrest of a man accused of the murder, the patient began to have recurrent nightmares and vivid memories of the night of the crime. In the dreams she frequently saw blood and imagined herself being pursued by ominous, cloaked figures. During the day, especially when walking somewhere alone, she often drifted off in daydreams, so that she forgot where she was going. Her friends noted that she began to startle easily and seemed to be preoccupied. She left her change or groceries at the store, or when waited on could not remember what she had come to buy. She began to sleep restlessly, and her work suffered because of poor concentration. She gradually withdrew from her friends and began to avoid work. She felt considerable guilt about her boyfriend's murder, although exactly why was not clear. (Spitzer, Skodol, Gibbon, & Williams, 1981, p. 17)

Posttraumatic stress disorder (PTSD), introduced as a diagnosis in DSM-III, reflects an extreme response to a severely stressful event. Increased anxiety, reexperiencing the trauma, avoidance of stimuli associated with the trauma, and a numbing of emotional responses are symptoms common to PTSD. Although there had been prior awareness that the stresses of combat could produce powerful and adverse effects on soldiers, the aftermath of the Vietnam War (see Focus Box 6.2) spurred the acceptance of the new diagnosis. Like other disorders in the DSM, PTSD is defined by a cluster of symptoms. Unlike the definitions of other psychological disorders, though, the definition of PTSD also includes its presumed cause, namely, a traumatic event directly experienced or witnessed by the person that involved actual or threatened death, serious injury, or a threat to physical integrity. PTSD differs from **acute stress disorder**, a new diagnosis in DSM-IV. Nearly everyone who encounters a trauma experiences stress, some-

acute stress disorder An *anxiety disorder* in which a traumatic event leads to symptoms similar to those exhibited by patients with *posttraumatic stress disorder* except that by definition acute stress disorder symptoms last less than a month after the occurrence of the trauma.

Comorbidity in the Anxiety Disorders

Patients with anxiety disorders often have symptoms of other mental disorders as well. This co-occurrence, called **comorbidity**, refers to the situation in which someone meeting diagnostic criteria for one disorder also meets criteria for another disorder. Some degree of comorbidity is inevitable unless one disorder actually protects you from others. For example, if 1% of the population had OCD and 5% had major depression, then by chance alone you would expect 1% of 5% (i.e., .0005, or 5 people in 10,000) of the population to have both OCD and major depression.

Of greater theoretical and clinical interest are pairs of disorders that co-occur more often than would be expected by chance. Descriptive research indicates that this is true of many anxiety disorders. Anxiety disorders frequently co-occur with depression. For example, co-occurrence of panic disorder and major depression is common (Breier, Charney, & Heninger, 1986), as is comorbidity between panic and generalized anxiety disorder (Sanderson, DiNardo, Rapee, & Barlow, 1990), alcoholism, and personality disorders (Johnson, Weiss-

man, & Klerman, 1990). Comorbidity is associated with poor outcomes in the treatment of panic disorder (Noyes et al., 1990).

Obsessive-compulsive disorder also shows substantial comorbidity with depression (Rachman & Hodgson, 1980). This overlap is illustrated by the case of Karen, which was presented in the beginning of this chapter and will be revisited after we consider the main theories of treatment of anxiety disorders. OCD shows comorbidity with other anxiety disorders as well, particularly panic and phobias (Austin, Lydiard, Forey, & Zealberg, 1990), and with various personality disorders (Baer et al., 1990; Mavissakalian, Hammen, & Jones, 1990).

There are many possible explanations of comorbidity (Klein & Riso, 1993), such as overlap in the symptoms included in each diagnostic category or the possibility that the same causal factor (e.g., being abused as a child) may contribute to both disorders. Also, depression, which is frequently associated with anxiety disorders, may sometimes be secondary, or caused by the anxiety problem. For example, to be housebound because of agoraphobia is likely to be a depressing state of affairs. The development of theories that address comorbidity is an important challenge for the future.

comorbidity   The co-occurrence of two disorders, as when a person is both depressed and alcoholic.

---

times to a considerable degree. This is normal. But people recover from acute stress disorder after a few days or weeks and go on to lead lives that are not marked by PTSD.

The symptoms for PTSD are grouped into three major categories. The diagnosis requires that symptoms in each category last longer than one month.

1. **Reexperiencing the traumatic event.** The event is frequently recalled, and nightmares about it are common. Intense distress is produced by stimuli that symbolize the event (e.g., thunder may remind a veteran of the battlefield) or by the anniversary of some specific experience. The importance of reexperiencing cannot be underestimated, for it is the likely source of the other categories of symptoms.
2. **Avoidance of stimuli associated with the event or numbing of responsiveness.** The person tries to avoid thinking about the trauma or encountering stimuli that bring it to mind. There may actually be amnesia for the event. Numbing refers to decreased interest in others, a sense of estrangement, and an inability to feel positive. Notice that the symptoms here seem almost contradictory to those in category 1. In PTSD there is fluctuation: the person goes back and forth between reexperiencing and numbing.
3. **Symptoms of increased arousal.** Included here are difficulty falling or staying asleep, difficulty concentrating, hypervigilance (being inordinately on the lookout for danger), and an exaggerated startle response. Laboratory studies have confirmed these clinical symptoms by documenting the heightened physiological reactivity of PTSD patients to combat imagery (e.g., Pitman et al., 1990).

Visiting the Vietnam War Memorial is an emotional experience for veterans.

![focus box banner] FOCUS BOX 6.2

Posttraumatic Stress Disorder and the Vietnam War

During war, military personnel must contend with devastating stress, and some of them break down. In World War I the term used was *shell shock*, reflecting the somatogenic belief that the soldier's brain suffered chronic concussions through the sudden and severe atmospheric pressure changes from nearby explosions. In World War II and the Korean War the great weariness of soldiers, their sleeplessness, tendency to startle at the slightest sounds, inability to speak, terror, and either stupor or agitated excitement were called exhaustion and then combat fatigue (Figley, 1978a), putting the blame clearly on the stressful circumstances of battle.

The Vietnam War was believed at first to have caused far fewer psychological casualties than did World War I or II—1.5% in Vietnam versus 10% in World War II—perhaps because battle duty was more intermittent and limited in time (Figley, 1978b). After veterans had been home for a few months or years, however, signs of great distress began to appear. In 1984, Congress commissioned The National Vietnam Veterans Readjustment Study (NVVRS), the first comprehensive investigation designed to determine the social and psychological consequences of a country's involvement in a war. The NVVRS found a much higher percentage of PTSD sufferers than originally thought—15.2% of the 3.14 million men who served in Vietnam have PTSD today (Keane, Gerardi, Quinn, & Litz, 1992). Rates are higher among African-Americans and Latinos than among whites, a finding attributable to the fact that these minorities saw more combat. Women also served in Vietnam, albeit not in direct combat situations; for them the rate of PTSD is close to 9%. All of these rates are much higher than for comparable groups of American adults who did not serve in Vietnam.

The listing of PTSD in DSM-III in 1980 eventually made it easier for Vietnam veterans to obtain help within the Veterans Administration system. They were acknowledged to have a recognized mental disorder. Their treatment centered on the combat stress itself and not on any emotional weakness presumed to have existed prior to the war.

Several factors contributed to the higher incidence of PTSD among Vietnam veterans than among veterans of other wars in recent history. The war in Vietnam was extremely unpopular and controversial, and it was a war that the United States did not win despite the infusion of billions of dollars, fatalities exceeding fifty-eight thousand, and many more seriously wounded and permanently maimed. Military personnel, after their one-year tour of duty, returned home alone and quickly, by jet. There were no battalions of soldiers arriving stateside together at war's end, no parades, no homecomings, indeed, none of the grateful celebration that all of us have seen in newsreels showing the end of World War II and, more recently, the Persian Gulf War. To make matters worse, the soldiers were subjected to criticism and sometimes abuse from those who regarded them as murderers for their participation in what many in the United States had gradually come to regard as an immoral war.

Existential philosophy teaches us that people must find meaning and purpose in their lives. Sheer survival is important, but men and women suffer distress and depression if they cannot develop some sense of self-worth in what they do. It is terrible enough for soldiers to see a friend torn up by shrapnel or to plunge a bayonet into the throat of a person designated as the enemy. How much worse are these experiences if soldiers know that back home people are protesting the morality of their being in the war in the first place?

A social worker with extensive experience treating Vietnam veterans provides a chilling and poignant ac-

Troops returning home from the Persian Gulf War were welcomed with parades instead of the hostility that greeted Vietnam veterans. The unpopularity of the Vietnam War may well have contributed to the high frequency of PTSD among its veterans.

count of how the particular nature of the war affected one soldier years afterward.

> Because of the guerrilla nature of the Vietnam war, the "enemy" could be anyone, including women and children. Thus, some stress responses are activated by closeness to women and the responsibility of marriage, a wife's pregnancy and the birth of a child. Veterans who have fought and killed women and children during combat often find it impossible to make a smooth transition to the roles of husband, protector and father. One veteran had warned his close friend, the squad medic, not to go near a crying baby lying in a village road until they had checked the area. In his haste to help the child, the medic raced forward and "was blown to bits" along with the child, who had been booby-trapped. The veteran came into treatment three years later, after a period of good adjustment, because he was made fearful and anxious by his eight-month-old daughter's crying. He had been unable to pick her up or hold her since her birth despite his conscious wish to "be a good father." (Haley, 1978, p. 263)

Why were there delays, sometimes years, before some of the combat-related PTSD symptoms began to show up in many returning Vietnam veterans? This may have happened because some of the stressors eliciting the symptoms did not occur until *after* the return home. The combat stressors themselves may have sensitized soldiers to react with great stress to the often hostile reception that awaited them after discharge. This lack of welcome (at best) may have robbed them of the healing effects that a warm and appreciative populace and family provided veterans who returned from more popular, or at least more widely accepted, wars.

When a person who has come through a traumatic event is in some way held responsible for what has happened—such as the rape victim who "brought it on herself" or the Vietnam veteran who is viewed as having promoted war—secondary stress, compounding that originally confronted, is the result (Foy, Resnick, Sipprelle, & Carroll, 1987).

This perspective implies that PTSD is virtually inevitable, with some people spared its worst effects because of social support and acceptance once the actual crisis is past. Rather than focusing on why some people develop PTSD after a stressor, we might consider why some do not. When we discuss the aftermath of rape

(Chapter 13), we will see that rape crisis intervention is actually based on this posttrauma perspective. Professional opinion holds that it is normal for a sexually abused individual to be traumatized and that therefore it is important to have in place readily available support systems to prevent the stressor from causing the development of PTSD. This view is also evidenced when crisis intervention professionals go to scenes of horror or destruction, for example, an unprovoked shooting spree at a school or other public place, immediately after the event and before any one individual seeks out mental health assistance.

The Veterans Administration, which had served veterans of World War II as well as those of the Korean War, was not prepared at first to address the psychological plight of Vietnam veterans. In 1971, the psychiatrist Robert Jay Lifton was approached by antiwar veterans from the New York–New Haven area to work with them in forming "rap groups." Initiated by the veterans themselves, these groups had a twofold purpose: a therapeutic one of healing themselves and a political one of forcing the American public to begin to understand the human costs of the war (Lifton, 1976). The rap groups spread outward from New York City until, in 1979, Congress approved a $25 million package establishing Operation Outreach, a network of ninety-one storefront counseling centers for psychologically distressed Vietnam veterans.

The rap groups focused on the residual guilt and rage felt by the veterans—guilt over what their status as soldiers had called on them to do in fighting a guerrilla war in which enemy and ally were often indistinguishable from one another; and rage at being placed in the predicament of risking their lives for a cause to which their country was not fully committed. Discussion extended as well to present-life concerns, such as relationships with women and feelings about masculinity, in particular, the macho view of physical violence. Although there is little in the way of actual research on these approaches, at least two factors have probably helped veterans in such programs. For perhaps the first time they could partake of the company of returned comrades in arms and feel the mutual support of others who had shared their war experiences. They were also able finally to begin confronting, in often emotional discussions, the combat events whose traumatic effects had been suppressed.

A major earthquake, such as the devastating one that struck Kobe, Japan, January 17, 1995, can result in symptoms of Posttraumatic Stress Disorder among some survivors.

Witnessing the death of others, as happened to these people who saw the Challenger *disaster, is among the types of stress related to posttraumatic stress disorder.*

Other problems often associated with PTSD are anxiety, depression, anger, guilt, substance abuse (self-medication to ease the distress), marital problems, and occupational impairment (Keane, Gerardi, Quinn, & Litz, 1992). Suicidal thoughts and plans are also common, as are incidents of explosive violence and stress-related psychophysiological problems, such as low back pain, headaches, and gastrointestinal disorders (Hobfoll et al., 1991).

The DSM alerts us to the fact that children can suffer from PTSD but may show it differently from adults. Children with PTSD may have trouble sleeping or may have nightmares. Often behavioral changes occur. For example, a previously outgoing youngster may become quiet and withdrawn, or a previously quiet youngster may become loud and aggressive. Some traumatized children begin to think that they will not become adults. In addition, some children may lose already acquired developmental skills, such as speech or toilet habits.

PTSD has a prevalence rate of about 1% in the general U.S. population (Helzer, Robins, & McEvoy, 1987). This figure represents about 2.4 million people. The rate rises to 3.5% among civilians who have been exposed to a physical attack and to 20% among those wounded in Vietnam. An even higher percentage of PTSD was found in a longitudinal study of rape victims (Rothbaum, Foa, Riggs, Murdock, & Walsh, 1992). The women were assessed weekly following the rape. At the twelfth week the rate of PTSD was 47%.

The character and duration of what some call rape trauma syndrome (Burgess & Holstrom, 1974) depend a great deal on the nature of the victim's life both prior to and following the attack. Such variables as marital status, partner's reactions, social support, prior psychological health, experiences testifying in court, and crisis intervention or longer term therapy can all worsen or mitigate the emotional consequences of rape (Atkeson, Calhoun, Resick & Ellis, 1982; Ruch & Leon, 1983) (see Chapter 13).

TO RECAP

Anxiety is experienced as an unpleasant feeling of fear. Anxiety disorders involve excessive, lasting anxiety about matters that do not warrant such concern. A phobia is an excessive, unrealistic fear, out of proportion to the danger actually associated with what is feared. Specific phobias concern particular objects or situations; agoraphobia involves fear of being in public places, especially on one's own, from which it would be difficult to escape; and social phobia is an irrational fear of situations in which one must interact with strangers or is otherwise subject to scrutiny and evaluation by other people. People with panic disorder experience repeated panic attacks, consisting of a sudden surge of intense anxiety along with multiple physical symptoms, such as heart palpitations, dizziness, or nausea, and thoughts of going crazy or even dying. Agoraphobia is a common complication of panic disorder.

Chronic worry is the core of generalized anxiety disorder (GAD). The patient is frequently tense and apprehensive about one or more situations or responsibilities. The GAD patient finds worry difficult to manage and as such is subject to multiple physical symptoms of tension and anxiety. People with obsessive-compulsive disorder (OCD) suffer from obsessions (intrusive, recurring thoughts, impulses, or images that seem uncontrollable) or compulsions (repetitive behaviors or mental acts that the person feels driven to perform in order to reduce distress or ward off disaster) or both. Common obsessions include doubts about whether a task was actually completed. Common compulsions include cleaning rituals and checking many times whether something was done. Posttraumatic stress disorder (PTSD) is an extreme response to a severely stressful event. To be diagnosed with PTSD, this response must last more than one month and include (a) re-experiencing the traumatic event, (b) avoiding stimuli associated with the trauma, and (c) signs of increased arousal, such as an exaggerated startle response.

Perspectives on the Causes and Treatment of Anxiety Disorders

Psychodynamic Perspectives: Conflict Between Id and Ego

Psychoanalytic theory regards anxiety as the result of an unconscious conflict between the ego and id impulses. The impulses, usually sexual or aggressive in nature, are struggling for expression, but the ego cannot allow their expression because it unconsciously fears that punishment will follow. Since the source of the anxiety is unconscious, the person experiences apprehension and distress without knowing why.

As we have seen, anxiety disorders vary. If unconscious conflict is the source of maladaptive anxiety, what would determine whether someone has, for instance, OCD versus a specific phobia? Two possibilities are the psychosexual stage at which the person's development is fixated and the nature of the defense mechanism the person employs in keeping the conflict unconscious.

OCD is believed to reflect fixation at the anal stage of development. Obsessions and compulsions are viewed as similar, resulting from instinctual sexual or aggressive forces that are not under control because of overly harsh toilet training. The symptoms observed represent the outcome of the struggle between the id and the defense mechanisms; sometimes the id predominates, sometimes the defense mechanisms. For example, when obsessive thoughts of killing intrude, the forces of the id are dominant. More often, however, the observed symptoms reflect the partially successful operation of one of the defense mechanisms. For example, an individual fixated at the anal stage may use the defense of reaction formation to resist the urge to soil, instead becoming compulsively neat, clean, and orderly.

Specific phobias may result from use of displacement as a defense mechanism. To avoid facing the unacceptable id impulses, the phobic patient displaces her or his anxiety onto a specific object or situation, which can then be avoided. According to Freud, the content of a phobia is not arbitrary. Anxiety is displaced from the feared id impulse to an object or situation that has some symbolic connection to it. These objects or situations—for example, elevators or enclosed spaces—then become the phobic stimuli. By avoiding them, the person is able to avoid dealing with repressed conflicts. The content of the phobia, coupled with information about the patient's life circumstances and childhood experiences, gives important clues to understanding the unconscious basis of what might otherwise seem an irrational and groundless fear.

Interpretation of the symbolic meaning of phobias is illustrated by a classic case of phobia, reported by Freud (1909).

A five-year-old boy, Little Hans, was afraid of horses and thus would not venture out of his home. Two years before the development of his phobia, when he was three, Hans was reported to have "a quite peculiarly lively interest in the part of his body which he used to describe as his widdler." When he was three and a half his mother caught him with his hand on his penis and threatened to have it cut off if he continued "doing that."

At age four and a half, while on summer vacation, Hans is described as having tried to "seduce" his mother. As his mother was powdering around his penis one day, taking care not to touch it, Hans said, "Why don't you put your finger there?" His mother answered, "Because that would be piggish." Hans replied, "What's that? Piggish? Why?" Mother: "Because it's not proper." Hans, laughing: "But it's great fun." These events were interpreted by Freud to mean that Hans had strong sexual urges, that they were directed toward his mother, and that they were repressed for fear of castration. According to psychoanalytic theory, this sexual frustration would ultimately be transformed into neurotic anxiety.

The first signs of the phobia appeared about six months later while Hans was out for a walk with his nursemaid. After a horse-drawn van had tipped over, he began crying, saying that he wanted to return home to "coax" (caress) with his mother. Later he indicated that he was afraid to go out because a horse might bite him, and he soon elaborated on his fears by referring to "black things around horses' mouths and the things in front of their eyes."

Freud considered this series of events to reflect Hans's oedipal desire to have his father out of the way so that he could possess his mother. His sexual excitement for his mother was converted into anxiety because he feared that he would be punished. Hans's father was considered the initial source of his son's fear, but the fear was then transposed to a symbol for his father—horses. The black muzzles and blinders on horses were viewed as symbolic representations of the father's mustache and eyeglasses. Thus, by fearing horses, Hans succeeded unconsciously in avoiding the fear of castration by his father while at the same time arranging to spend more time at home with his principal love object, his mother.

Psychodynamic Treatment: Confronting the Unconscious Conflict

Suppose that Freud's analysis of the basis of Hans's fear of horses is on target—what can be done about it? In general, psychodynamic treatments of anxiety disorders attempt to uncover the repressed conflicts that are assumed to underlie the extreme fear and avoidance characteristic of these disorders. The phobia or compulsion or anxious feelings are not dealt with directly because they are assumed to protect the person from repressed conflicts that are too painful to confront.

In treating agoraphobia, for example, a psychoanalyst might hypothesize that there is a repressed conflict between the patient's desire to be independent and an overanxious attachment to his or her mother or father. Therapy would aim at helping the patient recognize as unrealistic the belief that by leaving home and becoming independent the patient or the parents will not survive (Weiss & Sampson, 1986).

The analyst uses the techniques developed within the psychoanalytic tradition in various combinations to help lift the repression. During free association (see p. 39) the analyst listens carefully to what the patient mentions in connection with any references to the sources of the anxiety or situations that may have caused a generally anxious response. In the case of agoraphobia, the analyst might listen for expressions of ambivalence regarding independence and relationships. The analyst also attempts to discover clues to the repressed origins of the phobia in the manifest content of dreams.

These methods tend to be ineffective in treating OCD, which is one of the most difficult psychological problems to treat. Perhaps encouraging patients to free-associate but not necessarily to make direct behavioral changes merely feeds into their obsessiveness and their need for guaranteed correctness before any action can be taken (Salzman, 1980, 1985).

Contemporary dynamic therapists supplement free association and interpretation with suggestions that overlap the behavioral treatments discussed later in this chapter. Specifically, while continuing to view the fears as outgrowths of earlier problems, they encourage the patient to confront those fears. A "corrective emotional experience" is believed to result from the patient's confrontation with what is so desperately feared (Alexander & French, 1946). Indeed, Freud concluded that eventually analysts need to encourage patients to engage in the anxiety-provoking activities that they formerly avoided (Alexander & French, 1946).

Biological Perspectives

Biological perspectives on the causes and treatment of anxiety disorders contrast sharply with psychodynamic explanations and procedures. The biological view proposes specific biological vulnerabilities for the various disorders. Treatment relies heavily on using medications that attack anxiety symptoms directly, rather than focusing on theoretically related conflicts.

Genetic Influences on Anxiety Disorders

Family studies suggest that predisposition to anxiety disorders is to some extent heritable. The first-degree relatives of people with agoraphobia are at greater risk for it or one of the other anxiety disorders than are the first-degree relatives of nonanxious control subjects (Harris, Noyes, Crowe, & Chaudhry, 1983). Similar results have been obtained in family studies of OCD (Lenane et al., 1990; McKeon & Murray, 1987), panic disorder (Crowe, Noyes, Pauls, & Slymen, 1983), and social phobia (Fyer, Mannuzza, Chapman, Liebowitz, & Klein, 1993). These data are equivocal, however. Although close relatives share genes, they also have considerable opportunity to observe and influence one another. The fact that a son and his father are both afraid of heights may indicate not a genetic component but rather direct modeling of the son's behavior after that of his father, or both factors could be involved.

Twin studies are somewhat more compelling. Identical twins showed higher concordance than did fraternal twins for agoraphobia and for panic disorder (but not for GAD) (Torgersen, 1983) and for PTSD (True et al., 1993). Better still would be an adoption study, which would more conclusively differentiate genetic from environmental influences. In sum, although there is reason to believe that genetic factors may contribute to anxiety disorders, it is not yet clear to what extent they are important.

Biological Challenges and Panic

Another line of biological inquiry has focused on experimental manipulations that can induce panic attacks. One approach proposes that panic attacks are linked to hyperventilation or overbreathing (Ley, 1987). Hyperventilation may activate the autonomic nervous system, thus leading to the familiar somatic aspects of panic. Lactate (a product of muscular exertion) can also produce panic and may become elevated in patients with panic disorder because of chronic hyperventilation.

The various biological challenges (e.g., carbon dioxide, hyperventilation) that can induce panic tend to have this effect only on those already diagnosed with panic disorder. Although this situation could be interpreted as meaning that the challenges activate some kind of biological vulnerability in panic patients, these patients' physiological responses are actually very similar to those of control subjects. What distinguishes the two groups is that panic patients report much more fear induced by the biological challenge (Margraf, Ehlers, & Roth, 1986). Thus, as discussed later in the chapter, cognitive factors, such as perceived control, may be a key determinant of whether someone panics when exposed to stressors.

Neurobiology of Anxiety Disorders

Neurobiological research looks at the neurochemistry behind feelings of anxiety. It draws an important distinction between the physiology of panic anxiety and what is termed anticipatory anxiety, which is viewed as similar to the anxiety associated with GAD (J. A. Gray, 1982).

Panic anxiety appears to be linked to the noradrenergic system (that is, neurons that use norepinephrine as a neurotransmitter) and particularly to the locus coeruleus, a nucleus in the pons. The locus coeruleus is the major noradrenergic nucleus and has projections to many other brain areas—cortex, limbic system, and brain stem. Electrical stimulation of the locus coeruleus caused monkeys to respond with what appeared to be a panic attack, thus suggesting that naturally occurring panic might be based on noradrenergic overactivation (Redmond, 1977).

Subsequent research has indeed shown that drugs (e.g., yohimbine) that stimulate the locus coeruleus can elicit panic attacks, whereas drugs that reduce activity in the locus coeruleus (e.g., clonidine) reduce anxiety (e.g., Charney, Heninger, & Breier, 1984). Not all evidence supports this theory. Other measures of noradrenergic activation have failed to discriminate patients with panic disorder from those without it (Woods, Charney, Goodman, & Heninger, 1987), yet interest in the locus coeruleus as a source of anxiety responses remains active.

The most prevalent neurobiological model for generalized anxiety comes from looking at the effects of the benzodiazepines, a group of drugs used to treat anxiety. These drugs appear to ease anxiety by their effects on a receptor in the brain that is linked to an inhibitory neurotransmitter called gamma-aminobutyric acid (GABA) (see p. 55). It is believed that anxiety stimulates the neurons, and that the benzodiazepines enhance the release of GABA, thereby reducing the anxiety. Similarly, drugs that block or inhibit the GABA system lead to increases in anxiety (Insell, 1986).

Neurobiological research on OCD has focused on the neurotransmitter serotonin. Clomipramine and fluoxetine (Prozac), tricyclic antidepressants that block the reuptake of serotonin, have proven to be useful therapies for OCD (e.g., Pigott et al., 1990). Patients with high pretest levels of serotonin or its major metabolite improve most when treated with a serotonin reuptake blocker. The extent to which these drugs reduce levels of serotonin correlates with the degree to which they reduce feelings of anxiety and obsessional thinking (Lesch et al., 1991). Similarly, research with drugs that stimulate the serotonin receptor indicates that they can exacerbate the symptoms of OCD (e.g., Hollander et al., 1992). Encephalitis, head injuries, and brain tumors have also been associated with the development of OCD (Jenike, 1986).

Biological Perspectives on Treatment

As noted earlier, much of our understanding of the possible biological causes of anxiety comes from studies of the mechanisms by which antianxiety medication works. Drugs commonly used to treat depression may also help anxiety disorder patients.

Antidepressants, such as imipramine (Tofranil), appear to be useful in treating agoraphobia (e.g., Johnston, Troyer, & Whitsett, 1988), especially when depressed mood is part of the clinical picture (Marks, 1983). Both antidepressants and the benzodiazepines have shown some success in treating panic disorder. The evidence for the effectiveness of alprazolam, a benzodiazepine derivative, is particularly compelling, as it was obtained in a large-scale, multicenter study (Ballenger et al., 1988).

As indicated earlier tricyclic antidepressant medications, such as clomipramine, often help OCD patients (Clomipramine Collaborative Study Group, 1991). On the other hand, one study found that imipramine was not effective on OCD symptoms, although it did alleviate depression (Foa, Kozak, Steketee, & McCarthy, 1992). This is an important benefit, for behavioral treatment of OCD (discussed later in this chapter) appears to be less effective in alleviating depression, despite success in lowering anxiety, obsessions, and compulsions (Cox, Swinson, Morrison, & Lee, 1993).

Fluoxetine (Prozac), a relatively new antidepressant drug (discussed in Chapter 10), has been found to be effective for OCD (Cox et al., 1993). Interestingly, a comparison of fluoxetine and behavioral treatment found that improvement in OCD by *both* treatments was associated with the same changes in metabolic activity in the caudate nucleus (Baxter et al., 1992). Only those patients who improved clinically showed this change in brain activity as measured by PET scans (p. 121). Such findings suggest that markedly different therapies may work for similar reasons, as they are different ways of affecting the same factors in the brain.

Despite these favorable results with various anxiety disorders, there are grounds for caution in the use, especially as a sole treatment, of anxiolytic (anxiety-reducing) medications. First, benzodiazepines are addicting and produce a severe withdrawal syndrome (Schweizer, Rickels, Case, & Greenblatt, 1990). As with opiates, babies born of tranquilizer-dependent mothers are themselves dependent and suffer withdrawal. Second, all too often people calmed down by anxiolytics find themselves still fearful when weaned from the drugs (Barlow, 1988). This may be a result of the patient's (understandable) tendency to attribute the improvement to an external agent, the medication, rather than to internal changes and his or her own coping efforts (Davison & Valins, 1969). Thus patients continue to believe that the anxiety and the worrisome possibilities remain uncontrollable, and they tend to become dependent on the medications for long periods of time. In fact, in their efforts to reduce their anxiety, many phobics and other anxious people use anxiolytics or alcohol on their own. The use and abuse of drugs and alcohol are common among anxiety-ridden people. Finally, many tranquilizing drugs have undesirable side effects that argue against long-term use, ranging from drowsiness and depression to damage of certain bodily organs.

Behavioral Perspectives: Conditioned Fear and Avoidance

The primary assumption of all behavioral accounts of anxiety is that such reactions are learned. But the exact mechanisms by which the fear is learned and what is actually learned are viewed differently depending on the behavioral theory. We will look at three proposed mechanisms: avoidance conditioning, modeling, and operant conditioning.

The Avoidance Conditioning Model

Historically, Watson and Rayner's (1920) demonstration of the apparent conditioning of a fear or phobia in Little Albert (see p. 63) is considered the model of how a phobia may be acquired. Behavioral theorists contend that phobias develop via classical conditioning when a person learns to fear a neutral stimulus (the CS) because it is paired with an intrinsically painful or frightening event (the UCS). Then the person can learn to reduce this conditioned fear by escaping from or avoiding the CS. This second kind of learning is assumed to be operant conditioning, because the response is maintained by its reinforcing consequences.

Some phobias fit the avoidance conditioning model rather well. For example, a phobia of a specific object has sometimes been reported to have developed after a particularly painful experience with that object. Some people become intensely afraid of driving an automobile after a serious accident, or of descending stairs after a bad fall. Other phobias apparently originate in similar fashion.

However, avoidance conditioning is not a complete explanation of phobias. Some clinical reports suggest that phobias may develop *without* a prior frightening experience. Many individuals with severe fears of snakes, germs, airplanes, and heights tell clinicians that they have had no particularly unpleasant experiences with any of these objects or situations (Ost, 1987). In addition, many people who have had a harrowing automobile accident or a bad fall on stairs do *not* become phobic to automobiles or stairs. Thus the avoidance conditioning model cannot account for the acquisition of all phobias.

Another puzzling issue from the point of view of avoidance conditioning is why human beings tend to be afraid of only certain types of objects and events (Marks, 1969). People may have phobias of dogs, cats, and snakes, but few lamb phobics have been encountered. It is even more remarkable how few people phobically avoid electrical outlets, which do present certain dangers under specified circumstances. Research suggests that we may be more biologically prepared to be afraid of heights or dogs or snakes, and therefore these phobias are easily learned and not readily extinguished (Seligman & Hager, 1972).

Posttraumatic stress disorder also may be seen as arising from a classical conditioning of fear (Fairbank & Brown, 1987). In the case of rape, for example, the victim may come to fear walking in a certain neighborhood (the CS) that had previously caused her no second thoughts because of having been assaulted there (the UCS). Based on this classically conditioned fear, avoidance behavior arises. Avoidance is in turn negatively reinforced by the reduction of fear that comes from not being in the presence of the CS (Foy, Resnick, Carroll, & Osato, 1990).

Modeling

Phobic responses may also be learned by imitating the phobic reactions of others. As previously noted (see p. 65), a wide range of behavior, including emotional responses, may be learned by witnessing a model. An intriguing demonstration of the potential importance of modeling comes from a study of rhesus monkeys (Mineka, Davidson, Cook, & Keir, 1984). Adolescent rhesus monkeys were reared with parents who had an intense fear of snakes. During the observational learning sessions, the offspring saw their parents interact fearfully with real and toy snakes and interact nonfearfully with neutral objects. After six sessions, the level of fear of the adolescent monkeys was indistinguishable from that of the parents. A three-month follow-up showed that the fear was not extinguished.

As with classical conditioning, modeling fails to provide a complete explanation for all phobias. First, phobics who seek treatment do not often report that they became frightened after witnessing someone else's distress. Second, many people have been exposed to the bad experiences of others but have not themselves developed phobias.

Susan Mineka's research has shown that when monkeys observe another monkey display fear of a snake, they also acquire the fear. Observational learning may therefore play a role in causing phobias.

Operant Conditioning

Operant conditioning seems particularly relevant to understanding OCD. The idea is that compulsive behaviors are maintained by negative reinforcement, specifically, reduction of the anxiety aroused by obsessive thoughts (Meyer & Chesser, 1970). For example, compulsive hand washing reduces the anxiety associated with an obsessional preoccupation with contamination by dirt or germs. Therefore, the next time the person has an intrusive thought about contamination, hand washing is all the more likely to occur. Research has verified that compulsive behaviors do indeed sometimes reduce anxiety (e.g., Carr, 1971).

But where do obsessions come from in the first place? Most people occasionally experience unwanted ideas that are similar in content to obsessions (Rachman & deSilva, 1978). Among normal individuals, these thoughts are tolerated or dismissed. But the obsessive person may try to actively suppress these troubling thoughts. What happens, though, when you try *not* to think about something? Such a strategy often makes matters worse—it becomes impossible to get the idea or image out of your head. In one study two groups of college students were asked either to think about a white bear or not to think about one. One group thought about the white bear and then was told not to; the other group did the reverse. Thoughts were measured by having subjects voice their thoughts and also by having them ring a bell every time they thought about a white bear. Two findings are of particular note. First, the students were not completely able to stop themselves from thinking about a white bear. Second, the students who were first told not to think about the bear had more thoughts about it later (Wegner, Schneider, Carter, & White, 1987).

Trying to suppress a thought may therefore have the paradoxical effect of inducing preoccupation with it. This phenomenon may account for the durability of obsessive thinking. There are, of course, differences between trying not to think of a white bear, a relatively neutral topic chosen by the researcher, and trying not to think about an impulse to hurt a child, a greatly distressing thought arising from within (Kelly & Kahn, 1994). Further research is needed to determine whether the paradoxical effects of thought suppression can account for the development of obsessions in OCD.

Behavioral Perspectives on Treatment: Confronting the Feared Situation

Treatment of anxiety disorders from a behavioral perspective depends crucially on exposure to what is feared. The main differences from one disorder to another concern how such exposure is to be arranged and what sorts of situations the patient must confront.

A widely used behavioral treatment for phobias is systematic desensitization, which we discussed in Chapter 3 (Wolpe, 1958). The patient imagines a series of increasingly frightening scenes while in a state of deep relaxation. This technique is effective in eliminating or at least reducing many phobias (Wilson & O'Leary, 1980).

It is often necessary to supplement, or even replace, imagining the feared situation with actually confronting the phobic situation in real life (in vivo exposure). Evidence supports the value of treating agoraphobia, for instance, by graded exposures to real-life crowds and public places (Craske, Rapee, & Barlow, 1992). Involving patients' spouses in the treatment of agoraphobia may improve its effects. In one program, agoraphobic women participate with their spouses or with significant others in group meetings during which encouragement and exhortation are given for going out of the house between therapy sessions. Gradual forays away from the home are nurtured by the nonphobic participants and then discussed at the weekly group meetings. Although many of those who begin such exposure therapies drop out, and some of those who improve relapse, a considerable proportion do improve (Craske et al., 1992).

David Barlow, director of the Center for Stress and Anxiety Disorders at the State University of New York, Albany.

flooding A *behavior therapy* procedure in which a fearful person is exposed to what is frightening, in reality or in the imagination, for
extended periods of time and full intensity.

*In the most common treatment for
phobias, patients are exposed to
what they fear most, here, an enclosed space.*

Exposure to what the patient fears is the key strategy in treating PTSD as well
(Rothbaum & Foa, 1992a, 1992b). Many techniques have been employed. In one
well-designed study, Terence Keane and his associates compared a no-treatment
control group with a group of patients who visualized fearsome, trauma-related
scenes for extended periods of time. This technique, called **flooding**, exposes the
client to the source of the phobia at full intensity. Compared with controls, the
flooding group of PTSD Vietnam veterans showed significantly greater reductions in depression, anxiety, reexperiencing of the trauma, startle reactions, and
irritability (Keane, Fairbank, Caddell, & Zimering, 1989). Conducting such treatment is difficult for both patient and therapist, for it requires detailed review of
the traumatizing events. Patients may become temporarily worse in the initial
stages of therapy, and therapists themselves may become upset by hearing of the
horrifying events that their patients experienced (Keane et al., 1992).

The most widely used behavioral approach to treating OCD combines exposure with response prevention (Rachman & Hodgson, 1980). This approach involves having patients expose themselves to situations that elicit the compulsive
act—such as touching a dirty dish—and then refrain from performing the accustomed ritual—hand washing. The assumption is that the ritual reduces anxiety
that is aroused by some environmental stimulus or event, such as dust on a chair;
preventing the patients from performing the ritual will expose them to the anxiety-provoking stimuli, thereby allowing the anxiety to extinguish.

Controlled research (e.g., Foa, Steketee, & Ozarow, 1985) suggests that this is
an effective treatment. Although in the short term response prevention is very
unpleasant for clients, the extreme discomfort is believed worth enduring to alleviate these disabling problems. Clearly, however, conditions must be such that
the client can be persuaded to go along with the treatment. Indeed, refusal to enter treatment and dropping out are problems for all kinds of interventions for
OCD (Jenike, 1990). Sometimes control over obsessive-compulsive rituals is possible only in a hospital environment in which staff can make a concerted effort to
restrict the patient's opportunities to engage in ritualistic behaviors (V. Meyer,
1966).

Applying the exposure principle to social phobia carries some additional complications (G. Butler, 1985). For example, we can be relatively certain when helping an elevator phobic confront the feared situation that it is indeed not dangerous (and therefore the fear should extinguish as the CS is repeatedly not followed
by the UCS). With social phobics, though, the situation is not so clear-cut. If your
fear is that other people are scrutinizing you and thinking ill of you, then simply
entering the feared situation (talking to strangers, giving a speech, writing in
front of others) and surviving it is inconclusive. Perhaps they were privately
judging you negatively during this time; maybe they went home afterward and
phoned each other to compare notes on how ridiculous you were. Especially important in this respect is that, perhaps from lack of practice over the years, some
social phobics may indeed lack social skills and therefore behave in an awkward
manner that elicits negative feedback.

Accordingly, some behavior therapists emphasize encouraging socially phobic
patients first to role-play or rehearse in the consulting room how they might handle interpersonal encounters. Several studies attest to the effectiveness of such an
approach (e.g., Mattick, Peters, & Clarke, 1989). Such practice may expose the
fearful person, even when there is no social-skills deficit, to anxiety-provoking
cues, so that extinction of fear takes place. Whatever the mechanism of action, intensive real-life exposure appears to be effective. Benefits were maintained in a
six-month follow-up to a greater degree than with patients who received
atenolol, a beta-blocking medication sometimes used by stage performers to control rapid heartbeat, blushing, and other potentially embarrassing somatic indications of stage fright (Turner, Beidel, & Jacob, 1994).

> ## APPLYING CRITICAL THINKING SKILLS

THERAPY FOR SOCIAL PHOBIA

What works and why? As we just mentioned, practicing interpersonal encounters in the office and then extending this practice to the natural environment may work in the treatment of social phobia for more than one reason (skill building vs. extinction). Yet it is important to try to determine what it is about this approach to therapy that works, both to pinpoint the effective elements of treatment as well as for what that understanding might tell us about causes of the disorder. Critical thinking points to the direction research might take to resolve this issue and to further understanding of social phobia.

Frank Donaldson, a forty-year-old divorced man, sought treatment for social anxiety, which had resulted in his biting his fingers until they bled and in procrastinating at work. He reported feeling fairly comfortable interacting with others once he knew them or even if he had some legitimate pretext for seeing them, such as an appointment. He was terrified, however, if he had to speak to someone he did not know without a prearranged meeting. This posed a considerable problem, for Frank's job consisted mainly of cold sales calls to customers. He had been in psychotherapy for six years with no improvement in his anxiety. He believed the anxiety resulted from early socialization by his parents, who, he stated, were zealous in warning of the hazards associated with strangers yet at the same time critical of him for being an anxious child.

The therapist first suggested to Frank that instead of continued effort to become comfortable calling strangers, he might wish to find a different line of work. After all, six years of therapy is a lot, and many people without diagnosable social phobia would find telephone sales work uncomfortable. Frank was adamant that he wanted to try one more time, however, and the therapist agreed. Given that fear seemed to be the main problem (Frank's skills were apparently adequate once he relaxed, as in meetings for which he had an appointment), they tried systematic desensitization.

Once Frank became adept at relaxing while imagining the most difficult scenes on his anxiety hierarchy, between-session assignments for real-life exposure were added. For several months, Frank faithfully carried out exposure practice, but only at low levels of anxiety (e.g., calling prospective members of his staff to recruit them, making follow-up calls to previous customers). He did not tackle the more difficult items (cold calls to new customers). He was stuck at a plateau that represented some, but not sufficient, progress. Discussions of why he could not advance further and between-session phone calls with the therapist to check on progress did not help.

Finally, desperate to make additional headway, Frank suggested to his therapist that he needed a marathon session of calling new customers from the therapist's office, with the therapist available to consult between calls on the use of relaxation methods. The therapist agreed, cleared his schedule for an afternoon, and held a four-hour session along the lines of Frank's request. This appointment (and one similar follow-up session) seemed to break the logjam. Frank went on to stop biting his fingers, which healed completely, made the phone calls required by his job, on his own, with mild and tolerable anxiety, and reported significant improvement in occupational success and consequently in overall life satisfaction.

> *What conclusion does the evidence seem to support?* From a behavioral perspective, it would seem that the early in vivo exposure assignments, without therapist assistance, were too difficult. The therapist's presence was necessary and sufficient support for Frank to engage in this painful but therapeutic learning experience.

> *What other interpretations are plausible?* From a psychodynamic point of view, the details of exposure treatment (in imagination or in real life, with the

therapist present or not, for ten minutes or four hours) may have been largely irrelevant. Instead, the critical therapeutic process may have been in the patient–therapist relationship. In particular, Frank's wish for an unusual accommodation (extra-long session) from an authority figure was gratified.

One of the crucial dynamics in a psychotherapy relationship may be that the patient plays out with the therapist dysfunctional beliefs about relationships and unconsciously sets up tests for the therapist in an attempt to disconfirm these beliefs (J. Weiss, 1990). The patient makes demands of the therapist to see if the therapist can tolerate them or if the therapist will respond in the hurtful, rejecting manner she or he has come to expect from others.

Perhaps, then, in granting the long session, the therapist disconfirmed the pathogenic (illness-causing) belief, and in avoiding the trap of responding as others have, thereby showed the patient that the therapy relationship was a safe one in which to express and examine previously buried, perhaps shame-inducing, thoughts and wishes. In this case, Frank reported that he had often felt criticized by his parents for weakness and vulnerability, and he seemed pleased that showing his weakness to the therapist ("I need special help") evoked not criticism but support. The therapist in this sense passed the test, facilitating further productive and collaborative work.

According to Mahoney (1986), much of the impact of all psychotherapy techniques, not just the verbal interpretations associated with dynamic therapies, can be understood as communicative impact. Techniques communicate therapeutic messages about the patient (in this case, "You can handle it"), about the therapist ("I care about the pain and will stand by you"), and about the problem ("This is not hopeless"). These messages might fall flat if conveyed in so many words, in much the same way that the language of friendship is often more compelling when expressed implicitly (actually listening to someone) than when stated explicitly ("I'll always be there for you").

▶ *What other information would help choose among the alternative interpretations?* As usual, the uncontrolled case study is inconclusive when it comes to determining *why* a treatment worked (see Chapter 1). Further research might be able to distinguish the alternative interpretations if a situation could be arranged in which disconfirming the patient's pathogenic belief required doing something that would be expected to be unhelpful from a nonpsychodynamic theoretical perspective (e.g., avoid the feared situation). If the treatment still worked, it would provide stronger evidence in favor of the psychodynamic interpretation. If not, the behavioral interpretation would be bolstered.   ◀

Cognitive Perspectives: Misperceived Danger

Cognitive theorists view anxious people as hypersensitive to vulnerability and danger (Beck & Emery, 1985). Benign events are perceived as involving threats, and thinking focuses on anticipated future disasters (Beck, Brown, Steer, Eidelson & Riskind, 1987; Kendall & Ingram, 1989). The attention of anxious patients is easily drawn to stimuli that suggest possible harm or rejection (MacLeod, Matthews, & Tata, 1986). Relative to nonanxious people, anxious people are more apt to interpret ambiguous stimuli as threatening and to rate ominous events as more likely to occur to them (Butler & Mathews, 1983). From this perspective, the main differences among the various anxiety disorders involve *what* situations are perceived as especially dangerous and what sorts of misfortunes are expected to occur.

For example, OCD is believed to involve overestimating the likelihood that undesirable outcomes will occur (Carr, 1974) as well as an exaggerated sense of responsibility for these disasters (Salkovskis, 1989). In other words, the obsessive-compulsive person has an "If anything can go wrong, it will, and I am responsible" view of life. This belief motivates the patient to avoid the sources of threat and to check on whether this effort to ward off catastrophe has been successful, thus increasing the likelihood of obsessive-compulsive behavior.

Attentional and Memory Biases in Anxiety Disorders

What processes could underlie such overestimation of dangers? Biased attention and memory processes may provide part of the answer. For example, phobics have difficulty recalling and recognizing anxiety-inducing stimuli (Watts, Trezise, & Sharrock, 1986). The data seem inconsistent with the hypervigilance of phobics for the source of their anxiety, but another interpretation is possible. Perhaps, even though phobics are vigilant for stimuli related to their fears, once encountered, the stimuli are so quickly avoided that they are not fully processed and therefore not easily recalled. This would be an excellent avoidance mechanism for promoting the maintenance of the phobia.

Another line of investigation has special relevance to understanding checking compulsions. Specifically, it appears that compulsive checkers show poor memory for their own recent actions. This has been demonstrated both among college students scoring high on an index of compulsive checking (Rubenstein, Peynircioglu, Chambless, & Pigott, 1993) and among more disturbed psychiatric patients (Sher, Frost, Kushner, Crew & Alexander, 1989). If people have difficulty remembering accurately and with confidence whether or not they performed some necessary action (e.g., "Did I turn off the stove before leaving the house?"), it stands to reason that they would be at risk for compulsive checking.

Fear of Fear: When the Danger Is Internal

The cognitive perspective may help explain why panic disorder is so frequently associated with agoraphobia. The fear-of-fear hypothesis (Goldstein & Chambless, 1978) holds that agoraphobia is not a fear of public places per se, but a fear of fear, a fear of having a panic attack in public. One idea about why panic-disorder patients fear their own fear so acutely is that they misinterpret the physiological sensations associated with anxiety as being signs of impending disaster, which could then spiral into full-blown panic (Clark, 1988). For example, a skipped heartbeat may be taken to mean that one is about to have a heart attack.

Fear of Loss of Control

Another central theme in the cognitive perspective on panic is the concept of perceived control. People with GAD tend to perceive themselves as lacking control over stressors. They worry about a host of interconnecting future problems that might occur and that they do not consider themselves readily able to solve. Thus, the worries can reverberate in an unproductive cycle (Roemer & Borkovec, 1993). For example: What if I can't get a summer job? . . . Then I wouldn't have any money. . . . What if I can't find anything to do without any money? . . . What if not having a job this summer means I won't have the track record to get a good job later? . . . What if I end up being a failure my whole career? and so on.

The sense of being unable to control whether or not these problems develop is probably critical. In experimental work with human beings, stressful events over which the subjects can exert some control are less anxiety provoking than those over which no control can be exercised. Some research (e.g., Geer, Davison, & Gatchel, 1970) also suggests that in certain circumstances the control needs only to be perceived by the subject; it does not need to be real.

Patients with panic disorder also fear losing or not having control. In this case, though, the perceived-to-be-uncontrollable difficulty involves an imminent biological catastrophe, such as a heart attack, and not diffuse future problems; hence the greater surge of anxiety than in the case of GAD. Perceiving that one is in control, even if this is objectively not the case, can be helpful in warding off panic. This point was illustrated in a study that built on the knowledge that among patients with panic disorder, breathing carbon dioxide can precipitate an attack (Sanderson, Rapee, & Barlow, 1989). In the study, patients with panic disorder breathed carbon dioxide and were told that when a light came on they could turn a dial to reduce the concentration of the gas. For half the subjects the light was on continuously, whereas for the remainder it never came on. Turning the dial actually had no effect on carbon dioxide levels, so the perception of control over what happened was inaccurate. Only 20% of the group who thought they had control over carbon dioxide levels had a panic attack, compared with 80% of those who believed they did not have control.

Cognitive Treatment of Anxiety: Reevaluating the Risks

Cognitive therapies aim to change the misperceptions or irrational beliefs that underlie anxiety with more adaptive beliefs that promote the person's ability to cope with the feared situations or sensations. In some cases a logical reanalysis of the person's belief that something is dangerous is helpful. In other cases the most convincing evidence that feared catastrophes will not actually occur requires, as in behavioral exposure treatment, experiencing the feared situation. The commonality is using evidence and logic to change the patient's belief that what he or she fears is extremely dangerous and that he or she cannot cope with it.

If an otherwise well-functioning person is intensely afraid of something that, intellectually, he or she acknowledges is relatively harmless, of what use can it be to alter that person's thoughts about the feared object? One proposal derives from the rational-emotive theory (RET) of Ellis (1962) (see Chapter 3). RET suggests that a phobia is maintained by irrational beliefs, such as "If something seems dangerous or fearsome, you must be terribly occupied with and upset about it" or "It is easier to avoid than to face certain life difficulties." The RET patient is taught to dispute the irrational belief whenever the phobic object or situation is encountered. Disputing the belief does not substitute for exposure, but may help goad the patient into in vivo exposure. Indeed, there is no evidence that disputing irrational beliefs alone, without exposure to the fearsome situations, reduces phobic avoidance (Turner, Beidel, & Townsley, 1992).

Psychological treatment of panic has been derived from the view that patients may become unduly alarmed by noticing their fast heartbeats and that some people may attribute other sensations as well, such as hyperventilation, to an impending disaster. The observation that treating agoraphobia with exposure does not always reduce panic attacks (Michelson, Mavissakalian, & Marchione, 1985) has also been taken into account.

These factors have led to some innovative psychological therapies that incorporate cognitive methods. Barlow and his associates (e.g., Barlow & Cerny, 1988; Klosko, Barlow, Tassinari, & Cerny, 1990), for example, have developed a detailed and well-validated therapy that combines relaxation training with exposure to the internal cues that trigger panic.

The client practices in the consulting room behaviors that can elicit feelings associated with panic. For example, a person whose panic attacks begin with hyperventilation is asked to breathe fast for three minutes; someone who gets dizzy might be requested to spin in a chair for several minutes. When sensations such as dizziness, dry mouth, light-headedness, increased heart rate, and other signs of panic begin to be felt, the patient experiences them under safe conditions and applies previously learned cognitive and relaxation coping tactics (which can include breathing from the diaphragm rather than hyperventilating). With practice and encouragement and persuasion from the therapist, the client learns to reinterpret internal sensations from signals of loss of control and panic to cues that are intrinsically harmless and can be controlled with certain skills.

The intentional creation of these signs by the client, coupled with success in coping with them, reduces their unpredictability and their fearsome meaning for the client. Two-year follow-ups have shown that therapeutic gains from this cognitive and exposure therapy have been maintained and are superior to the use of alprazolam, a widely prescribed antipanic medication (Craske, Brown, & Barlow, 1991).

Because chronic worrying is central to GAD, it is not surprising that cognitive techniques have been employed in its treatment as well. Perhaps a person worries needlessly because he or she interprets ambiguous stimuli as threats or overestimates the likelihood that a negative event will occur (Butler & Mathews, 1983). Helping GAD sufferers reappraise situations may therefore help, and evidence suggests that it does (Durham & Turvey, 1987). Improvement tends to be well-maintained after the end of treatment (Borkovec & Costello, 1993).

Cognitive interventions are typically employed as a complement to, not a substitute for, behavioral methods in treating all these anxiety disorders. Learning to reinterpret the dangers associated with a situation might, for instance, bolster the person's willingness to enter that situation. Moreover, once exposure has been tried, cognitive interventions can be helpful in drawing conclusions from the experience (e.g., "I can manage it," as opposed to "I averted disaster . . . this time"). But there is really no substitute for exposure per se.

This viewpoint is consistent not only with clinical experience and empirical evidence, but also with common sense. Consider in this regard a strong fear you or someone you know has, strong enough that you avoid the object or situation (e.g., a roller coaster). You can logically analyze the safety of roller-coaster rides, think about the origins of this fear and the symbolic meanings for you of roller coasters, discuss the fear with empathic friends and family members, and so forth until the cows come home, but if you never get on a roller coaster, you are not really going to get over the fear.

Vulnerability-Stress Perspectives

Why do some people acquire unrealistic fears whereas others do not, given similar opportunities for learning? Alternatively, why would monozygotic twins ever be discordant for anxiety disorders? Vulnerability-stress perspectives can account for such phenomena by proposing that those who are adversely affected by stress have a preexisting vulnerability that predisposes them to be especially susceptible to anxiety.

In most instances, there are not yet well-elaborated and empirically tested vulnerability-stress models of specific anxiety disorders. One promising illustration, however, comes from research on PTSD (Breslau, Davis, Andreski, & Peterson, 1991). In this research a number of risk factors (vulnerabilities) for PTSD were identified. Predictors of PTSD given exposure to a traumatic event included early separation from parents, family history of a disorder, and a preexisting disorder (panic disorder, OCD, depression). In general, the likelihood of PTSD increases with the severity of the traumatic event; for example, the greater the exposure to combat the greater the risk. With a high degree of combat exposure, the rates of PTSD are the same in veterans with or without family members with other disorders. However, vulnerability to the disorder shows up in conditions of low combat among those with a family history of disorder, while those without this vulnerability do not develop PTSD (Foy et al., 1987).

To Recap

The main perspectives on psychopathology offer quite different explanations of anxiety disorders, varying in the level of detail as well as in the extent to which specific diagnostic categories are accounted for differently. Likewise, the perspec-

tives offer contrasting views of how anxiety disorders might best be treated. A brief review of the key features of each perspective is provided in the chapter summary.

The Case of Karen Rusa Revisited

We began this chapter with the case of Karen Rusa, whose anxiety took the form of obsessive thoughts and fears that centered on the health of her children. Her compulsive behaviors fall into a special type of checking ritual known as repeating. Repeaters perform an action, often a particular magical number of times, in an effort to prevent disastrous events from happening. Clearly, Karen's case exemplifies OCD.

The actual treatment process in any given case always depends on more than just making the diagnosis and looking up what is the best-supported treatment for this disorder. To illustrate such considerations and strategies more vividly, here and in subsequent chapters we discuss the selected case in more detail, beginning with a consideration of the patient's background and moving on to the treatment procedures used, their effects, and discussion of what alternative approaches might have been considered.

SOCIAL HISTORY

Karen was raised in New York City by Italian immigrant parents who were devout Roman Catholics. She attended parochial schools, and her memories of the severe practices of the church and school authorities were vivid. The formal rituals of the church played an important role in her life, as they did for the rest of her family. Beginning at a very early age, Karen was taught that she had to follow many specific guidelines that governed social behavior within the church (not eating meat on Fridays, going to confession regularly, etc.). She was told that her strict adherence to these norms would ensure the safety of her immortal soul and, conversely, that transgressions would be severely punished.

Karen remembered her parents as having been very strict disciplinarians. Her mother was apparently a cold, rigid person who had insisted on the maintenance of order and cleanliness in their household. When the children deviated from these guidelines, they were severely punished. Karen's most positive recollections of interaction with her mother centered on their mutual participation in prescribed church functions. She did not remember her parents ever demonstrating affection for each other in front of their children.

Shortly after she graduated from high school, Karen married Tony. He was two years older than she and had been working as a stock boy at a department store. Their courtship was hurried, and Karen became pregnant two months after their marriage. In retrospect, Karen wondered whether her interest in Tony had been motivated by a desire to escape from the confines of her parents' home.

Karen began experiencing repetitive, intrusive thoughts about injuring herself as a result of an accident she witnessed at about this time. While Karen was chatting with a friend, the woman's one-year-old daughter crawled off the porch and was run over by another child riding a bicycle. The girl was seriously injured and remained in the hospital for several weeks. Shortly thereafter, at unpredictable but frequent intervals throughout the day, Karen would find herself thinking about jumping out windows, walking in front of cars, and other similar dangerous behaviors. She attempted to get rid of these thoughts by quickly repeating a short prayer that she had learned as a child. This procedure was moderately successful as a temporary source of distraction, but it did not prevent the recurrence of a similar intrusive thought several hours later. These thoughts of self-injury gradually disappeared after the birth of her first child, Jennifer.

When Jennifer was nine months old, Karen once again became pregnant. She and

Tony moved to the suburbs, where they were able to afford a house with a yard in which the children could play. Although she was proud of their new home, Karen became somewhat depressed during this period because she missed her old friends. At this time Karen began to be disillusioned with the church as well. Her distress centered on a number of reforms that had been introduced by Pope John XXIII and the Ecumenical Council. For example, the Mass was no longer said in Latin, and nonclerical persons were allowed to administer various rites of the church. Most people found such changes refreshing, but Karen was horrified. The church's rituals had come to play a central role in her life. In deemphasizing the importance of traditional rituals, the church was depriving Karen of her principal means of controlling her own destiny. She was extremely uncomfortable with these new practices and soon stopped going to church altogether.

Karen's situation changed very little throughout the next few years, and she was generally unhappy. By the time she was twenty-five years old, she had four children. She found this responsibility overwhelming most of the time. Karen had established very specific guidelines for meals, bedtime, and so on, but found that she was unable to enforce these rules by herself. Tony refused to participate in what he considered unnecessarily rigid and complicated household regulations, particularly those dealing with the children's behavior.

Karen remained distant from Tony and resisted most of his attempts to display physical affection. They did maintain a sexual relationship, but it lacked spontaneity and genuine warmth. Since the birth of their fourth child, Karen had been particularly anxious about becoming pregnant again, and because artificial birth control was contrary to the teachings of the church, their sexual encounters had to be carefully scheduled to avoid the days surrounding ovulation. When they did engage in sexual activity, they followed a careful, routine sequence that was usually limited to the minimum physical stimulation necessary for Tony to achieve orgasm. On most occasions, Karen described herself as being tense and anxious at these times.

This unhappy yet tolerable equilibrium was disturbed by Tony's deteriorating health. One day, while he was working at the store, he experienced sudden chest pains and numbness in his extremities. His experience was diagnosed as a mild heart attack. Further testing revealed serious structural abnormalities in his heart. He was eventually discharged from the hospital, given a complete medical disability, and laid off from his job.

Karen became more and more depressed after Tony began staying home during the day. During this period her fears about the children's safety became clearly unreasonable, and she began to perform her counting rituals. Karen could not remember when she first began checking the order of items on a shelf or counting the number of cigarettes she smoked in sequence. She did realize that her situation was desperate because she felt that she had lost control of her own behavior and she experienced considerable anxiety whenever she attempted to resist performing the rituals. At this point she finally decided to seek professional help.

CONCEPTUALIZATION AND TREATMENT

The ritualistic behavior was seen by the therapist as one part of Karen's overall difficult situation. The counting obsession represented Karen's attempt to reintroduce a sense of personal control over her own life. In this sense, the rituals were being performed instead of either the more socially acceptable religious activities that she had employed as a child or the more effective social skills that she had apparently never developed. For example, she was unassertive in her relationship with Tony and markedly ineffective in her interactions with the children.

Treatment was therefore aimed at the development of interpersonal skills that would give Karen more control over her environment. It was hoped that as she was able to develop a more satisfactory relationship with her family, her increased competence would eliminate the necessity of turning to admittedly superstitious, ineffective attempts to achieve self-control.

During the course of their early sessions, it became evident to both Karen and her therapist that Karen was not behaving assertively, particularly with her husband. She and the therapist agreed to pursue a systematic program of assertion training. To determine the conditions under which Karen was unassertive, she kept a daily record of such situations, noting the people involved, the nature of their interaction, and her perception of the situation, including what she thought would happen if she did behave assertively.

Once they had identified typical problem situations, Karen and her therapist role-played several incidents as a way of introducing Karen to more appropriate responses. At first, the therapist played Karen's part and modeled appropriate behaviors for her. They then switched roles so that Karen could practice these new responses. After each role-playing sequence, the therapist provided Karen with feedback about the effectiveness of her behavior.

They also discussed some of Karen's irrational fears associated with assertion. These thoughts generally centered on her implicit belief that everyone should love her and that if she stood up for her own rights people would reject her. In many situations, these irrational beliefs were inhibiting the expression of assertive behaviors.

After assertion training had effected some positive results, the therapist began teaching Karen more effective child management skills. She was taught to ignore her daughters when they were quarreling and to reinforce them for playing together appropriately. Her efforts were initially channeled toward the behaviors that could be changed easily. The most difficult problems, such as getting the children to stop fighting at mealtimes, were left until Karen had mastered some of the general principles of child management.

In addition to these skill-training programs, the therapist also discussed with Karen her concerns about religion. It was clear that the church was still very important to her and that she experienced considerable guilt and anxiety over her failure to attend services regularly. The fact that her children were not involved in church activities also troubled Karen. She worried that if any harm came to one of them, God would not protect them. Therefore, Karen was encouraged to visit several priests at churches in her area in an effort to find one who held more conservative views compatible with her own.

Eventually Karen found an older priest at a church somewhat distant from her neighborhood who still adhered to several of the traditional rituals she had learned as a child. Karen felt much more comfortable with this priest than she did with the very liberal pastor who was in charge of the church in her immediate neighborhood. Within weeks she was once again attending church regularly with her four children.

The combination of assertion training, parent education, and a renewed interest in church activities led to an improvement in Karen's mood. After three months of treatment, she reported an increased sense of self-confidence and an improvement in her family life. There was also some reduction in her anxiety. She continued to observe her numbers rituals, but they were somewhat less frequent and, when she did fail to perform the counting routines, she was not as panic-stricken as she had been at the beginning of treatment.

At this point, the rituals were addressed directly through the combined use of flooding and response prevention. The therapist believed that this type of prolonged intense exposure to the anxiety-provoking situation without performing her rituals would lead to a reduction in Karen's anxiety.

Treatment was terminated after twenty sessions. Karen was no longer depressed and the frequency of her compulsive counting rituals had declined. The children were better behaved at home, and she had plans to institute still further changes in this regard. Her relationship with Tony was somewhat improved. Although he had become quite upset initially when Karen began to assert herself, he became more cooperative when he saw an improvement in her adjustment. Karen's reduced anxiety also led to some initial improvements in their sexual relationship, although this problem was not addressed directly in treatment. These improvements were still evident at a follow-up interview six months after termination.

DISCUSSION

Karen's upbringing in a strict, puritanical family setting, as well as her having been anxious as a child, is typical of OCD patients (Kringlen, 1970). Karen's family background is also consistent with the literature on OCD (e.g., Rasmussen & Tsuang, 1986). There is a relatively high incidence of psychological problems—particularly obsessional traits, anxious personalities, and other mood disturbances—among the biological relatives of obsessive-compulsive patients. In Karen's case, her mother's rigid, moralistic behavior may have had an important influence on the development of later symptoms. Karen's mother provided a very salient model for her daughter's subsequent compulsive behavior. She also reinforced early tendencies toward such response patterns.

Although the therapist in this case did not explicitly incorporate psychoanalytic techniques, the psychoanalytic explanation of OCD is compatible with Karen's situation. Her principal symptoms were compulsive rituals intended to protect her children from harm. But her feelings about her children were, in fact, ambivalent. It would not be unreasonable to assume that she was most often very angry with them, perhaps so much so that she might consider doing them physical harm. Of course, this impulse would be very anxiety provoking to the ego, which would convert it to its opposite form. Thus, instead of injuring the children, she would spend a good deal of her time every day performing irrational responses aimed at *protecting* them.

Behavioral theorists would view Karen's problems in a different fashion. Within this general model, two factors would be given primary consideration. Both involve the principle of negative reinforcement, which states that the probability of a response is increased if it leads to the termination of an aversive stimulus. Consider, for example, the net effect of Karen's rituals. Their performance ensured that she would be away from her home for extended periods of time. If she went to her neighbor's house for coffee, she would be gone for at least two hours before she could consume enough cups of coffee and smoke enough cigarettes to satisfy the rituals. Grocery shopping, which she did by herself, had also turned into a long, complicated process. Given that being at home with her family was mostly an aversive experience for Karen, her rituals might be seen as an operant response that was being maintained by negative reinforcement. The reduction in anxiety brought about by engaging in the compulsion was immediately reinforcing.

Some elements of the behavioral view were incorporated into Karen's treatment. In particular, by teaching her to be more assertive and to manage her children more effectively, the therapist was able to make her home life less aversive. She began to experience pleasurable interactions with her children and her husband. Thus one important source of negative reinforcement for her rituals was removed.

The cognitive perspective is also helpful in analyzing Karen's case. She clearly suffered as a result of irrational beliefs. As she gained more of an understanding of these beliefs and returned to the religious practices that the counting rituals were at least in part an effort to replace, she began to feel better and more in control of her environment.

Unfortunately, Karen's case is typical of OCD patients in that her treatment achieved only partial success. Regardless of treatment modality, OCD patients are seldom cured. While the improvement that many achieve in a variety of interventions can be significant, obsessive-compulsive tendencies usually persist to some degree, albeit under greater control and with less obtrusiveness in the conduct of their lives (White & Cole, 1990).

Visual Summary for Chapter 6:

Anxiety Disorders

Perspectives on the Causes of Anxiety Disorders

Psychodynamic ····▸ Anxiety disorders result from unconscious conflict between the id and the ego. For example, phobias are a defense against the anxiety produced by repressed id impulses and then displaced onto a situation or object symbolically connected to the impulses, whereas obsessive-compulsive disorder symptoms represent the oscillation of dominance in conflicts between the id (obsessions) and ego defense mechanisms (compulsions).

Behavioral ····▸ Anxiety-related behaviors are learned through classical conditioning, modeling, or operant conditioning. For instance, phobias or posttraumatic stress disorder symptoms can originate via classical conditioning (such that previously non-feared stimuli become feared because they co-occur with painful or frightening stimuli) and then be maintained by negative reinforcement of avoidance behavior. Animal research also supports the possibility that phobias can be learned by observing fearful behavior of others.

Cognitive ····▸ Anxiety disorders stem from exaggerated perceptions that situations are dangerous and that one's resources for controlling or coping with them are inadequate. The various disorders differ mainly according to what the dangerous consequence is perceived to be (e.g., humiliation in social phobia, death or nervous breakdown in panic disorder).

Biological ····▸ A predisposition to the anxiety disorders is to some degree genetically transmitted. Overactivation of the noradrenergic systems underlies panic, while generalized anxiety might be understandable in terms of inhibition of the gamma-aminobutyric acid system. Serotonin levels appear to be directly associated with obsessive-compulsive disorder symptoms.

Perspectives on the Treatment of Anxiety Disorders

Psychodynamic · · · ▶ *Treatment aims to lift repression and uncover the unconscious conflicts responsible for anxiety. In dealing with specific phobias and obsessive-compulsive disorder, some dynamic therapists believe that the usual procedures for achieving such goals need to be supplemented with more active encouragement to confront what is feared.*

Behavioral · · · ▶ *The core principle is the need for exposure to what is feared. This can be done in imagination (as in systematic desensitization) or in real life. The stimuli to which the patient is exposed can be objects (e.g., a dog, dirt), memories (e.g., of a trauma), or sensations (e.g., dizziness).*

Cognitive · · · ▶ *To supplement behavioral exposure methods, interview methods are used in helping patients reattribute (e.g., "I am short of breath because I have been hyperventilating, not because I am having a heart attack") or reappraise (e.g., "Just because something bad might happen does not mean it will happen") whatever they perceive to be dangerous and unmanageable.*

Biological · · · ▶ *Medications (e.g., benzodiazepines for panic disorder, clomipramine for obsessive-compulsive disorder) are often beneficial. Appropriate caution must be utilized in managing withdrawal symptoms and in preventing long-term dependence by teaching other skills for coping with anxiety once medication is discontinued.*

Chapter 7

Dissociative and Somatoform Disorders

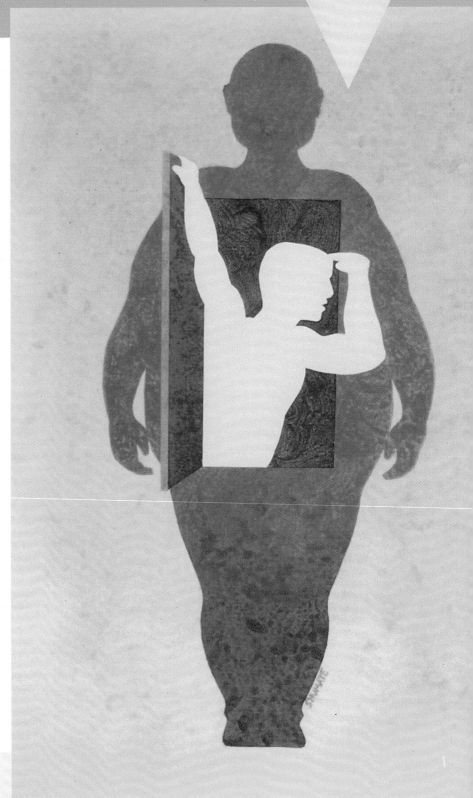

The Case of Paula Stewart ◀

Paula Stewart was thirty-eight years old, divorced, and the mother of an eighteen-year-old son and a fifteen-year old daughter. She was about ninety pounds overweight, but in other ways her appearance was unremarkable. For the past five years, she had been taking courses at the university and working part-time at a variety of secretarial positions on campus. She and her daughter lived together in a small, rural community located about twenty miles from the university—the same town in which Paula had been born. Her son had moved away from home and joined the marines after dropping out of high school. Paula's mother and father still lived in their home just down the street from Paula's.

The instructor in Paula's human sexuality course suggested that she talk to a psychologist. Although Paula was a good student, her behavior in class had been rather odd sometimes and was a cause for concern. She had earned A's on the first two exams, but she failed to appear for the third. When the instructor asked her where she had been, Paula said with apparent sincerity that she couldn't recall. Finally, she had handed in an essay assignment that described in rather vague, but sufficiently believable, terms the abusive, incestuous relationship that her father had forced on her from the age of five until well after she was married and had had her first child. All this led her professor to believe that Paula needed help. Fortunately, she agreed and made an appointment to talk to Dr. Harpin, a clinical psychologist at the student health center.

Over a series of sessions, Dr. Harpin noticed that Paula's behavior was often erratic. Her moods shifted quickly from anger and irritability to severe depression. When she was depressed, her movements became agitated and she experienced difficulty sleeping. She threatened suicide frequently, and had on several occasions made some attempts to harm herself. In addition, Paula often complained of severe headaches, dizziness, and breathing problems.

It also seemed that Paula abused alcohol, although the circumstances of abuse were not clear. This situation was clearly a source of distress and considerable confusion for her. She reported finding empty beer cans and whiskey bottles in the backseat of her car, but she denied drinking alcoholic beverages of any kind. Once every two or three weeks, she would wake up in the morning with terrible headaches as though she were hungover. Dr. Harpin attributed her confusion and other memory problems to her alcohol consumption.

Paula's relationships with other people were unpredictable. She would explode with little provocation and often argued that no one understood how serious her problems were. On occasion, she threatened to kill other people, including her mother and an older man, Cal, who lived nearby.

Paula's relationship with Cal was puzzling to both of them. They had known each other since she was an adolescent. Although he was fifteen years older than she and had been married to another woman for more than twenty years, he had persistently shown a romantic interest in Paula. He frequently came to her house saying that she had called. More often than not, this made Paula furious. At other times, however, she insisted that he was the only person who understood and cared for her.

Throughout the first year of treatment, Paula's memory problems became increasingly severe. The notes she wrote during classes were often incomplete, as though she had suddenly stopped listening in the middle of a lecture. She sometimes complained that she lost parts of days. On one occasion, for example, she told Dr. Harpin that she had gone home with a severe headache in the middle of the afternoon, then couldn't remember anything until she awakened the following morning.

Dr. Harpin decided to use hypnosis in an attempt to explore the frequent gaps in Paula's memory. Paula was easily hypnotized, but the hypnosis didn't help with the memory problem. On waking from a trance, Paula complained of a splitting headache. Then she placed her hands tightly over her eyes and slowly rubbed her face for a minute or two. Lowering her hands slightly so that she could peer over them while still covering her mouth and nose, she gazed slowly about the room as though she were lost. Dr. Harpin was puzzled. "Do you know where you are?" he asked. She said no. He asked if she knew who he was. Rather than provide a quick answer, she glanced around the room. She noticed his professional license hanging on the wall, read his name, and finally replied, "Yes. You're Dr. Harpin, the one who's working with Paula." This switch to the use of the third person struck Dr. Harpin as very odd and roused further curiosity about her state of mind.

"How do you feel?"

"Okay."

"Do you still have a headache?"

"No. *I* don't have a headache."

The way she emphasized the word *I* was unusual, so Dr. Harpin said, "You make it sound like somebody else has a headache." He was completely unprepared for her response.

"Yes. Paula does."

Over the course of the next few sessions, Dr. Harpin became acquainted with Sherry, an alter personality who had emerged at the time of a brutal rape.

Paula had frequently mentioned a day when she was fifteen years old. She couldn't remember the details, but it was clearly a source of considerable distress for her and seemed to involve her father and a neighbor, Henry. Dr. Harpin asked Paula to describe what she could remember about the day: where they were living at the time, what time of year it was, who was home, and so on. Paula filled in the details slowly and as best she could. Her father had grabbed her, hit her across the face, and dragged her toward the bedroom. No matter how hard she tried, she couldn't remember anything else. Paula said that she was getting a headache. Dr. Harpin suggested that she lean back in the chair and breathe slowly. She paused for a moment and closed her eyes. In a few moments, she opened her eyes and said, "She can't remember. She wasn't there. I was!" Sherry was back.

Paula's appearance had changed suddenly. She had been very tense, clutching the arms of the chair and sitting upright. She also had had an annoying, hacking cough. Now she eased down in the chair, folded her arms, and crossed her legs in front of her. The cough was gone. Sherry explained why Paula couldn't remember the incident with her father. As Sherry put it, when Paula was dragged into the bedroom, she simply decided to take off, leaving Sherry to experience the pain and humiliation of the ensuing rape.

Dr. Harpin interpreted this as meaning that Paula had experienced a dissociative episode. The incident was so extremely traumatic that she had completely separated the experience and its memory from the rest of her consciousness.

Eventually other personalities emerged. In addition to Sherry, who was in her thirties, there was Janet, who was fifteen and Caroline, who was five and remained devastated by the loss of a beloved stuffed dog given her by her grandfather and taken away by her parents as punishment.

Paula was not aware of the other personalities, but Sherry and Janet were aware of her and of Caroline. To begin to help Paula understand the problems that she faced, Dr. Harpin asked her to read *Sybil*. She reacted with interest and disbelief. She was still completely unable to remember those times when she spoke as if she were Sherry, Janet, or Caroline.

Dr. Harpin also used videotape to help Paula understand the problem. With her consent, he recorded her behavior during a sequence of three therapy sessions. She alternated among the various personalities several times during the course of these tapes. Paula was then asked to view the tapes and discuss her reactions to her own behavior. Again, she was surprised, interested, and puzzled, showing no signs of previous awareness of this behavior. She would often ask, "Did *I* say that?" or "Who am I? *What* am I?"

The disruption of consciousness experienced by Paula is characteristic of dissociative disorders. In this chapter we examine dissociative disorders as well as somatoform disorders, which create physical disabilities or cause physical pain. We will describe the symptoms of these disorders and then discuss their causes and treatment, focusing in more depth on those disorders about which more is known.

▶ *Dissociative Disorders*

In **dissociative disorders**, the individual experiences disruptions of consciousness, memory, or identity. We will address four dissociative disorders—dissociative amnesia, dissociative fugue, depersonalization disorder, and dissociative identity disorder, better known as multiple personality disorder. People with these disorders may be unable to recall important personal events or may temporarily forget their identity or even, as in the case of Paula, assume a new identity. In this section, we progress from the more specific, less complex dissociative disorders to the difficult and complicated problem posed by those, like Paula, whose identity has fragmented.

Dissociative Amnesia

A person with **dissociative amnesia** is suddenly unable to recall important personal information, usually after some stressful event such as witnessing the death of a loved one. The loss of memory is too extensive to be explained by ordinary forgetfulness. Most often the memory loss is for all events during a limited period of time following a traumatic experience. Far less frequently, the amnesia is for only selected events during a period of distress, or it is total, covering the person's entire life. During the period of amnesia, the person's behavior is otherwise unremarkable, except that the memory loss may bring some disorientation and aimless wandering. In the rare case of total amnesia, the patient does not recognize relatives and friends, but retains the ability to talk, read, and reason and perhaps also retains talents and previously acquired knowledge of the world and how to function in it. The amnesic episode may last several hours or as long as several years. It usually disappears as suddenly as it came on, with complete recovery and only a small chance of recurrence.

Memory loss is also common in many organic brain disorders as well as in substance abuse. But dissociative amnesia can be fairly easily distinguished from these other disorders. In degenerative brain disorders memory fails slowly over time. Memory loss following a brain injury (e.g., after an automobile accident) or substance abuse can be easily linked to the accident or the substance being abused.

Dissociative Fugue

If a person not only becomes totally amnesic but suddenly moves away from home and work and assumes a new identity, the diagnosis of **dissociative fugue** is made. Sometimes the assumption of the new identity can be quite elaborate, with the person taking on a new name, new home, new job, and even a new set of personality characteristics. The individual may succeed in establishing a fairly complex social life, all without questioning the inability to remember the past. More often, however, the new life does not develop to this extent, and the fugue consists for the most part of limited, but apparently purposeful, travel, during which social contacts are minimal or absent. (The word *fugue* comes from the Latin *fugere*, "to flee.") Fugues typically occur after a person has experienced

dissociative disorders Disorders in which the normal integration of consciousness, memory, or identity is suddenly altered; *dissociative amnesia, dissociative fugue, depersonalization disorder*, and *dissociative identity disorder*.

dissociative amnesia A *dissociative disorder* in which the person suddenly becomes unable to recall important personal information to an extent that cannot be explained by ordinary forgetfulness.

In the film Regarding Henry *Harrison Ford played the role of a man who experienced amnesia as a result of brain trauma suffered when he was shot in the head. In this scene he was still unable to remember his family members.*

dissociative fugue A *dissociative disorder* in which the person forgets important personal information and assumes a new identity, moving to a new location unexpectedly.

A person in a dissociative fugue moves away from home and work and assumes a new identity, unable to remember her or his past life. This condition usually occurs in the wake of severe stress.

some severe stress, such as having a major fight with a spouse, losing a job, or suffering through a natural disaster. Recovery, though varying in the time it takes, is usually complete. The person does not remember what took place during the fugue.

The nature of the patient's behavior in the fugue state may differ across cultures. *Pibloktoq*, for example, is a syndrome described among native peoples of the Arctic, in which the affected person suddenly shows a drastic increase in activity level, seems to be in a trance, and literally runs until exhaustion and sleep set in. As in other dissociative fugue states, the person does not remember what happened during the episode.

Depersonalization Disorder

depersonalization disorder A *dissociative disorder* in which the individual feels unreal and estranged from the self and surroundings enough to disrupt functioning. People with this disorder may feel that their extremities have changed in size or that they are watching themselves from a distance.

Depersonalization disorder involves a disruptive change in the person's perception or experience of the self. Memory is not disturbed as in the other dissociative disorders, but people lose their sense of self. They may have the impression that they are outside their bodies, viewing themselves from a distance or watching themselves in a movie. Sometimes they believe that the size of parts of their body has changed. They may feel mechanical, as though they are robots, or they may move as though in a dream, in a world that has lost its reality for them.

An *episode* of depersonalization is very common, affecting about half of all people at some point in their lives. Often the episode occurs after severe stress, such as being in an accident or in a similarly dangerous situation. Depersonalization disorder is distinguished from these normal experiences in that people with this diagnosis experience persistent or recurrent episodes of depersonalization that are severe enough to cause substantial distress or impairments in functioning.

Dissociative Identity Disorder (Multiple Personality Disorder)

Consider what it would be like to have multiple personalities, as did Paula, described in the chapter-opening case. People might tell you about things you did that seem out of character, events of which you have no memory. How could you explain these events? We all have days when we are not quite ourselves. This is assumed to be quite normal and is *not* what is meant by multiple personality.

According to DSM-IV, a proper diagnosis of **dissociative identity disorder (DID)** requires that a person have at least two separate ego states, or alters—different modes of being, feeling, and acting that exist independently of each other and come forth and are in control at different times. (We shall retain the traditional term **multiple personality disorder (MPD)** because it highlights the core feature of the disorder.) Gaps in memory are also common and are produced because at least one alter has no contact with the other. The existence of different alters must be chronic and severe (causing considerable disruption in the person's life); it cannot be a temporary change resulting from drug use, for example.

Each alter has its own behavior patterns, memories, and relationships. Each alter determines the nature and acts of the individual when it is in command. Usually the personalities are quite different, perhaps even opposites of one another. They may have different handedness, wear glasses with different prescriptions, and be allergic to different substances. The original and subordinate alters are all aware of lost periods of time, and the voices of the other alters may sometimes echo into their consciousness, even though they do not know to whom these voices belong. When an individual has more than two alters, each may be aware of the others to some extent, as Sherry was aware of Paula in our case.

Multiple personality disorder usually begins in early childhood, but it is rarely diagnosed until adolescence. It is more chronic and serious than other dissociative disorders, and recovery may be less complete. It is much more common in women than in men, perhaps because sexual abuse is so frequently a precondition for it, as we see shortly. The presence of other diagnoses—in particular, depression, borderline personality disorder, and somatization disorder—is frequent (Ross et al., 1990). In addition, MPD is commonly accompanied by headaches, substance abuse, phobias, suicidal ideas, and self-abusive behavior.

Cases of multiple personality are sometimes mislabeled as schizophrenic reactions in the popular press. Discussed in greater detail in Chapter 9, schizophrenia derives part of its name from the Greek root *schizo*, which means splitting away from. A split of the personality, wherein two or more fairly separate and coherent systems of being exist in the same person, the essence of MPD, is completely different from the severe disturbances in cognition (e.g., delusions), perception (e.g., hallucinations), and behavior that characterize schizophrenia.

Although formally recognized and included in the official diagnostic manual, the existence of MPD contradicts the basic belief that each body is inhabited by only one person. The idea that there could be, in effect, someone else in charge of one's actions at a given time also calls into question the nature of personal identity and personal responsibility. Should I, for instance, be held responsible for crimes committed by my body when it was in the control of a different alter? These issues are discussed in the Legal, Ethical, and Social Issues box.

Fluctuations in the Incidence of MPD

The incidence of MPD has fluctuated throughout history. The earliest mention of this disorder occurred in the nineteenth century. A review of the literature located a total of seventy-seven cases, most of them reported between 1890 and 1920 (Sutcliffe & Jones, 1962). After that period reports of MPD declined until the 1970s, when they increased substantially. One estimate is that more than six thousand cases of MPD were diagnosed during the 1980s (Ross, Norton, & Wozney, 1989).

dissociative identity disorder (DID) A *dissociative disorder* in which two or more fairly distinct and separate personalities (called alters) are present within the same individual, each with its own memories, relationships, and behavior patterns and only one of which is dominant at any given time. Formerly called *multiple personality disorder (MPD)*.

multiple personality disorder (MPD) See *dissociative identity disorder (DID)*.

Dissociative Identity Disorder (Multiple Personality Disorder) and the Insanity Defense

The **insanity defense** is the legal argument that a defendant should not be held responsible for an illegal act if his or her conduct is attributable to mental illness that interferes with rationality or that results in some other excusing circumstance, such as not knowing right from wrong. A staggering amount of material has been written on the insanity defense, even though it is pleaded in only about 2% of all cases that reach trial and is rarely successful (Steadman, 1979). For a person to be found not guilty by reason of insanity (NGRI) he or she must be so impaired as to be unable to exercise free will and thus to be responsible for his or her actions. Such impairment is difficult to prove.

The grounds accepted for establishing insanity defenses have changed many times. In the past decade there has been a new effort in the United States to clarify the legal defense of insanity. This effort was fueled by the controversy created by the NGRI verdict in the highly publicized trial of John Hinckley Jr. for attempted assassination of President Ronald Reagan. The judge who presided over the trial received a flood of mail. People were outraged that a would-be assassin of a U.S. president had not been held criminally responsible and had only been committed to an indefinite stay in a mental hospital until he was deemed mentally healthy enough for release.

Because of the publicity of the trial and the public outrage at the NGRI verdict, the insanity defense became a target of criticism. As a consequence of political pressures to get tough on criminals, Congress enacted in October 1984 the Insanity Defense Reform Act, addressing the insanity defense for the first time. This new law, which has been adopted in all federal courts (though not by every state), contains several provisions.

▶ The defendant must be found unable to appreciate the wrongfulness of his or her conduct.
▶ The mental disorder must be "severe." This has the effect of excluding insanity defenses on the bases of nonpsychotic disorders, such as antisocial personality disorder.
▶ Defenses relying on "diminished capacity" or "diminished responsibility," based on such mitigating circumstances as extreme passion or "temporary insanity," were ruled as inadmissible.

---

insanity defense   The legal argument that a defendant should not be held responsible for an illegal act if the conduct is attributable to mental illness.

Successful use of the insanity defense in the trial of John Hinckley, Jr., for attempting to assassinate U.S. President Ronald Reagan, prompted criticism of laws regarding the insanity defense and ultimately a revision of such laws.

▶ The burden of proof rests with the defense rather than with the prosecution. That is, rather than the prosecution's having to prove that the defendant was sane beyond a reasonable doubt at the time of the crime (the most stringent criterion, consistent with the constitutional requirement that people are considered innocent until proven guilty), the defense must prove that the defendant was not sane and must do so with "clear and convincing evidence" (a less stringent but still demanding standard of proof, designed to make it more difficult to relieve a defendant of moral and legal responsibility).
▶ If the person judged NGRI is later found to have recovered from mental illness, then instead of allowing release from the prison hospital, the period of incarceration can be extended to the maximum allowable for the actual crime.

As you read these criteria, you may have noted that multiple personality disorder is one of the few DSM diagnoses that could meet the criteria of the 1984 Insanity Defense Reform Act. In effect, a person suffering from MPD (now known as dissociative identity disorder) may not have been himself or herself at the time of the criminal act, but may have been an alter personality instead. However, the symptoms of MPD are also easier to feign than, say, those of schizophrenia (discussed in Chapter 9), another diagnosis that might yield an NGRI verdict. In addition, films, television shows, and books such as *Sybil* that have popularized MPD provide criminals with scripts for acting out their own self-serving versions of these stories. The nature of MPD makes it an attractive plea for criminals facing the death sentence or life in prison.

A well-known example involves the case of Kenneth Bianchi, also known as the Hillside Strangler. Several experienced clinicians interviewed Bianchi after he was arrested. With the aid of hypnosis, they discovered an alternate personality, Steve, who proudly claimed responsibility for several brutal rape-murders. The prosecution called Martin Orne, a hypnosis expert from the University of Pennsylvania, as an expert witness to examine Bianchi. Orne raised serious questions about the case. He indicated that the defendant was probably faking hypnosis during the interviews, and he demonstrated that Bianchi's symptoms changed dramatically as a result of subtle suggestions (Orne, Dinges, & Orne, 1984). He proposed that the defendant was faking symptoms of multiple personality in an attempt to avoid the death penalty. The court found Orne's skepticism persuasive, and Bianchi was eventually convicted of murder.

These circumstances are clearly rather extreme. Very few patients have such an obvious motive for faking a psychological disorder. The Bianchi case should not be taken to mean that all patients who exhibit signs of multiple personality are faking. Nevertheless, it does indicate that therapists should be cautious in evaluating the evidence for any diagnostic decision, particularly when the disorder is as difficult to define and evaluate as is multiple personality.

Other circumstances may produce a mistaken MPD diagnosis as well. A related hypothesis holds that multiple personality disorder can be a product of the therapist's influence on the client (Spanos, 1994). This is not to say that the patient is faking the disorder, but rather that patients respond to cues that are provided during the course of treatment (e.g., Sarbin & Coe, 1979). Clinicians have frequently noted, for example, that patients with multiple personality disorder are easily hypnotized and that the alternate personalities are often "discovered" during hypnosis. According to this view, some therapists may purposefully or inadvertently provide their patients with information and sugges-

Ken Bianchi, the Hillside Strangler, attempted an insanity defense for his serial killings but the court decided that he had merely tried to fake a multiple personality.

tions about multiple personality, subtly and unconsciously encourage them to behave in ways that are consistent with these expectations, and reward them with extra attention and care when they adopt the role. It is interesting to note in this regard that, whereas most clinicians work an entire career without seeing a single case of multiple personality, a small number of therapists each claim to have treated as many as fifty multiple personality patients (e.g., Allison, 1984).

The possibility that MPD could be faked or be an inadvertent product of therapists' suggestions is important from a scientific point of view. But it also has practical implications, particularly with respect to the legal system. For instance, if MPD is faked, then it cannot reasonably be used to excuse criminal behavior. Hence, the insanity defense failed in the Hillside Strangler trial of Ken Bianchi.

What has caused this apparent increase in the diagnosis of MPD? There are no sound epidemiological studies tracking the incidence of MPD over time, so it is not possible to tell whether MPD is actually becoming more common.

At least two alternative explanations could account for the increase in the number of reported cases even if there were no real increase in MPD. First, diagnostic practices may have changed. For example, publication of *Sybil*, which presented a dramatic case of MPD with sixteen personalities, attracted a great deal of attention and might have influenced clinicians to be more alert to the possibility of MPD when a patient showed otherwise puzzling symptoms.

A second explanation is that clinicians have always seen a similar number of cases of MPD but chose to report them only when interest in and acceptance of MPD seemed high. Such conduct would amount to a sort of bandwagon effect. Raising this possibility need not be seen as critical of clinicians; it just means that they are human and therefore sensitive to what others think. The current widespread publicity about MPD serves to make it a more legitimate, accepted diagnosis. To better appreciate the situation, suppose that you are a therapist treating a patient whom you sincerely believe to be an extraterrestrial seeking help in coping with the stress of living far from the home planet. You might not wish to write a report of the case (for an academic journal, at any rate). But in fifty years, if it has been established that large numbers of extraterrestrials are living on Earth, you might be viewed as having missed a valuable opportunity to report an important observation. In other words, the line between "new, fascinating" and "too unlikely to be believable" is drawn differently in different eras and in different cultures.

To Recap

Dissociative disorders are disruptions of consciousness, memory, or identity. An inability to recall important personal information, usually after some traumatic experience, is diagnosed as dissociative amnesia. In dissociative fugue, the person moves away from his or her home, assumes a new identity, and is amnesic for his or her previous life. In depersonalization disorder, the person's perception of the self is altered; he or she may have the experience of being outside the body or believe that the size of body parts has changed. The person with multiple personality disorder (MPD) [labeled dissociative identity disorder in DSM-IV] has two or more distinct and fully developed personalities, each with unique memories, behavior patterns, and relationships. MPD is usually associated with severe pathology. Reports of MPD have become more frequent in recent years, but it is unknown whether this situation reflects a real increase in incidence or simply an increase in reporting the disorder.

Perspectives on the Causes and Treatment of Dissociative Disorders

Psychodynamic Perspectives

Psychoanalytic theory views dissociative disorders as the result of massive repression, usually of unacceptable sexual wishes or of sexual or physical abuse. For example, patients may experience depersonalization because they view a certain sexual desire as unacceptable and so repress normal physical sensation. Dissociative disorders provide perhaps the best evidence available for the concept of repression. In three—amnesia, fugue, and multiple personality—people behave in ways that indicate that they have forgotten (repressed) earlier parts of their lives. Given that they may at the same time be unaware of having forgotten something, the hypothesis that they have repressed massive portions of their lives is a compelling one.

Severe trauma in childhood is regarded as a major cause of dissociative disorders.

Hypnosis is used as a treatment for dissociative disorders by trying to restore memory for the traumatic event that led to the dissociation.

Psychoanalytic treatment is chosen more often for dissociative disorders than for other psychological problems. The goal of therapy is clearly to lift repressions and integrate the unacceptable experiences. Using free association and often hypnosis, psychodynamic therapists encourage patients to reencounter the frightening, painful, and unacceptable thoughts and memories and to acknowledge them as part of themselves rather than as outside themselves. This reintegration can take a great deal of time, particularly in cases of multiple personality disorder, when current events or the emergence of another alter personality can upset any integration the patient has achieved. Since these patients have exerted a good deal of effort to protect themselves from these memories, just getting the forbidden material to surface can be extremely difficult and time-consuming. Hypnosis can help in some cases, but relapse is fairly common.

Biological Perspectives

Some physicians have used sodium amobarbital, "truth serum", to induce a hypnotic state. They assume that this state will bring forth painful, repressed memories and hence remove the need for the dissociative disorder. Several dramatic case studies in the clinical literature suggest that barbiturates, such as sodium amobarbital, can be helpful. However, there is little controlled research, and what exists is not encouraging. One comparison of sodium amobarbital and a placebo for amnesic patients showed no significant differences in the amount of new information recalled (Dysken, 1979).

Vulnerability-Stress Perspectives

Cases of multiple personality nearly always involve severe childhood traumas. For example, the results from a survey of therapists who work with multiple personalities indicated that 80% of their clients had suffered physical abuse in childhood and that almost 70% had been subjected to incest (Putnam, Post, & Guroff, 1983). Other estimates of physical and sexual abuse in childhood are even higher (Ross et al., 1990). Multiple personalities also appear to be very high in hypnotizability; that is, they can be more readily hypnotized than the average person (Bliss, 1983). For some individuals prone to lose themselves in fantasy, a highly traumatic and painful experience can precipitate creation of a fantasy self. This fantasy becomes very real to these people, because it protects them from such frightening and painful events.

General Approaches to Treatment of Multiple Personality Disorder

There is little controlled research on treatment of MPD from any of the perspectives just described, but several general principles or strategies are endorsed by most therapists with experience in this area (e.g., C. A. Ross, 1989).

- ▷ The goal is integration of the several personalities.
- ▷ Each alter has to be helped to understand that he or she is part of one person.
- ▷ All alters should be treated with fairness and empathy.
- ▷ The therapist should encourage empathy and cooperation among personalities.
- ▷ Gentleness and supportiveness are called for out of consideration for the childhood trauma that probably gave rise to the splits.

The general goal of any approach to MPD can be seen as trying to convince the person that forgetting or splitting into different personalities is no longer necessary to deal with traumatic events. In addition, on the assumption that MPD and the other dissociative disorders are in some measure an escape response to high levels of stress, teaching the patient to cope better with challenges can enhance treatment. The greater the number of personalities, the longer the treatment is likely to take (Putnam, Guroff, Silberman, Barban, & Post, 1986). In general, treatment is long term, typically lasting about two years and more than five hundred hours per patient. In a large sample (171 cases) of MPD patients treated by, or at least known to, one experienced therapist, Richard Kluft, about two-thirds were judged to have achieved integration of the personalities for at least three months and about one-third for at least two and a half years (Kluft, 1984).

To Recap

The psychodynamic explanation for dissociative disorders is that they arise from massive repression of unacceptable sexual desires or physical or sexual abuse. Treatment aims to overcome repression, sometimes by a method of encouraging the patient to retell his or her life story in detail, with free association to events preceding any large gaps in memory. Hypnosis may also be used. Biological approaches call for "truth serum" to override repression, but controlled studies have not supported the utility of this method. A vulnerability-stress model holds that MPD results from extreme trauma (e.g., sexual abuse) inflicted on a highly hypnotizable individual, who in effect uses self-hypnosis to cope with the trauma. Although research on treatment of MPD is sparse, clinical observations suggest that long-term psychotherapy should aim to integrate the personalities.

▶ The Case of Paula Stewart Revisited

Social History

Paula grew up in a small rural community. She had one older brother. Both parents were strict disciplinarians. They belonged to a fundamentalist Baptist church and were strongly opposed to drinking alcohol, playing cards, and dancing. When Paula was six years old, her father bought a small gasoline station in town. The Stewart family left their farm, and Paula was separated from a beloved grandfather, who was able to visit only on weekends.

Paula's father was a shy, withdrawn, unaffectionate man. For the first few years of her life, he ignored her completely. She desperately wanted his attention, but he was not interested. Then, when she was five years old, he suddenly began to demonstrate physical affection. He hugged and kissed her roughly, and when no one else was around, he fondled her genitals. Paula didn't know how to respond. His touches weren't pleasant or enjoyable, but she accepted whatever affection he was willing to provide.

When she was eleven, Mr. Stewart caught Paula making out with an adolescent boy. That evening, Mr. Stewart came to Paula's room and explained harshly that if she needed to be loved, he would be the source of her affection. Then he forced her to have intercourse with him.

When Paula was fifteen, their sexual encounters started to become violent. The pretense of affection and love was gone; her father wanted to hurt her. In one incident, which Paula and Dr. Harpin discussed frequently, her father dragged her into his bedroom by her hair and tied her to the bed. After slapping her repeatedly, he forced her to have intercourse with him while a neighbor, Henry, watched. Then Henry raped her. The incest and physical abuse continued until she was twenty years old.

Paula's mother often punished her by putting her hands in scalding water or locking her in a dark closet for hours on end. Mrs. Stewart was not a sympathetic listener and did not realize—or seem to care—that her husband was abusing Paula sexually. If she did know, she may have been afraid to intervene.

Perhaps in an effort to tear herself away from this abusive family, Paula pursued relationships with other men at an early age. Many of these men were older than she, including teachers and neighbors. The longest relationship of this sort was with Cal, the owner of a small construction business.

Paula met her husband, Roger, shortly after moving to Pittsburgh. He was in the air force and still married to another woman when he and Paula began having an affair. When Paula became pregnant, Roger agreed to get a divorce, but he couldn't marry her until the divorce became final. Then he was transferred to Japan. Paula moved back to live with her parents until the baby was born. Her sister-in-law provided some support during her pregnancy, but her mother was primarily interested in criticizing Paula for having a child out of wedlock. Several weeks after her son was born, Paula's father began to abuse her again. She also resumed her affair with Cal.

Two years later, Roger returned from Japan to stay with Paula and her parents during a forty-five-day leave. It was a momentous visit; they were married, and Paula became pregnant again. When his leave was over, Roger persuaded Paula to bring the children and move with him to an air force base in California where he was to receive further training before being reassigned to West Germany. One week after arriving in California, Paula decided that she could not stay married to Roger and did not want to leave the country. She returned home to live with her parents.

CONCEPTUALIZATION AND TREATMENT

Dr. Harpin's initial diagnostic impression, before the emergence of the alternate personalities, was that Paula suffered from both dysthymia and borderline personality disorder. Throughout the first year of treatment, he focused primarily on crisis management. Crises included numerous suicidal threats, fights with her mother and daughter, confusion and anger over her relationship—or lack of a relationship—with Cal, difficulties in her schoolwork and with her professors, and a variety of incidents involving her employers. When problems of this sort were not pressing, Paula usually wanted to talk about how her father had abused her. Her focus was on both the anger and the guilt that she felt about these incidents. She wondered whether in some way she hadn't encouraged his sexual advances.

After the appearance of the alternate personalities, it became clear that Paula was experiencing a genuine disruption of consciousness that was brought on by stress. Faced with an extremely threatening or unpleasant circumstance, Paula would often dissociate, repressing her awareness of that event. This pattern could be traced to the violent abuse received from her father during adolescence. By her own description, when these events began, she would usually "leave" the situation and Sherry would have to face her father. Over time, the extent of this fragmentation of conscious experience became more severe, and Paula's control over changes in her patterns of awareness decreased.

Dr. Harpin invited Paula to recall and explore these previous traumatic experiences that seemed to be responsible for particular splits in her consciousness. He especially encouraged her to remember the most salient of these episodes, her rape by her father and the neighbor Henry. The existence of Sherry suggested that the split could be traced to about this time, and the rape was an incident mentioned repeatedly by Sherry. Unfortunately, review of this memory did not seem to be useful. The episode continued to cause Paula extreme distress every time it was discussed, and there was no improvement with regard to Paula's control of the alternate personalities.

A different approach was needed. Dr. Harpin's main goal in the next several months of treatment was to discourage further fragmentation of Paula's conscious experience. This was done, in part, by having her read and discuss *Sybil* and allowing her to view videotapes of her own behavior. Dr. Harpin's hope was that the videotapes might jog Paula's memory and begin to break down the barriers that had been erected to prevent the exchange of information between the subdivisions of her conscious working memory.

It seemed to Dr. Harpin that each time they were beginning to make progress toward integration of the various personalities, another disruptive incident would occur. Also, the suicidal gestures continued and were sometimes more severe. One incident was particularly critical, because all the personalities became depressed at the same time. On this particular occasion, Dr. Harpin arranged an involuntary hospitalization to prevent Paula from taking her own life.

DISCUSSION

As mentioned earlier, most experts agree that integrating or fusing the alters is necessary in working with MPD patients (C. A. Ross, 1989). Dr. Harpin employed several techniques with this aim in mind. Fusion may eventually be accomplished if the main personality comes to share the memories and emotions of the alters. The first step toward integration is to facilitate recognition by the patient of the existence of alternate personalities. Videotapes of the alter's behavior, an approach used by Dr. Harpin, may help the patient recognize radical changes that are otherwise forgotten. It may also be important to help the patient understand the general nature of the problem as it has occurred in other people. This understanding may enable the patient to gain perspective on his or her own dilemma. Dr. Harpin had this goal in mind when he asked Paula to read *Sybil*. Finally, the most important step involves learning to react to conflict and stress in an adaptive manner rather than by dissociating.

One difficulty is that the process of therapy can create further fragmentation of the patient's behavior or personality. The act of questioning and exploring the independent personalities may encourage additional dissociative experiences. The use of separate names to describe and address alternate personalities may also serve to stabilize and condone their existence (Fahy, Abas, & Brown, 1989). Finally, although hypnosis can be a useful tool in attempting to facilitate the patient's recall of forgotten events, it can also lead to the emergence of additional personalities. None of these problems is easy to avoid.

▶ ## Somatoform Disorders

somatoform disorders Disorders in which physical symptoms suggest a physical problem but have no known physiological cause; they are therefore believed to be linked to psychological conflicts and needs but not voluntarily assumed. Examples are *somatization disorder, conversion disorder, pain disorder, hypochondriasis,* and *body dysmorphic disorder.*

In **somatoform disorders** the individual complains of bodily symptoms (*soma* means body) that suggest a physical dysfunction but for which no physiological basis can be found. Because the physical symptoms of somatoform disorders have no known physiological explanation and are not under voluntary control, they are assumed to be linked to psychological factors. DSM-IV includes five categories of somatoform disorders: pain disorder, body dysmorphic disorder, hypochondriasis, conversion disorder, and somatization disorder.

Pain Disorder

Pain disorder is diagnosed when psychological factors are associated with the onset, severity, or maintenance of pain that causes significant distress and impairment and that cannot be completely accounted for by a physical condition even after extensive investigation. Diagnosis is difficult because the subjective experience of pain is always psychologically influenced. Pain is not just a sensory experience in the same way in which vision and hearing are. Therefore, deciding when pain becomes somatoform pain is not easy.

pain disorder A *somatoform disorder* in which the person complains of severe and prolonged pain that is not explainable by organic pathology.

Body Dysmorphic Disorder

With **body dysmorphic disorder**, a person is preoccupied with an imagined or exaggerated defect in appearance, for example, facial wrinkles, excess facial hair, or the shape or size of the nose. These concerns are distressing and may lead to frequent consultations with plastic surgeons.

Concern about one's appearance is statistically common. A survey of college students found that 70% of them indicated at least some dissatisfaction with their appearance, with a higher percentage for women than for men (Fitts, Gibson, Redding, & Deiter, 1989). Body dysmorphic disorder is distinguished from typical concerns about appearance by its time-consuming, distressing, and maladaptive nature. For example, someone with body dysmorphic disorder does not just occasionally lament having a weak chin, but instead spends hours a day thinking about this defect or checking for it in mirrors. The person may imagine that oth-

body dysmorphic disorder A *somatoform disorder* in which the person is preoccupied with an imagined or exaggerated defect in appearance, for example, facial wrinkles or excess facial or body hair.

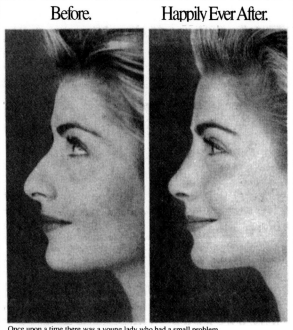

This ad illustrates the type of concern of someone with body dysmorphic disorder.

ers notice and perhaps discuss the alleged flaw, and he or she may even drop out of school or quit a job so as to be able to stay home more and avoid letting anyone see the defective body part.

Which body parts patients are excessively concerned about varies widely and may be influenced by culture. For instance, *koro*, a syndrome believed to be related to, but usually more temporary than, body dysmorphic disorder, is found mainly among men in Southeast Asia. The key fear in *koro* is that the penis is shrinking and will disappear into the abdomen, causing death.

Hypochondriasis

hypochondriasis A *somatoform disorder* in which the person, misinterpreting ordinary physical sensations, is preoccupied with fears of having a serious disease and is not dissuaded by medical opinion.

Hypochondriasis is a somatoform disorder in which individuals are preoccupied with fears of having a serious disease. They overreact to ordinary physical sensations and minor abnormalities—such as sweating, occasional coughing, or a stomachache—as evidence for this belief, and even medical reassurance cannot persuade them otherwise. For several reasons, hypochondriasis can be a very difficult problem for both patients and physicians (understandably, physicians are more likely to be in contact with these patients than are nonmedical psychotherapists).

For the patient, it is a disease of doubt. Unlike people with delusional disorder, somatic type, hypochondriacal patients are willing to consider the possibility that the feared disease is not present. However, they are never convinced that they do not have the disease. No medical tests are perfect. Many symptoms (muscle soreness, headaches, fatigue) are ambiguous in their implications—look them up in medical books, and you will find ample fodder for fear of unlikely-but-catastrophic diagnoses. DSM-IV thus notes that the most critical differential diagnostic issue with hypochondriasis is to ensure that the patient does not really have a general medical condition, perhaps the early stage of a neurological condition, such as multiple sclerosis. The physician's doubts may fuel the patient's doubts. Many patients who meet criteria for hypochondriasis receive medical diagnoses whose symptoms resemble their complaints (for example, irritable bowel syndrome, chronic fatigue syndrome, temporomandibular joint syndrome), and are treated accordingly (Noyes et al., 1993).

For both the patient and the physician, indeed for the entire health care team, hypochondriasis can be frustrating in that the patient is really suffering, and the providers are really providing treatment, but the patient is not getting better. There are no controlled studies that indicate that a particular treatment is effective. Compared with nonhypochondriacal patients of similar demographic characteristics and similar objective physical problems, hypochondriacal patients get more lab tests, take more medications, see more physicians, and are hospitalized more. Despite this extra (generally futile) care, they perceive their treatment as less adequate, their evaluations as less thorough and less clearly explained, and their physicians as less interested and caring (Noyes et al., 1993). Thus from the physician's point of view, the patient is demanding, does not have problems suited for treatment, uses treatment resources unproductively, and then is dissatisfied. From the patient's point of view, the physician is uncaring and ineffective. Clearly, development of valid explanations of, and effective treatments for, hypochondriasis (estimated to affect 4% to 9% of patients seen in general medical practice) is a high priority.

Conversion Disorder

conversion disorder A *somatoform disorder* in which sensory or muscular functions are impaired, usually suggesting neurological disease, even though the bodily organs themselves are sound; *anesthesias* and paralyses of limbs are examples.

The classic symptoms of **conversion disorder** suggest a physical illness of some sort, although medical examinations reveal that the bodily organs and nervous system are fine. Thus, physiologically normal people may experience partial or complete paralysis of arms or legs; seizures and coordination disturbances; a sensation of prickling, tingling, or creeping on the skin; insensitivity to pain; or the loss or impairment of sensations, called **anesthesia**. Vision may be seriously impaired; the person may become partially or completely blind or have tunnel vision. Other conversion disorders are *aphonia*, inability to speak except in a whisper; *anosmia*, loss or impairment of the sense of smell; and false pregnancy.

The nature of conversion symptoms suggests that they are linked to psychological factors. They usually appear suddenly in stressful situations, allowing the individual to avoid some activity or responsibility or to get badly wanted attention. The term *conversion* derived from Freud, who thought that the energy of a repressed instinct was diverted into sensorimotor channels and blocked functioning. Thus anxiety and psychological conflict were believed to be *converted* into physical symptoms.

Hysteria, the term originally used to describe what are now known as conversion disorders, has a history dating back to the earliest writings on abnormal behavior. Hippocrates thought that hysteria occurred only among women and was caused by the wandering of the uterus through the body. The Greek word *hystera* means womb. Presumably the wandering uterus symbolized the longing of the body to produce a child. Freud considered the specific nature of the hysterical symptom to relate either to the repressed instinctual urge itself or to the attempt to suppress the urge, representing it in disguised form. A hysterical convulsion, for example, might be the symbolic expression of a forbidden sexual wish.

Conversion symptoms usually develop in adolescence or early adulthood. An episode may end abruptly, but sooner or later the disorder is likely to return either in its original form or with a symptom of a different nature and site. More women than men are diagnosed as having conversion disorders (Viederman, 1986). During both world wars, however, a large number of men developed conversion-like difficulties in combat (Ziegler, Imboden, & Meyer, 1960).

Diagnostically, it is important to distinguish a conversion paralysis or sensory dysfunction from similar problems that have a true biological basis (see Figure 7.1). Because the majority of paralyses, analgesias (insensitivity to pain without

anesthesia An impairment or loss of sensation, usually of touch but sometimes of the other senses, that is often part of *conversion disorder*.

hysteria A disorder, known to the ancient Greeks, in which a physical incapacity, a paralysis, an anesthesia, or an analgesia, is not due to a physiological dysfunction; an older term for *conversion disorder*.

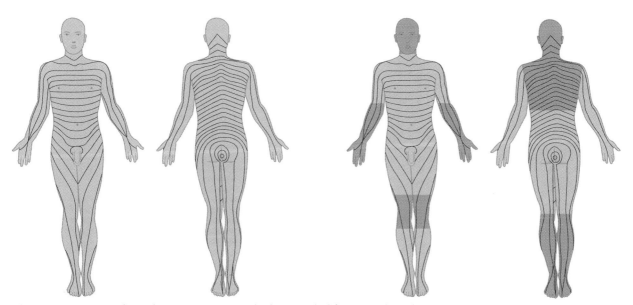

Figure 7.1 *Hysterical anesthesias can sometimes be distinguished from neurological dysfunctions. On the left are shown the patterns of neural innervation. On the right are superimposed typical areas of anesthesias in hysterical patients. The hysterical anesthesias do not make anatomical sense. Adapted from an original painting by Frank H. Netter, M.D. From* The CIBA Collection of Medical Illustrations, *copyright © by CIBA Pharmaceutical Company, Division of CIBA-GEIGY Corporation.*

loss of consciousness), and sensory failures have organic causes, true neurological problems may sometimes be misdiagnosed as conversion disorders. Slater and Glithero (1965) investigated this disturbing possibility in a follow-up of patients who nine years earlier had been diagnosed as suffering from conversion symptoms. An alarming proportion, 60%, of these individuals had either died in the meantime or developed symptoms of physical disease! A high proportion had diseases of the central nervous system. More recent studies also have found that many patients whose symptoms were considered conversion disorders actually had physical disorders (Fishbain & Goldberg, 1991). Clearly, it is not always possible to distinguish between psychologically and organically produced symptoms. It is sobering to contemplate the damage that can result from inappropriate diagnoses.

Another diagnostic problem with conversion disorder is distinguishing it from **malingering**, a DSM-IV category in which the individual fakes an incapacity in order to avoid a responsibility. Malingering is diagnosed when the conversion-like symptoms are under voluntary control, which is not thought to be the case in true conversion disorders. The problem is that it is difficult, if not impossible, to know for sure whether someone is voluntarily producing symptoms. One aspect of behavior that can sometimes help distinguish the two disorders is known as **la belle indifférence**, a relative lack of concern toward the symptoms that is out of keeping with their severity. Patients with conversion disorder sometimes demonstrate this behavior. They also appear willing and eager to talk endlessly and dramatically about their symptoms, but often without the concern that might be expected. In contrast, malingerers are likely to be more guarded and cautious, perhaps because they consider interviews a challenge or threat to the success of the lie.

Somatization Disorder

In 1859 the French physician Pierre Briquet described a syndrome that first bore his name, Briquet's syndrome, and now in DSM-IV is called **somatization disorder**. Patients diagnosed with somatization disorder have recurrent, multiple

malingering Faking a physical or psychological incapacity in order to avoid a responsibility or gain an end; the goal is readily recognized from the individual's circumstances. To be distinguished from *conversion disorder*, in which the incapacity is assumed to be beyond voluntary control.

la belle indifférence The blasé attitude people with *conversion disorder* sometimes have toward their symptoms.

somatization disorder A *somatoform disorder* in which the person continually seeks medical help for recurrent and multiple physical symptoms that have no discoverable physical cause. The medical history is complicated and dramatically presented. Formerly known as Briquet's syndrome.

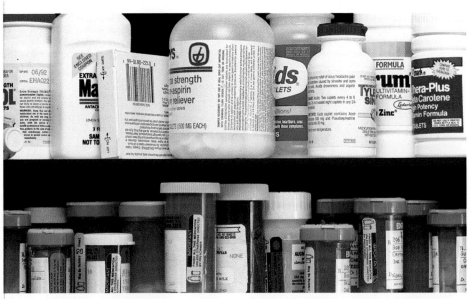

The medicine chest of a patient with a somatization disorder includes many drugs used to treat their numerous medical complaints.

physical complaints for which they seek medical attention but for which no physical cause can be found. Common complaints include headaches; abdominal, back, and chest pains; genitourinary symptoms, such as irregular menses; gastrointestinal symptoms, such as nausea and abdominal bloating; and symptoms suggestive of neurological conditions, such as muscular weakness or paralysis. Somatization disorder and conversion disorder share many of the same symptoms, and it is not uncommon for both diagnoses to be applicable to the same patient (e.g., Folks, Ford, & Regan, 1984). Visits to physicians, sometimes to several simultaneously, are frequent, as is the use of medication. Hospitalization and even surgery are common (Guze, 1967). Patients typically present their complaints in a histrionic, exaggerated fashion or as part of a long and complicated medical history. Many believe that they have been ailing all of their lives.

The lifetime prevalence of somatization disorder is estimated at 0.1% (Robins et al., 1984). The disorder is more frequent among women than among men (Viederman, 1986). Many patients with somatization disorder also meet criteria for anxiety disorders, mood disorders, and substance abuse (Golding, Smith, & Kashner, 1991).

Somatization disorder typically begins in late adolescence (Cloninger, Martin, Guze, & Clayton, 1986). A host of behavioral and interpersonal problems, such as truancy, poor work records, and marital difficulties, are frequently reported. The following case illustrates one woman's complaints.

Alice was referred to the psychological clinic by her physician, Joyce Williams. Dr. Williams had been Alice's physician for about six months and in that time had seen her twenty-three times. Alice had dwelt on a number of rather vague complaints—general aches and pains, bouts of nausea, tiredness, irregular menstruation, and dizziness. But various tests—complete blood workups, X rays, a spinal tap, and so on—had not revealed any pathology.

On meeting her therapist, Alice immediately let him know that she was a reluctant client. "I'm here only because I trust Dr. Williams and she urged me to come. I'm physically sick and don't see how a psychologist is going to help." But when Alice was asked to describe the history of her physical problems, she quickly warmed to the task. Alice reported that she had always been sick. As a child she had had episodes of high fever, frequent respiratory infections, convulsions, and her first two operations, an appendectomy and a tonsillectomy. As she continued the chronological account of her medical history, Alice described her problems more and more colorfully. "Yes, when I was in my early twenties I had some problems with vomiting. For weeks at a time I'd vomit up everything I ate. I'd even vomit up liquids, even water. Just the sight of food would make me vomit. The smell of food cooking was absolutely unbearable. I must have been vomiting every ten minutes." During her twenties, Alice had gone from one physician to another. She saw several gynecologists for her menstrual irregularity and dyspareunia (pain during intercourse) and had undergone dilatation and curettage (scraping the lining of the uterus). She had been referred to neurologists for her headaches, dizziness, and fainting spells, and they had performed EEGs, spinal taps, and even a CAT scan. Other physicians had ordered X rays to look for the possible causes of her abdominal pain and EKGs for her chest pains. Both rectal and gallbladder surgery had also been performed.

When the interview finally shifted away from Alice's medical history, it became apparent that she was a highly anxious person in many situations, particularly those in which she thought she might be evaluated by other people. Indeed, some of her physical complaints could be regarded as consequences of anxiety. Furthermore, her marriage was quite shaky, and she and her husband were considering divorce. Their marital problems seemed to be linked to sexual difficulties stemming from Alice's dyspareunia and her general indifference toward sex.

To Recap

Somatoform disorders involve complaints of bodily symptoms for which no physiological basis can be found. These include

▶ **pain disorder (pain causing distress and impairment but not linked to a known physical condition)**
▶ **body dysmorphic disorder (preoccupation with an imagined or exaggerated defect in physical appearance)**
▶ **hypochondriasis (preoccupation with fears of having a serious disease)**
▶ **conversion disorder (symptoms suggesting a physical disease, for example, paralysis or anesthesias, when medical tests show no damage)**
▶ **somatization disorder (multiple somatic complaints for which medical attention is sought but for which there is no apparent physical cause)**

Somatoform disorders are difficult to diagnose. In part, this is because of their subjective nature. For instance, the degree of dissatisfaction with one's appearance that would be required for a judgment of body dysmorphic disorder might vary from one diagnostician to another. The biggest issue, however, is the defining feature of somatoform disorders, the absence of an apparent biological basis for the symptoms. Because current knowledge of and diagnostic tests for physical diseases are imperfect, a patient's symptoms really may have an organic cause, even if one is not obvious. Thus, there is great potential with these disorders for misdiagnosis and ill-conceived treatment.

Perspectives on the Causes and Treatment of Somatoform Disorders

People with somatoform disorders understandably seek help from physicians far more often than from mental health professionals. Indeed, as in the case of Alice, they are often not receptive to psychological explanations of their predicaments, and they therefore resent referrals to "shrinks". This circumstance and the difficulties in diagnosis noted earlier contribute to the unfortunate reality that there is little solid information on the causes and treatment of somatoform disorders. Case reports and clinical speculation are, for now, the main sources of information on how to help people with these puzzling disorders. In this section, we examine the main theories of somatoform disorders.

Psychodynamic Perspectives

As with dissociative disorders, psychodynamic theory has a great deal to say about somatoform disorders. Conversion disorders first prompted Freud to explore the concept of the unconscious. Imagine that you are a neurologist, as Freud was. Consider for a moment how you might try to make sense of a patient's report that she awakened one morning with a paralyzed left arm. Your first reaction might be to give her a series of neurological tests to assess possible biological causes of the paralysis. Assume that these tests are negative, that no evidence of neurological disorder is present. You are now faced with choosing whether to believe or to doubt the patient's communication. On the one hand, she might be lying. She might know that her arm is not paralyzed, and she might be faking paralysis to achieve some end. This would be an example of malingering. But what if you believe the patient? You are almost forced to consider that unconscious processes are operating. On a conscious level, the patient is telling the truth. She believes and reports that her arm is paralyzed. Only on a level that is not conscious does she know that her arm is actually normal.

In their *Studies in Hysteria* (1895) Breuer and Freud proposed that a conversion disorder is caused by an experience that created great emotional arousal. The emotion was not expressed, and the memory of the event was cut off from conscious experience. They proposed two explanations for why the emotion associated with the experience was not expressed. The experience may have been so distressing that the person could not allow it to enter consciousness and therefore repressed it. Or the experience may have occurred while the person was in an abnormal psychological state, such as semihypnosis. In both situations, Breuer and Freud proposed, the specific conversion symptoms are causally related to the traumatic event that preceded them.

Anna O. (see p. 18), for example, while watching at the bedside of her seriously ill father, had dropped off into a waking dream with her right arm over the back of her chair. She saw a black snake emerge from the wall and come toward her sick father to bite him. She tried to ward it away, but her right arm had gone to sleep. When she looked at her hand, her fingers turned into little snakes with death's-heads. The next day a bent branch recalled her hallucination of the snake, and at once her right arm became rigidly extended. After that, her arm responded in the same way whenever some object revived her hallucination. Later, when Anna O. fell into her "absences" and took to her own bed, the contracture of her right arm became chronic and extended to paralysis and anesthesia of her right side.

In his later writings Freud formulated a theory of conversion disorder in which sexual impulses became primary. Specifically, because so many more women than men exhibited these symptoms, he hypothesized that conversion disorders are rooted in an early, unresolved Electra complex. The young female child becomes incestuously attached to her father, but these early impulses are repressed, producing both a preoccupation with sex and, at the same time, an avoidance of it. At a later period of her life, sexual excitement or some happenstance reawakens these repressed impulses, and they are transformed or converted into physical symptoms that represent them in distorted form.

With respect to treatment, the talking cure into which psychoanalysis developed (see Chapter 1, p. 19) was based on Freud's idea that repression had forced psychic energy to be transformed or converted into puzzling anesthesias or paralyses. The catharsis as the patient faced up to the infantile origins of the repression was assumed to help. Today efforts to uncover and lift repression are still commonly used to treat somatoform disorders.

> ## APPLYING CRITICAL THINKING SKILLS

TESTING PSYCHODYNAMIC VIEWS OF CONVERSION DISORDERS

As we have seen, one of the biggest criticisms of psychodynamic theory is that it is difficult to verify scientifically. How can we begin to test the idea that repressed emotions or thoughts actually can *cause* physical symptoms? One study of hysterical blindness offers some clues. Considering a particular case, and addressing the critical thinking questions introduced in earlier chapters, will help illustrate how some of the subtleties involved in psychodynamic theorizing can be tested.

A sixteen-year-old girl had experienced a sudden loss of peripheral vision, reporting that her visual field had become tubular and constricted (Theodor & Mandelcorn, 1973). All the neurological tests she took proved negative.

▶ *What conclusion does the evidence seem to support?* The negative neurological tests and sudden onset suggest that the blindness was hysterical. These factors are consistent with (albeit not direct proof of) the possibility that repression of some unacceptable memory associated with strong emotion caused the problem.

▶ *What other interpretations are plausible?* The major alternative interpretation is that the patient was suffering from ordinary blindness, a simple inability to see. That results of some tests were negative does not mean that all possible neurological causes are ruled out. Tests are fallible, and new conditions are constantly being discovered.

▶*What other information would help choose among the alternative interpretations?* In the ordinary course of daily life, it would be hard to choose between the two interpretations. Both positions are consistent with the patient's report that she had lost peripheral vision. What is needed is a situation or task in which different results might be obtained depending on which interpretation is accurate.

Theodor and Mandelcorn (1973) were able to create such a condition by devising a special visual test in which a bright, oval target was presented either in the center or in the periphery of the patient's visual field. On each trial there was a time interval, bounded by the sounding of a buzzer. A target was either illuminated during the intervals or not. The young woman's task was to report whether a target was present or not.

When the target was presented in the center of the visual field, the patient always correctly identified it. This result was expected, since she had not reported any loss of central vision. What happened when the oval was presented peripherally? The patient could be expected to be correct 50% of the time by chance alone. The authors reasoned that this would be the outcome if she were truly blind in peripheral vision. For the peripheral showings of the target, however, the young woman was correct only 30% of the time. She had performed significantly more poorly than would a person who was indeed blind! The clinicians reasoned that she must have been aware in some sense of the illuminated stimulus and that she wanted, consciously or unconsciously, to preserve her blindness by performing poorly on the test (Theodor & Mandelcorn, 1973).

Thus the results were consistent with the initial interpretation considered, that the vision problems were of psychological and perhaps psychodynamic origin. Is this different from malingering? Are the people who claim that they are blind and yet on another level respond to visual stimuli being truthful? Some patients with lesions in the visual cortex, rather than damage to the eye, say that they are blind and yet perform well on visual tasks (Sackeim, Nordlie, & Gur, 1979). They have vision, but they do not know that they can see. So it is possible for people to claim truthfully that they cannot see and at the same time give evidence that they can.   ◀

Biological Perspectives

Genetic factors do not appear to be of great importance in somatoform disorders. Although somatization disorder seems to run in families (Arkonac & Guze, 1963), more definitive twin studies do not support the conclusion that the disorder is inherited. For example, one study involved twelve identical and twelve fraternal pairs of twins, selected on the basis that one twin had conversion disorder (Slater, 1961) . *None* of the co-twins turned out to have conversion disorder. More recent twin research on somatization disorder, pain disorder, conversion disorder, and hypochondriasis also shows weak support for genetic factors (Torgersen, 1986).

More promising is a neurophysiological explanation of why emotions connected with conversion disorders remain unavailable to conscious awareness. Conversion symptoms are more likely to occur on the left side of the body than on the right side (Ford & Folks, 1985). In most instances these left-side body functions are controlled by the right hemisphere of the brain, which is believed to generate emotions, particularly unpleasant ones, more than does the left hemisphere. Conversion symptoms could thus be neurophysiologically linked to emotional arousal, though we do not as yet know exactly how. Furthermore, this same research indicates that the right hemisphere depends on the neural passageways of the corpus callosum for connection with the left hemisphere's verbal capacity to describe and explain emotions and thereby to gain awareness of them. In conversion disorders it may be that the left hemisphere somehow blocks impulses carrying painful emotional content from the right hemisphere. Thus individuals with a conversion disorder make no connection between it and their troubling circumstances or emotional needs.

Behavioral Perspectives

Behavioral perspectives on somatoform disorders focus on the reinforcement that the patient and others may give to localized feelings of tension or pain, thereby increasing and encouraging somatic symptoms. From this viewpoint, the various aches and pains, discomforts, and dysfunctions may begin as an indication of anxiety manifesting itself in particular bodily systems. Perhaps extreme tension localizes in stomach muscles, causing the individual to feel nauseous and even vomit, for example. Then, once normal functioning is disrupted, the maladaptive pattern may be strengthened because of the attention it receives or the excuses it provides. That is, a person might assume a disability if doing so is reinforced by reduced stress, concern from others, or other favorable consequences.

There is little direct evidence that these explanations of somatoform disorders are accurate, but some case studies suggest that treatment based on them can be effective. For instance, two patients with nausea stemming from psychological factors were encouraged to expose themselves to the situations that made them nauseous, much as a phobic person would confront a particular fear. The authors concluded that the favorable outcomes were due to extinction of the anxiety underlying the nausea (Lesage & Lamontagne, 1985).

An operant conditioning strategy that made it more rewarding for the patient to give up than to retain physical symptoms also was effective in one case (Liebson, 1967). A man left his job because of pain and weakness in the legs. The therapist helped the patient return to full-time work by persuading his family to refrain from reinforcing him for his idleness and by arranging for the man to receive a pay increase if he succeeded in getting to work.

An important part of any therapy for somatoform disorders is for the therapist to make certain that the patient finds a way to part with the disorder without losing face. The therapist should appreciate the possibility that the patient may feel humiliated by the success of psychological, rather than medical, treatment (Walen, Hauserman, & Lavin, 1977).

To Recap

There is little controlled research on the causes and treatment of somatoform disorders. Psychoanalytic theory proposes that conversion disorders result from repression of memories of traumatic experiences or incestuous sexual impulses. Treatment emphasizes lifting the repression through the catharsis produced by insights uncovered in psychoanalysis. Biological research suggests that conversion disorders might result when the left hemisphere of the brain blocks impulses carrying painful emotional content from the right hemisphere, so that the individual is unaware of the link between physical and emotional symptoms. Behavioral perspectives hold that physical symptoms might stem initially from anxiety and tension and then be maintained by the reinforcing consequences of being sick (e.g., escape from responsibilities). The recommended treatment is to extinguish the anxiety and create favorable consequences for giving up the symptoms.

Visual Summary for Chapter 7:

Dissociative and Somatoform Disorders

Dissociative Disorders (Disruptions of consciousness, memory, or identity)

Dissociative Amnesia	An inability to recall important personal information, usually after a trauma, is diagnosed as dissociative amnesia.
Dissociative Fugue	In dissociative fugue, the person moves away, assumes a new identity, and is amnesic for his or her former life.
Depersonalization Disorder	In depersonalization disorder, the person's perception of self is altered. He or she may experience being outside the body or perceive a change in the size of body parts.
Multiple Personality Disorder (MPD)	The person with multiple personality disorder (now called Dissociative Identity Disorder) has two or more distinct personalities, each with unique memories, behaviors, and relationships.

Perspectives on the Causes and Treatment of Dissociative Disorders

Psychodynamic	Cause	Psychodynamic theory views dissociative disorders as cases of repression of unacceptable sexual wishes or memories of sexual or physical abuse.
	Treatment	Using free association and often hypnosis, psychodynamic therapists encourage patients to reencounter the painful memories and to acknowledge them as part of themselves rather than outside themselves.
Biological		Some physicians have used truth serum to induce a hypnotic-like state in an attempt to elicit painful repressed memories. However, there is little controlled research on the efficacy of this method.
Vulnerability-Stress		Multiple personality disorder is viewed as self-hypnosis and a way of coping with intensely disturbing events. Two areas of evidence support this hypothesis: (1) individuals with MPD are highly hypnotizable; (2) individuals with MPD nearly always have experienced severe childhood trauma.

Somatoform Disorders *(Complaints of bodily symptoms for which no physiological basis can be found)*

Pain Disorder ····▶ *This diagnosis is given when someone experiences pain that causes distress and impairment, but the pain cannot be accounted for by a physiological condition.*

Body Dysmorphic Disorder ····▶ *The person is preoccupied with some imagined or exaggerated defect in appearance.*

Hypochondriasis ····▶ *The individual is preoccupied by fears of having a serious disease.*

Conversion Disorder ····▶ *Symptoms suggest a physical disease (e.g., paralysis), yet none can be detected.*

Somatization Disorder ····▶ *These individuals have multiple recurrent physical complaints for which they seek medical attention, yet no physical cause can be identified.*

Perspectives on the Causes and Treatment of Somatoform Disorders

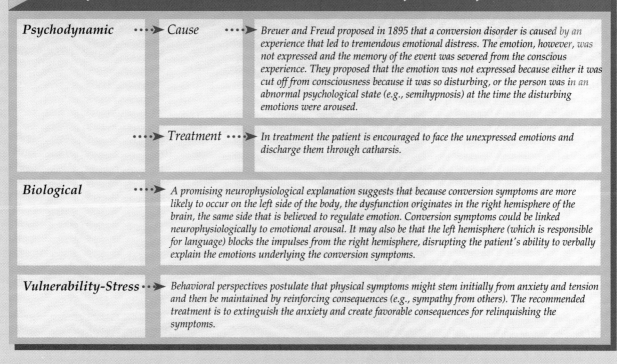

Psychodynamic ····▶ Cause ····▶ *Breuer and Freud proposed in 1895 that a conversion disorder is caused by an experience that led to tremendous emotional distress. The emotion, however, was not expressed and the memory of the event was severed from the conscious experience. They proposed that the emotion was not expressed because either it was cut off from consciousness because it was so disturbing, or the person was in an abnormal psychological state (e.g., semihypnosis) at the time the disturbing emotions were aroused.*

····▶ Treatment ····▶ *In treatment the patient is encouraged to face the unexpressed emotions and discharge them through catharsis.*

Biological ····▶ *A promising neurophysiological explanation suggests that because conversion symptoms are more likely to occur on the left side of the body, the dysfunction originates in the right hemisphere of the brain, the same side that is believed to regulate emotion. Conversion symptoms could be linked neurophysiologically to emotional arousal. It may also be that the left hemisphere (which is responsible for language) blocks the impulses from the right hemisphere, disrupting the patient's ability to verbally explain the emotions underlying the conversion symptoms.*

Vulnerability-Stress ··▶ *Behavioral perspectives postulate that physical symptoms might stem initially from anxiety and tension and then be maintained by reinforcing consequences (e.g., sympathy from others). The recommended treatment is to extinguish the anxiety and create favorable consequences for relinquishing the symptoms.*

Chapter 8

Stress
and Health

The Case of John Williams ◀

John Williams had been complaining of dizziness, fatigue, and occasional light-headedness that almost caused him to faint one day at the watercooler in the law office where he worked downtown. His boss had been after him for weeks to see a doctor, but John had stubbornly refused. He felt angry and frightened at the suggestion—angry because he interpreted it as condescending on his boss's part, and frightened because he had a sense that all was not right with him physically.

In fact, his hypertension, or high blood pressure, did not come to light until, during a visit to his dentist, the dental assistant took his blood pressure. John did not ask about the blood pressure reading until he was sitting across from the dentist's desk to discuss treatment plans. The dentist then told him that his blood pressure was dangerously high—165/110—putting him at risk for coronary heart disease. How have you been feeling? John was asked. Tired, irritable? How has the work been going? Under a lot of pressure lately? Although not a physician, John knew what high blood pressure might mean for a forty-year-old like himself, who was so driven to succeed professionally and financially. Certainly he would have to slow down.

Unfortunately, slowing down did not come naturally to John, and he had been under a lot of pressure not just lately. It seemed to him that pressure and conflict had been with him at least since college. John was born in 1939, the only child of a well-to-do African-American family in Atlanta. His father was a successful attorney, and his mother was a music teacher in one of the local high schools. Life was sweet in his childhood, and he had many friends in his neighborhood. In high school John excelled at everything he attempted. An A student and varsity athlete, he was popular socially and was elected president of his senior class. John's father was highly ambitious on his behalf and encouraged him to apply to the best colleges in the country. John was admitted to several and decided to go to Harvard.

At Harvard racial discrimination was apparent. John's roommate, a Jew from Brooklyn, told him years later that one month before school was to begin their freshman year, he received a letter from the housing office. According to the letter, the school was planning to assign him a room with an African-American student, but the assignment would be made only if he had no objection. John's roommate had been outraged, because he readily saw the prejudice behind the question. This incident, and others like it, prompted many discussions between the two roommates about the pressures on members of minority groups who elected to try to make it in society.

John was invited to join a prestigious social club at Harvard, and he became the only African-American member. When he looked back on things, the club seemed to symbolize much of the conflict he felt about his blackness in a white world. John had grown up proud of the fact that he was African-American and feeling that whatever barriers he might face in society were of lesser importance than his self-respect and pride. Being invited to join the social club seemed to confirm this sense. On the other hand, was it something to celebrate, or was he being treated as a token so that the other members could consider themselves liberal and fair by having one African-American person in the club?

The day of his initiation, John awoke with a terrible headache. He took three aspirins—a habit he had gotten into since arriving at college—and told himself to stop worrying about the party that evening. The welcome he received seemed genuine. And yet he could not shake the feeling that his new "brothers" were being too nice. His wine glass was never empty, always filled by a brother who, it struck John, smiled a bit too ingratiatingly. He tried to reassure himself that the cordiality was real, but he did not really know.

His membership in the club turned out to be a boon to his social standing, but an emotional disaster. Headaches became frequent. He hated himself for even being in the club, yet he prided himself on being the only African-American member. He was furious at the fact that so few Jews were members; he was also suspicious that there were no other African-Americans. Still, he found the young men in the club congenial and enjoyed spending time with them. But the clubs were by nature exclusionary, and John was coming to realize that he might be seen as an Uncle Tom for belonging to one.

The four years of college passed quickly. As his family and friends expected, John did very well academically and also managed to earn a varsity letter in baseball. His headaches continued, however. He was admitted to a first-rate law school, though he was uncertain whether he had been admitted solely on his academic merits or whether the schools wanted him primarily for his color. These conflicts continued through law school and created a need to excel that even his ambitious father regarded as unreasonable. John graduated at the top of his law school class in the middle 1960s. The developing social turmoil surrounding Vietnam and the civil rights movement increased John's conflict. He believed that he should be more involved, but his studies and his new job at a top law firm took precedence. He donated to some African-American civil rights groups, but it did not seem to assuage his guilt.

Most of us are subject to stress, whether from conflicts among our various roles, as John Williams experienced, or from economic pressures, losing a loved one, or even an accumulation of more minor difficulties, such as a long commute or work-related deadlines. All too often our physical health suffers as a result of such stress, as seems to be the case with John Williams, suffering from headaches and hypertension. In this chapter we consider what stress is, its association with physical illness, the details of a few of the many illnesses linked to stress (using asthma, hypertension, and coronary heart disease as illustrations), and theories of the causes and treatment of stress-related disorders.

▶ *What Is Stress?*

The term *stress* is used by professionals and the public alike to describe a wide range of situations and responses. There is no one universally accepted definition of stress. The various ways of defining stress suggest different means of measuring it and treating it.

Situational Definitions

stress Situational definitions focus on the objective nature of the event or circumstance; response-based definitions consider a pattern of behavioral, emotional, and biological reactions to events; relational definitions incorporate aspects of the event and the response to it.

Situational definitions depict **stress** as events or circumstances that involve a particular characteristic, such as threat or loss. Professionals who adopt a situational definition try, as objectively as possible, to identify stress according to what the environment is like. One influential attempt to measure stress is the Social Readjustment Rating Scale (SRRS) developed by Holmes and Rahe (1967). The situational definition used in the SRRS is that a stressful event is one that involves extensive change in a person's life.

Determining which events entail a great deal of change was accomplished by consensus. A large group of subjects rated a long list of events according to their intensity and how long it would take to adjust to them. Marriage was arbitrarily assigned a stress value of 500; all other items were evaluated using this reference point. The average ratings assigned to the events are shown in Table 8.1. In completing the SRRS the respondent checks off the life events experienced during the time period in question. The ratings for stressfulness of those events are then totaled for all the events actually experienced to produce a Life Change Unit (LCU) score. The LCU score has been correlated with several different illnesses, for example, heart attacks (Rahe & Lind, 1971) and onset of leukemia (Wold, 1968).

Table 8.1 ▶ *Social Readjustment Rating Scale*

Rank	Life Event	Mean Value	Rank	Life Event	Mean Value
1	Death of spouse	100	22	Change in responsibilities at work	29
2	Divorce	73	23	Child leaving home	29
3	Marital separation	65	24	Trouble with in-laws	29
4	Jail term	63	25	Outstanding personal achievement	28
5	Death of close family member	63	26	Spouse begins or stops work	26
6	Personal injury or illness	53	27	Begin or end school	26
7	Marriage	50[a]	28	Change in living conditions	25
8	Fired from work	47	29	Revision of personal habits	24
9	Marital reconciliation	45	30	Trouble with boss	23
10	Retirement	45	31	Change in work hours or conditions	20
11	Change in health of family member	44	32	Change in residence	20
12	Pregnancy	40	33	Change in schools	20
13	Sex difficulties	39	34	Change in recreation	19
14	New family member	39	35	Change in church activities	19
15	Business readjustment	39	36	Change in social activities	18
16	Change in financial state	38	37	Mortgage or loan less than $10,000	17
17	Death of close friend	37	38	Change in sleeping habits	16
18	Change to different line of work	36	39	Change in number of family get-togethers	15
19	Change in number of arguments with spouse	35	40	Change in eating habits	15
20	Mortgage over $10,000	31	41	Vacation	13
21	Foreclosure of mortgage or loan	30	42	Christmas	12
			43	Minor violations of the law	11

Source: From Holmes and Rahe (1967).

[a]Marriage was arbitrarily assigned a stress value of 500; no event was found to be any more than twice as stressful. Here the values are reduced proportionally and range up to 100.

The SRRS can be criticized for *assuming* that any change is stressful, whether it is a change usually regarded as negative, such as being fired from a job, or positive, such as marrying. Evidence seems to indicate that the undesirable aspects of events are what is particularly important, not just change itself (Sandler & Guenther, 1985).

More generally, a potential disadvantage of all situational definitions is that they do not take into account how stress actually works psychologically. *Physical* stimuli can be quantified objectively in a way that makes sense (e.g., the weight of a 200-lb barbell or the temperature of a 20-degree-Fahrenheit ice cream freezer is what it is, even though whether you can lift it or stand it for 2 minutes varies from person to person). But the psychological stressfulness of an event or circumstance is more nebulous. Is a flat tire very stressful, for instance? If it happens on a busy freeway, you do not have a spare tire, and you are late for a job interview, sure. If it happens on a Saturday, near your house on a quiet side street, and you have a spare tire, a jack, and the knowledge of how to fix it, maybe not. At the very least, the degree of stressfulness is not constant.

Some researchers (e.g., Brown & Harris, 1989) have tried to address this issue by measuring stressful events in a manner that takes more of the personal context into account. Rather than simply respond to a checklist item, such as "flat tire," "divorce," or "death of a relative," for example, the subject is interviewed about the details of her or his circumstances so that a "contextual threat" rating of stress can be made. The attempt is still to identify stress independently of the subject's personal response to it, but with more consideration for the context in which the event took place. That is, if you experienced the "death of a close relative who is young and had not been ill before suddenly expiring, leaving behind extensive

Experiencing major life events, such as marriage or starting school, statistically increases risk for illness. Research on the effects of these major stressors often assesses them with the Social Readjustment Rating Scale.

debts for you to settle," how well you handled the event remains an open question, but we can at least tell more about what sort of event it was.

Other investigators believe that no situational definition, no matter how rich, can capture the essence of psychological stress. They therefore define and study stress either as a response or as a relational concept.

Response-Based Definitions

Response-based definitions of stress consider that the essence of stress is a particular pattern of behavioral, emotional, or biological reactions to events. From this point of view, if you respond a certain way, it shows stress; if you do not respond that way, there was no stress, regardless of what events occurred. The best-known response-based approach to stress, introduced in 1936 by Hans Selye, is called the **general adaptation syndrome (GAS)**. The GAS was proposed first as a model to describe the biological reaction to sustained and unrelenting physical stress. The model has three phases (see Figure 8.1). During the first phase, the

general adaptation syndrome (GAS)
Hans Selye's model to describe the biological reaction of an organism to a sustained and unrelenting stressor; there are several stages, culminating in death in extreme circumstances.

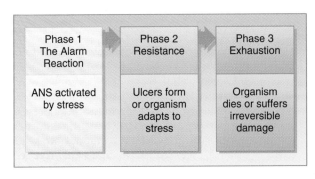

Phase 1 The Alarm Reaction	Phase 2 Resistance	Phase 3 Exhaustion
ANS activated by stress	Ulcers form or organism adapts to stress	Organism dies or suffers irreversible damage

Figure 8.1 *Selye's general adaptation syndrome.*

alarm reaction, the autonomic nervous system is activated by the stress. During the second phase, resistance, the organism adapts to the stress through available coping mechanisms. If the stressful event persists or the organism is unable to respond effectively, the third phase, a stage of exhaustion, follows, and the organism dies or suffers irreversible damage (Selye, 1950).

Eventually, Selye's concept of stress found its way into the psychological literature. Some researchers began to consider stress a response to environmental conditions, defined on the basis of such diverse criteria as emotional upset, deterioration of performance, or physiological changes, such as increased skin conductance or increases in the levels of certain hormones. To distinguish stress as a response from the events that might or might not cause it for a given person, those who adopt a response-based approach often use the term **stressor** for the events that can cause *stress*, the term applied to the response patterns themselves.

stressor An event that leads to *stress* responses.

An advantage of response-based definitions is that they can take individual differences into account. The fact that one person's divorce may be tremendously stressful, while another's is not, is not a problem. The people's responses presumably reflect this difference, and one response reflects stress, while the other does not. A disadvantage, however, is that studies of stress that use strictly response-based definitions shed little light on how people successfully manage potentially stressful events. If you handle a difficult situation well and never show typical stress responses, for example, your reaction might be very informative about your psychological makeup. But from the response-based point of view, no stress ever occurred.

Relational Definitions

The *relational* approach to defining stress takes the limitations of the other definitions into account (Lazarus, 1966). In this model, stress lies neither entirely in the event nor entirely in the person's response, but rather in the relation between the two. According to this view, stress is experienced when a situation is perceived or *appraised* as taxing or exceeding the person's adaptive resources. This is an important notion, for it helps to explain individual differences in how people respond to the same event. Taking a final examination may be incredibly stressful for some people and merely present a challenge for others.

This approach is not the same as a response-based definition, however. It is possible to appraise an event as stressful without showing any particular pattern of psychological or physiological response. You might see an examination, for instance, as taxing your resources (hence stressful), but you might cope with it sufficiently well (e.g., by studying well in advance) so that no negative physiological or subjective responses are evident.

TO RECAP

Stress can be defined in various ways. Those who employ situational definitions evaluate whether an event is stressful solely on the basis of features of the event, such as whether it entails change. Although more objective than other definitions, situational definitions do not reflect the wide variation in how people respond to stressors. Response-based definitions of stress consider the essence of stress to be a particular pattern of behavioral, emotional, or biological reactions to events. Although response-based definitions take individual differences into account, they do not illuminate how people effectively manage stress. In consideration of these difficulties with either purely situational or purely response-based approaches to stress, a relational model for defining stress was developed. In this model, stress is experienced when a situation is perceived as taxing or exceeding one's adaptive resources.

Headaches are among the physical illnesses that can be caused or made worse by stress.

Stress and Physical Illness

How one responds to stress psychologically can very much affect how great a physical toll such stress takes. As we saw in the case of John Williams, hypertension seemed to be caused by the stress of being the only African-American in many situations and the resulting conflicting feelings, including guilt, that John had about his success in white-dominated domains, such as the law. **Psychophysiological disorders**, such as asthma, ulcers, hypertension, headaches, and gastritis, are characterized by genuine physical symptoms that are caused or can be worsened by emotional factors, including stress. A psychophysiological disorder is a real disease that damages the body. The fact that such disorders are viewed as being caused by emotional factors does not make them imaginary.

Psychophysiological disorders as such do not appear in DSM-IV. Instead, DSM-IV requires a diagnostic judgment to indicate the presence of **psychological factors affecting a medical condition**. This approach reflects the current belief that all illnesses, not just a select few, can be affected by psychological factors.

Evidence Relating Stress to Illness

Some of the evidence for the view that illnesses can be stress related is provided by animal research. In one experiment, tumors were induced in mice with a transplant of cancerous tissue. Some of the animals were then exposed to stress in the form of electric shock. In these animals the tumors grew more rapidly, and the animals died earlier (Sklar & Anisman, 1979).

Although such research cannot be undertaken on human subjects, there is evidence that stress can affect physical health among humans as well. One line of research measures stress with the Assessment of Daily Experience (ADE; Stone & Neale, 1982), which improved on earlier stress measures such as the SRRS of Holmes and Rahe (1967). In the ADE people record and rate their experiences of just one day, which avoids the problem of possibly distorted memory for stressful events over a longer period of time. The ADE also includes both major events, such as those retrospectively reported in studies with the SRRS, and *hassles*, more mundane daily happenings that can also contribute to illness (Jandorf, Deblinger, Neale, & Stone, 1986). To ensure content validity (see Chapter 4) the specific categories of events included on the ADE were selected on the basis of daily diaries recorded for fourteen days by a group of twenty-six couples from the local community.

Using the ADE along with daily monitoring of physical symptoms and health-related behaviors over a twelve-week period, Stone, Reed, and Neale (1987) studied the relation between stress and respiratory illness—a cold or cough or sore throat, for example. After examining each subject's data, thirty (of a total of seventy-nine) were identified as having episodes of infectious illness. Next, the frequency of undesirable and desirable events that occurred from one to ten days before the start of an episode was examined. For each subject a set of control days without an episode was also selected, with the restriction that the control days had to match the others for day of the week. The data for desirable events are shown in Figure 8.2, for undesirable events in Figure 8.3.

It was expected that several days before a person became ill, he or she would have experienced an increase in undesirable events and a decrease in desirable events (symptoms of respiratory illness occur several days after exposure to a virus). The results indeed showed that desirable events decreased and undesirable events increased several days before an episode of respiratory illness.

Further support for the relation between stress and health comes from a study of the common cold (Cohen, Tyrell, & Smith, 1991). In this study, volunteers took nasal drops containing a mild cold virus and also completed a battery of mea-

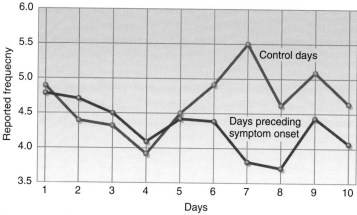

Figure 8.2 *Number of desirable events for the ten days preceding an episode of respiratory infection. After Stone, Reed, and Neale (1987).*

sures concerning recent stress. The advantage of this method was that exposure to the virus was an experimental variable, under the investigators' control. Increases in stress were clearly linked to the rate of infection. At the lowest level of recent stress, about 71% of subjects became infected; at the highest level the figure was more than 90%.

Immune Function as a Mediator of the Effects of Stress on Illness

There is evidence, then, both animal and human, correlational and experimental, linking stress and illness. While the evidence does establish a relationship, it does not give any information as to what the basis of that relationship is. It is important to determine the mechanisms linking stress and illness. A host of biological changes occur during encounters with stressors that could mediate the impact of stress on illness, for example, increases in heart rate and blood pressure and increases in hormone secretions. Recent research also suggests that stress affects the immune system, which is an important consideration in infectious diseases, cancer, and allergies (Zakowski, Hall, & Baum, 1992). This evidence has encouraged the development of the subspecialty of **psychoneuroimmunology**, in which researchers study both the adverse impact of stress on immune function and, conversely, the possibility of improving immune function by learning to manage stress more effectively (Kiecolt-Glaser & Glaser, 1992). We consider stress management later in this chapter. For now, it is important to note that several types of

Daily hassles like being stuck in traffic can be emotionally upsetting and also increase risk for illness.

psychoneuroimmunology The study of the impact of *stress* and ways of coping with stress on immune function.

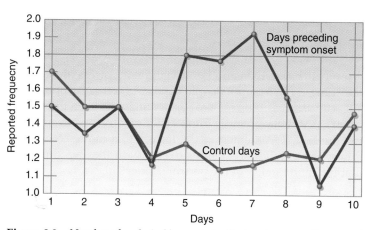

Figure 8.3 *Number of undesirable events for the ten days preceding an episode of respiratory infection. After Stone, Reed, and Neale (1987).*

studies indicate that stress can indeed have a negative effect on immune function, which may explain in part its association with physical illness.

Depression and bereavement have been shown to compromise immune function, (Linn, Linn, & Jensen, 1984; Schleifer, Keller, Camerino, Thornton, & Stein, 1983). A sense of loss may underlie immunological changes, for similar effects have been found in divorced people (Kiecolt-Glaser et al., 1988) and those who have lost their jobs (Arnetz et al., 1987). Other kinds of stress also hamper the functioning of the immune system, for example, examination anxiety (Kiecolt-Glaser & Glaser, 1987), caring for a spouse with dementia (Kiecolt-Glaser, Dura, Speicher, & Trask, 1991), and laboratory-induced stress (Zakowski, McAllister, Deal, & Baum, 1992). To illustrate, we will discuss one aspect of the immune system—secretory immunity—in some detail.

The secretory component of the immune system exists in the fluids (i.e., tears, saliva, and gastrointestinal, vaginal, nasal, and bronchial secretions) that bathe the mucosal surfaces of the body, where invading bacteria and viruses can enter. A substance found in these secretions, called immunoglobulin A, or IgA, contains antibodies that serve as the body's first line of defense against invading viruses and bacteria. They prevent the virus or bacterium from binding to mucosal tissues. A study by Stone, Cox et al. (1987) showed that changes in the number of antibodies in IgA were linked to changes in mood. Throughout an eight-week study period, a group of dental students came to the laboratory three times a week to have their saliva collected and a brief psychological assessment conducted. On days when the students experienced relatively high levels of negative mood, there were fewer antibodies present than on days when they experienced low levels of negative mood. Similarly, antibody level was higher on days with higher levels of positive mood.

Prior research (e.g., Stone & Neale, 1984) had shown that daily events affect mood. It is therefore quite possible that daily events affect the fluctuations in mood, which in turn suppress synthesis of the secretory IgA antibodies. The process could operate as follows. An increase in undesirable life events coupled with a decrease in desirable life events produces increased negative mood, which in turn depresses antibody levels in secretory IgA. If during this period a person is exposed to a virus, he or she will be at increased risk for the virus to infect the body. The symptoms of respiratory illness start to show up several days following infection.

In sum, there is evidence to support a role for stress in physical illness. Intensive short-term studies suggest that a causal chain explaining some of these effects may link stress to mood to immune function declines and ultimately to illness. However, whether stress-induced lessening of immune system functions actually leads to the more major and long-term negative clinical outcomes, such as early death from cancer, is uncertain (Zakowski, Hall, & Baum, 1992).

Individual Differences in the Consequences of Stress

What makes one person better able than another to handle the stress of making a sales presentation or taking a final exam? People differ in their susceptibility to the negative consequences of stress. A great deal of research has been directed at pinpointing those factors that determine the impact of a given stressor on an individual. At this time the best documented of the factors that moderate the impact of stress are (a) how the individual attempts to *cope* with the stressful situation and (b) the availability and quality of the person's *social support*.

Coping

With the approach of mid-terms or final exams, some students go to the library; others may talk over coffee about how nervous they are, decide to go to a movie to calm down, or pick up a copy of a favorite book or magazine. One of the factors influencing how severely people are affected by stress is how they cope with the event. There appear to be two main styles of coping that help reduce stress (Lazarus & Folkman, 1984). People who exhibit **problem-focused coping** take direct action to solve the problem or seek information that is relevant to the solution. An example of this type of coping is developing a study schedule to pace assignments over a semester and thereby reduce end-of-semester pressure. **Emotion-focused coping** refers to efforts to reduce negative emotional reactions to stress, even if the situation remains unchanged. For example, distracting oneself from the problem, relaxing, or seeking comfort from others are all emotion-focused coping tactics.

What coping tactics work best? It depends. A flexible coping repertoire may be most desirable. When a stressful situation is potentially under the person's control, problem-focused coping is probably better, whereas for unchangeable situations, emotion-focused coping might be better. Distraction, for instance, could be an effective way of dealing with fears regarding impending surgery, but it would be a poor way to handle the upset that would likely be produced by the discovery of a lump on one's breast (Lazarus & Folkman, 1984).

Social Support

Social support, the assistance of relatives and friends during times of stress, can help people achieve successful problem-focused or emotion-focused coping. Social support has two major aspects—structural and functional (Cohen & Wills, 1985). **Structural social support** refers to a person's network of social relationships, for example, marital status and number of friends. **Functional social support** is concerned more with the *quality* of a person's relationships. For example, does a person believe that he or she has friends to call on in time of need? And are those people able to provide the help necessary to decrease stress?

A lack of structural support has even been linked to death. Mortality has been associated with lower levels of structural support in an elderly population (Schoenbach, Kaplan, Fredman, & Kleinaum, 1986), in a large sample of members of a health maintenance organization (Vogt, Mullooly, Ernst, Pope, & Hollis, 1992), and among men who had experienced a heart attack (Ruberman, Weinblatt, Goldberg, & Chaudhary, 1984). On the whole, those with fewer friends died

problem-focused coping In response to stressful situations, taking direct action to improve the situation or seeking information that will yield a solution.

emotion-focused coping In response to stressful situations, taking steps to reduce one's negative emotional response, even if the situation stays the same.

structural social support A person's network of social relationships, for example, number of friends.

functional social support The quality of a person's relationships, for example, a good versus a distressed marriage.

Higher levels of social support reduce risk of illness. A close-knit family would be regarded as providing structural social support.

sooner than did those with a sizable network of friends and family. The role of functional support in predicting death, however, is unclear (S. Cohen, 1988).

Both structural and functional social support have been related to the onset of disease. For example, structural support correlates with various aspects of cardiovascular disease (Reed, McGhee, Yano, & Feinleib, 1983), and high functional support is linked with low rates of atherosclerosis (Seeman & Syme, 1987). Other studies have not shown such relations or have found mixed results. In one study, having fewer contacts with family and friends predicted onset of cancer and mortality from cancer for women, but not men (Reynolds & Kaplan, 1990).

To Recap

Psychophysiological disorders are physical diseases that are caused or worsened by emotional factors such as stress. Based on research on both animals and humans, it appears that illnesses can be affected by psychological factors. Stress probably increases susceptibility to illness through its impact on mood and mood's impact on various biological systems (e.g., hormonal, autonomic nervous system) as well as on the immune system. A person's susceptibility to the adverse effects of stress can be tempered by how that person attempts to cope with stress and by the quantity and quality of social support he or she has. Problem-focused coping includes taking direct action to solve a problem or seek information relevant to a solution. Emotion-focused coping refers to efforts to reduce emotional distress associated with the stressor. Two aspects of social support are structural, a person's network of social relationships, and functional, the quality of those relationships. Low levels of both forms of social support have been related to the onset of disease.

Illustrative Stress-Related Disorders

The picture of psychological influences on physical illness is clear on the surface, but fuzzy underneath. It is clear that stress is relevant to physical illness. But how it operates physically and the effect such variables as coping styles and social support systems have on whether these negative effects will occur is not precisely known. Stress and its effects may be so individual as to defy one all-encompassing explanation. There is evidence that stress plays a role in some specific illnesses, such as asthma, cancer, ulcers, and cardiovascular disorders. To give you a sense of how psychological investigators attempt to resolve complex questions about whether (and, if so, how) psychological factors affect physical health, we will look closely at two of these illnesses, asthma and cardiovascular disorders.

Asthma

asthma A disorder characterized by narrowing of the airways and increased secretion of mucus, which often cause breathing to be extremely labored and wheezy.

In **asthma**, the air passages and bronchioles are narrowed, causing breathing, particularly exhalation, to be wheezy and labored. In addition, there is an inflammation of lung tissue mediated by the immune system, resulting both in an increase in secretion of mucus and in edema (accumulation of fluid in the tissues).

It is estimated that between 2% and 5% of the population have asthma. One-third of asthma sufferers are children, and about two-thirds of these youngsters are boys (Graham, Rutter, Yule, & Pless, 1967; Purcell & Weiss, 1970). The earlier the disorder begins, the longer it is likely to last (Williams & McNicol, 1969). Asthma can be fatal if not treated appropriately, and for unknown reasons the mortality rate increased during the 1980s (Lehrer, Sargunaraj, & Hochron, 1992).

Description of Asthma

Asthma attacks occur intermittently and with variable severity. The frequency of some patients' attacks may increase seasonally when certain pollens are present. The airways are not continuously blocked; the respiratory system returns to normal or near normal either spontaneously or after treatment.

Most often, asthmatic attacks begin suddenly. The asthmatic individual has a sense of tightness in the chest, wheezes, coughs, and expectorates sputum. Subjective reactions can include panic, irritability, and fatigue (Kinsman, Spector, Shucard, & Luparello, 1974). A severe attack is a frightening experience indeed, even for onlookers. The asthma sufferer has immense difficulty getting air into and out of the lungs and feels as though he or she is suffocating. The raspy, harsh noise of the gasping, wheezing, and coughing compounds the terror. The sufferer may become exhausted by the exertion and fall asleep as soon as breathing is more normal.

The asthmatic takes a longer time than normal to exhale, and whistling sounds, referred to as rales, can be detected throughout the chest. Symptoms may last less than an hour or may continue for several hours or sometimes even days. Between attacks no abnormal signs may be detected when the individual is breathing normally, but forced, heavy expiration often allows the rales to be heard through a stethoscope.

The Multiple Causes of Asthma

Psychological factors likely play some role in causing asthma, but certainly do not tell the whole story. Allergies, respiratory infections, and environmental irritants, such as smoke and air pollution, are also influential. For example, in a study of 388 asthmatic children treated at an outpatient clinic, careful review of case histories, supplemented by laboratory tests, X rays, physical examinations, and behavioral observations, led to the conclusion that psychological factors—notably anxiety, anger, depression, or even pleasurable excitement, all of which may disturb the functioning of the respiratory system—were a dominant cause in about one-third of cases, a secondary cause in another one-third, and totally unimportant in the other one-third (Rees, 1964).

Intensive daily monitoring of respiratory functioning also supports the conclusion that emotional distress can bring on asthma attacks for some patients (Hyland, 1990). Consistent with Rees's data that psychological factors are relevant for about one-third of asthmatics, three of ten participants showed a strong relationship between mood and the amount of air they could exhale.

If asthma has a psychological component, is there a particular set of personality traits that predispose someone to develop asthma in response to stress? Research on personality factors in asthma is ambiguous, as noted in the following critical thinking exercise.

> ### APPLYING CRITICAL THINKING SKILLS

LINKING PERSONALITY TRAITS AND ASTHMA

It has often been suggested that particular personality traits are associated with asthma. Several investigators have found that asthmatic individuals possess many seemingly dysfunctional characteristics, such as dependency (J. Herbert, 1965), meekness, meticulousness, and perfectionism (Rees, 1964).

▶ *What conclusion does the evidence seem to support?* Given that there is a consistent association between personality traits and asthma, perhaps traits such as dependency and meekness play a role in causing asthma. The more bashful and less self-reliant child might, for instance, enjoy the extra attention and the opportunity to avoid challenging physical activities, such as sports. Asthma attacks, at least in some families, may fulfill these needs.

▶ *What other interpretations are plausible?* Maybe the direction of cause and effect is reversed. In other words, having asthma might cause dysfunctional personality characteristics. It seems reasonable that those who periodically experience extreme difficulty breathing might tend to become extremely cautious or anxious and dependent.

▶ *What other information would help choose among the alternative interpretations?* It would be useful to measure personality traits *before* asthma is apparent among a large, representative sample of children. These children would then need to be assessed repeatedly in order to determine which ones develop asthma and to monitor changes in personality. If personality traits cause asthma, then children who become asthmatic should appear more dependent, anxious, and meek at the initial evaluation while still healthy. If, instead, asthma causes the dysfunctional personality traits, then there should be no pre-existing personality differences, but differences should arise following the development of asthma.   ◀

The Possible Role of the Family.   Parent–child interactions may also be potential causes of asthma. In one investigation of 150 pregnant women with asthma, parents were interviewed three weeks after the children's births to determine attitudes toward and sensitivity to the infants, strategies for sharing parenting duties, and the presence of emotional disturbances (Mrazek, Klinnert, Mrazek, & Macey, 1991). Among the families who were rated as having problems, 25% of the children developed asthma in the next two years, as compared with only 8% of the children from the other families. Other research, however, has failed to show an association between parent–child relationships and asthma (Eiser, Eiser, Town, & Tripp, 1991). Research is thus not completely consistent regarding the role played by the home life of asthmatics in their illness.

Physiological Predisposition.   If dependency, excessive emotionality, or problematic parenting practices were shown more definitively to play a role in causing some proportion of asthma cases, we would still face the question of why everyone who is dependent, anxious, or the child of such a parent does not become asthmatic. In one study 86% of the asthmatics examined had a respiratory infection before asthma developed (Rees, 1964). Only 30% of control subjects had been so afflicted. Individuals whose asthma is primarily allergic may have an inherited hypersensitivity of the respiratory mucosa, which then overresponds to usually harmless substances, such as dust or pollen. Finally, asthmatics may have a less than normally responsive sympathetic nervous system (Miklich, Rewey, Weiss, & Kolton, 1973). Activation of the sympathetic nervous system reduces the intensity of an asthmatic attack.

Cardiovascular Disorders

cardiovascular disorders Medical problems involving the heart and blood circulation system, such as *essential hypertension* or *coronary heart disease*.

Cardiovascular disorders involve the heart and blood circulation system. Although the rate of death from cardiovascular disease has been decreasing since 1964, it remains a huge problem, accounting for almost half the deaths in the United States each year (Foreyt, 1990). In this section, we focus on the role of stress and personality in two forms of cardiovascular disease, hypertension and coronary heart disease.

Hypertension

essential hypertension A *psychophysiological disorder* characterized by high blood pressure that cannot be traced to a physical cause.

Hypertension, or high blood pressure, is one of the most serious psychophysiological disorders. It can lead to atherosclerosis (clogging of the arteries), heart attacks, and strokes, and it can also cause death through kidney failure. Only about 10% of all cases of hypertension in the United States have an identifiable physical cause. Hypertension without an evident physical cause is called **essential hypertension**. Recent estimates are that varying degrees of hypertension are found in 15% to 33% of the adult population of the United States. High blood pressure is

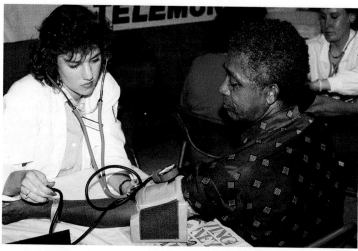

Because high blood pressure is typically not noticeable to the sufferer, regular checkups are recommended, especially for those at higher than average risk.

twice as frequent in African-Americans as in whites. As many as 10% of American college students have hypertension; most of them are unaware of their illness. Unless they check their blood pressure, people may go for years without knowing that they are hypertensive, which is why hypertension is often called "the silent killer."

Blood pressure is measured by two numbers: one represents **systolic pressure**, and the other represents **diastolic pressure**. The systolic measure is the amount of arterial pressure when the ventricles contract and the heart is pumping. The diastolic measure is the degree of arterial pressure when the ventricles relax and the heart is resting. A normal blood pressure in a young adult is 120 (systolic) over 80 (diastolic).

Various stressful conditions, ranging from confrontational interviews to natural disasters, have been found to produce short-term increases in blood pressure (e.g., Innes, Millar, & Valentine, 1959). How one responds to such stressors can also affect blood pressure. A series of laboratory studies was based on the hypothesis that inhibiting an aggressive response when angry would increase blood pressure. Subjects were given a task to perform. Then they were angered almost immediately by the interruptions of a supposed fellow subject, actually a confederate of the experimenter (e.g., Hokanson & Burgess, 1962). Later, half the subjects were given the opportunity to retaliate against the harasser. Harassment caused blood pressure to rise. Aggressing against the source of frustration then helped blood pressure to decrease.

More naturalistic studies in which people are asked how they would handle anger in a variety of situations also support the premise that holding anger in can be a cause of hypertension (e.g., Dimsdale et al., 1986). The case of John Williams, with which we began this chapter, seems to illustrate the dilemma of inhibited anger. Consider the mixed feelings he experienced on being invited to join an exclusive club and then being treated with seemingly excessive kindness. On the one hand, being patronized because of your race would of course provoke anger. On the other hand, what if (a) you are not absolutely sure that they are treating you differently on the basis of race; (b) what is overtly taking place is friendly behavior, not a confrontation or insult, and (c) your overall wish is to get along with the people in question? In such circumstances you might be strongly ambivalent about expressing your anger directly. Suppressing your anger may therefore be the logical choice, but the research on inhibited anger and hypertension suggests that it could be a costly one.

systolic pressure Amount of arterial pressure when the ventricles contract and the heart is pumping; for a young adult, 120 is normal.

diastolic pressure Amount of arterial pressure when the ventricles relax and the heart is resting; for a young adult, 80 is normal.

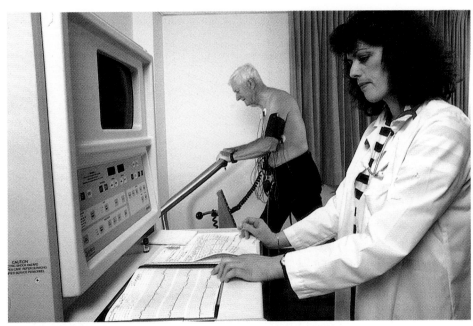

One test, used in both medical practice and in research on stress and illness, measures cardiovascular reactivity to exercise, such as walking on a treadmill.

How do short-term responses to stress, such as inhibited anger, lead to chronic hypertension? The most likely explanation is that the mechanism inducing long-term essential hypertension involves some structural changes, such as a thickening of the walls of the arteries. These structural changes might be the cumulative effects of many short-term increases in blood pressure in response to stress.

cardiovascular reactivity Temporary changes in measures of cardiovascular function, such as blood pressure, in response to specific events, such as *stressors*.

There has therefore been a great deal of interest in **cardiovascular reactivity**, the degree to which the cardiovascular system is reactive to stress, as a biological predisposition to hypertension. Results of studies that have tried to predict hypertension from reactivity vary, but those from several recent and well-conducted studies are positive (Adler & Matthews, 1994). For example, in one study cardiovascular measures were taken while subjects were threatened with shock if their responses were slow (Light, Dolan, Davis, & Sherwood, 1992). A follow-up ten to fifteen years later included a measure of cardiovascular functioning in a lab. Cardiovascular functioning was also measured during a day on which subjects wore a device that measured heart rate and blood pressure every hour. Assessment in the natural environment is important because some people, known as white coat hypertensives or office hypertensives, show much higher blood pressure in a physician's office than at home (e.g., Gerardi, Blanchard, Andrasik, & McCoy, 1985). Each of the cardiovascular reactivity measures taken earlier predicted blood pressure at the follow-up assessment.

Additional support for the importance of reactivity comes from research comparing individuals with and without a positive history for hypertension (e.g., Hastrup, Light, & Obrist, 1982). As anticipated, people with a positive family history showed greater blood pressure reactivity to stress. Coupled with other research showing the heritability of blood pressure reactivity (Matthews & Rakaczky, 1987) and the heritability of hypertension, blood pressure reactivity becomes a good candidate for a genetically transmitted vulnerability to hypertension.

Coronary Heart Disease

coronary heart disease (CHD) Angina pectoris, chest pains caused by insufficient supply of blood and thus oxygen to the heart; and myocardial infarction, or heart attack, in which the blood and oxygen supply are reduced so much that heart muscles are damaged.

Coronary heart disease (CHD) takes two main forms, angina pectoris and myocardial infarction, or heart attack. The symptoms of angina pectoris are periodic chest pains, frequently radiating into the left shoulder and arm. The major cause of these severe attacks of pain is an insufficient supply of oxygen to the heart. This deficiency, in turn, is traced to coronary atherosclerosis, a narrowing or plugging of the coronary arteries by deposits of fatty material. Angina is commonly relieved by rest or medication, and serious physical damage to the heart muscle rarely occurs.

Myocardial infarction is a much more serious disorder. It is the leading cause of death in the United States today. Like angina pectoris, myocardial infarction is caused by an insufficient supply of oxygen to the heart. The oxygen insufficiency, more extreme than in angina pectoris, results from coronary artery disease, a general reduction of the heart's blood supply through atherosclerosis, or from coronary occlusion, a sudden obstruction of a large coronary artery by deposits or a blood clot.

Risk factors for CHD include age, sex (men are at greater risk, though this difference is declining; see Focus Box 8.1 for more detailed discussion), cigarette smoking, elevated blood pressure, elevated serum cholesterol, increased size of the left ventricle of the heart, and diabetes (Adler & Matthews, 1994; Insull, 1973). These traditional, well-established risk factors do not fully account for CHD, however (Jenkins, 1976). Cross-cultural and subcultural comparisons illustrate the gap in our understanding of risk for CHD. For instance, in the Midwest, where diets are highest in saturated fats and smoking rates are especially high, the incidence of coronary heart disease is low compared with that in more industrialized parts of the United States. And anyone who has visited Paris is aware of the intemperate smoking and the fat-rich diets of the French population—yet CHD is relatively low there.

Type A Personality and CHD.   Therefore, there must be other causes of CHD. Psychological factors such as stress and personality are plausible candidates. In 1910 the Canadian physician Sir William Osler (1849–1919) described the typical angina patient as "vigorous in mind and body, and the keen and ambitious man, the indicator of whose engines is always set at full speed ahead" (Chesney, Eagleston, & Rosenman, 1980, p. 256). In 1958 two cardiologists, Meyer Friedman and Ray Rosenman, identified a coronary-prone behavior pattern, and called it **Type A behavior pattern**.

The Type A individual has an intense and competitive drive for achievement and advancement, an exaggerated sense of the urgency of passing time and of the need to hurry, and considerable aggressiveness and hostility toward others. Type A persons are overcommitted to their work, often attempt to carry on two activities at once, and believe that to get something done well, they must do it themselves. They cannot stand waiting in lines, and they play every game to win. Fast thinking, fast talking, and abrupt in gesture, they often jiggle their knees, tap their fingers, and blink rapidly. They are too busy to notice their surroundings or to be interested in things of beauty, and they tabulate success in life in numbers of articles written, projects under way, and material goods acquired. A second type of behavior pattern is called Type B. The Type B individual is less driven and relatively free of such pressures and hostility toward others.

The first convincing evidence that Type A behavior could be a cause of CHD was gathered in the Western Collaborative Group Study (WCGS) (Rosenman et al., 1975). A sample of about 3500 men aged thirty-nine to fifty-nine was followed over a period of eight and a half years. Some 3154 men completed the study. Those identified as Type A at the outset, based on their responses to a standardized interview, were more than twice as likely to develop CHD than were Type B men, even taking into account other risk factors, such as parental history of heart attacks, high blood levels of cholesterol, triglycerides, and lipids, diabetes, elevated blood pressure, cigarette smoking, lack of education, and lack of exercise.

These results do not mean that Type A men are highly likely to develop CHD. What the findings reveal is *relative* risk: Type A men were twice as likely as Type

Type A behavior pattern One of two contrasting psychological patterns revealed through studies seeking the cause of *coronary heart disease*. Type A people are competitive, rushed, hostile, and overcommitted to their work. Type As are believed to be at heightened risk for heart disease. People who fit the other pattern, Type B, are more relaxed and relatively free of pressure.

Sex Differences in Mortality

At every age from birth to eighty-five and older, more men die than women. In recent years, though, women's mortality advantage has been decreasing. The death rate from cardiovascular disease, for example, has declined among men in the last thirty years but has stayed about the same in women (Rodin & Ickovics, 1990).

What are some of the possible reasons for these findings? Tentative answers have been proposed from both biological and psychological points of view. From a biological vantage point it might be proposed that women have some mechanism that protects them from life-threatening diseases. For example, the female hormone, estrogen, may offer protection from cardiovascular disease. Several lines of evidence support this idea. First, postmenopausal women and those who have had their ovaries removed (in both cases lowering estrogen) have higher rates of cardiovascular disease than do premenopausal women. Furthermore, hormone replacement therapy lowers the rate of mortality from cardiovascular disease (Matthews et al., 1989).

Turning to a psychological proposal, women may be viewed as less likely than men to show Type A behavior pattern and less hostile than men (Weidner & Collins, 1993). Eisler and Blalock (1991) hypothesize that Type A is part of a rigid commitment to the traditional masculine gender role, which emphasizes achievement, mastery, competitiveness, refusal to ask for help or emotional support, an excessive need for control, and the tendency to become angry and to express anger when frustrated. They link these attributes to the tendency for men to be more prone to coronary problems and other stress-related health risks, such as hypertension (Harrison, Chin, & Ficarrotto, 1989).

Why is the gap between mortality rates in men and women decreasing? In the early twentieth century most deaths were due to epidemics and infection. Now most deaths result from diseases that are affected by lifestyle. One possibility, then, is that lifestyle differences between men and women account for the sex difference in mortality. As lifestyle differences decrease, the difference in mortality rates likewise decreases. Men smoke more than women and consume more alcohol. These

With improvements in control of most infectious diseases and birth complications in the twentieth century, lifestyle and behavioral risk factors have played an increasingly important role in mortality rates.

differences have been likely contributors to men's higher mortality from cardiovascular disease and lung cancer. In recent years, however, women have begun to smoke and drink more. These changes have been paralleled by increases in lung cancer and the failure of the mortality rate for cardiovascular disease to decrease among women (Rodin & Ickovics, 1990).

B men to develop CHD. But the overwhelming majority of Type A individuals do *not* develop CHD. By the late 1970s enough evidence had accumulated to lead a distinguished group of researchers to conclude that Type A is a major independent risk factor in CHD, at least for men (Review Panel on Coronary-Prone Behavior and Coronary Heart Disease, 1981). Further research identified and studied Type A women (Thoresen & Graff-Low, 1991), and the results appear to be equivalent (Miller, Turner, Tindale, Posavac, & Dugoni, 1991).

A striking trend is evident in recent research on the relation between Type A and CHD, however. Specifically, studies published in 1978 or earlier are far more likely than studies published in 1979 or later to show a significant relation (Miller et al., 1991). This does not necessarily mean, though, that the nature of heart disease changed in the late-1970's such that Type A personality characteristics no longer matter. A detailed review of studies that found Type A to be a risk factor and those that did not revealed some critical differences in research methods (Miller et al., 1991). In each case, earlier studies were more likely to employ the methods that tend to yield significant associations between Type A and CHD, so these research design issues might account for the change over time in research findings.

First, how Type A behavior pattern is measured makes a difference. Research using the Structured Interview technique (Rosenman et al., 1964) is more likely to find a relation with CHD than is research using questionnaire self-report measures of Type A. In the Structured Interview, questions about competition, achievement situations, and frustrating delays are asked in an intentionally provocative manner. For instance, the interviewer may deliberately stumble over words and thereby delay completing a question, may challenge the truthfulness of a subject's response, and so forth, all in an attempt to evoke impatience or hostility from the respondent if she or he is prone to such reactions. This method appears to be superior to more straightforward self-reports in identifying hostility and ultimately in predicting CHD (T. W. Smith, 1992).

Second, how the CHD criterion is defined makes a difference. No studies relating Type A to fatal myocardial infarction have found a predictive relationship. It appears that Type A people are more likely to suffer a heart attack, but that they actually survive longer after an attack than do Type B people who get heart attacks (e.g., Ragland & Brand, 1988). It is unclear why this is so. One possibility is that Type A behavior hastens the onset of CHD so that Type A's are younger than Type B's when they develop CHD. Other things being equal, of course, the young are likely to survive longer than the old. Or perhaps Type A subjects react to their first coronary event in a more adaptive fashion, for example, by altering some of their health habits in a more conscientious and effective manner.

In sum, the soundest studies support the conclusion that Type A behavior pattern is linked to increased risk of the onset of CHD. A further question is *how* such a relation occurs. Again, cardiovascular reactivity appears to be critical. Type A people generally have higher heart rate reactivity to stressful laboratory situations than do Type B people (Manuck & Krantz, 1986). Excessive changes in heart rate and the consequent alterations in the force with which blood is pumped through the arteries could injure arteries. Heart rate reactivity has been related to CHD in both animal (e.g., Manuck, Kaplan, Adams, & Clarkson, 1989) and human (Keys et al., 1971) research.

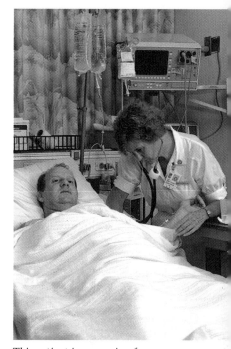

This patient is recovering from a heart attack. Type A Behavior Pattern has been linked to longer survival time after a heart attack, even though it may be a risk factor for having a heart attack in the first place.

TO RECAP

Research suggests that anxiety, anger, depression, and excitement are dominant causes in one-third of childhood asthma cases, secondary causes in another third, and irrelevant in the other third. Allergies, respiratory infections, and pollution are also believed to be causes. Asthma sufferers have some dysfunctional personality traits, but this may be a consequence rather than a cause of asthma. Physiological vulnerabilities, such as hypersensitivity of the respiratory mucosa, may serve as predisposing factors that, when aggravated by psychological stressors, produce asthma.

Essential hypertension (high blood pressure without an identifiable physical cause) may be influenced by psychological factors. Numerous stressful conditions produce short-term increases in blood pressure. People who suppress anger in response to frustration appear to be the most susceptible to such stress-related reactivity. Cardiovascular reactivity to experimentally induced stressors predicts blood pressure up to fifteen years later. Myocardial infarction (heart attack) is a serious form of coronary heart disease (CHD) thought to be influenced by psychological factors, such as Type A Behavior Pattern, in addition to other risk factors, such as cigarette smoking and high cholesterol. Studies assessing Type A behavior pattern on the basis of a provocative interview designed to evoke hostility and impatience often find a relation between Type A and CHD.

Perspectives on the Causes and Treatment of Stress-Related Disorders

Asthma and cardiovascular disorders illustrate how investigation into the physiological effects of psychological stress has proceeded from the basic idea that stress and other psychological factors can affect physical health to a more detailed understanding of some illnesses. In this section we take a step back to look at the big picture. Across disorders, how do the main perspectives of abnormal psychology explain the connection between stress and illness, and what do they have to say about how such disorders can be modified through treatment?

Psychodynamic Perspectives

According to one influential psychoanalytic theory of psychophysiological disorders, they are products of unconscious emotional states specific to each disorder (Alexander, 1950). For example, Alexander assumed that ulcer patients have repressed their longing for parental love in childhood and that this repressed impulse causes the overactivity of the autonomic nervous system and of the stomach, leading to ulcers. Physiologically, the stomach is continuously preparing to receive food, which the person has symbolically equated with parental love. Repressed hostile impulses, according to this view, are the psychological source of essential hypertension, which fits well with the research reviewed earlier on inhibited anger.

In treatment, traditional psychoanalysts who believe that anxiety underlies psychophysiological disorders employ techniques such as free association and dream analysis in their efforts to help the egos of their patients confront the origins of their fears. Ego analysts, however, like Franz Alexander, try to strengthen present functioning. Thus, for example, they would encourage patients with essential hypertension, viewed as laboring under a burden of undischarged anger, to learn to assert themselves, thereby alleviating the anger.

Biological Perspectives

somatic-weakness model The vulnerability of a particular organ or organ system to psychological *stress* and thereby to a particular *psychophysiological disorder.*

According to the **somatic-weakness model**, genetic factors, earlier illnesses, diet, and so on may disrupt a particular organ system, which may then become weak and vulnerable to stress. The connection between stress and a particular psychophysiological disorder is the weakness in a specific bodily organ. Like a tire that blows out at its weakest or thinnest portion, in the human body a congenitally weak respiratory system might predispose the individual to asthma, or a weak digestive system to ulcers.

Medications are available to treat many stress-related illnesses. For instance, several medications can reduce the constriction of the arteries and thereby lower the blood pressure of hypertensive patients. Asthma attacks can be alleviated by medications, taken either by inhalation or injection, that dilate the bronchial tubes. Although drug treatment can be helpful, there are sometimes negative side effects. Some antihypertensive drugs, for example, can cause drowsiness, light-headedness, and erectile difficulties for men. Even if side effects are not present, medications for the most part treat only the symptoms of a stress-related illness. In order to help patients get better and stay better, it is desirable to supplement this symptomatic relief with psychological interventions designed to develop new habits and attitudes conducive to handling stress effectively, as described next.

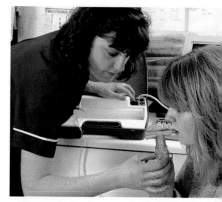

Asthma attacks are often treated by using a nebulizer to spray a fine mist of a bronchodilator into the bronchial tubes.

Cognitive and Behavioral Perspectives

Cognitive and behavioral perspectives are typically integrated in comprehensive programs for managing stress, so we shall discuss them together. In our general discussion of stress we saw that appraisal, how a person perceives a potential stressor, is central to how it affects that person. Therefore, people who continually appraise life experiences as exceeding their resources may be chronically stressed and at risk for the development of a psychophysiological disorder.

Perceiving threat is a mixed blessing, as we saw in Chapter 6 in regard to cognitive perspectives on anxiety. Humans perceive physical threats, such as a drunk driver weaving into their lane on the freeway. But we also perceive more nebulous psychosocial threats. We experience regrets about the past and worries about the future. All these perceptions stimulate sympathetic nervous system activity. But resentment and regret and worry cannot be fought or escaped as readily as can external threats, nor do they easily pass. They may keep the sympathetic system aroused and the body in a continual state of emergency, sometimes for far longer than it can bear. Under these circumstances, moreover, the necessary balancing of sympathetic and parasympathetic activity is made that much more difficult. Thus distressed thoughts bring about bodily changes that persist longer than the external threats that originally triggered them and that contribute to an imbalance between sympathetic and parasympathetic activity.

Stress Management

Unless you plan to live a very boring life, stress cannot be eliminated. It can be managed, though, and this is the aim of most therapies developed within the cognitive and behavioral perspectives. **Stress management** uses techniques designed to lower arousal, eliminate stress-producing thought patterns, teach coping skills, and improve individuals' social support systems (Davison & Thompson, 1988).

stress management A range of psychological procedures that help people control and reduce their *stress*.

Arousal Reduction. Teaching people to relax deeply and to apply these skills to real-life stressors can be helpful in lowering their stress levels. In arousal reduction the person is trained in muscle relaxation. There is some evidence that immune function (Jasnoski & Kugler, 1987), asthma (Steptoe, 1984), and hypertension (Kaufmann et al., 1988) can be improved via relaxation training. It is unclear, though, how enduring the effects of relaxation treatment are (Patel et al., 1985). Also, in some disorders, such as asthma, the average magnitude of the improvements resulting from relaxation alone are not considered sufficient (Lehrer et al., 1992). Relaxation training is often therefore considered an adjunctive treatment, to be used along with medications or with other techniques for stress management. Alternatively, it may be that there are subgroups of people for whom it is a sufficient treatment. One factor in determining the effectiveness of relaxation training is whether the person remains motivated to practice relaxation techniques regularly over the long haul.

Often used in conjunction with relaxation techniques, **biofeedback** provides

biofeedback Procedures that provide an individual immediate information on even minute changes in muscle activity, skin temperature, heart rate, blood pressure, and other bodily functions. It is assumed that voluntary control over these bodily processes can be achieved through this knowledge, thereby reducing to some extent certain *psychophysiological disorders*.

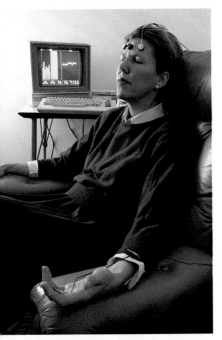

Biofeedback is often used in the treatment of psychophysiological disorders. Biofeedback can provide accurate information on physiological processes that, it is hoped, will allow the patient to gain better control of those processes.

people with prompt and exact information on heart rate, blood pressure, brain waves, skin temperature, and other bodily functions. Each of these physiological processes is monitored by a sensitive electronic recording device. The person knows instantaneously, through an auditory or visual signal, the rate of the process, whether it is too high or too low or just right. Numerous studies have shown that most people, if given the task, for example, of raising their heart rates or lowering their blood pressure, can do so with the help of biofeedback (Elmore & Tursky, 1978). In some instances, such as the treatment of migraine headaches, biofeedback has achieved a central place in stress management. In many areas, though, it is not clear that biofeedback adds anything to what can be achieved through relaxation training without biofeedback.

Cognitive Restructuring. In a general sense, cognitive approaches can be seen as focusing on the appraisal processes that Richard Lazarus identifies as critical in how people react to environmental stressors (e.g., Lazarus & Folkman, 1984). Cognitive restructuring methods, a central focus of rational-emotive therapy and cognitive therapy (see Chapter 3), involve changing people's belief systems. For example, one stress-management program for hostile Type A individuals targeted their common belief that "other people tend to be ignorant and inept" (Friedman & Ulmer, 1984, p. 223). Patients were encouraged to question the accuracy and usefulness of getting angry when others make mistakes (e.g., are there circumstances that might have contributed to this person's having difficulty?).

Behavioral Skills Training. Because it is natural to feel overwhelmed if one lacks the skills to execute a challenging task, stress management often includes instruction and practice in necessary skills as well as in general issues, such as time management. As an example of the complex interplay among behavior, emotion, and cognition, social-skills training can enhance a person's sense of self-efficacy (Bandura, 1986) by improving control over environmental stressors (Rodin, 1986). This enhanced control reduces stress.

Social-Support Enhancement. Because social support helps keep people healthy or helps them cope with illnesses, therapists often use supportive group therapy. Such interventions can help people cope with cancer. Groups providing emotional support, information about cancer and its medical treatment, relaxation training, and coping-skills training (such as practicing how to discuss decisions about care with family or medical staff) show positive effects in alleviating anxiety and depression, increasing the use of active, problem-focused coping rather than a more passive, defeatist approach to the disease, and improving some measures of immune system functioning (B. L. Andersen, 1992).

A particularly noteworthy research program, under the direction of David Spiegel, confirms the utility of psychosocial interventions in improving the quality of life and even in extending the survival time of patients with terminal cancer. Fatigue, anxiety, and depression in metastatic breast cancer patients were reduced by supportive weekly group therapy (Spiegel, Bloom, & Yalom, 1981). Patients offered understanding and comfort to each other, encouraged each other to live life as fully as possible in the face of death, openly discussed death and dying, and learned self-hypnosis techniques to control pain. Even more impressive are ten-year follow-up findings that this one-year supportive group intervention actually prolonged survival time by an average of a year and a half (Spiegel, Bloom, Kraemer, & Gottheil, 1989; Spiegel, 1990).

Speculating about these survival findings—which were not expected—Spiegel and his associates suggested that perhaps the therapy helped patients better comply with medical treatment or improved their appetite and diet by enhancing their mood. Ability to control pain might also have helped them be more

Supportive group therapy can improve quality of life and extend survival time according to research with breast cancer patients.

physically active. And, consistent with research reviewed earlier on how stress affects the immune system, the therapy might have improved immune function by controlling stress, with social support a key factor (House, Landis, & Umberson, 1988).

Multimethod Programs.   Stress-management programs often include more than one of the techniques just reviewed (Lehrer & Woolfolk, 1993). The relevance of multiple stress-management methods in coping with pediatric cancer is discussed in Focus Box 8.2. Another program integrating multiple strategies was directed at changing Type A Behavior Pattern among heart attack survivors—the Recurrent Coronary Prevention Project (Friedman et al., 1982). The overall purpose of this project was to change the Type A behavior of men who had suffered a heart attack in the direction of Type B, in the hope of preventing second heart attacks.

The treatment that was expected to help subjects the most attempted to alter their Type A behavior as well as the environmental, cognitive, and physiological factors believed to contribute to their hard-driving, hostile personalities. Patients practiced talking more slowly and listening to others more closely instead of interrupting. They were also encouraged to reduce excessive activities and demands and to relax more. They watched less television (an environmental switch), and they attempted to alter their self-talk by thinking that events are not necessarily direct challenges to them and by considering that Type A behavior may not be essential to success (a cognitive adjustment). They also complied with their physicians' drug and diet prescriptions to improve their physiological states.

Results were encouraging. Type A behavior was reduced. After three years of treatment, for men who had received Type A counseling the risk of a second heart attack was 7.2% annually, compared with 13.2% for men who received only cardiological counseling (Friedman et al., 1984; Powell, Friedman, Thoresen, Gill, & Ulmer, 1984; Thoresen, Friedman, Powell, Gill, & Ulmer, 1985). Reductions in

FOCUS BOX 8.2

Coping with Pediatric Cancer

In recent years, many forms of childhood cancer, such as acute lymphoblastic leukemia, have become treatable. Some types can be treated so effectively that they go into remission and the children are alive five years after the onset of cancer. With such improvement, however, come new challenges of a psychological nature for both patients and families—learning to live with the disease and its treatment.

Although many pediatric cancer patients and their families cope extremely well, it is undeniably stressful to live with a cancer diagnosis and the long-term medical care that is required. In one study, 17% of pediatric cancer patients met DSM criteria for depression, and separation anxiety was also common (Kashani & Hakami, 1982). Cognitive factors may be relevant in determining such emotional responses. Consistent with Lazarus's relational model of stress reviewed earlier in this chapter, pediatric cancer patients who appraised cancer or a recent cancer-related hassle (such as having to miss school or other activities because of the treatment regimen) as threatening or disruptive were more likely than others with the same disease severity to report high levels of anger, anxiety, and depressive symptoms (Burgess & Haaga, 1994).

Such descriptive and correlational research suggests that multifaceted stress management programs could be helpful for pediatric cancer patients and their families. Research and clinical experience have led to several guidelines for such interventions. First, concealing from a youngster the true nature of his or her illness and how life threatening it is increases rather than decreases anxiety (e.g., Spinetta, 1980). Open communication with the child is advocated. Research advises maintaining the child in his or her regular school as much as possible (Katz, 1980). Because cancer and its treatment can bring physical disfigurement, such as hair loss, the child should be taught to handle the teas-ing that often awaits any youngster who looks different. Assertion training and learning to ignore the hurtful remarks can be helpful.

Cancer does not have only long-term negative health implications. Pain accompanies both the diagnosis and the treatment of childhood cancer. A child with leukemia must undergo frequent and regular bone-marrow aspiration. The physician inserts a long needle into the middle of the thigh bone and extracts some marrow. It hurts. And it is not the kind of pain to which the person readily becomes habituated (Katz, Kellerman, & Siegel, 1980). The experience takes a toll on the young patient and on the parents as well. Hypnotic imagery techniques that teach the child to relax can help reduce the trauma of this inevitable medical event. Other interventions have also proven useful for this painful procedure. Jay, Elliott, Katz, and Siegel (1987) compared Valium with a cognitive-behavioral package that included breathing exercises and distraction from the pain. They found that the psychological intervention was superior to the tranquilizer in reducing behavioral and self-report measures of stress as well as pulse rate.

Children who develop anticipatory anxiety before undergoing other painful medical procedures have been helped by viewing films of other children coping with the procedure, thus providing a positive model (Jay, Elliott, Ozolins, & Olson, 1982). Systematic desensitization to situations associated with the pain, such as entering the hospital and sitting in the waiting room, can reduce the level of anxiety with which a patient comes to the medical procedure and thus, in turn, alleviate the pain. Reducing anxiety can be of more general importance. An extremely anxious child, for example, may avoid the medical procedure or may begin to lose weight, which decreases the chances of surviving cancer (Dewys, Begg, & Lavin, 1980).

---

hostility may have been particularly influential, consistent with its increasing importance in Type A research.

Ideally, the best approach to applying the results of this study would be to prevent Type A behavior pattern from developing in the first place, rather than waiting until after an initial heart attack. There are, however, many obstacles to reducing Type A patterns in our culture (Price, 1982). Being a Type A person is in many ways a cultural norm in the United States and in other countries as well. Often it takes a heart attack to force a Type A person to consider giving up the aggressive, individualistic struggle to gain as many material rewards as possible in the shortest amount of time and instead to treasure leisure time and to value people, including himself or herself, for their intrinsic worth rather than for their achievements and status.

To Recap

Different theoretical orientations have different conceptions about the causes of and treatments for stress-related disorders. Psychodynamic views of psychophysiological disorders are based on the assumption that they come about as the result of repressed emotions. The specific nature of the repression determines which organ is affected. Treatment involves helping patients confront the origins of their repressed conflict.

One biological perspective is the somatic-weakness model, which holds that the connection between stress and psychophysiological disorders is a weakness in a bodily organ. Biological factors such as genetics or previous illnesses create weaknesses that make certain organs or systems vulnerable to damage from stress. Biological treatment generally takes the form of medication for stress-related disorders such as hypertension and asthma. Cognitive perspectives emphasize that perceptions of psychosocial threat may keep the sympathetic nervous system chronically aroused, which could lead to organic damage. Cognitive and behavioral perspectives espouse stress-management treatments, which may involve training in relaxation, cognitive restructuring, behavioral skills, social-support enhancement, or often combinations of these methods.

The Case of John Williams Revisited ◀

Conceptualization and Treatment

Some weeks after the alarmingly high blood pressure reading in the dentist's office, John located a therapist, but the choice of whom to see—never an easy matter for anyone—presented special difficulties for him. Although he lived near a large city, there were few African-American psychiatrists or psychologists. He decided to work with a white psychologist.

"Well, what do you really want out of life?" asked Dr. Shaw, a distinguished and experienced clinical psychologist. "The same thing everyone else is after," was John's reply. "But what is that?" queried the psychologist.

The first couple of sessions were like this. Dr. Shaw tried to get John to examine what he really wanted, and John sparred with him, fending off the questions with generalities about "all other people." In Dr. Shaw's mind, John Williams did not want to confront the conflicts of playing a role in the white professional world. John identified with being an African-American, Dr. Shaw believed, but sensed a falseness about his life. He let racial slurs go by without comment. He hid from his law office colleagues his membership in several civil rights groups and his feeling that current civil rights leaders were somewhat too moderate.

During these early sessions, Dr. Shaw thought that he should pressure John more, but realized that he was holding back in a way he would not with a white client. Was it his right to suggest to John that he was at the same time proud and ashamed of his race, that he despised himself for hiding his feelings? Indeed, was it his duty? But how could he be certain? And wouldn't it be terrible if he intimated something to John that was off base? That, too, was something Dr. Shaw worried far less about with his white clients. Although no therapist is infallible, Dr. Shaw somehow felt that with John he had to be more certain about his interpretations.

A crisis took place in the fifth and final session. For months afterward Dr. Shaw wondered whether he had blundered so badly as to drive his client from therapy.

DR. SHAW: John, I've been wondering about what you've told me about your college days.

JOHN: What aspect of them?

DR. SHAW: Well, I guess I was thinking about the club.

JOHN: Well, what about the club?

DR. SHAW: Your feelings of being the only black.

JOHN: Well, I felt really good about it. I used to daydream about what my high school friends would think.

DR. SHAW: And what would they have thought?

JOHN: They'd have envied me. I mean, I must be doing something right.

DR. SHAW: Yes, I know you were quite proud about it. . . . But I wonder if you had any other feelings about it.

JOHN: What do you mean?

DR. SHAW: Well, lots of times people are conflicted about things that are important to them. Like the nervous bridegroom on the wedding day. He's eager for the honeymoon, but he knows he's giving up something.

JOHN: What do you think I was giving up?

DR. SHAW: You feel you were giving up something by being in the club?

JOHN: Come on, Doc, don't play games. You know damn well that *you* think I gave up something. What did I give up?

DR. SHAW: John, if anything was given up, it was you who gave it up, not I.

JOHN: I resent what you're implying.

DR. SHAW: Okay, but can you explore it, just hypothetically?

JOHN: Okay, Shaw, let me think of what I gave up. (*At this point there was a lengthy silence. John stared at his feet, Dr. Shaw at his notes, occasionally glancing up at John but not wanting to look at him too much.*)

DR. SHAW: John, can you share some of your thoughts with me?

JOHN: Doc, I can't do it. You're one of them.

DR. SHAW: One of whom?

JOHN: Doc, I can't talk to a white man about this. I can't talk to a black man about this. I'm too ashamed, too mixed up. (*Beginning to sob.*) I can't handle this.

DR. SHAW: This is hard for you, I know, John. But this is a place you can use to look at those feelings. Try to sort them out. Try to figure out what you really want. . . .

JOHN (*interrupting the psychologist*): No! It's not for you to tell me what I should be doing. *I'm* the one who has to decide.

(*Long silence again.*)

DR. SHAW: John, perhaps that's enough for today.

JOHN (*relieved*): Yes, that's right. That's enough . . . for today.

DR. SHAW: See you next week, same time.

JOHN: Yeah. Thanks. I'll see you next week.

John did not, however, return for another treatment session the following week, or ever.

DISCUSSION

In view of the research discussed earlier on the role of inhibited anger in hypertension, we can hypothesize that John Williams's habit of inhibiting anger and resentment played a role in the development of his high blood pressure.

African-Americans as a group have an especially high incidence of hypertension. Is there a genetic basis for this connected to race? Probably not. The causes may be found in social factors. A study of African-Americans and whites in two areas of Detroit—a poor neighborhood, with a high crime rate, overcrowding, and many marital breakups, and a middle-class neighborhood—found that blood pressure was higher among African-Americans than among whites. But African-Americans living in the poor neighborhood had higher blood pressure than did African-Americans living in the middle-class area. Thus, while race was one factor, also important were social class and the accompanying stress that comes with living in marginal circumstances. It would seem that

Research suggests that the crowding, crime, and economic hardship sometimes found in urban areas can contribute to hypertension.

the high blood pressure among African-Americans has a great deal to do with the socially created stress under which they live (Harburg et al., 1973).

In the case of John Williams, stress was not socioeconomic. Like many people, he succeeded in increasing his life pressures by his constant striving for perfection, over and above the pressure created as he suppressed feelings caused by the prejudice he encountered. His blood pressure apparently increased as well from the tremendous conflict he experienced as an African-American man who felt that he was at times being false to himself, compromising his beliefs and ideals in order to succeed in white society.

For African-Americans, the emotional challenges posed by discrepancies between the values, beliefs, norms, and behaviors of African-Americans and those of the majority white community represent a form of acculturative stress (L. P. Anderson, 1991). As with other minority groups, there are pressures on African-Americans to assimilate, while at the same time there are obstacles to their being truly accepted by the majority community.

Just as uncontrolled case studies do not prove why therapy is often successful, so, too, an unsuccessful case such as the one reported here is usually subject to multiple interpretations. One possibility is that Dr. Shaw was too abrupt in pushing John Williams to talk about issues of racial identity and acculturative stress. As important as these issues seem to have been in the case, it might have worked better (perhaps especially in view of the race difference between patient and therapist) to spend more time developing and communicating empathy for the patient's perspective before pushing a particular perspective on the internal conflict John needed to address. And yet, given the parallels between the therapeutic relationship and the stresses on John Williams, the therapy might have been marked by difficulties under any circumstances.

Visual Summary for Chapter 8:

Stress and Health

Definitions of Stress

There is no one universally accepted definition of stress. However, three ways of measuring and testing stress have evolved.

Situational ····▶ Defines stress as events or circumstances having a particular characteristic. ····▶ If Persons A and B witness a fatal accident, both are stressed.

Response-Based ····▶ Stress is a particular pattern of behavioral, emotional, or biological reactions. ····▶ Person B experiences no ill effects. Person A has nightmares. Person A is stressed; Person B is not.

Relational ····▶ Stress lies in the relationship between the situation and the person's response to it. ····▶ Emotions stirred up in Person A exceed coping abilities; Person A is stressed. Person B copes by seeking support from friends; B's stress is minimized.

Stress and Physical Illness

Psychophysiological disorders are physical diseases that are caused or worsened by psychological factors such as stress. Susceptibility to stress can be tempered by

Coping ····▶ Problem-focused
····▶ Emotion-focused

Social Support ····▶ Structural
····▶ Functional

Stress-Related Disorders

A vulnerability-stress model may be the best fit for psychophysiological disorders.

Predisposition	+	Psychological Factors	+	Other Factors	···▸	Disease
Respiratory Mucosa Hyperresponsive	+	Emotional Arousal (family? personality?)	+	Allergies, Environmental Irritants, etc.	···▸	Asthma
Cardiovascular Reactivity	+	Suppressed Anger	··············		▸	Hypertension
Enlarged Left Ventricle	+	Type A Personality	+	Smoking, Cholesterol, Inactivity	···▸	Coronary Heart Disease

Perspectives on Causes and Treatment of Stress-Related Disorders

Differing orientations have differing views of causes and treatment.

Orientation		Cause		Treatment
Biological	···▸	Somatic Weakness	···▸	Medication
Psychodynamic	···▸	Repressed Conflict	···▸	Confront Origins of Repressed Desire
Cognitive and Behavioral	···▸	Appraisal of Stressor as Exceeding Resources	···▸	•Arousal Reduction •Cognitive Restructuring •Behavioral Skills Training •Social-Support Enhancement

Chapter 9

Schizophrenia

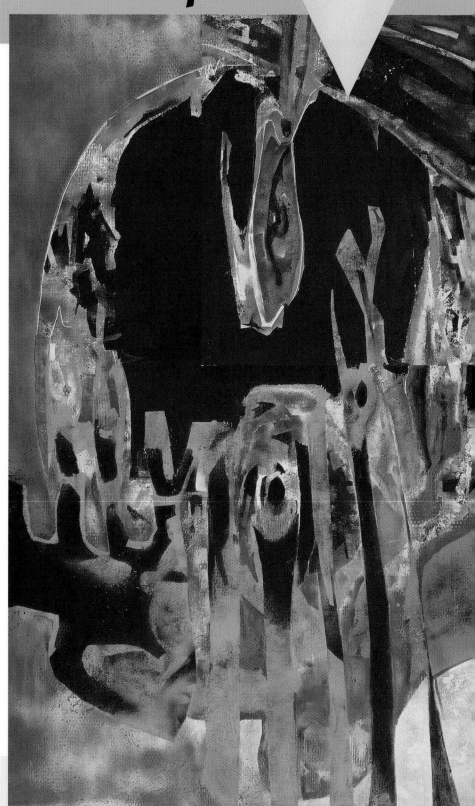

The Case of Bill McClary ◀

Bill McClary made his first appointment at the mental health center reluctantly. He was twenty-five years old, single, and unemployed. His sister, Colleen, with whom he had been living for eighteen months, had repeatedly encouraged him to seek professional help. She was concerned about his peculiar behavior and social isolation. He spent most of his time daydreaming, often talked to himself, and occasionally said things that made little sense. Bill acknowledged that he ought to keep more regular hours and assume more responsibility, but he insisted that he did not need psychological treatment. He finally made the appointment in an effort to please his sister and her husband.

During the first session, Bill spoke quietly and frequently hesitated. The therapist noted that Bill occasionally blinked and shook his head as though he was trying to clear his thoughts or return his concentration to the topic at hand. When the therapist commented on this unusual twitch, Bill apologized politely but denied that it held any significance. He was friendly, yet shy and ill at ease. The discussion centered on Bill's daily routine and his unsuccessful efforts to fit into the routine of Colleen's family. Bill assured the therapist that his problems would be solved if he could stop daydreaming. He also expressed a desire to become better organized.

Bill continued to be very guarded throughout the early therapy sessions. After several weeks, he began to discuss his social contacts and mentioned a concern about sexual orientation. Despite his lack of close friends, Bill had had some limited sexual experiences. These had been both heterosexual and homosexual. He was quite concerned about the possible meaning and consequences of his encounters with other men. This topic occupied much of the early phase of therapy.

A few months after Bill began attending the clinic, the therapist received a call from Bill's brother-in-law, Roger. Roger said that he and Bill had recently talked about some of Bill's unusual ideas, and Roger wanted to know how he should respond. The therapist asked Bill about these ideas at their next therapy session. He thereby became aware of an extensive delusional belief system that Bill held, which he described as follows,

> Shortly after moving to his sister's home, Bill realized that something strange was happening. He noticed that people were taking special interest in him and often felt that they were talking about him behind his back. These puzzling circumstances persisted for several weeks, during which Bill became increasingly anxious and suspicious. The pieces of the puzzle finally fell in place late one night as Bill sat in front of the television. In a flash of insight, Bill arrived at the belief that a group of conspirators had secretly produced and distributed a documentary film about his homosexual experiences. Several of his high school friends and a few distant relatives had presumably used hidden cameras and microphones to record each of his sexual encounters with other men. Bill believed that the film had grossed over $50 million at the box office and that this money had been sent to the Irish Republican Army to buy arms and ammunition. He therefore held himself responsible for the deaths of dozens of people who had died as the result of several recent bombings in Ireland.

This notion struck the therapist and Bill's brother-in-law as being preposterous, but Bill's conviction was genuine. He was visibly moved as he described his guilt concerning the bombings. He was also afraid that serious consequences would follow his confession. Bill believed that the conspirators had agreed to kill him if he ever found out about the movie. This imagined threat had prevented Bill from confiding in anyone previously. He now feared for his life.

Bill's fear was exacerbated by the voices he had been hearing for the past several weeks. He frequently heard male voices discussing his sexual behavior and arguing about what action should be taken to punish him. These voices terrified Bill.

schizophrenia A group of psychotic disorders characterized by major disturbances in thought, emotion, and behavior: disordered thinking in which ideas are not logically related; faulty perception and attention; bizarre disturbances in motor activity; flat or inappropriate emotions; and reduced tolerance for stress of interpersonal relations. The patient withdraws from people and reality, often into a fantasy life of *delusions* and *hallucinations*.

B ill's symptoms—the paranoid thinking and preposterous beliefs, the voices he heard—are a few of the wide variety of disturbances in thought, emotion, and behavior that characterize **schizophrenia**. Although the diagnosis of schizophrenia has existed now for about a century, and the disorder has spawned more research than any other, we are far from fully understanding this serious mental disorder. In this chapter we first provide descriptions of the diverse symptoms of schizophrenia. Next we consider the history of the diagnosis, and finally we examine research on the causes and treatment of schizophrenia.

Symptoms of Schizophrenia

The symptoms of schizophrenia involve disturbances in many areas of thinking, behavior, and emotional functioning. The range of problems of people diagnosed as schizophrenic is extensive, although patients who are so diagnosed typically have only *some* of them. Schizophrenia is unlike some of the other DSM diagnostic categories that we have considered in that there is no essential symptom that must be present, and schizophrenic patients differ substantially from one another.

positive symptoms In *schizophrenia*, behavioral excesses, such as *hallucinations* and bizarre behavior.

negative symptoms Behavioral deficits in *schizophrenia*, such as *flat affect* and apathy.

One way of categorizing the symptoms that has turned out to be useful in research (described later in the chapter) is to distinguish **positive symptoms** from **negative symptoms**. *Positive* does not mean "good" or "favorable" in this context. Instead, positive symptoms consist of excesses, such as hearing voices when no one is speaking, whereas negative symptoms consist of deficits, such as an inability to express a normal range of emotions.

Positive Symptoms

The excesses that characterize positive symptoms can affect how schizophrenics think, speak, and perceive. Many of the most noticeable of the mentally ill homeless exhibit positive symptoms of schizophrenia.

Disorganized Speech

disorganized speech Speech found in *schizophrenics* that is marked by problems in the organization of ideas and in speaking so that others can understand.

Disorganized speech refers to problems in the organization of ideas and in speaking so that a listener can understand. Here is an example:

> INTERVIEWER: Have you been nervous or tense lately?
> SCHIZOPHRENIC: No, I got a head of lettuce.
> INTERVIEWER: You got a head of lettuce? I don't understand.
> SCHIZOPHRENIC: Well, it's just a head of lettuce.
> INTERVIEWER: Tell me about lettuce. What do you mean?
> SCHIZOPHRENIC: Well . . . lettuce is a transformation of a dead cougar that suffered a relapse on the lion's toe. And he swallowed the lion and something happened. The . . . see, the . . . Gloria and Tommy, they're two heads and they're not whales. But they escaped with herds of vomit, and things like that.
> INTERVIEWER: Who are Tommy and Gloria?
> SCHIZOPHRENIC: Uh . . . there's Joe DiMaggio, Tommy Henrich, Bill Dickey, Phil Rizzuto, John Esclavera, Del Crandell, Ted Williams, Mickey Mantle, Roy Mantle, Ray Mantle, Bob Chance . . .
> INTERVIEWER: Who are they? Who are those people?
> SCHIZOPHRENIC: Dead people . . . that want to be fucked . . . by this outlaw.
> INTERVIEWER: What does all that mean?
> SCHIZOPHRENIC: Well, you see, I have to leave the hospital. I'm supposed to have an operation on my legs, you know. And it comes to me pretty sickly that I don't want to keep my legs. That's why I wish I could have an operation.

INTERVIEWER: You want to have your legs taken off?

SCHIZOPHRENIC: It's possible, you know.

INTERVIEWER: Why would you want to do that?

SCHIZOPHRENIC: I didn't have any legs to begin with. So I would imagine that if I was a fast runner, I'd be scared to be a wife, because I had a splinter inside of my head of lettuce. (Neale & Oltmanns, 1980, pp. 103–104)

This excerpt illustrates the incoherence sometimes found in the conversation of schizophrenics. Although the patient may make repeated references to central ideas or a theme, the images and fragments of thought are not connected. Thus it is quite difficult to understand exactly what the patient is trying to say.

Speech may also be characterized by **loose associations**. In this case the patient may be more successful in communicating with a listener, but he or she has difficulty sticking to one topic. The patient seems to drift off on a train of associations evoked by an idea from the past.

loose associations Typical of *schizophrenia*; the patient has difficulty sticking to one topic and drifts off on a train of associations evoked by an idea from the past.

Disturbances in speech at one time were regarded as the principal symptom of schizophrenia, and they remain one of the criteria for the diagnosis. But evidence indicates that the speech of many schizophrenics is not disorganized. Furthermore, the presence of disorganized speech does not discriminate well between schizophrenics and other psychotic patients, such as some patients with mood disorders (Andreasen, 1979). For example, many manic patients show as much loosening of associations as do schizophrenics.

Delusions

No doubt all of us at one time or another are concerned because we believe that others think ill of us. Many schizophrenics, however, are subject to **delusions**, holding beliefs that the rest of society would generally disagree with or view as misinterpretations of reality. Consider for a moment what life would be like if you were firmly convinced that many people did not like you, indeed, that they were plotting against you. Some of these persecutors have sophisticated listening devices that allow them to tune in on your most private conversations, and they are gathering evidence in a plot to discredit you. Not one of those around you, including your loved ones, is able to reassure you that these people are not spying on you. In fact, even your closest friends and confidants are gradually joining your tormentors and becoming members of the persecuting community. You are naturally quite anxious or angry about your situation, and you begin your own counteractions against the imagined persecutors. Any new room you enter must be carefully checked for listening devices. When you meet someone for the first time, you question your new acquaintance at great length to determine whether he or she is part of the plot against you.

delusions Beliefs contrary to reality, firmly held in spite of contradictory evidence. For example, delusions of persecution are beliefs that one is being plotted against or oppressed by others.

Delusions of persecution, such as those described here, were found in 65% of the sample in the World Health Organization's International Pilot Study of Schizophrenia (IPSS; Sartorius, Shapiro, & Jablonsky, 1974). Schizophrenics' delusions may take several other forms as well. Patients may believe that thoughts have been placed in their mind by an external source or that they are passive, unwilling recipients of bodily sensations imposed by an external agency. Other patients think that their thoughts are transmitted so that others know them, or that their own thoughts are stolen from their mind by an external force, suddenly and unexpectedly.

A twenty-two-year-old woman [described such an experience]. "I am thinking about my mother, and suddenly my thoughts are sucked out of my mind by a phrenological vacuum extractor, and there is nothing in my mind, it is empty. . . . " (Mellor, 1970, pp. 16–17)

Like speech disorganization, delusions are common among schizophrenics but not unique to them. They are found also among patients in other diagnostic categories, notably mania and delusional depression.

Disorders of Perception

hallucinations Perceptions in any sensory modality without relevant and adequate external stimuli.

Schizophrenic patients frequently report that the world seems somehow different or even unreal to them. Some mention changes in the way their bodies feel. Parts of their bodies may seem too large or too small, objects around them too close or too far away. Or they may experience numbness or tingling and electrical or burning sensations. Patients may feel as though snakes are crawling inside the abdomen. The body may become so depersonalized that it feels as though it is a machine. Some patients become hypersensitive to sights, sounds, and smells. They may find it torment to be touched. Light may seem blinding, and noise an agony. Others remark that their surroundings are not as they used to be, that everything appears flat and colorless.

The most dramatic distortions of perception are called **hallucinations**, sensory experiences in the absence of any stimulation from the environment. They can occur in any sensory modality but are most commonly found in hearing. Seventy-four percent of the IPSS sample reported having auditory hallucinations, often of voices arguing or commenting.

> A twenty-four-year-old male patient reported hearing voices coming from the nurse's office. One voice, deep in pitch and roughly spoken, repeatedly said "G.T. is a bloody paradox," and another higher in pitch said, "He is that, he should be locked up." A female voice occasionally interrupted, saying, "He is not, he is a lovely man." (Mellor, 1970, p. 16)

Negative Symptoms

In contrast to schizophrenics with mostly positive symptoms, those with primarily negative symptoms may appear less disturbed because they may be less noticeable. However, negative symptoms, though perhaps less immediately troubling to others, are nonetheless very serious and no less troubling to the disturbed individual. As we will see, they may also have a stronger genetic influence.

Avolition

avolition A *negative symptom* in *schizophrenia* in which the individual lacks interest and drive.

Avolition, or apathy, refers to a lack of energy and seeming absence of interest in what are usually routine activities. Patients may be inattentive to grooming and personal hygiene, with uncombed hair, unbrushed teeth, and disheveled clothes. They have difficulty persisting at work, school, or household chores and spend a lot of time just doing nothing.

Poverty of Speech and Poverty of Content

In *poverty of speech*, the amount of speech is greatly reduced. Alternatively, the amount of speech may be adequate, but convey little information, tending to be vague and repetitive. This *poverty of content of speech* is illustrated in the following excerpt.

> INTERVIEWER: O.K. Why is it, do you think, that people believe in God?
> PATIENT: Well, first of all because, He is the person that, is their personal savior. He walks with me and talks with me. And uh, the understanding that I have, a lot of peoples, they don't really know their personal self. Because they ain't, they all, just

don't know their personal self. They don't know that He uh, seems to like me, a lot of them don't understand that He walks and talks with them. And uh, show 'em their way to go. I understand also that, every man and every lady, is not just pointed in the same direction. Some are pointed different. They go in their different ways. The way that Jesus Christ wanted 'em to go. Myself. I am pointed in the ways of uh, knowing right from wrong, and doing it, I can't do any more, or not less than that. (American Psychiatric Association, 1987, pp. 403–404)

Flat Affect

In patients with **flat affect**, virtually nothing can elicit an emotional response. The patient may stare vacantly with lifeless eyes. When spoken to, he or she answers in a flat and toneless voice. Flat affect was found in 66% of the IPSS schizophrenics.

Flat affect refers only to the outward expression of emotion and not to the patient's inner experience, which may not be impoverished at all. In one study, schizophrenics and normal subjects watched excerpts from films while their facial reactions and skin conductance were recorded. After each film clip subjects reported the moods the films had elicited in them. As expected, schizophrenics were much less facially expressive than normal people, but they reported about the same amount of emotion and were even more physiologically aroused (Kring, 1991).

> **flat affect** A deviation in emotional response wherein virtually no emotion is expressed, whatever the stimulus.

Other Symptoms

Several other symptoms of schizophrenia do not fit neatly into the positive–negative scheme we have presented. One of these is catatonia. At one end of the spectrum is **catatonic immobility**: unusual postures are adopted and maintained for very long periods of time. A patient may stand on one leg, with the other tucked up toward the buttocks, and remain in this position virtually all day. Catatonic patients may also have **waxy flexibility**: another person can move the patient's limbs into strange positions that will then be maintained for long periods of time. At the other end of the spectrum is an unusual increase in the overall level of activity, including much excitement, wild flailing of the limbs, and a great expenditure of energy similar to that seen in mania.

Some schizophrenic patients show **inappropriate affect**. The emotional responses of these individuals are out of context—the patient may laugh on hearing that his or her mother just died or become enraged when asked a simple question about how a new garment fits. These schizophrenics are likely to shift rapidly from one emotional state to another for no discernible reason.

> **catatonic immobility** A fixity of posture, sometimes grotesque, maintained for long periods, with accompanying muscular rigidity, trancelike state of consciousness, and *waxy flexibility*.
>
> **waxy flexibility** An aspect of *catatonic immobility* in which the patient's limbs can be moved into a variety of positions and maintained thereafter for unusually long periods of time.
>
> **inappropriate affect** Emotional responses that are out of context, such as laughter when hearing sad news.

To Recap

Symptoms of schizophrenia involve disturbances in many areas of functioning. Positive symptoms (excesses) include disorganized speech that makes the schizophrenic difficult to comprehend; unshakable false beliefs (delusions), such as believing that one's thoughts are being stolen from one's mind; and hearing or seeing things that are not there (hallucinations). Negative symptoms (deficits) include apathy; poverty of content of speech, such that one's statements contain little information; and an inability to express emotion (flat affect). Other schizophrenic symptoms are inappropriate emotional reactions to events, and catatonic immobility, in which unusual postures may be adopted and then held for long periods. No one of these symptoms is found in all schizophrenics, and the particular symptoms vary from one patient to another.

▶ *History of Schizophrenia*

With the principal symptoms of schizophrenia described, we turn now to a review of the history of the concept, which has changed considerably over time.

Early Descriptions

The symptoms just detailed reflect the current conceptualization of the broad category of behaviors that are referred to as schizophrenia. Concepts of schizophrenia have changed over time and will probably continue to do so. This section traces the evolution of thinking about this severe mental disorder and concludes with the three main subtypes recognized by DSM-IV.

The concept of schizophrenia was formulated by two European psychiatrists, Emil Kraepelin and Eugen Bleuler. Kraepelin presented his concept of **dementia praecox**, the early term for schizophrenia, in 1898. Dementia praecox included several diagnostic concepts—dementia paranoides, catatonia, and hebephrenia—already singled out and regarded as distinct entities by clinicians in the preceding few decades. Although these disorders are symptomatically diverse, Kraepelin believed that they shared a common core. His term, dementia praecox, reflected what he believed the common core was—an early onset (praecox) and a progressive intellectual deterioration (dementia). Among the major symptoms that Kraepelin saw in such patients were hallucinations, delusions, negativism, attentional difficulties, stereotyped behavior, and emotional dysfunction. Thus Kraepelin focused on both the course and the symptoms in defining the disorder, with particular emphasis on the course.

Kraepelin defined schizophrenia narrowly and emphasized description over theorizing about causes. In the eighth edition of his textbook, he grouped the symptoms of dementia praecox into thirty-six major categories, assigning hundreds of symptoms to each. He made little effort to interrelate these separate symptoms and stated only that they all reflected dementia and a loss of the usual unity in thinking, feeling, and acting.

dementia praecox An older term for *schizophrenia*, chosen to describe what was believed to be an incurable and progressive deterioration of mental functioning beginning in adolescence.

Emil Kraepelin (1856–1926), a German psychiatrist, articulated descriptions of dementia praecox that have proved remarkably durable in the light of contemporary research.

Eugen Bleuler (1857–1939), a Swiss psychiatrist, contributed to our conceptions of schizophrenia and coined the term.

The view of the next major figure, Eugen Bleuler, however, represented both a specific attempt to define the core of the disorder and a move away from Krae-pelin's emphasis on prognosis in the definition. In describing schizophrenia, Bleuler differed from Kraepelin on two major points. He believed that the disor-der did not necessarily have an early onset and that it did not inevitably progress toward dementia. Thus the label dementia praecox was no longer considered ap-propriate, and in 1908 Bleuler proposed his own term, schizophrenia, from the Greek words *schizein*, "to split," and *phren*, "mind." This linguistic change was needed in view of Bleuler's disagreement with both points embedded in the term dementia praecox, but it may have inadvertently promoted confusion. The term schizophrenia is often erroneously used in the media today to mean multiple personality disorder (discussed in Chapter 7), or even simply ambivalence (as in "The President's policy on this issue seems schizophrenic").

The split referred to in Bleuler's introduction of the term schizophrenia, how-ever, is not between alter personality states or contradictory opinions. Instead, he used this term to signify what he considered the common core of the disorder, the metaphorical concept of the "breaking of associative threads." For Bleuler, associa-tive threads joined not only words but thoughts. Goal-directed, efficient thinking and communication were possible only when these hypothetical structures were intact. The notion that associative threads are disrupted in schizophrenics was then used to account for other problems. The attentional difficulties of schizophrenics, for example, were viewed by Bleuler as resulting from a loss of purposeful direc-tion in thought, which in turn caused passive responding to objects and people.

Although Kraepelin recognized that a small percentage of patients who origi-nally manifested symptoms of dementia praecox did not deteriorate, he pre-ferred to limit this diagnostic category to patients who had a poor prognosis. Bleuler's work, in contrast, led to a broader concept of schizophrenia and a more theoretical emphasis. He placed patients with a good prognosis in his group of schizophrenias and in addition included as schizophrenic "many atypical melan-cholias and manias of other schools, especially hysterical melancholias and ma-nias, most hallucinatory confusions, some 'nervous' people and compulsive and impulsive patients and many prison psychoses" (1923, p. 436).

The Broadened American Concept and Changes in the DSM-IV

Bleuler had a great influence on the American concept of schizophrenia. Over the first part of the twentieth century, its breadth was extended considerably. At the New York State Psychiatric Institute, for example, about 20% of the patients were diagnosed as schizophrenic in the 1930s. The numbers increased through the 1940s and in 1952 peaked at a remarkable 80%. In contrast, the European concept of schizophrenia remained narrower. The percentage of patients diagnosed as schizophrenic at the Maudsley Hospital in London stayed relatively constant, at 20%, for a forty-year period (Kuriansky, Deming, & Gurland, 1974).

Clearly, the diagnosis of schizophrenia was somewhat problematic. It is diffi-cult to make progress in studying the causes and treatment of a disorder when there is apparently great disagreement about how to define and identify it. One radical response to this state of affairs, adopted by some professionals and laypeople alike in the 1960s, contended that the diagnosis *was* the problem. In other words, labeling as schizophrenic someone who, for whatever reason, be-haves in an eccentric manner could shape others' reactions to that person, as well as his or her own self-conception, and lead to more permanent odd behavior. This point of view and its limitations are explored in Focus Box 9.1.

Subsequent to the publication of DSM-III, the more mainstream American con-cept of schizophrenia has shifted from the broad definition of DSM-II to a consid-erably narrower definition. This position holds that the diagnosis was applied

Focus Box 9.1

Labeling Theory and Schizophrenia

In a radical departure from the traditional conceptualization of schizophrenia, Thomas Scheff (1966) suggested that the disorder is a learned social role. This position, also known as *labeling theory*, argues that the crucial factor in schizophrenia is the act of assigning a diagnostic label to the individual. Presumably this label then influences the manner in which the person will continue to behave, based on the stereotypical notions of mental illness, and at the same time determines the reactions of other people to the individual's behavior.

The social role, therefore, *is* the disorder, and it is determined by the labeling process. Without the diagnosis, Scheff argues, deviant behavior—or to use his term, residual rule breaking—would not become stabilized. It would presumably be both transient and relatively inconsequential.

By residual rules Scheff means the rules that are left over after all the formal and obvious ones, about stealing and violence and fairness, have been laid down. The examples are endless. "Do not stand still staring vacantly in the middle of a busy sidewalk." "Do not talk to the neon beer sign in the delicatessen window." "Do not spit on the piano." Scheff believes that one-time violations of residual rules are fairly common. However, normal people, through poor judgment or bad luck, may be caught violating a rule and may be diagnosed as mentally ill. Once so judged, they are likely to accept this social role and will find it difficult to rejoin the sane. They will be denied employment, and other people will know about their pasts. In the hospital they will receive attention and sympathy and be free of all responsibilities. So once there, they actually perceive *themselves* as mentally ill and settle into acting crazy as they are expected to do.

Scheff's theory has some intuitive appeal. Most people who have worked for any amount of time at a psychiatric facility have witnessed abuses of the diagnostic process. Patients are sometimes assigned labels that are poorly justified.

This theory does have several serious problems, however. First, Scheff refers to deviance as residual rule breaking, and as described it is indeed merely that. However, calling schizophrenia residual rule breaking trivializes a very serious disorder. Second, very little evidence indicates that unlabeled norm violations are indeed transient, as Scheff implies. Third, information regarding the detrimental effects of the social stigma associated with mental illness is inconclusive (Gove, 1970).

An important correlate of the labeling position is the notion of cultural relativism, according to which definitions of abnormality should be very different in cultures different from our own because of the wide variation in social norms and rules. As an example, proponents of labeling theory might argue that the visions of a shaman are the same as the hallucinations of a schizophrenic, but that cultural differences allow a favorable response to shamans.

This and several other questions were addressed by Murphy (1976) in a report of her investigations of the Eskimo and Yoruba. Contrary to the labeling view, both cultures have a concept of being crazy that is similar to our definition of schizophrenia. The Eskimo call it *nuthkavihak*, and it includes talking to oneself, refusing to talk, delusional beliefs, and bizarre behavior. The Yoruba call the phenomenon *were* and include similar symptoms under this rubric. Notably, both cultures also have shamans, but draw a clear distinction between their behavior and that of crazy people.

In sum, a strong version of the labeling position, that schizophrenia is *only* role taking reinforced by the attitudes of diagnosticians and mental hospital staff, is not supported by evidence. A weaker version, that diagnostic labels can influence for good or ill how we view persons with mental disorders and how we react to them, seems more defensible. Just as one "alcoholic" or "cancer patient" is not the same as every other, knowing that someone like Bill McClary is "schizophrenic" provides only a start toward understanding him or her.

Some writers have held that the trances of shamans are the same as the hallucinations of schizophrenics. Murphy's research, however, finds that the behavior of shamans is clearly distinguishable from psychopathology.

too liberally in the United States in the wake of Bleuler's theorizing. The range of patients diagnosed as schizophrenic has been narrowed in four ways. *First*, the diagnostic criteria are presented in explicit and considerable detail. *Second*, patients with symptoms of a mood disorder are specifically *excluded*.

Third, DSM-IV requires at least six months of disturbance for the diagnosis. The six-month period must include at least one month of the active phase, defined by the presence of at least two of the following: delusions, hallucinations, disorganized speech, grossly disorganized or catatonic behavior, and negative symptoms. There need be only one of these symptoms if it is a bizarre delusion, an auditory hallucination in which the voice sustains a running commentary on the person's actions or thoughts, or an auditory hallucination in which two or more voices talk to each other. The remaining time required can be either a prodromal (before the active phase) or residual (after the active phase) period. Problems during either the prodromal or residual phases include social withdrawal, impaired role functioning, blunted or inappropriate affect, lack of initiative, vague and circumstantial speech, impairment in hygiene and grooming, odd beliefs or magical thinking, and unusual perceptual experiences. Thus are eliminated patients who have a brief, often stress-related, psychotic episode, and then recover quickly.

Fourth, what DSM-II regarded as mild forms of schizophrenia are now diagnosed as personality disorders (see Chapter 11). For example, patients with borderline personality disorder may experience paranoid delusions, but they are usually more short-lived than those in patients with schizophrenia. Also, patients with schizotypal personality disorder may show odd beliefs, suspiciousness, or constricted emotional expressiveness, but their symptoms are not as severe as the symptoms in schizophrenia.

Despite this return to a narrower definition, schizophrenia remains a heterogeneous diagnostic category. Accordingly, there have been many proposals over the years for subtype classifications of schizophrenia. Three subtypes included in DSM-IV are described next.

Disorganized Schizophrenia

Patients with **disorganized schizophrenia** may be subject to hallucinations and delusions—sexual, hypochondriacal, religious, or persecutory—and bizarre ideas, often involving deterioration of the body. Disorganized schizophrenics often speak incoherently, stringing together similar-sounding words and even inventing new words. They may have flat affect or be constantly changeable, breaking into inexplicable fits of laughter or crying. All in all, their behavior is extremely disorganized. These patients may tie a ribbon around a big toe or move incessantly, pointing at objects for no apparent reason. They frequently deteriorate to the point of incontinence, voiding anywhere and at any time, and completely neglect their appearance, never bathing, brushing their teeth, or combing their hair.

disorganized schizophrenia *Schizophrenia in which the person has rather diffuse and regressive symptoms; the individual is given to silliness, facial grimaces, and inconsequential rituals and has constantly changeable moods and poor hygiene.*

Catatonic Schizophrenia

The most obvious symptoms of **catatonic schizophrenia** are the motor disturbances discussed earlier. Individuals typically alternate between catatonic immobility and wild excitement, but one or the other type of motor symptom may predominate. These patients resist instructions and suggestions and often echo the speech of others. The onset of catatonic reactions may be more sudden than other forms of schizophrenia, although patients are likely to have previously exhibited some apathy and withdrawal from reality. The limbs of immobile catatonics may become stiff and swollen. Despite apparent obliviousness, these patients may later relate all that occurred during the stupor.

In the excited state, catatonics may shout and talk continuously and incoher-

catatonic schizophrenia *Schizophrenia in which the primary symptoms alternate between stuporous immobility and excited agitation.*

A schizophrenic with catatonic immobility adopts unusual and seemingly uncomfortable postures for long periods of time.

ently, all the while pacing with great agitation. This form of schizophrenia is seldom seen today, perhaps because drug therapy works effectively on these bizarre motor processes. Alternatively, the apparently high prevalence of catatonia during the early part of the century may have reflected misdiagnosis (Boyle, 1991). Similarities between encephalitis lethargica (sleeping sickness) and catatonic schizophrenia suggest that many cases of the former were misdiagnosed as the latter. This point was dramatized in the film *Awakenings*, based on the work of Oliver Sacks.

Paranoid Schizophrenia

paranoid schizophrenia *Schizophrenia in which the patient has numerous systematized* delusions, *such as* grandiose delusions *or* delusional jealousy, *as well as* hallucinations *and* ideas of reference. *He or she may also be agitated, angry, argumentative, and sometimes violent.*

grandiose delusions *An exaggerated sense of one's importance, power, knowledge, or identify.*

delusional jealousy *The unfounded conviction that one's mate is unfaithful. The individual may collect small bits of "evidence" to justify the* delusion.

ideas of reference *Reading personal significance into seemingly trivial remarks and activities of others and completely unrelated events.*

Paranoid schizophrenia involves prominent delusions, usually of persecution. Sometimes they may be **grandiose delusions**, when individuals have an exaggerated sense of their own importance, power, knowledge, or identity. Other paranoid schizophrenics may be plagued by **delusional jealousy**, believing their sexual partner to be unfaithful. Vivid auditory hallucinations may also accompany the delusions. These patients often develop what are referred to as **ideas of reference**. They incorporate events within a delusional framework, reading personal significance into the unrelated activities of others. Bill McClary's belief that bombings in Ireland pertained to his homosexual activities illustrates ideas of reference. Other patients may think that segments of overheard conversations apply to them, or that the frequent appearance of a person on a street where they customarily walk means that they are being watched.

Paranoid schizophrenics are agitated, argumentative, angry, and sometimes violent. However, they remain emotionally responsive, though they may be somewhat stilted, formal, and intense with others. They are more alert and verbal than other schizophrenics.

To Recap

Kraepelin's initial conception of dementia praecox emphasized early onset and progressive intellectual deterioration. Bleuler coined the term *schizophrenia*, rejecting Kraepelin's emphasis on inevitably early onset and deteriorating course. In-

stead, Bleuler considered the essence of schizophrenia to be a loosening of associative threads connecting one thought to another. This more expansive view of schizophrenia was influential in the United States, and prior to DSM-III many patients who probably had mood or personality disorders were considered schizophrenic. DSM-IV has returned to a narrower definition by using explicit criteria, excluding patients with mood disorders, and requiring a minimum six-month duration of illness. Subtypes recognized by current diagnostic criteria include disorganized, catatonic, and paranoid schizophrenics.

Perspectives on the Causes of Schizophrenia

We have considered how schizophrenics differ from others in the way in which they think, speak, perceive, and act. We are now ready to ask what can explain these severely disabling symptoms. Strictly psychological perspectives have not been very successful in explaining schizophrenia. For example, Freud had little contact with patients with this disorder and little to say about causes of schizophrenia. He did occasionally speculate on its origins. As a neurologist he did not rule out the possibility of a biochemical cause, but he also considered it possible that schizophrenics may have regressed to a state of primary narcissism, a phase early in the oral stage before the ego has differentiated from the id. There is thus no separate ego to engage in reality testing. By regressing to narcissism, schizophrenics have effectively lost contact with the world. They have withdrawn the libido from attachment to any objects external to themselves. Freud thought that the cause of the regression might be an increase in the intensity of id impulses, especially sexual ones. Systematic research support for this explanation of schizophrenia is lacking, however.

Biological Perspectives

There is strong evidence that schizophrenia has a substantial genetic component. This conclusion suggests that biochemicals should be investigated, for it is through the body chemistry and biological processes that heredity may have an effect. The genetics and biochemistry of schizophrenia have been explored for decades, and in this section we consider some of the main findings from these research efforts.

The Genetic Factor in Schizophrenia

All the major methods of behavior genetics research, including family, twin, and adoption studies (see Chapter 2), have been applied to schizophrenia. As we will see, any one study is usually subject to alternative, nongenetic interpretations, but the overall body of evidence strongly suggests that a vulnerability to schizophrenia is heritable.

Family Studies. The risk for schizophrenia in the general population is a little less than 1%, yet the risk of schizophrenia for children of schizophrenics is greater than 9%, and the risk of schizophrenia if one's identical twin has the disorder is 44% (see Table 9.1). Clearly, relatives of schizophrenics are at increased risk, and the risk increases as the genetic relationship with a schizophrenic patient becomes closer. Therefore, data gathered by the family method support the notion that a predisposition for schizophrenia can be transmitted genetically. Keep in mind, though, that closer relatives are also likely to be exposed to more similar environments, including the family environment. Therefore, the family method alone is not sufficient to document heritability conclusively.

Table 9.1 ▶ *Summary of Major European Family and Twin Studies of the Genetics of Schizophrenia*

Relation to Schizophrenic Patient	Percentage Schizophrenic
Spouse	1.00
Grandchildren	2.84
Nieces/nephews	2.65
Children	9.35
Siblings	7.30
DZ twins	12.08
MZ twins	44.30

Source: After Gottesman, McGuffin, & Farmer (1987).

APPLYING CRITICAL THINKING SKILLS

TWIN STUDIES

Concordance rates for identical, or monozygotic (MZ), and fraternal, or dizygotic (DZ), twins also appear in Table 9.1. The concordance rate for identical twins (44%) is less than 100%. This is significant, for if genetic transmission were solely responsible for schizophrenia and one twin was schizophrenic, the other twin would almost certainly have a similar fate because MZ twins are genetically identical. But even if genes do not provide the whole story, the question remains whether they play any role. Concordance for identical twins (44%) is clearly greater than that for fraternal twins (12%). This finding is the basis for the following critical thinking exercise.

▶ *What conclusion does the evidence seem to support?* Higher concordance rates for identical than for fraternal twins tend to support a conclusion that vulnerability to schizophrenia is genetically transmitted. The MZ twins are more similar genetically, and this may be why they are more often similar in the sense of both having schizophrenia if one does.

▶ *What other interpretations are plausible?* Studies of twins raised together remain somewhat ambiguous, though. Identical twins, perhaps because they look alike and are always of the same sex, may be exposed to more similar environments than are fraternal twins, and this could account for their higher concordance rates.

▶ *What other information would help choose among the alternative interpretations?* Several strategies for choosing between these interpretations have been attempted. In one variation on the standard twin study, Fischer (1971) reasoned that if vulnerability to schizophrenia is heritable, then children of even the discordant, or nonschizophrenic, identical co-twins of schizophrenics should be at high risk for schizophrenia. These nonschizophrenic twins would presumably have the genotype for schizophrenia, even though it was not expressed behaviorally, and thus would pass along an increased risk for the disorder to their children. In a study based on this reasoning, the rate of schizophrenia and schizophrenia-like psychoses in the children of nonschizophrenic co-twins of schizophrenics was nearly as high as it was among the children of the schizophrenics themselves. In both cases prevalence was substantially higher than that found in an unselected population (Fischer, 1971).

A follow-up report on this project eighteen years later confirmed these findings. Risk was just as high among the children of the nonschizophrenic identical twins of schizophrenics (Gottesman & Bertelsen, 1989). This finding makes sense from the standpoint of genetic vulnerability to schizophrenia. It would be very hard to explain from the standpoint of a purely environmental theory of schizophrenia, however. An environmental theory would likely predict that the children of the schizophrenic twin should have been exposed to more chaotic or otherwise damaging family environments than were the children of the nonschizophrenic twin, and rates of schizophrenia among the children should have differed accordingly.

Adoption Studies.   The study of children of schizophrenic mothers reared from early infancy by adoptive parents provides another angle on the role of genes in schizophrenia by eliminating the potential effects of a deviant environment. One such study looked at forty-seven people who had been born to schizophrenic mothers in a state mental hospital and were separated from their mothers at birth and raised by either foster or adoptive parents (Heston, 1966). The study also looked at the mental status of fifty control subjects from the same foundling homes that had placed the children of schizophrenic mothers. The control group was matched to the schizophrenics for sex, for where they were eventually placed, and for the length of time they spent in a child-care institution. All subjects were born between 1915 and 1945.

The control subjects were rated as less disabled than the children of schizophrenic mothers at a follow-up assessment in 1964. None of the control subjects was diagnosed as schizophrenic, but 17% of the offspring of schizophrenic mothers were so diagnosed. This study clearly supports the importance of genetic factors in the development of schizophrenia. Children reared without contact with their schizophrenic mothers were still more likely to become schizophrenic than were the controls.

Adoption studies in Denmark reached the same conclusion using a different method. Rather than starting with schizophrenic mothers, the focus was on schizophrenic adoptees. Their biological relatives, with whom they had lived only a few weeks on average after birth, were more likely to also have schizophrenia than were their adoptive families or the biological relatives of nonschizophrenic adoptees (Kety et al., 1994). Independent review of the interview records collected for this study, applying DSM-III rather than the original DSM-II criteria, confirmed the findings. Although applying narrower criteria lowered the overall frequency of schizophrenia diagnoses, there was still an excess rate among the biological relatives of schizophrenic adoptees (Kendler, Gruenberg, & Kinney, 1994).

Genetics and the Heterogeneity of Schizophrenia.   An analysis of the major twin studies according to the positive–negative symptom distinction compared schizophrenic patients whose twins did have schizophrenia with those whose twins did not (Dworkin & Lenzenweger, 1984; Dworkin, Lenzenweger, & Moldin, 1987). These two groups did not differ on positive symptoms. However, the patients whose twins did have schizophrenia were higher in negative symptoms than were those whose twins did not. Therefore, it appears that negative symptoms may have a stronger genetic component than do positive ones.

Biochemical Factors

Speculation concerning possible biochemical causes of schizophrenia began almost as soon as the syndrome was identified. Kraepelin, for instance, thought in terms of a chemical imbalance, for he believed that poisons secreted from the sex glands affected the brain to produce the symptoms. The search for possible biochemical causes of schizophrenia, however, faces a key difficulty. If an aberrant biochemical is found in schizophrenics and not in control subjects, it will not necessarily be a reflection of something inherent about schizophrenia. A difference in biochemical functioning could be produced by a third variable. There are two prominent third variables to consider.

First, most schizophrenic patients take psychoactive medication (discussed later). Although the effects of such drugs on behavior diminish quite rapidly once they are discontinued, traces of them may remain in the bloodstream for very long periods of time. Thus it would be difficult to attribute a biochemical difference between schizophrenic and control subjects to schizophrenia per se. Prolonged drug therapy may also lead to changes in the very process of neural transmission.

Second, schizophrenic patients are more likely than normal controls to have been institutionalized for substantial periods of time. Institutionalized patients may smoke more, drink more coffee, and have a less nutritionally adequate diet than do various control groups, and they may be relatively inactive. All these variables can produce biochemical differences between schizophrenic and control patients that confound attempts to seek deviant biochemicals in schizophrenics.

Nonetheless, the search for biochemical causes of schizophrenia proceeds at a rapid rate. Improved technology now allows a much greater understanding of the relation between biochemistry and behavior. At present, no biochemical theory has unequivocal support, but in the next subsection we review one of the best-researched of these theories.

Dopamine Activity. The theory that schizophrenia is related to activity of the neurotransmitter dopamine is based principally on the mode of action of drugs that are effective in treating schizophrenia. The phenothiazines (see p. 238) alleviate some symptoms of schizophrenia and produce side effects resembling Parkinson's disease. Since parkinsonism is known to be caused, in part, by low levels of dopamine in a particular nerve tract of the brain, it is hypothesized that phenothiazines lower dopamine activity. Because of their structural similarity to dopamine molecules, phenothiazine molecules (Figure 9.1) fit into and thereby block postsynaptic receptors in dopamine tracts. From this knowledge about the action of the drugs that help schizophrenics, it is inferred that schizophrenia may result from excess activity in dopamine nerve tracts. However, though the therapeutic effects of a drug may provide a *clue* to the causes of the disorder it helps to alleviate, treatment effects cannot logically prove what caused the problem in the first place. Other evidence must be considered as well.

Additional indirect support for the dopamine hypothesis is found in research on amphetamine psychosis. Amphetamines can produce a state that closely resembles paranoid schizophrenia, and they can exacerbate the symptoms of a schizophrenic (Angrist, Lee, & Gershon, 1974). The amphetamines are thought to act either by directly releasing catecholamines into the synaptic cleft or by preventing their inactivation (Snyder, Banerjee, Yamamora, & Greenberg, 1974). Furthermore, some postmortem studies of schizophrenics' brains as well as PET scans (see Chapter 5) of schizophrenics have revealed that dopamine receptors may have either increased in number or been hyperactive (e.g., Wong et al., 1986).

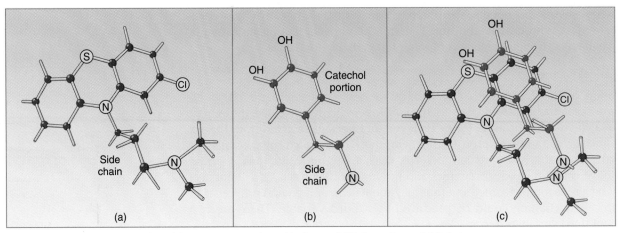

Figure 9.1   *Conformations of (a) chlorpromazine, a phenothiazine, and (b) dopamine and (c) their superimposition, determined by X-ray crystallographic analysis. Chlorpromazine blocks impulse transmission by dopamine by fitting into its receptor sites. Adapted from Horn and Snyder (1971).*

Other research on the excess dopamine activity theory has revealed, however, that it may not be applicable to all schizophrenics. Some studies have shown that amphetamines do not worsen the symptoms of all patients (e.g., Kornetsky, 1976), and one study has even reported that symptoms lessen after an amphetamine has been administered (van Kammen et al., 1977). Furthermore, phenothiazines have been shown to benefit only a subgroup of patients. These divergent results are related to the positive–negative symptom distinction. Amphetamines worsen positive symptoms and lessen negative ones. Phenothiazines lessen positive symptoms, but their effect on negative symptoms is less clear. Some studies show no benefit (e.g., Haracz, 1982) and others, a positive effect (e.g., van Kammen, Hommer, & Malas, 1987). The dopamine theory as originally formulated thus appears to apply mainly to the positive symptoms of schizophrenia.

More recent developments in the dopamine theory (e.g., Davis, Kahn, Ko, & Davidson, 1991) have expanded its scope. The key change involves the recognition of differences among the neural pathways that use dopamine as a transmitter. The excess dopamine activity that is thought to be most relevant to schizophrenia is localized in the mesolimbic pathway (see Figure 9.2). The therapeutic effects of phenothiazines on positive symptoms occur by blocking dopamine receptors there. The mesocortical dopamine pathway begins in the same brain region as the mesolimbic, but projects to the prefrontal cortex. The prefrontal cortex also projects to limbic areas that are innervated by dopamine. These dopamine neurons in the prefrontal cortex may be underactive and thus fail to inhibit the dopamine neurons in the limbic area adequately. The underactivity of the dopamine neurons in the prefrontal cortex may also be the cause of the negative

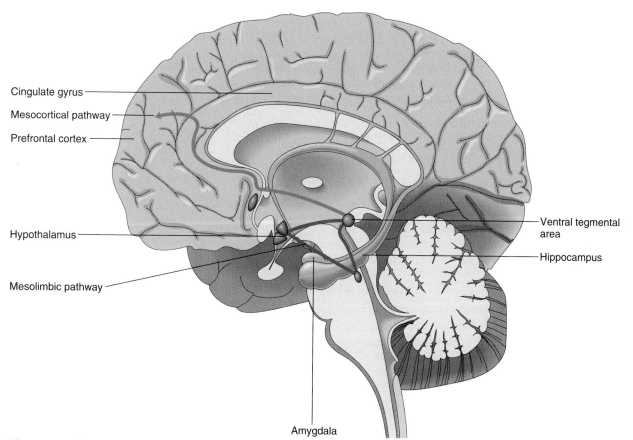

Figure 9.2 *The brain and schizophrenia. The mesocortical pathway begins in the ventral tegmental area and projects to the prefrontal cortex. The mesolimbic pathway also begins in the ventral tegmental area, but projects to the hypothalamus, amygdala, hippocampus, and nucleus accumbens.*

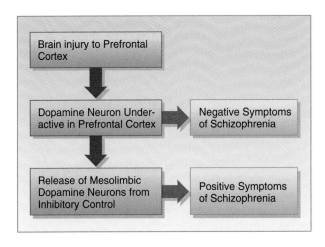

Figure 9.3 *Dopamine theory of schizophrenia.*

symptoms of schizophrenia (see Figure 9.3). This proposal has the advantage of allowing the simultaneous presence of positive and negative symptoms in a schizophrenic patient. Also, because phenothiazines do not have major effects on the dopamine neurons in the prefrontal cortex, we would expect them to be relatively ineffective as treatments for negative symptoms (and they are).

Despite these favorable developments, the dopamine hypothesis cannot be regarded as having been proven, for it has difficulty accounting for some other effects. For example, it takes a few weeks for phenothiazines to gradually lessen positive schizophrenic symptoms, but the drugs rapidly block dopamine receptors. This disparity has not been explained. After several weeks, tolerance for phenothiazines should develop and their effectiveness should diminish, yet this does not occur (Davis, 1978). This difference between the behavioral and pharmacological effects of phenothiazines is difficult to understand within the context of the theory. It is also puzzling that phenothiazines have to reduce dopamine levels or receptor activity to *below normal*, producing parkinsonian side effects, if they are to be therapeutically effective. According to the theory, reducing dopamine levels or receptor activity to normal should be sufficient for a therapeutic effect. Thus, although dopamine remains the most actively researched biochemical explanation for schizophrenia, it is not likely to provide a complete answer.

The Brain and Schizophrenia

The search for a brain abnormality that causes schizophrenia, like the search for a biochemical cause, began as early as schizophrenia was identified. But the research did not prove promising, for studies when replicated did not yield the same findings. Interest gradually waned over the years. In the last two decades, however, spurred by a number of methodological advances, the field has reawakened and yielded some promising evidence (Weinberger, Wagner, & Wyatt, 1983). A percentage of schizophrenics—the exact number cannot be specified—have been found to have observable brain pathology. The controversy is whether these abnormalities are localized in a small number of brain areas or are widespread.

Some of the evidence derives from images obtained in CAT scan and MRI studies. These images of living brain tissue show that some schizophrenics, especially men (Andreasen, Swayze, Flaum, Arndt, & McChesney 1990), have enlarged ventricles, suggesting deterioration or atrophy of brain tissue, particularly in the limbic areas. Large ventricles are in turn correlated with impaired performance on neuropsychological tests, poor premorbid adjustment, and poor response to drug treatment (Andreasen, Olsen, Dennert, & Smith, 1982; Weinberger, Cannon-Spoor, Potkin, & Wyatt, 1980).

A variety of data suggest that the prefrontal cortex is also of particular importance in schizophrenia. This area is often the site of atrophy (Doran et al., 1985).

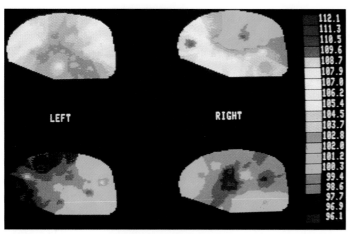

*Differences between schizophrenics (*bottom*) and normals (*top*) in regional cerebral blood flow for each hemisphere. The values shown were scored as the percentage change in cerebral blood flow from a control task to the Wisconsin Card Sort, which was expected to activate the prefrontal cortex. The normals showed greater prefrontal cortical activation as indexed by the "hotter" color of this brain region. From Weinberger et al. (1988).*

Schizophrenics show low metabolic rates in the prefrontal cortex (Buchsbaum, Kessler, King, Johnson, & Cappelletti, 1984) and perform poorly on tests that are believed to tap prefrontal function (Weinberger, Berman, & Illowsky, 1988).

Vulnerability-Stress Perspectives

Clearly, vulnerability to schizophrenia has something to do with genetics, and manifestations involve aberrant biochemistry and brain abnormalities. As we have seen, however, genetics cannot be everything, or all monozygotic twins of schizophrenics would be schizophrenic as well. Aside from this general point that diagnostic concordance is less than 100%, indeed, less than 50% (see Table 9.1), brain research on identical twins of schizophrenics provides additional support for the relevance of nongenetic factors. A study of fifteen pairs of identical (MZ) twins who were discordant for schizophrenia (only one had the disorder) found that the schizophrenic twin could be identified by simple visual inspection of an MRI scan in twelve of the fifteen pairs (Suddath, Christison, Torrey, Cassanova, & Weinberger, 1990). Because the twins were genetically identical, these data suggest that the origin of these brain abnormalities was not genetic.

If, as the evidence so far suggests, genetic factors can only predispose people to a behavioral disorder, the vulnerability-stress perspective seems to help make sense of research into the causes of schizophrenia. Data show that, like many of the disorders we have discussed, general life stress can precipitate a relapse of the condition (Ventura, Neuchterlein, Lukoff, & Hardesty, 1989). But more specific stressors have also played an important role in schizophrenia research. We now consider three—prenatal exposure to a virus, social class, and styles of interaction within families.

Prenatal Exposure to a Virus

Neurological abnormalities may result from infection by a virus that invades the brain and damages it. Some data suggest that an infection during fetal development is related to the development of schizophrenia later in life. During a five-week period in 1957, Helsinki experienced an epidemic of influenza virus. Researchers examined the rates of schizophrenia in adults who had been exposed to the virus during their mothers' pregnancies. They found that rates were much higher among those exposed during the second trimester of pregnancy than

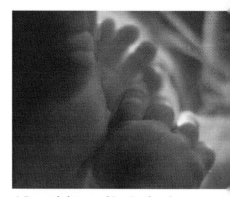

A 5-month fetus sucking its thumb. The second trimester of pregnancy is a critical stage for cortical development. Exposure during this period to a virus that invades the brain and damages it has been linked with later risk for schizophrenia.

Sarnoff Mednick is a psychologist at the University of Southern California who contributed to the hypothesis that a viral infection is implicated in schizophrenia.

sociogenic hypothesis Generally, an idea that seeks causes in social conditions, for example, that being in a low social class can cause one to become *schizophrenic*.

social-selection theory An attempt to explain the correlation between social class and *schizophrenia* by proposing that schizophrenics move downward in social status.

among those exposed in either of the other trimesters and among nonexposed controls (Mednick, Machon, Hottunen, & Bonett, 1988). This is an intriguing finding, especially since cortical development is in a critical stage of growth during the second trimester. Corroborating evidence has been reported by Barr, Mednick, and Munk-Jorgensen (1990), who found that the highest rates of birth of future schizophrenics coincided with elevated rates of influenza in the sixth month of gestation.

If schizophrenics' brains are damaged early in development, why does the disorder begin in adolescence or early adulthood? Weinberger (1987) proposed one answer to this question. He hypothesized that the brain injury interacts with normal brain development and that the prefrontal cortex is a brain structure that matures late, typically in adolescence. Thus, an injury to this area may remain silent until the period of development when the prefrontal cortex begins to play a larger role in behavior. Notably, dopamine activity also peaks in adolescence, which may further set the stage for the onset of schizophrenic symptoms.

Low Socioeconomic Status

Stress that occurs after birth may also be important. Numerous studies have shown a relation between social class and the diagnosis of schizophrenia. The highest rates of schizophrenia are found in urban areas inhabited by the lowest socioeconomic classes (e.g., Hollingshead & Redlich, 1958). The relationship between social class and schizophrenia does not show a continuous progression of higher rates of schizophrenia as the social class becomes lower. Rather, there is a sharp difference between the number of schizophrenics in the lowest social class and those in others. In their classic ten-year study of social class and mental illness in New Haven, Connecticut, Hollingshead and Redlich found that the rate of schizophrenia was twice as high in the lowest social class as in the next to the lowest social class. These findings have been confirmed cross-culturally by similar community studies carried out in such countries as Denmark, Norway, and England (Kohn, 1968).

What is less clear is how to interpret the relation between low social class and schizophrenia. Some believe that being in a low social class may in itself cause schizophrenia. This is called the **sociogenic hypothesis**. The degrading treatment a person receives from others, the low level of education, and the unavailability of rewards and opportunity, taken together, may make membership in the lowest social class such a stressful experience that it causes the individual to develop schizophrenia.

Another explanation of the correlation between schizophrenia and low social class is the **social-selection theory**. According to this theory, during the course of their developing psychosis, schizophrenics may drift into the poverty-ridden areas of the city. The growing cognitive and motivational problems besetting these individuals may so impair their earning abilities that they cannot afford to live elsewhere.

One way of resolving the conflict between these two differing hypotheses is to study the social mobility of schizophrenics. Three studies (Lystad, 1957; Schwartz, 1946; Turner & Wagonfeld, 1967) found that schizophrenics were downwardly mobile in occupational status. Other studies have not found such an effect (Clausen & Kohn, 1959; Dunham, 1965; Hollingshead & Redlich, 1958).

Another way of distinguishing the two explanations is to examine the social class of fathers of schizophrenics (Kohn, 1968). If they, too, are mainly in the lowest social class, this would support the sociogenic hypothesis, for class would be shown to precede schizophrenia. If the fathers are from a higher social class, the social-selection hypothesis would be favored. Here, too, the results are inconclusive. In one study, fathers of schizophrenics were more frequently from the lowest social class, supporting the sociogenic hypothesis. But at the same time, many of these schizophrenics were lower in occupational prestige than their fathers, supporting the selection hypothesis (Turner & Wagonfeld, 1967).

A recent study relevant to the two theories (Dohrenwend et al., 1992) employed a new method, simultaneously investigating both social class and ethnic background. The rates of schizophrenia were examined in Israeli Jews of European ethnic background as well as in more recent immigrants to Israel from North Africa and the Middle East. The latter group experiences considerable racial prejudice and discrimination. The sociogenic hypothesis would predict that, because they experience high levels of stress at all levels of social class, the members of the disadvantaged ethnic group would have consistently higher rates of schizophrenia at all levels of social class.

In contrast, the social-selection process should affect the two groups differently. Because of prejudice and discrimination, only the most healthy and able members of the disadvantaged ethnic group should be able to move upward in social class. Upward mobility should be easier and more frequent for the advantaged group, leaving more disabled members behind. According to the social-selection theory, then, the result should be that rates of schizophrenia are higher for the advantaged group. In fact, this pattern of results emerged. Thus some, but not all, of the relationship between social class and schizophrenia can be accounted for by the selection hypothesis. Social class also appears to play a role as a stressor, but the exact way in which the stresses associated with it exert their effect remains unknown.

Problematic Family Interactions

Many theorists have regarded family relationships, especially those between a mother and her son, as crucial in the development of schizophrenia. The view has been so prevalent that the term **schizophrenogenic mother** was coined for the supposedly cold and dominant, conflict-inducing parent who is said to produce schizophrenia in her offspring (Fromm-Reichmann, 1948). These mothers have also been characterized as rejecting, overprotective, self-sacrificing, impervious to the feelings of others, rigid and moralistic about sex, and fearful of intimacy.

schizophrenogenic mother A cold dominant, conflict-inducing mother once believed to cause *schizophrenia* in her child.

Another prominent early view was the **double-bind theory** proposed by Bateson and his colleagues (Bateson, Jackson, Haley, & Weakland, 1956). These writers believed that an important factor in the development of schizophrenic thought disorder is the constant subjection of an individual to a so-called double-bind situation, which includes the following elements.

double-bind theory An interpersonal situation in which an individual is confronted, over long periods of time, by mutually inconsistent messages to which she or he must respond, formerly believed by some theorists to cause *schizophrenia*.

1. The individual has an intense relationship with another, so intense that it is especially important to be able to understand communications from the other person accurately so that the individual can respond appropriately.
2. The other person expresses two messages when making a statement, one of which denies the other.
3. The individual cannot comment on the mutually contradictory messages and cannot withdraw from the situation or ignore the messages.

These theories were supported mainly by uncontrolled observation of families of schizophrenic patients. Such support is inadequate for two reasons: (a) a crucial piece of data, the proportion of *nonschizophrenic* people exposed to cold mothers, double-bind communications, and the like, is missing; and (b) a difference in communication style between the families of schizophrenics and the families of controls could be a result of having a disturbed child rather than a cause.

When controlled studies were done, the schizophrenogenic mother and double-bind theories were not supported. Despite their weak empirical basis, the theories were popular in professional and lay literature for decades, possibly be-

Table 9.2 ▶ *Adjustment of Adopted Children of Schizophrenic Parents Related to Maladjustment of Adoptive Families*

	Degree of Family Maladjustment		
Clinical Ratings of Children	None to Mild	Moderate	Severe
Healthy or mild disturbance	39	9	3
Moderate	10	9	24
Severe	0	11	16

Source: From Tienari et al. (1987). Adapted by permission.

cause their emphasis on environmental factors—especially a potential negative influence of the mother—fit with culturally dominant beliefs (Neill, 1990).

It seems unlikely that conflictual or confusing communication styles alone could provoke schizophrenia in someone otherwise not predisposed to it. Consistent with a vulnerability-stress model, however, family interaction styles might play a role in causing worse outcomes among those genetically vulnerable to, or already diagnosed with, schizophrenia. For example, an adoption study by Tienari and his colleagues (1987) is examining a large sample of adopted offspring of schizophrenic mothers. As of 1987, 112 children of schizophrenics and 135 controls had been assessed. Extensive data were collected on various aspects of family life in the adoptive families. Data on the adjustment of the children were related to data collected on their adoptive families. The families were categorized into levels of maladjustment based on material from clinical interviews as well as psychological tests. The major data are shown in Table 9.2. As the table shows, the more severe problems in adopted children of schizophrenics are clearly associated with more pathological environments. Also notable in this study was the fact that family environment was not related to psychopathology in the control adoptees. Both a genetic predisposition (vulnerability) and a noxious environment (stress) are therefore necessary to increase risk for schizophrenia.

A series of studies conducted in London indicates that the family can have an important impact on the adjustment of patients *after* they leave the hospital as well. Brown and his colleagues (Brown, Bone, Dalison, & Wing, 1966) undertook a nine-month follow-up study of a sample of schizophrenics who returned to live with their families after being discharged from the hospital. The researchers interviewed parents or spouses prior to the discharge and rated them for the number of critical comments made about the patient and for expressions of hostility toward or emotional overinvolvement with the patient. On the basis of this variable, called **expressed emotion (EE)**, families were divided into those revealing a great deal, high-EE families, and those revealing little, low-EE families. At the end of the follow-up period, 10% of the patients who returned to low-EE homes had relapsed. In marked contrast, 58% of the patients who returned to high-EE homes had gone back to the hospital in the same period! This research has since been replicated several times (Koenigsberg & Handley, 1986), indicating that the environment to which patients are discharged has great bearing on whether or not they are rehospitalized. Treatment implications of these studies are discussed later.

expressed emotion (EE) Originating in the literature on *schizophrenia*, the amount of hostility and criticism directed from other people to a patient, usually within a family.

To Recap

Biological perspectives on schizophrenia have pursued three main issues. First, family, twin, and adoption studies converge on the conclusion that vulnerability to schizophrenia is transmitted genetically, but at the same time nongenetic factors (such as stress) must play a role in determining which genetically vulnerable people will become schizophrenic. Second, research on the biochemistry of schizophrenia suggests that positive symptoms are associated with excess dopamine activity in the mesolimbic pathway, while negative symptoms stem from underactivity of dopamine neurons in the prefrontal cortex. Third, some schizophrenics show deterioration or atrophy of brain tissue, particularly in limbic areas or in the prefrontal cortex.

Researchers adopting a vulnerability-stress perspective have attempted to spell out what stressors in particular affect schizophrenia. One line of research suggests that a woman's exposure to a virus during the second trimester of pregnancy may cause damage to the prefrontal cortex of the fetus that is manifested in adolescence or early adulthood as schizophrenia. Low socioeconomic status is another stressor associated with schizophrenia, though the extent to which it plays a causal role remains controversial. Finally, the idea that poor parenting alone can cause schizophrenia has been discredited; but emotional overinvolvement with, or hostile criticism of, the patient on the part of family members predicts increased risk of relapse among schizophrenics.

Perspectives on the Treatment of Schizophrenia

The puzzling, often frightening array of phenomena that plague schizophrenics makes one wonder how they can possibly be helped. The history of psychopathology, reviewed in Chapter 1, is in many respects a history of humankind's efforts, often brutal and unenlightened, to deal with schizophrenia.

Biological Treatments

Shock and Psychosurgery

The general warehousing of severely disturbed patients in mental hospitals earlier in this century, coupled with the shortage of professional staff, created a climate that allowed, perhaps even subtly encouraged, experimentation with radical biological interventions. In the early 1930s, the practice of inducing a coma with large dosages of insulin was introduced (Sakel, 1938). Proponents claimed that up to three-quarters of schizophrenics showed significant improvement with this method. But later findings by others were less encouraging, and insulin coma therapy, which presented serious risks to health, including irreversible coma and death, was gradually abandoned.

In 1935 Moñiz, a Portuguese psychiatrist, introduced the **prefrontal lobotomy**, a surgical procedure that destroys the tracts connecting the frontal lobes to lower centers of the patient's brain. His initial reports, like those of Sakel for insulin coma therapy, claimed high rates of success (Moñiz, 1936). For twenty years thereafter thousands of patients underwent variations of psychosurgery, especially if their behavior was violent. Many of them did indeed quiet down and could even be discharged from hospitals. But during the 1950s this intervention, too, fell into disrepute for several reasons. Many patients suffered serious losses in their cognitive capacities—not surprising, given the destruction of parts of their brain believed responsible for thought—and became dull and listless; some even died. The principal reason for abandonment of this procedure, however, was the introduction of drugs that seemed to reduce the behavioral and emotional excesses of many patients.

prefrontal lobotomy A surgical procedure that destroys the tracts connecting the *frontal lobes* to lower centers of the brain; once believed to be an effective treatment for *schizophrenia*.

Drug Therapies

Without question the most important development in the treatment of schizophrenia was the advent in the 1950s of several drugs collectively referred to as antipsychotic medications. One of the more frequently prescribed antipsychotic

Antihistamines are commonly used by people suffering from colds. Historically, their tranquilizing effects were an important clue guiding work on the development of medications for schizophrenic patients.

drugs, *phenothiazine*, was first produced by a German chemist in the late nineteenth century and used to treat parasitic worm infections of the digestive system of animals. However, it was not until the discovery of the antihistamines in the 1940s that phenothiazines were given any attention. Antihistamines have a phenothiazine nucleus. Reaching beyond their use to treat the common cold and asthma, the French surgeon Laborit pioneered the use of antihistamines to reduce surgical shock. He noticed that they made his patients somewhat sleepy and less fearful about the impending operation. Laborit's work encouraged drug companies to reexamine antihistamines in light of their tranquilizing effects. Shortly thereafter a French chemist, Charpentier, prepared a new phenothiazine derivative and called it chlorpromazine. It proved effective in calming many schizophrenics.

Chlorpromazine (trade name Thorazine) was first used therapeutically in the United States in 1954 and rapidly became the preferred treatment for schizophrenics. By 1970 more than 85% of all patients in state mental hospitals were receiving chlorpromazine or one of the other phenothiazines. Over the last decade, two other classes of antipsychotic medication have also been given to schizophrenics, the *butyrophenones* (e.g., haloperidol, Haldol) and the *thioxanthenes* (e.g., navane, Taractan). Both seem generally as effective as the phenothiazines. These classes of drugs all reduce positive schizophrenic symptoms, but have less effect on the negative ones.

Side Effects.   Although the phenothiazine regimen reduces the positive symptoms of schizophrenia so that patients can be released from the hospital, it should not be viewed as a cure. Typically, patients are kept on *maintenance doses* of the drug—that is, just enough to continue the therapeutic effect. They take their medication and return to the hospital or clinic on occasion for adjustment of the dose level. But many released patients who are maintained on phenothiazine medication may make only marginal adjustment to the community. Reinstitutionalization is frequent. Although the use of phenothiazines reduced long-term institutionalization significantly, it also made the revolving-door pattern of admission, discharge, and readmission a reality. This situation is discussed in more detail in the Legal, Ethical, and Social Issues box.

Finally, the potentially serious side effects of phenothiazines must be noted. Patients generally report that taking the drug is disagreeable, causing dryness of the mouth, blurred vision, grogginess, and constipation. Among the other common side effects are low blood pressure and jaundice. Perhaps this unpleasantness is one of the reasons maintenance programs have proven so troublesome. It is difficult to get patients to take these drugs initially and to keep them on medication once they have left the hospital (Van Putten, May, Marder, & Wittman, 1981). Thus patients are now frequently treated with long-lasting antipsychotic medications (e.g., fluphenazine decanoate) that require an injection every few weeks.

Even more disturbing are the side effects that stem from dysfunctions of the nerve tracts that descend from the brain to spinal motor neurons. People taking phenothiazines have pill-rolling tremors of the fingers, a shuffling gait, muscular rigidity, and drooling. Other side effects include dystonia and dyskinesia, which cause arching of the back and a twisted posture of the neck and body. Some people pace constantly, fidget, and make chewing movements and other movements of the lips, fingers, and legs. These perturbing symptoms can be treated by drugs used with patients who have Parkinson's disease. In a muscular disturbance of older patients, called tardive dyskinesia, the mouth muscles involuntarily make sucking, lip-smacking, and chin-wagging motions. This syndrome affects from 10% to 20% of patients treated with phenothiazines for a long period of time (Kane et al., 1986) and has no effective treatment.

Because of these serious side effects some clinicians believe that it is unwise to take phenothiazines for extended periods of time. Current clinical practice calls for treating patients with the smallest possible doses of drugs.

Also, newer drugs are being developed. One, clozapine (Clozaril), can produce therapeutic gains in schizophrenics who do not respond positively to phenothiazines (Breier et al., 1994; Kane et al., 1988). Interestingly, clozapine does not appear to produce its therapeutic effect by blocking dopamine receptors and does not appear to produce Parkinson's side effects (Kane, Woerner, Pollack, Safferman, & Lieberman, 1993). Unfortunately, it can impair the functioning of the immune system, making patients vulnerable to infection, and it can produce seizures. It is therefore essential that patients taking clozapine be carefully monitored for adverse effects on the immune system. A second new medication for schizophrenia is risperidone (Risperidol), which blocks both serotonin and dopamine receptors. Research suggests that risperidone may be helpful with both positive and negative symptoms without causing severe side effects, though longer-term research is needed (Marder & Meibach, 1994).

Psychological Treatments

Although Freud did not advocate psychoanalysis as a treatment for schizophrenia, others have proposed adaptations. We will review some of them now, and we will also examine recent family and behavioral therapies for schizophrenics. At the end of this section we will see that it may be best to combine biological and psychological treatments in an integrated approach.

Psychodynamic Therapy

Freud believed that schizophrenics are ill suited for psychoanalysis, as they are incapable of establishing the close interpersonal relationship required. It was Harry Stack Sullivan, an American psychiatrist, who pioneered the use of psy-

Harry Stack Sullivan developed an interpersonal theory of, and therapy for, schizophrenia. His ideas were elaborated in Interpersonal Therapy for depression, discussed in Chapter 10.

Civil Liberties, Deinstitutionalization, and Homelessness

The nature of schizophrenia and the history of attempts to treat it raise challenging legal and ethical issues regarding the rights of patients. In general, adults are presumed to be competent to make decisions about their health care.

But what if you had lost touch with reality? Suppose that the nature of your disorder were such that you could not reason clearly about it, perhaps even holding the delusion that those who seek to help you with medication are actually out to poison you. In this case it might make more sense for those responsible for your care to overrule your judgment and insist that you be treated.

This is the situation faced by the families, friends, and professionals working with patients, such as those with schizophrenia, who are psychotic. Several legal issues arise. (1) Under what circumstances, if any, can someone be required, even against his or her will, to enter a hospital for treatment? (2) If someone is required to enter a hospital, is the state then obligated to ensure that appropriate treatment is provided there? (3) If the state is obligated to offer a treatment, is the patient obligated to accept it?

How such questions are answered in the United States has changed drastically over the last several decades, not always to the benefit of patients or of society. This recent history is reviewed below, beginning with some of the fundamental legal principles.

Least Restrictive Alternative

Civil commitment is a procedure in which someone is legally certified as mentally ill and may be hospitalized, even against her or his will. This procedure is based on presumed dangerousness to oneself or others. Dangerousness can vary, though, depending on the circumstances. Thus a person may be deemed dangerous if allowed to live in an apartment, but not dangerous if living in a boarding home and taking prescribed psychoactive drugs every day under medical supervision. In general terms, mental health professionals have to provide the treatment that restricts the patient's liberty to the least degree possible while still being viable.[1]

The **least restrictive alternative** to freedom is thus to be provided when treating disturbed people and protecting them from harming themselves and others. Several court rulings require that only mental patients who cannot be adequately looked after in less restrictive homes be confined in hospitals.[2] Thus commitment is no longer necessarily in an institution; a patient might well be required to reside in a supervised boarding home or in other sheltered quarters.

Right to Treatment

Related to the idea of civil commitment is the right to treatment, a principle first articulated by Birnbaum (1960). If a person is deprived of liberty because he or she is mentally ill and is a danger to self or others, the state is required to provide treatment to alleviate these problems. It is unconstitutional (not to mention indecent) to, in effect, incarcerate someone without afterward providing the help he or she is supposed to need.

Right to Refuse Treatment

Although a committed mental patient has the right to expect appropriate treatment, he or she also has a right to *refuse* treatment, or a particular kind of treatment; that is, a right to obtain treatment does not oblige the patient to *accept* treatment (Schwitzgebel & Schwitzgebel, 1980). Not surprisingly, the right of committed patients to refuse psychotropic drugs in particular is hotly debated. Although these drugs often reduce positive symptoms of schizophrenia, they do not address all of the patient's psychosocial problems. In addition, their side effects can be very aversive to the patient and sometimes harmful and irreversible. Yet anti-psychotic drugs are often the only kind of treatment a patient in a state hospital receives with any regularity.

If the patient has the right to refuse certain forms of treatment, how far should the courts go in ensuring

---

least restrictive alternative   The legal principle according to which a committed mental patient must be treated in a setting that imposes as few restrictions as possible on his or her freedom.

[2]*Lessard v. Schmidt*, 349 F. Supp. 1078 (E.D. Wisc. 1972), *vacated and remanded on other grounds*, 94 S. Ct. 712 (1974), *reinstated* 413 F. Supp. 1318 (E.D. Wisc. 1976).

---

civil commitment   A procedure whereby a person can be legally certified as mentally ill and hospitalized, even against his or her will.

[1]*In Re: Tarpley*, 556 N.E. 2d 71, superseded by 581 N.E. 2d 1251 (1991).

this right, remaining at the same time realistic about the state's ability to provide alternatives? When should the judgment of a professional override the wishes of a patient, especially one who is considerably out of touch with reality? Are the patient's best interests always served if he or she can veto the plans of those responsible for care (A. A. Stone, 1975)?

Although patients have the right to refuse a particular treatment, this right is not unlimited. For example, it was ruled in a 1987 case that forcing a psychoactive drug on a former mental patient did not violate his constitutional rights because he had been threatening to assassinate the president of the United States, posed a threat to his own safety, and could be shown by clear and convincing evidence to be seriously mentally impaired.[3]

When a patient is believed to be too psychotic to give informed consent about a treatment, mental health law sometimes invokes the doctrine of *substituted judgment*, the decision that the patient *would have made* if he or she had been able or competent to make a decision.[4] Obviously, this principle creates problems as well as solves them.

Deinstitutionalization

The cumulative impact of such court rulings has been to put mental health professionals on notice to be more careful about keeping people in mental hospitals against their will and to attend more to the specific treatment needs of committed patients. Pressure has been placed on state governments in particular to upgrade the quality of care in mental institutions. In view of the abuses that have been documented in hospital care, these are surely encouraging trends.

But the picture is not all that rosy. For judges to declare that patient care must meet certain minimal standards does not automatically translate into that praiseworthy goal. There is not an unlimited supply of money, and care of the mentally ill has never been one of government's high priorities.

Over the past thirty years, particularly with the development of anti-psychotic drugs, many states have embarked on a policy of deinstitutionalization, discharging as many patients as possible from mental hospitals and also discouraging admissions. As we have just mentioned, civil commitment is more difficult to achieve now than it was forty and more years ago, and even if committed, patients are able to refuse much of the treatment made available to them in the hospital. At its peak in the 1950s, state mental hospitals housed almost half a million patients. By the late 1980s, the population had dropped to about 130,000. The maxim has become "Treat them in the community," the assumption being that virtually anything is preferable to institutionalization.

The Homeless Mentally Ill

The irony is that deinstitutionalization may be contributing to the very problem it was designed to alleviate, chronic mental illness. Indeed, deinstitutionalization may be a misnomer. Transinstitutionalization may be more apt, for declines in the census of public mental hospitals have occasioned *increases* in the presence of mentally ill people in jails and prisons, nursing homes, and the mental health departments of nonpsychiatric hospitals (Kiesler, 1991). These settings are by and large not equipped to handle the particular needs of mental patients. The revolving-door syndrome is seen in the increase in readmission rates from 25% before the

Deinstitutionalization policies have contributed to the increased prevalence of homeless mentally ill persons.

---

[3]*Dautremont v. Broadlawns Hospital*, 827 F. 2d 291 (8th Cir. 1987)
[4]*Guardianship of Weedon*, 565 N.E. 2d 432, 409 Mass. 196 (1991).

deinstitutionalization movement to around 80% by the 1980s (Paul & Menditto, 1992).

Many discharged mental patients are eligible for benefits from the Veterans Administration and for Social Security Disability Insurance, but a large number are not receiving them. Homeless persons do not have fixed addresses and need assistance in establishing eligibility and residency for the purpose of receiving benefits. An old but still accurate study by the Community Service Society (Baxter & Hopper, 1981), a long-established and respected social agency in New York City, found homeless people living in the streets, in train and bus terminals, in abandoned buildings, on subways, in cavernous steam tunnels running north from Grand Central Station in Manhattan, and in shelters operated by public agencies, churches, and charitable organizations. The lives of these homeless are desperate.

The relationship between homelessness and mental health was analyzed by a committee of the National Academy of Sciences (NAS; Committee on Health Care for Homeless People, 1988). It is estimated that 25% to 40% of the homeless are alcoholics, with similar proportions suffering from some form of serious mental illness, usually schizophrenia. Such problems are probably aggravated by their nomadic and dangerous existence. Homeless people, especially women, are likely victims of violence and rape, even when living in shelters for the homeless (D'Ercole & Struening, 1990). Children, too, are among the homeless, a fact that the NAS committee termed "a national disgrace," for these youngsters are forced to live their formative years in chaotic and dangerous situations, with parents under severe stress.

Do such appalling facts justify reversing the policy of deinstitutionalization? The NAS committee thinks not because, in their view, the problem lies with the failure of communities to provide suitable living and rehabilitation conditions. In Chapter 16 we discuss a few of the community programs that have grown up in response to deinstitutionalization, as well as the financial difficulties that have prevented these community programs from being fully effective.

chotherapy with schizophrenic patients. Sullivan established a ward at the Sheppard and Enoch Pratt Hospital in Towson, Maryland, in 1923. There he developed a psychoanalytic treatment reported to be markedly successful. He held that schizophrenia reflects a return to early childhood forms of communication. The fragile ego of the schizophrenic, unable to handle the extreme stress of interpersonal challenges, regresses.

Therapy therefore requires the patient to learn adult forms of communication and achieve insight into the role that the past has played in current problems. Sullivan advised the very gradual, nonthreatening development of a trusting relationship. For example, he recommended that the therapist sit somewhat to the side of the patient in order not to force eye contact, which is deemed too frightening in the early stages of treatment. After many sessions, and with the establishment of greater trust and support, the analyst begins to encourage the patient to examine his or her interpersonal relationships.

Evaluation of analytically oriented psychotherapy with schizophrenics thus far justifies little enthusiasm for applying it with these severely disturbed people, however (Feinsilver & Gunderson, 1972). For example, results from a long-term follow-up of patients bearing a diagnosis of schizophrenia and discharged after treatment between 1963 and 1976 at the New York State Psychiatric Institute suggest a lack of success (M. H. Stone, 1986). These patients had received drugs in addition to what was described as analytically oriented therapy. An analysis of data from half the sample of more than five hundred indicated that the patients were doing poorly. It may be, as Stone hypothesized, that gaining psychoanalytic insight into one's problems and illness may even worsen a schizophrenic patient's psychological condition.

Behavior Therapy

Behavior therapy techniques, such as token economies based on operant conditioning principles, have been employed in mental hospitals. Hundreds of hospitalized patients, most of them carrying a diagnosis of schizophrenia, have lived in a token economy. Such programs have been instituted to eliminate specific behavior, such as hoarding towels, to teach more socially appropriate responses, such as combing hair and arriving on time at dining halls, and to encourage activity, such as doing chores on the ward (Ayllon & Azrin, 1968). A study by Paul and Lentz (1977), described in more detail in Chapter 16, demonstrated the potential of a carefully designed program based on learning principles. Some seriously ill schizophrenics were released to shelter care or to independent living. As in the case of medication, the changes brought about by behavior therapy are seldom so thoroughgoing that we can speak of curing schizophrenics.

Family Therapy

Family therapy has attempted to help schizophrenics discharged from a mental hospital remain at home. Since high levels of expressed emotion have been linked with relapse, some family therapists try to lower the emotional intensity of the households to which schizophrenics return.

In one closely studied effort, family therapy sessions took place in the patients' homes, with family and patient participating together (Falloon et al., 1985). The importance of the patient's taking medication regularly was stressed. The family was also instructed in ways to express both positive and negative feelings in a constructive, empathic manner and to defuse tense, personal conflicts through collaborative problem solving. The patient's symptoms were explained to the family, and ways of coping with them and of reducing emotional turmoil in the home were suggested. To alleviate the guilt that patients and families may feel as a result of the stigma of schizophrenia, the fact that schizophrenia is primarily a biological illness was made clear. The idea that proper medication and the kind of psychosocial treatment they were receiving could reduce stress on the patient and prevent relapses was emphasized repeatedly. Treatment in this study extended over the first nine months after the patient returned home.

The results of this family treatment were compared with an individual therapy in which the patient was seen alone at a clinic, with supportive discussions centering on problems in daily living and on developing a social network. Family members of patients in this control group were seldom seen, and when they were, it was not in conjoint home sessions with the patients. These control patients received the typical, individual, supportive management in widespread use in aftercare programs for schizophrenics. All patients, including the controls, were maintained on antipsychotic medication.

In all, thirty-six patients were treated over a two-year period, eighteen in the family therapy group and eighteen in the individual therapy control group. Those receiving family therapy fared much better. Nine of the eighteen control patients were returned to the hospital, whereas only two of the eighteen family therapy patients had to return.

Family therapy programs are sometimes combined with behavioral techniques aimed at improving the social skills of the schizophrenic patients themselves. Social skills training is complementary to efforts to reduce family criticism of the patient. The idea is that if schizophrenic patients can handle conflict better and avoid behavior in social interactions that might upset their families and others, the overall emotional temperature of their interactions will be lowered. In one study, after one year, patient-focused social-skills treatment achieved low relapse results equal to those of family therapy. In a treatment group that combined family therapy with patient-focused social-skills training, there were no relapses whatsoever after a year (Hogarty et al., 1986).

Thus, family therapy, by itself or perhaps especially in combination with social-skills training for the individual patient, is a promising approach to schizophrenia, but it is not a panacea. For one thing, long-term effects are not always positive. In the study by Hogarty, for instance, the positive one-year results did not hold up after two years of treatment. Relapse rates no longer differed among groups (Hogarty et al., 1991). It is also important to bear in mind when interpreting the Hogarty study as well as all others that the actual real-life adjustment of the nonrelapsing patients remained marginal. Prevention or delay of rehospitalization are very worthwhile goals, but these patients do not, as a rule, become fully functioning members of society. They continue to require care and treatment.

Integrating Biological and Psychological Treatments

Enthusiasm for drugs that reduce hallucinations and delusions and even sometimes improve the clarity of thought of schizophrenic patients is certainly justified. However, it runs the risk of ignoring psychological methods that are necessary for effective and humane intervention. As we will see when we return to the case of Bill McClary, biological and psychological approaches need to be integrated. Long-term use of phenothiazines and other anti-psychotic medications can have seriously negative side effects, such as tardive dyskinesia. Moreover, anti-psychotic medications have only modest effects on negative symptoms, such as social withdrawal and behavioral deficits. Many schizophrenics need to learn or relearn ways of interacting with their world, of dealing with the emotional challenges that all people face as they negotiate life.

Therefore, though medication is clearly at the core of treatment for schizophrenia, an emerging trend in attitudes toward and treatment of schizophrenia is a consensus that psychological methods must be included as well. Only a generation ago many, if not most, mental health professionals and laypeople believed that the primary culprit was the psychological environment, and most especially the family, because the seeds for schizophrenia were seen as having been sown in early childhood. The thinking now is that a biological, and probably a genetic, factor predisposes a person to become schizophrenic. In our view, the most promising contemporary approaches to treatment make good use of this increased understanding.

Families and patients need above all to be given information about current scientific knowledge. For best treatment results, this information must include a realistic view of schizophrenia as a disability that can be controlled, but that is probably lifelong. Every effort must be made to avoid making parents or other family members feel that something in the patient's upbringing has caused the problem.

In addition, the stressful conditions facing the patient on discharge must be kept to a minimum. Hostility, overinvolvement or intrusiveness, and critical comments by the family must be reduced, and medication must be provided to help the patient think more clearly. Finally, networking among families of schizophrenics helps reduce the isolation and stigma associated with having a schizophrenic family member (Greenberg et al., 1988). Support groups are increasingly available to help families cope with the stress of having a member who is schizophrenic.

TO RECAP

Historically, biological treatments of schizophrenia included very invasive, dangerous interventions, such as induction of coma with insulin and prefrontal lobotomies. Since the 1950s, these methods have given way to anti-psychotic medications. These medications tend to be effective in reducing positive symptoms, but they do not always improve social adjustment and they have annoying and sometimes serious side effects. A new drug, clozapine, can help patients who do not respond to phenothiazines. Clozapine does not cause the most serious side effects, such as tardive dyskinesia, but it can impair the immune system and therefore necessitates close monitoring. Psychological treatment alone is generally not successful for schizophrenia. Dynamic therapy appears to be ineffective. As a complement to medication, though, behavioral skills training or family therapy aimed at reducing expressed emotion and providing information and support for family members can improve the functioning of schizophrenics.

The Case of Bill McClary Revisited ◄

SOCIAL HISTORY

Bill was the youngest of four children. He grew up in New York City, where his father worked as a fire fighter. Both his parents were first-generation Irish Americans and came from large families. Bill's childhood memories were filled with stories about the family's Irish heritage.

Bill was always much closer to his mother than to his father, whom he remembered as being harsh and distant. As the youngest child, he was treated protectively by his mother. When his parents fought, which they did frequently, Bill often found himself caught in the middle. Mr. McClary accused his wife of lavishing all her affection on Bill and seemed to blame Bill for their marital disharmony. Mrs. McClary, on the other hand, pointed out that her husband spent all his time with their oldest son and excluded Bill from their activities. Neither parent seemed to make a serious effort to improve their relationship. Bill later learned that his father had carried on an extended affair with another woman. His mother depended on her own mother, who lived in the same neighborhood, for advice and support and frequently took Bill with her to stay at her parents' apartment after particularly heated arguments.

Bill grew to hate his father, but felt guilty about his feelings. Mr. McClary became gravely ill when Bill was twelve years old, and Bill remembered wishing that his father would die. His wish came true. Years later, Bill looked back on this time with considerable ambivalence and dismay.

Bill could not remember having any close friends as a child. Most of his social contacts were with cousins, nephews, and nieces. He did not enjoy their company or the games that other children played. He remembered himself as a clumsy, effeminate child who preferred to be alone or with his mother instead of with other boys.

He was a good student and finished near the top of his class in high school. His mother and the rest of the family seemed certain that he would go on to college, but Bill could not decide on a course of study. The prospect of selecting a profession struck Bill as an ominous task. How could he be sure that he wanted to do the same thing for the rest of his life? He decided that he needed more time to ponder the matter and took a job as a bank clerk after graduating from high school.

Bill moved to a small efficiency apartment and seemed to perform adequately at the bank. His superiors noted that he was reliable, though somewhat eccentric. He was described as polite and quiet, bordering on being socially withdrawn. He did not associate with any of the other employees and rarely spoke to them beyond the usual exchange of social pleasantries. Although he was not in danger of losing his job, Bill's chances for advancement were remote. This did not bother him because he did not aspire to promotion in the banking profession. It was only a way of forestalling a serious career decision. After two years at the bank, Bill resigned. He had decided that the job did not afford him enough time to think about his future.

He was soon able to find a position as an elevator operator. Here, he reasoned, was a job that provided time for thought. Over the next several months, he gradually became more aloof and disorganized. He was frequently late to work and seemed unconcerned about the reprimands that he began receiving. Residents at the apartment house described him as peculiar. His appearance was always neat and clean, but he seemed preoccupied most of the time. On occasion he seemed to mumble to himself, and he often forgot to which floor number he had been directed. These problems continued to mount until he was fired after one year.

Bill had had his first sexual experience while working at the bank. A man in his middle forties who often did business at the bank invited Bill to his apartment for a drink, and they became intimate. The experience was moderately enjoyable, but primarily anxiety provoking. Bill decided not to see this man again. Over the next two years, Bill had sexual relationships with a small number of other men as well as with a few women. In each case, it was Bill's partner who took the initiative. Only one relationship lasted more than a few days. He became friends with a woman named Patty, who was about his own age, divorced, and the mother of a three-year-old daughter. Bill enjoyed being with Patty and her daughter and occasionally spent evenings at their apartment watching television and drinking wine. Despite their occasional sexual encounters, this relationship never developed beyond a casual stage.

After he was fired from the job as an elevator operator, Bill moved back into his mother's apartment. He later recalled that they made each other very nervous. Rarely leaving the apartment, Bill sat around the apartment daydreaming in front of the television. When his mother returned from work, she would clean, cook, and coax him unsuccessfully to enroll in various kinds of job-training programs. His social isolation was a constant cause of concern for her. The tension eventually became too great for both of them, and Bill decided to move in with his sister, Colleen, her husband, and their three young children.

CONCEPTUALIZATION AND TREATMENT

Bill's problems were obviously extensive. He had experienced serious difficulties in the development of social and occupational roles. He was unable to experience pleasure and seldom, if ever, had any fun. Even his sexual experiences were described in a detached, intellectual manner. He might indicate, for example, that he had performed well or that his partner seemed satisfied, but he never seemed delighted about it. He strongly preferred to be alone. When Colleen and Roger had parties, Bill became anxious and withdrew to his room, explaining that he felt ill.

Bill's ambivalence toward other people was evident in his relationship with his therapist. He never missed an appointment; in fact, he was always early and seemed to look forward to the visits. Despite this apparent dependence, he seemed to distrust the therapist and was often guarded in his response to questions. He seemed to want to confide in the therapist and was simultaneously fearful of the imagined consequences. The therapist decided initially to address Bill's problems from a behavioral perspective. Treatment eventually also involved biological and cognitive approaches.

The first several therapy sessions were among the most difficult. Bill was tense, reserved, and more than a bit suspicious. Therapy had been his sister's idea, not his own. The therapist adopted a passive, nondirective manner and concentrated on the difficult goal of establishing a trusting relationship with Bill.

Many of the early sessions were spent discussing Bill's concerns about homosexuality. The therapist listened to Bill's thoughts and concerns and shared various bits of information about sexuality and homosexual behavior in particular. Bill was afraid that homosexual behavior per se was a direct manifestation of psychological disturbance. The therapist took the position that the gender of one's sexual partner was less important than the quality of the sexual relationship. In fact, the therapist was most concerned about Bill's apparent failure to enjoy sexual activity and his inability to establish lasting relationships.

As their relationship became more secure, the therapist adopted a more directive role. Specific target problems were identified. The first area of concern was Bill's daily schedule. The therapist enlisted Colleen's support. Together with Bill they instituted a sequence of contingencies designed to integrate his activities with those of the family. For example, Colleen called Bill once for breakfast at 7:30 A.M. If he missed eating with everyone else, Colleen went on with other activities and did not make him a late brunch as had been her custom. In general, the therapist taught Colleen to reinforce appropriate behavior and to ignore inappropriate behavior as much as possible. Over the initial weeks, Bill did begin to keep more regular hours and to be more helpful around the house.

At this point, the therapist decided to address two problems that were somewhat more difficult: Bill's lack of social contacts with peers and his annoying habit of mumbling to himself while daydreaming. This behavior seemed to occur most frequently when Bill was alone or thought he was alone. The therapist decided to try a stimulus control procedure. Bill was instructed to select one place in the house in which he would daydream and talk to himself. Whenever he felt the urge to daydream, he was to go to this specific spot, the laundry room, before engaging in these behaviors. It was hoped that this procedure would severely restrict the environmental stimuli that were associated with these asocial behaviors and thereby reduce their frequency. Colleen was encouraged to prompt Bill whenever she noticed him engaging in self-talk outside the laundry room. The program seemed to have modest, positive results, but it did not eliminate self-talk entirely.

Interpersonal behaviors were also addressed from a behavioral perspective. Since moving to his sister's home, Bill had not met any people his own age and had discontinued seeing his friends in New York City. He was encouraged to call his old friends and, in particular, to renew his friendship with Patty. The therapist spent several sessions with Bill rehearsing telephone calls and practicing conversations that might take place. Although Bill was generally aware of what things he should say, he was anxious about social contacts. This form of behavioral rehearsal was seen as a way of exposing him gradually to the anxiety-provoking stimuli. He was also given weekly homework assignments involving social contacts at home. This aspect of the treatment program was modestly effective. Bill called Patty several times and arranged to stay with his mother for a weekend so that he could visit with Patty and her daughter. Although he was somewhat anxious at first, the visit was very successful and seemed to lift Bill's spirits. He was more animated during the following therapy session and seemed almost optimistic about changing his current situation.

It was at about this time that Bill first mentioned the imagined movie to Roger. When the therapist learned of these ideas, and the auditory hallucinations, he modified the treatment plan. He had initially rejected the idea of antipsychotic medication because there was no clear-cut evidence of schizophrenia. Now that there was such evidence, Bill's therapist arranged an appointment with a psychiatrist, who prescribed a moderate dosage of Mellaril, one of the standard phenothiazines. Because Bill's behavior was not considered dangerous and his sister was able to supervise his activities closely, hospitalization was not necessary. All the other aspects of the program were continued.

Bill's response to the medication was positive, but not dramatic. His self-talk was reduced considerably over a four-week period. His delusions remained intact, however, despite the therapist's attempt to encourage a rational consideration of the evidence.

One of Bill's ideas, for example, was that his picture had been on the cover of *Time* magazine. This seemed like a simple idea to test, and Bill expressed a willingness to try. Together they narrowed the range of dates to the last eight months. The therapist then asked Bill to visit the public library before their next session and check all issues of *Time* during this period. Of course, Bill did not find his picture. Nevertheless, his conviction seemed even stronger than before. He had convinced himself that the conspirators had seen him on his way to the library, beaten him there, and switched magazine covers before he could discover the original. Every effort to introduce contradictory evidence was met by this same stubborn resistance.

Overall, the medication had a positive effect on Bill's behavior, but it also produced some bothersome side effects. Many of these were minor in nature, such as a dry mouth and drowsiness. The most annoying side effect involved muscular rigidity. Bill said that his arms and legs felt stiff and that his hands sometimes trembled involuntarily. These motor disturbances were counteracted by having Bill supplement his Mellaril with an anti-Parkinson drug, Cogentin.

Over the next several weeks, Bill became somewhat less adamant about his beliefs. He conceded that there was a *chance* that he had imagined the whole thing. It seemed to him that the plot probably did exist and that the movie was, in all likelihood, still playing around the country, but he was willing to admit that the evidence for this belief was less than overwhelming. Although his suspicions remained, the fear of observation and the threat of death were less immediate, and he was able to concentrate more fully on the other aspects of the treatment program. Hospitalization did not become necessary, and he was able to continue living with Colleen's family. Despite important improvements, it was clear that Bill would continue to need a special supportive environment and it seemed unlikely that he would soon assume normal occupational and social roles.

DISCUSSION

Bill clearly fit diagnostic criteria for paranoid schizophrenia. Prior to the expression of his complex delusional scheme, he exhibited several of the characteristics of a prodromal phase. He had been socially isolated since moving to his sister's home. In fact, he had never been particularly active socially, even during his childhood. His occupational performance had deteriorated long before he was fired from his job as an elevator operator. Several neighbors had complained about his peculiar behavior.

The data regarding expressed emotion are consistent with Bill's experience. Bill remembered that when he and his mother were living together, they made each other very nervous. His descriptions of her behavior indicate that her emotional involvement was excessive, given that he was an adult and capable of greater independence. She was always worried about his job, or his friends, or what he was doing with his time. Her constant intrusions and coaxing finally led him to seek refuge with his sister's family. The supportive environment provided by Colleen and her family and their willingness to tolerate many of Bill's idiosyncrasies were undoubtedly helpful in allowing Bill to remain outside a hospital during his psychotic episode.

Bill's case illustrates the desirability of involving the family in treatment of schizophrenic patients, as well as the importance of combining psychological methods with maintenance medication. His sister's family would not have been considered high in expressed emotion. Direct intervention focused on family patterns of communication was therefore unnecessary. The therapist did, however, spend time talking with Colleen and Roger about Bill's situation in an effort to help them cope with his idiosyncratic behavior. Bill's therapist also directed his attention to the development of social skills, with mixed success.

With the benefit of hindsight it might have been better to instigate the medication earlier. Using a direct, active psychological approach to increase the level of social interaction among chronic schizophrenic patients may have adverse effects on other areas of the patient's adjustment (e.g., Schooler & Spohn, 1982). It may be that patients who are not on medication cannot handle the increase in stress that is probably associated with a directive form of social intervention. This phenomenon may have been evident in Bill's case. He was not receiving medication until after the therapist became aware of his extensive delusional system. His response to the behavioral program seemed to be more positive after the introduction of antipsychotic medication.

Visual Summary for Chapter 9:

Schizophrenia

Positive Symptoms of Schizophrenia

- Disorganized Speech
- Delusions
- Perceptual Distortions (e.g., hallucinations)

Major Events in the History of Schizophrenia

Kraepelin defined dementia praecox.	Bleuler broadened concept to "schizophrenia."	American psychiatrists broadened the concept even more. In the 1930s, 20% of psychiatric patients were diagnosed as schizophrenic.

| 1890 | 1898 | 1908 | 1930 | 1940 |

Theories About the Cause of Schizophrenia

Biological

- **Genetics** — Family, twin, and adoption studies suggest that vulnerability to schizophrenia is genetically transmitted.
- **Biochemistry** — Antipsychotics block dopamine receptors, suggesting that schizophrenia is caused by a problem in the dopamine system.
- **Neuroanatomy** — Brain abnormalities (e.g., enlarged ventricles) are found among schizophrenic patients.

Vulnerability –Stress

- Prenatal exposure to a virus?
- The sociogenic hypothesis posits that the stress of living in lower social classes can trigger schizophrenia in vulnerable individuals. In contrast, the social-selection hypothesis argues that patients suffering from schizophrenia are downwardly mobile.

Family Interaction

- Notion of the schizophrenogenic mother and double-bind theory are not considered credible.
- Households high in expressed emotion (critical, hostile, emotionally overinvolved) are believed capable of worsening a schizophrenic condition.

Negative Symptoms of Schizophrenia

- *Avolition*
- *Poverty of Speech*
- *Poverty of Content*
- *Flat Affect*

By the 1950s, 80% of psychiatric patients were diagnosed as schizophrenic.

DSM-IV has narrower definition:
- *Explicit criteria*
- *Mood disorders excluded*
- *At least 6 months duration*
- *Mild forms excluded*

DSM-IV subtypes:
- *Disorganized*
- *Catatonic*
- *Paranoid*

1950   **1990**   **1994**

Effective Treatments for Schizophrenia

Medication

Antipsychotic medications can alleviate the positive symptoms of schizophrenia, but often have serious side effects that mimic neurological diseases. Clozaril (a recently developed antipsychotic) helps some who did not benefit from traditional antipsychotics, but can impair immune system functioning.

Psychological Therapies

Family therapy can provide support, information, and can help reduce detrimental levels of expressed emotion.

Behavioral therapies (e.g., social-skills training) can reduce behaviors that might elicit hostility and criticism from friends or family.

Chapter 10

Mood Disorders

The Case of George Lawler

By the time he was admitted to the hospital, George Lawler was talking a mile a minute. He harangued the other patients and ward staff, declaring that he was the coach of the U.S. Olympic track team and offering to hold tryouts for the other patients in the hospital. His movements were rapid and somewhat erratic as he paced the halls of the ward and explored every room. At the slightest provocation, he flew into a rage. When an attendant blocked his entrance to the nursing station, he threatened to report her to the president of the Olympic committee. He had not slept for three nights.

His life had changed drastically over the past two weeks. George was thirty-five years old, married, and the father of two young children. He worked at a small junior college, where he taught physical education and coached the men's and women's track teams. Until his breakdown, the teams had been having an outstanding season.

This was not the first time that George had experienced psychological problems. His first serious episode had occurred during his junior year in college. It did not seem to be triggered by any particular incident. In fact, things had been going well. George was majoring in physical education and playing defensive back on the university football team. He was in good academic standing and fairly popular with the other students. Nevertheless, during the spring semester, George found that he was losing interest in everything. It was not surprising that he did not look forward to classes or studying. He had never been an outstanding student, but he noticed that he no longer enjoyed going out with his friends. They said he seemed depressed all the time.

George said that he just did not care anymore. He began avoiding his girlfriend and, when they were together, he found fault with almost everything she did. Most of his time was spent in his apartment in front of the television. When George did not show up for spring football practice, the coach called him to the office for a long talk. George said that he did not have the energy to play football. Recognizing that the problem was more than a simple lack of motivation, the coach persuaded George to visit a psychiatrist at the student health clinic. George began taking antidepressant medication and attending individual counseling sessions. Within several weeks he was back to his normal level of functioning.

George had also experienced intervals of unusual ambition and energy. As a student, George had frequently spent several days cramming for exams at the end of a semester. Many of his friends took amphetamines to stay awake, but George seemed able to summon endless, internal reserves of energy.

The behavior that brought George to the hospital began suddenly. Two days before the conference meet, his wife, Cheryl, noticed that he was behaving strangely. There was a driven quality about his preparation for the meet. He was working much longer hours and demanding more from the athletes. When he was home, he talked endlessly about the team, bragging about their chances for national recognition and planning intricate strategies for particularly important events. Cheryl was worried about this change in George's behavior, but she attributed it to the pressures of his job and assured herself that he would return to normal when the season was over.

George was clearly losing control over his own behavior. After his team won the conference meet easily, George did not return home. He stayed in his office, working straight through the night in preparation for the regional meet. Cheryl was finally able to locate him by phoning his friend who worked in the office next door. She and his colleagues tried to persuade him to slow down, but he would not listen. The next morning George was approached by a reporter from the school newspaper. Here, George thought, was the perfect opportunity to expound on his ability as a coach and to publicize his exciting plans for future competition. The interview turned into a grandiose tirade, with George rambling uninterrupted for three hours.

This incident became a professional disaster for George. Among other things, he boasted that he was going to send the star high jumper from the women's team to the

NCAA national meet in Oregon. He planned to go along as her chaperon and said that he would pay for their trip with the proceeds of a recent community fund-raising drive. This announcement was startling in two regards. First, the money in question had been raised with the athletic department's assurance that it would be used to improve the college's track facilities and to sponsor running clinics for local youngsters. George did not have the authority to reroute the funds. Second, the prospect of a married male coach chaperoning a female athlete promised to create a minor scandal. Recognizing the sensitive nature of these plans, the reporter asked George if he might want to reconsider his brash announcement. George replied—asking the reporter to quote him—that it was not every year that he had the opportunity to take a free trip with a pretty woman, and he was not about to pass it up.

The article appeared, along with a picture of George, on the front page of the school paper the next morning. His disheveled appearance and outrageous remarks raised an instant furor in the athletic department and the school administration. The head of the department finally located George making a series of long-distance calls in his office. The director demanded an explanation, and immediately found himself in the midst of a shouting match. George claimed that he had just been named head coach of the Olympic track team. He was now calling potential assistant coaches and athletes around the country to organize tryouts for the following month. Any interference, he claimed, would be attributed to foreign countries that were reluctant to compete against a team led by a coach with such a distinguished record. The department head realized that George was not kidding and that he could not reason with him. He returned to his own office and phoned Cheryl. When she arrived, they were unable to convince George that he needed help. They eventually realized that their only option was to call the police, who then took George to a psychiatric hospital. Following an intake evaluation, George was committed for three days of observation.

▶ *Description of Mood Disorders*

George Lawler was suffering from what is often called manic-depression. This mood disorder is formally known as bipolar disorder, because individuals experiencing it have periods of intense energy and exuberance alternating with periods of lethargy and depression. **Mood disorders** involve disabling disturbances in emotion. Two major mood disorders are listed in DSM-IV, major depressive disorder and bipolar disorder. We cover the characteristics of depression first, and then consider the more complicated symptoms of bipolar disorder.

mood disorders   Disorders in which there are disabling disturbances in emotion.

Major Depressive Disorder

Everyone feels down or depressed occasionally. For most, these feelings are not cause for alarm. Even so, major depressive disorder is one of the most widespread of the disorders considered in this book. Specific estimates vary, but the recent National Comorbidity Survey reported a lifetime prevalence of 17% (Blazer, Kessler, McGonagle, & Swartz, 1994). Epidemiological studies from around the world show increased risk for major depressive disorder in people born more recently (Cross-National Collaborative Group, 1992). Major depressive disorder is about twice as common in women as in men. This sex difference in depression emerges in early adolescence. Prior to about age thirteen, boys and girls report equal levels of depression (Nolen-Hoeksema & Girgus, 1994).

Major depressive disorder tends to be recurrent. Fortunately, most depression dissipates with time. But an average untreated episode may stretch on for six to eight months or even longer. When depression becomes chronic—recurring regularly and frequently—the patient does not always snap back to an earlier level of functioning between bouts.

Because we all feel sad or depressed from time to time, it may be hard to appreciate how overwhelming a bona fide major depressive episode may be. The following eloquent account is that of a person suffering from profound depression. Clearly, anxiety plays a part in deepening the despair.

> I was seized with an unspeakable physical weariness. There was a tired feeling in the muscles unlike anything I had ever experienced. A peculiar sensation appeared to travel up my spine to my brain. I had an indescribable nervous feeling. My nerves seemed like live wires charged with electricity. My nights were sleepless. I lay with dry, staring eyes gazing into space. I had a fear that some terrible calamity was about to happen. I grew afraid to be left alone. The most trivial duty became a formidable task. Finally mental and physical exercises became impossible; the tired muscles refused to respond, my "thinking apparatus" refused to work, ambition was gone. My general feeling might be summed up in the familiar saying "What's the use?" I had tried so hard to make something of myself, but the struggle seemed useless. Life seemed utterly futile. (Reid, 1910, pp. 612–613)

As we see in this example, symptoms of **major depressive disorder** include more than just profoundly sad mood. There are also disturbances of appetite, weight, sleep, and activity level.

> *major depressive disorder* A disorder of individuals who have experienced episodes of depression but not of *mania*.

The DSM-IV diagnosis of a major depressive episode requires that a person exhibit at least five of the following symptoms nearly every day for at least two weeks. Either depressed mood or loss of interest and pleasure must be one of the five symptoms.

- Sad, depressed mood.
- Loss of interest and pleasure in usual activities.
- Difficulties in sleeping (insomnia); not falling asleep initially, not returning to sleep after awakening in the middle of the night, and early morning awakenings; or, in some patients, a desire to sleep a great deal of the time.
- Shift in activity level, becoming either lethargic (psychomotor retardation) or agitated.
- Poor appetite and weight loss, or increased appetite and weight gain.
- Loss of energy, great fatigue.
- Negative self-concept; self-reproach and self-blame; feelings of worthlessness and guilt.
- Complaints or evidence of difficulty in concentrating, such as slowed thinking and indecisiveness.
- Recurrent thoughts of death or suicide.

These symptoms can occur in response to another psychological or medical problem. Alcohol abusers, for instance, may be depressed by their inability to control their drinking or drinking-related problems. Our chief focus in this chapter is on people for whom depression is the *primary* problem.

There is some variation in the symptoms and signs of depression across the life span. As we discuss in Chapters 14 and 15, depression in children sometimes results in their being overly active, irritable, and aggressive; in adolescents, it is sometimes manifested by negativism, antisocial behavior, and a feeling of being misunderstood; and in older adults, depression is often characterized by distractibility and memory loss.

Bipolar Disorder

The critical symptoms of **bipolar disorder** are the elated or irritable mood, talkativeness, and hyperactivity of mania, as well as episodes of depression, both shown by George Lawler. These symptoms must be severe enough to cause serious impairment in social or occupational functioning or to require hospitaliza-

> *bipolar disorder* A term applied to the disorder of people who experience episodes of both *mania* and depression or of mania alone.

tion. The symptoms for a depressive episode are the same as those just listed for major depressive disorder. A diagnosis of a manic episode requires the presence of elevated or irritable mood and three additional symptoms (four if the mood is only irritable) from the following list.

▷ Increase in activity level—at work, socially, or sexually.
▷ Unusual talkativeness, rapid speech.
▷ A feeling that one's thoughts are racing.
▷ Less than the usual amount of sleep needed.
▷ Inflated self-esteem or grandiosity; a belief that one has special talents, powers, and abilities.
▷ Distractibility; attention easily diverted.
▷ Excessive involvement in pleasurable activities that are likely to have undesirable consequences, such as reckless spending or promiscuity.

Although there are clinical reports of individuals who experience episodes of **mania** but not depression, such a condition is apparently quite rare.

"Unusual talkativeness" or "increase in activity level" are accurate descriptions of the behavior of George Lawler. In a sense, though, they are too tame to convey the out-of-control nature of a manic episode. The manic stream of remarks is loud and incessant, full of puns, jokes, plays on words, rhyming, and interjections about nearby objects and happenings that have attracted the speaker's attention. This speech is very difficult to interrupt and reveals the manic's so-called flight of ideas. Although small bits of talk are coherent, the individual shifts rapidly from topic to topic. The manic need for activity may cause the individual to be sociable to the point of being intrusive, constantly and sometimes purposelessly busy, and, unfortunately, oblivious to the obvious pitfalls of his or her endeavors. Any attempt to curb this momentum can bring quick anger and even rage. Mania usually comes on suddenly, over the period of a day or two. Untreated episodes may last from a few days to several months.

Bipolar disorder occurs less often than major depressive disorder, with a prevalence rate of about 1% of the population (Myers et al., 1984). The average age of onset is thirty, and it occurs equally often in men and in women. Like major depressive disorder, bipolar disorder tends to recur. Over 50% of cases have four or more episodes.

Variation Among Mood Disorders

These two basic patterns, major depressive disorder and bipolar disorder, have been recognized (albeit by different names) for thousands of years. It has long been clear, however, that they are not homogeneous categories. Accordingly, many subclassification schemes have been proposed to account for variation among people with mood disorders. Some of the subtypes proved to be difficult to judge reliably. Some lacked validity in the sense that they did not make a clear difference from the standpoint of predicting the course of the disorder or selecting the best treatment for a patient. In this section we describe some of the subtypes currently considered useful in classifying patients with mood disorders.

Seasonal Affective Disorders

Both bipolar disorder and major depressive disorder can be subdiagnosed as seasonal in DSM-IV if there is a regular relationship between an episode and a particular time of the year. Most research on these **seasonal affective disorders (SAD)** has been conducted on patients who experienced depression in the winter

mania An emotional state of intense but unfounded elation evidenced in talkativeness, racing thoughts and distractibility, grandiose plans, and spurts of purposeless activity.

Patty Duke has experienced episodes of both mania and depression and therefore would be regarded as having bipolar disorder.

seasonal affective disorders (SAD) Mood disorders recurring regularly at a particular time of year; for example, bipolar disorder with winter depressive episodes and manic episodes in spring or summer.

Seasonal depression is one of the subtypes of major depressive disorders. This woman is demonstrating light therapy, an effective treatment for patients whose seasonal depression occurs during the winter.

and mania in the spring or summer (e.g., Rosenthal et al., 1986). The most likely explanation is that the mood disorders were linked to changes in the length of daylight hours. Indeed, therapy for these winter depressions involves exposing the patients to bright, white light (Blehar & Rosenthal, 1989; Rosenthal et al., 1985).

Chronic Mood Disorders: Cyclothymic Disorder and Dysthymic Disorder

DSM-IV lists two long-lasting, or chronic, disorders in which mood disturbances are predominant. Although the symptoms of these disorders must have been evident for at least two years, they are not severe enough to warrant a diagnosis of major depressive or manic episode. In **cyclothymic disorder**, the person has frequent periods of depressed mood and **hypomania**, elevated mood and behavior that are not as extreme as mania. These periods may alternate with periods of normal mood lasting as long as two months. During depression patients feel inadequate; during hypomania their self-esteem is inflated. They withdraw from people, then seek them out in an uninhibited fashion. They sleep too much and then too little. Depressed cyclothymic patients have trouble concentrating, and their productivity decreases. During hypomania their thinking becomes sharp and creative, and their productivity increases. Patients with cyclothymic disorder may also experience full-blown episodes of mania and depression.

People with **dysthymic disorder** are chronically depressed. Besides feeling blue and losing pleasure in usual activities, they experience several other signs of depression, such as insomnia or sleeping too much; feelings of inadequacy, ineffectiveness, and lack of energy; pessimism; an inability to concentrate and to think clearly; and the desire to avoid the company of others. Data have shown that dysthymia appears to be a particularly debilitating disorder (Klein, Taylor, Dickstein, & Harding, 1988). Many dysthymics are chronically depressed and have episodes of major depressive disorder as well.

cyclothymic disorder Swings between elation and depresssion not severe enough to warrant the diagnosis of *bipolar disorder*.

hypomania An above-normal elevation of mood, but not as extreme as *mania*.

dysthymic disorder State of depression that is long lasting but not severe enough for the diagnosis of *major depressive disorder*.

Psychotic Depression

Some severely depressed patients show the psychotic features of delusions and hallucinations (discussed in Chapter 9 in the context of schizophrenia). Typically, the content of the delusions or hallucinations is consistent with the depressed person's negative mood. For example, the person might hold an extreme, unrealistic belief that she or he is personally responsible for someone else's misfortune. The presence of delusions appears to be a useful distinction among major depressives (e.g., Johnson, Horvath, & Weissman, 1991). Depressed patients with delusions do not generally respond well to the usual drug therapies for depression, but they do respond favorably to these drugs when they are combined with the drugs commonly used to treat other psychotic disorders, such as schizophrenia.

Comorbid Depression

Many depressed people also meet criteria for other disorders, such as panic disorder, posttraumatic stress disorder, and eating disorders. The overlap between depression and anxiety is so common that a new diagnosis of mixed anxiety-depressive disorder was proposed for DSM-IV. Not an official DSM diagnosis, it is listed in an appendix as providing guidelines for further study. Consideration of such a blended diagnosis reflects the belief that comorbid depressions may differ in important ways from pure depressions (in which the person meets criteria for major depressive disorder and nothing else). For example, lower education and lower income were associated with greater risk for comorbid depression but not for pure depression in the study by Blazer and his colleagues (1994). The authors speculated that comorbid depressions may be tied more closely than pure major depressive disorders to environmental adversities, which can also prompt comorbid conditions such as alcohol abuse or anxiety.

To Recap

The two major mood disorders listed in DSM-IV are major depressive disorder and bipolar disorder. Major depressive disorder involves very sad mood and/or loss of interest and pleasure in usual activities along with changes in activity level, difficulty sleeping, changes in appetite, negative self-concept, difficulty concentrating, and thoughts of death or suicide. Major depressive disorder is a common, recurrent disorder, affecting about twice as many women as men. Patients with bipolar disorder also experience depressive episodes, but these periods alternate with episodes of mania. Mania is marked by racing thoughts, increased activity level, decreased need for sleep, inflated self-esteem, distractibility, and recklessness or poor judgment. Bipolar disorder is recurrent, less common than major depressive disorder, and equally common in men and women. There are several variations on these two main disorders. In seasonal affective disorders, there is a predictable relationship between time of year and mood disturbance (e.g., depression in winter and mania in spring or summer). Cyclothymic disorder is a less severe variant of bipolar disorder, and dysthymic disorder is a less acutely severe, but chronic, depressive disorder. Finally, psychotic depression is a major depressive disorder in which delusions and hallucinations are present.

Perspectives on the Causes and Treatment of Mood Disorders

Several psychological theories and therapies of depression have been developed and tested, but psychological perspectives have had little impact on research on mania. Biological perspectives, however, have provided integrated analyses of both depression and mania. Because stressful events, specifically significant loss experiences, such as the death of a family member or being laid off from a job (Brown, 1993; Shrout et al., 1989), have been linked to major depressive disorder, the main theories of depression are, in effect, vulnerability-stress theories. None of the perspectives denies the relevance of stressful events. The perspectives differ with respect to what vulnerabilities make some people more susceptible than others to becoming depressed after such events.

Psychodynamic and Interpersonal Perspectives

In his celebrated paper "Mourning and Melancholia," Freud (1917/1950) wrote of the potential for depression being created early in childhood. He theorized that during the oral period a child's needs may be insufficiently or excessively gratified, causing the person to continue to be dependent on the instinctual gratifications particular to this stage.

Given this fixation at the oral stage, the person may develop a tendency to be excessively dependent on other people for the maintenance of self-esteem. Subsequently, when losses or rejections are suffered, the person is especially vulnerable to depression. The reasoning can be illustrated most readily by considering the case of depression after bereavement. Freud hypothesized that after the loss of a loved one, the mourner first **introjects**, or incorporates, the lost person. He or she identifies with the lost one, perhaps in a fruitless attempt to undo the loss. The loss may also be symbolic. For example, a child whose parents get divorced or do not express much love or physical affection may unconsciously interpret the divorce or lack of affection as a personal rejection and a total withdrawal of love.

introject In psychoanalytic theory, the idea that a person unconsciously incorporates the values, attitudes, and qualities of another person into the individual's own personality.

Because, as Freud asserted, we unconsciously harbor negative feelings toward those we love, the mourner or deserted one now becomes the object of his or her own hate and anger. In addition, he or she resents being deserted and feels guilt for real or imagined sins against the deceased or otherwise departed. The period of introjection is followed by the period of *mourning work*, when the mourner recalls memories of the lost one and thereby separates himself or herself from the person who has died or departed and loosens the bonds imposed by introjection.

The grief work can go astray in overly dependent individuals and develop into an ongoing process of self-abuse, self-blame, and depression. Like the child angered by the mother's leaving, the dependent person who has suffered a loss is angry, but feels guilty about being angry and so becomes depressed. Thus, depression is seen as involving anger turned against the self.

Research on depression supports some but not all aspects of psychoanalytic theory. Consistent with the theory, excessive dependence on the approval of others to bolster one's self-esteem does appear to increase the risk of depression (Bornstein, 1992). Likewise, parents' divorce or marital discord seems to make children more prone to depression later in life, which is consistent with the concept of symbolic loss of a loved one as contributing to depression (Parker, 1992).

The "anger directed inward" aspect of psychoanalytic theory has fared less well in research. Dreams and projective tests should theoretically be means of expressing unconscious needs and fears. An analysis of the dreams of depressed people showed themes of loss and failure, but not of anger and hostility (Beck & Ward, 1961). An examination of responses to projective tests established that depressives identify with the victim, not the aggressor. Also, if depression derived from anger turned inward, we would expect depressed people to express little hostility toward others, but they often express intense anger toward people close to them (Biglan et al., 1985; Weissman, Klerman, & Paykel, 1971).

Interpersonal Aspects of Depression

In view of these findings that depressed persons have conflictual relationships as opposed to directing all their anger at themselves, many researchers have focused attention on the real, current social relationships in which depressed peo-

Depressed people often have sparse social-support networks and may even elicit negative reactions from others. Both these factors can contribute to the onset and maintenance of depression.

ple find themselves. In Chapter 8 we discussed the role of social support in coping with stress and maintaining physical health. The concept has also been applied to research on depression. Depressives tend to have few friends and regard those they do have as not very supportive (Kendler, Kessler, Neale, Heath, & Eaves, 1993). This reduced social support may lessen the individual's ability to handle negative life events (Billings, Cronkite, & Moos, 1983).

Is it mere bad luck that confronts the depressive with an inadequate level of social support? Perhaps, but it is also possible that the depressed person himself or herself plays a role. A longitudinal study of major depressives confirmed that they experience much stress (particularly of an interpersonal nature) and that their own behavior contributes to the high levels of stress that they experience (Hammen, 1991). Depressed people rate themselves, and are rated by observers in laboratory experiments, as lower in overall social competence than nondepressed people. A number of studies have examined what, in particular, depressed people do to create this negative impression. Research shows that they speak slower, more quietly and hesitantly, in a more monotonous fashion, engage in less eye contact, and engage in more self-disclosure of negative information about themselves and their feelings (Segrin & Abramson, 1994).

These dysfunctional social behaviors of depressed people tend to elicit negative reactions from others (Coyne, 1976). This possibility has been studied under a variety of circumstances, including telephone conversations with depressed patients, audiotapes of depressed patients, and even face-to-face interactions. The data show that depressives are often difficult to get along with, and their behavior encourages rejection from others. For example, the roommates of depressed college students rated social contacts with them as low in enjoyment, and they reported high levels of aggression toward their depressed roommates (Hokanson, Rubert, Welker, Hollander, & Hedeen, 1989). Also, mildly depressed college students were likely to be rejected by their roommates (Joiner, Alfano, & Metalsky 1992).

Negative interpersonal styles may precede the onset of depression. For example, the classroom behavior of elementary-school children of depressed parents was rated negatively by both teachers and peers (Weintraub, Liebert, & Neale, 1975; Weintraub, Prinz, & Neale, 1978). Interpersonal behavior appears to play a major role in depression.

Psychodynamic Therapies for Depression

Psychoanalysis. Because depression is considered to result from a repressed sense of loss and from anger about that loss unconsciously turned inward, psychoanalytic treatment tries to help the patient achieve insight into the repressed conflict and often encourages outward release of the hostility directed inward. The goal is to uncover the motivations for the patient's depression. A person may, for example, blame himself or herself for a parent's rejecting behavior, and feel inadequate and depressed instead of angry about the parent's lack of love and attention. The therapist must first guide the patient to confront the fact that he or she holds this belief. Then the therapist can help the patient realize that the self-blame is unfounded. The recovery of memories and the reexperiencing of childhood feelings of disappointment or longing toward the inadequate parent should also help. Research on the effectiveness of psychoanalytic treatment in alleviating depression is sparse (Craighead, Evans, & Robins, 1992) and not very favorable (e.g., Covi, Lipman, Derogatis, Smith, & Pattison, 1974).

Interpersonal Therapy. A newer form of psychodynamic therapy concentrates on present-day interactions between the depressed person and the social environment, just as the descriptive research on depression suggests that it may be maintained in part by difficulties in current relationships. Interpersonal therapy (IPT; Klerman, Weissman, Rounsaville, & Chevron, 1984) is an insight-oriented approach that focuses on current problems and interpersonal relationships. It emphasizes better understanding of the interpersonal problems assumed to give rise to depression and aims at improving relationships with others. As such, the focus is on better communication with others, reality testing, developing more effective social skills, and meeting present social-role requirements.

IPT therapists remain nondirective as interpersonal problems are discussed. Yet they also encourage exploration and expression of unacknowledged negative feelings, improvement of both verbal and nonverbal communications, and problem solving. For example, a man depressed over difficulties in dealing assertively with a domineering father might be encouraged by the therapist to initiate frank discussions with his father. In this respect, IPT resembles assertion and social-skills training therapies, which originated within the behavioral perspective and have proven useful in treating depression (Hersen, Bellack, Himmelhoch, & Thase, 1984; Lewinsohn, 1974). Findings from large-scale research projects suggest that IPT is quite effective for alleviating major depressive disorder (Elkin et al., 1989; see Focus Box 10.1) as well as for maintaining treatment gains (Frank et al., 1990).

To Recap

Psychoanalytic theory explains depression as resulting from anger turned inward against the self in response to loss (literal or symbolic) of a loved one with whom the depressed person identifies. This process is believed to be likely if one's needs were insufficiently or excessively gratified during the oral stage, resulting in fixation and excessive dependency on others for maintaining self-esteem. Interpersonal researchers shift the focus from how depression-prone people have internalized past relationships to the nature of the actual relationships in which they find themselves today. Depressed people show a range of social-skill deficits (e.g., poor eye contact), which may result in others rejecting them. This rejection, in turn, is depressing.

Psychoanalytic therapy tries to help depressed patients gain insight into their loss and repressed anger. A variation that focuses on present-day social interactions and relationships (interpersonal therapy) appears to be quite effective.

NIMH Treatment of Depression Collaborative Research Program

In 1977 the National Institute of Mental Health under-took a large, complex, three-site study of cognitive therapy (CT), interpersonal therapy (IPT), and pharma-cotherapy for depression, the Treatment of Depression Collaborative Research Program (TDCRP; Elkin, Parloff, Hadley, & Autry, 1985).

Therapies

The effectiveness of two therapies, cognitive and inter-personal, was studied. Imipramine (Tofranil), a tricyclic drug widely regarded as a standard therapy for depres-sion, was used as a reference against which to evaluate the two psychotherapies. A fourth and final condition was a placebo–clinical management group, against which to judge the efficacy of imipramine. It was also conceived of as a partial control for the two psy-chotherapies because of the presence of strong support and encouragement.

All treatments lasted sixteen weeks. Throughout all therapies, patients were closely monitored, and all pro-fessional safeguards were employed to minimize risk, for example, excluding imminently suicidal patients and, in general, maintaining close and regular contact during the study. These considerations were particu-larly important in the placebo condition.

Selection and Training of Therapists

An important feature of this study was the care and thoroughness of therapist selection and training. This phase took almost two years, beginning with careful

screening of recruits for general clinical competence and some experience in one of the treatments under study. Altogether twenty-eight therapists were se-lected—ten each for interpersonal therapy and drug therapy and eight for cognitive therapy.

Training took months and was very rigorous, involv-ing 119 patients. The selection and training phase itself constituted an achievement in psychotherapy research (Rounsaville, Chevron, & Weissman, 1984; Shaw, 1984; Waskow, 1984). This lengthy procedure was followed to ensure the integrity of the independent variable, the therapy each subject received. The training and super-vision efforts were successful. Although IPT and cogni-tive therapy overlap in their emphasis on improving accuracy of perception and efficacy in social behavior, they differ sufficiently that a comparison of their effec-tiveness on the dependent variables was meaningful (Hill, O'Grady, & Elkin, 1992).

Selection of Patient Subjects

The overall design of the study called for 240 pa-tients, 60 in each of the four conditions. They had to meet the criteria for major depressive disorder but could not be imminently suicidal or have medical con-traindications for the use of imipramine (in case they were assigned to the drug condition). All were outpa-tients, nonbipolar and nonpsychotic. Seventy percent of the sample were female. Of those who began treat-ment, 162, or 68%, completed at least fifteen weeks and twelve sessions.

Cognitive Perspectives

Perhaps the most actively studied psychological theories of depression are cogni-tive theories. We describe two in this subsection—hopelessness theory and Beck's cognitive theory of depression.

Hopelessness Theory of Depression

Hopelessness theory developed originally as a result of animal research. In this section we discuss the evolution of the theory. Actually, we will be describing three theories, the original learned helplessness theory; its subsequent, more cog-nitive, attributional version; and, finally, its transformation into the hopelessness theory (see Figure 10.1 for a summary of the three).

learned helplessness theory   An in-dividual's passivity and sense of be-ing unable to act and to control his or her life, acquired through the ineffec-tiveness of the individual's efforts to control unpleasant and traumatic ex-periences; according to Seligman's original theory, this brings on de-pression.

Learned Helplessness.   The basic premise of the **learned helplessness theory** is that an individual's passivity and sense of being unable to act and control his or

Types of Assessments

Many assessments were made at pre- and posttreatment, as well as three times during treatment and again at six-, twelve-, and eighteen-month follow-ups. Assessment instruments included those that tapped the perspectives of the patient, the therapist, an independent clinical evaluator blind to treatment condition, and, whenever possible, a significant other from the patient's life, for example, a spouse. In addition to measuring depressive symptoms, assessments covered overall life functioning and functioning related to particular treatment approaches (e.g., the Dysfunctional Attitudes Scale of Weissman and Beck [1978], to assess cognitive change).

Results

Results may be summarized as follows (Elkin et al., 1989; Gibbons et al., 1993; Imber et al., 1990; Shea, Elkin, et al., 1992; Watkins et al., 1993)

▷ There were no significant differences in reduction of depression or improvement in overall functioning between cognitive therapy (CT) and interpersonal therapy (IPT) or between either of them and imipramine plus clinical management. In general, then, the three active treatments achieved significant *and equivalent* degrees of success. The placebo plus clinical management subjects also showed significant improvement. Imipramine was faster than the other treatments in reducing depressive symptoms. By the end of sixteen weeks, however, the two psychotherapies had caught up with the drug.

▷ On some measures the less severely depressed placebo subjects were doing as well at termination as were the less depressed people in the three active treatment conditions.

▷ Severely depressed patients did not fare as well in the placebo condition as did those in the three active treatments.

▷ There was little evidence that particular treatments were specifically effective in changing the aspects of depression that they emphasized the most. For instance, IPT patients did not show any greater improvement in social functioning than did imipramine or CT patients.

▷ Eighteen months after the end of treatment, the different treatment conditions did *not* differ significantly. Of those patients across the four conditions who had markedly improved immediately at the end of treatment, only between 20% and 30% remained nondepressed.

Much remains to be learned about effecting even short-term improvement in depressed patients. Even less is known about how to maintain this improvement over the long haul. One of the lasting effects of the TD-CRP will likely be to increase the methodological standards of psychotherapy outcome research, making it easier to achieve conclusive answers concerning the effects of treatment (see Chapter 16).

her own life is acquired through unpleasant experiences and traumas that the individual tried unsuccessfully to control. This perceived inability to effect control brings on depression. Initially, this theory was used to explain the behavior of dogs who received inescapable electric shocks. Soon after receiving the first shocks, the dogs stopped running around in a distressed manner. They seemed to give up and to accept passively the painful stimulation. In a subsequent part of the experiment the shocks could be avoided, but the dogs did not learn to do so as efficiently and effectively as did the control animals. Most of them lay down in a corner and whined. The researcher, Martin Seligman (1974), proposed that animals can acquire a sense of helplessness when confronted with uncontrollable aversive stimulation. This helplessness later tends to affect negatively their performance in stressful situations that *can* be controlled.

On the basis of this and other work on the effects of uncontrollable stress, Seligman concluded that learned helplessness in animals could provide a model for at least certain forms of human depression.

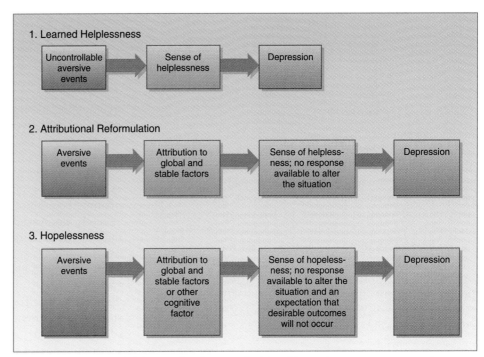

Figure 10.1   *The three helplessness/hopelessness theories of depression.*

Experiments with human beings have yielded results similar to those of experiments with animals. People who are subjected to inescapable noise or inescapable shock or who are confronted with unsolvable problems fail later to escape noise and shock and to solve simple problems (e.g., Hiroto & Seligman, 1975). Moreover, the performance of tasks by depressed subjects is similar to that of nondepressed subjects earlier subjected to these same helplessness-inducing experiences (Miller, Seligman, & Kurlander, 1975).

Attribution and Learned Helplessness.   By 1978, several limitations of the theory had become apparent. Some studies with humans, for example, had indicated that helplessness inductions actually led to subsequent facilitation of performance (e.g., see Wortman & Brehm, 1975). In addition, many depressed people hold themselves responsible for their failures. If they regard themselves as helpless, how can they blame themselves?

A revised version of the learned helplessness model was proposed by Lyn Abramson, Martin Seligman, and John Teasdale in 1978. The essence of the revised theory lies in the concept of **attribution**—the explanation a person has for his or her experiences (Weiner et al., 1971)—and in this way it blends cognitive and behavioral elements. Given a situation in which the individual has experienced failure, for example, he or she tries to attribute the failure to some cause. In Table 10.1 the Abramson, Seligman, and Teasdale formulation is applied to indicate the ways in which a college student might attribute failure on the mathematics portion of the Graduate Record Examination (GRE). Three questions are asked in this theory. Are the reasons for failure believed to be internal (personal) or external (environmentally caused)? Is the cause believed to be stable or unstable? How global or specific is the cause of failure perceived to be?

The attributional revision of the helplessness theory postulates that the way in which a person explains failure, the attribution he or she makes about it, will determine its subsequent effects. The more global the attribution, the more widespread the effects of failure. Attributions to stable factors make the effects long-term. Attributing the failure to internal characteristics is more likely to

attribution The explanation a person has for his or her experience.

Table 10.1 ▶ **Attributions and Depression: Why I Failed My GRE Math Exam**

Degree	Internal (Personal)		External (Environmental)	
	Stable	Unstable	Stable	Unstable
Global	I lack intelligence.	I am exhausted.	These tests are all unfair.	It's an unlucky day, Friday the thirteenth.
Specific	I lack mathematical ability.	I am fed up with math.	The math tests are unfair.	My math test was numbered "13."

Source: Adapted from Abramson, Seligman, and Teasdale (1978).

diminish self-esteem, particularly if the personal fault is also global and persistent.

People become depressed, the theory suggests, when they attribute negative life events to stable and global causes. Whether self-esteem collapses, too, depends on whether they blame the bad outcome on their own inadequacies. The depression-prone individual is also thought to show a "depressive attributional style," a tendency to attribute bad outcomes to personal, global, stable faults of character. When persons with this style (a vulnerability) have adverse experiences (stressors), they become depressed, and their self-esteem is shattered (Peterson & Seligman, 1984; see Focus Box 10.2).

Some research gives direct support to the reformulated theory. Many studies show that, on average, depressed people do more often attribute failure to personal, global, and persistent inadequacies than do nondepressed people (Sweeney, Anderson, & Bailey, 1986). There is also some evidence to support the view that the coexistence of a depressive attributional style and stressful events predicts subsequent depressive symptoms (Dixon & Ahrens, 1992; Metalsky, Halberstadt, & Abramson, 1987).

Other research, however, indicates that making attributions is not a universal process (Downey, Silver, & Wortman, 1990; Hanusa & Schulz, 1977). This second version of learned helplessness theory focused too narrowly on attributions as the sole cognitive vulnerability to depression.

Hopelessness Theory. The latest version of the theory (Abramson, Metalsky, & Alloy, 1989) has broadened its focus to include other vulnerabilities besides attributional style. A subtype of depression called **hopelessness depression** is regarded as caused by an expectation that desirable outcomes will not occur or that undesirable ones will occur and that the person can do nothing to change this situation. (The latter part of the definition of hopelessness, of course, refers to helplessness, the central concept of earlier versions of the theory.) As in the attributional reformulation, negative life events (stressors) are seen as interacting with vulnerabilities to yield hopelessness. One vulnerability is the attributional style pattern already described, attributing negative events to stable and global factors. However, this revised theory considers the possibility that there are other vulnerabilities—a tendency to infer that negative life events will have severe negative consequences and a tendency to draw negative inferences about the self. Returning to the example of doing poorly on the math GRE (Table 10.1), someone who draws negative inferences about the self might conclude, "this kind of thing only happens to losers," while someone who infers negative consequences might think "this will permanently ruin my chances for a professional career." These conclusions could fuel hopelessness and depression, even if the person thinks the exam failure itself resulted from an unfortunate fluke (I was sick and could not study enough) rather than a stable, global cause.

As discussed earlier, anxiety disorders occur frequently with depression. Accounting for this pattern poses a major challenge for many theories, for they

hopelessness depression A subtype of depression believed to be caused by the expectation that desirable outcomes will not occur or that undesirable ones will occur and that nothing one can do will change this state of affairs. These expectations in turn are caused by the interaction of stressful events with any of several cognitive vulnerabilities, according to the theory of Abramson, Metalsky, and Alloy.

Depression in Women: A Consequence of Learned Helplessness and Style of Coping?

Depression occurs more often in women than in men. Research involving both patients in treatment and surveys of community residents consistently yields a 2:1 female-to-male ratio (Nolen-Hoeksema, 1987). Understanding the cause of this sex difference may yield some further clues to the causes of depression. Radloff (1975) speculates that the higher levels of depression among women are best explained as a consequence of learned helplessness.

Some feminist scholars would agree (e.g., Chesler, 1972), for they consider the greater incidence of some mental problems among women a reflection of their lack of personal and political power. Feminists take the position that more women than men become depressed because their social roles do not encourage them to feel competent. What women do seems not to count compared with the greater power that men have in society. In fact, it may be that little girls are *trained* to be helpless (Broverman, Broverman, & Clarkson, 1970). Consistent with these speculations are data showing that girls' behavior is less likely than that of boys to elicit consequences both from parents (Maccoby & Jacklin, 1974) and from teachers (Dweck, Davidson, Nelson, & Enna 1978). Furthermore, girls are more likely to attribute success to luck or to the favors of others (unstable factors) and failures to global and stable factors (Dweck, 1975).

Another element may also be at work. In her research on factors influencing the duration of depressive episodes, Nolen-Hoeksema (1987, 1990) proposed an equally plausible account of these sex differences, referring to "response style," the different ways in which men and women tend to cope with negative emotions. When responding to sadness, men typically engage in activities that distract them from their mood, for example, exercise or watching television. Women, on the other hand, tend to ruminate about their situation and blame themselves for being sad (e.g., Kleinke, Staneski, & Mason, 1982). This ruminative reaction is then seen as amplifying the state of depression and negative mood, perhaps by interfering with attempts to solve problems.

Many studies support this hypothesis, including controlled laboratory experiments and naturalistic studies of people's moods in the wake of severe stressors, such as bereavement or major earthquakes (for a review, see Nolen-Hoeksema, 1991). People who report a tendency to ruminate over problems are less likely to engage in efforts at problem solving (Carver, Scheier, & Weintraub, 1989; Nolen-Hoeksema & Morrow, 1991b), and this tendency to ruminate over rather than to solve problems is associated with longer periods of depression (Morrow & Nolen-Hoeksema, 1990; Nolen-Hoeksema & Morrow, 1991a). Women tend to ruminate more than men when depressed and to have longer periods of depressed mood (Nolen-Hoeksema, Parker, & Larson, 1994). This response style view of depression is concerned with the ways in which people cope with a depressed mood once it is evident, rather than with the reasons that people develop negative moods in the first place.

How does it come about that women have more of a ruminative response style to stress and sadness than

concern only a single diagnosis. One advantage of the hopelessness theory is that it can deal directly with comorbidity of depression and anxiety disorders. There are several important features of this comorbidity (Alloy, Kelly, Mineka, & Clements, 1990). First, cases of anxiety without depression are relatively common, but pure depression is rare. Second, longitudinal studies reveal that anxiety diagnoses typically precede depression (e.g., Rohde, Lewinsohn, & Seeley, 1991). On the basis of a good deal of prior evidence (e.g., Mandler, 1972), Alloy and her colleagues proposed that an expectation of helplessness creates anxiety. When the expectation of helplessness becomes certain, a syndrome with elements of both depression and anxiety ensues. Finally, if the perceived probability of the occurrence of negative events becomes certain, hopelessness develops.

Although the hopelessness theory is promising, research is just beginning to address its specific predictions. In particular, it is not yet clear how to distinguish

According to Susan Nolen-Hoeksema's theory and research, men are more likely to cope with negative moods by distracting themselves, for instance by watching TV. Conversely, women are more prone to ruminating about their bad feelings and what caused them, which can have the unintended effect of prolonging or exacerbating negative moods.

men? Nolen-Hoeksema seeks answers in sex-role learning that begins during childhood. It is part of the masculine stereotype to be active and coping rather than to reflect on one's feelings and the reasons for them. Men learn to be less emotionally tuned in than women. By the same token, this sex-linked learning may teach women that they are by nature more emotional and that therefore depressive episodes are natural and unavoidable.

The implications for treatment are clear according to this view. Depressed women—and men—should be encouraged to increase their coping and pleasure-producing activity rather than to dwell on their moods and search for causes of depression. Problem-solving skills should also be nurtured. In a preventive vein, Nolen-Hoeksema suggests that parents and other caretakers encourage girls to adopt active behavior in response to negative moods.

hopelessness depressions from depression in general and thereby provide precise tests of the theory's predictions (Spangler, Simons, Monroe, & Thase, 1993). Much of the initial supporting research (e.g., Metalsky, Joiner, Hardin, & Abramson, 1993) concerns depressive mood reactions among college students to minor stressors, such as a poor midterm exam grade. Although there may be continuity between the factors responsible for significant sadness when setbacks occur and those responsible for clinical depression (Vredenburg, Flett, & Krames, 1993), it is not safe to make this assumption (Coyne, 1994).

Beck's Cognitive Theory of Depression

A separate cognitive theory of depression, developed by Aaron Beck (1967, 1987), was directly based on observation of clinically depressed patients and what they said about their lives in therapy sessions. Beck's central thesis was that depressed individuals feel as they do because their thinking is biased toward negative inter-

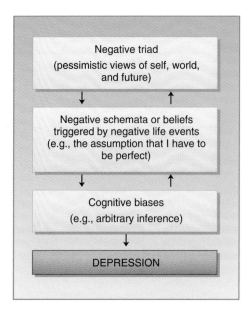

Figure 10.2   *Beck's theory of depression, showing the interrelationships among different kinds of cognitions.*

pretations. Figure 10.2 illustrates the interactions among three levels of cognitive activity believed by Beck to underlie depression.

According to Beck, in childhood and adolescence, depressed individuals acquired dysfunctional beliefs (see Chapter 3) through the loss of a parent, an unrelenting succession of tragedies, the social rejection of peers, the criticisms of teachers, or the depressive attitude of a parent. The negative beliefs acquired by depressed persons are activated whenever they encounter new situations that resemble in some way, perhaps only remotely, the conditions in which the beliefs were learned. Moreover, the negative beliefs of depressives fuel, and are fueled by, certain cognitive biases which lead these sufferers to misperceive reality. Thus a tendency to believe that they are inept can make depressives expect to fail most of the time.

negative triad In Beck's theory of depression, a person's negative views of the self, the world, and the future.

The negative beliefs, together with cognitive biases or distortions, maintain what Beck called the **negative triad**: negative views of the self, the world, and the future. The "world" refers here to the individual's personal environment and the demands it presents, not the political world, international trade, or the like. Similarly, the negative view of the future concerns the depressed person's own future, not necessarily the future of the economy, the environment, or other global concerns. The following list illustrates some of the cognitive biases that are believed to maintain these negative views among depressed people.

1. **Arbitrary Inference.** A conclusion drawn in the absence of sufficient evidence or of any evidence at all. For example, a man concludes that he is worthless because it is raining the day that he is hosting an outdoor party.
2. **Selective Abstraction.** A conclusion drawn on the basis of but one of many elements in a situation. A worker feels worthless when a product fails to function, even though she is only one of many people who contributed to its production.
3. **Overgeneralization.** A sweeping conclusion drawn on the basis of a single, perhaps trivial, event. A student regards his poor performance in a single class on one particular day as final proof of his worthlessness and stupidity.

These biases could, of course, be used within a schema of positive self-evaluation by people who bias what they see so as to *enhance* their view of self. For example, a person can selectively abstract from the success of a project undertaken with many others the conclusion that he or she has great ability and was primarily responsible for the good outcome. The depressed person, however, by these

According to Beck's theory, someone who is likely to develop depression will magnify or overgeneralize a negative experience, such as scoring poorly on the SAT.

errors in thinking, confirms the self-deprecatory schema and feels unworthy and responsible for calamities.

In Beck's theory, then, our emotional reactions are considered primarily a function of the way we think about our world. Beck sees depressives as the victims of their own illogical, negative self-judgments.

Evaluation of Beck's Theory. At least two points need to be demonstrated when evaluating Beck's theory. First, depressed patients, in contrast with nondepressed individuals, must actually judge themselves in the biased ways enumerated by Beck. This point was initially confirmed by Beck's clinical observations, which suggested that depressed patients do, in fact, manifest at least some of these biases (Beck, 1967).

Further support for this general proposition is provided by several sources. Questionnaires can assess depressives' cognitive biases in their reactions to stories about college students in problematic situations (Krantz & Hammen, 1979) or allow subjects to report negative thoughts reflecting the cognitive triad (Hollon & Kendall, 1980). In general, depressives' responses to these questionnaires agree with expectations based on Beck's theory (e.g., Dobson & Shaw, 1986). Furthermore, a study employing the Articulated Thoughts During Simulated Situations procedure (see Chapter 5) found that the thinking of depressive patients was biased, as Beck postulated (White, Davison, Haaga, & White, 1992).

A challenge for researchers is to demonstrate that the cognitive bias of depressives does not result from an emotional disturbance, that it does in fact *cause* the depressed mood. Many studies in experimental psychology have in a general way shown that a person's mood can be influenced by how he or she construes events. But manipulating emotion has also been shown to change thinking (e.g., Isen, Shaiken, Clark, & Karp, 1978). No study that we know of directly demonstrates that the various emotional and physical aspects of depression are truly a function of the negative schemata and biases that Beck believes operate in this disorder. Beck and others have found that depression and certain kinds of thinking are *correlated*, but a specific causal relationship cannot be determined from such data. Depression could cause negative thoughts, or negative thoughts could cause depression; indeed, both could be true.

Cognitive Therapy of Depression

In keeping with their cognitive theory of depression, Aaron Beck and his associates devised a cognitive therapy (CT) aimed at altering maladaptive thought patterns. The therapist tries to persuade the depressed person to change his or her opinions of events and of the self. When a client states that he or she is worthless because "nothing goes right. Everything I try to do ends in a disaster," the therapist offers examples contrary to this overgeneralization, such as abilities and accomplishments that the client is either overlooking or discounting. The therapist also instructs the patient to monitor private monologues with himself or herself and to identify all patterns of thought that contribute to depression. The therapist then teaches the patient to think through negative prevailing beliefs to understand how they prevent making more realistic and positive assumptions and interpreting adversity more accurately.

CT also includes behavioral techniques. Especially when patients are severely depressed, they are encouraged to *do* things, such as get out of bed in the morning or go for a walk, even if they are pessimistic about the value of such tasks. One of the purposes of behavioral assignments in CT is to help patients get in the habit of looking at their expectations for what they can and cannot do, or what will make them feel better, as hypotheses to be tested, not facts to be assumed. Activity assignments are thus a win–win situation. If a change in overt behavior helps the patient feel better or think more favorably about himself or herself, fine. If not, then the patient can try other behavioral tasks and use the failure experience to practice more logical ways of drawing inferences about setbacks (e.g., failing to read the whole newspaper does not necessarily mean I am stupid, but may mean that being depressed is temporarily interfering with my concentration skills, so I need to try a smaller task tomorrow).

Over the past two decades considerable research has been conducted on Beck's therapy (Hollon & Beck, 1994). A quantitative review of outcome studies of CT for depression concluded that it achieves greater short-term improvement than no treatment, common antidepressant medications, non-cognitive-behavioral treatments, and a heterogeneous group of other psychotherapies (Dobson, 1989). Particularly encouraging are findings indicating that patients treated with CT remained improved longer than did patients treated with antidepressant medication that was then discontinued (maintaining medication indefinitely also seems to improve long-term outcomes) (Evans et al., 1992).

One major test of CT was the widely publicized comparative outcome study sponsored by the National Institute of Mental Health (Elkin et al., 1985), a study that supported its utility but, unlike earlier research, did not find CT superior to a drug therapy and interpersonal psychotherapy (see Focus Box 10.1).

To Recap

Hopelessness theory contends that a subtype of depression (hopelessness depression) is caused by a feeling of hopelessness, which arises when negative events happen to someone with one or more of the following tendencies: (a) to attribute negative events to stable, global causes; (b) to infer that negative events will have severe consequences; and (c) to draw negative inferences about the self from the occurrence of negative events.

Beck's cognitive theory explains depression in terms of tacit dysfunctional beliefs or schemata (e.g., that one is unworthy and defective). When triggered by relevant stressful events (e.g., failure), these schemata fuel biased perceptions, such as overgeneralizing the implications of a setback, and thus sustain the person's negative outlook on self, the future, and the environment, which in turn maintains the depressed mood.

Cognitive therapy is based on Beck's theory of depression and teaches patients how to question and evaluate, rather than automatically accept, their depressing

negative thoughts. It appears to be as effective as standard antidepressant medications in the short term, possibly more so when it comes to long-term maintenance of improvement.

Biological Perspectives

Biological processes are known to have large effects on moods, so it is not surprising that researchers have looked for biological causes for depression and mania. We review here some of the findings in the areas of genetics, neurochemistry, and the neuroendocrine system.

Genetic Influences on Mood Disorders

As we will see, a family history of bipolar disorder was one of the facts supporting George Lawler's diagnosis. Several lines of evidence substantiate the view that vulnerability to bipolar disorder is genetically transmitted. The frequency of mood disorders in first-degree relatives of patients with bipolar disorder ranges from about 10% to 20% (e.g., Perris, 1969), much higher than the rate of about 1% among the general population. Twin studies also suggest that vulnerability to bipolar disorder is heritable. Overall, concordance rates for bipolar disorder in identical twins were 72% and in fraternal twins only 14% (Allen, 1976).

Genetic factors, though important, are not as decisive in major depressive disorder as they are in bipolar disorder. Relatives of people with major depressive disorder are at increased risk, but less so than are relatives of bipolar patients (Andreasen et al., 1987). Studies of major depressive disorder in twins usually report monozygotic concordances of about 40% and dizygotic concordances of about 11% (Allen, 1976).

Family and twin studies together thus suggest that both bipolar disorder and major depressive disorder have heritable components. This conclusion is further supported by several small-scale studies using the adoption method. Mood disorders occur more frequently in the biological parents than in the adoptive parents of bipolar adoptees (Mendlewicz & Rainer, 1977). Mood disorders are similarly more common in adopted children whose biological parents had a mood disorder (Cadoret, 1978). Finally, one study found that the biological relatives of adopted probands were eight times more likely than controls to have a mood disorder (Wender et al., 1986).

A recent development in genetic research on mood disorders is the use of **linkage analysis**. This technique involves studying the occurrence of mood disorders over several generations in a family and simultaneously assessing some other characteristic—a genetic marker—for which the genetics are fully understood (e.g., red-green color blindness is known to result from mutations on the X chromosome). When the genes for mood disorder and the genetic marker are linked, that is, when they are sufficiently close together on a chromosome, the family pedigree tends to show that the two traits being examined are inherited together. In a linkage study of the Old Order Amish, Egeland and her colleagues (1987) found evidence favoring the hypothesis that bipolar disorder results from a dominant gene on the eleventh chromosome. Unfortunately, the Egeland study and other apparently successful linkage studies have failed to be replicated (e.g., Berrittini et al, 1990). These inconsistencies may result because mood disorders are produced by different genes in different people.

linkage analysis A technique in genetic research whereby occurrence of a disorder in a family is evaluated alongside a known genetic marker.

Neurochemistry and Mood Disorders

Numerous attempts have been made to link mood disorders to various neurotransmitters. We will describe one line of research involving the neurotransmitter norepinephrine and another involving serotonin. The theory involving norepinephrine is that a low level of norepinephrine leads to depression and a high level to mania. The serotonin theory suggests that a low level of serotonin, which frequently serves to modulate neural activity in other neurochemical systems, allows wild fluctuations in the activity of other neurotransmitters, thereby producing both mania and depression.

Low Norepinephrine in Depression and High Norepinephrine in Mania. The view that norepinephrine levels can account for mania and depression is supported by several observations.

1. **Drugs that increase brain levels of norepinephrine lower depression.** The actions of drugs provided the initial clue on which the norepinephrine theory is based. In the 1950s two groups of drugs, tricyclics and monoamine oxidase inhibitors (MAOIs), were found effective in relieving depression. Both tricyclics and MAOIs increase the levels of norepinephrine in the brains of animals.

2. **A drug that reduces norepinephrine sometimes results in depression as a side effect.** Another piece of evidence favoring the norepinephrine theory was provided by reserpine, a drug sometimes used in the treatment of hypertension. Reserpine was isolated in the 1950s by a research team working in Switzerland. It is an alkaloid of the root of *Rauwolfia serpentina*, a shrub that grows in India. Hindu physicians have for centuries administered powdered rauwolfia as a treatment for mental illness. Reserpine and chlorpromazine were given to schizophrenics to calm their agitation. Reserpine did indeed relax them but was soon contraindicated, since depression was a serious side effect in about 15% of the patients taking it (e.g., Lemieux, Davignon, & Genest, 1956). Reserpine was discovered to reduce levels of norepinephrine by impairing the process by which it is stored within the synaptic vesicles, allowing the norepinephrine to become degraded by monoamine oxidase.

3. **Depressed bipolar patients have generally been shown to have low levels of urinary MHPG, norepinephrine's principal metabolite.** The amount of MHPG in the urine of patients with major depressive disorder, however, does not differ from that of controls (e.g., Muscettola, Potter, Pickar, & Goodwin, 1984), so evidence is mixed. MHPG levels are higher in bipolar manics than in depressed bipolar patients or normal people, consistent with the theory (Goodwin & Jamison, 1990).

4. **Urinary levels of norepinephrine decrease as bipolar patients become depressed and increase during mania.** These observations (Bunney, Goodwin, & Murphy, 1972; Bunney, Murphy, Goodwin & Borge, 1970) are an important extension of points 1 and 2 concerning drug effects because they showed more directly a link between norepinephrine and mood disorders. Inferring such a connection from drug effects alone would be hazardous, because drugs generally have multiple effects. Therefore, it is potentially misleading to attribute an effect on depression or mania to the specific drug effect (such as on level of norepinephrine) predicted by a theory.

5. **Deliberately increasing norepinephrine levels can lead to a manic episode.** Stimulating a norepinephrine increase can precipitate a manic episode in a bipolar patient (Silberman, Reus, Jimerson, Lynott, & Post, 1981). This effect means that mania is preceded by a rise in norepinephrine levels rather than causing them. This finding is an important supplement to points 3 and 4 (tracking urinary levels of norepinephrine or its metabolites). The urinary levels alone are consistent with the theory but do not prove it, because it is also possible that the clinical syndrome causes the change in norepinephrine level. For example, people in manic episodes have increased activity levels, which can lead to an increase in norepinephrine activity.

Low Serotonin in Mood Disorders. Very similar types of evidence have accumulated in support of the serotonin theory. First, tricyclic drugs and MAOIs also increase brain levels of serotonin, so their effectiveness in alleviating depression is consistent with the possibility that low serotonin is responsible for depression. Second, reserpine reduces serotonin in the same manner in which it reduces norepinephrine. Third, fluoxetine (Prozac) sometimes lessens depression, and it blocks reuptake of serotonin. Fluoxetine is much more selective than tricyclics or MAOIs: it affects serotonin but does not have an effect on norepinephrine. Therefore, its effectiveness is particularly supportive of the serotonin hypothesis.

Third, metabolite data on major depressive disorder support the theory. Studies of serotonin examine 5-hydroxyindoleacetic acid (5-HIAA), a major metabolite of serotonin that is present in cerebrospinal fluid. A fairly consistent body of data indicates that 5-HIAA levels are low in the cerebrospinal fluid of depressives (McNeal & Cimbolic, 1986), indicating low serotonin levels.

Finally, manipulating serotonin levels has the expected effects on depression. For example, ingestion of *l*-tryptophan, an amino acid from which serotonin is created, relieves depression, especially when used in combination with other drugs (Coppen, Prange, Whybrow, & Noguera, 1972; Mendels, Stinnett, Burns & Frazer, 1975). Also, when tryptophan in recovered depressives was reduced with a special diet, 67% experienced a return of their symptoms (Delgado et al., 1990). When their normal diet was resumed, a gradual remission followed.

Evaluation of Neurochemical Theories. There is considerable evidence to support a role for neurotransmitters in mood disorders. However, the theories are probably incomplete. Ironically, just as the clinical effectiveness of antidepressant medication formed the initial support for norepinephrine and serotonin theories of mood disorders, so, too, drug effects have been crucial in highlighting the limitations of the theories.

In brief, the explanation of why antidepressant medications work is not as straightforward as it seemed at first. The therapeutic effects of tricyclics and monoamine oxidase inhibitors do not depend solely on an increase in levels of neurotransmitters. The earlier findings were correct: tricyclics and MAOIs do indeed increase levels of norepinephrine and serotonin *when they are first taken*. But after several days the levels of neurotransmitters return to what were earlier.

This information is crucial because it does not fit with data on how much time must pass before antidepressants become effective. Both tricyclics and MAOIs take from seven to fourteen days to relieve depression! By that time, the neurotransmitter level has already returned to its previous level. It would seem, then, that a simple increase in norepinephrine or serotonin is not a sufficient explanation for why the drugs alleviate depression (Heninger, Charney, & Menkes, 1983).

Another key discovery that has prompted a move away from the original theories of a simple increase in serotonin and norepinephrine levels comes from studies of new antidepressants. Mianserin, for example, is an effective antidepressant (Cole, 1988), but does not simply increase the amount of norepinephrine or serotonin. This and similar findings are leading researchers to examine whether tricyclics and MAOIs act against depression by altering postsynaptic receptors. Results are contradictory and unclear, and many hypotheses remain under investigation (Delgado, Price, Heninger, & Charney, 1992).

The Neuroendocrine System

Research also suggests a role in depression for the neuroendocrine system, the brain's control over endocrine glands. The limbic area of the brain is closely linked to emotion and also has effects on the hypothalamus. The hypothalamus, in turn, controls various endocrine glands and thus the levels of hormones they secrete. Hormones secreted by the hypothalamus also affect the pituitary gland and the hormones it produces. Because of its relevance to the vegetative symptoms of depression, such as disturbances in appetite and sleep, the hypothalamic–pituitary–adrenal cortical axis is thought to be overactive in depression.

Various findings support this proposition. Levels of cortisol (an adrenocortical hormone) are high in depressives. This discovery even led to the development of a biological test for depression—the dexamethasone suppression test (DST). Dexamethasone suppresses cortisol secretion. When given dexamethasone during an overnight test, some depressives did not experience cortisol suppression (e.g., Poland, Rubin, Lesser, Lane, & Hart, 1987). The interpretation is that the failure of dexamethasone to suppress cortisol reflects overactivity in the hypothalamic–pituitary–adrenal cortical axis of depressive subjects. Another finding linking high levels of cortisol to depression is that patients with Cushing syndrome show an increased rate of depression. Abnormal growths on the adrenal cortex lead to oversecretion of cortisol in these patients.

Oversecretion of cortisol may also be linked to the neurotransmitter theories of mood disorders discussed in the prior subsection. High levels of cortisol may lower the density of serotonin receptors (Roy, Everett, Pickar, & Paul, 1987) and impair the function of noradrenergic receptors (Price, Charney, Rubin, & Heninger, 1986).

Finally, the hypothalamic-pituitary-thyroid axis is of possible relevance to bipolar disorder. Disorders of thyroid function are often seen in bipolar patients, and thyroid hormones can induce mania in these patients (Goodwin & Jamison, 1990).

Table 10.2 ▶ Drugs for Treating Mood Disorders

Category	Generic Name	Trade Name	Side Effects
Tricyclic antidepressants	Imipramine Amitriptyline	Tofranil Elavil	Heart attack, stroke, hypotension, blurred vision, anxiety, fatigue, dry mouth, constipation, gastric disorders, erectile failure, weight gain
MAO inhibitors	Tranylcyronize	Parnate	Possibly fatal hypertension, dry mouth, dizziness, nausea, headaches
Second-generation antidepressants	Fluoxetine	Prozac	Nervousness, fatigue, gastrointestinal complaints, dizziness, headaches, insomnia
	Buproprion	Wellbutin	Agitation, dry mouth, insomnia, headaches, constipation, tremors, seizures, weight loss
Lithium	Lithium	Lithium	Tremors, gastric distress, lack of coordination, dizziness, cardiac arrhythmia, blurred vision, fatigue

Biological Therapies

There are a variety of biological therapies for depression and mania. Medications are the most commonly used treatments for mood disorders. They do not work for all people, however, and side effects are sometimes serious (see Table 10.2). Determination of proper dosages can also be tricky.

Antidepressant Medication. As we have seen, antidepressant medications played a crucial role historically in research on the neurochemistry of mood disorders. The two major categories of antidepressant drugs are the tricyclics, such as imipramine (Tofranil) and amitriptyline (Elavil), and the monoamine oxidase inhibitors (MAOIs), such as Parnate. Since the MAOI's have by far the more serious side effects, for example, possibly fatal hypertension, the tricyclics are more extensively used. These medications have been generally accepted as effective on the basis of the results of many double-blind studies (Davidson, Giller, Zisook, & Overall, 1988.)

There is some controversy about the interpretation of the study results, however. Most double-blind, placebo-controlled studies use chemically inert substances as the placebo, with the idea that effects of simply expecting that one will get better (or, from an interviewer's perspective, that the patient will get better) are thereby estimated, and any greater effect of the active drug (in this case, tricyclic antidepressant) indicates a specific biological effect. However, a major complication to this logic is that the vast majority of studies on the issue indicate that double-blind studies of psychotropic drugs are not really double-blind. Both investigators and patients are likely to know more often than would be expected by chance whether a patient is receiving the drug or a placebo (Fisher & Greenberg, 1993). This situation may be a reflection of the treatment effect (i.e., patients who are getting better are, correctly on average, viewed as getting the drug), but it may also be a reflection of side effects (e.g., patients who develop dry mouth are judged to be on the drug). Attempts to modify the double-blind design in such a way as to make the results less subject to these complications find tricyclic antidepressants less effective than previously believed (Greenberg, Bornstein, Greenberg, & Fisher, 1992).

MAOIs and tricyclics are not the only options. In recent years several new antidepressants have been introduced. Two that appear to offer therapeutic advantages relative to previous medications are buproprion (Wellbutin) and fluoxetine (Prozac). Prozac has achieved considerable notoriety. Hailed as a breakthrough drug, it appeared on the cover of *Newsweek* (March 26, 1990). Then, numerous anecdotal reports of serious side effects (especially a severe preoccupation with suicide and other violent acts) propelled the drug further into the public eye and even onto the talk-show circuit.

> APPLYING CRITICAL THINKING SKILLS

PROZAC AND VIOLENCE

One study described six patients who appeared to develop a preoccupation with suicidal and violent thoughts when they started taking Prozac (Teicher, Glod, & Cole, 1990). Others taking Prozac also claimed that it caused them to act violently or self-destructively and filed suit against the manufacturer, Eli Lilly & Co.

▶ *What conclusion does the evidence seem to support?* Certainly some people taking Prozac have been violent or suicidal. One possibility is that the drug caused these thoughts and behaviors.

▶ *What other interpretations are plausible?* A major alternative interpretation is

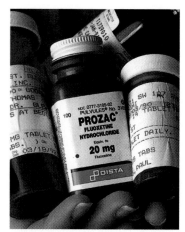

Prozac selectively blocks reuptake of serotonin and has shown effectiveness in reducing depression. It has also generated controversy based on case reports of negative side effects such as preoccupation with violent or suicidal thoughts.

that the disorder for which people were taking Prozac caused their preoccupation with thoughts of suicide or violence.

▶ **What other information would help choose among the alternative interpretations?** To choose between these interpretations it is necessary to compare the behavior of patients taking Prozac with that of comparable patients who are not taking it. If the rates of violence, self-destructiveness, and suicide or thinking about suicide are higher for Prozac patients, this would support the view that the drug influences these behaviors. If both groups show similar problems, it would support the view that the disorder, not Prozac, is the cause.

A review of controlled studies (involving a total of more than three thousand depressed patients) found that less than one-half of 1% of patients on Prozac became significantly worse during treatment (defined as at least a 50% increase in depressive symptoms) (Tollefson, Rampey, Enas, & Potvin, 1993). This rate of negative effects was equivalent to the rate for the placebo and for tricyclic antidepressants. Although the study is not conclusive, it tentatively suggests that Prozac is not especially likely to make depressed patients worse. Instead, it is unfortunately true that some depressed people get worse anyway, and if the treatment is ineffective for them, the worsening will occur while they are receiving treatment (whether Prozac or something else).

Although the various antidepressants hasten a patient's recovery from an episode of depression, relapse is still common after the drugs are withdrawn. Continuing to use an antidepressant after remission is of value in preventing recurrence—provided that maintenance doses are as high as the effective treatment doses (instead of lower, as is usually the case) and that the patient was involved during the drug therapy in a psychosocial treatment, such as interpersonal therapy (Frank et al., 1990).

Even if a chemical agent manages to alleviate a bout of depression only temporarily, that benefit in itself should not be underestimated, given the potential for suicide in depression and given the extreme anguish and suffering borne by the individual and usually by the family as well. Moreover, the judicious use of a drug may make hospitalization unnecessary.

Medication Treatment of Bipolar Disorder.   Wellbutin appears effective in the treatment of bipolar disorder, as it successfully reduces psychomotor retardation and is less likely than other antidepressants to induce a manic episode (Goodwin & Jamison, 1990). The possibility that use of the incorrect medication can cause mania is one of the reasons accurate diagnosis of major depressive disorder versus the depressed phase of a bipolar disorder is essential.

lithium carbonate   A drug useful in treating both *mania* and depression in *bipolar disorder.*

The major medication treatment for bipolar disorder, though, is lithium, an element, taken in a salt form, **lithium carbonate**. Because the effects of lithium occur gradually, therapy typically begins with both lithium and an antipsychotic, such as Haldol, which has an immediate calming effect. While a number of hypotheses are being pursued concerning how lithium works, none has good support at this time (e.g., Manji et al., 1991).

Because of possibly serious, even fatal, side effects, such as damage to kidney function, lithium has to be prescribed and used very carefully. Furthermore, although it has great value in the elimination of a manic episode, discontinuation of lithium actually increases a person's risk for recurrence (Suppes, Baldessarini, Faedda, & Tohen, 1991). Thus, it is recommended that lithium be used continually. Well-controlled studies have shown that lithium is effective in preventing the recurrence of manic episodes and probably effective in preventing recurrent depression in bipolar patients (e.g., Prien et al., 1984).

The major role for psychological interventions in bipolar disorder may lie in facilitating compliance to lithium treatment. A six-session individual treatment for bipolar-disorder patients based on cognitive therapy significantly lowered the rate of major noncompliance with lithium treatment and the likelihood of repeat hospitalization during a six-month follow-up period (Cochran, 1984). Challenging cognitions associated with noncompliance is important, because many bipolar patients perceive the illness (hypomanic periods in particular) as beneficial, making them more sensitive, more productive, more creative, and more outgoing (Jamison, Gerner, Hammen, & Padesky, 1980). Adhering to lithium treatment, therefore, may be analogous to quitting smoking—you have to give up something you like in the short run in order to achieve long-term benefits, not a trade-off people find easy to make.

Electroconvulsive Therapy. Perhaps the most dramatic, and controversial, treatment for depression is **electroconvulsive therapy (ECT)**. ECT was originated by two Italian physicians, Cerletti and Bini, in the early twentieth century. Cerletti had been interested in epilepsy and was seeking a means by which its seizures could be experimentally induced. The solution became apparent to him during a visit to a slaughterhouse, where he saw seizures and unconsciousness induced in animals by electric shocks administered to the head. He found that by applying electric shocks to the sides of the human head, he could produce full epileptic seizures. Shortly thereafter, in 1938 in Rome, he used the technique on a schizophrenic patient.

In the decades that followed, ECT was administered to both schizophrenic and psychotically depressed patients, usually in hospital settings. For the most part its use now is restricted to profoundly depressed individuals for whom other treatments have been ineffective. ECT entails the deliberate induction of a seizure and momentary unconsciousness by passing a current of between 70 and 130 volts through the patient's brain. Electrodes were formerly placed on each side of the forehead, which allowed the current to pass through both hemispheres (**bilateral ECT**). Today, **unilateral ECT**, in which the current passes through the non-dominant cerebral hemisphere only (e.g., Abrams, Swartz, & Vedak, 1991), is more commonly used. In the past the patient was usually awake until the current triggered the seizure, and the electric shock often created frightening contortions of the body, sometimes even causing bone fractures. Now the patient is given a short-acting anesthetic, then an injection of a strong muscle relaxant before the current is applied. The convulsive spasms of the body muscles are barely perceptible to onlookers, and the patient awakens a few minutes later, remembering nothing about the treatment.

Inducing a seizure remains a drastic procedure, however. Why should anyone in his or her right but depressed mind agree to undergo such radical therapy, or how could a parent or a spouse consent to such treatment if the patient is judged legally incapable of giving consent? The answer is simple. Although we do not know why, ECT may be the most effective treatment for certain forms of severe depression (Klerman, 1988). There are risks, though—confusion and sometimes prolonged memory loss. However, unilateral ECT to the nondominant hemisphere now erases fewer memories than did bilateral ECT, and no detectable changes in brain structure result (Coffey et al., 1991). Clinicians typically resort to ECT only after less drastic treatments have been tried and found wanting. In considering *any* treatment that has negative side effects, the person making the decision must be aware of the consequences of not providing any treatment at all. Given that suicide is a real possibility among depressed people, and given a moral stance that values the preservation of life, the use of ECT, at least after other treatments have failed, is regarded by many as defensible and responsible.

TO RECAP

Biological research indicates that vulnerability to the major mood disorders is in part genetically transmitted, especially for bipolar disorder. The main theories of the neurochemistry of mood disorders are that a low level of norepinephrine leads to depression and a high level to mania; and that a low level of serotonin allows

electroconvulsive therapy (ECT) A treatment that produces a convulsion by passing electric current through the brain. Though an unpleasant and occasionally dangerous procedure, it can be useful in alleviating profound depression.

bilateral ECT Electroconvulsive therapy in which electrodes are placed on each side of the forehead and an electrical current is passed through both hemispheres of the brain.

unilateral ECT Electroconvulsive therapy in which electrodes are placed on one side of the forehead so that current passes through only one brain hemisphere.

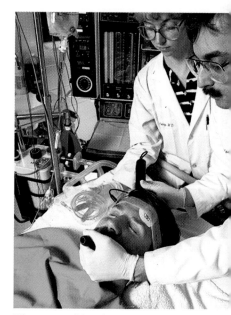

Electroconvulsive therapy (ECT) is an effective treatment for depression. Using unilateral shock, anesthetics, and muscle relaxants has reduced its undesirable side effects.

wild fluctuations in the activity of other neurotransmitters, thereby producing both mania and depression. These theories are supported by diverse lines of research, but are incomplete and unable to account for some aspects of drug therapy for mood disorders. The hypothalamic–pituitary–adrenal cortical axis appears to be overactive in depression, whereas disorders of thyroid function may play a role in bipolar disorder.

Biological interventions include medications, such as tricyclic antidepressants for major depressive disorder and lithium carbonate for bipolar disorder. These can be highly effective but require careful monitoring for side effects and indefinitely continued treatment; otherwise, relapse is likely after withdrawal of the medication. Electroconvulsive therapy, while safer now than in the past, is used as a last resort for severely depressed people who fail to respond to other treatments.

The Case of George Lawler Revisited

SOCIAL HISTORY

Psychological problems were evident on both sides of George's family. His father was an alcoholic, though abstinent for the past ten years. During George's childhood the alcohol abuse had led to erratic behavior on his father's part and frequent conflict between the parents. On his mother's side of the family, George's uncle Ralph had also experienced serious adjustment problems and had been hospitalized twice following periods of rather wild, maniclike behavior.

CONCEPTUALIZATION AND TREATMENT

When George was admitted to the hospital, he was racing in high gear despite the fact that he had not slept for several days. The psychiatrist prescribed a moderate dosage of haloperidol (Haldol), an antipsychotic drug. George was also started on a dose of 900 milligrams of lithium on the first day. The dosage was increased to 1800 milligrams per day over the next two weeks.

The hospital nursing staff took blood tests every third day to ensure that the blood lithium level did not exceed 1.4 milliequivalents per liter—the point at which toxic effects might be expected. After three weeks, the Haldol was discontinued, but George continued to receive maintenance doses of lithium. George and his wife, Cheryl, were given very specific instructions pertaining to the potential hazards of taking lithium. The importance of a proper diet, and particularly a normal level of salt intake, was stressed.

George was involved in various additional therapeutic activities as well. He and the other patients on the ward met daily for group psychotherapy. The patients could choose from several recreational and occupational activities according to their own interests. Visits by family members and close friends were encouraged during the evening hours. When George's behavior improved, he was taken off restricted status and allowed to leave the ward for short periods of time.

George was discharged from the hospital after twenty-seven days. His behavior had improved dramatically. The first few days in the hospital had been very difficult for everyone. He had been so excited that the entire ward routine had been disrupted. Mealtimes were utterly chaotic and, when the patients were supposed to go to sleep for the night, George shouted and ran around. After a few days, though, he became thoroughly exhausted and slept most of the next several days. Subsequently, he was more subdued. He gave up the grandiose notion about Olympic fame and seemed to be in better control of himself. But he had not returned to normal. He was still given to rambling speeches and continued to flirt with the female staff members. His mood was unstable, fluctuating between comical amusement and quick irritation. These residual symptoms dissipated gradually over the next two weeks. He now recognized the severity of his previous condition. In retrospect, the events that had struck him as exhilarating and amusing seemed like a nightmare. He said that his thoughts had been racing a mile a minute.

Following his discharge, George was kept on a maintenance dosage of lithium. He attended the hospital's outpatient clinic regularly for individual psychotherapy, and his blood levels of lithium were carefully monitored. George and Cheryl also began couples therapy sessions. Unfortunately, this aspect of treatment was unsuccessful. Cheryl had been seriously embarrassed by George's behavior during the manic episode, especially his announcement (via the newspaper) of affection for another woman. This incident seemed to create an insurmountable degree of tension and mistrust between George and Cheryl. They both made a serious effort to improve their relationship, but to no avail. Cheryl finally decided that the situation was hopeless and, six months after George was discharged from the hospital, she filed for divorce.

George was shaken by this development and also by the subsequent loss of his coaching position, but managed to avoid becoming seriously depressed. His friends from work were an important source of social support, particularly during the first weeks after Cheryl and the children moved to another apartment. He also met more frequently with his therapist during this period and continued to take lithium carbonate.

DISCUSSION

George had exhibited manic as well as depressive symptoms and clearly merited the diagnosis of bipolar disorder. His case was typical with respect to the course of the illness. He showed an early onset of symptoms and a relatively complete remission between episodes. On the other hand, though his symptoms remitted between episodes, his behavior was so disruptive during each manic episode that it had serious long-term consequences, notably loss of his job and his marriage.

That George's maternal uncle had also experienced manic episodes is consistent with the literature concerning genetic factors in bipolar disorders. A vulnerability-stress perspective may be more helpful than an exclusive focus on genetics in understanding the case, however. It suggests that bipolar patients inherit some unidentified form of predisposition to the disorder and that the expression of this predisposition depends on subsequent events. In George's case it would be reasonable to wonder whether the excitement and highly competitive atmosphere associated with college coaching might have triggered the onset of his manic symptoms or his depressive episodes. The weeks preceding his manic episode were busier than usual. His teams had been winning, and the athletic department's administration seemed to be putting considerable emphasis on the final meets of the season. Viewed from George's perspective, this amounted to enormous pressure.

George's relationship with his family illustrates the complex interactive nature of mood disorders. Although his marital problems may not have resulted solely from his bipolar disorder, the disorder certainly made an already difficult situation virtually impossible. Research shows that bipolar patients are much more likely to get divorced than are patients with major depressive disorder or people in the general population (Brodie & Leff, 1971). The emotional atmosphere within a family is also related to the patient's social functioning and the course of the disorder. In one study, patients who lived in a stressful family environment were much more likely to relapse than were others during the nine months after discharge (Miklowitz, Goldstein, Nuechterlein, Snyder, & Mintz, 1988). George's situation was probably typical of the problems experienced by manic patients. Cheryl was forced by his erratic behavior to act as a buffer between George and the community. When he acted strangely at work, his colleagues called her to see if she could explain his behavior. She often found herself making up excuses for him in order to avoid the unpleasant necessity of disclosing the personal details of his problems. Her efforts were then "rewarded" by his continued excesses. Cheryl gradually came to see herself as a victim. The incident with the undergraduate student was the last straw.

In terms of treatment, George's case is also typical in that he responded favorably to lithium during his hospitalization. Continuing on prescribed drugs is a serious problem with all forms of psychopharmacological treatment. Every effort is made to educate the patient in this regard. The cooperation of family members is often enlisted to assist in the regulation of daily doses. In spite of these measures, many patients fail to follow medication schedules designed to prevent relapse.

Suicide

Suicide must always be considered a danger when people are profoundly depressed. The risk of suicide is about equal in bipolar disorder and major depressive disorder (Lester, 1993). Sometimes the sole reason a depressed individual does *not* attempt suicide is that he or she cannot summon the energy to formulate and implement a suicide plan. In working with a seriously depressed individual, clinicians therefore are particularly vigilant as the patient emerges from the low point of depression because at this time they may still wish to kill themselves and may begin to have enough energy to do so.

A significant number of people who are not depressed, however, make suicidal attempts, sometimes completing suicide. Other disorders are also associated with suicide, including alcohol dependence (Kessel & Grossman, 1961), schizophrenia (Roy, 1982), and panic disorder (J. Johnson et al., 1990). Our focus in this section is on issues in suicide that transcend specific diagnoses. We discuss first some of the basic facts about suicide, including demographics, cross-national comparisons, and methods used. Next we review current theories of the causes of suicide, followed by methods of suicide prevention.

Prevalence and Demographics

In imagining a suicide, we usually think of a person deliberately performing a dramatic act obviously intended to end life almost immediately—the woman swallowing a lethal dose of barbiturates, the man with the gun next to his temple, and so on—perhaps with a suicide note left behind explaining her or his despair. Some suicides certainly fit such a pattern and are readily recognized as suicides. But other cases are more ambiguous, such as fatal single-car accidents when road conditions are not particularly bad; or people who act in self-destructive ways that can cause serious injury or death after a prolonged period of time, such as a diabetic who neglects insulin and a dietary regimen. Sometimes termed *subintentioned death*, these tragedies are viewed by many investigators as a form of suicide and complicate the task of understanding and compiling data on suicide (Shneidman, 1973). In light of these ambiguities, data on suicide must be considered tentative. The information provided here is based on the best available estimates (Fremouw, Perczel, & Ellis, 1990; National Center for Health Statistics, 1988).

Prevalence

There are more than 30,000 completed suicides per year in the United States, about 12.8 per 100,000 people. For every completed suicide in the United States, between eight and twenty people have made an attempt. About half of those who commit suicide have made at least one previous attempt, but two-thirds of attempters never make another attempt. Estimates of the number of people who have ever thought about committing suicide range from 40% to 80% of the population.

Demographics

Suicide rates vary with age, race, nation, and sex. The rate rises in old age. Between the ages of seventy-five and eighty-four, it reaches 25.2 per 100,000, twice as high as the overall rate for the population. Though far below the suicide rate of older adults, the rates of suicide for adolescents and children in the United States are increasing dramatically. Attempts are made by children as young as six.

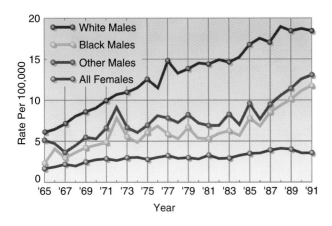

Figure 10.3 *Rates of suicide among white and black adolescents (15–19 years old), 1965–1991. Source: Shaffer, Gould, & Hicks, 1994.*

The rates for suicide among white youths are higher than those for African-American youths, although the suicide rate among young African-American men is rising more rapidly in recent years than among young white men in the United States (Shaffer, Gould, & Hick, 1994), as is depicted in Figure 10.3. The highest rates of suicide in the United States are for white men over age fifty. Hungary has the highest rate of suicide in the world. The Czech Republic, Finland, Sweden, Japan, and Austria also have high incidences. The countries with the lowest rates are Greece, Ireland, and Italy.

Men are three to four times more likely to kill themselves than are women. Conversely, about three times as many women as men attempt to kill themselves but do not die. Thus, male suicide attempters are considerably more likely to complete suicide than are female suicide attempters. This difference may relate to sex differences in the means of attempting suicide. Men usually choose to shoot or hang themselves; women are more likely to use sleeping pills. Taking overdoses of sleeping pills is not a safe behavior, but relative to shooting oneself it affords a somewhat better chance of survival.

Facts about the demographics of suicide are inherently interesting. They also set

Suicide involving violent death, such as jumping off a building, is more common among men than women.

constraints on our thinking about causes of suicide. For example, any theory that ascribed suicide to a characteristic more common among young people than among the elderly would have a hard time accounting for the high rate of completed suicide among those seventy-five years of age or older. By themselves, the demographics do not provide satisfactory explanations of suicide. They cannot tell us *why* white men over fifty or citizens of Hungary are at elevated risk, nor why some members of these groups kill themselves while most do not. The perspectives described in the following section attempt to provide the missing explanations.

Perspectives on the Causes of Suicide

As complicated as it is to be certain of how many people consider, attempt, or complete suicide, it is still more difficult to determine the causes of suicide. By the nature of the act, those who have completed suicide are not available to help us understand their perceptions of the causes. Even those who attempt suicide but do not complete it are imperfect sources. They may differ in some ways from those who complete suicide, and they are no doubt changed by the experience of the suicide attempt. In the absence of definite information, many myths about suicide have arisen, including that it is influenced by the phases of the moon, that Catholics do not kill themselves, or that people who attempt but do not complete suicide must not have been serious about it. There is no evidence in support of these views (Fremouw et al., 1990). Several lines of theory and research have shown more promise, however.

Psychodynamic and Interpersonal Perspectives

Freud's hypothesis, extending his theory of depression, basically views suicide as murder. When a person loses someone whom he or she has ambivalently loved and hated, and introjects that person, aggression is directed inward. If these feelings are strong enough, the person will commit suicide.

Suicide notes are a source of information for evaluating the aggression-turned-inward hypothesis. In one study, genuine suicide notes were contrasted with simulated notes prepared by individuals who were *not* suicidal, but who were matched to the suicides on such demographic variables as age, sex, and social class (Shneidman & Farberow, 1970). The genuine notes contained significantly more hostility than did the simulated notes.

Paralleling the trends noted earlier in this chapter in psychodynamic approaches to understanding and treating depression, research on suicide has modified the concept of aggression turned inward by noting that suicide can actually represent an aggressive act motivated by hostility toward others. To the extent that this is the motivation, suicide is all too effective. Indeed, no other kind of death leaves in friends and relatives such long-lasting feelings of distress, shame, guilt, puzzlement, and general disturbance.

Cognitive Perspectives

Cognitive theories focus on the suicidal person's reasoning processes. In effect, suicide is viewed as a (very poor) decision about how to solve current problems and eliminate intolerable psychological pain. The theories differ somewhat in emphasis on what makes the decision-making process go awry.

Escape from Self-awareness.   Some suicides are believed to arise from a person's strong desire to escape from aversive self-awareness, that is, from the painful awareness of his or her self-perceived shortcomings and self-induced lack of success (Baumeister, 1990). This awareness is assumed to produce severe emotional suffering. Oblivion through death can appear more tolerable than a continuation of the painful awareness of one's deficiencies. Having unrealistically high expectations—and therefore being likely to be disappointed—plays a central role in this explanation of suicide. Of particular importance is a discrepancy between high expectations for intimacy and a reality that falls short, for example, being rejected by a loved one (Stephens, 1985). The person considers emotional life so negative as to be intolerable. There is considerable research in support of this hypothesis. For example, chronic poverty or being single is associated with slight if any increase in suicide rate, but a recent downturn in one's economic fortunes or a recent separation or divorce increases risk of suicide greatly (Baumeister, 1990). Thus, it appears that dashed expectations, more so than just any unfavorable conditions, play a role in suicide.

Hopelessness. Several studies have found significant correlations between suicide intent and hopelessness. Especially noteworthy are Aaron Beck's findings that hopelessness is a significant predictor of completed suicide (Beck, Brown, Berchick, Stewart, & Steer, 1990; Beck, Steer, Kovacs, & Garrison, 1985), more so than is depression (Beck, Kovacs, & Weissman, 1975). The expectation that in the future things will be no better than they are right now seems to be more instrumental than depression per se in propelling a person to take his or her life.

Problem-Solving Deficiencies. Among the cognitive deficits that may contribute to hopelessness and suicide is a rigid approach to problem solving under severe stress (Neuringer, 1964). The individual shows tunnel vision, being able to see only a narrow range of alternatives, of which suicide appears the most viable (Linehan & Shearin, 1988). In a sense, suicide may be a defective, inflexible attempt to cope rather than an unmitigated wish to be dead.

This view regards suicide as (almost always) a conscious effort to seek a solution to a problem that is causing intense suffering (Shneidman, 1987). To the sufferer, this solution ends consciousness and unendurable pain—what Melville in *Moby Dick* termed an "insufferable anguish." At the same time, most suicides are

According to the cognitive perspective, one problem contributing to the risk for suicide is tunnel vision, an inability to conceive of a range of alternatives to suicide as a way to solve or escape from overwhelming problems.

ambivalent (Shneidman, 1987). One indicator of this ambivalence is that about three-fourths of those who take their lives have communicated their intention beforehand, sometimes as a cry for help, contrary to the myth that people who talk about suicide will not commit the act (Fremouw et al., 1990).

In the study of genuine and simulated suicide notes mentioned earlier (Shneidman & Farberow, 1970), evidence consistent with the view that suicide relates to tunnel vision was obtained. The genuine notes contained a greater number of instructions, such as suggestions about raising the children and explicit orders about how to dispose of the body. Other research also shows a higher degree of concreteness and specificity in genuine suicide notes than in simulated ones (Black, 1993; Ogilvie, Stone, & Shneidman, 1983). Lacking in real suicide notes is the kind of general and philosophical content that characterizes those written by simulators. For example, "Be sure to pay the electric bill" would more likely appear in a real suicide note than "Be good to others" (Baumeister, 1990).

Tunnel vision and rigidity may account for why people who commit suicide have a hard time thinking of many alternatives for solving their problems. But if a person can only focus on a narrow range of solutions, why would suicide come to mind, and why would it seem like a viable solution? One possibility is that publicity about other suicides may influence a desperate person to attempt suicide. It appears that media reports of suicide may spark an increase in suicides. This disturbing prospect is supported by several pieces of evidence (Bandura, 1986; D. P. Phillips, 1974, 1977, 1985): (a) suicides rose by 12% in the month following Marilyn Monroe's death; (b) publicized accounts of self-inflicted deaths of people other than the famous also are followed by significant increases in suicides (suggesting that it is publicity rather than the fame of the suicide that is important); (c) publicized accounts of murder-suicides are followed by increases in auto and plane crashes in which the driver and others are killed; and, finally, (d) media reports of natural deaths of famous people are not followed by increases in suicide, suggesting that it is not grief itself that is influential.

Biological Perspectives

Although there is no evidence of genetic vulnerability to suicide, there has been promising research on neurochemistry and suicide. Earlier we described the serotonin theory of depression. Research has also established a link between serotonin, suicide, and impulsivity. Low levels of serotonin's major metabolite, 5-HIAA, have been found in suicide victims in several diagnostic categories—depression, schizophrenia, and various personality disorders (Brown & Goodwin, 1986). Furthermore, postmortem studies of the brains of people who committed suicide have revealed increased numbers of serotonin receptors (presumably a response to a decreased level of serotonin itself). The link between 5-HIAA levels and suicide is especially compelling in the case of violent and impulsive suicide. Finally, 5-HIAA levels are correlated with questionnaire measures of both aggression and impulsivity (Brown & Goodwin, 1986).

Suicide Prevention

Suicide-prevention centers usually provide round-the-clock consultation to persons who are suicidal. Workers are typically nonprofessional volunteers under professional supervision (Shneidman, Farberow, & Litman, 1970). As they take phone calls from people in suicidal crises, they have before them a checklist that guides their questioning of each caller. They must immediately assess how great the risk of suicide may be. For example, a caller would be regarded as a lethal risk if he were male, middle-aged, divorced, and living alone and had a history of previous suicide attempts. Those with detailed and concrete suicide plans are also viewed as high risk.

Assessment of risk is important, but by no means an easy task on a case-by-case basis. It is hard to predict with accuracy a very infrequent event like suicide. The prediction of suicide is inexact (Fremouw et al., 1990). For example, subjects rated as high in hopelessness are far more likely to kill themselves than are those low in hopelessness, yet most hopeless people do not kill themselves. In one study, 11% of those judged high in hopelessness committed suicide during a five-to-ten year follow-up period (Beck, Brown, & Steer, 1989). In outpatient (nonhospitalized) samples, the figure is closer to 1% to 2% (Beck, Brown, et al., 1990). Still, even if something is less likely to happen than not to happen, it is important to know the risks. If we knew that 10% of people crossing a given intersection got run over, for instance, it would be odd and heartless to conclude "it's pretty safe—most people don't get hit."

Community mental health centers often provide a 24-hour-a-day hot line for people who are considering suicide.

What can be done for a hot-line caller, or for any suicidal patient for that matter, given that risk has tentatively been assessed as high? In the most general sense, any intervention that reduces relevant risk factors is potentially applicable. Hot-line volunteers usually first try to get people talking. They usually refer callers to a professional for treatment. If medication is called for, the clinician would want the dose to provide adequate therapeutic benefit without being enough to make possible an intentional overdose.

There is widespread agreement, regardless of therapeutic orientation, that clinicians should not hesitate to inquire directly whether a client has thought of suicide. It is also important to be empathic, to view the suicidal person's situation as he or she sees it, rather than to convey in any way that the patient is a fool or is crazy to have settled on suicide as a solution to his or her woes.

Based on the problem-solving view of suicide, a number of additional intervention goals are suggested. Shneidman's (1985, 1987) approach to suicide prevention, for instance, is based on three strategies: (a) try to reduce the intense psychological pain and suffering; (b) encourage the person to pull back even a little from the idea of suicide; and (c) lift the blinders, or expand the constricted view, by helping the individual see options other than the extremes of continued suffering or death.

 Reducing the psychological pain and suffering is essentially the goal of all therapies discussed in this chapter and throughout the book, not a unique aspect of suicide prevention. Encouraging the person to pull back even a bit may be facilitated by, in effect, flipping the question around. Instead of focusing on the person's motives for wanting to die, one can ask, "Why live?" A self-report test called the Reasons for Living (RFL) Inventory (Linehan, 1985) may be useful in this context. Clusters of items tap things that are important to the individual, such as responsibility to family and concerns about children. The approach taken here is different from one focused exclusively on understanding and trying to reduce pessimism. Knowing what there is in a person's life that could potentially persuade that person not to commit suicide may enable the counselor to be more productive.

Finally, helping the suicidal person take a broader perspective can sometimes be as simple as concretely and systematically doing so with him or her in session. Shneidman gives the example of a wealthy college student who was single, pregnant—and suicidal, with a clearly formed plan. The only solution she could think of besides suicide was never to have become pregnant, even to be virginal again.

I took out a sheet of paper and began to widen her blinders. I said something like, "Now, let's see: You could have an abortion here locally." She responded, "I couldn't do that." I continued, "You could go away and have an abortion," "I couldn't do that." "You could bring the baby to term and keep the baby." "I couldn't do that." "You could have the baby and adopt it out." Further options were similarly dismissed. When I said, "You can always commit suicide, but there is obviously no

LEGAL, ETHICAL, AND SOCIAL ISSUES

An Argument Against Coercive Suicide Prevention

In a controversial article on coercive suicide prevention, Thomas Szasz (1986) argues that it is both impractical and immoral to prevent a person from committing suicide. It is impractical because we cannot really force people to live if they are intent on committing suicide unless—and this is where morality becomes an issue—we are prepared not only to commit them but to enslave them via heavy psychotropic medication or even physical restraints.

Arguing further in terms of morality, Szasz asserts that health professionals *should not* assume such responsibility—even if it were practical to do so—because all people, those seriously disturbed as well, should be accorded freedom to make choices, including the choice to end their lives. He allows one exception for what he calls impulsive suicide, when people are temporarily agitated, perhaps truly deranged, and need to be protected for a short while from their uncontrollable impulses. He draws an analogy with patients coming out of general anesthesia, when it is common medical practice to strap them down lest their flailing about involuntarily lead to unintended and preventable harm. This qualifier raises the question of how we can know when we are dealing with an impulsive act rather than an act that the person has been thinking about and planning for a period of time.

Szasz is not against advising a person not to commit suicide or otherwise treating problems, like depression, which might have a good deal to do with self-destructive thinking. It is forcible prevention that he opposes. Indeed, he believes that if professionals exclude coercive suicide prevention from their intervention options, they will be able to be more empathic with their patients and perhaps more helpful. He also suggests a psychiatric will. A patient, when not feeling suicidal, would agree about how to be treated if, later on, he or

Noted psychiatrist, Thomas S. Szasz, argues strongly against coercive suicide prevention.

she wished to commit suicide. If the patient opted for coercive prevention in this will, then it would be all right.

Szasz's analysis should be scrutinized with care. What about the fact that many, if not most, people who somehow weather suicidal crises, including those forcibly prevented from killing themselves, are grateful afterwards for another chance at life? It may be the case that if we were to follow Szasz's urging, we would miss opportunities to save savable lives. Szasz's rejoinder might be that one of the strongest predictors of a suicide attempt is a prior attempt. In other words, many people try more than once to kill themselves. We would therefore be repeatedly challenged to decide how drastically we were prepared to limit freedom (and sometimes degrade the person by restraints of one kind or another) in the hopes of forestalling what may be inevitable. There are no easy answers here, but it is important to raise the questions.

need to do that today," there was no response. "Now," I said, "let's look at this list and rank them in order of your preference, keeping in mind that none of them is optimal." (Shneidman, 1987, p. 171)

Just drawing up the list had a calming effect. The drive to kill herself very soon receded, and she was able to rank the list even though she found something wrong with each item. *But* an important goal had been achieved: she had been pulled back from the brink and was in a frame of mind to consider courses of action other than dying or being a virgin again. "We were then simply 'haggling' about life, a perfectly viable solution" (p. 171).

Although the range of strategies just discussed represent standard current practice in suicide prevention, Thomas Szasz has argued that such interventions are inappropriate if applied against the patient's will. His analysis is considered in the Legal, Ethical, and Social Issue box.

TO RECAP

There are more than thirty thousand completed suicides per year in the United States, and at least eight times as many suicide attempts. Women are more likely to attempt suicide, men to complete it. Psychoanalytic theory hypothesizes that suicide results from excessive anger at an introjected loved one. Cognitive perspectives implicate (a) the desire to escape from painful awareness of a discrepancy between reality and one's high expectations (e.g., for intimate relationships), (b) the expectation that things will get no better in the future, and (c) a rigid, inflexible approach to problem solving as determinants of suicide attempts. Imitation may be a factor in making suicide seem like a solution to one's problems, for media reports of suicides appear to provoke increased suicide rates. Decreased levels of serotonin may also relate to suicide, especially violent and impulsive suicides. The main strategies for working with acutely suicidal people are to assess suicide risk, help them expand their vision of possible solutions to their problems, underscore their own personally motivating reasons for living, and, in the long run, reduce the sources of despair and hopelessness.

Visual Summary for Chapter 10:

Mood Disorders

> *Mania*

- Increased Activity
- Talkativeness
- Racing Thoughts
- Decreased Sleep
- Inflated Self-Esteem
- Distractibility
- Risky Behavior

> *Depression*

- Sad Mood
- Loss of Interest and Pleasure
- Sleep Disturbances
- Changes in Activity Level
- Appetite Disturbances
- Loss of Energy
- Self-Reproach
- Difficulty Concentrating
- Thoughts of Death or Suicide

> *Perspectives on the Causes of Mood Disorders*

Psychodynamic ···> Orally fixated, overly dependent persons harbor hostility toward introjected loved ones who have died or otherwise been lost, such as an ex-partner. Thus depression equals anger turned inward.

Interpersonal ····> Depressed people have less than adequate levels of social support and tend to elicit negative reactions from others. Some evidence suggests that interpersonal difficulties precede depression.

Cognitive ····> **Learned Helplessness** ····> A person's passivity and sense of being unable to control his or her life is acquired through unpleasant experiences and traumas that the person unsuccessfully tried to control.

Attributions and Learned Helplessness ····> People become depressed when they attribute negative events to stable and global causes.

Hopelessness Theory ····> A subtype of depression (hopelessness depression) is caused by the expectation that undesirable events will occur and the person cannot influence the situation.

····> **Beck's Theory** ····> Negative schemata and cognitive biases lead people to misperceive reality and maintain the negative triad: negative views about self, world, and future.

Biological ····> **Genetics** ····> Family, twin, and adoption studies indicate that vulnerability to mood disorders, especially bipolar disorder, is heritable.

····> **Neurochemistry** ····> Biological evidence suggests that serotonin and/or norepinephrine are at below-normal levels during depression. Medication that boosts levels of these neurotransmitters alleviates depression. Drugs that decrease levels cause depression. Other evidence suggests that norepinephrine levels are above normal during mania.

····> **Neuroendocrine** ····> The hypothalamic–pituitary–adrenal cortical axis may be overactive in depression. Cortisol levels (an adrenocortical hormone) are high in depression. Thyroid disorders are also seen in bipolar disorders.

Treatment for Depression

Talk Therapies

Psychodynamic ••➤ Achieve insight into repressed conflict and facilitate release of inner-directed hostility.

Interpersonal ••➤ Understand interpersonal problems and improve relationships. May incorporate behavioral methods for improving social interactions, such as assertiveness and social-skills training.

Cognitive ••➤ Identify and change negative cognitive patterns that contribute to depression.

Biological Treatments

Medication ••➤ Tricyclics, monoamine oxidase inhibitors, and more recently developed drugs, such as buproprion and fluoxetine, are used for depression. Lithium is the main medication for bipolar disorder.

Electroconvulsive therapy (ECT) ••➤ Deliberate induction of a seizure by passing an electrical current through the patient's brain. It may be the most effective treatment for severe depression.

Suicide

Risk is elevated in mood disorder as well as other disorders and varies with **sex** (men are more likely to commit suicide) and **age** (the elderly are at increased risk, though adolescent suicide is increasing).

Perspectives on Causes

Psychodynamic/ Interpersonal ••➤ Freud argued that if anger at an introjected loved one is too strong, it could lead to suicide.

Cognitive ••➤ One view suggests suicide is an escape from awareness of failures. Another view sees suicide as a result of hopelessness. A third perspective sees suicide as an attempt to solve a problem that is causing intense anguish. Modeling may play a role in making suicide seem like a solution.

Biological ••➤ Low levels of serotonin metabolites are found in the brains of suicide victims.

Suicide Prevention ••➤ Suicide-prevention centers provide round-the-clock consultation to persons who are suicidal. Therapists should:
1. Try to reduce psychological pain (the overarching goal of therapy).
2. Encourage the suicidal person to pull back a little from the idea of suicide.
3. Help expand the range of solutions available to the person.

Chapter 11

Personality Disorders

The Case of Alice Siegel

Alice Siegel was twenty-two years old when she reluctantly agreed to interrupt her college education in midsemester and admit herself for the eighth time to a psychiatric hospital. Of most concern to her psychologist, Dr. Swenson, and her psychiatrist, Dr. Smythe, were brief episodes in which Alice felt that her body was not real. Terrified, she would cut herself with a knife in order to feel pain and thereby feel real. During the first part of the admission interview at the hospital, Alice angrily denied that she had done anything self-destructive. She did not stay angry, however, and was soon in tears as she described her fear that she would fail her midterm examinations and be expelled from college. The admitting psychiatrist noted that at times, Alice behaved in a flirtatious manner and asked inappropriately personal questions.

On arrival at the inpatient unit, Alice again became quite angry. She protested loudly, using obscene language when a nurse searched her luggage for illegal drugs and sharp objects. These impulsive outbursts of anger had become typical of Alice over the past several years. She often expressed intense anger far out of proportion to the situation. At such times she did and said things she later regretted, such as yelling at a close friend.

The same day on which she was admitted, Alice filed a 3-Day Notice, expressing her intention to leave the hospital within seventy-two hours. Dr. Swenson told Alice that if she did not agree to remain in the hospital voluntarily, he would initiate legal proceedings for her involuntary commitment on the grounds that she was a threat to herself. Two days later, Alice retracted the 3-Day Notice, and her anger seemed to lessen.

Over the next two weeks, Alice seemed to be getting along well. Despite some complaints of feeling depressed, she was always well dressed and groomed. Except for occasional episodes when she became verbally abusive and slammed doors, Alice appeared and acted like a staff member. Indeed, she began taking on a "therapist" role with other patients, listening intently to their problems and suggesting solutions. She would often serve as a spokesperson for disgruntled patients, expressing their complaints to administrators. With the help of her therapist, Alice wrote a contract stating that she did not feel like hurting herself and that she would notify staff members if that situation changed. She was allowed a number of passes off the unit with other patients and friends.

Alice became particularly attached to several staff members and arranged private talks with them, using this time to complain about alleged inadequacies of other staff members. She would tell whomever she was talking with that he or she was one of the few who knew her well enough to be helpful. These talks usually ended with flattery from Alice as to how understanding and helpful she found that particular staff person. These overtures made it difficult for some staff members to confront Alice on issues such as violations of the rules of the treatment unit. For instance, when Alice returned late from a pass off grounds, it was often overlooked. If she was confronted, especially by someone with whom she felt she had a special relationship, she felt betrayed and would angrily accuse that person of being "just like the rest of them."

By the end of the third week of hospitalization, Alice no longer appeared to be in acute distress, so discussions were begun concerning her discharge from the hospital. At about this time Alice began to drop hints in her therapy sessions with Dr. Swenson that she had been withholding some kind of secret. Dr. Swenson encouraged her to be more direct. Alice then revealed that since her second day in the hospital, she had been receiving illegal street drugs from two friends who visited her. In addition to occasionally using the drugs herself, Alice had been giving them to other patients on the unit. This situation was quickly brought to the attention of all the other patients on the unit in a meeting called by Dr. Swenson. During the meeting Alice protested that the other patients had forced her to bring them drugs. Dr. Swenson interpreted this as meaning that Alice had found it intolerable to be rejected by other people and would go to any lengths to avoid such rejection.

Soon after this incident came to light, Alice experienced another episode of feeling as if she were unreal, and cut herself a number of times across her wrists with a soda can she had broken in half. The cuts were deep enough to draw blood but were not life threatening. In contrast to previous occasions, she did not try to keep this hidden. Several staff members concluded that Alice was malingering—that is, exaggerating the severity of her problems so that she could remain in the hospital longer. The members of Alice's treatment team then met to decide the best course of action. Not everyone agreed that Alice was malingering. Although she was undoubtedly self-destructive and possibly suicidal and, therefore, in need of further hospitalization, Alice had been sabotaging the treatment of other patients and might do so again. With the members of her treatment team split on the question of whether or not Alice should be allowed to remain in the hospital, designing a coherent treatment program would prove difficult.

Introduction to Personality Disorders

personality disorders A heterogeneous group of disorders, listed separately on Axis II, regarded as long-standing, inflexible, and maladaptive patterns of inner experience and behavior that cut across many situations and impair social and occupational functioning.

The case of Alice Siegel illustrates borderline personality disorder, a syndrome we will discuss shortly. It is one of several **personality disorders**, a diverse group of long-standing, inflexible, and maladaptive patterns of inner experience and behavior that cut across many situations, impair social or occupational functioning, and deviate significantly from the expectations of the person's culture. Each of us develops some means of dealing with life's challenges over the years and through this a certain style of relating to other people. One person may be challenging and aggressive; another is very shy and avoids social contact; and another is so concerned with his or her appearance and status that relating honestly and intimately with others seems of little importance. These individuals would not be diagnosed as having personality disorders unless the patterns of behavior were dysfunctional, long-standing, and pervasive.

In DSM-IV, personality disorders are indicated on Axis II. They were placed on a separate axis to ensure that diagnosticians would pay greater attention to their possible presence. Sometimes, a diagnostic interview will point directly to the presence of a personality disorder. Often, however, someone who has come to a clinic has an Axis I disorder, such as panic disorder, which, quite naturally is a primary focus of attention. The patient may also exhibit the characteristics of a dependent personality. Placing the personality disorders on Axis II is meant to guide the clinician to consider routinely whether a personality disorder is also present.

Over the years, personality disorders have been difficult to diagnose reliably, despite attempts to improve the clarity of their definitions. In the field trials of DSM-III, for example, although personality disorders were diagnosed in more than 50% of the patients, the reliabilities of many of the individual personality disorders were inadequate (American Psychiatric Association, 1980). These low reliabilities may have been caused by the lack of a good assessment device in the DSM-III field trials. More recent work with structured interviews specially designed for assessing personality disorders indicates that good reliabilities can be achieved (Zimmerman, 1994).

Cultural Influences on Diagnosis

Conceptions of which personality traits are maladaptive, inflexible, and a source of any distress or impaired role functioning have been based largely on the study of highly educated, middle-class white people from North America or northern Europe (Lewis-Fernandez & Kleinman, 1994). To some extent this sampling bias characterizes all of our study of abnormal behavior, but it seems especially relevant and troubling when it comes to the personality disorders. For example, what might strike a Western diagnostician as pathological dependency and deficient development of a sense of self-identity could represent a normal, healthy personality from the standpoint of other cultures. Cultural psychologists have described Chinese society, among many other cultures, as placing a greater emphasis than does the U.S. culture on the family and one's belonging in a network of social relationships as a source of self-worth and identity (Markus & Kitayama, 1991; Shweder & Sullivan, 1990). So, though it is encouraged by his or her culture, the dependency of a Chinese-American might be evaluated negatively by a Western clinician.

Categorical versus Dimensional Classification

Thus, the validity of personality disorder criteria, not just the reliability of their application, is in question. A further sign of problems with the validity of personality disorders is that it is often difficult to diagnose someone with a single, specific personality disorder. Many disordered people exhibit a wide range of characteristics that make several Axis II diagnoses applicable (e.g., Widiger, Frances, & Trull, 1987).

Such considerations suggest that the categorical diagnostic system of the DSM may not be ideal for classifying personality disorders. In a *categorical* classification system you either have the disorder or you do not. Some personality disorders may lend themselves instead to a *dimensional* system, in which the *degree* to which personality problems are present is rated (Livesley, Schroeder, Jackson, & Jang, 1994). The best model may vary across personality disorders. Research suggests that borderline personality disorder, for instance, may fit a dimensional model (Trull et al., 1990), whereas psychopathy may fit the categorical model (Harris, Rice, & Quinsey, 1994).

In a dimensional model, what are now called personality disorders are seen as extreme or rigid expressions of normal human tendencies present to some extent in most people. A dimensional system was considered for inclusion in both DSM-III-R and DSM-IV, but consensus could not be reached on which dimensions to include (Widiger, Frances, Spitzer, & Williams, 1988) (see Focus Box 11.1 for an introduction to one dimensional scheme).

The possible utility of a dimensional model notwithstanding, research on personality disorders conducted so far has been based on the categorical approach used in the DSM. Personality disorders are grouped into three clusters in DSM-IV: odd/eccentric; anxious/fearful; and dramatic/emotional. There is more information available on dramatic/emotional personality disorders, especially antisocial personality disorder, than on other categories, so they receive the most attention in this chapter.

Chinese society typically places a strong emphasis on family connections. A person's cultural background must be considered in evaluating their adult personality features as normal versus disordered.

To Recap

Personality disorders consist of long-standing, inflexible, maladaptive inner experience and behaviors that impair functioning. They are diagnosed on a separate axis (Axis II) of the DSM to ensure that they are considered for all cases. They are grouped into three clusters (odd/eccentric, anxious/fearful, dramatic/emotional). Historically, personality disorders have been difficult to diagnose reliably, but reliability appears to have improved with the development of structured interviews. Several concerns about the validity of DSM-IV personality disorder criteria remain, including (a) whether they are universal or specific to Western cultures, (b) the fact that the various diagnoses overlap a great deal, resulting in high comorbidity, and (c) the possibility that personality pathology should be evaluated along continuous dimensions, such as those in the five-factor model of normal personality, rather than with categorical (present/absent) diagnoses.

> ◢ FOCUS BOX 11.1

Personality Disorders and the Five-Factor Model

The most promising dimensional system for describing personality pathology may be the five-factor model (FFM), which is widely accepted as capturing the main dimensions of normal personality (e.g., Digman, 1990). The five factors are depicted in Table 11.1. They represent in effect the primary colors of personality. Other traits can be described in terms of where they fall on these five dimensions, just as a particular place on Earth can be described by its longitude, latitude, and elevation.

Several studies have related criteria for diagnosing personality disorders to measures of the five factors shown in the table. Borderline personality disorder (BPD) patients, for instance, stand out particularly for very high scores on neuroticism and, to a lesser degree, for low scores on agreeableness and conscientiousness (Clarkin, Hull, Cantor, & Sanderson, 1993). High neuroticism is characteristic of many personality (and other) disorders, which may help explain the high comorbidity of BPD with other disorders (Widiger & Costa, 1994). The five-factor model can also be useful for describing differences among related disorders. Both schizoid and avoidant personality disorders, for instance, are associated with low extraversion, but they differ in that schizoid personality disorder is unrelated to neuroticism, whereas avoidant personality disorder is positively correlated with neuroticism. Simply reporting a person's relative standing on extraversion and neuroticism might be more informative and realistic than setting what amounts to an arbitrary cutoff on the neuroticism dimension for deciding which introverted people will be called schizoid and which avoidant. This is a difficult distinction required by the current categorical system (Widiger & Costa, 1994).

Table 11.1 ▶ *Five-Factor Model of Personality*

Dimension	Descriptors	
	Low Scores	*High Scores*
1. *Extraversion*	Quiet	Talkative
	Reserved	Assertive
	Shy	Active
	Withdrawn	Energetic
	Retiring	Outgoing
2. *Agreeableness*	Fault finding	Sympathetic
	Cold	Kind
	Unfriendly	Appreciative
	Quarrelsome	Affectionate
	Hard-hearted	Soft-hearted
3. *Conscientiousness*	Careless	Organized
	Disorderly	Thorough
	Frivolous	Planful
	Irresponsible	Efficient
	Slipshod	Responsible
4. *Neuroticism*	Stable	Tense
	Calm	Anxious
	Content	Touchy
	Assured	Moody
	Unemotional	Worrying
5. *Openness*	Commonplace	Imaginative
	Narrow	Wide
	interests	interests
	Simple	Curious
	Shallow	Sophisticated
	Conventional	Original

Source: Adapted from John (1990).

> ◢ *Odd/Eccentric Cluster*

Odd/eccentric behavior and subjective experiences, such as unwarranted suspiciousness or extreme detachment from other people, characterize this cluster. The paranoid, schizoid, and schizotypal personality disorders fall into this grouping.

Paranoid Personality Disorder

paranoid personality This person, expecting to be mistreated by others, becomes suspicious, secretive, jealous, and argumentative. He or she will not accept blame.

We all find ourselves being suspicious from time to time—certain that the guy at the gas station has shortchanged us or that a professor knows we have not read the chapter. The person with a **paranoid personality** routinely *expects* to be mistreated or exploited by others. He or she thus becomes secretive and is continually on the lookout for possible signs of trickery and abuse. Such people are reluctant to confide in others and tend to blame others even when they themselves are at fault. They are extremely jealous and may unjustifiably question the fidelity of their partner.

Paranoid personalities are also preoccupied with doubts about the loyalty or trustworthiness of others. Once they perceive someone as having violated their trust, they are prone to bearing grudges and acting in a hostile manner toward them. Paranoid people read hidden messages into events. For example, they may believe that a neighbor's dog deliberately barks in the early morning to disturb them. Paranoid personality disorder overlaps most strongly with borderline and avoidant personality disorders (Morey, 1988). It is more common among the first-degree relatives of patients with delusional disorder and schizophrenia, suggesting a genetic relationship with these disorders (Kendler, Masterson, & Davis, 1985). However, paranoid personality disorder is not the same as paranoid schizophrenia. In particular, paranoid personalities are not subject to delusions and hallucinations (see Chapter 9).

Schizoid Personality Disorder

The **schizoid personality** does not desire or enjoy social relationships and usually has few if any close friends, preferring solitary activities. He or she appears dull and aloof and without warm, tender feelings for other people. These patients rarely report or display strong emotions, are not interested in sex, and experience few pleasurable activities. Indifferent to praise, criticism, and the sentiments of others, people with this disorder are extreme loners. Schizoid personality disorder is not the same as schizophrenia (Chapter 9) despite the similar name. Schizoid personality disorder lacks the psychotic symptoms of schizophrenia such as delusions and hallucinations.

schizoid personality This person, emotionally aloof and indifferent to the praise, criticism, and feelings of others, is usually a loner with few, if any, close friends and with solitary interests.

Schizotypal Personality Disorder

The modern concept of schizotypal personality disorder grew out of Danish studies of the adopted children of schizophrenics (Kety, Rosenthal, Wender, & Schulsinger, 1968). While some of these children developed full-blown schizophrenia as adults, an even larger number developed what seemed to be an attenuated form of schizophrenia. The diagnostic criteria for schizotypal personality disorder were developed to describe these people (Spitzer, Endicott, & Gibbon, 1979).

The **schizotypal personality** usually has the same interpersonal difficulties as the schizoid personality, as well as excessive social anxiety. Other, more eccentric symptoms are present as well, although they are not severe enough to warrant a diagnosis of schizophrenia (see Chapter 9). Schizotypal personalities may have *odd beliefs* or *magical thinking*, such as superstitiousness or a belief that they are clairvoyant and telepathic. One patient believed that seeing pigeons brought him good luck and that on such lucky days his touch would have the power to cure others' medical ailments. Schizotypal people may also show recurrent *illusions*—they may sense the presence of a force or a person not actually there. They may use words in an unusual and unclear fashion. They may talk to themselves or wear dirty and disheveled clothing. They may exhibit suspiciousness, paranoia, and ideas of reference, the belief that events have a particular and unusual meaning for them. Their emotions appear to be constricted and flat. In view of these characteristics, it is not surprising that schizotypal personalities usually have trouble fitting in with others and are considered odd or awkward socially.

schizotypal personality This eccentric individual has oddities of thought and perception, speaks digressively and with overelaborations, and is usually socially isolated. Under stress, he or she may appear psychotic.

The prevalence of schizotypal personality disorder is estimated at about 3%. It is slightly more frequent in men than in women (Zimmerman & Coryell, 1989).

The relatives of people with schizotypal personality disorder are themselves at increased risk for the disorder (Siever et al., 1990).

Patients with the disorder are also similar to schizophrenics on some biological measures, such as low levels of monoamine oxidase (M. Baron, Levitt, Gruen, Kane, & Asnis, 1984). Schizotypal personality disorder and schizophrenia may be related to each other through genetic transmission of a predisposition. More first-degree relatives of schizophrenics are given the diagnosis than are relatives of individuals in control groups; the disorder may thus be a mild form of schizophrenia (Spitzer et al., 1979).

The biggest problem facing this diagnosis is its continuing overlap with other personality disorder diagnoses. Morey (1988), for example, found that 33% of DSM-III-R diagnosed schizotypal personalities met the diagnostic criteria for borderline personality disorder, 33% for narcissistic personality disorder, 59% for avoidant personality disorder, 59% for paranoid personality disorder, and 44% for schizoid personality disorder. Clearly, these are unsatisfactory figures if we want to consider schizotypal personality disorder as a discrete diagnostic entity.

To Recap

Paranoid personalities are suspicious of others, mistrustful, secretive, and jealous. There appears to be a familial relationship between paranoid personality disorder and delusional disorder. Schizoid personalities are aloof and unemotional loners, uninterested in social relationships. Schizotypal personalities are socially anxious and unemotional and show odd beliefs, perceptions, and use of language. This disorder is genetically related to schizophrenia and may constitute a mild form of it. Schizotypal personality also overlaps other personality disorders to a great extent.

Anxious/Fearful Cluster

The disorders in this cluster—avoidant, dependent, and obsessive-compulsive personality disorders—involve *anxious/fearful* reactions, such as being preoccupied with the possibility that others will criticize you or lacking the self-confidence to make your own decisions.

Avoidant Personality Disorder

avoidant personality Individuals with an avoidant personality have poor self-esteem and thus are extremely sensitive to potential rejection and remain aloof, even though they very much desire affiliation and affection.

Avoidant personality disorder is diagnosed when people are keenly sensitive to the possibility of criticism, rejection, or disapproval and are therefore reluctant to enter into relationships unless they are sure they will be liked. These people believe they are incompetent and inferior to others. They typically exaggerate the dangers or difficulties involved in doing something outside their usual routine. In social situations, they are afraid of saying something foolish or of being embarrassed by blushing or other signs of anxiety. Work or school functioning can also be affected. Avoidant personalities may forego projects or promotions that would give them more responsibilities and set them up for criticism from colleagues.

Avoidant personality disorder thus shares with schizoid personality disorder the feature of social isolation and withdrawal. The key difference is that the schizoid patient remains alone because of a lack of interest in social interaction, whereas the avoidant patient desires relationships but is afraid of rejection by others (see Focus Box 11.1). As we shall see, there is also considerable overlap between the features of avoidant personality disorder and those of dependent personality disorder (Trull, Widiger, & Frances, 1987) and borderline personality disorder (Morey, 1988).

Dependent Personality Disorder

The **dependent personality** lacks self-confidence and self-reliance. Such individuals passively allow their spouses or partners to assume responsibility for deciding where they should live, what jobs they should hold, with whom they should be friendly. They agree with others even when they know others are wrong, and they have difficulty initiating any activities on their own. Dependent personalities feel uncomfortable when alone and are often preoccupied with fears of being left to take care of themselves. They are unable to make demands on others, and they subordinate their own needs to ensure that they do not break up the protective relationships they have established. When close relationships end, they urgently seek another relationship to replace the old one.

Dependent personality overlaps strongly with borderline and avoidant personality disorders (Morey, 1988) and is linked to several Axis I diagnoses, notably depression (Bornstein, 1992), as well as to poor physical health (Greenberg & Bornstein, 1988).

dependent personality Lacking in self-confidence, people with a dependent personality passively allow others to run their lives and make no demands on them so as not to endanger these protective relationships.

> ### APPLYING CRITICAL THINKING SKILLS

SEX DIFFERENCES IN DEPENDENCY

Sex differences in dependency traits vary with the method of assessment. Women score higher than men on objective self-report tests of dependency (see Chapter 5). That is, women are more likely to agree with such statements as "I easily get discouraged when I don't get what I need from others" (Hirschfeld et al., 1977). But on projective tests of dependency men and women score equally on average (Bornstein, Manning, Krukonis, Rossner, & Mastrosimone, 1993). For example, they are equally likely to see in Rorschach cards (see Chapter 5) images of gift giving or food and drink, which are linked with dependency in psychoanalytic theory.

▶*What conclusion does the evidence seem to support?* Men and women may have equivalent psychological dependency needs, just as we are all biologically dependent at the start of life. These needs are reflected in their responses to subtle projective tests that have no apparent (to the test taker) relevance to dependency. Men, or at least those who endorse traditionally masculine sex roles, may be less willing to admit dependency (Bornstein, 1992). Therefore, they score lower on transparent questionnaire measures.

▶*What other interpretations are plausible?* It may be that projective tests are not valid measures of dependency and therefore do not show the (true) sex difference revealed by objective tests.

▶*What other information would help choose among the alternative interpretations?* If the second interpretation is correct, that projective tests are invalid and objective tests are valid, then the projective tests should fare worse in predicting dependency-related behaviors, dependency-related psychological and physical disorders, and so forth. Moreover, objective and projective tests of dependency should correlate poorly with one another.

If the first interpretation (men are just as dependent, but unwilling to admit it) is accurate, then objective dependency test scores should be correlated with sex-role attitudes. People who endorse traditionally masculine sex roles should score low on objective tests of dependency.

Research along these lines so far favors the first interpretation. Specifically, objective dependency test scores correlate positively with feminine sex-role orientation and negatively with masculine orientation, among both male and female subjects (Bornstein, 1992). In other words, people with a high "masculine" score on tests of sex-role orientation tend to score low on dependency. Also, the idea that projective tests are invalid (the second possible interpretation) and so would not correlate positively with objective measures is not supported by research (Bornstein et al., 1993). The two types of measures correlate positively, though more so among women. Taken together, these findings suggest that men, and more particularly anyone endorsing conventionally masculine sex role attitudes, are unlikely to acknowledge dependency. However, men and women are probably equally dependent in reality.   ◀

Obsessive-Compulsive Personality Disorder

obsessive-compulsive personality People with this disorder have inordinate difficulty making decisions, are overly concerned with details and efficiency, and relate poorly to others because they demand that things be done their way. They are perfectionistic, unduly conventional, serious, and formal.

The **obsessive-compulsive personality** is a perfectionist, preoccupied with details, rules, schedules, and the like. These people are work rather than pleasure oriented. Ironically, their focus on work does not necessarily enhance productivity, for obsessive-compulsive personalities have inordinate difficulty making decisions, allocating time, and delegating tasks. They may get so immersed in details and procedures that projects are never completed or the actual point of an activity is lost. Their interpersonal relationships are also often poor because they demand that everything be done their way. They are generally serious, formal, and inflexible, especially regarding moral issues. Obsessive-compulsive personalties are unable to discard worn-out and useless objects, even if the objects have no sentimental value, and they are likely to hoard money. This dysfunctional attention to work and productivity is found about twice as often in men as in women.

Obsessive-compulsive personality disorder is quite different from obsessive-compulsive disorder (OCD; see Chapter 6), despite the similar name. A person with OCD is at the mercy of obsessive thoughts and compulsive behavior to allay anxiety. The obsessive-compulsive personality is generally rigid, but does not have the obsessions and compulsions that define OCD.

To Recap

Avoidant personalities are socially withdrawn. Unlike schizoid personalities, they desire social interaction but are fearful of rejection by others and consider themselves inferior. Dependent personalities lack self-confidence and self-reliance, allowing others to make key decisions for them. Dependency appears more common among women, but evidence suggests that this appearance may be misleading. It may result from traditionally masculine individuals' unwillingness to report dependency on others. The obsessive-compulsive personality is a detail-oriented, rule-governed perfectionist who has trouble with setting priorities, making decisions, and being flexible enough to get along with others. This disorder is especially common among men.

Histrionic personalities are highly emotionally expressive and long to be the center of attention.

▶ Dramatic/Emotional Cluster

Some people exhibit symptoms that are best characterized as *dramatic/emotional*. The disorders in this cluster—histrionic, narcissistic, borderline, and antisocial personality disorders—frequently involve erratic, extreme, and sometimes destructive behavior.

Histrionic Personality Disorder

histrionic personality This person is overly dramatic, attention seeking, given to emotional excess, and immature.

The **histrionic personality** is overly dramatic and attention seeking. Although histrionic people display emotion extravagantly, they are actually emotionally shallow, and their relationships generally are not as intimate as they believe.

They are self-centered, overly concerned with physical attractiveness, and uncomfortable when not the center of attention. Histrionic patients can be inappropriately sexually provocative, using their appearance to call attention to themselves, and they are easily influenced by others. Their speech tends to be impressionistic or vague, with few details.

One histrionic patient was distressed by a lack of satisfying relationships and by feelings of insecurity about others' opinions of her (Turkat & Maisto, 1985). However, she reported being easily bored by her children, interacting with men mainly by flirting with them, and viewing all women as potentially in competition with her for men's attention. If things did not go her way, she threw temper tantrums to try to manipulate others. This situation illustrates the often self-defeating nature of personality disorders. The patient's goals, such as positive social attention and close relationships, were obstructed by the very behaviors she used in pursuing them, in this case, tantrums and competitiveness.

The diagnosis of histrionic personality disorder is more common among women in hospital samples (Reich 1987), but this appears to be the result of sampling bias, as the rates for men and women were equal (2.1%) in a community survey (Nestadt, Romanowski, Chahal, & Merchant, 1990). The frequency of the disorder is higher among separated and divorced people, and it is associated with high rates of depression and poor physical health (Nestadt et al., 1990). The major overlap is with borderline personality disorder.

Narcissistic Personality Disorder

People with a **narcissistic personality** have a grandiose view of their own uniqueness and abilities, and they are preoccupied with fantasies of great success. To say that they are self-centered is an understatement. They require almost constant attention and admiration and believe that they can only be understood by other special (though not equal!) people. Their need to be the center of attention is similar to that of histrionic people, but the quality of the recognition desired is different. Histrionic people crave attention and may act out any role that will procure it, including the role of victim or person in need of help. Narcissists want admiring attention for being superior. Their interpersonal relationships are disturbed by their lack of empathy, their feelings of envy, and their arrogance. Narcissists take advantage of others because they feel entitled. They expect others to do special, not-to-be-reciprocated favors for them. If thwarted, narcissists are prone to extreme anger.

As narcissists are self-centered and grandiose, they are unlikely to perceive themselves as disturbed and in need of change. Therapists are most apt to see them when their behavior patterns have created significant interpersonal or occupational difficulties. From the patient's perspective, these difficulties are the problem, not the narcissism itself. For example, one patient began therapy having lost three jobs in the prior year. In each case, she had talked her way into getting a position for which she was marginally qualified. As pressures and responsibilities mounted, she became angry and complained of unfairness and the incompetence of others. Ultimately she was fired. She got over feeling bad about losing her job by concluding that the problem was that her supervisor was jealous of her talent and attractiveness and was unable to cope with that jealousy.

The diagnosis of narcissistic personality disorder was formally introduced in DSM-III. From DSM-III to DSM-III-R the frequency of the diagnosis increased markedly. It overlaps greatly with borderline personality disorder (Morey, 1988) (see Focus Box 11.1).

Narcissistic personality disorder draws its name from Narcissus of Greek mythology. He fell in love with his own reflection, was consumed by his own desire, and was then transformed into a flower.

narcissistic personality Extremely selfish and self-centered, people with a narcissistic personality have a grandiose view of their uniqueness, achievements, and talents and an insatiable craving for admiration and approval from others. They are exploitative to achieve their own goals and expect much more from others than they themselves are willing to give.

Borderline Personality Disorder

borderline personality This impulsive and unpredictable person has an uncertain self-image, intense and unstable social relationships, and extreme swings of mood.

Persons diagnosed as having **borderline personality** disorder are unstable in their relationships, mood, and self-image. For example, their attitudes and feelings toward other people may vary considerably and inexplicably over short periods of time. Emotions are also erratic and can shift abruptly, particularly to anger. This feature was especially evident in Alice Siegel, the borderline personality disorder case with which we opened this chapter. Borderline personalities are argumentative, irritable, and sarcastic. Their unpredictable and impulsive behavior, such as gambling, spending, sex, and eating sprees, is potentially self-damaging. These individuals have not developed a clear and coherent sense of self and remain uncertain about their values, loyalties, and choice of career. They cannot bear to be alone and have fears of abandonment. They tend to have a series of intense one-on-one relationships that are usually stormy, as they alternate between idealizing loved ones and devaluing them. Subject to chronic feelings of depression and emptiness, these individuals may make manipulative attempts at suicide. Paranoid thinking and dissociative symptoms may appear during periods of high stress. Of these symptoms, unstable and intense interpersonal relationships are a critical feature (Modestin, 1987).

The character portrayed by Glenn Close in the film Fatal Attraction *had many characteristics of the borderline personality.*

Therapists have used the term *borderline personality* for some time, but they have given it many meanings. Originally, the term implied that the patient was on the borderline between neurosis and schizophrenia. The DSM concept of borderline personality no longer has this connotation. Borderline personality disorder is considered a unique syndrome, not necessarily at the border of two others.

Borderline personality disorder has a prevalence of about 2% and typically begins in adolescence (McGlashan, 1983). It also runs in families (Baron, Risch, Levitt, & Gruen, 1985). Borderline personality disorder is more often diagnosed in women than in men (Swartz, Blazer, George, & Winfield, 1990). Conversely, antisocial personality disorder (discussed next) is more often diagnosed in men than in women (Morey & Ochoa, 1989).

These sex differences may reflect sex biases in diagnosis. Making a clear case for diagnostic bias, however, presents some thorny problems. For example, it may be that the characteristics of borderline personality are, for sociocultural reasons, *normally* found more often among women than among men, and the opposite may be true for antisocial personality disorder (Widiger & Spitzer, 1991). Society may shape women and men in these different directions. Thus, diagnoses may not themselves be biased; rather, they may be telling us something about our society that itself merits attention. For example, borderline personalities report a high frequency of childhood physical and sexual abuse (Ogata et al., 1990), and this may account for the disorder's greater prevalence among women.

Borderline personalities are very likely to have an Axis I mood disorder (Manos, Vasilopoulou, & Sotiriou, 1987), and their relatives are more likely than average to have mood disorders (Pope, Jones, Hudson, Cohen, & Gunderson, 1983).

Antisocial Personality Disorder (Psychopathy)

antisocial personality Also called a psychopath, a person with this disorder is superficially charming and a habitual liar, has no regard for others, shows no remorse after hurting others, has no shame for behaving in an outrageously objectionable manner, is unable to form relationships and take responsibility, and does not learn from punishment.

Antisocial personality disorder begins in adolescence as a conduct disorder (see Chapter 14), which involves truancy, running away from home, frequent lying, theft, arson, and deliberate destruction of property. This pattern is then continued by antisocial behavior in adulthood. The adult antisocial personality shows irresponsible and antisocial behavior by not working consistently, breaking laws, being irritable and physically aggressive, defaulting on debts, and being reckless. He or she is impulsive and fails to plan ahead. In addition, the antisocial personality is manipulative and shows no regard for truth nor remorse for misdeeds.

Continuity of antisocial behavior from childhood to adulthood is thus thematic, revolving around disregard for conventional norms and others' interests and well-being. It is not literal, in the sense of the same behaviors simply recurring throughout the life span.

About 6% of adult American men and 1% of women are antisocial personalities (Kessler et al., 1994). It is common for antisocial personalities to break the law, since they are for the most part amoral. But pimps, confidence artists, murderers, and drug dealers are by no means the only antisocial personalities (and not all of them are). Business executives, professors, politicians, physicians, plumbers, salespeople, carpenters, and bartenders can be antisocial personalities as well. Nevertheless, income and years of education are inversely correlated with being diagnosed as having antisocial personality disorder (Kessler et al., 1994).

Psychologist Elton McNeil (1967) was a personal friend of an antisocial personality, Dan.

Dan was a wealthy actor and disc jockey who lived in an expensive house in an exclusive suburb and generally played his role as a personality to the hilt. One evening, when he and McNeil were out for dinner, Dan made a great fuss over the condition of the shrimp de Johnge he had ordered. McNeil thought that Dan deliberately contrived the whole scene for the effect it might produce, and he said to his companion, "I have a sneaking suspicion this whole scene came about just because you weren't really hungry." Dan laughed loudly in agreement and said, "What the hell, they'll be on their toes next time." "Was that the only reason for this display?" "No," he replied, "I wanted to show you how gutless the rest of the world is. If you shove a little they all jump. Next time I come in, they'll be all over me to make sure everything is exactly as I want it. That's the only way they can tell the difference between class and plain ordinary. When I travel I go first class."

"Yes, . . . but how do you feel about you as a person—as a fellow human being?"

"Who cares?" he laughed. "If they were on top they would do the same to me. The more you walk on them, the more they like it. It's like royalty in the old days. It makes them nervous if everyone is equal to everyone else. Watch. When we leave I'll put my arm around that waitress, ask her if she still loves me, pat her on the fanny, and she'll be ready to roll over any time I wiggle my little finger." (p. 85)

Another incident occurred when a friend of Dan's committed suicide. Most of the other friends whom Dan and McNeil had in common were concerned and called McNeil to see whether he could provide any information about why the man had taken his life. Dan did not. Later, when McNeil mentioned the suicide to him, all he could say was, "That's the way the ball bounces." In his public behavior, however, Dan's attitude toward the incident appeared quite different. He was the one who collected money and presented it personally to the widow. In keeping with his character, however, Dan remarked that the widow had a sexy body that really interested him.

These two incidents convey the flavor of Dan's behavior. McNeil had witnessed a long succession of similar events, which led him to conclude that

> [The incidents] painted a grisly picture of lifelong abuse of people for Dan's amusement and profit. He was adept at office politics and told me casually of an unbelievable set of deceptive ways to deal with the opposition. Character assassination, rumor mongering, modest blackmail, seduction, and barefaced lying were the least of his talents. He was a jackal in the entertainment jungle, a jackal who feasted on the bodies of those he had slaughtered professionally. (p. 91)

In his conversations with Dan, McNeil was also able to inquire into Dan's life history. One early and potentially important event was related by Dan.

Some of the psychopath's antisocial behavior seems to be motivated by thrill seeking, but in a more pervasive and intense way than simply engaging in bungee jumping.

I can remember the first time in my life when I began to suspect I was a little different from most people. When I was in high school my best friend got leukemia and died and I went to his funeral. Everybody else was crying and feeling sorry for themselves and as they were praying to get him into heaven I suddenly realized that I wasn't feeling anything at all. He was a nice guy but what the hell. That night I thought about it some more and found that I wouldn't miss my mother and father if they died and that I wasn't too nuts about my brothers and sisters for that matter. I figured there wasn't anybody I really cared for but, then, I didn't need any of them anyway so I rolled over and went to sleep. (p. 87)

(Copyright 1967. Adapted by permission of Prentice-Hall.)

Antisocial personality disorder has some similarity to *psychopathy*, a concept closely linked to the writings of Hervey Cleckley, including his classic book, *The Mask of Sanity* (1976). On the basis of his clinical experience, Cleckley formulated a set of criteria by which to recognize psychopathy. Unlike the DSM criteria for antisocial personality disorder, Cleckley's criteria for psychopathy refer less to antisocial behavior itself and more to the psychopath's state of mind. For example, one of the key characteristics of the psychopath is poverty of emotions, both positive and negative. Psychopaths have no sense of shame, and any seemingly positive feelings for others are merely an act. The psychopath is superficially charming and manipulates others for personal gain. The lack of negative emotions, such as anxiety, may make it impossible for psychopaths to learn from their mistakes, and the lack of positive emotions leads them to behave irresponsibly toward others. Another key point in Cleckley's description is that the antisocial behavior of the psychopath is inadequately motivated. This behavior is not due, for example, to a need for something, like money, but is performed impulsively, as much for thrills as anything else. Psychopathy often occurs in conjunction with abuse of alcohol and other drugs (Smith & Newman, 1990).

Thus we have two related but not identical concepts—antisocial personality disorder (APD) and psychopathy. Some researchers (e.g., Hare et al., 1991) are critical of current APD criteria because, over time, they have drifted away from the core concept of psychopathy discussed by Cleckley. The drift is understandable in view of the desire to make DSM diagnoses reliable. It is easier to agree on the meaning of "running away from home" or "sets fires deliberately" (APD childhood behavior items) than to agree on how to measure whether someone is "superficially charming" or "lacks remorse" (adult psychopathic characteristics). Accordingly, APD is among the most reliable (both across raters and over time) of the DSM personality disorder diagnoses (Zimmerman, 1994).

However, as discussed in Chapter 4, trying at all costs to improve reliability can have the unintended side effect of decreasing validity, and the transformation of psychopathy into current APD criteria may be an instance of this problem. For example, the APD criteria rely heavily on reports of specific behaviors in childhood. Although we may well be able to rate people's reports about such events reliably, is it realistic to trust the reports of events that took place many years ago by people who are believed to be habitual liars? Also, from the standpoint of discriminant validity, it is important that APD not mean simply criminal behavior, yet 75% to 80% of convicted felons meet the criteria for antisocial personality disorder. In contrast, the corresponding figure for psychopaths is 15% to 25% (Hart & Hare, 1989). Therefore, the concept of psychopathy seems to have some distinct advantages, even if it is difficult to define some of its features concretely.

To Recap

People with histrionic personality disorder are overly dramatic and self-centered, wanting to be the center of attention. Those with narcissistic personality disorder lack empathy for others and possess a grandiose sense of their own special impor-

tance and entitlement. Borderline personalities show unstable emotions and are easily angered, impulsive, and desperate to avoid abandonment by others, and they lack a clear sense of identity. This disorder is often associated with mood disorders. Borderline personal disorder is more prevalent among women than among men, possibly because one of the causes seems to be childhood physical and sexual abuse.

Antisocial personalities show a childhood history of conduct disorder as well as antisocial behavior in adulthood, such as law-breaking or physical aggressiveness. They are deceitful and lack remorse for misdeeds. This disorder is much more prevalent among men than among women. Cleckley's concept of psychopathy differs from current antisocial personality disorder criteria by deemphasizing antisocial behavior and emphasizing emotional features, such as a lack of anxiety, that make it difficult for them to learn from the negative consequences of actions.

Perspectives on the Causes and Treatment of Personality Disorders

Considering how long clinicians have been interested in the personality disorders, surprisingly little is known about their causes or how to treat them. Progress toward understanding the causes of personality disorders was long impeded by the low reliability of diagnoses. It remains complicated by the extensive overlap among personality disorders and between them and Axis I mental disorders. As we will see, there are clinically derived theories concerning several of the personality disorders, and a more extensive tradition of research on psychopathy.

If personality disorders are challenging to study, they are even more difficult to treat. Therapeutic outcomes are often poor, and the stress of treating patients with personality disorders is great (McGlashan, 1983). A majority of borderline personality disorder patients, for instance, have engaged in parasuicidal behaviors, including suicide attempts or other self-mutilation, such as cutting or burning themselves (Clarkin, Widiger, Frances, Hurt, & Gilmore, 1983). Apart from suicide threats or acts, the intense anger experienced by borderline patients may become directed at their therapists, adding to the stressfulness of treating them (Linehan & Kehrer, 1993). The tendency of borderline personalities to test the reliability of the therapist with threats and other demands, their low tolerance for intimacy and yet exquisite sensitivity to rejection, and the presentation in each session of constantly emergent crises make focusing on a manageable set of goals extremely difficult (Beck, Freeman et al., 1990).

Psychopathy is often regarded as virtually impossible to treat (Cleckley, 1976; McCord & McCord, 1964). It may be that people with the classic symptoms listed by Cleckley are, by their very natures, largely incapable of benefiting from psychotherapy, as they are unable to form any sort of trusting, honest relationship with a therapist. People who lie almost without knowing it, who care little for the feelings of others and understand their own even less, who appear not to realize that what they are doing is morally wrong, who lack any motivation to obey society's laws and mores, and who, living only for the present, have no concern for the future are extremely poor candidates for therapy.

In addition to studying the issue of how to treat a personality disorder, investigators have considered how the presence of a personality disorder affects treatment of Axis I disorders, and vice versa. Across a wide range of diagnoses and therapies, personality disorders are associated with worse outcomes in the treatment of Axis I conditions (Reich & Vasile, 1993). For example, with the possible exception of cognitive therapy, both psychological and biological treatments for depression are less effective if the depressed patient also has a personality disorder (Shea, Widiger, & Klein, 1992).

The reverse is not necessarily true, however. An interesting exception to the general principle that having more disorders makes treatment less successful involves antisocial patients who are also depressed. A study of male opiate addicts found that those who were both depressed and antisocial benefited from psychotherapy (whether cognitive or psychodynamic) in terms of drug use, employment, and other measures, whereas nondepressed antisocial patients experienced little improvement (Woody, McLellan, Luborsky, & O'Brien, 1985). For antisocial patients it may be that depression serves to motivate them to adhere to treatment recommendations and change their behavior accordingly.

Bearing in mind the tentative state of knowledge about causes and effective treatment, we next survey the main perspectives on personality disorders.

Psychodynamic Perspectives: Object Relations Theory

Psychodynamic theorists typically locate the source of personality disorders in childhood experiences. A particularly influential approach is *object relations theory*. This branch of psychoanalytic theory deals with the nature and development of mental representations of the self and others (the objects) as well as with the interaction between the self and others. The theory concerns not only the content of the representations, such as whether the self is viewed as defective or other people as malicious, but also the fantasies and emotions attached to these representations and how these affect real-life interpersonal functioning. Certainly one's relationships are not helped by regarding others as malicious. Object relations theorists stress the impact of deprivation and abuse during childhood, resulting in mistrust of the child's earliest love object. Prominent contemporary object relations theorists include Heinz Kohut, a specialist in narcissism, and Otto Kernberg, who has written extensively about the borderline personality.

Kohut and the Narcissistic Personality

From a psychodynamic perspective, the narcissist's remarkable sense of self-importance, complete self-absorption, and fantasies of limitless success may mask a very fragile self-esteem. Constantly seeking attention and adulation, narcissistic personalities are, underneath, extremely sensitive to criticism and deeply fearful of failure. Sometimes they seek out others whom they can idealize because they are disappointed in themselves, but they generally do not allow anyone to be genuinely close to them. Their personal relationships are few and shallow. When people inevitably fall short of their unrealistic expectations, they become angry and rejecting.

Heinz Kohut (1971, 1977) has proposed that narcissism is the result of unsatisfying relations with a primary caretaker, usually one or both parents. His basic idea is that parents must respond to their children with respect, warmth, and empathy if the children are to acquire a normal sense of self-worth. But parents may further their own needs rather than being empathic with their children.

> A little girl comes home from school, eager to tell her mother about some great successes. But this mother, instead of listening with pride, deflects the conversation from the child to herself [and] begins to talk about her own successes which overshadow those of her little daughter (Kohut & Wolf, 1978, p. 418)

Children neglected in this way may develop into narcissistic personalities. They strive to bolster their sense of self through unending quests for love and approval from others, the love and approval they sought and did not receive from their parents.

According to Kohut's theory, children who fail to receive the kind of warm and affirming response to their accomplishments illustrated here are at risk for narcissistic personality disorder.

Kernberg's Object Relations Therapy for Borderline Personality Disorder

Otto Kernberg (1985) operates from the basic assumption that borderline personalities have weak egos and therefore inordinate difficulty tolerating the regression (probing of childhood conflicts) that occurs in psychoanalytic treatment. His opinion that such patients are inappropriate subjects for classical psychoanalysis is consistent with a long-term study conducted at the Menninger Clinic (M. H. Stone, 1987). The weak ego fears reexperiencing long-repressed desires and disappointments from childhood and the angry or sexual feelings that attend them. Kernberg's modified analytic treatment has the overall goal of strengthening the patient's ego. Therapy involves analysis of a principal defense of the borderline person, namely, splitting, or dichotomizing into all good or all bad and not integrating positive and negative aspects of a person into a whole. Splitting is attributed to an inability to form complex object representations that do not fit a simple good–bad dichotomy.

For example, suppose someone's mother was kind and well-meaning but not able to tolerate conflict and discuss it candidly. A complex object representation would include both the positive and negative features, but a borderline patient engaged in splitting would vacillate between viewing the mother as saintly and seeing her as phony and superficial.

Splitting protects the borderline personality's weak ego from intolerable anxiety by providing the veneer of certainty. But seeing the world or specific people in black-and-white terms ultimately takes a toll, for it makes regulating emotions extremely difficult. Splitting may have played a role in the anger and betrayal that Alice Siegel felt when one of the staff members whom she had idealized and taken into her confidence confronted her about violations of hospital rules. From this point of view, in trying to empathize with the patient, it is helpful to understand that these extreme reactions—"you are all good and take my side in any disputes no matter what I do" versus "you are all bad and go out of your way to oppose me just like the rest of them"—constitute Alice's genuine psychological experience. This does not mean that she is right about hospital staff, nor that she should never be confronted. It means that her divisive, erratic behavior and intense emotional reaction should not be seen simply as manipulation of others through ingratiation and intimidation to obtain more privileges.

Kernberg's treatment approach for borderline patients is more directive than that of most analysts. He gives patients concrete suggestions for behaving more adaptively and advocates hospitalizing patients whose behavior becomes dangerous to either themselves or others.

Biological Perspectives

Research on the possible biological bases of most DSM-IV personality disorders is just beginning. There has been some research on heritability, as well as research on biological factors in psychopathy.

Genetics of Personality Disorders

Although extensive research on the genetics of normal-range personality dimensions has been conducted, evidence on the genetics of most of the personality disorders is sparse (Nigg & Goldsmith, 1994). Vulnerability to schizotypal personality disorder appears to be at least in part heritable, and family studies suggest that the same may be true of borderline personality disorder. The evidence on borderline personality disorder is mixed, however. One conjecture about the equivocal findings is that current borderline criteria may be tapping at least two distinct phenomena, with one syndrome genetically related to mood disorders (Nigg & Goldsmith, 1994).

Central Nervous System Activity and Psychopathy

The nervous systems of psychopaths appear to differ from those of nonpsychopaths. Brain-wave activity in psychopaths has been studied using an electroencephalograph (EEG). Fluctuations in voltage are recorded, and these fluctuations are amplified so that they can be viewed. Most studies report rather high frequencies of EEG abnormalities in psychopaths (Syndulko, 1978). The most frequent form of abnormality is slow-wave activity, which is typical of infants and young children but not of normal adults. The slow waves are widespread throughout the brain. Also common are positive spikes. These spikes occur in the

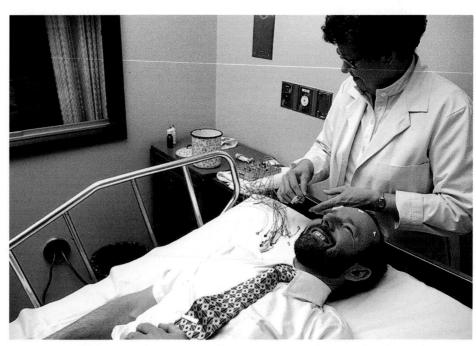

Electroencephalographic (EEG) recordings of brain-wave activity have revealed abnormalities in some psychopaths.

temporal area of the brain and consist of bursts of activity with frequencies of six to eight and fourteen to sixteen cycles per second (cps).

Not all psychopaths show EEG abnormalities, however, and it is unclear whether those who do differ in any other way from those who do not. Furthermore, the brain waves of psychopaths are not abnormally slow in all experimental contexts. For example, one study found the usual high levels of slow-wave activity when psychopaths were resting. Later, when they played an exciting video game, their brain waves were the same as those of normal subjects (Hare & Jutai, 1983). The high frequency of slow-wave activity may indicate a dysfunction in inhibitory mechanisms, which, in turn, lessens the psychopath's ability to learn to forestall actions that are likely to get him or her into trouble (Hare, 1970).

Underarousal and Impulsivity among Psychopaths

Psychopaths are often described as responding unemotionally when confronted with familiar or new situations that most people would find stressful or unpleasant (e.g., Cleckley, 1976). For example, if caught in a lie, a psychopath is calm and indifferent, whereas a normal person might show heightened arousal. In resting situations, psychopaths have lower than normal levels of skin conductance. Also, their skin conductance is less reactive when they are confronted with intense or aversive stimuli or when they anticipate an aversive stimulus (Harpur & Hare, 1990). A different picture emerges when heart rate is examined. The heart rate of psychopaths is similar to that of normal people under resting conditions, and their heart rate reactivity to neutral stimuli is also unremarkable. But in situations in which psychopaths anticipate a stressful stimulus, their hearts beat faster than those of normal people anticipating stress.

Taken together, these findings indicate that the psychopath is not simply underaroused, for measurements of skin conductance and heart rate are inconsistent. One interpretation focuses on the *pattern* of psychophysiological responses of psychopaths (Hare, 1978). The faster heartbeats may be a reflection of the psychopath's reducing sensory input and thus lowering cortical arousal. The increased heart rate of psychopaths anticipating an aversive stimulus indicates that they are tuning it out. Their skin conductance is then less reactive to an aversive stimulus, because they have been able effectively to ignore it. That is, anxiety (as reflected by skin conductance) does not increase among psychopaths after expected aversive stimulation because they have already dealt with it by screening it out. This interpretation of the physiological reactions of psychopaths has been directly confirmed in subsequent research (Ogloff & Wong, 1990).

Treatment from the Biological Perspective

Biological methods of treating psychopathy—electroconvulsive shock, drugs such as Dilantin, stimulants, and sedatives, and psychosurgery—appear ineffective for the most part. There is some evidence that large doses of antianxiety medications can reduce hostility in psychopaths (Kellner, 1982). And psychopaths who had attention-deficit disorder (see Chapter 14) as children might benefit from the drug Ritalin, which has had some positive effects with hyperactive youngsters (Stringer & Josef, 1983).

Various drugs have been used in the treatment of other personality disorders as well. In the case of borderline personality disorder, most researchers have tried antidepressant and antipsychotic medications. Results suggest that these medications can be helpful with respect to some aspects of borderline personality disorder. For example, the impulsive or aggressive behavior associated with the disorder has been treated with some success with lithium (Links, Steiner, Boiago, & Irwin, 1990), carbamazepine (Cowdry & Gardner, 1988), and fluoxetine (Prozac) (Cornelius, Soloff, Perel, & Ulrich, 1990). With drug therapies it is important to be alert to the possibility that the therapeutic drug might be abused by a borderline patient as part of a suicide attempt (Linehan & Kehrer, 1993).

Family Systems Perspectives

Because psychopathy so clearly reflects inadequate socialization, many investigators have understandably focused on a primary agent of socialization, the family. McCord and McCord (1964) concluded, on the basis of a review of the literature, that lack of affection and severe parental rejection contribute to causing psychopathic behavior. Several other studies have related psychopathic behavior to parents' inconsistencies in disciplining their children and in teaching them responsibility toward others (I. Bennett, 1960).

retrospective reports Recollections by an individual of past events.

Because these data on early rearing were gathered from **retrospective reports**, individual recollections of past events, they are of questionable value. When people are asked to recollect the early events in the life of someone who is now known to be a psychopath, their knowledge of that person's adult status may affect what they remember or report about childhood events. Deviant incidents are more likely to be recalled, whereas more typical or normal incidents that do not match with the person's current behavior may be overlooked.

A major study avoided this problem of retrospective data. A large number of individuals who as children had been seen at child-guidance clinics were followed up in adulthood. Very detailed clinical records had been kept on the children, including the type of problem that had brought them to the clinic and considerable information relating to the family (Robins, 1966). Ninety percent of an initial sample of 584 cases were located thirty years after their referral to the clinic, a remarkable feat in itself. In addition to the clinic cases, 100 control subjects, who had lived in the same geographic area served by the clinic but who had not been referred to it, were also interviewed in adulthood. Both inconsistent discipline and no discipline at all predicted psychopathic behavior in adulthood.

A more recent prospective study also found a link between childhood experiences and adult antisocial personality (Luntz & Widom, 1994). Children who were physically or sexually abused and/or neglected by their parents at some time between 1967 and 1971, as identified from criminal court records, were interviewed twenty years later. Also interviewed was a comparison group matched to the abuse and/or neglect victims for age, sex, race, and the hospital at which they were born. Of the abuse/neglect victims, about 14% met criteria for antisocial personality disorder according to the follow-up interviews, roughly double the rate found in the comparison group.

These *prospective* studies are more convincing than retrospective studies in suggesting that parental mistreatment may affect antisocial personality disorder. We must caution, however, that poor socialization has been implicated in the cause of several disorders, and that many individuals who come from what appear to be similarly disturbed social backgrounds do not become psychopaths or develop any other behavior disorders. This point is important. Adults may have no problems whatsoever in spite of the inconsistent and otherwise undesirable manner of their upbringing. Thus, although family experience may be significant in the development of psychopathic behavior, it is probably *not* the sole factor.

Behavioral Perspectives

As described in Chapter 3, behavioral perspectives tend to attribute abnormal behavior to features of the environment rather than to stable aspects of the individual, such as personality characteristics. Given this emphasis, how can behavioral theorists make sense of personality disorders, which entail stable, maladaptive personality traits evident across many different situations? One approach to this problem is to think of dysfunctional traits in terms of deficient capacities for learning. To illustrate this type of theorizing, we describe in the following section an explanation of certain features of psychopathy in terms of deficits in the ability to learn from punishments available in many natural environments.

Avoidance Learning, Punishment, and Psychopathy

By definition, psychopaths are unable to profit from experience. They do not try to avoid the negative consequences of social misbehavior. They are seldom anxious. It may be that psychopaths have few inhibitions about committing antisocial acts because they experience so little anxiety (Lykken, 1957). One source of support for this conclusion is that increasing their anxiety by injecting adrenalin helped psychopaths learn to shun punishment (Schachter & Latané, 1964).

Subsequent research on avoidance learning in psychopaths has qualified this conclusion, though. It is not so much that psychopaths suffer from a general deficit in the ability to learn, as that only certain punishments have meaning for them (Schmauk, 1970). For punishment to have an effect on psychopaths, it must be made very noticeable (Newman & Kosson, 1986). For example, psychopaths were just as successful as controls in learning from punishment in a discrimination learning task if there were no rewards for correct answers but only punishments for errors. Yet if errors were punished *and* correct answers rewarded, reducing the extent to which punishment experiences stood out against a background of the absence of consequences, psychopaths were as deficient in learning from punishment as in the earlier research (Newman & Kosson, 1986). Getting the psychopath's attention may be what is needed for a punishment to be effective. In situations in which both rewards and punishments are present, psychopaths focus on the rewards rather than balancing their attention between rewards and punishments (Scerbo et al., 1990).

Although the avoidance learning theory of psychopathy is promising, it is also incomplete (Gorenstein, 1991). It fails to account for some important aspects of psychopathy, such as gratuitous lying, insensitivity to others, and failure to follow a life plan.

Treatment from the Behavioral Perspective

Behavior therapists, in keeping with their attention to situations rather than to traits, have had little to say until recently about specific treatments for personality disorders. They have instead focused on the problems that, taken together, reflect a personality disorder. For example, a person diagnosed as having a paranoid personality is very sensitive to criticism. This sensitivity may be treated by systematic desensitization. The person's hostility when disagreeing with others both pushes the others away and provokes counterattacks from them. The behavior therapist may help the paranoid patient learn more adaptive ways of disagreeing with other people. Social-skills training in a support group might be considered a way to encourage avoidant personalities to be bolder in initiating contacts with other people. This technique may help them cope when their efforts to reach out do not succeed, as is bound to happen at times (Turkat & Maisto, 1985).

Dialectical Behavior Therapy for Borderline Personality Disorder.   One approach that combines the empathic qualities of person-centered therapy with behavioral problem solving has shown promise with borderline patients. Developed by Marsha Linehan (1987), **dialectical behavior therapy (DBT)** centers on the therapist's full acceptance of borderline personalities with all their contradictions and acting out. The therapist empathically validates the patients' (distorted) beliefs with a matter-of-fact attitude toward their suicidal and other dysfunc-

dialectical behavior therapy (DBT) A therapeutic approach to *borderline personality* disorder that combines empathy and acceptance with behavioral problem solving, social-skills training, and limit setting.

Marsha Linehan created dialectical behavior therapy, which combines cognitive behavior therapy with Zen and Rogerian notions of acceptance.

tional behavior. The behavioral aspect of the treatment involves helping patients learn to solve problems, that is, to acquire more effective and socially acceptable ways of handling their daily living problems and controlling their emotions. Patients also work on improving their interpersonal skills and controlling their anxieties. After many months of intensive treatment, limits are set on their behavior.

It is imperative to fully accept the patient as she or he is. The borderline personality is so extremely sensitive to rejection and criticism as well as so emotionally unstable that even gentle encouragement to behave or think differently leads to high levels of emotional arousal and subsequent misinterpretation of suggestions as a serious rebuke (Linehan, 1993a). The therapist who a moment earlier was revered, is now rejected. Thus, while observing limits—"I would be very sad if you killed yourself so I hope very much that you won't"—the therapist must convey to the borderline patient that he or she is fully accepted, even while threatening suicide and making everyone else's (including the therapist's!) life miserable. This complete acceptance of the patient does not mean that the DBT therapist *approves* of everything the patient is doing, only that the therapist accepts the situation for what it is.

In one study, patients were randomly assigned to dialectical behavior therapy or to treatment as usual, meaning any therapy available in the community (Seattle, Washington). At the end of one year of treatment, and again six and twelve months later, patients in the two groups were compared on a variety of measures (Linehan, Heard, & Armstrong, 1993). The findings immediately after treatment revealed that the group treated with DBT showed less intentional self-injurious behavior, including suicide attempts; had fewer dropouts from treatment; and had fewer inpatient hospital days. At the follow-ups, these improvements were maintained. Additionally, DBT patients had better work histories, reported less anger, and were judged as overall better adjusted than the comparison therapy patients.

Cognitive Perspectives

The cognitive view of personality disorders focuses on the thoughts and assumptions underlying a particular disorder (Beck, Freeman, et al., 1990). For example, among the dysfunctional beliefs said to be associated with antisocial personality disorder are justification (merely wanting something justifies any actions to attain it), personal infallibility (believing that one always makes good choices), the impotence of others (what others think doesn't matter), and low-impact consequences (negative outcomes may happen, and if they do, it will not matter). Borderline personality disorder is believed to reflect an approach to life based on one or more of the following three negative beliefs: the world is dangerous and malevolent; the person himself or herself is vulnerable and powerless; and the person is unacceptable to others.

In cognitive therapy for personality disorders, many of the same techniques found promising in the treatment of depression are applied (Beck, Freeman, et al., 1990) (see Chapter 10). For example, patients are encouraged to identify and test the validity of automatic thoughts associated with experiences of painful negative emotions.

The application of cognitive therapy to personality disorders differs in some ways from its application to mood or anxiety disorders. As in psychodynamic therapy, great emphasis is placed on the patient–therapist relationship itself, as opposed to plans for or results of between-session activities designed to change behavior or thinking. Transference reactions are even considered. The therapeutic relationship can present opportunities for personality-disordered patients to clarify and challenge their maladaptive beliefs about other people, but it can also undermine the effectiveness of therapy if not handled well. Therefore, cognitive therapists tend to be far more flexible when dealing with borderline patients and emphasize establishing trust with them as a crucial goal.

TO RECAP

Psychodynamic perspectives trace personality disorders to early childhood. The object relations view is that deprivation or abuse by parents in childhood caused the patient to see others (the generalized object) as malicious. For example, Kohut hypothesizes that narcissism is the result of a defensive reaction to underlying low self-esteem, which results from parents' failure to respond to the child with respect, warmth, and empathy. Kernberg attributes borderline personality disorder to a weak ego and overuse of the defense mechanism of splitting to protect the ego from excessive anxiety caused by intensely positive and negative feelings about the love object. Therapy from these object relations perspectives is more supportive and directive than classical psychoanalysis.

Biological research suggests that vulnerability to personality disorders may be at least in part hereditary. The evidence is strongest for schizotypal personality disorder. Psychopathy is often associated with EEG abnormalities, including slow-wave activity when at rest, suggesting dysfunction in inhibition. Heart rate and skin conductance reactivity to stress are consistent with a view that psychopaths screen out anticipated aversive stimuli and therefore do not become as anxious as do normal people when the stimuli occur. Biological treatments have generally been ineffective for psychopaths, though several medications show some utility in treating impulsive behavior associated with borderline personality disorder.

Family systems perspectives focus on poor parenting practices as sources of the stress that may translate vulnerability into actual personality disorders. Although much of the literature is based on possibly biased retrospective reports, sounder studies also suggest that abuse, extreme neglect, or inconsistent or inadequate discipline during childhood can predict increased risk of adult antisocial personality disorder. Behavioral perspectives on psychopathy converge with the biological research by indicating that psychopaths fail to learn to avoid unpleasant stimuli because they are insufficiently anxious and do not normally pay attention to punishments. A promising treatment from the behavioral perspective is dialectical behavior therapy (DBT). In treating borderline personality disorder, DBT teaches skills for emotion regulation and problem solving in a context of unconditional acceptance of the patient.

Cognitive therapists ascribe personality disorders to maladaptive beliefs about the self, others, and the environment. Relative to cognitive therapy of mood or anxiety disorders, treatment is longer term and makes greater use of the patient–therapist relationship as a vehicle for changing beliefs about the self and others.

The Case of Alice Siegel Revisited ◀

SOCIAL HISTORY

Alice was the older by two years of two girls born to a suburban middle-class family. Alice's parents divorced when she was six, and the girls lived with their mother. Financial problems were severe, as Alice's father provided little in the way of child support. He remarried soon afterward and was generally unavailable to his original family. When Alice was seven years old, her mother began working as a waitress in a neighborhood restaurant. Neighbors checked in on Alice and her younger sister, Jane, after school, but the children were left largely unattended until their mother returned home from work in the evening. Thus at a very early age, Alice was in a caretaker role for her sister. Over the next few years Alice took on several household responsibilities more appropriate for an adult or much older child, such as baby-sitting, regular meal preparation, and shopping.

Her mother married a man whom she had dated for about three months when Alice was thirteen years old. The man, Arthur Siegel, had a sixteen-year-old son named Michael, who joined the household on a somewhat sporadic basis. Michael had been moving back and forth between his mother's and father's homes since their divorce four years earlier. His mother had legal custody. But she was unable to manage his more abusive and aggressive behaviors, and so she frequently sent him to live with his father for several weeks or months. Because she still entertained the fantasy that her mother and father would remarry, Alice resented the intrusion of these new people into her house and was quite upset when her mother changed her and her children's last name to Siegel.

The first indications that Alice had any emotional problems occurred shortly after the marriage. Alice had been doing very well academically in the seventh grade when she started to skip class. Her grades fell, and she began spending time with peers who experimented with alcohol and street drugs. Alice became a frequent user of these drugs, even though after taking them she experienced some frightening symptoms, such as vivid visual hallucinations and strong feelings of paranoia. By the end of the eighth grade, Alice's grades were so poor and her school attendance so erratic that it was recommended that she be evaluated by a psychologist. Alice was found to be extremely intelligent yet quite disturbed, harboring considerable anger. Of even more concern was that Alice gave a number of bizarre and confused responses on projective tests (see Chapter 5). When people report what they see in the Rorschach inkblots, it is usually easy for the tester to share the client's perception. Several of Alice's responses just did not match any discernible features of the inkblots. This type of response is usually seen in serious disorders, such as schizophrenia.

Family therapy was recommended. Alice and her mother and sister saw a social worker at their community mental health center for several months. Mr. Siegel was distrustful of therapy and refused to attend. The social worker tried to teach Mrs. Siegel more effective methods of discipline and to help Alice see the importance of attending school on a regular basis, but the therapy ended with only marginal success. Although Mrs. Siegel was a highly motivated client and diligently followed the therapist's suggestions, Alice remained a reluctant participant in the therapy and was unwilling to open up.

One very serious problem that Alice had been experiencing was not even brought to light. She was being sexually abused by her stepbrother, Michael. The abuse had started soon after her mother's marriage to Mr. Siegel. Michael had told Alice that it was important for her to learn about sex, and, after having sexual intercourse with her, threatened that if she ever told anyone he would tell all her friends that she was a slut. This pattern of abuse continued whenever Michael was living with his father. Even though Alice found these encounters aversive, she felt unable to refuse participation or to let anyone know what was occurring. At the time Mr. and Mrs. Siegel divorced, when Alice was fifteen years old, these instances of sexual abuse were the extent of Alice's sexual experience. She was left feeling depressed and guilty.

When Alice began high school, she continued her association with the same peer group she had known in junior high. As a group, they regularly abused drugs. It was under the influence of drugs that Alice began to have her first experiences of feeling unreal and dissociated from her surroundings. She felt that she was ghostlike, that she was transparent and could pass through objects or people. Alice also began a pattern of promiscuous sexual activity within the peer group, sometimes involving sadomasochistic activities, especially when she was under the influence of drugs.

By the time Alice was sixteen years old, she found that she rarely, if ever, wanted to spend time alone. She was often bored and depressed, particularly if she had no plans for spending time with anyone else. One night while cruising in a car with friends, a siren and flashing lights appeared. The police stopped the car because it had been stolen by one of her friends. Street drugs were found in the car. Alice claimed that she did not know that the car was stolen. The judge who subsequently heard the case was provided with information concerning Alice's recent history at home and school. He was quite concerned with what appeared to be a progressive deterioration in Alice's academic and social functioning. Because previous outpatient treatment had failed, he recommended inpatient treatment as a means of helping her gain some control over her impulses and preventing future legal and psychological problems.

During this first hospitalization, Alice's emotional experiences seemed to intensify. She vacillated between outbursts of anger and feelings of emptiness and depression. She showed some signs of depression, such as lack of appetite and insomnia. She spent most of her time with one of the hospital's male patients. Alice idealized him and had fantasies of marrying him. When he was discharged from the hospital and severed the relationship, Alice had her first non-drug-induced episode of feeling unreal (derealization). She subsequently cut herself with a kitchen knife in order to feel real. She began making suicide threats over the telephone to the former patient, saying that if he did not take her back she would kill herself.

During this first hospitalization and shortly thereafter, several interventions (psychodynamic therapy, antidepressant medication, antipsychotic medication) were attempted with little success. Alice continued to exhibit the symptoms that had developed over the past several years, including drug abuse, promiscuity, depression, feelings of boredom, episodes of intense anger, suicide threats, derealization, and self-mutilation (cutting herself). Hospitalization was required several times, when Alice's threats or self-mutilation became particularly intense or frequent. These incidents were usually precipitated by stressful interpersonal events, such as breaking up with a boyfriend or discussing emotionally charged issues, for example, her past sexual abuse, in psychotherapy. Most of the hospital stays were relatively brief (two to four weeks), and Alice was able to leave after the precipitating crisis had been resolved.

During one hospitalization, when Alice was nineteen years old, she was introduced to Dr. Swenson, a psychologist, and she began individual behavior therapy with him.

CONCEPTUALIZATION AND TREATMENT

Together, Alice and Dr. Swenson identified several problem areas: (1) lack of direction or goals, (2) feelings of depression, (3) poor impulse control, and (4) excessive anger. Specific interventions were designed for each area. Concerning the first problem, Alice had done so poorly in her schoolwork and was so far behind that going back to high school was not realistic. Alice therefore decided to study for the examination for a graduate equivalency diploma, which would then allow her to pursue further education or job training. Alice was able to pass the exam after studying for approximately four months. This success enhanced her self-esteem, since she had never before maintained the self-discipline necessary to accomplish any but the most short-term goals.

To help Alice become more aware of the thoughts that might make her more vulnerable to depression, she was asked to keep a written record of her mood three times daily. Next to her mood, she wrote down what she was thinking, particularly those thoughts that involved predictions about how a given situation might turn out. Through this exercise, Alice came to realize that she often made predictions about events and subsequently felt sad and depressed.

In order to learn to restructure, or "talk back" to, these negative thoughts, Alice was given another exercise. When faced with an anxiety-provoking situation, Alice was to write up three different scenarios for the situation: (1) a worst-case scenario, in which everything that could go wrong did go wrong, (2) a best-case scenario, in which events turned out just as she wanted, and (3) a scenario that she believed, after appropriate reflection, was most likely to occur. The actual outcome was then compared with the three different predicted outcomes. More often than not, the actual events were markedly different from either the best- or worst-case predictions. With time, this exercise helped Alice control some of her more negative thoughts and replace them with more adaptive and realistic ways of thinking based on her own experiences.

For example, Alice had a history of difficulty in holding a job, partly because she assumed that people would reject her, and so she rejected them first. After obtaining a part-time job in a supermarket, but before starting work, Alice devised the following scenarios.

1. **Worst case.** I'll show up to work, and nobody will like me. Nobody will show me how to do my job, and they will probably make fun of me because I'm new there. I'll probably quit after one day.
2. **Best case.** This will be a job that I can finally do well. It will be the kind of work I have always wanted, and I'll be promoted quickly, and earn a high salary. Everyone at work will like me.
3. **Most likely.** I'm new at work, but everyone else was new at one time too. Some people may like me, and some may not—but that's the way it is with everyone. Some conflict with other people is inevitable. I can still do my job even if everyone does not like me. One bad day at work does not mean I have to quit.

Alice was instructed to rehearse the most likely scenario daily, especially when she felt like quitting. This helped her to keep the part-time job in the supermarket for one and one-half years, substantially longer than she had kept previous jobs.

Using these and other concrete techniques for behavioral and cognitive change, Alice made noticeable progress over the first few months of therapy with Dr. Swenson and showed a marked decline in her symptoms. She felt optimistic for the first time in a long while. However, this feeling soon deteriorated in the face of conflicts at home. For example, Alice did not want to help maintain the household, either financially or by doing work around the house. She insisted that it was her mother's responsibility to take care of her. She also wanted her boyfriends to be able to spend the night with her, which her mother would not allow. Alice's mother then asked her to move out of the house, but Alice refused. Instead, she threatened suicide, superficially cut her wrists with a razor blade, and had to be rehospitalized. Alice followed this same pattern over the next few years, making apparent gains in therapy for a month or so and then falling back in the face of interpersonal conflict.

When Alice was twenty-two years old, she decided to attend college on a full-time basis while living at home. Dr. Swenson was opposed to this move because Alice had not shown enough psychological stability to complete even a semester of college, let alone a degree program. Alice went to college anyway and soon became sexually involved with another student. As with previous relationships, Alice idealized this boyfriend and became quite dependent on him. After an argument in which Alice smashed plates and glasses on the floor, her boyfriend left her. Alice once again became suicidal and self-destructive. This episode led to the hospitalization described at the beginning of this chapter.

Alice's treatment team at the hospital noted that none of the interventions attempted with Alice had shown any lasting impact. Alice had a mediocre employment history and showed little evidence that she would be able to support herself independently in the foreseeable future. The team also feared that she might continue to deteriorate, perhaps winding up in a state hospital on a long-term basis. It was decided that Dr. Swenson needed help in managing Alice's symptoms, especially since they tended to worsen after dealing with difficult issues in therapy. She was referred to a day-treatment program at a local hospital. There she would have regular access to staff members who could provide therapy and support while she was living outside the hospital and possibly working part-time at an entry-level, unskilled job. The treatment team realized that it would require a great deal of work to convince Alice to accept these recommendations, since accepting them would be an admission that she was more seriously disturbed than she cared to admit. Even if she did follow the recommendations, Alice's prognosis was guarded.

DISCUSSION

Alice clearly showed many of the features of borderline personality disorder—unstable and intense relationships, self-damaging impulsivity, inability to control anger, recurrent suicidal threats or gestures, chronic feelings of boredom or emptiness, and desperate efforts to avoid abandonment by others.

Alice's therapists faced a common dilemma encountered with borderline patients. Should treatment be aimed at structural intrapsychic change or simply at better adaptation to the environment (Gordon & Beresin, 1983)? A retrospective study found that relatively few borderline patients complete the process of intensive psychotherapy, often terminating when an impasse in therapy occurs (Waldinger & Gunderson, 1984).

While Alice's treatment seemed largely unsuccessful, it should not be assumed that all borderlines are equally impaired. Indeed, there is a great deal of heterogeneity within the domain of borderline personality disorder. Many patients are able to continue in outpatient psychotherapy without ever being admitted to a hospital, and the outcome of therapy is not invariably negative. One of the major differences between hospitalized and nonhospitalized borderlines is that the latter group is involved in significantly fewer incidents of self-mutilation (Koenigsberg, 1982). Not all borderline patients are as self-destructive as Alice.

Nevertheless, borderline personalities present a daunting challenge to anyone who treats them. As with Alice, treatment is likely to span several years. In the long run, though, the outlook is relatively promising. Several long-term studies have painted a fairly consistent picture of what patients like Alice can expect. Patients hospitalized with borderline personality disorder in early adulthood often improve considerably in their thirties and thereafter (Stone, Hurt, & Stone, 1987). Approximately 8% to 10% of borderline patients kill themselves, however, with maximum risk during their twenties. Good long-term outcome seems to be associated with the patient's having a stable, supportive relationship with a single therapist or treatment staff during his or her twenties. Important as well is an emphasis on practical problem solving regarding relationship problems, rather than an attempt to explore psychodynamics stemming from childhood (M. H. Stone et al., 1987).

Visual Summary for Chapter 11:

Personality Disorders

Personality disorders are enduring, inflexible maladaptive patterns of behavior and subjective experience. They vary greatly and overlap, both with each other and with other categories of disorders. They are indicated on Axis II of DSM-IV and may be diagnosed along with Axis I disorders, such as anxiety disorders and mood disorders.

Issues in Diagnosis and Classification

Because they overlap with each other and co-occur with other disorders personality disorders are difficult to classify.

Can raters agree? ····▶	*Yes, especially via structured interviews.*
Are the criteria universal or culture specific? ····▶	*There is not enough research to be able to answer this question. DSM-IV specifies that the personality patterns should deviate from the expectations of the individual's culture, but the listed criteria are based mainly on research and clinical observations derived from Western cultures.*
Would dimensional ratings be more valid than yes/no diagnoses? ····▶	*Some personality disorder criteria (e.g., borderline) may represent extremes of normal personality dimensions present in varying degrees in everyone. Others (e.g., psychopathy) may be categorical, in that one has these characteristics or one does not. Lack of consensus on which dimensions to include has prevented the incorporation of dimensional rating schemes in the DSM so far.*
Are differences in prevalence between the sexes valid or a result of assessment biases? ····▶	*Dependent, borderline, and histrionic personality disorders are more prevalent for women, while antisocial personality and psychopathy are more prevalent in men. Evidence from studies using projective tests suggests that greater dependency among women may only reflect a traditionally masculine unwillingness to acknowledge dependency. Other differences between the sexes such as those in borderline and antisocial personality disorder may be valid reflections of differences between men and women as a result of different societal pressures and expectations.*

Clusters and Specific Disorders and their Basic Characteristics

Odd /Eccentric		Anxious /Fearful		Dramatic /Emotional	
Paranoid ····▶	suspicious, mistrustful	**Avoidant** ····▶	sensitive, easily embarrassed	**Histrionic** ····▶	theatrical, superficial
Schizoid ····▶	aloof, tend to be loners	**Dependent** ····▶	clingy, lack initiative, other-reliant	**Narcissistic** ····▶	grandiose, self-absorbed, unempathic
Schizotypal ····▶	socially isolated, prone to odd behavior and beliefs	**Obsessive-compulsive** ····▶	perfectionistic, indecisive	**Borderline** ····▶	unstable, impulsive
				Antisocial ····▶	remorseless, manipulative

Perspectives on Causes and Treatment

Perspective	Causes	Treatment
Psychodynamic ·▶	Disturbed mental representations of self and others, stemming from childhood ···▶ mistreatment (e.g., child ignored by self-absorbed parents sees the self as fragile and unacceptable and compensates by becoming narcissistic).	Uncover the origins of the disorder but also emphasize support and practical guidance.
Biological ····▶	Biological abnormalities, such as slow brain waves at rest, have been noted ····▶ among psychopaths. Genetically transmitted vulnerabilities also appear to influence the appearance of schizotypal and at least some forms of borderline personality disorder.	Medication such as Prozac for impulsive borderlines.
Family Systems ·▶	Poor parenting (e.g., inadequate discipline, abuse) can predict increased risk of ··▶ personality disorders, with prospective studies supporting a link to antisocial personality disorder.	Family therapy, or ideally prevention through better education for, and support of, parents.
Behavioral ····▶	Defective learning repertoires (e.g., psychopaths' failure to attend to ···▶ punishment).	Identify and repair specific skill deficits (e.g., dialectical behavior therapy for borderlines).
Cognitive ····▶	Biased negative beliefs regarding the self, others, and the environment (e.g., ····▶ psychopath: I am infallible; others are irrelevant; consequences do not matter).	Challenge dysfunctional beliefs gradually and with careful attention to patient–therapist relationship.

Chapter 12

Substance-Related Disorders

The Case of Gary Jackson

Gary Jackson was a thirty-three-year-old hardware store manager with a fifteen-year history of excessive use of alcohol. He usually had his first drink at 7:30 in the morning at home, before his wife was up. Whether or not he had a drink at home, he typically took two or three cans of beer to drink on the train on his way to work. During the day he drank about eight cans of beer at the rate of one every hour or so, depending on the workload. He attempted to hide his drinking from his customers and employees by using a strong breath freshener. In the evening, at home, he drank another five to eight cans of beer, falling asleep by 10 P.M. He followed this pattern of drinking seven days a week.

Over the years, as his drinking increased, Gary became quite tolerant of the effects of alcohol. He rarely appeared to be drunk to others, but he had begun to notice a few problems. If he did not drink through the day, he suffered trembling hands, perspiration, and nausea. Also, he regularly experienced sexual dysfunction, specifically, an inability to sustain an erection, which aggravated problems in his marriage. Finally, Gary suffered increasingly severe memory problems, which had begun to affect his work performance.

Gary visited his general practitioner for advice about the memory problem and sexual dysfunction, though he did not at first disclose his drinking habit. The physician noted Gary's bloodshot eyes and dilated facial capillaries and became suspicious. Confronted directly, Gary acknowledged his long-standing alcohol abuse. He told the physician that he had always been shy and had avoided social activities generally. When he had to be involved in them, he found the use of alcohol helped him to cope.

(Source: Mattick, R. P. (1992). Psychoactive substance dependence and associated states. In S. Schwartz (Ed.), *Case studies in abnormal psychology* (pp. 155–179). Brisbane, Australia: Wiley)

Introduction to Substance-Related Disorders

Almost all peoples, from prehistoric times forward, have discovered, as Gary did, some intoxicant that affects the central nervous system, relieving physical and mental discomfort or producing euphoria. Whatever the aftermath of taking such substances into the body, their initial effects are usually pleasing.

Many if not most of us use drugs on awakening (coffee or tea), throughout the day (cigarettes, certain soft drinks), as a way to relax (alcohol), and to reduce pain (aspirin). The widespread availability and frequent use of various drugs set the stage for the potential abuse of drugs, the topic of this chapter. Data on the frequency of use of several drugs, both legal and illegal, are given in Table 12.1. These figures do not represent the frequency of abuse, which is presented in the discussion of individual drugs, but simply provide an indication of how pervasive drug use is in the United States.

Many of those who abuse drugs use more than one at any given time (Wilkinson, Leigh, Cordingley, Martin, & Lei, 1987). This multiple usage, called **polysubstance abuse**, poses a serious health problem because the effects of some drugs when taken together interact to produce an especially strong reaction. For example, mixing barbiturates, powerful sedatives, with alcohol is a common means of suicide, intentional or accidental. Alcohol is believed to have contributed to deaths from heroin, because alcohol can dramatically reduce the amount of narcotic that makes a dose lethal. The pathological use of substances that affect the central nervous system falls into two categories: *substance abuse* and *substance de-*

polysubstance abuse The misuse of more than one drug at a time, such as drinking heavily and taking *cocaine.*

Polysubstance abuse involves the use of multiple drugs. Alcohol and nicotine are a frequent combination, although most people who smoke and drink in social situations do not become substance abusers.

Table 12.1 ▷ Use of Various Drugs in One Month

Substance	U.S. Population Reporting Use, %
Alcohol	50.9
Cigarettes	27.0
Marijuana	4.8
Smokeless tobacco	3.4
Psychotherapeutics[a]	1.5
Cocaine	0.9
Inhalants	0.6
Hallucinogens	0.3
Crack	0.2
PCP	0.2

Source: From National Institute on Drug Abuse (1991).

[a]Includes tranquilizers, sedatives, stimulants, and analgesics.

pendence. Together these constitute the major DSM-IV category substance-related disorders.

Substance Abuse and Substance Dependence

In **substance abuse** a person repeatedly uses a drug to such an extent that it creates significant problems, but there is no physiological dependence or pattern of compulsive use. **Substance dependence** is more severe abuse of a drug. It involves drug taking that is out of control, and it is often accompanied by a physiological dependence on the substance, made evident by tolerance and withdrawal symptoms. **Tolerance** is a physiological process whereby greater and greater amounts of an addictive drug are required to produce the same effect. **Withdrawal symptoms** are negative physiological and psychological reactions, such as tremors and dysphoria, experienced when a person suddenly stops taking an addictive drug.

Thus, both abuse and dependence involve maladaptive patterns of drug use, but they are not identical concepts. Someone might, for instance, abuse marijuana by smoking it from time to time and missing work as a result. To be considered dependent on marijuana, though, the person would need to show signs of being unable to control his or her use of it. For example, she or he might use marijuana daily, spending a good deal of time obtaining it or smoking it, might use more than intended on a given day, and might have failed to quit or decrease marijuana use despite trying to do so.

To meet criteria for a diagnosis of substance abuse the person must experience one of the following problems resulting from recurrent use of the drug.

▷ Failure to fulfill major obligations, for example, absences from work or neglect of children.

▷ Exposure to physical dangers, such as operating machinery or driving while intoxicated.

▷ Legal problems, such as arrests for disorderly conduct or traffic violations.

▷ Persistent social or interpersonal problems, such as arguments with spouse.

DSM-IV delineates the criteria for a diagnosis of substance *dependence* as the presence of at least three of the following:

▷ Tolerance develops, indicated by (a) the need for larger doses of the substance

substance abuse The use of a drug to such an extent that the person fails in important obligations, engages in dangerous behavior, or has persistent interpersonal or social problems, but where there is no physiological dependence.

substance dependence Severe abuse of a drug, often accompanied by a physiological dependence on it, often made evident by *tolerance* and *withdrawal* symptoms.

tolerance A physiological process in which greater and greater amounts of an addictive drug are required to produce the same effect.

withdrawal symptoms Negative physiological and psychological reactions evidenced when a person suddenly stops taking an addictive drug.

to produce the desired effect, or (b) a marked lessening of the effects of the drug if the usual amount is taken.

▷ Withdrawal symptoms develop when the person stops taking the substance or reduces the amount. The person may also use the substance to relieve or avoid withdrawal symptoms.

▷ The person uses more of the substance or uses it for a longer time than intended.

▷ The person recognizes excessive use of the substance. He or she may have tried to reduce it but has been unable to do so.

▷ Much of the person's time is spent in efforts to obtain the substance, use it, or recover from its effects.

▷ Substance use continues despite psychological or physical problems caused or made worse by the drug. For example, someone who smokes despite having emphysema would meet this criterion.

▷ Many activities (work, recreation, socializing) are given up or reduced in frequency because of the use of the substance.

Major substance-related disorders include cigarette smoking; the use of marijuana, sedatives, amphetamines, cocaine, and hallucinogens; and alcoholism. Each can take a terrible toll on those who use them and on their families and society in general in terms of accidents, injuries, days lost from work, and reduced longevity. Drug dependence can have different causes in different people, and it is notoriously difficult to treat. As we shall see, though, progress has been made in understanding how dependence develops and how it can be changed or prevented.

To Recap

Through the ages and within all societies, using substances that affect the central nervous system in the hope of feeling better or reducing pain has proven attractive. Unfortunately, abusing drugs is also a fairly common problem. Many drug abusers use more than one drug at any given time (polysubstance abuse), which can cause serious health problems. The DSM-IV designates substance abuse as the recurrent use of a drug leading to legal, social, or occupational problems. Substance dependence is severe drug abuse that the person cannot control and can involve physiological dependence as well.

Nicotine Dependence

Nicotine is the addicting agent in tobacco. Some idea of the addictive qualities of tobacco can be appreciated by considering how much people have historically been willing to sacrifice in order to maintain their supplies. In sixteenth-century England, for example, tobacco was exchanged for silver ounce for ounce.

nicotine The principal addicting agent of tobacco.

Prevalence and Consequences of Smoking

The threat to health posed by cigarette smoking has been documented convincingly by the surgeon general of the United States in a series of reports since 1964. Among the medical problems associated with, and almost certainly caused or exacerbated by, long-term cigarette smoking are lung cancer, emphysema, cancer of the larynx and of the esophagus, and a number of cardiovascular diseases. The most probable harmful components in the smoke from burning tobacco are nicotine, carbon monoxide, and tar. Tar consists primarily of certain hydrocarbons, many of which are known carcinogens (Jaffe, 1985). The socioeconomic cost is considerable: each year smokers compile over 80 million extra days of lost work and 145 million extra days of disability.

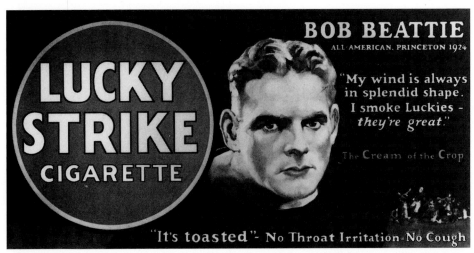

Prior to the Surgeon General's report of 1964, advertisements associating cigarette smoking with physical well-being were much more direct than would currently be credible.

Over a period of five to ten years following cessation of smoking, health risks are reduced dramatically to levels only slightly above those of nonsmokers, although the destruction of lung tissue is not reversible (Jaffe, 1985). For cigarette smokers who switch to smoking pipes, the mortality risks remain higher than for those who stop smoking altogether (Ben-Shlomo, Smith, Shipley, & Marmot, 1994).

Reports from the surgeon general (U.S. Department of Health and Human Services, 1989) and the Centers for Disease Control (Cimons, 1992) have drawn several conclusions about trends in cigarette smoking since its health risks first became well known. The prevalence of habitual smoking among American adults decreased from a little over 40% in 1965 to about 25% in 1990—almost half of all living adults who ever smoked have quit. College graduates show the lowest prevalence rates, while prevalence remains high among Native Americans, African-Americans, and blue-collar workers. However, some of the sharpest de-

This 1926 photograph predates recent declines in the prevalence of cigarette smoking in the United States.

clines have occurred among African-American men since 1965. Prevalence has declined much less among women of all races than among men. In Asia and Eastern Europe, however, cigarette smoking is much more prevalent than in the United States and shows no signs of diminishing (Levin, 1994).

The reports also note that cigarette smoking is responsible in some way for one of every six deaths in the United States, killing about one thousand people each day. It remains the single biggest preventable cause of premature death. The risks are significantly less for cigar and pipe smokers, because they seldom inhale the smoke into their lungs, but cancers of the mouth and lips are enhanced by such consumption.

Secondhand Smoke

The health hazards of smoking are not restricted to smokers themselves (W. Bennett, 1980). The smoke coming from the burning end of a cigarette, so-called secondhand smoke, contains higher concentrations of ammonia, carbon monoxide, nicotine, and tar than does the smoke actually inhaled by the smoker. Nonsmokers can suffer lung damage, possibly permanent, from extended exposure to cigarette smoke. For example, women who were never smokers themselves showed a 30% greater risk of lung cancer if their husbands smoked than if not, and the excess risk was greater the more their husbands smoked (Fontham et al., 1994). Findings are not significant in every single study, but a review of the entire body of research led the Environmental Protection Agency to classify environmental tobacco smoke as a cause of lung cancer in humans, responsible for an estimated three thousand lung cancer deaths per year in nonsmokers in the United States (U.S. Environmental Protection Agency, 1992).

Babies of women who smoke during pregnancy are more likely to be born prematurely, to have low birth weights, and to have birth defects. Children whose mothers smoked during pregnancy show lower lung function even in childhood (ages eight to twelve), regardless of whether the mother continued to smoke at the time of the study (Cunningham, Dockery, & Speizer, 1994). In recent years, many local governments have passed ordinances regulating cigarette smoking in public places and work settings.

Anti-smoking campaigns have made use of public-service announcements in addition to interventions targeted at the individual smoker.

To Recap

Long-term cigarette smoking is associated with, and probably causes, many medical problems, including lung cancer, emphysema, and cardiovascular diseases. Quitting smoking causes a decline in health risks. Since the 1964 surgeon general's report on adverse health consequences of smoking, the prevalence of regular smoking has declined among American adults from more than 40% to about 25%. Cigarette smoking is a massive public health problem, killing about one thousand people per day in the United States. Antismoking legislation, including workplace and restaurant restrictions, appears to have gained momentum from research that documents the negative health consequences for people other than the smoker. These include greater risk of low birth weight or birth defects among the babies of women who smoke during pregnancy, as well as lung damage to those exposed to secondhand smoke.

▶ *Marijuana*

Marijuana consists of the dried and crushed leaves and flowering tops of the hemp plant, *Cannabis sativa*. It is most often smoked, but it may be chewed, prepared as a tea, or eaten in baked goods. It has been known for thousands of years, but until 1920 was little seen in the United States. With the passage of the Eighteenth Amendment prohibiting the sale of alcohol, some people began to

marijuana A drug derived from the dried and ground leaves and stems of the female hemp plant, *Cannabis sativa*.

smoke marijuana brought across the border from Mexico. Unfavorable reports in the press attributing crimes to marijuana use led to the enactment of a federal law against the sale of the drug in 1937. It is today illegal in most countries (Goodwin & Guze, 1984).

Prevalence and Effects of Marijuana Use

Periodically the National Institute on Drug Abuse publishes the results of surveys on drug use. These studies suggest that the use of marijuana peaked in 1979 and declined from 1979 to 1992. For example, the following percentages of respondents between the ages of twelve and seventeen reported having used marijuana at least once: 14% in 1972, 31% in 1979, 24% in 1985, and 13% in 1991 (Kozel & Adams, 1986; *Marijuana Research Findings*, 1980; National Institute on Drug Abuse, 1979, 1982, 1991). Similar trends were evident in older age groups as well.

One possible source of the decline in marijuana use was an increase in the perception that it is harmful. Among high school seniors, daily use of marijuana peaked at 11% in 1978. At that time only 12% of seniors believed there was risk associated with occasional use and 35% believed there was risk with regular use. By 1985, daily use had plummeted to 5%; 25% of high school seniors then believed marijuana was harmful if used occasionally, and 70% believed that regular use was harmful (Kozel & Adams, 1986). In 1993 and 1994, both of these trends reversed. Marijuana use is again increasing among high school students, whereas the belief that marijuana harms health is declining (Drug use and problems continue to rise, 1994).

Effects of Marijuana

A great deal of research has been conducted on marijuana. Though marijuana is often perceived as benign, it is not without risks.

Psychological Effects of Marijuana. The intoxicating effects of marijuana, as of most drugs, depend in part on potency and size of the dose. The major active chemical in marijuana is delta-9-tetrahydrocannabinol (THC). Since 1974 the marijuana available in the United States has been very potent, as much as ten times stronger than that sold earlier. Smokers of marijuana find it makes them feel relaxed and sociable. Large doses have been reported to bring rapid shifts in emotion, to dull attention, fragment thoughts, and impair memory. Extremely heavy doses have sometimes been found to induce hallucinations and other effects similar to those of LSD, including extreme panic. People who have had psychological problems before using any psychoactive drug, a drug that has major effects on thought or emotion, are generally believed to be at highest risk for negative reactions.

Marijuana interferes with a wide range of cognitive functions. A number of tests—digit-symbol substitution (substituting symbols for numbers), reaction time tests, repeating series of digits forward and backward, arithmetic calculations, reading comprehension and speech tests—all revealed intellectual impairment (*Marijuana Research Findings*, 1980). Of special significance are loss of short-term memory and state-dependent learning—the inability, when straight, to recall material learned when high.

Being high on marijuana also diminishes complex psychomotor skills necessary for driving. Highway fatality and driver arrest figures indicate that marijuana plays a role in a significant proportion of accidents and arrests. Marijuana has similarly been found to impair manipulation of flight simulators. Some performance decrements measurable after smoking one or two joints can persist for up to eight hours after a person believes that he or she is no longer high, creating the danger that people will attempt to drive or to fly when they are not functioning adequately.

Somatic Effects of Marijuana.   In the short term, marijuana makes the eyes bloodshot and itchy, dries the mouth and throat, increases appetite, and may raise blood pressure somewhat. There is no evidence that smoking marijuana has untoward effects on the normal heart. The drug apparently does pose a danger to people with already abnormal heart function because it elevates heart rate, sometimes dramatically.

Long-term use of marijuana may seriously impair lung structure and function. Most marijuana smokers inhale more deeply and retain smoke in their lungs for much longer periods than do cigarette smokers. Also, since marijuana cigarettes are generally homemade, they are not filtered. Thus the smoke contains significantly higher levels of tar, which, like the tar from conventional cigarettes, has been found to cause cancer when applied to the skin of laboratory animals. Moreover, marijuana smoke contains 70% more benzopyrene, another known cancer-causing agent, and 50% more carcinogenic polyaromatic hydrocarbons than does the smoke from regular cigarettes (S. Cohen, 1981).

Is marijuana addictive? It indeed may be. Contrary to early impressions of the drug, heavy use of marijuana can lead to tolerance. The development of tolerance began to be suspected when U.S. service personnel returned from Vietnam accustomed to concentrations of THC that would be toxic to domestic users. Controlled observations have confirmed that habitual use of marijuana does produce tolerance (e.g., Compton, Dewey, & Martin, 1990). Whether long-term users suffer physical withdrawal when accustomed amounts of marijuana are not available is less clear.

To Recap

Marijuana use declined from the late 1970s to the early 1990s, possibly as a result of more information on its associated risks. Since 1992, use has increased. Although marijuana smokers find it makes them feel relaxed and sociable, it can impair, at least temporarily, short-term memory and other intellectual functions, as well as psychomotor skills needed for driving. Marijuana also elevates heart rate and is dangerous for those with existing heart problems. Chronic marijuana use may lead to tolerance.

Sedatives

The major **sedatives**, or downers, slow the activities of the body and reduce its responsiveness. In this group of drugs are the organic narcotics—opium and its derivatives morphine, heroin, and codeine—and the synthetic barbiturates, such as Seconal.

Narcotics

Narcotics represent a group of addictive sedatives that in moderate doses relieve pain and induce sleep. Foremost of the narcotics is **opium**, originally the principal drug of illegal international traffic and known to the people of the Sumerian civilization as far back as 7000 B.C. Opium is a mixture of about eighteen alkaloids, but until 1806 people had no knowledge of these substances to which so many natural drugs owe their potency.

In that year the alkaloid **morphine**, named after Morpheus, the Greek god of dreams, was separated from raw opium. This bitter-tasting powder proved to be a powerful sedative and pain reliever. In the middle of the nineteenth century, when the hypodermic needle was introduced in the United States, morphine began to be injected directly into the veins to relieve pain. Many soldiers wounded

sedatives Drugs that slow bodily activities, especially those of the central nervous system; used to reduce pain and tension and to induce relaxation and sleep.

narcotics Addictive *sedative* drugs, for example, *morphine* and *heroin*, that in moderate doses relieve pain and induce sleep.

opium The dried milky juice obtained from the immature fruit of the opium poppy. This addictive *narcotic* produces euphoria and drowsiness and reduces pain.

morphine An addictive narcotic alkaloid extracted from *opium*, used primarily as an analgesic and as a *sedative*.

in battle and those suffering from dysentery during the Civil War were treated with morphine and returned home addicted to the drug.

Concerned about administering a drug that could disturb the later lives of patients, scientists began studying morphine. In 1874 they found that morphine could be converted into another powerful pain-relieving drug, which they named **heroin**. Initially, heroin was used as a cure for morphine addiction and substituted for morphine in cough syrups and other patent medicines. So many maladies were treated with heroin that it came to be known as G.O.M., or "God's own medicine" (Brecher et al., 1972). Heroin proved to be even more addictive and more potent than morphine, however, acting more quickly and with greater intensity.

heroin An extremely addictive *narcotic* drug derived from *morphine*.

It is difficult to gather accurate data, but expert opinion is that there are more than a million heroin addicts in the United States. Most of these began using heroin in the 1960s and have continued to use it (Kozel & Adams, 1986). Among young adults aged eighteen to twenty-five, the frequency of heroin addiction has declined steadily from 4.6% in 1972 to 1.2% in 1982 and 0.6% in 1990 (HHS News, 1990).

Opium and its derivatives morphine and heroin produce euphoria, drowsiness, reverie, and sometimes a lack of coordination. Heroin has an additional initial effect, the rush, a feeling of warm, suffusing ecstasy immediately following an intravenous injection. The addict has great self-confidence for four to six hours, but then experiences letdown, bordering on stupor. Because these drugs are central nervous system depressants, they relieve pain. All three clearly induce dependence, for users show both increased tolerance of the drugs and withdrawal symptoms when they are unable to obtain another dose.

Even more serious than the physical effects are the social consequences of narcotic addiction. The drug and obtaining it become the center of the abuser's existence, governing all activities and social relationships. Since narcotics are illegal, addicts must deal with the underworld to maintain their habits. The correlation between addiction and criminal activities is high. In recent years, an additional problem associated with intravenous drug use is exposure, through the sharing of needles, to the human immunodeficiency virus (HIV), which causes AIDS (see Chapter 16).

Withdrawal Symptoms.   Reactions to not having a dose of heroin may begin within eight hours of the last injection. During the next few hours the individual typically has muscle pain, sneezes, sweats, becomes tearful, and yawns a great deal; the symptoms resemble those of influenza. Within thirty-six hours the withdrawal symptoms become more severe. There may be uncontrollable muscle twitching, cramps, chills alternating with excessive flushing and sweating, and a rise in heart rate and blood pressure. The addict vomits, is unable to sleep, and has diarrhea. These symptoms typically persist for about seventy-two hours and then diminish gradually over a five- to ten-day period.

Barbiturates

barbiturates A class of synthetic *sedative* drugs that are addictive and in large doses can cause death by almost completely relaxing the diaphragm.

Barbiturates were first synthesized as aids for sleeping and relaxation in 1903. Although there are hundreds of derivatives of barbituric acid, two types are usually distinguished—long-acting barbiturates for prolonged sedation, and short-acting barbiturates for prompt sedation and sleep. The short-acting drugs are usually viewed as addicting. Initially, the drugs were prescribed frequently. In the 1940s, however, they were discovered to be addicting, and physicians began to prescribe them less often.

Barbiturates (pentobarbital, secobarbital, and amobarbital) relax the muscles and in small doses produce a mildly euphoric state. Methaqualone, a sedative sold under the trade names Quaalude and Sopor, is similar in effect to barbiturates and has become a popular street drug. Besides being addictive, it poses other dangers—internal bleeding, coma, and even death from overdose. With excessive doses of barbiturates, speech becomes slurred and gait unsteady. Impairment of judgment, concentration, and ability to work may be extreme. The user loses emotional control and may become irritable and combative before falling into a deep sleep. Very large doses can be fatal, because the diaphragm muscles relax to such an extent that the individual suffocates. As discussed in Chapter 10, barbiturates are frequently chosen as a means of suicide. But many users accidentally kill themselves by drinking alcohol, which magnifies the depressant effects of barbiturates. With continued excessive use the brain can become damaged and personality deteriorates.

Prolonged use of barbiturates induces tolerance. Withdrawal reactions after abrupt termination are particularly severe and long lasting and can even cause sudden death. The delirium, convulsions, and other symptoms resemble those following abrupt withdrawal of alcohol.

Three types of abusers can be distinguished. The first group fits the stereotype of the illicit drug abuser: adolescents and young adults, usually male and often antisocial, who use the drugs to alter their moods and consciousness, sometimes mixing them with other drugs. The second group consists of middle-aged, middle-class individuals who begin their use of sedatives under a physician's orders, to alleviate sleeplessness and anxiety, and then come to use larger and larger doses until they are addicted. The third group consists of health professionals, physicians and nurses who have easy access to these drugs and often use them to self-medicate for anxiety-related problems (Liskow, 1982; Shader, Caine, & Meyer, 1975).

To Recap

Sedatives relax people and slow physiological activity. Sedatives include narcotics, such as opium, morphine, and heroin. These drugs are useful painkillers, but they are highly addicting. Barbiturates can be safe and effective when prescribed and taken properly. However, they can be dependency inducing and are especially dangerous when taken in conjunction with alcohol.

Amphetamines

Amphetamines, such as Benzedrine, Dexedrine, and Methedrine, are stimulants, or uppers, which act on the brain and the sympathetic nervous system to increase alertness and motor activity. They are taken orally or intravenously and can be addicting. Wakefulness is heightened, intestinal functions are inhibited, and appetite is reduced—hence their use in dieting. The heart rate quickens and blood vessels in the skin and mucous membranes constrict. The individual becomes alert, euphoric, and more outgoing and is possessed with seemingly boundless energy and self-confidence. Larger doses can make a person nervous, agitated, and confused, subjecting him or her to palpitations, headaches, dizziness, and sleeplessness. Sometimes the high-level user becomes so suspicious and hostile that he or she can be dangerous to others. Large doses taken over a period of time can cause brain damage or induce a state quite similar to paranoid schizophrenia, including its delusions. This state can persist beyond the time that the drug is present in the body.

Tolerance develops rapidly so that a large amount of the drug is required to produce the stimulating effect. As tolerance increases, the user may stop taking pills and inject Methedrine, the strongest of the amphetamines, directly into the

amphetamines A group of stimulating drugs that produce heightened levels of energy and, in large doses, nervousness, sleeplessness, and paranoid *delusions*.

veins. So-called speed freaks give themselves repeated injections of the drug and maintain intense and euphoric activity for a few days, without eating or sleeping, after which they are exhausted and depressed and sleep for several days. Then the cycle starts again. After several repetitions of this pattern, the physical and social functioning of the individual deteriorates considerably. Behavior is erratic and hostile, and the speed freak may become a danger to self and to others. Fortunately, the use of stimulants has been declining over the past several years (National Institute on Drug Abuse, 1991), although the abuse of a smokable form of methamphetamine (ice) has increased. (Focus Box 12.1 discusses a more prevalent and less risky stimulant—caffeine.)

Cocaine

cocaine A pain-reducing, stimulating, and addictive drug, obtained from coca leaves, which increases mental powers, produces euphoria, heightens sexual desire, and in large doses causes *paranoia* and *hallucinations*.

The Spanish conquistadores introduced coca leaves to Europe. Whereas the Indians of the Andean uplands, to which the coca shrubs are native, chew the leaves, the Europeans chose to brew them instead in beverages. The alkaloid **cocaine** was extracted from the leaves of the coca plant in 1844 and has been used since then as a local anesthetic.

An early product that used coca leaves in its manufacture was Coca-Cola, concocted by an Atlanta druggist in 1886. For the next twenty years Coke was the real thing, but in 1906 the Pure Food and Drugs Act was passed and the manufacturer switched to coca leaves from which the cocaine had been removed.

In addition to its pain-reducing effects, cocaine acts rapidly on the cortex of the brain, heightening sensory awareness and inducing a thirty-minute state of euphoria. Sexual desire is accentuated, and feelings of self-confidence, well-being, and high energy pervade the user's consciousness. An overdose may bring on chills, nausea, and insomnia, as well as paranoia and terrifying hallucinations of insects crawling beneath the skin. Chronic use often leads to changes in personality that include heightened irritability, impaired social relationships, paranoid thinking, and disturbances in eating and sleeping ("Scientific Perspectives", 1987). As they take larger and larger doses of the purer forms of cocaine now available, an increasing number of users are rushed to emergency rooms and may die of overdoses, typically from heart attacks (Kozel, Crider, & Adams, 1982). Because of its strong vasoconstricting properties, cocaine may pose special dangers in pregnancy by causing the blood supply to the developing fetus to be compromised.

Cocaine can be sniffed (snorted), smoked in pipes or cigarettes, swallowed, or even injected into the veins like heroin. Some heroin addicts mix the two drugs in combination. In the 1970s users in this country adopted a practice similar to that used in parts of South America for enhancing the effects of the drug. To separate, or free, the most potent component of cocaine, they heated cocaine with ether. When purified by this chemical process, the cocaine base—or freebase—is extremely powerful. It is usually smoked in a water pipe or sprinkled on a tobacco or marijuana cigarette. It is rapidly absorbed into the lungs and carried to the brain in a few seconds, inducing an intense, two-minute high, followed by restlessness and discomfort. Some freebase smokers go on marathon binges lasting up to four days (Goodwin & Guze, 1984). The freebasing process is hazardous, however, because ether is flammable.

In the mid-1980s a new form of freebase, called crack, appeared. Because it was available in small, relatively inexpensive doses, younger and less-affluent buyers began to experiment with the drug and to become addicted (Kozel & Adams, 1986).

Cocaine use increased more than 260% between 1974 and 1985 (Kozel &

Our Tastiest Addiction—Caffeine

What may be the world's most popular drug is seldom viewed as a drug at all, and yet it has strong effects, produces tolerance in people, and even subjects habitual users to withdrawal (Hughes, Gust, Skoog, Keenan, & Fenwick, 1991). Users and nonusers alike joke about it, and most readers of this book have probably had some this very day. We are, of course, referring to caffeine, a substance found in coffee, tea, cocoa, candies, cola and other soft drinks, some cold remedies, and some diet pills.

Two cups of coffee, containing between 150 and 300 milligrams of caffeine, affect most people within half an hour. Metabolism, body temperature, and blood pressure increase. Urine production goes up, as most of us will attest. There may be hand tremors, appetite can diminish, and, most familiar of all, sleepiness is warded off. Panic disorder can be exacerbated by caffeine, not surprising in light of the heightened sympathetic nervous system arousal occasioned by the drug. Extremely large doses of caffeine can cause headaches, diarrhea, nervousness, severe agitation, and even convulsions and death. Death, though, is virtually impossible unless the individual grossly overuses tablets that contain caffeine, because caffeine is excreted by the kidneys without any appreciable accumulation.

It has long been recognized that drinkers of very large amounts of coffee daily can experience withdrawal symptoms when consumption ceases. Recent research indicates that people who drink as few as two cups of coffee a day can suffer from clinically significant headaches, fatigue, and anxiety if caffeine is withdrawn from their daily diet (Silverman, Evans, Strain, & Griffiths, 1992), and these symptoms can markedly interfere with social and occupational functioning. These findings are disturbing because more than three-quarters of Americans consume over two cups of coffee a day (Roan, 1992).

Although parents usually deny their children access

Coffee drinking is extremely common, and caffeine is addictive; even low doses can prompt withdrawal symptoms once the person stops ingesting caffeine.

to coffee and tea, often they do allow them to imbibe caffeine-laden cola drinks, hot chocolate, and cocoa, and to eat chocolate candy and coffee and chocolate ice cream. Thus our addiction to caffeine can begin to develop as early as six months of age, the form of it changing as we move from childhood to adulthood.

Adams, 1986), but has dramatically decreased since then (Golub & Johnson, 1994). Cocaine can take a tenacious hold of people. For example, a cocaine-addicted executive sustained for months a pattern of freebasing all weekend, then reducing or eliminating use throughout the week in order to function acceptably at work (Washton, Stone, & Hendrickson, 1988). However, her work performance began to suffer, as she would miss or arrive late for work after staying up all night freebasing, and she refused important business trips for fear of being without cocaine or being caught transporting it.

Developing fetuses are markedly and negatively affected in the womb by the mother's use of cocaine during pregnancy, and many babies are born addicted to the drug. The mass media frequently report on the social, psychological, economic, and legal damage to which people will subject themselves in order to continue taking the drug.

To Recap

Amphetamines and cocaine are stimulant drugs. Cocaine use has declined since the mid-1980s, but remains a major social problem. For instance, many babies are born addicted to cocaine as a result of their mothers' use of cocaine during pregnancy.

▶ *LSD and Other Hallucinogens*

First synthesized in 1938, the effects of *d*-lysergic acid diethylamide, or **LSD**, were not known until Albert Hofmann, the Swiss chemist who manufactured it, accidentally ingested some in 1943.

> At home, I lay down and sank into a not unpleasant delirium, which was characterized by extremely exciting fantasies. In a semiconscious state with my eyes closed . . . fantastic visions of extraordinary realness and with an intense kaleidoscopic play of colors assaulted me. (cited in Cashman, 1966, p. 31)

Reasoning that he might have unknowingly ingested some LSD and that this was the cause of his unusual experience, Hofmann deliberately took a dose and confirmed his hypothesis. Eventually the term *psychedelic*, from the Greek words for "soul" and "to make manifest," was applied to emphasize the subjectively experienced expansion of consciousness reported by users of LSD. LSD and similar drugs are also called **hallucinogens**, a word that describes one of the main effects of these drugs, producing hallucinations.

Two other hallucinogens are mescaline and psilocybin. In 1896 **mescaline**, an alkaloid and the active ingredient of peyote, was isolated from small growths of the top of the peyote cactus. The drug has been used for centuries in the religious rites of Native American peoples living in the Southwest and in northern Mexico. **Psilocybin** is a crystalline powder that Hofmann isolated from the mushroom *Psilocybe mexicana* in 1958.

The use of LSD and other hallucinogens peaked in the 1960s. By the 1980s and into the 1990s only 1% or 2% of people could be classified as regular users (National Institute on Drug Abuse, 1983; *HHS News*, 1990). There is no evidence of withdrawal symptoms during abstinence and only equivocal evidence of tolerance (Jaffe, 1985).

A newer hallucinogen, **Ecstasy**, refers to two very similar synthetic compounds. MDA (methylenedioxyamphetamine) and MDMA (methylenedioxymethamphetamine) are chemically similar to mescaline and the amphetamines. MDA is the psychoactive agent in nutmeg. Although first synthesized in 1910, Ecstasy's psychedelic properties came to the attention of the drug-using, consciousness-expanding generation of the 1960s. It was made illegal in 1985, but is popular on some college campuses. Users report that the drug enhances intimacy and insight, elevates mood, and promotes aesthetic awareness. However, it can also cause muscle tension, rapid eye movements, nausea, faintness, chills or sweating, and anxiety, depression, and confusion. A number of deaths have been reported from accidental overdose (Climko, Roehrich, Sweeney, & Al-Razi, 1987).

LSD   A drug derived from lysergic acid, *d*-lysergic acid diethylamide, synthesized in 1938 and discovered to be a *hallucinogen* in 1943. It is the principal constituent of the alkaloids of ergot, a grain fungus that in earlier centuries brought on epidemics of spasmodic ergotism, a nervous disorder sometimes marked by *psychotic* symptoms.

hallucinogens   Drugs or chemicals whose effects include *hallucinations*. Hallucinogenic drugs are often called psychedelic.

mescaline   A *hallucinogen* that is the active ingredient of peyote.

psilocybin   A psychedelic drug extracted from the mushroom *Psilocybe mexicana*.

Ecstasy   A relatively new *hallucinogen* that is chemically similar to *mescaline* and the *amphetamines*.

Effects of Hallucinogens

The effects of LSD and mescaline usually last about twelve hours and those of psilocybin about six hours. Many psychological effects of hallucinogens are possible. One's sense of time may be altered so that time seems to pass very slowly. A frightening loss of the distinction between oneself and the environment may occur. The drug user may experience rapidly shifting moods, sometimes intense anxiety, and intrusive thoughts. After a few hours, some may feel a pleasant sense of detachment from mundane concerns and a heightened sensitivity to feelings and creative ideas (Jaffe, 1985).

The effects of the hallucinogens, like those of other kinds of drugs, depend on a number of psychological variables in addition to the dose itself. A person's frame of mind—attitudes, motives, and expectations—can affect his or her reaction to hallucinogens. Among the most prominent dangers of taking LSD is the bad trip: some aspect of experience after taking the drug creates anxiety, which escalates and can sometimes develop into a full-blown panic attack. Often the specific fear is of going crazy. These panics are usually short-lived and subside as the drug is metabolized. A minority of people, however, go into a psychotic state that can require hospitalization and extended treatment (see Focus Box 12.2).

To Recap

Hallucinogens, such as LSD, mescaline, psilocybin, and Ecstasy, can produce hallucinations as well as a subjective sense of expanded consciousness, slowed passage of time, and a loss of boundaries between the sense of self and the environment. Dangers include a panic reaction to the unusual sensory experience, and even the development of a psychotic episode.

◢ Alcohol

Written reports of the use of wine, beer, and other alcoholic beverages date back to 3000 B.C. About 800 B.C. the distillation process was applied to fermented beverages, making possible the preparation of the highly potent liquors that are available today. Alcohol consumption was on the rise in the United States and in most other countries until about ten years ago (Hasin, Grant, Harford, Hilton, & Endicott, 1990). In 1940, for example, 30% of the U.S. population were drinkers. By 1970, 68% of the population drank (Caddy, 1983). In 1984, 70% of the U.S. population aged eighteen and over had consumed alcohol within the past year, but this figure had declined to 65% by 1990 (Midanik & Clark, 1994).

Similarly, the proportion of U.S. adults drinking at least once a week for the past year declined (from 36% to 29% from 1984 to 1990), as did the proportion of people having at least five drinks on a single occasion at least weekly (from 6% to 4%) (Midanik & Clark, 1994). Alcohol sales data suggest that consumption declined about 11% during the 1980s (Williams, Stinson, Clem, & Noble, 1992). Some of the decline in alcohol use is attributable to aging; that is, young people are more likely to drink alcohol, and the U.S. population is aging (see Chapter 15). However, within a given age range decline in use is still evident, so aging does not provide a complete explanation (Midanik & Clark, 1994). Changing attitudes toward alcohol are probably relevant as well.

Lifetime prevalence rates for alcohol dependence have been estimated in an epidemiological study in the United States as 20% for men and 8% for women (Kessler et al., 1994). For alcohol abuse without dependence the rates were lower, 12% for men and 6% for women. The same survey estimated one-year prevalence rates, the proportion of people who have experienced a disorder within the prior year, as much lower, ranging from one-fourth to one-half of the corresponding

FOCUS BOX 12.2

Not an Upper or a Downer but an Inside-Outer

In 1956 Parke-Davis and Company, a large pharmaceutical firm, synthesized a new anesthetic. Although effective in large doses, it was found to cause agitation and disorientation as a patient regained consciousness. When administered in smaller doses, it induced a psychoticlike state. In 1965 this new drug, **phencyclidine (PCP)**, was taken off the market, and by 1978 its legal manufacture was discontinued in the United States.

The effects of PCP depend largely on the dosage. The user generally has jerky eye movements alternating with a blank stare, is unable to walk heel to toe in a straight line, and has great rigidity of the muscles. Some users experience hallucinations and delusions. All the sensory systems become overly sensitive so that users are extremely susceptible to any stimulation and are best left alone. When touched, they are likely to flail and become so agitated and combative that it takes several people to restrain them. Their incoherence and lack of communicativeness do not allow them to be talked down from their high. Very large dosages usually result in a deep and prolonged coma, seizures, apnea or periods of no breathing, sustained high blood pressure, and sometimes even death from heart and lung failure or from ruptured blood vessels in the brain. No medication to reverse the effects of PCP has yet been found. People seldom remember afterward what happened while they were on the drug.

Phencyclidine is not an upper or a downer, nor is it a psychedelic. Some workers refer to it as an inside-outer, a term that to some extent conveys the bizarre and extreme nature of its effects. The dosage and the way in which it is ingested seem to play a role in how long the effects of PCP last. Onset is usually between one and five minutes after smoking a treated cigarette. Effects peak after about half an hour and may not dissipate for up to two days. Since PCP remains in the body for several days, it can accumulate if ingested repeatedly. Chronic users who have taken the drug several times a week for six months may experience cognitive distortions and disorientation for several months afterward, or even for as long as two years after use has ceased. In addition, personality often changes, there can be memory loss, and the user may experience severe anxiety, depression, and aggressive urges (Aniline & Pitts, 1982).

Death is a potential consequence. Fatalities may come about in a variety of ways. One man who was swimming drowned because he lost his spatial orientation. Others have died because of severe respiratory depression or an uncontrollable increase in body temperature.

Those who use PCP are typically very young, averaging fifteen years of age. Abusers tend to be arrested more often for substance-related offenses than are abusers of the other drugs discussed in this chapter. PCP abusers also tend to overdose more often. In light of how terrifying and dangerous the drug is, it is not surprising that its popularity declined in the 1980s. More surprising perhaps is that it is enjoying a resurgence in the 1990s.

---

lifetime prevalence rates (Kessler et al., 1994). That only one-fourth to one-half of those ever meeting DSM criteria for an alcohol-related diagnosis have met the criteria within the past year suggests that alcohol problems, though difficult to overcome, need not last forever.

Alcohol abuse and dependence show substantial comorbidity with other psychological disorders, including antisocial personality disorder, mania, schizophrenia, and panic disorder (Robins, Helzer, Przybec, & Regier, 1988). Alcohol is often part of a pattern of polysubstance abuse. Cigarette smoking is especially common in association with heavy drinking (e.g., DiFranza & Guerrera, 1990). In addition, alcohol is believed to be a contributing cause in one-third of all suicides.

Alcohol abuse is a costly societal problem in other ways as well, playing a role in fatalities from automobile accidents, in airplane crashes, in industrial accidents, and in mishaps in the home. Homicide is an alcohol-related crime—it is believed that over half of all murders are committed under its influence—and so, too, are parental child abuse, spouse abuse, and sexual offenses (Brecher et al., 1972; National Institute on Alcohol Abuse and Alcoholism, 1983).

Alcohol is implicated in vehicular accidents. The driver of this New York subway train, which derailed, killing 5 and injuring more than 100, was intoxicated.

Characteristics of Alcohol Dependence

Alcohol dependence is well illustrated by the case of Gary Jackson with which this chapter began. Gary's tolerance and withdrawal reactions, such as morning shakes and malaise, which can be relieved only by taking a drink, are evidence of physical dependence on alcohol.

Alcohol's Short-Term Physical Effects

When a person takes a drink, a small part of the alcohol ingested passes immediately into the bloodstream through the stomach walls, but most of it goes into the small intestines, from which it is absorbed into the blood. It is then broken down, primarily in the liver, which can metabolize about one ounce of one hundred proof (that is, 50% alcohol) whiskey per hour. Quantities in excess of this amount remain in the bloodstream. While the body absorbs alcohol rapidly, it is slow to shed it. The effects of alcohol vary directly with its concentration in the bloodstream. The concentration depends on the amount ingested in a particular period of time, the presence or absence of food in the stomach to retain the alcohol and reduce its absorption rate, the size of the person's body, and the efficiency of the liver. A bottle of beer on an empty stomach has a stronger effect than on a full one.

Alcohol depresses the central nervous system, but its initial effect is stimulating. Tensions and inhibitions are reduced, and the drinker may experience an expansive feeling of sociability and well-being. Larger amounts of alcohol interfere with complex thought processes. Motor coordination, balance, speech, and vision are also impaired. At this stage of intoxication, some individuals become depressed and withdrawn. Other people, though, become suspicious and even violent. Alcohol is capable of blunting pain and, in larger doses, of inducing sedation and sleep.

Long-Term Effects of Alcohol Abuse

For some time the life histories of alcoholics were thought to have a common progression. Based on an extensive survey of two thousand alcoholic men, Jellinek (1952) came to view the alcoholic as passing through four stages. In the *prealcoholic* phase a person drinks socially and on occasion rather heavily to relieve tension and forget about problems. In the *prodromal* stage the drinking may become secretive and may also be marked by blackouts. The drinker remains conscious, talks coherently, and carries on other activities without appearing to be greatly intoxicated, but later has no recall of the occasion. Alcohol begins to be used more as a drug and less as a beverage.

Jellinek termed the third phase *crucial*, because alcoholics in this stage are in severe danger of losing everything that they value. At this stage they have lost control of their drinking. Once they take a single drink, they continue to consume alcohol until they are too sick or in too much of a stupor to drink anymore. Social adjustment begins to deteriorate. The alcoholic starts to drink during the day, and the drinking becomes evident to employers, family, and friends. In this stage the alcoholics neglect their diet, have their first bender—a several-day period of excessive drinking—and may experience hallucinations and delirium when they stop drinking. The individual still has the ability to abstain. It is possible to give up alcohol for several weeks or even months at a time, but if the person has just one drink, the whole pattern begins again.

In the final, *chronic*, stage drinking is continual and benders are frequent. The individual lives only to drink. The bodily systems have become so accustomed to alcohol that its absence triggers withdrawal reactions. If liquor is not available, the person consumes any liquid he or she can find that contains alcohol—shaving lotion, hair tonic, whatever. These people suffer from malnutrition and other physiological changes. They neglect their personal appearance and, having lost their self-esteem, feel little remorse about any aspect of their behavior. Finally, they cease to care at all about family and home, friends, occupation, and social status.

▶ *APPLYING CRITICAL THINKING SKILLS*

GENERALIZATIONS ABOUT THE COURSE OF ALCOHOLISM

Jellinek's description will certainly sound familiar to those who have lived with alcoholic relatives or treated alcoholics. It has been widely cited and influential. However, even if an idea seems intuitively right, understanding what we can conclude from it calls for critical thinking.

▶ *What conclusion does the evidence seem to support?* The apparent implication of Jellinek's research is that there is a common sequence of four increasingly severe stages of alcoholism. This sort of sequential model is implicit in statements such as that alcoholism is a "progressive disease" or that one typically must "hit bottom" before getting better.

▶ *What other interpretations are plausible?* Jellinek's sample of alcoholics was large, but it is important in evaluating research to consider the representativeness of a sample alongside its size. In this case, an obvious sampling bias is that all the alcoholics studied were men, and a plausible alternative interpretation of the results is that this pattern fits male, but not necessarily female, alcoholics.

▶ *What other information would help choose among the alternative interpretations?* Research on the course of alcohol dependence among women would help determine whether Jellinek's description of the stages of alcoholism is universal or limited to men.

Results of such research suggest that, as would probably be the case with any description of *the* course of alcoholism, Jellinek's model is oversimplified, for alcohol problems develop in different ways for different drinkers. Alcoholism usually begins at a later age in women than in men and very often after an inordinately stressful experience, such as the death of a husband or a serious family crisis. For women the time interval between the onset of problem drinking and alcoholism is briefer. Alcoholic women tend more than men to be steady drinkers and to drink alone; they are also less likely to engage in binge drinking (Hill, 1980; Wolin, 1980).

Even apart from these sex differences in average drinking patterns, it is clear that alcoholism is more heterogeneous than implied by Jellinek's model. For example, many alcoholics have never experienced a blackout (Goodwin, Crane, & Guze, 1969). Moreover, a single drink does not necessarily stimulate an irresistible impulse to continue drinking. Alcoholics primed with an initial drink, one they believed to be nonalcoholic, later consumed no more alcohol than did social drinkers (Marlatt, Demming, & Reid, 1973).

Research also shows that alcoholism does not always follow a steadily worsening course. There is considerable fluctuation in many drinkers, from heavy drinking for periods of time to abstinence or lighter drinking at other times (Clark & Cahalan, 1976). Patterns of maladaptive use of alcohol also vary. Heavy use of the drug may be restricted to weekends, or long periods of abstinence may be interspersed with binges of continual drinking for several weeks (Robins et al., 1988). Thus, while alcoholism can be progressive, the rate of progression and the way in which it progresses are not uniform across drinkers.

Biological Effects of Chronic Alcohol Abuse

In addition to psychological deterioration, almost every tissue and organ of the body is harmed by prolonged consumption of alcohol. Because alcohol provides calories—a pint of eighty proof spirits supplies about half a day's caloric requirements—alcoholics often reduce their intake of food. But the calories provided by alcohol are empty. They do not supply the nutrients essential for health. Alcohol also contributes directly to malnutrition by impairing the digestion of food and absorption of vitamins. In older chronic alcoholics, a deficiency of B-complex vitamins can cause *amnestic syndrome,* a severe loss of memory for both recent and long-past events. These memory gaps are often filled in by reporting imaginary events (confabulation) that are highly improbable.

A drastic reduction in the intake of protein as well as alcohol itself contributes to the development of cirrhosis of the liver, a disease in which some liver cells become engorged with fat and protein, impeding their function, and some cells die, triggering an inflammatory process. When scar tissue develops, blood flow is obstructed. Cirrhosis ranks ninth among causes of death in the United States (U.S. Department of Health and Human Services, 1990). It is more common in female than in male alcoholics.

Other common physiological effects of chronic alcohol abuse include damage to the endocrine glands and pancreas, heart failure, hypertension, and capillary hemorrhages, which are responsible for the swelling and redness in the face, and especially of the nose, of chronic alcoholics. Prolonged use of alcohol appears to damage brain cells, especially those in the frontal lobes, causing cortical atrophy and other changes in structure (Parsons, 1975). Alcohol also reduces the effectiveness of the immune system, resulting in increased susceptibility to infection.

Heavy alcohol consumption during pregnancy can retard the growth of the fetus and infant and can cause cranial, facial, and limb anomalies as well as mental retardation, a condition known as **fetal alcohol syndrome**. Even moderate drinking can produce less severe but undesirable effects on the fetus. In 1989 a law was

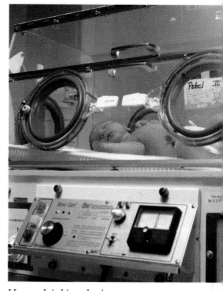

Heavy drinking during pregnancy can lead to premature birth as well as physical and mental abnormalities in the fetus. This condition is called fetal alcohol syndrome.

fetal alcohol syndrome Retarded growth of the developing fetus; cranial, facial, and limb anomalies and *mental retardation* caused by heavy consumption of alcohol by the mother during pregnancy.

enacted requiring the inclusion of warnings about birth defects on packaging for all alcoholic beverages (NIAAA, 1990).

Biological Effects of Withdrawal

The effects of the abrupt withdrawal of alcohol from an alcoholic may be rather dramatic, because the body has become accustomed to the drug. Subjectively, the patient is often anxious, depressed, weak, restless, and unable to sleep. Tremors of the muscles, especially of the small muscles of the fingers, face, eyelids, lips, and tongue, may be marked, and there is an elevation of pulse, blood pressure, and temperature. In relatively rare cases an alcoholic who has been drinking for a number of years may also suffer from **delirium tremens (DTs)** when the level of alcohol in the blood drops suddenly. The person becomes delirious as well as tremulous and suffers from hallucinations that are primarily visual but may be tactile as well. Unpleasant and very active creatures—snakes, cockroaches, spiders, and the like—may appear to be crawling up the wall or all over the alcoholic's body, or they may fill the room. Feverish, disoriented, and terrified, the alcoholic may claw frantically at his or her skin to get rid of the vermin or may cower in the corner to escape an advancing army of fantastic animals.

In addition to these withdrawal symptoms, increased tolerance is also possible. Some alcoholics can drink a quart of bourbon a day without showing signs of drunkenness. Moreover, levels of alcohol in the blood of these people were unexpectedly low after what would usually be viewed as excessive drinking (Mello & Mendelson, 1970).

Although changes in the liver enzymes that metabolize alcohol can account to some extent for tolerance, most researchers now believe that the central nervous system is implicated. Alcohol can, for example, increase the fluidity of nerve cell membranes and by this process alter electrical conduction in the brain (NIAAA, 1983).

delirium tremens (DTs) A set of *withdrawal symptoms* when a period of heavy alcohol consumption is terminated; marked by fever, sweating, trembling, cognitive impairment, and *hallucinations*.

To Recap

About 20% of American male adults have at some point met criteria for alcohol dependence (more than twice the proportion among women). Comorbidity with other disorders is common. Alcohol abuse increases suicide risk and is associated with numerous adverse social consequences, such as highway fatalities, homicide, and elevated health care costs. Short-term effects of alcohol depend on the amount consumed. They may include an initial feeling of relaxation and sociability, but at higher doses impairment of thought processes and motor coordination. The course of alcoholism is highly variable. Long-term effects can include malnutrition, memory loss, and death from cirrhosis of the liver. Alcohol consumption during pregnancy is dangerous, with heavy consumption creating risk for fetal alcohol syndrome. At its most severe, withdrawal from alcohol after chronic drinking stops may bring on delirium and hallucinations.

Perspectives on the Causes of Substance-Related Disorders

There are many possible causes of drug addiction. One case of alcohol dependence might be traced to a genetically influenced tolerance for alcohol, facilitating heavy drinking. Another addiction might result from culturally shaped expectations about the usefulness of drugs for managing one's mood or getting along with other people. Indeed, it is likely that a combination of factors underlies the substance-related problem of any individual.

Personality Perspectives

Researchers have long attempted to find an addictive personality, a set of character traits that might predispose people to drug dependence. Drug addicts have been found to be deviant on various personality questionnaire measures. But these personality characteristics may not precede or cause the addiction; they could be effects of addiction. For example, we might find that drug addicts tend to be more suspicious than nonusers. To conclude that suspiciousness contributes to the use of drugs would not be justified, for it might well be the addict's *reaction* to his or her illegal status as a drug user.

Several longitudinal studies have found that antisocial personality traits predict alcohol abuse (e.g., M. C. Jones, 1968). If antisocial personality disorder patients are excluded from the analysis, other personality measures do not predict the development of alcohol dependence (Schuckit, Klein, Twitchell, & Smith, 1994). Thus, most personality differences between alcohol-dependent people and others are probably *effects* of alcohol problems rather than causes of them.

The relevance of personality traits in predicting drug problems may vary from one drug to another, however. A longitudinal study of heavy marijuana users (Shedler & Block, 1990) found that as early as age seven they had difficulty getting along well with others. They tended to be indecisive, untrustworthy, and undependable, unable to admit to negative feelings, and lacking in confidence and self-esteem. At age eleven these same children were emotionally erratic and inattentive, were unable to concentrate, and lacked involvement in activities.

Biological Perspectives

Much of the research on biological factors in substance abuse has addressed the possibility that a genetically transmitted alteration in some biological process serves as a predisposition for alcoholism.

Alcoholism runs in families. Studies indicating greater concordance for alcoholism (e.g., McGue, Pickens, & Svikis, 1992) in identical twins than in fraternal twins point toward a possible role of heredity, as do adoption studies (Goodwin, Schulsinger, Hermansen, Guze, & Winokur, 1973).

These results suggest that a predisposition toward alcoholism can be inherited. Such a conclusion might be oversimplified, however. For one thing, the genetic transmission of alcoholism may apply only to men. In one twin study, the concordance rate for male MZ pairs was 76% and for DZ pairs, 54%. The corresponding figures for women (39% for MZs and 41% for DZs) did not show evidence of heritability (McGue et al., 1992).

Also, large-scale adoptee research conducted in Sweden raised the possibility that there are subtypes of alcoholism with different genetic bases (Cloninger, Bohman, & Sigvardsson, 1981). Adoptees whose alcoholic biological parents started drinking in adulthood and tended toward episodic or binge drinking seemed to need both genes and environment (exposure to heavy drinking in the adoptive home) to produce the disorder. In contrast, a genetic effect alone was evident in the children whose biological parents continually used alcohol. This effect held only for male adoptees. A subsequent twin study also showed that genetic factors were much more important in the case of early-onset alcoholism (McGue et al., 1992). Thus, genetic factors may be especially important when the parents began drinking heavily early in life and continued to do so into adulthood.

A further question arises as to *what* in particular is inherited as a vulnerability. One possibility is an ability to tolerate alcohol (Goodwin, 1979). To become an alcoholic, a person first has to be able to drink a lot, in other words, has to be able to tolerate large quantities of alcohol. Some ethnic groups, notably Asians, may have a low rate of alcoholism because of their physiological intolerance, which is caused by a deficiency in an enzyme that metabolizes alcohol. Indeed, about three-quarters of Asians experience unpleasant effects from small quantities of alcohol. Noxious effects of the drug may then protect a person from alcoholism.

Goodwin's hypothesis focuses on short-term effects, possibly on how alcohol is metabolized or on how the central nervous system responds to alcohol. Animal research indicates that genetic components are at work in both these processes (Schuckit, 1983). More recently, these findings have been corroborated in human research. Sons of alcoholics reported less intoxication than controls after a dose of alcohol and showed a smaller hormonal response to the alcohol (Schuckit & Gold, 1988). A quantitative review of studies using similar procedures suggests that these effects are reliable (Pollock, 1992).

A small response to alcohol may set the stage for heavier than normal drinking. This reasoning was supported in a nine-year follow-up of subjects from the Schuckit and Gold (1988) study comparing sons of alcoholics (not yet alcohol dependent) with controls matched on demographics, drug use, and personal drinking history. Subjects who went on to develop alcohol abuse or alcohol dependence by the time of follow-up (at an average age of thirty-three) were more likely to have shown at the initial testing low subjective intoxication and low levels of change in motor coordination (body sway) in response to a standard dose of alcohol (Schuckit, 1994).

Behavioral Perspectives

Because drugs are used to alter mood, the behavioral view is that they are reinforcing, either by enhancing positive mood states or by diminishing negative ones. Such drugs as alcohol, marijuana, sedatives, nicotine, and caffeine are thought to reduce anxiety and distress and to be relaxing, while stimulants and narcotics promote positive feelings.

Early experiments showed that animals under the influence of alcohol were less quick to learn an *avoidance response*, usually regarded as evidence of anxiety

The tension reduction theory argues that people become heavy drinkers because of alcohol's stress-reducing properties. The stock market crash of 1987 apparently drove many financiers to the nearest bar. Although some came to read and some to talk, others undoubtedly had an extra drink or two.

(Conger, 1951), supporting the idea of alcohol as tension reducing. Some later experiments with humans also indicated that alcohol can reduce tension in people who are not yet alcoholic (e.g., Sher & Levenson, 1982). But there are conflicting findings as well (e.g., Thyer & Curtis, 1984).

Cognitive Perspectives

One factor reflected in these inconsistent results may be the situation in which alcohol is consumed. Alcohol may produce its tension-reducing effect by reducing the intoxicated person's cognitive capacity so that he or she cannot maintain an activity and worry at the same time. If a distracting activity is available, attention will be diverted to it rather than focused on worrisome thoughts, with a resultant decrease in anxiety (Steele & Josephs, 1988). However, this effect can backfire in some situations. For example, discouraged people can become even more depressed while drinking alone because they find it harder to distract themselves from their depressing thoughts. Also, alcohol may not be a potent tension reducer in situations in which it is consumed after stress (Sayette & Wilson, 1991).

The cognitive perspective emphasizes that people use alcohol after stress not because it reduces distress directly but because they *expect* it will. In support of this idea, studies of college undergraduates (Rather, Goldman, Roehrich, & Brannick, 1992) and children of alcoholic parents (Sher, Walitzer, Wood, & Brent, 1991) demonstrate that people who expect alcohol to reduce stress and anxiety are those likely to be frequent users. Indeed, positive expectancies about a drug's effects predict drug use in general (Stacy, Newcomb, & Bentler, 1991).

Sociocultural Perspectives

Cultural and subcultural attitudes toward drugs also have a profound effect on drug use. Alcohol consumption varies tremendously across cultures (see Figure 12.1). It cannot be assumed, however, that these cross-national differences always reflect sociocultural factors. Low rates of alcohol dependence among Japanese or Korean people, for instance, may result from low physiological tolerance for alcohol, as discussed earlier. More typically, though, national variations in consumption patterns and ethnic variations, such as elevated prevalence of alcohol problems among Native Americans, are attributed to differences in attitudes toward the acceptability of drug use. For example, members of religions that forbid the use of psychoactive drugs, such as the Amish or Mormons, are rarely addicted

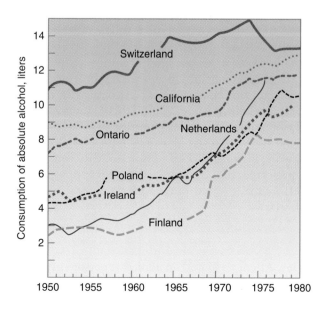

Figure 12.1 *Total consumption of alcoholic beverages (in liters of absolute alcohol per head) of population aged 15 years and over from 1950 to 1980. After Mäkelä et al. (1981).*

Alcoholism is highest in countries in which alcohol use is heavy, such as vinicultural societies. Note that everyone is drinking wine in this French bar.

(Trimble, 1994). Conversely, high levels of alcoholism are found among sailors, railroad workers, and people in the drink trade—restaurant owners, bartenders, and liquor dealers—where heavy drinking is part of the culture surrounding the job (Fillmore & Caetano, 1980). Of course, people may become bartenders in part because they like to drink.

Similarly, tobacco use among high school students is highest among a particular subculture: those with poor grades, behavior problems, and a taste for heavy metal music (Sussman et al., 1990) as well as those who have little adult supervision after school (Richardson et al., 1989). Also, heroin and crack use is most common in ghettos, and marijuana and hallucinogen use was common among those drawn to the social activism and other pursuits of the late 1960s. In all these cases, members of a subcultural group are likely to be exposed to multiple models of drug use, peer pressure to conform, and substances that are readily available.

In addition to local influences such as peer pressure, it is important to consider in this context deliberate attempts to foster drug use via the culture of the mass media. We are bombarded with advertisements in which drinking beer or smoking cigarettes is (paradoxically) linked with being athletic, physically fit, attractive, and socially skilled. For example, elementary and high school students have been the targets of the Joe Camel campaign, which was launched in 1988 to create a new generation of smokers lured by Joe's resemblance to James Bond or the character played by Don Johnson in *Miami Vice.* Prior to the campaign (1976–1988) Camels were the preferred brand of less than 0.5% of seventh through twelfth graders. By 1991 Camel's share of this *illegal* market had increased to 33% (DiFranza et al., 1991)!

To Recap

Drug addiction has multiple origins. Attempts to find an addictive personality have been plagued by ambiguity, but there is some more compelling evidence relating antisocial attitudes and behaviors to subsequent drug abuse. Biological fac-

Permissive attitudes toward drug use formed a part of late-1960's youth culture in many areas.

tors tend to focus on alcoholism as at least partly hereditary, especially among men with a family history of early-onset, chronic alcoholism. An early marker of inherited vulnerability in the sons of alcoholics appears to be high tolerance for the effects of alcohol, which facilitates heavy drinking.

Behavioral perspectives see drug use as a learned behavior reinforced by the mood changes associated with the drug. Research on the hypothesis that alcohol is negatively reinforced by reducing anxiety, however, shows mixed results. This ambiguity may reflect the fact that reinforcing effects of alcohol are themselves affected by cognitive factors, such as a person's expectations about the effects of alcohol.

Cultural factors shape drug use, as indicated by wide variation in alcohol consumption over time and across nations, religious groups, and occupations. Mass media advertising represents a deliberate attempt to foster drug use through cultural influence.

Perspectives on the Treatment of Alcoholism

The havoc created by alcoholism, both for the drinkers and for their families, friends, employers, and communities, makes this problem a serious public health issue. Accordingly, treatment efforts are diverse and intensive. Industry spends large sums of money in support of various alcohol rehabilitation programs for employees. Television and radio carry public service messages about the dangers of alcoholism in attempts to discourage people from beginning to drink excessively and to encourage those already affected to own up to their problem and seek help.

Public and private hospitals worldwide have for many years provided retreats for alcoholics, sanctums where people can dry out and avail themselves of a variety of individual and group therapies. The withdrawal from alcohol—**detoxification**—can be difficult, both physically and psychologically, and usually takes about one month. Tranquilizers are sometimes given to ease the anxiety and general discomfort of withdrawal. However, because many alcoholics misuse tranquilizers, some clinics try gradual tapering off without tranquilizers rather than a sudden cutoff of alcohol. Alcoholics also need carbohydrate solutions, B vitamins, and, perhaps, anticonvulsants.

detoxification The initial stage in weaning an addicted person from a drug; involves medical supervision of the sometimes painful *withdrawal*.

The number of for-profit hospitals treating alcoholism increased almost four-fold from 1978 to 1984, fueled by the fact that such treatment is covered in large measure by both private insurance companies and the federal government (Holder, Longabaugh, Miller, & Rubonis, 1991). Inpatient treatment is much more expensive than outpatient treatment, but its higher costs are not matched by higher degrees of effectiveness (Miller & Hester, 1986). Detoxification can be safely managed on an outpatient basis for most people, and, in general, the therapeutic results of hospital treatment are not superior to those of outpatient treatment.

There are also many forms of psychotherapy, medication, and self-help aimed at treating alcohol dependence. The treatment of alcoholics is very difficult, not only because of the addictive nature of the drug but also because many other psychological problems are likely to be present, for example, depression, anxiety, and severe disruptions in the person's social and occupational functioning. Risk of suicide is also elevated (Galanter & Castaneda, 1985). Although some of these problems may have preceded, indeed, contributed to, the abuse of alcohol, by the time an alcoholic is treated it is seldom possible to know what is cause and what is effect. What *is* certain is that the person's life is usually a shambles. Regardless of the kind of intervention, the first step, and a difficult one, is to admit the problem and decide to do something about it.

Mutual Help: Alcoholics Anonymous

The largest and most widely known self-help group in the world is Alcoholics Anonymous (AA), founded in 1935 by two recovered alcoholics. It currently has thirty thousand chapters and membership numbering more than a million people in the United States and ninety-one other countries throughout the world. An AA chapter runs regular and frequent meetings at which newcomers rise to announce that they are alcoholics and older, sober members give testimonials, relating the stories of their alcoholism and indicating how their lives have changed for the better. The group provides emotional support, understanding, and counseling for the alcoholic as well as a social life to relieve isolation. Members are urged to call on one another around-the-clock when they need companionship and encouragement not to relapse. The belief is instilled in each AA member that alcoholism is a disease one is never cured of and that continuing vigilance is necessary to resist taking even a single drink, lest uncontrollable drinking begin all over again. Also important is the spiritual aspect of AA, which is evident in the twelve steps of AA shown in Table 12.2.

Unfortunately, the claims made by AA about the effectiveness of its treatment have rarely been subjected to scientific scrutiny. Findings from uncontrolled studies must be viewed with caution. AA has high drop-out rates, and the dropouts are not factored into the results (Edwards, Hensman, Hawker, & Williamson, 1967). In addition, there is a lack of long-term follow-up of AA clients. Results from the best controlled study to date are mixed (Walsh & Hingson, 1991). Alcoholics who were given a choice of treatment and chose AA did well in the study; those who were randomly *assigned* to AA did not. Many people who choose AA and stay with it for more than three months—a select group—remain abstinent for at least a few years (Emerick, Lassen, & Edwards, 1977). The needs of such people seem to be met by the fellowship and support of AA. For them it becomes a way of life. As with other forms of intervention, it remains to be determined for whom this particular mode is best suited.

Biological Treatment: Antabuse

Antabuse (Trade name for disulfiram)   A drug that makes the drinking of alcohol produce nausea and other unpleasant effects.

Among the treatments available for alcoholics is disulfiram, or **Antabuse**, a drug that discourages drinking by causing violent vomiting if alcohol is ingested. As you can imagine, adherence to an Antabuse regimen can be a problem. Indeed, *if*

Table 12.2 ▶ *Twelve Suggested Steps of Alcoholics Anonymous*

1. We admitted we were powerless over alcohol—that our lives had become unmanageable.
2. Came to believe that a power greater than ourselves could restore us to sanity.
3. Made a decision to turn our will and our lives over to the care of God *as we understood Him.*
4. Made a searching and fearless moral inventory of ourselves.
5. Admitted to God, to ourselves, and to another human being the exact nature of our wrongs.
6. Were entirely ready to have God remove all these defects of character.
7. Humbly asked Him to remove our shortcomings.
8. Made a list of all persons we had harmed, and became willing to make amends to them all.
9. Made direct amends to such people wherever possible, except when to do so would injure them or others.
10. Continued to take personal inventory and, when we were wrong, promptly admitted it.
11. Sought through prayer and meditation to improve our conscious contact with God *as we understood Him,* praying only for knowledge of His will for us and the power to carry that out.
12. Having had a spiritual awakening as the result of these steps, we tried to carry this message to alcoholics and to practice these principles in all our affairs.

an alcoholic is able or willing to take the drug every morning as prescribed, it would seem that drinking would lessen because of its negative consequences (Sisson & Azrin, 1989). However, in a large, multicenter study with placebo controls, Antabuse was not shown to have any specific benefit (Fuller, 1988; Fuller et al., 1986).

Psychodynamic Perspectives

Insight-oriented psychotherapists see the need for active and directive intervention when it comes to treating alcoholics and other substance abusers (Galanter & Castaneda, 1990). Unlike traditional insight-oriented treatment—but similar to the approach used with suicidal patients—the therapist is available between sessions to provide support and understanding as the patient wrestles with the challenge of living without alcohol.

If the patient has a social support system, such as a spouse, companion, or relative, that person is involved as well in treatment as part of a network to discourage drinking. Insight-oriented therapists often use Antabuse as well as attendance at AA meetings to ensure abstinence. The patient's social network is enlisted to make sure the patient complies with these assignments, for example, by having a spouse watch the patient take the Antabuse each morning. With these rather behavioral aspects in place, an insight therapist can proceed with exploration of conflicts that might underlie the need to abuse alcohol (Galanter & Castaneda, 1990).

Behavioral Perspectives

Aversion Therapy

Behavioral researchers have been studying the treatment of alcoholism for many years. One of the earliest articles on behavior therapy concerned aversive "conditioning" of alcoholism (Kantorovich, 1930). With these procedures a problem drinker is shocked or made nauseous while looking at, reaching for, or beginning to drink alcohol. The aversive stimulus may also be vividly imagined in a procedure called **covert sensitization** (Cautela, 1966). Using a hierarchy of scenes, the alcoholic is instructed to imagine being made violently and disgustingly sick by his or her drinking.

covert sensitization   A form of *aversion therapy* in which the subject is told to imagine the undesirably attractive situations and activities at the same time that unpleasant feelings are also induced by imagery.

Aversion therapies are best implemented in the context of broadly based programs that attend to the patient's particular life circumstances, for example, marital conflict, social fears, and other factors often associated with problem drinking (Tucker, Vuchinich, & Downey, 1992).

Other Behaviorial Techniques

Job clubs have been used to help patients develop or enhance employment-seeking skills and social networks for recreational activities that do not include alcohol. Assertiveness training for refusing drinks is also provided. This community reinforcement approach has generated promising results (Azrin, Sisson, Meyers, & Godley, 1982; Keane, Foy, Nunn, & Rychtarik, 1984).

Still other behavioral treatment techniques emphasize patient self-control. Patients may be encouraged to narrow the situations in which they allow themselves to drink, for example, with others on a special occasion. Or they may change what and how they drink, for example, having only mixed drinks and taking small sips rather than gulps. Self-reinforcement is also important. Patients might allow themselves a nonalcoholic treat if they resist the urge to drink (Tucker et al., 1992).

The behavioral therapies summarized have been tested in many studies. A review of controlled alcohol-treatment outcome research concluded that covert sensitization, the community reinforcement approach, and self-control strategies were among the small group of treatments with good evidence of effectiveness (Holder et al., 1991). Behavioral treatments also tend to fare well in cost comparisons but are less widely employed in clinical practice than other methods, such as twelve-step programs and inpatient detoxification, that are either less proven with respect to effectiveness, more expensive, or both (W. R. Miller, 1993).

Controlled Drinking

Until recently it was generally agreed that alcoholics had to abstain completely if they were to be cured, for they were said to have no control over their imbibing once they had taken that first drink. Research calls this assumption into question. Drinkers' *beliefs* about themselves and alcohol may be as important as the physiological addiction to the drug (e.g., Wilson & Lawson, 1976).

Considering the difficulty in our society of avoiding alcohol altogether, it may be useful to teach some problem drinkers to imbibe with moderation. A drinker's self-esteem should benefit from being able to control a problem and from feeling in charge of his or her life.

Controlled drinking refers to a pattern of alcohol consumption that is moderate and avoids the extremes of total abstinence and inebriation. Note that controlled drinking is, strictly speaking, an outcome of treatment (whether intentionally sought or not), not a specific method. Not all behavior therapy programs strive to achieve controlled drinking, and not all controlled drinkers achieved this status via behavior therapy. Still, it is reasonable to discuss controlled drinking in an evaluation of this perspective, for most of the research on deliberate attempts to bring about controlled drinking has focused on behavior therapies such as the self-control strategies described earlier.

controlled drinking A pattern of alcohol consumption that is moderate and avoids the extremes of total abstinence and of inebriation.

Findings of one well-known treatment program suggest that at least some alcoholics can learn to control their drinking and improve other aspects of their lives as well (Sobell & Sobell, 1976, 1978). Alcoholics attempting to control their drinking were given shocks when they chose straight liquor rather than mixed drinks, gulped their drinks down too fast, or took large swallows rather than sips. They were given problem-solving and assertiveness training to help them better handle situations that might prompt them to drink. They also increased their awareness by watching videotapes of themselves inebriated and identifying the situations precipitating their drinking so that they could settle on a less self-destructive course of action. Their improvement was greater than that of alcoholics who tried for total abstinence and were given shocks for any drinking at all.

In contemporary controlled drinking treatment programs, patients are taught to resist social pressures to drink, using assertiveness, relaxation, and stress-management training, sometimes including biofeedback and meditation. Exercise and improved diets are also part of the treatment and help bolster patients physically. They are taught that a lapse will not inevitably precipitate a total relapse and should be regarded as a learning experience (Marlatt & Gordon, 1985). Sources of stress in their work, family, and relationships are examined. To be able to control their drinking, they must become active and responsible in anticipating and resisting situations that might tempt excesses (Marlatt, 1983; Sobell, Toneatto, & Sobell, 1990).

Controlled drinking is controversial, however (e.g., Searles, 1993; Wallace, 1993), for it contradicts strongly held beliefs that abstinence is the *only* proper goal for problem drinkers. Controlled drinking is much more widely accepted in Canada and Europe than it is in the United States.

A Rand Corporation study (Armor, Polich, & Stambul, 1978) offered a way to resolve the controversy by suggesting that abstinence is a better goal for older, more addicted drinkers, while moderation is viable for younger, less dependent drinkers. Findings published in the late 1980s of well-controlled studies with at least a twelve-month follow-up indicated that controlled drinking is often a viable outcome even when the original goal was abstinence. Success at controlled drinking is associated with younger age and lighter drinking, as suggested by the Rand study (Miller & Hester, 1986; Sobell et al., 1990). The patient's ability to choose his or her own goals may also improve outcome (Sanchez-Craig & Wilkinson, 1987).

Eclectic Treatment

A general problem with attempts to treat alcoholism has been the therapist's often unstated assumption that all people who drink to excess do so for the same reasons. For example, a behavior therapist favoring aversive treatment believes that reducing the attraction alcohol or its taste has for drinkers will help them abstain. Excessive drinking is a complex human problem, though, and it may be too simple to assume that all people drink for the same reason (A. A. Lazarus, 1965).

A more comprehensive clinical assessment considers the place that drinking occupies in the person's life (Tucker et al., 1992). A woman in a desperately unhappy marriage, with time on her hands now that her children are in school and no longer need her constant attention, may seek the numbing effects of alcohol just to help the time pass and to avoid facing life. Making the taste of alcohol unpleasant for this patient by pairing it with shock or an emetic seems insufficient. Treatment should concentrate on the marital and family problems prompting her to drink, and on trying to reduce the psychological pain that permeates her existence. She will also need help in tolerating the withdrawal symptoms that come with reduced consumption. Without alcohol as a reliable anesthetic, she will need to mobilize other resources to confront her hitherto avoided problems. Social-skills or assertiveness training may be helpful. Again, there is tremendous variation among individuals.

In addition, alcoholism is sometimes associated with other mental disorders, in particular, mood disorders and psychopathy (Goodwin, 1982). The clinician must conduct a broad-spectrum assessment of the patient's problem, for if heavy drinking stems from the desperation of deep depression, a regimen of Antabuse or any other treatment focused only on alcohol is unlikely to be of lasting value.

Even with the many treatment programs available to help alcoholics live without their drug, it has been estimated that no more than 10% of alcoholics are ever in professional treatment and that upwards of 40% cure themselves. How does such spontaneous recovery take place? Among the apparent factors are a new marriage, a new job, a religious or spiritual experience or conversion, a near-fatal auto accident while driving drunk, or being shaken by a serious illness. What is not clear is why some people can stop drinking after a serious crisis while others react by seeking the solace of the bottle (Vaillant, 1983).

TO RECAP

Alcoholism treatment is difficult, and many approaches have been tried for those who enter formal programs. Detoxification can usually be managed safely on an outpatient basis, and inpatient treatment in general appears to be costly and not uniquely helpful. Alcoholics Anonymous is a mutual-help group in which recovering alcoholics attend chapter meetings and provide one another with emotional support and advice about staying sober. Its general principles are encapsulated in a sequence of twelve steps, which include a strong emphasis on the spiritual aspects of recovery.

Psychodynamic therapies try to address the personality conflicts believed to underlie alcoholism, along with taking practical measures to discourage drinking. Antabuse is a drug treatment that discourages drinking by causing violent vomiting if one does drink alcohol. Behavioral therapies have received the most extensive scrutiny in research. Effective procedures include covert sensitization (vividly imagining aversive consequences of drinking), community reinforcement (getting significant others to reinforce drinking-incompatible behaviors, as well as teaching job-seeking skills and social skills), and self-control training (for example, gradually narrowing the situations in which one drinks).

A controversial aspect of behavior therapy is that some of the programs aim at a goal of controlled drinking rather than abstinence. Younger age, lower pretreatment drinking rate, and a preference for controlled drinking as a goal have all been associated with success in controlled drinking programs. Eclectic treatments recognize the heterogeneous nature of the population of alcoholics. Techniques are selected according to an individualized assessment of the role of drinking in the patient's life and the availability of social support systems.

The Case of Gary Jackson Revisited ◀

SOCIAL HISTORY

Gary's first experience of drinking alcohol came at age sixteen, when he tagged along with a group of school friends who were able to get served in a bar. Initially Gary did not enjoy the taste of alcohol, but he gradually developed a taste for it. By age twenty he was drinking daily, though not excessively. He met and married his wife when he was twenty-three.

Gary had always been sensitive to the opinions of others, and shortly after his marriage this became a problem with his work friends. The morning after one especially heavy evening of drinking with them, Gary was hungover. He was visibly shaking and suffered diarrhea, so much so that at work he was heading to the toilet every few minutes. Some of his friends there laughed at him because of the shaking. Nobody would likely enjoy such an incident, but Gary found it particularly difficult. He became self-conscious about doing even ordinary things in front of other people. At first he was slightly afraid of writing in front of others, for fear that he would shake and that they might notice. This fear gradually grew, to the extent that he found many routine activities, such as eating or writing, difficult in the presence of others.

CONCEPTUALIZATION AND TREATMENT

Gary's principal diagnosis was alcohol dependence, but his social phobia also would have to be considered in treatment. Given Gary's high level of alcohol dependence it was concluded that total abstinence should be the treatment goal. It was anticipated that withdrawal symptoms could be severe, and detoxification was conducted on an inpatient basis over a four-day period. Diazepam, a benzodiazepine tranquilizer, was given by intravenous injection to assist in this process. During detoxification Gary was introduced to the ideas of Alcoholics Anonymous. He responded unfavorably and refused to attend any AA meetings after discharge.

After detoxification Gary was seen, along with his wife, on an outpatient basis by a drug and alcohol team that consisted of a psychologist, a psychiatrist, and a social worker. To help manage the difficult early stages of returning to his daily activities without alcohol, Gary was given Antabuse. He accepted the need for some external control, at least temporarily, over his drinking, and he wished to abstain completely. Gary was prepared to be supervised while taking his Antabuse doses, which appears to be essential for the treatment to be helpful (Mattick & Jarvis, 1992).

In an attempt to bolster Gary's motivation and compliance, the therapist explained in detail the negative effects (flushing, dizziness, nausea, breathlessness) he could expect if he drank alcohol while on Antabuse. Gary's wife was at first reluctant to take on the role of supervising his intake of the drug. She saw this as inappropriately placing responsibility for the drinking on her shoulders, and she had long since given up on the idea that she could control Gary's drinking. The therapist acknowledged that she had a point, but emphasized that her role was only to observe Gary taking the Antabuse, not to stop him from drinking alcohol altogether.

In addition, Gary entered individual psychotherapy. The basic approach was to conceptualize alcohol use as an overdeveloped, maladaptive coping strategy that Gary had used to manage his anxiety around others. The overall goal was to relieve Gary's social phobia and to teach more functional coping skills to achieve the same aims without drinking (Monti, Abrams, Kadden, & Cooney, 1989). Gary learned to say no to offers of alcohol or pressure from others to drink, without hesitation and without making excuses. He was taught to speak directly to the person making the offer and not feel guilty about it. For someone like Gary, whose social life and acquaintanceships revolved around drinking and who overvalued others' opinions of him, this was indeed a difficult issue.

In addition, Gary needed help with some of the basic, taken-for-granted skills for living among others—listening accurately and communicating effectively, talking about personal feelings in intimate relationships, giving and receiving compliments and criticism. Particularly in view of the early onset and long history of his chronic, heavy drinking, it is not surprising that he had failed to develop healthy means of relating to other people while sober.

As one way to manage anxiety, Gary was taught deep muscle relaxation and the use of relaxing images, such as being at the beach on a pleasant day. He and his wife attended some sessions together to focus specifically on their ability to communicate clearly with one another. Alcohol dependence often leaves in its wake a legacy of resentment and frustration on the part of family members and guilt and shame on the part of the alcoholic. These feelings are understandable, but if left unexpressed and lingering may maintain problems in living even after the drinking has stopped.

DISCUSSION

Gary succeeded in attaining and maintaining abstinence for a period of six months after the end of the daily Antabuse dosing and the psychological intervention. During that time his relationship with his wife improved markedly, as did his self-esteem and general mood. His social phobia also improved, though he still had significant concerns over others' opinions of him and remained basically shy and unsure of himself socially. He was happier at work and performed his job better.

It is possible that Gary's continuing social discomfort could require a longer-term intervention. At some point it might become necessary to think in terms of accepting himself as a shy, relatively asocial person, rather than attempting to alter this basic personality disposition.

The therapist's belief that Gary would not be a good candidate for controlled drinking was based on the research reviewed earlier, which indicates that this approach is more feasible for lighter, less dependent drinkers. This prediction seemed to be borne out by Gary's experience during the posttreatment period. On two occasions he decided to test himself to see if he could drink just a little with his friends. He became quite drunk both times. This clear evidence that he still lacked control over his drinking, coupled with a threat from his wife that she would leave him for good, convinced Gary that complete abstinence was the only appropriate goal for him.

Perspectives on the Treatment of Illicit Drug Abuse

Central to the treatment of those who use illegal drugs is detoxification, withdrawal from the drug itself. Heroin withdrawal reactions range from relatively mild periods of anxiety, nausea, and restlessness for several days, to more severe and frightening bouts of delirium and apparent madness, depending primarily on the purity of the heroin that the individual has been using. Someone high on amphetamines can be brought down by appropriate dosages of one of the phenothiazines, a class of drugs more commonly used to treat schizophrenics (see Chapter 9). Withdrawal reactions from barbiturates, as already noted, are especially severe, even life threatening. They begin about twenty-four hours after the last dose and reach their maximum two or three days later. They usually abate by the end of the first week, but they may last a month if doses have been large. Withdrawal from these drugs is best done gradually and under close medical supervision (Honigfeld & Howard, 1978).

Detoxification is but the first step by which therapists try to help an addict. Finding a way to enable the drug user to function without drugs is an even more arduous task.

Mutual Help and Residential Communities

Self-help residential homes or communities are the most widespread psychological approach to dealing with heroin addiction and other drug abuse. These residences are designed to radically restructure the addict's outlook on life and put him or her in an environment in which illicit drugs have no place. Phoenix House and other drug rehabilitation homes offer a total environment in which drugs are not available. Continuing support is offered to ease the transition from regular drug use to a drug-free existence. This approach has the benefit of separating addicts from previous social contacts, on the assumption that these relationships have been instrumental in fostering an addictive lifestyle.

Another aspect of this environment is the presence of often charismatic role models who serve as counselors, former addicts who are meeting life's challenges without drugs. Residential programs use group therapy, in which addicts are confronted directly and urged to accept responsibility for their problems and drug habits and to take charge of their lives. However, this confrontation occurs in a setting in which addicts are respected as human beings, rather than stigmatized as failures or criminals.

Since entry to residential drug-treatment programs is voluntary, and only a small minority of those dependent on drugs enter such settings, it is difficult to evaluate their effectiveness (Jaffe, 1985). Furthermore, because the drop-out rate is high, those who remain cannot be regarded as representative of the population of people addicted to illicit drugs. (We have already seen these problems with evaluations of AA.) Their motivation to go straight is probably much higher than average. Thus any improvement they make reflects in part their uncommon desire to rid themselves of their habit rather than the specific qualities of the treatment program. Moreover, the role of mental health professionals is either nonexistent or marginal. As such, adequately designed research on the outcomes of these programs has not been undertaken. Such self-regulating residential communities, however, may help a large number of those who stay in them for a year or so (Jaffe, 1985).

Biological Perspectives

Treatments for Heroin Addiction

Two widely used drug therapy programs for heroin addiction are the administration of **heroin substitutes**, narcotics that can replace the body's craving for heroin, and of **heroin antagonists**, drugs that prevent the user from experiencing the heroin high. The first category includes **methadone** and methadyl acetate, both synthetic narcotics designed to take the place of heroin. Since they are themselves narcotics, successful treatment converts the heroin addict into a methadone addict. This conversion occurs because methadone acts on the same central nervous system receptors as heroin and becomes a substitute for the original dependency.

Abrupt discontinuation of methadone also causes withdrawal reactions, but these are not as severe as those of heroin, hence its potential therapeutic properties for weaning the addict altogether from drug dependence (Jaffe, 1985). The addict must come to a clinic and swallow the drug in the presence of a staff member, once a day for methadone and three times a week for methadyl acetate. Many methadone users manage to hold jobs, commit no crimes, and stay away from other illicit drugs (Cooper, 1983), but many others do not.

Since methadone does not give the addict a euphoric high, many return to heroin if it becomes available to them (Maddux & Desmond, 1992). In addition, when methadone is injected, rather than taken orally as it is supposed to be, its effects on some addicts are similar to those of heroin (Honigfeld & Howard, 1978). In this era of AIDS and the transmission of the human immunodeficiency

heroin substitutes Narcotics, like *methadone*, that replace the body's craving for *heroin*.

heroin antagonists Drugs, like naxolone, that prevent a *heroin* user from experiencing any high.

methadone A synthetic addictive *heroin substitute* for treating *heroin* addicts that acts as a substitute for *heroin* by eliminating its effects and the craving for it.

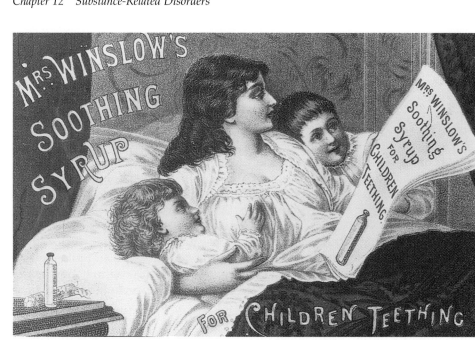

Heroin was synthesized from opium in 1874 and soon was being added to a variety of medicines that could be purchased without prescription. The ad shown here is for a teething remedy containing heroin. It probably worked.

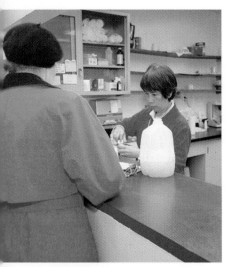

Methadone is a synthetic narcotic substitute. Former heroin addicts come to clinics each day and swallow their dose.

virus through shared needles (p. 478), the fact that methadone *can* be swallowed is a big advantage. Not surprisingly, an illegal market in methadone has developed, which would seem to be defeating the purpose of its use. Finally, a great many people drop out of methadone programs, in part because of side effects such as insomnia, constipation, excessive sweating, and diminished sexual function.

After being gradually weaned from heroin, addicts often receive increasing dosages of cyclazocine or naloxone, which prevent them from experiencing any high should they later take heroin. The drugs occupy the receptors in the brain that heroin usually binds to without stimulating them, and heroin molecules have no place to go. The antagonist, then, changes the whole nature of heroin. It simply will not produce the euphoric effect that the addict seeks. As with methadone, however, addicts must make frequent and regular visits to a clinic, which requires motivation and responsibility. In addition, addicts do not lose the actual craving for heroin for some time. Therefore, patient compliance is very poor with opiate antagonists (Ginzburg, 1986).

Treatments for Cocaine

Investigators are searching for medications that will ease the symptoms of withdrawal from cocaine and perhaps also attack the physical basis of the addiction. While some favorable results were reported with the antidepressants imipramine (Tennant & Rawson, 1982) and desipramine (Gawin et al., 1989), the findings from two more recent and better controlled studies were decidedly less positive (Arndt, Dorozynsky, Woody, McLellan, & O'Brien, 1992; Kosten, Morgan, Falcione, & Schottenfeld, 1992). Desipramine, though, may be useful as a first step in treatment. One study showed a significant advantage over a placebo in reducing cocaine use in the first six weeks of treatment, although the advantage disappeared by the end of the twelve-week study (Carroll et al., 1994).

Behavioral Perspectives

People turn to drugs for many reasons. Even though in most instances drug use is controlled primarily by a physical addiction, the entire pattern of the user's existence is bound to be influenced by the drug and must therefore command the attention of whoever would hope to remove the drug from the user's life. The difficulty of maintaining abstinence is attributable in a major way to environmental stimuli that can influence the recovering addict. The behavioral view is that the presence of needles, neighborhoods, and others with whom a person used to take drugs can readily come to elicit a craving for the substance (Wikler, 1980). Alcoholics and cigarette smokers have similar experiences in their local bars or while talking on the telephone.

While behavioral treatment is taking place there is some reduction in drug use, but this improvement does not usually last. Somewhat better results are emerging with cognitive-behavioral approaches (Sobell et al., 1990). Results may depend on patient characteristics. A study of cocaine abusers showed cognitive-behavioral strategies superior to minimal treatment only among the more severely addicted (Carroll et al., 1994).

To Recap

The first critical issue to face in treatment of addiction to illicit drugs is detoxification. Withdrawal from heroin or barbiturates, for instance, can be extremely uncomfortable or even life threatening and requires careful medical supervision. After this difficult period, strategies vary. Residential mutual-help programs entail moving the addict out of his or her previous environment and into a drug-free residence organized by recovering addicts. In these settings, addicts are encouraged to take responsibility for developing sober lifestyles.

Biological treatment strategies include the use of medications (a) to ease withdrawal symptoms (for example, desipramine may be useful in the early stages of cocaine-abuse treatment); (b) to substitute for the effects of the original drug (methadone satisfies the craving for heroin without providing the euphoric high, for instance); and (c) to nullify the effects of the original drug with an antagonist (for example, naloxone occupies receptors to which heroin usually binds and thereby prevents the user from experiencing a high if heroin is taken). Such medications have a place in drug treatment, but they may not be sufficient. Drop-out and noncompliance rates are high, and the immediate environment continues to exert a strong influence on the person to return to drug use.

Behavioral treatments include contingency management strategies such as making rewards dependent on drug-free urine testing. Such programs have yet to show long-term maintenance of improvement.

Perspectives on the Treatment of Nicotine Dependence

Self-Help and Advice

Most people who quit smoking do so without professional help (U. S. Department of Health and Human Services, 1989). Each year more than 30% of cigarette smokers try to quit with minimal outside assistance. They may read a brochure describing strategies often employed in smoking cessation programs or follow a friend's advice, but fewer than 10% succeed (Fiore et al., 1990). Those who smoke less and who are less addicted (Curry, 1993) or who experience less stress (Carey, Kalra, Carey, Halperin, & Richards, 1993) are the most likely to be able to quit smoking on their own.

Each year millions of smokers are told by their physicians to stop smok-

Preventing Abuse

It is generally acknowledged that by far the best way to deal with drug abuse is to *prevent* it in the first place. In recent years we have seen well-known sports and entertainment figures urge audiences not to experiment with drugs. The message in the 1960s and the 1970s was often that certain drugs—especially the psychedelics—would help people realize their potential or at least provide an escape from the humdrum and the stressful. The message in the 1990s, however, is that mind-altering drugs interfere with achievement and with emotional functioning and that, above all, these drugs are harmful to the body. "Just say no" has replaced "Turn on, tune in, drop out."

Adequate prevention requires more knowledge of the developmental paths to drug use. Such information will not only help clinical researchers target subgroups toward whom preventive efforts can be most fruitfully directed, but can also shed light on the whys and hows of people's initiation into and continuation of substance abuse and dependence.

In the 1980s and 1990s, several programs were developed to try to prevent substance abuse. These programs, typically directed at elementary school children, provide information on the harmful effects of drugs.

ing. There is some evidence that a physician's advice alone can get some people (an estimated 7% to 10%) to stop smoking (Fiore, Jorenby, Baker, & Kenford, 1992). However, much more needs to be learned about the nature of the advice, the manner in which it is given, its timing, and other factors that must surely play a role in whether an addicted individual is prepared and able to alter his or her behavior when advised by a physician to do so. Also, before a physician can help someone quit smoking, she or he must know which patients are in fact smokers. Only about one-half of smokers report ever having been asked by their physicians whether they smoke (Fiore et al., 1992).

Some smokers attend smoking clinics or consult with professionals for specialized smoking reduction programs. The American Cancer Society, the American Lung Association, and the Church of the Seventh Day Adventists have been especially active in offering programs to help people stop smoking. As mentioned earlier, an increasing number of nonsmokers object to people smoking in restaurants, trains, airplanes, and public buildings. The social context, then, provides more incentive and support to stop smoking than existed in 1964, when the surgeon general first warned of the serious health hazards associated with cigarette smoking. Even so, it is estimated that not more than half of those who go through smoking cessation programs succeed in quitting by the time the program is over. And only about one-third of those who succeed in the short term actually remain nonsmokers after a year (Schwartz, 1987). One response to such potentially dis-

A particularly well-studied application of drug prevention is the prevention of cigarette smoking among children. In recent years scores of school-based programs have aimed at preventing the onset of tobacco use by young people. A review of 143 such programs indicates marked success in delaying the onset of smoking (Tobler, 1986). Several components are found in such efforts (Hansen, Johnson, Flay, Graham, & Sobel, 1988).

▷ **Peer Pressure Resistance Training.** Instruction is given about the nature of peer pressure and ways to say no. The idea is to teach assertive ways to refuse invitations to smoke, not an easy matter for young people, for whom peer approval and acceptance are acutely important. Resistance training appears to work (Schinke & Gilchrist, 1985), more so for girls than for boys (Graham, Johnson, Hansen, Flay, & Gee, 1990).

▷ **Correction of Normative Expectations.** Many young people believe that cigarette smoking is more prevalent (and by implication, more acceptable) than it actually is. To counter this misinformation, some programs provide facts about prevalence rates as part of an attempt to convey the message that it is *not* okay to smoke cigarettes (or drink alcohol or use marijuana). Changing young people's sense of the societal norms appears to be a powerful tool in discouraging adolescents from indulging (Hansen & Graham, 1991).

▷ **Information about Parental Influences.** Since it is known that parental smoking is strongly correlated with smoking by their children, some programs point out this fact and argue that this aspect of one's parents' behavior does not have to be imitated.

▷ **Peer Leadership.** Most programs involve peers of recognized status to enhance the impact of the nonsmoking messages being conveyed.

▷ **Self-Image Enhancement.** A number of programs focus on the idea that intrapsychic factors, such as poor self-image and inability to cope with stress, underlie the onset of smoking in young people. However, this approach appears far less effective in preventing the use of tobacco, alcohol, and marijuana than the other methods listed (Hansen et al., 1988). In fact, there were indications that a program with this emphasis actually *increased* drug use over a period of three years, perhaps by unintentionally suggesting drug experimentation to deal with life stress.

couraging statistics is to try to develop improved programs based on what theory and research tell us about what maintains nicotine dependence. We review such efforts in the next several subsections. Another approach is to conclude that quitting smoking is difficult, so why not try to prevent people from starting in the first place (see Focus Box 12.3)?

Biological Strategies: Nicotine Replacement

Two biological treatments aim to satisfy the smoker's need for nicotine without the adverse effects of smoking: nicotine gum and nicotine patches.

Nicotine Gum

Nicotine is the addictive substance in tobacco. Each of the thousands of puffs that a smoker takes each day during the consumption of a pack or two of cigarettes delivers nicotine to the brain in seven seconds. Gum containing nicotine, available in the United States since 1984 by doctor's prescription, may help smokers endure the nicotine withdrawal that accompanies any effort to stop smoking. The nicotine in gum is absorbed much more slowly and steadily. Also, it helps disconnect the act of smoking from the nicotine hit, which disconnects the act of quitting smoking from the nicotine fit, or withdrawal. The long-term goal, of course,

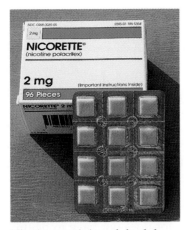

Nicotine gum is intended to help smokers who are trying to quit, by lessening the symptoms of withdrawal from nicotine.

is for the former smoker to be able to cut back on the use of the gum as well, eventually eliminating reliance on nicotine altogether.

Ex-smokers can become dependent on this gum. Moreover, the gum can produce cardiovascular changes, such as increased blood pressure, that can be dangerous to people with cardiovascular diseases. Nevertheless, even prolonged, continued use of the gum may be healthier than obtaining nicotine by smoking because at least the poisons in the smoke and damage to the lungs are avoided.

Clinical support is important. This entails monitoring the use of the gum for the first week, daily encouragement, and advice regarding coping with the urge to smoke. The gum must be chewed slowly as well as intermittently and then discarded after about twenty minutes. Enough must be chewed to provide relief from withdrawal—as many as fifteen pieces a day. This regimen may last for several months, with a gradual tapering off, and the gum should be kept on hand for emergencies after that (Schneider, 1987). The best results occur when the gum is combined with a behaviorally oriented treatment (Killen, Fortmann, Newman, & Varady, 1990). A quantitative review of thirty-three studies estimated one-year abstinence rates averaging 35% for intensive treatments including nicotine gum and 22% for the same treatments with placebo gum or no gum (Cepeda-Benito, 1993). When nicotine gum is prescribed in a minimal treatment context, for instance, as part of a physician's *unsolicited* advice to stop smoking, it seems to have no long-term effect (Cepeda-Benito, 1993; Hughes, Gust, Keenan, Fenwick, & Healey, 1989).

Nicotine Patches

The nicotine patch, a polyethylene patch taped to the arm, provides a transdermal nicotine delivery system that slowly and steadily releases the drug through the skin, into the bloodstream, and thence to the brain. These patches began to be sold in December 1991. An advantage of this method over nicotine gum is that the person need only apply a patch each day and not remove it, making it easier to use properly. Marketed directly to consumers, who were instructed to ask their physicians about "the patch," nicotine patches immediately became a billion dollar a year industry (Fiore et al., 1992).

The patch is designed to be used over a period of six to eight weeks, with the dose decreasing as treatment progresses (Fiore et al., 1992). A person who continues smoking while wearing the patch risks increasing the amount of nicotine in the body to dangerous levels.

Studies comparing the patch with a placebo show that the patch is effective in helping smokers abstain and reduces their craving for nicotine (Abelin, Buehler, Mueller, Vesanen, & Imhof, 1989). The advantage of the patch over a placebo is maintained at six-month follow-up, with average success rates of about 25% for the patch and 15% for the placebo (Fiore et al., 1992). In other words, the patch is helpful, but not a panacea. As in the case of nicotine gum, it is hypothesized that results will be best if the patch is combined with therapies aimed at finding other ways for the ex-smoker to relax, to concentrate, to have something to do, to maintain a personally acceptable body weight, and so forth—all the functions cigarettes serve in addition to warding off nicotine withdrawal (Hughes, 1993). Patch manufacturers state that the patch is to be used only as part of a psychological smoking-cessation program, and then for not more than three months at a time. The manufacturers offer psychological support via free 800 telephone numbers.

Behavioral Perspectives

Many efforts have been made within behavioral frameworks to reduce or eliminate cigarette smoking. Although short-term results are often very encouraging, longer term results are more modest. Regardless of how well things look when an intervention ends, on any given attempt to quit the overwhelming majority of smokers return to their drug dependence within a year. This evidence does not deny the fact that a substantial minority of smokers can be helped. As with other efforts to change behavior, though, the task is not an easy one.

The idea behind some behavioral techniques is to make smoking unpleasant, even nauseating. For a while in the 1970s, there was considerable interest in *rapid-smoking treatment,* a kind of aversion therapy in which a smoker sits in a poorly ventilated room and puffs much faster than normal, perhaps as often as every six seconds (e.g., Lando, 1977). Newer variations include *rapid puffing* (rapid smoking without inhaling), *focused smoking* (in which the person smokes for a long period of time but at a normal rate), and *smoke holding* (retaining smoke in the mouth for several minutes but without inhaling). Although such treatments reduce smoking and foster abstinence more than no-treatment control conditions, they usually do not differ from each other or from other credible interventions. They also show high rates of relapse at follow-ups of several months to a year (Schwartz, 1987; Sobell et al., 1990).

Cognitive Perspectives

Cognitive therapists have tried to encourage more control in the smoker. Treatments teach various coping skills, such as relaxation and positive self-talk, when confronted with tempting situations, for example, following a meal or sitting down to read a book. Results with such interventions alone have not been very promising (Schwartz, 1987).

Cognitive therapy may have an increasingly important specialized role to play in smoking cessation, however, by virtue of its utility in the treatment of depression (see Chapter 10). Depression and nicotine dependence are positively correlated, and people with a history of major depression have greater difficulty quitting smoking than do others (Hall, Munoz, Reus, & Sees, 1993). As an adjunctive treatment, a mood-management program incorporating principles and techniques of cognitive therapy significantly increased the effectiveness of nicotine gum *only* for smokers with a history of major depression (Hall, Munoz, & Reus, 1994).

To Recap

Most people who have quit smoking have done so on their own, though most unaided quitters, especially heavier smokers, fail on a given attempt. Physician advice to quit is sometimes effective in its own right and has great potential as a public health measure, since such a high percentage of people (especially smokers) have occasion to see physicians. Nicotine replacement therapies include nicotine gum and the nicotine patch. These items are designed to decouple the habit of smoking from the intake of nicotine and gradually to wean the nicotine addict in such a way as to minimize withdrawal symptoms. These methods appear more successful than placebo controls at six-to-twelve month follow-ups, especially if they are used along with behavioral strategies.

Behavioral methods, such as rapid smoking, attempt to link smoking with unpleasant consequences. As with most methods of intervention, long-term results are modest. Cognitive therapy has had little impact in smoking cessation, though it may prove useful for those with a history of depression, who otherwise tend to have particular difficulty quitting.

Visual Summary for Chapter 12:

Substance-Related Disorders

Substance abuse: *Recurrent use of a drug resulting in impaired social or occupational functioning.*
Substance dependence: *Out-of-control drug taking often accompanied by physiological dependence.*

Selected Addictive Drugs

Drug	Effects	Comments
Nicotine	*Sympathetic arousal but feelings of relaxation in addicted smokers; lung cancer, emphysema, heart disease, birth defects in offspring.*	*Prevalence has declined greatly as publicity about health consequences, legal restrictions on, and social disapproval of smoking in public have increased.*
Marijuana	*Relaxing, impairs cognitive functioning (e.g., short-term memory) and motor skills, damages lung functioning, increases heart rate.*	*Prevalence declining since late 1970's although recently rising. Seems to induce tolerance.*
Sedatives	*Pain relief, drowsiness, euphoria. Barbiturates can be fatal in combination with alcohol.*	*Severe withdrawal syndrome.* **Examples:** *Opium, morphine, heroin, barbiturates. Illegal and expensive nature of narcotics links addiction to them with criminality.*
Amphetamines	*Increased alertness, motor activity, energy, euphoria. In large doses can induce psychosis.*	*Severe addicts may have euphoric binges of several days' duration with periods of crashing.*
Cocaine	*Feelings of exhilaration; creates risk of heart attacks and retardation in offspring.*	*Prevalence has declined since mid-1980s, following a decade of rapid increase.*
Hallucinogens	*Hallucinations, odd sensory distortions, unstable mood, panic about going crazy.*	**Examples:** *LSD, mescaline, psilocybin, Ecstasy. Effects may depend on setting and expectancies, not just type of drug and dose.*
Alcohol	*Initially stimulating, then depressing. Impairs coordination, cognitive processes. Contributes to work absences, auto accidents, child and spouse abuse, homicide. In the long run, may lead to amnestic syndrome, cirrhosis, heart disease, birth defects in offspring.*	*Legal, available, **used** by most people, dependence much more common among men.*

Perspective on Causes of Addiction

Personality	*Character defects (e.g., antisocial personality, low self-esteem) cause vulnerability to addiction.*
Biological	*Vulnerability to at least some forms of addiction (e.g., early-onset chronic alcoholism among men, perhaps mediated by low responsiveness to the intoxicating effects of alcohol) is genetically transmitted.*

Behavioral ••••>	Drugs make us feel better, or in some cases make us feel less bad (less bored, less anxious, etc.). Such effects are reinforcing and override the negative consequences for people who lack alternative skills for mood self-regulation.
Cognitive ••••>	Drugs are uniquely reinforcing, and therefore used or abused, to the extent that we **expect** them to be. These expectations may be independent of pharmacological effects.
Sociocultural ••>	Drug use varies by nation, religion, subculture, and historical period. Peers, opinion leaders, and the mass media shape attitudes that favor or inhibit drug use, which is a prerequisite for drug dependence.

Treatments for Addiction

Perspective	General Strategy	Example	Effects
Biological ••••>	Alleviate withdrawal and ••> craving, often via substitute medication.	Nicotine patch for cigarette ••••> smokers.	Useful component of treatment, perhaps especially for the more severely dependent, but singly insufficient because of failure to provide skills for long-term drug-free living.
Behavioral ••••>	Make abstinence more ••••> reinforcing and drug use less so. Bolster skills for obtaining nondrug reinforcements.	Rapid smoking for nicotine ••••> dependence.	Little impact on illicit drug abuse or on nicotine dependence in the long term. Positive results for several techniques in treating alcoholism.
Psychodynamic •>	Support and practical ••••> advice to achieve abstinence, followed by exploration of unconscious conflicts underlying addiction.	Individual dynamic therapy ••••> for alcoholism in conjunction with advice to attend AA.	Generally unknown.
Cognitive ••••>	Alter thoughts about ••••> consequences of drug use, reduce emotional distress that may underlie drug use.	Cognitive restructuring for ••••> cocaine relapse prevention.	Modest overall. Some data suggesting relevancy for subgroups of addicts.
Eclectic ••••>	Tailor strategy to suit ••••> individual and circumstances. Most relevant interventions depend on which skills are currently lacking, presence of comorbid disorders, drug-use history, associated life problems and so on.	Minimal advice for young, ••••> low-dependence smokers, but nicotine replacement and cognitive-skills training for mood management if highly dependent.	Some specific studies look promising, but no well-validated, all-purpose decision rules.
Mutual help •••>	Each one, teach one (i.e., •••> get better yourself by sharing experiences and emotional support with fellow addicts).	Anonymous fellowship groups, •••> such as AA.	Generally unknown. Probably requires freely choosing the group, staying with it, and making its spiritual and social aspects a centerpiece of one's life.

Chapter 13

Sexual and Gender Identity Disorders

The Case of Barbara Garrison

Barbara Garrison's principal complaint when she arrived for her first appointment at the mental health center was an inability to achieve orgasm during sexual intercourse with her husband, Frank. They were both thirty-three and had been married for fifteen years. Frank was a police detective, and Barbara had recently resumed her college education.

Barbara experienced orgasms by masturbating, which she did once or twice a week, but never during sexual activity with Frank. She found him sexually attractive and did become aroused, though, during their sexual encounters. They had intercourse two or three times a month, usually late at night after their two children, ages fifteen and twelve, had gone to sleep. Their foreplay seldom lasted more than five minutes. Frank always reached orgasm quickly after penetration and often fell asleep shortly thereafter, leaving Barbara frustrated. Sometimes she would slip out of the bedroom to the TV room, where she would secretly masturbate to orgasm.

This situation was very distressing to Barbara. She felt guilty about masturbating, especially after sexual intercourse, as she thought it was a very deviant practice. She was also concerned about the fantasies in which she engaged during masturbation, which involved having intercourse with several men—usually strangers, but sometimes friends to whom she was attracted. She believed that these promiscuous fantasies might mean that she was a latent nymphomaniac.

Barbara's anxieties about her sexual interests and arousal were also a problem during intercourse with Frank. She was self-conscious about what he would think of her and whether she was performing adequately. The combination of fear of loss of control of her sexual impulses and continual worry about her perceived inadequacy as a sexual partner prompted Barbara to seek professional help.

In addition to the sexual problem, Barbara and Frank were not getting along as well as they had in the past. Frank had not completed his college education, and he was threatened by the possibility that Barbara might finish her degree. He was uncomfortable around her friends from the university. They also had more financial concerns than before. Tuition was expensive, and they had taken out a loan to build an addition to their home. In order to make more money, Frank had been working more overtime hours. When he was home, Barbara resented the fact that he spent most of his spare time working on the new rooms in their house. Finally, they disagreed about matters of discipline, such as whether their daughter should be allowed to be alone with her boyfriend without adult supervision. Barbara was stricter on this issue, being preoccupied with fears that Bonnie would become pregnant as a teenager.

Despite their conflicts, Barbara and Frank were both committed to their marriage. Neither was happy, but they were not considering divorce. Barbara thought that their relationship would be improved if she could overcome her orgasmic dysfunction. Frank was less concerned about that matter in particular, but agreed that Barbara might feel better if a therapist could "help her understand *her* problem."

Of all the aspects of human behavior that command the attention of psychopathologists and clinicians, few touch the lives of more people than problems involving sex. As we see in the case of Barbara Garrison, sexual problems both influence and are influenced by other aspects of a relationship. Sexual difficulties can create problems in a marriage. Often, though, other stresses, such as unemployment or parenting difficulties, can cause sexual problems. This chapter considers the full range of human sexual thoughts, feelings, and actions that are generally regarded as abnormal and are listed in DSM-IV as sexual and gender identity disorders (See Table 13.1 for an outline of the disorders described in this chapter).

Table 13.1 ▶ **Sexual and Gender Identity Disorders**

A. Sexual Dysfunctions
    1. Sexual desire disorders
        a. Hypoactive sexual desire disorder
        b. Sexual aversion disorder
    2. Sexual arousal disorders
        a. Female sexual arousal disorder
        b. Male erectile disorder
    3. Orgasmic disorders
        a. Female orgasmic disorder
        b. Male orgasmic disorder
        c. Premature ejaculation
    4. Sexual pain disorders
        a. Dyspareunia
        b. Vaginismus
B. Gender Identity Disorders
C. Paraphilias
    1. Pedophilia
    2. Fetishism
    3. Voyeurism
    4. Exhibitionism
    5. Sexual sadism
    6. Sexual masochism

We discuss first *sexual dysfunctions*, disruptions in normal sexual functioning found in many people who are in otherwise reasonably sound psychological health. We then turn to *gender identity disorder*, characterized by strong identification with the opposite sex and a sense of discomfort with one's own sex. *Paraphilias* involve intense, persistent sexual attraction to nonhuman objects or to children or other nonconsenting people, or suffering or humiliation of oneself or a partner. The final two sections of the chapter deal with rape and homosexuality. Rape is not a separate category in DSM-IV but clearly merits attention from psychopathologists. Homosexuality is not considered a disorder, but it has a controversial history in the DSM that can shed light on some issues in the study of sexuality and abnormal behavior in general.

 ## Sexual Dysfunctions

sexual dysfunctions Recurrent, distressing inhibitions in the normal sexual response cycle.

Many people have problems that interfere with conventional sexual enjoyment. In the most general terms, such **sexual dysfunctions** are defined as inhibitions in the normal sexual response cycle. To be considered a dysfunction, the difficulty should be persistent and recurrent, a clinical judgment acknowledged in the DSM as somewhat subjective. New in DSM-IV is the requirement that the disturbance cause marked distress or interpersonal problems. This change allows the person's *own* reactions to, say, having no interest in sex, to play a role in whether he or she should be diagnosed. Barbara Garrison came to treatment because her relationship with her husband had deteriorated, and she was experiencing distress regarding their sexual relations. Sexual dysfunctions are not diagnosed if the problems are believed to be due entirely to a medical illness (such as advanced diabetes, which can cause erectile problems in men) or if they are believed to be due to another Axis I disorder (such as major depressive disorder).

A psychological problem such as sexual dysfunction has consequences not

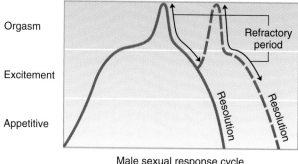

Male sexual response cycle

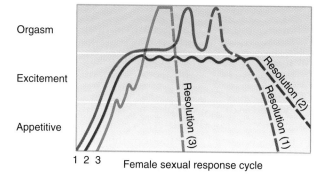

Female sexual response cycle

Figure 13.1 *The stages of the human sexual response cycle. Note the different patterns for men and women.*

only for the individual but also for those with whom he or she is involved. A marriage is bound to suffer if one or both of the partners fear sex. And most of us, for better and for worse, base part of our self-concept on our sexuality. Do we please the people we love, do we gratify ourselves, or, more simply, are we able to enjoy the fulfillment and relaxation that can come from a pleasurable sexual experience? Sexual dysfunctions can be so severe that tenderness itself is lost, let alone the more intense satisfaction of sexual activity.

We look first at the human sexual response cycle as it normally functions and then at sexual dysfunctions and their causes and treatment.

The Human Sexual Response Cycle

Most conceptualizations of the sexual response cycle are a distillation of proposals by Havelock Ellis (1906), Masters and Johnson (1966), and Helen Singer Kaplan (1974). The work of Masters and Johnson in particular signaled a revolution in the nature and intensity of research in and clinical attention to human sexuality. They extended the earlier interview-based breakthroughs of the Kinsey group (Kinsey, Pomeroy, Main, & Gebbard, 1953; Kinsey, Pomeroy, & Martin, 1948) to make direct observations and physiological measurements of people masturbating and having sexual intercourse.

Based on this research, four phases in the human sexual response cycle are typically identified (see Figure 13.1).

1. **Appetitive.** This stage refers to initial sexual interest or desire, often associated with sexually arousing fantasies (Kaplan, 1974).
2. **Excitement.** This stage is a subjective experience of sexual pleasure associated with physiological changes brought about by increased blood flow. This **tumescence**—the flow of blood into tissues—shows up in men as erection of the penis and in women as enlargement of the breasts and changes in the vagina, such as increased lubrication.

The pioneering work of the sex therapists William H. Masters and Virginia Johnson helped launch a more candid and scientific appraisal of human sexuality.

3. **Orgasm.** In this phase sexual pleasure peaks. In men, ejaculation feels inevitable and indeed almost always occurs (in rare instances some men can have an orgasm without ejaculating and can ejaculate without experiencing orgasm). In women, the walls of the outer third of the vagina contract. In both sexes there is general muscle tension and involuntary pelvic thrusting.

4. **Resolution.** This last stage refers to the relaxation and sense of well-being that usually follow an orgasm. In men, there is an associated refractory period during which further erection and arousal are not possible (but for varying periods of time across individuals and even within the same person across occasions). Women, however, are often able to respond again with sexual excitement almost immediately.

Specific Dysfunctions

It is important that people do not assume that they need treatment simply because they sometimes experience one or more disturbances in the sexual response cycle. The prevalence of disturbances in the cycle just described is high. For example, in a survey of married heterosexual couples, almost half the men reported erectile and ejaculatory problems and more than half the women reported arousal or orgasmic problems—yet 80% of the couples regarded their marital and sexual relations as positive and satisfying (Frank, Anderson, & Rubenstein, 1978). In the diagnostic criteria for each sexual dysfunction, the phrase "persistent or recurrent" is included to underscore the fact that a problem must be serious indeed before a diagnosis of dysfunction is made. A given individual's responses can differ noticeably from the population average and yet not be considered abnormal (see Focus Box 13.1). Problems can and do occur at every stage of the response cycle. Even those persistent enough to merit the label "dysfunction" can often be successfully treated. Beginning with dysfunctions based on the first stage of the sexual response cycle, we look at some of the ways in which normal functioning can be impaired, perspectives on why such dysfunctions occur, and the treatments that have been developed to restore normal sexual functioning.

Sexual Desire Disorders

hypoactive sexual desire disorder The absence of or deficiency in sexual fantasies and urges.

sexual aversion disorder Avoidance of nearly all genital contact with other people.

DSM-IV distinguishes two kinds of sexual desire disorders. In **hypoactive sexual desire disorder**, usually referred to as low sex drive, sexual fantasies and urges are deficient or absent. In **sexual aversion disorder** the person actively avoids nearly all genital contact with another. In making either diagnosis the clinician should take into consideration the patient's age, health, and life circumstances. Among people seeking treatment for sexual dysfunctions, more than half complain of low desire. Of these, 60% are men (Spector & Carey, 1990).

As indicated in the DSM-IV, hypoactive sexual desire disorder is a diagnosis resting heavily on clinical judgment, for there are no objective criteria for how often a person *should* want sex. Diagnosis is also complicated by the interpersonal nature of sexual dysfunction. One partner might seem to have deficient sexual desire only because his or her sexual desire is low in comparison with the other partner's particularly high sexual desire. The hypoactive desire category appeared for the first time in DSM-III in 1980. This diagnosis may reflect increasingly high expectations that people have about being sexual. In general, the importance of sex in someone's life can vary tremendously. Unlike hunger and thirst, an appetite for sex does not need to be satisfied or even to exist in order for the individual to survive and, it seems, to live happily.

Little is known about the causes of either hypoactive sexual desire or sexual aversion disorder. Hypothesized causes include religious orthodoxy, trying to have sex with a partner of the nonpreferred gender, fear of loss of control, fear of

Helen Singer Kaplan is the noted sex therapist who introduced the appetitive phase to the sexual response cycle.

◣ FOCUS BOX 13.1

Some Sexual Myths Dispelled by Masters and Johnson

Masters and Johnson's work had considerable impact in contributing to our knowledge of the physiology of human sexuality and helped to legitimize the scientific study of sex. The laboratory circumstances in which Masters and Johnson gathered their findings limit their generality somewhat, however. We should be mindful as well that their physiological research can tell us little about the *psychological* components of human sexuality, particularly the romantic aspects of a relationship. Masters and Johnson nonetheless provided useful data on certain controversial points and were able to dispel a few myths.

▶ Although the **clitoris** (the small, heavily innervated erectile structure located above the vaginal opening) is very important in transmitting sexual stimulation in the female, it has been a mistake to advise continual stimulation during intercourse. During the excitement phase the clitoris retracts, making access to it extremely difficult and even painful for some women. In fact, it is very difficult to have intercourse without stimulating the clitoris *indirectly*, which is the type of stimulation that some women prefer.

▶ Orgasms in women obtained from stimulation of the clitoris, without entrance into the vagina, are as in-

tense as, indeed, physiologically indistinguishable from, orgasms obtained by having an erect penis in the vagina.

▶ Having simultaneous orgasms, a goal held up in numerous marriage manuals as indicating true love and compatibility, is not a mark of superior sexual achievement. In fact, working toward such a goal can often distract the partners from their own sexual pleasure. In any case, some experts believe that simultaneous orgasms are actually rare (Wincze & Carey, 1991).

▶ Most women do not object to intercourse during menstruation. Recent laboratory evidence reported by Meuwissen and Over (1992) shows little variation in the ability to become sexually aroused across different phases of the menstrual cycle.

▶ The size of a man's erect penis is not a key factor in the enjoyment he can derive himself or impart to his sexual partner. For the most part, the vagina is a potential, not an actual, space; that is, it distends just enough to accommodate the penis. Hence a very large penis really does not create more friction for the man or the woman than does a smaller one. Furthermore, penises that are small when flaccid may double in size when erect, whereas penises that are large in the limp state increase less proportionately. In other words, there does not seem to be as much variation in the size of the *erect* penis as was formerly assumed.

clitoris The small, heavily innervated structure located above the vaginal opening; the primary site of female responsiveness to sexual stimulation.

---

pregnancy, depression, side effects from medications such as antihypertensives and tranquilizers, couples conflict, lack of attraction to the partner (LoPiccolo & Friedman, 1988), past history of sexual trauma such as rape (Stuart & Greer, 1984), and fears of contracting AIDS (Katz, Gipson, Kearl, & Kriskovich, 1989).

Sexual Arousal Disorders

Difficulties at the next stage of sexual response, sexual arousal disorders, include **female sexual arousal disorder** and **male erectile disorder**, which used to be called by the pejorative terms *frigidity* and *impotence*, respectively. Arousal disorders and orgasmic disorders (discussed later) assume that the person has adequate sexual stimulation. In other words, if the situation is simply that the person's partner does not do what the person *likes*, the diagnosis is not made.

In female sexual arousal disorder, there is inadequate vaginal lubrication for comfortable completion of intercourse. In male erectile disorder there is failure to attain or maintain an erection through completion of the sexual activity. The prevalence of female sexual arousal disorder is estimated to be around 11%

female sexual arousal disorder The inability of a woman to reach or maintain the lubrication stage of sexual excitement or the inability to enjoy a subjective sense of pleasure or excitement during sexual activity.

male erectile disorder A recurrent and persistent inability to attain or maintain an erection until completion of sexual activity.

The Accused *depicted a gang rape and its legal aftermath. A traumatic event like this is regarded by Masters and Johnson as a possible cause of sexual dysfunction.*

(Spector & Carey, 1990). For male erectile disorder prevalence is estimated at between 3% and 9% (e.g., Frank et al., 1978) and increases greatly in older adults (Kinsey et al., 1948). Arousal problems account for about half the complaints of men and women who seek help with sexual dysfunctions (Renshaw, 1988).

In addition to the fear of performance and the spectator role discussed later as general causes of sexual dysfunctions, some specific causes are believed to underlie female arousal problems. A woman may not have learned adequately what she finds sexually arousing and may even lack knowledge about her own anatomy. Coupled with a shyness about communicating her needs, she may find the behavior of her partner unstimulating or even aversive.

Erectile problems vary widely (Kaplan, 1974). Some men get an erection easily but lose it as they enter the woman's vagina. Others are flaccid when intercourse is imminent but maintain an erection easily during fellatio. Some men have erect penises when the partner dominates the situation, others when they themselves are in control. Some are unable to maintain an erection under any circumstances. Others have problems only with people they care for deeply. A woman can go through the motions of lovemaking, but sexual intercourse is usually stalemated if the man is not erect. Thus, a great deal is at stake if the penis becomes flaccid when it "should" be erect, thereby increasing the psychological stressfulness of male erectile disorder.

As many as two-thirds of erectile problems have some organic basis, usually combined with psychological factors (LoPiccolo, 1992a). In general, any disease or hormonal imbalance that can affect the nerve pathways or blood supply to the penis can contribute to erectile problems (Geer, Heiman, & Leitenberg, 1984). These include certain drugs, such as some antihypertensive medications, and illnesses, such as diabetes and chronic alcoholism.

Orgasmic Disorders

For some people, the orgasmic phase presents a problem. Three kinds of orgasmic disorders are described in DSM-IV, female orgasmic disorder, male orgasmic disorder, and premature ejaculation in men.

Female Orgasmic Disorder.   **Female orgasmic disorder** refers to absence of orgasm after a period of normal sexual excitement. Stimulation can come from masturbation or from having sex with a partner. How prevalent a problem is this in women? Answering that question has proved difficult for researchers.

female orgasmic disorder A recurrent and persistent absence of orgasm in a woman during sexual activity adequate in focus, intensity, and duration; in many instances the woman may nonetheless experience considerable sexual excitement.

> APPLYING CRITICAL THINKING SKILLS

ASSESSING THE PREVALENCE OF FEMALE ORGASMIC DISORDER

Information on prevalence rates for any and all sexual dysfunctions, or indeed for sexual behaviors in general, is of questionable accuracy and must be interpreted with care. The prevalence of female orgasmic disorder provides an excellent example.

The classic Kinsey study reported that 10% of all women said that they had never experienced an orgasm (Kinsey et al., 1953). A quarter of a century later Levine and Yost (1976) found that only 5% were nonorgasmic over their lifetimes. What this shift means and how to account for it pose an interesting problem.

▶*What conclusion does the evidence seem to support?* The most straightforward conclusion would be that the prevalence of being nonorgasmic declined among women in the third quarter of the twentieth century, perhaps as a result of more widespread dissemination of accurate information about sexuality.

▶*What other interpretations are plausible?* One or both of the prevalence estimates might be wrong. It is not easy to obtain a representative sample in this sort of study. People who are willing to respond to surveys about sexuality may be especially uninhibited, or perhaps especially concerned or distressed about sex. Any such tendency among respondents could cause underestimates or overestimates of sexual dysfunctions. Such sampling biases are a notorious difficulty with sex surveys and form the grounds for criticism of the work of Shere Hite (1976), which is based on anecdotes from people who responded to magazine ads.

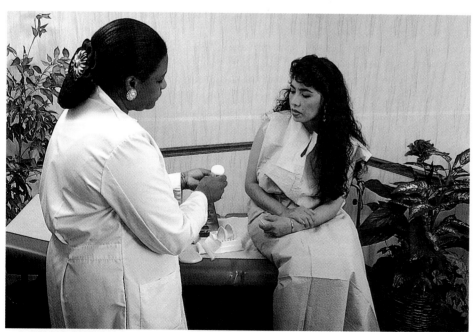

Information about sexuality and birth control is disseminated in health care settings as well as schools and via mass media. The increase in this information may have contributed to lowering the frequency of female orgasmic disorder.

Another potential source of error in these prevalence rates is that even if people are willing to respond, there is no guarantee that they are responding honestly to questions about such sensitive material as sexual problems. The vast majority of studies on sex rely on self-reports. It might realistically be conceded that we have far more information on *reported* sexual behaviors than on sexual behaviors themselves (Oliver & Hyde, 1993). If social mores that affect willingness to respond, and respond honestly, to questions about sex dysfunctions changed between 1953 and 1976, it could explain the differing results of the two studies of the prevalence of nonorgasmic women. Perhaps inhibited women were uncomfortable reporting that they had orgasms. Or perhaps the sexual mores of the 1970s made some women uncomfortable reporting their *lack* of response.

▶ **What other information would help choose among the alternative interpretations?** Since it is unlikely that researchers would receive permission to unobtrusively observe the sexual encounters of a random sample of women on a continuous basis throughout their lifetimes, and equally unlikely that researchers would have an infallible observational measure of the occurrence of orgasm, it is difficult to imagine how one might conclusively study the prevalence of female orgasmic disorder. It might be possible, though, to use multiple methods to test whether changes in prevalence over time are real changes in sexual experience or only changes in reporting. One could, for example, repeatedly survey women about whether they have ever had an orgasm, but do so in different ways. One method could foster honest responding, such as clearly guaranteeing confidentiality of written responses, while another does not, such as asking for immediate answers spoken to an interviewer. If the confidential written survey shows no change over time, while the interview does, it would support the hypothesis that discussion of orgasms has changed more than orgasms themselves.   ◼◀

While the specific percentages are elusive, clearly a proportion of women have never experienced an orgasm and a greater proportion have orgasms only rarely (Spector & Carey, 1990). However, as reflected in the case of Barbara Garrison, being nonorgasmic does not mean being unaroused or unresponsive during lovemaking. To the contrary, most women with female orgasmic disorder are responsive sexually (Kaplan, 1974).

Numerous explanations for female orgasmic disorder have been proposed. Lack of sexual knowledge appears to play a role. Many nonorgasmic women are unaware of their own genital anatomy and therefore have trouble knowing what their needs are and communicating them to a partner. Chronic use of alcohol may contribute to orgasmic dysfunction in some women (Wilsnak, 1984).

Women also have different thresholds for orgasm. Although some have orgasms quickly and without much clitoral stimulation, others seem to need intense and prolonged stimulation during foreplay or intercourse. Because a man may conclude that he and his penis are inadequate if the woman asks for manual stimulation of her clitoris during intercourse, the reaction of a woman's partner can contribute to the problem.

Another factor, seemingly relevant in the chapter-opening case, may be fear of losing control. The French have an expression for orgasm, *la petite mort*, "the little death." Some women fear that they will begin screaming uncontrollably, make fools of themselves, or faint. A related source of inhibition is a belief, perhaps poorly articulated, that to let go and allow the body to take over from the conscious, controlling mind is somehow unseemly. The state of a relationship is also important. Although some women can enjoy making love to a person with whom they are angry, most hold back under such circumstances.

male orgasmic disorder   A recurrent and persistent delay or absence of ejaculation after an adequate phase of sexual excitement.

Male Orgasmic Disorder.   The DSM-IV diagnosis of **male orgasmic disorder** is applied to problems ejaculating during intercourse, masturbation, manual or oral manipulation by a partner, or anal intercourse. Difficulty ejaculating is relatively rare. Hypothesized causes include fear of impregnating a female partner, withholding love, expressing hostility, and, as with female orgasmic disorder, fear of letting go. In rare cases the problem may be traced to a physical source, such as taking certain tranquilizers (Munjack & Kanno, 1979).

Premature Ejaculation. **Premature ejaculation** was defined by Masters and Johnson (1970) as a man's inability to inhibit his orgasm long enough for his partner to climax in 50% of their sexual encounters. Many people were concerned about couching the problem in terms of a *partner's* responsiveness. In DSM-IV these concerns were addressed by including the man's own desires and preferences as well as such factors as his age and the novelty of the sexual partner or situation. Thus, there is no specific numerical definition in DSM-IV regarding when ejaculation is premature. Sometimes the man ejaculates before he penetrates the vagina, but more usually within a few seconds of penetration.

Premature ejaculation is probably the most prevalent sexual dysfunction among males, a problem for 30% of men at any given time. Men with such problems ejaculate at lower levels of sexual arousal and have longer periods of abstinence from climactic sex than do other men (Spiess, Geer, & O'Donohue, 1984). In general, premature ejaculation is associated with considerable anxiety.

Concern about ejaculating too soon may be regarded as part and parcel of the undue emphasis placed on coitus as the ultimate in sexual behavior. The problem for couples who prize conventional sexual intercourse above all other sexual activities is that erection is slowly lost after an ejaculation, with many men finding continued stimulation unpleasant and sometimes painful. If lovemaking stops when the penis is no longer hard, ejaculation may indeed sometimes be premature. But if, as sex therapists advise, couples expand their repertoire of activities to include techniques not requiring an engorged penis, gratification of the partner is eminently possible *after* the man has climaxed. Indeed, when the focus is removed from penile-vaginal intercourse, a couple's anxieties about sex usually diminish sufficiently to permit greater ejaculatory control in the man and sexual intercourse of longer duration.

Sexual Pain Disorders

Two pain disorders associated with sex are listed in the DSM, dyspareunia and vaginismus. **Dyspareunia** is diagnosed when there is recurrent pain before, during, or after sexual intercourse. In women the diagnosis is not made when the pain is believed to be due to lack of vaginal lubrication (when presumably female sexual arousal disorder would be diagnosed). It is also not diagnosed when the pain is judged to result from the second pain disorder, **vaginismus**, which is marked by involuntary spasms of the outer third of the vagina to such a degree that intercourse is uncomfortable or even impossible. Prevalence of dyspareunia in women has been estimated at 8% (Schover, 1981). It is far less common among men, affecting perhaps 1% (Bancroft, 1989). Estimates for vaginismus vary widely but are not based on good epidemiological data. It is believed to be rare (Wincze & Carey, 1991).

One theory of vaginismus is that the woman wishes, perhaps unconsciously, to deny herself, her partner, or both the pleasures of sexual intimacy. Evidence does not support this theory, however. Indeed, women with vaginismus can often have sexually satisfying lives through clitoral stimulation. Clinical reports also suggest that vaginismus can be caused by fear of pregnancy or by negative attitudes about sex in general that stem from having been raped or molested in childhood (LoPiccolo & Stock, 1987). Masters and Johnson found that for a number of couples the man's inability to maintain an erection preceded the develop-

premature ejaculation Inability of the male to inhibit his orgasm long enough for mutually satisfying sexual relations.

dyspareunia Recurrent pain before, during, or after sexual intercourse.

vaginismus Painful, spasmodic contractions of the outer third of the vagina, which make insertion of the penis impossible or extremely difficult.

ment of vaginismus. For some women, then, the sexual problems of their partners are so anxiety provoking that a condition such as vaginismus may develop.

TO RECAP

Sexual dysfunctions involve persistent, distressing inhibitions in the normal sexual response cycle of appetitive, excitement, orgasm, and resolution phases. Depending on definitional criteria, these dysfunctions appear to be relatively common, but solid information on their prevalence and causes is sparse. Sexual dysfunctions include sexual desire disorders, deficient sexual urges or even active aversion to genital contact; sexual arousal disorders, in which either a woman's vagina does not become adequately lubricated, or a man's penis does not become and stay erect long enough for completion of intercourse; orgasmic disorders, absence of orgasm after a period of normal sexual excitement or, for men, ejaculating sooner than is preferred; and sexual pain disorders. Specific sexual dysfunctions may be caused to varying degrees by organic factors, such as medication side effects, and by psychological factors, such as a relationship problem or a fear of letting go and losing control.

▶ Perspectives on the Causes and Treatment of Sexual Dysfunctions

Sexual dysfunctions almost always involve a complicated set of biological, interpersonal, and individual psychological processes. Similarly, effective treatment is usually multifaceted, approaching the problem from a number of vantage points. Prior to modern research, though, a simpler message prevailed. Sexual dysfunctions were generally viewed as a result of moral degeneracy (LoPiccolo, 1992a). von Krafft-Ebing (1902) and Havelock Ellis (1910), two early sex researchers, postulated that early masturbation damaged the sexual organs and exhausted a finite reservoir of sexual energy, resulting in lessened abilities to function sexually in adulthood. Even in adulthood excessive sexual activity was thought to cause such problems as erectile failure, and the general Victorian view was to restrain dangerous sexual appetite. To discourage handling of the genitals by children, metal mittens were promoted. To distract adults from too much sex, outdoor exercise and a bland diet were recommended. Kellogg's Corn Flakes and graham crackers were developed as foods that would lessen sexual interest. They did not.

Psychodynamic Perspectives

Psychodynamic theorists hypothesize that sexual dysfunctions are symptoms of repressed conflicts. The analyst considers the symbolic meaning of the symptom both to understand its cause and to guide treatment. Since sexual dysfunctions bring discomfort and psychological pain to both the individual and his or her partner, and since unimpaired sexuality is inherently pleasurable, repressed anger and aggression competing with the gratification of sexual needs is often considered a possible cause. Thus a man who ejaculates so quickly that he frustrates his female partner may be expressing repressed guilt or hostility toward women who remind him unconsciously of his mother.

Many contemporary dynamic therapists supplement interpretive methods with more directive cognitive-behavioral techniques (LoPiccolo, 1977). Conversely, cognitive-behavioral therapists are coming to appreciate the role of psychodynamic themes in what used to be straightforward behavioral treatments (cf. p. 482). For example, a man may not at first admit that he cannot have an erection, in which case the therapist must listen for clues in what he says. A woman may be reluctant to initiate sexual encounters because, although she may not verbalize it to the therapist, she considers such assertiveness unseemly and inappropriate to her traditional female role. In such instances the psychodynamic hypothesis that patients are often unable to express clearly to their therapists what truly bothers them can help in proper assessment and planning for any sort of treatment.

Biological Perspectives

Some dysfunctions are attributable to physical damage. For example, clitoral or vaginal infections, scar tissue at the vaginal opening from incisions made during childbirth, and—especially in postmenopausal women—insufficient lubrication of the vagina may make intercourse painful for women. Infection of the glans of the penis may cause dyspareunia in men. Some men with erectile problems suffer from metabolic disturbances caused by diabetes. In others, sexual arousal is dulled by the use of tranquilizers.

As more is discovered about organic factors in sexual dysfunctions, it becomes increasingly important for therapists to consider the possible utility of medical interventions (LoPiccolo, 1992b). When depression is part of the clinical picture along with severely diminished sex drive, for example, antidepressant drugs can be helpful. The drug yohimbine has been used with some success with male patients in whom biological factors are suspected as the cause of erectile dysfunction (Sonda, Mazo, & Chancellor, 1990). It is believed to work by increasing blood flow into the penis and reducing outflow from it (J. J. Meyer, 1988).

Integrative Perspectives

Therapy for sexual dysfunctions often involves the use of diverse techniques from a variety of perspectives. Cognitive and behavioral methods have been notably successful (e.g., D'Amicis, Goldberg, LoPiccolo, Friedman, & Davies, 1985; LoPiccolo, Heiman, Hogan, & Roberts, 1985), and a range of strategies from these and other perspectives are applied depending on the case.

The Perspective of Masters and Johnson

Performance Fears and the Spectator Role.   The integrative treatment advocated by Masters and Johnson (1970) is based on their analysis of the causes of sexual dysfunctions. In their view, **fears about performance** and the adoption of a **spectator role** are the two main current sources of sexual dysfunction. Fears about performance are excessive concerns about the adequacy of one's behavior during sexual contact with a partner. The spectator role is a closely related concept, meaning that someone concerned about sexual performance begins to focus on his or her own behavior, almost as if watching rather than participating in the sexual experience. This inward direction of attention tends to distract people from what is actually pleasurable about sex and therefore impairs sexual responsiveness. The chapter-opening case exemplified these problems. Given that Barbara was thinking about how she was responding to her husband, or what her fantasies might mean about her as a person, it is small wonder that she could not relax and respond fully.

Performance fears and the spectator role were hypothesized by Masters and Johnson to result from one or more of several historical factors (see Figure 13.2). One or both partners may, for instance, have negative attitudes toward sex because they were brought up with strict religious beliefs that denigrate sexual enjoyment. Alternatively, some patients trace their fears of sexual contact to particularly frightening or degrading experiences during early sexual encounters. One woman could date her vaginismus to a gang rape from which she suffered severe

fears about performance Being overly concerned with one's behavior during sexual contact with another, postulated by Masters and Johnson as a major factor causing *sexual dysfunction.*

spectator role As applied by Masters and Johnson, a pattern of behavior in which the individual's focus on and concern with sexual performance impedes his or her natural sexual responses.

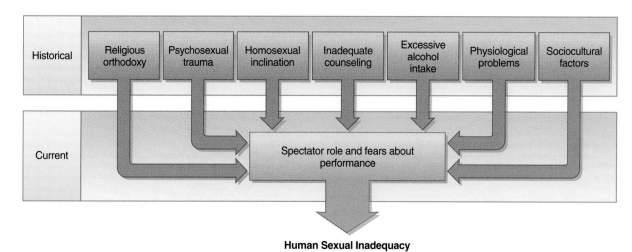

Human Sexual Inadequacy

Figure 13.2   *Historical and current causes of human sexual inadequacies according to Masters and Johnson.*

physical and psychological damage. Men with erectile problems and nonorgasmic women may be unable to enjoy heterosexual relations because they have homosexual inclinations.

Bad advice from professionals may also create or worsen sexual dysfunctions. Some men are told by physicians that erectile problems are incurable or that they are a natural part of the aging process (see Chapter 15). An erectile problem sometimes begins with undue concern about a normal reduction in sexual responsiveness brought on by excessive drinking.

Especially in female dysfunctions, cultural biases may also play a role. "Sociocultural influence more often than not places the woman in a position in which she must adapt, sublimate, inhibit, or even distort her natural capacity to function sexually in order to fulfill her genetically assigned role. Herein lies a major source of woman's sexual dysfunction" (Masters & Johnson, 1970, p. 218). The man has the blessing of society to develop sexual expressiveness, but the woman, at least until recently, has not had this freedom, and her needs have often been ignored.

Treatment.   Depending on what seems to underlie the sexual dysfunction in a given case, treatment can involve any of a number of techniques. If, as is common, the couple with sexual problems also has more general relationship problems, couples therapy (discussed in Chapter 16) is part of the therapy for sexual dysfunctions.

Because many sexually dysfunctional people are ignorant of basic facts about human sexuality, most therapists devote time and effort to educating their clients in sexual anatomy and the physiological processes of intercourse. An important effect of such instruction is to legitimize the explicit discussion of sex, taking it out of the realm of unspoken taboo and mystery and reducing some of the anxiety and embarrassment surrounding this topic.

Systematic exposure to anxiety-provoking aspects of the sexual situation can also be useful. Wolpe's systematic desensitization and in vivo desensitization (that is, desensitization by real-life encounters) have been highly successful (Andersen, 1983), especially when combined with skills training. People who are very anxious about sex have often failed to learn to do a number of necessary and preliminary things, such as engaging in foreplay or romantic conversation.

Directed masturbation involves persuading the patient of the propriety and normality of masturbation (often, women who have never had an orgasm have never masturbated) and encouraging the patient to stroke himself or herself in pleasurable ways. Finally, exploring those masturbation methods that are most effective in bringing the patient to high levels of sexual arousal and to orgasm can be very helpful (LoPiccolo & Lobitz, 1972).

In **sensory-awareness procedures**, patients are encouraged to tune in to the pleasant sensations that accompany even incipient sexual arousal. One way of opening the individual to sensual and sexual feelings is to use **sensate focus**. The couple is instructed to choose a time when they feel "a natural sense of warmth, unit compatibility . . . or even a shared sense of gamesmanship" (Masters & Johnson, 1970, p. 71). They are to undress and give each other pleasure by touching each other's bodies. One marital partner is assigned to do the first "pleasuring," or "giving"; the partner who is "getting" is simply to enjoy being touched. The one being touched, however, is *not required* to feel a sexual response and, moreover, is responsible for immediately telling the partner if something becomes distracting or uncomfortable. Then the roles are switched. Attempts at intercourse are forbidden. The sensate-focus assignment may promote contact where none has existed for years. If it does, it is a first step toward gradually reestablishing sexual intimacy.

Sensate focusing may uncover deep animosities that have previously remained hidden. Most of the time, however, partners begin to realize that encounters in bed can be intimate without necessarily being a prelude to sexual intercourse. Later, the partner being pleasured is instructed to give specific encouragement and direction by placing his or her hand on the hand of the giving partner in order to regulate pressure and rate of stroking. The touching of genitals and breasts is also now allowed. Still, however, there is no mention of an orgasm, and the prohibition on intercourse remains in effect.

Integrative Treatment of Sexual Desire Disorders

The techniques just described, developed by Masters and Johnson and others, proved to be very effective for patients who wanted to have sex but whose functioning was impaired by lack of knowledge, lack of skill, or fear. As noted earlier in this chapter, though, sexual dysfunction can instead take the form of deficient interest in, or aversion to, sexual activity. For such patients these established procedures did not work as well. In a sense, training in foreplay, directed masturbation, and the like are premature if someone is not intrinsically motivated to engage in sexual activity. Sex therapists have therefore developed integrative treatments for low sexual desire that use insight-oriented techniques before the behavioral interventions.

A first step entails *sensory awareness exercises* with the purpose of helping the low-desire or sex-aversive partner become more aware of his or her actual feelings about sex. It turns out in clinical cases that the problem much more often involves an actual *aversion* (fear, anger, disgust, embarrassment) to sex rather than a lack of interest in it. The person is more often negative than neutral, a very important finding, for it can suggest leads to work on later in the therapy.

The second stage, often undertaken in conjunction with the first, entails *insight* into the reasons for the negative feelings. For example, a sixty-year-old man may believe that this is "just the way I am," perhaps because of his age, whereas it may appear to the therapist that his hypoactive sexual desire is due (more) to his anger at his partner for things having nothing to do with sex. The therapist may also use empathy statements in the manner of Rogers's person-centered therapy to help the patient become more comfortable with these feelings and aware of the factors that might underlie the sexual problem.

Once these inhibiting factors have been identified, specific self-statements are created for the patient to counteract these ideas. For example, a coping self-statement, such as "Just because I feel sexy does not mean I am a bad person," could

sensory-awareness procedures Often used in sex therapy, techniques that help clients tune into their feelings and sensations, as in *sensate focus* exercises, and to be open to new ways of experiencing and feeling.

sensate focus A term applied to exercises prescribed at the beginning of the Masters and Johnson sex therapy program; partners are instructed to fondle each other to give pleasure but to refrain from intercourse, thus reducing anxiety about sexual performance.

make sense for a person who learned that sexuality made him or her unworthy of respect and love. It is not easy for patients to accept these more constructive self-statements or beliefs. One of the continuing challenges for any cognitive intervention is to understand how people internalize new ideas that can help them function better.

The fourth and final treatment stage involves *behavioral interventions*. For example, a person with little experience in frankly sexual situations can be expected to need instruction and support in particular sexual techniques for pleasuring his or her partner. Encouragement, indeed, permission, to view erotic films and read erotic books can further legitimize sex and can also serve to prime the pump. As with more traditional Masters and Johnson therapy, the partner of the patient is best involved in the treatment, for he or she is an inextricable part of the problem and therefore a necessary part of the solution.

To Recap

Psychodynamic theorists view sexual dysfunctions as reflections of repressed conflict, such as the conflict between wanting to enjoy sexual pleasure and wanting to aggress against a partner toward whom one is unconsciously hostile, perhaps as a result of experiences with and feelings toward the opposite sex parent. This approach serves as a useful reminder to all therapists to consider the possibility of psychological sources of sexual dysfunction of which the patient is not aware.

Sexual dysfunctions are sometimes caused by biological problems. Sexual pain disorders can result from infections, for instance. Biological treatments include yohimbine for male erectile disorder, which works by increasing blood flow to the penis and decreasing outflow. Masters and Johnson attribute sexual dysfunctions to performance fears and adoption of a spectator role that preclude full involvement and responsiveness in sexual activity. These in turn may stem from misinformation, cultural biases, religious teachings about sex that generate inhibition, or other sources. Treatment strategies based on this view draw from a number of perspectives (especially cognitive and behavioral) and include information giving, desensitization, directed masturbation, sensate focus, and other means of improving people's knowledge of, comfort with, and skill at sexual functioning. Integrative treatment of sexual desire disorders employs many of the same behavioral techniques, but also requires more use of insight-oriented techniques to lay the groundwork for such interventions.

> ## The Case of Barbara Garrison Revisited

Social History

Barbara's parents were in their mid-forties when she was born. They had one other child, a boy, five years older than Barbara. Her father was a police officer, and her mother took care of the children full-time at home. Both parents were conservative, devoutly religious people. Barbara's parents clearly cared for each other and for the children, but they were not affectionate. Barbara remembered growing up in a quiet, peaceful household in which emotional displays of any kind were generally discouraged.

Her parents and her older brother were very protective of her. As the baby of the family she was always closely supervised, and it seemed to Barbara that she was not allowed to do many of the things her friends' parents permitted. For instance, until she was 16, Barbara was not allowed to go to parties if boys were also invited.

Barbara's knowledge about and experiences with sexual activity were extremely limited during childhood and adolescence. Neither of her parents made an effort to provide her with information about her own body or reproductive functions. After she began menstruating at the age of eleven, her mother gave her a book that explained the basic organs and physiology of the human reproductive system, but she avoided any personal discussion of Barbara's questions about sexuality. The implicit message conveyed by her parents' behaviors and attitudes was that sex was a mysterious and dangerous phenomenon.

After she graduated from high school, Barbara continued to live at home and took classes at the local junior college. During her first semester she met Frank, who was also eighteen and then a student at the police academy. Perhaps because her father was a police officer too, Barbara's parents liked Frank and gradually began to allow her more freedom than before.

Barbara and Frank's sexual relationship progressed rapidly. Although she was initially apprehensive and shy, Barbara found that she enjoyed heavy petting. She refused to have intercourse with Frank for several months, finally agreeing one evening after they had both been drinking at a party. She later remembered being disappointed by the experience, which foreshadowed much of their subsequent sexual relationship. Frank had climaxed quickly, but she had not reached orgasm. A sense of guilt about this incident was replaced by shock several weeks later when Barbara learned she was pregnant. She and Frank agreed to marry as soon as possible, and Bonnie was born six months afterward. Barbara dropped out of college and did not return to school for many years.

CONCEPTUALIZATION AND TREATMENT

Perhaps the most critical issue that the therapist faced in treating the sexual problem described by Barbara was getting her and, especially, Frank to see this as a couples problem rather than as Barbara's problem alone. It was evident from Barbara's description of the problem that she knew little about sexual behavior, but it was also apparent that she and Frank did not communicate well with one another about sexual activity and that this would need to be a main focus of treatment.

Reluctantly, Frank agreed to attend the second treatment session. Once the therapist made clear that the therapy goal was to increase the satisfaction each of them felt with their sexual relationship, and not to assign Frank blame for existing problems, Frank became a willing participant in therapy. Both Frank and Barbara had complete physical examinations, which revealed no likely medical causes of sexual dysfunction.

During the third session, the therapist explored many of Barbara's and Frank's attitudes and beliefs about sexual behavior, with the goal of encouraging them to communicate frankly and of opening up a discussion about sexuality in which possibly mistaken beliefs could be corrected. For example, both Barbara and Frank believed that vaginal stimulation should be the main source of sexual pleasure for women and that orgasm during coitus depends solely on such stimulation. The therapist explained that the clitoris is, in fact, more sensitive than the vagina and that female orgasm seems to depend on both direct and indirect stimulation of the clitoris during both masturbation and intercourse.

Considerable time was also spent discussing the Garrisons' attitudes toward and use of sexual fantasies. The therapist's matter-of-fact tone and preliminary statement that most adults engage in sexual fantasies helped both Frank and Barbara reveal to one another previously secret fantasies in which they had engaged.

The next step in treatment was to help Barbara and Frank overcome the self-consciousness they usually experienced during sex, which interfered considerably with their enjoyment. Frank had been concerned about delaying ejaculation long enough for Barbara to become more aroused, while Barbara had felt pressure to reach orgasm. To establish a less-pressured atmosphere, the therapist asked Barbara and Frank *not*, under any circumstances, to have intercourse during the next few weeks. Instead, they practiced sensate focus to gain experience in simply giving and receiving pleasurable sensations and learning more about each other's reactions.

Barbara and Frank responded well to this initial exercise. They described these extended periods of touching and caressing as very relaxing and pleasurable. They both said that they had felt a sense of warmth and closeness that had disappeared from their relationship years ago. Barbara also expressed some relief that she was able to focus on the pleasure of Frank's touch without worrying about whether she would have an orgasm.

Building on this early success, the therapist added new elements each week to Barbara and Frank's between-session exercises. Frank developed greater awareness of his own responses and greater ejaculatory control. For instance, in a "start–stop" procedure, Barbara stimulated his penis manually, while Frank concentrated on his own level of arousal and signalled her when he experienced the sensation that immediately precedes ejaculation. She would discontinue stimulation at that point, to resume only when Frank no longer felt that ejaculation was imminent. The cycle was repeated for up to fifteen or twenty minutes.

By practicing such exercises as the start-stop technique and Frank's manually stimulating Barbara while she engaged in favored sexual fantasies, they soon improved considerably in their ability to communicate what each enjoyed sexually and to become less self-conscious with one another.

Ultimately the prohibition against intercourse was lifted, and Barbara and Frank alternated periods of insertion with periods of Frank's manually stimulating Barbara's clitoris. Only during the latter periods did Barbara experience orgasm. The therapist assured them that this was not uncommon, and the Garrisons were quite satisfied with this degree of progress.

After fifteen sessions, Barbara and Frank discontinued couples sex therapy. They were pleased to note that to some extent the emphasis on clearer communication with one another had generalized to other areas of life. Although problems remained, particularly with regard to conflicts about how to balance issues of freedom and responsibility for their teenage daughter, Barbara and Frank were learning to talk to one another more openly about such conflicts and felt closer in the relationship as a result.

DISCUSSION

The case of Barbara Garrison exemplifies the complexity of diagnostic judgments in the area of sexual dysfunction. Besides asking if the problem is sufficiently persistent and pervasive to warrant a diagnosis, one must ask whether the problem centers on one partner or the other. In the Garrisons' situation, for instance, it was not clear whether Barbara's inability to reach orgasm during intercourse could be attributed to Frank's difficulty in delaying or controlling his ejaculatory response rather than to any dysfunction of her own. In any case, sexual dysfunction is clearly most easily defined in the context of the relationship rather than as an individual problem.

The positive outcome that the Garrisons obtained with sex therapy is not uncommon. Both premature ejaculation and female orgasmic disorder have favorable prognoses when directive approaches are applied. For instance, about 85% of women who had never had an orgasm prior to treatment were able to reach orgasm when stimulated directly by their partners (LoPiccolo & Stock, 1986). Consistent with Barbara Garrison's experience, however, 60% did not become able to reach orgasm during intercourse. The goals of treatment therefore obviously play a role in determining one's appraisal of success rates. The degree of personal satisfaction and renewed intimacy that Barbara and Frank felt after sex therapy must be taken strongly into account in this respect.

Barbara and Frank Garrison experienced one variety of sexual disorder, a problem that impeded an aspect of the sexual response cycle. Other people exhibit another kind of sexual disorder, variations of sexual functioning apart from the normal sexual response cycle. It is to these, gender identity disorders and paraphilias, that we now turn. Afterwards, we address the serious societal problem of rape.

▶ *Gender Identity Disorder*

"Are you a boy or a girl?" "Are you a man or a woman?" For virtually all people—even those with serious mental disorders such as schizophrenia—the answer to such questions is immediate and obvious. Also clear is that others will agree with the answer given. Our sense of ourselves as male or female, our **gender identity**, is so deeply ingrained from childhood that, no matter what happens later, most people are certain beyond a doubt of their gender.

Some people, however, men more often than women, feel deep within themselves from early childhood that they are of the opposite sex. The evidence of their anatomy—normal genitals and the usual secondary sex characteristics, such as beard growth for men and developed breasts for women—does not persuade them that they are what others see them as. A man, for instance, might look at himself in a mirror, see a biological man, and yet announce to himself that he is a woman.

Gender identity disorder can be diagnosed in children or adults. Among children, the disorder is evident in either profoundly feminine boys or profoundly masculine girls, youngsters whose behavior, likes, and dislikes do not fit our culture's ideas of what is appropriate for the two sexes.

As with several disorders discussed in this chapter, culture-specific attitudes play a role in our concepts of abnormality. If a boy dislikes rough-and-tumble play, prefers the company of little girls, dresses up in women's clothing, finds his penis and testes disgusting, and insists that he will grow up to be a girl, he is now viewed as having gender identity disorder. The same behaviors and feelings in the nineteenth century in some Native American tribes in the western United States would have identified the child as a shaman, a special, honored person with healing powers (Wade & Travis, 1994). This cultural and historical relativism does not negate the genuine distress of children with gender identity disorder. Presumably, few would be reassured by being told "Don't worry about it. In a different culture, you would have fit in quite well." It does, however, remind us that ideas of what is appropriate masculine or appropriate feminine behavior are largely cultural inventions.

In adults, gender identity disorder is not, of course, identified on the basis of play styles or enjoying the company of members of the opposite sex. Rather, an adult with gender identity disorder, or a **transsexual**, is one who experiences persistent discomfort with his or her sex or gender role and identifies strongly with the opposite sex to the point of believing that he or she really is the opposite sex. Such a person often tries to pass as a member of the opposite sex and frequently desires to have his or her sex changed surgically. The prevalence rates for transsexualism are slight, one in thirty thousand for men and one in one hundred thousand for women.

Most transsexuals report that as children they dressed in clothes typical of the opposite sex (e.g., Tsoi, 1990). However, most gender identity disordered children do not become transsexual in adulthood, even without professional intervention (Zucker, Finegan, Deering, & Bradley, 1984). According to DSM-IV, about three-fourths of boys with gender identity disorder indicate by late adolescence a homosexual or bisexual orientation, and the other one-fourth indicate a heterosexual orientation. Corresponding percentages for girls are unknown.

Transsexuals generally suffer from anxiety and depression, not surprising in light of their psychological predicament. A male transsexual's interest in men will be interpreted by him as a conventional heterosexual preference, given that he considers himself really a woman. Predictably, transsexuals often arouse the disapproval of others when they choose to cross-dress in clothing of the other sex. Indeed, for a man to dress as a woman is illegal in many states. Cross-dressing is somewhat less of a problem for female-to-male transsexuals be-

gender identity The deeply ingrained sense a person has of being either a man or a woman.

The transsexual shown here was running for mayor of a town in California.

transsexual A person who experiences persistent discomfort with his or her sex and identifies with the opposite sex, to the point of believing that he or she is opposite in sex to his or her biological endowment.

cause contemporary fashions allow women to wear clothing similar to that worn by men.

Note that cross-dressing is not unique to transsexuals. Some heterosexual or bisexual men (who would be diagnosed with the paraphilia transvestic fetishism in DSM-IV) wear women's clothes as part of sexual activity (usually masturbation) and fantasies. Unlike transsexuals, they do not wish to dress as women all the time or actually to live as women.

To Recap

Gender identity disorder involves a strong identification with the opposite sex and a sense of discomfort with being one's own sex. It is diagnosed among children who exhibit strong attitudes and preferences associated with the opposite sex. In adulthood this disorder is evident in transsexuals, who believe themselves to be of the opposite sex. Transsexuals, who are usually men, often cross-dress and may desire sex-reassignment surgery to bring their bodies into line with their sense of themselves.

Perspectives on the Causes and Treatment of Gender Identity Disorder

The main explanations for and treatments of gender identity disorder are provided by the biological or behavioral perspectives.

Biological Perspectives

Hormone Abnormalities

Some evidence suggests that gender identity disorder can result from a physical disturbance. For example, girls whose mothers took synthetic progestins to prevent uterine bleeding during pregnancy were found to be tomboyish during their preschool years (Ehrhardt & Money, 1967). Progestins are considered precursors of androgens, the male sex hormones. Other young tomboys also had genitalia with male characteristics (though this is quite rare), which suggests a link between the progestins taken by their mothers and male physical features (Green, 1976). Young boys whose mothers ingested female hormones during pregnancy were found to engage less in rough-and-tumble play than their male peers (Yalom, Green, & Fisk, 1973). Although such children were not necessarily abnormal in their gender identity, the mother's ingestion of prenatal sex hormones did give them higher than usual levels of cross-gender interests and behavior.

Conversely, the hypothesis that levels of sex hormones could account for gender identity disorder has not been supported by research on adult transsexuals. There are few, if any, differences in hormone levels between transsexuals and others (e.g., Gladue, 1985). Efforts to find differences in brain structure between transsexuals and control subjects have likewise been negative (Emory, Williams, Cole, Amparo, & Meyer, 1991).

Sex-Reassignment Surgery

sex-reassignment surgery An operation removing existing genitalia of a *transsexual* and constructing a substitute for the genitals of the opposite sex.

For adults with gender identity disorders the main biological treatment is **sex-reassignment surgery**, an operation in which the existing genitalia of a transsexual are altered and a substitute for the genitals of the opposite sex is constructed. Reassignment surgery is an interesting case of an intervention that accommodates what is perceived as a psychologically disturbed attitude. Whereas, for example, people who are irrationally fearful of dogs (see Chapter 6) are encouraged to reduce the fear rather than to move to a country with fewer dogs, reassign-

James Morris (in a 1960 picture) became Jan Morris (in a 1974 photograph) after sex-reassignment surgery.

ment surgery holds out the hope that the attitude can be left in place while the body is brought into line with it. It is important to remember, however, that such surgery does *not* biologically transform a man or woman into the opposite sex.

For male-to-female reassignment surgery, the male genitalia are almost entirely removed, with some of the tissue retained to form an artificial vagina. At least a year before the operation, the patient takes appropriate female hormones to develop the breasts, soften the skin, and change the body in other ways. These hormones have to be taken indefinitely after the surgery (Green & Money, 1969). Most male-to-female transsexuals have to undergo extensive and costly electrolysis to remove beard and body hair and receive training to raise the pitch of their voices. Some male-to-female transsexuals also have plastic surgery on their chins, noses, and Adam's apples to rid them of masculine largeness. At the same time the transsexual begins to live as a female member of society in order to experience as fully as possible what it is like. The genital surgery itself is usually not done until a one- or two-year trial period has been completed. Conventional heterosexual intercourse is possible for male-to-female transsexuals, although pregnancy is not.

For female-to-male reassignment surgery, the process is more arduous. The penis that can be constructed is small and not capable of normal erection. Artificial supports are therefore needed for conventional sexual intercourse. The male hormones prescribed drastically alter fat distribution and stimulate the growth of beard and body hair.

Evaluating Sex-Reassignment Surgery.   Over the years, controversy has existed over the benefits of sex-reassignment surgery. One of the first outcome studies (Meyer & Reter, 1979) found no advantage to the individual "in terms of social rehabilitation" (p. 1015). The findings of this study led to the termination of the Johns Hopkins University School of Medicine sex-reassignment program, the largest such program in the United States. However, subsequent studies indicated an overall improvement in social adaptation resulting from sex-reassignment surgery, with female-to-male transsexuals showing somewhat greater success than male-to-female transsexuals (Abramovitz, 1986). The relatively greater ease of the female-to-male change may come in part from our society's lesser focus on the physical attributes of men. A small, soft-spoken man may be more acceptable to society than a large, hulking woman.

Besides this sex difference, other predictors of good outcome have been identified. Patients who seem to adjust most successfully after sex-reassignment surgery are emotionally stable, adapt well to their new gender identity during the year prior to surgery, understand the limitations of the surgery, and receive psychotherapy as part of an established gender identity program (Green & Fleming, 1990).

For any patient, sex-reassignment surgery is a drastic step, the last resort. Often, such patients cut ties to their previous lives and confront challenges to adjustment that are extremely difficult. Therapists are generally wary of a patient who says, "If only. . . . " The variations are legion. "If only I were not so fat. . . . " "If only I were not so nervous. . . . " "If only I had not left school before graduation. . . . " Following each "if only" clause is some statement indicating that life would be far better, even wonderful . . . if only. Most of the time the hopes expressed are an illusion. Things are seldom so simple. The transsexual, understandably focusing on the discrepancy between gender identity and biological makeup, blames present dissatisfactions on the horrible trick nature has played. But he or she usually finds that sex reassignment falls short of solving life's problems. It may handle this one set of them, but it usually leaves untouched other difficulties to which all human beings are subject, such as conflicts at work, with intimates, and even within oneself.

Behavioral Perspectives

Behavioral therapists and researchers have largely focused on the ways in which gender-appropriate and gender-inappropriate behavior and dress are encouraged in children who exhibit gender identity disorders. Interviews with the parents of children who have developed gender identity problems frequently reveal that these parents did not discourage, and in many instances clearly encouraged, cross-dressing behavior. Many mothers, aunts, and grandmothers found it cute when the boys dressed in Mommy's old dresses and high-heeled shoes, and very often they instructed the youngsters on how to apply makeup. Family albums often contained photographs of the young boys attired in women's clothing. Such reinforcing reactions on the part of the family to an atypical child may contribute to the conflict between his or her anatomical sex and the acquired gender identity (Green, 1974).

These findings, however, should *not* be interpreted to mean that encouraging gentleness in a little boy or assertiveness, even aggressiveness, in a little girl will probably lead to a gender identity disorder. There is a substantial difference between enjoying activities or personal styles more typical of the opposite sex and actually believing that one *is* of the opposite sex.

Because gender identity was assumed to be too deep-seated to alter, sex-reassignment operations used to be considered the only viable treatment for gender identity disorders. Some successful behavior therapy procedures for altering gender identity, particularly in children, have been reported, however. Behavior therapy seeks to help patients become more comfortable with their biological sex, primarily by using rewards. One five-year-old boy had been cross-dressing since age two and showing other signs of gender identity disorder. His parents began, as instructed by his therapist, to compliment and otherwise support him whenever he played with traditionally male toys, rather than those commonly preferred by girls, and whenever he engaged in other traditionally male activities.

After six months of intensive treatment, the boy was typically masculine, and he was still so at a two-year follow-up (Rekers & Lovaas, 1974).

TO RECAP

While children of mothers who took prenatal sex hormones of the sex opposite that of the child show higher than usual cross-gender interests and behavior, biological factors have not been shown to account for transsexualism. Early studies of sex-reassignment surgery were discouraging. However, recent research suggests that surgery (especially female-to-male operations) usually leads to improved social adaptation, especially if the patient was reasonably stable emotionally to begin with and realizes that the surgery will not be a complete cure for all problems. Behavioral perspectives attribute gender identity disorders in part to early encouragement by family members of a child's cross-gender dress and interests. Treatment in this approach relies on systematically rewarding the behaviors and mannerisms associated with the patient's biological sex.

Paraphilias

The **paraphilias** are a group of disorders in which sexual attraction is to nonhuman objects, to children or other nonconsenting people, or to the suffering or humiliation of oneself or one's partner. The DSM-IV diagnosis is made only if the attraction is intense and has lasted at least six months and the person has acted on these urges or is experiencing significant distress because of them. People can have the same fantasies and urges that a paraphiliac has (e.g., exhibiting the genitals to an unsuspecting stranger) but not be diagnosed as having a sexual disorder if the fantasies are not recurrent and intense and if he or she has never acted on the urges or is not markedly distressed by them.

Paraphilias often occur together and can be an aspect of other mental disorders, such as schizophrenia or one of the personality disorders. Paraphiliacs are almost always men. Only in masochism are there appreciable numbers of women, but even then men outnumber women by a ratio of twenty to one. That some paraphiliacs seek nonconsenting partners indicates that there are often legal consequences to the disorders.

paraphilias Sexual attraction to unusual objects, children or other nonconsenting people, or suffering or humiliation of oneself or one's partner.

Pedophilia

Pedophiles are adults, usually men, who derive sexual gratification through physical and often sexual contact with prepubertal children. The DSM-IV diagnosis of this paraphilia requires that the offender be at least sixteen years old and at least five years older than the child. The pedophile can be either heterosexual or homosexual. Violence is seldom a part of the molestation, although some pedophiles frighten the child by, for example, killing a pet and threatening further harm if the youngster tells his or her parents. Sometimes pedophiles are content to stroke the child's hair, but they may also manipulate the child's genitalia, encourage the child to manipulate theirs, and, less often, attempt intercourse. The molestations may be repeated over a period of weeks, months, or years if they are not discovered by other adults or if the child does not protest.

Pedophiles are often rigidly religious and moralistic. As with most aberrant sexual behavior, a strong sense of attraction draws the pedophile to the child. Pedophiles generally know the children they molest; they are neighbors or friends of the family (Gebhard, Gagnon, Pomeroy, & Christenson, 1965). Pedophiles tend to be low in social maturity, self-esteem, impulse control, and social skills (Finkelhor & Araji, 1986; Kalichman, 1991). Most older, heterosexual pedophiles are or have been married at some time in their lives.

pedophiles People with a preference for obtaining sexual gratification through contact with youngsters defined legally as underage; pedophilia is a *paraphilia*.

The widespread belief that pedophilia is caused by having been sexually abused in childhood has very little support from research (Freund, Watson, & Dickey, 1990). Child sexual abuse often has very harmful consequences (Kendall-Tackett, Williams, & Finkelhor, 1993), but these consequences are probably not specific to the creation of yet another generation of molesters.

Incest

incest Sexual relations between close relatives, most often between daughter and father or between brother and sister.

In some cases the pedophile's interest is in a child in the same family. The taboo against **incest**, sexual relations between close relatives for whom marriage is forbidden, seems virtually universal in human societies (Ford & Beach, 1951). It may have adaptive evolutionary significance (Geer et al., 1984). The offspring from a father–daughter or a brother–sister union has a greater probability of inheriting a pair of recessive genes, one from each parent. For the most part, recessive genes have negative biological effects, such as serious birth defects.

Most incest victims tend to be older than the objects of other pedophiles' desires. It is more often the case that a father becomes interested in his daughter when she begins to mature physically, whereas other pedophiles are interested in the youngster precisely because he or she is sexually immature.

Men who engage in incest with their daughters tend to be very devout, moralistic, and fundamentalist in their religious beliefs (Gebhard et al., 1965) and are apt to be somewhat neglectful as parents and emotionally distant from their children (Madonna, Van Scoyk, & Jones, 1991), as in the case of Paula Stewart, discussed in Chapter 7. These correlational data do not necessarily mean that being religious, even rigidly so, predisposes one to committing incest. Different interpretations are possible. For instance, perhaps some people, overcome by the intensity of their attraction to their own children, seek solace and forgiveness in religion.

Fathers who commit incest may be sexually frustrated in their marriage yet feel constrained, for religious reasons, from seeking gratification through masturbation, prostitutes, or extramarital affairs. (This in no way implies that it is the wife's fault for not sexually satisfying her husband.) However, recent evidence suggests that it is not sexual dissatisfaction so much as it is lack of a satisfying emotional relationship with his wife that is associated with incest by the father (Lang, Flor, & Frenzel, 1990). Other factors associated with increased risk for being subjected to this type of incest are a child's having a stepfather, having a mother who did not graduate from high school, having a poor relationship with his or her mother, and having fewer than two close friends in childhood (Finkelhor, 1983).

Incest is now acknowledged to occur much more often than was earlier assumed. A study of 796 college students found that an astounding 19% of the women and 8.6% of the men had been sexually victimized as children. Of the victimized women, 28% had had incestuous relations; of the men, 23% (Finkelhor, 1979). More recent survey data confirm these findings (Siegel, Sorenson, Golding, Burnam, & Stein, 1987). One of the reasons the prevalence of incest has historically been underestimated is that it is a secretive problem and understandably difficult for children to report. More detailed discussion of the effects of incest and pedophilia, including some of the legal complications in prosecuting these offenses, appears in the Legal, Ethical, and Social Issues box.

Fetishism

fetishism Reliance on an inanimate object for sexual arousal.

Fetishism involves reliance on an inanimate object for sexual arousal. During adolescence, the fetishist, almost always a man, develops recurrent and intense sexual urges toward nonliving objects, called fetishes. The fetish is strongly preferred or even necessary for sexual arousal to occur.

Beautiful shoes, sheer stockings, gloves, toilet articles, fur garments, and especially underpants are common sources of arousal for fetishists. One twenty-six-year-old man was aroused by other people's sneezing (King, 1990). Some can carry on their fetishism by themselves in secret by fondling, kissing, smelling, or merely gazing at the adored object as they masturbate. Others need their partner to don the fetish as a stimulant for intercourse. Fetishists sometimes become primarily interested in making a collection of the desired objects, and they may commit burglary week after week to add to their hoard.

The attraction felt by the fetishist toward the object is involuntary and irresistible. That the fetishist focuses almost exclusively on the fetish and needs it for sexual arousal distinguishes fetishisms from the ordinary attraction that high heels and sheer stockings may hold for heterosexual men.

Voyeurism

Voyeurism is a marked preference for obtaining sexual gratification by watching others in a state of undress or having sexual relations. The looking, or peeping, is what helps the individual become sexually aroused and is sometimes essential for arousal. The voyeur's orgasm is achieved by masturbation, either while watching or later, remembering what he or she saw. Sometimes the voyeur fantasizes about having sexual contact with the observed person, but it remains a fantasy. In voyeurism, there is seldom contact between the observer and the observed. A true voyeur, almost always a man, does not find it particularly exciting to watch a woman who is undressing for his special benefit. The element of risk seems important, for the voyeur is excited by the anticipation of how the woman would react if she knew he was watching.

voyeurism Marked preference for obtaining sexual gratification by watching others in a state of undress or having sexual relations.

As with all categories of behavior that are against the law, frequencies of occurrence are difficult to assess. From what we know, voyeurs tend to be young, single, submissive, and fearful of more direct sexual encounters with others (McCary, 1973). Their peeping serves as a substitute gratification and possibly gives them a sense of power over those watched. They do not seem to be otherwise disturbed, however. That voyeurs have an impoverished social life and engage in surreptitious peeping instead of making conventional sexual and social contacts with women suggests another way to understand their preference for spying on unaware women. If the woman were aware of the man's actions and continued nonetheless to allow herself to be watched, the man might well conclude that she had some personal interest in him. This possibility would be very threatening to the voyeur and, because of his fear, less sexually arousing.

Exhibitionism

Exhibitionism is a recurrent, marked preference for obtaining sexual gratification by exposing one's genitals to an unwilling stranger. As with voyeurism, there is seldom an attempt to have actual contact with the stranger. Sexual arousal comes from fantasizing that one is exposing himself or from actually doing so, and the exhibitionist masturbates either while fantasizing or even during the actual exposure. In most cases there is a desire to shock or embarrass the observer. Voyeurism and exhibitionism together account for close to a majority of all sexual offenses that come to the attention of the police. Again, the frequency of exhibitionism is much greater among men.

exhibitionism Marked preference for obtaining sexual gratification by exposing one's genitals to an unwilling observer.

The urge to expose seems overwhelming and virtually uncontrollable to the exhibitionist and is apparently triggered by anxiety and restlessness as well as by sexual arousal. One exhibitionist persisted in his practices even after suffering a spinal cord injury that left him without sensation or movement from the waist down (DeFazio & Cunningham, 1987). Because of the compulsive nature of the urge, the exposures may be repeated rather frequently and even in the same

Child Sexual Abuse

Both pedophilia and incest are forms of **child sexual abuse**. They should be distinguished from nonsexual child abuse. Both can have very negative consequences and are reportable offenses, and sometimes they co-occur. Nonsexual child abuse includes such things as neglecting the child's physical and mental welfare, for example, punishing the child unfairly; belittling the child; intentionally withholding suitable shelter, food, and medical care; and striking or otherwise inflicting physical pain and injury.

Child sexual abuse generally refers to such physical contact as penetration of the child's vagina or anus with the perpetrator's penis, finger, or other object; fellatio, cunnilingus, or anilingus; and fondling or caressing. Also included are exhibitionism and child pornography, which may not involve actual sexual activity between an adult and a child (Wolfe, 1990). Most child sexual abuse victims are female. There is evidence attesting to the long-term adverse effects of incest and pedophilia. A study of college women, for instance, found that those who had suffered incest as children had more severe problems than did others in dating relationships, in general social adjustment, in sexual satisfaction, in self-esteem, and with depression (Jackson, Calhoun, Amick, Maddever, & Habif, 1990). Other research implicates incest in subsequent prostitution, sexual promiscuity, substance abuse, anxiety disorders, and sexual dysfunctions (Burnam et al., 1988).

In recent years many communities have developed programs to reduce the incidence of child sexual abuse. The programs are reminiscent of the warnings that most of us (even those old enough to be the parents of most readers of this book) recall: "Don't talk to strangers" and "Don't take candy from strangers." Few of us had the image of this dangerous stranger as being other than a man, and the data bear this out, for very

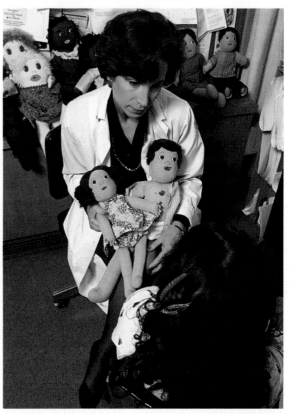

Great sensitivity is required when interviewing a child about the possibility of sexual abuse. Anatomically correct dolls are often used to facilitate the process.

few child sexual abusers are women. But few of us were told that a molester was usually *not* a stranger, that it could be an uncle, a father, a brother, a teacher, a coach, a neighbor, or even a cleric. These are very difficult things to discuss with a child, difficult also to confront for ourselves. But the child molester is often a male adult whom the child knows and probably also

child sexual abuse   Sexual contact with a minor.

place and at the same time of day. Apparently exhibitionists are so strongly driven that, at the time of the act, they are usually oblivious to the social and legal consequences of what they are doing (Stevenson & Jones, 1972). In the desperation and tension of the moment, they may suffer headaches and palpitations and have a sense of unreality. Afterward they flee in trembling and remorse (Bond & Hutchinson, 1960). Generally exhibitionists have difficulty in relationships. Over half of exhibitionists are married, but their sexual relationships with their spouses are not satisfactory (Mohr, Turner, & Jerry, 1964).

trusts. The betrayal of this trust is part of what makes this crime so damaging.

Sexual abuse prevention efforts have focused on elementary schools. While content varies from program to program, common elements include teaching children how to recognize inappropriate adult behavior, to resist inducements, to leave the situation quickly, and to report the incident to an appropriate adult (Wolfe, 1990). Children are taught to say no in a firm, assertive way when an adult talks to or touches them in a way that makes them feel uncomfortable. Instructors use such things as comic books, films, and descriptions of risky situations to try to teach about the nature of sexual abuse and how children can protect themselves.

Evaluations of school programs suggest that they increase awareness of sexual abuse among children, but less is known about whether the children are able to translate what they have learned into overt behavior and whether such changes reduce the problem (Wolfe, 1990). At the very least, programs seem to legitimize discussion of the problem at home (Wurtele & Miller-Perrin, 1987) and might therefore achieve one important goal, namely, to increase the *reporting* of the crime by encouraging and empowering children to tell their parents or guardians that an adult has made a sexual overture to them.

And yet, it is not a straightforward matter for a child or developing adolescent to report molestation. Because a child feels helpless and dependent, he or she will find it very frightening to tell Mommy or Daddy that he or she has been fondled by a brother or grandfather. Probably even more threatening are advances from Daddy himself, for the child is likely to be torn by allegiance to and love for his or her father on the one hand and by fear and revulsion on the other, coupled with the knowledge that what is happening is wrong. And when, as sometimes is the case, the mother suspects what is happening to her child and yet allows it to continue, the victim's complaints to the mother can be met with lack of support, with disbelief, and even with hostility.

Great skill is required in questioning a child about possible sexual abuse to ensure that the report is accurate, to avoid biasing the youngster one way or the other, and to minimize the stress that is inevitable in recounting a disturbing experience, especially if a decision is made to prosecute.

Taking formal legal action is still relatively rare, but some jurisdictions use innovative procedures that can reduce the stress on the victim while still protecting the rights of the accused. These measures include videotaped testimony, closed-courtroom trials, closed-circuit televised testimony, and special assistants and coaching sessions to explain courtroom etiquette and what to expect (Wolfe, 1990). Having the child play with anatomically correct dolls can be useful in getting at the truth, but it should be but one part of an assessment because many nonabused children will portray such dolls having sexual intercourse (Jampole & Weber, 1987). The professional consensus is that very few cases of sexual abuse are fabricated by children. Still, it is little wonder that many, perhaps most, occurrences of child molestation within families go unreported and become a developing adult's terrible secret that can lower self-esteem, distort what could otherwise be positive relationships, and even contribute to serious mental disorders.

After the immediate crisis is past, many children may still need professional attention (Wolfe, 1990). Like adult victims of rape (p. 388), they may suffer posttraumatic stress disorder. Many interventions are similar to those used for PTSD in adults (p. 152). The emphasis is on exposure to memories of the trauma through discussion in a safe and supportive therapeutic atmosphere (D. R. Johnson, 1987). As with rape, an important focus is externalizing the blame for what happened, changing the victim's attribution of responsibility from an "I was bad" self-concept to "He/she was bad."

Sexual Sadism and Sexual Masochism

A strong preference for obtaining or increasing sexual gratification by inflicting pain or psychological suffering (e.g., humiliation) is the key characteristic of **sexual sadism**. Preference for obtaining or increasing sexual gratification through subjection to pain or humiliation is the key characteristic of **sexual masochism**. Both these disorders are found in heterosexual and homosexual relationships, though it is estimated that more than 85% of people with these disorders are exclusively or predominantly heterosexual (Moser & Levitt, 1987). Some sadists

sexual sadism A marked preference for obtaining or increasing sexual gratification by inflicting pain or humiliation on another person.

sexual masochism A marked preference for obtaining or increasing sexual gratification through subjection to pain or humiliation.

The sexual sadist obtains sexual gratification from inflicting pain or humiliation on another person, often a sexual masochist who is aroused by being dominated or humiliated.

and masochists are women. The disorders seem to begin by early adulthood, and most sadists and masochists are relatively comfortable with their unconventional sexual practices (Spengler, 1977).

The majority of sadists establish relationships with masochists to derive mutual sexual gratification. Moser and Levitt (1987) estimated that millions of Americans engage in sexual practices that involve the infliction of pain or humiliation (though far fewer engage in such practices often or intensively enough to be diagnosed as sadists or masochists). The majority of sadists and masochists lead otherwise conventional lives, and they are above average in income and educational status (Moser & Levitt, 1987; Spengler, 1977).

The sadist may derive full orgasmic pleasure by inflicting pain on his or her partner, and the masochist may be completely gratified by being subjected to pain. For other partners the sadistic and masochistic practices are a prelude to or aspect of sexual intercourse. Manifestations of sexual masochism are varied. Examples include restraint (physical bondage), blindfolding (sensory bondage), spanking, whipping, electrical shocks, cutting, and humiliation (such as being urinated or defecated on, being forced to bark like a dog, or being subjected to verbal abuse). The term *infantilism* refers to a desire to be treated like a helpless infant and clothed in diapers. An especially dangerous form of masochism, called hypoxyphilia, involves sexual arousal by oxygen deprivation brought about by a noose, plastic bag, chest compression, or a chemical that produces a temporary decrease in brain oxygenation by reducing blood flow to the brain (American Psychiatric Association, 1994).

The shared activities of a sadist and a masochist are heavily scripted. Pain, humiliation and domination, or both take place as part of a story that the two agree to act out together. Themes of submission–domination appear to be as important as inflicting physical pain. The activities of the masochist and sadist assume for both parties a certain fictional *meaning* that heightens sexual arousal. The masochist, for example, may be a mischievous child who must be punished by a discipline-minded teacher.

Some sadists do murder and mutilate and are among sex offenders who are imprisoned for torturing victims, mostly strangers, and deriving sexual satisfaction from this (Dietz, Hazelwood, & Warren, 1990). Most of the time, however, sadism and masochism are restricted to fantasies. They are not then regarded as disorders according to the DSM unless the person is "markedly distressed by them." This is a constant theme in DSM-IV—it is okay to have very unconventional fantasies provided that one does not act on them or that one is not bothered by them.

TO RECAP

The paraphilias involve enduring, intense sexual attraction to nonhuman objects, to children or other nonconsenting people, or to the suffering or humiliation of oneself or one's partner. To be diagnosed with one of these disorders the person must have acted on the unusual urges or must be significantly distressed by them. Examples of paraphilias and the object of sexual interest they involve include pedophilia (children, in one's own family in the case of incest); fetishism (inanimate objects, such as underpants); voyeurism (watching others undress or have sex when they do not know they are being watched), exhibitionism (exposing one's genitals to an unwilling stranger); sexual sadism (inflicting pain or psychological suffering); and sexual masochism (being subjected to pain or psychological suffering). Most paraphiliacs are men who lack social skills and maturity and who experience their unusual sexual attraction as involuntary and irresistible.

Perspectives on the Causes and Treatment of Paraphilias

Psychodynamic Perspectives

In general, psychoanalytic theories depict paraphilias as defensive responses to repressed fears and personal inadequacies. For example, pedophiles are seen as having debilitating anxiety about adult sexual relationships and a sense of having failed socially and professionally in the adult world (Lanyon, 1986). Therefore, their only means of achieving a sense of mastery interpersonally is with helpless victims. Exhibitionism is believed to result from a repressed fear of castration and the male exhibitionist's need to reassure himself that he is still a man. Male sexual sadists are likewise believed to fear castration and to inflict pain to assure themselves of their power and masculinity. At this point there is little research support for these hypotheses (which are quite difficult to test definitively).

Biological Perspectives

In the legal, ethical, and social issues essay, we discussed child sexual abuse from the victim's perspective. Efforts to reduce its prevalence and severity must, however, focus on the sex offender. A variety of medical interventions have been tried with sex offenders based on the general idea that paraphilias must involve some abnormality in the brain. Brain surgery, usually lesioning parts of the hypothalamus in the midbrain, was attempted primarily by a group of surgeons in Germany. The results were mainly negative, sometimes producing serious unintended side effects, such as loss of intellect or even death (Muller, Roeder, & Orthner, 1973). Too little is known about the role of the hypothalamus in complex human sexual behavior to justify such radical and irreversible interventions.

Some efforts to control paraphiliac behavior among sex offenders have employed certain drugs. For example, Medroxyprogesterone acetate (MPA) is believed to reduce testosterone levels in men and to reduce the frequency of erections and ejaculations. It is hypothesized, therefore, that MPA would inhibit unconventional sexual arousal and consequent disapproved behavior. After periods of MPA administration ranging from five to twenty years, seventeen of twenty sex offenders did not engage in paraphiliac behaviors. However, when the drug was discontinued, most reverted to their paraphilias (Berlin & Meinecke, 1981). From a scientific point of view, this relapse to prior behaviors is actually useful in the sense of clarifying that the earlier improvements resulted from taking MPA. Clinically, of course, the effect is discouraging, suggesting that MPA may have to be taken indefinitely. Long-term use would be problematic, for side effects can include infertility and diabetes.

With respect to short-term use of MPA, findings are mixed. Short-term administration of the drug might bring paraphiliac behavior under enough control in some individuals to permit psychological intervention that might have a more enduring effect (Marshall, Jones, Ward, Johnston, & Barbaree, 1991).

Behavioral Perspectives

Behavioral theorists usually invoke classical conditioning to explain fetishism. For example, a young man may, early in his sexual experiences, masturbate to pictures of women dressed in black leather. In an experiment consistent with this reasoning, male subjects were repeatedly shown slides of attractive nude women interspersed with slides of women's boots (Rachman, 1966). The subjects were eventually aroused by the boots alone.

However, the fetishistic attraction was weak and transient, and it is not clear that such conditioning experiences can or do account for the development of a substantial proportion of clinically significant paraphilias. Moreover, if mere association with sexual stimulation were all there was to acquiring a fetishism, one would expect objects such as ceilings and pillows to be high on the list of fetishes, but they are not (Baron & Byrne, 1977). Just as people may be prepared to learn to become phobic of certain objects (see Chapter 6), people may also be prepared to learn to be sexually stimulated by certain classes of stimuli.

With respect to sadism and masochism the classical conditioning explanation proposes that some sort of sadomasochistic elements were present at a prior time when the person experienced orgasm. There are as yet no data to support this theory. A related hypothesis suggests that the physiological arousal from inflicting and experiencing pain is not, in fact, dissimilar to sexual excitement. In the early stages of being sexualized, discriminations may be difficult to make, especially if the pain-inducing act also includes sexual elements. In this way the individual may learn to label pain-produced arousal as sexual. This hypothesis is also speculative at this time.

In efforts to alter paraphilias, behavior therapists often try a combination of approaches. The main emphasis is on using conditioning methods to change the particular pattern of unconventional sexuality.

Aversion Therapy

One early tactic was aversion therapy. Thus a shock or an emetic would be given to a boot fetishist when looking at a boot, to a transvestite when cross-dressing, to a pedophile when gazing at a photograph of a nude child, and so on. Sometimes these negative treatments were supplemented by training in social skills and assertion to bolster patients' capacities for relating effectively with others. Aversion therapy can have beneficial effects on pedophilia, exhibitionism, and fetishism (Marks & Gelder, 1967; Marks, Gelder, & Bancroft, 1970; Marshall & Barbaree, 1990), though it is unlikely that such techniques work in accordance with the conditioning principles on which they were originally based. Although aversion therapy may not actually eliminate the attraction, it does in some cases provide the patient with a greater measure of control over the overt behavior (McConaghy, 1990).

Orgasmic Reorientation and Desensitization

orgasmic reorientation A *behavior therapy* technique for altering classes of stimuli to which people are sexually attracted; individuals are confronted by a conventionally arousing stimulus while experiencing orgasm for another, undesirable reason.

Increasing conventional arousal seems to depend more on positive therapeutic approaches. **Orgasmic reorientation** is one such behavioral technique used to alter classes of stimuli to which people are sexually attracted (Brownell, Hayes, & Barlow, 1977; Davison, 1968). Paraphiliacs, for instance, are confronted with a conventionally arousing stimulus while they are responding sexually for other, undesirable reasons, in the hope that an association will be formed between sexual arousal and the conventional stimulus.

Family Systems Perspectives

Incest is increasingly viewed as involving an entire family—the victim, the spouse, and siblings as well—and the entire family is therefore included in therapy. Sessions are primarily insight oriented, aimed at helping all members understand why the father (in most instances) turns to a daughter for emotional support and sexual gratification. The best-known program of this kind is the Child Sexual Abuse Treatment Program in Santa Clara County, California, which reports that more than 90% of fathers can be returned to their families and that there is only a 1% recidivism rate (Giarretto, 1982). Considerable research is needed, however, to replicate these findings and to uncover why this complex (and expensive) treatment approach effects beneficial change (Lanyon, 1986).

To Recap

Psychodynamic theories see paraphilias as defensive responses to childhood experiences and subsequent repressed fears and doubts about personal adequacy. Biological approaches to treatment of paraphiliac sex offenders have included psychosurgery, which proved ineffective, and medication. Medroxyprogesterone acetate (MPA), a drug that reduces testosterone levels in men, appears to work in most cases, but only while the drug is being administered, and it can have serious side effects. Behavioral theories typically attribute paraphilias to classical conditioning. Although there is no convincing evidence for this explanation, aversion therapies based on this rationale seem helpful in reducing deviant behavior. Comprehensive behavioral treatment also entails reconditioning to increase sexual arousal to more conventional stimuli. Family systems treatments for incest survivors and their families show promising results, but conclusive information is lacking on what aspects of treatment reliably produce long-term success.

Rape

We have mentioned rape several times in this chapter already, for example, as a possible source of sexual dysfunction. In this section we focus specifically on rape as a problem in its own right. Though not a separate category in the DSM, rape is an important aspect of human behavior and, in our opinion, is properly studied in a textbook such as this.

Few other antisocial acts are viewed with more disgust and anger than **forcible rape**, sexual intercourse with an unwilling partner. A second category, statutory rape, refers to sexual intercourse between a man and a girl under the age of consent. The typical age of consent, as decided by state statutes, is eighteen years. It is assumed that a younger person should not be held responsible for her sexual activity. Statutory rape does not necessarily involve force. The charge can be made even if it is proven that the girl entered into the situation willingly, so long as she is too young. We focus here on forcible rape.

forcible rape The legal term for *rape*, to force sexual intercourse or other sexual activity on another person. Statutory rape is sexual intercourse between an adult male and someone who is under the age of consent, as fixed by local statute.

The Crime

Rape is considered as much an act of violence and aggression as a sexual act. In many jurisdictions the definition of rape includes not only vaginal penetration but oral and anal entry as well. If one focuses on the victim's reactions—helplessness, fear, humiliation—rather than on the specifics of the perpetrator's acts, *any* act of sexual domination can be construed as rape (Calhoun & Atkeson, 1991). This expanded definition may be useful for purposes of helping victims, but is different from legal definitions. In our discussion, we will distinguish whenever possible rape that involves penile penetration or oral sex from unwanted sexual activity that does not, such as sexually harassing remarks in the workplace or coerced stroking of the breasts or buttocks (even though these may be traumatic also). Also, though men can be victims of sexual assault, our discussion focuses on women, because rape is primarily an act of men against women.

As many as 25% of American women will be raped during their lifetimes (Kilpatrick & Best, 1990). The majority of sexual assaults are not reported. Expanding the purview to coerced sexual activity that stops short of rape, as many as 75% of female college students have been subjected to unwanted sexual activity (Koss, 1985).

The Victim

A prevalent belief is that the victims of rape are always young and attractive. This is a myth. Although many victims do indeed fit this description, many others do not. Age and physical appearance are no barriers to some rapists. They might choose children as young as one year old or women in their eighties.

Rape victims are often traumatized by the experience, both physically and mentally (Resick, Veronen, Calhoun, Kilpatrick, & Atkeson, 1986). In the minutes or seconds preceding rape, the woman begins to recognize her dangerous situation but can scarcely believe what is about to happen to her. During the moments of the attack, she is first and foremost in great fear for her life. The physical violation of her body and the ripping away of her freedom of choice are enraging. But the victim also feels her vulnerability in not being able to fight off her stronger attacker and usually finds her capacity for resistance seriously compromised by her terror. For weeks or months following the rape, many victims suffer from posttraumatic stress (p. 140). They are extremely tense and deeply humiliated. They may feel guilty because they were unable to fight harder and have angry thoughts of revenge. Many have nightmares about the rape.

In a study of women admitted to a large city hospital for emergency treatment immediately following rape, Burgess and Holmstrom (1974) found that half ultimately changed their place of residence or their telephone number. Such changes can seriously disrupt social relationships, lead to loss of time at work and even loss of employment, and contribute to depression because such dislocations can reduce contacts with friends, relatives, and other sources of social support (Calhoun & Atkeson, 1991).

Women who have been raped are more likely to have trouble in sexual relationships with their husbands or lovers. For some women, even though frequency of sex and of orgasms may not be diminished, satisfaction with sex can be reduced for years (Feldman-Summers, Gordon, & Meagher, 1979). Some victims of rape develop phobias about being outdoors or indoors or in the dark, depending on where the rape took place. They may also fear being alone or in crowds or having anyone behind them.

Without intervention, posttraumatic symptoms of anxiety and depression can persist in some women for years following an assault (Calhoun & Atkeson, 1991). They are also at higher risk for suicide (Cohen & Roth, 1987) and substance abuse (Burnam et al., 1988), which is probably an attempt to self-medicate to reduce anxiety and depression. We have already seen that multiple personality disorder (p. 169) and borderline personality disorder (p. 300) have been linked to sexual trauma in childhood. Moreover, consistent with research on the effects of stress on physical health, rape victims can suffer a variety of somatic problems and tend to increase their use of medical services (Phelps, Wallace, & Waigant, 1989).

A secondary source of stress for rape victims may be people's reactions after the rape. Many feminist groups object to the classification of rape as a *sexual* crime at all. This classification can mask the basically assaultive and typically brutal nature of the act and creates an atmosphere in which the sexual motives of the *victim* are questioned. Although a person who is beaten and robbed (without being sexually abused) is hardly suspected of secretly wanting to be attacked, by cruel irony the victims of rape must often prove their moral purity to husbands, friends, police—even to themselves. What, after all, did *they* do that might have contributed to the incident, especially if the rapist is not a complete stranger?

The Rapist

The vast majority of rapes are planned. Rape is not the spontaneous act of a man whose sexual impulses have gone out of control (Harrington & Sutton-Simon, 1977). The rapist may have a sadistic streak, but unlike the sexual sadist, he often does not know the victim beforehand and he attacks someone who is unwilling. Moreover, a sadist usually has an established, ongoing relationship with a masochist that involves voluntary mutual exchange of sexually pleasurable pain. **Sadistic rape** involves the infliction of serious physical harm on the victim's body, such as inserting foreign objects into the vagina. Some rapists murder and mutilate (Holmstrom & Burgess, 1980).

sadistic rape Acts of rape that involve the infliction of serious physical harm on the victim's body.

Many rapists experience sexual dysfunction during rape. Interviews with 170 men convicted of sexual assault revealed that three-fourths experienced sexual dysfunction (such as erectile failure or premature ejaculation) during their criminal act, though almost none reported having these problems in consenting sexual relations (Groth & Burgess, 1977). Rapists often abuse alcohol, so the frequency of erectile failure might be due in part to the inhibitory effects of alcohol on sexual arousal (Wilson & Lawson, 1976).

Who is the rapist? Is he primarily the psychopath who seeks the thrill of dominating and humiliating a woman through intimidation and often brutal assault? Is he an ordinarily unassertive man with a fragile ego who, feeling inadequate after disappointment and rejection in work or love, takes out his frustrations on an unwilling stranger? Or is he the teenager, provoked by a seductive and apparently available young woman who, it turns out, was not as interested as he in sexual intimacy? Is he a man whose inhibitions against expressing anger have been dissolved by alcohol? The best answer is that the rapist is all these men.

What many rapists seem to have in common is unusually high hostility toward women, arising from beliefs of having been betrayed, deceived, or demeaned by them. From a sociological perspective, the more a society accepts interpersonal violence as a way to handle conflict and solve problems, the higher the frequency of rape (Sanday, 1981).

Men arrested for rape tend to be young—usually between fifteen and twenty-five years of age—poor, unskilled, and not well educated. About half of them are married and living with their wives at the time of the crime. One-fourth to one-third of all rapes are carried out by two or more men. Given the knowledge that rape is seriously underreported, however, it would be a mistake to generalize too confidently about rapists from these arrest records. Indeed, in some instances the rapist is the victim's husband

Exposure to certain forms of pornography may dispose some men to act aggressively toward women in sexual situations. In a review of research on the topic, Bandura (1986) concluded that whereas pleasant erotica does not increase sexual aggressiveness, erotica that demeans women or entails violence toward and domination of them does (Malamuth, Feshbach, & Jaffe, 1977). Hard-core pornography—which typically derogates women—leads male viewers to become more lenient in their thinking about rape offenders (Linz, Donnerstein, & Penrod, 1988). Violent pornography that portrays women as initially resisting but then enjoying rape fosters the idea that women like to be sexually assaulted (Malamuth & Check, 1981). One-third of a sample of college men admitted that they might rape if they could avoid arrest, and they tended to subscribe to the myth that women who are raped ask for it by the way they dress and act (Malamuth, 1981) (See Focus Box 13.2 for a review of what we know today as date rape or acquaintance rape.)

Therapy for Rapists and Rape Victims

Unlike most of the disorders dealt with in this book, rape presents two different challenges to the mental health professional: treating the man who has committed the act and treating the woman who has been the victim.

> ### Focus Box 13.2

Acquaintance Rape

Rape between two people who know each other and may even be dating is called **acquaintance rape** or **date rape**. Such attacks may outnumber those between strangers by as much as three to one (Kilpatrick & Best, 1990).

Date rapes are the least reported type of rape (Warshaw, 1988). In part this underreporting may result from victims' not labeling what happened to them as rape. According to a survey conducted by *Ms Magazine*, only one-quarter of women who said that they had had sexual intercourse against their will said that they had ever been raped (Warshaw, 1988). Also, victims of date rape are more likely to blame themselves for what happened, believing that since they permitted the man to embrace them and kiss them, they implicitly gave him permission to have intercourse or to engage in other intimate sexual acts with them. Those who have been working to increase women's awareness of acquaintance rape urge women to consider that either party in a sexual situation always has the right to say no. There is no justification in the claim that the man has been all stirred up by the woman's alleged seductiveness and can't help himself.

It may be that some acts of rape are committed through faulty communication between the man and the woman. The woman's "maybe" is interpreted as "yes" by the man, who proceeds on the assumption that the woman really wants to be intimate, only to be sorely disappointed and unable to accept her ultimate refusal (Gagnon, 1977; Margolin, 1990). This view of rape would of course apply only to instances in which the two people know each other. Nor does this view account for the extreme brutality that is often part of the assault.

Alcohol consumption seems to affect both the occurrence of date rape and perceptions of it. Many acquaintance rapes involve alcohol consumption by the victim, the rapist, or both (Norris & Cubbins, 1992). On reading a story depicting an acquaintance rape, both men and women were less likely to perceive the man's behavior as rape if both the rapist and the victim had been drinking. The victim's drinking alone did not have this effect. "The implication is that a woman and a man drinking together may signify an expectation that sexual activity will occur. In contrast, if only a woman has been drinking, the man may be viewed as taking advantage of a women who is in a vulnerable or weakened condition" (Norris & Cubbins, 1992, pp. 188–189).

There may be a message here that can reduce date rape. In addition to being more assertive and demanding if they feel unwanted pressure being applied, women can learn to understand the risks associated with alcohol and the different scripts from which men and women often operate. Women can thereby become

---

acquaintance (date) rape Forcible sex between two people who know each other, sometimes occurring on a date.

Treating Rapists

Several therapy programs have been developed to reduce the tendency of men to rape. In some prisons confrontational group therapy has been employed in efforts to encourage convicted rapists to take responsibility for their violence toward women and to explore more decent ways of handling their anger and of relating to the opposite sex. But the effectiveness of these programs has not been adequately studied. Most rapists perpetrate their assaults many times in their lives, and prison terms have a limited effect on reducing the future incidence of rape. Therapists who try to help men who rape have to consider a wide range of causes that might underlie the problem—loneliness, deficient social skills (Overholser & Beck, 1986), fear of dealing with women in conventional ways, hatred of women, inability or unwillingness to delay gratification, especially after excessive drinking, and exaggerated conceptions of masculinity that relegate women to an inferior status.

Biological interventions, such as surgical castration and the chemical lowering of testosterone, rest on the assumption that rape is primarily a sexual act. It should be kept in mind, however, that erectile capacity is not necessary for rape.

Many colleges provide educational workshops in the hope of lowering the incidence of rape, including date rate.

more mindful of the possibility that some of their messages can be received and interpreted by men in unintended ways. This is not to shift the responsibility to the woman, rather to provide her with some tools that can improve communication and lessen the chances of misunderstanding. Certainly any preventive efforts directed at women have to be complemented by educational programs for men. Men need to examine their attitudes and practices in dealing with women as possible sexual partners (rather than as objects) and need to understand the different scripts as well.

The violent behavior itself is not directly addressed by these drastic medical measures (Geer et al., 1984).

Treating Rape Victims

Considerable effort is devoted to helping the victims of sexual assaults. Many rape crisis centers and telephone hot lines have been established across the country, some of them associated with hospitals and clinics, others operating on their own. Staffed by both professionals and volunteers, these centers offer support and advice within what is called a crisis intervention framework. The focus is on helping the rape victim accept her emotional reactions—"Everyone goes through this emotional turmoil after an assault"; encouraging her to talk about her feelings; helping her meet immediate needs, such as arranging for child care or improving the security arrangements in her home; and, generally, helping her solve problems and cope with the immediate aftermath of the trauma (Calhoun & Atkeson, 1991; Sorenson & Brown, 1990).

Women are encouraged not to withdraw. Reporting the rape to the police is also urged as a way of taking action and overcoming some of the sense of

Being raped produces powerful emotional effects on the victim. In recent years, rape counseling centers have been established to help victims deal with these traumatic aftereffects.

helplessness such an attack causes. Women from the crisis center can accompany the rape victim to the hospital and to the police station, where they help her with the legal procedures and with recounting the events of the attack. They may later arrange for examinations for pregnancy and venereal disease and for psychological counseling. The possibility of HIV infection also has to be addressed. The empathic companions from the crisis center help the victim get started in expressing her feelings about her ordeal, and they prompt her to continue her venting with her own relatives and friends. If the attacker or attackers have been apprehended, the women from the center urge the victim to go through with the prosecution. They attend her meetings with the district attorney as well as the trial.

As already indicated, rape victims, far more than victims of other violent crimes, tend to examine their own role in provoking or allowing the attack. Counseling, therefore, must concentrate on alleviating the woman's feelings of responsibility and guilt (Frazier, 1990). When long-term therapy is available, its work often involves relieving this guilt and helping the woman with her ongoing relationships, which may be disrupted or negatively affected by the rape. Friends and family, especially spouses and lovers, also need attention—to help them handle their own emotional distress so that they can provide the kind of nonjudgmental support that rape victims need.

Coping with the Trauma of Rape.   One of the most serious effects of rape is anxiety. Victims need help coping with their fears. Although anxiety-reduction approaches vary, they share in common with the treatment of PTSD (Keane et al., 1989) the idea that the victim must reencounter the fearsome events of the attack so that the anxiety can be extinguished (Rothbaum & Foa, 1992b). As with other kinds of anxiety, it is no easy task to encourage the person to reflect on her fears, because denial and avoidance are the usual coping methods used by rape victims—for the most part unsuccessfully.

Coping with the Criminal Justice System.   Attitudes and support systems now encourage the victim to report rape and pursue the prosecution of the alleged rapist, but the legal situation is still problematic. Rape continues to be one of the most underreported of crimes. A national crime survey conducted by the U.S. Bureau of Justice estimates that not more than 53% of rapes committed between 1973 and 1987 were reported to the police. The actual figure is probably much lower. Interviews with half a million women indicated three reasons for reluctance to report rape: considering the rape a private matter, fearing reprisals from the rapist or his family or friends, and believing that the police would be inefficient, ineffective, or insensitive (Wright, 1991). Furthermore, estimates are that only a very small percentage of rapists are convicted of their crimes. Any familiarity of the victim with her assailant argues strongly against his ultimate conviction. And even though many rapists rape hundreds of times, they are only occasionally imprisoned for an offense. The victim's role in her own assault continues to be examined, though there are indications that the stigma of rape is being lessened by more enlightened views.

TO RECAP

About 25% of American women are raped at some point in their lives. Posttraumatic consequences of this terrifying act of violence can include physical health problems, anxiety, depression, substance abuse, rage, and difficulties in relationships in general and sexual functioning in particular. The underreporting of rape makes it difficult to draw conclusions about the characteristics of rapists. Available arrest records suggest that a typical rapist would be a young man of low socioeconomic status. Psychologically, rapists seem to be diverse, but the common denominator is high hostility toward women. Usually the rapist has a sense of having been demeaned by women and considers violence an acceptable way to resolve such conflicts. Exposure to violent pornography appears to increase such attitudes. Attempts to prevent recurrence among rapists have included (a) group therapies aimed at changing attitudes toward women and teaching other ways to deal with anger and (b) biological interventions such as chemical lowering of testosterone. Evidence of effectiveness is limited.

Therapy for rape victims usually begins in the context of a rape crisis center or hot line. The immediate goals include encouraging the victim to discuss her feelings about the trauma and to report the crime as well as helping her cope with the legal system and get medical attention. Longer-term therapy typically focuses on (a) relationship problems that may have resulted from the rape, (b) reexposure in imagination to the trauma so as to lower anxiety, and (c) any guilt the victim may feel about her own role in the attack.

▶ *Homosexuality: Evolving Views*

Some of the behaviors described in this chapter, such as rape and incest, would surely be considered deviant by nearly everyone. With these exceptions, however, what is defined as normal and desirable in human sexual behavior varies with time and place. A striking illustration of the historical and cultural relativity of sexual norms, and the resulting impact on diagnostic classification, is the recent history of the classification of homosexuality.

From the publication of DSM-II in 1968 until 1973, **homosexuality**, sexual desire or activity directed toward a member of one's own sex, was listed as one of the sexual deviations. In 1973, the Nomenclature Committee of the American Psychiatric Association, under pressure from many professionals and particularly from gay activist groups, recommended to the general membership the elimination of the category homosexuality and the substitution of *sexual orientation disturbance*. This new diagnosis was to be applied to gay men and women who are "disturbed by, in conflict with, or wish to change their sexual orientation." The members of the psychiatric association voted on the issue, in itself a

homosexuality Sexual desire or activity directed toward a member of one's own sex.

In DSM-II, homosexuality was listed as one of several sexual deviations. In subsequent editions of the DSM, homosexuality was gradually dropped as a mental disorder, in part because of pressure from gay rights groups.

ego-dystonic homosexuality According to DSM-III, a disorder of people who are persistently dissatisfied with their *homosexuality* and wish instead to be attracted to members of the opposite sex.

comment on the degree to which the evaluation of sexual behavior is political rather than scientific. The change was approved. But there were vehement protests from some renowned psychiatrists who had for some time been identified with the traditional view that homosexuality reflects a fixation at an early stage of psychosexual development and is inherently abnormal.

The controversy continued among mental health professionals, but DSM-III (American Psychiatric Association, 1980) maintained the tolerant stance toward homosexuality that had become evident in 1973. The DSM-III category **ego-dystonic homosexuality** referred to a person who is homosexually aroused, finds that this arousal is a persistent source of distress, and wishes to become heterosexual.

DSM-III-R and now DSM-IV contain no specific mention of homosexuality as a disorder in its own right. In the years following publication of DSM-III in 1980, very little use was made by mental health professionals of the ego-dystonic homosexuality diagnosis. It is impossible to establish the exact reasons, but by the time the American Psychiatric Association was ready in 1987 to publish DSM-III-R, it had decided that even the watered-down diagnosis of ego-dystonic homosexuality should not be included. Instead, the catchall category of sexual disorder not otherwise specified referred to "persistent and marked distress about one's sexual orientation" (p. 296). This language is used in DSM-IV also.

It is noteworthy that this definition does not specify a particular sexual orientation. Thus, while the door is still open for a diagnosis of ego-dystonic homosexuality, the DSM now appears to allow as well for ego-dystonic *hetero*sexuality. Our own expectation is that neither diagnosis will be made often. Further, as we saw in the first part of this chapter, DSM-IV criteria for sexual dysfunctions do not state whether the sexual partner is of the opposite sex or the same sex, another sign of the growing liberalization of the attitude of the mental health professions toward homosexuality.

This brief history of the classification of homosexuality in the DSM illustrates the complexity of the issue with which this book began, the definition of abnormality. As noted in Chapter 1, there is no perfect definition to which we can appeal when trying to decide if homosexuality, compulsive eating, or any other condition is abnormal, but clearly the extent to which the person's behavior violates social norms is a commonly considered criterion. Sexuality is of such great interest in society that norms loom large in diagnosing problems. Therapists and researchers need to remain aware of the culture-relative aspects of diagnostic criteria, such as the norms for masculinity and femininity from which some children's gender identity is considered too discrepant.

Visual Summary for Chapter 13:

Sexual and Gender Identity Disorders

Sexual Dysfunctions

Disruptions in the normal sexual response cycle of appetitive, excitement, orgasm, and resolution phases. Must be recurrent and distressing.

Examples

Sexual Desire Disorders	····▷ Low desire for or active aversion to sex.
Sexual Arousal Disorders	····▷ Either lubrication (female) or erection (male) insufficient to complete intercourse.
Orgasmic Disorders	··▷ Orgasm absent after a period of normal sexual excitement. More common among men is ejaculating sooner than desired.
Sexual Pain Disorders	····▷ Pain before, during, or after intercourse. Among women one type is vaginismus, involuntary spasms of the outer third of the vagina that make intercourse painful or impossible.

Perspectives on Sexual Dysfunctions

	Causes	Treatment
Psychodynamic ···▷	Dysfunction symbolizes repressed conflict about sexual feelings. Premature ejaculation may, for instance, stem from repressed hostility toward one's partner. ····▷	Interpret the nature of the conflict, providing insight and the possibility of using healthier, less defensive coping tactics. Usually supplemented with directive sex therapy methods.
Biological ····▷	Infections can cause sexual pain disorders. Illnesses such as diabetes and medications such as antihypertensive drugs can cause male erectile disorder. ····▷	Medications, such as yohimbine for male erectile disorder. Surgery, such as sex reassignment for adult transsexuals.
Integrative ····▷	Multiple past and present causes are possible. For instance, Masters and Johnson's model attributes much of sexual dysfunction to fears about performance and adoption of a spectator role, which in turn can result from traumatic sexual experiences or negative attitudes toward sex learned from the family or the wider culture. ····▷	Depends on the case and is usually multifaceted. May include couples therapy, education about sex, skills training, along with sensate focus and other procedures for increasing awareness of sexual preferences and decreasing self-imposed performance pressure. For problems of low desire, directive procedures may need to be preceded by an insight-oriented phase aimed at understanding why desire is low.

Gender Identity Disorder

Discomfort with one's biological sex and identification with opposite sex, often called transsexualism.

Age-Specific Features

Childhood ····► Adopts attitudes, play styles, preferences considered by the culture appropriate for the opposite sex. Prefers company of opposite sex.

Adulthood ····► Believes he (far more prevalent in males) is a member of the opposite sex, cross-dresses, may desire to have sex changed surgically.

Perspectives on Gender Identity Disorder

	Causes	Treatment
Biological	Hormone abnormalities, but not well supported by research with adults.	Sex-reassignment surgery but with mixed results, possibly more favorable for female-to-male operations.
Behavioral	Opposite-sex clothing, activities, and preferences were rewarded with attention and encouragement in childhood.	Compliments and other rewards are given specifically for behaviors and mannerisms associated with the person's biological sex.

Paraphilias

Intense, persistent attraction to nonhuman objects, to children or other nonconsenting people, or to suffering or humiliation, either acted upon or causing great distress.

Pedophilia ····► Attraction is to children; in the case of incest, to children in one's family.

Fetishism ····► Attraction to specific inanimate objects, often articles of women's clothing.

Voyeurism ····► Watching unsuspecting others undress or have sex.

Exhibitionism ····► Exposing one's genitals to unwilling strangers.

Sexual Sadism ····► Sexual arousal from inflicting pain or humiliation.

Sexual Masochism ··► Sexual arousal from being subjected to pain or humiliation.

Perspectives on Paraphilias

	Causes	Treatment
Psychodynamic ····▶	*Defensive responses to perceived personal inadequacies, such as inability to sustain adult, mature sexual relationships. Recreating the dynamics of one's relationship with one or both parents.* ····▶	*Develop awareness of, and more adaptive means of overcoming, the unconscious self-doubt.*
Biological ····▶	*Brain abnormalities.* ····▶	*Lesioning parts of the hypothalamus; not effective. Later, a drug (MPA) for reducing testosterone levels; effective only as long as the drug is being given and has negative side effects.*
Behavioral ····▶	*Association of sexual arousal or orgasm with unconventional objects, such as a specific type of women's clothing, or with unconventional feelings, such as pain.* ····▶	*Break the association through relearning experiences. Pair the deviant source of arousal with shock or another unpleasant stimulus. Introduce conventional sexual stimuli at a time when the person is already aroused.*
Family Systems ····▶	*Applied mainly to incest. Maladaptive family relationships and ways of communicating that have resulted in father turning to daughter for emotional and sexual gratification with no one effectively stopping this situation.* ····▶	*Insight-oriented family therapy designed to reveal the maladaptive patterns and see the options for changing them.*

Rape

Consequences to Victim	Rapist Characteristics	Treatments
•*Anxiety (PTSD)* •*Depression* •*Substance abuse* •*Rage* •*Sexual dysfunction* •*Relationship problems*	•*Young and uneducated* •*Male* •*Hostile toward women* •*Tolerant of violence*	**For rapist:** *Training in healthier means of coping with and expressing anger.* **For victim:** *Emotional support, practical support (e.g., in coping with legal and medical aspects), reexposure to trauma cues to extinguish fear.*

Classification of Homosexuality as a Function of Changing Social Norms

Your sexual orientation is disordered if...	You are homosexual.	You are homosexual and distressed about it and want to change.	You are either homosexual or heterosexual and distressed about it and want to change.
	1968–1973	*1973–1987*	*1987–*

Chapter 14

Developmental Disorders and Eating Disorders

The Case of Ginny Nelson

Ginny Nelson was referred to the university counseling center by her gymnastics coach because she was binge eating and then vomiting nearly every day. This practice had become obvious to some of her teammates who lived in the same dorm, and they had shared their concerns with their coach. Ginny was a twenty-one-year-old college junior who was 5 feet 3 inches tall and weighed 110 pounds.

Ginny reluctantly agreed to contact the student counseling center. Though she realized that her eating patterns were unusual, she was not certain that they were harmful to her health. After talking for a while with Dr. R., a psychologist, Ginny admitted that she was concerned that she might be losing control over her eating habits and that she was relieved that others had pressured her to come to the center.

Until recently, Ginny had felt that she could control the binging and purging (vomiting), and she believed that purging helped her maintain her weight at a level that was beneficial for her sport. However, the gymnastics season had ended, and she was gradually gaining weight despite the regular purging. Ginny revealed that she always felt guilty and disgusted with herself after she binged and vomited. She also had to deal with other negative feelings because she had done poorly in gymnastics during the past season. These bad feelings about previous binges and other situations tended to trigger still more binge–purge episodes. Because these cycles were becoming more frequent, Ginny was eager for help.

Introduction to Developmental Disorders and Eating Disorders

Ginny's binging and purging, an eating disorder known as bulimia, had begun in adolescence. Until now we have discussed psychological problems that affect the adult population. As upsetting as it may be to have a friend or adult relative who suffers from depression or from unpredictable bouts of anxiety, it is still more disturbing to see such problems in a child or adolescent. Because they are young, children and adolescents have fewer emotional resources with which to cope with problems. The dependency of troubled children on their parents and guardians adds to the sense of responsibility that these people feel.

Most clinicians view childhood experience and development as critically important to adult mental health. In addition, they regard children as better able to change than adults and thus more amenable to treatment. We might therefore expect the disorders of children to have been the focus of voluminous research. Until recently, however, they have received considerably less attention than adult problems.

Prior to DSM-III, children were often given diagnoses that had been created for adults. A developmentally oriented diagnostic system, tailored specifically to childhood disorders, was incorporated into DSM-III and expanded in DSM-III-R and DSM-IV. These revisions reflect the growing influence of the field of developmental psychopathology, which studies disorders of childhood within the context of normal life-span development. Understanding normal developmental changes allows us to identify behaviors that are appropriate at one stage but are considered disturbed at another. For example, although defiant behavior is quite common at age two or three, the persistence of such behavior at ages five or six is considered much more problematic.

Whereas in most cases adults identify *themselves* as having a problem, children are generally so identified *by others*. The difference between "I have a problem" (adult disorders) and "You have a problem" (childhood disorders) is great. When adults are referred for treatment, we can be reasonably sure that they have problems for which they desire help. When a child is referred for treatment, all we really know is that someone perceives this child as disordered. Why does the person see this child as needing treatment? Is this boy really unmanageable, or does he just remind his mother of her divorced husband? Is this girl really distractible, or is she merely bored by school? Although the child's actual behavior plays a major role in how adults perceive him or her, many other factors also enter into the perception (A. O. Ross, 1981).

In discussing several of the childhood disorders recognized by DSM-IV, we organize them according to two broad clusters of childhood symptoms that have emerged in research but have not been included explicitly in the DSM. Children with symptoms from one cluster are called **undercontrolled**, or externalizers, and show behavior excesses. Children who have symptoms from the other cluster are said to be **overcontrolled**, or internalizers, or to have behavior deficits and emotional inhibitions (Achenbach & Edelbrock, 1978). Across cultures, undercontrol problems are found more often among boys, overcontrol among girls (Weisz, Suwanlert, Chaiyasit, & Walter 1987). Focus Box 14.1 discusses the possible role of culture in the varying degrees of prevalence of undercontrolled and overcontrolled behavior problems in children. These two groupings are addressed first, followed by a discussion of learning disabilities, mental retardation, and autism. Finally, we describe eating disorders in this chapter because they usually begin in adolescence, though they are included in a separate section of DSM-IV.

> *undercontrolled (behavior)* In reference to childhood disorders, problem behavior of the child that involves excesses, such as unwarranted aggressiveness.

> *overcontrolled (behavior)* In reference to childhood disorders, problems that involve behavioral deficits and emotional inhibitions, such as *anxiety* and social withdrawal.

Disorders of Undercontrolled Behavior

The undercontrolled child has less control over behavior than is expected in a given setting and at a given age. Her or his behavior is frequently aggravating to both adults and peers. Two general categories of undercontrolled behavior are frequently differentiated, attention-deficit/hyperactivity disorder and conduct disorder.

Attention-Deficit/Hyperactivity Disorder

Children with **attention-deficit/hyperactivity disorder (ADHD)** have great difficulty concentrating. These inattentive children seem to have particular difficulty controlling their activity in situations that call for sitting still, such as at school or at mealtimes. When required to be quiet, they appear unable to stop moving or talking. They are constantly moving, disorganized, erratic, tactless, and bossy. Their activities and movements seem haphazard. They quickly wear out their shoes and clothing, smash their toys, and soon exhaust their family, teachers, and friends. ADHD is more common in boys than in girls. Very few studies of girls with ADHD have been conducted, but few differences between girls and boys with ADHD have been found thus far (e.g., Breen, 1989).

> *attention-deficit/hyperactivity disorder (ADHD)* A disorder in children marked by difficulties in focusing adaptively on the task at hand and by inappropriate fidgeting and antisocial behavior.

ADHD does not refer to simply being rambunctious or a bit distractible, for in the early school years children are often so. ADHD as a diagnosis refers to truly extreme and persistent cases, not to children who are merely more lively and more difficult to control than a parent or teacher would like.

Because the symptoms of ADHD described in DSM-III-R represented such a heterogeneous group of behaviors, DSM-IV separates those children with both attention deficits *and* hyperactivity from those with predominantly one feature or the other. Research indicates that ADHD children (with attentional problems *and* hyperactivity) are more likely to develop conduct problems and oppositional behavior (habitually going against what adults want them to do), to be placed in special classes for behavior-disordered children, and to have difficulties getting along with their peers (Barkley, DuPaul, & McMurray, 1990). ADD children (with attentional problems but with normal activity levels) appear to have more prob-

Culture and Childhood Problems

The values of a culture play a role in whether a certain pattern of child behavior develops or is considered a problem. In a study comparing clinic referrals in Thailand with those in the United States, problems of overcontrol (for example, fearfulness) were reported more often for Thai than for American youngsters, whereas problems of undercontrol (for example, fighting) were reported more often for American than for Thai children (Weisz et al., 1987).

Thailand's chief religion, Buddhism, disapproves of and discourages aggression. As a result, parents do not tolerate undercontrolled behavior such as disrespect and aggression. The additional finding that within Thailand problems of overcontrol were reported at clinics more often for adolescents than for children may be

due to the fact that Buddhist strictures are especially strong in the teen years, when young men may serve as novices in the temples.

The underlying assumption of this study is that because undercontrol is actively discouraged, Thai children, virtually by default, are more likely than American children to develop problems of overcontrol. As we will see later in this chapter, Western industrialized countries have emphasized thinness as a standard for feminine beauty and perhaps as a result have seen this standard emerge in exaggerated form in eating disorders.

In a similar manner, Thai emphasis on inhibiting aggression may in general be healthy, but could also cause an overreaction in some cases and consequently problems of undercontrol.

lems with focused attention or speed of information processing (Barkley, Grodzinsky, & DuPaul, 1992). These studies suggest that it may be best to think of these as two separate disorders (Barkley, 1990). Most of the theory and research, however, does not yet make this distinction.

Not surprisingly, the inattention and impulsiveness of ADHD children are often associated with academic difficulties. About 20% to 25% of children with ADHD have been found to have a learning disability (see p. 413) (Barkley et al., 1990), and many ADHD children are placed in special educational programs because of their difficulty in adjusting to a typical classroom environment.

ADHD can be difficult to distinguish from conduct disorder (discussed later). Since an overlap of 30% to 90% between the two categories has been found (Hinshaw, 1987), some researchers have asserted that the two types of undercontrolled behavior, ADHD and conduct disorder, are actually the same disorder (Quay, 1979). However, hyperactivity is associated more with behavior in school that is irrelevant to the assigned task, with cognitive and achievement deficits, and with a better long-term prognosis. Conversely, children with conduct problems and aggression are more likely to have antisocial parents, family hostility, low socioeconomic status, and a much higher risk for delinquency and substance abuse in adolescence (Hinshaw, 1987; Loney, Langhorne, & Paternite, 1978). Thus these are probably two separate but related disorders (Hinshaw, 1987).

Although many preschoolers are considered inattentive and overactive by their parents and teachers, the majority of these youngsters are going through a normal developmental stage that will not become a persistent pattern of ADHD (Campbell, 1990). Still, most children who *do* go on to develop ADHD exhibit excessive activity and temperamental behavior quite early in life. Although the preschool years are stressful for parents coping with ADHD, the problems are most obvious when the children enter school and are suddenly expected to comply with demands that they sit in their seats for long periods of time, complete assignments independently, and negotiate with peers on the playground.

Many hyperactive children have inordinate difficulties getting along with peers and establishing friendships (Whalen & Henker, 1985). Although these children are usually friendly and talkative, they often miss subtle social cues, misinterpret peers' intentions, and make unintentional social mistakes. ADHD children are often knowledgeable about correct social actions in hypothetical situations, but do not translate this knowledge into appropriate behavior in real-life social interactions. This ineptitude, often combined with impulsive aggressiveness, leads hyperactive children to be rejected by their peers (Whalen & Henker, 1985).

At one time it was thought that hyperactivity simply went away by adolescence. However, this belief has been challenged by longitudinal research. In one study, for instance, more than 70% of children with ADHD were found to meet criteria for the disorder in adolescence (Barkley et al., 1990). Table 14.1 provides a catalogue of behaviors found more often among ADHD adolescents than among controls. In addition to these fidgety, distractible, impulsive behaviors, adolescents with ADHD are far more likely to drop out of high school. Though most are employed and financially independent in adulthood, they generally reach a lower level of socioeconomic status than expected and change jobs more frequently. Most adults with a history of ADHD continue to exhibit some symptoms of the disorder, but most also learn to adapt to these symptoms, perhaps by finding a niche for themselves in the working world.

Perspectives on the Causes and Treatment of ADHD

The search for causes and effective treatments of ADHD is complicated by the heterogeneity of children given this diagnosis. Any factor found to be associated with the syndrome, or any treatment found to reduce its symptoms, may apply to only some of those carrying the diagnosis.

Biological Perspectives.   A predisposition toward ADHD is probably inherited. In a study of 238 twin pairs, Goodman and Stevenson (1989) found concordance for clinically diagnosed hyperactivity in 51% of identical twins and in 33% of fraternal twins.

But what is it that ADHD children inherit? Preliminary studies suggest that defects in the frontal-limbic system may be the biological basis for the disorder. PET scans demonstrate that adults with childhood-onset ADHD have reduced cerebral glucose metabolism; their brains were less active than the brains of normal adults during an auditory-attention task (Zametkin et al., 1990). The difference was most striking in those regions of the brain involved in self-regulation of

Table 14.1 ▶ *Prevalence of Symptoms in ADHD and Normal Adolescents*

Symptom	ADHD, %	Normal, %
Fidgets	73.2	10.6
Difficulty remaining seated	60.2	3.0
Easily distracted	82.1	15.2
Difficulty waiting turn	48.0	4.5
Blurts out answers	65.0	10.6
Difficulty following instructions	83.7	12.1
Difficulty sustaining attention	79.7	16.7
Shifts from one uncompleted task to another	77.2	16.7
Difficulty playing quietly	39.8	7.6
Talks excessively	43.9	6.1
Interrupts others	65.9	10.6
Doesn't seem to listen	80.5	15.2
Loses things needed for tasks	62.6	12.1
Engages in physically dangerous activities	37.4	3.0

Source: Adapted from Barkley et al. (1990).

motor functions and attentional systems. ADHD children also show poorer performance on neuropsychological tests of frontal lobe functioning. This result provides further support for the theory that a basic deficit in this part of the brain may be related to the symptoms of the disorder (Chelune, Ferguson, Koon, & Dickey, 1986).

Popular theories of ADHD over the years have also proposed a role for environmental toxins such as food additives (Feingold, 1973) and refined sugar (Wolraich, Milich, Stumbo, & Schultz, 1985), but research has not shown either to cause ADHD. Although some evidence suggests that lead poisoning may be associated to a small degree with symptoms of hyperactivity and attentional problems (Thompson et al., 1989), most children with ADHD do not show elevated levels of lead in the blood. Thus, environmental toxins have not proven a productive avenue in the search for the cause of most cases of ADHD.

Biological treatment in the form of stimulant medications, especially Ritalin (methylphenidate), is commonly used for children with ADHD. Recently, prescription of these medications has continued into adolescence for many youngsters in light of the accumulating evidence that the symptoms of ADHD often do not disappear with the passage of time.

Several controlled studies comparing stimulants with placebos in double-blind designs indicate dramatic short-term improvements in concentration, goal-directed activity, classroom behavior, and fine-motor activity and reduced aggressive behavior and impulsivity in many ADHD children (G. Weiss, 1983). However, such drugs may not improve academic achievement over the long haul (G. Weiss, 1983).

The success of stimulant medication in treating hyperactive children was once considered evidence in support of a biological theory of hyperactivity. Amphetamines heighten the adult's sense of energy, yet they increase attention and decrease activity level in hyperactive children. This apparently paradoxical effect was taken as evidence for abnormal biological processes in hyperactive children. Such an interpretation is no longer viable, for some evidence demonstrates that normal children also respond to amphetamines with increased attention and decreased activity (Rapoport et al., 1978). The once presumed paradoxical effect has proven to be the normal response of children to stimulant drugs.

Behavioral Perspectives.   Learning might also figure in hyperactivity. Hyperactivity may be modeled on the behavior of parents and siblings (Ross & Ross, 1982). Or, hyperactivity could be reinforced by the attention it elicits. Parents of hyperactive children give them more commands and have more negative interactions with them. However, when stimulant medication is used to improve attention and lessen hyperactivity, the parents' commands and negative behavior decrease (Barkley, 1990), suggesting that aberrant parental behavior may be more a result than a cause of ADHD.

Even if poor parenting does not cause ADHD, deliberate changes in the consequences provided for the child's behavior can be an effective treatment. Treatments of ADHD based on behavioral principles have demonstrated at least short-term success in improving both social and academic behavior. In these treatments, the behavior of the children is monitored both at home and in school, and they are reinforced for doing the appropriate thing, such as working on assignments. Point systems and star charts are frequently a part of these programs. Youngsters earn points or stars for behaving in certain ways, and they can later spend their earnings for rewards.

These operant programs focus on improving academic work, completing household tasks, or learning specific social skills, rather than on reducing the signs of hyperactivity, such as running around and jiggling (O'Leary, Pelham, Rosenbaum, & Price, 1976). The therapists who devise these interventions conceptualize hyperactivity as a deficit in certain skills rather than as an excess of disruptive behavior. Although hyperactive children have proven very responsive to such programs, the optimal treatment for ADHD may require the use of both stimulants and behavior therapy (Barkley, 1990).

Conduct Disorder

Conduct disorder encompasses a wide variety of undercontrolled behavior, including aggression, lying, destructiveness, cruelty to animals, vandalism, arson, theft, and truancy. The connecting thread in this array of behaviors is the violation of societal norms and the basic rights of others. The severity of the acts goes beyond the mischief and pranks common among children and adolescents. The diagnosis is made only if the child shows a persistent pattern of at least three of the different categories of misbehavior. Many youngsters who are diagnosed as conduct disordered run afoul of the law and are judged to be juvenile delinquents by our system of juvenile justice. A young person with a conduct disorder, however, might well evade legal detection.

Perhaps more than any other childhood disorder, conduct problems are defined by the impact of the child's behavior on others. Schools, parents, and peers usually decide what undercontrolled behavior is unacceptable conduct. Thus the diagnosis of conduct disorder is especially subjective and difficult to define with precision.

An excerpt from the case history of Tom serves to illustrate the difficulty of defining conduct disorders in terms of behavior alone.

> He entered the church, now, with a swarm of clean and noisy boys and girls, proceeded to his seat and started a quarrel with the first boy who came handy. The teacher, a grave, elderly man, interfered; then turned his back a moment and Tom pulled a boy's hair in the next bench, and was absorbed in his book when the boy turned around; stuck a pin in another boy, presently, in order to hear him say "Ouch!" and got a new reprimand from his teacher.

Based on this sample of Tom's behavior, are we to conclude that he has a conduct disorder? Certainly he is aggressive and disobedient, and the impact of Tom's behavior on his companions and the Sunday school session is disruptive. This excerpt was taken from *The Adventures of Tom Sawyer*, by Mark Twain (1876). For more than one hundred years Tom has been considered the prototypical all-American boy. Something about Tom, perhaps his cleverness and his affection for Becky, keeps us from thinking of him as a boy with conduct problems. More generally, what causes the actions of one child to be considered a conduct problem and the same actions of another to be accepted as normal is largely unknown.

This is not to say that conduct disorder is only in the eye of the beholder, however. Many qualities of the child's behavior itself must be considered in the diagnosis of conduct disorders. Perhaps the two most important criteria for deciding whether a given act is aggressive or problematic are the *frequency* with which it occurs and the *intensity* of the behavior (M. Herbert, 1978). Thus one fight in a year is not a problem, but one fight per week is. Similarly, whereas stealing a candy bar may be viewed (by some) as a minor incident, stealing a car is not.

Many children with conduct disorders display other problems as well. We have already discussed the high degree of overlap between conduct disorder and attention-deficit/hyperactivity disorder. Substance abuse is another behavior that commonly co-occurs with conduct problems. Investigators from the Pittsburgh Youth Study, a longitudinal study of conduct problems in boys, found a strong association between substance use and delinquent acts (Van Kammen, Loeber, & Stouthamer-Loeber, 1991). For example, among seventh graders who reported having tried marijuana, more than 30% had attacked someone with a weapon and 43% admitted to the offense of breaking and entering. Fewer than 5% of children who reported no substance use had committed these acts.

conduct disorder A pattern of extreme disobedience in youngsters, including theft, vandalism, lying, and early drug use; may be a precursor of *antisocial personality disorder*.

Conduct disorders are identified by the frequent occurrence of antisocial behaviors, such as aggression, theft, vandalism, and truancy.

With respect to prognosis, it appears that conduct problems in childhood are usually a necessary condition for antisocial behavior in adulthood, but they do not inevitably predict adult antisocial behavior. The vast majority of highly antisocial adults were highly antisocial as children, though more than half the antisocial children did *not* go on to become antisocial adults (Robins, 1978).

Conduct disorder is much more commonly diagnosed among boys than among girls, and almost all the research in this area has been conducted with boys. However, one study followed for several years fifty-five hospitalized adolescent girls with conduct disorder (Zoccolillo & Rogers, 1991). As with boys, the majority of these subjects had a history of substance use, and most also met diagnostic criteria for depression or an anxiety disorder. The outcome for these girls paralleled the poor prognosis found in male subjects. For example, 41% dropped out of school, and 32% became pregnant before age seventeen.

Perspectives on the Causes and Treatment of Conduct Disorder

Genetic Vulnerability.   Familial transmission is suggested by data that show a high prevalence of antisocial personality disorder in both mothers and fathers of children with conduct disorder (Lahey et al., 1988). Since adoptive parents of conduct-disordered children have *not* been found to have antisocial problems or alcoholism (Jary & Stewart, 1985), the connection between parents' and children's conduct problems may be at least partly genetic. Furthermore, twin studies show consistently higher concordance rates for antisocial behavior in identical pairs than in fraternal pairs (Eysenck, 1975).

Moral Awareness and the Superego.   An important part of normal child development is the growth of moral awareness, a sense of what is right and wrong and the ability, even desire, to abide by rules and norms. Most people refrain from hurting others, not only because it is illegal, but also because it would make them feel guilty to do so. Research into the backgrounds of conduct-disordered youngsters has shown a pattern of family life lacking in factors believed to be central to the development of a strong moral sense. Such factors include affection between child and parents, making firm moral demands on the child, using sanctions in a consistent manner, punishing psychologically rather than physically to induce anxiety and guilt rather than anger, and reasoning and explaining things to the child (M. Herbert, 1982).

Conduct-disordered children, like the psychopaths discussed in Chapter 11, seem to view antisocial acts as exciting and rewarding, indeed as central to their very self-concept (Ryall, 1974). Some psychodynamic theorists have thus explained conduct problems and delinquency as "disorder(s) in the functioning of the superego" (Kessler, 1966, p. 303). That is, the superego is failing to intercede in the sometimes destructively aggressive impulses of the id.

The treatment of conduct disorder poses a formidable challenge. Some of the young people with conduct disorder are the psychopaths of tomorrow. Just as precious little in the way of effective psychological treatment has been found for psychopathy, so are there few ways to reach young people who commit violent and antisocial acts with little remorse or emotional involvement.

Modeling Aggressive Behavior.   Behavioral theories that look to both modeling and operant conditioning have received considerable attention as explanations of the development and maintenance of conduct problems. Children can learn aggressiveness from parents who behave aggressively (Bandura & Walters, 1963). Children may also imitate aggressive acts that are seen elsewhere, such as on television (Liebert, Neale, & Davidson, 1973). Since aggression is an effective, albeit unpleasant, means of achieving a goal, it is likely to be reinforced. Thus, once imitated, aggressive acts will probably be maintained.

A good deal of evidence indicates that modeling is involved in increasing aggressiveness. Viewing televised violence is one way in which this can occur.

Conduct problems are often rewarded in families (Patterson, 1986).

> Chris was an eight-year-old boy brought to the clinic by his mother, who described him as unmanageable. Whenever his mother refused to comply with Chris's requests, he became upset. At these times Chris would be stubborn, uncooperative, and verbally abusive. Occasionally he would throw a temper tantrum and lie down on the floor, kicking his feet and screaming. His mother usually ignored Chris's behavior for a few minutes, but she gave in to his demands when his tantrums became too difficult for her to bear. This sequence of agitation and giving in had become habitual, particularly when the mother was busy. When she felt rushed and perturbed, she gave in to Chris almost immediately.

Both Chris and his mother are rewarded in this sequence of events. Chris is rewarded by getting his own way, his mother by the cessation of Chris's obnoxious behavior. Through this mutual rewarding, both Chris's conduct problems and his mother's acquiescence are likely to be maintained. Note that this model does not explain how obstreperous behavior develops in the first place.

Some of the most promising approaches to treating conduct disorders involve intervening with families in an attempt to change their responses to antisocial behavior. In essence, rather than directly focusing on the difficult aim of enhancing the child's moral awareness, the therapist tries to help parents create conditions such that prosocial behavior has more favorable consequences for the child. Gerald Patterson and his colleagues have developed and tested a behavioral program of parent training along these lines. Parents are taught to use techniques such as positive reinforcement when the child exhibits positive behaviors and time-out and loss of privileges for aggressive or antisocial behavior. Sessions include practicing the techniques and discussing difficulties the parents may encounter when applying the methods to an antisocial child.

Research has demonstrated the effectiveness of this program (Patterson, 1982). Parent management training has even been shown to improve the behavior of siblings and reduce depression in mothers involved in the program (Kazdin, 1985). However, it is less effective in families with low socioeconomic status or marital discord and when there is psychopathology in one or both parents (Kazdin, 1985).

Cognitive Biases. Research by Dodge and Frame (1982) implicates cognitive biases as possibly underlying antisocial behavior. They found that aggressive boys interpret ambiguous acts (such as being bumped in line) as hostile. This biased view may lead such boys to retaliate aggressively to actions that may not have been intended to be provocative. Their peers, remembering these aggressive acts, may tend to aggress more often against them, further angering the aggressive children. This cycle can lead to peer rejection and further aggression.

Cognitive therapy methods may help disrupt such unproductive cycles and enhance children's ability to control anger. In a version of the old strategy of counting to ten, children learned to withstand verbal attacks without responding aggressively using distracting techniques such as humming a tune, saying calming things to themselves, or turning away (Hinshaw, Henker, & Whalen, 1984). The children practiced these self-control methods while a peer provoked and insulted them. Learning problem-solving skills and empathy and the ability to take the perspective of others can also be helpful for those with conduct disorder (Kazdin, Bass, Siegel, & Thomas, 1989).

To Recap

Undercontrolled behavior problems include attention-deficit/hyperactivity disorder (ADHD) and conduct disorder. ADHD involves difficulty concentrating on tasks and excessive non-goal-directed activity. It is associated with problems in academic settings and in peer relations. ADHD is more common in boys, and some symptoms persist into adulthood. Deficits in frontal lobe functioning may underlie ADHD. Ritalin, a stimulant medication, and operant conditioning programs are useful in treatment.

Conduct disorders cover a range of behaviors, such as aggression, lying, and vandalism, all involving violation of others' rights. Though genetic factors may play a role in causing conduct disorder, it appears that modeling violent, aggressive, domineering behavior from parents, peers, or the media also can contribute to conduct disorder. Conduct problems may be inadvertently maintained by family members' paying more attention to and reinforcing the child's obnoxious behavior. Treatment may involve teaching parents to differentially reinforce prosocial behavior and teaching children empathy for others and nonaggressive means of solving their problems.

Disorders of Overcontrolled Behavior

Overcontrolled behavior problems involve inhibitions, fears, and sadness. Children with problems of overcontrol frequently complain of bothersome fears and tenseness; of feelings of shyness or of being unhappy and unloved; and of being inferior to other children. Their difficulties are painful, yet they may be less obvious to other people, such as parents or teachers, than are the overt maladaptive behaviors of undercontrolled children. Symptoms of overcontrolled behavior are generally similar to those of the adult problems of anxiety and depression, but there are some age-specific features as well. Anxiety and depression are frequently found in the same child (Brady & Kendall, 1992).

We describe three examples of overcontrolled behavior problems in this section. Separation anxiety disorder is listed in the DSM-IV section on childhood disorders. Social withdrawal and depression are not separate childhood diagnoses. Children with these problems are diagnosed (provided that the criteria are met) with social phobia or major depressive disorder, respectively, in the adult sections of DSM-IV.

Separation Anxiety Disorder

separation anxiety disorder A disorder in which the child feels intense fear and distress when away from someone on whom he or she is very dependent; it is said to be an important cause of *school phobia*.

Separation anxiety disorder involves persistent, excessive, age-inappropriate anxiety about being (or anticipating being) away from home or a caregiver to whom the child is attached. "Age-inappropriate" and "excessive" are critical aspects of this definition. An infant's or young toddler's crying when her or his mother leaves the room does not justify this diagnosis. Indeed, being distressed about separation can be a healthy sign of attachment to a primary caregiver (typically but not necessarily the mother), starting usually in the second six months of life.

Determining when separation anxiety is excessive for the child's age requires subjective judgment, but there are several signs besides the emotion of fear. Physical symptoms may include headaches, stomachaches, or nausea. Cognitive symptoms include children's worries that something terrible will happen to them (e.g., being kidnapped) or to their caregiver (e.g., being in an accident) during periods of separation. Also, children with separation anxiety disorder may experience recurrent nightmares about being apart from the caregiver.

Perhaps the clearest signal of separation anxiety disorder is the child's behavior. These children may refuse to sleep alone and end up in their parents' bed most nights, may refuse to go to camps or overnight parties or endure such separations only with great distress and perhaps frequent telephone calls home, and may almost literally cling to a parent, following him or her closely from room to room throughout the day. Finally, such children may exhibit **school phobia** (sometimes called school refusal), refusing to go to school for fear of being apart from the caregiver.

school phobia An irrational dread of attending school, usually for fear of being away from the caregiver.

School Phobia

School phobia is disabling to the child and disruptive to the household. It has obvious potential for causing impairment in occupational and social functioning given that the primary occupation of young children is going to school and that school is typically the main arena of peer interaction.

The frequency of school phobia has been estimated at seventeen per one thousand children per year (Kennedy, 1965). The beginning of school is sometimes the first circumstance that requires lengthy and frequent separations of children and their parents. It has been hypothesized that the child's refusal or extreme reluctance to go to school stems from some difficulty in the mother–child relationship. Perhaps the mother communicates her own separation anxieties and unwit-

School phobia is most commonly associated with separation anxiety disorder, an intense fear of being away from parents or other attachment figures.

tingly reinforces the child's dependent and avoidant behavior. One study found that 75% of children who had school refusal caused by separation anxiety had mothers who had also refused school in childhood (Last & Strauss, 1990). Recent events such as moving, being sick, or the death of a relative can also precipitate separation anxiety problems.

School refusal also occurs, though less commonly, in the absence of separation anxiety disorder. In these cases the child shows a true phobia of school—either a fear specifically related to school or a more general social phobia. These school phobics generally begin refusing to go to school later in life and have more severe avoidance of school. Their fear is more likely to be related to specific aspects of the school environment, such as worries about academic failure or discomfort with peers (see Chapter 6 for a general discussion of phobias).

Social Withdrawal

selective mutism A pattern of continually refusing to speak in almost all social situations, including school, even though the child understands spoken language and is able to speak.

Most classrooms have in attendance at least one or two children who are extremely quiet and shy. Often these children will play only with family members or familiar peers, avoiding strangers both young and old. Their shyness may prevent them from acquiring skills and participating in a variety of activities enjoyed by most of their age-mates. They avoid playgrounds and games played by neighborhood children. Although some youngsters who are shy may simply be slow to warm up, withdrawn children never do. Extremely shy children may refuse to speak at all in unfamiliar social circumstances; this is called **selective mutism**. In crowded rooms they cling and whisper to their parents, hide behind the furniture, and cower in corners. At home they ask their parents endless questions about situations that worry them. Withdrawn children usually have warm and satisfying relationships with family members and family friends, and they show an eagerness for affection and acceptance.

Some children exhibit intense anxiety in specific social situations, showing social phobia similar to that of adults (see p. 136). When such children were asked to keep daily diaries of anxiety-producing events, they reported experiencing anxiety three times more frequently than did a normal control group. They had concerns about such activities as reading aloud before a group, writing on the board, and performing in front of others. When faced with these events, they reported using negative coping strategies, such as crying, avoidance, and somatic complaints. When these socially phobic children were asked to read *Jack in the Beanstalk* aloud before a small audience of research assistants, they showed dramatic increases in pulse rate (Beidel, 1991).

The causes of social withdrawal vary. Clearly, anxiety may interfere with social interaction and thus cause the child to avoid social situations. Or withdrawn children may simply not have the social know-how that facilitates interaction with their age-mates. Also, research by developmental psychologist Jerome Kagan (1994) strongly indicates a biological predisposition for extreme shyness in children.

Treatment of Anxiety among Children

How are childhood anxiety problems overcome? Some simply dissipate with time, requiring no specific treatment. Moreover, it is important to clarify whether a child's fear is truly irrational or instead a realistic appraisal of danger. If, for instance, a child is afraid of going to school because gangs are shooting people along the route to school, then realistic precautions would be preferable to merely trying to eliminate the fear.

If the fear persists and is an appropriate treatment target, perhaps the most widespread treatment is to expose children gradually to the feared object, often while acting simultaneously to inhibit their anxiety. If a little girl fears people with whom she is unfamiliar, a parent takes her by the hand and walks her slowly toward the new person. Modeling has also proven effective when a child whom the fearful child is likely to imitate demonstrates fearless behavior (e.g., Bandura, Grusec, & Menlove, 1967).

Modeling can also help shy children who lack specific social skills needed for peer interaction. Skills such as asking questions (Ladd, 1981), giving compliments, and starting conversations with age-mates may be taught in small groups or pairs, with interactions videotaped so the child and coach can observe and modify the new behaviors (Michelson, Sugai, Wood, & Kazdin, 1983).

Behavioral treatment of specific phobias among children is very effective, with gains maintained at follow-up assessments a year or two after the end of treatment (e.g., Blagg & Yule, 1984; Hampe, Noble, Miller, & Barrett, 1973). Less-directive treatments appear to be insufficient to achieve concrete progress in overcoming phobias, but they may be useful for breaking the ice in interacting with a child and for fostering rapport (see Focus Box 14.2).

Depression in Childhood and Adolescence

Considering our typical image of children as happy-go-lucky, it is distressing to observe that major depression and dysthymia occur in children and adolescents as well as in adults. DSM-IV includes mood disorders in children under the adult criteria, while allowing for age-specific features such as irritability instead of depressed mood.

There are similarities as well as differences between the symptoms of children and those of adults with major depression (Mitchell et al., 1988). Like depressed adults, children and adolescents ages seven to seventeen show depressed mood, fatigue, concentration problems, suicidal ideation, and a loss of the ability to experience pleasure. Depressed children and adolescents are more likely to attempt suicide than are adults, and express more feelings of guilt. Adults have more terminal insomnia (waking up early in the morning), loss of appetite and weight loss, and early morning depression.

As with adults, depression in children is recurrent. Longitudinal studies have demonstrated that both children and adolescents with major depression are likely to continue to exhibit significant depressive symptoms when assessed even four to eight years later (Garber, Kriss, Koch, & Lindholm, 1988; McGee & Williams, 1988).

The diagnosis of depression in children often co-occurs with other disorders. Several studies have estimated that the overlap between depression and separation anxiety is close to 50% (e.g., Puig-Antich & Rabinovich, 1986). Depression also is frequently associated with conduct disorder (e.g., Puig-Antich, 1982).

Depression in young people heightens suicide risk, especially for those between the ages of fifteen and nineteen. But even at much younger ages children can become so despondent, so completely without hope of things becoming better, that they attempt to end their lives. However, as previously discussed (see p. 280), suicide is not always linked to depression. Adolescents apparently commit suicide far less from depression than from personal conflicts and developmental crises, such as the breakup of a love affair (Achenbach, 1982), arguments with parents, and problems at school (Hoberman & Garfinkel, 1988).

Causes and Treatment of Childhood Depression

What causes a child to become depressed? Several theories have been suggested. As discussed in Chapter 10, evidence supports the role of a genetic factor in adult depression. Perhaps genetics are implicated in childhood depression as well. However, studies of children have also focused on family relationships.

Parents of depressed children communicate with them less and show less warmth and more hostility. They spend less time in activities with their children. Outside the family, depressed children are less able to maintain close friendships

Play Therapy

Many of the childhood disorders discussed in this chapter are treated by **play therapy**, the use of play as a means of uncovering what is troubling a child and of establishing rapport. Children are usually less verbal than adults, at least in the sense that is needed for psychodynamic or humanistic therapies. Through the pioneering work of Melanie Klein (1932) and Anna Freud (1946), play became an analytic vehicle for delving into a child's unconscious, taking the place of the free association and recounting of dreams that are important in analytic treatment of adults. It is assumed that in play therapy a child will express his or her feelings about problems, parents, teachers, and peers.

A play therapy room is equipped with such objects as puppets, blocks, games, puzzles, drawing materials, paints, water, sand, clay, toy guns and soldiers, and a large inflated rubber clown to punch. It is hoped that these toys will help draw out inner tensions and concerns. A dollhouse inhabited by parent and child dolls is a common fixture. The therapist may encourage a young male patient to place the figures in "any room you wish," to position the dolls in a way "that makes you feel good." The child may assemble members of the family in the living room, except for the father, who is placed in the study. "What is Daddy doing?" the therapist will ask. "He's working. If he weren't such a meanie, he'd come out and play with the kids." The therapist will then, as he or she would for an adult, interpret for the boy the wish he seems reluctant to express openly.

In nondirective play therapy, such as that practiced by Virginia Axline (1964), the relationship between the therapist and child developed through play is used to

Because children are often less verbal than adults, play therapy was developed to help them better express their concerns as they play with a toy house and dolls that represent their parents and siblings.

provide a corrective emotional experience for the child. Rather than interpreting the child's symbolic expressions, the therapist responds to the child's words and actions in an empathic manner, demonstrating unconditional acceptance.

There has been little controlled research to evaluate the claims made for play therapy by its adherents. Whatever ultimate purposes may be served by play therapy, at the very least it is likely to help the adult therapist establish rapport with a youngster. Therapists of varying persuasions commonly use a playroom to establish a relationship with a young patient and perhaps also to determine from what the child says and does with toys the youngster's perspective on the problem.

---

play therapy   The use of play as a means of uncovering what is troubling a child and of establishing *rapport*.

---

and are more likely to be teased by their peers. The sibling relationships of depressed children are especially difficult (Puig-Antich et al., 1985). It is not yet clear whether poor social bonds cause depression in children, whether depression produces persistent impairments in social relationships, or whether some third variable causes both depression and interpersonal difficulties.

In terms of therapy, far less research has been done with depressed children and adolescents than with depressed adults (Kaslow & Racusin, 1990). Nearly all the literature is composed of uncontrolled case reports. Research with some measure of experimental control indicates that the use of antidepressant drugs has little support (Puig-Antich et al., 1987). Social-skills training shows promise in providing depressed youngsters the behavioral and verbal means to gain access to pleasant, reinforcing environments, for example, by making friends and getting along with peers (Frame, Matson, Sonis, Fialkov, & Kazdin, 1982).

To Recap

Children who are overcontrolled experience painful feelings, such as anxiety and depression, rather than aggravating others with their actions, which is more typical of children with undercontrolled behavior problems. Examples of overcontrolled behavior problems include separation anxiety disorder, sometimes manifested as school phobia; social withdrawal; and depression. School phobia can also stem from fear of the school situation itself (for instance, social anxiety around peers or academic worries) rather than from separation anxiety. For anxiety problems exposing the child gradually to the object or situation that is feared is helpful, as is social-skills training for shy and withdrawn children. Treatments for child and adolescent depression have not been well studied, but there is some indication that social-skills training may be particularly helpful for depressed children, who often experience highly conflictual family relationships and difficulty making friends.

Learning Disabilities

Learning disabilities involve inadequate development in a specific area of academic, language, speech, or motor skills. The deficits are not due to mental retardation, autism, a demonstrable physical or neurological disorder, or deficient educational opportunities.

Children with learning disabilities are usually of average or above average intelligence but have difficulty learning some specific skill, such as arithmetic or reading. In the category of learning disabilities we are grouping together three disorders that appear in DSM-IV: learning disorders, communication disorders, and motor skills disorder. In each of these a child fails to develop a specific skill to the degree expected on the basis of his or her general intellectual level.

Learning disabilities are usually identified and treated within the school system rather than through mental health clinics. The disorders are from two to four times more common in males than in females. Though learning-disabled individuals usually cope with their problems, their academic and social development is affected, sometimes quite seriously. They are often depressed and suffer from low self-esteem.

Learning Disorders

DSM-IV divides learning disorders into three categories: reading disorder, mathematics disorder, and disorder of written expression. None of these diagnoses is appropriate if the disability can be accounted for by a sensory deficit, such as visual or auditory problems.

Children with **reading disorder,** better known as dyslexia, have trouble recognizing words, understanding what they have read, and, typically, spelling words correctly. When reading orally, they omit, add, or distort the pronunciation of words to an unusual extent for their age. In adulthood, problems with fluent oral reading, comprehension, and written spelling persist (Bruck, 1987). This disorder, present in 2% to 8% of school-age children, does not preclude great achievements. For example, Nelson Rockefeller, former vice president of the United States, suffered from dyslexia.

reading disorder (dyslexia) A disturbance in the ability to read; a learning disorder.

In **mathematics disorder**, the child's math ability falls far below what would be expected on the basis of education, general intelligence, and age. The child may experience difficulties such as coding written problems into mathematical symbols (linguistic skills), recognizing numerical symbols (perceptual skills), remembering to add in "carried" numbers (attention skills), counting objects or following sequences of mathematical steps (mathematical skills).

mathematics disorder Difficulty dealing with arithmetic symbols and operations beyond what would be expected on the basis of education, general intelligence, and age.

disorder of written expression Difficulty writing without errors in spelling, grammar, or punctuation.

Disorder of written expression describes an impairment in the ability to compose the written word (including spelling errors, errors in grammar and punctuation, and poor paragraph organization) that is serious enough to interfere significantly with academic achievement or daily activities that entail writing skills. Few systematic data have been collected on the prevalence of this disorder.

Communication Disorders

receptive language disorder Difficulty understanding spoken language.

expressive language disorder Difficulty expressing oneself in speech.

phonological disorder A learning disability in which some words sound like baby talk because the person is not able to make certain speech sounds.

motor skills disorder A learning disability characterized by marked impairment in the development of motor coordination that is not accounted for by a physical disorder.

In **receptive language disorder**, the child has trouble understanding spoken language and may be so deficient in comprehending what is being said that he or she appears to be deaf. In **expressive language disorder**, the child has difficulty expressing himself or herself in speech. A child with expressive language disorder may seem eager to communicate but have inordinate difficulty finding the right words. By age four, the child speaks only in short phrases. Old words are forgotten when new ones are learned, and the use of grammatical structures is far below age level.

Unlike children who have trouble understanding or finding words, youngsters with **phonological disorder** both comprehend and are able to use a substantial vocabulary, but their words sound like baby talk. *Blue* comes out *bu*, and *rabbit* sounds like *wabbit*. They have not learned articulation of the later acquired speech sounds, such as *r, sh, th, f, z, l*, and *ch*. With speech therapy, complete recovery occurs in almost all cases, and milder cases may recover spontaneously by age eight.

Motor Skills Disorder

In **motor skills disorder** children show marked impairment in the development of motor coordination that is not explainable by mental retardation or a known physical disorder, such as cerebral palsy. The young child may have difficulty tying shoelaces and buttoning shirts and, when older, with model building, playing ball, and printing or handwriting. The diagnosis is made only if the impairment interferes significantly with academic achievement or other daily activities.

A speech therapist works with a child with phonological disorder by having him practice the sounds he finds difficult.

Causes of Learning Disabilities

Twin studies two decades ago confirmed the heritability of learning disabilities (Matheny, Dolan, & Wilson, 1976), and more recent research has begun to pinpoint which specific learning problems are inherited. Evidence reviewed by Pennington and Smith (1988) suggests that whereas simple word reading and spelling skills are genetically influenced, reading comprehension seems not to be.

Neurological problems may be responsible for learning disabilities. Autopsies of the brains of eight individuals with childhood dyslexia revealed microscopic abnormalities in the location, number, and organization of neurons. The anomalies were predominantly located in the language regions of the left hemisphere (Galaburda, 1989). The source of these developmental defects remains unknown.

Structural or hormonal differences between male and female brains account for some of the greater prevalence of learning disabilities among boys. For example, damage to the left hemisphere causes more deficits in language in males than in females; females have a greater representation of language in the right hemisphere than do males (Kimura, 1983). This finding suggests that boys are more vulnerable to language and reading disabilities in the wake of left-hemisphere damage.

In the past, psychological theories have focused on visual perceptual deficits as the basis for dyslexia. One popular hypothesis suggested that children with reading problems perceive letters in reverse order, or mirror image, mistaking, for example, a *d* for a *b*. However, research fails to support this notion (Calfee, Fisk, & Piontkowski, 1975; McGuiness, 1981).

Treatment of Learning Disabilities

Several methods are used to treat learning disabilities. In young children, *readiness skills*, such as discriminating letters and learning the sounds that correspond to each letter, may need to be taught before explicit instruction in reading is attempted. Dyslexic individuals often can succeed in college with the aid of instructional supports, such as tape-recorded lectures, tutors, writing editors, and untimed tests (Bruck, 1987).

In recent years researchers have focused on the possibility that some learning-disabled children lack specific, teachable skills rather than an overall ability to learn and plan (Braswell & Kendall, 1988). The implication of this assumption is important, for it suggests that one can help such children learn better by teaching them problem-solving techniques or strategies. For example, Karen Harris (1986) videotaped children putting together a puzzle of a superhero (Shazam) and observed their private speech during the task. Compared with normally achieving children, the self-talk of the learning-disabled youngsters was marked by irrelevant comments, such as wordplay ("a dogie, dogie, dogie"), descriptions of irrelevant stimuli ("that's a funny noise"), noisemaking ("criminy," "pheweee"), and negative evaluations of their performance or the task ("This is a stupid puzzle"; "I can't do this"). In contrast, the control children were more likely to employ useful self-talk to guide themselves through the task. Explicitly teaching the use of constructive self-talk helped the learning-disabled children to persist at the task for longer periods.

For all children, but especially for those with learning disabilities, an approach geared to producing small, accumulating successes is essential. Most learning-disabled children have probably experienced a great deal of frustration and failure that erode their motivation and confidence. Behavioral programs that reward small steps can be helpful in increasing the child's motivation, focusing attention on the learning task, and reducing behavioral problems caused by frustration.

TO RECAP

Learning disabilities signify inadequate development in a specific area of academic, language, speech, or motor skills that is not due to mental retardation, autism, a known neurological disorder, or inadequate educational opportunity. These disorders can affect academic and social adjustment, particularly if undiagnosed. With specific instructional accommodations, however, it is often possible for the individual to cope well with the problem. Examples include reading disorder, mathematics disorder, communication disorders, and motor skills disorder. Some learning disabilities involving word reading and spelling skills appear to be genetically influenced. Damage to left-hemispheric language regions has been found in autopsies of dyslexic individuals, which is consistent with the observed sex difference in learning disabilities (boys predominate).

▶ *Mental Retardation*

In DSM-IV **mental retardation** is defined as significantly subaverage intellectual functioning along with deficits in adaptive behavior, both occurring prior to age eighteen. The first component of this definition requires a judgment of intelligence. Scores on most IQ tests are standardized in such a way that 100 is the mean and 15 or 16 is the standard deviation (a measure of how scores are dispersed both above and below the average). This means that approximately two-thirds of the population receive scores between 85 and 115. Those with a score below 70 are two standard deviations below the mean of the population and are considered to have "significant subaverage general intellectual functioning" and therefore evidence of mental retardation. Approximately 2.5% of the population falls into this category.

mental retardation Significantly subaverage intellectual functioning along with deficits in adaptive behavior, both occurring prior to age eighteen.

Table 14.2 ▶ *Sample Items from the Vineland Adaptive Behavior Scales*

Age Level	Adaptive Ability
2 years	Says at least fifty recognizable words.
	Removes front-opening coat, sweater, or shirt without assistance.
5 years	Tells popular story, fairy tale, lengthy joke, or plot of television program.
	Ties shoelaces into a bow without assistance.
8 years	Keeps secrets or confidences for more than one day.
	Orders own meal in a restaurant.
11 years	Uses the telephone for all kinds of calls without assistance.
	Watches television or listens to radio for information about a particular area of interest.
16 years	Looks after own health.
	Responds to hints or indirect cues in conversation.

Source: From Sparrow, Balla, and Cicchetti (1984).

The adaptive functioning aspect of mental retardation refers to skills needed for successful independent functioning in one's environment. In childhood these would include such skills as learning to tell time and count money and understand how it works, using tools, shopping, and taking public transportation. Adaptive functioning also encompasses becoming socially responsive and self-directive. Several tests have been constructed to assess adaptive behavior. One of the best known is the Vineland Adaptive Behavior Scales (Sparrow, Balla, & Cicchetti, 1984) (see Table 14.2).

Finally, the definition of mental retardation requires that it be manifest before age eighteen. This rules out classifying as mental retardation any deficits in intelligence and adaptive behavior resulting from traumatic accidents or illnesses that occur later in life.

Levels of Mental Retardation

Four levels of mental retardation are recognized by DSM-IV, each of them a specific subaverage range of measured intelligence. The IQ ranges given are not the sole basis of diagnosis, for some persons falling in the mildly retarded range based on IQ may have no deficits in adaptive behavior and thus would not be considered mentally retarded. The following is a summary of how individuals at each level of mental retardation are described (Robinson & Robinson, 1976).

Mild Mental Retardation (IQ 50–55 to 70)

About 85% of all those who have IQs less than 70 are classified as having **mild mental retardation**. With IQs of 50–55 to 70, they can usually learn academic skills at about a sixth-grade level by their late teens. Such children can often be mainstreamed, or taught in regular classrooms, with careful planning of teaching programs. This issue is explored in the Legal, Ethical, and Social Issues box.

As adults, the mildly mentally retarded are likely to be able to maintain themselves in unskilled jobs or in sheltered workshops, although they may need help

In addition to low intelligence, the diagnosis of mental retardation requires the presence of deficits in adaptive behavior, a set of skills including self-care.

mild mental retardation A limitation in mental development measured on IQ tests at between 50–55 and 70; children with such a limitation are considered the educable mentally retarded and are placed in special classes.

Public Laws 94-142 and 99-457: Educating and Mainstreaming

In 1975 the United States Congress passed Public Law 94-142, the Education for All Handicapped Children Act. Passage of this law represented substantial gains for the educational rights of children with disabilities and secured their integration into the community. The law guarantees children between the ages of three and twenty-one a free, appropriate public education in the least restrictive environment. Such an environment is one that allows the disabled student to develop mentally, physically, and socially with the fewest barriers while providing necessary support. The goals for each child are set forth in an individual educational program (IEP) that is evaluated annually.

Public Law 99-457, passed in 1986, extended the earlier statute by requiring that all public schools serve disabled preschoolers by 1991 or lose their federal funding. This law has led to agreements between Head Start centers and public schools, resulting in more extensive services for young children not previously involved in the educational system.

These laws apply to all children with exceptional needs, including those with mental retardation, autism, and learning disabilities, as well as to children with speech, hearing, or visual impairments, gifted and talented children, and those with serious emotional disturbances that interfere with their school progress. Overall, programs that are sensitive to the problems inherent in mainstreaming (integrating children with special needs into regular public schools as much as possible) appear likely to yield positive results for students both with and without disabilities (Gottlieb, 1990; Zigler, Hodapp, & Edison, 1990). Normal children can learn early in life that there is tremendous diversity among human beings and that a child may be different in some very important ways and yet be worthy of respect and friendship. With support from parents and teachers, normal children may reach adulthood without the burden of the prejudice of earlier generations. Such an effect would benefit normal children as well as emotionally or cognitively disadvantaged children.

---

with social and financial problems. They may marry and have children of their own. Only about 1% are ever institutionalized, usually in adolescence for behavior problems. Most of the mildly retarded show no signs of brain pathology and are members of families whose formal education and intelligence test scores are low.

Moderate Mental Retardation (IQ 35–40 to 50–55).

About 10% of people with IQs less than 70 are classified as having **moderate mental retardation** and have IQs from 35–40 to 50–55. Often they have brain damage and other pathologies. The moderately retarded may have physical defects and neurological dysfunctions that hinder fine motor skills, such as grasping and coloring within lines, and gross motor skills, such as running and climbing. During childhood these individuals are eligible for special classes that emphasize the development of self-care skills rather than academic achievement. The moderately retarded are unlikely to progress beyond the second-grade level in academic subjects and can manage this learning only in later childhood or as adults. Many are institutionalized. Although most can do useful work, few hold jobs except in sheltered workshops or in family businesses. Most live dependently within the family or in supervised group homes. Few have friends of their own, but they may be left alone without supervision for several hours at a time.

moderate mental retardation A limitation in mental development measured on IQ tests at between 35–40 and 50–55; children with this degree of retardation are often institutionalized, and their training is focused on self-care rather than on development of intellectual skills.

Severe Mental Retardation (IQ 20–25 to 35–40)

Of those with IQs less than 70, about 3% to 4% fall under the category of **severe mental retardation**. They have IQs from 20–25 to 35–40 and commonly have congenital physical abnormalities and limited sensorimotor control. Genetic disorders and environmental insults, such as severe oxygen deprivation at birth, account for

severe mental retardation A limitation in mental development measured on IQ tests at between 20–25 and 35–40. Individuals so afflicted often cannot care for themselves, communicate only briefly, and are listless and inactive.

most of this degree of retardation. Most of the severely mentally retarded are institutionalized and require constant aid and supervision. For children in this group to be able to speak and take care of their own basic needs requires prolonged training. As adults the severely retarded may be friendly, but can usually communicate only briefly on a very concrete level. They engage in very little independent activity and are often lethargic. Their severe brain damage leaves them relatively passive, and the circumstances of their lives allow them little stimulation. They may be able to perform very simple work under close supervision.

Profound Mental Retardation (IQ below 20–25)

profound mental retardation A limitation in mental development measured on IQ tests at less than 20–25; children with this degree of retardation require total supervision of all their activities.

One to two percent of the retarded are classified as having **profound mental retardation** (with IQs below 20–25), requiring total supervision and often nursing care all their lives. Intensive training may improve motor development, self-care, and communication skills. Many have severe physical deformities as well as neurological damage and cannot get around on their own. The profoundly mentally retarded have a very high mortality rate during childhood.

Causes of Mental Retardation

The more severe forms of mental retardation are primarily biological disorders. The known organic causes of mental retardation include genetic conditions, infectious diseases, accidents, prematurity, chemicals, and environmental hazards.

Genetic or Chromosomal Anomalies

Chromosomal abnormalities occur in about 4% of pregnancies, many of which result in miscarriages. A significant proportion of these infants die soon after birth. Of the babies that survive, the largest proportion have **Down syndrome**, or **trisomy 21**.

Down syndrome (trisomy 21) A form of *mental retardation* generally caused by an extra *chromosome*. Physical characteristics are distinctive, most notably slanted eyes.

The IQs of people with Down syndrome are in the mild to moderate range of mental retardation. There are distinctive physical signs of the syndrome: short and stocky stature; oval, upward-slanting eyes; the epicanthic fold, a prolongation of the fold of the upper eyelid over the inner corner of the eye; sparse, fine, straight hair; a wide and flat nasal bridge; square-shaped ears; a large, furrowed tongue, protruding because the mouth is small and its roof low; short, broad hands with stubby fingers; a general loose-jointedness, particularly in the ankles; and a broad-based walk.

At autopsy, brain tissue generally shows deterioration similar to that in Alzheimer's disease (p. 444). Despite their mental retardation, most of these children can learn to read, write, and do math.

Down syndrome is named after the British physician Langdon Down, who first described the clinical signs in 1866. In 1959 the French geneticist Jerome Lejeune and his colleagues identified its genetic basis. Human beings usually possess forty-six chromosomes, inheriting twenty-three from each parent by means of the germ cells. Individuals with Down syndrome almost always have forty-seven chromosomes. During maturation of the egg, something goes wrong so that the two chromosomes of pair 21, the smallest ones, fail to separate. If this egg is fertilized, uniting with a sperm, there will be three of chromosome 21 (see Figure 14.1); thus the technical term *trisomy 21*.

Recessive-Gene Diseases

phenylketonuria (PKU) A genetic disorder that, through a deficiency in a liver enzyme, phenylalanine hydroxylase, causes severe *mental retardation* unless phenylalanine can be largely restricted from the diet until the age of six.

When a pair of defective recessive genes misdirects the formation of an enzyme, metabolic processes are disturbed. The problem may affect development of the embryo in the uterus or become important only much later in life.

In **phenylketonuria (PKU)** the infant, born normal, soon suffers from a deficiency of a liver enzyme, phenylalanine hydroxylase, which is needed to convert

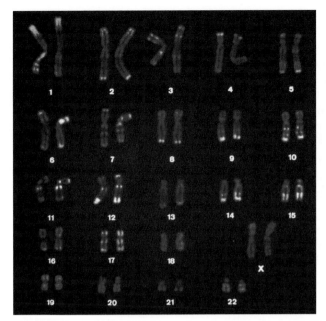
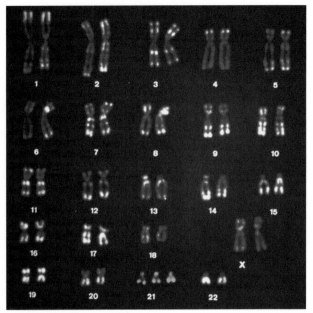

Figure 14.1 *Left: The normal complement of chromosomes is 23 pairs. Right: In Down syndrome there is a trisomy of chromosome 21.*

phenylalanine, an amino acid of protein food, to tyrosine. Phenylalanine and its derivative phenylpyruvic acid build up in the body fluids, ultimately causing irreversible brain damage. The unmetabolized amino acid interferes with the process of myelination, the sheathing of neuron axons. This sheathing is essential for the rapid transmittal of impulses and thus of information. The neurons of the frontal lobes are particularly affected. Little wonder that mental retardation is profound.

Although PKU is a rare disease, with an incidence of about one in fourteen thousand live births, it is estimated that one person in seventy is a carrier of the recessive gene. There is a blood test for prospective parents who have reason to suspect that they might be carriers. Fortunately, too, after the PKU newborn has

Through genetic counseling, parents can learn whether their family history suggests they may be carriers of recessive genes that cause mental retardation.

consumed milk for several days, an excess amount of unconverted phenylalanine can be detected in its blood. State laws require that the necessary test be given. If the test is positive, the parents are urged to provide the infant a diet low in phenylalanine. If the diet is restricted as early as the third month and until the age of six, when brain differentiation is relatively complete, cognitive development improves, sometimes to within the normal range (*Collaborative Study of Children Treated for Phenylketonuria*, 1975).

Prenatal and Postnatal Risks

While in the uterus, the fetus is at increased risk of mental retardation from certain maternal infectious diseases. The consequences of these diseases are more serious during the first trimester of pregnancy, when the fetus has no detectable immunological response. In addition, the first trimester is a critical period in the development of the brain. Cytomegalovirus, toxoplasmosis, rubella, herpes simplex, and syphilis are all maternal infections that may cause both physical deformities and mental retardation of the fetus.

After birth, infectious diseases can also affect a child's developing brain. Encephalitis and meningococcal meningitis may cause irreversible brain damage and even death if contracted in infancy or early childhood. These infections in adulthood are usually far less serious, probably because the brain is largely developed by about the age of six. There are several forms of childhood meningitis, a disease in which the protective membranes of the brain are acutely inflamed and fever is very high. Even if the child survives and is not severely retarded, moderate or mild retardation is likely.

Accidents.   In the United States accidents are the leading cause of severe disability and death in children over one year of age. Falls and automobile accidents are among the most common mishaps in early childhood and may cause varying degrees of head injuries and mental retardation.

Prematurity.   A baby is considered premature if delivered three or more weeks before term. Premature infants who survive have an increased risk of developing mental retardation. Although the relation between prematurity and mental retardation is quite high, it is difficult to isolate prematurity itself as a cause. Many factors—poverty, teenage motherhood, inadequate nutrition, alcohol and drug abuse, and poor prenatal care—all figure in prematurity. Additionally, premature infants may develop other medical problems that place them at increased risk for mental retardation. Of course, many children born prematurely grow up quite normally.

Environmental Hazards.   Several environmental pollutants can cause poisoning and mental retardation. These include mercury, which may be transmitted through affected fish, and lead, which is found in lead-based paints, smog, and the exhaust from automobiles that burn leaded gasoline. Lead poisoning can cause kidney and brain damage as well as anemia, mental retardation, seizures, and death. Lead-based paint is now illegal, but it is still found in older homes, where it may be flaking.

Mental Retardation with No Identifiable Cause

In general, persons with severe or profound mental retardation have an identifiable organic brain defect, whereas persons with less severe mental retardation do not. Persons whose mental retardation is associated with identifiable organic impairments are found in much the same percentages throughout all socioeconomic, ethnic, and racial groups. In contrast, persons with mild or moderate mental retardation are overrepresented in the lower socioeconomic classes.

There are two main possible explanations for cases of mental retardation in which there is no identified organic impairment. One is that damage to the brain,

Although lead-based paint is now illegal, it can still be found in older homes. Eating lead-paint chips can cause lead poisoning and mental retardation.

for example, from trauma during birth, has occurred but is too slight to be detected by currently available methods (Baumeister & MacLean, 1979). This slight impairment might be sufficient to cause retardation if combined with a disadvantageous environment. The second hypothesis is that less severe forms of mental retardation may not represent a specific brain pathology at all. Instead, this term may simply be describing people who are at the very low end of the distribution of inherited intellectual potential and do not develop their full potential because of environmental factors (Zigler, 1967). Environmental factors could include the social deprivation and lack of stimulation sometimes associated with institutions for the retarded, as well as the demoralizing impact of a history of failure and the resulting decline in motivation.

Prevention of Mental Retardation

Preventing mental retardation depends on understanding its causes. The known organic causes present a fairly straightforward challenge and opportunity, and many of them can now be counteracted. For the majority of cases in which the cause of retardation is not as obvious, prevention becomes considerably more problematic.

Prevention of mild mental retardation depends on early identification and training of susceptible people. Certainly the best-known, large-scale effort to raise the achievement and intellectual level of disadvantaged children is Project Head Start. Its purpose is to prepare children socially and culturally to succeed in the regular school setting by giving them experiences that they are missing at home.

The core of the Head Start program is community-based preschool education, focusing on the development of early cognitive and social skills. In addition, Head Start contracts with professionals in the community to provide children with health and dental services, including vaccinations, hearing and vision testing, medical treatment, and nutrition information (North, 1979). Mental health services are also an important component of Head Start programs. Psychologists may assist in identifying children with psychological problems and consult with teachers and staff to help make the preschool environment sensitive to psychological issues. For example, they may share knowledge of child development,

Early intervention, exemplified by Head Start programs, is a way of counteracting the impoverished environments of retarded children.

Training in vocational skills is an important component of the education of the mentally retarded. Even children with moderate retardation can acquire work skills.

consult on an individual case, or help staff address parents' concerns (Cohen, Solnit, & Wohlford, 1979).

In a comparison of Head Start children with other disadvantaged children who attended either a different preschool or no preschool, the Head Start children improved significantly more than both control groups on social-cognitive ability and motor impulsivity (Lee, Brooks-Gunn & Schnur, 1988). Although the Head Start program succeeded in enhancing the functioning of the neediest children, the authors note that these children were still behind their peers in terms of absolute cognitive levels after one year in the program.

Early Intervention and Mental Retardation

Whereas programs such as Head Start may help prevent mild mental retardation in disadvantaged children, other early intervention programs have been developed to improve the eventual level of functioning of more seriously retarded individuals (without preventing the retardation). Pilot projects with Down syndrome children start in infancy and early childhood to attempt to improve their functioning by teaching them language skills, fine and gross motor skills, self-care, and how to relate to others. Specific behavioral objectives are defined, and children are taught in small, sequential steps (e.g., Clunies-Ross, 1979).

Results of these programs indicate consistent improvements in fine motor skills, social acceptance, and self-help skills. Unfortunately, the programs appear to have little effect on gross motor skills and linguistic abilities, and long-term improvements in IQ and school performance have not been demonstrated. It is not yet clear whether the benefits of the programs are greater than what parents can provide in the home without special training (Gibson & Harris, 1988).

TO RECAP

Mental retardation is indicated by significantly below-average intellectual functioning (IQ below 70) and deficits in adaptive behavior, with onset before age eighteen. The majority of cases show mild mental retardation (IQ 50–55 to 70). Typically there is no clear sign of brain pathology, though this situation may be merely a reflection of insensitivity of current measures to subtle damage. Moderate, severe, and profound mental retardation usually have a known organic cause, such as genetic or chromosomal abnormalities, maternal infectious diseases during the first trimester of pregnancy, a head injury suffered in an accident, premature birth, or ingestion of toxins, such as lead-based paint. The known causes sometimes permit prevention. For example, a special diet helps babies with PKU develop near normally, and lead-based paint is illegal in new houses. Efforts to help the mildly mentally retarded or those seen as at risk include preschool education programs such as Head Start, aimed at providing health services and improving readiness for school, educational plans to foster mainstreaming, and operant conditioning to teach adaptive behaviors.

▶ Autistic Disorder

If you were to walk into a community group home for children with developmental disabilities, you would probably notice some minor or major physical signs of retardation among many residents. One child has slanted eyes and a flat nose, characteristic of Down syndrome. Another makes spastic movements, signs of cerebral palsy. A third child may call to you from a wheelchair with grunting noises and communicate with a combination of hand gestures and pictures. So far the children are as you might expect from your readings.

However, you might have difficulty placing the child standing in front of the fish tank. He has graceful, deft movements and a dreamy, remote look in his eye, making him hauntingly attractive.

From the time it was first distinguished, **autistic disorder** has seemed to have

autistic disorder A *pervasive developmental disorder* involving profound aloneness and difficulty in relating to others, severe communication problems, and ritualistic behavior; often associated with *mental retardation*.

a mystical aura. The syndrome was first identified in 1943 by a psychiatrist, Leo Kanner, who noticed that eleven disturbed children behaved in ways that were not common in children with mental retardation or schizophrenia. He named the syndrome *early infantile autism*, because he observed that "there is from the start an *extreme autistic aloneness* that, whenever possible, disregards, ignores, shuts out anything that comes to the child from the outside" (Kanner, 1943). Kanner considered autistic aloneness the most fundamental symptom, but he also found that these eleven children had been unable from the beginning of life to relate to people in a normal way, were severely limited in language, and had an obsessive desire for everything around them to remain exactly the same.

Autism begins in early childhood and indeed can be evident in the first weeks of life. It occurs relatively infrequently, in approximately three or four infants in ten thousand. About four times more boys than girls have autism.

Description and Classification

Social Adjustment

The social adjustment of autistic children is noteworthy from early infancy. In a sense, autistic children do not withdraw from society—they never join it to begin with. Normal infants show signs of attachment, usually to their mothers, as early as three months of age. In autistic children this early attachment is virtually absent. They do not smile or reach out or look at their mothers when being fed. Autistic infants may reject parents' affection by refusing to be held or cuddled, arching their backs when picked up to minimize the contact normal infants— and parents—love. Although normal infants often coo or cry or fret to attract parental attention, autistic children seldom initiate contact with the caregiver, except when hungry or wet. Indeed, such children are often described as unusually good babies because they make few demands. Autistic infants are generally content to sit quietly in their playpens, completely self-absorbed, never noticing the comings, goings, and doings of other people. However, by age two or three many autistic children do form some emotional attachment to their parents or to other caregivers, though they may continue to shun physical contact.

Impaired attachment to parents is not the only way in which the autistic child's social development is poor. The child rarely approaches others and may look through or past people or turn his or her back on them. When play is initiated by someone else, however, the autistic child may be compliant and engage in the selected activity for a period of time. Physical play, such as tickling and wrestling, may actually appear to be enjoyable to the child. Observations of spontaneous play in an unstructured setting demonstrate that children with autism spend much less of their time engaged in symbolic play, such as making a doll drive to the store or pretending that a block is a car, than do either mentally retarded or normal children of comparable mental age (Sigman, Ungerer, Mundy, & Sherman, 1987).

Few autistic children may be said to have friends. Not only do they seldom initiate play with other children, but potential companions, like parents, usually receive little responsiveness from the autistic child. Autistic infants may avert their gaze if parents try to communicate with them, and they are described as engaging in less eye contact than their peers. The sheer amount of gazing may sometimes be relatively normal, but not the way in which it is used. Normal children gaze to gain someone's attention or to direct the other person's attention to an object. The autistic child generally does not do this (Mirenda, Donnellan, & Yoder, 1983).

Communication Problems

Autistic children typically experience many language problems. Even before the period when language is usually acquired, autistic children have deficits in communication. Babbling is less frequent in infants with autism and conveys less information than does that of other infants (Ricks, 1972).

By two years of age, most normally developing children use words to represent objects in their surroundings and construct one- and two-word sentences to express more complex thoughts. About 50% of autistic children never learn to speak at all (Rutter, 1966). When they do learn to speak, their speech often has peculiarities, among them **echolalia**. The child echoes, usually with remarkable fidelity and in a high-pitched monotone, what he or she has heard another person say.

Another abnormality common in the speech of autistic children is **pronoun reversal**. The children refer to themselves as "he" or "you," or by their own proper names. Pronoun reversal is closely linked to echolalia. Since autistic children often use echolalic speech, they refer to themselves as they have heard others speak of them. Children with autism are also very literal in their use of words. If a father provided positive reinforcement by putting the child on his shoulders when he or she learned to say the word yes, then the child might say yes to mean that he or she wants to be lifted onto the father's shoulders.

Communication deficiencies may leave a lasting mark of social retardation on the child. The link between social skills and language is made evident by the often spontaneous appearance of affectionate and dependent behavior in these children after they have been trained to speak (Churchill, 1969). Even after they learn to speak, however, people with autism often lack verbal spontaneity and are sparse in their verbal expression and less than entirely appropriate in their use of language (R. Paul, 1987).

Desire for Sameness and Ritualistic Acts

Autistic children become extremely upset over changes in daily routine and their surroundings. An offer of milk in a different drinking cup or a rearrangement of furniture may make them cry or bring on a temper tantrum. Autistic children are also given to stereotypical behavior, peculiar ritualistic hand motions and other rhythmic movements such as endless body rocking, hand flapping, and walking on tiptoe. At times their repetitive behaviors may be self-destructive, such as banging their heads against the wall or biting their own fingers.

Other stereotypical behavior patterns and interests are, at least physically, innocuous. Autistic children may spin and twirl string, crayons, sticks, and plates, or twiddle their fingers in front of their eyes. Often they use toys in a compulsive and ritualistic manner. Attention seems to be highly selective. An autistic child may be preoccupied with and stare for a long time at a specific object, such as a spinning fan or a part of an object, such as a button on a shirt. These children may also become preoccupied with manipulating a mechanical object and become very upset when interrupted.

Autism and Mental Retardation

About 80% of autistic children score below 70 on standardized intelligence tests. Autism is not the same as mental retardation, however. Although retarded children usually score consistently poorly on all parts of an intelligence test, the scores of autistic children may have a more differentiated pattern. In general, autistic children do worse on tasks that require abstract thought, symbolism, or sequential logic, all of which may be associated with language. They usually obtain better scores on items that entail visual-spatial skills (DeMyer, 1975). In addition, they may have isolated skills that reflect great talent, such as the ability to multiply two four-digit numbers rapidly in their heads. Retarded children are much more delayed in areas of gross motor development, such as learning to walk. In contrast, autistic children, who may show severe and profound deficits in cognitive abilities, can be quite graceful and adept at swinging, climbing, or balancing.

echolalia A speech problem in which the person repeats back exactly what she or he has heard another say; often found in the speech of children with *autistic disorder*.

pronoun reversal A speech problem in which the child refers to himself or herself as "he," "she," "you," and and "I" or "me" in referring to others; often found in the speech of children with *autistic disorder*.

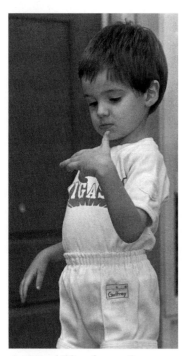

Autistic children frequently engage in stereotypical behaviors, such as ritualistic hand movements at which they stare.

Prognosis in Autistic Disorder

What happens to such severely disturbed children when they reach adulthood? Kanner (1973) reported on the adult status of nine of the eleven children whom he had described in his original paper on autism. Two had developed epileptic seizures: one of them died, and the other was in a state mental hospital. Four others had spent most of their lives in institutions. Of the other three, one remained mute but was working on a farm and as an orderly in a nursing home. The last two had made at least somewhat satisfactory recoveries. Although both still lived with their parents and had little social life, they were gainfully employed and had some recreational interests. Other follow-up studies corroborate the generally gloomy picture of adult autistics (Lotter, 1978) (see Focus Box 14.3). However, most of the autistic children followed into adulthood have not had the benefit of intensive educational interventions or the kind of intensive behavioral program described later (p. 427). New follow-up studies are needed to determine whether the prognosis for autism will remain as poor.

Other Severe Developmental Disorders

Autistic disorder is classified in DSM-IV under **pervasive developmental disorders**, a category of disorders in which several areas of development, such as communication and social interaction, are greatly impaired from early childhood. The other disorders in this category are less well understood than autistic disorder.

Rett's disorder has been diagnosed only among girls. Children with this condition are usually also severely or profoundly mentally retarded. They appear to develop normally in the first five months of life but then show slowed head growth between five months and four years of age. They lose already developed motor skills involving their hands between five and thirty months of age and develop repetitive hand movements similar to hand-wringing or hand washing, as well as generally poor coordination. Their language development is very poor, as in autistic disorder. The main differences from autistic disorder are the sex distribution, the early period of normal development, and, at least during preschool years, a greater interest in the social environment.

Childhood disintegrative disorder is less common than autistic disorder and occurs among both boys and girls. Children with this condition are usually severely mentally retarded. The symptoms are similar to those of autistic disorder, but the course is different. In childhood disintegrative disorder, development is normal in all areas for at least the first two years. Sometime between the ages of two and ten (typically at age three or four), these children lose previously developed skills in several areas, such as language, social interaction, bowel and bladder control, or motor skills.

Finally, **Asperger's disorder** is similar to autistic disorder in two respects. First, these children have problems in social interaction; for example, they may be unable to sustain eye contact or play with others in an interactive manner. Second, they develop repetitive, stereotyped patterns of behavior or interests, such as repeatedly making the same motion with their hands. The main differences from autistic disorder are that children with Asperger's disorder show basically normal language and cognitive development, as well as normal adaptive behavior and ability to care for themselves.

Perspectives on the Causes and Treatment of Autistic Disorder

More information is available on the causes and treatment of autistic disorder than on the other pervasive developmental disorders. Although biological factors appear much more likely than environmental problems (e.g., poor parenting) to cause the disorder, behavioral methods can play a key role in improving the functioning of these children.

---

pervasive developmental disorders Severe childhood problems marked by profound disturbances in social relations and oddities in behavior. *Austistic disorder* is one.

Rett's disorder A *pervasive developmental disorder* affecting girls. Development is normal in the first five months, but some time in the next few years head growth slows and motor skills involving the hands deteriorate; language development is poor.

childhood disintegrative disorder A *pervasive developmental disorder* in which the child is usually severely mentally retarded; similar to *autistic disorder* except that development is normal for the first two years.

Asperger's disorder A *pervasive developmental disorder* involving difficulty in social interaction and stereotyped behaviors. Unlike *autistic disorder*, language and cognitive development and self-care skills are normal.

▶ FOCUS BOX 14.3

A First-Person Account of an Adult Autistic Man

Excerpted here, with some punctuation and spelling corrections made by the professionals who published the account (Volkmar & Cohen, 1985), is a first-person report by a twenty-two-year-old man who had been treated for autism. This depiction is unusual because autistic children seldom acquire enough cognitive and linguistic abilities to communicate in this way.

When examined at twenty-six months of age, "Tony" did not speak, exhibited bizarre behavior, and showed no interest in others. After treatment he was able to enter a special education program in a public school and was even able to attend a private high school until the tenth grade. His IQ at the time he wrote his autobiographical account was 93, which placed him just a little below the average. When he contacted the center to gain access to his records, he was employed as an assembler in a local industry. Eventually, Tony succeeded in obtaining a driver's license and enlisting in the army.

Autism: "The Disease of Abomination" Tony W.

I was living in a world of daydreaming and Fear revolving about my self I had no care about Human feelings or other people. I was afraid of everything! I was terrified to go in the water swimming, (and of) loud noises; in the dark I had severe, repetitive Nightmares and occasionally hearing electronic noises with nightmares. I would wake up so terrified and disoriented I wasnt able to Find my way out of the room for a few miniuts. It felt like I was being draged to Hell. I was afraid of simple things such as going into the shower, getting my nails cliped, soap in my eyes. . . . I like machanical Battery Power toys or electronic toys. Regular toys such as toy trucks, cars that wernt battery powered didnt turn me on at all. I was terrified to learn to ride the bybycle. One thing I loved that not even the Fear could stop was Airplanes. I saw an air show the planes—f4s—were loud. I was allway(s) Impressed by Airplanes. I drew picutres and had severeal Airplane models. The Test came when we went to D.C. I was so Anxious and Hyper to go on the plane I drove my Parents nut. The only peace they had is when I heard the turbines reving at the end of the runway. Then I knew we were taking off. Soon as the plane took off I was amazed. I started to yell y(a)h HO! I loved every minuit of it. . . . I dont or didnt trust anybody but my self—that still (is) a problem today. And (I) was and still (am) verry insucure! I was very cold Harted too. I(t) was impossible for me to Give or Receive love from anybody. I often Repulse it by turning people off. Thats is still a problem today and relating to other people. . . . (Volkmar & Cohen, 1985, pp. 49–52)

Psychological Perspectives

One of the best-known psychological theories of autism was formulated by Bruno Bettelheim (1967). His basic idea was that autism closely resembles the apathy and hopelessness found among inmates of German concentration camps during World War II. Bettelheim hypothesized that the young infant has rejecting parents and is able to perceive their negative feelings. The infant finds that his or her own actions have little impact on their unresponsiveness. The child comes to believe "that [his or her] own efforts have no power to influence the world because of the earlier conviction that the world is insensitive to [his or her] reactions" (p. 46). Thus, the autistic child never really enters the world, but builds the "empty fortress" of autism against pain and disappointment.

Some behavioral theorists also believed that certain childhood learning experiences could cause autism. For example, Ferster (1961) suggested that the inattention of the parents, especially of the mother, prevents establishment of the associations that make human beings reinforcers. And because the parents have not become reinforcers, they cannot control the child's behavior; the result is autistic disorder.

Systematic investigations have failed to confirm these hypotheses. For example, the parents of autistic children were compared with those of children with receptive aphasia, a disorder in understanding speech (Cox, Rutter, Newman, & Bartak, 1975). The two groups did *not* differ in warmth, emotional demonstrativeness, responsiveness, and sociability. This and other studies (e.g., Cantwell,

Baker, & Rutter, 1978) indicate that there is nothing remarkable about the parents of autistic children.

Because of the difficulty that autistic children have in relating to others, treatment of them is more educational than psychotherapeutic. Educational programs for autistic children usually try to relieve their symptoms and improve their communication, social skills, and adaptive behavior so that they can become more independent. Teaching autistic children is challenging, however. They do not adjust normally to changes in routines, and efforts to teach necessarily involve such changes. Their behavior problems may interfere with effective teaching. A further impediment to learning of autistic children is their overselectivity of attention. That is, they can fixate on one aspect of a situation, such as color, and overlook other features. Despite these difficulties, educational programs for students with autism have achieved some positive results.

Autistic children have been helped through modeling and operant conditioning. Behavior therapists have taught autistic children to talk (Hewett, 1965), modified their echolalic speech (Carr, Schreibman, & Lovaas, 1975), encouraged them to play with other children (Romanczyk, Diament, Goren, Trundeff, & Harris, 1975), and helped them become more generally responsive to adults (Davison, 1964).

Ivar Lovaas, a leading clinical researcher at the University of California at Los Angeles, has had success with an intensive program with very young (under four years) autistic children (Lovaas, 1987). Therapy encompassed all aspects of the children's lives for more than forty hours a week over more than two years. Parents were trained extensively, so that treatment could continue during almost all the children's waking hours. The goal of the program was to mainstream the children, the assumption being that autistic children, as they improve, benefit more from being with normal peers than by remaining by themselves or with other seriously disturbed children.

Ivar Lovaas, a behavior therapist, is noted for his operant conditioning treatment of autistic children.

The results were quite dramatic and encouraging for the intensive therapy group. Their measured IQs averaged 83 in first grade (after about two years in the intensive therapy) compared with about 55 for the controls who did not receive intensive therapy. Twelve of the nineteen reached the normal range, compared with only two (of forty) in the control group. Furthermore, nine of the nineteen who received intensive attention were promoted to second grade in a regular public school, whereas only one of the much larger control group achieved this level of normal functioning. This ambitious program confirms the need for heavy involvement of both professionals and parents in dealing with the extreme challenge of autistic disorder.

There is reason to believe that the education provided by parents is more beneficial to the child than is clinic- or hospital-based treatment. After only twenty-five to thirty hours of training by parents, autistic children's improvements on standardized tests and behavioral measures were similar to those of other autistic children who had received more than two hundred hours of direct clinic treatment (Koegel, Schreibman, Britten, Burkey, & O'Neill, 1982). It may be that parent training is superior in generalizing learning because parents are present in many different situations.

Biological Perspectives

While parents can play a pivotal role in teaching their autistic children, there is no indication that parenting style caused the disorder in the first place. Evidence increasingly points to a biological basis for the disorder.

Genetic Factors.   Genetic studies of autism are difficult to conduct because the disorder is so rare. Indeed, the family method presents special problems, because autistic persons almost never marry. Twin studies indicate that genetic factors are important in the development of autism. One study found 91% concordance in monozygotic twins and zero percent in dizygotic twins (Steffenberg et al., 1989).

Neurological Factors. Early EEG studies of autistic children indicated that many had abnormal brain-wave patterns (e.g., Hutt, Huff, Lee, & Ountsted, 1964). Other types of neurological examination also revealed signs of damage in many autistic children (e.g., Gillberg & Svendsen, 1983). Further evidence supporting the possibility of neurological dysfunction includes a study using magnetic resonance scans of the brain, which found that portions of the cerebellum were underdeveloped in autistic children (Courchesne, Yeung-Courchesne, Press, Hesselink, & Jernigan, 1988). This abnormality was present in fourteen of eighteen autistic subjects.

The degree of neurological abnormality or central nervous system dysfunction seems to be related to the severity of autistic symptoms. Thirty percent of those who had severe autistic symptoms as children begin having epileptic seizures in adolescence. Furthermore, the prevalence of autism in children whose mothers had rubella during the prenatal period is approximately ten times higher than that in the general population of children. A syndrome similar to autism may follow in the aftermath of meningitis, encephalitis, and tuberous sclerosis, all of which may affect central nervous system functioning. These findings, plus the presence of mental retardation, would seem to link autism and brain damage.

Several medications have been tried in attempts to help children with autistic disorder. One current strategy is to use an opioid receptor antagonist, naltrexone, which has been found to reduce self-injurious behavior (for example, hitting one's head against the wall) and to reduce hyperactivity, increase attention span, and reduce the severity of autistic behaviors (Campbell et al., 1989). The first double-blind, placebo-controlled study of naltrexone produced mixed results. Although the children on naltrexone improved more than the placebo group in terms of global ratings by staff, more specific behavioral ratings did not show significant differences in favor of the drug (Campbell et al., 1990). Clearly, more controlled studies are needed to determine whether naltrexone will prove to be a helpful medication for use with autistic children.

To Recap

Autistic disorder begins in early childhood. Autistic people show difficulties in relating to other people (autistic aloneness) as well as communication problems, such as failure to learn any language at all, or speech problems like echolalia and pronoun reversal. They also experience an obsessive desire for sameness and routine. Early psychological theories conjecturing that cold, aloof, insensitive parenting caused the disorder have been discredited. The most promising treatments of autism have used modeling and operant conditioning procedures. Although the prognosis for autistic children remains poor in general, intensive behavioral treatments with substantial family involvement may enable some autistic children to function at a normal level. There is no certain biological basis, but evidence for such a basis is found in very early onset, data showing a genetic predisposition, abnormalities on neurological tests, and the fact that a syndrome like autism sometimes follows diseases that affect central nervous system functioning.

▶ *Eating Disorders*

eating disorders Severe disturbance in eating behavior accompanied by distorted perception of body shape and weight.

Eating disorders are severe disturbances in eating behavior accompanied by distorted perception of body shape and weight. One form of eating disorder is *anorexia nervosa*, characterized by semistarvation and an extreme fear of being fat. Another, reflected in the case of Ginny Nelson, is *bulimia nervosa*, involving recurrent episodes of binge eating along with unhealthy means of compensating for the binge, such as self-induced vomiting to prevent weight gain.

Eating disorders most often affect women and usually begin in adolescence, a period during which young women are subject to greatly increased focus on their physical appearance. Eating disorders are included in this chapter because they typically begin during adolescence. However, it should be noted that in DSM-IV eating disorders are classified in their own section.

The incidence of eating disorders in several Western countries has risen in recent years, prompting researchers to look for influences contributing to this change. One study in Switzerland (Willi & Grossman, 1983) found that the incidence of anorexia nervosa in women age twelve to twenty-five more than quadrupled from 1956 to 1975. Similar increases have been documented in other Western industrialized nations (Garner, Garfinkel, & Olmstead, 1983). Research suggests that bulimia also has become more prevalent (Pyle, Halvorson, Neuman, & Mitchell, 1986).

Eating disorders tend to be found in the upper social classes (Garner et al., 1983), whereas obesity is more common in lower social classes. Why is this an epidemic of young, usually white, economically privileged women?

One proposed explanation has to do with the relative accessibility of food in a particular culture at a particular time.

> In societies in which there are not sufficient calories to provide an adequate diet, such as in times of famine, everyone will be thin and many will die prematurely. As the amount of food increases, food, still being a relatively scarce commodity, will become the pursuit of the wealthy and thus the upper social strata will be fat. Europe in the Middle Ages provides an example of this distribution of fatness. Curiously, though, as the amount of food further increases to become a common and hence less desirable commodity, the wealthy become thinner and those in the lower social classes become increasingly overweight. The pursuit of thinness by social-opinion leaders may account in part for the recent emergence of bulimia as a widespread problem, and for the increasing prevalence of anorexia nervosa (Agras, 1987, p. 2)

Anorexia Nervosa

Anorexia nervosa is a life-threatening disorder characterized by semistarvation unaccounted for by any known physical disease, as well as intense fear of being fat. The term *anorexia* means severe loss of appetite, and *nervosa* indicates for emotional reasons. The word *anorexia* is a misnomer, because many anorexics initially do not so much lose their appetites as fear gaining weight (Achenbach, 1982). They refuse to eat enough to maintain minimal weight and have an intense fear of becoming obese. An essential feature of anorexia is a distorted body image. Despite their protruding ribs and hipbones, their skull-like faces, and their broomstick limbs, anorexics do not view themselves as too thin. Rather, in frequent scrutiny of their figures in mirrors, they either continue to see themselves (or some specific part of the body, such as the hips) as too fat or feel that they have finally arrived at an attractive weight (Garner, Olmstead, & Polivy, 1984).

The self-starvation imposed by anorexics brings about physiological changes that are sometimes difficult to reverse. Estimates vary, but approximately 5% of anorexics die from suicide or from the medical consequences of starvation. Another 25% of anorexics continue in the unremitting course of their disorder at two-year follow-ups, and the remainder gain weight back as a result of treatment (Hsu, 1980).

Approximately 0.5% to 1% of young women in late adolescence or early adulthood meet diagnostic criteria for anorexia nervosa. The disorder is apparently much more common among women than among men (e.g., Whitaker et al., 1990). Onset of the weight loss often occurs during early adolescence, shortly after the beginning of menstruation. Amenorrhea, failure to menstruate regularly, is a characteristic feature of anorexia nervosa that frequently starts before weight loss

anorexia nervosa A disorder in which a person is unwilling to eat or to retain any food or suffers a prolonged and severe diminution of appetite. The individual has an intense fear of becoming obese, feels fat even when emaciated, and refuses to maintain a minimal body weight.

Anorexia nervosa is defined by major weight loss and fear of becoming fat. Karen Carpenter, a popular singer, died from it.

has become extreme. Other physiological manifestations of anorexia include dry, cracking skin, fine downy hair on the face and neck, brittle fingernails, yellowish discoloration of the skin, slowed heart rate, constipation, reduced body temperature, and muscular weakness (Kaplan & Woodside, 1987). Anorexics may take laxatives and exercise extensively and frantically to lose weight. The manic energy expended in excessive physical activity is amazing, considering their emaciation.

Some anorexics are preoccupied with food, even when they are struggling not to ingest it. They become interested in its preparation, collecting cookbooks, trying new recipes, and planning and cooking elaborate meals of many courses and special dishes for others. Many anorexics do not admit to feeling any hunger. Others say they do feel hungry but force themselves not to eat. Anorexics typically deny having a problem that needs treatment. Psychological treatment is therefore usually at the instigation of someone else, such as a relative or friend who is alarmed by the anorexic person's weight loss.

Perspectives on the Causes of Anorexia Nervosa

A variety of biological explanations for anorexia have been offered. Abnormal functioning of the part of the hypothalamus known to control eating, sexual activity, and menstruation is perhaps the leading physiological theory, but cause-and-effect relations are unclear. A disturbance in hypothalamic functioning may cause anorexia, may result from the weight loss and caloric restriction, or may result from the emotional distress of the patient (Garfinkel & Garner, 1982).

Some psychological explanations of anorexia nervosa have been based on Freud's notion that eating can be a substitute for sexual expression. Thus the anorexic's refusal to eat is thought to indicate fear of increasing sexual desires or perhaps of oral impregnation (J. L. Ross, 1977). Some view anorexia as a reflection of the conflict between wanting to attain independence and a fear of growing up. The girl who feels ineffective in general and is struggling with adjustment to the demands of adolescence may seek refuge in one area of life (food intake and weight) that appears to permit effective control and thereby a sense of accomplishment (Goodsitt, 1985).

Personality research indicates that anorexic patients are consistently depicted as conforming, obsessional, perfectionistic, and shy (Vitousek & Manke, 1994). However, these studies involve patients who are already anorexic, so it is unclear whether these personality features caused the anorexia. Normal men subjected to semistarvation for experimental purposes showed similar obsessional behavior as a consequence of their lack of food intake (Keys, Brozek, Henschel, Mickelsen, & Taylor, 1950). In other words, severely restricting food intake may be responsible for the observed personality features, not the other way around. Studies of what the patient was like before anorexia have been based on recollections and are of unknown validity.

Perspectives on the Treatment of Anorexia Nervosa

Therapy for anorexia is a two-tiered process. The immediate goal is to help the anorexic gain weight in order to avoid medical complications and the possibility of death. Hospitalization may be necessary to ensure that the patient ingests some food. The anorexic is often so weak and physiological functioning so disturbed that hospital treatment is imperative. Intravenous feeding provides necessary nourishment in life-threatening situations. Some success in producing immediate increases in body weight has been achieved by behavior therapy programs in which the hospitalized anorexic is isolated as much as possible and given mealtime company, then access to a television set, radio, or stereo, walks with a student nurse, mail, and visitors as rewards for eating and gaining weight (Hsu, 1986).

Family Therapy.   One mode of treatment that may be able to produce longer-term gains for anorexics is family therapy. Like most other treatments, family therapy has been insufficiently studied for its long-term effects. One report, however, found that 86% of fifty anorexic daughters treated with their families were still functioning well when assessed at times ranging from three months to four years after treatment (Rosman, Minuchin, & Liebman, 1975). Salvador Minuchin and his colleagues, who represent but one of several schools of family therapy, have done considerable work on anorexia nervosa.

Minuchin's family treatment is based on the assumption that sick family members, especially children, serve to deflect attention away from underlying conflict in family relationships. The illness is the family psychopathology become manifest. Members of these families are both rigid and deeply enmeshed in one another's lives. They overprotect their children and do not acknowledge conflicts. By providing an alternative focus of attention, the illness lessens the tension among family members. Minuchin believes that troubled families therefore act in a way that keeps the sick family member in the patient role (Minuchin et al., 1975). Studies of the family interactions of anorexia nervosa patients provide some support for this view (Kog & Vandereycken, 1985).

To treat the disorder, Minuchin attempts to redefine it as interpersonal rather than individual and to bring the family conflict to the fore. Thus, it is theorized, the symptomatic family member is freed from having to maintain his or her problem, for it no longer deflects attention from the dysfunctional family.

Families of anorexics are seen by the therapist during mealtime, since the conflicts related to anorexia are believed to be most evident then. There are three major goals for these family lunch sessions: (1) changing the patient role of the anorexic; (2) redefining the eating problem as an interpersonal one; and (3) preventing the parents from using their child's anorexia as a means of avoiding conflict. One strategy is to instruct each parent to try individually to force the child to eat. The other parent may leave the room. The individual efforts are expected to fail, but through this failure and the frustration of each, the parents may now work *together* to persuade the child to eat. Thus, rather than being a focus of conflict, the child's eating will produce cooperation and increase parental effectiveness in dealing with him or her (Rosman et al., 1975).

Bulimia Nervosa

For some time **bulimia nervosa** was regarded as an occasional accompaniment to anorexia, but it is recognized in DSM-IV as an eating disorder separate from anorexia nervosa. Often referred to as the binge–purge syndrome, it consists of episodes of gross overeating followed by some means of compensating for the enormous amount of food ingested. This compensation process can take the form of excessive exercise or fasting, but typically the bulimic person purges food by taking laxatives or inducing vomiting. Unlike the anorexic, the bulimic does not necessarily have abnormally low weight, but patients with both disorders do share an abnormal concern with body size, having a morbid fear of becoming fat.

The foods bulimics choose, such as ice cream or cookies, have a texture or size that allows them to be eaten rapidly. They gobble them down in huge amounts in a short span of time. Unlike anorexics, bulimics are painfully aware that their uncontrollable eating pattern is abnormal. They often feel disgust, helplessness, and panic during a binge. The purge is a source of relief for most victims. It may be that bulimics purge to reduce the anxiety caused by a binge (Rosen & Leitenberg, 1985). Their vomiting helps free them from normal inhibitions against overeating. Thus, binges often become more extreme after the individual has discovered the use of purging to control the previous anxiety about overeating.

Estimates of the prevalence of bulimia nervosa vary depending on the re-

bulimia nervosa Episodic uncontrollable eating binges, often followed by purging, either by vomiting or by taking laxatives.

search methods used, but probably about 1% to 2% of college women meet DSM criteria for the disorder (Fairburn & Beglin, 1990). Very few studies have been conducted other than on college campuses. About one-tenth of bulimic people are men. In her review of the bulimia literature, Schlesier-Stropp (1984) provided a portrait of the typical binge eater. She is likely to be a white woman in her mid-twenties who began overeating at about age eighteen and began purging, usually by vomiting, about a year later. She is typically within the normal weight range for her age and height, and her family history has an unusually high incidence of obesity and alcoholism. She may binge and purge as seldom as once a week or as often as thirty times a week. To meet DSM-IV criteria the frequency must be at least twice a week on average for at least three months.

Bulimics also frequently suffer periods of depression (Hinz & Williamson, 1987) and anxiety as well as guilt over their inability to control their binges. This feature was evident in the case of Ginny Nelson we described at the beginning of this chapter. Their costly binge–purge behavior can take up so much time that bulimics' social activities are restricted and financial resources squandered (Mitchell, Hatsukami, Eckert, & Pyle, 1985). Many bulimics are suicidal as well.

Bulimia has serious physiological consequences, especially if the purging is done by vomiting. Sore throats, swollen salivary glands, and destruction of tooth enamel by the acidic vomitus have been reported in a significant number of bulimics. Intestinal damage, nutritional deficiencies, and dehydration can also result. Decreased levels of potassium and electrolyte abnormalities can be life threatening. Bulimics have been known to experience heart failure leading to sudden death (Kaplan & Woodside, 1987).

Perspectives on the Causes of Bulimia Nervosa

Psychodynamic Perspectives. One hypothesized cause of bulimia is sexual abuse. Both sexual abuse victims and bulimic patients show low self-esteem and negative attitudes toward their bodies and toward sexuality. This possibility recalls an early idea of Freud's. Freud postulated that the cause of his patients' neurotic problems was sexual abuse in childhood, typically rape by the father. His views elicited outrage from his colleagues, and, perhaps as a result (Masson, 1984), he eventually came to believe that many of his patients' accounts were fantasies. Contemporary evidence on the frequency of child sexual abuse and its effects suggests that Freud's initial theory may have been more accurate than the revised fantasy theory.

> APPLYING CRITICAL THINKING SKILLS

INTERPRETING THE RELATIONSHIP BETWEEN SEXUAL ABUSE AND BULIMIA

Several clinical reports have indicated a more specific link between childhood sexual abuse and the development of eating disorders, including bulimia nervosa, than was evident in Freud's time (Oppenheimer, Howells, Palmer, & Chaloner, 1985).

▶ *What conclusion does the evidence seem to support?* Being sexually abused as a child, perhaps by way of its impact on self-image and especially on body image, may create vulnerability to bulimia.

▶ *What other interpretations are plausible?* Numerous alternative interpretations are possible, and we will consider two. First, sexual abuse may be a risk factor for psychological disorders in general, not for eating disorders in particular (Pope & Hudson, 1992). Second, perhaps the apparent link between sexual abuse and bulimia nervosa is an illusion created because most of the research has been conducted in clinical settings. Most people with bulimia nervosa are not in treatment. It may be that people are more likely to seek treatment if they have both an eating disorder *and* a history of sexual abuse. If so, then the two would appear to be associated in studies of clinical samples even if there were no correlation between them in the population at large (P. Bell, 1992).

▶ ***What other information would help choose among the alternative interpretations?*** To see if sexual abuse is associated with bulimia specifically or with psychological disorders in general, patients with bulimia and patients with other disorders have to be included in the same study of sexual abuse and compared with a group of nondisturbed people. To evaluate the possibility that sampling bias creates the correlation between sexual abuse and bulimia, it would help to study bulimics who are not in treatment as well as those who are.

Each of these comparisons was conducted in a study of young adult women in England (Welch & Fairburn, 1994). Fifty women with bulimia nervosa and fifty with other disorders (mainly depression) were identified on the basis of two measures. Screening questionnaires were sent to women between the ages of sixteen and thirty-five who were on the case registers of a group of physicians (such registers include nearly everybody in England), and follow-up diagnostic interviews were conducted with those who seemed likely to meet the criteria. Most (90%) of the bulimic women identified in this manner were *not* in treatment. Another sample of fifty bulimic women were recruited from clinics. The final comparison group was one hundred nondistressed women matched to the community sample of bulimics in age and parental socioeconomic status.

Sexual abuse (prior to the onset of the eating disorder) was reported by 26% of the community bulimic sample. By contrast, only 10% of the nondistressed control group reported having been sexually abused. The rate of sexual abuse was no higher in the clinical sample of bulimics than in the community sample. Thus, referral bias does not seem able to account for the correlation of bulimia nervosa with sexual abuse. However, the community sample with other disorders were as likely as the bulimics to have been sexually abused (24%).

That a minority of bulimics were sexually abused, and no higher a proportion than in the case of other disorders, indicates that sexual abuse may be one factor in the development of bulimia (as well as other disorders), but other causal factors must be relevant as well. ◀

Sociocultural Perspectives. Cultural pressures to be thin may play a critical role in causing bulimia and anorexia. The core similarity of the disorders, in this view, is an overconcern about weight and shape and an excessive desire to be thin. The image of the beautiful woman as being impossibly thin is extensively modeled and emulated by our society (Bemis, 1978). In order to achieve the same figure as Barbie, the doll who represents the ideal body to many young girls, the average American woman (who weighs 124 pounds) would have to increase her bust by twelve inches, reduce her waist by ten inches, and reach seven feet two inches in height (Moser, 1989)!

Given such cultural standards, it is not surprising that most American women are dissatisfied with their bodies (L. Harris, 1987). Using figure drawings (see Figure 14.2) designed by Stunkard, Sorensen, and Schulsinger (1980), a study by Fallon and Rozin (1985) found that women rate their ideal figure and the figure they think men find attractive as much thinner than they judge their own current figure. Men, in contrast, rate their current, ideal, and attractive figures as virtually the same.

Unfortunately, the cultural pressure on women to be thin shows no sign of disappearing (see Focus Box 14.4). To the extent that it leads young women to diet, which usually does not work, this can be the start of a maladaptive cycle. Unsuccessful attempts to maintain desired weight by restricting intake set the stage for

FOCUS BOX 14.4

Cultural Expectations of Thinness in Women as a Factor in Eating Disorders

A preoccupation with thinness (and recently, fitness) appears to influence the rise in the rate of eating disorders among affluent women. It also appears to be disseminated through the media. A study covering 1959 to 1978 showed a decrease in the average weights of *Playboy* magazine centerfolds and Miss America Pageant contestants (Garner, Garfinkel, Schwartz, & Thompson, 1980). To the extent that it is safe to consider *Playboy* centerfolds and Miss America representatives of societal standards of feminine beauty (which is debatable), this study suggests a trend toward a thinner standard. At the same time researchers found that typical weights for American women were actually *increasing*, making the ideal doubly unrealistic for the average woman. These investigators also counted "diet for weight loss" articles in six popular women's magazines during the period from 1959 to 1978 and found that the number of such articles had steadily increased.

A more recent investigation of the period from 1979 to 1988 indicated that *Playboy* centerfolds and Miss America contestants had body weights 13% to 19% below the expected weight for women of their ages (Wiseman, Gray, Mosimann, & Ahrens, 1992). The trend described first by Garner and his colleagues continued its downward trajectory and leveled off toward the end of the ten-year period studied.

As for magazine articles, the proportion of diet, exercise, and diet/exercise articles has increased steadily over the past thirty years. The number of exercise articles surpassed diet articles in the 1980s, and the number of articles that combined diet and exercise jumped dramatically, almost doubling in the 1980s.

A related project found that the number of television commercials for diet food and diet products shown on major U.S. networks also rose steadily in the 1980s (Wiseman, Gunning, & Gray, 1993). Ironically, these commercials may exacerbate the difficulties experienced by those trying to diet by reminding them of failures in their attempts to restrain eating. In a laboratory experiment, women attempting to restrict their food consumption ate more M & M's or peanuts (ostensibly being used for a taste test) after consuming a high-calorie milk shake and then viewing a sad film that included diet ads than they did if neutral ads or no ads were shown (Strauss, Doyle, & Kreipe, 1994). Women who were not prone to restraining their eating did not show such a response to diet ads.

Although the mass media is widely influential, we still need to bear in mind that not all young women exposed to such messages become anorexic or bulimic. Therefore, media influences cannot account by themselves for eating disorders. Individual factors must be operating to explain why only a minority of young women succumb in this extreme manner to societal pressures as transmitted by the media.

---

overeating when one's determination lapses, which prompts purging in order to feel less guilty and avoid weight gain (Vitousek & Manke, 1994).

Treatment of Bulimia Nervosa

The major treatments for bulimia are antidepressant medication and cognitive behavior therapy. Double-blind, placebo-controlled studies show that antidepressant medications such as fluoxetine, desipramine, and amitriptyline reduce binge eating and purging, but this treatment has limitations as well. Drop-out rates are higher than for psychotherapies, perhaps because of side effects, and relapse rates are high after treatment is discontinued (G. T. Wilson, 1993).

Cognitive behavior therapy combines cognitive restructuring with exposure to forbidden foods followed by prevention of the usual response of purging (Agras, 1987). One of the first tasks for the therapist is to explain the rationale for treatment. This involves, among other things, discussion of the social pressure on women to lose weight, the often unrealistic nature of such ideals, and the ways in which dieting can encourage out-of-control binge eating and purging.

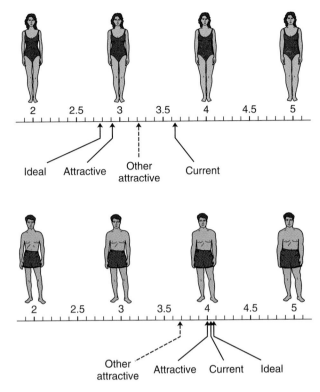

Figure 14.2 *Ratings by women (top) and men (bottom) of their own figures: ideal, attractive to the opposite sex, and current. Other attractive represents the figure rated by the opposite sex as most attractive. From "Use of the Danish Adoption Register for the Study of Obesity and Thinness" by A. Stunkard, T. Sorensen, and F. Schulsinger, in* The Genetics of Neurological and Psychiatric Disorders, *edited by S. Kety, 1980, p. 119. Copyright 1983 by Raven Press. Adapted by permission.*

The patients monitor the foods they eat as well as all binges and purges. This helps both patient and therapist understand the exact nature of the problem and monitor the effectiveness of treatment. The next objective of therapy is to establish a normal eating pattern. Eating three meals a day decreases the level of hunger and in turn decreases the probability of binging and purging. As therapy progresses, patients are asked to bring into the therapy session small amounts of forbidden foods (just enough to create the urge to vomit when eaten). The in-session minibinge is followed by a period of relaxation as the desire to purge abates. Cognitive distortions are elicited after the minibinge and challenged in session. The goal is to challenge those self-statements that are unrealistic and to substitute realistic coping statements.

In the final sessions, patient and therapist use records accumulated during self-monitoring to examine events that trigger binging and purging. The aim at this point is to assist the client in recognizing triggers and practicing coping responses in the natural environment to replace purging.

Controlled research suggests the value of this treatment. Binge-eating and purging frequency are reduced by 70% to 90% on average, with about one-half of patients becoming abstinent from binging and purging. There are other benefits as well—depression eases; self-esteem and social functioning increase; dysfunctional attitudes toward weight and shape are reduced; and eating patterns become more regular. Especially important is that improvement is well-maintained at six-month and twelve-month follow-ups (G. T. Wilson, 1993).

To Recap

Anorexia nervosa is a life-threatening disorder, found mainly among young women, that involves deliberate self-starvation, extreme fear of obesity, and a distorted body image. Anorexics tend to be conforming and perfectionistic, but it is unknown whether these traits predate the onset of the disorder. Therapy starts with feeding, intravenously if necessary. Family therapy is often used to resolve

family conflicts, on the theory that the anorexia may be maintained because it functions as a distracter from family problems.

Bulimia nervosa consists of episodes of gross overeating followed by induced vomiting or other means of compensating for overeating in the hope of feeling better and preventing weight gain. Bulimics may have a normal weight but share with anorexics the extreme fear of becoming fat. Bulimics and anorexics are typically white women of high socioeconomic status. Depression commonly accompanies both disorders as do a variety of medical problems. A history of sexual abuse is more common among bulimics than among nonbulimics without other psychological disorders and may be a contributing factor to the disorder. Cultural pressures on women to strive for virtually impossible standards of thinness may also contribute to both eating disorders. Cognitive-behavioral treatments geared toward normalizing eating habits and disputing such beliefs as that self-worth is a function of thinness have proven highly effective. These treatments are discussed next in relation to the case with which we began this chapter.

▶ The Case of Ginny Nelson Revisited

SOCIAL HISTORY

The roots of Ginny's eating problem were set down in adolescence. She was the third of four children and grew up in a medium-sized midwestern city. Her father managed a discount store, and her mother worked part-time as a supermarket cashier. Her father had a chronic drinking problem, which caused considerable conflict between her parents. Ginny's mother would criticize her husband about his drinking, and he would get angry and deny that he drank too much. When Ginny was twelve years old her father moved out of the house for two months after a particularly bad period of conflict. He returned, but more because Ginny's mother had found the separation financially stressful than because anything had been resolved. Her entire family seemed to argue a great deal about nearly everything. The only time she could recall things going smoothly between her and her parents was when she was involved in activities related to school sports.

Throughout her involvement in gymnastics, Ginny reported that coaches told her and her teammates that they would be better athletes if they kept their weight as low as possible. Very strict dieting seemed to be encouraged. During high school, Ginny had little trouble maintaining her weight, thanks to her regular exercise. Her mother overate during times of stress and frequently used crash diets to try to control her weight, which could fluctuate as much as thirty pounds. Ginny began to follow her mother's pattern of dieting by severely restricting food intake. She also used over-the-counter diet pills to make dieting easier. However, she indicated that trying to lose weight in this manner made her feel extremely hungry and irritable. Sometimes, after upsetting fights with her parents, she would soothe her bad feelings by "pigging out."

Ginny did well in gymnastics during her first two years of college, which pleased her greatly. She noticed, however, that her periods of overeating when under stress were becoming more of a problem, and that part of the stress was caused by the effort involved in maintaining her weight at 105 pounds.

Eventually the episodes of overeating began to take on a different quality. In the summer between her sophomore and junior years in college, Ginny at times felt driven to eat whatever food was available. Afterward, she felt guilty and disgusted with herself for eating so much. She also began to induce vomiting after binge episodes, concealing the sound from others by closing the bathroom door and running water in the sink.

The junior year was not a good one for Ginny. She did not do well in gymnastics and felt disappointed and embarrassed about her performance. After the season she did not exercise regularly, and her weight increased to 128 pounds. She felt desperate and tried to keep her daily food intake down to one thousand calories with the help of diet pills.

But this method was not successful, and Ginny had numerous episodes of binge eating and vomiting. On one occasion she was studying for a final exam and became increasingly scared about how far behind she was in the course. She felt so uncomfortable that she left her room to buy several boxes of doughnuts, cookies, candy, and popcorn. She ate everything within one hour. She said that she felt out of control, as if she would have kept on eating so long as a morsel of food was available.

Ginny's menstrual cycle had become irregular. She had had only one menstrual period lasting three days during the previous six months. She told Dr. R. that she felt that her whole body was "messed up." The more she talked to Dr. R., the more Ginny realized she needed help.

CONCEPTUALIZATION AND TREATMENT

Ginny agreed to participate in a ten-week group therapy program for women with eating disorders. The program offered by Dr. R. was based largely on cognitive-behavior therapy principles. The group searched for and examined the beliefs that seemed to motivate their binging and purging. A common maladaptive belief expressed by patients in the group was that they would gain a significant amount of weight by eating just one doughnut or one cookie. This belief often resulted in a full-blown binge, for patients would assume that as long as they had eaten one cookie, they had blown it anyway and might as well keep on eating.

In addition to challenging such thinking in group discussions, patients were asked to monitor their food intake, including binges and purges, along with the emotional and social circumstances in which they ate and their thoughts about these situations. The goal was to identify patterns of negative thinking about problems at home or at work that might precipitate negative emotions and prompt a binge episode.

The group worked together to try to identify more effective ways to deal with such problem situations and to practice these alternative behaviors between sessions. They also discussed the unrealistically low societal standards of ideal weight for women and the sex-role stereotyping that pushed them to define their self-worth in terms of physical appearance. Finally, Dr. R. worked with each patient individually to develop a plan for regular, nutritionally balanced meals and strategies for how to regain control of her eating if she should slip and engage in an eating binge.

At the end of treatment Ginny had not binged in two weeks and had adopted more regular eating patterns. By the time of her individual six-month follow-up appointment, Ginny weighed 113 pounds, exercised regularly but not to excess, and felt she was making progress in controlling her eating and in managing her life in general. She had experienced four binge–purge episodes in the course of six months. She had been able to discuss her bulimia with her parents and found them to be supportive of her attempts to deal with the problem and more generally to be understanding of her need to become more assertive and independent.

DISCUSSION

Ginny's case is typical of bulimia nervosa in several respects, including the family history of obesity and alcoholism (Schlesier-Stropp, 1984). She had imitated the behavior of her parents, dealing with conflict and bad feelings by, in effect, self-medicating through the ingestion of substances. In addition to her difficult family environment, Ginny was also subjected to societal (and subcultural within the world of gymnastics) pressure to be thin.

Ginny was fortunate in having friends and a coach who became aware of her problems and concerned about her well-being. The fact that she was not bulimic for a very long time may have contributed to her overall favorable response to treatment. Still, her prognosis remains uncertain. She has mastered some basic self-control skills, but in the long run she will also need to divorce her self-worth from her athletic success or her physical appearance, something not easily accomplished in this culture.

Visual Summary for Chapter 14:

Developmental Disorders and Eating Disorders

Descriptions of Developmental Disorders

Category	Definition	Examples
Undercontrolled Behavior	Behavioral excesses, such as too much activity, destructiveness, lying.	**Attention-Deficit/Hyperactivity Disorder** Excess activity in situations in which it is inappropriate; deficient ability to concentrate.
		Conduct Disorder Persistent violation of others' rights through such behaviors as destructiveness, lying, theft, arson, and vandalism.
Overcontrolled Behavior	Behavioral deficits and inhibitions, such as anxiety and depression.	**Separation Anxiety Disorder** Persistent, excessive, age-inappropriate fear of being away from home or from a primary caregiver.
		Social Withdrawal Extreme shyness and anxiety about being around peers or strangers.
		Depression Sadness, fatigue, poor concentration, suicidal tendencies, inability to feel pleasure, guilt.
Learning Disabilities	Lagging development in a specific area of academic, communication, or motor skills.	**Learning Disorders** Reading, mathematics, or writing skills are impaired relative to general intellectual level and education.
		Communication Disorders Difficulties in understanding spoken language or in oral expression.
		Motor Skills Disorder Impaired coordination.
Mental Retardation	Far below average intellectual functioning and deficits in adaptive behavior.	**Mild, Moderate, Severe, and Profound levels of retardation**, with varying degrees of subaverage intellectual functioning.
Pervasive Developmental Disorders	Impairments in several areas of development, such as language and social interaction, from early childhood.	**Autistic Disorder** Aloofness from others, severe language problems, repetitive, ritualistic behaviors, obsessive preoccupations with specific objects.

Descriptions of Eating Disorders

Category	Definition	Examples
Eating Disorders	Disturbances in eating behavior and distorted perceptions of body shape and weight.	**Anorexia Nervosa** Self-starvation, with extreme fear of being fat.
		Bulimia Nervosa Recurrent binge-eating episodes followed by an attempt to compensate for the binge, most commonly by self-induced vomiting.

Causes and Treatment of Developmental Disorders

Disorder	Most Likely Causes	Best-Documented Treatments
ADHD	Frontal lobe deficits.	Stimulant medication, such as Ritalin; operant conditioning programs providing positive reinforcement for sustained work on tasks and apt social behaviors.
Conduct Disorder	Genetic link with adult antisocial behavior; parenting style that does not foster moral awareness; modeling aggressive behavior; bias to perceive others as hostile.	Parent training to learn deliberate use of reinforcement and punishment to evoke more prosocial behavior; child therapy that teaches problem-solving skills and empathy.
Separation Anxiety Disorder	Recent stresses that threaten sense of security (e.g., moving); parental insecurity.	Gradual exposure to feared situation; modeling competent social behavior.
Social Withdrawal	Biological predisposition to shy temperament; lack of social skills.	Gradual exposure to feared situation; modeling competent social behavior.
Depression	Genetic vulnerability; poor peer and family relationships.	Social-skills training to foster better peer relations.
Learning Disabilities	Left hemisphere damage.	Reading readiness training for young dyslexic students; various instructional supports, such as untimed tests for older students.
Mental Retardation	Chromosomal abnormalities, such as in Down syndrome; recessive-gene diseases, as in PKU; maternal infectious diseases, such as rubella, during the prenatal period and especially during the first trimester.	Prevention of the known causes, such as a special diet for babies with PKU; early intervention programs, such as Head Start, to bolster cognitive, medical, and social functioning.
Autistic Disorder	Neurological abnormalities.	Intensive early educational efforts involving parents and professionals, using modeling and operant conditioning to promote language development and social behavior.

Causes and Treatment of Eating Disorders

Disorder	Most Likely Causes	Best-Documented Treatments
Anorexia Nervosa	Malfunctioning of the hypothalamus; cultural standards of beauty; need for control.	Feeding, forced if necessary, to gain weight; family therapy may help with long-term outcome, based on the premise that dealing openly with family conflicts will reduce the need for the anorexia as a focus of family attention.
Bulimia Nervosa	Sexual abuse or cultural standards equating beauty with thinness can prompt dieting, which often fails and leads to more desperate attempts to compensate when binges occur.	Antidepressant medication; cognitive behavior therapy to learn normal eating habits, prevent purging after binges, and change attitudes toward weight and shape.

Chapter 15

Aging and Psychological Disorders

The Case of Helen Kay

Helen Kay, age seventy-three, was huddled against a wooden piling, an empty pint of whiskey in her left hand. The police officer thought at first that she was dead, but she was still breathing, faintly. He took her to the emergency room of the county hospital.

By the time they arrived, Mrs. Kay was mumbling incoherently to herself and once there, she occasionally jumped up to run wildly about the examining room. The physician in charge was tempted to administer a tranquilizer just to quiet her down, but refrained from doing so, noting her state of apparent alcohol intoxication and wary of the hypersensitivity of many older people to drugs.

Mrs. Kay had failed to appear in the dining room of her retirement hotel for breakfast one Monday morning. The manager, careful about such incidents among his elderly clientele, sent one of the waiters upstairs to check on her. The waiter returned thirty minutes later to report that Mrs. Kay had pulled him into her room with a frightened look on her face and then screamed at him, "I did what I could!" The waiter managed to get away and report the situation to his boss, who went to Mrs. Kay's room himself. She refused to come downstairs to eat, but she did agree to eat the breakfast that was brought up to her room.

Over the preceding months Mrs. Kay had occasionally acted peculiarly. She was agitated and hostile at times, lethargic and depressed at others. This moodiness seemed to be related to the fact that she had begun to drink heavily by herself in her room. The staff had come to expect verbal abuse from her within a few hours of her return from the store. On this particular morning, the manager noticed a strong odor of alcohol while he was persuading her to eat some breakfast. He concluded that she had been drinking earlier that morning.

Later that evening Mrs. Kay was herself again, sober and, unfortunately, very depressed. Sadness was not unheard of among other residents of the hotel, but Mrs. Kay's concerned and angered the other guests. For example, at dinner that same day, Mrs. Kay went on and on about her aching back and feet, her poor eyesight, and generally about the woes that God had inflicted on her. A woman sitting beside her walked only with the aid of a four-pointed cane, was almost completely blind, and was otherwise in poorer physical health than Mrs. Kay—and exclaimed that to her angrily. Mrs. Kay's reaction was to sulk and brood even more, eventually excusing herself before dessert was served and retreating to her room to drink herself into a stupor once again.

The following morning saw a repeat of her refusal to come down for breakfast, but this time she also refused to open her door to the manager. Just before dinnertime, a couple from the hotel saw her walking morosely by herself in the park across the street from the hotel. Occasionally stopping to gaze at the ocean, she had a liquor bottle dangling from one hand. Their impulse to approach was suppressed by their expectation of verbal abuse from her.

Mrs. Kay did not return to her hotel that evening. Chilled by the night ocean breezes, she found her way to the pier and settled herself against a piling to finish her bottle. Hours later she was discovered by the police officer.

Social and Cultural Factors in Psychological Disorders Among the Elderly

When one thinks of the problems that affect older people, it is physical, rather than psychological, problems that come to mind. As the case of Helen Kay illustrates, however, the physical and environmental changes associated with aging can have psychological consequences. On the other hand, physical factors can, as with younger people, play little if any role in their psychological problems.

A Chinese grandfather helping his grandson with his writing. The generally lower status of the elderly in society in the United States relative to most Asian countries can be a source of stress for elderly immigrants.

ageism Prejudice and discrimination based on age.

gerontology The interdisciplinary study of aging.

In contrast to the esteem in which the elderly are held in most Asian countries, they are generally not treated very well in the United States. Indeed, the lower level of status and respect accorded old people in the United States has been identified as a significant source of stress for elderly people who immigrate to the United States from Southeast Asian countries (Uba, 1994). Lack of regard for senior citizens may stem from our own fear of growing old. The old person with serious infirmities is an unwelcome reminder that some of us may one day walk with a less steady gait, see less clearly, enjoy sex less frequently, and fall victim to some of the many diseases and maladies that are the lot of many old people. The less desirable physical changes associated with aging are made considerably worse by society's negative attitudes about them. These attitudes can affect mental health as well.

Older adults often suffer from **ageism**, which can be defined as discrimination against any person, young or old, based on chronological age. In this chapter, our focus is on ageism as it relates to prejudicial attitudes and behavior toward older adults. Ageism can be seen, for instance, when a person older than seventy-five is ignored in a social gathering on the assumption that she or he has nothing to contribute to the conversation. Like any prejudice, ageism ignores the diversity among people (Gatz & Pearson, 1988).

Another important consideration in studying older adults is that issues of sexism and racism do not suddenly become irrelevant. Elderly individuals from minority ethnic groups may experience a double jeopardy: African-American and Mexican-American elders have considerably lower income and poorer health, as well as lower life satisfaction, than do their white counterparts (Dowd & Bengston, 1978; Gerber, 1983). And societal biases against women contribute to what some consider triple jeopardy, with elderly minority women running the greatest risk of economic dependency and associated problems (Blau, Oser, & Stephens, 1979).

Mental health professionals have only recently begun to consider the relation between social stereotypes about aging and the behavioral and emotional problems of the elderly. Certain widely held misconceptions, such as the belief that intellectual deterioration is prevalent and inevitable, or that depression among old people is widespread and untreatable, may influence mental health workers. Although those who provide mental health services are probably not extremely ageist (Gatz & Pearson, 1988), they nevertheless merit attention because their attitudes and practices influence the people they treat as well as policies that affect the lives of older adults. In the past decade research and training in **gerontology**, the study of aging, have been introduced into the curricula of many schools that prepare people for the health professions. However, there are still comparatively few professionals who are committed primarily to gerontology (Gatz & Smyer, 1992).

This relative neglect of older adults is problematic, considering their growing numbers. In 1900 only 4% of the U.S. population was over age sixty-five. Today, this figure is more than 12% and it is expected to be between 21% and 25% by 2040 (Guralnik, Yanagashita, & Schneider, 1988; U.S. Bureau of the Census, 1986). The increase is attributable to many causes, especially decreased infant, childhood, and maternal mortality, as well as people living longer as a result of improved sanitation and more effective control of many infectious diseases. Thus it is especially important to examine what we know about the psychological and neuropsychological problems of older adults.

In this chapter we examine the problems of aging that produce psychological effects. In some cases, disease produces brain disorders. In others, a mix of sociocultural and emotional factors combines to cause psychological disorders. Most of these we have already discussed, but here we consider them with a particular focus on how they are manifest in old age and how they might be treated.

The elderly are usually defined as those over the age of sixty-five. The decision to use this age was set largely by social policies, not because age sixty-five is some critical point at which the physiological and psychological processes of aging suddenly begin. To have some rough demarcation points for better describing the diversity of the elderly, gerontologists usually divide those over age sixty-five into three groups: the young-old, those aged sixty-five to seventy-four; the old-old, those aged seventy-five to eighty-four; and the oldest-old, those over age eighty-five. The health of these groups differs in important ways.

To Recap

The psychological problems of older people are as important to consider as their physical problems. In fact, each may influence the other. As the proportion of people who live beyond age sixty-five continues to grow, it is important to learn about the disorders suffered and the social and cultural stereotypes that can influence both how the elderly feel about themselves and how they are treated by mental health professionals.

▶ Brain Disorders

Brain disorders are psychological abnormalities presumed to be caused by temporary or permanent brain malfunctions. Although the majority of older people do not have brain disorders, these problems account for more admissions and hospital inpatient days than any other condition of older adults (Christie, 1982). There are two principal types of brain disorders, dementia and delirium.

brain disorders Psychological abnormalities presumed to be caused by brain malfunctions.

Dementia

Sometimes called senility, **dementia** is a gradual deterioration of intellectual abilities to the point that social and occupational functioning are impaired. Dementia can result from a variety of diseases, for example, Alzheimer's disease or Huntington's chorea. People with dementia have difficulty remembering things, especially recent events. They may leave tasks unfinished because they forget to return to them after an interruption. A person who has started to fill a kettle at the sink leaves the water running. A parent may be unable to remember the name of a daughter or son and later may not even recall that he or she has children. Hygiene may be poor and appearance slovenly because the person forgets to bathe or how to dress adequately. Dementia patients also get lost, even in familiar surroundings.

dementia Deterioration of mental faculties—of memory, judgment, abstract thought, control of impulses, intellectual ability—that impairs social and occupational functioning and eventually changes the personality.

Various cognitive processes are impaired as well. Patients may have difficulty producing the names of objects and individuals. Speech becomes vague. They are unable to recognize familiar objects and have difficulty carrying out simple motor actions (e.g., waving good-bye) even though their motor functioning itself is not impaired.

Judgment may also become faulty, and the person may have difficulty making plans or decisions. The demented also lose their standards and control of their impulses. They may use coarse language, tell inappropriate jokes, shoplift, or make sexual advances to strangers. The ability to deal with abstract ideas, for example, discussing the political significance of a current news event, also declines. Disturbances in the emotions are common, including both flatness of affect and sporadic emotional outbursts. The course of dementia may be progressive (getting worse as time goes on), static, or remitting (getting better as time goes on), depending on the cause. Eventually, many with progressive dementia become withdrawn and apathetic. In the last stages of the progressive form of the illness, the personality loses its sparkle and integrity. Relatives and friends say that the person is just not himself or herself anymore. Social involvement with others becomes more and more limited. In the end, the person is oblivious to his or her surroundings.

The prevalence of definite cases of dementia in the aged has been estimated at approximately 2% to 5% among noninstitutionalized adults, and another 2% to 3% is added when considering the institutionalized aged (Folstein, Bassett, Anthony, Romanoski and Nestadt, 1991; Gurland & Cross, 1982). Only a small proportion of persons under age sixty suffer from dementia, but approximately 30% of people over the age of eighty do (Heston & White, 1991; LaRue, Dessonville, & Jarvik, 1985).

Causes of Dementia

There are many possible causes of dementia. The most common, Alzheimer's disease, accounts for 50% of dementia in the elderly. It is usually referred to as dementia of the Alzheimer's type (DAT), because a definitive diagnosis can be made only by microscopic examination of the brain tissue after death. When the person is alive, a diagnosis of Alzheimer's is made by exclusion, that is, by ruling out other possible causes of the person's symptoms.

Alzheimer's disease A *dementia* involving a progressive atrophy of cortical tissue and marked by concentration and memory impairment, disorientation, and progressive intellectual deterioration.

In **Alzheimer's disease** the brain tissue irreversibly deteriorates. On average, women die four years, and men three, after diagnosis of Alzheimer's disease. Some evidence of symptoms precedes formal diagnosis by an average of four or five years (Ernst & Hay, 1994). About 100,000 Americans die each year from the disease. As of 1991 it was estimated that 1.35 million elderly Americans had Alzheimer's disease (Ernst & Hay, 1994). The disorder is somewhat more prevalent among women than among men. The disease was first described by the German neurologist Alois Alzheimer in 1860. It starts with difficulties in concentration and memory for newly learned material. The individual appears absentminded and irritable. The person blames others for personal failings, and has delusions of being persecuted. Memory continues to deteriorate, and the person becomes increasingly disoriented and agitated.

The primary physiological change in the brain, evident at autopsy, is a general atrophy of the cerebral cortex as neurons are lost, particularly axons and dendrites rather than the cell bodies themselves (Kowall & Beal, 1988). The fissures widen and the ridges become narrower and flatter. The ventricles also become enlarged. Moreover, senile plaques—small, round areas consisting of the remnants of the lost neurons and amyloid, a waxy substance deposited when protein synthesis is disturbed—are scattered throughout the cortex (see Figure 15.1). Tangled abnormal protein filaments, neurofibrillary tangles, accumulate within the cell bodies of neurons. These plaques and tangles are present throughout the cerebral cortex and the hippocampus. The cerebellum, spinal cord, and sensory areas of the cortex are less affected, which is why Alzheimer's patients do not appear to have anything physically wrong with them until late in the disease process. They can walk around normally, and overlearned habits, such as making small talk, remain intact for some time so that in short encounters, strangers may not notice that there is anything amiss.

Although neural pathways that use different transmitters (e.g., serotonin, norepinephrine) deteriorate (Lawlor et al., 1989; Wester, Eriksson, Forsell, Puu, & Adolfsson, 1988), those using acetylcholine are of particular importance. There is evidence that anticholinergic drugs (which block acetylcholine activity) can produce in normal subjects memory impairments similar to those found in Alzheimer's patients. The number of acetylcholine terminals are reduced in the brains of DAT patients (Strong et al., 1991), and levels of the major metabolite of acetylcholine are low and are related to the extent of the patient's mental deterioration (Wester et al., 1988).

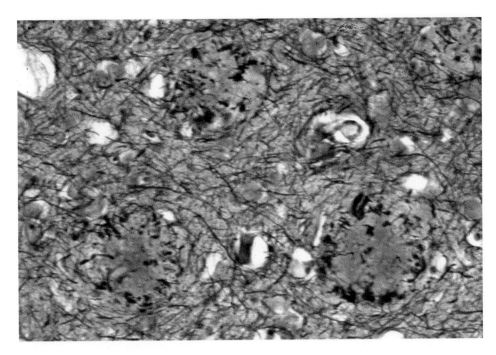

Figure 15.1 *Brain tissue from a patient with Alzheimer's disease. The waxy amyloid shows up in this photograph as areas of dark pink.*

In first-degree relatives of afflicted individuals, the risk for Alzheimer's is considerably higher than in the rest of the population (Mohs, Breftner, Silverman, & Davis, 1987), and among some families the pattern of inheritance suggests the operation of a single dominant gene. Furthermore, the gene that controls the protein responsible for the formation of plaques has been shown to be on the long arm of chromosome 21, and one linkage study has demonstrated an association between this gene and the expression of the disease (Tanzi et al., 1987). Although another linkage study did not confirm these results (Schellenberg et al., 1988), it involved patients of a much younger age. Therefore, early and late onset of Alzheimer's may have different causes (Nyth, Gottfries, Blennow, Brane, & Wallin, 1991; Small et al., 1989) and only a subset of cases of DAT may be genetically linked to chromosome 21.

Aluminum may play a role in some Alzheimer's type dementias. Animal research shows that aluminum can induce lesions such as those found in DAT and is present in excess quantity in the brains of DAT patients (Heston & White, 1991). Finally, the immune system may be involved. The amyloid found in the brains of patients with DAT is also present in other diseases in which the immune system plays a significant role. Some researchers have reported finding a novel antigen in the brains of DAT patients that could be attacking the brain (Bisette et al., 1991). However, we are far from understanding the causes of Alzheimer's.

Several infectious diseases can also produce irreversible dementias. *Encephalitis*, a generic term for any inflammation of brain tissue, is caused by viruses that enter the brain either from other parts of the body (e.g., the sinuses or ears) or from the bites of mosquitoes or ticks. *Meningitis*, an inflammation of the membranes covering the outer brain, is usually caused by a bacterial infection. The organism (*Treponema pallidum*) that produces the venereal disease syphilis can also invade the brain and cause dementia.

Other diseases that affect the brain, such as *Huntington's chorea*, can produce dementia as well. Huntington's is caused by a single dominant gene located on chromosome 4 and is diagnosed principally by the presence of writhing (choreiform) movements. Similarly, *Parkinson's disease*, marked by muscle tremors, muscular rigidity, and akinesia (an inability to initiate movement) can lead to dementia. It is the result of degeneration of the nigrostriatal pathway. In *normal pressure hydrocephalus*, an impairment in the circulation of the cerebrospinal fluid leads to an accumulation in the brain's ventricles (water on the brain). Pressure builds and cre-

FOCUS BOX 15.1

Cerebrovascular Diseases—Stroke and Its Aftermath

The blood vessels that supply the brain are subject to several types of malfunction. In atherosclerosis, deposits of fatty material narrow the lumen, or inner passageway, of the arteries of the body. When those in the brain are affected, some areas may receive insufficient blood and hence insufficient oxygen and glucose. If the shortage is prolonged, the brain tissue, which is particularly dependent on receiving adequate supplies, softens, degenerates, and may even be destroyed. The effects of cerebral atherosclerosis vary widely, depending on what area of the brain has clogged arteries and whether it is also supplied by nonaffected blood vessels. About three million Americans are presently incapacitated in some way by cerebral atherosclerosis.

In **cerebral thrombosis** a blood clot forms at a site narrowed by atherosclerosis and blocks circulation. Carbon dioxide builds up and damages the neural tissues. The loss of consciousness and control is referred

In recovering from a stroke, patients need therapy to help them regain lost skills such as fine motor control.

cerebral thrombosis The formation of a blood clot in a cerebral artery that blocks circulation in that area of brain tissue and causes paralysis, loss of sensory functions, and possibly death.

ates dementia as well as difficulty standing and walking. The condition is reversible with surgery to restore normal circulation of cerebrospinal fluid.

Dementias can arise from other diseases or conditions, some of which are reversible. Depression, particularly one that includes psychomotor retardation, is a significant cause (Heston & White, 1991). When the depression lifts, the dementia lifts also. Other causes of dementia include hormonal imbalances (e.g., hypothyroidism), drugs (including alcohol), vitamin deficiencies, and atherosclerosis (see Focus Box 15.1). In the case of atherosclerosis, *multi-infarct dementias* (also called vascular dementias) develop gradually and have a variable course (brain tissue can partially recover from the damage caused by a series of small strokes). The specific symptoms of multi-infarct dementia depend on whether the infarcts affect the cerebral cortex or subcortical areas. Various infections (e.g., pneumonia, infections of the urinary system) can result in dementia. HIV infection and AIDS can cause irreversible dementia, though this kind of brain damage is usually associated with younger people.

Treatment of Dementia

If the dementia has a reversible cause, appropriate medical treatment should begin immediately, for example, to correct a hormonal imbalance. To date no clinically significant treatment has been found for Alzheimer's disease. It is a degenerative disease, resulting in continued deterioration of the patient.

to as apoplexy, or **stroke**. The patient may suffer paralysis or decreased sensation on one side of the body or on an arm or leg, lose other motor and sensory functions, or die. The impairments of the patients who survive may disappear spontaneously, or they may be lessened through therapy and determined effort. Usually there is some residual damage. When only a small vessel is suddenly blocked, the patient suffers transient confusion and unsteadiness. A succession of these small strokes brings cumulative damage, however.

In **cerebral hemorrhage** a blood vessel ruptures because of a weakness in its wall, damaging the brain tissue on which the blood spills. Cerebral hemorrhages are frequently associated with hypertension. The psychological disturbance produced depends on the size of the vessel that has ruptured and on the extent and the location of the damage. Often the person suffering a cerebral hemorrhage is overtaken suddenly and rapidly loses consciousness. When a large vessel ruptures, the person suffers a major stroke. All functions of the brain are generally disturbed—speech, memory, reasoning, orientation, and balance. The person usually lapses into a coma, sometimes with convulsions, and may die within two to fourteen days. If the person survives, he or she will probably have some paralysis and difficulties with speech and memory, though in some cases appropriate rehabilitation restores nearly normal functioning.

A frequent impairment is **aphasia**, a disturbance of the ability to use words. The cause of this damage may be a clot in the middle cerebral artery that supplies the parietotemporal region, usually of the dominant cerebral hemisphere. A right-handed person depends on the parietotemporal region in the left hemisphere for language skills; a left-handed person may depend on this region in the right hemisphere or in the left.

---

stroke A sudden loss of consciousness and control followed by paralysis; caused when a blood clot obstructs an artery or by hemorrhage into the brain when an artery ruptures.

cerebral hemorrhage Bleeding onto brain tissue from a ruptured blood vessel.

aphasia The loss or impairment of the ability to use language because of lesions in the brain.

Because of the death of brain cells that secrete acetylcholine in DAT, various studies have attempted to increase the levels of this neurotransmitter. Research using choline (a precursor of the enzyme that catalyzes the reaction producing acetylcholine) and physostigmine (a drug that prevents the breakdown of acetylcholine) have been disappointing. Tetrahydroaminoacridine (THA), which also prevents the breakdown of acetylcholine, has yielded positive effects on short-term memory, but it is not known if any longer-term benefits will be produced (Heston & White, 1991). In March 1993, the Food and Drug Administration approved the marketing of the drug, also known as tacrine, in recognition of the lack of promising alternatives in the treatment of this fatal disease. Long-term strategies focus on slowing the progression of the disease. Growth factors and other drugs that prevent alterations in cell metabolism offer hope of actually preventing neural degeneration (Whitehouse, 1991), underscoring the importance of ongoing efforts to develop tests for early detection of Alzheimer's. Management of other symptoms of DAT includes many of the drugs previously discussed, for example, phenothiazines for paranoia, diazepine for anxiety, and sedatives for sleep difficulties.

Counseling the impaired person is difficult and, with the more severely deteriorated, of apparently little long-term benefit because of their cognitive losses. But some patients seem to enjoy and be reassured by occasional conversations with professionals and with others not directly involved in their lives. It is important not to discount entirely their ability to participate in discussions of ways to cope with the problems they face, although their inherent cognitive limitations must be appreciated. In many ways it is unwise to get patients to admit to their problems, for their denial may be the most effective coping mechanism available (Zarit, 1980).

Perhaps the most heartrending decision is whether or when to institutionalize the impaired person. At some point the nursing needs may become so onerous and the mental state of the person so deteriorated that placement in a nursing home is the only realistic option, for the benefit not only of the person but of the family. The conflicts encountered in making this decision are substantial. The counselor can provide information about nearby facilities as well as support for making and implementing the decision (Zarit, 1980).

Treating Caregivers and Family Members. Caring for a person with Alzheimer's disease is especially stressful (Anthony-Bergstone, Zarit, & Gatz, 1988). Alzheimer's patients in the early stages may benefit from psychotherapy with respect to coming to terms with their disease, but it is their families for whom psychological treatment is most beneficial. For every individual with a severely disabling dementia living in an institution, there are two living in the community (Gurland & Cross, 1982), usually supported by a spouse, daughter, or other family member. Adult children and spouses caring for their demented parents or spouses have a far greater chance of becoming clinically depressed and anxious than do noncaregivers (Dura, Stukenberg, & Kiecolt-Glaser, 1991; Schulz & Williamson, 1991). Studies have also found more physical illness (Haley, Levine, Brown, Berry, & Hughes, 1987; Potashnik & Pruchno, 1988) and decreased immune functioning (Kiecolt-Glaser et al., 1991) among them. In many instances the disorders seem to be attributable to the stresses of caregiving. Prior to these challenges, the families of caregivers usually did not experience psychological difficulties (Gatz, Bengston, & Blum, 1990). The severity of the patient's memory loss and other problems, the family's or caregiver's sense of isolation or

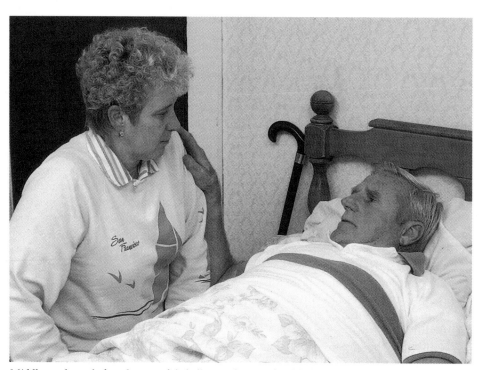

Middle-aged people face the stressful challenge of caring for elderly parents, often at the same time that they have young children of their own.

lack of social support, and financial concerns during the long, debilitating, and often expensive illness all increase the likelihood that depression and anxiety will occur.

A critical goal of psychological treatment of caregivers is to support them so that they can be as effective as possible in continuing to help the demented patient. One important method of providing this support is to furnish caregivers a chance to discuss the illness, its practical consequences, and its emotional consequences for all concerned (Zarit, 1980).

Another form of support for caregivers is accurate information on the nature of the patient's problems (Zarit, 1980). For example, because people with Alzheimer's have great difficulty placing new information into memory, they can engage in a reasonable conversation but forget a few minutes later what has been discussed. A caregiver may become impatient unless he or she understands that this impairment is to be expected because of the underlying brain damage.

Families can be taught how to help their relatives cope with lost functions. It is much easier for the elderly patient with dementia to respond to "Was the person you just spoke to on the phone Harry or Tom?" than to "Who just called?" Labels on drawers, appliances, and rooms also help orient them. If the individual has lost the ability to read, pictures can be used instead of verbal labels. Prominent calendars, clocks, and strategic notes can also help, as can an automatic dialer on a telephone.

Therapy for caregivers emphasizes safety issues as well. Patients do not always appreciate their limitations and may attempt to engage in activities beyond their abilities, sometimes in a dangerous manner. Although it is not advisable for families to coddle patients, it is important for them to set limits in light of the demented person's obliviousness to his or her own problems and impairments.

Sometimes, however, it is the caregiver's reactions to the patient's problems that require attention. In one case, the daughter-in-law of a woman was offended by the woman's color combinations in clothing and wished to take over responsibility for coordinating her wardrobe, even though the patient was capable of dressing herself adequately. The caregiver was urged not to impose her standards and taste on the patient, and to understand that her ability to dress herself

The task of caring for demented patients often falls on their families, who themselves need support and information on how to cope.

Providing memory aids is one way of combating the severe memory loss of dementia.

delirium   A state of great mental confusion in which consciousness is clouded, attention cannot be sustained, and the stream of thought and speech is incoherent. The person is disoriented, emotionally erratic, restless or lethargic, and often has illusions, *delusions*, and *hallucinations*.

and to take responsibility for her clothes was more important than adherence to conventional standards of fashion (Zarit, 1980).

Thus, different caregivers' needs differ. One issue is how long the person has been caring for the impaired relative. Treatment of depressed caregivers with highly structured cognitive and behavioral methods was especially effective for those who had had at least three and a half years of caregiving experience. Conversely, those who had been caregivers for less time obtained more benefit from psychodynamic therapy (Gallagher-Thompson & Steffen, 1994). Perhaps people who become depressed early in the caregiving process may be responding to a sense of loss as they anticipate the future of their relationship with a deteriorating spouse or parent. Psychodynamic therapy for caregivers focuses on this sense of loss as well as any unresolved conflicts in the relationship between the caregiver and the patient. Conversely, people who become depressed after several years of caregiving may be in effect worn out from the ongoing strains of taking care of a very needy patient. Cognitive and behavioral methods help such caregivers find practical ways to manage their own moods and thus cope better with the extraordinarily difficult and emotionally draining job of caregiving.

Delirium

Delirium is a state of severe mental confusion. The term **delirium** is derived from the Latin words *de,* "from" or "out of," and *lira,* "furrow" or "track." The term thus implies being off track, or deviating from the individual's usual state (Wells & Duncan, 1980). Between one-third and one-half of all the hospitalized elderly are likely to be delirious at some point during their stay (Lipowski, 1983), indicating that delirium is a serious health problem for older adults. There is a high rate of mortality among delirious patients, either from the underlying condition or from exhaustion (Rabins & Folstein, 1982). In fact, the fatality rate over a one-year period is higher for delirium (37.5%) than for dementia (16%).

Clinical Description

Delirium is typically described as a "clouded state of consciousness." The patient, sometimes rather suddenly, has great trouble concentrating and cannot maintain a coherent and directed stream of thought. In the early stages of delirium, the person is frequently restless, particularly at night. The sleep–waking cycle becomes disturbed so that the person is drowsy during the day and awake, restless, and agitated during the night. The individual is generally worse during sleepless nights and in the dark. Vivid dreams and nightmares are common.

Delirious patients may be impossible to engage in conversation because of their wandering attention and fragmented thinking. Words are slurred, or they have difficulty finding them, and handwriting and spelling may become impaired. In severe delirium, speech is sparse or pressured and incoherent. Bewildered and confused, delirious individuals may become disoriented for time, place, and sometimes for person. Very often they are so inattentive that they cannot be questioned about orientation. In the course of a twenty-four-hour period, however, they do have lucid intervals and become alert and coherent. These fluctuations help distinguish delirium from other syndromes, especially dementia, which has no such fluctuation.

Delusions and Hallucinations.   Perceptual disturbances are common in delirium. Individuals mistake the unfamiliar for the familiar. For example, they state that they are in a hotel instead of a hospital, and see the attending nurse as a room clerk. Moreover, they may see objects as too small, too big, misshapen, or duplicated. Although illusions and hallucinations are common, particularly visual and mixed visual-auditory ones, they are not always present in delirium. Paranoid delusions have been noted in 40% to 70% of the delirious aged. These delusions tend to be poorly worked out, fleeting, changeable, and tied to the surroundings.

Emotional and Behavorial Symptoms. Accompanying their disordered thoughts and perceptions are swings in activity and mood. Delirious people can be erratic, ripping their clothes one moment and sitting lethargically the next. They may shift rapidly from one emotion to another. Fever, flushed face, dilated pupils, rapid tremors, rapid heartbeat, elevated blood pressure, and incontinence are also common. If the delirium proceeds, the person completely loses touch with reality and may become stuporous (Lipowski, 1983; Strub & Black, 1981).

Frequent Misdiagnosis.   The accurate diagnosis of delirium and its differentiation from conditions that resemble it are obviously critical to the welfare of older persons, yet it appears that it is frequently overlooked as a diagnosis. One study found that of 133 consecutive admissions to an acute medical ward, there were fifteen cases of delirium, but only one of these had been detected by the admitting physician (Cameron, Thomas, Mulvhill, & Bronheim, 1987). Older adults are frequently mistaken for senile, and therefore beyond hope. A decision for long-term institutional care is all too often viewed as the only sound one, despite the fact that the person may have a reversible condition. The older adult who has cognitive impairment must be examined thoroughly for all possible reversible causes of the disorder, such as drug intoxication, infection, fever, malnutrition, and head trauma, and then treated accordingly.

Causes of Delirium

Delirium in the aged can be the result of any one or a combination of several general causes: drug intoxication, metabolic and nutritional imbalance, infection or fever, neurological disorder, or the stress of a change in the person's surroundings (Habot & Libow, 1980; Lipowski, 1980). It may also occur following major surgery. It is especially common after hip surgery (Gustafson et al., 1988), and

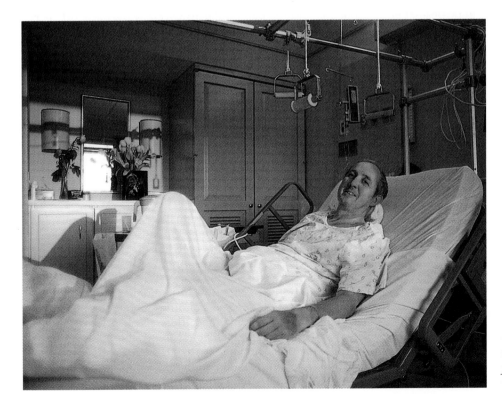

Delirium can result from major surgery such as the hip replacement from which this man is recuperating.

delirium predicts poor outcome in these cases. Delirium was the strongest predictor of death in the following month in a study of elderly Medicare patients admitted to nursing homes following a hip fracture. Relative to patients who were not disoriented at admission, delirious patients were nearly four times as likely to die and only one-third as likely to be able to return home within a month (Kiel, Eichorn, Intrator, Silliman, & Mor, 1994).

Delirium can occur during drug withdrawal or following head trauma or seizures. Common physical illnesses that cause delirium in this age group include congestive heart failure, pneumonia, urinary tract infection, cancer, uremia, malnutrition, dehydration, and cerebrovascular accidents or strokes. Probably the single most frequent cause of delirium in the aged is intoxication with prescription drugs (Lipowski, 1983). In most cases, however, the delirium has more than one cause (Sloane, 1980).

Although delirium usually develops swiftly, within a matter of hours or days, the speed of onset depends on the cause. Delirium resulting from a toxic reaction or concussion has an abrupt onset. When infection or metabolic disturbance underlies delirium, the onset of symptoms is gradual.

Why are the elderly especially vulnerable to delirium? Many explanations have been offered: the physical declines of aging, the increased general susceptibility to chronic diseases, the many medications prescribed for older patients, and vulnerability to stress. One other factor, brain damage, increases the risk of delirium. The elderly with dementing disorders appear to be the most susceptible of all. A retrospective review of one hundred hospital admissions of people of all ages who had a diagnosis of delirium revealed that 44% had a delirium superimposed on another brain malfunction (Purdie, Honigman, & Rosen, 1981).

Treatment of Delirium

As already indicated, complete recovery from delirium is possible if it is correctly identified and the underlying cause promptly and effectively treated. Generally, the condition takes one to four weeks to clear, although it takes longer in the elderly than in the young. If the underlying cause is not treated, however, the brain can be permanently damaged and the patient may die.

One often neglected aspect of the care of delirium is educating the family of a demented patient to recognize the symptoms of delirium and its reversible nature. They may interpret the onset of delirium as a new stage of a progressive dementing condition. For example, a patient with Alzheimer's disease may run a high fever from an internal infection and begin to hallucinate and otherwise act bizarrely. These new symptoms, superimposed on the intellectual deterioration to which members of the family have become accustomed, may alarm them into concluding that the patient is losing ground fast and irreversibly. Proper diagnosis and treatment, however, can usually return the person to the earlier state.

To Recap

In dementia the person's intellectual functioning gradually declines; memory, language, abstract thinking, and judgment deteriorate. Eventually the patient seems like a different person altogether and in the end is oblivious to her or his surroundings. A variety of diseases can cause dementia. Among the most prominent is Alzheimer's disease, in which cortical cells waste away.

In delirium there is sudden clouding of consciousness and other problems in thinking, feeling, and behaving—fragmented and undirected thought, incoherent speech, inability to sustain attention, hallucinations, illusions, disorientation, lethargy or hyperactivity, and mood swings. Delirium is reversible if the underlying cause is self-limiting or is identified and adequately treated. Possible causes include overmedication, congestive heart failure, high fevers, nutritional imbalances, head trauma, and cerebrovascular accidents or strokes.

If delirium is suspected, there should be a search for the cause so that the condition can possibly be reversed. Dementia usually cannot be treated, but the patient and his or her family can be counseled on how to make the patient's remaining time manageable and even rewarding.

Old Age and Psychological Disorders

Older adults often believe that their aging body is the source of all problems. The same is true for others' explanations of elders' problems. The most obvious characteristic of a seventy-five-year-old man is that he is old. If he is cranky, it is because he is old. If he is depressed, it is because he is old. Even when he is happy, it is assumed to be because of his age. Moreover, the old-age explanation is generally a somatic one, even if this is not made explicit. Some ill-defined physical deterioration is assumed to underlie not only the physical problems of old people but all their psychological problems as well.

Although a psychological disorder at any age may have at least a partial physical explanation, this explanation can be problematic with older adults because it can blind us to other important causes. Most psychopathology found in the aged has *not* been directly linked to the physiological processes of aging. Whether the person brings maladaptive personality traits and inadequate coping skills into old age plays a role, as do health, genetic predisposition, and life stressors. With these considerations in mind, we will first look at how common mental disorders are in late life and then describe several of them as they appear in old age.

Overall Prevalence of Mental Disorders in Late Life

The DSM criteria for various disorders are basically the same for older adults as for younger ones. The manifestations of mental disorders are apparently assumed to be the same in adulthood and in old age, even though little research supports this assumption (LaRue et al., 1985). We often do not know what certain symptoms of older adults mean because we have few specifics about psychopathology in the elderly (Zarit, Eiler, & Hassinger, 1985). For example, complaints about aches and pains are generally more prevalent in late life, but these symptoms are also evident in depression in older adults. Are the somatic symptoms of a depressed older adult necessarily a part of depression? Or might they (also) reflect physical decline?

Comprehensive and systematic research on the incidence and prevalence of various psychiatric disorders in late adulthood is just beginning (LaRue et al., 1985). Current prevalence rates indicate that persons over age sixty-five have the lowest overall rates of all age groups when the disorders are grouped together. For example, schizophrenia is extremely rare in people in the upper age ranges. The primary problem of old age is *cognitive impairment*. In the National Institute of Mental Health (NIMH) study mentioned in Chapter 1, rates for mild cognitive impairment were about 14% for elderly men and women; rates for severe cognitive impairment were 5.5% for men and 4.7% for women (Myers et al., 1984). These rates tell us only the overall prevalence of cognitive impairment in the aged, not whether the causes were reversible or irreversible. As we have seen, this is an important issue.

The majority of persons sixty-five years of age and older are free from serious psychopathology, but 10% to 20% do have psychological problems severe enough to warrant professional attention (Gurland, 1991). Although many psychological disorders become less prevalent as we age, depression, substance abuse, and sexual dysfunction can develop partly as a consequence of aging—as was illustrated in the case of Helen Kay.

Depression

Mood disorders in general are less common in older adults than in younger adults (Eaton et al., 1989; Regier et al., 1988); major depression is much more common in the elderly than is bipolar depression (Regier et al., 1988). For this reason, our discussion addresses only major depression in older adults.

Depression in older adults is somewhat different from that in younger adults. The depressed elderly are less likely to feel guilt, but more likely to voice somatic complaints, as illustrated in the case of Helen Kay with which this chapter began. Also, older depressed patients show greater motor retardation, more weight loss, and more of a general physical decline. While hostility is often part of depression in younger adults, this is less the case in the elderly. Finally, memory complaints—not necessarily actual memory problems—are more common in older than in younger depressed individuals (O'Connor, Pollitt, Roth, Brook, & Reiss, 1990).

Sources of Depression in the Aged

As might be expected, many aged in poor physical health are depressed. In one study, 44% of people with depressive symptoms were found to be medically ill (Blazer & Williams, 1980). Physicians who care for elderly medical patients are often insensitive to the likelihood of depression coexisting with physical illnesses and therefore are likely to fail to diagnose and treat the psychological condition (Rapp, Parisi, & Walsh, 1988). This oversight can worsen not only the depression, but the medical problem itself.

Physical illness and depression are linked for reasons other than the disheartening aspects of an illness. Medications prescribed to treat a chronic condition can cause a depression to start or can aggravate a depression that already exists (Klerman, 1983). The drugs most likely to do this are antihypertensive medications. Hormones, corticosteroids, and antiparkinsonian medications may also affect mood. On the other side of the coin, individuals who are already depressed may be predisposed to develop physical illness (Vaillant, 1979).

Few older people appear to develop a disabling depressive illness following an expected loss of a loved one. Longitudinal studies have found relatively low rates of depression in the bereaved, and the symptoms of depression in bereft individuals are generally less severe and fewer than are those in individuals institutionalized for depression (Gallagher, Breckenridge, Thompson, Dessonville & Amaral, 1982). Similarly, though retirement has also been assumed to have negative consequences for a person, research does not generally support this assumption (Atchley, 1980). Any ill effects of retirement may have to do with the poor health and low incomes of some retirees. Each older person brings to late life a developmental history that makes his or her reactions to common problems unique. The person's coping skills and personality determine how effectively he or she will respond to new events (Butler & Lewis, 1982).

Treatment of Depression

Cognitive, behavioral, and brief psychodynamic psychotherapies have all been found equally effective for older depressed individuals (Gallagher & Thompson, 1982, 1983). A review of all forms of psychotherapy of depression in elderly people found the effectiveness of therapy to be virtually identical to the effects of psychotherapy for depression in younger adult samples (Scogin & McElreath, 1994).

The use of antidepressant drugs with older adults, however, is complicated by side effects. Some patients treated with tricyclic antidepressants become dizzy and fall when they stand up. There is also risk to the cardiovascular system, including the danger of a heart attack. Moreover, older people are at high risk for toxic reactions to medications generally. Since the efficacy of antidepressants with older adults is in question (Gerson, Plotkin, & Jarvik, 1988), psychotherapy for the depressed elderly is particularly important.

Sexuality and Aging

Bias against the expression of sexuality in old age and disbelief in the capacity for sex among older people have abounded in our culture. Men and women alike have been expected to lose interest in and capacity for sex once they reach their senior years.

The facts are that most older people have considerable sexual interest and capacity. This holds true even for many healthy eighty- to one-hundred-year-old individuals, the preferred activities being caressing and masturbation, with some occasions of sexual intercourse as well (Bretschneider & McCoy, 1988). As we review the data, it will be important to bear in mind that sexual interest and activity vary greatly in younger adults. Disinterest or infrequent sex on the part of an older person cannot necessarily be taken as evidence that older people are inherently asexual.

Contrary to the stereotypes, many older people maintain an active interest in sex. Studies indicate that the frequency of sexual activity among those in their seventies is as high as among middle-aged people.

> ## APPLYING CRITICAL THINKING SKILLS

AGING AND THE FREQUENCY OF SEXUAL ACTIVITY

How can we accurately assess the sexual behavior of the elderly? Early studies, such as the famous Kinsey reports (Kinsey et al., 1948; 1953), noted a decline in heterosexual intercourse, masturbation, and homosexual intercourse beginning around age thirty and continuing across the life span. A critical look at this research reveals some interesting variables that may have influenced these findings.

▶ **What conclusion does the evidence seem to support?** These data suggest that on average, sex becomes less important to people in their middle years and in old age. This interpretation describes an **age effect**, a consequence of being a certain age.

▶ **What other interpretations are plausible?** As we showed in Chapter 13, interpretation of data in sex research is not always simple. There are at least two alternative interpretations of these data. One is that at the time these studies were conducted, cultural attitudes toward sexuality among the elderly were repressive. Older adults were therefore less willing to discuss their sexual interests and activities with researchers (regardless of how sexually active they in fact were, i.e., regardless of whether there was any real age effect). This interpretation exemplifies a **time-of-measurement effect**, a possible confound in research whereby events at a particular point in time can affect the variable that the researcher wishes to study over time.

Another interpretation is that at the time of these early studies, older people were indeed less sexually active (not just saying so), but that this situation may have been unique to their generation, not a universal feature of human aging. They may have grown up during a time of widespread negative stereotypes about sexuality and aging. Or they may have been less physically healthy than old people are now. These possibilities describe **cohort effects**, the consequences of having been born in a given year and having grown up during a particular time period with its own unique pressures, challenges, and opportunities.

▶ **What other information would help choose between the alternative interpretations?** The two alternative interpretations highlight issues in aging research that have received considerable attention. In general, the easiest way to study aging is

age effect The consequences of being a given chronological age. Compare with *cohort effects*.

time-of-measurement effects A possible confound in *longitudinal studies*, whereby conditions at a particular point in time can have a specific effect on a variable that is being studied over time.

cohort effects The consequences of having been born in a given year and having grown up during a particular time period with its own unique pressures, problems, challenges, and opportunities.

Cohort effects refer to the fact that people of the same chronological age may differ considerably depending on when they were born.

cross-sectional study   A study in which different age groups are compared at the same time. Compare with *longitudinal study*.

to conduct a **cross-sectional study** comparing people of different age groups at the same time on the variable of interest. Unfortunately, this is also the most ambiguous research design. If, for example, seventy-year-olds differ in sexual behavior from thirty-year-olds in a cross-sectional study conducted in 1996, one cannot tell whether this result reveals (a) how humans change on average as they age from thirty to seventy (age effect), (b) how prevailing conditions in 1996 affect the measurement of sexual behavior differentially across age groups (time-of-measurement effect), or (c) how people born in the 1920s (and growing up during the Great Depression, World War II, etc.) differ from people born in the 1960s (cohort effect).

longitudinal study   An investigation that collects information on the same individuals repeatedly over time, perhaps over many years, in an effort to determine how phenomena change.

One way to clarify matters is to conduct a **longitudinal study**, in which researchers select one group of individuals and study them over time. In this manner it is possible to study change in the same people. A longitudinal study covering the years 1968 to 1974 (George & Weiler, 1981) indicated no decline in the sexual activity of people between the ages forty-six and seventy-one. In fact, 15% of older persons increased their sexual activity as they aged. This research suggests that the Kinsey findings of declining sexual activity with aging probably do not represent a pure age effect.

Physiological Changes in Sexual Response with Aging

Despite some of the problems just described, a good deal of useful research has been done on aging and sexuality. Among the volunteer subjects studied by Masters and Johnson (1966) were several older adults. We know a great deal about sexuality in older adults both from their physiological research and from later work (e.g., O'Donohue, 1987). There are wide individual differences in sexual capacity and behavior among older adults. The following sections describe differences found between older and younger adults.

Men.   Older men take longer to have an erection, even when they are being stimulated in a way they like. They can maintain an erection longer before ejaculating than younger men, however, and the feeling that ejaculation is inevitable may disappear. It is not known whether physiological changes or control learned over the years explains this. During the orgasm phase, contractions are less intense and fewer in number, and less seminal fluid is expelled under less pressure. Once orgasm has occurred, the capacity for another erection cannot be regained as quickly as in younger men. In fact, the refractory period begins to lengthen in men in their twenties (Rosen & Hall, 1984).

Older men are capable of the same pattern of sexual activity as younger men. The major difference is that for older men, things take longer to happen, and when they do, there is less urgency. Unfortunately, normal changes that occur with aging are often misinterpreted as evidence that older men are becoming sexually dysfunctional (LoPiccolo, 1991). If, for example, a man or his partner reacts with alarm to a slow buildup of sexual arousal, these performance fears may provoke sexual dysfunction.

Women.   Like younger women, older women are capable of at least as much sexual activity as are men. But like men, older women need more time to become sexually aroused. Vaginal lubrication is slower and reduced because estrogen levels are lower, and there may be vaginal itching and burning. Steroid replacement can reduce many of these symptoms and also help protect against osteoporosis, a disease that causes brittleness of the bones. There are risks to this treatment, such as developing endometrial (uterine) cancer. Vaginal contractions during orgasm are fewer in number compared with those of younger women. Spastic contractions of the vagina and uterus, rather than the rhythmic ones of orgasm in younger women, can cause discomfort and even pain in the lower abdomen and legs. Estrogen deficiency, which can be corrected, can change skin sensitivity such that caressing of the breast and having a penis inside the vagina may not feel as pleasurable as when the woman was younger (Morokoff, 1988).

Age-Related Problems.   Physical illness can interfere with sex in older people as it can in younger people. Because the elderly suffer from many chronic ailments, the potential for interference from illness and medications is greater (Mulligan, Retchin, Chinchilli, & Bettinger, 1988). This is particularly true for men. Any disease that disrupts male hormone balance, the nerve pathways to the pelvic area, or blood supply to the penis can prevent erection. Diabetes is one such disease, and it affects men and women similarly in terms of nerve damage and reduction of blood supply to the genitalia.

Tranquilizers and antihypertensive drugs can bring about sexual dysfunction, as can fatigue and excessive drinking and eating (Moss & Procci, 1982). Fears of resuming sexual activities after a heart attack or coronary bypass surgery have inhibited older adults and their lovers, but for most of them the fears are exaggerated (J. M. Friedman, 1978). The situation for patients with congestive heart failure, in which the heart is unable to maintain an adequate circulation of blood in the tissues of the body or to pump out blood returned by the venous circulation, can create a risk in intercourse, but less strenuous sexual activity is usually not a problem (Kaiser et al., 1988).

Although women experience fewer physical problems than men, they are subject to all the myths about aging women's sexuality (Gatz, Pearson, & Fuentes, 1984). The sexual activity of older women is sometimes less than that of older men because they lack a partner (Caven, 1973) or because, if they are married, their husbands may be older and have significant health problems.

Treatment of Sexual Dysfunction

Making the facts of sexuality in old age available to the general public and to health professionals is likely to benefit many older people. As with younger adults, a degree of permission giving is useful, especially in light of widespread societal stereotypes of the asexuality of seniors.

Some older people prefer not to be sexually active. For older adults who are experiencing and are troubled by sexual dysfunctions, indications are that they are good candidates for the type of sex therapy devised by Masters and Johnson (Berman & Lief, 1976), with particular attention to providing the kind of information we have just reviewed about normal age-related changes in sexual functioning.

As with younger adults, problems in a relationship or problems in general can be both a cause and an effect of sexual problems. The situation can be particularly complex with older partners, who must deal with transitions arising from retirement and illness. Many couples who have been together for decades encounter distress in their relationship for the first time in their senior years.

Delusional (Paranoid) Disorders

Paranoia is a general complaint of many elderly psychiatric patients (Pfeiffer, 1977). One study of geriatric inpatients found that 32% of them had paranoid symptoms associated with some other form of mental illness (Whanger, 1973).

> A sixty-six-year-old married woman claimed her husband sprayed the house with a fluid that smelled like "burned food." She complained that he sprayed the substance everywhere around the house, including draperies and furniture, although she had never seen him do it. She could smell the substance almost constantly, and it affected her head, chest, and rectum. She also complained that someone in the neighborhood had been throwing bricks and rocks at her house. In addition, she suspected her husband of having affairs with other women, whose footprints she claimed to have seen near home. (Varner & Gaitz, 1982, p. 108)

In addition to the distress experienced by the patient, paranoia may have a disturbing and immediate impact on others, often bringing angry reactions and contributing to a decision to institutionalize the older adult (Berger & Zarit, 1978). Assessments of eight hundred older patients at the Texas Research Institute of Mental Science for a period of five years revealed a 2% prevalence for outpatients and a 4.6% prevalence for inpatients (Varner & Gaitz, 1982).

Causes of Paranoia

Paranoia in the elderly may be the continuation of a disorder that began earlier in life. It may also accompany brain disorders, such as delirium and dementia. Paranoia may serve a function for the demented, filling in the gaps caused by memory loss. Instead of admitting, "I can't remember where I left my keys," they think, "Someone must have come in and taken my keys" (Zarit, 1980). Paranoid thinking has also been linked to sensory losses, in particular to loss of hearing. Older people with severe paranoid disorders tend to have long-standing hearing loss in both ears (Post, 1980). An older person who is deaf may believe that other people are whispering about him or her, so that he or she cannot hear what is being said. The person's paranoid reactions may be an attempt to fill in the blanks caused by sensory loss (Pfeiffer, 1977; Zimbardo, Andersen, & Kabat, 1981; Zimbardo, LaBerge, & Butler, 1993).

By explaining bewildering events, paranoid delusions are in a sense adaptive and understandable. Often the earlier social adjustment of paranoid patients has been poor. The onset of their symptoms may follow a period in which they have become increasingly isolated. And isolation itself limits a person's opportunities to check his or her suspicions about the world, making it easier for delusions to take hold.

Unrecognized hearing loss may lead some elderly people to conclude that others are whispering about them and therefore to the development of delusions.

In some cases the delusional ideas have a basis in reality. Older people may be talked about behind their backs, or even to their faces, as though they were not present, and they may be taken advantage of by others in many ways. There is thus a danger that a complaint of persecution from an older person will be quickly dismissed as a sign of late-life paranoia. An older client of one of the authors complained bitterly about being followed by a detective hired by her evil husband. Inquiry revealed that the husband was worried that she was having an affair and had indeed hired someone to follow her!

Treatment of Paranoia

The treatment of paranoia in older adults is much the same as it is in younger adults. Although controlled data are lacking, clinicians suggest that a patient, supportive approach is best. The therapist should provide empathic understanding of the person's concerns. Directly challenging the paranoid delusion or attempting to reason the person out of his or her beliefs is seldom effective. Rather, recognition of the distress caused by the paranoia is more likely to promote a therapeutic relationship with the patient. When the patient trusts and feels safe with the therapist, the delusions can gradually be questioned.

If the person has a hearing or sight problem, a hearing aid or corrective lenses may alleviate some of the symptoms. If the individual is socially isolated, efforts can be made to increase his or her activities and contacts. Regular supportive therapy may help the patient in reestablishing relations with family members and friends. Attention should be provided for appropriate behavior. Even if these straightforward measures do not relieve paranoia, they may be beneficial in other areas of the person's life. Delusions in the elderly can be treated successfully with phenothiazines (Post, 1980). Unfortunately, paranoid individuals are generally suspicious of the motives of those who give them drugs. Toxicity from medications must also be considered, given the particular sensitivity of older people to drugs.

Substance-Related Disorders

Alcohol Abuse and Dependence

Alcoholism is generally less prevalent in the elderly than in younger adults. In the NIMH Epidemiological Catchment Area study of one-month prevalence rates (Regier et al., 1988), only 0.9% of community-dwelling adults aged sixty-five and over were found to be abusing alcohol. This rate was much lower than for younger adults. More men than women had alcohol problems. Many problem drinkers do not survive to old age. The peak years for death from cirrhosis are between fifty-five and sixty-four years of age. Older people may also develop a physiological intolerance for alcohol, counteracting its positive effects on mood (Gurland & Cross, 1982).

It is believed that older alcoholics fall into two groups, the two-thirds or more who began drinking in early or middle adulthood and who continued their pattern into late life, and the small percentage who took to drink after age fifty (Rosin & Glatt, 1971). Alcoholics like Helen Kay, who started late, either had intermittent drinking problems in the past and now abuse alcohol regularly in late life or had no history of alcohol problems until their late years (Zimberg, 1987). The late-starting abuser is more likely to be separated or divorced, to live alone, and to have serious health difficulties (Schuckit & Moore, 1979). Age-related circumstances, such as retirement, may have provoked some of them to drink (Rosin & Glatt, 1971).

Though not all researchers support this distinction (Borgatta, Montgomery, &

Medication misuse is a serious problem among the aged and can cause delirium.

Borgatta, 1982), one conclusion that *can* be drawn from research is that alcoholism is not a self-limiting problem. If a person is a problem drinker in the younger years, chances are that he or she will remain so later in life (if the person lives that long).

As people age, their tolerance for alcohol is reduced, for they metabolize it more slowly. Thus the drug may cause greater changes in their brain chemistry than in that of the young and may more readily bring on toxic effects, such as delirium. Neuropsychological studies have shown that cognitive deficits associated with alcohol abuse are likely to be more pronounced in the aged alcoholic than in younger individuals with comparable drinking histories (Brandt, Buffers, Ryan, & Bayog, 1983). Although some intellectual functioning is recovered with abstinence, residual effects may remain long after the older person has stopped drinking.

Medication Misuse

Because they are more likely to use legal drugs (Warheit, Arey, & Swanson, 1976), the elderly are also more likely than younger adults to misuse them. The misuse of prescription and over-the-counter medicines is a much greater problem in the aged population than is drug or alcohol abuse (LaRue et al., 1985). Since all phases of drug intake are altered in the elderly—absorption, distribution, metabolism, and excretion—they are more likely to react adversely to medications even in normal doses and to experience side effects to a wide range of drugs.

Abuse of prescription or legal drugs can be deliberate or inadvertent. Some people may seek drugs to abuse, obtaining medications from several sources. Others may not take medications as they are prescribed, perhaps through misunderstanding, ignorance, or limited financial resources. An interview study of 141 well-functioning middle-class elderly people living in their own homes found that almost half reported having misused prescription or over-the-counter drugs at least once over a period of six months (Folkman, Bernstein, & Lazarus, 1987). The chance for misuse is believed to increase the greater the number of medications and the more complex the instructions. Dependence on medications can develop, particularly in anxious, depressed, and hypochondriacal older adults (LaRue et al., 1985).

People of any age need to understand why they are taking a drug, what it is called, when and how often they should take it, and under what conditions, for example, after meals, on an empty stomach, and so on. Their comprehension of the instructions should be tested. An older woman who had been given an antibiotics prescription that cautioned against taking it before or after meals came to the attention of one of the authors. She believed that this warning meant she could not eat at all while taking the medication!

Hypochondriasis

Older adults complain of a multitude of physical problems, among them sore feet and backs, poor digestion, constipation, labored breathing, and cold extremities. All are to be taken seriously by responsible health professionals. But some of the elderly only believe themselves to be ill and complain unendingly about aches and pains for which there are no plausible physical causes.

The prevalence of hypochondriasis is *not* greater in old age than at any other age (Siegler & Costa, 1985). The elderly as a group tend to *under*report somatic symptoms and often fail to seek help for serious illnesses (Besdine, 1980). Perhaps they are concerned about health care costs or perhaps they believe—probably with reason—that aches and pains are an inevitable part of aging and may not reflect a medical problem as such.

Longitudinal survey data indicate that health concerns remain fairly stable over the life span; since actual health *problems* do increase with age without accompanying increases in *concerns* about health, such data support the idea that people do not become more hypochondriacal as they get older (Costa et al., 1987). As Siegler and Costa (1985) stated, older persons who have many physical complaints have long-standing personality traits that predict such complaining. Their excessive somatic complaints appear to be associated with neuroticism or poor adjustment, which are not associated with age.

Insomnia

Insomnia is a frequent complaint among the elderly. One national survey found serious sleep disturbances in 25% of respondents aged sixty-five to seventy-nine, as compared with 14% in the group aged eighteen to thirty-four. Another 20% have less serious but still problematic insomnia (Mellinger, Balter, & Uhlenhuth, 1985).

The most common problems are awakening often at night, frequent early-morning awakenings, difficulty falling asleep, and daytime fatigue (Miles & Dement, 1980). These complaints have been found to parallel the physiological changes that occur normally in the sleep patterns of older adults (Bootzin, Engle-Friedman, & Hazelwood, 1983). For example, the total time that the elderly devote to sleep appears to be somewhat less than or the same as that of younger age groups. But sleep is more often spontaneously interrupted as people grow older. In addition, the elderly spend less absolute time in a phase known as rapid eye movement (REM) sleep, and stage 4 sleep, the deepest, is virtually absent. In general, elderly men appear to have more sleep disturbances than do women, a difference found to a lesser extent in young adults (Dement, Laughton, & Carskadon, 1981).

Causes of Insomnia

Besides the ordinary changes in sleep associated with aging, various illnesses, medications, caffeine, stress, anxiety, depression, lack of activity, and poor sleep habits may make insomniacs of older adults. Depressed mood—even in the absence of a full-blown mood disorder—has been shown to be related to sleep disturbances, especially early-morning awakening, in older adults (Rodin, McAvay, & Timko, 1988). Pain, particularly that of arthritis, is a principal disrupter of their sleep (Prinz & Raskin, 1978). Whatever the cause of insomnia at any age, it is worsened by self-defeating actions such as worrying about it and counting the number of hours slept and those spent waiting to fall asleep. Sleeping problems can also be worsened by medications used to deal with them, as noted next.

Older people sleep less than do young adults. There are also qualitative differences in sleep; elderly people wake up more during the night.

Treatment of Insomnia

The elderly are major consumers of sleep aids, yet these rapidly lose their effectiveness, and with continuous use, they may even make sleep light and fragmented. REM–rebound sleep, an increase in REM sleep after prolonged reliance on drugs, is fitful (Bootzin et al., 1983). Medications can bring about what is called a drug-dependent insomnia. These so-called aids can also cause drug hangovers and increase respiratory difficulties. Side effects of such tranquilizers as the benzodiazepines (e.g., Valium) include problems in learning new information—anterograde amnesia—and serious difficulties in thinking clearly the following day (Ghoneim & Mewaldt, 1990).

There is considerable evidence that sleep medication is not the appropriate treatment for the chronic insomniac of any age, but particularly not for the elderly insomniac. Still, sleep medications are prescribed for most nursing home residents. In many instances they are administered daily, even without evidence of a sleep disturbance (Cohen et al., 1983).

Nonpharmacological treatment of sleep disorders in the elderly has not been researched much (Bootzin & Engle-Friedman, 1987), but improvement is possible. Explaining the nature of sleep and the changes that take place as a normal part of the aging process can reduce the worry that older persons have about their sleep patterns, concern that itself can interfere with sleep. The therapist should also reassure patients that going without sleep is not a calamity. It will not cause irreversible brain damage or insanity, as some people fear. Some individuals are given relaxation training to help them fall asleep and instructions to help them develop good sleep habits. Such instructions include rising at the same time every day; avoiding activities at bedtime that are inconsistent with falling asleep, such as watching television and reading; lying down only when sleepy, and, if unable to go to sleep, getting up and going into another room. All these tactics can loosen the grip of insomnia in adults of all ages (Morin & Azrin, 1988).

Suicide

Several factors put people in general at especially high risk for suicide: serious physical illness, feelings of hopelessness, social isolation, loss of loved ones, dire financial circumstances, and depression (see Chapter 10). Because these problems are widespread among the elderly, we should not be surprised to learn that suicide rates for people over age sixty-five are high, perhaps three times greater than the rate for younger individuals (Manton, Blazer, & Woodbury, 1987).

Rates of suicide in white men increase sharply during old age, and rates for white women decline somewhat. Throughout the life span men have higher suicide rates than women, but the difference is most notable in the very old. Marked increases have also been noted among nonwhite men (Manton et al., 1987).

Older persons communicate their intentions to commit suicide less often than do the young and make fewer attempts. When they do make an attempt, however, they are more often successful in killing themselves (Butler & Lewis, 1982).

Intervention to prevent the suicide of an older person is similar to that discussed in Chapter 10 (p. 284). Generally, the therapist tries to persuade the person to regard his or her problems in less desperate terms. Mental health professionals, who are usually younger and healthier, may unwittingly try less hard to prevent an older person's suicide attempt. But even an older person, once the crisis has passed, is usually grateful to have another chance at life.

To Recap

Older people suffer from the entire spectrum of psychological disorders, but the overall prevalence of disorders appears to be lower than in younger age groups. Poor physical health makes geriatric depression more likely to occur. Symptoms of depression in the elderly center on somatic complaints more so than in younger depressed patients. Sexuality among the elderly has been the subject of much misinformation. Research suggests that most older people have considerable sexual interest and capacity, though there are characteristic physiological changes in sexual responding with aging. Physical illnesses and the medications taken for them are common causes of sexual dysfunctions found among the elderly.

Paranoia can be caused by dementia or delirium, or by a loss of hearing. An older person who is hard of hearing may believe that others are whispering about him or her so as not to be heard. Paranoid reactions then may be an attempt to explain this phenomenon. Other psychological disorders experienced in old age include substance abuse (especially medication misuse), hypochondriasis, and insomnia. White men are at increasing risk of suicide as they enter old age. Older persons in general are more likely to complete suicide if they attempt it than are young people.

The Case of Helen Kay Revisited

SOCIAL HISTORY

Helen Kay was the daughter of a well-to-do family from the Midwest. She had grown up in a small town and was popular with peers. She was successful enough in school to be admitted to Radcliffe.

Her college years were pivotal. Although subject to the sexism taken for granted in the 1920s, she nonetheless learned to value her own intelligence and drive, deciding—to her family's dismay—that she would forge a career for herself after college and not marry immediately.

But it was not just her ambition that characterized her college years. She found herself subject to occasional profound depressive episodes, some of them serious enough to have her roommates take her to the university health service. Nevertheless, she managed to cope well on her own, without formal therapy, and excelled socially and academically. After graduation she obtained a position with a prestigious literary magazine in New York. Her boyfriend, Harold Kay, visited her often. After his own graduation from law school, he got a job with a good firm in New York City, and two years later they married.

The marriage was a generally happy one. They had three children, all of them ultimately successful in their respective careers and lives; two careers, not a common occurrence at that time; considerable income from both their jobs; and reasonably good physical health. Three years after they married, they moved to Los Angeles, where Mr. Kay had received an offer from a noted law firm, and Mrs. Kay took an editorial position with a leading city newspaper. Mrs. Kay continued to experience episodes of depression, however. In general, she seemed to take inordinate responsibility for anything bad that happened to her children or to her husband, an approach to life that became particularly problematic when Mr. Kay developed a chronic illness.

Mr. Kay retired at the age of seventy-two. A cancerous lung was removed, but its removal did not halt the spread of the disease. In addition, Mr. Kay suffered from intellectual deterioration, diagnosed as dementia due to Alzheimer's disease, which progressed month after month. He was bedridden for the remaining three years of his life.

Against her children's wishes Mrs. Kay insisted on looking after her husband at home. Her depressions were more frequent now and frighteningly intense, accompanied by sleeplessness, poor appetite, and thoughts of suicide.

In one horrible moment of insight she acknowledged that her husband had no idea who she was or who he was and seemed to have little in common with the man to whom she had been married for more than 50 years. She had been warned of this aspect of Alzheimer's disease, yet she hated herself for having these thoughts. Who knows what is going on in his mind? she would ask herself. Surely he needs and appreciates my personal care each day and night. Family, friends, and Mr. Kay's own physician had been urging her for months to let Mr. Kay be hospitalized, but she could not bear the thought. She was finally persuaded to allow his hospitalization on the basis of medical needs that the physician insisted could not be met at home. One day later Mr. Kay died.

Although the death was hardly unanticipated, Mrs. Kay was devastated. At the funeral, she interrupted the minister's eulogy repeatedly with declamations of her responsibility for her husband's death. Mrs. Kay's son and daughter-in-law took her to live with them and their children, but she could not accept their hospitality comfortably. She complained at meals every day of what a burden she was to the family, and no amount of reassurance changed her mind. Ironically, her very act of complaining was the most burdensome aspect of her living with them. She began, several months after her husband's death, to beseech her son to find her a place where she could live on her own. He reluctantly did so.

Mrs. Kay moved into a spacious single room on the fourth floor of the Hotel Gregorian, "A Retirement Hotel for the Active Retired." At first she did well in her new surroundings. The other residents were mostly widows like herself. A few women befriended Mrs. Kay, finding her an intelligent and worldly woman. There were many stories to be told about going to college back East, working and living in New York, traveling with her husband, and about her children and grandchildren.

A few months after her arrival at the Gregorian, however, a change became evident. Mrs. Kay would sometimes come down to breakfast sullen and depressed. Deflecting inquiries about her health, she would eat quietly and then leave as soon as the meal was over, withdrawing to her room for most of the day and evening. Even more worrisome were her daily, almost furtive exits in the late afternoon, to return thirty minutes later with a paper bag. The strong odor of alcohol that one of the residents noted one day when she came to get Mrs. Kay for dinner confirmed the growing suspicion that she had begun drinking—heavily, regularly, and by herself—a habit she had developed during her husband's long illness.

CONCEPTUALIZATION AND TREATMENT

The first therapeutic task was to keep Mrs. Kay from dying. Her bizarre behavior in the emergency room of the hospital to which the police officer had taken her suggested delirium from a reversible malfunction of the brain. The examining physician made this diagnosis because of Mrs. Kay's obvious state of alcohol intoxication and because of her age. He also made the judgment that her diet might not have been adequate in recent days or weeks, given her disheveled appearance and the tendency for alcohol abuse and malnourishment to go together.

Her son's name and phone number were listed in her wallet. Within a few hours he arrived at the hospital and was at his mother's bedside. Mr. Kay wanted to take her home immediately and take care of her, but the doctor cautioned him about the danger she was in and the need to restore her to a normal state of brain function through withdrawal from alcohol and a proper diet.

Not yet known to the family was Mrs. Kay's intent when she left the hotel that evening with her bottle of scotch to get as drunk as possible and then walk as far as she could into the nearby surf and drown herself. When she came to her senses several days later to find herself still alive, she experienced the kind of shame and guilt often felt by people who have made an unsuccessful suicide attempt.

Mrs. Kay returned to the Gregorian two weeks after attempting suicide, having agreed to see a therapist regularly and to allow a social worker to check on her several times a week. Her therapist was a woman in her late forties. Dr. Gardner, a clinical psychologist, had devoted special study to the physical and psychological problems of older people.

Mrs. Kay described the reasons for her suicide attempt candidly. As the story unfolded, Mrs. Kay initially liked the retirement hotel because she knew she was no longer "bothering" her son's family and, in a more positive vein, she enjoyed the privacy and increased feeling of independence. The other residents of the hotel all shared some common experiences that could be discussed at meals and on other social occasions. However, after the initial positive period of a few weeks, her guilt about the death of her husband returned. It was only because he had worked so hard all his life that she could now afford to live out her life in these comfortable surroundings. She made no mention of her own contributions to the family's estate. If she had not been so selfish and weak, he would not have been hospitalized and allowed to die, alone among strangers.

Mrs. Kay had suffered a great loss. Selling her home to move in with her son's family engendered still further feelings that her life was getting out of control. Reality, then, was providing some reason to feel helpless and blue. But the conclusions Mrs. Kay drew from the facts seemed exaggerated and distorted.

The following transcript of part of one therapy session illustrates the kinds of discussions Dr. Gardner had with her client over a period of several months.

DR. GARDNER: We were talking last week about why your husband died.

MRS. KAY *(eyes cast downward)*: Yes, I was to blame for it.

DR. GARDNER: I understand you feel that way, Helen, but let's talk about other aspects of his illness some more. You said he'd had an operation six months earlier to remove a cancerous lung?

MRS. KAY *(sobbing):* Yes. . . . The only reason he got cancer was because of me.

DR. GARDNER: What do you mean?

MRS. KAY: He smoked a lot till he was almost sixty. When we first met he was smoking two packs a day. Of course, in those days, the 1920s, no one worried about cancer from cigarettes. Still, I never liked it and told him so. . . .

DR. GARDNER: Tell me, was it your fault that he had begun smoking in the first place?

MRS. KAY: Well, not really. . . . Well, I guess not, you see, he'd already been smoking for several years before we met.

DR. GARDNER: Okay, so you were not responsible for his taking up the habit.

MRS. KAY: I don't see how I could have been. But certainly I could have made him stop.

DR. GARDNER: Tell me.

MRS. KAY: What do you mean?

DR. GARDNER: Can you tell me how you could have made him stop? How did you fail him in those early parts of your relationship?

MRS. KAY: Well, I didn't mean to say I failed him or anything. I just . . . well. . . . *(Flustered.)*

DR. GARDNER: Oh, sorry. I must have misunderstood. I thought I heard you say or at least imply that you were responsible for his smoking.

MRS. KAY: I guess I did. I guess I have felt that way for a long time.

DR. GARDNER: Is it possible that *he* might have been the responsible one? Or is it possible that he was just addicted to the nicotine?

MRS. KAY: Yes, he tried [to quit] many times. But it didn't work, somehow. He seemed able to do most anything he set out to do, but that smoking was something he never could handle.

DR. GARDNER: So he tried, but he didn't make it.

MRS. KAY: No. But he was a good man.

DR. GARDNER: Of course. I agree a person can be good and still fail at things.

MRS. KAY: Now, doctor, are you making a point about me?

DR. GARDNER *(smiling)*: Well, now that you mention it, I guess I am.

Many more such discussions were held on issues such as the decision to hospitalize Mr. Kay the day before he died—before Helen could stop blaming herself for her husband's death. Gradually, Mrs. Kay admitted to herself that there were some things "even she" could not do, and that she could not reasonably blame herself for her husband's demise. Because the heavy drinking seemed to be due to her depression, no specific treatment was undertaken for this aspect of her problem. Nevertheless, Mrs. Kay was provided with some information on how a temporary state of delirium could be produced in an older person by excessive alcohol consumption. The psychologist also warned her about drug interactions.

Mrs. Kay had a total of thirty therapy sessions. After six months, she was reasonably comfortable and taking a more active interest than before in the many social functions available to older people in her community. She had also stopped drinking.

DISCUSSION

Life problems alone would not explain Mrs. Kay's depression. After all, most older people suffer losses *without* becoming profoundly depressed. The case material reveals a long tendency on her part to blame herself for negative events in her life and the lives of others close to her. She also insisted that she excel without help from others. In terms of Beck's cognitive theory of depression (Chapter 10), the schema she was operating in was one of self-deprecation and self-blame (A. T. Beck, 1967). This pattern was reflected in her tendency to construe as her fault unfortunate events, such as her husband's chronic cigarette smoking, his contracting lung cancer, and his dying in the hospital after her agreement to cease taking care of him at home. Her therapy was aimed at

LEGAL, ETHICAL, AND SOCIAL ISSUES

Loss of Control and Mindlessness in Nursing Homes

Lack of control over life circumstances may well be related to the deterioration in both physical and mental health often found in some of the elderly. Since we know that a perceived or actual lack of control leads to deterioration in adaptive behavior, at least some of what we regard as senility—the inactivity of elderly people and their poor adjustment to changing circumstances—may be caused by loss of control rather than by progressive brain disease (Langer, 1981). Indeed, the loss of a sense of effectiveness and control appears to have especially negative effects in the elderly (Rodin, 1986).

Ellen Langer points out that our society actually teaches the elderly—and sometimes the nonelderly as well!—that older adults are incompetent, or at least far less competent than they were before they became old. In our eagerness to help them, we seem to protect old people from having to make decisions that they might, in fact, be able to make. In our concern to protect them from physical harm, we arrange environments that require little effort to control. These practices, especially in a society that values competence and activity, do much to destroy an elderly person's belief that he or she is still effective and that life is indeed worthwhile.

The crucial problem in nursing homes is loss of opportunity to exercise control and personal responsibility (Langer & Rodin, 1976). In one study, patients were assigned a particular fifteen-minute period during

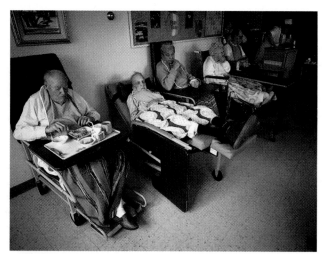

Nursing homes play a major role in the institutional care of the aged, providing for people with a variety of physical and psychological needs. They have often been severely criticized for the poor care they provide. While conditions and care can differ widely across dif-

ferent homes, advances in knowledge about the processes of aging have aided many homes in better meeting the needs of all their residents.

uncovering these unspoken beliefs, examining them openly, considering their validity, and offering other, presumably more realistic, ways of viewing events.

Mrs. Kay was lucky in many ways. Her son's family cared about her and remained willing to have her live with them. She had her physical health and was therefore less dependent on others for taking care of basic needs, such as dressing, eating, shopping, and so forth. She also had money, unlike many older people. She entered her senior years with a sharp, active mind and wide interests, which made her interesting to be around and probably contributed to her popularity in her retirement hotel. People in their eighties have usually outlived their friends and spouses, and new social contacts are often not as easy to make as was the case with Mrs. Kay.

which the nurse would be on call specifically for them, thus increasing each individual's control over his or her own caretaking. The health of these patients improved more than that of the control group, and they were more sociable (Rodin, 1980).

In another study, one group of residents was given a variety of decisions to make, instead of the staff's making decisions for them. They were also given plants to take care of. A control group was told how eager the staff was to take care of them and that the plants they were given would be looked after by the staff. Although initially matched on variables such as health, within three weeks members of the group given enhanced responsibility—and presumably a sense of greater control—tested superior on measures of alertness, happiness, and general well-being. Even more impressive was the finding eighteen months later that only half as many of the experimental group as of the control group had died, seven of forty-seven compared with thirteen of forty-four. Moreover, the group given responsibilities continued to show better psychological and physical health (Rodin & Langer, 1977).

Other research generally shows that people who feel in greater control actually do more things that enhance their health, such as complying with medical regimens, losing weight, and engaging in other self-care behaviors (Rodin, 1986).

Increased control is not positive under all circumstances and for all individuals, however (Rodin, 1986). With increased control comes more responsibility. Some people may convert this responsibility into self-blame when such an internal attribution is not warranted, for example, blaming themselves for a dementing illness caused by biological factors beyond their control. And if the actual environment is not supportive of increased efforts to exert control and assume responsibility, people are also likely to feel worse. With

this qualifier in mind, Judith Rodin concludes that health professionals as well as family members should look for ways to enhance control in older adults, including those in institutional settings such as nursing homes.

Not only may our treatment of old people engender in them a sense of lost control, but their repetitious, unchallenging environments—especially the surroundings of those who are hospital patients or who live in nursing homes—may encourage a mode of automatic information processing that Langer termed *mindlessness*. This mode of thinking is adaptive when people are in situations that recur frequently, for example, remembering a familiar sequence such as how to tie one's shoes.

The clinical implications of too much mindlessness are that the elderly may be afforded too few opportunities to be thoughtful and to maintain an alert state of mind. Because of the restricted mobility of nursing home residents and hospital patients and because little is demanded of them, their experiences tend to be repetitious and boring. The Langer and Rodin nursing home research may well demonstrate that conscious *thinking* per se as well as perceived control are essential in maintaining emotional and physical well-being. Accordingly, in a study of aged (average age of eighty-one years) nursing home residents, a three-month intervention teaching the practice of transcendental meditation, and to a lesser extent a simple program of mindfulness training (e.g., practicing thinking of unfamiliar uses for familiar objects), led to decreased anxiety and blood pressure, increased cognitive flexibility, and increased survival rates in the following three years. Control groups included a no-treatment condition and a passive relaxation condition lacking mindfulness training (Alexander, Langer, Newman, Chandler, & Davies, 1989).

General Issues in Treatment and Care of the Elderly

In spite of improvements in recent years, older adults still do not receive their just share of mental health services (Gatz, Karel, & Wolkenstein, 1991). This underservice is especially serious for minority and rural elderly. Why is there an apparent underservice to the mental health needs of older adults? One difficulty may be therapists' own expectations. Clinicians do not expect to treat the elderly as successfully as they treat the young (e.g., Settin, 1982). In one study older patients were rated by therapists as having more severe psychopathology, less motivation for treatment, a poorer prognosis, and less insight than younger patients (Karasu, Stein, & Charles, 1979). If the elderly are viewed as having limited possibilities for improvement, they may not be treated. Ironically, research does not indicate that older adults are any more reluctant to seek therapy (Knight, 1983) or any less likely to benefit from psychotherapy (Knight, Kelly, & Gatz, 1992; Scogin & McElreath, 1994) than their younger counterparts.

Most elderly people with severe chronic illnesses and mental disorders are cared for in nursing homes (Gatz & Smyer, 1992). Some of the psychological challenges faced in these settings are discussed in the Legal, Ethical, and Social Issues box. Other elderly people are seen in outpatient psychotherapy. Although generalizations are hazardous in view of the diversity of backgrounds and personalities among the elderly (Smyer, Zarit, & Qualls, 1990), there are a few common issues important to consider in the conduct of therapy with older people.

The incidence of brain disorders increases with age. As we have seen, though, other mental health problems of older adults are not that different from those experienced earlier in life. Although the clinician should appreciate how physical incapacities and medications may intensify psychological problems, consistency and continuity from earlier decades of the older person's life should be noted too.

The clinician must also bear in mind that the emotional distress of older adults may be a realistic reaction to problems in living (Zarit, 1980). Medical illnesses can create irreversible difficulties in walking, seeing, and hearing. Finances may be a problem, particularly for the older woman who lives alone. Older women suffer doubly as psychotherapy patients. Not only ageist, but also sexist, attitudes can negatively influence the direction of psychotherapy. For example, stress in an older couple can increase when the husband retires. A common therapeutic goal is for the woman to accommodate to the husband's loss of status and to learn to spend more time with him each day. But less often does the woman get to retire from her long-standing role as homemaker (Steuer, 1982).

The older person's worries about impending death are another realistic source of stress. Much psychological turmoil about dying can be reduced by encouraging the client to attend to such concrete details as a will, funeral or cremation plans, and the desirability of artificial life-support treatments sometimes applied in cases of terminal illness. Family members are wisely included in discussions, for their own concerns about death often influence their dealings with the old person (Zarit, 1980).

The technique of life review (R. N. Butler, 1963) seems to be a psychotherapeutic approach uniquely suitable for older adults (Knight et al., 1992). It reflects the influence of Erik Erikson's (1950) life-span developmental theory, which postulated stages of conflict and growth extending well into the senior years. Life review basically facilitates what appears to be a natural tendency of older adults to reflect on their lives and to try to make sense of what has happened to them. In Erikson's terms, it helps the person address the conflict between integrity, the feeling that one's life is whole and full, and despair. Methods include having the patient bring in old photographs, travel to a childhood home, and write an autobiography. This kind of therapy can cause people to feel worse as well as better. The therapist needs considerable skill to guide the patient to a positive view of life and to the coming end of existence.

An aspect of psychotherapy, regardless of theoretical orientation, that is highlighted by working with elders is reminiscent of the analytic concept of countertransference. Therapists, usually many years younger than these patients, can be troubled by the patients' problems. These patients' difficulties can touch on sensitive personal areas of their own, such as unresolved conflicts with their own parents, worries about their own aging process, and a reluctance to deal with issues of death and dying (Knight et al., 1992).

To Recap

Older adults have been underserved by the mental health professions, in part because therapists have held unwarranted negative expectancies about the usefulness of psychotherapy for the elderly. Many older people benefit from psychotherapy, but several issues specific to their treatment should be kept in mind. The emotional distress of the elderly sometimes stems from realistic problems in living (e.g., physical illness, financial problems, impending death) and should not automatically be attributed to psychopathology. It is also important for therapists to avoid letting their own concerns about aging interfere with the process of treatment. On the whole, outcome research suggests that the same systems of psychotherapy useful for younger adults are beneficial for older adults.

Visual Summary for Chapter 15:

Aging and Psychological Disorders

Psychological disorders of the elderly have historically received insufficient attention in part because of negative stereotypes about their responsiveness to treatment. This situation is changing as the elderly constitute a larger proportion of the population. Mental health issues regarding aging are becoming more prominent.

Brain Disorders

Disorder	Key Features	Possible Causes	Course	Treatments
Dementia	Deterioration of intellectual functioning, including memory, abstract thinking, judgment.	• Alzheimer's disease • Parkinson's disease • Vitamin deficiencies • Cerebrovascular diseases • Alcoholism • AIDS • Depression	Depends on cause. If dementia is caused by depression, for instance, it should improve when the depression lifts. If caused by Alzheimer's disease, it is irreversible and fatal (an average of about 8 years after symptom onset).	Again, depends on cause. If reversible, medical treatment may be rationally selected (e.g., correction of hormonal imbalance). For Alzheimer's disease, tacrine bolsters short-term memory, but in general only symptom management is possible. Psychological treatment is directed to caregivers to provide education, support, stress management, and a chance to discuss emotional reactions to changes in the relationship with the patient.
Delirium	Sudden clouding of consciousness, disorientation, confusion, mood swings, hallucinations.	• Drug intoxication • Infections or fevers • Dehydration • Aftermath of surgery	Usually rapid onset, within days; can show complete recovery in 1 to 4 weeks if treated effectively. Can be fatal if not.	Treatment is basically medical. The keys are recognizing delirium and systematically searching for the underlying cause.

Prevalence of Psychological Disorders in Old Age

- The elderly are less likely, overall, to have psychological disorders than are other age groups.

- Some disorders are less common than in younger adults (e.g., depression, alcohol abuse, schizophrenia).

- Cognitive impairment is much more common among the elderly.

- Several other problems (e.g., insomnia, paranoia, medication misuse) appear to increase with age as well.

- Completed suicide rates are also higher among the elderly.

Emergent Themes from the Review of Specific Disorders

- Diagnostic criteria are typically the same for the elderly as for younger adults, but there is not enough research yet to be sure that this observation is valid.

- Biological changes with normal aging, or illnesses correlated with aging, may be the sources of disorders (e.g., hearing loss can lead to paranoia, chronic illness to depression, diabetes to sexual dysfunction).

- The complete picture of physical and psychological difficulties and treatments must be considered for proper evaluation of a patient. One disorder may result from another (e.g., insomnia caused by the pain associated with arthritis) or even the intervention used in treating another (e.g., sexual dysfunction secondary to antihypertensive medication, delirium secondary to medication misuse).

- Focusing on interpersonal (e.g., stress and burden associated with caregiving) and societal (e.g., rampant ageism in Western cultures and attendant myths about the limitations of elders) contexts is critical to understanding and effective treatment of psychological disorders of the elderly.

- In many cases, disorders among the elderly reflect a continuation of problems from earlier in life; just because an aged person has a problem does not mean that aging caused the problem.

- Overall, elderly people are as likely to be interested in, and to benefit from, psychotherapy as are younger adults, though for some specific conditions (e.g., dementia) psychotherapy is not an adequate treatment.

Chapter 16

Issues in Intervention

Throughout our account of the various psychopathologies, we have considered the ways in which therapists attempt to prevent or reduce emotional suffering. Our descriptions in Chapters 2 and 3 of several perspectives on treatment—psychodynamic, biological, humanistic and existential, behavioral, and cognitive—covered the fundamentals of various approaches to this task. In Chapters 6 through 15, we learned that some forms of intervention are more appropriate than others for particular problems. For example, because of advances in our understanding of biological processes, new parents now have means to halt or at least reduce certain forms of genetically transmitted mental retardation. And through better understanding of the process of learning, retarded children now acquire more cognitive, social, and self-care skills than was formerly thought possible. Psychoanalytic theory helps therapists treat dissociative disorders, for it alerts them to the possibility that an amnesic patient, for example, cannot remember because the pain of certain past events forced them to be repressed.

In this concluding chapter we take a closer look at general issues in intervention. Psychological intervention can take many forms, including attempts to prevent problems from developing in the first place. Prevention represents an ideal for all the health professions, and as we will see, psychologists have made some progress in learning to prevent mental and even physical health problems. However, no foolproof mental health vaccines have been developed, so it remains important to study and improve the effectiveness of treatment techniques. The second section of this chapter attempts to broaden the picture of the field of psychotherapy painted by our discussion so far. We will consider how therapists may draw from several different perspectives in deciding how to help a given patient. Also discussed is the importance of considering whether a patient is a member of an ethnic minority group or whether the patient might be a couple, an entire family, or even a group of strangers. Finally, we end the chapter and the text with an overview of answers to perhaps the most basic set of questions one can ask about psychotherapy: How effective is it? Under what conditions is it most effective? How confident can we be of the answers to questions about the effects of psychotherapy?

▶ *Prevention and Community Psychology*

The movement known as **community psychology** places a great emphasis on preventing disorders. Though three types of prevention strategies have been distinguished (Caplan, 1964), community psychologists are primarily concerned with two of them: primary and secondary prevention. The third, **tertiary prevention**, seeks to reduce the long-term consequences of having a disorder and so is only modestly preventive. For example, mental health workers who help those who have recovered from mental illness to participate fully in the occupational and social life of the community are engaging in tertiary prevention, as they seek to prevent rehospitalization. **Secondary prevention** targets at-risk populations in order to help them lower the risk of actually developing a disorder. For example, community mental health centers might offer programs to help children whose parents have recently divorced to adjust emotionally to this stressor, with the aim of preventing more serious or chronic distress.

Finally, **primary prevention** involves attempts to reduce the incidence of new cases of disorders in a population. Such efforts are targeted at the currently well population, not just at those known to have problems or to be at unusually high risk for problems. Many primary prevention programs involve social and political efforts to improve living conditions. Another aspect of primary prevention particularly related to community psychology involves strengthening individu-

community psychology An approach to therapy that emphasizes prevention and the seeking out of potential difficulties rather than waiting for troubled individuals to initiate consultation. The location for professional activities tends to be in the person's natural surroundings rather than in the therapist's office.

prevention Primary prevention refers to efforts in *community psychology* to reduce the incidence of new cases of psychological disorder by such means as altering stressful living conditions and genetic counseling; **secondary prevention** applies to efforts to target at-risk populations in order to help them lower the risk of actually developing a disorder; **tertiary prevention** encompasses efforts to reduce the long-term consequences of having a disorder, equivalent in most respects to therapy.

Peer counseling groups for children of alcohol abusers exemplify a secondary prevention strategy in which at-risk individuals are helped in the hope of preventing severe disturbances.

waiting mode An approach to the delivery of therapy in which one treats only those who initiate the request for services.

seeking mode An approach to the delivery of therapy in which one seeks out those in need of services; found in *community psychology*.

als so that they can resist stress and cope with the adversity they face. Some examples of primary prevention measures include attention to neighborhood recreation, school curricula, prenatal care for mothers, and preventing child abuse.

Nearly all the therapies reviewed thus far are administered by professional persons with advanced degrees who make themselves available by appointment in offices, clinics, and hospitals. These professionals provide assistance to individuals who initiate the contact themselves or are referred by the courts. This method of delivery of services has been referred to as the **waiting mode** (Rappaport & Chinsky, 1974). In contrast, community psychology operates in the **seeking mode**. In other words, those who are troubled or are likely one day to be so are sought out by community workers, some of whom are paraprofessionals supervised by professionals. Mental health services are often provided outside offices and clinics, in the schools, businesses, and factories of the person's own community.

Part of the impetus for the community psychology movement was a practical one. In 1955 Congress authorized the Joint Commission on Mental Illness and Health to examine the state mental hospitals. On the basis of its six-year survey, the commission concluded that the care offered was largely custodial and that steps must be taken to provide effective treatment. Its 1961 report recommended that no additional large hospitals be built and that instead community mental health clinics be established. In 1963 President Kennedy sent a message to Congress calling for a "bold new approach," proposing the Community Mental Health Centers Act to provide comprehensive services in the community and to establish programs for the prevention and treatment of mental disturbances. The act was passed. For every one hundred thousand people there would be a **community mental health center (CMHC)**.

community mental health center (CMHC) A center for delivery of services to needy, underserved groups. Services include outpatient therapy, short-term inpatient care, day hospitalization, twenty-four-hour emergency services, and consultation and education for other community agencies, such as the police.

The principal objective of a CMHC is to provide outpatient mental health care in a person's own community and at an affordable cost. A twenty-four-hour walk-in crisis service offers emergency consultation around the clock and rap sessions for members of the community served by a CMHC. Another function of CMHCs is consultation and education. The aim is to educate other community workers, teachers, clergy, and police in the principles of preventive mental health and in how to extend help themselves.

In practice, CMHCs may have fallen short of their ambitious aims. As we saw in Chapter 9, the departure of many patients from psychiatric hospitals did not necessarily result in adequate care for them. CMHCs failed to fill the gap in services created by deinstitutionalization. Part of the problem has more to do with funding priorities than with what the CMHCs have done. In particular, fewer than eight hundred of the two thousand community mental health centers envisioned by Congress have been established. Moreover, CMHCs were based on a good set of ideas, but the implementation was sometimes poor (Holden, 1972). Often the centers were controlled by professionals whose training and outlook were tied to traditional one-to-one therapy. More recent data suggest a positive change in CMHCs. For example, child-oriented services show greater attention to specific pressing problems, such as prevention of child abuse (Jerrell & Larsen, 1986).

Selected Prevention Programs

CMHCs played an important historical role in the community psychology movement, but they are no longer at the leading edge of community psychology. Today community psychology is mainly concerned with primary and secondary prevention based on creating healthier institutions and social environments.

In this section we consider a few noteworthy examples of community psychology programs. We focus on projects whose effectiveness has been evaluated in research and on topics that give a flavor for the scope of this field.

Suicide-Prevention Centers

Many suicide-prevention centers are modeled after the Los Angeles Suicide Prevention Center, founded in 1958 by Farberow and Shneidman. There are now more than two hundred such centers in the United States. Staffed largely by nonprofessionals under the supervision of psychologists or psychiatrists, these centers attempt to provide twenty-four-hour consultation to people in suicidal crises. Usually the initial contact is made by telephone. The center's phone number is well publicized in the community. The worker tries to assess the likelihood that the caller will actually attempt suicide and, most important, tries to establish personal contact and dissuade the caller from a suicide attempt.

Most suicides give warnings before taking their lives (see Chapter 10), and many are ambivalent about living or dying (Shneidman, 1976). Usually their pleas are directed first to relatives and friends, but many potential suicides are isolated from these sources of emotional support. A hot-line service can therefore be extremely valuable in saving lives. However, a review of five studies on the effectiveness of suicide-prevention centers failed to demonstrate that suicide rates decline after the implementation of services (Dew, Bromet, Brent, & Greenhouse, 1987). By the same token, there is no indication that suicide prevention centers do harm, and the real possibility that they save lives justifies continuing support of them.

Suicide prevention centers provide hotline numbers for those in crisis to call at any time of day or night. Center staff and volunteers try to establish personal contact with the caller and help the caller pull back from the brink of suicide.

The Use of Media and Mass Education to Change Harmful Lifestyles

Cardiovascular diseases, such as high blood pressure and coronary heart disease, are responsible for more deaths in the United States than is any other single group of illnesses. In many respects the lifestyle of an affluent, industrialized society increases the risk of premature cardiovascular diseases. A group of researchers in the Stanford Heart Disease Prevention Program, led by Nathan Maccoby (Maccoby & Altman, 1988), developed and tested ways to educate large numbers of people about the desirability of altering their lifestyles to reduce their risk of cardiovascular diseases.

For the Three Communities Project they chose a media campaign and a direct,

Health fairs provide information and screening tests such as blood pressure and cholesterol assessments. Providing such information is part of community psychology's emphasis on prevention.

intensive, instructional program (Maccoby, Farquhar, Wood, & Alexander, 1977). Three towns in northern California were studied. Watsonville and Gilroy were the two experimental towns, and Tracy was the control town. For two years both experimental towns were bombarded by a mass media campaign to inform citizens about cardiovascular diseases. The campaign consisted of television and radio spots, weekly newspaper columns, and newspaper advertisements and stories, all urging people to stop smoking, exercise more, and eat foods low in cholesterol. Posters in buses and in stores conveyed briefly and graphically such vital information as the desirability of eating fewer eggs, since yolks are rich in cholesterol.

The control town, Tracy, had media services that were quite different from those of the two experimental towns. Tracy is separated from Watsonville and Gilroy by a range of low mountains and therefore had entirely separate local television stations. The inhabitants of Tracy were not imprisoned in their hometown for the duration of the two-year study, but for the most part they did not receive through their media the messages conveyed to the citizens of the two experimental towns.

The findings revealed that citizens of Watsonville and Gilroy significantly increased their knowledge of cardiovascular risk factors, whereas people in the control town did not gain in such knowledge. Egg consumption was reduced more in Watsonville and Gilroy than in Tracy. Clinically significant blood pressure decreases were observed in the two experimental towns, in contrast with small increases in the control town. Finally, the researchers considered the townspeople's overall measure of risk, a weighted average of the several known physical risk factors—high blood levels of cholesterol, smoking cigarettes, and not exercising enough—and found highly significant drops in risk in the people in the experimental towns.

> APPLYING CRITICAL THINKING SKILLS

INTERPRETING THE RESULTS OF COMMUNITY-WIDE PREVENTION EFFORTS

A follow-up experiment, the Stanford Five-City Project, built on the encouraging initial results of the Three Communities Project. The follow-up study exposed Modesto and Salinas, California, to extensive, interrelated health-education efforts. One aspect of this massive project was an attempt to reduce the prevalence of cigarette smoking. Over the first five years of the study (1980–85) prevalence of cigarette smoking among adults in these two cities declined about 1.5% per year.

> *What conclusion does the evidence seem to support?* It would appear that community-wide intervention can indeed lower the percentage of adults in an area who smoke cigarettes. Creative use of mass media, contests, work-site smoking-cessation groups, and the like all played a role in this public health effort.

> *What other interpretations are plausible?* Cigarette smoking was in decline during the early 1980s in the United States anyway (see Chapter 12). It may be that the educational efforts of the Stanford project researchers were irrelevant and that the decline in smoking prevalence noted in this study was simply a reflection of this general antismoking trend in the culture.

> *What other information would help choose among the alternative interpretations?* As we have seen throughout the text, control groups can help shed light on the meaning of the results of interventions. This is just as true of community-wide projects as it is of laboratory experiments in psychopathology or small therapy outcome studies. If comparable communities not exposed to the educational intervention show steady smoking rates, this would support the inference that the decline in smoking in Modesto and Salinas resulted from the intervention. If, instead, they showed the same decrease in smoking rates, it would suggest that smoking rates would have declined even without the special intervention.

The design of the Stanford project took this issue into account. Three control cities in California were not targeted for health education. These cities did show a decline in smoking prevalence during the study period, but only about one-half the decline in the experimental cities (Fortmann, Taylor, Flora, & Jatulis, 1993). Thus it appears that both interpretations of the basic findings are partly right. Some of the decline in smoking in experimental cities probably reflects a general historical trend, but some of the effect can be attributed to the intervention itself.

Competence Enhancement and Family Problems

The negative effects of nonsexual child abuse on perpetrators, the victim, and other family members make this another problem of considerable social and psychological importance. Several approaches to preventing child abuse have been studied (Rosenberg & Reppucci, 1985). One method emphasizes competence enhancement, that is, instruction in parenting skills so that the various challenges of child rearing are more familiar and less daunting. If parents know what to expect in child development—that contrariness and self-centeredness are normal in two- and three-year-olds, for example—they may react less negatively when their children act in these ways. Also, learning ways to cope with their children's behavior and to guide them in positive ways may help parents be less emotionally and physically punitive. Some programs utilize live or videotaped skits that model such skills (E. B. Gray, 1983, reported in Rosenberg & Reppucci, 1985). Results from several large-scale programs suggest positive attitudinal changes, but the actual impact on lessening child abuse has yet to be determined.

Better validation exists for secondary prevention efforts directed specifically at high-risk groups, such as teenage-mother and single-parent families. One such study (Olds, 1984, reported in Rosenberg & Reppucci, 1985) added regular visits by a nurse to other services during the child's first two years of life. Special intervention included parent education and enhancement of social-support networks. Results indicated that nurse-visited mothers had fewer conflicts with their children and punished them less. Most important, the frequency of child abuse and neglect was less than in the control group.

Children of divorced couples have also been targeted by community researchers in an effort to prevent, or at least to minimize, the adjustment difficulties they so often have. In one study, school-based groups of fourth, fifth, and sixth graders discussed common concerns in a supportive group atmosphere and learned useful skills such as anger control (Pedro-Carroll, Cowen, Hightower, & Guare, 1986). A subsequent program also involved some of the youngsters serving on an expert panel, fielding questions from peers about coping with their parents' divorce. Results generally demonstrated fewer classroom adjustment problems and lower anxiety levels as compared with control groups. What remains unexamined, in this and in most other prevention studies, is the degree to which they truly reduce the incidence of psychopathology. This is a tall order indeed, but perhaps the ultimate test of community psychology programs.

AIDS Prevention

AIDS (acquired immunodeficiency syndrome) A fatal disease transmitted by transfer of the human immunodeficiency virus, usually during sexual relations or by using needles previously infected by an HIV-positive person; it compromises the person's immune system to such a degree that he or she ultimately dies from cancer or one of a number of infections.

There is no greater public health threat today than **AIDS (acquired immunodeficiency syndrome)**. AIDS is a disease in which the body's immune system is severely compromised, putting the individual at high risk for opportunistic diseases, such as Kaposi's sarcoma, rare forms of lymph cancer, and a wide range of dangerous fungal, viral, and bacterial infections. Medical authorities suspect AIDS when an otherwise healthy person presents with an illness that he or she would not likely have with a properly functioning immune system. This typically fatal illness has two unique, interrelated characteristics that make it appropriate for discussion in an abnormal psychology textbook: (1) it is not presently curable or preventable by medical means; and (2) it *is* preventable by psychological means in that by changing one's behavior, one can prevent contraction of the AIDS virus.

First identified in 1981, AIDS has emerged as the most serious infectious epidemic of modern times. AIDS was first proclaimed in this country to be a disease of homosexuals. As of the late 1980s, almost 75% of AIDS patients were homosexual men, with intravenous drug users accounting for approximately 20%. Before blood screening began in 1985, many hemophiliacs received contaminated blood transfusions that ultimately resulted in their contracting AIDS. But AIDS is by no means a homosexual disease. Indeed, in Africa and parts of Latin America, AIDS is found primarily among heterosexuals, and throughout the world infected women are giving birth to babies who are HIV (human immunodeficiency virus) positive, for the virus can cross the placental barrier and infect the developing fetus.

Although millions are being spent on developing a vaccine against HIV, the focus is now squarely on behavioral science research and practice for prevention and control. The core of the problem is risky sexual practices, not sexual orientation. HIV is present only in blood, semen, and vaginal secretions and can be transmitted only when infected liquids get into the bloodstream. AIDS cannot be caught through casual social contact or even by living with an AIDS or HIV-positive person, provided that reasonable care is taken to avoid contact with blood. Unprotected receptive anal intercourse (i.e., having a penis inserted into one's anus) is the riskiest of sexual practices (Kingsley et al., 1987). Less risky but

Intervention programs in Africa have been successful in reducing the incidence of HIV infection.

still to be avoided in a nonmonogamous relationship is vaginal intercourse without a condom, and probably also unprotected oral-genital contact and finger or hand insertion into the anus or vagina. The use of alcohol and drugs during sex increases the probability of risky sexual practices (Stall, McKusick, Wiley, Coates, & Ostrow, 1986). Another category of extremely risky behavior is found among intravenous drug users. Sharing unsterilized needles can introduce HIV-carrying blood into the bloodstream of another.

The primary focus in prevention of sexually transmitted AIDS is on changing sexual practices. Exposure can be eliminated by being in a monogamous relationship with a partner who tests negative for HIV. However, monogamous relationships are rare among young people, and are not invariably found among married people or those in other committed relationships. Prevention may be best directed at encouraging sexually active people to use condoms, which are about 90% effective in preventing HIV infection. Employing sophisticated probability modeling techniques, Reiss and Leik (1989) demonstrated that risk is far more significantly reduced by using condoms—even though they are less than 100% effective—than by reducing the number of partners with whom a person has sex. Of course, the safest strategy would be to use condoms in a monogamous relationship. Prevention for intravenous drug users should also include the use of new or sterilized needles. The best precaution would be getting off drugs altogether.

Kelly and St. Lawrence (1988a, 1988b) drew on social psychological theory and research to suggest principles that can form the basis of effective AIDS prevention programs. Educational messages should (1) emphasize the risk of certain behaviors; (2) make clear the vulnerability of people who engage in such behaviors; (3) demonstrate how changes in behavior can reduce risk; and (4) persuade people that the benefits of making behavioral changes outweigh any inconvenience and loss of satisfaction. The information needs to be presented so that people know exactly what they should be doing and why. Communication must be frequent and conveyed in a supportive, optimistic (yet realistic) way by respected persons with whom the audience can identify.

Interventions implementing these principles led to reductions in unprotected anal intercourse and increased use of condoms in gay and bisexual men (Kelly, St. Lawrence, Betts, Brasfield, & Hood, 1990; Kelly, St. Lawrence, Hood, & Brasfield, 1989). Such efforts are having a positive impact in reducing the spread of HIV infection among homosexuals. For example, in the San Francisco Men's Health Study, unprotected anal intercourse was reported by about 35% of gay men in 1985 but by only 2% to 4% in 1988 (Ekstrand & Coates, 1990).

To Recap

Community psychologists emphasize primary (reducing the incidence of new cases of psychopathology in the population) and secondary prevention (helping high-risk groups learn to cope better and thereby avoid the onset of a disorder), rather than treatment of existing disorders. They try to change organizations and institutions in ways that promote psychological and physical health. Historical influences on the development of the community approach include federal funding for community mental health centers as a response to inadequate mental health care in state hospitals. Primary and secondary prevention efforts are illustrated by suicide-prevention centers, mass media education efforts about cardiovascular health, educational and skills-training efforts to help children and families, and AIDS prevention efforts aimed at reducing risky sexual practices and unsafe intravenous drug use. Evaluations of some of these programs are encouraging, but in most instances the ultimate goal of primary prevention has yet to be demonstrated.

General Issues in Psychotherapy

Psychotherapy is a diverse field. In this section we elaborate on our earlier reviews of theories and disorders by considering (a) therapists' efforts to apply insights from more than one theoretical perspective, (b) issues in psychotherapy with members of ethnic minority groups, (c) psychotherapy with more than one patient at a time (i.e., couples, family, and group therapy), and (d) psychotherapy in hospital or halfway house settings rather than in the customary outpatient office.

Eclecticism and Integration

Although theoretical perspectives are important, serving to focus research and to describe basic assumptions to which researchers and clinicians subscribe, many psychotherapists believe that no one perspective on psychological disorders can adequately guide treatment. A survey of clinical and counseling psychologists found that nearly half (41%) called themselves **eclectic**, meaning that they employed concepts and procedures from more than one theoretical system in their practices (D. Smith, 1982). Since the 1970s, there has been a rapid acceleration in scholarly and professional interest in eclecticism and a related concept, **psychotherapy integration**. Integration shares with eclecticism the characteristic of combining multiple points of view, but it implies an effort to blend the original approaches into a new theoretical perspective. Eclecticism, on the other hand, means using methods from different orientations without necessarily blending them in a new, expanded therapy.

By analogy, suppose that your ideal for friendship includes (a) shared interests and activities (for instance, you and your friend both like television situation comedies) and (b) honest feedback (for example, your friend will tell you directly when you are behaving obnoxiously, choosing the wrong person to date, or what have you). An eclectic set of friends would comprise some friends with whom you shared interests and some you could count on to be candid with you. These qualities might well not be found in one person, and, depending on what you most need now, you might choose one or the other type of friend to see this evening. An integrative friendship would be one that combined candor and shared interests in the same person, such as a friend who would tell you honestly when you both need to stop watching TV and study.

Eclecticism and integration do not define a single way to practice psychotherapy. Indeed, as would seem fitting for an approach born of dissatisfaction with the "one true way" of conceptualizing psychopathology and treatment, there are multiple perspectives on how best to go beyond the bounds of the approaches reviewed in Chapters 2 and 3 (Arkowitz, 1989). Three major strategies are technical eclecticism, common factors, and theoretical integration.

Technical Eclecticism

Arnold Lazarus, trained as a behavior therapist by Joseph Wolpe in the late 1950s in South Africa, has long advocated what he called **technical eclecticism**, a willingness to use whatever techniques work best for a particular patient or disorder, without regard to the theoretical approach from which they are drawn. He has applied technical eclecticism in an approach called **multimodal therapy** (Lazarus, 1973, 1989). The basic premise of multimodal therapy is that people are a composite of seven dimensions, according to the acronym BASIC ID: Behavior, Affective processes, Sensations, Imagery, Cognitions, Interpersonal relationships, and Drugs (biological functions).

Effective therapy, according to Lazarus, must assess problems in all or in some subset of these areas, decide the order in which problems should be treated, and

---

eclectic In *psychotherapy*, an approach that draws on concepts or methods from more than one theoretical perspective.

psychotherapy integration An attempt to blend aspects of existing theoretical perspectives on *psychotherapy* in such a way as to create a new, coherent theory.

technical eclecticism Use of whatever techniques will work in *psychotherapy*, regardless of the theoretical perspective from which they derive or whether the original theories can be sensibly integrated; found in *multimodal therapy*.

multimodal therapy A therapy, introduced by Arnold Lazarus, based on *technical eclecticism*; it employs techniques from diverse approaches in an effort to help people make positive changes in their BASIC ID, or behavior, affects, sensations, images, cognitions, interpersonal relationships, and drugs/biological functioning.

then apply to each problem area the techniques that are best suited to it. If, for example, a patient's duress seems to be triggered by aberrant thought processes, attention should focus on the *C*, for cognition, and procedures that clinical and experimental research suggest are well suited to altering how people think about things should be applied. But *B*, behavior, might also be problematic and might require specific attention in and of itself via procedures quite different from those applied to aberrant thoughts.

For each patient, Lazarus draws up a Modality Profile, which helps him and the patient see the areas from the BASIC ID that merit attention. Besides its comprehensive, structured approach to assessment, perhaps the main distinction between multimodal therapy and the noneclectic behavioral approach that Lazarus practiced initially is that in multimodal therapy the decision to use a given technique is not based on theoretical perspective. Instead, an open-minded consideration of data regarding what works is the guide. If a technique from psychodynamic therapy or humanistic therapy could be more beneficial than a cognitive therapy technique for changing a particular dysfunctional belief, then use it, Lazarus suggests. Use whatever works is the operating principle of the technical eclectic.

It is not clear yet whether multimodal therapy is any more effective than the more circumscribed approaches from which it draws its techniques. There are no controlled studies of this issue (Lambert, 1992). Although it might seem virtually a logical necessity that selecting "what works" would be more effective than any other strategy, what needs empirical testing is a specific way of deciding on the basis of multimodal assessment which techniques should be applied. It may not be as simple, for instance, as applying behavioral methods for problem behaviors, interpersonal therapy for interpersonal problems, and so on. Techniques that appear to target one mode of functioning are often just as likely to affect others (e.g., Haaga et al., 1994; Imber et al., 1990).

Arnold Lazarus, Rutgers psychologist and master clinician, who developed multimodal therapy.

Common Factors

A **common factors** approach (e.g., J. D. Frank, 1961; Goldfried, 1980) bases therapeutic practice on strategies and principles shared by all the major perspectives on therapy. The premise is that, in a sort of survival of the fittest, the most powerful ideas are those that have managed to gain acceptance from clinicians who hold different perspectives and therefore perhaps different biases about psychotherapy (Goldfried, 1980). Some possible commonalities across therapies are a positive relationship with a respected therapist, the patient's engaging in new learning experiences, and the patient's receiving direct feedback from the therapist about how he or she comes across (e.g., Brady et al., 1980). An example of feedback would be the therapist's informing a patient that the tendency not to react to his or her partner's angry outbursts conveys the impression that he or she doesn't care about the partner.

A key contribution of the common factors approach is that by its nature it calls attention to the insights of all the major perspectives. Thus the tendency to ignore work from outside the favored perspective is reduced. This approach is limited, however, for at least two reasons. First, different proponents of the importance of common factors have provided very different lists of what they are (Grencavage & Norcross, 1990). Second, the common factors approach by itself does not tell therapists what to do to help patients. For example, if a good therapeutic relationship is important, what should be done to foster one?

common factors In psychotherapy, the attempt to base practice on the strategies and principles shared by all major perspectives.

Theoretical Integration

The third major approach within the realm of eclecticism and integration is theoretical integration. This approach synthesizes not only techniques but theories. The resulting theory is itself something different because of the blending of the original perspectives. Theoretical integration can be illustrated by Paul Wachtel's *cyclical psychodynamics* The reciprocal relations between current behavior and repressed conflicts, such that they mutually reinforce each other.

(1982) **cyclical psychodynamics**, an integration of psychoanalysis and behavior therapy.

Traditionally, these two perspectives have been seen as largely incompatible. For example, psychoanalysts have been skeptical of the wisdom of behavior therapy's emphasis on working directly on how people act and feel in the present. This approach might mean that patients would not recover memories of repressed childhood conflicts. Wachtel, however, suggests that the therapist should help the patient change current behavior, not only so that he or she can feel better in the here and now, but indeed so that the patient can change those childlike fears from the past. Wachtel believes that people maintain repressed problems by their current behavior and the feedback it brings from their social relations. Although their problems were set in motion by past repressed events, people keep acting in ways that maintain them.

For example, consider a young man who has repressed his extreme rage at his mother for having mistreated his father years ago, when he was still a child. To control this rage, as a youngster he developed defenses that took the form of overpoliteness and deference to women. Today this solicitousness and unassertiveness encourage some women to take advantage of him, but he also misperceives situations in which women are genuinely nice to him. Misinterpreting their friendly overtures as condescending insults, he comes to resent women even more and retreats still further. In this fashion his submissiveness, originating in his buried problem of long ago, creates difficulties in the present and revives his repressed rage. This present-day confirmation of the belief from childhood turns back on the buried conflict and keeps it alive. The cycle continues, with the young man's own behavior and misconceptions confirming the nastiness of women.

The implications for therapy are to alter current behavioral patterns both for their own sake, as in behavior therapy, and for the purpose of uncovering the underlying psychodynamics. One could, for instance, give the deferential young man some assertion training, in the hope of breaking into the vicious cycle by changing his here-and-now relations with women. Such training might give him a chance to see that not all women will object to his asserting himself as well as providing the positive experience of confronting those who are taking advantage of him. Once his belief that all women want to take advantage of him is repeatedly disconfirmed, he can begin to understand the repressed conflict of love–hate with his mother.

Conversely, Wachtel's integrated theory suggests that behavior therapists can learn much from the psychoanalytic perspective as well, especially concerning the kinds of problems people tend to develop. For example, psychoanalytic theory tells us that children have strong and usually ambivalent feelings about their parents and that, presumably, some of these are so unpleasant that they are repressed, or at least are difficult to focus on and talk about openly.

Cyclical psychodynamics is a coherent model that blends insights of psychoanalysis regarding the likely origins and contents of psychological problems with insights of behavior therapy about the role of the current environment in maintaining problems and providing leverage for modifying them. It is an integration, not an eclectic approach that suggests, for instance, trying psychoanalysis for patients with personality disorders and behavior therapy for those with anxiety disorders. Cyclical psychodynamics is plausible, but to date there is no research indicating that it is effective.

To Recap

More therapists are eclectic, drawing on multiple perspectives, than adhere to any one approach. The main strategies for using multiple perspectives are technical eclecticism (borrowing effective techniques from other orientations without necessarily subscribing to the theories that developed them), common factors (basing

therapy on strategies shared by all the main perspectives on psychotherapy), and theoretical integration (combining aspects of existing theories to form one new, coherent model).

Cultural and Racial Factors in Psychotherapy

Most systems of psychotherapy have been developed without explicit reference to culture or race. There is no rational-emotive theory of the psychopathology of northern European peoples or counterconditioning principles applicable to Asian-Americans. Nevertheless, just because a theory or therapy fails to attend to cultural and racial diversity does not mean that they are irrelevant. Most of the perspectives covered in Chapters 2 and 3, for instance, could be said to have been initiated by white men from the United States of some western European background, and the methods they devised may reflect this homogeneity to some degree. To practice effectively in highly heterogeneous countries, such as the United States and Canada, therefore requires careful consideration of whether and in what ways the traditional approaches require modification when patients are members of minority groups. This issue has received less research attention than it should, but there is some relevant information, discussed here.

First, a disclaimer. Our discussion of racial factors in intervention runs the risk of stereotyping because we review generalizations that experts make about how certain groups of people react to psychological assistance. People from minority groups, however, are individuals who can differ as much from each other as their racial group differs from another racial group. Still, a consideration of group characteristics is potentially helpful.

African-Americans and Psychological Intervention

Several studies have examined the effects of race on therapy relationships. African-American patients on average prefer African-American counselors to white counselors, engage in more self-exploration with counselors of their own race, and in general feel more positively toward African-American than toward white helpers. At the same time, race differences are *not* insurmountable barriers to understanding between counselor and patient. Therapists with considerable

A match in race between therapist and client may facilitate the formation of a positive working relationship but is not necessary for successful treatment. More directly crucial is that the therapist be, and be perceived as, empathic and able to understand the client.

empathy are perceived as more helpful by patients, regardless of the racial mix (Jackson, 1973), and successful treatment outcome does not appear to depend strongly on the racial similarity of patient and therapist (Sue, Zane, & Young, 1994).

Some African-Americans react differently to whites than to other African-Americans. With African-Americans they are more open and spontaneous, whereas with whites they tend to be more guarded and less talkative (Ridley, 1984). Virtually all African-Americans have encountered prejudice and racism, and many must often wrestle with their anger at a majority culture that is sometimes insensitive to and unappreciative of the emotional consequences of growing up as a feared, resented, and sometimes hated minority. Therapists must remain sensitive to the effects of such social oppression without letting this sensitivity translate into a paternalistic attitude that removes personal responsibility and individual empowerment from African-American patients (Greene, 1985).

Latinos/Latinas and Psychological Intervention

Findings about how Latinos/Latinas react to non-Latino/Latina therapists are mixed. However, a well-designed series of three interrelated studies showed that Mexican-Americans reported a clear preference for ethnically similar therapists, especially when the clinical problem related to ethnic concerns (such as a woman's feeling pressure from Mexican parents to marry and forego a career) (Lopez, Lopez, & Fong, 1991). Therapy with most Latinos/Latinas should appreciate their hesitancy to express psychological concerns. Latino men in particular may have great trouble expressing weakness and fear.

Asian-Americans and Psychological Intervention

As with other minority groups, there is considerable variability among those identified as Asian-Americans, who comprise more than two dozen distinct subgroups, including Filipinos and Filipinas, Chinese, Japanese, and Vietnamese. Asian-Americans differ also on such dimensions as how well they speak English, whether they immigrated to the United States or came as refugees from war or terrorism in their homeland, and the degree to which they identify with their native land or that of their parents if they were born in the United States (Sue & Sue, 1992). Therapists should be aware of greater tendencies among these groups than among whites to be ashamed of emotional suffering and, coupled with a relative lack of assertiveness, to seek out professional help with great reluctance. Above all, the stereotype of Asian-Americans as having made it, as invariably being highly educated, earning good salaries, and being well-adjusted emotionally, is belied by the facts. The discrimination suffered by Asians in this and many other countries appears to be as severe as that endured by other racial and ethnic minority groups (Sue & Sue, 1992).

All these factors have many implications for how to conduct psychotherapy with Asian-Americans. Sue and Sue (1992) advise therapists to be sensitive to the personal losses that many Asian refugees have suffered and, especially in light of the great importance that family connections have for them, to the likelihood that they are very stressed from these losses. Therapists should also be aware that Asian-Americans have a tendency to "somaticize," that is, to experience and to talk about stress in physical terms, such as headaches and fatigue. Also, the values of Asian-Americans are quite different from the Western values of the majority culture in our country. For example—and allowing for considerable individual variation—Asians respect structure and formality in interpersonal relationships, whereas a Western therapist is likely to favor informality and a less authoritative attitude. Respect for authority may take the form of agreeing readily to what the therapist does and proposes—and perhaps, rather than discussing differences openly, just not showing up for the next session. Indeed, the very acceptability of psychotherapy as a way to handle stress is likely to be much lower among Asian-Americans, who tend to see emotional duress as something to be handled on one's own and through willpower (Kinzie, 1985).

Asian-Americans may consider some areas off-limits for discussion with a therapist, for example, the nature of the marital relationship, and especially sex. Like many other immigrant groups, Asian-Americans born in the United States are often caught between two cultures. One form of resolving this conflict is to identify vigorously with majority values and to denigrate anything Asian, a kind of racial self-hate. Others are torn by conflicting loyalties, experiencing (poorly expressed) rage at a discriminatory Western culture but at the same time questioning aspects of their Asian background. Finally, the therapist may have to be more directive and active than he or she otherwise might be, given the preference of many Asian-Americans for a structured approach over a reflective one, as in Rogerian therapy (Atkinson, Maruyama, & Matsui, 1978).

Native Americans and Psychological Intervention

As with other minority groups, Native Americans are a highly heterogeneous group, with about five hundred tribes residing in the United States. With due regard for individual differences, some generalizations can be made (Sue & Sue, 1992). Because Native American children are often looked after in the households of different relatives, the pattern of a child or young adult moving around in different households is not necessarily a sign of trouble. A youngster's avoidance of eye contact is a traditional sign of respect, but may be misconstrued by someone unfamiliar with the culture as quite the opposite and regarded as a problem to be remedied (Everett, Proctor, & Cartmell, 1989). As with other minorities, conflicts about identification can be severe—young people can be torn between traditional values and those of the (decidedly more privileged) majority culture, which may underlie the high rates of truancy, substance abuse, and suicide among Native American young people (Red Horse, 1982). Value placed on cooperativeness rather than on competitiveness can be misinterpreted by a culturally unaware therapist as lack of motivation. The importance of family may make it advisable to conduct treatment in the home, with family members present and an integral part of the intervention.

Extended family, such as grandparents, are often closely involved in the upbringing of Native American children.

To Recap

Perspectives on psychotherapy have typically been developed without explicit consideration of cultural and racial diversity. Clinicians and scholars have begun to address this limitation by describing issues involved in working with members of minority groups. Whereas generalizations can be useful for forming hypotheses about patients, the vast individual differences among members of minority groups make it critical not to assume that they apply in every case.

Beyond Individual Therapy

In this section, we examine treatment approaches applied to more than one patient at a time, proceeding from couples and families to groups of unrelated people.

Couples and Family Therapy

Couples therapy refers to attempts to help couples improve their distressed relationships. It is largely replacing the earlier term *marital therapy* because an increasing number of couples, both happy and unhappy, heterosexual as well as homosexual, live together in committed relationships but are not married. More-

couples therapy Any professional intervention that treats the relationship problems of a couple.

Couples therapy deals with relationship problems. It can take a number of forms, ranging from psychoanalytic to behavioral.

over, many couples who enter therapy to deal with problems in their relationship have children. Sometimes the problems that parents have with a child arise from conflicts in the marriage. At other times a child's behavior creates distress in an otherwise well-functioning couple. The line between couples therapy and **family therapy**, efforts to help an entire family function better, is often blurred. We discuss them together, distinguishing between the two when useful.

family therapy A form of therapy in which members of a family are helped to relate better to one another

Other than the basic point that a couple or family, rather than one individual, is the patient, there is no set procedure associated with family therapy or couples therapy. How the therapist views the problem, what techniques are chosen, how often members of the couple or family are seen, and whether children and even grandparents are included all vary. What these approaches share is a set of assumptions distinguishing them from individual therapy, in particular, (a) pathology often resides in a system of interactions among people rather than in just one of them, and (b) some degree of conflict among members of a family or couple is normal, perhaps even essential.

Family Systems Perspectives.   As an overall approach, family and couples therapy strives to identify faulty communication patterns, uneasy relationships, and inflexibility within the family (J. E. Bell, 1961). Members of the family are shown how their behavior affects their relations with others. They then devote their energies to making specific changes. Family therapists are relatively unconcerned with past history, and few believe that working with only one member of the family can be fruitful. Whatever the clinical problem, the family therapist takes a **family systems approach**, a general view of psychopathology and treatment that focuses on the complex interrelationships within families. As such, treatment is viewed as most effective within this group context. We introduced an example of a family systems approach with Minuchin's family therapy for anorexia nervosa in Chapter 14.

family systems approach A general approach to psychopathology and treatment that focuses on the complex interrelationships within families.

Another illustration of the value of a systems perspective comes from the field of sex therapy. Early sex therapy treated a sexual problem of one or both partners directly, expecting that whatever other difficulties the couple might have—anger, resentment—would dissipate thereafter. This pattern undoubtedly holds for many sexually distressed couples. But, as mentioned in Chapter 13, the increasing popularity of sex therapy since the publication of Masters and Johnson's *Hu-*

Family therapists consider it essential to assess, and ultimately to change, patterns of communication among all members of a family system, even if only one is diagnosed with a psychological disorder.

man Sexual Inadequacy in 1970 has brought to the attention of sex therapists many troubled couples for whom the sexual problem is but one aspect of a more complex system (Heiman & Verhulst, 1990). Couples and family therapy looks for these systems. The case history depicted in Focus Box 16.1 exemplifies such a system, one in which a sexual dysfunction served the paradoxical purpose of helping to maintain a couple's relationship. In this case, therapeutic interventions to improve sexual functioning, ordinarily a sensible tactic, temporarily worsened the overall relationship.

Viewing Conflict as Normal. Conflict is inevitable in any long-term relationship. The aura of the honeymoon phase passes when the couple makes unromantic decisions about where to live, where to seek employment, how to budget money, sharing household chores, dealing with relatives, and so forth. How couples deal with the conflicts that arise is likely to determine the quality and duration of their relationship (e.g., Schwartz & Schwartz, 1980).

A strategy that some couples adopt, deliberately or unconsciously, is to avoid acknowledging conflicts. Because they believe in the reality of the fairy-tale ending, "and they lived happily ever after," any sign that their own relationship is not going smoothly is so threatening that it must be ignored. Unfortunately, dissatisfaction and resentment usually develop and take their toll as time goes by. Because the partners do not quarrel, they may appear to be a perfect couple to outside observers. But without opening the lines of communication, they may drift apart emotionally.

Influence of Individual Therapy Perspectives. Couples and family therapy methods vary. Some methods derive from extending and modifying perspectives used in individual therapy. For example, psychoanalytic marital therapists focus on the person's seeking or avoiding a partner who resembles, to his or her unconscious, the opposite-sexed parent (Segraves, 1990). Frustrated and unsatisfied

FOCUS BOX 16.1

Case Illustration of a Dysfunctional Marital System

"A couple with a marriage of twenty years' duration sought treatment for the male's problem of total inability to have an erection. This had been a problem for over nineteen of their twenty years of marriage. Successful intercourse had only taken place in the first few months of the marriage. The woman in this couple was also unable to reach an orgasm, and indeed had never had an orgasm from any form of stimulation, in her entire life. However, she reported that she greatly enjoyed sex and was extremely frustrated by her husband's inability to have an erection.

"In treating this couple, through techniques [based on those of Masters and Johnson], very rapid progress was made. The husband very quickly began to have erections in response to his wife's manual stimulation of his genitals.

"She also learned to have orgasm, first through her own masturbation and then through her husband's manual and oral stimulation of her genitals. By session 10 of weekly therapy, the couple was able to engage in normal intercourse with both of them having orgasm. Thus, the case was essentially "cured" within ten sessions. However, at this point, something rather peculiar happened. Rather than continuing intercourse after this success, the couple discontinued all sexual activity for the next several weeks. Upon careful exploration by the therapist a rather interesting picture emerged. First, it became clear that the husband had a great need to remain distant and aloof from his wife. He had great fears of being overwhelmed and controlled by her, and found closeness to be very uncomfortable. He himself had had a rather disturbed relationship with his mother, with her being extremely controlling, manipulating, and intrusive in his life, well into his adulthood.

For him, the inability to have an erection served to keep his wife distant from him, and to maintain his need for privacy, separateness, and autonomy in the relationship. In exploring the situation with the wife, [the therapist found] in contrast to her overt statements. . . an extremely ambivalent attitude toward sex. She had been raised in a very anti-sexual family. While she claimed to have rejected these anti-sexual teachings in her own late adolescence and adulthood, in point of fact this rejection had occurred only at a superficial intellectual level. Emotionally, she still had a great deal of difficulty in accepting her sexual feelings. She had fears of being overwhelmed by uncontrollable sexual urges if she allowed herself to enjoy sex. Thus, her husband's erectile problems served to protect her from her own fears about sex. Furthermore, over the nineteen years of her husband being unable to attain an erection, she had come to have a very powerful position in the relationship. She very often reminded her husband that he owed her a lot because of her sexual frustration. Thus, she was essentially able to win all arguments with him, and to get him to do anything that she wanted.

"For this couple, the rapid resolution of their sexual dysfunction threatened elements in both their own personalities and in the way their relationship was structured. In exploring their inability to continue having intercourse once they had succeeded, they came to realize the [link] between their sexual problems and the structure of their [marriage]. With several additional weeks of therapy focused on resolving these individual and relationship factors, they were able to resume sexual activity successfully." (LoPiccolo & Friedman, 1985, pp. 465–466)

by his love-seeking attempts as a child, the adult man may unconsciously seek maternal nurturance from his wife and make excessive, even infantile, demands of her. Much of the discussion in therapy then centers on the conflicts he is having with his wife and the repressed striving for maternal love that underlies his immature ways of relating to her. These unconscious forces are examined, with the wife assisting and possibly revealing some of her own unresolved yearnings for her father. Notice that the transference examined in analytic marital therapy is that between the two partners rather than between the patient and the therapist. The overall goal is to help each partner see the other as he or she actually is rather than as a symbolic parent (Fitzgerald, 1973). Positive findings in treating couples in distress have been reported for psychodynamic couples therapy (Snyder & Wills, 1989) and for a humanistic therapy (Greenberg & Johnson, 1988; Johnson & Greenberg, 1985), though only a few such studies have been published.

The most thoroughly tested method of couples therapy, behavioral couples therapy, extends principles derived from the behavioral and cognitive perspectives on individual treatment. Behavioral couples therapists generally adopt a view of couples' interactions that is based on exchange theory (Thibaut & Kelley, 1959). According to this view, people value others if they receive a high ratio of benefits to costs, that is, if they see themselves getting at least as much from the other person as they have to expend. Furthermore, people are assumed to be more disposed to continue a given relationship if other alternatives are less attractive to them, promising fewer benefits and costing more. Although it can sound more economic than romantic when put this way, there is empirical support for the basic point that "the relative rates of pleasant and unpleasant interactions determine the subjective quality of the relationship" (Wood & Jacobson, 1985).

In trying to help distressed couples, behavioral couples therapists therefore encourage a mutual dispensing of rewards. One strategy is the "caring days" idea of Richard Stuart (1976). One partner agrees to devote himself or herself to doing nice things for the other partner on a given day, without expecting anything in return. On another day the roles are reversed. If successful, this strategy accomplishes at least two important things: first, it breaks the cycle of distance and mutual suspicion, and second, it shows the giving partner that he or she is able to affect the other partner in a positive way. This enhanced sense of positive control is achieved simply by pleasing the partner.

Giving can later be more reciprocal and spontaneous. Couples are taught communication skills with an eye toward becoming able to listen better and thereby perhaps to be better attuned to what might be done for and with one another that would be pleasing. Cognitive change is also seen as important, for couples often need encouragement to acknowledge when positive changes are occurring. Distressed couples frequently have inaccurate perceptions of the ratio of positive to negative exchanges, tending to overlook the positive and to emphasize the negative (e.g., Baucom & Lester, 1986).

Beneficial effects of behavioral couples therapy (BCT) have been demonstrated in more than two dozen studies (Hahlweg & Markman, 1988). BCT can also be useful in treating what seem like individual problems in one of the partners. For example, depression in at least one of the partners is often a part of a distressed couple's relationship, and relapse into depression is more likely if the formerly depressed partner is in a troubled relationship (Hooley & Teasdale, 1989). Accordingly, researchers have studied BCT as a treatment for depression (e.g., Jacobson, Dobson, Fruzzetti, Schmaling, & Salusky, 1991; O'Leary & Beach, 1990). BCT was just as effective as individualized cognitive therapy for the depressed partner in alleviating depression and more effective in enhancing satisfaction with the relationship. This result suggests that someone who is depressed and is also in a troubled relationship might be helped as much by a systems-oriented approach to the relationship as by an individualized intervention—with the advantage of also deriving benefit for relationship problems.

Even though improvement is evident, BCT and other forms of couples therapy are not panaceas. Across all studies, no more than half the treated couples were as satisfied with their relationships at the end of treatment as are typical nondistressed couples (Alexander, Holtzworth-Munroe, & Jameson, 1994). Furthermore, few studies have examined long-term effects after treatment is concluded. Those that have conducted follow-up assessments have found frequent relapse (Jacobson, Schmaling, & Holtzworth-Munroe, 1987). Thus, current methods of couples therapy usually result in some benefits, but it is important to continue to try to improve them so as to achieve stronger and more lasting effects. One such ongoing effort is described in Focus Box 16.2.

FOCUS BOX 16.2

Acceptance in Behavioral Couples Therapy

A recent development in behavioral couples therapy (BCT) is a growing appreciation of acceptance of the partner while trying to encourage and support change. Based on earlier work by person-centered (Chapter 2) and rational-emotive (Chapter 3) therapists and on Marsha Linehan's (1993a, 1993b) dialectical behavior therapy (see Chapter 11), Neil Jacobson (1992), in collaboration with Andrew Christensen (Jacobson & Christensen, in press), argues that behavior therapists have overlooked the importance of people in a committed relationship being able to accept their partner while at the same time hoping for and encouraging change.

In following up the results from an earlier outcome study (Jacobson, 1984), Jacobson found that after two years, of the two-thirds of couples who had benefited from BCT, one-third had relapsed (Jacobson et al., 1987). Thus, although BCT was very effective for almost half the couples, it was not effective for the other half over an extended (two-year) period of time. This finding led to the question of what might be wrong or missing from BCT.

Predictors of poor outcome from BCT include being married for a long time, emotional disengagement, high severity of distress in the relationship, and rigidly held gender roles. It seemed to Jacobson and Christensen that a theme common to these negative predictors might be an unwillingness to compromise with and accommodate to the other person. And since BCT requires compromise—by, for example, trying to meet the partner's wishes in exchange for certain reinforcers—it makes sense that BCT would be less effective for people who cannot readily accommodate to the desires of their partners.

This should not be news to anyone who has tried to mediate in a marital problem or who has been in a distressed relationship. When a couple has been together for many years, there can be an accumulation of anger, hurt, resentment, and betrayal that makes it a challenge even to decide what restaurant to go to on a Friday evening. Good will is gone. Motives are constantly questioned. If a negative interpretation can be placed on a seemingly positive behavior, it will be. And if a behavior therapist asks the partners to do something nice for each other, the kind of couple Jacobson and Christensen are talking about will either not budge or, if they do make a specific change, will readily attribute it to the therapist's instruction, for example, "He doesn't *really* appreciate me for my good work at the office today; he's complimenting me only because Dr. Smith told me to."

Acceptance, in Jacobson and Christensen's terms, is "a letting go of the struggle to change and in some cases even embracing those aspects of a partner which have . . . been precipitants of conflict . . . [it] implies that some conflicts cannot be resolved, and it attempts to turn areas of conflict into sources of intimacy and closeness" (Jacobson, 1992, p. 497). Of course, as Jacobson points out, acceptance does imply change—but the change is in the partner who is giving up efforts to change the other! It is even possible that giving up on trying to change the partner can lower the resistance on her or his part to making such changes (see Focus Box 16.4).

Is acceptance tantamount to resignation, to accepting a status quo that keeps one or both partners in a destructive relationship, one that perhaps demeans one partner in order to satisfy the selfish demands of the other? Jacobson argues that acceptance is actually affirmative, holding out the promise of even greater intimacy. And as suggested here, some behavioral changes that were formerly—and unsuccessfully—worked toward in BCT only by direct attempts to change might be facilitated by embedding such efforts within a context of acceptance.

Group Therapy

group therapy A method of treating psychological disorders whereby several persons are seen simultaneously.

Group therapy involves a single therapist (or sometimes two cotherapists) meeting simultaneously with multiple patients. It differs from family therapy in that the patients are unrelated. Indeed, some group therapists consider it critical that the group members should not know each other apart from the group. This arrangement makes it easier to preserve the confidentiality of what goes on in the group, which is essential for honest communication but more difficult to preserve than in individual therapy.

Group therapy began in the early twentieth century. As psychotherapists ex-

Peer support groups are important in helping the friends and family of someone who has committed suicide cope with its aftermath.

perimented with therapy in groups, they discovered that for many patients it was as good as individual therapy (Wolf & Kutash, 1990) and therefore more efficient in terms of resources, including the therapist's time and the patient's money.

Most group therapists regard this form of treatment as uniquely appropriate for accomplishing certain goals. Group members can learn vicariously when attention is focused on another participant. Social pressures, too, can be surprisingly strong in groups. If a therapist tells an individual patient that his or her behavior seems hostile even when hostility is not intended, the message may be rejected. However, if three or four other group members agree with the interpretation, the person may find it much more difficult to dismiss. In addition, many people derive comfort and support simply from knowing that others have problems similar to their own (Yalom, 1985).

As far as technique is concerned, much of group therapy practice is derived from perspectives used in treating individual patients. Thus there are psychoanalytic groups (Slavson, 1950), person-centered groups (Rogers, 1970), behavior therapy groups (Upper & Ross, 1980), and so on.

Psychoanalytic group therapists employ such Freudian concepts and methods as transference, free association, dream analysis, resistance, the power of the unconscious, and the importance of past history all in an effort to move patients toward an understanding of intrapsychic processes. Some therapists (e.g., Wolf & Kutash, 1990) concentrate on the psychodynamics of each individual group member. Others (e.g., Bion, 1959) conceive of the group itself as having a kind of collective set of psychodynamics, manifested in such ways as a group transference to the therapist. Sometimes the therapist sees each of the group members for many sessions of individual psychoanalysis or psychoanalytically oriented therapy prior to group therapy. Interpretations of what members say are offered not only by the therapist but by other members of the group. What all such approaches have in common is the belief that increased self-understanding and deep emotional change can take place in the individual within the context of a group and that the group itself can facilitate these curative psychoanalytic processes.

Behavior therapy groups are sometimes conducted in a manner that is very similar to individual therapy except that, for reasons of efficiency, it is carried out with multiple patients at the same time (A. A. Lazarus, 1968). For example, systematic desensitization could be conducted simultaneously for a number of people with the same specific phobia. What is lost in the individual tailoring of the hierarchy of anxiety-provoking scenes may be gained in efficiency.

Other behavior therapy groups make more use of the group setting. A prime example is social-skills training groups, in which members have a ready-made opportunity to practice the skills they are learning (e.g., job interview or conversational skills) in the group context. Efforts are usually made to keep together people whose skill levels prior to treatment are comparable, so that an appropriate pace can be maintained for all involved (Bartzokis, Liberman, & Hierholzer, 1990). Participants rehearse jointly the skills they are learning and thus provide one another unique and appropriate help in changing behavior. Groups of depressed people, for example, have learned social skills likely to bring them more reinforcement from others (Teri & Lewinsohn, 1986). Other social-skills training groups have helped hospitalized schizophrenic patients cope with the interpersonal challenges they face when discharged (Liberman, DeRisi, & Mueser, 1989). Finally, for some patients, the group setting itself provides a good analogue of the very situations they find most problematic and is thus ideal as a context for therapeutic work. Social phobics, for instance, can practice giving speeches in front of group members and coping with the anxiety that results.

Little research on group therapy meets the basic standards of psychological research. Lacking are random assignment of subjects to different treatments and clear specifications of what was done in each treatment (Bednar & Kaul, 1994). Tentative evidence indicates that group therapies of different kinds appear to have beneficial effects on a wide variety of patients, and in some instances these favorable outcomes endure at several months' follow-up. Pregroup training, that is, teaching general skills about participating in group therapy and instilling positive attitudes toward the experience, can help people get more from group therapy experiences.

To Recap

Couples, family, and group therapies all involve more than one patient at a time. In each case principles and techniques vary, typically depending on the theoretical perspective of the therapist, but certain assumptions are held in common. Family and couples therapists, for instance, assume that problems can stem from faulty communication and interaction patterns among family members rather than from pathology located within one individual. Also assumed is that some degree of conflict among family members is normal. Group therapies use the group setting to enhance therapeutic benefits by offering patients feedback from more than one person about their interpersonal style and multiple partners with whom they can try out new social skills. Perhaps most important, group therapy gives patients the sense that their problems are not unique. In general, couples, family, and group therapies have been subjected to less scientific scrutiny than have individual therapies. The most extensive empirical support exists for behavioral couples therapy, which helps couples act in more reinforcing ways toward one another. This treatment is not sufficient for everyone, however, and is being modified and expanded accordingly.

Intervention Beyond the Outpatient Setting

Some of the most severe psychological disorders are treated not in discrete therapy sessions in clinicians' offices but in therapeutic environments removed from the ordinary routines of daily life. In recent years, the nature of these inpatient programs has diversified, with the development of such strategies as twenty-eight-day inpatient programs for adolescents with eating disorders, day hospitalization for alcohol abusers, resortlike retreats for overweight people who wish to achieve drastic changes in their health habits, and so on. The mainstays of intensive treatment, however, remain inpatient hospital care and halfway houses for the severely mentally ill, most notably patients with schizophrenia. In this section we review the typical nature of such care, as well as some as-yet-atypical but highly promising alternative methods.

Inpatient Hospitalization

Each year more than two million Americans are hospitalized for mental disorders. Treatment in public mental institutions is primarily custodial in nature, and the existence of patients is monotonous and sedentary for the most part.

Mental hospitals in the United States are usually funded either by the federal government or by the state. Some Veterans Administration hospitals and general medical hospitals also contain psychiatric wards. In addition, there are private mental hospitals. The physical facilities and professional care in private institutions tend to be superior to those of state hospitals because the private hospitals have more money. Costs to patients in these private institutions can exceed $1000 per day. Although some patients may have medical insurance, usually with a ninety-day limit, such hospitals are clearly beyond the means of most citizens.

Even in the best hospitals, patients usually have little contact with psychiatrists or clinical psychologists. Direct observations have led to estimates that most patients have no contact with staff for 80% to 90% of their waking hours and that the clinical staff spend less than 25% of their working time in contact with patients (Paul, 1988). Most of a patient's days and evenings are spent either alone or in the company of other patients and of aides. As with imprisonment, the overwhelming feeling is of helplessness. Patients sit for endless hours in hallways waiting for dining halls to open, for medication to be dispensed, and for consultations with psychologists, social workers, and vocational counselors to begin. Except for the most severely disturbed, patients have access to the various facilities of a hospital, ranging from woodworking shops to swimming pools, from gymnasiums to basket-weaving shops.

Most hospitals require patients to attend group therapy. For some patients there are a few sessions alone with a professional therapist. For the most part, however, traditional hospital treatment over the past forty years has been biologically oriented, with these other activities used primarily to occupy the patients' time until drugs have taken effect. The institutional setting itself is used as a way to provide supportive care and to protect and care for patients whose condition makes it virtually impossible for them to look after themselves or makes them an unreasonable burden or threat to others (Paul & Menditto, 1992).

Social Learning and Milieu Therapy in Institutions. There are, however, effective examples of a more systematic psychological approach to inpatient care. Research supports in particular the usefulness of methods derived from the behavioral perspective (Chapter 3). These can be illustrated by reviewing the procedures and results of an ambitious project undertaken by Gordon Paul and Robert Lentz (1977).

The long-term, regressed, and chronic schizophrenic patients involved in the study by Paul and Lentz (1977) are among the most severely debilitated institutionalized adults ever studied systematically. Some of these patients screamed for long periods, some were mute; many were incontinent, a few assaultive. Most of them no longer used silverware, and some buried their faces in their food. The patients were matched for age, sex, socioeconomic background, symptoms, and length of hospitalization and then assigned to one of three wards—social-learning therapy, milieu therapy, and routine hospital management. Each ward had twenty-eight residents. The social-learning and milieu wards shared ambitious objectives: to teach self-care, housekeeping, communication, and vocational skills; to reduce symptomatic behavior; and to release patients to the community. The routine hospital management ward served as a control group.

Social-Learning Ward.   Located in a new mental health center, the social-learning ward was operated on a token economy (as described in Chapter 3), which embraced all aspects of the residents' lives. Their appearance had to pass muster each morning, in eleven specific ways, in order to earn a token. Well-made beds, good behavior at mealtime, classroom participation, and socializing during free periods were other means of earning tokens. Residents learned through modeling, shaping, prompting, and instructions. They were also taught to communicate better with one another and participated in problem-solving groups. Tokens could be used to purchase meals and small luxuries. In addition to living by the rules of the token economy, individuals received behavioral treatments tailored to their needs. Residents were kept busy 85% of their waking hours learning to behave better.

Milieu Therapy Ward.   Another ward of the center operated on the principles of Maxwell Jones's (1953) therapeutic community. These residents, too, were kept busy 85% of their waking hours. Both individually and as a group they were expected to act responsibly and to participate in decisions about how the ward was to function. In general, they were treated more as normal individuals than as incompetent mental patients. Staff members impressed on the residents their positive expectations and praised them for doing well. When they behaved symptomatically, staff members stayed with them, making clear the expectation that they would soon behave more appropriately.

Routine Hospital Management.   These patients continued their accustomed hospital existence in an older state institution, receiving custodial care and antipsychotic medication. Except for the 5% of their waking hours occupied by occasional activity, and recreational, occupational, and individual and group therapies, these people were on their own.

Over the four and a half years of hospitalization and the one and a half years of follow-up, the patients were evaluated at regular six-month intervals by structured interviews and by direct behavioral observations. Both social-learning and milieu therapy reduced positive and negative symptoms of schizophrenia (p. 218), with the social-learning ward achieving better results than the milieu ward on several measures. The residents also acquired self-care, housekeeping, social, and vocational skills. The behavior of members of these two groups within the institution was superior to that of the residents of the hospital ward. By the end of treatment, more of them had been discharged. Over 10% of the social-learning patients left the center for independent living; 7% of the milieu patients achieved this goal; and none of the routine hospital management patients did.

Considering how poorly these patients had been functioning before this treatment project, these results are remarkable. The fact that the social-learning program was superior to the milieu program is also significant, for milieu treatment is used in many mental hospitals. Paul and Lentz never claimed that any one of these patients was cured, however. Although they were able to live outside the hospital, most continued to manifest many signs of mental disorder, and few of them had gainful employment or participated in the social activities that most people take for granted. The outcome, though, is not to be underestimated. Chronic mental patients, those typically shut away on back wards and forgotten by society, can be resocialized and taught self-care. They can learn to behave normally enough to be discharged from mental institutions in some instances. Reports published since the Paul and Lentz study support the effectiveness of social-learning programs (Paul & Menditto, 1992).

Halfway Houses and Aftercare

Some people function too well to remain in a psychiatric hospital and yet do not function independently enough to live on their own or with their own families. For such individuals there are **halfway houses**. These are protected living units, typically located in large, formerly private residences. Here patients discharged from a mental hospital live, take their meals, and gradually return to ordinary community life by holding a part-time job or going to school. Living arrangements may be relatively unstructured. Some houses set up money-making enterprises that help to train and support the residents. Depending on how well funded the halfway house is, the staff may include psychiatrists or clinical psychologists. The most important staff members are paraprofessionals, often graduate students in the mental health professions, who live in the house and act both as administrators and as friends to the residents. Group meetings, at which residents talk out their frustrations and learn to relate to others constructively, are often part of the routine.

halfway houses Homelike residences for people who are considered too disturbed to remain in their accustomed surroundings but do not require the total care of a mental institution.

The need for effective halfway houses in the United States is great, especially in light of deinstitutionalization efforts, reviewed in Chapter 9, that have seen tens of thousands of patients discharged from mental hospitals who thirty years ago would have remained in the protected hospital setting. Ex-patients often need follow-up community-based services (**aftercare**), and these are scarce. A model of what aftercare can be is again provided by the Paul and Lentz (1977) study. When patients were discharged they usually went to live in nearby boarding homes. These homes were staffed by workers who had been trained by the Paul–Lentz project to treat the formerly hospitalized patients according to social-learning principles, including positive reinforcement of appropriate and independent behavior.

aftercare Follow-up community-based services for patients who have been discharged from psychiatric hospitals.

Results were as positive as those of the social-learning ward program. More than 90% of the patients discharged from the social-learning ward were able to remain continuously in the community residences during the year-and-a-half follow-up period. Some had been living in the community residences for over five years. Finally, in a finding critical in these days of diminishing public funds, the social-learning program was much less expensive than the institutional care such patients usually receive.

Encouraging findings on milieu-therapy community programs in nonhospital residential settings have also been reported by Mosher and Burti (1989). They found results equivalent to those of a well-staffed inpatient unit relying mainly on psychotropic medication. The patients were young adults experiencing their first psychotic episodes (and therefore very different from the chronic patients in the Paul–Lentz project). The positive outcomes for the community-based program indicate that hospitalization may not even be necessary for some acutely disturbed patients.

To Recap

Deinstitutionalization efforts of the 1970s have reduced their numbers, but millions of Americans are still treated in mental hospitals. These are predominantly publicly funded institutions in which access to mental health professionals for anything other than administering medications is often scarce. A study by Paul and Lentz (1977) found that a social-learning program for chronic schizophrenic

patients, based in part on a token economy in which patients were rewarded for positive social and self-care behaviors, was far more beneficial than routine institutional care. A milieu-therapy program was also effective, albeit less so than social-learning therapy. Aftercare programs, in which the patients lived in community settings but continued to receive support and positive reinforcement of desired behaviors, helped sustain the benefits of the treatment.

▶ *Psychotherapy: How Effective?*

For much of its history, psychotherapy was the object of little scientific evaluation. Much like the teaching profession today, in which choices among alternative methods, such as lecture versus group discussion, are usually made on the basis of personal preference or tradition rather than data on what helps students learn, so, too, psychotherapy was practiced but not evaluated in research. Indeed, many considered it impossible to study, for both ethical and scientific reasons. Ethically, treatment was considered confidential and therefore not open to objective scrutiny. Scientifically, psychotherapy methods were considered too individual-specific and not sufficiently standardized. This argument amounts to viewing psychotherapy more as an art than as a scientific treatment.

The problem with this situation is that clinicians, and for that matter consumers of psychotherapy services, are left with no basis for evaluating the claims made by advocates of different therapies; for example, when Arthur Janov, originator of primal therapy, states that "primal therapy has become a phenomenon. The reason for its success is that it is true. . . . By implication, this renders all other psychological theories obsolete and invalid" (Gross, 1978, p. 278), should everyone rush out to be trained in or helped by primal therapy? Maybe, but it might make sense instead to wonder about his objectivity in reaching this conclusion, to want to hear more specifics about the observations on which it is based and how those observations were made.

As noted in Chapter 2, Carl Rogers was especially influential in making the case that the effectiveness of therapy, and the manner in which it works, should be studied formally. It is now widely accepted as ethical to report on processes and outcomes of therapy provided that patients have given informed consent to participate in research and patients' confidentiality is protected. Methodological challenges in studying psychotherapy have been more difficult to overcome, as we shall see. We begin this final section of the chapter with an overview of the average effectiveness of psychotherapy.

Impact of Psychotherapy

By the mid-1970s the problem with psychotherapy research was not a lack of studies but an overwhelming amount of data. Making sense of all the information would exceed the capacity of even the most dedicated scholar. Apart from the sheer quantity of information, its diversity makes it difficult to interpret. If one study uses measure x for patients with panic disorder (as diagnosed with the SCID; see Chapter 5) and finds an average of 5 points improvement after treatment with psychodynamic therapy, while a second study uses measure y with panic patients (diagnosed by a new method devised just for this study) and finds 3 points improvement on average using cognitive therapy, how can these results be compared? How would you answer the seemingly simple question of which treatment you should use with your panic patients (assuming that you are competent in both)? How would you describe the results to a panic patient? Are these treatments highly effective, somewhat effective, or barely effective at all?

A set of statistical procedures known generically as **meta-analysis** has been developed to aid in interpreting the results of multiple studies of similar topics.

meta-analysis Quantitative methods of analyzing and comparing the results of various scientific studies.

The mathematical foundations of such work were well established by the 1950s, but the use of meta-analysis was rare until the late 1970s. It is now widely used in evaluating psychotherapy as well as other areas of psychological research (Hunter & Schmidt, 1990). Meta-analysis was first used in the evaluation of psychotherapy by Smith, Glass, and Miller (1980). The results of different studies (in this case controlled treatment outcome experiments) are combined statistically to provide an overall picture of therapy effectiveness.

The great advantage of meta-analysis is that it quantifies the extent of therapy effects in a common way that can be applied across studies conducted in different settings by different investigators at different times (Kazdin, 1986). Using this common scale, investigators can combine studies and compare the effectiveness of various kinds of therapy.

In their original report, Smith and colleagues (1980) meta-analyzed 475 psychotherapy outcome studies involving more than 25,000 subjects and came to the conclusion that a wide range of therapies produce much better results than no treatment. Moreover, positive effects of psychotherapy tend to be maintained for many months following termination (Lambert & Bergin, 1994; Nicholson & Berman, 1983).

These data from controlled studies on the average effects of psychotherapy at posttreatment and follow-up are clearly heartening. At this general level, it can be said that practitioners of psychotherapy may feel confident that they are offering services documented to be beneficial. There is no basis for complacency, however. For one thing, there is considerable variability in therapy effects. Although treatment on average leads to significant improvement, there are patients who get no better or even get worse (Lambert & Bergin, 1994).

The possibility that therapy can actually harm patients, labeled the **deterioration effect** by Bergin (1971), is particularly troubling to mental health professionals. Deterioration may be especially likely when fragile patients, such as those with borderline personality disorder or schizophrenia, are matched with highly confrontational, emotionally arousing therapists (Lambert & Bergin, 1994). But it is difficult to reach specific conclusions about how common the deterioration effect is or what causes it (Mays & Franks, 1980). The main problem in studying deterioration effects is that we do not have extensive, reliable data on the frequency of **spontaneous deterioration**, or getting worse in the absence of treatment (Lambert & Bergin, 1994). If 5% of patients get worse during three months of psychotherapy, this in itself does not mean that the treatment harmed them. Indeed, it could be that the treatment *reduced* negative effects. Perhaps 25% of patients would have gotten worse over the course of three months in the absence of therapy.

Effects of psychotherapy, then, are typically positive but can vary substantially for different patients. To a large extent the impact of psychotherapy no doubt depends on who the therapist is (Lambert, 1989), but it has proven surprisingly difficult to identify what characteristics make a therapist especially effective (Beutler, Machado, & Neufeldt, 1994). Even seemingly obvious signs, such as the therapist's having received professional training or having many years of experience, do not correlate substantially with effectiveness (e.g., Christensen & Jacobson, 1994). Thus, from the consumer perspective, the choice of a therapist is important but not simple. We examine the choice of therapist further in Focus Box 16.3. In the next subsection we describe some of the other factors that might account for variability in the outcome of psychotherapy.

deterioration effect A harmful outcome from being in *psychotherapy.*

spontaneous deterioration Getting worse in the absence of treatment.

Some Factors Affecting the Effectiveness of Psychotherapy

The Amount of Therapy

We often assume that if something is good, more of it would be better. Few therapists would be optimistic about a course of treatment in which the patient would

Choosing a Therapist

The first issue to consider in choosing a therapist is whether you (or someone you know, perhaps a friend or family member) should be in treatment at all. People sometimes perceive their problems as too insignificant to merit formal help, or they think that they should be able to solve all their problems on their own and are embarrassed about considering therapy. However, everyone faces difficulties at some point or other, and there is really no reason to be ashamed of wanting or needing the insights and assistance of others. Often these "others" can be friends, relatives, or perhaps teachers or coworkers. Sometimes, though, you may wish to consult a professional therapist. Perhaps the problems are difficult to manage informally, or you want to confer with someone who can be objective about your situation because she or he is not involved in it, or you are uncomfortable discussing sensitive issues with people you know.

If so, you are far from alone. The National Comorbidity Survey (NCS; Kessler et al., 1994) found that 28% of a representative sample of U.S. adults reported having received mental health services of one kind or another from a professional. Mental health care is not only for those with severe disorders, such as major depression or bulimia nervosa, either. The NCS indicated that 42% of people who had ever qualified for a diagnosis of a psychological disorder had received treatment at some point, and that 15% of those who had never qualified for a diagnosis had received treatment. Many people have benefited from therapy during difficult transitions in their lives, such as the end of a romantic relationship, a major setback in academic progress, or a parent's progressive decline due to dementia, regardless of whether a formal DSM diagnosis was warranted.

In the event that you decide to seek treatment, your next decision will be, from whom? There are a variety of ways in which to proceed and no one right answer. At many universities, student health centers offer low-cost or even free confidential counseling services for students. This can be an excellent option. If, for whatever reason, no one at such a clinic is suitable for you,

the staff is likely to have extensive information on local therapists, some of whom may be willing to accept reduced fees if, as is the case for most students, financial resources are modest. In addition, mental health centers listed in the Yellow Pages can provide referrals. Or, if the problem is specific and definable, there may be specialty referral services, such as that offered by the Anxiety Disorders Association of America, that can suggest therapists in your area.

Once you have a name or two or three, you can arrange an initial consultation if the hours and fees the therapist offers suit your needs. Rapport with the therapist is important. However, unless you are adamant that the therapist be of a particular age, sex, race, or what have you, it would be unwise to prejudge whether you can work with someone on the basis of such characteristics. A skilled therapist can transcend differences and understand and help clients with very distinct backgrounds. One does not need to be African-American to help African-Americans, or a woman to help women, or a recovering alcoholic to help people dependent on alcohol. What is needed is an ability to communicate well, understand clients, see the nature of problems clearly, and give sound suggestions and strong support for coping with the problems. Identifying therapists with these skills as they apply to your troubles may best be achieved by giving it a try.

Giving it a try does not mean that in one meeting you can expect resolution of all difficulties. Talking honestly about personal problems and feelings may even make you more uncomfortable temporarily. But, as noted elsewhere in this chapter, it is also not necessary to wait years to find out whether the therapy is helping. In most instances (provided that you are working hard along with your therapist) you can anticipate that a successful match will result in noticeable improvement within about eight or ten sessions. Even sooner, you should be able to tell whether you are "clicking" with your therapist personally and feel able to confide honestly in him or her. If not, try another. No one therapist is ideal for every client.

agree only to a "dose" of five minutes' interaction. But surely there are limits to this principle and some point at which we would get diminishing returns for trying more and more therapy. How much is enough? Although many laypeople assume that patients usually spend many months, even years, in psychotherapy, more than one-half of therapies actually last fewer than ten sessions (Garfield, 1994).

There are many reasons for the short duration of therapy. People set realistic goals, understanding that while psychotherapy may not cure all problems, it can help troubled individuals learn to deal better with life's inevitable stressors. Insurance companies set limits on the reimbursement provided for psychotherapy, which encourages or even requires people to seek brief treatment. Also, active, focused treatments based on behavioral and cognitive perspectives have shown that brief treatment can be successful. Briefer forms of psychodynamic therapy show promise as well.

But are ten sessions enough? An analysis of fifteen different sets of data on individual outpatient psychotherapy, covering a total of 2431 patients, suggests that the answer is often yes (Howard, Kopta, Krause, & Orlinsky, 1986). It was estimated that approximately 50% of patients are measurably improved within eight sessions, and about 75% within twenty-six sessions. This information is potentially useful for consumers who want to know how soon they can expect to see noticeable benefits from therapy as well as for third-party payers who want to establish reasonable time limits for reimbursable outpatient psychotherapy.

There are uncertainties in making inferences from these data, though (Howard et al., 1986). The results were from time-unlimited therapy. If a twenty-six-session time limit were set on therapy, the therapist and patient might feel excessive pressure and the results might be worse. Or the results might be better if the therapist and patient felt more motivated to work hard and efficiently. Also, the research reviewed by Howard et al. (1986) spanned a thirty-year period from the early 1950s to the early 1980s and represented primarily psychodynamic therapy. The findings might differ for behavioral or cognitive treatments, which are more directive, and for the newer, intentionally brief, dynamic therapies (see p. 42). Finally, while on average a particular amount of psychotherapy might be needed, no particular patient is average. Depressed patients, for example, showed more rapid improvement, followed by anxious patients, while borderline patients were the slowest to improve.

Who Benefits from Therapy?

Regardless of how long a treatment is conducted, some patients will not benefit much. What sort of patients benefit most from psychotherapy? There is surprisingly little solid information on this point, even though it is widely believed that some people are better candidates for therapy than others. Much of the accumulated research tends to disconfirm traditional lore. Demographic factors such as age, sex, and social class, for example, have not consistently related to therapy outcome (Garfield, 1994).

One area of research has shown clearer predictive power. Patients in treatment for Axis I clinical syndromes who also have Axis II personality disorders tend to show poorer results (Reich & Vasile, 1993). Studies supporting this conclusion span inpatient and outpatient settings, a range of disorders (major depression, panic disorder, obsessive-compulsive disorder, alcohol dependence), and a range of treatments (interpersonal therapy, cognitive therapy, behavior therapy, and a variety of medications).

A further question is whether certain types of patients benefit not from therapy in general, but from a particular form of therapy. If so, therapists might be able to prescribe on a rational basis what sort of treatment a person with, say, panic disorder should get. In an **aptitude-treatment interaction (ATI) study**, more than one treatment condition is employed. Rather than focus solely on which treatment is more effective on average, this approach tests whether preexisting characteristics of patients (generically called aptitudes) interact with the type of treatment being offered in determining outcome. For instance, if one type of patient does better in psychodynamic therapy while another does better in person-centered therapy, there might be no overall advantage for either type of

aptitude-treatment interaction (ATI) study A study of whether different treatments are especially effective for subtypes of clients distinguished by their pretherapy characteristics.

> ## Focus Box 16.4

You're Changed If You Do and Changed If You Don't: An Example of Aptitude-Treatment Interactions

Have you ever tried to persuade a friend to do something by asking him or her not to do it? Intuition tells us that this sneaky ploy might be effective when a person is spiteful or doesn't like to be controlled by others. The thinking of such an individual might be as follows: "So, he wants me to continue arriving late, huh? I'll show him—I'll start arriving early!"

Since the publication of *Pragmatics of Human Communication*, a book by Watzlawick, Beavin, and Jackson (1967) on complex communication and interaction, some psychotherapists have been drawn to what have come to be called **paradoxical interventions**. These attempts to effect change have in common a request or prescription by the therapist for the patient to continue the problem behavior or to increase its severity or frequency. Thus, if a patient cannot go to sleep, he or she is asked to remain awake. If a patient cannot stop thinking of a disturbing event, he or she is asked to think of it more often.

Research by Varda Shoham-Salomon and her co-workers tested an ATI hypothesis about the sort of person for whom paradoxical interventions should work

best (Shoham-Salomon, Avner, & Neeman, 1989), people who are highly reactant. **Reactance** refers to a motivational state aroused when people perceive that their range of freedom is being limited, with the result that they then make efforts to restore their freedom (Brehm & Brehm, 1981). Thus a reactant patient, when asked by the therapist to become more anxious, might see this symptom prescription as an infringement of freedom and protect himself or herself from this perceived threat by becoming less anxious.

This prediction was confirmed in research on college students suffering from procrastination (Shoham-Salomon et al., 1989). First, students were divided into reactant and nonreactant groups, using procedures that detected spitefulness in tone of voice. Then, the experimenters had the subjects undergo one of two treatments, each conducted for two weekly sessions.

In the *paradoxical intervention*, the therapist explained to the subjects that they needed to understand their procrastination problem better and become more aware of it. To this end, they were to observe the problem carefully by trying to procrastinate deliberately.

paradoxical interventions   Attempts to change behavior by indirect methods, such as requesting that the patient increase the frequency of the problem behavior.

reactance   A motivational state in which people perceive their freedom to be limited and try to restore it, for instance, by acting contrary to therapists' requests.

patient and no overall advantage for either type of therapy, yet the interaction information would be useful in making decisions about treatment.

The importance of ATI studies has long been recognized, and many have been conducted. Unfortunately, the yield of clear indications for how to match therapy approach with type of patient has been very small (Dance & Neufeld, 1988). It may be, though, that results will be superior if theoretically promising ATIs are pursued as opposed to a more scattershot exploratory approach (Smith & Sechrest, 1991). One promising ATI project following a theoretically guided strategy is described in Focus Box 16.4.

To Recap

Broad-gauge consideration of the effectiveness of psychotherapy leads to the following conclusions: (a) psychotherapy is on average considerably more effective than no treatment, but results vary a good deal across cases; (b) individual therapists differ widely in impact, yet the most obvious and plausible markers of who would be a good therapist (such as professional training and years of experience) are weakly related to effectiveness; (c) the amount of therapy that a patient receives is positively related to the benefits of therapy, but the needed dose is not always

Subjects were instructed to gather all their study materials on their desks but not to study for half an hour, to resist any impulse to study, and to concentrate on procrastinating, for example, by ruminating about the problem as they usually did when procrastination occurred normally. *Studying at these times was not permitted.* If they succeeded in this unusual observation task for six days, then on the seventh day they could either study or not study, as they wished and whenever they wished.

At the second therapy session, subjects discussed this assignment. Those who were able to do it were congratulated and reminded that their not studying had allowed them to better understand their problem and therefore to begin to deal with it. If a subject reported having studied more, he or she was not praised. In fact, the change was regarded with skepticism by the therapist as probably only temporary. If subjects did not schedule procrastination time, the therapist exhorted them to try it again in the coming week. Above all, subjects were not encouraged to procrastinate less or to study more.

The contrasting intervention was one of *self-control.* Procrastination was described to the subjects as a learned habit. The subjects needed to develop new behaviors incompatible with procrastination. They were directed to select a place in which they could study more effectively and to try to study as much as possible there, the idea being that these new conditions would become associated with improved study habits. Any reported successes were praised by the therapist.

Results showed that study time was improved via both treatments, but the really interesting results concern interactions between individual levels of reactance and the modality of treatment. As expected, those with higher reactance improved in study habits (less procrastination) more than did low-reactance students in the paradoxical treatment. Thus, subjects who were motivated to restore freedom that they saw as being threatened engaged in behavior that went against the instructions of the therapist—told to study less, they studied more.

Conversely, being highly reactant was *not* an advantage in the self-control treatment, which in fact worked just as well for low-reactance students.

Further research with more clinically disturbed subjects and with long follow-ups needs to be conducted. But this research provides support for the idea that, for some people, telling them not to change their problematic behaviors may be more effective than, as is usual, encouraging them to work directly on behavioral changes.

high—about one-half of patients are measurably improved within just eight sessions; (d) patients with personality disorders benefit less than do others from treatments aimed at their Axis I clinical syndromes; (e) people from all age ranges, both sexes, and all socioeconomic status levels can benefit from psychotherapy; and (f) there are few solid leads on how to select treatments for particular types of patients in order to maximize effectiveness.

How Confident Can We Be?

To arrive at the conclusions just listed, extensive research efforts have been made. Despite the formidable difficulties of conducting well-controlled research, the achievements of therapy researchers are considerable. Nonetheless, we would be remiss to leave the impression that all these conclusions are known to be true without qualification. Psychotherapy research methods are subject to several limitations that require us to be tentative with conclusions about the effects of treatment.

To maximize the validity of studies, many projects implement features that detract from their generalizability to the ordinary clinic situation. For instance, patients are often recruited for treatment via advertisements and the like, rather than having sought it out in the normal course of events; samples are selected to be homogeneous, and exclusion/inclusion criteria are used to promote this feature even if it means including in the study only a small percentage of interested patients; therapists are trained immediately before the study in the exact procedures to be used and are required to stick closely to these procedures. This set of conditions, none of which obtains in ordinary clinical settings, characterizes what Weisz, Weiss, and Donenberg (1992) called "research therapy." Positive results from studies conducted in these ways may not generalize to the regular clinical setting. There is some preliminary evidence from studies of therapy with children that ordinary clinical therapy is less effective than research therapy (Weisz et al., 1992).

In the original meta-analysis of psychotherapy outcome studies, the researchers concluded that the magnitude of effects did not differ for different psychotherapy perspectives (Smith et al., 1980). Their conclusion was controversial, in part because of differences of opinion about how they classified treatments according to theoretical perspective (Eysenck, 1994; Rachman & Wilson, 1980). Meta-analytic studies conducted since the initial work have shown small but statistically reliable advantages on average for cognitive and behavioral methods relative to psychodynamic and humanistic therapies (Lambert & Bergin, 1994).

Proponents of dynamic and humanistic therapies criticize the evidence that behavioral and cognitive therapies are more effective, however. The main problem is that there is a bias favoring behavioral and cognitive approaches because advocates of these methods conduct most of the therapy outcome research (Lambert, Shapiro, & Bergin, 1986). For example, a meta-analysis of controlled experiments on family and marital therapy from 1963 to 1988 included forty studies testing behavioral treatments and one study of psychodynamic treatment (Shadish et al., 1993). This is troublesome because meta-analyses find larger effect sizes for those techniques to which the investigator had a prior allegiance (Robinson, Berman, & Neimeyer, 1990; Smith et al., 1980). This situation may be due to the fact that investigators are able to do a better job of training therapists to perform these preferred methods competently.

As noted earlier, meta-analysis has been very helpful for managing the overload of information on psychotherapy. It does, however, have a notable limitation. The statistics used in meta-analysis (called effect sizes) are in part a function of variability. They do not tell directly whether the patients got healthy or even whether they improved a lot (Jacobson & Truax, 1991). For instance, if a sample of cigarette smokers treated with the nicotine patch (see Chapter 12) reduced intake from an average of thirty to an average of twenty-nine cigarettes a day, while control subjects showed no decline on average, and if variability within groups was small, there would be a large effect size even though the result is not very good. New methods are therefore being devised to try to measure the **clinical significance**, or practical relevance, of psychotherapy effects.

Finally, the constraints of outcome research require that the same dependent measure be utilized for each patient in order to compare equitably treated patients with untreated controls, patients treated with person-centered therapy with those treated with interpersonal therapy, and so on. This requirement leads to the use of broad-gauge indexes that can be assumed to be relevant to most or all patients (number of panic attacks, interviewer-rated depressive symptom severity, etc.) (Persons, 1991).

When we focus attention on individual people, however, it quickly becomes clear that we need to ask *what* effects therapy is intended to have in that particular case and how they might best be measured. If someone still has three panic attacks a month but is much less afraid of them between times and does not restrict travel accordingly, is this a failed therapy? If someone becomes far less anxious

clinical significance The practical relevance of research findings such as psychotherapy effects.

around others but consequently feels free to (and does) abuse them verbally for their shortcomings, is this a successful therapy?

Considering such questions brings us full circle, back to our struggles in Chapter 1 to define abnormal behavior. There is no escaping the conclusion that *values*, not just scientific issues such as research design or statistics or reliability of measurement, play a role in determining our judgments of what constitutes a good outcome in therapy.

Choice of Goals in Psychotherapy

Ideally, the patient sets the goals for therapy. In practice, though, it would be naive to assume that some goals are not imposed by the therapist and may even go against the wishes of the patient. This issue was addressed by Seymour Halleck (1971), a psychiatrist who asserts that the neutrality of the therapist is a myth. In his opinion, therapists influence their patients in ways that are subtle, yet powerful.

> At first glance, a model of psychiatric [or psychological] practice based on the contention that people should just be helped to learn to do the things they want to do seems uncomplicated and desirable. But it is an unobtainable model. Unlike a technician, a psychiatrist [or psychologist] cannot avoid communicating and at times imposing his own values upon his patients. The patient usually has considerable difficulty in finding the way in which he would wish to change his behavior, but as he talks to the psychiatrist his wants and needs become clearer. In the very process of defining his needs in the presence of a figure who is viewed as wise and authoritarian, the patient is profoundly influenced. He ends up wanting some of the things the psychiatrist thinks he should want. (p. 19)

Psychologists agree and research supports the contention that patients are indeed influenced by the values of their therapists (Kelly, 1990). A person not only seeks out a therapist who suits his or her taste and meets what the person believes are his or her needs but also adopts some of the ideals, sometimes even the mannerisms, of the therapist. Most therapists are keenly aware of this modeling after themselves, which surely increases the already heavy responsibilities of their professional role. Perry London (1964, 1986) even suggested that therapists are contemporary society's secular priests, purveyors of values and ethics to help patients live "the good life." Implications of this view for the treatment of homosexual patients are explored in the Legal, Ethical, and Social Issues box.

To Recap

Inferences derived from psychotherapy outcome research must be tentative because of several limitations of existing research. First, outcome studies may be unrepresentative of ordinary clinical practice in terms of such factors as the exclusion criteria used to produce homogeneous samples, reliance on a limited set of techniques in which the therapists have just received special training, and treatment of solicited volunteers rather than of ordinary clinical referrals. Second, most research is conducted by adherents of behavioral or cognitive perspectives, which may bias comparative studies in favor of these approaches. Third, most commonly used methods of analyzing outcome data tell us whether a group of patients improved to a statistically reliable degree but do not tell us whether they improved much, or whether they got well. Finally, most studies use the same assessment methods for all patients, which enhances the comparability of results across patients but ignores the idiosyncratic aspects of goal selection in therapy. Values (including the values of the therapist), not just science, underlie the choice of goals in individual cases of psychotherapy.

LEGAL, ETHICAL, AND SOCIAL ISSUES

An Opinion on the Treatment of Homosexuality

Because social pressures against homosexuality may influence homosexuals to attempt to become heterosexual, some psychologists argue that the small minority of people who consult therapists for help in changing their sexual orientation from same-sex to opposite-sex partners may not be acting based on their own desires, but rather on those of society (Begelman, 1975; Davison, 1974, 1976; Silverstein, 1972). In this case, then, what is the therapist's proper response? Should he or she accede to the person's stated goal or embark on a therapeutic course geared more toward having the patient accept the person he or she is?

There are obviously extensive pressures on homosexuals to become heterosexual (see Chapter 13). It has been suggested that the mere availability of change-of-orientation programs serves to condone the prejudice against homosexuality (Davison, 1976). Clinicians work to develop procedures and study their effects only if they first perceive a "problem" to be dealt with by their techniques. The therapy literature contains relatively little material on helping homosexuals develop as individuals without changing their sexual orientation, in contrast with the many articles and books on how best to discourage homosexual behavior and substitute for it heterosexual patterns. Aversion therapy used to be the most widely used behavioral technique for treating people who wished to end their attraction to the same sex. (Davison & Wilson, 1973; Henkel & Lewis-Thomé, 1976). "What are we really saying to our clients when, on the one hand, we assure them that they are not abnormal and on the other hand, present them with an array of techniques, some of them painful, which are aimed at eliminating that set of feelings and behavior that we have just told them is okay?" (Davison, 1976, p. 161)

In view of these issues it has been proposed that therapists not help homosexuals become heterosexual even when such treatment is requested. This obviously

Homosexuality is not considered a psychological disorder, and many psychologists oppose the development and promotion of therapies for changing homosexual people's sexual orientation.

extreme proposal has evoked some strong reactions. Gay-activist groups are understandably pleased, considering the suggestion concrete support for the belief that homosexuality per se is not a mental disorder. But many therapists are concerned about limiting the choices available to people seeking therapy. Why should a therapist decide for potential patients which options should be available? Do not therapists have a responsibility to satisfy the needs expressed by their patients (Sturgis & Adams, 1978)? A reply to this important criticism would be that therapists already decide what therapy they will offer when they refuse to take as patients people with whose goals they disagree. The request of a patient for a certain kind of treatment has never been sufficient justification for providing it (Davison, 1978).

Efforts to change sexual orientation have shown little success (Haldeman, 1994), but some people have asserted that continued research could help develop sex-reorientation programs that are more effective (Sturgis & Adams, 1978). To discourage such work would deprive today's homosexuals of promising therapies and tomorrow's homosexuals of improved treatments. This objection, however, is not definitive. The fact that we *can do* something does not indicate that we *should*. The proposal to deny sexual-reorientation therapy is ethical, not empirical, in nature. The decision whether we should change sexual orientation will have to be made on moral grounds.

Will numbers of people be hurt by eliminating the sex-reorientation option? Some have raised the specter of an upsurge in suicides among homosexuals if therapists refuse to help them switch. These are very serious concerns, but they overlook the possibility, some would say the fact, that far greater numbers of people have been hurt over the years by the availability of sex-reorientation programs. As already argued, the existence of these treatments is consistent with societal prejudices and discrimination against homosexuals.

It is noteworthy that since 1975 there has been a dramatic reduction in the use of aversion therapy to change homosexual orientation to heterosexual (Rosen & Beck, 1988) and a sharp decrease also in reports of other procedures for altering homosexuality. Additional signs of increased acceptance of homosexuality as a lifestyle are the elimination of ego-dystonic homosexuality from the DSM and the establishment within the American Psychological Association of the Division of Lesbian and Gay Psychologists and the Committee on Lesbian and Gay Concerns on the Board of Social and Ethical Responsibility. This trend is not universal, however. Some recent programs, including religion-based efforts to convert homosexuals into heterosexuals, have been reviewed by Haldeman (1994).

The proponents who wish to terminate change-of-orientation programs believe that much good can come of their proposal. Homosexuals would be helped to think better of themselves, and greater efforts could be directed toward the problems homosexuals have, rather than toward the issue of homosexuality.

> It would be nice if an alcoholic homosexual, for example, could be helped to reduce his or her drinking without having his or her sexual orientation questioned. It would be nice if a homosexual fearful of interpersonal relationships, or incompetent in them, could be helped without the therapist assuming that homosexuality lies at the root of the problem. It would be nice if a nonorgasmic or impotent homosexual could be helped as a heterosexual would be rather than [being guided] to change-of-orientation regimens . . . the hope [is] that therapists will concentrate their efforts on such human problems rather than focusing on the most obvious "maladjustment"—loving members of one's own sex. (Davison, 1978, p. 171)

Visual Summary for Chapter 16:

Issues in Intervention

Prevention

Tertiary

Reduce long-term consequences of having a disorder (e.g., teach a young patient with schizophrenia skills needed to hold a job and prevent decline in socioeconomic status).

Secondary

Reduce incidence of disorder by targeting high-risk groups (e.g., lower incidence of child depression by providing support for children whose parents are going through a divorce).

Primary

Reduce incidence of disorder by eliminating the cause of the problem in entire population (e.g., lower incidence of mental retardation by outlawing lead-based paint).

A Sample of Prevention Programs

Suicide-Prevention Centers ····> *Provide 24-hour telephone hot line for people in suicidal crises.*

Mass Media Programs to Promote Cardiovascular Health ····> *Use posters, ads, television and radio programs, and so on to encourage low-cholesterol diet, smoking cessation, and increased exercise. Controlled studies suggest that such interventions targeted at entire communities can lower risk factors for coronary heart disease.*

Promoting Family Competence ····> *Provide coping-skills training and information about child rearing aimed at lowering prevalence of child abuse. Intensive interventions with high-risk families (i.e., secondary prevention) show the clearest effect.*

AIDS Prevention ····> *Use persuasive messages to describe which sexual practices are associated with the highest or lowest risk of transmitting HIV and suggest that the benefits of lower-risk sex outweigh any perceived costs. Reductions in unprotected anal intercourse and increases in condom use have resulted.*

General Issues in Psychotherapy

Eclecticism and Integration ····> *The modal psychotherapist is eclectic, drawing on more than one theoretical perspective at a time. The therapist may (e.g., Paul Wachtel's cyclical psychodynamics blends psychoanalysis and behavior therapy) or may not (e.g., Arnold Lazarus's multimodal therapy defines a range of problem areas for each patient and then selects any technique known to be effective for a given one of the problems) attempt to blend and integrate the contributing theories into a new conceptual whole.*

Cultural and Racial Factors ····> *Some studies show an overall preference of minority group members for therapists of the same race or ethnicity, but racial differences between therapist and patient do not preclude the possibility of effective therapy.*

Effective Therapy with Culturally Diverse Patients

•Communicate understanding and empathy, but not condescension or stereotyping.

•Learn as much as possible about diverse cultures to facilitate accurate interpretation rather than overpathologizing of behaviors and attitudes that vary substantially across cultures, such as willingness to disclose emotions or attitudes toward family relationships.

•Be aware of culture-specific stresses, such as experiencing race-based oppression or fleeing political oppression and becoming an immigrant.

•Bear in mind that such generalizations provide possible clues to understanding a patient, but that individuals are individuals. Knowing that a patient is a Native American does not dictate that his or her problems must be **X** or the best intervention **Y** any more than does knowing that a patient is a woman, is thirty years old, or is a Unitarian-Universalist.

Beyond Individual Therapy ••••▶ Couples therapy and family therapy assume that a system of interactions within the family may be a better target for change than are the behaviors and cognitive processes of any one member of the family.
Conflict within the family is considered inevitable, but how it is managed is a critical aspect of family functioning.
Group therapies include multiple unrelated patients, sometimes just for efficiency but sometimes to take advantage of group processes, such as group support, peer feedback, and awareness that one's problems are not unique.

Beyond the Outpatient Setting •••▶ Inpatient hospitalization has typically involved medication, group therapy, and not a great deal of interaction with therapists. Some more active psychological intervention programs, such as Paul and Lentz's application of social learning principles in an inpatient setting, have proven effective.
Halfway houses try to bridge the gap between inpatient hospitalization and completely independent functioning for patients who need extra support and structure but do not necessarily need hospitalization.

Does Psychotherapy Help People?

Apparently so. Hundreds of controlled experiments indicate positive effects on average.

Does it Help Everyone? •••▶ No. Effects are variable, depending on the therapist, possibly (though this is more controversial) the theory guiding the therapist's work, the patient (e.g., presence of a comorbid personality disorder tends to worsen results), the fit between therapist and patient, and the length of treatment (about eight sessions seems to be a median length needed to show effects).

Does it Help Enough? •••▶ This is hard to say and depends on the goals (the patient's, the therapist's, and society's goals for therapy). Many researchers are adopting ways of evaluating therapy that stress the practical importance of its effects, as distinct from their statistical reliability. Such evaluations tend to paint a less flattering picture and encourage the search for improvements to current techniques.

Glossary

abnormal behavior Patterns of emotion, thought, and action deemed pathological for one or more of the following reasons: infrequent occurrence, violation of norms, personal distress, disability or dysfunction, and unexpectedness.

accurate empathic understanding In person-centered therapy, an essential quality of the therapist, referring to the ability to see the world through the client's eyes.

acquaintance (date) rape Forcible sex between two people who know each other, sometimes occurring on a date.

acute stress disorder An *anxiety disorder* in which a traumatic event leads to symptoms similar to those exhibited by patients with *posttraumatic stress disorder* except that by definition acute stress disorder symptoms last less than a month after the occurrence of the trauma.

advanced empathy A form of empathy in which the therapist infers concerns and feelings that lie behind what the client is saying.

aftercare Follow-up community-based services for patients who have been discharged from psychiatric hospitals.

age effect The consequences of being a given chronological age. Compare with *cohort effects*.

ageism Prejudice and discrimination based on age.

agoraphobia A cluster of fears centering on being in open spaces and leaving the home.

AIDS (acquired immunodeficiency syndrome) A fatal disease transmitted by the human immunodeficiency virus, usually during sexual relations or by using needles previously infected by an HIV-positive person; it compromises the person's immune system to such a degree that he or she ultimately dies from cancer or one of a number of infections.

Alzheimer's disease A *dementia* involving a progressive atrophy of cortical tissue and marked by concentration and memory impairment, disorientation, and progressive intellectual deterioration.

amphetamines A group of stimulating drugs that produce heightened levels of energy and, in large doses, nervousness, sleeplessness, and paranoid *delusions*.

analogue experiment An experimental study of a phenomenon different from but related to the actual interests of the investigator.

anal personality In *psychoanalytic theory*, an adult whose traits, such as stinginess, are assumed to be caused by *fixation* through either excessive or inadequate gratification of id impulses during the *anal stage* of *psychosexual development*.

anal stage In *psychoanalytic theory*, the second *psychosexual stage*, occurring during the second year of life, during which the anus is considered the principal site of gratification.

analytical psychology A variation of Freud's *psychoanalysis* introduced by Carl Jung and focusing less on biological drives and more on such factors as self-fulfillment, *collective unconscious*, and religious symbolism

anesthesia An impairment or loss of sensation, usually of touch but sometimes of the other senses, that is often part of *conversion disorder*.

anorexia nervosa A disorder in which a person is unwilling to eat or to retain any food or suffers a prolonged and severe diminution of appetite. The individual has an intense fear of becoming obese, feels fat even when emaciated, and refuses to maintain a minimal body weight.

Antabuse (Trade name for disulfiram) A drug that makes the drinking of alcohol produce nausea and other unpleasant effects.

antisocial personality Also called a psychopath, a person with this disorder is superficially charming and a habitual liar, has no regard for others, shows no remorse after hurting others, has no shame for behaving in an outrageously objectionable manner, is unable to form relationships and take responsibility, and does not learn from punishment.

anxiety An unpleasant feeling of fear and apprehension accompanied by increased physiological arousal and avoidance behavior.

anxiety disorders Disorders in which fear or tension is overriding and the primary disturbance: *phobias, panic disorder, generalized anxiety disorder, obsessive-compulsive disorder, posttraumatic stress disorder*, and *acute stress disorder*.

aphasia The loss or impairment of the ability to use language because of lesions in the brain.

aptitude test An assessment of a person's intellectual functioning that is supposed to predict how he or she will perform at a later time; well-known examples include the

Scholastic Aptitude Test and the Graduate Record Examination.

aptitude-treatment interaction (ATI) study   A study of whether different treatments are especially effective for subtypes of clients distinguished by their pretherapy characteristics.

Asperger's disorder   A *pervasive developmental disorder* involving difficulty in social interaction and stereotyped behaviors. Unlike *autistic disorder*, language and cognitive development and self-care skills are normal.

assertiveness training   *Behavior therapy* procedures that attempt to help a person express more easily thoughts, wishes, beliefs, and legitimate feelings of resentment or approval.

asthma   A disorder characterized by narrowing of the airways and increased secretion of mucus, which often cause breathing to be extremely labored and wheezy.

asylums   Refuges established in western Europe in the fifteenth century to confine and care for the mentally ill; the forerunners of the mental hospital.

attention-deficit/hyperactivity disorder (ADHD)   A disorder in children marked by difficulties in focusing adaptively on the task at hand and by inappropriate fidgeting and antisocial behavior.

attribution   The explanation a person has for his or her experience.

autistic disorder   A *pervasive developmental disorder* involving profound aloneness and difficulty in relating to others, severe communication problems, and ritualistic behavior; often associated with *mental retardation*.

automatic thoughts   In Beck's theory, the things people picture or tell themselves as they make their way in life.

avoidant personality   Individuals with an avoidant personality have poor self-esteem and thus are extremely sensitive to potential rejection and remain aloof, even though they very much desire affiliation and affection.

avolition   A *negative symptom* in *schizophrenia* in which the individual lacks interest and drive.

barbiturates   A class of synthetic *sedative* drugs that are addictive and in large doses can cause death by almost completely relaxing the diaphragm.

behavioral perspective   As applied in abnormal psychology, a set of assumptions that *abnormal behavior* is learned in the same way as other human behavior.

behavior genetics   The study of individual differences in behavior that are attributable in part to differences in genetic makeup.

behaviorism   The school of psychology associated with John B. Watson, who proposed that observable behavior, not consciousness, is the proper subject matter of psychology.

behavior therapy   A branch of *psychotherapy* relying mainly on the application of learning principles to the alteration of clinical problems.

bilateral ECT   *Electroconvulsive therapy* in which electrodes are placed on each side of the forehead and an electrical current is passed through both hemispheres of the brain.

biofeedback   Procedures that provide an individual immediate information on even minute changes in muscle activity, skin temperature, heart rate, blood pressure, and other bodily functions. It is assumed that voluntary control over

these bodily processes can be achieved through this knowledge, thereby reducing to some extent certain *psychophysiological disorders*.

biological perspective   A broad theoretical view that holds that mental disorders are caused by some aberrant bodily process or defect.

bipolar disorder   A term applied to the disorder of people who experience episodes of both *mania* and depression or of mania alone.

body dysmorphic disorder   A *somatoform disorder* in which the person is preoccupied with an imagined or exaggerated defect in appearance, for example, facial wrinkles or excess facial or body hair.

borderline personality   This impulsive and unpredictable person has an uncertain self-image, intense and unstable social relationships, and extreme swings of mood.

brain disorders   Psychological abnormalities presumed to be caused by brain malfunctions.

brain stem   The part of the brain connecting the spinal cord with the *cerebrum*. It contains the *pons* and *medulla oblongata* and functions as a neural relay station.

brief dynamic therapies   Short-term therapy approaches based on such Freudian concepts as *defense mechanisms*, but with a more active approach and more attention to present problems and relationships.

bulimia nervosa   Episodic uncontrollable eating binges, often followed by purging, either by vomiting or by taking laxatives.

cardiovascular disorders   Medical problems involving the heart and blood circulation system, such as *essential hypertension* or *coronary heart disease*.

cardiovascular reactivity   Temporary changes in measures of cardiovascular function, such as blood pressure, in response to specific events, such as *stressors*.

case study   The collection of historical or biographical information on a single individual, often including experiences in therapy.

catatonic immobility   A fixity of posture, sometimes grotesque, maintained for long periods, with accompanying muscular rigidity, trancelike state of consciousness, and *waxy flexibility*.

catatonic schizophrenia   *Schizophrenia* in which the primary symptoms alternate between stuporous immobility and excited agitation.

categorical classification   An approach to assessment in which the basic decision is whether a person is or is not a member of a discrete grouping.

CAT scan   Computerized axial tomography, a method of assessment employing X rays taken from different angles and then analyzed by computer to produce a representation of the part of the body in cross section. Often used on the brain.

cathartic method   A therapeutic procedure introduced by Breuer and developed further by Freud in the late nineteenth century whereby a patient recalls and relives an earlier emotional catastrophe and reexperiences the tension and unhappiness, with the goal of relieving emotional suffering.

cerebellum   An area of the hindbrain concerned with balance, posture, and motor coordination.

cerebral cortex   The thin outer covering of each of the *cerebral hemispheres*; it is highly convoluted and composed of nerve cell bodies, which constitute the gray matter of the brain.

cerebral hemispheres   The two halves that make up the cerebrum, the anterior part of the brain.

cerebral hemorrhage   Bleeding onto brain tissue from a ruptured blood vessel.

cerebral thrombosis   The formation of a blood clot in a cerebral artery that blocks circulation in that area of brain tissue and causes paralysis, loss of sensory functions, and possibly death.

childhood disintegrative disorder   A *pervasive developmental disorder* in which the child is usually severely mentally retarded; similar to *autistic disorder* except that development is normal for the first two years.

child sexual abuse   Sexual contact with a minor.

civil commitment   A procedure whereby a person can be legally certified as mentally ill and hospitalized, even against his or her will.

classical conditioning   A basic form of learning, sometimes referred to as Pavlovian conditioning, in which a neutral stimulus is paired with another stimulus (called the **unconditioned stimulus, or UCS**) that naturally elicits a certain desired response (called the **unconditioned response or UCR**). After repeated trials the neutral stimulus becomes a *conditioned stimulus* (CS) and evokes the same or a similar response, now called the **conditioned response (CR)**.

clinical interview   General term for conversation between a clinician and a patient, aimed at determining diagnosis, history, causes of problems, and possible treatment options.

clinical psychologist   A specialist in the area of psychology concerned with the study of *psychopathology*, its causes, prevention, and treatment.

clinical significance   The practical relevance of research findings such as psychotherapy effects.

clinician   A health professional authorized to provide diagnostic and therapeutic services.

clitoris   The small, heavily innervated structure located above the vaginal opening; the primary site of female responsiveness to sexual stimulation.

cocaine   A pain-reducing, stimulating, and addictive drug, obtained from coca leaves, which increases mental powers, produces euphoria, heightens sexual desire, and in large doses causes *paranoia* and *hallucinations*.

cognition   The process of knowing; the thinking, judging, reasoning, and planning activities of the human mind.

cognitive perspective   General view that people can best be understood by studying how they perceive and structure their experiences.

cognitive therapy (CT)   A therapy associated with the psychiatrist Aaron T. Beck, concerned with changing negative *schemata* and certain cognitive biases or distortions that underlie and reinforce the person's symptoms.

cohort effects   The consequences of having been born in a given year and having grown up during a particular time period with its own unique pressures, problems, challenges, and opportunities.

collective unconscious   Jung's concept that every human being has inherited the wisdom, ideas, and strivings of those who have come before.

common factors   In psychotherapy, the attempt to base practice on the strategies and principles shared by all major perspectives.

community mental health center (CMHC)   A center for delivery of services to needy, underserved groups. Services include outpatient therapy, short-term inpatient care, day hospitalization, twenty-four-hour emergency services, and consultation and education for other community agencies, such as the police.

community psychology   An approach to therapy that emphasizes prevention and the seeking out of potential difficulties rather than waiting for troubled individuals to initiate consultation. The location for professional activities tends to be in the person's natural surroundings rather than in the therapist's office.

comorbidity   The co-occurrence of two disorders, as when a person is both depressed and alcoholic.

compulsion   The irresistible impulse to repeat an irrational behavior or mental act over and over again.

concordance   As applied in *behavior genetics*, the similarity in psychiatric diagnosis or in other traits within a pair of twins.

concurrent validity   A kind of *criterion-related validity*, the extent to which common current features are found (e.g., the same socioeconomic status) among patients with the same diagnosis.

conduct disorder   A pattern of extreme disobedience in youngsters, including theft, vandalism, lying, and early drug use; may be a precursor of *antisocial personality disorder*.

content validity   The extent to which all important aspects of the characteristic are included in appropriate proportions in a measure.

control group   The subjects in an *experiment* who form a baseline against which the effects of the manipulation of the experimental group can be evaluated.

controlled drinking   A pattern of alcohol consumption that is moderate and avoids the extremes of total abstinence and of inebriation.

conversion disorder   A *somatoform disorder* in which sensory or muscular functions are impaired, usually suggesting neurological disease, even though the bodily organs themselves are sound; *anesthesias* and paralyses of limbs are examples.

coronary heart disease (CHD)   Angina pectoris, chest pains caused by insufficient supply of blood and thus oxygen to the heart; and myocardial infarction, or heart attack, in which the blood and oxygen supply are reduced so much that heart muscles are damaged.

corpus callosum   The large band of nerve fibers connecting the two *cerebral hemispheres*.

correlational method   Research that establishes whether two or more variables are related.

counseling psychologists   Mental health professionals whose training is similar to that of *clinical psychologists*, though usually with less emphasis on research and *psychopathology*.

counterconditioning   Relearning achieved by eliciting a new response in the presence of a particular stimulus.

countertransference   Feelings that the analyst unconsciously directs to the patient, stemming from his or her own emotional vulnerabilities and unresolved conflicts.

couples therapy Any professional intervention that treats the relationship problems of a couple.

covert sensitization A form of *aversion therapy* in which the subject is told to imagine the undesirably attractive situations and activities at the same time that unpleasant feelings are also induced by imagery.

criterion-related validity The extent to which diagnostic criteria or scores on a test are systematically related to other important information about a person (the criterion).

critical thinking A habit of thinking involving questioning assumptions, evaluating the soundness of evidence for claims people make, and exploring alternative hypotheses.

cross-sectional study A study in which different age groups are compared at the same time. Compare with *longitudinal study*.

cyclical psychodynamics The reciprocal relations between current behavior and repressed conflicts, such that they mutually reinforce each other.

cyclothymic disorder Swings between elation and depression not severe enough to warrant the diagnosis of *bipolar disorder*.

defense mechanism In *psychoanalytic theory*, reality-distorting strategies unconsciously adopted to protect the *ego* from anxiety.

delirium A state of great mental confusion in which consciousness is clouded, attention cannot be sustained, and the stream of thought and speech is incoherent. The person is disoriented, emotionally erratic, restless or lethargic, and often has illusions, *delusions*, and *hallucinations*.

delirium tremens (DTs) A set of *withdrawal symptoms* when a period of heavy alcohol consumption is terminated; marked by fever, sweating, trembling, cognitive impairment, and *hallucinations*.

delusional jealousy The unfounded conviction that one's mate is unfaithful. The individual may collect small bits of "evidence" to justify the *delusion*.

delusions Beliefs contrary to reality, firmly held in spite of contradictory evidence. For example, delusions of persecution are beliefs that one is being plotted against or oppressed by others.

dementia Deterioration of mental faculties—of memory, judgment, abstract thought, control of impulses, intellectual ability—that impairs social and occupational functioning and eventually changes the personality.

dementia praecox An older term for *schizophrenia*, chosen to describe what was believed to be an incurable and progressive deterioration of mental functioning beginning in adolescence.

demonology The doctrine that a person's abnormal behavior is caused by an evil spirit.

denial *Defense mechanism* in which objective events are kept out of conscious awareness.

dependent personality Lacking in self-confidence, people with a dependent personality passively allow others to run their lives and make no demands on them so as not to endanger these protective relationships.

dependent variable In a psychological *experiment*, the behavior that is measured and expected to change with manipulation of the *independent variable*.

depersonalization An alteration in perception of the self in which the individual loses a sense of reality and feels estranged from the self and perhaps separated from the body.

depersonalization disorder A *dissociative disorder* in which the individual feels unreal and estranged from the self and surroundings enough to disrupt functioning. People with this disorder may feel that their extremities have changed in size or that they are watching themselves from a distance.

derealization Loss of the sense that the surroundings are real.

deterioration effect A harmful outcome from being in *psychotherapy*.

detoxification The initial stage in weaning an addicted person from a drug; involves medical supervision of the sometimes painful *withdrawal*.

dialectical behavior therapy (DBT) A therapeutic approach to *borderline personality* disorder that combines empathy and acceptance with behavioral problem solving, social-skills training, and limit setting.

diastolic pressure Amount of arterial pressure when the ventricles relax and the heart is resting; for a young adult, 80 is normal.

diencephalon The lower area of the forebrain, containing the *thalamus* and *hypothalamus*.

dimensional classification An approach to assessment according to which a person is placed on a continuum.

directionality problem A difficulty in the *correlational method* of research whereby it is known that two variables are related, but it is unclear which is causing the other.

disorder of written expression Difficulty writing without errors in spelling, grammar, or punctuation.

disorganized schizophrenia *Schizophrenia* in which the person has rather diffuse and regressive symptoms; the individual is given to silliness, facial grimaces, and inconsequential rituals and has constantly changeable moods and poor hygiene.

disorganized speech Speech found in *schizophrenics* that is marked by problems in the organization of ideas and in speaking so that others can understand.

discriminative stimulus An event that informs an organism that if a particular response is made, *reinforcement* will follow.

dissociative amnesia A *dissociative disorder* in which the person suddenly becomes unable to recall important personal information to an extent that cannot be explained by ordinary forgetfulness.

dissociative disorders Disorders in which the normal integration of consciousness, memory, or identity is suddenly altered; *dissociative amnesia, dissociative fugue, depersonalization disorder*, and *dissociative identity disorder*.

dissociative fugue A *dissociative disorder* in which the person forgets important personal information and assumes a new identity, moving to a new location unexpectedly.

dissociative identity disorder (DID) A *dissociative disorder* in which two or more fairly distinct and separate personalities (called alters) are present within the same individual, each with its own memories, relationships, and behavior patterns and only one of which is dominant at any given time. Formerly called *multiple personality disorder (MPD)*.

dizygotic (DZ) twins   Birth partners who have developed from separate fertilized eggs and who are only 50% alike genetically, no more so than siblings born from different pregnancies; sometimes called fraternal twins.

double-bind theory   An interpersonal situation in which an individual is confronted, over long periods of time, by mutually inconsistent messages to which she or he must respond, formerly believed by some theorists to cause *schizophrenia*.

Down syndrome (trisomy 21)   A form of *mental retardation* generally caused by an extra *chromosome*. Physical characteristics are distinctive, most notably slanted eyes.

dream analysis   A key psychoanalytic technique in which the unconscious meanings of dream material are uncovered.

DSM-IV   The current *Diagnostic and Statistical Manual of the American Psychiatric Association*.

dysfunctional beliefs   In Beck's theory, attitudes, of which a person may be unaware, that constitute vulnerability to *psychopathology*.

dyspareunia   Recurrent pain before, during, or after sexual intercourse.

dysthymic disorder   State of depression that is long lasting but not severe enough for the diagnosis of *major depressive disorder*.

eating disorders   Severe disturbance in eating behavior accompanied by distorted perception of body shape and weight.

echolalia   A speech problem in which the person repeats back exactly what she or he has heard another say; often found in the speech of children with *autistic disorder*.

eclectic   In *psychotherapy*, an approach that draws on concepts or methods from more than one theoretical perspective.

eclecticism   In psychology, the view that more is to be gained by employing concepts from various theoretical systems than by restricting oneself to a single theory.

Ecstasy   A relatively new *hallucinogen* that is chemically similar to *mescaline* and the *amphetamines*.

ego   In *psychoanalytic theory*, the predominantly conscious part of the personality responsible for decision making and for dealing with reality.

ego-dystonic homosexuality   According to DSM-III, a disorder of people who are persistently dissatisfied with their *homosexuality* and wish instead to be attracted to members of the opposite sex.

electroconvulsive therapy (ECT)   A treatment that produces a convulsion by passing electric current through the brain. Though an unpleasant and occasionally dangerous procedure, it can be useful in alleviating profound depression.

emotion-focused coping   In response to stressful situations, taking steps to reduce one's negative emotional response, even if the situation stays the same.

epidemiology   The study of the frequency and distribution of illness in a population.

essential hypertension   A disorder characterized by high blood pressure that cannot be traced to a physical cause.

exhibitionism   Marked preference for obtaining sexual gratification by exposing one's genitals to an unwilling observer.

exorcism   The casting out of evil spirits by ritualistic chanting or torture.

experiment   The most powerful research technique for determining causal relationships, requiring the manipulation of an *independent variable*, the measurement of a *dependent variable*, and the *random assignment* of subjects to the several different conditions being investigated.

experimental effect   A difference between groups experiencing different manipulations of the *independent variable*.

experimental hypothesis   What the investigator believes will happen in a scientific investigation if particular variables are manipulated.

expressed emotion (EE)   Originating in the literature on *schizophrenia*, the amount of hostility and criticism directed from other people to a patient, usually within a family.

expressive language disorder   Difficulty expressing oneself in speech.

extinction   The elimination of a classically *conditioned response* by the omission of the *unconditioned stimulus*. In *operant conditioning*, the elimination of the *conditioned response* by the omission of *reinforcement*.

family studies   A research strategy in *behavior genetics* in which the frequency of a trait or of abnormal behavior is determined in relatives who have varying percentages of shared genetic background.

family systems approach   A general approach to psychopathology and treatment that focuses on the complex interrelationships within families.

family systems therapy   A general approach to treatment that focuses on the complex interrelationships within families.

family therapy   A form of therapy in which members of a family are helped to relate better to one another.

fears about performance   Being overly concerned with one's behavior during sexual contact with another, postulated by Masters and Johnson as a major factor causing *sexual dysfunction*.

female orgasmic disorder   A recurrent and persistent absence of orgasm in a woman during sexual activity adequate in focus, intensity, and duration; in many instances the woman may nonetheless experience considerable sexual excitement.

female sexual arousal disorder   The inability of a woman to reach or maintain the lubrication stage of sexual excitement or the inability to enjoy a subjective sense of pleasure or excitement during sexual activity.

fetal alcohol syndrome   Retarded growth of the developing fetus; cranial, facial, and limb anomalies and *mental retardation* caused by heavy consumption of alcohol by the mother during pregnancy.

fetishism   Reliance on an inanimate object for sexual arousal.

fixated (fixation)   In *psychoanalytic theory*, arrested *psychosexual* development at a particular stage because of too much or too little gratification at that stage.

flat affect   A deviation in emotional response wherein virtually no emotion is expressed, whatever the stimulus.

flooding   A *behavior therapy* procedure in which a fearful person is exposed to what is frightening, in reality or in the imagination, for extended periods of time and full intensity.

forcible rape   The legal term for *rape,* to force sexual intercourse or other sexual activity on another person. Statutory rape is sexual intercourse between an adult male and someone who is under the age of consent, as fixed by local statute.

free association   A key psychoanalytic procedure in which the patient is encouraged to give free rein to thoughts and feelings, verbalizing whatever comes into the mind without monitoring its content. The assumption is that, over time, hitherto *repressed* material will come forth for examination by the patient and analyst.

frontal lobe   The forward or upper half of each *cerebral hemispheres,* in front of the central sulcus, active in reasoning and other higher mental processes.

functional social support   The quality of a person's relationships, for example, a good versus a distressed marriage.

gender identity   The deeply ingrained sense a person has of being either a man or a woman.

general adaptation syndrome (GAS)   Hans Selye's model to describe the biological reaction of an organism to a sustained and unrelenting stressor; there are several stages, culminating in death in extreme circumstances.

generalized anxiety disorder (GAD)   One of the *anxiety disorders,* where worry is chronic, uncontrollable, and excessive. The individual is jittery and strained, distractible, and apprehensive that something bad is about to happen. A pounding heart, fast pulse and breathing, sweating, flushing, muscle aches, a lump in the throat, and an upset gastrointestinal tract are some of the bodily indications of this disorder.

general paresis   Infection of the central nervous system by a spirochete which destroys brain tissue; marked by eye disturbances, tremors, and disordered speech as well as severe intellectual deterioration and *psychotic* symptoms.

genes   Ultramicroscopic areas of the *chromosome.* The gene is the smallest physical unit of the DNA molecule that carries a piece of hereditary information.

genital stage   In *psychoanalytic theory,* the final *psychosexual stage,* reached in adulthood, in which heterosexual interests predominate.

genotype   An individual's unobservable, physiological genetic constitution; the totality of *genes* possessed by an individual.

genuineness   In *person-centered therapy,* an essential quality of the therapist, referring to openness and authenticity.

germ theory (of disease)   The general view in medicine that disease is caused by infection of the body by minute organisms and viruses.

gerontology   The interdisciplinary study of aging.

grandiose delusions   An exaggerated sense of one's importance, power, knowledge, or identity.

group therapy   A method of treating psychological disorders whereby several persons are seen simultaneously.

gyri   Ridges or convolutions of the *cerebral cortex.*

halfway houses   Homelike residences for people who are considered too disturbed to remain in their accustomed surroundings but do not require the total care of a mental institution.

hallucinations   Perceptions in any sensory modality without relevant and adequate external stimuli.

hallucinogens   Drugs or chemicals whose effects include *hallucinations.* Hallucinogenic drugs are often called psychedelic.

heritability   The extent to which *genes* contribute to the likelihood that a person will develop a particular disorder or condition.

heroin   An extremely addictive *narcotic* drug derived from *morphine.*

heroin antagonists   Drugs, like naloxone, that prevent a *heroin* user from experiencing any high.

heroin substitutes   Narcotics, like *methadone,* that replace the body's craving for *heroin.*

histrionic personality   This person is overly dramatic, attention seeking, given to emotional excess, and immature.

homosexuality   Sexual desire or activity directed toward a member of one's own sex.

hopelessness depression   A subtype of depression believed to be caused by the expectation that desirable outcomes will not occur or that undesirable ones will occur and that nothing one can do will change this state of affairs. These expectations in turn are caused by the interaction of stressful events with any of several cognitive vulnerabilities, according to the theory of Abramson, Metalsky, and Alloy.

humanistic and existential perspectives   A generic term for theories that emphasize the individual's subjective experiences, free will, and ever-present ability to decide on a new life course.

hypoactive sexual desire disorder   The absence of or deficiency in sexual fantasies and urges.

hypochondriasis   A *somatoform disorder* in which the person, misinterpreting ordinary physical sensations, is preoccupied with fears of having a serious disease and is not dissuaded by medical opinion.

hypomania   An above-normal elevation of mood, but not as extreme as *mania.*

hypothalamus   A collection of nuclei and fibers in the lower part of the *diencephalon* concerned with the regulation of many visceral processes, such as metabolism, temperature, water balance, and so on.

hypothesis   What the investigator believes will happen in a scientific investigation if certain conditions are met or particular variables are manipulated.

hysteria   A disorder, known to the ancient Greeks, in which a physical incapacity, a paralysis, an anesthesia, or an analgesia, is not due to a physiological dysfunction; an older term for *conversion disorder.*

id   In *psychoanalytic theory,* that part of the personality present at birth, composed of all the energy of the mind and expressed as biological urges that strive continually for gratification.

ideas of reference   Reading personal significance into seemingly trivial remarks and activities of others and completely unrelated events.

identity crisis   A developmental period in adolescence marked by concerns about who one is and what one is going to do with his or her life.

inappropriate affect   Emotional responses that are out of context, such as laughter when hearing sad news.

incest   Sexual relations between close relatives, most often between daughter and father or between brother and sister.

incidence   In *epidemiological* studies of a particular disorder, the rate at which new cases occur in a given period of time.

independent variable   In a psychological *experiment*, the factor, experience, or treatment that is under the control of the experimenter and that is expected to have an effect on the subjects as assessed by changes in the *dependent variable*.

intelligence test   A standardized means of assessing a person's current mental ability, for example, the Stanford–Binet test and the Wechsler Adult Intelligence Scale.

internal consistency reliability   The extent to which scores on different parts of a measure, such as different test items or diagnostic criteria, are consistent with one another.

interpretation   In *psychoanalysis*, a key procedure in which the *psychoanalyst* points out to the patient where *resistances* exist and what certain dreams and verbalizations reveal about impulses repressed in the *unconscious*.

interrater reliability   The relationship between the judgments that at least two raters make independently about a phenomenon.

interview   Any conversation in which one person uses language to find out about another.

introject   In psychoanalytic theory, the idea that a person unconsciously incorporates the values, attitudes, and qualities of another person into the individual's own personality.

introspection   A procedure whereby trained subjects are asked to report on their conscious experiences. This was the principal method of study in early twentieth-century psychology.

irrational beliefs   Self-defeating assumptions that are assumed by *rational-emotive* therapists to underlie psychological distress.

la belle indifférence   The blasé attitude people with *conversion disorder* sometimes have toward their symptoms.

latency period   In *psychoanalytic theory*, the years between ages six and twelve, during which *id* impulses play a minor role in motivation.

latent content   In dreams, the presumed true meaning hidden behind the *manifest content*.

law of effect   A principle of learning that holds that behavior is acquired by virtue of its consequences.

learned helplessness theory   An individual's passivity and sense of being unable to act and to control his or her life, acquired through the ineffectiveness of the individual's efforts to control unpleasant and traumatic experiences; according to Seligman's original theory, this brings on depression.

least restrictive alternative   The legal principle according to which a committed mental patient must be treated in a setting that imposes as few restrictions as possible on his or her freedom.

lifetime prevalence rate   The proportion of a sample that has ever had a disorder.

limbic system   The lower parts of the *cerebrum*, made up of primitive cortex; it controls visceral and bodily changes associated with emotion and regulates drive-motivated behavior.

linkage analysis   A technique in genetic research whereby occurrence of a disorder in a family is evaluated alongside a known genetic marker.

lithium carbonate   A drug useful in treating both *mania* and depression in *bipolar disorder*.

longitudinal study   An investigation that collects information on the same individuals repeatedly over time, perhaps over many years, in an effort to determine how phenomena change.

loose associations   Typical of *schizophrenia*; the patient has difficulty sticking to one topic and drifts off on a train of associations evoked by an idea from the past.

LSD   A drug derived from lysergic acid, *d*-lysergic acid diethylamide, synthesized in 1938 and discovered to be a *hallucinogen* in 1943. It is the principal constituent of the alkaloids of ergot, a grain fungus that in earlier centuries brought on epidemics of spasmodic ergotism, a nervous disorder sometimes marked by *psychotic* symptoms.

major depressive disorder   A disorder of individuals who have experienced episodes of depression but not of *mania*.

male erectile disorder   A recurrent and persistent inability to attain or maintain an erection until completion of sexual activity.

male orgasmic disorder   A recurrent and persistent delay or absence of ejaculation after an adequate phase of sexual excitement.

malingering   Faking a physical or psychological incapacity in order to avoid a responsibility or gain an end; the goal is readily recognized from the individual's circumstances. To be distinguished from *conversion disorder*, in which the incapacity is assumed to be beyond voluntary control.

mania   An emotional state of intense but unfounded elation evidenced in talkativeness, racing thoughts and distractibility, grandiose plans, and spurts of purposeless activity.

manifest content   The immediately apparent, conscious content of dreams. Compare with *latent content*.

marijuana   A drug derived from the dried and ground leaves and stems of the female hemp plant, *Cannabis sativa*.

mathematics disorder   Difficulty dealing with arithmetic symbols and operations beyond what would be expected on the basis of education, general intelligence, and age.

medulla oblongata   An area in the *brain stem* through which nerve-fiber tracts ascend to or descend from higher brain centers.

meninges   The three layers of nonneural tissue that envelop the brain and spinal cord.

mental retardation   Significantly subaverage intellectual functioning along with deficits in adaptive behavior, both occurring prior to age eighteen.

mescaline   A *hallucinogen* that is the active ingredient of peyote.

meta-analysis   Quantitative methods of analyzing and comparing the results of various scientific studies.

methadone   A synthetic addictive *heroin substitute* for treating *heroin* addicts that acts as a substitute for *heroin* by eliminating its effects and the craving for it.

midbrain   The middle part of the brain that consists of a mass of nerve-fiber tracts connecting the spinal cord and *pons, medulla,* and *cerebellum* to the *cerebral cortex*.

mild mental retardation   A limitation in mental development measured on IQ tests at between 50–55 and 70; children with such a limitation are considered the educable mentally retarded and are placed in special classes.

minimize   To underestimate the severity of a clinical problem by attributing the problem behavior to the patient's cultural background.

Minnesota Multiphasic Personality Inventory (MMPI)   A lengthy *personality inventory* by which individuals are diagnosed through their true–false replies to groups of statements that indicate states such as *anxiety*, *depression*, and *paranoia*.

modeling   Learning by observing the behavior of others.

moderate mental retardation   A limitation in mental development measured on IQ tests at between 35–40 and 50–55; children with this degree of retardation are often institutionalized, and their training is focused on self-care rather than on development of intellectual skills.

monozygotic (MZ) twins   Genetically identical siblings who have developed from a single fertilized egg; sometimes called identical twins.

mood disorders   Disorders in which there are disabling disturbances in emotion.

moral treatment   A therapeutic regimen, introduced by Philippe Pinel during the French Revolution, whereby mental patients were released from their restraints and treated with compassion and dignity.

morphine   An addictive narcotic alkaloid extracted from *opium*, used primarily as an analgesic and as a *sedative*.

motor skills disorder   A learning disability characterized by marked impairment in the development of motor coordination that is not accounted for by a physical disorder.

multiaxial classification   Classification having several dimensions, each of which is employed in categorizing; the *DSM-IV* is an example.

multimodal therapy   A therapy, introduced by Arnold Lazarus, based on *technical eclecticism*; it employs techniques from diverse approaches in an effort to help people make positive changes in their BASIC ID, or behavior, affects, sensations, images, cognitions, interpersonal relationships, and drugs/biological functioning.

multiple personality disorder (MPD)   See *dissociative identity disorder (DID)*.

narcissistic personality   Extremely selfish and self-centered, people with a narcissistic personality have a grandiose view of their uniqueness, achievements, and talents and an insatiable craving for admiration and approval from others. They are exploitative to achieve their own goals and expect much more from others than they themselves are willing to give.

narcotics   Addictive *sedative* drugs, for example, *morphine* and *heroin*, that in moderate doses relieve pain and induce sleep.

negative reinforcement   The strengthening of a tendency to behave by virtue of the fact that previous responses in that situation have been rewarded by the removal of an aversive stimulus.

negative symptoms   Behavioral deficits in *schizophrenia*, such as *flat affect* and apathy.

negative triad   In Beck's theory of depression, a person's negative views of the self, the world, and the future.

nerve impulse   A change in the electric potential of a *neuron*; a wave of depolarization spreads along the *neuron* and causes the release of the *neurotransmitter*.

neurologist   A physician who studies the nervous system, especially its structure, functions, and abnormalities.

neuron   A single nerve cell.

neuropsychological tests   Psychological tests, such as the *Luria–Nebraska*, that can detect impairment in different parts of the brain.

neuropsychologist   A psychologist concerned with the relationships among cognition, affect, and behavior on the one hand, and brain function on the other.

neurotransmitters   Chemical substances important in transferring a *nerve impulse* from one *neuron* to another.

nicotine   The principal addicting agent of tobacco.

normal curve   As applied in psychology, the bell-shaped distribution of a measurable trait depicting most people in the middle and few at the extremes.

nuclear magnetic response imaging (NMR)   A biological assessment that entails placing a person inside a large magnet. When force is turned on, hydrogen atoms move; when force is turned off they return to their original positions. This process produces an electromagnetic signal that a computer can translate into black-and-white pictures of living tissue.

obsession   Intrusive and recurring thought that seems irrational and uncontrollable to the person experiencing it.

obsessive-compulsive disorder (OCD)   An *anxiety disorder* in which the mind is flooded with persistent and uncontrollable thoughts or the individual is compelled to repeat certain acts again and again, causing significant distress and interference with everyday functioning.

obsessive-compulsive personality   People with this disorder have inordinate difficulty making decisions, are overly concerned with details and efficiency, and relate poorly to others because they demand that things be done their way. They are perfectionistic, unduly conventional, serious, and formal.

occipital lobe   The forward or upper half of each *cerebral hemisphere*, situated behind the central sulcus and above the lateral sulcus; the receiving center for sensations of the skin and of bodily positions.

Oedipus complex   In Freudian theory, the desire and conflict of the four-year-old male child, who wants to possess his mother sexually and eliminate the father rival. The threat of punishment from the father causes *repression* of these *id* impulses. Girls have a similar sexual desire for the father, which is repressed in analogous fashion, called the *Electra complex*.

operant conditioning   The acquisition or elimination of a response as a function of the environmental contingencies of *reinforcement* and *punishment*.

opium   The dried milky juice obtained from the immature fruit of the opium poppy. This addictive *narcotic* produces euphoria and drowsiness and reduces pain.

oral stage   In *psychoanalytic theory*, the first *psychosexual stage*, extending into the second year, during which the mouth is the principle erogenous zone.

orgasmic reorientation   A *behavior therapy* technique for altering classes of stimuli to which people are sexually attracted; individuals are confronted by a conventionally arousing stimulus while experiencing orgasm for another, undesirable reason.

overcontrolled (behavior)   In reference to childhood disorders, problems that involve behavioral deficits and emotional inhibitions, such as *anxiety* and social withdrawal.

overpathologize   To misinterpret a normal behavior as pathological by ignoring the patient's cultural background.

pain disorder   A *somatoform disorder* in which the person complains of severe and prolonged pain that is not explainable by organic pathology.

panic disorder   An *anxiety disorder* in which the individual has sudden and inexplicable attacks of jarring symptoms, such as difficulty breathing, heart palpitations, dizziness, trembling, terror, and feelings of impending doom. In DSM-IV, said to occur with or without *agoraphobia*.

paradoxical interventions   Attempts to change behavior by indirect methods, such as requesting that the patient increase the frequency of the problem behavior.

paranoid personality   This person, expecting to be mistreated by others, becomes suspicious, secretive, jealous, and argumentative. He or she will not accept blame.

paranoid schizophrenia   *Schizophrenia* in which the patient has numerous systematized *delusions*, such as *grandiose delusions* or *delusional jealousy*, as well as *hallucinations* and *ideas of reference*. He or she may also be agitated, angry, argumentative, and sometimes violent.

paraphilias   Sexual attraction to unusual objects, children or other nonconsenting people, or suffering or humiliation of oneself or one's partner.

parietal lobe   The middle division of each *cerebral hemisphere*, situated behind the central sulcus and above the lateral sulcus; the receiving center for sensations of the skin and of bodily positions.

pedophiles   People with a preference for obtaining sexual gratification through contact with youngsters defined legally as underage; pedophilia is a *paraphilia*.

personality   A person's habitual ways of feeling, thinking, and acting.

personality disorders   A heterogeneous group of disorders, listed separately on Axis II, regarded as long-standing, inflexible, and maladaptive patterns of inner experience and behavior that cut across many situations and impair social and occupational functioning.

personality inventory   A self-report questionnaire by which an examinee indicates whether statements assessing habitual tendencies apply to him or her.

person-centered   A theory and *humanistic-existential therapy* developed by Carl Rogers that emphasizes the importance of the therapist's understanding a person's subjective experiences and assisting him or her to reduce anxieties as well as fostering actualization of the person's potential.

pervasive developmental disorders   Severe childhood problems marked by profound disturbances in social relations and oddities in behavior. *Austistic disorder* is one.

PET scan   Computer-assisted motion pictures of the living brain, created by analysis of radioactive particles from isotopes injected into the bloodstream.

phallic stage   In *psychoanalytic theory*, the third *psychoxexual stage*, extending from ages three to six, during which maximal gratification is obtained from genital stimulation.

phencyclidine (PCP)   This very powerful and hazardous drug causes profound disorientation, agitated and often violent behavior, and even seizures, coma, and death.

phenotype   The totality of observable characteristics of a person.

phenylketonuria (PKU)   A genetic disorder that, through a deficiency in a liver enzyme, phenylalanine hydroxylase, causes severe *mental retardation* unless phenylalanine can be largely restricted from the diet until the age of six.

phobia   An *anxiety disorder* in which there is intense fear and avoidance of specific objects and situations, recognized as irrational by the individual.

phonological disorder   A learning disability in which some words sound like baby talk because the person is not able to make certain speech sounds.

play therapy   The use of play as a means of uncovering what is troubling a child and of establishing *rapport*.

pleasure principle   In *psychoanalytic theory*, the demanding manner by which the *id* operates, seeking immediate gratification of its needs.

polysubstance abuse   The misuse of more than one drug at a time, such as drinking heavily and taking *cocaine*.

pons   An area in the *brain stem* containing nerve-fiber tracts that connect the *cerebellum* with the spinal cord and with motor areas of the *cerebrum*.

positive reinforcement   The strengthening of a tendency to behave by virtue of the fact that previous responses in that situation have been followed by presentation of a desired reward.

positive symptoms   In *schizophrenia*, behavioral excesses, such as *hallucinations* and bizarre behavior.

posttraumatic stress disorder (PTSD)   An *anxiety disorder* in which a particularly stressful event, such as military combat, rape, or a natural disaster, brings in its aftermath intrusive reexperiencings of the trauma, a numbing of responsiveness to the outside world, estrangement from others, a tendency to be easily startled, and nightmares, recurrent dreams, and otherwise disturbed sleep.

predictive validity   A kind of *criterion-related validity*, the extent to which being diagnosed in a particular way predicts some future criterion such as response to treatment.

prefrontal lobotomy   A surgical procedure that destroys the tracts connecting the *frontal lobes* to lower centers of the brain; once believed to be an effective treatment for *schizophrenia*.

premature ejaculation   Inability of the male to inhibit his orgasm long enough for mutually satisfying sexual relations.

prevalence   In *epidemiological* studies of a disorder, the percentage of a population that has it at a given time.

prevention   **Primary prevention** refers to efforts in *community psychology* to reduce the incidence of new cases of psychological disorder by such means as altering stressful living conditions and genetic counseling; **secondary prevention** applies to efforts to target at-risk populations in order to help them lower the risk of actually developing a disorder; **tertiary prevention** encompasses efforts to reduce the long-term consequences of having a disorder, equivalent in most respects to therapy.

primary empathy   A form of empathy in which the therapist understands the content and feeling of what the client is saying and expressing from the client's point of view.

primary process   In *psychoanalytic theory*, one of the *id*'s means of reducing tension, by imagining what it desires.

problem-focused coping   In response to stressful situations, taking direct action to improve the situation or seeking information that will yield a solution.

profound mental retardation   A limitation in mental development measured on IQ tests at less than 20–25; children with this degree of retardation require total supervision of all their activities.

projective test   A psychological assessment device employing a set of standard but ambiguous stimuli on the assumption that such material will allow unconscious motivations and conflicts to be uncovered. The *Rorschach* series of inkblots is an example.

pronoun reversal   A speech problem in which the child refers to himself or herself as "he," "she," "you," and "I" or "me" in referring to others; often found in the speech of children with *autistic disorder*.

psilocybin   A psychedelic drug extracted from the mushroom *Psilocybe mexicana*.

psychiatrist   A physician (M.D.) who has taken specialized postdoctoral training, called a residency, in the diagnosis, treatment, and prevention of mental and emotional disorders.

psychiatric social worker   A mental health professional who holds a master of social work (M.S.W.) degree.

psychoanalysis   A term applied primarily to the therapeutic procedures pioneered by Freud.

psychoanalyst   A therapist who has taken specialized postdoctoral training in psychoanalysis after earning either an M.D. or a Ph.D. degree.

psychoanalytic theory   Sigmund Freud's theory of the way in which *psychodynamics* influence normal and abnormal behavior.

psychodynamic perspectives   A general view that *psychopathology* results from the interplay among *unconscious* forces.

psychodynamics   In *psychoanalytic theory*, the interplay of mental and emotional forces and processes that develop in early childhood and affect behavior and mental states.

psychogenesis   Development from psychological origins as distinguished from somatic origins.

psychological factors affecting a medical condition   A diagnosis indicating in DSM-IV that a physical illness is caused (in part) or exacerbated by psychological *stress*.

psychoneuroimmunology   The study of the impact of *stress* and ways of coping with stress on immune function.

psychopathologists   Mental health professionals who conduct research into the nature and development of mental and emotional disorders.

psychopathology   The study of the nature and development of mental disorders.

psychophysiological disorders   Disorders with physical symptoms that may involve actual tissue damage, usually in one organ system, and that are produced in part by *stress*. Hives and ulcers are examples. No longer listed in DSM-IV in a separate category, such disorders are now diagnosed on

Axis I as *psychological factors affecting a medical condition;* on Axis III the specific physical condition is given.

psychosexual stages (psychosexual development)   In *psychoanalytic theory*, critical developmental phases through which an individual passes, each stage characterized by the body area providing maximal erotic gratification. The adult personality is formed by the pattern and intensity of instinctual gratification at each stage.

psychosocial stages of development   In Erik Erikson's theory, phases of personality development, each of which is associated with a particular challenge or crisis.

psychotherapy   A primarily verbal means of helping troubled individuals change their thoughts, feelings, and behavior to reduce distress and to achieve greater life satisfaction.

psychotherapy integration   An attempt to blend aspects of existing theoretical perspectives on *psychotherapy* in such a way as to create a new, coherent theory.

punishment   In psychological experiments, any noxious stimulus imposed on the animal or person to reduce the probability that it will behave in an undesired way.

random assignment   A method of assigning subjects to groups in an *experiment* that gives each subject an equal chance of being in each group.

rational-emotive theory (RET)   The model that explains *psychopathology* as a result of negative experiences occurring to someone who holds *irrational beliefs* about their implications.

rational-emotive therapy (RET)   A therapy introduced by Albert Ellis and based on the assumption that much disordered behavior is rooted in absolutistic demands that people make on themselves. The therapy aims to alter the unrealistic, self-defeating goals individuals set for themselves, such as "I must be universally loved."

rationalization   A *defense mechanism* in which a socially acceptable reason is unconsciously invented by the *ego* to protect itself from confronting the real reason for an action, thought, or emotion.

reactance   A motivational state in which people perceive their freedom to be limited and try to restore it, for instance, by acting contrary to therapists' requests.

reactivity (of behavior)   The phenomenon whereby the object of observation is changed by the very fact that it is being observed.

reading disorder (dyslexia)   A disturbance in the ability to read; a learning disorder.

reality principle   In *psychoanalytic theory*, the manner in which the *ego* delays gratification and otherwise deals with the environment in a planned, rational fashion.

receptive language disorder   Difficulty understanding spoken language.

receptors   Proteins embedded in the membrane covering a neural cell that interact with one or more *neurotransmitters*.

reliability   The extent to which a test, measurement, or classification system is consistent in that it produces the same observation each time it is applied.

repression   A *defense mechanism* whereby impulses and thoughts unacceptable to the *ego* are pushed into the *unconscious*.

resistances   During *psychoanalysis*, the defensive tendency of the unconscious part of the *ego* to ward off from conscious- ness particularly threatening *repressed* material.

retest reliability The relationship between the scores that a person achieves when he or she takes the same test at two separate times.

retrospective reports Recollections by an individual of past events.

Rett's disorder A *pervasive developmental disorder* affecting girls. Development is normal in the first five months, but some time in the next few years head growth slows and motor skills involving the hands deteriorate; language de- velopment is poor.

risk factors Conditions or variables that, if present, increase the likelihood of developing a disorder.

Rorschach Inkblot Test A *projective test* in which the exami- nee is instructed to interpret a series of ten inkblots repro- duced on cards.

sadistic rape Acts of rape that involve the infliction of seri- ous physical harm on the victim's body.

schema A mental structure for organizing information about the world (*Pl.* schemata)

schizoid personality This person, emotionally aloof and in- different to the praise, criticism, and feelings of others, is usually a loner with few, if any, close friends and with soli- tary interests.

schizophrenia A group of psychotic disorders character- ized by major disturbances in thought, emotion, and be- havior: disordered thinking in which ideas are not logi- cally related; faulty perception and attention; bizarre disturbances in motor activity; flat or inappropriate emo- tions; and reduced tolerance for stress of interpersonal relations. The patient withdraws from people and reality, often into a fantasy life of *delusions* and *hallucina- tions*.

schizophrenogenic mother A cold dominant, conflict-induc- ing mother once believed to cause *schizophrenia* in her child.

schizotypal personality This eccentric individual has oddi- ties of thought and perception, speaks digressively and with overelaborations, and is usually socially isolated. Un- der stress, he or she may appear psychotic.

school phobia An irrational dread of attending school, usu- ally for fear of being away from the caregiver.

seasonal affective disorders (SAD) *Mood disorders* recurring regularly at a particular time of year; for example, *bipolar dis- order* with winter depressive episodes and manic episodes in spring or summer.

secondary process The reality-based decision-making and problem-solving activities of the *ego*.

sedatives Drugs that slow bodily activities, especially those of the central nervous system; used to reduce pain and ten- sion and to induce relaxation and sleep.

seeking mode An approach to the delivery of therapy in which one seeks out those in need of services; found in *community psychology*.

selective mutism A pattern of continually refusing to speak in almost all social situations, including school, even though the child understands spoken language and is able to speak.

self-actualization Fulfilling one's potential as an always growing human being; believed by *person-centered therapists* to be the master motive.

self-monitoring A procedure whereby the individual observes and reports certain aspects of his or her own behavior, thoughts, or emotions.

sensate focus A term applied to exercises prescribed at the beginning of the Masters and Johnson sex therapy pro- gram; partners are instructed to fondle each other to give pleasure but to refrain from intercourse, thus reducing anx- iety about sexual performance.

sensory-awareness procedures Often used in sex therapy, techniques that help clients tune into their feelings and sen- sations, as in *sensate focus* exercises, and to be open to new ways of experiencing and feeling.

separation anxiety disorder A disorder in which the child feels intense fear and distress when away from someone on whom he or she is very dependent; it is said to be an im- portant cause of *school phobia*.

severe mental retardation A limitation in mental develop- ment measured on IQ tests at between 20–25 and 35–40. Individuals so afflicted often cannot care for themselves, communicate only briefly, and are listless and inactive.

sex-reassignment surgery An operation removing existing genitalia of a *transsexual* and constructing a substitute for the genitals of the opposite sex.

sexual aversion disorder Avoidance of nearly all genital contact with other people.

sexual dysfunctions Recurrent, distressing inhibitions in the normal sexual response cycle.

sexual masochism A marked preference for obtaining or in- creasing sexual gratification through subjection to pain or humiliation.

sexual sadism A marked preference for obtaining or in- creasing sexual gratification by inflicting pain or humilia- tion on another person.

social phobia Persistent, irrational fear of situations in which one is exposed to scrutiny by others or interaction with unfamiliar people.

social-selection theory An attempt to explain the correla- tion between social class and *schizophrenia* by proposing that schizophrenics move downward in social status.

sociogenic hypothesis Generally, an idea that seeks causes in social conditions, for example, that being in a low social class can cause one to become *schizophrenic*.

somatic-weakness model The vulnerability of a particular organ or organ system to psychological *stress* and thereby to a particular *psychophysiological disorder*.

somatization disorder A *somatoform disorder* in which the person continually seeks medical help for recurrent and multiple physical symptoms that have no discoverable physical cause. The medical history is complicated and dramatically presented. Formerly known as Briquet's syn- drome.

somatoform disorders Disorders in which physical symp- toms suggest a physical problem but have no known physi- ological cause; they are therefore believed to be linked to psychological conflicts and needs but not voluntarily as- sumed. Examples are *somatization disorder, conversion disor- der, pain disorder, hypochondriasis*, and *body dysmorphic disor- der*.

somatogenesis　Development from bodily origins as distinguished from psychological origins.

specific phobia　An unwarranted fear and avoidance of a specific object or circumstance, for example, fear of nonpoisonous snakes or fear of heights.

spectator role　As applied by Masters and Johnson, a pattern of behavior in which the individual's focus on and concern with sexual performance impedes his or her natural sexual responses.

spontaneous deterioration　Getting worse in the absence of treatment.

standardization　The process of constructing an assessment procedure so that norms can be established and research conducted on its *reliability* and *validity*. Test administration procedures and instructions are fixed.

stress　Situational definitions focus on the objective nature of the event or circumstance; response-based definitions consider a pattern of behavioral, emotional, and biological reactions to events; relational definitions incorporate aspects of the event and the response to it.

stress management　A range of psychological procedures that help people control and reduce their *stress*.

stressor　An event that leads to *stress* responses.

stroke　A sudden loss of consciousness and control followed by paralysis; caused when a blood clot obstructs an artery or by hemorrhage into the brain when an artery ruptures.

structural social support　A person's network of social relationships, for example, number of friends.

structured interview　An *interview* in which the sequence and wording of questions is prearranged.

substance abuse　The use of a drug to such an extent that the person fails in important obligations, engages in dangerous behavior, or has persistent interpersonal or social problems, but where there is no physiological dependence.

substance dependence　Severe abuse of a drug, often accompanied by a physiological dependence on it, often made evident by *tolerance* and *withdrawal* symptoms.

sulci　Shallow furrows in the *cerebral cortex* separating adjacent convolutions, or *gyri*.

superego　In *psychoanalytic theory*, the part of the personality that acts as the conscience and reflects society's moral standards.

synapse　A small gap between two *neurons* where the nerve impulse passes from the axon of the first to the dendrites, cell body, or axon of the second.

syndrome　A group of *symptoms* that tend to occur together in a particular disease.

systematic desensitization　A major *behavior therapy* procedure in which a fearful person, while deeply relaxed, imagines a series of progressively more fearsome situations. The two responses of relaxation and fear are incompatible, and fear is dispelled.

systolic pressure　Amount of arterial pressure when the ventricles contract and the heart is pumping; for a young adult, 120 is normal.

technical eclecticism　Use of whatever techniques will work in *psychotherapy*, regardless of the theoretical perspective from which they derive or whether the original theories can be sensibly integrated; found in *multimodal therapy*.

temporal lobe　A large area of each *cerebral hemisphere* situated below the lateral sulcus and in front of the *occipital lobe*; contains primary auditory projection and association areas and general association areas.

Thematic Apperception Test (TAT)　A *projective test* consisting of a set of black-and-white pictures reproduced on cards, each depicting a potentially emotion-laden situation. The examinee, presented with the cards one at a time, is instructed to make up a story about each situation.

third-variable problem　The difficulty in the *correlational method* of research whereby the relationship between two variables may be attributable to a third factor.

time-of-measurement effects　A possible confound in *longitudinal studies*, whereby conditions at a particular point in time can have a specific effect on a variable that is being studied over time.

token economy　A *behavior therapy* procedure, based on *operant conditioning* principles, in which patients are given tokens, such as poker chips, for desired behaviors. The tokens can be exchanged for desirable items and activities.

tolerance　A physiological process in which greater and greater amounts of an addictive drug are required to produce the same effect.

transference　The venting of the patient's emotions, either positive or negative, by treating the analyst as the symbolic representative of someone important in the past. An example is the patient's becoming angry with the analyst to release emotions actually felt toward his or her father.

transsexual　A person who experiences persistent discomfort with his or her sex and identifies with the opposite sex, to the point of believing that he or she is opposite in sex to his or her biological endowment.

treatment utility　The extent to which knowing the results of an assessment procedure improves the outcome of treatment.

tumescence　The flow of blood into the genitals.

twin study　A research strategy in *behavior genetics* in which *concordance* rates of *monozygotic twins* and *dizygotic twins* are compared.

Type A behavior pattern　One of two contrasting psychological patterns revealed through studies seeking the cause of *coronary heart disease*. Type A people are competitive, rushed, hostile, and overcommitted to their work. Type As are believed to be at heightened risk for heart disease. People who fit the other pattern, Type B, are more relaxed and relatively free of pressure.

unconditional positive regard　According to Rogers, a crucial attitude for the *person-centered* therapist to adopt toward the client, who needs to feel complete acceptance as a person in order to evaluate the extent to which current behavior contributes to *self-actualization*.

unconscious　In *psychoanalytic theory*, the repository of instinctual forces and emotions of which the person is unaware.

undercontrolled (behavior)　In reference to childhood disorders, problem behavior of the child that involves excesses, such as unwarranted aggressiveness.

unilateral ECT　*Electroconvulsive therapy* in which electrodes are placed on one side of the forehead so that current passes through only one brain hemisphere.

vaginismus   Painful, spasmodic contractions of the outer third of the vagina, which make insertion of the penis impossible or extremely difficult.

validity   The extent to which a test or diagnosis measures what it is intended to measure.

voyeurism   Marked preference for obtaining sexual gratification by watching others in a state of undress or having sexual relations.

vulnerability-stress perspective   As applied in *psychopathology*, a view that assumes that individuals predisposed toward a particular mental disorder will be particularly affected by stress and will then manifest *abnormal behavior*.

waiting mode   An approach to the delivery of therapy in which one treats only those who initiate the request for services.

waxy flexibility   An aspect of *catatonic immobility* in which the patient's limbs can be moved into a variety of positions and maintained thereafter for unusually long periods of time.

white matter   The neural tissue, particularly of the brain and spinal cord, consisting of tracts or bundles of myelinated (sheathed) nerve fibers.

withdrawal symptoms   Negative physiological and psychological reactions evidenced when a person suddenly stops taking an addictive drug.

References

Abelin, T., Buehler, A., Mueller, P., Vesanen, K., & Imhof, P. R. (1989, January 7). Controlled trial of transdermal nicotine patch in tobacco withdrawal. *Lancet*, 7–10.

Abramovitz, S. I. (1986). Psychosocial outcomes of sex reassignment surgery. *Journal of Consulting and Clinical Psychology , 54*, 183–189.

Abrams, R., Swartz, C. M., & Vedak, C. (1991). Antidepressant effects of high-dose right unilateral electroconvulsive therapy. *Archives of General Psychiatry, 48*, 746–748.

Abramson, L. Y., Metalsky, G. I., & Alloy, L. B. (1989). Hopelessness depression: A theory-based subtype of depression. *Psychological Review, 96*, 358–372.

Abramson, L. Y., Seligman, M. E. P., & Teasdale, J. D. (1978). Learned helplessness in humans: Critique and reformulation. *Journal of Abnormal Psychology, 87*, 49–74.

Achenbach, T. M. (1982). *Developmental psychopathology* (2nd ed.). New York: Wiley.

Achenbach, T. M., & Edelbrock, C. S. (1978). The classification of child psychopathology: A review of empirical efforts. *Psychological Bulletin, 85*, 1275–1301.

Achenbach, T. M., & Edelbrock, C. S. (1983). *Manual for the child behavior checklist*. Burlington, VT: Author.

Adler, N., & Matthews, K. (1994). Health psychology: Why do some people get sick and some stay well? *Annual Review of Psychology, 45*, 229–259.

Agras, W. S. (1987). *Eating disorders: Management of obesity, bulimia, and anorexia nervosa*. Oxford: Pergamon.

Akhter, S., Wig, N. N., Varma, V. K., Pershad, D., & Varma, S. K. (1975). A phenomenological analysis of symptoms in obsessive-compulsive neurosis. *British Journal of Psychiatry, 127*, 342–348.

Alexander, C. N., Langer, E. J., Newman, R. I., Chandler, H. M., & Davies, J. L. (1989). Transcendental meditation, mindfulness, and longevity: An experimental study with the elderly. *Journal of Personality and Social Psychology, 57*, 950–964.

Alexander, F. (1950). *Psychosomatic medicine*. New York: Norton.

Alexander, F., & French, T. M. (1946). *Psychoanalytic therapy*. New York: Ronald Press.

Alexander, J. F., Holtzworth-Munroe, A., & Jameson, P. B. (1994). The process and outcome of marital and family therapy: Research review and evaluation. In A. E. Bergin & S. L. Garfield (Eds.), *Handbook of psychotherapy and behavior change* (4th ed., pp. 595–630). New York: Wiley.

Allen, M. G. (1976). Twin studies of affective illness. *Archives of General Psychiatry, 33*, 1476–1478.

Allison, R. B. (1984). Difficulties diagnosing the multiple personality syndrome in a death penalty case. *International Journal of Clinical and Experimental Hypnosis, 32*, 102–117.

Alloy, L. B., Kelly, K. A., Mineka, S., & Clements, C. M. (1990). Comorbidity in anxiety and depressive disorders: A helplessness/hopelessness perspective. In J. D. Maser & C. R. Cloninger (Eds.), *Comorbidity in anxiety and mood disorders*. Washington, DC: American Psychiatric Press.

American Psychiatric Association. *Diagnostic and statistical manual of mental disorders*. First edition, 1952; second edition, 1968; third edition, 1980; revised, 1987; fourth edition 1994. Washington, DC: Author.

Anastasi, A. (1988). *Psychological testing* (6th ed.). New York: Macmillan.

Andersen, B. L. (1983). Primary orgasmic dysfunction: Diagnostic considerations and review of treatment. *Psychological Bulletin, 93*, 105–136.

Andersen, B. L. (1992). Psychological interventions for cancer patients to enhance quality of life. *Journal of Consulting and Clinical Psychology, 60*, 552–568.

Anderson, L. P. (1991). Acculturative stress: A theory of relevance to black Americans. *Clinical Psychology Review, 11*, 685–702.

Andreasen, N. C. (1979). Thought, language, and communication disorders: 2. Diagnostic significance. *Archives of General Psychiatry, 36*, 1325–1330.

Andreasen, N. C., Olsen, S. A., Dennert, J. W., & Smith, M. R. (1982). Ventricular enlargement in schizophrenia: Relationship to positive and negative symptoms. *American Journal of Psychiatry, 139*, 297–302.

Andreasen, N. C., Rice, J., Endicott, J., Coryell, W., Grove, W. W., & Reich, T. (1987). Familial rates of affective disorder. *Archives of General Psychiatry, 44*, 461–472.

Andreasen, N. C., Swayze, V. W., Flaum, M., Arndt, S., & McChesney, C. (1990). Ventricular enlargement in schizophrenia evaluated with computed tomographic scanning: Effects of gender, age, and stage of illness. *Archives of General Psychiatry, 47*, 1008–1015.

Angrist, B., Lee, H. K., & Gershon, S. (1974). The antagonism of amphetamine-induced symptomatology by a neuroleptic. *American Journal of Psychiatry, 131*, 817–819.

Aniline, O., & Pitts, F. N., Jr. (1982). Phencyclidine (PCP): A review and perspectives. *CRC Critical Review of Toxicology, 10*, 145–177.

Anthony-Bergstone, C., Zarit, S. H., & Gatz, M. (1988). Symptoms of psychological distress among caregivers of dementia patients. *Psychology and Aging, 3*, 245–248.

Arkonac, O., & Guze, S. B. (1963). A family study of hysteria. *New England Journal of Medicine, 268*, 239–242.

Arkowitz, H. (1989). The role of theory in psychotherapy integration. *Journal of Integrative and Eclectic Psychotherapy, 8*, 8–16.

Armor, D. J., Polich, J. M., & Stambul, H. B. (1978). *Alcoholism and treatment.* New York: Wiley.

Arndt, I. O., Dorozynsky, L., Woody, G. E., McLellan, A. T., & O'Brien, C. P. (1992). Desipramine treatment of cocaine dependence in methadone-maintained patients. *Archives of General Psychiatry, 49*, 888–893.

Arnetz, B. B., Wasserman, J., Petrini, B., Brenner, S. O., Levy, L., Eneroth, P., Salovaara, H., Hjelm, R., Salovaara, L., Theorell, T., & Petterson, I. L. (1987). Immune function in unemployed women. *Psychosomatic Medicine, 49*, 3–12.

Atchley, R. (1980). Aging and suicide: Reflection of the quality of life. In S. Haynes & M. Feinleib (Eds.), *Proceedings of the Second Conference on the Epidemiology of Aging.* National Institute of Health, Washington, DC: U.S. Government Printing Office.

Atkeson, B. M., Calhoun, K. S., Resick, P. A., & Ellis, E. M. (1982). Victims of rape: Repeated assessment of depressive symptoms. *Journal of Consulting and Clinical Psychology, 50*, 96–102.

Atkinson, D. R., Maruyama, M., & Matsui, S. (197 counselor race and counseling approach on Asian Americans' perception of counselor credibility and utility. *Journal of Counseling Psychology, 25*, 76–83.

Austin, L. S., Lydiard, R. B., Forey, M. D., & Zealberg, J. J. (1990). Panic and phobic disorders in patients with obsessive compulsive disorder. *Journal of Clinical Psychiatry, 51*, 456–458.

Axline, V. M. (1964). *Dibs: In search of self.* New York: Ballantine.

Ayllon, T., & Azrin, N. H. (1968). *The token economy: A motivational system for therapy and rehabilitation.* New York: Appleton-Century-Crofts.

Azrin, N. H., Sisson, R. W., Meyers, R., & Godley, M. (1982). Alcoholism treatment by disulfiram and community reinforcement therapy. *Journal of Behavior Therapy and Experimental Psychiatry, 13*, 105–112.

Baer, L., Jenike, M. A., Ricciardi, J. N., Holland, A. D., Seymour, R. J., Minichiello, W. E., & Buttolph, M. L. (1990). Standardized assessment of personality disorders in obsessive compulsive disorder. *Archives of General Psychiatry, 47*, 826–831.

Baker, R. C., & Kirschenbaum, D. S. (1993). Self-monitoring may be necessary for successful weight control. *Behavior Therapy, 24*, 377–394.

Ballenger, J. C., Burrows, G. O., DuPont, R. L., Lesser, M., Noyes, R. C., Pecknold, J. C., Rifkin, A., & Swinson, R. P. (1988). Alprazolam in panic disorder and agoraphobia: Results from a multicenter trial. *Archives of General Psychiatry, 45*, 413–421.

Bancroft, J. H. (1989). *Human sexuality and its problems* (2nd ed.). Edinburgh: Churchill Livingstone.

Bandura, A. (1986). *Social foundations of thought and action: A social cognitive theory.* Englewood Cliffs, NJ: Prentice-Hall.

Bandura, A., Blanchard, E. B., & Ritter, B. (1969). Relative efficacy of desensitization and modeling approaches for inducing behavioral, affective, and attitudinal changes. *Journal of Personality and Social Psychology, 13*, 173–199.

Bandura, A., Grusec, J. E., & Menlove, F. L. (1967). Vicarious extinction of avoidance behavior. *Journal of Personality and Social Psychology, 5*, 16–23.

Bandura, A., & Menlove, F. L. (1968). Factors determining vicarious extinction of avoidance behavior through symbolic modeling. *Journal of Personality and Social Psychology, 8*, 99–108.

Bandura, A., & Walters, R. H. (1963). *Social learning and personality development.* New York: Holt, Rinehart & Winston.

Barber, J. P., & DeRubeis, R. J. (1989). On second thought: Where the action is in cognitive therapy for depression. *Cognitive Therapy and Research, 13*, 441–457.

Barkley, R. A. (1981). *Hyperactive children: A handbook for diagnosis and treatment.* New York: Guilford.

Barkley, R. A. (1990). *Attention-deficit hyperactivity disorder: A handbook for diagnosis and treatment.* New York: Guilford.

Barkley, R. A., & Cunningham, C. E. (1979). The effects of methylphenidate on the mother–child interactions of hyperactive children. *Archives of General Psychiatry, 36*, 201–208.

Barkley, R. A., DuPaul, G. J., & McMurray, M. B. (1990). A comprehensive evaluation of attention deficit disorder with and without hyperactivity defined by research criteria. *Journal of Consulting and Clinical Psychology, 58*, 775–789.

Barkley, R. A., Grodzinsky, G., & DuPaul, G. J. (1992). Frontal lobe functions in attention deficit disorder with and without hyperactivity: A review and research report. *Journal of Abnormal Child Psychology, 20*, 163–188.

Barlow, D. H. (1988). *Anxiety and its disorders: The nature and treatment of anxiety and panic.* New York: Guilford.

Barlow, D. H., & Cerny, J. A. (1988). *Psychological treatment of panic.* New York: Guilford.

Baron, M., Levitt, M., Gruen, R., Kane, J., & Asnis, L. (1984). Platelet monoamine oxidase activity and genetic vulnerability to schizophrenia. *American Journal of Psychiatry, 141*, 836–842.

Baron, M., Risch, N., Levitt, M., & Gruen, R. (1985). Familial transmission of schizotypal and borderline personality disorders. *American Journal of Psychiatry, 142*, 927–934.

Baron, R. A., & Byrne, D. (1977). *Social psychology: Understanding human interaction* (2nd ed.). Boston: Allyn & Bacon.

Barr, C. E., Mednick, S. A., & Munk-Jorgensen, P. (1990). Exposure to influenza epidemics during gestation and adult schizophrenia: A 40-year study. *Archives of General Psychiatry, 47*, 869–874.

Bartzokis, G., Liberman, R. P., & Hierholzer, R. (1990). Behavior therapy in groups. In I. L. Kutash & A. Wolf (Eds.), *The group psychotherapist's handbook: Contemporary theory and technique.* New York: Columbia University Press.

Bates, G. W., Campbell, T. M., & Burgess, P. M. (1990). Assessment of articulated thoughts in social anxiety: Modification of the ATSS procedure. *British Journal of Clinical Psychology, 29*, 91–98.

Bateson, G., Jackson, D. D., Haley, J., & Weakland, J. (1956). Toward a theory of schizophrenia. *Behavioral Science, 1*, 251–264.

Baucom, D. H., & Lester, G. W. (1986). The usefulness of cognitive restructuring as an adjunct to behavioral marital therapy. *Behavior Therapy, 17*, 385–403.

Baumeister, A. A., & Maclean, W. E., Jr. (1979). Brain damage and mental retardation. In N. R. Ellis (Ed.), *Handbook of mental deficiency; Psychological theory and research* (2nd ed.). Hillsdale, NJ: Erlbaum.

Baumeister, R. F. (1990). Suicide as escape from self. *Psychological Review, 97*, 90–113.

Baxter, E., & Hopper, K. (1981). *Private lives/public places: Homeless adults on the streets of New York City.* New York: Community Service Society.

Baxter, L. R., Schwartz, J. M., Bergman, K. S., Szuba, M. P., Guze, B. H., Mazziotta, J. C., Alazraki, A., Selin, C. E., Ferng, H., Munford, P., & Phelps, M. E. (1992). Caudate glucose metabolic rate changes with both drug and behavior therapy for obsessive-compulsive disorder. *Archives of General Psychiatry, 49*, 681–689.

Beck, A. T. (1967). *Depression: Clinical, experimental and theoretical aspects.* New York: Harper & Row.

Beck, A. T. (1976). *Cognitive therapy and the emotional disorders.* New York: International Universities Press.

Beck, A. T. (1987). Cognitive models of depression. *Journal of Cognitive Psychotherapy: An International Quarterly, 1*, 5–37.

Beck, A. T., Brown, G., Berchick, R. J., Stewart, B. L., & Steer, R. A. (1990). Relationship between hopelessness and ultimate suicide: A replication with psychiatric outpatients. *American Journal of Psychiatry, 147*, 190–195.

Beck, A. T., Brown, G., & Steer, R. A. (1989). Prediction of eventual suicide in psychiatric inpatients by clinical ratings of hopelessness. *Journal of Consulting and Clinical Psychology, 57,* 309–310.

Beck, A. T., Brown, G., Steer, R. A., Eidelson, J. I., & Riskind, J. H. (1987). Differentiating anxiety and depression: A test of the cognitive content-specificity hypothesis. *Journal of Abnormal Psychology, 96,* 179–183.

Beck, A. T., & Emery, G. (1985). *Anxiety disorders and phobias: A cognitive perspective.* New York: Basic Books.

Beck, A. T., Freeman, A., and Associates (1990). *Cognitive therapy of personality disorders.* New York: Guilford.

Beck, A. T., Kovacs, M., & Weissman, A. (1975). Hopelessness and suicidal behavior: An overview. *Journal of the American Medical Association, 234,* 1146–1149.

Beck, A. T., Steer, R. A., Kovacs, M., & Garrison, B. (1985). Hopelessness and eventual suicide: A 10–year prospective study of patients hospitalized with suicidal ideation. *American Journal of Psychiatry, 142,* 559–563.

Beck, A. T., & Ward, C. H. (1961). Dreams of depressed patients: Characteristic themes in manifest content. *Archives of General Psychiatry, 5,* 462–467.

Bednar, R. L., & Kaul, T. J. (1994). Experiential group research: Can the canon fire? In A. E. Bergin & S. L. Garfield (Eds.), *Handbook of psychotherapy and behavior change* (4th ed.). New York: Wiley.

Begelman, D. A. (1975). Ethical and legal issues of behavior modification. In M. Hersen, R. Eisler, & P. M. Miller (Eds.), *Progress in behavior modification.* New York: Academic Press.

Beidel, D. C. (1991). Social phobia and overanxious disorder in school-age children. *Journal of the American Academy of Child and Adolescent Psychiatry, 30,* 545–552.

Bell, J. E. (1961). *Family group therapy.* Washington, DC: U.S. Department of Health, Education, and Welfare.

Bell, P. (1992). Sexual abuse and referral bias [letter]. *British Journal of Psychiatry, 160,* 717.

Bemis, K. M. (1978). Current approaches to the etiology and treatment of anorexia nervosa. *Psychological Bulletin, 85,* 593–617.

Bennett, I. (1960). *Delinquent and neurotic children.* London: Tavistock.

Bennett, W. (1980). The nicotine fix. *Harvard Magazine, 82,* 10–14.

Ben-Porath, Y. S., & Butcher, J. N. (1989). The comparability of MMPI and MMPI-2 scales and profiles. *Psychological Assessment, 1,* 345–347.

Ben-Shlomo, Y., Smith, G. D., Shipley, M. J., & Marmot, M. G. (1994). What determines mortality risk in male former cigarette smokers? *American Journal of Public Health, 84,* 1235–1242.

Berger, K. S., & Zarit, S. H. (1978). Late life paranoid states: Assessment and treatment. *American Journal of Orthopsychiatry, 48,* 528–537.

Bergin, A. E. (1971). The evaluation of therapeutic outcomes. In A. E. Bergin & S. L. Garfield (Eds.), *Handbook of psychotherapy and behavior change: An empirical analysis.* New York: Wiley.

Berlin, F. S., & Meinecke, C. F. (1981). Treatment of sex offenders with antiandrogenic medication: Conceptualization, review of treatment modalities, and preliminary findings. *American Journal of Psychiatry, 138,* 601–607.

Berman, E. M., & Lief, H. I. (1976). Sex and the aging process. In W. W. Oaks, G. A. Melchiode, & I. Ficher (Eds.), *Sex and the life cycle.* New York: Grune & Stratton.

Berrettini, W. H., Goldin, L. R., Gelernter, J., Gejman, P. V., Gershon, E. S., & Detera-Wadleigh, S. (1990). X-chromosome markers and manic-depressive illness: Rejection of linkage to Xq28 in nine bipolar pedigrees. *Archives of General Psychiatry, 47,* 366–373.

Besdine, R. W. (1980). Geriatric medicine: An overview. In C. Eisodorfer (Ed.), *Annual review of gerontology and geriatrics.* New York: Springer.

Bettelheim, B. (1967). *The empty fortress.* New York: Free Press.

Beutler, L. E., Crago, M., & Arizmendi, T. G. (1986). Therapist variables in psychotherapy process and outcome. In S. L. Garfield & A. E. Bergin (Eds.), *Handbook of psychotherapy and behavior change* (3rd ed.). New York: Wiley.

Beutler, L. E., Machado, P. P. P., & Neufeldt, S. A. (1994). Therapist variables. In A. E. Bergin & S. L. Garfield (Eds.), *Handbook of psychotherapy and behavior change* (4th ed., pp. 229–269). New York: Wiley.

Biglan, A., Hops, H., Sherman, L., Friedman, L., Arthur, J., & Osteen, V. (1985). Problem-solving interactions of depressed women and their husbands. *Behavior Therapy, 16,* 431–451.

Billings, A. G., Cronkite, R. C., & Moos, R. H. (1983). Social-environmental factors in unipolar depression: Comparisons of depressed patients and nondepressed controls. *Journal of Abnormal Psychology, 92,* 119–133.

Bion, W. (1959). *Experiences in groups.* New York: Basic Books.

Birnbaum, M. (1960). The right to treatment. *American Bar Association Journal, 46,* 499–505.

Bisette, G., Smith, W. H., Dole, K. C., Crain, B., Ghanbari, B., Miller, B., & Nemeroff, C. B. (1991). Alterations in Alzheimer's disease-associated protein in Alzheimer's disease frontal and temporal cortex. *Archives of General Psychiatry, 48,* 1009–1011.

Black, S. T. (1993). Comparing genuine and simulated suicide notes: A new perspective. *Journal of Consulting and Clinical Psychology, 61,* 699–702.

Blagg, N. R., & Yule, W. (1984). The behavioural treatment of school refusal: A comparative study. *Behaviour Research and Therapy, 22,* 119–127.

Blake, W. (1973). The influence of race on diagnosis. *Smith College Studies in Social Work, 43,* 184–192.

Blashfield, R. K., & Livesley, W. J. (1991). Metaphorical analysis of psychiatric classification as a psychological test. *Journal of Abnormal Psychology, 100,* 262–270.

Blashfield, R., Sprock, J., & Fuller, A. (1990). Suggested guidelines for including/excluding categories in the DSM-IV. *Comprehensive Psychiatry, 31,* 15–19.

Blau, Z. S., Oser, G. T., & Stephens, R. C. (1979). Aging, social class, and ethnicity: A comparison of Anglo, Black, and Mexican-American Texans. *Pacific Sociological Review, 22,* 501–525.

Blazer, D., Hughes, D., & George, L. K. (1987). Stressful life events and the onset of a generalized anxiety syndrome. *American Journal of Psychiatry, 144,* 1178–1183.

Blazer, D. G., Kessler, R. C., McGonagle, K. A., & Swartz, M. S. (1994). The prevalence and distribution of major depression in a national community sample: The National Comorbidity Survey. *American Journal of Psychiatry, 151,* 979–986.

Blazer, D. G., & Williams, C. D. (1980). Epidemiology of dysphoria and depression in the elderly population. *American Journal of Psychiatry, 137,* 439–444.

Blehar, M. C., & Rosenthal, N. E. (1989). Seasonal affective disorders and phototherapy: Report of a National Institute of Mental Health–sponsored workshop. *Archives of General Psychiatry, 46,* 469–474.

Bleuler, E. (1923). *Lehrbuch der Psychiatrie* (4th ed.). Berlin: Springer.

Bliss, E. L. (1983). Multiple personalities, related disorders, and hypnosis. *American Journal of Clinical Hypnosis, 26,* 114–123.

Bockhoven, J. (1963). *Moral treatment in American psychiatry.* New York: Springer.

Boll, T. J. (1985). Developing issues in clinical neuropsychology. *Journal of Clinical and Experimental Neuropsychology, 7,* 473–485.

Bond, I. K., & Hutchinson, H. C. (1960). Application of reciprocal inhibition therapy to exhibitionism. *Canadian Medical Association Journal, 83,* 23–25.

Bootzin, R. R., & Engle-Friedman, M. (1987). Sleep disturbances. In L. L. Carstensen & B.A. Edelstein (Eds.), *Handbook of clinical gerontology.* New York: Pergamon.

Bootzin, R. R., Engle-Friedman, M., & Hazelwood, L. (1983). Sleep disorders and the elderly. In P. M. Lewinsohn & L. Teri (Eds.), *Clinical geropsychology: New directions in assessment and treatment*. New York: Pergamon.

Borgatta, E. F., Montgomery, R. J. Y., & Borgatta, M. L. (1982). Alcohol use and abuse, life crisis events, and the elderly. *Research on Aging, 4*, 378–408.

Borkovec, T. D., & Costello, E. (1993). Efficacy of applied relaxation and cognitive-behavioral therapy in the treatment of generalized anxiety disorder. *Journal of Consulting and Clinical Psychology, 61*, 611–619.

Bornstein, R. F. (1992). The dependent personality: Developmental, social, and clinical perspectives. *Psychological Bulletin, 112*, 3–23.

Bornstein, R. F. (1993). Implicit perception, implicit memory, and the recovery of unconscious material in psychotherapy. *Journal of Nervous and Mental Disease, 181*, 337–344.

Bornstein, R. F., Leone, D. R., & Galley, D. J. (1987). The generalizability of subliminal mere exposure effects: Influence of stimuli perceived without awareness on social behavior. *Journal of Personality and Social Psychology, 53*, 1070–1079.

Bornstein, R. F., Manning, K. A., Krukonis, A. B., Rossner, S. C., & Mastrosimone, C. C. (1993). Sex differences in dependency: A comparison of objective and projective measures. *Journal of Personality Assessment, 61*, 169–181.

Boyle, M. (1991). *Schizophrenia: A scientific delusion?* New York: Routledge.

Brady, E. U., & Kendall, P. C. (1992). Comorbidity of anxiety and depression in children and adolescents. *Psychological Bulletin, 111*, 244–255.

Brady, J. P., Davison, G. C., DeWald, P. A., Egan, G., Fadiman, J., Frank, J. D., Gill, M. M., Hoffman, I., Kempler, W., Lazarus, A. A., Raimy, V., Rotter, J. B., & Strupp, H. H. (1980). Some views on effective principles of psychotherapy. *Cognitive Therapy and Research, 4*, 269–306.

Brandt, J., Buffers, N., Ryan, C., & Bayog, R. (1983). Cognitive loss and recovery in chronic alcohol abusers. *Archives of General Psychiatry, 40*, 435–442.

Bransford, J. D., & Johnson, M. K. (1973). Considerations of some problems of comprehension. In W. G. Chase (Ed.), *Visual information processing*. New York: Academic Press.

Braswell, L., & Kendall, P. C. (1988). Cognitive-behavioral methods with children. In K. S. Dobson (Ed.), *Handbook of cognitive-behavioral therapies*. New York: Guilford.

Brecher, E. M., & the Editors of *Consumer Reports*. (1972). *Licit and illicit drugs*. Mount Vernon, NY: Consumers Union.

Breen, M. J. (1989). Cognitive and behavioral differences in ADHD boys and girls. *Journal of Child Psychology and Psychiatry, 30*, 711–716.

Brehm, S. S., & Brehm, J. W. (1981). *Psychological reactance: A theory of freedom and control*. New York: Academic Press.

Breier, A., Buchanan, R. W., Kirkpatrick, B., Davis, O. R., Irish, D., Summerfelt, A., & Carpenter, W. T., Jr. (1994). Effects of clozapine on positive and negative symptoms in outpatients with schizophrenia. *American Journal of Psychiatry, 151*, 20–26.

Breier, A., Charney, D. S., & Heninger, G. R. (1986). Agoraphobia with panic attacks. *Archives of General Psychiatry, 43*, 1029–1036.

Breslau, N., Davis, G. C., Andreski, P., & Peterson, E. (1991). Traumatic events and posttraumatic stress disorder in an urban population of young adults. *Archives of General Psychiatry, 48*, 216–222.

Bretschneider, J. G., & McCoy, N. L. (1988). Sexual interest and behavior in healthy 80- to 102-year-olds. *Archives of Sexual Behavior, 17*, 109–129.

Breuer, J., & Freud, S. (1982). *Studies in hysteria*. (J. Strachey, Trans. and Ed., with the collaboration of A. Freud). New York: Basic Books. (Original work published 1895)

Brickman, A. S., McManus, M., Grapentine, W. L., & Alessi, N. (1984). Neuropsychological assessment of seriously delinquent adolescents. *Journal of the American Academy of Child Psychiatry, 23*, 453–457.

Brodie, H. K. H., & Leff, M. J. (1971). Bipolar depression: A comparative study of patient characteristics. *American Journal of Psychiatry, 127*, 1086–1090.

Brookfield, S. D. (1987). *Developing critical thinkers: Challenging adults to explore alternative ways of thinking and acting*. San Francisco: Jossey-Bass.

Broverman, J. K., Broverman, D. M., & Clarkson, F. E. (1970). Sexual stereotypes and clinical judgments of mental health. *Journal of Consulting and Clinical Psychology, 34*, 1–7.

Brown, G. L., & Goodwin, F. K. (1986). Cerebrospinal fluid correlates of suicide attempts and aggression. *Annals of the New York Academy of Science, 487*, 175–188.

Brown, G. W. (1993). Life events and affective disorder: Replications and limitations. *Psychosomatic Medicine, 55*, 248–259.

Brown, G. W., Bone, M., Dalison, B., & Wing, J. K. (1966). *Schizophrenia and social care*. London: Oxford University Press.

Brown, G. W., & Harris, T. O. (1989). *Life events and illness*. New York: Guilford.

Brownell, K. D., Hayes, S. C., & Barlow, D. H. (1977). Patterns of appropriate and deviant sexual arousal: The behavioral treatment of multiple sexual deviations. *Journal of Consulting and Clinical Psychology, 45*, 1144–1155.

Bruck, M. (1987). The adult outcomes of children with learning disabilities. *Annals of Dyslexia, 37*, 252–263.

Buchsbaum, M. S., Kessler, R., King, A., Johnson, J., & Cappelletti, J. (1984). Simultaneous cerebral glucography with positron emission tomography and topographic electroencephalography. In G. Pfurtscheller, E. J. Jonkman, & F.H. Lopes da Silva (Eds.), *Brain ischemia: Quantitative EEG and imaging techniques*. Amsterdam: Elsevier.

Buchwald, A. M., & Rudick-Davis, D. (1993). The symptoms of major depression. *Journal of Abnormal Psychology, 102*, 197–205.

Buglass, D., Clarke, J., Henderson, A. S., Kreitman, N., & Presley, A. S. (1977). A study of agoraphobic housewives. *Psychological Medicine, 7*, 73–86.

Bunney, W. E., Goodwin, F. K., & Murphy, D. L. (1972). The "Switch Process" in manic-depressive illness. *Archives of General Psychiatry, 27*, 312–317.

Bunney, W. E., Murphy, D. L., Goodwin, F. K., & Borge, G. F. (1970). The switch process from depression to mania: Relationship to drugs which alter brain amines. *Lancet, 1*, 1022–1027.

Burgess, A. W., & Holmstrom, L. L. (1974). *Rape: Victim of crisis*. Bowie, MD: Robert J. Brady.

Burgess, E. S., & Haaga, D. A. F. (1994, November). *Appraisals, coping responses, and attributions as predictors of individual differences in negative emotions among adolescents with cancer*. Paper presented at the 28th annual convention of the Association for Advancement of Behavior Therapy, San Diego.

Burnam, M. A., Stein, J. A., Golding, J. M., Siegel, J. M., Sorenson, S. B., Forsythe, A. B., & Telles, C. A. (1988). Sexual assault and mental disorders in a community population. *Journal of Consulting and Clinical Psychology, 56*, 843–850.

Butcher, J. N., Dahlstrom, W. G., Graham, J. R., Tellegen, A., & Kraemer, B. (1989). *Minnesota Multiphasic Personality Inventory-2: Manual for administration and scoring*. Minneapolis: University of Minnesota Press.

Butler, G. (1985). Exposure as a treatment for social phobia: Some instructive difficulties. *Behaviour Research and Therapy, 23*, 651–657.

Butler, G., & Mathews, A. (1983). Cognitive processes in anxiety. *Advances in Behaviour Research and Therapy, 5*, 51–62.

Butler, R. N. (1963). The life review: An interpretation of reminiscence in the aged. *Psychiatry, 119*, 721–728.

Butler, R. N., & Lewis, M. I. (1982). *Aging and mental health: Positive psychosocial approaches* (3rd ed.). St. Louis: Mosby.

Cacioppo, J. T., Glass, C. R., & Merluzzi, T. V. (1979). Self-statements and self-evaluations: A cognitive-response analysis of heterosexual social anxiety. *Cognitive Therapy and Research, 3,* 249–262.

Caddy, G. R. (1983). Alcohol use and abuse. In B. Tabakoff, P. B. Sutker, & C. L. Randell (Eds.), *Medical and social aspects of alcohol use.* New York: Plenum.

Cadoret, R. J. (1978). Evidence for genetic inheritance of primary affective disorder in adoptees. *American Journal of Psychiatry, 135,* 463–466.

Calfee, R. C., Fisk, L., & Piontkowski, D. (1975). "On–Off" tests of cognitive skills in reading acquisition. In M. P. Douglass (Ed.), *Claremont Reading Conference 39th Yearbook 1975.* Claremont, CA: Claremont Graduate School.

Calhoun, K. S., & Atkeson, B. M. (1991). *Treatment of rape victims.* Elmsford, NY: Pergamon.

Cameron, D. J., Thomas, R. I., Mulvhill, M., & Bronheim, H. (1987). Delirium: A test of the Diagnostic and Statistical Manual III criteria on medical inpatients. *Journal of the American Geriatrics Society, 35,* 1007–1010.

Campbell, M., Anderson, L. T., Small, A. M., Locascio, J. J., Lynch, N. S., & Choroco, M. C. (1990). Naltrexone in autistic children: A double-blind and placebo controlled study. *Psychopharmacology Bulletin, 26,* 130–135.

Campbell, M., Overall, J. E., Small, A. M., Sokol, M. S., Spencer, E. K., Adams, P., Foltz, R. L., Monti, K. M., Perry, R., Nobler, M., & Roberts, E. (1989). Naltrexone in autistic children: An acute dose range tolerance trial. *Journal of the American Academy of Child and Adolescent Psychiatry, 28,* 200–206.

Campbell, S. B. (1990). *Behavioral problems in preschoolers: Clinical and developmental issues.* New York: Guilford.

Cantwell, D. P., Baker, L., & Rutter, M. (1978). Family factors. In M. Rutter & E. Schopler (Eds.), *Autism: A reappraisal of concepts and treatment.* New York: Plenum.

Caplan, G. (1964). *Principles of preventive psychiatry.* New York: Basic Books.

Caporael, L. (1976). Ergotism: The satan loosed in Salem? *Science, 192,* 21–26.

Carey, M. P., Kalra, D. L., Carey, K. B., Halperin, S., & Richards, C. S. (1993). Stress and unaided smoking cessation: A prospective investigation. *Journal of Consulting and Clinical Psychology, 61,* 831–838.

Carr, A. T. (1971). Compulsive neurosis: Two psychophysiological studies. *Bulletin of the British Psychological Society, 24,* 256–257.

Carr, A. T. (1974). Compulsive neurosis: A review of the literature. *Psychological Bulletin, 81,* 311–319.

Carr, E. G., Schreibman, L., & Lovaas, O. I. (1975). Control of echolalic speech in psychotic children. *Journal of Abnormal Child Psychology, 3,* 331–351.

Carroll, K. M., Rounsaville, B. J., Gordon, L. T., Nich, C., Jatlow, P., Bisighini, R. M., & Gawin, F. H. (1994). Psychotherapy and pharmacotherapy for ambulatory cocaine abusers. *Archives of General Psychiatry, 51,* 177–187.

Carver, C. S., Scheier, M. F., & Weintraub, J. K. (1989). Assessing coping strategies: A theoretically based approach. *Journal of Personality and Social Psychology, 56,* 267–283.

Cashman, J. A. (1966). *The LSD story.* Greenwich, CT: Fawcett.

Caspi, A., & Herbener, E. S. (1990). Continuity and change: Assortative marriage and the consistency of personality in adulthood. *Journal of Personality and Social Psychology, 58,* 250–258.

Cautela, J. R. (1966). Treatment of compulsive behavior by covert sensitization. *Psychological Record, 16,* 33–41.

Caven, R. S. (1973). Speculations on innovations to conventional marriage in old age. *The Gerontologist, 13,* 409–411.

Cepeda-Benito, A. (1993). Meta-analytical review of the efficacy of nicotine chewing gum in smoking treatment programs. *Journal of Consulting and Clinical Psychology, 61,* 822–830.

Chambless, D. L., & Gillis, M. M. (1993). Cognitive therapy of anxiety disorders. *Journal of Consulting and Clinical Psychology, 61,* 248–260.

Charney, D. S., Heninger, G. R., & Breier, A. (1984). Noradrenergic function in panic attacks. *Archives of General Psychiatry, 41,* 751–763.

Chelune, G. J., Ferguson, W., Koon, R., & Dickey, T. O. (1986). Frontal lobe disinhibition in attention deficit disorder. *Child Psychiatry and Human Development, 16,* 264–281.

Chesler, P. (1972). *Women and madness.* Garden City, NY: Doubleday.

Chesney, M. A., Eagleston, J. R., & Rosenman, R. H. (1980). The Type A structured interview: A behavioral assessment in the rough. *Journal of Behavioral Assessment, 2,* 255–272.

Christensen, A., & Jacobson, N. S. (1994). Who (or what) can do psychotherapy: The status and challenge of nonprofessional therapies. *Psychological Science, 5,* 8–14.

Christie, A. B. (1982). Changing patterns in mental illness in the elderly. *British Journal of Psychiatry, 140,* 154–159.

Churchill, D. W. (1969). Psychotic children and behavior modification. *American Journal of Psychiatry, 125,* 1585–1590.

Cimons, M. (1992, May 22). Record number of Americans stop smoking. *Los Angeles Times,* p. A4.

Clark, D. A. (1988). The validity of measures of cognition: A review of the literature. *Cognitive Therapy and Research, 12,* 1–20.

Clark, W. B., & Cahalan, D. (1976). Changes in drinking behavior over a four-year span. *Addictive Behaviors, 1,* 251–259.

Clarkin, J. F., Hull, J. W., Cantor, J., & Sanderson, C. (1993). Borderline personality disorder and personality traits: A comparison of SCID-II BPD and NEO-PI. *Psychological Assessment, 5,* 472–476.

Clarkin, J. F., Widiger, T. A., Frances, A. J., Hurt, S. W., & Gilmore, M. (1983). Prototypic typology and the borderline personality disorder. *Journal of Abnormal Psychology, 92,* 263–275.

Clausen, J. A., & Kohn, M. L. (1959). Relation of schizophrenia to the social structure of a small city. In B. Pasamanick (Ed.), *Epidemiology of mental disorder.* Washington, DC: American Association for the Advancement of Science.

Cleckley, H. (1976). *The mask of sanity* (5th ed.). St. Louis: Mosby.

Climko, R. P., Roehrich, H., Sweeney, D. R., & Al-Razi, J. (1987). Ecstasy: A review of MDMA and MDA. *International Journal of Psychiatry in Medicine, 16,* 359–372.

Clomipramine Collaborative Study Group (1991). Clomipramine in the treatment of patients with obsessive-compulsive disorder. *Archives of General Psychiatry, 48,* 730–738.

Cloninger, R. C., Bohman, M., & Sigvardsson, S. (1981). Inheritance of alcohol abuse: Cross-fostering analysis of adopted men. *Archives of General Psychiatry, 38,* 861–868.

Cloninger, R. C., Martin, R. L., Guze, S. B., & Clayton, P. L. (1986). A prospective follow-up and family study of somatization in men and women. *American Journal of Psychiatry, 143,* 713–714.

Clunies-Ross, G. G. (1979). Accelerating the development of Down's syndrome infants and young children. *The Journal of Special Education, 13,* 169–177.

Cochran, S. D. (1984). Preventing medical noncompliance in the outpatient treatment of bipolar affective disorders. *Journal of Consulting and Clinical Psychology, 52,* 873–878.

Coffey, C. E., Weiner, R. D., Djang, W. T., Figiel, G. S., Soady, S. A. R., Patterson, L. J., Holt, P. D., Spritzer, C. E., & Wilkinson, W. E. (1991). Brain anatomic effects of electroconvulsive therapy: A prospective magnetic resonance imaging study. *Archives of General Psychiatry, 48,* 1009–1012.

Cohen, D., Eisdorfer, C., Prinz, P., Breen, A., Davis, M., & Gadsby, A. (1983). Sleep disturbances in the institutionalized aged. *Journal of the American Geriatrics Society, 31,* 79–82.

Cohen, D. J., Solnit, A. J., & Wohlford, P. (1979). Mental health services in Head Start. In E. Zigler & J. Valentine (Eds.), *Project Head Start*. New York: Free Press.

Cohen, L. J., & Roth, S. (1987). The psychological aftermath of rape: Long-term effects and individual differences in recovery. *Journal of Social and Clinical Psychology, 5*, 525–534.

Cohen, S. (1981). Adverse effects of marijuana: Selected issues. *Annals of the New York Academy of Science, 362*, 119–124.

Cohen, S. (1988). Psychosocial models of the role of social support in the etiology of physical disease. *Health Psychology, 7*, 269–297.

Cohen, S., Tyrell, D. A. J., & Smith, A. P. (1991). Psychological stress and susceptibility to the common cold. *New England Journal of Medicine, 325*, 606–612.

Cohen, S., & Wills, T. A. (1985). Stress, social support, and the buffering process. *Psychological Bulletin, 98*, 310–357.

Cole, J. D. (1988). Where are those new antidepressants we were promised? *Archives of General Psychiatry, 45*, 193–194.

Collaborative study of children treated for phenylketonuria, preliminary report 8. (1975, February). R. Koch, principal investigator. Presented at the Eleventh General Medicine Conference, Stateline, NV.

Committee on Health Care for Homeless People. (1988). *Homelessness, health, and human needs*. Washington, DC: National Academic Press.

Compton, D. R., Dewey, W. L., & Martin, B. R. (1990). Cannabis dependence and tolerance production. *Advances in Alcohol and Substance Abuse, 9*, 129–147.

Conger, J. J. (1951). The effects of alcohol on conflict behavior in the albino rat. *Quarterly Journal of Studies on Alcohol, 12*, 129.

Conners, C. K. (1969). A teacher rating scale for use in drug studies with children. *American Journal of Psychiatry, 126*, 884–888.

Cooper, J. R. (1983). *Research on the treatment of narcotic addiction: State of the art*. Rockville, MD: U.S. Department of Health and Human Services, Public Health Service, Alcohol, Drug Abuse, and Mental Health Administration, National Institute on Drug Abuse.

Coppen, A., Prange, A. J., Whybrow, P. C., & Noguera, R. (1972). Abnormalities in indoleamines in affective disorders. *Archives of General Psychiatry, 26*, 474–478.

Cornelius, J. R., Soloff, P. H., Perel, J. M., & Ulrich, R. F. (1990). Fluoxetine trial in borderline personality disorder. *Psychopharmacology Bulletin, 26*, 151–154.

Costa, P. T., Jr., Zonderman, A. B., McCrae, R. R., Cornoni-Huntley, J., Locke, B. Z., & Barbano, H. E. (1987). Longitudinal analyses of psychological well-being in a national sample: Stability of mean levels. *Journal of Gerontology, 42*, 50–55.

Costello, C. G. (1993). Cognitive causes of psychopathology. In C. G. Costello (Ed.), *Basic issues in psychopathology* (pp. 320–355). New York: Guilford.

Courchesne, E., Yeung-Courchesne, R., Press, G. A., Hesselink, J. R., & Jernigan, T. L. (1988). Hypoplasia of cerebellar vermal lobules VI and VII in autism. *New England Journal of Medicine, 318*, 1349–1354.

Covi, L., Lipman, R. S., Derogatis, L. R., Smith, J. E., & Pattison, J. H. (1974). Drugs and group psychotherapy in neurotic depression. *American Journal of Psychiatry, 131*, 191–197.

Cowdry, R. W., & Gardner, D. L. (1988). Pharmacotherapy of borderline personality disorder: Alprazolam, carbamazepine, trofluoperazine, and tranylcypromine. *Archives of General Psychiatry, 45*, 802–803.

Cox, A., Rutter, M., Newman, S., & Bartak, L. (1975). A comparative study of infantile autism and specific developmental language disorders: II. Parental characteristics. *British Journal of Psychiatry, 126*, 146–159.

Cox, B. J., Swinson, R. P., Morrison, B., & Lee, P. S. (1993). Clomipramine, fluoxetine, and behavior therapy in the treatment of obsessive-compulsive disorder: A meta-analysis. *Journal of Behavior Therapy and Experimental Psychiatry, 24*, 149–153.

Coyne, J. C. (1976). Depression and the response of others. *Journal of Abnormal Psychology, 85*, 186–193.

Coyne, J. C. (1994). Self-reported distress: Analog or ersatz depression? *Psychological Bulletin, 116*, 29–45.

Craighead, W. E., Evans, D. D., & Robins, C. J. (1992). Unipolar depression. In S. M. Turner, K. S. Calhoun, & H. E. Adams (Eds.), *Handbook of clinical behavior therapy* (2nd ed., pp. 99–116). New York: Wiley.

Craske, M. G., Brown, T. A., & Barlow, D. H. (1991). Behavioral treatment of panic disorder: A two-year follow-up. *Behavior Therapy, 22*, 289–304.

Craske, M. G., Rapee, R. M., & Barlow, D. H. (1992). Cognitive-behavioral treatment of panic disorder, agoraphobia, and generalized anxiety disorder. In S. M. Turner, K. S. Calhoun, & H. E. Adams (Eds.), *Handbook of clinical behavior therapy* (2nd ed., pp. 39–65). New York: Wiley.

Crits-Christoph, P. (1992). The efficacy of brief dynamic psychotherapy: A meta-analysis. *American Journal of Psychiatry, 149*, 151–158.

Cross-National Collaborative Group (1992). The changing rate of major depression: Cross-national comparisons. *Journal of the American Medical Association, 268*, 3098–3105.

Crowe, R. R., Noyes, R., Pauls, D. L., & Slymen, D. J. (1983). A family study of panic disorder. *Archives of General Psychiatry, 40*, 1065–1069.

Crumbaugh, J. C. (1968). Cross-validation of Purpose in Life Test based on Frankl's concepts. *Journal of Individual Psychology, 24*, 74–81.

Crumbaugh, J. C., & Maholick, L. T. (1964). An experimental study in existentialism: The psychometric approach to Frankl's concept of noogenic neurosis. *Journal of Clinical Psychology, 20*, 200–207.

Cunningham, J., Dockery, D. W., & Speizer, F. E. (1994). Maternal smoking during pregnancy as a predictor of lung function in children. *American Journal of Epidemiology, 139*, 1139–1152.

Curry, S. J. (1993). Self-help interventions for smoking cessation. *Journal of Consulting and Clinical Psychology, 61*, 790–803.

D'Amicis, L., Goldberg, D., LoPiccolo, J., Friedman, J., & Davies, L. (1985). Clinical follow-up of couples treated for sexual dysfunction. *Archives of Sexual Behavior, 14*, 461–483.

Dance, K. A., & Neufeld, R. W. J. (1988). Aptitude-treatment interaction research in the clinical setting: A review of attempts to dispel the "patient uniformity" myth. *Psychological Bulletin, 104*, 192–213.

Dauphinais, P., & King, J. (1992). Psychological assessment with American Indian children. *Applied and Preventive Psychology, 1*, 97–110.

Davidson, J. T. R., Giller, E. L., Zisook, S., & Overall, J. E. (1988). An efficacy study of isocarboxazid in depression and its relationship to depressive nosology. *Archives of General Psychiatry, 45*, 120–128.

Davis, J. M. (1978). Dopamine theory of schizophrenia: A two-factor theory. In L. C. Wynne, R. L. Cromwell, & S. Matthysse (Eds.), *The nature of schizophrenia*. New York: Wiley.

Davis, K. L., Kahn, R. S., Ko, G., & Davidson, M. (1991). Dopamine and schizophrenia: A review and reconceptualization. *American Journal of Psychiatry, 148*, 1474–1486.

Davison, G. C. (1964). A social learning therapy programme with an autistic child. *Behaviour Research and Therapy, 2*, 146–159.

Davison, G. C. (1968). Elimination of a sadistic fantasy by a client-controlled counterconditioning technique. *Journal of Abnormal Psychology, 73*, 84–90.

Davison, G. C. (1974). *Homosexuality: The ethical challenge*. Presidential address to the Eighth Annual Convention of the Association for Advancement of Behavior Therapy, Chicago.

Davison, G. C. (1976). Homosexuality: The ethical challenge. *Journal of Consulting and Clinical Psychology, 44*, 157–162.

Davison, G. C. (1978). Not can but ought: The treatment of homosexuality. *Journal of Consulting and Clinical Psychology, 46*, 170–172.

Davison, G. C., Haaga, D. A. F., Rosenbaum, J., Dolezal, S. L., & Weinstein, K. A. (1991). Assessment of self-efficacy in articulated thoughts: "States of Mind" analysis and association with speech anxious behavior. *Journal of Cognitive Psychotherapy: An International Quarterly, 5,* 83–92.

Davison, G. C., Robins, C., & Johnson, M. K. (1983). Articulated thoughts during simulated situations: A paradigm for studying cognition in emotion and behavior. *Cognitive Therapy and Research, 7,* 17–40.

Davison, G. C., & Thompson, R. F. (1988). Stress management. In D. Druckman & J.A. Swets (Eds.), *Enhancing human performance: Issues, theories, and techniques.* Washington, DC: National Academic Press.

Davison, G. C., & Valins, S. (1969). Maintenance of self-attributed and drug-attributed behavior change. *Journal of Personality and Social Psychology, 11,* 25–33.

Davison, G. C., & Wilson, G. T. (1973). Attitudes of behavior therapists toward homosexuality. *Behavior Therapy, 4,* 686–696.

Davison, G. C., & Zighelboim, V. (1987). Irrational beliefs in the articulated thoughts of college students with social anxiety. *Journal of Rational-Emotive Therapy, 5,* 238–254.

DeFazio, A., & Cunningham, K. A. (1987). A paraphilia in a spinal-cord-injured patient: A case report. *Sexuality-and-Disability, 8,* 247–254.

Delgado, P. L., Charney, D. S., Price, L. H., Aghajanian, G. K., Landis, H., & Heninger, G. R. (1990). Serotonin function and the mechanism of antidepressant action: Reversal of antidepressant-induced remission by rapid depletion of plasma tryptophan. *Archives of General Psychiatry, 47,* 411–418.

Delgado, P. L., Price, L. H., Heninger, G. R., & Charney, D. S. (1992). Neurochemistry. In E. S. Paykel (Ed.), *Handbook of affective disorders* (2nd ed., pp. 219–253). Edinburgh: Churchill Livingstone.

Dement, W. C., Laughton, E., & Carskadon, M. A. (1981). "White paper" on sleep and aging. *Journal of the American Geriatrics Society, 30,* 25–50.

DeMyer, M. (1975). The nature of the neuropsychological disability of autistic children. *Journal of Autism and Childhood Schizophrenia, 5,* 109–127.

Depue, R. A., & Monroe, S. M. (1978). Learned helplessness in the perspective of the depressive disorders: Conceptual and definitional issues. *Journal of Abnormal Psychology, 87,* 3–20.

D'Ercole, A., & Struening, E. (1990). Victimization among homeless women: Implications for service delivery. *Journal of Community Psychology, 18,* 141–152.

Deutsch, A. (1949). *The mentally ill in America.* New York: Columbia University Press.

Dew, M. A., Bromet, E. J., Brent, D., & Greenhouse, J. B. (1987). A quantitative literature review of the effectiveness of suicide prevention centers. *Journal of Consulting and Clinical Psychology, 55,* 239–244.

Dewys, W. D., Begg, C., & Lavin, P. T. (1980). Prognostic effect of weight loss prior to chemotherapy in cancer patients. *American Journal of Medicine, 69,* 491–497.

Dietz, P. E., Hazelwood, R. R., & Warren, J. (1990). The sexually sadistic criminal and his offenses. *Bulletin of the American Academy of Psychiatry and the Law, 18,* 163–178.

DiFranza, J. R., & Guerrera, M. P. (1990). Alcoholism and smoking. *Journal of Studies on Alcohol, 51,* 130–135.

DiFranza, J. R., Richards, J. W., Paulman, P. M., Wolf-Gillespie, N., Fletcher, C., Jaffe, R. D., & Murray, D. (1991). RJR Nabisco's cartoon camel promotes Camel cigarettes to children. *Journal of the American Medical Association, 266,* 3149–3153.

Digman, J. M. (1990). Personality structure: Emergence of the five-factor model. *Annual Review of Psychology, 41,* 417–440.

Dimsdale, J. E., Pierce, C., Schoenfeld, D., Brown, A., Zusman, R., & Graham, R. (1986). Suppressed anger and blood pressure: The effects of race, sex, social class, and age. *Psychosomatic Medicine, 48,* 430–436.

DiNardo, P. A., & Barlow, D. H. (1988). *Anxiety Disorders Interview Schedule—Revised (ADIS-R).* Center for Stress and Anxiety Disorders, State University of New York at Albany.

Dixon, J. F., & Ahrens, A. H. (1992). Stress and attributional style as predictors of self-reported depression in children. *Cognitive Therapy and Research, 16,* 623–634.

Dobson, K. S. (1989). A meta-analysis of the efficacy of cognitive therapy for depression. *Journal of Consulting and Clinical Psychology, 57,* 414–419.

Dobson, K. S., & Shaw, B. F. (1986). Cognitive assessment with major depressive disorders. *Cognitive Therapy and Research, 10,* 13–29.

Dodge, K. A., & Frame, C. L. (1982). Social cognitive biases and deficits in aggressive boys. *Child Development, 53,* 620–635.

Dohrenwend, B. P., Levav, P. E., Schwartz, S., Naveh, G., Link, B. G., Skodol, A. E., & Stueve, A. (1992). Socioeconomic status and psychiatric disorders: The causation-selection issue. *Science, 255,* 946–952.

Doran, A. R., Pickar, D., Boronow, J., et al. (1985). *CT scans in schizophrenics, medical and normal controls.* Paper presented at the annual meeting of the American College of Neuropsychopharmacology, Maui, HI.

Dowd, J. J., & Bengston, V. L. (1978). Aging in minority populations: An examination of the double jeopardy hypothesis. *Journal of Gerontology, 33,* 427–436.

Downey, G., Silver, R. C., & Wortman, C. B. (1990). Reconsidering the attribution-adjustment relation following a major negative event: Coping with the loss of a child. *Journal of Personality and Social Psychology, 59,* 925–940.

Draguns, J. G. (1989). Normal and abnormal behavior in cross-cultural perspective: Specifying the nature of their relationships. In J. J. Berman (Ed.), *Nebraska symposium on motivation.* Lincoln: University of Nebraska Press.

Drug use and problems continue to rise. (1994, Sept./Oct.). *Prevention Pipeline* (pp. 48–50). Rockville, MD: Center for Substance Abuse Prevention.

Dunham, H. W. (1965). *Community and schizophrenia: An epidemiological analysis.* Detroit: Wayne State University Press.

Dura, J. R., Stukenberg, K. W., & Kiecolt-Glaser, J. K. (1991). Anxiety and depressive disorders in adult children caring for demented parents. *Psychology and Aging, 6,* 467–473.

Durham, R. C., & Turvey, A. A. (1987). Cognitive therapy versus behaviour therapy in the treatment of chronic general anxiety. *Behaviour Research and Therapy, 25,* 229–234.

Dweck, C. S. (1975). The role of expectation and attributions in the alleviation of learned helplessness. *Journal of Personality and Social Psychology, 31,* 674–685.

Dweck, C. S., Davidson, W., Nelson, S., & Enna, B. (1978). Sex differences in learned helplessness: II. The contingencies of evaluative feedback in the classroom and III. An experimental analysis. *Developmental Psychology, 14,* 268–276.

Dworkin, R. H., & Lenzenweger, M. F. (1984). Symptoms and the genetics of schizophrenia: Implications for diagnosis. *American Journal of Psychiatry, 141,* 1541–1546.

Dworkin, R. H., Lenzenweger, M. F., & Moldin, S. O. (1987). Genetics and the phenomenology of schizophrenia. In P. D. Harvey & E. F. Walker (Eds.), *Positive and negative symptoms of psychosis.* Hillsdale, NJ: Erlbaum.

Dysken, M. W. (1979). Clinical usefulness of sodium amobarbital interviewing. *Archives of General Psychiatry, 36,* 789–794.

Eaton, W. W., Kramer, M., Anthony, J. C., Dryman, A., Shapiro, S., & Locke, B. Z. (1989). The incidence of specific DIS/DSM-III mental disorders: Data from the NIMH Epidemiologic Catchment Area Programs. *Acta Psychiatrica Scandinavica, 79,* 163–178.

Edwards, G., Hensman, C., Hawker, A., & Williamson, V. (1967). Alcoholics Anonymous: The anatomy of a self-help group. *Social Psychiatry, 1*, 195–204.

Egan, G. (1975). *The skilled helper*. Monterey, CA: Brooks/Cole.

Egeland, J. A., Gerhard, D. S., Pauls, D. L., Sussex, J. N., Kidd, K. K., Allen, C. R., Hosterer, A. M., & Housman, D. E. (1987). Bipolar affective disorders linked to DNA markers on chromosome 11. *Nature, 325*, 783–787.

Ehrhardt, A., & Money, J. (1967). Progestin-induced hermaphroditism: IQ and psychosexual identity in a study of ten girls. *Journal of Sex Research, 3*, 83–100.

Eiser, C., Eiser, R. J., Town, C., & Tripp, J. (1991). Discipline strategies and parental perceptions of preschool children with asthma. *British Journal of Medical Psychology, 64*, 45–53.

Eisler, R. M., & Blalock, J. A. (1991). Masculine gender role stress: Implications for the assessment of men. *Clinical Psychology Review, 11*, 45–60.

Ekstrand, M., & Coates, T. J. (1990). Maintenance of safer sexual behaviors and predictors of risky sex: The San Francisco Men's Health Study. *American Journal of Public Health, 80*, 973–977.

Elkin, I., Parloff, M. B., Hadley, S. W., & Autry, J. H. (1985). NIMH Treatment of Depression Collaborative Research Program. *Archives of General Psychiatry, 42*, 305–316.

Elkin, I., Shea, M. T., Watkins, J. T., Imber, S. D., Sotsky, S. M., Collins, J. F., Glass, D. R., Pilkonis, P. A., Leber, W. R., Docherty, J. P., Fiester, S. J., & Parloff, M. B. (1989). NIMH Treatment of Depression Collaborative Research Program: I. General effectiveness of treatments. *Archives of General Psychiatry, 46*, 971–983.

Ellis, A. (1962). *Reason and emotion in psychotherapy*. New York: Lyle Stuart.

Ellis, A. (1993). Changing rational-emotive therapy (RET) to rational emotive behavior therapy (REBT). *The Behavior Therapist, 16*, 257–258.

Ellis, H. (1906). *Studies in the psychology of sex*. New York: Random House.

Ellis, H. (1910). *Studies in the psychology of sex*. Philadelphia: F. A. Davis.

Elmore, A. M., & Tursky, B. (1978). The biofeedback hypothesis: An idea in search of a theory and method. In A. A. Sugerman & R. E. Tarter (Eds.), *Expanding dimensions of consciousness*. New York: Springer.

Emerick, C., Lassen, D. L., & Edwards, M. T. (1977). Nonprofessional peers as therapeutic agents. In A. M. Razin, & A. S. Gurman (Eds.), *Effective psychotherapy: A handbook of research*. New York: Pergamon.

Emory, L. E., Williams, D. H., Cole, C. M., Amparo, E. G., & Meyer, W. J. (1991). Anatomic variation of the corpus callosum in persons with gender dysphoria. *Archives of Sexual Behavior, 20*, 409–417.

Erdberg, P., & Exner, J. E., Jr. (1984). Rorschach assessment. In G. Goldstein & M. Hersen (Eds.), *Handbook of psychological assessment*. New York: Pergamon.

Erikson, E. H. (1950). *Childhood and society*. New York: Norton.

Erikson, E. H. (1959). *Identity and the life cycle: Selected papers*. New York: International Universities Press.

Ernst, R. L., & Hay, J. W. (1994). The U.S. economic and social costs of Alzheimer's disease revisited. *American Journal of Public Health, 84*, 1261–1264.

Evans, M. D., Hollon, S. D., DeRubeis, R. J., Piasecki, J. M., Grove, W. M., Garvey, M. J., & Tuason, V. B. (1992). Differential relapse following cognitive therapy and pharmacotherapy for depression. *Archives of General Psychiatry, 49*, 802–808.

Everett, F., Proctor, N., & Cartmell, B. (1989). Providing psychological services to American Indian children and families. In D. R. Atkinson, G. Morten, & D. W. Sue (Eds.), *Counseling American minorities* (3rd ed.). Dubuque, IA: W.C. Brown.

Exner, J. E., Jr. (1978). *The Rorschach: A comprehensive system: Vol. 2. Current research and advanced interpretation*. New York: Wiley.

Exner, J. E., Jr. (1986). *The Rorschach: A comprehensive system: Vol. 1. Basic foundations* (2nd ed.). New York: Wiley.

Exner, J. E., Jr. (1991). *The Rorschach: A comprehensive system: Vol. 2. Interpretation* (2nd ed.). New York: Wiley.

Eysenck, H. J. (1975). Crime as destiny. *New Behaviour, 9*, 46–49.

Eysenck, H. J. (1994). The outcome problem in psychotherapy: What have we learned? *Behaviour Research and Therapy, 32*, 477–495.

Fahy, T. A., Abas, M., & Brown, J. C. (1989). Multiple personality: A symptom of psychiatric disorder. *British Journal of Psychiatry, 154*, 99–101.

Fairbank, J. A., & Brown, T. A. (1987). Current behavioral approaches to the treatment of posttraumatic stress disorder. *The Behavior Therapist, 3*, 57–64.

Fairburn, C. G., & Beglin, S. J. (1990). Studies of the epidemiology of bulimia nervosa. *American Journal of Psychiatry, 147*, 401–408.

Fallon, A. E., & Rozin, P. (1985). Sex differences in perceptions of desirable body shape. *Journal of Abnormal Psychology, 94*, 102–105.

Falloon, I. R. H., Boyd, J. L., McGill, C. W., Williamson, M., Razani, J., Moss, H. B., Gilderman, A. M., & Simpson, G. M. (1985). Family management in the prevention of morbidity of schizophrenia. *Archives of General Psychiatry, 42*, 887–896.

Farina, A. (1976). *Abnormal psychology*. Englewood Cliffs, NJ: Prentice-Hall.

Feingold, B. F. (1973). *Introduction to clinical allergy*. Springfield, IL: Charles C. Thomas.

Feinsilver, D. B., & Gunderson, J. G. (1972). Psychotherapy for schizophrenics—Is it indicated? *Schizophrenia Bulletin, 1*, 11–23.

Feldman-Summers, S., Gordon, P. E., & Meagher, J. R. (1979). The impact of rape on sexual satisfaction. *Journal of Abnormal Psychology, 88*, 101–105.

Ferster, C. B. (1961). Positive reinforcement and behavioral deficits of autistic children. *Child Development, 32*, 437–456.

Figley, C. R. (1978a). Introduction to C. R. Figley (Ed.), *Stress disorders among Vietnam veterans*. New York: Brunner/Mazel.

Figley, C. R. (1978b). Psychosocial adjustment among Vietnam veterans: An overview of the research. In C. R. Figley (Ed.), *Stress disorders among Vietnam veterans*. New York: Brunner/Mazel.

Fillmore, K. M., & Caetano, R. (1980, May 22). *Epidemiology of occupational alcoholism*. Paper presented at the National Institute on Alcohol Abuse and Alcoholism's Workshop on Alcoholism in the Workplace, Reston, VA.

Finkelhor, D. (1979). *Sexually victimized children*. New York: Free Press.

Finkelhor, D. (1983). Removing the child—Prosecuting the offender in cases of sexual abuse: Evidence from the national reporting system for child abuse and neglect. *Child Abuse and Neglect, 7*, 195–205.

Finkelhor, D., & Araji, S. (1986). Explanations of pedophilia: A four-factor model. *Journal of Sex Research, 22*, 145–161.

Finn, S. E. (1982). Base rates, utilities, and DSM-III: Shortcomings of fixed-rule systems of psychodiagnosis. *Journal of Abnormal Psychology, 91*, 294–302.

Fiore, M. C., Jorenby, D. E., Baker, T. B., & Kenford, S. L. (1992). Tobacco dependence and the nicotine patch: Clinical guidelines for effective use. *Journal of the American Medical Association, 268*, 2687–2694.

Fiore, M. C., Novotny, T. F., Pierce, J. P., Giovino, G. A., Hatziandreu, E. J., Newcomb, P. A., Surawicz, T. S., & Davis, R. M. (1990). Methods used to quit smoking in the United States: Do cessation programs help? *Journal of the American Medical Association, 263*, 2760–2765.

Fischer, M. (1971). Psychoses in the offspring of schizophrenic monozygotic twins and their normal co-twins. *British Journal of Psychiatry, 118*, 43–52.

Fishbain, D. A., & Goldberg, M. (1991). The misdiagnosis of conversion disorder in a psychiatric emergency service. *General Hospital Psychiatry, 13*, 177–181.

Fisher, S., & Greenberg, R. P. (1993). How sound is the double-blind design for evaluating psychotropic drugs? *Journal of Nervous and Mental Disease, 181,* 345–350.

Fitts, S. N., Gibson, P., Redding, C. A., & Deiter, P. J. (1989). Body dysmorphic disorder: Implications for its validity as a DSM-III-R clinical syndrome. *Psychological Reports, 64,* 655–658.

Fitzgerald, R. V. (1973). *Conjoint marital therapy.* New York: Jason Aronson.

Foa, E. B., Kozak, M. J., Steketee, G. S., & McCarthy, P. R. (1992). Treatment of depressive and obsessive-compulsive symptoms in OCD by imipramine and behavior therapy. *British Journal of Clinical Psychology, 31,* 279–292.

Foa, E. B., Steketee, G. S., & Ozarow, B. J. (1985). Behavior therapy with obsessive-compulsives: From theory to treatment. In M. Mavissakalian, S. M. Turner, & L. Michelson (Eds.), *Obsessive-compulsive disorder: Psychological and pharmacological treatment.* New York: Plenum.

Folkman, S., Bernstein, L., & Lazarus, R. S. (1987). Stress processes and the misuse of drugs in older adults. *Psychology and Aging, 2,* 366–374.

Folks, D. G., Ford, C. V., & Regan, W. M. (1984). Conversion symptoms in a general hospital. *Psychosomatics, 25,* 285–295.

Folstein, M. F., Bassett, S. S., Anthony, J. C., Romanoski, A. J., & Nestadt, G. R. (1991). Dementia: case ascertainment in a community survey. *Journal of Gerontology, 46,* 132–138.

Fontham, E. T. H., Correa, P., Reynolds, P., Wu-Williams, A., Buffler, P. A., Greenberg, R. S., Chen, V. W., Alterman, T., Boyd, P., Austin, D. F., & Liff, J. (1994). Environmental tobacco smoke and lung cancer in nonsmoking women: A multicenter study. *Journal of the American Medical Association, 271,* 1752–1759.

Ford, C. S., & Beach, F. A. (1951). *Patterns of sexual behavior.* New York: Harper.

Ford, C. V., & Folks, D. G. (1985). Conversion disorders: An overview. *Psychosomatics, 26,* 371–383.

Foreyt, J. P. (1990). Behavioral medicine. In C. M. Franks, G. T. Wilson, P. C. Kendall, & J. P. Foreyt (Eds.), *Annual review of behavior therapy: Theory and practice* (Vol. 12). New York: Guilford.

Fortmann, S. P., Taylor, C. B., Flora, J. A., & Jatulis, D. E. (1993). Changes in adult cigarette smoking prevalence after five years of community health education: The Stanford Five-City Project. *American Journal of Epidemiology, 137,* 82–96.

Foy, D. W., Resnick, H. S., Carroll, E. M., & Osato, S. S. (1990). Behavior therapy. In A. S. Bellack, & M. Hersen (Eds.), *Handbook of comparative treatments for adult disorders* (pp. 302–315). New York: Wiley.

Foy, D. W., Resnick, H. S., Sipprelle, R. C., & Carroll, E. M. (1987). Premilitary, military, and postmilitary factors in the development of combat-related posttraumatic stress disorder. *The Behavior Therapist, 10,* 3–9.

Frame, C., Matson, J. L., Sonis, W. A., Fialkov, M. J., & Kazdin, A. E. (1982). Behavioral treatment of depression in a prepubertal child. *Journal of Behavior Therapy and Experimental Psychiatry, 3,* 239–243.

Frank, E., Anderson, C., & Rubenstein, D. (1978). Frequency of sexual dysfunctions in "normal" couples. *New England Journal of Medicine, 299,* 111–115.

Frank, E., Kupfer, D. J., Perel, J. M. , Cornes C., Jarrett, D. B., Mallinger, A. G., Thase, M. E., McEachian, A. B., & Grochocinski, V. J. (1990). Three-year outcomes for maintenance therapies in recurrent depression. *Archives of General Psychiatry, 47,* 1093–1099.

Frank, G. (1992). The response of African Americans to the Rorschach: A review of the research. *Journal of Personality Assessment, 59,* 317–325.

Frank, J. D. (1961). *Persuasion and healing.* Baltimore: Johns Hopkins University Press.

Frazier, P. A. (1990). Victim attributions and post-rape trauma. *Journal of Personality & Social Psychology, 59,* 298–304.

Fremouw, W. J., Perczel, W. J., & Ellis, T. E. (1990). *Suicide risk: Assessment and response guidelines.* Elmsford, NY: Pergamon.

Freud, A. (1946). *The psychoanalytic treatment of children: Lectures and essays.* London: Imago.

Freud, A. (1966). *The ego and the mechanisms of defense.* New York: International Universities Press.

Freud, S. (1909). Analysis of a phobia in a five-year-old boy. In *Collected works of Sigmund Freud* (Vol. 10). London: Hogarth Press.

Freud, S. (1950). Mourning and melancholia. In *Collected papers* (Vol. 4). London: Hogarth and the Institute of Psychoanalysis. (Original work published 1917)

Freund, K., Watson, R., & Dickey, R. (1990). Does sexual abuse in childhood cause pedophilia: An exploratory study. *Archives of Sexual Behavior, 19,* 557–568.

Friedman, J. M. (1978). Sexual adjustment of the postcoronary male. In J. LoPiccolo & L. LoPiccolo (Eds.), *Handbook of sex therapy.* New York: Plenum.

Friedman, M., Thoresen, C. E., Gill, J. J., Powell, L. H., Ulmer, D., Thompson, L., Price, V. A., Rabin, D. D., Breall, W. S., Dixon, T., Levy, R., & Bourg, E. (1984). Alteration of type A behavior and reduction in cardiac recurrences in postmyocardial infarction patients. *American Heart Journal, 108,* 237–248.

Friedman, M., Thoresen, C. E., Gill, J. J., Ulmer, D., Thompson, L., Powell, L., Price, A., Elek, S. R., Rabin, D. D., Breall, W. S., Piaget, G., Dixon, T., Bourg, E., Levy, R., & Tasto, D. I. (1982). Feasibility of altering type A behavior pattern after myocardial infarction. *Circulation, 66,* 83–92.

Friedman, M., & Ulmer, D. (1984). *Treating Type A behavior—and your heart.* New York: Fawcett Crest.

Friman, P. C., Allen, K. D., Kerwin, M. L. E., & Larzelere, R. (1993). Changes in modern psychology: A citation analysis of the Kuhnian displacement thesis. *American Psychologist, 48,* 658–664.

Fromm-Reichmann, F. (1948). Notes on the development of treatment of schizophrenics by psychoanalytic psychotherapy. *Psychiatry, 11,* 263–273.

Fuller, R. K. (1988). Disulfiram treatment of alcoholism. In R. M. Rose & J. E. Barrett (Eds.), *Alcoholism: Treatment and outcome.* New York: Raven.

Fuller, R. K., Branchey, L., Brightwell, D. R., Derman, R. M., Emrick, C. D., Iber, F. L., James, K. E., & Lacoursiere, R. B. (1986). Disulfiram treatment of alcoholism: A Veterans Administration cooperative study. *Journal of the American Medical Association, 256,* 1449–1455.

Furnham, A. (1988). *Lay theories: Everyday understanding of problems in the social sciences.* Oxford: Pergamon.

Fyer, A. J., Mannuzza, S., Chapman, T. F., Liebowitz, M. R., & Klein, D. F. (1993). A direct interview family study of social phobia. *Archives of General Psychiatry, 50,* 286–293.

Gagnon, J. H. (1977). *Human sexualities.* Chicago: Scott, Foresman.

Galaburda, A. M. (1989). Ordinary and extraordinary brain development: Anatomical variation in developmental dyslexia. *Annals of Dyslexia, 39,* 67–80.

Galanter, M., & Castaneda, R. (1985). Self-destructive behavior in the substance abuser. *Psychiatric Clinics of North America, 8,* 251–261.

Galanter, M., & Castaneda, R. (1990). Psychotherapy. In A. S. Bellack, & M. Hersen (Eds.), *Handbook of comparative treatments for adult disorders* (pp. 463–478). New York: Wiley.

Gallagher, D., Breckenridge, J. N., Thompson, L. W., Dessonville, C., & Amaral, P. (1982). Similarities and differences between normal grief and depression in older adults. *Essence, 5,* 127–140.

Gallagher, D., & Thompson, L. W. (1982). *Elders' maintenance of treatment benefits following individual psychotherapy for depression: Results of a pilot study and preliminary data from an ongoing replication study.*

Paper presented at the annual meeting of the American Psychological Association, Washington, DC.

Gallagher, D., & Thompson, L. W. (1983). Cognitive therapy for depression in the elderly. A promising model for treatment and research. In L. D. Breslau & M. R. Haug (Eds.), *Depression and aging: Causes, care and consequences.* New York: Springer.

Gallagher-Thompson, D. & Steffen, A. M. (1994). Comparative effects of cognitive-behavioral and brief psychodynamic psychotherapies for depressed family caregivers. *Journal of Consulting and Clinical Psychology, 62,* 543–549.

Garber, J., Kriss, M. R., Koch, M., & Lindholm, L. (1988). Recurrent depression in adolescents: A follow-up study. *Journal of the American Academy of Child and Adolescent Psychiatry, 27,* 49–54.

Garfield, S. L. (1994). Research on client variables in psychotherapy. In A. E. Bergin & S. L. Garfield (Eds.), *Handbook of psychotherapy and behavior change* (4th ed., pp. 190–228). New York: Wiley.

Garfield, S. L., & Kurtz, R. (1974). A survey of clinical psychologists: Characteristics, activities, and orientations. *The Clinical Psychologist, 28,* 7–10.

Garfinkel, P. E., & Garner, D. M. (1982). *Anorexia nervosa: A multidimensional perspective.* New York: Brunner/Mazel.

Garner, D. M., Garfinkel, P. E., & Olmstead, M. P. (1983). An overview of sociocultural factors in the development of anorexia nervosa. In P. L. Darby, P. E. Garfinkel, D. M. Garner, & D. V. Coscina (Eds.), *Anorexia nervosa: Recent developments in research* (pp. 65–82). New York: Alan R. Liss.

Garner, D. M., Garfinkel, P. E., Schwartz, D., & Thompson, M. (1980). Cultural expectations of thinness in women. *Psychological Reports, 47,* 483–491.

Garner, D. M., Olmstead, M. P., & Polivy, J. (1984). Comparison between weight-preoccupied women and anorexia nervosa. *Psychosomatic Medicine, 46,* 255–266.

Gatz, M., Bengston, V. L., & Blum, M. J. (1990). Caregiving families. In J. E. Birren & K. W. Schaie (Eds.), *Handbook of the psychology of aging* (3rd ed., pp. 404–426). New York: Academic Press.

Gatz, M., Karel, M. J., & Wolkenstein, B. (1991). Survey of providers of psychological services to older adults. *Professional Psychology: Research and Practice, 5,* 413–415.

Gatz, M., & Pearson, C. G. (1988). Ageism revised and the provision of psychological services. *American Psychologist, 43,* 184–188.

Gatz, M., Pearson, C., & Fuentes, M. (1984). Older women and mental health. In A.U. Rickel, M. Gerrard, & I. Iscoe (Eds.), *Social and psychological problems of women: Prevention and crisis intervention.* Washington, DC: Hemisphere.

Gatz, M., & Smyer, M. A. (1992). The mental health system and older adults in the 1990s. *American Psychologist, 47,* 741–751.

Gawin, F. H., Kleber, H. D., Byck, R., Rounsaville, B. J., Kosten, T. R., Jatlow, P. I., & Morgan, C. (1989). Desipramine facilitation of initial cocaine abstinence. *Archives of General Psychiatry, 46,* 117–121.

Gebhard, P. H., Gagnon, J. H., Pomeroy, W. B., & Christenson, C. V. (1965). *Sex offenders.* New York: Harper & Row.

Geer, J. H., Davison, G. C., & Gatchel, R. I. (1970). Reduction of stress in humans through nonveridical perceived control of aversive stimulation. *Journal of Personality and Social Psychology, 16,* 731–738.

Geer, J. H., Heiman, J., & Leitenberg, H. (1984). *Human sexuality.* Englewood Cliffs, NJ: Prentice-Hall.

George, L. K., & Weiler, S. J. (1981). Sexuality in middle and late life: The effects of age, cohort, and gender. *Archives of General Psychiatry, 38,* 919–923.

Gerardi, R. J., Blanchard, E. B., Andrasik, F., & McCoy, G. C. (1985). Psychological dimensions of "office hypertension." *Behaviour Research and Therapy, 23,* 609–612.

Gerber, L. M. (1983). Ethnicity still matters: Socio-demographic profiles of the ethnic elderly in Ontario. *Canadian Ethnic Studies, 15,* 60–80.

Gerson, S. C., Plotkin, D. A., & Jarvik, L. F. (1988). Antidepressant drug studies, 1964 to 1986: Empirical evidence for aging patients. *Journal of Clinical Psychopharmacology, 8,* 311–322.

Ghoneim, M. M., & Mewaldt, S. P. (1990). Benzodiazepines and human memory: A review. *Anesthesiology, 72,* 926–938.

Giarretto, H. (1982). A comprehensive child sexual abuse treatment program. *Child Abuse and Neglect, 6,* 263–278.

Gibbons, R. D., Hedeker, D., Elkin, I., Waternaux, C., Kraemer, H. C., Greenhouse, J. B., Shea, M. T., Imber, S. D., Sotsky, S. M., & Watkins, J. T. (1993). Some conceptual and statistical issues in analysis of longitudinal psychiatric data: Application to the NIMH Treatment of Depression Collaborative Research Program dataset. *Archives of General Psychiatry, 50,* 739–750.

Gibson, D., & Harris, A. (1988). Aggregated early intervention effects for Down's syndrome persons: Patterning and longevity of benefits. *Journal of Mental Deficiency Research, 32,* 1–17.

Gillberg, C., & Svendsen, P. (1983). Childhood psychosis and computed tomographic brain scan findings. *Journal of Autism and Developmental Disorders, 13,* 19–32.

Ginzburg, H. M. (1986). Naltrexone: Its clinical utility. In B. Stimmel (Ed.), *Advances in alcohol and substance abuse* (pp. 83–101). New York: Haworth.

Gladue, B. A. (1985). Neuroendocrine response to estrogen and sexual orientation. *Science, 230,* 961.

Golden, C. J. (1981). The Luria–Nebraska Children's Battery: Theory and formulation. In G. W. Hynd & J. E. Obrzut (Eds.), *Neuropsychological assesssment and the school-age child: Issues and procedures.* New York: Grune & Stratton.

Golden, C. J., Hammeke, T., & Purisch, A. (1978). Diagnostic validity of a standardized neuropsychological battery derived from Luria's neuropsychological test. *Journal of Consulting and Clinical Psychology, 46,* 1258–1265.

Goldfried, M. R. (1980). Toward the delineation of therapeutic change principles. *American Psychologist, 35,* 991–999.

Goldfried, M. R., & Davison, G.C. (1976). *Clinical behavior therapy.* New York: Holt, Rinehart & Winston.

Golding, J. M., Smith, G. R., & Kashner, T. M. (1991). Does somatization disorder occur in men? Clinical characteristics of women and men with unexplained somatic symptoms. *Archives of General Psychiatry, 48,* 231–235.

Goldstein, A. J., & Chambless, D.L. (1978). A reanalysis of agoraphobic behavior. *Behavior Therapy, 9,* 47–59.

Golub, A., & Johnson, B. D. (1994). A recent decline in cocaine use among youthful arrestees in Manhattan, 1987 through 1993. *American Journal of Public Health, 84,* 1250–1254.

Gomez, F. C., Piedmont, R. L., & Fleming, M. Z. (1992). Factor analysis of the Spanish version of the WAIS: The Escala de Inteligencia Wechsler para Adultos (EIWA). *Psychological Assessment, 4,* 317–321.

Goodman, R., & Stevenson, J. (1989). A twin study of hyperactivity: II. The aetiological role of genes, family relationships, and perinatal adversity. *Journal of Child Psychology and Psychiatry, 30,* 691–709.

Goodsitt, A. (1985). Self psychology and treatment of anorexia nervosa. In D. M. Garner & P. E. Garfinkel (Eds.), *Handbook of psychotherapy for anorexia nervosa and bulimia* (pp. 55–82). New York: Guilford.

Goodwin, D. W. (1979). Alcoholism and heredity: A review and hypothesis. *Archives of General Psychiatry, 36,* 57–61.

Goodwin, D. W. (1982). Substance induced and substance use disorders: Alcohol. In J. H. Griest, I. W. Jefferson, & R. L. Spitzer (Eds.), *Treatment of mental disorders.* New York: Oxford University Press.

Goodwin, D. W., Crane, J. B., & Guze, S. B. (1969). Alcoholic "blackouts": A review and clinical study of 100 alcoholics. *American Journal of Psychiatry, 26,* 191–198.

Goodwin, D. W., & Guze, S. B. (1984). *Psychiatric diagnosis* (3rd ed.). New York: Oxford University Press.

Goodwin, D. W., Schulsinger, F., Hermansen, L., Guze, S. B., &

Winokur, G. A. (1973). Alcohol problems in adoptees raised apart from alcoholic biological parents. *Archives of General Psychiatry, 128,* 239–243.

Goodwin, F., & Jamison, K. (1990). *Manic-depressive illness.* New York: Oxford University Press.

Gordon, C., & Beresin, E. (1983). Conflicting treatment models for the inpatient management of borderline patients. *American Journal of Psychiatry, 140,* 979–983.

Gorenstein, E. E. (1991). A cognitive perspective on antisocial personality. In P. A. Magaro (Ed.), *Cognitive bases of mental disorders.* Newbury Park, CA: Sage.

Gotlib, I. H., & Avison, W. R. (1993). Children at risk for psychopathology. In C. G. Costello (Ed.), *Basic issues in psychopathology* (pp. 271–319). New York: Guilford.

Gottesman, I. I., & Bertelsen, A. (1989). Confirming unexpressed genotypes for schizophrenia: Risks in the offspring of Fischer's Danish identical and fraternal discordant twins. *Archives of General Psychiatry, 46,* 867–872.

Gottesman, I. I., McGuffin, P., & Farmer, A. E. (1987). Clinical genetics as clues to the "real" genetics of schizophrenia. *Schizophrenia Bulletin, 13,* 23–47.

Gottlieb, J. (1990). Mainstreaming and quality education. *American Journal on Mental Retardation, 95,* 16.

Gove, W. R. (1970). Societal reaction as an explanation of mental illness: An evaluation. *American Sociological Review, 35,* 873–884.

Gove, W. R., & Fain, T. (1973). The stigma of mental hospitalization. *Archives of General Psychiatry, 28,* 494–500.

Graham, J. R. (1988). *Establishing validity of the revised form of the MMPI.* Symposium presentation at the 96th Annual Convention of the American Psychological Association, Atlanta.

Graham, J. R. (1990). *MMPI-2: Assessing personality and psychopathology.* New York: Oxford University Press.

Graham, J. W., Johnson, C. A., Hansen, W. B., Flay, B. R., & Gee, M. (1990). Drug use prevention programs, gender, and ethnicity: Evaluation of three seventh-grade Project SMART cohorts. *Preventive Medicine, 19,* 305–313.

Graham, P. J., Rutter, M. L., Yule, W., & Pless, I. B. (1967). Childhood asthma: A psychosomatic disorder? Some epidemiological considerations. *British Journal of Preventive Medicine, 21,* 78–85.

Gray, E. B. (1983). *Final report: Collaborative research of community and minority group action to prevent child abuse and neglect: Vol. 3. Public awareness and education using the creative arts.* Chicago: National Committee for Prevention of Child Abuse.

Gray, J. A. (1982). *The neuropsychology of anxiety: An enquiry into the functions of the septo-hippocampal system.* Oxford: Oxford University Press.

Green, R. (1974). *Sexual identity conflict in children and adults.* New York: Basic Books.

Green, R. (1976). One hundred ten feminine and masculine boys: Behavioral contrasts and demographic similarities. *Archives of Sexual Behavior, 5,* 425–446.

Green, R., & Fleming, D. T. (1990). Transsexual surgery follow-up: Status in the 1990s. In J. Bancroft, C. Davis, & D. Weinstein (Eds.), *Annual review of sex research* (pp. 163–174). Society for the Scientific Study of Sex.

Green, R., & Money, J. (1969). *Transsexualism and sex reassignment.* Baltimore: Johns Hopkins University Press.

Greenberg, L., Elliott, R., & Lietaer, G. (1994). Research on experiential psychotherapies. In A. E. Bergin & S. L. Garfield (Eds.), *Handbook of psychotherapy and behavior change* (4th ed.). New York: Wiley.

Greenberg, L., Fine, S. B., Cohen, C., Larson, K., Michaelson-Baily, A., Rubinton, P., & Glick, I. D. (1988). An interdisciplinary psychoeducation program for schizophrenic patients and their families in an acute care setting. *Hospital and Community Psychiatry, 39,* 277–281.

Greenberg, L. S., & Johnson, S. M. (1988). *Emotionally focused couples therapy.* New York: Guilford.

Greenberg, R. P., & Bornstein, R. F. (1988). The dependent personality: I. Risk for physical disorders. *Journal of Personality Disorders, 2,* 126–135.

Greenberg, R. P., Bornstein, R. F., Greenberg, M. D., & Fisher, S. (1992). A meta-analysis of antidepressant outcome under "blinder" conditions. *Journal of Consulting and Clinical Psychology, 60,* 664–669.

Greene, R. M. (1985). A study of the relationship between divorced mothers' attitude towards their ex-husbands, perceived supportive and coercive behavior in mother-son interactions, and aggressive behavior in boys. *Dissertation Abstracts International, 45,* 2039.

Greenwald, A. G. (1992). New Look 3: Unconscious cognition reclaimed. *American Psychologist, 47,* 766–779.

Grencavage, L. M., & Norcross, J. C. (1990). Where are the commonalities among the therapeutic common factors? *Professional Psychology: Research and Practice, 21,* 372–378.

Gross, M. L. (1978). *The psychological society: A critical analysis of psychiatry, psychotherapy, psychoanalysis and the psychological revolution.* New York: Simon & Schuster.

Groth, N. A., & Burgess, A. W. (1977). Sexual dysfunction during rape. *New England Journal of Medicine, 297,* 764–766.

Guarnaccia, P. J., Canino, G., Rubio-Stipec, M., & Bravo, M. (1993). The prevalence of ataque de nervios in the Puerto Rico disaster study: The role of culture in psychiatric epidemiology. *Journal of Nervous and Mental Disease, 181,* 157–165.

Guralnik, J. M., Yanagashita, M., & Schneider, E. L. (1988). Projecting the older population of the United States: Lessons from the past and prospects for the future. *The Milbank Quarterly, 66,* 283–308.

Gurland, B. (1991). Epidemiology of psychiatric disorders. In J. Sadavoy & L. F. Jarvik (Eds.), *Comprehensive review of geriatric psychiatry* (pp. 25–40). Washington, DC: American Psychiatric Press.

Gurland, B. J., & Cross, P. S. (1982). Epidemiology of psychopathology in old age. In L. F. Jarvik & G. W. Small (Eds.), *Psychiatric Clinics of North America.* Philadelphia: Saunders.

Gustafson, Y., Berggren, D., Bucht, B., Norberf, A., Hansson, L. I., & Winblad, B. (1988). Acute confusional states in elderly patients treated for femoral neck fracture. *Journal of the American Geriatrics Society, 36,* 525–530.

Guze, S. B. (1967). The diagnosis of hysteria: What are we trying to do? *American Journal of Psychiatry, 124,* 491–498.

Haaga, D. A. F. (1989). Articulated thoughts and endorsement procedures for cognitive assessment in the prediction of smoking relapse. *Psychological Assessment: A Journal of Consulting and Clinical Psychology, 1,* 112–117.

Haaga, D. A. F., Davison, G. C., Williams, M. E., Dolezal, S. L., Haleblian, J., Rosenbaum, J., Dwyer, J. H., Baker, S., Nezami, E., & DeQuattro, V. (1994). Mode-specific impact of relaxation training for hypertensive men with Type A Behavior Pattern. *Behavior Therapy, 25,* 209–223.

Haaga, D. A. F., Dyck, M. J., & Ernst, D. (1991). Empirical status of cognitive theory of depression. *Psychological Bulletin, 110,* 215–236.

Habot, B., & Libow, L. S. (1980). The interrelationship of mental and physical status and its assessment in the older adult: Mind–body interaction. In J. E. Birren & R. B. Sloane (Eds.), *Handbook of mental health and aging.* Englewood Cliffs, NJ: Prentice-Hall.

Hahlweg, K., & Markman, H. J. (1988). The effectiveness of behavioral marital therapy: Empirical status of behavioral techniques in preventing and alleviating marital distress. *Journal of Consulting and Clinical Psychology, 56,* 440–447.

Haldeman, D. C. (1994). The practice and ethics of sexual orientation conversion therapy. *Journal of Consulting and Clinical Psychology, 62,* 221–227.

Haley, S. A. (1978). Treatment implications of post-combat stress response syndromes for mental health professionals. In C. R. Figley

(Ed.), *Stress disorders among Vietnam veterans*. New York: Brunner/Mazel.

Haley, W. E., Levine, E. G., Brown, S. L., Berry, J. W., & Hughes, G. H. (1987). Psychological, social, and health consequences of caring for a relative with senile dementia. *Journal of the American Geriatrics Society, 35*, 405–411.

Hall, S. M., Munoz, R. F., & Reus, V. I. (1994). Cognitive-behavioral intervention increases abstinence rates for depressive-history smokers. *Journal of Consulting and Clinical Psychology, 62*, 141–146.

Hall, S. M., Munoz, R. F., Reus, V. I., & Sees, K. L. (1993). Nicotine, negative affect, and depression. *Journal of Consulting and Clinical Psychology, 61*, 761–767.

Halleck, S. L. (1971). *The politics of therapy*. New York: Science House.

Hammen, C. L. (1991). Generation of stress in the course of unipolar depression. *Journal of Abnormal Psychology, 100*, 555–561.

Hampe, E., Noble, H., Miller, L. C., & Barrett, C. L. (1973). Phobic children one and two years posttreatment. *Journal of Abnormal Psychology, 82*, 446–453.

Hansen, W. B., & Graham, J. W. (1991). Preventing alcohol, marijuana, and cigarette use among adolescents: Peer pressure resistance training versus establishing conservative norms. *Preventive Medicine, 20*, 414–430.

Hansen, W. B., Johnson, C. A., Flay, B. R., Graham, J. W., & Sobel, J. (1988). Affective and social influence approaches to the prevention of multiple substance abuse among seventh grade students. *Preventive Medicine, 17*, 135–154.

Hanusa, B. H., & Schulz, R. (1977). Attributional mediators of learned helplessness. *Journal of Personality and Social Psychology, 35*, 602–611.

Haracz, J. L. (1982). The dopamine hypothesis: An overview of studies with schizophrenic patients. *Schizophrenia Bulletin, 8*, 438–469.

Harburg, E., Erfurt, J. C., Hauenstein, L. S., Chape, C., Schull, W. J., & Schork, M. A. (1973). Socioecological stress, suppressed hostility, skin color, and black–white male blood pressure: Detroit. *Psychosomatic Medicine, 35*, 276–296.

Hare, R. D. (1970). *Psychopathy: Theory and research*. New York: Wiley.

Hare, R. D. (1978). Electrodermal and cardiovascular correlates of sociopathy. In R. D. Hare & D. Schalling (Eds.), *Psychopathic behaviour: Approaches to research*. New York: Wiley.

Hare, R. D., Hart, S. D., & Harpur, T. J. (1991). Psychopathy and the DSM-IV criteria for antisocial personality disorder. *Journal of Abnormal Psychology, 100*, 391–398.

Hare, R. D., & Jutai, J. W. (1983). Psychopathy and electrocortical indices of perceptual processing during selective attention. *Psychophysiology, 20*, 146–151.

Harpur, T. J., & Hare, R. D. (1990). Psychopathy and attention. In J. Enns (Ed.), *The development of attention: Research and theory*. Amsterdam: New Holland.

Harrington, A., & Sutton-Simon, K. (1977). Rape. In A. P. Goldstein, P. J. Monti, T. J. Sardino, & D. J. Green (Eds.), *Police crisis intervention*. Kalamazoo, MI: Behavior-Delia.

Harris, E. L., Noyes, R., Crowe, R. R., & Chaudhry, D. R. (1983). Family study of agoraphobia: Report of a pilot study. *Archives of General Psychiatry, 40*, 1061–1064.

Harris, G. T., Rice, M. E., & Quinsey, V. L. (1994). Psychopathy as a taxon: Evidence that psychopaths are a discrete class. *Journal of Consulting and Clinical Psychology, 62*, 387–397.

Harris, K. R. (1986). The effects of cognitive-behavior modification on private speech and task performance during problem solving among learning-disabled and normally achieving children. *Journal of Abnormal Child Psychology, 14*, 63–67.

Harris, L. (1987). *Inside America*. New York: Vintage Books.

Harrison, J., Chin, J., & Ficarrotto, T. (1989). Warning: Masculinity may be dangerous to your health. In M. S. Kimmel, & M. A. Messner (Eds.), *Men's lives* (pp. 296–309). New York: Macmillan.

Hart, S. D., & Hare, R. D. (1989). Discriminant validity of the Psychopathy Checklist in a forensic psychiatric population. *Psychological Assessment, 1*, 211–218.

Hasin, D., Grant, B., Harford, T., Hilton, M., & Endicott, J. (1990). Multiple alcohol-related problems in the United States: On the rise? *Journal of Studies on Alcohol, 51*, 484–493.

Hastrup, J. L., Light, K. C., & Obrist, P. A. (1982). Parental hypertension and cardiovascular response to stress in healthy young adults. *Psychophysiology, 19*, 615–622.

Hathaway, S. R., & McKinley, J. C. (1943). *MMPI manual*. New York: Psychological Corporation.

Hayes, S. C. (1987). Contextual determinants of "volitional action": A reply to Howard and Conway. *American Psychologist, 42*, 1029–1030.

Hayes, S. C., Nelson, R. O., & Jarrett, R. B. (1987). The treatment utility of assessment: A functional approach to evaluating assessment quality. *American Psychologist, 42*, 963–974.

Haynes, S. N., & Horn, W. F. (1982). Reactivity in behavioral observation: A review. *Behavioral Assessment, 4*, 369–385.

Heiman, J. R., & Verhulst, J. (1990). Sexual dysfunction and marriage. In F. D. Fincham & T. N. Bradbury (Eds.), *The psychology of marriage: Basic issues and applications* (pp. 299–322). New York: Guilford.

Helzer, J. E., Robins, L. N., & McEvoy, L. (1987). Post-traumatic stress disorder in the general population. *New England Journal of Medicine, 317*, 1630–1634.

Heninger, G. R., Charney, D. S., & Menkes, D. B. (1983). Receptor sensitivity and the mechanism of action of antidepressant treatment. In P. J. Clayton & J. E. Barrett (Eds.), *Treatment of depression: Old controversies and new approaches*. New York: Raven.

Henkel, H., & Lewis-Thomé, J. (1976). *Verhaltenstherapie bei männlichen Homosexuellen*. Diplomarbeit der Studierenden der Psychologie, University of Marburg, Germany.

Herbert, J. (1965). Personality factors and bronchial asthma. A study of South African Indian children. *Journal of Psychosomatic Research, 8*, 353–364.

Herbert, M. (1978). *Conduct disorders of childhood and adolescence*. New York: Wiley.

Herbert, M. (1982). Conduct disorders. In B. B. Lahey & A. E. Kazdin (Eds.), *Advances in clinical child psychology* (Vol. 5). New York: Plenum.

Hersen, M., & Barlow, D. H. (1976). *Single-case experimental designs*. Elmsford, NY: Pergamon.

Hersen, M., Bellack, A. S., Himmelhoch, J. M., & Thase, M. E. (1984). Effects of social skills training, amitriptyline, and psychotherapy in unipolar depressed women. *Behavior Therapy, 15*, 21–40.

Heston, L. L. (1966). Psychiatric disorders in foster home reared children of schizophrenic mothers. *British Journal of Psychiatry, 112*, 819–825.

Heston, L. L., & White, J. A. (1991). *The vanishing mind*. New York: Freeman.

Heumann, K. A., & Morey, L. C. (1990). Reliability of categorical and dimensional judgments of personality disorder. *American Journal of Psychiatry, 147*, 498–500.

Hewett, F. M. (1965). Teaching speech to an autistic child through operant conditioning. *American Journal of Orthopsychiatry, 33*, 927–936.

Hill, C. E., O'Grady, K. E., & Elkin, I. (1992). Applying the Collaborative Study Psychotherapy Rating Scale to rate therapist adherence to cognitive-behavior therapy, interpersonal therapy, and clinical management. *Journal of Consulting and Clinical Psychology, 60*, 73–79.

Hill, J. H., Liebert, R. M., & Mott, D. E. W. (1968). Vicarious extinction of avoidance behavior through films: An initial test. *Psychological Reports, 12*, 192.

Hill, S. Y. (1980). Introduction: The biological consequences. In *Alco-*

holism and alcohol abuse among women: Research issues. Rockville, MD: National Institute on Alcohol Abuse and Alcoholism.

Hinshaw, S. P. (1987). On the distinction between attentional deficits/hyperactivity and conduct problems/aggression in child psychopathology. *Psychological Bulletin, 101,* 443–463.

Hinshaw, S. P., Henker, B., & Whalen, C. K. (1984). Self-control in hyperactive boys in anger-inducing situations: Effects of cognitive-behavioral training and of methylphenidate. *Journal of Abnormal Child Psychology, 12,* 55–77.

Hinz, L. D., & Williamson, D. A. (1987). Bulimia and depression: A review of the affective variant hypothesis. *Psychological Bulletin, 102,* 150–158.

Hiroto, D. S., & Seligman, M. E. P. (1975). Generality of learned helplessness in man. *Journal of Personality and Social Psychology, 31,* 311–327.

Hirschfeld, R. M. A., Klerman, G. L., Gough, H. G., Barrett, J., Korchin, S. J., & Chodoff, P. (1977). A measure of interpersonal dependency. *Journal of Personality Assessment, 41,* 610–618.

Hite, S. (1976). *The Hite Report: A nationwide study of female sexuality.* New York: Dell.

Hoberman, H. M., & Garfinkel, B. D. (1988). Completed suicide in children and adolescents. *Journal of the American Academy of Child and Adolescent Psychiatry, 27,* 689–695.

Hobfoll, S. E., Spielberger, C. D., Breznitz, S., Figley, C., Folkman, S., Lepper-Green, B., Meichenbaum, D., Milgram, N. A., Sandler, I., Sarason, I., & van der Kolk, B. (1991). War-related stress: Addressing the stress of war and other traumatic events. *American Psychologist, 46,* 848–855.

Hogarty, G. E., Anderson, C. M., Reiss, D. J., Kornblith, S. J., Greenwald, D. P., Javna, C. D., & Madonia, M. J. (1986). Family psychoeducation, social skills training, and maintenance chemotherapy in the aftercare treatment of schizophrenia: 1. One year effects of a controlled study on relapse and expressed emotion. *Archives of General Psychiatry, 43,* 633–642.

Hogarty, G. E., Anderson, C. M., Reiss, D. J., Kornblith, S. J., Greenwald, D. P., Ulrich, R. F., Carter, M., & The Environmental-Personal Indicators in the Course of Schizophrenia (EPICS) Research Group. (1991). Family psychoeducation, social skills training, and maintenance chemotherapy in the aftercare treatment of schizophrenia. *Archives of General Psychiatry, 48,* 340–347.

Hokanson, J. E., & Burgess, M. (1962). The effects of three types of aggression on vascular processes. *Journal of Abnormal and Social Psychology, 65,* 446–449.

Hokanson, J. E., Rubert, M. P., Welker, R. A., Hollander, G. R., & Hedeen, C. (1989). Interpersonal concomitants and antecedents of depression among college students. *Journal of Abnormal Psychology, 98,* 209–217.

Holden, C. (1972). Nader on mental health centers: A movement that got bogged down. *Science, 177,* 413–415.

Holder, H., Longabaugh, R., Miller, W. R., & Rubonis, A. V. (1991). The cost effectiveness of treatment for alcoholism: A first approximation. *Journal of Studies on Alcohol, 52,* 517–540.

Hollander, E., DeCaria, C. M., Nitescu, A., Gully, R., Suckow, R. F., Cooper, T. B., Gorman, J. M., Klein, D. F., & Liebowitz, M. R. (1992). Serotonergic function in obsessive-compulsive disorder: Behavioral and neuroendocrine responses to oral m-chlorophenylpiperazine and fenfluramine in patients and healthy volunteers. *Archives of General Psychiatry, 49,* 21–27.

Hollingshead, A. B., & Redlich, F. C. (1958). *Social class and mental illness: A community study.* New York: Wiley.

Hollon, S. D., & Beck, A. J. (1986). Cognitive and cognitive-behavioral therapies. In S. L. Garfield & A. E. Bergin (Eds.), *Handbook of psychotherapy and behavior change* (3rd ed). New York: Wiley

Hollon, S. D., & Beck, A. T. (1994). Cognitive and cognitive-behavioral therapies. In A. E. Bergin & S. L. Garfield (Eds.), *Handbook of psychotherapy and behavior change* (4th ed). New York: Wiley.

Hollon, S. D., & Kendall, P. C. (1980). Cognitive self-statements in depression: Development of an automatic thoughts questionnaire. *Cognitive Therapy and Research, 4,* 383–395.

Holmes, T. H., & Rahe, R. H. (1967). The social readjustment rating scale. *Journal of Psychosomatic Research, 11,* 213–218.

Holmstrom, L. L., & Burgess, A. W. (1980). Sexual behavior during reported rapes. *Archives of Sexual Behavior, 9,* 427–439.

Honigfeld, G., & Howard, A. (1978). *Psychiatric drugs: A desk reference* (2nd ed.). New York: Academic Press.

Hooley, J. M., & Teasdale, J. D. (1989). Predictors of relapse in unipolar depressives: Expressed emotion, marital distress, and perceived criticism. *Journal of Abnormal Psychology, 98,* 229–235.

Horn, A. S., & Snyder, S. H. (1971). Chlorpromazine and dopamine: Conformational similarities that correlate with the anti-schizophrenic activity of phenothiazine drugs. *Proceedings of the National Academy of Sciences, 68,* 2324–2328.

Horowitz, M. J. (1988). *Introduction to psychodynamics: A new synthesis.* New York: Basic Books.

House, J. S., Landis, K. R., & Umberson, D. (1988). Social relationships and health. *Science, 241,* 540–544.

Howard, G. S., & Conway, C. G. (1986). Can there be an empirical science of volitional action? *American Psychologist, 41,* 1241–1251.

Howard, G. S., & Myers, P. R. (1990). Predicting human behavior: Comparing idiographic, nomothetic, and agentic methodologies. *Journal of Counseling Psychology, 37,* 227–233.

Howard, K. I., Kopta, S. M., Krause, M. S., & Orlinsky, D. E. (1986). The dose-effect relationship in psychotherapy. *American Psychologist, 41,* 159–164.

Hsu, L. K. G. (1980). Outcome of anorexia nervosa: A review of the literature (1954 to 1978). *Archives of General Psychiatry, 37,* 1041–1046.

Hsu, L. K. G. (1986). The treatment of anorexia nervosa. *American Journal of Psychiatry, 143,* 573–581.

Hughes, J. R. (1993). Pharmacotherapy for smoking cessation: Unvalidated assumptions, anomalies, and suggestions for future research. *Journal of Consulting and Clinical Psychology, 61,* 751–760.

Hughes, J. R., Gust, S. W., Keenan, R. M., Fenwick, J. W., & Healey, M. L. (1989). Nicotine versus placebo gum in general medical practice. *Journal of the American Medical Association, 261,* 1300–1305.

Hughes, J. R., Gust, S. W., Skoog, K., Keenan, R. M., & Fenwick, J. W. (1991). Symptoms of tobacco withdrawal: A replication and extension. *Archives of General Psychiatry, 48,* 52–61.

Hunter, J. E., & Schmidt, F. L. (1990). *Methods of meta-analysis: Correcting error and bias in research findings.* Newbury Park, CA: Sage.

Hutt, C., Hutt, S. J., Lee, D., & Ounsted, C. (1964). Arousal and childhood autism. *Nature, 204,* 908–909.

Hyland, M. E. (1990). The mood-peak flow relationship in adult asthmatics: A pilot study of individual differences and direction of causality. *British Journal of Medical Psychology, 63,* 379–384.

Imber, S. D., Elkin, I., Watkins, J. T., Collins, J. F., Shea, M. T., Leber, W. R., & Glass, D. R. (1990). Mode-specific effects among three treatments for depression. *Journal of Consulting and Clinical Psychology, 58,* 352–359.

Innes, G., Millar, W. M., & Valentine, M. (1959). Emotion and blood pressure. *Journal of Mental Science, 105,* 840–851.

Insell, T. R. (1986). The neurobiology of anxiety. In B. F. Shaw, Z. V. Segal, T. M. Vallis, & F. E. Cashman (Eds.), *Anxiety disorders.* New York: Plenum.

Insull, W. (Ed.). (1973). *Coronary risk handbook.* New York: American Heart Association.

Isen, A. M., Shaiken, T. F., Clark, M., & Karp, L. (1978). Affect, accessibility of material in memory, and behavior: A cognitive loop? *Journal of Personality and Social Psychology, 36,* 1–12.

Jackson, A. M. (1973). Psychotherapy: Factors associated with the race of the therapist. *Psychotherapy: Theory, Research, and Practice, 10*, 273–277.

Jackson, J. L., Calhoun, K. S., Amick, A. E., Maddever, H. M., & Habif, V. L. (1990). Young adult women who report childhood intrafamilial sexual abuse: Subsequent adjustment. *Archives of Sexual Behavior, 19*, 211–221.

Jacobson, N. S. (1984). A component analysis of behavioral marital therapy: The relative effectiveness of behavior exchange and problem solving training. *Journal of Consulting and Clinical Psychology, 52*, 295–305.

Jacobson, N. S. (1992). Behavioral couple therapy: A new beginning. *Behavior Therapy, 23*, 493–506.

Jacobson, N. S., & Christensen, A. (in press). *Couple therapy: An integrative approach*. New York: Norton.

Jacobson, N. S., Dobson, K., Fruzzetti, A. E., Schmaling, K. B., & Salusky, S. (1991). Marital therapy as a treatment for depression. *Journal of Consulting and Clinical Psychology, 59*, 547–557.

Jacobson, N. S., Schmaling, K. B., & Holtzworth-Munroe, A. (1987). Component analysis of behavioral marital therapy: Two-year follow-up and prediction of relapse. *Journal of Marital and Family Therapy, 13*, 187–195.

Jacobson, N. S., & Truax, P. (1991). Clinical significance: A statistical approach to defining meaningful change in psychotherapy research. *Journal of Consulting and Clinical Psychology, 59*, 12–19.

Jaffe, J. H. (1985). Drug addiction and drug abuse. In *Goodman and Gilman's the pharmacological basis of therapeutic behavior*. New York: Macmillan.

Jamison, K. R., Gerner, R. H., Hammen, C., & Padesky, C. (1980). Clouds and silver linings: Positive experiences associated with primary affective disorders. *American Journal of Psychiatry, 137*, 198–202.

Jampala, V. L., Sierles, F. S., & Taylor, M. A. (1988). The use of DSM-III in the United States: A case of not going by the book. *Comprehensive Psychiatry, 29*, 39–47.

Jampole, L., & Weber, M. K. (1987). An assessment of the behavior of sexually abused and nonsexually abused children with anatomically correct dolls. *Child Abuse and Neglect, 11*, 187–192.

Jandorf, L., Deblinger, E., Neale, J. M., & Stone, A. A. (1986). Daily versus major life events as predictors of symptom frequency. *Journal of General Psychology, 113*, 205–218.

Jary, M. L., & Stewart, M. A. (1985). Psychiatric disorder in the parents of adopted children with aggressive conduct disorder. *Neuropsychobiology, 13*, 7–11.

Jasnoski, M. L., & Kugler, J. (1987). Relaxation, imagery, and neuroimmunomodulation. *Annals of the New York Academy of Sciences, 496*, 722–730.

Jay, S. M., Elliott, C. H., Katz, E., & Siegel, S. E. (1987). Cognitive-behavioral and pharmacologic interventions for children's distress during painful medical procedures. *Journal of Consulting and Clinical Psychology, 55*, 860–865.

Jay, S. M., Elliott, C. H., Ozolins, M., & Olson, R. A. (1982). *Behavioral management of children's distress during painful medical procedures*. Paper presented at the annual meeting of the American Psychological Association, Washington, DC.

Jellinek, E. M. (1952). Phases of alcohol addiction. *Quarterly Journal of Studies on Alcohol, 13*, 673–684.

Jenike, M. A. (1986). Theories of etiology. In M. A. Jenike, L. Baer, & W. E. Minichiello (Eds.), *Obsessive-compulsive disorders*. Littleton, MA: PSG Publishing.

Jenike, M. A. (1990). Psychotherapy. In A. S. Bellack & M. Hersen (Eds.), *Handbook of comparative treatments for adult disorders* (pp. 245–255). New York: Wiley.

Jenkins, C. D. (1976). Recent evidence supporting psychologic and social risk factors for coronary disease. *New England Journal of Medicine, 294*, 987–994, 1033–1038.

Jerrell, J. M., & Larsen, J. K. (1986). Community mental health centers

in transition: Who is benefitting? *American Journal of Orthopsychiatry, 56*, 78–88.

John, O. P. (1990). The "Big Five" factor taxonomy: Dimensions of personality in the natural language and in questionnaires. In L. A. Pervin (Ed.), *Handbook of personality: Theory and research*. New York: Guilford.

Johnson, A. B. (1990). *Out of Bedlam: The truth about deinstitutionalization*. New York: Basic Books.

Johnson, D. R. (1987). The role of the creative arts therapist in the diagnosis and treatment of psychological trauma. *The Arts in Psychotherapy, 14*, 7–13.

Johnson, J., Horvath, E., & Weissman, M. M. (1991). The validity of depression with psychotic features based on a community study. *Archives of General Psychiatry, 48*, 1075–1081.

Johnson, J., Weissman, M. M., & Klerman, G. L. (1990). Panic disorder and suicide attempts. *Archives of General Psychiatry, 47*, 805–808.

Johnson, R. H. (1992). The problem of defining critical thinking. In S. P. Norris (Ed.), *The generalizability of critical thinking: Multiple perspectives on an educational ideal* (pp. 38–53). New York: Teachers College Press.

Johnson, S. M., & Greenberg, L. S. (1985). Differential effects of experiential and problem-solving interventions in resolving marital conflict. *Journal of Consulting and Clinical Psychology, 53*, 175–184.

Johnston, D. G., Troyer, I. E., & Whitsett, S. F. (1988). Clomipramine treatment of agoraphobic women. *Archives of General Psychiatry, 45*, 453–459.

Joiner, T. E., Alfano, M. S., & Metalsky, G. I. (1992). When depression breeds contempt: Reassurance seeking, self-esteem, and rejection of depressed college students by their roommates. *Journal of Abnormal Psychology, 101*, 165–173.

Jones, M. (1953). *The therapeutic community*. New York: Basic Books.

Jones, M. C. (1924). A laboratory study of fear: The case of Peter. *Pedagogical Seminary, 31*, 308–315.

Jones, M. C. (1968). Personality correlates and antecedents of drinking patterns in males. *Journal of Consulting and Clinical Psychology, 32*, 2–12.

Jung, C. G. (1928). *Contributions to analytical psychology*. New York: Harcourt Brace Jovanovich.

Kagan, J. (1994). *Galen's prophecy: Temperament in human nature*. New York: Basic Books.

Kaiser, F. E., Viosca, S. P., Morley, J. E., Mooradian, A. D., Davis, S. S., & Korenman, S. G. (1988). Impotence and aging: Clinical and hormonal factors. *Journal of the American Geriatrics Society, 36*, 511–519.

Kalichman, S. C. (1991). Psychopathology and personality characteristics of criminal sexual offenders as a function of victim age. *Archives of Sexual Behavior, 20*, 187–198.

Kane, J., Honigfeld, G., Singer, J., Meltzer, H., and The Clozaril Collaborative Study Group. (1988). Clozapine for treatment resistant schizophrenics. *Archives of General Psychiatry, 45*, 789–796.

Kane, J. M., Woerner, M. G., Pollack, S., Safferman, A. Z., & Lieberman, J. A. (1993). Does clozapine cause tardive dyskinesia? *Journal of Clinical Psychiatry, 54*, 327–330.

Kane, J. M., Woerner, M. G., Weinhold, P., Wegner, J., Kinon, B., & Bernstein, M. (1986). Incidence of tardive dyskinesia: Five-year data from a prospective study. *Psychopharmacology Bulletin, 20*, 387–389.

Kane, R. L., Parsons, D. A., & Goldstein, G. (1985). Statistical relationships and discriminative accuracy of the Halstead-Reitan, Luria-Nebraska, and Wechsler IQ scores in the identification of brain damage. *Journal of Clinical and Experimental Neuropsychology, 7*, 211–223.

Kanner, L. (1943). Autistic disturbances of affective contact. *Nervous Child, 2*, 217–250.

Kanner, L. (1973). Follow-up of eleven autistic children originally reported in 1943. In L. Kanner (Ed.), *Childhood psychosis: Initial studies and new insights*. Washington, DC: Winston-Wiley.

Kantorovich, N. V. (1930). An attempt at associative-reflex therapy in alcoholism. *Psychological Abstracts, 4*, 493.

Kaplan, A. S., & Woodside, D. B. (1987). Biological aspects of anorexia nervosa and bulimia nervosa. *Journal of Consulting and Clinical Psychology, 55*, 645–653.

Kaplan, H. S. (1974). *The new sex therapy.* New York: Brunner/Mazel.

Karasu, T. B., Stein, S. P., & Charles, E. S. (1979). Age factors in the patient-therapist relationship. *Journal of Nervous and Mental Disease, 167*, 100–104.

Kashani, J., & Hakami, N. (1982). Depression in children and adolescents with malignancy. *Canadian Journal of Psychiatry, 27*, 474–477.

Kaslow, N. J., & Racusin, G. R. (1990). Childhood depression: Current status and future directions. In A. S. Bellack, M. Hersen, & A. E. Kazdin (Eds.), *International handbook of behavior modification and therapy* (2nd ed.). New York: Plenum.

Katz, E. R. (1980). Illness impact and social reintegration. In J. Kellerman (Ed.), *Psychological aspects of childhood cancer.* Springfield, IL: Charles C. Thomas.

Katz, E. R., Kellerman, J., & Siegel, S. E. (1980). Behavioral distress in children with leukemia undergoing bone marrow aspirations. *Journal of Consulting and Clinical Psychology, 48*, 356–365.

Katz, R. C., Gipson, M. T., Kearl, A., & Kriskovich, M. (1989). Assessing sexual aversion in college students: The Sexual Aversion Scale. *Journal of Sex and Marital Therapy, 15*, 135–140.

Kaufmann, P. G., Jacob, R. G., Ewart, C. K., Chesney, M. A., Muenz, L. R., Doub, N., Mercer, W., & HIPP Investigators. (1988). Hypertension intervention pooling project. *Health Psychology, 7*, 209–224.

Kazdin, A. E. (1985). *Treatment of antisocial behavior in children and adolescents.* Homewood, IL: Dorsey Press.

Kazdin, A. E. (1986). Research designs and methodology. In S. L. Garfield & A. E. Bergin (Eds.), *Handbook of psychotherapy and behavior change* (3rd ed.). New York: Wiley.

Kazdin, A. E., Bass, D., Siegel, T., & Thomas, C. (1989). Cognitive-behavioral therapy and relationship therapy in the treatment of children referred for antisocial behavior. *Journal of Consulting and Clinical Psychology, 57*, 522–535.

Keane, T. M., Fairbank, J. A., Caddell, J. M., & Zimering, R. T. (1989). Implosive (flooding) therapy reduces symptoms of PTSD in Vietnam combat veterans. *Behavior Therapy, 20*, 245–260.

Keane, T. M., Foy, D. W., Nunn, B., & Rychtarik, R. G. (1984). Spouse contracting to increase antabuse compliance in alcoholic veterans. *Journal of Clinical Psychology, 40*, 340–344.

Keane, T. M., Gerardi, R. J., Quinn, S. J., & Litz, B. T. (1992). Behavioral treatment of post-traumatic stress disorder. In S. M. Turner, K. S. Calhoun, & H. E. Adams (Eds.), *Handbook of clinical behavior therapy* (2nd ed., pp. 87–97). New York: Wiley.

Keiser, R. E., & Prather, E. N. (1990). What is the TAT? A review of ten years of research. *Journal of Personality Assessment, 55*, 800–803.

Kellner, R. (1982). Disorders of impulse control (not elsewhere classified). In J. H. Griest, J. W. Jefferson, & R. L. Spitzer (Eds.), *Treatment of mental disorders.* New York: Oxford University Press.

Kelly, A. E., & Kahn, J. H. (1994). Effects of suppression of personal intrusive thoughts. *Journal of Personality and Social Psychology, 66*, 998–1006.

Kelly, J. A., & St. Lawrence, J. S. (1988a). *The AIDS health crisis: Psychological and social interventions.* New York: Plenum.

Kelly, J. A., & St. Lawrence, J. S. (1988b). AIDS prevention and treatment: Psychology's role in the health crisis. *Clinical Psychology Review, 8*, 255–284.

Kelly, J. A., St. Lawrence, J. S., Betts, R., Brasfield, T., & Hood, H. (1990). A skills training group intervention model to assist persons in reducing risk behaviors for HIV infection. *AIDS Education and Prevention, 2*, 24–35.

Kelly, J. A., St. Lawrence, J. S., Hood, H., & Brasfield, T. (1989). Behav-

ioral intervention to reduce AIDS risk activities. *Journal of Consulting and Clinical Psychology, 57*, 60–67.

Kelly, T. A. (1990). The role of values in psychotherapy: Review and methodological critique. *Clinical Psychology Review, 10*, 171–186.

Kendall, P. C., Haaga, D. A. F., Ellis, A., Bernard, M., DiGiuseppe, R., & Kassinove, H. (1995). Rational-emotive therapy in the 1990s and beyond: Current status, recent revisions and research questions. *Clinical Psychology Review, 15*, 169-185.

Kendall, P. C., & Ingram, R. E. (1989). Cognitive-behavioral perspectives: Theory and research on depression and anxiety. In P. C. Kendall & D. Watson (Eds.), *Anxiety and depression: Distinctive and overlapping features* (pp. 27–54). New York: Academic Press.

Kendall-Tackett, K. A., Williams, L. M., & Finkelhor, D. (1993). Impact of sexual abuse on children: A review and synthesis of recent empirical studies. *Psychological Bulletin, 113*, 164–180.

Kendler, K. S., Gruenberg, A. M., & Kinney, D. K. (1994). Independent diagnoses of adoptees and relatives as defined by DSM-III in the provincial and national samples of the Danish adoption study of schizophrenia. *Archives of General Psychiatry, 51*, 456–468.

Kendler, K. S., Kessler, R. C., Neale, M. C., Heath, A. C., & Eaves, L. J. (1993). The prediction of major depression in women: Toward an integrated etiologic model. *American Journal of Psychiatry, 150*, 1139–1148.

Kendler, K. S., Masterson, C. C., & Davis, K. L. (1985). Psychiatric illness in first degree relatives of patients with paranoid psychosis, schizophrenia and medical controls. *British Journal of Psychiatry, 147*, 524–531.

Kennedy, W. A. (1965). School phobia: Rapid treatment of 50 cases. *Journal of Abnormal Psychology, 70*, 285–289.

Kenrick, D. T., & Funder, D. C. (1988). Profiting from controversy: Lessons from the person-situation debate. *American Psychologist, 43*, 23–34.

Kernberg, O. F. (1985). *Borderline conditions and pathological narcissism.* Northvale, NJ: Jason Aronson.

Kessel, N., & Grossman, G. (1961). Suicide in alcoholics. *British Medical Journal, 2*, 1671–1672.

Kessler, J. (1966). *Psychopathology of childhood.* Englewood Cliffs, NJ: Prentice-Hall.

Kessler, R. C., McGonagle, K. A., Zhao, S., Nelson, C. B., Hughes, M., Eshleman, S., Wittchen, H-U., & Kendler, K. S. (1994). Lifetime and 12–month prevalence of DSM-III-R psychiatric disorders in the United States: Results from the National Comorbidity Survey. *Archives of General Psychiatry, 51*, 8–19.

Kety, S. S., Rosenthal, D., Wender, P. H., & Schulsinger, F. (1968). The types and prevalence of mental illness in the biological and adoptive families of adopted schizophrenics. In D. Rosenthal & S. S. Kety (Eds.), *The transmission of schizophrenia.* Elmsford, NY: Pergamon.

Kety, S. S., Wender, P. H., Jacobsen, B., Ingraham, L. J., Jansson, L., Faber, B., & Kinney, D. K. (1994). Mental illness in the biological and adoptive relatives of schizophrenic adoptees: Replication of the Copenhagen study in the rest of Denmark. *Archives of General Psychiatry, 51*, 442–455.

Keys, A., Brozek, J., Henschel, A., Mickelsen, O., & Taylor, H. L. (1950). *The biology of human starvation.* Minneapolis: University of Minnesota Press.

Keys, A., Taylor, H. L., Blackburn, H., Brozek, J., Anderson, J. T., & Simonson, E. (1971). Mortality and coronary heart disease among men studied for 23 years. *Archives of Internal Medicine, 128*, 201–214.

Kiecolt-Glaser, J., Dura, J. R., Speicher, C. E., & Trask, O. (1991). Spousal caregivers of dementia victims: Longitudinal changes in immunity and health. *Psychosomatic Medicine, 54*, 345–362.

Kiecolt-Glaser, J. K., & Glaser, R. (1987). Psychosocial moderators of immune function. *Annals of Behavioral Medicine, 9*, 16–20.

Kiecolt-Glaser, J. K., & Glaser, R. (1992). Psychoneuroimmunology:

Can psychological interventions modulate immunity? *Journal of Consulting and Clinical Psychology, 60,* 569–575.

Kiecolt-Glaser, J. K., Kennedy, S., Malkoff, S., Fisher, L., Speicher, D. E., & Glaser, R. (1988). Marital discord and immunity in males. *Psychosomatic Medicine, 50,* 213–229.

Kiel, D. P., Eichorn, A., Intrator, O., Silliman, R. A., & Mor, V. (1994). The outcomes of patients newly admitted to nursing homes after hip fracture. *American Journal of Public Health, 84,* 1281–1286.

Kiesler, C. A. (1991). Changes in general hospital psychiatric care. *American Psychologist, 46,* 416–421.

Kihlstrom, J. F., Barnhardt, T. M., & Tataryn, D. J. (1992). The psychological unconscious: Found, lost, and regained. *American Psychologist, 47,* 788–791.

Killen, J. D., Fortmann, S. P., Newman, B., & Varady, A. (1990). Evaluation of a treatment approach combining nicotine gum with self-guided behavioral treatments for smoking relapse prevention. *Journal of Consulting and Clinical Psychology, 58,* 85–92.

Kilpatrick, D. G., & Best, C. L. (1990, April). *Sexual assault victims: Data from a random national probability sample.* Paper presented at the annual convention of the Southeastern Psychological Association, Atlanta.

Kimura, D. (1983). Sex differences in cerebral organization for speech and praxic functions. *Canadian Journal of Psychology, 37,* 19–35.

King, M. B. (1990). Sneezing as a fetishistic stimulus. *Sexual and Marital Therapy, 5,* 69–72.

Kingsley, L. A., Kaslow, R., Rinaldo, C. R., Detre, K., Odaka, N., Van-Raden, M., Detels, R., Polk, B. F., Chmiel, J., Kelsey, S. F., Ostrow, D., & Visscher, B. (1987). Risk factors for seroconversion to human immunodeficiency virus among male homosexuals. *Lancet, 1,* 345–348.

Kinsey, A. C., Pomeroy, W. B., Main, C. E., & Gebbard, P. H. (1953). *Sexual behavior in the human female.* Philadelphia: Saunders.

Kinsey, A. C., Pomeroy, W. B., & Martin, C. E. (1948). *Sexual behavior in the human male.* Philadelphia: Saunders.

Kinsman, R. A., Spector, S. L., Shucard, D. W., & Luparello, T. J. (1974). Observations on patterns of subjective symptomatology of acute asthma. *Psychosomatic Medicine, 36,* 129–143.

Kinzie, J. D. (1985). Overview of clinical issues in the treatment of Southeast Asian refugees. In T. C. Owan (Ed.), *Southeast Asian mental health treatment, prevention services, training, and research.* Washington, DC: National Institute of Mental Health.

Klein, D. N., & Riso, L. P. (1993). Psychiatric disorders: Problems of boundaries and comorbidity. In C. G. Costello (Ed.), *Basic issues in psychopathology* (pp. 19–66). New York: Guilford.

Klein, D. N., Taylor, E. B., Dickstein, S., & Harding, K. (1988). Primary early-onset dysthymia: Comparison with primary nonbipolar nonchronic major depression on demographic, clinical, familial, personality, and socioenvironmental characteristics and short-term outcome. *Journal of Abnormal Psychology, 97,* 387–398.

Klein, M. (1932). *The psychoanalysis of children.* London: Hogarth.

Kleinke, C. L., Staneski, R. A., & Mason, J. K. (1982). Sex differences in coping with depression. *Sex Roles, 8,* 877–889.

Klerman, G. L. (1983). Problems in the definition and diagnosis of depression in the elderly. In M. Hauge & L. Breslau (Eds.), *Depression in the elderly: Causes, care, consequences.* New York: Springer.

Klerman, G. L. (1988). Depression and related disorders of mood (affective disorders). In A. M. Nicholi, Jr. (Ed.), *The new Harvard guide to psychiatry.* Cambridge: Harvard University Press.

Klerman, G. L., Weissman, M. M., Rounsaville, B. J., & Chevron, E. S. (1984). *Interpersonal psychotherapy of depression.* New York: Basic Books.

Klosko, J. S., Barlow, D. H., Tassinari, R., & Cerny, J. A. (1990). A comparison of alprazolam and behavior therapy in treatment of panic disorder. *Journal of Consulting and Clinical Psychology, 58,* 77–84.

Kluft, R. P. (1984). An introduction to multiple personality disorder. *Psychiatric Annals, 7,* 19–24.

Knight, B. (1983). An evaluation of a mobile geriatric team. In M. A. Smyer & M. Gatz (Eds.), *Mental health and aging: Programs and evaluations.* Beverly Hills, CA: Sage.

Knight B. G., Kelly, M., & Gatz, M. (1992). Psychotherapy and the older adult. In D. K. Freedheim (Ed.), *History of psychotherapy: A century of change* (pp. 528–551). Washington, DC: American Psychological Association.

Koegel, R. L., Schreibman, L., Britten, K. R., Burkey, J. C., & O'Neill, R. E. (1982). A comparison of parent training to direct child treatment. In R. L. Koegel, A. Rincover, & A. L. Egel (Eds.), *Educating and understanding autistic children.* San Diego, CA: College-Hill.

Koenigsberg, H. W. (1982). A comparison of hospitalized and nonhospitalized borderline patients. *American Journal of Psychiatry, 139,* 1292–1297.

Koenigsberg, H. W., & Handley, R. (1986). Expressed emotion: From predictive index to clinical construct. *American Journal of Psychiatry, 143,* 1361–1373.

Kog, E., & Vandereycken, W. (1985). Family characteristics of anorexia nervosa and bulimia: A review of the research literature. *Clinical Psychology Review, 5,* 159–180.

Kohn, M. L. (1968). Social class and schizophrenia: A critical review. In D. Rosenthal & S. S. Kety (Eds.), *The transmission of schizophrenia.* Elmsford, NY: Pergamon.

Kohut, H. (1971). *The analysis of the self.* New York: International Universities Press.

Kohut, H. (1977). *The restoration of the self.* New York: International Universities Press.

Kohut, H., & Wolf, E. S. (1978). The disorders of the self and their treatment: An outline. *International Journal of Psychoanalysis, 59,* 413–425.

Kornetsky, C. (1976). Hyporesponsivity of chronic schizophrenic patients to dextroamphetamine. *Archives of General Psychiatry, 33,* 1425–1428.

Koss, M. P. (1985). The hidden rape victim: Personality, attitudinal, and situational characteristics. *Psychology of Women Quarterly, 9,* 193–212.

Koss, M. P., & Butcher, J. N. (1986). Research on brief psychotherapy. In S. L. Garfield & A. E. Bergin (Eds.), *Handbook of psychotherapy and behavior change* (3rd ed.). New York: Wiley.

Koss, M. P., & Shiang, J. (1994). Research on brief psychotherapy. In A. E. Bergin, & S. L. Garfield (Eds.), *Handbook of psychotherapy and behavior change* (4th ed.). New York: Wiley.

Kosten, T. R., Morgan, C. M., Falcione, J., & Schottenfeld, R. S. (1992). Pharmacotherapy for cocaine-abusing methadone-maintained patients using amantadine or desipramine. *Archives of General Psychiatry, 49,* 894–898.

Kowall, N. K., & Beal, M. F. (1988). Cortical somatostatin, neuropeptide Y, and NADPH diaphorase neurons: Normal anatomy and alterations in Alzheimer's disease. *Annals of Neurology, 23,* 105–114.

Kozel, N. J., & Adams, E. H. (1986). Epidemiology of drug abuse: An overview. *Science, 234,* 970–974.

Kozel, N. J., Crider, R. A., & Adams, E. H. (1982). National surveillance of cocaine use and related health consequences. *Morbidity and Mortality Weekly Report 31, 20,* 265–273.

Krantz, S., & Hammen, C. L. (1979). Assessment of cognitive bias in depression. *Journal of Abnormal Psychology, 88,* 611–619.

Kring, A. M. (1991). *The relationship between emotional expression, subjective experience, and autonomic arousal in schizophrenia.* Unpublished doctoral thesis, State University of New York at Stony Brook.

Kringlen, E. (1970). Natural history of obsessional neurosis. *Seminars in Psychiatry, 2,* 403–419.

Kuhn, T. S. (1962). *The structure of scientific revolutions.* Chicago: University of Chicago Press.

Kuriansky, J. B., Deming, W. E., & Gurland, B. J. (1974). On trends in the diagnosis of schizophrenia. *American Journal of Psychiatry, 131,* 402–407.

Ladd, G. W. (1981). Effectiveness of a social learning method for enhancing children's social interaction and peer acceptance. *Child Development, 52,* 171–178.

Lahey, B. B., Piacentini, J. C., McBurnett, K., Stone, P., Hartdagen, S., & Hynd, G. (1988). Psychopathology in the parents of children with conduct disorder and hyperactivity. *Journal of the American Academy of Child and Adolescent Psychiatry, 27,* 163–170.

Lambert, M. J. (1989). The individual therapist's contribution to psychotherapy process and outcome. *Clinical Psychology Review, 9,* 469–485.

Lambert, M. J. (1992). Psychotherapy outcome research: Implications for integrative and eclectic therapists. In J. C. Norcross & M. R. Goldfried (Eds.), *Handbook of psychotherapy integration* (pp. 94–129). New York: Basic Books.

Lambert, M. J., & Bergin, A. E. (1994). The effectiveness of psychotherapy. In A. E. Bergin & S. L. Garfield (Eds.), *Handbook of psychotherapy and behavior change* (4th ed., pp. 143–189). New York: Wiley.

Lambert, M. J., Shapiro, D. A., & Bergin, A. E. (1986). The effectiveness of psychotherapy. In S. L. Garfield & A. E. Bergin (Eds.), *Handbook of psychotherapy and behavior change* (3rd ed.). New York: Wiley.

Lando, H. A. (1977). Successful treatment of smokers with a broad-spectrum behavioral approach. *Journal of Consulting and Clinical Psychology, 45,* 361–366.

Lang, R. A., Flor, H. P., & Frenzel, R. R. (1990). Sex hormone profiles in pedophilic and incestuous men. *Annals of Sex Research, 3,* 59–74.

Langer, E. J. (1981). Old age: An artifact? In J. McGaugh & S. Kiesler (Eds.), *Aging: Biology and behavior.* New York: Academic Press.

Langer, E. J., & Rodin, J. (1976). The effects of choice and enhanced personal responsibility for the aged. *Journal of Personality and Social Psychology, 34,* 191–198.

Lanyon, R. I. (1986). Theory and treatment of child molestation. *Journal of Consulting and Clinical Psychology, 54,* 176–182.

LaRue, A., Dessonville, C., & Jarvik, L. F. (1985). Aging and mental disorders. In J. E. Birren & K. W. Schaie (Eds.), *Handbook of psychology of aging* (2nd ed.). New York: Van Nostrand-Reinhold.

Last, C. G., & Strauss, C. C. (1990). School refusal in anxiety-disordered children and adolescents. *Journal of the American Academy of Child & Adolescent Psychiatry, 29,* 31–35.

Lawlor, B. A., Sunderland, T., Mellow, A. M., Hill, J. L., Molchan, S. E., & Murphy, D. L. (1989). Hyperresponsivity to the serotonin agonist m-chlorophenylpiperazine in Alzheimer's disease. *Archives of General Psychiatry, 46,* 542–548.

Lazarus, A. A. (1965). Behavior therapy, incomplete treatment, and symptom substitution. *Journal of Nervous and Mental Disease, 140,* 80–86.

Lazarus, A. A. (1968). Behavior therapy in groups. In G. M. Gazda (Ed.), *Basic approaches to group psychotherapy and counseling.* Springfield, IL: Charles C. Thomas.

Lazarus, A. A. (1973). Multimodal behavior therapy: Treating the basic I D. *Journal of Nervous and Mental Disease, 156,* 404–411.

Lazarus, A. A. (1989). *The practice of multimodal therapy.* Baltimore: Johns Hopkins University Press.

Lazarus, A. A., & Davison, G. C. (1971). Clinical innovation in research and practice. In A. E. Bergin & S. L. Garfield (Eds.), *Handbook of psychotherapy and behavior change.* New York: Wiley.

Lazarus, R. S. (1966). *Psychological stress and the coping process.* New York: McGraw-Hill.

Lazarus, R. S., & Folkman, S. (1984). *Stress, appraisal, and coping.* New York: Springer.

Lee, V. E., Brooks-Gunn, J., & Schnur, E. (1988). Does Head Start work? A 1-year follow-up comparison of disadvantaged children attending Head Start, no preschool, and other preschool programs. *Developmental Psychology, 24,* 210–222.

Lehrer, P. M., Sargunaraj, D., & Hochron, S. (1992). Psychological approaches to the treatment of asthma. *Journal of Consulting and Clinical Psychology, 60,* 639–643.

Lehrer, P. M., & Woolfolk, R. L. (1993) *Principles and practice of stress management.* (2nd ed.) New York: Guilford.

Lemieux, G., Davignon, A., & Genest, J. (1956). Depressive states during rauwolfia therapy for arterial hypertension. *Canadian Medical Association Journal, 74,* 522–526.

Lenane, M. C., Swedo, S. E., Leonard, H., Pauls, D. L., Sceery, W., & Rapoport, J. L. (1990). Psychiatric disorders in first degree relatives of children and adolescents with obsessive compulsive disorder. *Journal of the American Academy of Child and Adolescent Psychiatry, 29,* 407–412.

Lesage, A., & Lamontagne, Y. (1985). Paradoxical intention and exposure *in vivo* in the treatment of psychogenic nausea: Report of two cases. *Behavioral Psychotherapy, 13,* 69–75.

Lesch, K.P., Hoh, A., Disselkamp-Tietze, J., Weismann, M., Osterheider, M., & Schulte, H. M. (1991). 5-Hydroxytryptamine$_{1A}$ receptor responsivity in obsessive-compulsive disorder: Comparison of patients and controls. *Archives of General Psychiatry, 48,* 540–547.

Lester, D. (1993). Suicidal behavior in bipolar and unipolar affective disorders: A meta-analysis. *Journal of Affective Disorders, 27,* 117–121.

Levin, M. (1994, November 17). Targeting foreign smokers. *Los Angeles Times,* pp. A1, A15.

Levine, E. S., & Padilla, A. M. (1980). *Crossing cultures in therapy: Counseling for the Hispanic.* Monterey, CA: Brooks/Cole.

Levine, S. B., & Yost, M. A. (1976). Frequency of sexual dysfunction in a general gynecological clinic: An epidemiological approach. *Archives of Sexual Behavior, 5,* 229–238.

Lewinsohn, P. M. (1974). A behavioral approach to depression. In R. J. Friedman & M. M. Katz (Eds.), *The psychology of depression: Contemporary theory and research.* Washington, DC: Winston-Wiley.

Lewis-Fernandez, R., & Kleinman, A. (1994). Culture, personality, and psychopathology. *Journal of Abnormal Psychology, 103,* 67–71.

Ley, R. (1987). Panic disorder: A hyperventilation interpretation. In L. Michelson & L. M. Asher (Eds.), *Anxiety and stress disorders.* New York: Guilford.

Liberman, R. P., DeRisi, W. J., & Mueser, K. T. (1989). *Social skills training for psychiatric patients.* Elmsford, NY: Pergamon Press.

Liebert, R. M., Neale, J. M., & Davidson, E. S. (1973). *The early window.* Elmsford, NY: Pergamon.

Liebowitz, M. R., Salman, E., Jusino, C. M., Garfinkel, R., Street, L., Cardenas, D. L., Silvestre, J., Fyer, A. J., Carrasco, J. L., Davies, S., Guarnaccia, P., & Klein, D. F. (1994). Ataque de nervios and panic disorder. *American Journal of Psychiatry, 151,* 871–875.

Liebson, I. (1967). Conversion reaction: A learning theory approach. *Behaviour Research and Therapy, 7,* 217–218.

Lifton, R. J. (1976). Advocacy and corruption in the healing profession. In N. L. Goldman & D. R. Segal (Eds.), *The social psychology of military service.* Beverly Hills, CA: Sage.

Light, K. C., Dolan, C. A., Davis, M. R., & Sherwood, A. (1992). Cardiovascular responses to an active coping challenge as predictors of blood pressure patterns 10 to 15 years later. *Psychosomatic Medicine, 54,* 217–230.

Linehan, M. M. (1985). The reasons for living inventory. In P. Keller & L. Ritt (Eds.), *Innovations in clinical practice: A sourcebook.* Sarasota, FL: Professional Resource Exchange.

Linehan, M. M. (1987). Dialectical behavior therapy for borderline personality disorder. *Bulletin of the Menninger Clinic, 51,* 261–276.

Linehan, M. M. (1993a). *Cognitive behavioral treatment of borderline personality disorder.* New York: Guilford.

Linehan, M. M. (1993b). *Skills training manual for treating borderline personality disorder*. New York: Guilford.

Linehan, M. M., Heard, H. L., & Armstrong, H. E. (1993) Naturalistic follow-up of a behavioral treatment for chronically parasuicidal borderline patients. *Archives of General Psychiatry, 50*, 971–974.

Linehan, M. M., & Kehrer, C. A. (1993). Borderline personality disorder. In D. H. Barlow (Ed.), *Clinical handbook of psychological disorders: A step-by-step treatment manual* (2nd ed., pp. 396–441). New York: Guilford.

Linehan, M. M., & Shearin, E. N. (1988). Lethal stress: A social-behavioral model of suicidal behavior. In S. Fisher & J. Reason (Eds.), *Handbook of life stress, cognition, and health*. New York: Wiley.

Links, P. S., Steiner, M., Boiago, I., & Irwin, D. (1990). Lithium therapy for borderline patients: Preliminary findings. *Journal of Personality Disorders, 4*, 173–181.

Linn, M. W., Linn, B. S., & Jensen, J. (1984). Stressful events, dysphoric mood, and immune responsiveness. *Psychological Reports, 54*, 219–222.

Linz, D. G., Donnerstein, E., & Penrod, S. (1988). Effects of long-term exposure to violent and sexually degrading depictions of women. *Journal of Personality and Social Psychology, 55*, 758–768.

Lipowski, Z. J. (1980). *Delirium: Acute brain failure in man*. Springfield, IL: Charles C. Thomas.

Lipowski, Z. J. (1983). Transient cognitive disorders (delirium and acute confusional states) in the elderly. *American Journal of Psychiatry, 140*, 1426–1436.

Liskow, B. (1982). Substance induced and substance use disorders: Barbiturates and similarly acting sedative hypnotics. In J. H. Greist, J. W. Jefferson, & R. L. Spitzer (Eds.), *Treatment of mental disorders*. New York: Oxford University Press.

Livesley, W. J., Schroeder, M. L., Jackson, D. N., & Jang, K. L. (1994). Categorical distinctions in the study of personality disorder: Implications for classification. *Journal of Abnormal Psychology, 103*, 6–17.

London, P. (1964). *The modes and morals of psychotherapy*. New York: Holt, Rinehart & Winston.

London, P. (1986). *The modes and morals of psychotherapy* (2nd ed.). New York: Hemisphere.

Loney, J., Langhorne, J. E., Jr., & Paternite, C. E. (1978). An empirical basis for subgrouping the hyperkinetic-minimal brain dysfunction syndrome. *Journal of Abnormal Psychology, 87*, 431–441.

Lopez, S. R. (1989). Patient variable biases in clinical judgment: Conceptual overview and methodological considerations. *Psychological Bulletin, 106*, 184–203.

Lopez, S. R., & Hernandez, P. (1986). How culture is considered in evaluations of psychopathology. *Journal of Nervous and Mental Disease, 176*, 598–606.

Lopez, S. R., Lopez, A. A., & Fong, K. T. (1991). Mexican Americans' initial preferences for counselors: The role of ethnic factors. *Journal of Counseling Psychology, 38*, 487–496.

Lopez, S., & Nunez, J. A. (1987). Cultural factors considered in selected diagnostic criteria and interview schedules. *Journal of Abnormal Psychology, 96*, 270–272.

Lopez S. R., & Taussig, I. M. (1991). Cognitive-intellectual functioning of Spanish-speaking impaired and nonimpaired elderly: Implication for culturally sensitive assessment. *Psychological Assessment: A Journal of Consulting and Clinical Psychology, 3*, 448–454.

LoPiccolo, J. (1977). Direct treatment of sexual dysfunction in the couple. In J. Money & H. Musaph (Eds.), *Handbook of sexology*. New York: Elsevier/North-Holland.

LoPiccolo, J. (1991). Counseling and therapy for sexual problems in the elderly. *Clinics in Geriatric Medicine, 7*, 161–179.

LoPiccolo, J. (1992a). Post-modern sex therapy for erectile failure. In R. C. Rosen & S. R. Leiblum (Eds.), *Erectile failure: Assessment and treatment*. New York: Guilford.

LoPiccolo, J. (1992b). Psychological evaluation of erectile failure. In R.

Kirby, C. Carson, & G. Webster (Eds.), *Diagnosis and management of male erectile failure dysfunction*. Oxford: Butterworth-Heinemann.

LoPiccolo, J., & Friedman, J. M. (1985). Sex therapy: An integrated model. In S. J. Lynn & J. P. Garskee (Eds.), *Contemporary psychotherapies: Models and methods*. New York: Merrill.

LoPiccolo, J., & Friedman, J. (1988). Broad-spectrum treatment of low sexual desire: Integration of cognitive, behavioral, and systemic therapy. In S. Leiblum & R. C. Rosen (Eds.), *Sexual desire disorders*. New York: Guilford.

LoPiccolo, J., Heiman, J., Hogan, D., & Roberts, C. (1985). Effectiveness of single therapists versus co-therapy teams in sex therapy. *Journal of Consulting and Clinical Psychology, 53*, 287–294.

LoPiccolo, J., & Lobitz, W. C. (1972). The role of masturbation in the treatment of orgasmic dysfunction. *Archives of Sexual Behavior, 2*, 163–171.

LoPiccolo, J., & Stock, W. E. (1986). Treatment of sexual dysfunction. *Journal of Consulting and Clinical Psychology, 54*, 158–167.

LoPiccolo, J., & Stock, W. E. (1987). Sexual function, dysfunction, and counseling in gynecological practice. In Z. Rosenwaks, F. Benjamin, & M. L. Stone (Eds.), *Gynecology*. New York: Macmillan.

Lotter, V. (1978). Follow-up studies. In M. Rutter & E. Schopler (Eds.), *Autism: A reappraisal of concepts and treatment*. New York: Plenum.

Lovaas, O. I. (1987). Behavioral treatment and normal educational and intellectual functioning in young autistic children. *Journal of Consulting and Clinical Psychology, 55*, 3–9.

Luborsky, L., & DeRubeis, R. J. (1984). The use of psychotherapy treatment manuals: A small revolution in psychotherapy research style. *Clinical Psychology Review, 4*, 5–14.

Luntz, B. K., & Widom, C. S. (1994). Antisocial personality disorder in abused and neglected children grown up. *American Journal of Psychiatry, 151*, 670–674.

Lykken, D. T. (1957). A study of anxiety in the sociopathic personality. *Journal of Abnormal and Social Psychology, 55*, 6–10.

Lystad, M. M. (1957). Social mobility among selected groups of schizophrenics. *American Sociological Review, 22*, 288–292.

Maccoby, E. E., & Jacklin, C. N. (1974). *The psychology of sex differences*. Stanford, CA: Stanford University Press.

Maccoby, N., & Altman, D. G. (1988). Disease prevention in communities: The Stanford Heart Disease Prevention Program. In R. H. Price, E. L. Cowen, R. P. Lorion, & J. Ramos-McKay (Eds.), *14 ounces of prevention: A casebook for practitioners* (pp. 165–174). Washington, DC: American Psychological Association.

Maccoby, N., Farquhar, J. W., Wood, P. D., & Alexander, J. (1977). Reducing the risk of cardiovascular disease: Effects of a community-based campaign on knowledge and behavior. *Journal of Community Health, 3*, 100–114.

MacLeod, C., Mathews, A., & Tata, P. (1986). Attentional bias in emotional disorders. *Journal of Abnormal Psychology, 95*, 15–20.

MacPhillamy, D. J., & Lewinsohn, P. M. (1974). Depression as a function of levels of desired and obtained pleasure. *Journal of Abnormal Psychology, 83*, 651–657.

Maddux, J. F., & Desmond, D. P. (1992). Methadone maintenance and recovery from opioid dependence. *American Journal of Drug and Alcohol Abuse, 18*, 63–74.

Madonna, P. G., Van Scoyk, S., & Jones, D. B. (1991). Family interactions within incest and nonincest families. *American Journal of Psychiatry, 148*, 46–49.

Mahoney, M. J. (1986). The tyranny of technique. *Counseling and Values, 30*, 169–174.

Malamuth, N. M. (1981). Rape proclivity among males. *Journal of Social Issues, 37*, 138–157.

Malamuth, N. M., & Check, J. V. P. (1981). The effects of mass media exposure on acceptance of violence against women: A field experiment. *Journal of Research in Personality, 15*, 436–446.

Malamuth, N. M., Feshbach, S., & Jaffe, Y. (1977). Sexual arousal and aggression: Recent experiments and theoretical issues. *Journal of Social Issues, 33*, 110–133.

Malgady, R. G., Rogler, L. H., & Constantino, G. (1987). Ethnocultural and linguistic bias in mental health evaluation of Hispanics. *American Psychologist, 42*, 228–234.

Mandler, G. (1972). Helplessness: Theory and research in anxiety. In C. D. Spielberger (Ed.), *Anxiety: Current trends in theory and research.* New York: Academic Press.

Manji, H. K., Hsiao, J. K., Risby, E. D., Oliver, J., Rudorfer, M. V., Potter, W. Z. (1991). The mechanisms of action of lithium: I. Effects on serotonergic and noradrenergic systems in normal subjects. *Archives of General Psychiatry, 48*, 505–512.

Manos, N., Vasilopoulou, E., & Sotiriou, M. (1987). DSM-III diagnoses of borderline disorder and depression. *Journal of Personality Disorders, 1*, 263–268.

Manson, S. M., Walker, R. D. & Kivlahan, D. R. (1987). Psychiatric assessment and treatment of American Indians and Alaskan natives. *Hospital and Community Psychiatry, 38*, 165–173.

Manton, K. G., Blazer, D. G., & Woodbury, M. A. (1987). Suicide in middle age and later life: Sex and race specific life table and cohort analyses. *Journal of Gerontology, 42*, 219–227.

Manuck, S. B., Kaplan, J. R., Adams, M. R., & Clarkson, T. B. (1989). Behaviorally elicited heart rate reactivity and atherosclerosis in female cynomolgus monkeys (*Macaca fascicularis*). *Psychosomatic Medicine, 51*, 306–318.

Manuck, S. B., & Krantz, D. S. (1986). Psychophysiologic reactivity in coronary heart disease and essential hypertension. In K. A. Matthews, S. M. Weiss, T. Detre, T. M. Dembroski, B. F. Faulkner, S. B. Manuck, & R. B. Williams (Eds.), *Handbook of stress, reactivity, and cardiovascular disease.* New York: Wiley.

Marder, S. R., & Meibach, R. C. (1994). Risperidone in the treatment of schizophrenia. *American Journal of Psychiatry, 151*, 825–835.

Margolin, L. (1990). Gender and the stolen kiss: Social support of male and female to violate a partner's sexual consent in a noncoercive situation. *Archives of Sexual Behavior, 19*, 281–291.

Margraf, J., Ehlers, A., & Roth, W. T. (1986). Sodium lactate infusions and panic attacks: A review and critique. *Psychosomatic Medicine, 48*, 23–51.

Marijuana research findings. (1980). Washington, DC: U.S. Government Printing Office.

Marks, I. M. (1969). *Fears and phobias.* New York: Academic Press.

Marks, I. M. (1983). Behavioral psychotherapy for anxiety disorders. *Psychiatric Clinics of North America, 8*, 25–34.

Marks, I. M., & Gelder, M. G. (1966). Different ages of onset in varieties of phobias. *American Journal of Psychiatry, 123*, 218–221.

Marks, I. M., & Gelder, M. G. (1967). Transvestism and fetishism: Clinical and psychological changes during faradic aversion. *British Journal of Psychiatry, 113*, 711–729.

Marks, I. M., Gelder, M. G., & Bancroft, J. (1970). Sexual deviants two years after electrical aversion. *British Journal of Psychiatry, 117*, 73–85.

Markus, H. R., & Kitayama, S. (1991). Culture and the self: Implications for cognition, emotion, and motivation. *Psychological Review, 98*, 224–253.

Marlatt, G. A. (1983). The controlled drinking controversy: A commentary. *American Psychologist, 38*, 1097–1110.

Marlatt, G. A., Demming, B., & Reid, J. B. (1973). Loss of control drinking in alcoholics: An experimental analogue. *Journal of Abnormal Psychology, 81*, 233–241.

Marlatt, G. A., & Gordon, J. R. (Eds.). (1985). *Relapse prevention.* New York: Guilford.

Marmar, C. R., Horowitz, M. J., Weiss, D. S., Wilner, N. R., & Kaltreider, N. B. (1988). A controlled trial of brief psychotherapy and mutual-help group treatment of conjugal bereavement. *American Journal of Psychiatry, 145*, 203–209.

Marshall, W. L., & Barbaree, H. E. (1990). Outcome of comprehensive cognitive-behavioral treatment programs. In W. L. Marshall, D. R. Laws, & H. E. Barbaree (Eds.), *Handbook of sexual assault: Is-* *sues, theories, and treatment of the offender* (pp. 257–275). New York, Plenum.

Marshall, W. L., Jones, R., Ward, T., Johnston, P., & Barbaree, H. E. (1991). Treatment outcome with sex offenders. *Clinical Psychology Review, 11*, 465–485.

Maruish, M. E., Sawicki, R. F., Franzen, M. D., & Golden, C. J. (1984). Alpha coefficient reliabilities for the Luria–Nebraska Neuropsychological Battery summary and localization scales by diagnostic category. *The International Journal of Clinical Neuropsychology, 7*, 10–12.

Marziali, E. (1984). Prediction of outcome of brief psychotherapy from therapist interpretive interventions. *Archives of General Psychiatry, 41*, 301–304.

Masling, J. (1960). The influences of situational and interpersonal variables in projective testing. *Psychological Bulletin, 57*, 65–85.

Masson, J. M. (1984). *The assault on truth: Freud's suppression of the seduction theory.* New York: Farrar, Strauss, Giroux.

Masters, W. H., & Johnson, V. E. (1966). *Human sexual response.* Boston: Little, Brown.

Masters, W. H., & Johnson, V. E. (1970). *Human sexual inadequacy.* Boston: Little, Brown.

Matarazzo, J. D. (1972). *Wechsler's measurement and appraisal of adult intelligence* (5th ed.). Baltimore: Williams & Wilkins.

Matheny, A. P., Jr., Dolan, A. B., & Wilson, R. S. (1976). Twins with academic learning problems: Antecedent characteristics. *American Journal of Orthopsychiatry, 46*, 464–469.

Matthews, K. A., Meilan, E., Kuller, L. H., Kelsey, S. F., Caggiula, A. W., & Wing, R. R. (1989). Menopause and risk factors in coronary heart disease. *New England Journal of Medicine, 321*, 641–646.

Matthews, K. A., & Rakaczky, C. J. (1987). Familial aspects of type A behavior and physiologic reactivity to stress. In T. Dembroski and T. Schmidt (Eds.), *Behavioral factors in coronary heart disease.* Heidelberg: Springer-Verlag.

Mattick, R. P. (1992). Psychoactive substance dependence and associated states. In S. Schwartz (Ed.), *Case studies in abnormal psychology* (pp. 155–179). Brisbane, Australia: Wiley.

Mattick, R. P., & Jarvis, T. (1992). *An outline for the management of alcohol dependence and abuse.* Canberra: Australian Government Publishing Service.

Mattick, R. P., Peters, L., & Clarke, J. C. (1989). Exposure and cognitive restructuring for severe social phobia. *Behavior Therapy, 20*, 3–23.

Mavissakalian, M., Hammen, M. S., & Jones, B. (1990). DSM-III personality disorders in obsessive-compulsive disorder. *Comprehensive Psychiatry, 31*, 432–437.

Mays, D. T., & Franks, C. M. (1980). Getting worse: Psychotherapy or no treatment—The jury should still be out. *Professional Psychology, 11*, 78–92.

McCary, J. L. (1973). *Human sexuality* (2nd ed.). New York: Van Nostrand-Reinhold.

McConaghy, N. (1990). Sexual deviation. In A. S. Bellack, M. Hersen, & A. E. Kazdin (Eds.), *International handbook of behavior modification and therapy* (2nd ed., pp. 565–580). New York: Plenum.

McCord, W., & McCord, J. (1964). *The psychopath: An essay on the criminal mind.* New York: Van Nostrand-Reinhold.

McFall, R. M., & Hammen, C. L. (1971). Motivation, structure, and self-monitoring: Role of nonspecific factors in smoking reduction. *Journal of Consulting and Clinical Psychology, 37*, 80–86.

McGee, R., & Williams, S. (1988). A longitudinal study of depression in nine-year-old children. *Journal of the American Academy of Child and Adolescent Psychiatry, 27*, 49–54.

McGlashan, T. M. (1983). The borderline syndrome: I. Testing three diagnostic systems. *Archives of General Psychiatry, 40*, 1311–1318.

McGrady, A. V., & Bernal, G. A. A. (1986). Relaxation based treatment of stress induced syncope. *Journal of Behavior Therapy and Experimental Psychiatry, 17*, 23–27.

McGue, M., Pickens, R. W., & Svikis, D. S. (1992). Sex and age effects on the inheritance of alcohol problems: A twin study. *Journal of Abnormal Psychology, 101,* 3–17.

McGuiness, D. (1981). Auditory and motor aspects of language development in males and females. In A. Ansara (Ed.), *Sex differences in dyslexia.* Towson, MD: The Orton Dyslexia Society.

McKeon, P., & Murray, R. (1987). Familial aspects of obsessive-compulsive neurosis. *British Journal of Psychiatry, 151,* 528–534.

McMullen, S., & Rosen, R. C. (1979). Self-administered masturbation training in the treatment of primary orgasmic dysfunction. *Journal of Consulting and Clinical Psychology, 47,* 912–918.

McNeal, E. T., & Cimbolic, P. (1986). Antidepressants and biochemical theories of depression. *Psychological Bulletin, 99,* 361–374.

McNeil, E. (1967). *The quiet furies.* Englewood Cliffs, NJ: Prentice-Hall.

Mednick, S. A., Machon, R., Hottunen, M. O., & Bonett, D. (1988). Fetal viral infection and adult schizophrenia. *Archives of General Psychiatry, 45,* 189–192.

Meehl, P. E., & Golden, R. (1982). Taxometric methods. In P. Kendall & J. Butcher (Eds.), *Handbook of research methods in clinical psychology* (pp. 127–181). New York: Wiley.

Melamed, B. G., Hawes, R. R., Heiby, E., & Glick, J. (1975). Use of filmed modeling to reduce uncooperative behavior of children during dental treatment. *Journal of Dental Research, 54,* 797–801.

Mellinger, G. D., Balter, M. B., & Uhlenhuth, E. H. (1985). Insomnia and its treatment. *Archives of General Psychiatry, 42,* 225–232.

Mello, N. K., & Mendelson, J. H. (1970). Experimentally induced intoxication in alcoholics: A comparison between programmed and spontaneous drinking. *Journal of Pharmacology and Experimental Therapy, 173,* 101.

Mellor, C. S. (1970). First rank symptoms of schizophrenia. *British Journal of Psychiatry, 117,* 15–23.

Mendels, J., Stinnett, J. L., Burns, D., & Frazer, A. (1975). Amine precursors and depression. *Archives of General Psychiatry, 32,* 22–30.

Mendlewicz, J., & Rainer, J. D. (1977). Adoption study supporting genetic transmission in manic-depressive illness. *Nature, 268,* 327–329.

Metalsky, G. I., Halberstadt, L. J., & Abramson, L. Y. (1987). Vulnerability and invulnerability to depressive mood reactions: Toward a more powerful test of the diathesis-stress and causal mediation components of the reformulated theory of depression. *Journal of Personality and Social Psychology, 52,* 386–393.

Metalsky, G. I., Joiner, T. E., Jr., Hardin, T. S., & Abramson, L. Y. (1993). Depressive reactions to failure in a naturalistic setting: A test of the hopelessness and self-esteem theories of depression. *Journal of Abnormal Psychology, 102,* 101–109.

Meuwissen, I., & Over, R. (1992). Sexual arousal across phases of the human menstrual cycle. *Archives of Sexual Behavior, 21,* 101–119.

Meyer, G. J. (1992). Response frequency problems in the Rorschach: Clinical and research implications with suggestions for the future. *Journal of Personality Assessment, 58,* 231–244.

Meyer, J. J. (1988). Impotence: Assessment in the private-practice office. *Postgraduate Medicine, 84,* 87–91.

Meyer, J. J., & Reter, D. J. (1979). Sex reassignment follow-up. *Archives of General Psychiatry, 36,* 1010–1015.

Meyer, V. (1966). Modification of expectations in cases with obsessional rituals. *Behaviour Research and Therapy, 4,* 273–280.

Meyer, V., & Chesser, E. S. (1970). *Behavior therapy in clinical psychiatry.* Baltimore: Penguin.

Michelson, L. K., & Marchione, K. (1991). Behavioral, cognitive, and pharmacological treatments of panic disorder with agoraphobia: Critique and synthesis. *Journal of Consulting and Clinical Psychology, 59,* 100–114.

Michelson, L., Mavissakalian, M., & Marchione, K. (1985). Cognitive and behavioral treatments of agoraphobia: Clinical, behavioral, and psychophysiological treatments of agoraphobia. *Journal of Consulting and Clinical Psychology, 53,* 913–925.

Michelson, L., Sugai, D. P., Wood, R. P., & Kazdin, A. E. (1983). *Social skills assessment and training with children: An empirically based handbook.* New York: Plenum.

Midanik, L. T., & Clark, W. B. (1994). The demographic distribution of U.S. drinking patterns in 1990: Description and trends from 1984. *American Journal of Public Health, 84,* 1218–1222.

Miklich, D. R., Rewey, H. H., Weiss, J. H., & Kolton, S. (1973). A preliminary investigation of psychophysiological responses to stress among different subgroups of asthmatic children. *Journal of Psychosomatic Research, 17,* 1–8.

Miklowitz, D. J., Goldstein, J. J., Nuechterlein, K. H., Snyder, K. S., & Mintz, J. (1988). Family factors and the course of bipolar affective disorder. *Archives of General Psychiatry, 45,* 225–231.

Miles, L. E., & Dement, W. C. (1980). Sleep and aging. *Sleep, 3,* 119–220.

Miller, T. Q., Turner, C. W., Tindale, R. S., Posavac, E. J., & Dugoni, B. L. (1991). Reasons for the trend toward null findings in research on Type A behavior. *Psychological Bulletin, 110,* 469–485.

Miller, W. R. (1993). Behavioral treatments for drug problems: Lessons from the alcohol treatment outcome literature. In L. S. Onken, J. D. Blaine, & J. J. Boren (Eds.), *Behavioral treatments for drug abuse and dependence* (NIDA Research Monograph 137, pp. 167–180, NIH Publication No. 93–3684). Rockville, MD: U. S. Department of Health and Human Services.

Miller, W. R., & Hester, R. K. (1986). Inpatient alcohol treatment: Who benefits? *American Psychologist, 41,* 794–805.

Miller, W. R., Seligman, M. E. P., & Kurlander, H. M. (1975). Learned helplessness, depression, and anxiety. *Journal of Nervous and Mental Disease, 161,* 347–357.

Mineka, S., Davidson, M., Cook, M., & Keir, R. (1984). Observational conditioning of snake fear in rhesus monkeys. *Journal of Abnormal Psychology, 93,* 355–372.

Minuchin, S., Baker, L., Rosman, B. L., Liebman, R., Milman, L., & Todd, T. C. (1975). A conceptual model of psychosomatic illness in children: Family organization and family therapy. *Archives of General Psychiatry, 32,* 1031–1038.

Mirenda, P. L., Donnellan, A. M., & Yoder, D. E. (1983). Gaze behavior: A new look at an old problem. *Journal of Autism and Developmental Disorders, 13,* 397–409.

Mischel, W. (1968). *Personality and assessment.* New York: Wiley.

Mitchell, J., McCauley, E., Burke, P. M., & Moss, S. J. (1988). Phenomenology of depression in children and adolescents. *Journal of the American Academy of Child and Adolescent Psychiatry, 27,* 12–20.

Mitchell, J. E., Hatsukami, D., Eckert, E. D., & Pyle, R. L. (1985). Characteristics of 275 patients with bulimia. *American Journal of Psychiatry, 142,* 482–485.

Modestin, J. (1987). Quality of interpersonal relationships: The most characteristic DSM-III BPD characteristic. *Comprehensive Psychiatry, 28,* 397–402.

Mohr, J. W., Turner, R. E., & Jerry, M. B. (1964). *Pedophilia and exhibitionism.* Toronto: University of Toronto Press.

Mohs, R. C., Breftner, J. C. S., Silverman, J. M., & Davis, K. L. (1987). Alzheimer's disease: Morbid risk among first-degree relatives approximates 50% by 90 years of age. *Archives of General Psychiatry, 44,* 405–408.

Moñiz, E. (1936). *Tentatives operatoires dans le traitement de certaines psychoses.* Paris: Masson.

Monti, P. M., Abrams, D. B., Kadden, R. M., & Cooney, N. L. (1989). *Treating alcohol dependence: A coping skills training guide.* New York: Guilford.

Morey, L. C. (1988). Personality disorders in DSM-III and DSM-III-R: Convergence, coverage, and internal consistency. *American Journal of Psychiatry, 145,* 573–577.

Morey, L. C., & Ochoa, E. S. (1989). An investigation of adherence to diagnostic criteria: Clinical diagnosis of the DSM-III personality disorders. *Journal of Personality Disorders, 3,* 180–192.

Morin, C. M., & Azrin, N. H. (1988). Behavioral and cognitive treatments of geriatric insomnia. *Journal of Consulting and Clinical Psychology, 56,* 748–753.

Morokoff, P. J. (1988). Sexuality in perimenopausal and post-menopausal women. *Psychology of Women Quarterly, 12,* 489–511.

Morrow, J., & Nolen-Hoeksema, S. (1990). Effects of responses to depression on the remediation of depressive affect. *Journal of Personality and Social Psychology, 58,* 519–527.

Moser, C., & Levitt, E. E. (1987). An exploratory-descriptive study of a sadomasochistically oriented sample. *Journal of Sex Research, 23,* 322–337.

Moser, P. W. (1989, January). Double vision: Why do we never match up to our mind's ideal? *Self Magazine,* pp. 51–52.

Moses, J. A. (1983). Luria–Nebraska Neuropsychological Battery performance of brain dysfunctional patients with positive or negative findings on current neurological examination. *International Journal of Neuroscience, 22,* 135–146.

Mosher, L. R., & Burti, L. (1989). *Community mental health: Principles and practice.* New York: Norton.

Moss, H. B., & Procci, W. R. (1982). Sexual dysfunction associated with oral antihypertensive medication: A critical survey of the literature. *General Hospital Psychiatry, 4,* 121–129.

Mrazek, D. A., Klinnert, M. D., Mrazek, P., & Macey, T. (1991). Early asthma onset: Consideration of parenting issues. *Journal of the American Academy of Child and Adolescent Psychiatry, 30,* 277–282.

Muller, D., Roeder, F., & Orthner, H. (1973). Further results of stereotaxis in human hypothalamus in sexual deviations: First use of this operation in addition to drugs. *Neurochirurgia, 16,* 113–126.

Mulligan, T., Retchin, S. M., Chinchilli, V. M., & Bettinger, C. B. (1988). The role of aging and chronic disease in sexual dysfunction. *Journal of the American Geriatrics Society, 36,* 520–524.

Munjack, D. J., & Kanno, P. H. (1979). Retarded ejaculation: A review. *Archives of Sexual Behavior, 8,* 139–150.

Murphy, J. (1976). Psychiatric labeling in cross-cultural perspective. *Science, 191,* 1019–1028.

Murray, H. A. (1943). *Thematic Apperception Test Manual.* Cambridge: Harvard University Press.

Muscettola, G., Potter, W. Z., Pickar, D., & Goodwin, F. K. (1984). Urinary 3–methoxy-4–hydroxyphenylglycol and major affective disorders. *Archives of General Psychiatry, 41,* 337–342.

Myers, J. K., Weissman, M. M. Tischler, G. L., Holzer, C. E., Leaf, P. J., Orvaschel, H. A., Anthony, J. C., Boyd, J. H., Burke, J. E., Kramer, M., & Stoltzman, R. (1984). Six-month prevalence of psychiatric disorders in three communities: 1980–1982. *Archives of General Psychiatry, 41,* 959–967.

National Center for Health Statistics. (1988). Advance report of final mortality statistics, 1986. *Monthly Vital Statistics Report, 37* (Suppl. 6).

National Commission on Testing and Public Policy. (1990). *From gatekeeper to gateway: Transforming testing in America.* Chestnut Hill, MA: Boston College.

National Institute on Alcohol Abuse and Alcoholism. (1983). *Special report to the U.S. Congress on alcohol and health.* Washington, DC: U.S. Government Printing Office.

National Institute on Alcohol Abuse and Alcoholism. (1990). *Seventh special report to the U.S. Congress on alcohol and health* (DHHS Publication No. ADM 90–1656). Washington, DC: U.S. Government Printing Office.

National Institute on Drug Abuse. (1979). *National Survey on Drug Abuse.* Washington, DC: Author.

National Institute on Drug Abuse. (1982). *National Survey on Drug Abuse.* Washington, DC: Author.

National Institute on Drug Abuse. (1983). *National Survey on Drug Abuse: Main Findings 1982* (DHHS Publication No. ADM 83–1263). Washington, DC: U.S. Government Printing Office.

National Institute on Drug Abuse. (1991). *National household survey on drug abuse: Population estimates, 1991.* Washington, DC.

Neale, J. M., & Liebert, R. M. (1986). *Science and behavior: An introduction to methods of research* (3rd ed.). Englewood Cliffs, NJ: Prentice-Hall.

Neale, J. M., & Oltmanns, T. F. (1980). *Schizophrenia.* New York: Wiley.

Neill, J. (1990). Whatever became of the schizophrenogenic mother? *American Journal of Psychotherapy, 44,* 499–505.

Neisser, U. (1976). *Cognition and reality.* San Francisco: Freeman.

Nelson, R. O., Lipinski, D. P., & Black, J. L. (1976). The reactivity of adult retardates' self-monitoring: A comparison among behaviors of different valences, and a comparison with token reinforcement. *Psychological Record, 26,* 189–201.

Nelson-Gray, R. O. (1991). DSM-IV: Empirical guidelines from psychometrics. *Journal of Abnormal Psychology, 100,* 308–315.

Nemeroff, C. J., & Karoly, P. (1991). Operant methods. In F. H. Kanfer & A. P. Goldstein (Eds.), *Helping people change: A textbook of methods* (4th ed.). Elmsford, NY: Pergamon Press.

Nestadt, G., Romanowski, A. J., Chahal, R., & Merchant, A. (1990). An epidemiological study of histrionic personality disorder. *Psychological Medicine, 20,* 413–422.

Neugebauer, R. (1979). Medieval and early modern theories of mental illness. *Archives of General Psychiatry, 36,* 477–484.

Neuringer, C. (1964). Rigid thinking in suicidal individuals. *Journal of Consulting Psychology, 28,* 54–58.

Newman, J. P., & Kosson, D. S. (1986). Passive avoidance learning in psychopathic and nonpsychopathic offenders. *Journal of Abnormal Psychology, 95,* 257–263.

Nicholson, R. A., & Berman, J. S. (1983). Is follow-up necessary in evaluating psychotherapy? *Psychological Bulletin, 93,* 261–278.

Nigg, J. T., & Goldsmith, H. H. (1994). Genetics of personality disorders: Perspectives from personality and psychopathology research. *Psychological Bulletin, 115,* 346–380.

Nisbett, R. E., & Wilson, T. D. (1977). Telling more than we can know: Verbal reports on mental processes. *Psychological Review, 84,* 231–259.

Nolen-Hoeksema, S. (1987). Sex differences in unipolar depression: Evidence and theory. *Psychological Bulletin, 101,* 259–282.

Nolen-Hoeksema, S. (1990). *Sex differences in depression.* Stanford, CA: Stanford University Press.

Nolen-Hoeksema, S. (1991). Responses to depression and their effects on the duration of depressive episodes. *Journal of Abnormal Psychology, 100,* 569–582.

Nolen-Hoeksema, S., & Girgus, J. S. (1994). The emergence of gender differences in depression during adolescence. *Psychological Bulletin, 115,* 424–443.

Nolen-Hoeksema, S., & Morrow, J. (1991a). *The effects of rumination and distraction on naturally occurring depressed moods.* Manuscript submitted for publication.

Nolen-Hoeksema, S., & Morrow, J. (1991b). A prospective study of depression and distress following a natural disaster: The 1989 Loma Prieta earthquake. *Journal of Personality and Social Psychology, 61,* 115–121.

Nolen-Hoeksema, S., Parker, L. E., & Larson, J. (1994). Ruminative coping with depressed mood following loss. *Journal of Personality and Social Psychology, 67,* 92–104.

Norris, J., & Cubbins, L. A. (1992). Dating, drinking, and rape: Effects of victim's and assailant's alcohol consumption on judgments of their behavior and traits. *Psychology of Women Quarterly, 16,* 179–191.

North, A. F. (1979). Health services in Head Start. In E. Zigler & J. Valentine (Eds.), *Project Head Start.* New York: Free Press.

Noshirvani, H. F., Kasvikis, Y., Marks, I. M., Tsakiris, F., & Monteiro, W. O. (1991). Gender-divergent factors in obsessive-compulsive disorder. *British Journal of Psychiatry, 158,* 260–263.

Noyes, R., Kathol, R. G., Fisher, M. M., Phillips, B. M., Suelzer, M. T., & Holt, C. S. (1993). The validity of DSM-III-R hypochondriasis. *Archives of General Psychiatry, 50,* 961–970.

Noyes, R., Reich, J., Christiansen, J., Suelzer, M., Pfohl, B., & Coryell,

W. A. (1990). Outcome of panic disorder: Relationship to diagnostic subtypes and comorbidity. *Archives of General Psychiatry, 47,* 809–818.

Nyth, A. L., Gottfries, C. G., Blennow, F., Brane, G., & Wallin, A. (1991). Heterogeneity in the course of Alzheimer's disease: A differentiation of subgroups. *Dementia, 2,* 18–24.

O'Conner, M. C. (1989). Aspects of differential performance by minorities on standardized tests: Linguistic and sociocultural factors. In B. R. Gifford (Ed.), *Test policy and test performance: Education, language, and culture* (pp. 129–181). Boston: Kluwer Academic Publishers.

O'Connor, D. W., Pollitt, P. A., Roth, M., Brook, P. B., & Reiss, B. B. (1990). Memory complaints and impairment in normal, depressed, and demented elderly persons identified in a community survey. *Archives of General Psychiatry, 47,* 224–227.

O'Donohue, W. T. (1987). The sexual behavior and problems of the elderly. In L. L. Carstensen & B. A. Edelstein (Eds.), *Handbook of clinical gerontology.* New York: Pergamon.

Ogata, S. N., Silk, K. R., Goodrich, S., Lohr, N. E., Westen, D., & Hill, E. M. (1990). Childhood sexual and physical abuse in adult patients with borderline personality disorder. *American Journal of Psychiatry, 147,* 1008–1013.

Ogilvie, D. M., Stone, P. J., & Shneidman, E. S. (1983). A computer analysis of suicide notes. In E.S. Shneidman, N. Farberow, & R. Litman (Eds.), *The psychology of suicide* (pp. 249–256). New York: Jason Aronson.

Ogloff, J. R., & Wong, S. (1990). Electrodermal and cardiovascular evidence of a coping response in psychopaths. *Criminal Justice and Behavior, 17,* 231–245.

Olds, D. L. (1984). *Final report: Prenatal/early infancy project.* Washington, DC: Maternal and Child Health Research, National Institute of Health.

O'Leary, K. D., & Beach, S. R. H. (1990). Marital therapy: A viable treatment for depression and marital discord. *American Journal of Psychiatry, 147,* 183–186.

O'Leary, K. D., Pelham, W. E., Rosenbaum, A., & Price, G. H. (1976). Behavioral treatment of hyperkinetic children: An experimental evaluation of its usefulness. *Clinical Pediatrics, 15,* 510–515.

Oliver, M. O., & Hyde, J. S. (1993). Gender differences in sexuality: A meta-analysis. *Psychological Bulletin, 114,* 29–51.

Oppenheimer, R., Howells, K., Palmer, R. L., & Chaloner, D. A. (1985). Adverse sexual experience in childhood and clinical eating disorders: A preliminary description. *Journal of Psychiatric Research, 19,* 357–361.

Orne, M. T., Dinges, D. F., & Orne, E. C. (1984). The differential diagnosis of multiple personality in the forensic court. *International Journal of Clinical and Experimental Hypnosis, 32,* 118–169.

Ost, L-G. (1987). Age of onset in different phobias. *Journal of Abnormal Psychology, 96,* 223–229.

Ost, L-G. (1992). Blood and injection phobia: Background and cognitive, physiological, and behavioral variables. *Journal of Abnormal Psychology, 101,* 68–74.

Ost, L-G., Sterner, U., & Fellenius, J. (1989). Applied tension, applied relaxation, and the combination in the treatment of blood phobia. *Behaviour Research and Therapy, 27,* 109–121.

Overholser, J. C., & Beck, S. (1986). Multimethod assessment of rapists, child molesters, and three control groups on behavioral and psychological measures. *Journal of Consulting and Clinical Psychology, 54,* 682–687.

Parker, G. (1992). Early environment. In E. S. Paykel (Ed.), *Handbook of affective disorders* (2nd ed., pp. 171–183). Edinburgh: Churchill Livingstone.

Parks, C. V., Jr., & Hollon, S. D. (1988). Cognitive assessment. In A. S. Bellack & M. Hersen (Eds.), *Behavioral assessment* (3rd ed.). Elmsford, NY: Pergamon.

Parsons, O. A. (1975). Brain damage in alcoholics: Altered states of consciousness. In M. M. Gross (Ed.), *Alcohol intoxication and withdrawal.* New York: Plenum.

Patel, C., Marmot, M. G., Terry, D. J., Carruthers, M., Hunt, B., & Patel, M. (1985). Trial of relaxation in reducing coronary risk: Four year follow-up. *British Medical Journal, 290,* 1103–1106.

Patterson, G. R. (1982). *Coercive family process.* Eugene, OR: Castalia.

Patterson, G. R. (1986). Performance models for antisocial boys. *American Psychologist, 41,* 432–444.

Patterson, G. R., Ray, R. S., Shaw, D. A., & Cobb, J. A. (1969). *Manual for coding of family interactions.* New York: ASIS/NAPS, Microfiche Publications.

Paul, G. L. (1988). *Observational assessment instrumentation for service and research—The Staff-Resident Interaction Chronograph: Assessment in residential treatment settings* (Part 3). Champaign, IL: Research Press.

Paul, G. L., & Lentz, R. J. (1977). *Psychosocial treatment of chronic mental patients: Milieu versus social learning programs.* Cambridge: Harvard University Press.

Paul, G. L., & Menditto, A. A. (1992). Effectiveness of inpatient treatment programs for mentally ill adults in public psychiatric facilities. *Applied and Preventive Psychology: Current Scientific Perspectives, 1,* 41–63.

Paul, R. (1987). *Communication.* In D. J. Cohen, A. M. Donnellan, & R. Paul (Eds.), *Handbook of autism and pervasive developmental disorders* (pp. 61–84). New York: Wiley.

Peck, E. (1974). The relationship of disease and other stress to second language. *International Journal of Social Psychiatry, 20,* 128–133.

Pedro-Carroll, J. L., Cowen, E. L., Hightower, A. D., & Guare, J. C. (1986). Preventive intervention with latency-aged children of divorce: A replication study. *American Journal of Community Psychology, 14,* 277–290.

Pennebaker, J., Kiecolt-Glaser, J. K., & Glaser, R. (1988). Disclosure of traumas and immune function: Health implications for psychotherapy. *Journal of Consulting and Clinical Psychology, 56,* 239–245.

Pennington, B. F., & Smith, S. D. (1988). Genetic influences on learning disabilities: An update. *Journal of Consulting and Clinical Psychology, 56,* 817–823.

Perris, L. (1969). The separation of bipolar (manic-depressive) from unipolar recurrent depressive psychoses. *Behavioral Neuropsychiatry, 1,* 17–25.

Persons, J. B. (1991). Psychotherapy outcome studies do not accurately represent current models of psychotherapy: A proposed remedy. *American Psychologist, 46,* 99–106.

Peterson, C., & Seligman, M. E. P. (1984). Causal explanations as a risk factor for depression: Theory and evidence. *Psychological Review, 91,* 347–374.

Pfeiffer, E. (1977). Psychopathology and social pathology. In J. E. Birren & K. W. Schaie (Eds.), *Handbook of psychology and aging.* New York: Van Nostrand-Reinhold.

Phelps, L., Wallace, D., & Waigant, A. (1989, August). *Impact of sexual assault: Post-assault behavior and health status.* Paper presented at the annual convention of the American Psychological Association, New Orleans.

Phillips, D. P. (1974). The influence of suggestion on suicide: Substantive and theoretical implications of the Werther effect. *American Sociological Review, 39,* 340–354.

Phillips, D. P. (1977). Motor vehicle fatalities increase just after publicized suicide stories. *Science, 196,* 1464–1465.

Phillips, D. P. (1985). The found experiment: A new technique for assessing impact of mass media violence on real-world aggressive behavior. In G. Comstock (Ed.), *Public communication and behavior* (Vol. 1). New York: Academic Press.

Pigott, T. A., Pato, M. T., Bernstein, S. E., Grover, G. N., Hill, J. L., Tolliver, T. J., & Murphy, D. L. (1990). Controlled comparison of clomipramine and fluoxetine in the treatment of obsessive-compulsive disorder. *Archives of General Psychiatry, 47,* 926–932.

Pitman, R. K., Orr, S. P., Forgue, D. F., Altman, B., deJong, J. B., & Herz, L. R. (1990). Psychophysiologic responses to combat imagery of Vietnam veterans with post-traumatic stress disorder versus other anxiety disorders. *Journal of Abnormal Psychology, 99,* 49–54.

Poland, R. E., Rubin, R. T., Lesser, I. M., Lane, L. A., & Hart, P. J. (1987). Neuroendocrine aspects of primary endogenous depression. *Archives of General Psychiatry, 44,* 790–796.

Pollard, C. A., Pollard, H. J., & Corn, K. J. (1989). Panic onset and major events in the lives of agoraphobics: A test of contiguity. *Journal of Abnormal Psychology, 98,* 318–321.

Pollock, V. E. (1992). Meta-analysis of subjective sensitivity to alcohol in sons of alcoholics. *American Journal of Psychiatry, 149,* 1534–1538.

Pope, H. G., & Hudson, J. I. (1992). Is childhood sexual abuse a risk factor for bulimia nervosa? *American Journal of Psychiatry, 149,* 455–463.

Pope, H. G., Jonas, J. M., Hudson, J. I., Cohen, B. M., & Gunderson, J. G. (1983). The validity of DSM-III borderline personality disorder. *Archives of General Psychiatry, 40,* 23–30.

Post, F. (1980). Paranoid, schizophrenia-like and schizophrenic states in the aged. In J. E. Birren & R. B. Sloane (Eds.), *Handbook of mental health and aging.* Englewood Cliffs, NJ: Prentice-Hall.

Potashnik, S., & Pruchno, R. (1988, November). *Spouse caregivers: Physical and mental health in perspective.* Paper presented at the meeting of the Gerontological Society of America, San Francisco.

Powell, L. H., Friedman, M., Thoresen, C. E., Gill, J. J., & Ulmer, D. K. (1984). Can the type A behavior pattern be altered after myocardial infarction? A second year report from the Recurrent Coronary Prevention Project. *Psychosomatic Medicine, 46,* 293–313.

Price, L. H., Charney, D. S., Rubin, A. L., & Heninger, G. R. (1986). Alpha-2 adrenergic receptor function in depression. *Archives of General Psychiatry, 43,* 849–860.

Price, V. A. (1982). *Type A behavior pattern: A model for research and practice.* New York: Academic Press.

Prien, R. F., Kupfer, D. J., Mansky, P. A., Small, J. G., Tuason, V. B., Voss, C. B., & Johnson, W. E. (1984). Drug therapy in the prevention of recurrences in unipolar and bipolar affective disorders. *Archives of General Psychiatry, 41,* 1096–1104.

Prinz, P., & Raskin, M. (1978). Aging and sleep disorders. In R. Williams & R. Karacan (Eds.), *Sleep disorders: Diagnosis and treatment.* New York: Wiley.

Prochaska, J. O. (1984). *Systems of psychotherapy* (2nd ed.). Homewood, IL: Dorsey Press.

Puig-Antich, J. (1982). Major depression and conduct disorder in prepuberty. *Journal of the American Academy of Child and Adolescent Psychiatry, 21,* 118–128.

Puig-Antich, J., Lukens, E., Davies, M., Goetz, D., Brennan-Quattrock, J., & Todak, G. (1985). Psychosocial functioning in prepubertal major depressive disorders: 1. Interpersonal relationships during the depressive episode. *Archives of General Psychiatry, 42,* 500–507.

Puig-Antich, J., Perel, J. M., Lupatkin, W., Chambers, W. J., Tabrizi, M. A., King, J., Goetz, R., Davies, M., & Stiller, R. L. (1987). Imipramine in prepubertal major depressive disorders. *Archives of General Psychiatry, 44,* 81–89.

Puig-Antich, J., & Rabinovich, H. (1986). Relationship between affective and anxiety disorders in childhood. In R. G. Helman (Ed.), *Anxiety disorders of childhood.* New York: Guilford.

Purcell, K., & Weiss, J. H. (1970). Asthma. In C. G. Costello (Ed.), *Symptoms of psychopathology: A handbook.* New York: Wiley.

Purdie, F. R., Honigman, T. B., & Rosen, P. (1981). Acute organic brain syndrome: A view of 100 cases. *Annals of Emergency Medicine, 10,* 455–461.

Putnam, F. W., Guroff, J. J., Silberman, E. K., Barban, L., & Post, R. M. (1986). The clinical phenomenology of multiple personality disor-

der: Review of 100 recent cases. *Journal of Clinical Psychiatry, 47,* 285–293.

Putnam, F. W., Post, R. M., & Guroff, J. J. (1983). *One hundred cases of multiple personality disorder.* Paper presented at the annual meeting of the American Psychiatric Association, New York.

Pyle, R. L., Halvorson, A., Neuman, P. A., & Mitchell, J. E. (1986). The increasing prevalence of bulimia in freshman college students. *International Journal of Eating Disorders, 5,* 631–648.

Quay, H. C. (1979). Classification. In H. C. Quay & J. S. Werry (Eds.), *Psychopathological disorders of childhood* (2nd ed.). New York: Wiley.

Rabins, P. V., & Folstein, M. F. (1982). Delirium and dementia: Diagnostic criteria and fatality rates. *British Journal of Psychiatry, 140,* 149–153.

Rabkin, J. G. (1974). Public attitudes toward mental illness: A review of the literature. *Schizophrenia Bulletin,* 9–33.

Rachman, S. J. (1966). Sexual fetishism: An experimental analogue. *Psychological Record, 16,* 293–296.

Rachman, S., & deSilva, P. (1978). Abnormal and normal obsessions. *Behaviour Research and Therapy, 16,* 233–248.

Rachman, S. J., & Hodgson, R. J. (1980). *Obsessions and compulsions.* Englewood Cliffs, NJ: Prentice-Hall.

Rachman, S. J., & Wilson, G. T. (1980). *The effects of psychological therapy* (2nd ed.). Elmsford, NY: Pergamon.

Radloff, L. (1975). Sex differences in depression: The effects of occupation and marital status. *Sex Roles, 1,* 249–265.

Ragland, D. R., & Brand, R. J. (1988). Type A behavior and mortality from coronary heart disease. *The New England Journal of Medicine, 318,* 65–69.

Rahe, R. H., & Lind, E. (1971). Psychosocial factors and sudden cardiac death: A pilot study. *Journal of Psychosomatic Research, 15,* 19–24.

Rapoport, J. L., Buchsbaum, M. S., Zahn, T. P., Weingartner, H., Ludlow, D., & Mikkelson, E. J. (1978). Dextroamphetamine: Cognitive and behavioral effects in normal prepubertal boys. *Science, 199,* 560–563.

Rapp, S. R., Parisi, S. A., & Walsh, D. A. (1988). Psychological dysfunction and physical health among elderly medical inpatients. *Journal of Consulting and Clinical Psychology, 56,* 851–855.

Rappaport, J., & Chinsky, J. M. (1974). Models for delivery of service from a historical and conceptual perspective. *Professional Psychology, 5,* 42–50.

Rasmussen, S. A., & Tsuang, M. T. (1986). Clinical characteristics and family history in DSM-III obsessive-compulsive disorder. *American Journal of Psychiatry, 143,* 317–322.

Rather, B. C., Goldman, M. S., Roehrich, L., & Brannick, M. (1992). Empirical modeling of an alcohol expectancy memory network using multidimensional scaling. *Journal of Abnormal Psychology, 101,* 174–183.

Red Horse, Y. (1982). A cultural network model: Perspectives for adolescent services and paraprofessional training. In S. Manson (Ed.), *New directions in prevention among American Indians and Alaskan Native communities.* Portland: Oregon Health Sciences University.

Redmond, D. E. (1977). Alterations in the function of the nucleus locus coeruleus. In I. Hanin & E. Usdin (Eds.), *Animal models in psychiatry and neurology.* New York: Pergamon.

Reed, D., McGhee, D., Yano, K., & Feinleib, M. (1983). Social networks and coronary heart disease among Japanese men in Hawaii. *American Journal of Epidemiology, 119,* 356–370.

Rees, L. (1964). The importance of psychological, allergic and infective factors in childhood asthma. *Journal of Psychosomatic Research, 7,* 253–262.

Regier, D. A., Boyd, J. H., Burke, J. D., Jr., Rae, D. S., Myers, J. K., Kramer, M., Robins, L. N., George, L. K., Karno, M., & Locke, B. Z. (1988). One-month prevalence of mental disorders in the United States. *Archives of General Psychiatry, 45,* 977–986.

Reich, J. (1987). Sex distribution of DSM-III personality disorders in psychiatric outpatients. _American Journal of Psychiatry, 144,_ 485–488.

Reich, J. H., & Vasile, R. G. (1993). Effect of personality disorders on the treatment outcome of Axis I conditions: An update. _Journal of Nervous and Mental Disease, 181,_ 475–484.

Reid, E. C. (1910). Autopsychology of the manic-depressive. _Journal of Nervous and Mental Disease, 37,_ 606–620.

Reiss, D., Plomin, R., & Hetherington, E. M. (1991). Genetics and psychiatry: An unheralded window on the environment. _American Journal of Psychiatry, 148,_ 283–291.

Reiss, I. L., & Leik, R. K. (1989). Evaluating strategies to avoid AIDS: Number of partners versus use of condoms. _Journal of Sex Research, 26,_ 411–433.

Reitan, R. M., & Wolfson, D. (1985). _The Halstead–Reitan neuropsychological test battery: Theory and clinical interpretation._ Tucson, AZ: Neuropsychology Press.

Rekers, G. A., & Lovaas, O. I. (1974). Behavioral treatment of deviant sex role behaviors in a male child. _Journal of Applied Behavioral Analysis, 7,_ 173–190.

Renshaw, D. C. (1988). Profile of 2376 patients treated at Loyola Sex Clinic between 1972 and 1987. _Sexual and Marital Therapy, 3,_ 111–117.

Resick, P. A., Veronen, L. J., Calhoun, K. S., Kilpatrick, D. G., & Atkeson, B. M. (1986). Assessment of fear reactions in sexual assault victims: A factor-analytic study of the Veronen–Kilpatrick Modified Fear Survey. _Behavioral Assessment, 8,_ 271–283.

Review Panel on Coronary-Prone Behavior and Coronary Heart Disease. (1981). Coronary-prone behavior and coronary heart disease: A critical review. _Circulation, 63,_ 1199–1215.

Reynolds, P., & Kaplan, G. A. (1990). Social connections and risk for cancer: Prospective evidence from the Alameda County Study. _Behavioral Medicine, 9,_ 101–110.

Richardson, J. L., Dwyer, K. M., McGuigan, K., Hansen, W. B., Dent, C. W., Johnson, C. A., Sussman, S. Y., Brannon, B., & Flay, B. (1989). Substance use among eighth grade students who take care of themselves after school. _Pediatrics, 84,_ 556–566.

Ricks, D. M. (1972). _The beginning of vocal communication in infants and autistic children._ Unpublished doctoral dissertation, University of London.

Ridley, C. R. (1984). Clinical treatment of the nondisclosing black client. _American Psychologist, 39,_ 1234–1244.

Rimland, B. (1964). _Infantile autism._ New York: Appleton-Century-Crofts.

Roan, S. (1992, October 15). Giving up coffee tied to withdrawal symptoms. _Los Angeles Times,_ p. A26.

Roberts, M. C., Wurtele, S. K., Boone, R. R., Ginther, L. J., & Elkins, P. D. (1981). Reduction of medical fears by use of modeling: A preventive application in a general population of children. _Journal of Pediatric Psychology, 6,_ 293–300.

Robins, L. N. (1966). _Deviant children grown up._ Baltimore: Williams & Wilkins.

Robins, L. N. (1978). Sturdy childhood predictors of adult antisocial behavior: Replications from longitudinal studies. _Psychological Medicine, 8,_ 611–622.

Robins, L. N., Helzer, J. E., Przybec, T. R., & Regier, D. A. (1988). Alcohol disorders in the community: A report from the Epidemiologic Catchment Area. In R. M. Rose & J. E. Barrett (Eds.), _Alcoholism: Origins and Outcome._ New York: Raven.

Robins, L. N., Helzer, J. E., Weissman, M. M., Orvaschel, H., Gruenberg, E., Burke, J. D., & Regier, D. A. (1984). Lifetime prevalence of specific psychiatric disorders in three sites. _Archives of General Psychiatry, 41,_ 942–949.

Robinson, L. A., Berman, J. S., & Neimeyer, R. A. (1990). Psychotherapy for the treatment of depression: A comprehensive review of controlled outcome research. _Psychological Bulletin, 108,_ 30–49.

Robinson, N. M., & Robinson, H. B. (1976). _The mentally retarded child_ (2nd ed.). New York: McGraw-Hill.

Rodin, J. (1980). Managing the stress of aging: The control of control and coping. In H. Ursin & S. Levine (Eds.), _Coping and Health._ New York: Academic Press.

Rodin, J., (1986). Aging and health: Effects of the sense of control. _Science, 233,_ 1271–1276.

Rodin, J. & Ickovics, J. R. (1990). Women's health: Review and research agenda as we approach the 21st century. _American Psychologist, 45,_ 1018–1034.

Rodin, J., & Langer, E. J. (1977). Long-term effects of a control-relevant intervention with the institutionalized aged. _Journal of Personality and Social Psychology, 35,_ 897–902.

Rodin, J., McAvay, G., & Timko, C. (1988). A longitudinal study of depressed mood and sleep disturbances in elderly adults. _Journal of Gerontology: Psychological Sciences, 43,_ 45–53.

Roemer, L., & Borkovec, T. D. (1993). Worry: Unwanted cognitive activity that controls unwanted somatic experience. In D. M. Wegner & J. W. Pennebaker (Eds.), _Handbook of mental control_ (pp. 220–238). Englewood Cliffs, NJ: Prentice-Hall.

Rogers, C. R. (1951). _Client-centered therapy._ Boston: Houghton Mifflin.

Rogers, C. R. (1961). _On becoming a person: A therapist's view of psychotherapy._ Boston: Houghton Mifflin.

Rogers, C. R. (1970). _Carl Rogers on encounter groups._ New York: Harper & Row.

Rogler, L. H., & Hollingshead, A. B. (1985). _Trapped: Families and schizophrenia_ (3rd ed.). Maplewood, NJ: Waterfront Press.

Rohde, P., Lewinsohn, P. M., & Seeley, J. R. (1991). Comorbidity of unipolar depression: II. Comorbidity with other mental disorders in adolescents and adults. _Journal of Abnormal Psychology, 100,_ 214–222.

Romanczyk, R. G., Diament, C., Goren, E. R., Trundeff, G., & Harris, S. L. (1975). Increasing isolate and social play in severely disturbed children: Intervention and postintervention effectiveness. _Journal of Autism and Childhood Schizophrenia, 43,_ 730–739.

Rosen, J. C., & Leitenberg, H. C. (1985). Exposure plus response prevention treatment of bulimia. In D. M. Garner & P. E. Garfinkel (Eds.), _Handbook of psychotherapy for anorexia nervosa and bulimia._ New York: Guilford.

Rosen, R. C., & Beck, J. G. (1988). _Patterns of sexual arousal: Psychophysiological processes and clinical applications._ New York: Guilford.

Rosen, R. C., & Hall, E. (1984). _Sexuality._ New York: Random House.

Rosenberg, M. S., & Reppucci, N. D. (1985). Primary prevention of child abuse. _Journal of Consulting and Clinical Psychology, 53,_ 576–585.

Rosenman, R. H., Friedman, M., Straus, R., Wurm, M., Kositichek, R., Hahn, W., & Werthessen, N. T. (1964). A predictive study of coronary heart disease. _Journal of the American Medical Association, 189,_ 103–110.

Rosenman, R. H., Brand, R. J., Jenkins, C. D., Friedman, M., Straus, R., & Wurm, M. (1975). Coronary heart disease in the Western Collaborative Group Study: Final follow-up experience of eight years. _Journal of the American Medical Association, 233,_ 872–877.

Rosenthal, N. E., Carpenter, C. J., James, S. P., Parry, B. L., Rogers, S. L. B., & Wehr, T. A. (1986). Seasonal affective disorder in children and adolescents. _American Journal of Psychiatry, 143,_ 356–358.

Rosenthal, N. E., Sack, D. A., Carpenter, C. J., Parry, B. L., Mendelson, W. B., & Wehr, T. A. (1985). Antidepressant effects of light in seasonal affective disorder. _American Journal of Psychiatry, 142,_ 163–170.

Rosin, A. J., & Glatt, M. M. (1971). Alcohol excess in the elderly. _Quarterly Journal of Studies on Alcoholism, 32,_ 53–59.

Rosman, B. L., Minuchin, S., & Liebman, R. (1975). Family lunch session: An introduction to family therapy in anorexia nervosa. _American Journal of Orthopsychiatry, 45,_ 846–853.

Ross, A. O. (1981). _Psychological disorders of childhood: A behavioral ap-_

proach to theory, research, and practice (2nd ed.). New York: McGraw-Hill.

Ross, C. A. (1989). *Multiple personality disorder: Diagnosis, clinical features, and treatment.* New York: Wiley.

Ross, C. A., Miller, S. D., Reagor, P., Bjornson, L., Fraser, G. A., & Anderson, G. (1990). Structured interview data on 102 cases of multiple personality disorder from four centers. *American Journal of Psychiatry, 147*, 596–600.

Ross, C. A., Norton, G. R., & Wozney, K. (1989). Multiple personality disorder: An analysis of 236 cases. *Canadian Journal of Psychiatry, 34*, 413–418.

Ross, D. M., & Ross, S. A. (1982). *Hyperactivity: Research, theory, and action.* New York: Wiley.

Ross, J. L. (1977). Anorexia nervosa: An overview. *Bulletin of the Menninger Clinic, 41*, 418–436.

Rothbaum, B. O., & Foa, E. B. (1992a). Cognitive-behavioral treatment of posttraumatic stress disorder. In P. A. Saigh (Ed.), *Posttraumatic stress disorder: A behavioral approach to assessment and treatment.* Boston: Allyn & Bacon.

Rothbaum, B. O., & Foa, E. B. (1992b). Exposure therapy for rape victims with post-traumatic stress disorder. *The Behavior Therapist, 15*, 219–222.

Rothbaum, B. O., Foa, E. B., Riggs, D. S., Murdock, T., & Walsh, W. (1992). A prospective examination of post-traumatic stress disorder in rape victims. *Journal of Traumatic Stress, 5*, 455–475.

Rounsaville, B. J., Chevron, E. S., & Weissman, M. M. (1984). Specification of techniques in Interpersonal Psychotherapy. In J. B. W. Williams & R. L. Spitzer (Eds.), *Psychotherapy research: Where are we and where should we go?* New York: Guilford.

Roy, A. (1982). Suicide in chronic schizophrenics. *British Journal of Psychiatry, 141*, 171–177.

Roy, A., Everett, D., Pickar, D., & Paul, S. M. (1987). Platelet tritiated imipramine binding and serotonin uptake in depressed patients. *Archives of General Psychiatry, 44*, 320–327.

Rubenstein, C. S., Peynircioglu, Z. F., Chambless, D. L., & Pigott, T. A. (1993). Memory in sub-clinical obsessive-compulsive checkers. *Behaviour Research and Therapy, 31*, 759–765.

Ruberman, W., Weinblatt, E., Goldberg, J. D., & Chaudhary, B. S. (1984). Psychosocial influences on mortality after myocardial infarction. *New England Journal of Medicine, 311*, 552–559.

Ruch, L. O., & Leon, J. J. (1983). Sexual assault trauma and trauma change. *Women and Health, 8*, 5–21.

Rutter, M. (1966). Prognosis: Psychotic children in adolescence and early adult life. In J. K. Wing (Ed.), *Childhood autism: Clinical, educational, and social aspects.* Elmsford, NY: Pergamon.

Ryall, R. (1974). Delinquency: The problem for treatment. *Social Work Today, 15*, 98–104.

Sabin, J. E. (1975). Translating despair. *American Journal of Psychiatry, 132*, 197–199.

Sackeim, H. A., Nordlie, J. W., & Gur, R. C. (1979). A model of hysterical and hypnotic blindness: Cognition, motivation and awareness. *Journal of Abnormal Psychology, 88*, 474–489.

Sakel, M. (1938). The pharmacological shock treatment of schizophrenia. *Nervous and Mental Disease Monograph*, 62.

Salkovskis, P. M. (1989). Cognitive-behavioral factors and the persistence of intrusive thoughts in obsessional problems. *Behaviour Research and Therapy, 27*, 677–682.

Salzman, L. (1980). *Psychotherapy of the obsessive personality.* New York: Jason Aronson.

Salzman, L. (1985). Psychotherapeutic management of obsessive-compulsive patients. *American Journal of Psychotherapy, 39*, 323–330.

Salzman, L., & Thaler, F. H. (1981). Obsessive-compulsive disorders: A review of the literature. *American Journal of Psychiatry, 138*, 286–296.

Sanchez-Craig, M., & Wilkinson, D. A. (1987). Treating problem drinkers who are not severely dependent on alcohol. *Drugs and Society, 1*, 39–67.

Sanday, P. R. (1981). The socio-cultural context of rape: A cross-cultural study. *The Journal of Social Issues, 37*, 5–27.

Sanderson, W. C., DiNardo, P. A., Rapee, R. M., & Barlow, D. H. (1990). Syndrome comorbidity in patients diagnosed with a DSM-IIIR anxiety disorder. *Journal of Abnormal Psychology, 99*, 308–312.

Sanderson, W. C., Rapee, R. M., & Barlow, D. H. (1989). The influence of an illusion of control on panic attacks induced via inhalation of 5.5% carbon dioxide-enriched air. *Archives of General Psychiatry, 46*, 157–162.

Sandler, I. N., & Guenther, R. T. (1985). Assessment of life stress events. In P. Karoly (Ed.), *Measurement strategies in health psychology* (pp. 555–600). New York: Wiley.

Sarbin, T. R., & Coe, W. C. (1979). Hypnosis and psychopathology: Replacing old myths with fresh metaphors. *Journal of Abnormal Psychology, 88*, 506–526.

Sartorius, N., Shapiro, R., & Jablonsky, A. (1974). The international pilot study of schizophrenia. *Schizophrenia Bulletin, 2*, 21–35.

Sayette, M. A., & Wilson, G. T. (1991). Intoxication and exposure to stress: Effects of temporal patterning. *Journal of Abnormal Psychology, 100*, 56–62.

Scerbo, A., Raine, A., O'Brien, M., Chan, C. J., Rhee, C., & Smiley, N. (1990). Reward dominance and passive avoidance learning in adolescent psychopaths. *Journal of Abnormal Child Psychology, 18*, 451–463.

Schachter, S., & Latané, B. (1964). Crime, cognition, and the autonomic nervous system. In D. Levine (Ed.), *Nebraska symposium on motivation* (Vol. 12). Lincoln: University of Nebraska Press.

Scheff, T. J. (1966). *Being mentally ill: A sociological theory.* Chicago: Aldine.

Schellenberg, G. D., Bird, T. D., Wijsman, E. M., Moore, D. K., Boehkne, E. M., Bryant, E. M., Lampe, T. H., Nochlin, D., Sumi, S. M., Deeb, S. S., Bayreuther, K., & Martin, G. M. (1988). Absence of linkage of chromosome 21q21 markers to familial Alzheimer's disease. *Science, 241*, 1507–1510.

Schinke, S. P., & Gilchrist, L. D. (1985). Preventing substance abuse with children and adolescents. *Journal of Consulting and Clinical Psychology, 53*, 596–602.

Schleifer, S. J., Keller, S. E., Camerino, M., Thornton, J. C., & Stein, M. (1983). Suppression of lymphocyte stimulation following bereavement. *Journal of the American Medical Association, 250*, 374–377.

Schlesier-Stropp, B. (1984). Bulimia: A review of the literature. *Psychological Bulletin, 95*, 247–257.

Schmauk, F. J. (1970). Punishment, arousal, and avoidance learning in sociopaths. *Journal of Abnormal Psychology, 76*, 443–453.

Schneider, N. G. (1987). Nicotine gum in smoking cessation: Rationale, efficacy, and proper use. *Comprehensive Therapy, 13*, 32–37.

Schoenbach, V., Kaplan, B. H., Fredman, L., & Kleinaum, D. G. (1986) Social ties and mortality in Evans County, Georgia. *American Journal of Epidemiology, 123*, 577–591.

Schoeneman, T. J. (1977). The role of mental illness in the European witch-hunts of the sixteenth and seventeenth centuries: An assessment. *Journal of the History of the Behavioral Sciences, 13*, 337–351.

Schooler, C., & Spohn, H. E. (1982). Social dysfunction and treatment failure in schizophrenia. *Schizophrenia Bulletin, 8*, 85–98.

Schover, L. R. (1981). Unpublished research. As cited in Spector & Carey (1990).

Schuckit, M. A. (1983). The genetics of alcoholism. In B. Tabakoff, P. B. Sulker, & C. L. Randall (Eds.), *Medical and social aspects of alcohol use.* New York: Plenum.

Schuckit, M. A. (1994). Low level of response to alcohol as a predictor of future alcoholism. *American Journal of Psychiatry, 151*, 184–189.

Schuckit, M. A., & Gold, E. O. (1988). A simultaneous evaluation of multiple ethanol challenges to sons of alcoholics and controls. *Archives of General Psychiatry, 45,* 211–216.

Schuckit, M. A., Klein, J., Twitchell, G., & Smith, T. (1994). Personality test scores as predictors of alcoholism almost a decade later. *American Journal of Psychiatry, 151,* 1038–1042.

Schuckit, M. A., & Moore, M. A. (1979). Drug problems in the elderly. In O. J. Kaplan (Ed.), *Psychopathology of aging.* New York: Academic Press.

Schulz, R., & Williamson, G. M. (1991). A two-year longitudinal study of depression among Alzheimer's caregivers. *Psychology and Aging, 6,* 569–578.

Schwartz, J. L. (1987). *Review and evaluation of smoking cessation methods: The United States and Canada 1978–1985* (NIH Publication No. 87–2940). U.S. Department of Health and Human Services, National Institutes of Health.

Schwartz, M. S. (1946). *The economic and spatial mobility of paranoid schizophrenics.* Unpublished master's thesis, University of Chicago.

Schwartz, R., & Schwartz, L. J. (1980). *Becoming a couple.* Englewood Cliffs, NJ: Prentice-Hall.

Schweizer, E., Rickels, K., Case, W. G., & Greenblatt, D. J. (1990). Long-term therapeutic use of benzodiazepines: Effects of gradual taper. *Archives of General Psychiatry, 47,* 908–915.

Schwitzgebel, R. L., & Schwitzgebel, R. K. (1980). *Law and psychological practice.* New York: Wiley.

Scientific perspectives on cocaine abuse. (1987). *Pharmacologist, 29,* 20–27.

Scogin, F., & McElreath, L. (1994). Efficacy of psychosocial treatments for geriatric depression: A quantitative review. *Journal of Consulting and Clinical Psychology, 62,* 69–74.

Searles, J. S. (1993). Science and fascism: Confronting unpopular ideas. *Addictive Behaviors, 18,* 5–8.

Seeman, T. E., & Syme, S. L. (1987). Social networks and coronary artery disease: A comparison of the structure and function of social relations as predictors of disease. *Psychosomatic Medicine, 49,* 381–406.

Segraves, R. T. (1990). Theoretical orientations in the treatment of marital discord. In F. D. Fincham & T. N. Bradbury (Eds.), *The psychology of marriage: Basic issues and applications* (pp. 281–298). New York: Guilford.

Segrin, C., & Abramson, L. Y. (1994). Negative reactions to depressive behaviors: A communication theories analysis. *Journal of Abnormal Psychology, 103,* 655–668.

Seligman, M. E. P. (1974). Depression and learned helplessness. In R. J. Friedman & M. M. Katz (Eds.), *The psychology of depression: Contemporary theory and research.* Washington, DC: Winston-Wiley.

Seligman, M. E. P., & Hager, M. (Eds.). (1972). *Biological boundaries of learning.* New York: Appleton-Century-Crofts.

Selling, L. S. (1940). *Men against madness.* New York: Greenberg.

Selye, H. (1950). *The physiology and pathology of exposure to stress.* Montreal: Acta.

Settin, J. M. (1982). Clinical judgment in geropsychology practice. *Psychotherapy: Theory, Research and Practice, 19,* 397–404.

Shader, R. I., Caine, E. D., & Meyer, R. E. (1975). Treatment of dependence on barbiturates and sedative hypnotics. In R. I. Shader (Ed.), *Manual of psychiatric therapeutics: Practical psychopharmacology and psychiatry.* Boston: Little, Brown.

Shadish, W. R., Montgomery, L. M., Wilson, P., Wilson, M. R., Bright, I., & Okwumabua, T. (1993). Effects of family and marital psychotherapies: A meta-analysis. *Journal of Consulting and Clinical Psychology, 61,* 992–1002.

Shaffer, D., Gould, M., & Hicks, R. C. (1994). Worsening suicide rate in black teenagers. *American Journal of Psychiatry, 151,* 1810–1812.

Shaw, B. F. (1984). Specification of the training and evaluation of cognitive therapists for outcome studies. In J. B. W. Williams & R. L.

Spitzer (Eds.), *Psychotherapy research: Where are we and where should we go?* New York: Guilford.

Shea, M. T., Elkin, I., Imber, S. D., Sotsky, S. M., Watkins, J. T., Collins, J. F., Pilkonis, P. A., Beckham, E., Glass, D. R., Dolan, R. T., & Parloff, M. B. (1992). Course of depressive symptoms over follow-up: Findings from the National Institute of Mental Health Treatment of Depression Collaborative Research Program. *Archives of General Psychiatry, 49,* 782–787.

Shea, M. T., Widiger, T. A., & Klein, M. H. (1992). Comorbidity of personality disorders and depression: Implications for treatment. *Journal of Consulting and Clinical Psychology, 60,* 857–868.

Shedler, J., & Block, J. (1990). Adolescent drug use and psychological health: A longitudinal inquiry. *American Psychologist, 45,* 612–630.

Shedler, J., Mayman, M., & Manis, M. (1993). The illusion of mental health. *American Psychologist, 48,* 1117–1131.

Sher, K. J., Frost, R. O., Kushner, M., Crew, T. M., & Alexander, J. E. (1989). Memory deficits in compulsive checkers in a clinical sample. *Behaviour Research and Therapy, 27,* 65–69.

Sher, K. J., & Levenson, R. W. (1982). Risk for alcoholism and individual differences in the stress-response-dampening effects of alcohol. *Journal of Abnormal Psychology, 91,* 350–367.

Sher, K. J., Walitzer, K. S., Wood, P. K., & Brent, E. F. (1991). Characteristics of children of alcoholics: Putative risk factors, substance use and abuse, and psychopathology. *Journal of Abnormal Psychology, 100,* 427–448.

Shneidman, E. S. (1973). Suicide. In *Encyclopedia Britannica.* Chicago: Encyclopedia Britannica.

Shneidman, E. S. (1976). A psychological theory of suicide. *Psychiatric Annals, 6,* 51–66.

Shneidman, E. S. (1985). *Definition of suicide.* New York: Wiley.

Shneidman, E. S. (1987). A psychological approach to suicide. In G. R. VandenBos & B. K. Bryant (Eds.), *Cataclysms, crises, and catastrophes: Psychology in action.* Washington, DC: American Psychological Association.

Shneidman, E. S., & Farberow, N. L. (1970). A psychological approach to the study of suicide notes. In E. S. Shneidman, N. L. Farberow, & R. E. Litman (Eds.), *The psychology of suicide.* New York: Jason Aronson.

Shneidman, E. S., Farberow, N. L., & Litman, R. E. (Eds.). (1970). *The psychology of suicide.* New York: Jason Aronson.

Shoham-Salomon, V., Avner, R., & Neeman, R. (1989). You're changed if you do and changed if you don't: Mechanisms underlying paradoxical interventions. *Journal of Consulting and Clinical Psychology, 57,* 590–598.

Shrout, P. E., Link, B. G., Dohrenwend, B. P., Skodol, A. E., Stueve, A., & Mirotznik, J. (1989). Characterizing life events as risk factors for depression: The role of fateful loss events. *Journal of Abnormal Psychology, 98,* 460–467.

Shweder, R. A., & Sullivan, M. A. (1990). The semiotic subject of cultural psychology. In L. A. Pervin (Ed.), *Handbook of personality: Theory and research* (pp. 399–416). New York: Guilford.

Siegel, J. M., Sorenson, S. B., Golding, J. M., Burnam, M. A., & Stein, J. A. (1987). The prevalence of childhood sexual assault: The Los Angeles Epidemiological Catchment Area Project. *American Journal of Epidemiology, 126,* 1141–1153.

Siegler, I. C., & Costa, P. T., Jr. (1985). Health behavior relationships. In J. E. Birren & K. W. Schaie (Eds.), *Handbook of the psychology of aging* (2nd ed.). New York: Van Nostrand-Reinhold.

Siever, L. J., Silverman, J. M., Horvath, T. B., Klar, H., Loccaro, E., Keefe, R., Pinkham, N., Rinaldi, P., Mohs, R., & Davis, K. (1990). Increased morbid risk for schizophrenia-related disorders in relatives of schizotypal personality disordered patients. *Archives of General Psychiatry, 47,* 634–640.

Sigman, M., Ungerer, J. A., Mundy, P., & Sherman, T. (1987). Cognition in autistic children. In D. J. Cohen, A. M. Donnellan, & R. Paul

(Eds.), *Handbook of autism and pervasive developmental disorders* (pp. 103–120). New York: Wiley.

Silberman, E. K., Reus, V. I., Jimerson, D. C., Lynott, A. M., & Post, R. M. (1981). Heterogeneity of amphetamine response in depressed patients. *American Journal of Psychiatry, 138,* 1302–1307.

Silverman, K., Evans, S. M., Strain, E. C., & Griffiths, R. R. (1992). Withdrawal syndrome after the double-blind cessation of caffeine consumption. *New England Journal of Medicine, 327,* 1109–1114.

Silverstein, C. (1972). *Behavior modification and the gay community.* Paper presented at the annual convention of the Association for Advancement of Behavior Therapy, New York.

Sisson, R. W., & Azrin, N. H. (1989). The community-reinforcement approach. In R. K. Hester & W. R. Miller (Eds.), *Handbook of alcoholism treatment approaches: Effective alternatives* (pp. 242–258). New York: Pergamon.

Skinner, B. F. (1953). *Science and human behavior.* New York: Macmillan.

Sklar, L. A., & Anisman, H. (1979). Stress and coping factors influence tumor growth. *Science, 205,* 513–515.

Slater, E. (1961). The thirty-fifth Maudsley lecture: Hysteria 311. *Journal of Mental Science, 107,* 358–381.

Slater, E., & Glithero, E. (1965). A followup of patients diagnosed as suffering from hysteria. *Journal of Psychosomatic Research, 9,* 9–13.

Slavson, S. R. (1950). *Analytic group psychotherapy with children, adolescents and adults.* New York: Columbia University Press.

Sloane, R. B. (1980). Organic brain syndrome. In J. E. Birren & R. B. Sloane (Eds.), *Handbook of mental health and aging.* Englewood Cliffs, NJ: Prentice-Hall.

Small, G. W., Kuhl, D. E., Riege, W. H., Fujikawa, D. G., Ashford, J. W., Metter, E. J., & Mazziotta, J. C. (1989). Cerebral glucose metabolic patterns in Alzheimer's disease: Effects of gender and age at dementia onset. *Archives of General Psychiatry, 46,* 527–533.

Smith, B., & Sechrest, L. (1991). Treatment of aptitude X treatment interactions. *Journal of Consulting and Clinical Psychology, 59,* 233–244.

Smith, D. (1982). Trends in counseling and psychotherapy. *American Psychologist, 37,* 802–809.

Smith, M. L., Glass, G., & Miller, T. (1980). *The benefits of psychotherapy.* Baltimore: Johns Hopkins University Press.

Smith, S. S. & Newman, J. P. (1990). Alcohol and drug dependence in psychopathic and nonpsychopathic criminal offenders. *Journal of Abnormal Psychology, 99,* 430–439.

Smith, T. W. (1989). Assessment in rational-emotive therapy: Empirical access to the ABCD model. In M. E. Bernard & R. DiGiuseppe (Eds.), *Inside rational-emotive therapy: A critical appraisal of the theory and therapy of Albert Ellis* (pp. 135–153). San Diego, CA: Academic Press.

Smith, T. W. (1992). Hostility and health: Current status of a psychosomatic hypothesis. *Health Psychology, 11,* 139–150.

Smyer, M. A., Zarit, S. H., & Qualls, S. H. (1990). Psychological interventions with the aging individual. In J. E. Birren & K. W. Schaie (Eds.), *Handbook of the psychology of aging* (3rd ed., pp. 375–403). New York: Academic Press.

Snyder, D. K., & Wills, R. M. (1989). Behavioral versus insight-oriented marital therapy: Effects of individual and interspousal functioning. *Journal of Consulting and Clinical Psychology, 57,* 39–46.

Snyder, S. H., Banerjee, S. P., Yamamora, H. I., & Greenberg, D. (1974). Drugs, neurotransmitters, and schizophrenia. *Science, 184,* 1243–1253.

Sobell, L. C., Toneatto, A., & Sobell, M. B. (1990). Behavior therapy. In A. S. Bellack & M. Hersen (Eds.), *Handbook of comparative treatments for adult disorders* (pp. 479–505). New York: Wiley.

Sobell, M. B., & Sobell, L. C. (1976). Second-year treatment outcome of alcoholics treated by individualized behavior therapy: Results. *Behaviour Research and Therapy, 14,* 195–215.

Sobell, M. B., & Sobell, L. C. (1978). *Behavioral treatment of alcohol problems: Individualized therapy and controlled drinking.* New York: Plenum.

Sonda, P., Mazo, R., & Chancellor, M. B. (1990). The role of yohimbine for the treatment of erectile impotence. *Journal of Sex and Marital Therapy, 16,* 15–21.

Sorenson, S. B., & Brown, V. B. (1990). Interpersonal violence and crisis intervention on the college campus. *New Directions for Student Services, 49,* 57–66.

Span, P. (1993, July 8). The politics of a very bad mood: After tomorrow, many women may be told they're plain crazy. *The Washington Post,* pp. C1–C2.

Spangler, D. L., Simons, A. D., Monroe, S. M., & Thase, M. E. (1993). Evaluating the hopelessness model of depression: Diathesis-stress and symptom components. *Journal of Abnormal Psychology, 102,* 592–600.

Spanos, N. P. (1978). Witchcraft in histories of psychiatry: A critical analysis and an alternative conceptualization. *Psychological Bulletin, 85,* 417–439.

Spanos, N. P. (1994). Multiple identity enactments and multiple personality disorder: A sociocognitive perspective. *Psychological Bulletin, 116,* 143–165.

Sparrow, S. S., Balla, D. A., & Cicchetti, D. V. (1984). *Vineland Adaptive Behavior Scales.* Circle Pines, MI: American Guidance Service.

Spector, I. P., & Carey, M. P. (1990). Incidence and prevalence of the sexual dysfunctions: A critical review of the empirical literature. *Archives of Sexual Behavior, 19,* 389–408.

Spence, D. P. (1982). *Narrative truth and historical truth: Meaning and interpretation in psychoanalysis.* New York: Norton.

Spengler, A. (1977). Manifest sadomasochism of males: Results of an empirical study. *Archives of Sexual Behavior, 6,* 441–456 .

Spiegel, D. (1990). Can psychotherapy prolong cancer survival? *Psychosomatics, 31,* 361–366.

Spiegel, D., Bloom, J. R., Kraemer, H. C., & Gottheil, E. (1989). Effect of psychosocial treatment on survival of patients with metastatic breast cancer. *Lancet, 2,* 888–891.

Spiegel, D., Bloom, J. R., & Yalom, I. (1981). Group support for patients with metastatic cancer: A randomized prospective outcome study. *Archives of General Psychiatry, 38,* 527–534.

Spiess, W. F. J., Geer, J. H., & O'Donohue, W. T. (1984). Premature ejaculation: Investigation of factors in ejaculatory latency. *Journal of Abnormal Psychology, 93,* 242–245.

Spinetta, J. J. (1980). Disease-related communication: How to tell. In J. Kenerman (Ed.), *Psychological aspects of childhood cancer.* Springfield, IL: Charles C. Thomas.

Spitzer, R. L., Endicott, J., & Gibbon, M. (1979). Crossing the border into borderline personality and borderline schizophrenia. *Archives of General Psychiatry, 36,* 17–24.

Spitzer, R. L., Skodol, A. E., Gibbon, M., & Williams, J. B. W. (1981) *DSM-III casebook.* Washington, DC: American Psychiatric Press.

Spitzer, R. L., Williams, J. B. W., Gibbon, M., & First, M. B. (1992). The Structured Clinical Interview for DSM-III-R (SCID): I. History, rationale, and description. *Archives of General Psychiatry, 49,* 624–629.

Sprock, J., & Blashfield, R. K. (1991). Classification and nosology. In M. Hersen, A. E. Kazdin, & A. S. Bellack (Eds.), *The clinical psychology handbook* (2nd ed., pp. 329–344). Elmsford, NY: Pergamon.

Stacy, A. W., Newcomb, M. D., & Bentler, P. M. (1991). Cognitive motivation and drug use: A nine-year longitudinal study. *Journal of Abnormal Psychology, 100,* 502–515.

Stall, R. D., McKusick, L., Wiley, J., Coates, T., & Ostrow, D. (1986). Alcohol and drug use during sexual activity and compliance with safe sex guidelines for AIDS: The AIDS Behavioral Research Project. *Health Education Quarterly, 13,* 359–371.

Steadman, H. J. (1979). *Beating a rap: Defendants found incompetent to stand trial.* Chicago: University of Chicago Press.

Steele, C. M., & Josephs, R. A. (1988). Drinking your troubles away:

II. An attention-allocation model of alcohol's effects on psychological stress. *Journal of Abnormal Psychology, 97,* 196–205.

Steffenberg, S., Gillberg, C., Hellgren, L., Andersson, L., Gillberg, I. C., Jakobssohn, G., & Bohman, M. (1989). A twin study of autism in Denmark, Finland, Iceland, Norway and Sweden. *Journal of Child Psychology and Psychiatry and Allied Disciplines, 30,* 405–416.

Stephens, B. J. (1985). Suicidal women and their relationships with husbands, boyfriends, and lovers. *Suicide and Life-Threatening Behavior, 15,* 77–89.

Steptoe, A. (1984). Psychological aspects of bronchial asthma. In S. Rachman (Ed.), *Contributions to medical psychology* (Vol. 3, pp. 7–32). Elmsford, NY: Pergamon.

Steuer, J. L. (1982). Psychotherapy with older women: Ageism and sexism in traditional practice. *Psychotherapy: Theory, research and practice, 19,* 429–436.

Stevenson, J., & Jones, I. H. (1972). Behavior therapy technique for exhibitionism: A preliminary report. *Archives of General Psychiatry, 27,* 839–841.

Stone, A. A. (1975). *Mental health and law: A system in transition.* Rockville, MD: National Institute of Mental Health.

Stone, A. A., Cox, D. S., Valdimarsdottir, H., Jandorf, L., & Neale, J. M. (1987). Evidence that secretory IgA antibody is associated with daily mood. *Journal of Personality and Social Psychology, 52,* 988–993.

Stone, A. A., & Neale, J. M. (1982). Development of a methodology for assessing daily experiences. In A. Baum and J. Singer (Eds.), *Environment and health.* Hillsdale, NJ: Erlbaum.

Stone, A. A., & Neale, J. M. (1984). The effects of "severe" daily events on mood. *Journal of Personality and Social Psychology, 46,* 137–144.

Stone, A. A., Reed, B. R., & Neale, J. M. (1987). Changes in daily event frequency precede episodes of physical symptoms. *Journal of Human Stress, 13,* 70–74.

Stone, M. H. (1986). Exploratory psychotherapy in schizophrenia-spectrum patients: A reevaluation in the light of long-term follow-up of schizophrenic and borderline patients. *Bulletin of the Menninger Clinic, 50,* 287–306.

Stone, M. H. (1987) Psychotherapy of borderline patients in light of long-term follow-up. *Bulletin of the Menninger Clinic, 51,* 231–247.

Stone, M. H., Hurt, S. W., & Stone, D. K. (1987). The PI 500: Long-term follow-up of borderline inpatients meeting DSM-III criteria: I. Global outcome. *Journal of Personality Disorders, 1,* 291–298.

Strauss, J., Doyle, A. E., & Kreipe, R. E. (1994). The paradoxical effect of diet commercials on reinhibition of dietary restraint. *Journal of Abnormal Psychology, 103,* 441–444.

Stringer, A. Y., & Josef, N. C. (1983). Methylphenidate in the treatment of aggression in two patients with antisocial personality disorder. *American Journal of Psychiatry, 140,* 1365–1366.

Strong, R., Huang, J. S., Huang, S. S., Chung, H. D., Hale, C., & Burke, W. J. (1991). Degeneration of the cholinergic innervation of the locus ceruleus in Alzheimer's disease. *Brain Research, 542,* 23–28.

Strub, R. L., & Black, F. W. (1981). *Organic brain syndromes: An introduction to neurobehavioral disorders.* Philadelphia: F.A. Davis.

Stuart, I. R., & Greer, J. G. (Eds.). (1984). *Victims of sexual aggression: Treatment of children, women and men.* New York: Van Nostrand-Reinhold.

Stuart, R. B. (1976). An operant interpersonal program for couples. In D. H. L. Olson (Ed.), *Treating relationships.* Lake Mills, IA: Graphic Publishing Company.

Stunkard, A., Sorensen, T., & Schulsinger, F. (1983). Use of the Danish Adoption Register for the study of obesity and thinness. In S. Kety (Ed.), *The genetics of neurological and psychiatric disorders.* New York: Raven Press.

Sturgis, E. T., & Adams, H. E. (1978). The right to treatment: Issues in the treatment of homosexuality. *Journal of Consulting and Clinical Psychology, 46,* 165–169.

Suddath, R. L., Christison, G. W., Torrey, E. F., Cassanova, M. F., & Weinberger, D. R. (1990). Anatomical abnormalities in the brains of monozygotic twins discordant for schizophrenia. *New England Journal of Medicine, 322,* 789–793.

Sue, D. W., & Sue, D. (1992). *Counseling the culturally different* (2nd ed.). New York: Wiley.

Sue, S., Zane, N., & Young, K. (1994). Research on psychotherapy with culturally diverse populations. In A. E. Bergin & S. L. Garfield (Eds.), *Handbook of psychotherapy and behavior change* (4th ed., pp. 783–817). New York: Wiley.

Suppes, T., Baldessarini, R. J., Faedda, G. L., & Tohen, M. (1991). Risk of recurrence following discontinuation of lithium treatment in bipolar disorder. *Archives of General Psychiatry, 48,* 1082–1088.

Sussman, S. S., Dent, C. W., Stacy, A. W., Burciaga, C., Raynor, A., Turner, G. E., Charlin, V., Craig, S., Hansen, W. B., Burton, D., & Flay, B. R. (1990). Peer-group association and adolescent tobacco use. *Journal of Abnormal Psychology, 99,* 349–352.

Sutcliffe, J. P., & Jones, J. (1962). Personal identity, multiple personality, and hypnosis. *International Journal of Clinical and Experimental Hypnosis, 10,* 231–269.

Swartz, M., Blazer, D., George, L., & Winfield, I. (1990). Estimating the prevalence of borderline personality in the community. *Journal of Personality Disorders, 1990,* 257–272.

Sweeney, P. D., Anderson, K., & Bailey, S. (1986). Attributional style in depression: A meta-analytic review. *Journal of Personality and Social Psychology, 50,* 974–991.

Sweet, J. J., Carr , M. A., Rossini, E., & Kasper, C. (1986). Relationship between the Luria–Nebraska Neuropsychological Battery and the WISC-R: Further examination using Kaufman's factors. *International Journal of Clinical Neuropsychology, 8,* 177–180.

Syndulko, K. (1978). Electrocortical investigations of sociopathy. In R.D. Hare & D. Schalling (Eds.), *Psychopathic behaviour: Approaches to research.* New York: Wiley.

Szasz, T. S. (Ed.). (1974). *The age of madness: The history of involuntary hospitalization.* New York: Jason Aronson.

Szasz, T. (1986). The case against suicide prevention. *American Psychologist, 41,* 806–812.

Tanzi, R. E., Gusella, F., Watkins, P. C., Bruns, G. A. P., St. George-Hyslop, P., Van Keunen, M. L., Patterson, D., Pagan, S., Kurnit, D. M., & Neve, R. L. (1987). Amyloid B protein gene: cDNA, mRNA distribution, and genetic linkage near the Alzheimer locus. *Science, 235,* 880–884.

Teicher, M. H., Glod, C., & Cole, J. O. (1990). Emergence of intense suicidal preoccupation during fluoxetine treatment. *American Journal of Psychiatry, 147,* 207–210.

Tennant, F., & Rawson, R. A. (1982). Cocaine and amphetamine dependence treated with desipramine. In *Problems of drug dependence.* Washington, DC: National Institute of Drug Abuse.

Teri, L., & Lewinsohn, P. M. (1986). Individual and group treatment of unipolar depression: Comparison of treatment outcome and identification of predictors of successful treatment outcome. *Behavior Therapy, 17,* 215–228.

Theodor, L. H., & Mandelcorn, M. S. (1973). Hysterical blindness: A case report and study using a modern psychophysical technique. *Journal of Abnormal Psychology, 82,* 552–553.

Thibaut, J. W., & Kelley, H. H. (1959). *The social psychology of groups.* New York: Wiley.

Thompson, G. O. B., Raab, G. M., Hepburn, W. S., Hunter, R., Fulton, M. & Laxen, D. P. H. (1989). Blood-lead levels and children's behaviour—Results from the Edinburgh lead study. *Journal of Child Psychology and Psychiatry, 30,* 515–528.

Thompson, L. W., Gallagher, D., & Breckenridge, J. S. (1987). Comparative effectiveness of psychotherapies for depressed elders. *Journal of Consulting and Clinical Psychology, 55*, 385–390.

Thoresen, C. E., Friedman, M., Powell, L. H., Gill, J. J., & Ulmer, D. K. (1985). Altering the type A behavior pattern in postinfarction patients. *Journal of Cardiopulmonary Rehabilitation, 5*, 258–266.

Thoresen, C. E., & Graff-Low, K. (1991). Women and the Type A behavior pattern: Review and commentary. In M. Strube (Ed.), *Type A behavior.* (pp. 117–133). Newberry Park, CA: Sage.

Thorndike, R. L., Hagen, E. P., & Sattler, J. M. (1986). *The Stanford–Binet Intelligence Scale: Fourth edition, guide for administering and scoring.* Chicago: Riverside.

Thyer, B. A., & Curtis, G. C. (1984). The effects of ethanol on phobic anxiety. *Behaviour Research and Therapy, 22*, 599–610.

Tienari, P., Sorri, A., Lahti, I., Naarala, M. N., Wahlberg, E., Moring, J., Pohjola, J., & Wynne, L. C. (1987). Genetic and psychosocial factors in schizophrenia: The Finnish adoptive family study. *Schizophrenia Bulletin, 13*, 477–484.

Tillich, P. (1952). *The courage to be.* New Haven, CT: Yale University Press.

Tobler, N. (1986). Meta-analysis of 143 adolescent drug prevention programs: Quantitative outcome results of program participants compared to a control or comparison group. *Journal of Drug Issues, 16*, 537–568.

Tollefson, G. D., Rampey, A. H., Jr., Enas, G. G., & Potvin, J. H. (1993). Does pharmacotherapy induce paradoxical worsening in some patients? *Depression, 1*, 105–107.

Torgersen, S. (1983). Genetic factors in anxiety disorders. *Archives of General Psychiatry, 40*, 1085–1089.

Torgersen, S. (1986). Genetics of somatoform disorder. *Archives of General Psychiatry, 43*, 502–505.

Trimble, J. E. (1994). Cultural variations in the use of alcohol and drugs. In W. J. Lonner & R. Malpass (Eds.), *Psychology and culture* (pp. 79–84). Boston: Allyn & Bacon.

True, W. R., Rice, J., Eisen, S. A., Health, A. C., Goldberg, J., Lyons, M. J., & Nowak, J. (1993). A twin study of genetic and environmental contributions to liability for posttraumatic stress symptoms. *Archives of General Psychiatry, 50*, 257–264.

Trull, T. J., Widiger, T. A., & Frances, A. (1987). Covariation of criteria for avoidant, schizoid, and dependent personality disorders. *American Journal of Psychiatry, 144*, 767–771.

Trull, T. J., Widiger, T. A., & Guthrie, P. (1990). Categorical versus dimensional status of borderline personality disorder. *Journal of Abnormal Psychology, 99*, 40–48.

Tsoi, W. F. (1990). Developmental profile of 200 male and 100 female transsexuals in Singapore. *Archives of Sexual Behavior, 19*, 595–605.

Tucker, J. A., Vuchinich, R. E., & Downey, K. K. (1992). Substance abuse. In S. M. Turner, K. S. Calhoun, & H. E. Adams (Eds.), *Handbook of clinical behavior therapy* (pp. 203–223). New York: Wiley.

Turkat, I. D., & Maisto, S. A. (1985). Personality disorders: Application of the experimental method to the formulation and modification of personality disorders. In D. H. Barlow (Ed.), *Clinical handbook of psychological disorders.* New York: Guilford.

Turner, R. J., & Wagonfeld, M. O. (1967). Occupational mobility and schizophrenia. *American Sociological Review, 32*, 104–113.

Turner, S. M., Beidel, D. C., & Jacob, R. G. (1994). Social phobia: A comparison of behavior therapy and atenolol. *Journal of Consulting and Clinical Psychology, 62*, 350–358.

Turner, S. M., Beidel, D. C., & Townsley, R. M. (1992). Behavioral treatment of social phobia. In S. M. Turner, K. S. Calhoun, & H. E. Adams (Eds.), *Handbook of clinical behavior therapy* (2nd ed., pp. 13–37). New York: Wiley.

Uba, L. (1994). *Asian Americans: Personality patterns, identity, and mental health.* New York: Guilford Press.

Upper, D., & Ross, S. M. (Eds.). (1980). *Behavioral group therapy 1980: An annual review.* Champaign, IL: Research Press.

U.S. Bureau of the Census. (1986). *Statistical brief.* Washington, DC: U.S. Government Printing Office.

U.S. Department of Health and Human Services. (1989). *Reducing the health consequences of smoking: 25 years of progress. A report of the surgeon general, executive summary* (DHHS Publication No. CDC 89–8411). Washington, DC: U.S. Government Printing Office.

U.S. Department of Health and Human Services, National Center for Health Statistics. (1990, August). *Monthly vital statistics.* Hyattsville, MD.

U.S. Environmental Protection Agency, Office of Health and Environmental Assessment, Office of Research and Development. (1992). *Respiratory health effects of passive smoking: Lung cancer and other disorders.* Washington, DC: Author.

Vaillant, G. E. (1979). Natural history of male psychologic health: Effects of mental health on physical health. *New England Journal of Medicine, 301*, 1249–1254.

Vaillant, G. E. (1983). *The natural history of alcoholism: Causes, patterns, and paths to recovery.* Cambridge, MA: Harvard University Press.

Vaillant, G. E. (1994). Ego mechanisms of defense and personality psychopathology. *Journal of Abnormal Psychology, 103*, 44–50.

Van Kammen, D. P., Bunney, W. E., Docherty, J. P., Jimerson, D. C., Post, R. M., Sivis, S., Ebart, M., & Gillin, J. C. (1977). Amphetamine-induced catecholamine activation in schizophrenia and depression. *Advances in Biochemical Psychopharmacology, 16*, 655–659.

Van Kammen, D. P., Hommer, D. W., & Malas, K. L. (1987). Effects of pimozide on positive and negative symptoms in schizophrenic patients: Are negative symptoms state dependent? *Neuropsychobiology, 18*, 113–117.

Van Kammen, W. B., Loeber, R., & Stouthamer-Loeber, M. (1991). Substance use and its relationship to conduct problems and delinquency in young boys. *Journal of Youth and Adolescence, 20*, 399–413.

Van Putten, T., May, P. R. A., Marder, S. R., & Wittman, L. A. (1981). Subjective response to antipsychotic drugs. *Archives of General Psychiatry, 38*, 187–190.

Varner, R. V., & Gaitz, C. M. (1982). Schizophrenic and paranoid disorders in the aged. In L. F. Jarvik & G. W. Small (Eds.), *Psychiatric clinics of North America.* Philadelphia: Saunders.

Ventura, J., Neuchterlein, K. H., Lukoff, D., & Hardesty, J. D. (1989). A prospective study of stressful life events and schizophrenic relapse. *Journal of Abnormal Psychology, 98*, 407–411.

Viederman, M. (1986). Somatoform and factitious disorders. In A. M. Cooper, A. J. Frances, & M. H. Sacks (Eds.), *The personality disorders and neuroses.* Philadelphia: Lippincott.

Vitousek, K., & Manke, F. (1994). Personality variables and disorders in anorexia nervosa and bulimia nervosa. *Journal of Abnormal Psychology, 103*, 137–147.

Vogt, T., Mullooly, J., Ernst, D., Pope, C., & Hollis, J. (1992). Social networks as predictors of ischemic heart disease, cancer, stroke and hypertension: Incidence, survival and mortality. *Journal of Clinical Epidemiology, 45*, 659–666.

Volkmar, F., & Cohen, D. J. (1985). The experience of infantile autism: A first-person account by Tony W. *Journal of Autism and Developmental Disorders, 15*, 47–54.

von Krafft-Ebing, R. (1902). *Psychopathia sexualis.* Brooklyn, NY: Physicians and Surgeons Books.

Vredenburg, K., Flett, G. L., & Krames, L. (1993). Analogue versus clinical depression: A critical reappraisal. *Psychological Bulletin, 113*, 327–344.

Wachtel, P. L. (1977). *Psychoanalysis and behavior therapy: Toward an integration.* New York: Basic Books.

Wachtel, P. L. (1982). Vicious circles: The self and the rhetoric of emerging and unfolding. *Contemporary Psychoanalysis, 18*, 259–273.

Wade, C., & Travis, C. (1994). The longest war: Gender and culture. In

W. J. Lonner & R. Malpass (Eds.), *Psychology and culture* (pp. 121–126). Boston: Allyn & Bacon.

Wahl, O. F., & Harrman, C. R. (1989). Family views of stigma. *Schizophrenia Bulletin, 15,* 131–139.

Wakefield, J. (1992). Disorder as dysfunction: A conceptual critique of DSM-III-R's definition of mental disorder. *Psychological Review, 99,* 232–247.

Waldinger, R. J., & Gunderson, J. G. (1984). Completed psychotherapies with borderline patients. *American Journal of Psychotherapy, 38,* 190–202.

Walen, S., Hauserman, N. M., & Lavin, P. J. (1977). *Clinical guide to behavior therapy.* Baltimore: William & Wilkins.

Wallace, J. (1993). Fascism and the eye of the beholder: A reply to J. S. Searles on the controlled intoxication issue. *Addictive Behaviors, 18,* 239–251.

Walsh, D. C., & Hingson, R. W. (1991). A randomized trial of treatment options for alcohol abusing workers. *New England Journal of Medicine, 325,* 775–782.

Ward, C. H., Beck, A. T., Mendelson, M., Mock, E., & Erbaugh, J. K. (1962). The psychiatric nomenclature: Reasons for diagnostic disagreement. *Archives of General Psychiatry, 7,* 198–205.

Warheit, G. J., Arey, S. A., & Swanson, E. (1976). Patterns of drug use: An epidemiologic overview. *Journal of Drug Issues, 6,* 223–237.

Warshaw, R. (1988). *I never called it rape.* New York: Harper & Row.

Washton, A. M., Stone, N. S., & Hendrickson, E. C. (1988). Cocaine abuse. In D. M. Donovan & G. A. Marlatt (Eds.), *Assessment of addictive behaviors* (pp. 364–389). New York: Guilford.

Waskow, I. E. (1984). Specification of the technique variable in the NIMH Treatment of Depression Collaborative Research Program. In J. B. W. Williams & R. L. Spitzer (Eds.), *Psychotherapy research: Where are we and where should we go?* New York: Guilford.

Watkins, J. T., Leber, W. R., Imber, S. D., Collins, J. F., Elkin, I., Pilkonis, P. A., Sotsky, S. M., Shea, M. T., & Glass, D. R. (1993). Temporal course of change of depression. *Journal of Consulting and Clinical Psychology, 61,* 858–864.

Watson, J. B. (1913). Psychology as the behaviorist views it. *Psychological Review, 20,* 158–177.

Watson, J. B., & Rayner, R. (1920). Conditioned emotional reactions. *Journal of Experimental Psychology, 3,* 1–14.

Watts, F. N., Trezise, L., & Sharrock, R. (1986). Processing of phobic stimuli. *British Journal of Clinical Psychology, 25,* 253–259.

Watzlawick, P., Beavin, J., & Jackson, D. D. (1967). *Pragmatics of human communication: A study of interactional patterns, pathologies, and paradoxes.* New York: Norton.

Wechsler, D. (1968). *Escala de Inteligencia Wechsler para Adultos.* New York: Psychological Corporation.

Wegner, D. M., Schneider, D. J., Carter, S. R., & White, T. L. (1987). Paradoxical effects of thought suppression. *Journal of Personality and Social Psychology, 53,* 5–13.

Weidner, G., & Collins, R. L. (1993). Gender, coping, and health. In H. W. Krohne (Ed.), *Attention and avoidance: Strategies in coping with aversiveness.* (pp. 241–265). Gottingen, Federal Republic of Germany: Hogrefe & Huber Publishers.

Weinberger, D. R. (1987). Implications of normal brain development for the pathogenesis of schizophrenia. *Archives of General Psychiatry, 44,* 660–669.

Weinberger, D. R., Berman, K. F., & Illowsky, B. P. (1988). Physiological dysfunction of dorsolateral prefrontal cortex in schizophrenia: III. A new cohort and evidence for a monoaminergic mechanism. *Archives of General Psychiatry, 45,* 609–615.

Weinberger, D. R., Cannon-Spoor, H. E., Potkin, S. G., & Wyatt, R. J. (1980). Poor premorbid adjustment and CT scan abnormalities in chronic schizophrenia. *American Journal of Psychiatry, 137,* 1410–1413.

Weinberger, D. R., Wagner, R. L., & Wyatt, R. J. (1983). Neuropathological studies of schizophrenia: A selective review. *Schizophrenia Bulletin, 9,* 193–212.

Weiner, B., Frieze, L., Kukla, A., Reed, L., Rest, S., & Rosenbaum, R. M. (1971). *Perceiving the causes of success and failure.* New York: General Learning Press.

Weintraub, S., Liebert, D. E., & Neale, J. M. (1975). Teacher ratings of children vulnerable to psychopathology. *American Journal of Orthopsychiatry, 45,* 838–845.

Weintraub, S., Prinz, R., & Neale, J. M. (1978). Peer evaluations of the competence of children vulnerable to psychopathology. *Journal of Abnormal Child Psychology, 6,* 461–473.

Weiss, G. (1983). Long-term outcome: Findings, concepts, and practical implications. In M. Rutter (Ed.), *Developmental neuropsychiatry.* New York: Guilford.

Weiss, J. (1990, March). Unconscious mental functioning. *Scientific American, 262,* 103–109.

Weiss, J., & Sampson, H. (1986). *The psychoanalytic process.* New York: Guilford.

Weissman, A. N., & Beck, A. T. (1978). *Development and validation of the Dysfunctional Attitude Scale: A preliminary investigation.* Paper presented at the annual meeting of the American Educational Research Association, Toronto.

Weissman, M. M., Klerman, G. L., & Paykel, E. S. (1971). Clinical evaluation of hostility in depression. *American Journal of Psychiatry, 128,* 261–266.

Weisz, J. R., Suwanlert, S., Chaiyasit, W., & Walter, B. R. (1987). Over- and undercontrolled referral problems among children and adolescents from Thailand and the United States: The *wat* and *wai* of cultural differences. *Journal of Consulting and Clinical Psychology, 55,* 719–726.

Weisz, J. R., Weiss, B., & Donenberg, G. R. (1992). The lab versus the clinic: Effects of child and adolescent psychotherapy. *American Psychologist, 47,* 1578–1585.

Welch, S. L., & Fairburn, C. G. (1994). Sexual abuse and bulimia nervosa: Three integrated case control comparisons. *American Journal of Psychiatry, 151,* 402–407.

Wells, C. E., & Duncan, G. W. (1980). *Neurology for psychiatrists.* Philadelphia: F.A. Davis Co.

Wender, P. H., Kety, S. S., Rosenthal, D., Schulsinger, F., Ortmann, J., & Lunde, I. (1986). Psychiatric disorders in the biological and adoptive families of adopted individuals with affective disorders. *Archives of General Psychiatry, 43,* 923–929.

Westen, D. (1990). Psychoanalytic approaches to personality. In L. A. Pervin (Ed.), *Handbook of personality: Theory and research* (pp. 21–65). New York: Guilford.

Wester, P., Eriksson, S., Forsell, A., Puu, G., & Adolfsson, R. (1988). Monoamine metabolite concentrations and cholinesterase activities in cerebrospinal fluid of progressive dementia patents: Relation to clinical parameters. *Acta Neurologica Scandinavica, 77,* 12–21.

Whalen, C. K., & Henker, B. (1985). The social worlds of hyperactive (ADHD) children. *Clinical Psychology Review, 5,* 447–478.

Whanger, A. D. (1973). Paranoid syndrome of the senium. In E. Eisdorfer & W. E. Fann (Eds.), *Psychopharmacology—Aging.* New York: Plenum.

Whitaker, A., Johnson, J., Shaffer, D., Rapoport, J. L., Kalikow, K., Walsh, B. T., Davies, M., Braiman S., & Dolinsky, A. (1990). Uncommon troubles in young people: Prevalence estimates of selected psychiatric disorders in a nonreferred adolescent population. *Archives of General Psychiatry, 47,* 487–496.

White, J., Davison, G. C., Haaga, D. A. F., & White, K. (1992). Cognitive bias in the articulated thoughts of depressed and nondepressed psychiatric patients. *Journal of Nervous and Mental Disease, 180,* 77–81.

White, K., & Cole, J. O. (1990). Pharmacotherapy. In A. S. Bellack &

M. Hersen (Eds.), *Handbook of comparative treatments for adult disorders* (pp. 266–284). New York: Wiley.

Whitehouse, P. J. (1991). Treatment of Alzheimer disease. *Alzheimer Disease and Associated Disorders, 5*, Suppl. 1, 532–536.

Widiger, T. A., & Costa, P. T., Jr. (1994). Personality and personality disorders. *Journal of Abnormal Psychology, 103*, 78–91.

Widiger, T. A., Frances, A. J., Pincus, H. A., Davis, W. W., & First, M. B. (1991). Toward an empirical classification for the DSM-IV. *Journal of Abnormal Psychology, 100*, 280–288.

Widiger, T. A., Frances, A., Spitzer, R. L., & Williams, J. B. W. (1988). The DSM-III-R personality disorders: An overview. *American Journal of Psychiatry, 145*, 786–795.

Widiger, T. A., Frances, A., & Trull, T. J. (1987). A psychometric analysis of the social-interpersonal and cognitive-perceptual items for the schizotypal personality disorder. *Archives of General Psychiatry, 44*, 741–745.

Widiger, T. A., & Spitzer, R. L. (1991). Sex bias in the diagnosis of personality disorders: Conceptual and methodological issues. *Clinical Psychology Review, 11*, 1–22.

Wikler, A. (1980). *Opioid dependence.* New York: Plenum.

Wilkinson, D. A., Leigh, G. M., Cordingley, J., Martin, G. W., & Lei, H. (1987). Dimensions of multiple drug use and a typology of drug users. *British Journal of Addiction, 82*, 259–273.

Willi, J., & Grossman, S. (1983). Epidemiology of anorexia nervosa in a defined region of Switzerland. *American Journal of Psychiatry, 140*, 564–567.

Williams, G. D., Stinson, F. S., Clem, D., Noble, J. *Apparent per Capita Consumption: National, State and Regional Trends: 1977–1990.* Washington, DC: US Dept of Health and Human Services; 1992:1–17. DHHS publication ADM 281-89-0001. Surveillance report No. 23.

Williams, H., & McNicol, K. N. (1969). Prevalence, natural history and relationship of wheezy bronchitis and asthma in children: An epidemiological study. *British Medical Journal, 4*, 321–325.

Williams, J. B. W., Gibbon, J., First, M. B., Spitzer, R. L., Davies, M., Borus, J., Howes, M. J., Kane, J., Pope, H. G., Rounsaville, B., & Wittchen, H. (1992). The Structured Clinical Interview for DSM-III-R (SCID): II. Multisite test–retest reliability. *Archives of General Psychiatry, 49*, 630–636.

Wilsnak, S. C. (1984). Drinking, sexuality, and sexual dysfunction in women. In S. C. Wilsnak & L. J. Beckman (Eds.), *Alcohol problems in women: Antecedents, consequences, and intervention* (pp. 189–227). New York: Guilford.

Wilson, G. T. (1993). Psychological and pharmacological treatments of bulimia nervosa: A research update. *Applied and Preventive Psychology, 2*, 35–42.

Wilson, G. T., & Davison, G. C. (1971). Processes of fear reduction in systematic desensitization. Animal studies. *Psychological Bulletin, 76*, 1–14.

Wilson, G. T., & Lawson, D. M. (1976). The effects of alcohol on sexual arousal in women. *Journal of Abnormal Psychology, 85*, 489–497.

Wilson, G. T., & O'Leary, K. D. (1980). *Principles of behavior therapy.* Englewood Cliffs, NJ: Prentice-Hall.

Wilson, W. R. (1975). *Unobtrusive induction of positive attitudes.* Unpublished doctoral dissertation, University of Michigan. Ann Arbor, MI.

Wincze, J. P., & Carey, M. P. (1991). *Sexual dysfunction: A guide for assessment and treatment.* New York: Guilford.

Winters, K. C., Weintraub, S., & Neale, J. M. (1981). Validity of MMPI code types in identifying DSM-III schizophrenics, unipolars and bipolars. *Journal of Consulting and Clinical Psychology, 49*, 486–487.

Wiseman, C. V., Gray, J. J., Mosimann, J. E., & Ahrens, A. H. (1992). Cultural expectations of thinness in women: An update. *International Journal of Eating Disorders, 11*, 85–89.

Wiseman, C. V., Gunning, F. M., & Gray, J. J. (1993). Increasing pressure to be thin: 19 years of diet products in television commercials. *Eating Disorders, 1*, 52–61.

Wittchen, H-U., Zhao, S., Kessler, R. C., & Eaton, W. W. (1994). DSM-III-R generalized anxiety disorder in the National Comorbidity Survey. *Archives of General Psychiatry, 51*, 355–364.

Wold, D. A. (1968). *The adjustment of siblings to childhood leukemia.* Unpublished medical thesis, University of Washington, Seattle.

Wolf, A., & Kutash, I. L. (1990). Psychoanalysis in groups. In I. L. Kutash & A. Wolf (Eds.), *The group psychotherapist's handbook: Contemporary theory and technique.* New York: Columbia University Press.

Wolfe, V. V. (1990). Sexual abuse of children. In A. S. Bellack, M. Hersen, & A. E. Kazdin (Eds.), *International handbook of behavior modification and therapy* (2nd ed.). New York: Plenum.

Wolin, S. J. (1980). Introduction: Psychosocial consequences. In *Alcoholism and alcohol abuse among women: Research issues.* Rockville, MD: National Institute on Alcohol Abuse and Alcoholism.

Wolpe, J. (1958). *Psychotherapy by reciprocal inhibition.* Stanford, CA: Stanford University Press.

Wolraich, M., Milich, R., Stumbo, P., & Schultz, F. (1985). The effects of sucrose ingestion on the behavior of hyperactive boys. *Journal of Pediatrics, 106*, 675–682.

Wong, D. F., Wagner, H. N., Tune, L. E., Dannals, R. F., Pearlson, G. D., Links, J. M., Tamminga, C. A., Broussolle, E. P., Ravert, H. T., Wilson, A. A., Toung, J. K. T., Malat, J., Williams, J. A., O'Tuama, L. A., Snyder, S. H., Kuhar, M. J., & Gjedde, A. (1986). Positron emission tomography reveals elevated D_2 dopamine receptors in drug-naive schizophrenics. *Science, 234*, 1558–1562.

Wood, L. F., & Jacobson, N. S. (1985). Marital distress. In D. H. Barlow (Ed.), *Clinical handbook of psychological disorders.* New York: Guilford.

Woods, S. W., Charney, D. S., Goodman, W. K., & Heninger, G. R. (1987). Carbon dioxide induced anxiety. *Archives of General Psychiatry, 44*, 365–375.

Woody, G. E., McLellan, T., Luborsky, L., & O'Brien, C. P. (1985). Sociopathy and psychotherapy outcome. *Archives of General Psychiatry, 42*, 1081–1086.

Wortman, C. B., & Brehm, J. W. (1975). Responses to uncontrollable outcomes: An integration of the reactance theory and the learned helplessness model. In L. Berkowitz (Ed.), *Advances in social psychology.* New York: Academic Press.

Wright, M. J. (1991). Identifying child sexual abuse using the Personality Inventory for Children. *Dissertation Abstracts International, 52*, 1744.

Wurtele, S. K., & Miller-Perrin, C. L. (1987). An evaluation of side-effects associated with participation in a child sexual abuse prevention program. *Journal of School Health, 57*, 228–231.

Yalom, I. D. (1985). *The theory and practice of group psychotherapy* (3rd ed.). New York: Basic Books.

Yalom, I. D., Green, R., & Fisk, N. (1973). Prenatal exposure to female hormones: Effect on psychosexual development in boys. *Archives of General Psychiatry, 28*, 554–561.

Zakowski, S., Hall, M. H., & Baum, A. (1992). Stress, stress management, and the immune system. *Applied and Preventive Psychology, 1*, 1–13.

Zakowski, S. G., McAllister, C. G., Deal, M., & Baum, A. (1992). Stress, reactivity, and immune function in healthy men. *Health Psychology, 11*, 223–232.

Zametkin, A. J., Nordahl, T. E., Gross, M., King, A. C., Semple, W. E., Rumsey, J., Hamburger, S., & Cohen, R. M. (1990). Cerebral glucose metabolism in adults with hyperactivity of childhood onset. *The New England Journal of Medicine, 20*, 1361–1366.

Zarit, S. H. (1980). *Aging and mental disorders: Psychological approaches to assessment and treatment.* New York: Free Press.

Zarit, S. H., Eiler, J., & Hassinger M. (1985). Clinical assessment. In J. E. Birren & K. W. Schaie (Eds.), *Handbook of psychology of aging* (2nd ed.). New York: Van Nostrand-Reinhold.

Ziegler, F. J., Imboden, J. B., & Meyer, E. (1960). Contemporary conversion reactions: A clinical study. *American Journal of Psychiatry, 116*, 901–910.

Zigler, E. (1967). Familial mental retardation: A continuing dilemma. *Science, 155*, 292–298.

Zigler, E., Hodapp, R. M., & Edison, M. R. (1990). From theory to practice in the care and education of mentally retarded individuals. *American Journal on Mental Retardation, 95*, 1–12.

Zilboorg, G., & Henry, G. W. (1941). *A history of medical psychology.* New York: Norton.

Zimbardo, P. G., Andersen, S. M., & Kabat, L. G. (1981). Paranoia and deafness: An experimental investigation. *Science, 212*, 1529–1531.

Zimbardo, P. G., LaBerge, S., & Butler, L. D. (1993). Psychophysiological consequences of unexplained arousal: A post-hypnotic suggestion paradigm. *Journal of Abnormal Psychology, 102*, 466–473.

Zimberg, S. (1987). Alcohol abuse among the elderly. In L. L. Carstensen & B. A. Edelstein (Eds.), *Handbook of clinical gerontology* (pp. 57–65). Elmsford, NY: Pergamon.

Zimmerman, M. (1994). Diagnosing personality disorders: A review of issues and research methods. *Archives of General Psychiatry, 51*, 225–245.

Zimmerman, M., & Coryell, W. (1989). DSM-III personality disorder diagnoses in a nonpatient sample. *Archives of General Psychiatry, 46*, 682–689.

Zoccolillo, M., & Rogers, K. (1991). Characteristics and outcome of hospitalized adolescent girls with conduct disorder. *Journal of the American Academy of Child and Adolescent Psychiatry, 30*, 973–981.

Zucker, K. J., Finegan, J. K., Deering, R. W., & Bradley, S. J. (1984). Two subgroups of gender-problem children. *Archives of Sexual Behavior, 13*, 27–39.

Quotation Credits

Permission was obtained for use of the following copyrighted material

Page 21, table 1.1: Myers, J. K., Weissman, M. M., Tischler, G. L., Holzer, C. E., Leaf, P. J., Orvaschel, H. A., Anthony, J. C., Boyd, J. H., Burke, J. E., Kramer, M., & Stoltzman, R. (1984). Six-month prevalence of psychiatric disorders in three communities: 1980–1982. *Archives of General Psychiatry, 41,* 959–967. Copyright © 1984, American Medical Association.

Page 23, figure 1.2: Pennebaker, J. W., Kiecolt-Glaser, J. K., & Glaser, R. (1988). Disclosure of trauma and immune function: Health implications for psychotherapy. *Journal of Consulting and Clinical Psychology, 56,* 239–245. Copyright © 1988 by the American Psychological Association. Reprinted by permission.

Pages 84–85, table 4.1: American Psychiatric Association: *Diagnostic and Statistical Manual of Mental Disorders, Fourth Edition.* Washington, DC, American Psychiatric Association, 1994.

Page 97, table 4.3: American Psychiatric Association: *Diagnostic and Statistical Manual of Mental Disorders, Fourth Edition.* Washington, DC, American Psychiatric Association, 1994.

Page 108, figure 5.1: Spitzer, R. L., & Williams, J. B. W. (1985). *Structured clinical interview for DSM-III-R. Patient version.* New York: New York State Psychiatric Institute Biometrics Research Division. Reprinted by permission of New York State Psychiatric Institute Biometrics Research Division.

Chapters 6, 7, 8, 9, 10, 11, 13 and 15, featured case studies: Oltmanns, T. F., Neale, J. M., Davison, G. C. (1991). *Case studies in abnormal psychology* (3rd ed.). John Wiley & Sons, Inc. Reprinted by permission of John Wiley & Sons, Inc.

Page 191, table 8.1: Holmes, T. H., & Rahe, R. H. (1967). The Social Readjustment Rating Scale. *Journal of Psychosomatic Research, 11,* 213–218. Elsevier Science Ltd., Pergamon Imprint, Oxford, England.

Page 195, figures 8.2 and 8.3: Stone, A. A., Reed, B. R., & Neale, J. M. (1987). Changes in daily event frequency precede episodes of physical symptoms. *Journal of Human Stress, 13,* 70–74, Reprinted with permission of the Helen Dwight Reid Educational Foundation. Published by Heldref Publications, 1319 18th Street, N.W. Washington, DC 20036-1802. Copyright © 1987.

Pages 219–220, quotations: Mellor, C. S. (1970). First rank symptoms of schizophrenia. *British Journal of Psychiatry, 117,* 15–23. Copyright © 1970. Reprinted by permission of the Royal College of Psychiatrists.

Page 228, table 9.1: McGue, Gottesman, Rao. *American Journal of Human Genetics, 35,* 1161–1178. Copyright © 1983 by University of Chicago Press.

Page 230, Figure 9.1: Horn, A. S., & Snyder, S. H. (1971). Chlorpromazine and dopamine: Conformational similarities that correlate with the anti-schizophrenic activity of phenothiazine drugs. *Proceedings of the National Academy of Sciences, 68,* 2324–2328. Copyright © 1971. Reprinted by permission of Solomon H. Snyder, M.D.

Page 236, table 9.2: Adapted from Tienari, P., Sorri, A., Lahti, I., Naarala, M. N., Wahlberg, E., Moring, J., Pohjola, J., & Wynne, L. C. (1987). Genetic and psychosocial factors in schizophrenia: The Finnish adoptive family study. *Schizophrenia Bulletin, 13*(3), 484, 1987, by permission.

Page 255, quotation: Reid, E. C. (1910). Autopsychology of the manic-depressive. *Journal of Nervous and Mental Disease, 37,* 606–620.

Page 265, table 10.1: Abramson, L. Y., Seligman, M. E. P., & Teasdale, J. D. (1978). Learned helplessness in humans: Critique and reformulation. *Journal of Abnormal Psychology 87,* 49–74. Copyright © 1978 by the American Psychological Association. Adapted by permission.

Page 281, figure 10.3: Shaffer, D., Gould, M., & Hicks, R. C. (1994). Worsening suicide rate in Black teenagers. *American Journal of Psychiatry, 151,* 1810–1812. Copyright © 1994, the American Psychiatric Association. Reprinted by permission.

Page 294, table 11.1: Adapted with permission from John, O. P. (1990). The "Big Five" factor taxonomy: Dimensions of personality in the natural language and in questionnaires. In L. A. Pervin (Ed.), *Handbook of personality: Theory and research* (pp. 66–100). New York: Guilford.

Pages 301–302, case: Elton B. McNeil, *The Quiet Furies: Man and disorder,* copyright © 1967, pp. 83–91. Adapted by permission of Prentice Hall, Englewood Cliffs, New Jersey.

Pages 319, and 347–348, case: Mattick, R. P. (1992). Psychoactive substance dependence and associated states. In S. Schwartz (Ed.), *Case studies in abnormal psychology* (pp. 155–179). Brisbane, Australia: Wiley. Adapted from a case study by Richard Mattick, from S. Schwartz (Ed.), *Case studies in abnormal psychology.* John Wiley & Sons, Brisbane.

Page 343, table 12.2: The Twelve Steps are reprinted with permission of Alcoholics Anonymous World Services, Inc. Permission to reprint this material does not mean that A. A. has reviewed or approved the contents of this publication, nor that A. A. agrees with the views expressed herein. A. A. is a program of recovery from alcoholism *only*—use of the Twelve Steps in connection with programs and activities which are patterned after A. A., but which address other problems, does not imply otherwise.

Page 361, figure 13.1: Masters, W. H., & Johnson, V. E. (1966). *Human sexual response.* Copyright © 1966 by the Masters and Johnson Institute. Reprinted by permission of the Masters and Johnson Institute.

Page 400, and 436–437 case: Leon, G. R. (1990). *Case histories of psychopathology* (4th ed.). Needham Heights, MA: Allyn & Bacon. From Gloria R. Leon, *Case histories of psychopathology*. Copyright © 1990 by Allyn and Bacon. Adapted by permission.

Page 403, table 14.1: Barkley, R. A., Fischer, M., Edelbrock, C. S., & Smallish, L. The adolescent outcome of hyperactive children diagnosed by research criteria, I: An 8 year prospective follow-up study. *Journal of the American Academy of Child and Adolescent Psychiatry, 29,* 546–557. Copyright © 1990 by Williams & Wilkins.

Page 416, table 14.2: Sparrow, S. S., Balla, D. A., & Cicchetti, D. V. (1984). Vineland Adaptive Behavior Scales. Copyright © 1984 by the American Guidance Service, Inc.

Page 426, quotations: Volkmar, F., & Cohen, D. J. (1985). The experience of infantile autism. *Journal of Autism and Developmental Disorders, 15,* 47–54. Reprinted by permission.

Page 435, figure 14.2: Stunkard, A., Sorensen, T., & Schulsinger, F. (1983). Use of the Danish Adoption Register for the study of obesity and thinness. In S. Kety (Ed.), *The genetics of neurological and psychiatric disorders,* 119. New York: Raven Press. Copyright © 1983 by Raven Press. Reprinted by permission of A. Stunkard.

Page 488, case: LoPiccolo, J., & Friedman, J. M. (1985). Sex therapy: An integrated model. In S. J. Lynn & J. P. Garske (Eds.), *Contemporary psychotherapies: Models and methods.* Copyright © 1985 S. J. Lynn & J. P. Garske. Reprinted by permission.

Endpapers: American Psychiatric Association: *Diagnostic and Statistical Manual of Mental Disorders, Fourth Edition.* Washington, DC, American Psychiatric Association, 1994.

Photo Credits

Chapter 10
Opener: David Chambers/Tony Stone Images/New York, Inc. Page 256: Everett Collection, Inc. Page 257: Griffin/The Image Works. Page 260: Sybil Shackman/Monkmeyer Press Photo. Page 267: Robert Goldstein/Photo Researchers. Page 269: COMSTOCK, Inc. Page 276: Tom McCarthy/PhotoEdit. Page 277: Will & Deni McIntyre/Photo Researchers. Page 281: Murray & Associates/Tony Stone Images/ New York, Inc. Page 283: Marc Romanelli/The Image Bank. Page 285: Mark Antman/The Image Works. Page 286: AP/Wide World Photos.

Chapter 11
Opener: Astromujoff/The Image Bank. Page 293: Cary Wolinsky/Tony Stone World Wide. Page 298: Grecco/Stock, Boston. Page 299: Culver Pictures, Inc. Page 300: Jerry Ohlinger's Movie Material Store. Page 302: Douglas Mason/Woodfin Camp & Associates. Page 305: Dan Bosler/Tony Stone Images/ New York, Inc. Page 306: Michaud Grapes/Photo Researchers. Page 310: Courtesy Marsha Linehan.

Chapter 12
Opener: Izumi Ohta/The Image Bank. Page 320: Chuck Nacke/Picture Group. Page 322: Bettmann Archive. Page 323: Tony Freeman/PhotoEdit. Page 329: Willie Hill/Stock, Boston. Page 333: Reuters/Bettmann Archive. Page 335: Yoav Levy/Phototake. Page 338: J.P. Laffont/Sygma. Page 340: Eric Brissaud/Gamma Liaison. Page 341: UPI/Bettmann. Page 350 (top): National Library of Medicine/Photo Researchers. Page 350 (bottom): John Giordano/Picture Group. Page 352: Grant LeDuc/Monkmeyer Press Photo. Page 354: Michael Newman/PhotoEdit.

Chapter 13
Opener: John Oresnik/The Image Bank. Page 361: Ira Wyman/Sygma. Page 362 (top): Bernard Gotfryd/Woodfin Camp & Associates. Page 362 (bottom): Everett Collection, Inc. Page 365: Blair Seitz/Photo Researchers. Page 375: Kermani/Gamma Liaison. Page 377 (left): Bettmann Archive. Page 377 (right): Robin Laurence/New York Times Pictures. Page 382: Jacques Chenet/Woodfin Camp & Associates. Page 384: Alon Reininger/Contact Press Images, Inc. Page 391: Tony Freeman/PhotoEdit. Page 392: Rhoda Sidney/Monkmeyer Press Photo. Page 394: Chuck Nacke/Picture Group.

Chapter 14
Opener: Phil Borges/Tony Stone Images/New York, Inc. Page 405: Doris De Witt/Tony Stone Images/New York, Inc. Page 407: Rick Kopstein/Monkmeyer Press Photo. Page 409: Laura Dwight/Peter Arnold, Inc. Page 412: M. Siluk/The Image Works. Page 414: Hattie Young/Science Photo Library/Photo Researchers. Page 416: Stephen Frisch/Stock, Boston. Figure. 14.1: Kunkel/Phototake. Page 419 (bottom): Will and Deni McIntyre/Photo Researchers. Page 420: Jeff Albertson/Stock, Boston. Page 421: Jacques Chenet/Woodfin Camp & Associates. Page 422: Greenlar/The Image Works. Page 424: Glassman/The Image Works. Page 427: Susan Oliver Young/Courtesy of Ivar Lovaas. Page 429: Steve Schapiro/Sygma.

Chapter 15
Opener: Masahiro Sano/The Stock Market. Page 442: Ken Lax/Photo Researchers. Figure 15.1: Martin Rotker/Phototake. Page 446: Blair Seitz/Photo Researchers. Page 448: Richard Pasley/Stock, Boston. Page 449: Ira Wyman/Sygma. Page 450: Freda Leinwand/ Monkmeyer Press Photo. Page 451: Frank Siteman/Stock, Boston. Page 455: Frank Siteman/Monkmeyer Press Photo. Page 456 (left): Jackson Archives/The Image Works. Page 456 (right): Bob Daemmrich/The Image Works. Page 458: Leonard Lessin/Peter Arnold, Inc. Page 460: Bob Daemmrich/Stock, Boston. Page 461: Ted Spagna/ Science Source/Photo Researchers. Page 466 (left): Charles Harbutt/Actuality. Page 466 (right): Don & Pat Valenti/Tony Stone Images/ New York, Inc.

Chapter 16
Opener: Ellen Schuster/The Image Bank. Page 474: Bob Daemmrich/Stock, Boston. Page 475: Mary Kate Denny/PhotoEdit. Page 476: Tony Freeman/PhotoEdit. Page 478: Betty Press/Woodfin Camp & Associates. Page 481: Courtesy Dr. Arnold Lazarus. Page 483: Michael Newman/PhotoEdit. Page 485: Lawrence Migdale/Photo Researchers. Page 486: Ann Chwatsky/Phototake. Page 487: David Young-Wolff/PhotoEdit. Page 491: Rob Nelson/Picture Group. Page 504: Lord/The Image Works.

Index

Name Index

Subject Index